C++ Programming:

Program Design Including Data Structures

Third Edition

D.S. Malik

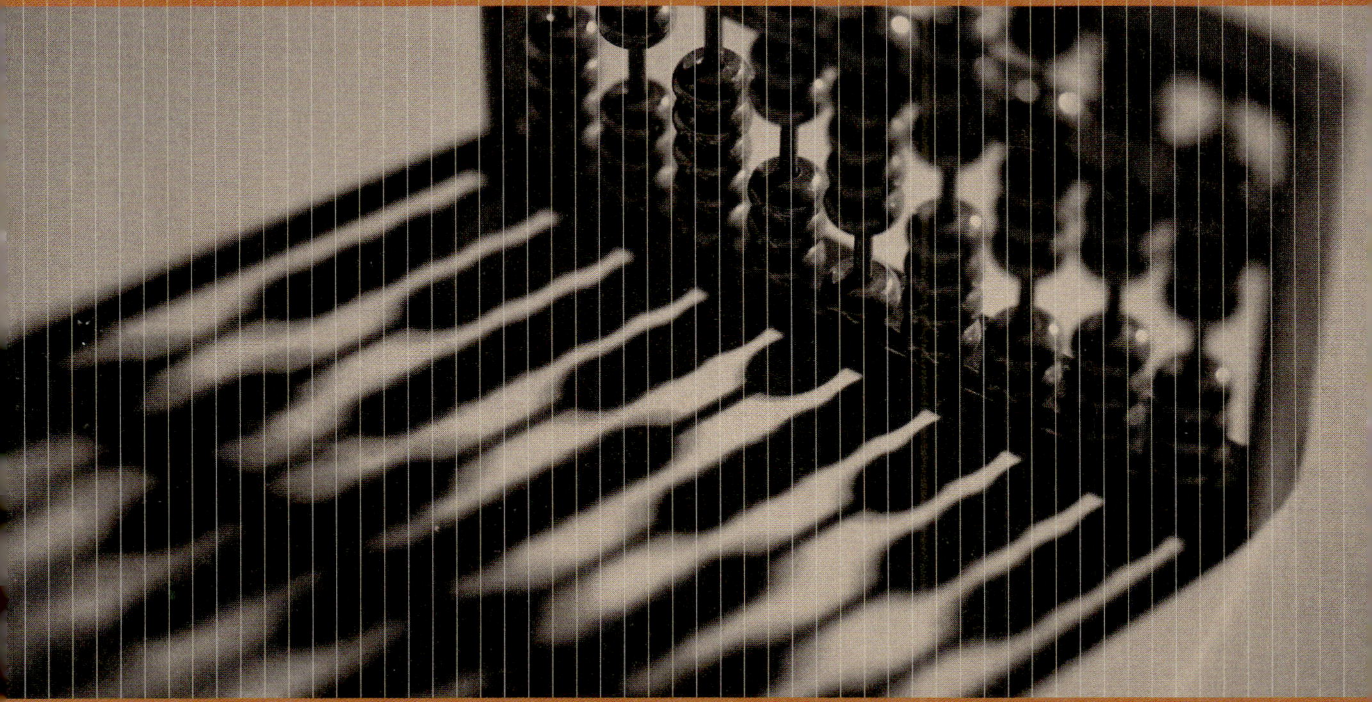

THOMSON
COURSE TECHNOLOGY

Australia | Canada | Mexico | Singapore | Spain | United Kingdom | United States

C++ Programming: Program Design Including Data Structures, Third Edition

by D.S. Malik

Senior Product Manager:
Alyssa Pratt

Managing Editor:
Mary Franz

Production Manager:
Aimee Poirier

Editorial Assistant:
Allison Murphy

Senior Manufacturing Coordinator:
Justin Palmeiro

Cover Designer:
Abby Scholz

Compositor:
Integra

TO

My Parents

BRIEF CONTENTS

	PREFACE	xxxiii
1.	An Overview of Computers and Programming Languages	1
2.	Basic Elements of C++	29
3.	Input/Output	115
4.	Control Structures I (Selection)	167
5.	Control Structures II (Repetition)	231
6.	User-Defined Functions I	309
7.	User-Defined Functions II	345
8.	User-Defined Simple Data Types, Namespaces, and the `string` Type	419
9.	Arrays and Strings	473
10.	Records (`structs`)	551
11.	Classes and Data Abstraction	591
12.	Inheritance and Composition	667
13.	Pointers, Classes, Virtual Functions, Abstract Classes, and Lists	733
14.	Overloading and Templates	817
15.	Exception Handling	907
16.	Recursion	945
17.	Linked Lists	981
18.	Stacks and Queues	1075
19.	Searching and Sorting Algorithms	1183
20.	Binary Trees	1273

21. Graphs   1333

22. Standard Template Library (STL)   1373

APPENDIX A   Reserved Words   1489

APPENDIX B   Operator Precedence   1491

APPENDIX C   Character Sets   1493

APPENDIX D   Operator Overloading   1497

APPENDIX E   Additional C++ Topics   1499

APPENDIX F   Header Files   1519

APPENDIX G   Memory Size on a System and Random
              Number Generator   1529

APPENDIX H   References   1531

APPENDIX I   Answers to Odd Numbered Exercises   1533

INDEX   1559

TABLE OF CONTENTS

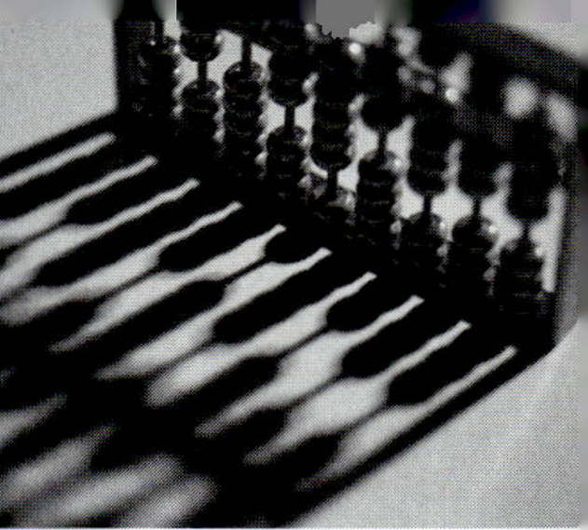

Preface   xxxiii

1 AN OVERVIEW OF COMPUTERS AND PROGRAMMING LANGUAGES   1

Introduction   2

A Brief Overview of the History of Computers   2

Elements of a Computer System   3
Hardware   3
Central Processing Unit   3
Main Memory   4
Secondary Storage   5
Input/Output Devices   5
Software   6

The Language of a Computer   6

The Evolution of Programming Languages   8

A C++ Program   9

Processing a C++ Program   12

Programming with the Problem Analysis–Coding–Execution Cycle   14

Programming Methodologies   22
Structured Programming   22
Object-Oriented Programming   22

ANSI/ISO Standard C++   24

Quick Review   24

Exercises   26

2 BASIC ELEMENTS OF C++ — 29

The Basics of a C++ Program — 30
Special Symbols — 32
Word Symbols — 32
Identifiers — 32

Data Types — 34
Simple Data Types — 34
Floating-Point Data Types — 37

Arithmetic Operators and Operator Precedence — 39
Order of Precedence — 43

Expressions — 44
Mixed Expressions — 45

Type Conversion (Casting) — 47

string Type — 50

Input — 51
Allocating Memory with Constants and Variables — 51
Putting Data into Variables — 54
Assignment Statement — 54
Saving and Using the Value of an Expression — 56
Declaring and Initializing Variables — 57
Input (Read) Statement — 58
Variable Initialization — 62

Increment and Decrement Operators — 68

Output — 70

Preprocessor Directives — 78
namespace and Using cin and cout in a Program — 79
Using the string Data Type in a Program — 79

Creating a C++ Program — 80

Program Style and Form	84
Syntax	84
Use of Blanks	85
Use of Semicolons, Brackets, and Commas	85
Semantics	85
Naming Identifiers	85
Prompt Lines	86
Documentation	87
Comments	87
Form and Style	87
More on Assignment Statements	89
Programming Example: Convert Length	91
Programming Example: Make Change	95
Quick Review	98
Exercises	100
Programming Exercises	109

3 INPUT/OUTPUT — 115

I/O Streams and Standard I/O Devices	116
`cin` and the Extraction Operator >>	117
Using Predefined Functions in a Program	123
`cin` and the `get` Function	125
`cin` and the `ignore` Function	126
The `putback` and `peek` Functions	128
The Dot Notation Between I/O Stream Variables and I/O Functions: A Precaution	130
Input Failure	131
The `clear` Function	133

Output and Formatting Output — 135
`setprecision` Manipulator — 135
`fixed` Manipulator — 136
`showpoint` Manipulator — 136
`setw` — 138
`flush` Manipulator — 141

Additional Output Formatting Tools — 141
`setfill` Manipulator — 142
`left` and `right` Manipulators — 143

Input/Output and the `string` Type — 146

File Input/Output — 147

Programming Example: Movie Ticket Sale and Donation to Charity — 150

Programming Example: Student Grade — 156

Quick Review — 159

Exercises — 161

Programming Exercises — 164

4 CONTROL STRUCTURES I (SELECTION) — 167

Control Structures — 168

Relational Operators — 169
Relational Operators and Simple Data Types — 171
Relational Operators and the `string` Type — 173

Logical (Boolean) Operators and Logical Expressions — 175
Order of Precedence — 177
Short-Circuit Evaluation — 181
`int` Data Type and Logical (Boolean) Expressions — 182
`bool` Data Type and Logical (Boolean) Expressions — 183

Selection: `if` and `if...else` ... 184

One-Way Selection ... 185

Two-Way Selection ... 187

Compound (Block of) Statements ... 191

Multiple Selections: Nested `if` ... 192

Comparing `if...else` Statements with
a Series of `if` Statements ... 195

Using Pseudocode to Develop, Test, and Debug
a Program ... 196

Input Failure and the `if` Statement ... 199

Confusion Between the Equality Operator (==) and
the Assignment Operator (=) ... 202

Conditional Operator (? :) ... 203

`switch` Structures ... 204

**Terminating a Program with the
`assert` Function** ... 211

Programming Example: Cable Company Billing ... 214

Quick Review ... 219

Exercises ... 221

Programming Exercises ... 226

5 CONTROL STRUCTURES II (REPETITION) ... 231

Why Is Repetition Needed? ... 232

`while` Looping (Repetition) Structure ... 233

Case 1: Counter-Controlled `while` Loops ... 236

Case 2: Sentinel-Controlled `while` Loops ... 238

Case 3: Flag-Controlled `while` Loops ... 243

Case 4: EOF-Controlled `while` Loops ... 247

`eof` Function 248

More on Expressions in `while` Statements 249

Programming Example: Checking Account Balance 250

Programming Example: Fibonacci Number 259

`for` **Looping (Repetition) Structure** 264

Programming Example: Classifying Numbers 270

`do...while` **Looping (Repetition) Structure** 274

`break` **and** `continue` **Statements** 279

Nested Control Structures 281

Quick Review 289

Exercises 291

Programming Exercises 302

6 USER-DEFINED FUNCTIONS I 309

Predefined Functions 310

User-Defined Functions 313

Value-Returning Functions 314

Syntax: Value-Returning function 316

Syntax: Formal Parameter List 316

Function Call 316

Syntax: Actual Parameter List 316

`return` Statement 317

Syntax: `return` Statement 317

Function Prototype 320

Syntax: Function Prototype 321

Flow of Execution 327

Programming Example: Largest Number   328

Programming Example: Cable Company   329

Quick Review   335

Exercises   337

Programming Exercises   341

7 USER-DEFINED FUNCTIONS II   345

Void Functions   346
Void Functions Without Parameters   346
Void Functions with Parameters   349
Value Parameters   354

Reference Variables as Parameters   355

Value and Reference Parameters and Memory Allocation   360

Reference Parameters and Value-Returning Functions   375

Scope of an Identifier   375

Global Variables, Named Constants, and Side Effects   379

Static and Automatic Variables   380

Function Overloading: An Introduction   382

Functions with Default Parameters   384

Programming Example: Classify Numbers   387

Programming Example: Data Comparison   392

Quick Review   402

Exercises   404

Programming Exercises   411

8 USER-DEFINED SIMPLE DATA TYPES, NAMESPACES, AND THE string TYPE — 419

Enumeration Type — 420
Declaring Variables — 422
Assignment — 422
Operations on Enumeration Types — 423
Relational Operators — 423
Input/Output of Enumeration Types — 424
Functions and Enumeration Types — 426
Declaring Variables When Defining the Enumeration Type — 428
Anonymous Data Types — 428
typedef Statement — 429

Programming Example: The Game of Rock, Paper, and Scissors — 430

Namespaces — 441

string Type — 446
Additional string Operations — 450
length Function — 450
size Function — 452
find Function — 453
substr Function — 456
swap Function — 458

Programming Example: Pig Latin Strings — 458

Quick Review — 464

Exercises — 467

Programming Exercises — 470

9 ARRAYS AND STRINGS — 473

Arrays — 475
Accessing Array Components — 476
Processing One-Dimensional Arrays — 479

Array Index Out of Bounds 483
Array Initialization During Declaration 484
Partial Initialization of Arrays During Declaration 484
Some Restrictions on Array Processing 485
Arrays as Parameters to Functions 486
Constant Arrays as Formal Parameters 487
Base Address of an Array and Array in Computer Memory 489
Functions Cannot Return a Value of the Type array 492
Integral Data Type and Array Indices 495
Other Ways to Declare Arrays 495

c-strings (Character Arrays) 496
String Comparison 498
Reading and Writing Strings 500
String Input 500
String Output 501
Specifying Input/Output Files at Execution Time 502
string Type and Input/Output Files 502

Parallel Arrays 503

Two- and Multidimensional Arrays 504
Accessing Array Components 506
Two-Dimensional Array Initialization During Declaration 507
Two-Dimensional Arrays and Enumeration Types 507
Initialization 511
Print 511
Input 511
Sum by Row 512
Sum by Column 512
Largest Element in Each Row and Each Column 512
Reversing Diagonal 513
Passing Two-Dimensional Arrays
as Parameters to Functions 515
Arrays of Strings 518
Arrays of Strings and the string Type 518
Arrays of Strings and c-Strings (Character Arrays) 519

Another Way to Declare a Two-Dimensional Array 520

Multidimensional Arrays 521

Programming Example: Code Detection 522

Programming Example: Text Processing 529

Quick Review 536

Exercises 538

Programming Exercises 543

10 RECORDS (structS) 551

Records (structs) 552

Accessing struct Members 554

Assignment 556

Comparison (Relational Operators) 557

Input/Output 558

struct Variables and Functions 558

Arrays versus structs 559

Arrays in structs 560

structs in Arrays 562

structs within a struct 565

Programming Example: Sales Data Analysis 569

Quick Review 585

Exercises 586

Programming Exercises 588

11 CLASSES AND DATA ABSTRACTION 591

Classes 592

Unified Modeling Language Class Diagrams 595

Variable (Object) Declaration 596

Accessing Class Members 597

Built-in Operations on Classes 598

Assignment Operator and Classes   599
Class Scope   600
Functions and Classes   600
Reference Parameters and Class Objects (Variables)   601
Implementation of Member Functions   601
Accessor and Mutator Functions   606
Order of `public` and `private` Members of a Class   612
Constructors   614
Invoking a Constructor   616
Invoking the Default Constructor   616
Invoking a Constructor with Parameters   617
Constructors and Default Parameters   620
Classes and Constructors: A Precaution   622
Arrays of Class Objects (Variables) and Constructors   623
Destructors   625

Data Abstraction, Classes, and Abstract Data Types   626
A `struct` Versus a `class`   628

Information Hiding   629

Executable Code   633

Static Members of a Class   636

Programming Example: Candy Machine   642

Quick Review   657

Exercises   659

Programming Exercises   664

12 INHERITANCE AND COMPOSITION   667

Inheritance   668
Redefining (Overriding) Member Functions of the Base Class   671
Constructors of Derived and Base Classes   678
Multiple Inclusions of a Header File   686

C++ Stream Classes 688

Protected Members of a Class 689

Inheritance as `public`, `protected`, or `private` 689

Composition 693

Object-Oriented Design (OOD) and Object-Oriented Programming (OOP) 698

Identifying Classes, Objects, and Operations 700

Programming Example: Grade Report 701

Quick Review 721

Exercises 722

Programming Exercises 728

13 POINTERS, CLASSES, VIRTUAL FUNCTIONS, ABSTRACT CLASSES, AND LISTS 733

Pointer Data Type and Pointer Variables 734

Declaring Pointer Variables 734

Address of Operator (&) 735

Dereferencing Operator (*) 736

Classes, Structs, and Pointer Variables 742

Initializing Pointer Variables 745

Dynamic Variables 745

Operator `new` 746

Operator `delete` 747

Operations on Pointer Variables 749

Dynamic Arrays 751

Functions and Pointers 754

Pointers and Function Return Values 754

Dynamic Two-Dimensional Arrays 755

Shallow versus Deep Copy and Pointers — 758

Classes and Pointers: Some Peculiarities — 760
Destructor — 761
Assignment Operator — 762
Copy Constructor — 764

Inheritance, Pointers, and Virtual Functions — 771
Classes and Virtual Destructors — 778

Abstract Classes and Pure Virtual Functions — 778

Array-Based Lists — 786

Unordered Lists — 794

Ordered Lists — 800

Address of Operator and Classes — 801

Quick Review — 804

Exercises — 807

Programming Exercises — 814

14 OVERLOADING AND TEMPLATES — 817

Why Operator Overloading Is Needed — 818

Operator Overloading — 819
Syntax for Operator Functions — 820
Overloading an Operator: Some Restrictions — 820
Pointer `this` — 821
Friend Functions of Classes — 826
Operator Functions as Member Functions
    and Nonmember Functions — 829
Overloading Binary Operators — 832
Overloading the Stream Insertion (<<) and
    Extraction (>>) Operators — 838
Overloading the Assignment Operator (=) — 843

Overloading Unary Operators   851
Operator Overloading: Member versus Nonmember   857
Classes and Pointer Member Variables (Revisited)   858
Operator Overloading: One Final Word   858

Programming Example: `clockType`   858

Programming Example: Complex Numbers   866

Overloading the Array Index (Subscript) Operator ([])   872

Programming Example: `newString`   874

Function Overloading   880

Templates   881
Function Templates   881
Class Templates   883
Array-Based Lists (Revisited)   886

Quick Review   892

Exercises   895

Programming Exercises   899

15 EXCEPTION HANDLING   907

Handling Exceptions within a Program   908
C++ Mechanisms of Exception Handling   912
`try`/`catch` Block   912
Using C++ Exception Classes   919

Creating Your Own Exception Classes   923
Rethrowing and Throwing an Exception   929

Exception Handling Techniques   933
Terminate the Program   933
Fix the Error and Continue   934
Log the Error and Continue   935

Stack Unwinding 935

Quick Review 939

Exercises 941

Programming Exercises 944

16 RECURSION 945

Recursive Definitions 946
Direct and Indirect Recursion 949
Infinite Recursion 949

Problem Solving Using Recursion 950
Tower of Hanoi: Analysis 961

Recursion or Iteration? 962

Programming Example: Converting a Number from Binary to Decimal 963

Programming Example: Converting a Number from Decimal to Binary 968

Quick Review 972

Exercises 973

Programming Exercises 976

17 LINKED LISTS 981

Linked Lists 982
Linked Lists: Some Properties 983
Building a Linked List 992

Linked List as an ADT 996
Structure of Linked List Nodes 998
Member Variables of the `class linkedListType` 998

Linked List Iterators 998
Print the List 1005
Length of a List 1005
Retrieve the Data of the First Node 1006
Retrieve the Data of the Last Node 1006
Begin and End 1006
Copy the List 1007
Destructor 1008
Copy Constructor 1008
Overloading the Assignment Operator 1009

Unordered Linked Lists 1009
Search the List 1010
Insert the First Node 1011
Insert the Last Node 1012
Header File of the Unordered Linked List 1017

Ordered Linked Lists 1018
Search the List 1020
Insert a Node 1020
Insert First and Insert Last 1025
Delete a Node 1026
Header File of the Ordered Linked List 1027

**Print a Linked List in Reverse Order
(Recursion Revisited)** 1030
printListReverse 1032

Doubly Linked Lists 1033
Default Constructor 1036
isEmptyList 1036
Destroy the List 1036
Initialize the List 1037
Length of the List 1037
Print the List 1037
Reverse Print the List 1037

Search the List 1038
First and Last Elements 1038

Circular Linked Lists 1044

Programming Example: Video Store 1045

Quick Review 1064

Exercises 1065

Programming Exercises 1069

18 STACKS AND QUEUES 1075

Stacks 1076
Stack Operations 1078

Implementation of Stacks as Arrays 1080
Initialize Stack 1083
Empty Stack 1084
Full Stack 1084
Push 1084
Return the Top Element 1086
Pop 1086
Copy Stack 1088
Constructor and Destructor 1088
Copy Constructor 1089
Overloading the Assignment Operator (=) 1089
Stack Header File 1090

Programming Example: Highest GPA 1094

Linked Implementation of Stacks 1098
Default Constructor 1101
Empty Stack and Full Stack 1102
Initialize Stack 1102
Push 1103

Return the Top Element   1105
Pop   1105
Copy Stack   1107
Constructors and Destructors   1108
Overloading the Assignment Operator (=)   1108
Stack as Derived from the `class`
   `unorderedLinkedList`   1110

Application of Stacks: Postfix Expressions Calculator   1112
Main Algorithm   1117
Function `evaluateExpression`   1117
Function `evaluateOpr`   1119
Function `discardExp`   1121
Function `printResult`   1121

**Removing Recursion: Nonrecursive Algorithm
to Print a Linked List Backward**   1124

Queues   1131
Queue Operations   1131
Implementation of Queues as Arrays   1133
Linked Implementation of Queues   1144
Queue Derived from the `class`
   `unorderedLinkedListType`   1149

Application of Queues: Simulation   1150
Designing a Queuing System   1151
Customer   1152
Server   1155
Server List   1158
Waiting Customers Queue   1163
Main Program   1165

Quick Review   1170

Exercises   1171

Programming Exercises   1177

19 SEARCHING AND SORTING ALGORITHMS — 1183

Searching and Sorting Algorithms — 1184

Search Algorithms — 1184
Sequential Search — 1185
Binary Search — 1187
Performance of Binary Search — 1192
Binary Search Algorithm and the `class`
   `orderedArrayListType` — 1195

Asymptotic Notation: Big-O Notation — 1195
Lower Bound on Comparison-Based Search Algorithms — 1204

Sorting Algorithms — 1204

Sorting a List: Bubble Sort — 1205
Analysis: Bubble Sort — 1209
Bubble Sort Algorithm and the `class`
   `unorderedArrayListType` — 1210

Selection Sort: Array-Based Lists — 1211
Analysis: Selection Sort — 1215

Insertion Sort: Array-Based Lists — 1215
Analysis: Insertion Sort — 1222

Lower Bound on Comparison-Based Sort Algorithms — 1223

Quick Sort: Array-Based Lists — 1224
Analysis: Quick Sort — 1231

Merge Sort: Linked List-Based Lists — 1232
Divide — 1234
Merge — 1236
Analysis: Merge Sort — 1240

Programming Example: Election Results — 1242

Quick Review 1264

Exercises 1265

Programming Exercises 1268

20 BINARY TREES 1273

Binary Trees 1274
Copy Tree 1281
Binary Tree Traversal 1282

Implementing Binary Trees 1286

Binary Search Trees 1295
Binary Search Tree: Analysis 1309

Nonrecursive Binary Tree Traversal Algorithms 1310
Nonrecursive Inorder Traversal 1310
Nonrecursive Preorder Traversal 1312
Nonrecursive Postorder Traversal 1313

Binary Tree Traversal and Functions as Parameters 1314

Programming Example: Video Store (Revisited) 1318

Quick Review 1327

Exercises 1328

Programming Exercises 1331

21 GRAPHS 1333

Introduction 1334

Graph Definitions and Notations 1335

Graph Representation 1338
Adjacency Matrix 1338
Adjacency Lists 1339

Operations on Graphs — 1340

Graphs as ADTs — 1341

Graph Traversals — 1345
Depth First Traversal — 1345
Breadth First Traversal — 1347

Shortest Path Algorithm — 1349
Shortest Path — 1351

Minimal Spanning Tree — 1357

Quick Review — 1367

Exercises — 1369

Programming Exercises — 1371

22 STANDARD TEMPLATE LIBRARY (STL) — 1373

Components of the STL — 1374
Container Types — 1375
Sequence Containers — 1375
Sequence Container: vector — 1375
Member Functions Common to All Containers — 1384
Member Functions Common to Sequence Containers — 1386
The copy Algorithm — 1387
Sequence Container: deque — 1391
Sequence Container: list — 1395

Iterators — 1402
Types of Iterators — 1402
Stream Iterators — 1408

Associative Containers — 1408
Associative Containers: set and multiset — 1409
Declaring set or multiset Associative Containers — 1409
Item Insertion and Deletion from set/multiset — 1411

Container Adapters 1415

Stack 1415

Queue 1417

Containers, Associated Header Files, and Iterator Support 1418

Algorithms 1419

STL Algorithm Classification 1420

Function Objects 1422

Insert Iterator 1428

STL Algorithms 1430

The Functions `fill` and `fill_n` 1430

The Functions `generate` and `generate_n` 1432

The Functions `find`, `find_if`, `find_end`, and `find_first_of` 1434

The Functions `remove`, `remove_if`, `remove_copy`, and `remove_copy_if` 1439

The Functions `replace`, `replace_if`, `replace_copy`, and `replace_copy_if` 1442

The Functions `swap`, `iter_swap`, and `swap_ranges` 1446

The Functions `search`, `search_n`, `sort`, and `binary_search` 1449

The Functions `adjacent_find`, `merge`, and `inplace_merge` 1453

The Functions `reverse`, `reverse_copy`, `rotate`, and `rotate_copy` 1457

The Functions `count`, `count_if`, `max`, `max_element`, `min`, `min_element`, and `random_shuffle` 1460

The Functions `for_each` and `transform` 1464

The Functions `includes`, `set_intersection`, `set_union`, `set_difference`, and `set_symmetric_difference` 1467

The Functions `accumulate`, `adjacent_difference`, `inner_product`, and `partial_sum` 1475

Quick Review 1480

Exercises 1484

Programming Exercises 1486

APPENDIX A: RESERVED WORDS 1489

APPENDIX B: OPERATOR PRECEDENCE 1491

APPENDIX C: CHARACTER SETS 1493

ASCII (American Standard Code for Information Interchange) 1493

EBCDIC (Extended Binary Coded Decimal Interchange Code) 1494

APPENDIX D: OPERATOR OVERLOADING 1497

APPENDIX E: ADDITIONAL C++ TOPICS 1499

Binary (Base 2) Representation of a Non-Negative Integer 1499
  Converting a Base 10 Number to a Binary Number (Base 2) 1499
  Converting a Binary Number (Base 2) to Base 10 1501

More on File Input/Output 1502
  Binary Files 1502
  Random File Access 1508

APPENDIX F: HEADER FILES 1519

Header File `cassert` (`assert.h`) 1519

Header File `cctype` (`ctype.h`) 1520

Header File `cfloat` (`float.h`) 1521

Header File `climits` (`limits.h`) 1522

Header File `cmath` (`math.h`) 1524
   Header File `cstddef` (`stddef.h`) 1525
   Header File `cstring` (`string.h`) 1525

APPENDIX G: MEMORY SIZE ON A SYSTEM AND RANDOM NUMBER GENERATOR   1529

Random Number Generator 1530

APPENDIX H: REFERENCES   1531

APPENDIX I: ANSWERS TO ODD NUMBERED EXERCISES   1533

Chapter 1 1533

Chapter 2 1535

Chapter 3 1537

Chapter 4 1538

Chapter 5 1539

Chapter 6 1540

Chapter 7 1541

Chapter 8 1542

Chapter 9 1542

Chapter 10 1543

Chapter 11 1544

Chapter 12 1546

Chapter 13 1547

Chapter 14 1548

Chapter 15 1549

Chapter 16 1550

Chapter 17 1551

Chapter 18 1551

Chapter 19 1553

Chapter 20 1555

Chapter 21 1557

Chapter 22 1558

INDEX 1559

WELCOME TO THE THIRD EDITION OF *C++ Programming: Program Design Including Data Structures*. Designed for a two semester (CS1 and CS2) C++ course, this text will provide a breath of fresh air to you and your students. The CS1 and CS2 courses serve as the cornerstone of the Computer Science curriculum. My primary goal is to motivate and excite all introductory programming students, regardless of their level. Motivation breeds excitement for learning. Motivation and excitement are critical factors that lead to the success of the programming student. This text is a culmination and development of my classroom notes throughout more than fifty semesters of teaching successful programming to Computer Science students.

C++ Programming: Program Design Including Data Structures started as a collection of brief examples, exercises, and lengthy programming examples to supplement the books that were in use at our university. It soon turned into a collection large enough to develop into a text. *The approach taken in this book is, in fact, driven by the students' demand for clarity and readability.* The material was written and rewritten until the students felt comfortable with it. Most of the examples in this book resulted from student interaction in the classroom.

As with any profession, practice is essential. Cooking students practice their recipes. Budding violinists practice their scales. New programmers must practice solving problems and writing code. This is not a C++ cookbook. We do not simply list the C++ syntax followed by an example; we dissect the "why" behind all the concepts. The crucial question of "why?" is answered for every topic when first introduced. This technique offers a bridge to learning C++. Students must understand the "why?" in order to be motivated to learn.

Traditionally, a C++ programming neophyte needed a working knowledge of another programming language. This book assumes no prior programming experience. However, some adequate mathematics background such as college algebra is required.

Changes in the Third Edition

In the third edition, the following changes have been implemented:

- In Chapter 1, a new section on processing a C++ program has been added. This chapter also contains additional examples and exercises on problem analysis and algorithm design.

- Examples in Chapter 2 also contain C++ programs showing the effect of certain C++ statements. The chapter contains several new programming exercises.

- Chapter 4 contains several new programming exercises.

- In Chapter 5, examples have been added to illustrate flag control loops as well as `do...while` loops. Moreover, this chapter contains several new programming exercises, including some that are related to engineering.

- Chapter 9 contains a new section on how arrays are stored in computer memory.

- In Chapter 13, a section on creating and manipulating dynamic two-dimensional arrays and a new section on abstract classes is included.

- To create generic code to process data in linked lists, Chapter 17 uses the concept of abstract classes to capture the basic properties of linked lists and then derive two separate classes to process unordered and ordered lists.

- Chapter 18 uses the concept of abstract classes to capture the basic properties of stacks and queues and then discusses various implementations of stacks and queues.

- Searching and sorting algorithms, discussed in Chapter 19, are stand-alone algorithms. Array-based searching and sorting algorithms are written as function templates and are not tied with any class. They can be used with buit-in types, such as `int`, as well as with user-defined data types, such as classes. This chapter also includes the heap sort algorithm, which is provided as a separate section and is available on the Web site accompanying this book.

- Chapter 20 uses the concept of abstract classes to define the basic properties of a binary tree and then derives the class to implement the basic operations on a binary search tree. This chapter also includes a detailed discussion of AVL (height-balanced) trees, which is provided as a separate section and is available on the Web site accompanying this book.

- Graph algorithms in Chapter 21 are slightly modified so that the graphs can be traversed using iterators on linked lists. The classes to implement the graph algorithms are no longer templates because the nodes of a graph are typically labeled as non-negative integers. This chapter also includes breadth-first topological ordering, which is provided as a separate section and is available on the Web site accompanying this book.

- In Appendix E, a new section on converting a number from decimal to binary and binary to decimal is added.

These changes were implemented based on comments from the Third Edition text reviewers and readers of the Second Edition.

Approach

The programming language C++, which evolved from C, is no longer considered an industry-only language. Numerous colleges and universities use C++ for their first programming language course. C++ is a combination of structured programming and object-oriented programming, and this book addresses both types.

This book is intended for a two-semester course, CS1 and CS2, in Computer Science. The first eleven or twelve chapters can be covered in the first course and the remaining in the second course.

In July 1998, ANSI/ISO Standard C++ was officially approved. This book focuses on ANSI/ISO Standard C++. Even though the syntax of Standard C++ and ANSI/ISO Standard C++

is very similar, Chapter 8 discusses some of the features of ANSI/ISO Standard C++ that are not available in Standard C++.

Chapter 1 briefly reviews the history of computers and programming languages. The reader can quickly skim through this chapter and become familiar with some of the hardware components and the software parts of the computer. This chapter contains a section on processing a C++ program. This chapter also describes structured and object-oriented programming.

Chapter 2 discusses the basic elements of C++. After completing this chapter, students become familiar with the basics of C++ and are ready to write programs that are complicated enough to do some computations. Input/output is fundamental to any programming language. It is introduced early, in Chapter 3, and is covered in detail.

Chapters 4 and 5 introduce control structures to alter the sequential flow of execution. Chapters 6 and 7 study user-defined functions. It is recommended that readers with no prior programming background spend extra time on Chapters 6 and 7. Several examples are provided to help readers understand the concepts of parameter passing and the scope of an identifier.

Chapter 8 discusses the user-defined simple data type (enumeration type), the `namespace` mechanism of ANSI/ISO Standard C++, and the `string` type. The earlier versions of C did not include the enumeration type. Enumeration types have very limited use; their main purpose is to make the program readable. This book is organized such that readers can skip the section on enumeration types during the first reading without experiencing any discontinuity, and then later go through this section.

Chapter 9 discusses arrays in detail. Chapter 10 introduces records (`struct`s). The introduction of `struct`s in this book is similar to C `struct`s. This chapter is optional; it is not a prerequisite for any of the remaining chapters.

Chapter 11 begins the study of object-oriented programming (OOP) and introduces classes. The first half of this chapter shows how classes are defined and used in a program. The second half of the chapter introduces abstract data types (ADTs). This chapter shows how classes in C++ are a natural way to implement ADTs. Chapter 12 continues with the fundamentals of object-oriented design (OOD) and OOP, and discusses inheritance and composition. It explains how classes in C++ provide a natural mechanism for OOD and how C++ supports OOP. Chapter 12 also discusses how to find the objects in a given problem.

Chapter 13 studies pointers in detail. After introducing pointers and how to use them in a program, this chapter highlights the peculiarities of classes with pointer data members and how to avoid them. Moreover, this chapter also discusses how to create and work with dynamic two-dimensional arrays. Chapter 13 also discusses abstract classes and a type of polymorphism accomplished via virtual functions.

Chapter 14 continues the study of OOD and OOP. In particular, it studies polymorphism in C++. Chapter 14 specifically discusses two types of polymorphism—overloading and templates.

Chapter 15 discusses exception handling in detail. Chapter 16 introduces and discusses recursion. This is a stand-alone chapter, so it can be studied any time after Chapter 10.

Chapters 17 and 18 are devoted to the study of data structures. Discussed in detail are linked lists in Chapter 17 and stacks and queues in Chapter 18. The programming code developed in these chapters is generic. These chapters effectively use the fundamentals of OOD.

Chapter 19 discusses various searching and sorting algorithms. In addition to showing how these algorithms work, it also provides relevant analysis and results concerning the performance of the algorithms. The algorithm analysis allows the user to decide which algorithm to use in a particular application. This chapter also includes several sorting algorithms. The instructor can decide which algorithms to cover.

Chapter 20 provides an introduction to binary trees. Various traversal algorithms, as well as the basic properties of binary trees, are discussed and illustrated. Special binary trees, called binary search trees, are introduced. Searching, as well as item insertion and deletion from a binary search tree, are described and illustrated. Chapter 20 also discusses nonrecursive binary tree traversal algorithms. Furthermore, to enhance the flexibility of traversal algorithms, it shows how to construct and pass functions as parameters to other functions. This chapter also discusses AVL (height balanced) trees in detail. Due to text length considerations, discussion on AVL trees is provided as a separate section and is available on the Web site accompanying this book.

Graph algorithms are discussed in Chapter 21. After introducing the basic graph theory terminology, the representation of graphs in computer memory is discussed. This chapter also discusses graph traversal algorithms, the shortest path algorithm, and the minimal spanning tree algorithm. Topological sort is also discussed in this chapter and is available on the Web site accompanying this book.

C++ is equipped with a powerful library—the Standard Template Library (STL)—of data structures and algorithms that can be used effectively in a wide variety of applications. Chapter 22 describes the STL in detail. After introducing the three basic components of the STL, it shows how sequence containers are used in a program. Special containers, such as stack and queue, are also discussed. The latter half of this chapter shows how various STL algorithms can be used in a program. This chapter is fairly long; depending on the availability of time, the instructor can at least cover the sequence containers, iterators, the classes `stack` and `queue`, and certain algorithms.

Appendix A lists the reserved words in C++. Appendix B shows the precedence and associativity of the C++ operators. Appendix C lists the ASCII (American Standard Code for Information Interchange) and EBCDIC (Extended Binary Coded Decimal Interchange Code) character sets. Appendix D lists the C++ operators that can be overloaded.

Appendix E has three objectives. First, we discuss how to convert a number from decimal to binary and binary to decimal. We then discuss binary and random access files in detail. Finally, we describe the naming conventions of the header files in both ANSI/ISO Standard C++ and Standard C++. Appendix F discusses some of the most widely used library routines, and includes the names of the standard C++ header files. The programs in Appendix G show how to print the memory size for the built-in data types on your system as well as how to use a random number generator. Appendix H gives selected references for further study. Appendix I provides the answers to odd numbered exercises in the book.

How to Use the Book

This book can be used in various ways. Figure 1 shows the dependency of the chapters.

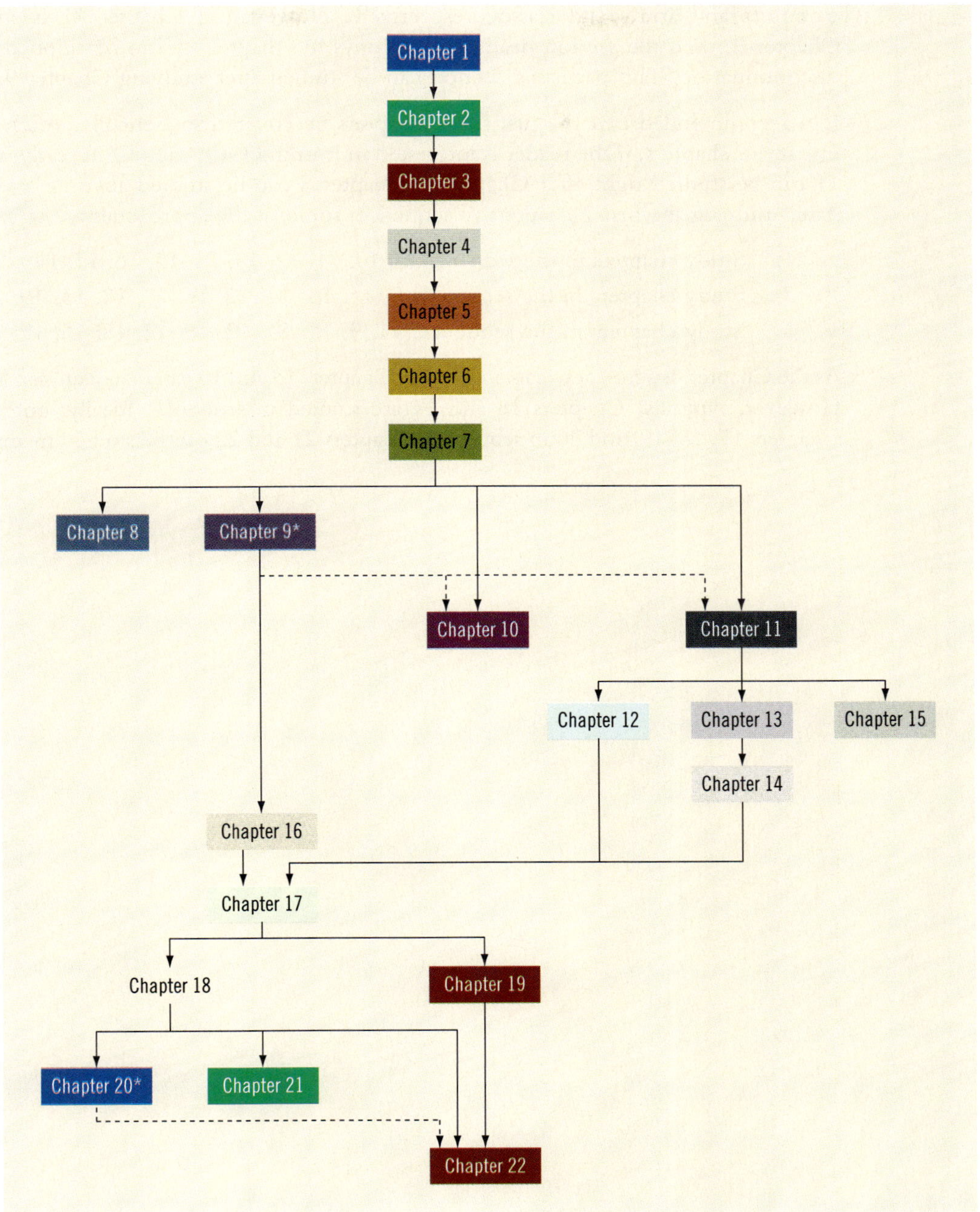

FIGURE 1 Chapter dependency diagram

In Figure 1, dotted lines mean that the preceding chapter is used in one of the sections of the chapter and is not necessarily a prerequisite for the next chapter. For example, Chapter 9 covers arrays in detail. In Chapters 10 and 11, we show the relationship between arrays and `struct`s and arrays and classes, respectively. However, if Chapter 11 is studied before Chapter 9, then the section dealing with arrays in Chapter 11 can be skipped without any discontinuation. This particular section can be studied after studying Chapter 9.

It is recommended that the first seven chapters be covered sequentially. After covering the first seven chapters, if the reader is interested in learning OOD and OOP early, then Chapter 11 can be studied right after Chapter 7. Chapter 8 can be studied anytime after Chapter 7. After studying the first 7 chapters in sequence, some of the approaches are:

1. Study chapters in the sequence: 9, 10, 11, 12, 13, 14, 15, 16, 17, 18, 19, 20, 21, 22.
2. Study chapters in the sequence: 9, 11, 13, 14, 12, 16, 17, 18, 15, 19, 20, 21, 22.
3. Study chapters in the sequence: 11, 9, 13, 14, 12, 16, 17, 18, 15, 19, 20, 21, 22.

As the Chapter dependency diagram shows, Chapters 18 and 19 can be covered in any sequence. However, typically, Chapters 18 and 19 are studied in sequence. Ideally, one should study Chapters 17, 18, 19, and 20 in sequence. Chapters 21 and 22 can be studied in any sequence.

From beginning to end, the concepts are introduced at a pace that is conducive to learning. *The writing style of this book is simple and straightforward, and it parallels the teaching style of a classroom.* Before introducing a key concept, we explain why certain elements are necessary. The concepts introduced are then described using examples and small programs.

Each chapter has two types of programs. The first type are small programs that are part of the numbered Examples (*e.g.*, Example 4-1), and are used to explain key concepts. In these examples, each line of the programming code is numbered. The program, illustrated through a Sample Run, is then explained line-by-line. The rationale behind each line is discussed in detail.

The Programming Examples form the backbone of the book and are designed to be methodical and user-friendly. Each Programming Example starts with a Problem Analysis and is followed by the Algorithm Design. Every step of the algorithm is then coded in C++. In addition to teaching problem-solving techniques, these detailed programs show the user how to implement concepts in an actual C++ program. I strongly recommend that students study the Programming Examples very carefully in order to effectively learn C++.

Quick Review sections at the end of each chapter reinforce learning. After reading the chapter, students can quickly walk through the highlights of the chapter and test themselves using the ensuing Exercises. Many readers refer to the Quick Review as an easy way to review the chapter before an exam.

The features of the text are clearly illustrated on the following pages.

FEATURES OF THE BOOK


```cpp
using namespace std;

int main()
{
    ifstream inFile;      //input file stream variable
    ofstream outFile;     //output file stream variable

    double test1, test2, test3, test4, test5;
    double average;

    string firstName;
    string lastName;

    inFile.open("a:\\test.txt"); //open the input file

    if (!inFile)
    {
        cout << "Cannot open the input file. "
             << "The program terminates." << endl;
        return  1;
    }

    outFile.open("a:\\testavg.out");   //open the output file

    outFile << fixed << showpoint;
    outFile << setprecision(2);

    cout << "Processing data" << endl;

    inFile >> firstName >> lastName;
    outFile << "Student name: " << firstName
            << " " << lastName << endl;

    inFile >> test1 >> test2 >> test3
           >> test4 >> test5;
    outFile << "Test scores: " << setw(4) << test1
            << setw(4) << test2 << setw(4) << test3
            << setw(4) << test4 << setw(4) << test5
            << endl;

    average = (test1 + test2 + test3 + test4 + test5) / 5.0;

    outFile << "Average test score: " << setw(6)
            << average << endl;

    inFile.close();
    outFile.close();

    return 0;
}
```

Four-color interior design shows accurate C++ code and related comments.

Chapter 2 defined a program as a sequence of statements whose objective is to accomplish some task. The programs you have examined so far were simple and straightforward. To process a program, the computer begins at the first executable statement and executes the statements in order until it comes to the end. In this chapter and Chapter 5, you will learn how to tell a computer that it does not have to follow a simple sequential order of statements; it can also make decisions and repeat certain statements over and over until certain conditions are met.

Control Structures

A computer can process a program in one of three ways: in sequence; selectively, by making a choice, which is also called a branch; or repetitively, by executing a statement over and over, using a structure called a loop (as shown in Figure 4–1). The programming examples in Chapters 2 and 3 included simple sequential programs. With such a program, the computer starts at the beginning and follows the statements in order. No choices are made; there is no repetition. Control structures provide alternatives to sequential program execution and are used to alter the sequential flow of execution. The two most common control structures are selection and repetition. In selection, the program executes particular statements depending on some condition(s). In repetition, the program repeats particular statements a certain number of times based on some condition(s).

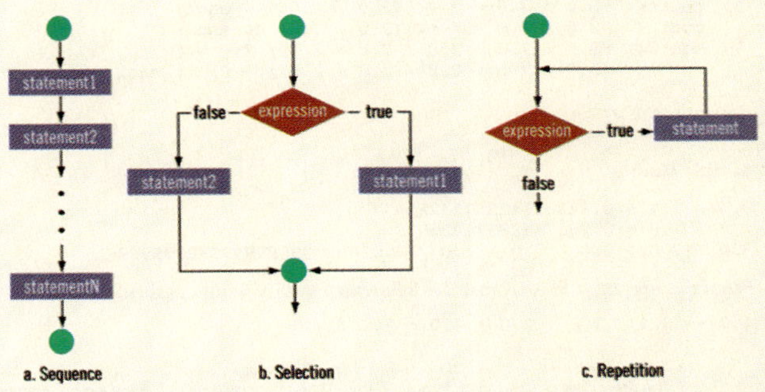

FIGURE 4-1 Flow of execution

Relational Operators and Simple Data Types

You can use the relational operators with all three simple data types. For example, the following expressions use both integers and real numbers:

Expression	Meaning	Value
8 < 15	8 is less than 15	true
6 != 6	6 is not equal to 6	false
2.5 > 5.8	2.5 is greater than 5.8	false
5.9 <= 7.5	5.9 is less than or equal to 7.5	true

> **NOTE** It is important to remember that the comparison of real numbers for equality may not behave as you would expect; see Example 4-1.

EXAMPLE 4-1

```cpp
#include <iostream>
#include <iomanip>

using namespace std;

int main()
{
    cout << fixed << showpoint << setprecision(17);

    cout << "3.0 / 7.0 = " << (3.0 / 7.0) << endl;
    cout << "2.0 / 7.0 = " << (2.0 / 7.0) << endl;
    cout << "3.0 / 7.0 + 2.0 / 7.0 + 2.0 / 7.0 = "
         << (3.0 / 7.0 + 2.0 / 7.0 + 2.0 / 7.0) << endl;

    return 0;
}
```

Sample Run:

```
3.0 / 7.0 = 0.42857142857142855
2.0 / 7.0 = 0.28571428571428570
3.0 / 7.0 + 2.0 / 7.0 + 2.0 / 7.0 = 0.99999999999999989
```

From the output, it follows that the following equality would evaluate to false.

```
1.0 == 3.0 / 7.0 + 2.0 / 7.0 + 2.0 / 7.0
```

> **NOTE** The preceding program and its output show that you should be careful when comparing floating-point numbers for equality. One way to check whether two floating-point numbers are equal is to check whether the absolute value of their difference is less than a certain tolerance.

PROGRAMMING EXAMPLE: Cable Company Billing

This programming example demonstrates a program that calculates a customer's bill for a local cable company. There are two types of customers: residential and business. There are two rates for calculating a cable bill: one for residential customers and one for business customers. For residential customers, the following rates apply:

- Bill processing fee: $4.50
- Basic service fee: $20.50
- Premium channels: $7.50 per channel.

For business customers, the following rates apply:

- Bill processing fee: $15.00
- Basic service fee: $75.00 for first 10 connections, $5.00 for each additional connection
- Premium channels: $50.00 per channel for any number of connections.

The program should ask the user for an account number (an integer) and a customer code. Assume that R or r stands for a residential customer, and B or b stands for a business customer.

Input   The customer's account number, customer code, number of premium channels to which the user subscribes, and, in the case of business customers, number of basic service connections.

Output   Customer's account number and the billing amount.

PROBLEM ANALYSIS AND ALGORITHM DESIGN   The purpose of this program is to calculate and print the billing amount. To calculate the billing amount, you need to know the customer for whom the billing amount is calculated (whether the customer is residential or business) and the number of premium channels to which the customer subscribes. In the case of a business customer, you also need to know the number of basic service connections and the number of premium channels. Other data needed to calculate the bill, such as the bill processing fees and the cost of a premium channel, are known quantities. The program should print the billing amount to two decimal places, which is standard for monetary amounts. This problem analysis translates into the following algorithm:

1. Set the precision to two decimal places.
2. Prompt the user for the account number and customer type.

EXERCISES

1. Mark the following statements as true or false.

   a. The result of a logical expression cannot be assigned to an `int` variable.

   b. In a one-way selection, if a semicolon is placed after the expression in an `if` statement, the expression in the `if` statement is always `true`.

   c. Every `if` statement must have a corresponding `else`.

   d. The expression in the `if` statement:

   ```
   if (score = 30)
       grade = 'A';
   ```

   always evaluates to `true`.

   e. The expression:

   ```
   (ch >= 'A' && ch <= 'Z')
   ```

   evaluates to `false` if either ch < 'A' or ch >= 'Z'.

   f. Suppose the input is 5. The output of the code:

   ```
   cin >> num;
   if (num > 5)
       cout << num;
       num = 0;
   else
       cout << "Num is zero" << endl;
    is:  Num is zero
   ```

   g. The expression in a `switch` statement should evaluate to a value of the simple data type.

   h. The expression `!(x > 0)` is `true` only if **x** is a negative number.

   i. In C++, both `!` and `!=` are logical operators.

   j. The order in which statements execute in a program is called the flow of control.

2. Circle the best answer.

   a.
   ```
   if (6 < 2 * 5)
       cout << "Hello";
       cout << " There";
   ```

   outputs the following:

   (i) Hello There   (ii) Hello   (iii) Hello   (iv) There
                                                        There

11. The following program contains errors. Correct them so that the program will run and output **w = 21**.

```cpp
#include <iostream>

using namespace std;

const int ONE = 5

main ()
{
    int x, y, w, z;
    z = 9;

    if z > 10
        x = 12; y = 5, w = x + y + ONE;
    else
        x = 12; y = 4, w = x + y + ONE;

    cout << "w = " << w << endl;
}
```

PROGRAMMING EXERCISES

1. Write a program that prompts the user to input a number. The program should then output the number and a message saying whether the number is positive, negative, or zero.

2. Write a program that prompts the user to input three numbers. The program should then output the numbers in ascending order.

3. Write a program that prompts the user to input an integer between 0 and 35. If the number is less than or equal to 9, the program should output the number; otherwise, it should output A for 10, B for 11, C for 12, ..., and Z for 35. (*Hint:* Use the cast operator, `static_cast<char> ( )`, for numbers >= 10.)

4. The cost of an international call from New York to New Delhi is calculated as follows: Connection fee, $1.99; $2.00 for the first three minutes; and $0.45 for each additional minute. Write a program that prompts the user to enter the number of minutes the call lasted and outputs the amount due. Format your output with two decimal places.

5. In a right triangle, the square of the length of one side is equal to the sum of the squares of the lengths of the other two sides. Write a program that prompts the user to enter the lengths of three sides of a triangle and then outputs a message indicating whether the triangle is a right triangle.

6. A box of cookies can hold 24 cookies and a container can hold 75 boxes of cookies. Write a program that prompts the user to enter the total number of cookies, the number of cookies in a box, and the number of cookie

SUPPLEMENTAL RESOURCES

The following supplemental materials are available when this book is used in a classroom setting. All instructor materials as outlined below are available on a single CD-ROM.

Electronic Instructor's Manual

The Instructor's Manual that accompanies this textbook includes:

- Additional instructional material to assist in class preparation, including suggestions for lecture topics.
- Solutions to all the end-of-chapter materials, including the Programming Exercises.

ExamView®

This textbook is accompanied by ExamView, a powerful testing software package that allows instructors to create and administer printed, computer (LAN-based), and Internet exams. ExamView includes hundreds of questions that correspond to the topics covered in this text, enabling students to generate detailed study guides that include page references for further review. These computer-based and Internet testing components allow students to take exams at their computers, and save the instructor time because each exam is graded automatically.

PowerPoint Presentations

This book comes with Microsoft PowerPoint slides for each chapter. These are included as a teaching aid for classroom presentations, either to make available to students on the network for chapter review, or to be printed for classroom distribution. Instructors can add their own slides for additional topics that they introduce to the class.

Distance Learning

Thomson Course Technology is proud to present online courses in WebCT and Blackboard to provide the most complete and dynamic learning experience possible. When you add online content to one of your courses, you're adding value to your course: Topic Reviews, Practice Tests, Review Questions, Assignments, PowerPoint presentations, and, most of all, a gateway to the 21st century's most important information resource. We hope you will make the most of your course, both online and offline. For more information on how to bring distance learning to your course, contact your local Thomson Course Technology sales representative.

Source Code

The source code, in ANSI/ISO Standard C++, is available at www.course.com, and is also available on the Teaching Tools CD-ROM. The input files needed to run some of the programs are also included with the source code. However, the input files should first be stored on a floppy disk in drive A:.

Solution Files

The solution files for all programming exercises, in ANSI/ISO C++, are available at www.course.com, and are also available on the Teaching Tools CD-ROM. The input files needed to run some of the programming exercises are also included with the solution files. However, the input files should first be stored on a disk or CD in drive A:.

Student Online Companion

This robust Web site, accessible at www.course.com/malik/cpp, offers students a plethora of review and self-assessment options. Each chapter includes a Concepts Review, Chapter Summary, Key Terms, Self-Tests, and Assignments. In addition, the Online Companion features related Web links, source code for all chapters, and compiler tutorials.

ACKNOWLEDGEMENTS

There are many people that I must thank who, one way or another, contributed to the success of this book. First, I would like to thank all the students who, during the preparation, were spontaneous in telling me if certain portions needed to be reworded for better understanding and clearer reading. Next, I would like to thank those who e-mailed numerous comments to improve upon the second edition. I am thankful to Professors S.C. Cheng, Randall Crist, John N. Mordeson, and Vasant Raval for constantly supporting this project. I must thank Lee I. Fenicle, Director, Office of Technology Transfer, Creighton University, for his involvement, support, and for providing encouraging words when I needed them. I am also very grateful to the reviewers who reviewed earlier versions of this book and offered many critical suggestions on how to improve it.

I owe a great deal to the following reviewers, who patiently read each page of every chapter of the current version and made critical comments to improve on the book: Stefano Basagni, Northeastern University; Ron Davidson, Highline Community College; Amar Raheja, California State Polytechnic University, Pomona; and Sylvia Unwin, Bellevue Community College. Additionally, I would like to thank the reviewers of the proposal package: Ali Berrachad, University of Houston—Downtown; Ray Hawkins, North Carolina Agricultural and Technical State University; and Mark E. Lehr, Riverside Community College. The reviewers will recognize that their criticisms have not been overlooked and, in fact, made this a better book. All this would not have been possible without the careful planning of Senior Product Manager Alyssa Pratt. My sincere thanks go to Alyssa Pratt for her work on this text. Aimee Poirier, Production Manager, checks and double or triple checks to make sure that the corrections are in place and the project stays on schedule. I, therefore, extend my sincere thanks to Aimee. I would like to thank Chris Scriver and Serge Palladino of the Thomson Course Technology QA department for patiently and carefully testing the code and discovering typos and errors.

I am thankful to my parents for their blessings, to whom this book is dedicated.

Finally, I am thankful for the support of my wife Sadhana and especially my daughter Shelly. They cheered me up whenever I was overwhelmed during the writing of this book. I welcome any comments concerning the text. Comments may be forwarded to the following e-mail address: malik@creighton.edu.

D. S. Malik

AN OVERVIEW OF COMPUTERS AND PROGRAMMING LANGUAGES

IN THIS CHAPTER, YOU WILL:

- Learn about different types of computers
- Explore the hardware and software components of a computer system
- Learn about the language of a computer
- Learn about the evolution of programming languages
- Examine high-level programming languages
- Discover what a compiler is and what it does
- Examine a C++ program
- Explore how a C++ program is processed
- Learn what an algorithm is and explore problem-solving techniques
- Become aware of structured design and object-oriented design programming methodologies
- Become aware of Standard C++ and ANSI/ISO Standard C++

Introduction

Today we live in an era where information is processed almost at the speed of light. Through computers, the technological revolution has drastically changed the way we live and communicate with one another. Terms such as "the Internet," which was unfamiliar just a few years ago, are very common today. With the help of computers you can send letters to and receive letters from loved ones within seconds. You no longer need to send a résumé by mail to apply for a job; in many cases you can simply submit your job application via the Internet. You can watch how stocks perform in real time and instantly buy and sell them. Students regularly "surf" the Internet and use computers to design their classroom projects. They also use powerful word processing software to complete their term papers. Many people maintain and balance their checkbooks on computers.

These examples are some of the ways that computers have greatly affected our daily lives. They are all made possible by the availability of different software, which are computer programs. For example, word processing software is a program that enables you to write term papers, create impressive-looking résumés, and even write a book. This book, for example, was created with the help of a powerful word processor. Without software, a computer is of no use. Software is developed with the help of programming languages. The programming language C++ is especially well suited for developing software to accomplish a specific task.

Until the early 1990s, instructors spent the first few weeks of a programming language course teaching their students how to use computers. Today, by the time students graduate from high school they know very well how to work with a computer. This book is not concerned with explaining how to use computers. Rather, it teaches you how to write programs in the language called C++. It is useful, however, to understand some of the basic terminology and different components of a computer before you begin programming. This chapter briefly describes the main components of a computer system, the history and evolution of computer languages, and some fundamental ideas about how to solve problems with computer programming.

A Brief Overview of the History of Computers

In the 1950s, computers were large devices accessible only to a very few people. All work—including accounting, word processing, and calculations—was done without the aid of computers. In the 1960s, multimillion-dollar computers emerged, and only large companies were able to afford them. These computers were very large in size, and only computer experts were allowed to use them. During the mid-1970s, computers became cheaper and smaller. By the mid-1990s, people from all walks of life were able to afford them. During the late 1990s, small computers became even less expensive and much faster. There are several categories of computers, such as main-frame, midsize, and micro, yet all computers share some basic elements.

Elements of a Computer System

A computer is an electronic device capable of performing commands. The basic commands that a computer performs are input (get data), output (display result), storage, and performance of arithmetic and logical operations.

In today's market, personal computers are sold with descriptions such as Pentium 4 Processor 2.80 GHz, 512MB RAM, 100GB HD, VX750 17" Silver Flat CRT Color Monitor, preloaded software such as operating systems, games, encyclopedias, and application software such as word processors or money management programs. These descriptions represent two categories: hardware and software. Items such as "Pentium 4 Processor 2.80 GHz, 512MB RAM, 100GB HD, VX750 17" Silver Flat CRT Color Monitor" fall into the hardware category; items such as "operating systems, games, encyclopedias, and application software" fall into the software category. Let's look at the hardware first.

Hardware

Major hardware components include the central processing unit (CPU); main memory (MM), also called random access memory (RAM); input/output devices; and secondary storage. Some examples of input devices are the keyboard, mouse, and secondary storage. Examples of output devices are the screen, printer, and secondary storage. Let's look at each of these components in more detail.

Central Processing Unit

The **central processing unit (CPU)** is the brain of the computer and the single most expensive piece of hardware in a personal computer. The more powerful the CPU, the faster the computer. The main components of the CPU are the control unit (CU), arithmetic logic unit (ALU), and registers. Figure 1-1 shows how certain components of the CPU fit together.

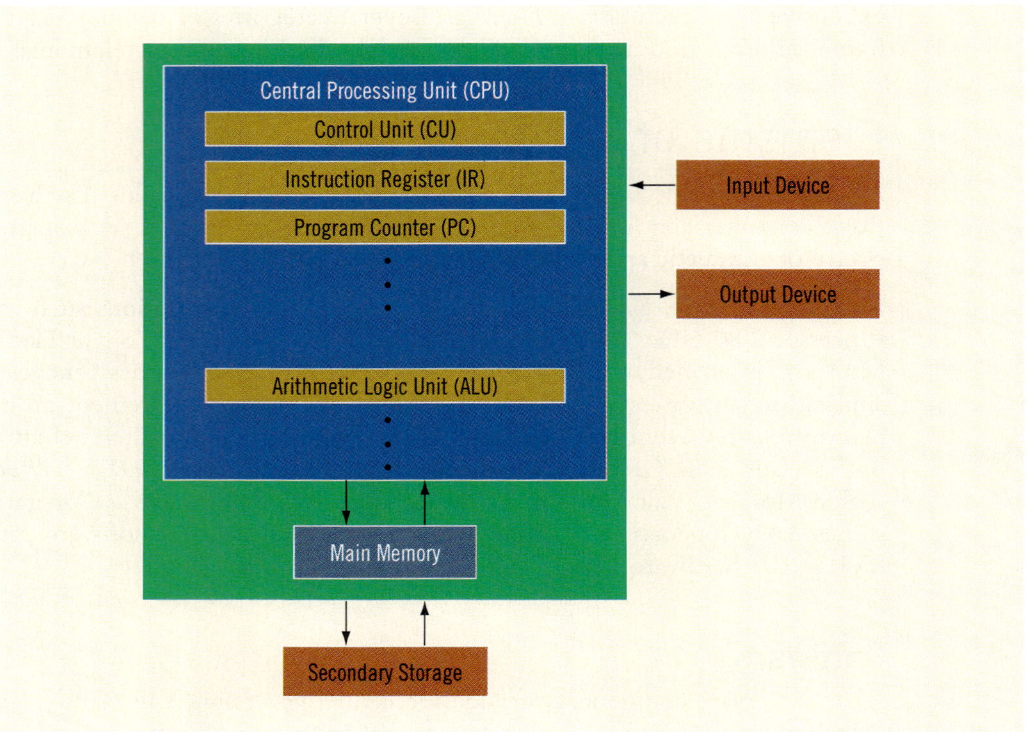

FIGURE 1-1   Hardware components of a computer

- The **control unit (CU)** has three main functions: fetch and decode the instructions, control the flow of information (instructions or data) in and out of main memory, and control the operation of the CPU's internal components.

- The **arithmetic logic unit (ALU)** carries out all arithmetic and logical operations.

- The CPU contains various registers. Some of these registers are for special purposes. For example, the **instruction register (IR)** holds the instruction currently being executed. The **program counter (PC)** points to the next instruction to be executed. All registers provide temporary storage.

Main Memory

The **main memory** is directly connected to the CPU. All programs must be loaded into main memory before they can be executed. Similarly, all data must be brought into main memory before a program can manipulate it. When the computer is turned off, everything in main memory is lost for good.

The main memory is an ordered sequence of cells, called **memory cells**. Each cell has a unique location in main memory, called the **address** of the cell. These addresses help you access the information stored in the cell. Figure 1-2 shows main memory with 100 storage cells.

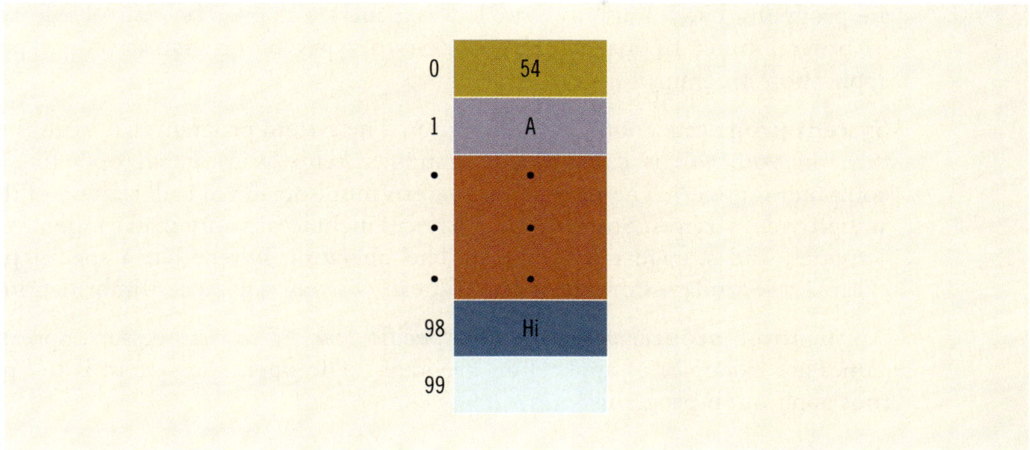

FIGURE 1-2 Main memory with 100 storage cells

Today's computers come with main memory consisting of millions to billions of cells. The content of a cell can be either a programming instruction or data. Figure 1-2 shows data stored in cells.

Secondary Storage

Because programs and data must be stored in main memory before processing and because everything in main memory is lost when the computer is turned off, information stored in main memory must be transferred to some other device for permanent storage. The device that stores information permanently (unless the device becomes unusable or you change the information by rewriting it) is called **secondary storage**. To be able to transfer information from main memory to secondary storage, these components must be directly connected to each other. Examples of secondary storage are hard disks, flash drives, floppy disks, ZIP disks, CD-ROMs, and tapes.

Input/Output Devices

For a computer to perform a useful task, it must be able to take in data and programs and display the results of calculations. The devices that feed data and programs into computers are called **input devices**. The keyboard, mouse, and secondary storage are examples of input devices. The devices that the computer uses to display results are called **output devices**. A monitor, printer, and secondary storage are examples of output devices.

Software

Software are programs written to perform specific tasks. For example, word processors are programs that you use to write letters, papers, and even books. All software is written in programming languages. There are two types of programs: system programs and application programs.

System programs control the computer. The system program that loads first when you turn on your PC is called the operating system. Without an operating system, the computer is useless. The **operating system** monitors the overall activity of the computer and provides services. Some of these services include memory management, input/output activities, and storage management. The operating system has a special program that organizes secondary storage so that you can conveniently access information.

Application programs perform a specific task. Word processors, spreadsheets, and games are examples of application programs. The operating system is the program that runs application programs.

The Language of a Computer

When you press **A** on your keyboard the computer displays **A** on the screen, but what is actually stored inside the computer's main memory? What is the language of the computer? How does it store whatever you type on the keyboard?

Remember that a computer is an electronic device. Electrical signals are used inside the computer to process information. There are two types of electrical signals: analog and digital. **Analog signals** are continuous wave forms used to represent such things as sound. Audio tapes, for example, store data in analog signals. **Digital signals** represent information with a sequence of 0s and 1s. A 0 represents a low voltage, and a 1 represents a high voltage. Digital signals are more reliable carriers of information than analog signals and can be copied from one device to another with exact precision. You might have noticed that when you make a copy of an audio tape, the sound quality of the copy is not as good as the original tape. This is because the analog signals may not be copied with exact precision. Therefore, of the two electrical signals, the computer uses digital signals.

Because digital signals are processed inside a computer, the language of a computer, called **machine language**, is a sequence of 0s and 1s. The digit 0 or 1 is called a **binary digit**, or **bit**. Sometimes a sequence of 0s and 1s is referred to as a **binary code** or a **binary number**.

Bit: A binary digit 0 or 1.

A sequence of eight bits is called a **byte**. Moreover, 2^{10} bytes = 1,024 bytes is called a **kilobyte (KB)**. Table 1-1 summarizes the terms used to describe various numbers of bytes.

TABLE 1-1 Binary Units

Unit	Symbol	Bits/Bytes
Byte		8 bits
Kilobyte	KB	2^{10} bytes = 1,024 bytes
Megabyte	MB	1024 KB = 2^{10} KB = 2^{20} bytes = 1,048,576 bytes
Gigabyte	GB	1024 MB = 2^{10} MB = 2^{30} bytes = 1,073,741,824 bytes
Terabyte	TB	1024 GB = 2^{10} GB = 2^{40} bytes = 1,099,511,627,776 bytes

Every letter, number, or special symbol (such as * or {) on your keyboard is encoded as a sequence of bits, each having a unique representation. The most commonly used encoding scheme on personal computers is the *seven-bit* **American Standard Code for Information Interchange (ASCII)**. The ASCII data set consists of 128 characters numbered 0 through 127. That is, in the ASCII data set, the position of the first character is 0, the position of the second character is 1, and so on. In this scheme, A is encoded as the binary number 1000001. In fact, A is the 66th character in the ASCII character code, but its position is 65 because the position of the first character is 0. Furthermore, the binary number 1000001 is the binary representation of 65. The character 3 is encoded as 0110011. Note that in the ASCII character set, the position of the character 3 is 51, so the character 3 is the 52nd character in the ASCII set. It also follows that 0110011 is the binary representation of 51. For a complete list of the printable ASCII character set, refer to Appendix C.

NOTE The number system that we use in our daily life is called the **decimal system** or **base 10**. Because everything inside a computer is represented as a sequence of 0s and 1s, that is, binary numbers, the number system that a computer uses is called **binary** or **base 2**. We indicated in the preceding paragraph that the number 1000001 is the binary representation of 65. Appendix E describes how to convert a number from base 10 to base 2 and vice versa.

Inside the computer, every character is represented as a sequence of *eight* bits, that is, as a byte. Now the eight-bit binary representation of 65 is 01000001. Note that we added 0 to the left of the seven-bit representation of 65 to convert it to an eight-bit representation. Similarly, the eight-bit binary representation of 51 is 00110011.

Now ASCII is a seven-bit code. Therefore, to represent each ASCII character inside the computer, you must convert the seven-bit binary representation of an ASCII character to an eight-bit binary representation. This is accomplished by adding 0 to the left of the seven-bit ASCII encoding of a character. Hence, inside the computer, the character A is represented as 01000001, and the character 3 is represented as 00110011.

There are other encoding schemes, such as EBCDIC (used by IBM) and Unicode, which is a more recent development. EBCDIC consists of 256 characters; Unicode consists of 65,536 characters. To store a character belonging to Unicode, you need two bytes.

The Evolution of Programming Languages

The most basic language of a computer, the machine language, provides program instructions in bits. Even though most computers perform the same kinds of operations, the designers of the computer may have chosen different sets of binary codes to perform the operations. Therefore, the machine language of one machine is not necessarily the same as the machine language of another machine. The only consistency among computers is that in any modern computer, all data is stored and manipulated as binary codes.

Early computers were programmed in machine language. To see how instructions are written in machine language, suppose you want to use the equation:

```
wages = rate · hours
```

to calculate weekly wages. Further suppose that the binary code 100100 stands for load, 100110 stands for multiplication, and 100010 stands for store. In machine language, you might need the following sequence of instructions to calculate weekly wages:

```
100100 010001
100110 010010
100010 010011
```

To represent the weekly wages equation in machine language, the programmer had to remember the machine language codes for various operations. Also, to manipulate data, the programmer had to remember the locations of the data in the main memory. This need to remember specific codes made programming not only very difficult, but also error-prone.

Assembly languages were developed to make the programmer's job easier. In assembly language, an instruction is an easy-to-remember form called a **mnemonic**. For example, Table 1-2 shows some examples of instructions in assembly language and their corresponding machine language code.

TABLE 1-2 Examples of Instructions in Assembly Language and Machine Language

Assembly Language	Machine Language
LOAD	100100
STOR	100010
MULT	100110
ADD	100101
SUB	100011

Using assembly language instructions, you can write the equation to calculate the weekly wages as follows:

```
LOAD   rate
MULT   hours
STOR   wages
```

As you can see, it is much easier to write instructions in assembly language. However, a computer cannot execute assembly language instructions directly. The instructions first have to be translated into machine language. A program called an **assembler** translates the assembly language instructions into machine language.

Assembler: A program that translates a program written in assembly language into an equivalent program in machine language.

Moving from machine language to assembly language made programming easier, but a programmer was still forced to think in terms of individual machine instructions. The next step toward making programming easier was to devise **high-level languages** that were closer to natural languages, such as English, French, German, and Spanish. Basic, FORTRAN, COBOL, Pascal, C, C++, C#, and Java are all high-level languages. You will learn the high-level language C++ in this book.

In C++, you write the weekly wages equation as follows:

```
wages = rate * hours;
```

The instruction written in C++ is much easier to understand and is self-explanatory to a novice user who is familiar with basic arithmetic. As in the case of assembly language, however, the computer cannot directly execute instructions written in a high-level language. To run on a computer, these C++ instructions first need to be translated into machine language. A program called a **compiler** translates instructions written in high-level languages into machine code.

Compiler: A program that translates instructions written in a high-level language into the equivalent machine language.

A C++ Program

In Chapter 2, you will learn the basic elements and concepts of the C++ programming language to create C++ programs. In addition to giving examples to illustrate various concepts, we will also show C++ programs to clarify them. In this section, we provide an example of a C++ program. At this point, you need not be too concerned with the details of this program. You only need to know the effect of an *output* statement, which is introduced in this program.

Consider the following C++ program:

```cpp
#include <iostream>

using namespace std;

int main()
{
    cout << "My first C++ program." << endl;
    cout << "The sum of 2 and 3 = " << 5 << endl;
    cout << "7 + 8 = " << 7 + 8 << endl;

    return 0;
}
```

Sample Run: (When you compile and execute this program, the following three lines are displayed on the screen.)

```
My first C++ program.
The sum of 2 and 3 = 5
7 + 8 = 15
```

These lines are displayed by the execution of the following three statements.

```cpp
cout << "My first C++ program." << endl;
cout << "The sum of 2 and 3 = " << 5 << endl;
cout << "7 + 8 = " << 7 + 8 << endl;
```

Next we explain how this happens. Let us first consider the following statement:

```cpp
cout << "My first C++ program." << endl;
```

This is an example of a C++ *output* statement. It causes the computer to evaluate the *expression* after the pair of symbols << and display the result on the screen.

Usually, a C++ program contains various types of expressions such as arithmetic and strings. For example, 7 + 8 is an arithmetic expression. Anything in double quotes is a *string*. For example, "My first C++ program." and "7 + 8 = " are strings. Typically, a string evaluates to itself. Arithmetic expressions are evaluated according to rules of arithmetic operations, which you typically learn in an algebra course. Chapter 2 explains how arithmetic expressions and strings are formed and evaluated.

Also note that in an output statement, endl *causes the insertion point to move to the beginning of the next line.* (On the screen, the insertion point is where the cursor is.) Therefore, the preceding statement causes the system to display the following line on the screen.

```
My first C++ program.
```

Let us now consider the following statement:

```cpp
cout << "The sum of 2 and 3 = " << 5 << endl;
```

This output statement consists of two expressions. The first expression, (after the first <<), is `"The sum of 2 and 3 = "` and the second expression, (after the second <<), consists of the number 5. The expression `"The sum of 2 and 3 = "` is a string and evaluates to itself. (Notice the space after =.) The second expression, which consists of the number 5 evaluates to 5. Thus, the output of the preceding statement is:

```
The sum of 2 and 3 = 5
```

Let us now consider the following statement:

```
cout << "7 + 8 = " << 7 + 8 << endl;
```

In this output statement, the expression `"7 + 8 = "`, which is a string, evaluates to itself. Let us consider the second expression, 7 + 8. This expression consists of the numbers 7 and 8, and the C++ arithmetic operator +. Therefore, the result of the expression 7 + 8 is the sum of 7 and 8, which is 15. Thus, the output of the preceding statement is:

```
7 + 8 = 15
```

The last statement, that is,

```
return 0;
```

returns the value 0 to the operating system when the program terminates. We will elaborate on this statement in Chapter 2.

In the next chapter, until we explain how to properly construct a C++ program, we will be using output statements such as the preceding ones to explain various concepts. After finishing Chapter 2, you should be able to write C++ programs good enough to do some computations and show results.

Before leaving this chapter, let us note the following about the preceding C++ program. A C++ program is a collection of functions, one of which is the function `main`. Roughly speaking, a *function* is a set of statements whose objective is to accomplish something. The preceding program consists of the function `main`.

The first line of the program, that is,

```
#include <iostream>
```

allows us to use the (predefined object) `cout` to generate output and the (manipulator) `endl`.

The second line, which is

```
using namespace std;
```

allows you to use `cout` and `endl` without the prefix `std::`. It means that if you do not include this statement, then `cout` should be used as `std::cout` and `endl` should be used as `std::endl`. We will elaborate on this in Chapter 2.

The third line consists of the following line:

```
int main()
```

This is the heading of the function `main`. The fourth line consists of a left brace. This marks the beginning of the (body) of the function `main`. The right brace (at the last line of the program) matches this left brace and marks the end of the body of the function `main`. We will explain the meaning of the other terms, such as the ones shown in blue, later in this book. Moreover, in C++, << is an operator, called the *stream insertion operator*.

Processing a C++ Program

In the preceding sections, we discussed machine language and high-level languages and showed a C++ program. Because a computer can understand only machine language, you are ready to review the steps required to process a program written in C++.

The following steps, as shown in Figure 1-3, are necessary to process a C++ program.

1. You use a text editor to create a C++ program following the rules, or *syntax*, of the high-level language. This program is called the **source code** or **source program**. The program must be saved in a text file that has the extension `.cpp`. For example, if you saved the preceding program in the file named `FirstCPPProgram`, then its complete name is `FirstCPPProgram.cpp`.

   Source program: A program written in a high-level language.

2. The C++ program given in the preceding section contains the statement `#include <iostream>`. In a C++ program, statements that begin with the symbol `#` are called preprocessor directives. These statements are processed by a program called **preprocessor**.

3. After processing preprocessor directives, the next step is to verify that the program obeys the rules of the programming language—that is, the program is syntactically correct—and translate the program into the equivalent machine language. The *compiler* checks the source program for syntax errors and, if no error is found, translates the program into the equivalent machine language. The equivalent machine language program is called an **object program**.

   Object program: The machine language version of the high-level language program.

4. The programs that you write in a high-level language are developed using a software development kit (SDK). The SDK contains many programs that are useful in creating your program. For example, it contains the necessary code (program) to display the results of the program and several mathematical functions to make the programmer's job somewhat easier. Therefore, if certain code is already available, you can use this code rather than writing your own code. Once the program is developed and successfully compiled, you must still bring the code for the resources used from the SDK into your program to produce a final program that the computer can execute. This prewritten code (program) resides in a place called the **library**. A program

called a **linker** combines the object program with the programs from libraries.

Linker: A program that combines the object program with other programs in the library, and used in the program to create the executable code.

5. You must next load the executable program into main memory for execution. A program called a **loader** accomplishes this task.

Loader: A program that loads an executable program into main memory.

6. The final step is to execute the program.

Figure 1-3 shows how a typical C++ program is processed.

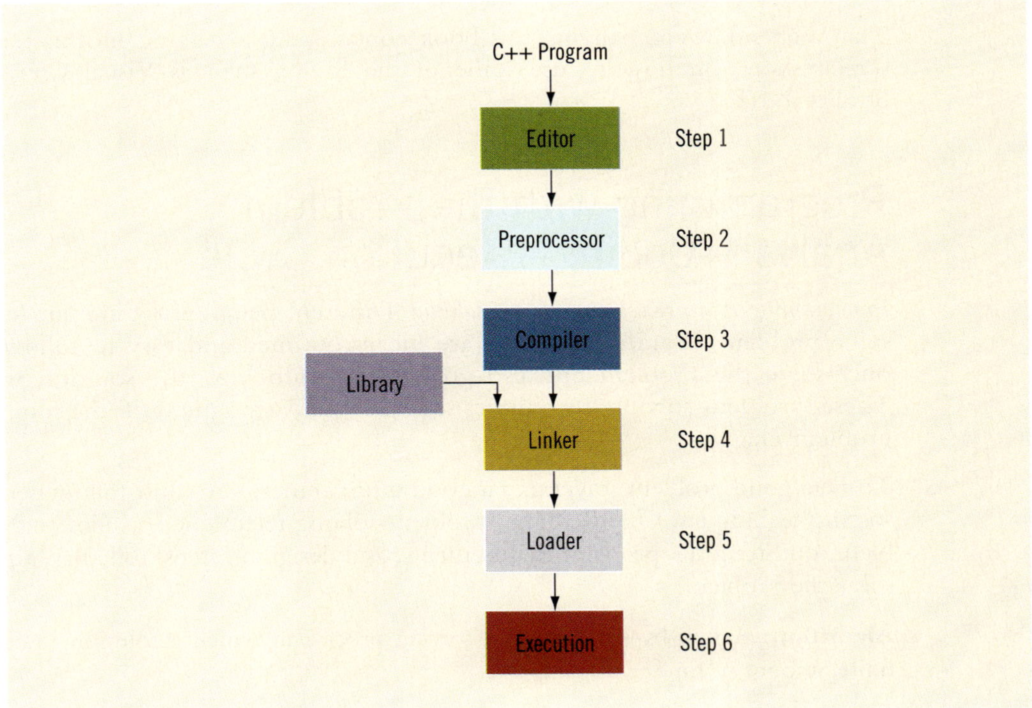

FIGURE 1-3   Processing a C++ program

As a programmer, you need to be concerned only with Step 1. That is, you must learn, understand, and master the rules of the programming language to create source programs.

As noted earlier, programs are developed using an SDK. Well-known SDKs used to create programs in the high-level language C++ include Visual C++ and Visual Studio .NET (from Microsoft), C++ Builder (from Borland), and CodeWarrior (from Metrowerks).

These SDKs contain a text editor to create the source program, a compiler to check the source program for syntax errors, a program to link the object code with the SDK resources, and a program to execute the program.

These SDKs are quite user-friendly. When you compile your program, the compiler not only identifies the syntax errors but also typically suggests how to correct them. Moreover, with just a simple command, the object code is linked with the resources used from the SDK. The command that does the linking on Visual C++ and Visual Studio .NET is **Build** or **Rebuild**; on C++ Builder, it is **Build** or **Make**; and on CodeWarrior, it is **Make**. (For further clarification regarding the use of these commands, check the documentation of these SDKs.) If the program is not yet compiled, each of these commands first compiles the program and then links and produces the executable code.

The Web site accompanying this book contains the necessary information, including screen shots, on how to use some of the SDKs, such as Visual C++ and Visual Studio .NET.

Programming with the Problem Analysis–Coding–Execution Cycle

Programming is a process of problem solving. Different people use different techniques to solve problems. Some techniques are nicely outlined and easy to follow. They not only solve the problem but also give insight into how the solution was reached. These problem-solving techniques can be easily modified if the domain of the problem changes.

To be a good problem solver and a good programmer, you must follow good problem-solving techniques. One common problem-solving technique includes analyzing a problem, outlining the problem requirements, and designing steps, called an **algorithm**, to solve the problem.

Algorithm: A step-by-step problem-solving process in which a solution is arrived at in a finite amount of time.

In a programming environment, the problem-solving process requires the following three steps:

1. Analyze the problem, outline the problem and its solution requirements, and design an algorithm to solve the problem.
2. Implement the algorithm in a programming language, such as C++, and verify that the algorithm works.
3. Maintain the program by using and modifying it if the problem domain changes.

Figure 1-4 summarizes this three-step programming process.

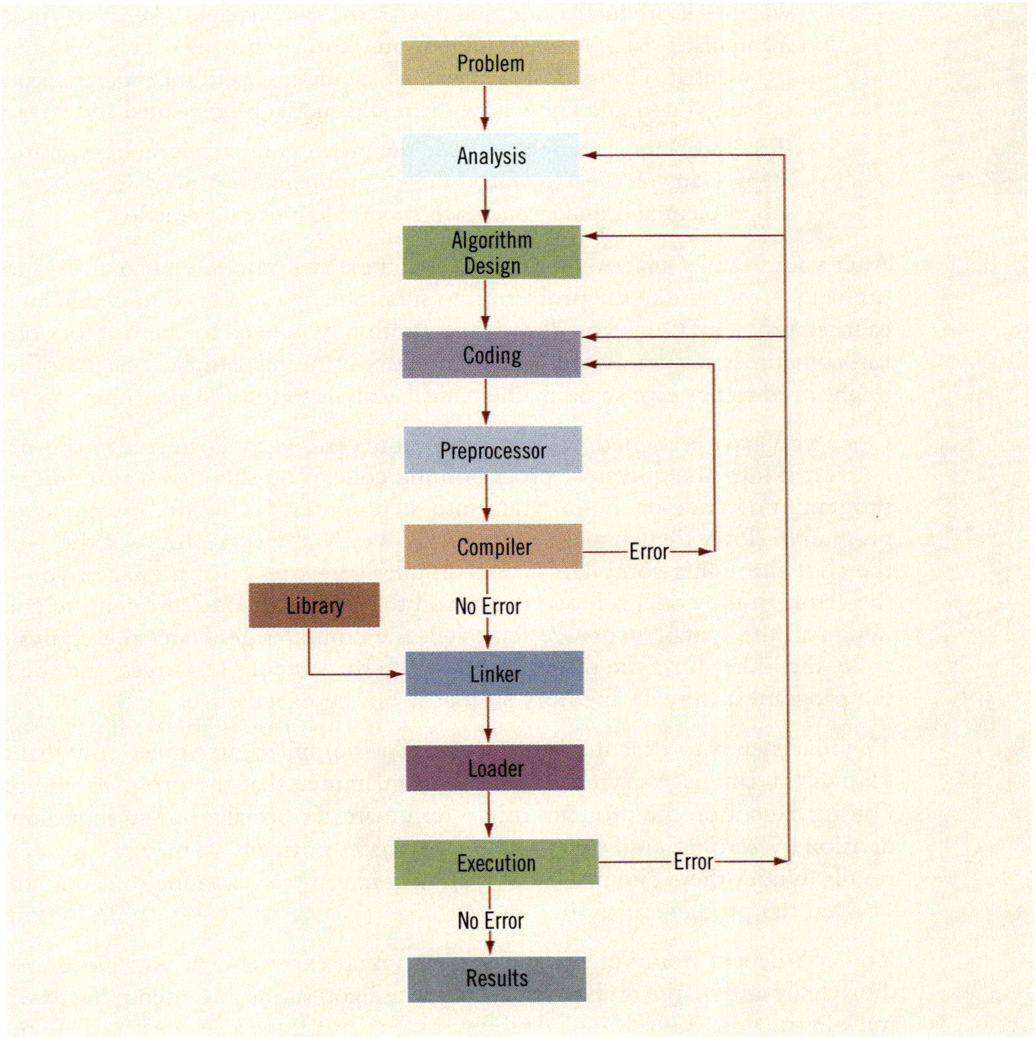

FIGURE 1-4   Problem analysis–coding–execution cycle

To develop a program to solve a problem, you start by analyzing the problem. You then design the algorithm; write the program instructions in a high-level language, or code the program; and enter the program into a computer system.

Analyzing the problem is the first and most important step. This step requires you to do the following:

1.   Thoroughly understand the problem.

2.   Understand the problem requirements. Requirements can include whether the program requires interaction with the user, whether it manipulates data,

whether it produces output, and what the output looks like. If the program manipulates data, the programmer must know what the data is and how it is represented. That is, you need to look at sample data. If the program produces output, you should know how the results should be generated and formatted.

3. If the problem is complex, divide the problem into subproblems and repeat Steps 1 and 2. That is, for complex problems, you need to analyze each subproblem and understand each subproblem's requirements.

After you carefully analyze the problem, the next step is to design an algorithm to solve the problem. If you broke the problem into subproblems, you need to design an algorithm for each subproblem. Once you design an algorithm, you need to check it for correctness. You can sometimes test an algorithm's correctness by using sample data. At other times, you might need to perform some mathematical analysis to test the algorithm's correctness.

Once you have designed the algorithm and verified its correctness, the next step is to convert it into an equivalent programming code. You then use a text editor to enter the programming code or the program into a computer. Next, you must make sure that the program follows the language's syntax. To verify the correctness of the syntax, you run the code through a compiler. If the compiler generates error messages, you must identify the errors in the code, remove them, and then run the code through the compiler again. When all the syntax errors are removed, the compiler generates the equivalent machine code, the linker links the machine code with the system's resources, and the loader places the program into main memory so that it can be executed.

The final step is to execute the program. The compiler guarantees only that the program follows the language's syntax. It does not guarantee that the program will run correctly. During execution the program might terminate abnormally due to logical errors, such as division by zero. Even if the program terminates normally, it may still generate erroneous results. Under these circumstances, you may have to re-examine the code, the algorithm, or even the problem analysis.

You will benefit from your overall programming experience if you spend enough time to thoroughly analyze the problem and design the algorithm before attempting to write programming instructions. Usually, you do this work on paper using a pen or pencil. Taking this careful approach to programming has a number of advantages. It is much easier to discover errors in a program that is well analyzed and well designed. Furthermore, a carefully analyzed and designed program is much easier to follow and modify. Even the most experienced programmers spend a considerable amount of time analyzing a problem and designing an algorithm.

Throughout this book, you will not only learn the rules of writing programs in C++, but you will also learn problem-solving techniques. Each chapter provides several Programming Examples that discuss programming problems. These Programming Examples teach techniques of how to analyze and solve problems, design algorithms, code the algorithms into C++, and also help you understand the concepts discussed in the chapter. To gain the full benefit of this book, we recommend that you work through the Programming Examples at the end of each chapter.

Next, we provide examples of various problem-analysis and algorithm-design techniques.

EXAMPLE 1-1

In this example, we design an algorithm to find the perimeter and area of a rectangle.

To find the perimeter and area of a rectangle, you need to know the rectangle's length and width.

The perimeter and area of the rectangle are then given by the following formulas:

```
perimeter = 2 · (length + width)
area = length · width
```

The algorithm to find the perimeter and area of the rectangle is:

1. Get the length of the rectangle.
2. Get the width of the rectangle.
3. Find the perimeter using the following equation:

   ```
   perimeter = 2 · (length + width)
   ```

4. Find the area using the following equation:

   ```
   area = length · width
   ```

EXAMPLE 1-2

In this example, we design an algorithm that calculates the sales tax and the price of an item sold in a particular state.

The sales tax is calculated as follows: The state's portion of the sales tax is 4% and the city's portion of the sales tax is 1.5%. If the item is a luxury item, such as a car over $50,000, then there is a 10% luxury tax.

To calculate the price of the item, we need to calculate the state's portion of the sales tax, the city's portion of the sales tax, and, if it is a luxury item, the luxury tax. Suppose `salePrice` denotes the selling price of the item, `stateSalesTax` denotes the state's sales tax, `citySalesTax` denotes the city's sales tax, `luxuryTax` denotes the luxury tax, `salesTax` denotes the total sales tax, and `amountDue` the final price of the item.

To calculate the sales tax, we must know the selling price of the item and whether the item is a luxury item.

The `stateSalesTax` and `citySalesTax` can be calculated using the following formulas:

```
stateSalesTax = salePrice · 0.04
citySalesTax = salePrice · 0.015
```

Next, you can determine `luxuryTax` as follows:

```
if (item is a luxury item)
    luxuryTax = salePrice · 0.1
otherwise
    luxuryTax = 0
```

Next, you can determine `salesTax` as follows:

```
salesTax = stateSalesTax +  citySalesTax + luxuryTax
```

Finally, you can calculate `amountDue` as follows:

```
amountDue = salePrice + salesTax
```

The algorithm to determine `salesTax` and `amountDue` is, therefore:

1. Get the selling price of the item.

2. Determine whether the item is a luxury item.

3. Find the state's portion of the sales tax using the formula:

   ```
   stateSalesTax = salePrice · 0.04
   ```

4. Find the city's portion of the sales tax using the formula:

   ```
   citySalesTax = salePrice · 0.015
   ```

5. Find the luxury tax using the following formulas:

   ```
   if (item is a luxury item)
       luxuryTax = salePrice · 0.1
   otherwise
       luxuryTax = 0
   ```

6. Find `salesTax` using the formula:

   ```
   salesTax = stateSalesTax + citySalesTax + luxuryTax
   ```

7. Find `amountDue` using the formula:

   ```
   amountDue = salePrice + salesTax
   ```

EXAMPLE 1-3

In this example, we design an algorithm that calculates the monthly paycheck of a salesperson at a local department store.

Every salesperson has a base salary. The salesperson also receives a bonus at the end of each month, based on the following criteria: If the salesperson has been with the store for five years or less, the bonus is $10 for each year that he or she has worked there. If the salesperson has been with the store for more than five years, the bonus is $20 for each year that he or she has worked there. The salesperson can earn an additional bonus as follows: If the total sales made by the salesperson for the month are more than $5,000 but less than $10,000, he or she receives a 3% commission on the sale. If the total sales made by the salesperson for the month are at least $10,000, he or she receives a 6% commission on the sale.

To calculate a salesperson's monthly paycheck, you need to know the base salary, the number of years that the salesperson has been with the company, and the total sales made by the salesperson for that month. Suppose `baseSalary` denotes the base salary, `noOfServiceYears` denotes the number of years that the salesperson has been with the store, `bonus` denotes the bonus, `totalSales` denotes the total sales made by the salesperson for the month, and `additionalBonus` denotes the additional bonus.

You can determine the bonus as follows:

```
if (noOfServiceYears is less than or equal to five)
    bonus = 10 · noOfServiceYears
otherwise
    bonus = 20 · noOfServiceYears
```

Next, you can determine the additional bonus of the salesperson as follows:

```
if (totalSales is less than 5000)
    additionalBonus = 0
otherwise
    if (totalSales is greater than or equal to 5000 and
                    totalSales is less than 10000)
        additionalBonus = totalSales · (0.03)
    otherwise
        additionalBonus = totalSales · (0.06)
```

Following the above discussion, you can now design the algorithm to calculate a salesperson's monthly paycheck:

1. Get `baseSalary`.

2. Get `noOfServiceYears`.

3. Calculate bonus using the following formula:

   ```
   if (noOfServiceYears is less than or equal to five)
       bonus = 10 · noOfServiceYears
   otherwise

   bonus = 20 · noOfServiceYears
   ```

4. Get `totalSales`.

5. Calculate `additionalBonus` using the following formula:

   ```
   if (totalSales is less than 5000)
       additionalBonus = 0
   otherwise
     if (totalSales is greater than or equal to 5000 and
           totalSales is less than 10000)
        additionalBonus = totalSales · (0.03)
     otherwise
        additionalBonus = totalSales · (0.06)
   ```

6. Calculate `payCheck` using the equation:

```
payCheck = baseSalary + bonus + additionalBonus
```

EXAMPLE 1-4

In this example, we design an algorithm to play a number-guessing game.

The objective is to randomly generate an integer greater than or equal to 0 and less than 100. Then prompt the player (user) to guess the number. If the player guesses the number correctly, output an appropriate message. Otherwise, check whether the guessed number is less than the random number. If the guessed number is less than the random number generated, output the message, "Your guess is lower than the number. Guess again!"; otherwise, output the message, "Your guess is higher than the number. Guess again!". Then prompt the player to enter another number. The player is prompted to guess the random number until the player enters the correct number.

The first step is to generate a random number, as described above. C++ provides the means to do so, which is discussed in Chapter 5. Suppose `num` stands for the random number and `guess` stands for the number guessed by the player.

After the player enters the `guess`, you can compare the `guess` with the random number as follows:

```
if (guess is equal to num)
   Print "You guessed the correct number."
otherwise
  if guess is less than num
     Print "Your guess is lower than the number. Guess again!"
otherwise
     Print "Your guess is higher than the number. Guess again!"
```

You can now design an algorithm as follows:

1. Generate a random number and call it `num`.

2. *Repeat* the following steps until the player has guessed the correct number:

   a. Prompt the player to enter `guess`.

   b.

   ```
   if (guess is equal to num)
       Print "You guessed the correct number."
   otherwise
     if guess is less than num
        Print "Your guess is lower than the number. Guess again!"
   otherwise
        Print "Your guess is higher than the number. Guess again!"
   ```

In Chapter 5, we use this algorithm to write a C++ program to play guessing the number game.

EXAMPLE 1-5

There are 10 students in a class. Each student has taken five tests and each test is worth 100 points. We want to design an algorithm to calculate the grade for each student, as well as the class average. The grade is assigned as follows: If the average test score is greater than or equal to 90, the grade is **A**; if the average test score is greater than or equal to 80 and less than 90, the grade is **B**; if the average test score is greater than or equal to 70 and less than 80, the grade is **C**; if the average test score is greater than or equal to 60 and less than 70, the grade is **D**; otherwise the grade is **F**. Note that the data consists of students' names and their test scores.

This is a problem that can be divided into subproblems as follows: There are five tests, so you design an algorithm to find the average test score. Next, you design an algorithm to determine the grade. The two subproblems are to determine the average test score and to determine the grade.

Let us first design an algorithm to determine the average test score. To find the average test score, add the five test scores and then divide the sum by 5. Therefore, the algorithm is:

1.   Get the five test scores.

2.   Add the five test scores. Suppose **sum** stands for the sum of the test scores.

3.   Suppose average stands for the **average** test score. Then:

    average = sum / 5;

Next, you design an algorithm to determine the grade. Suppose **grade** stands for the grade assigned to a student. The following algorithm determines the grade:

```
if average is greater than or equal to 90
    grade = A
otherwise
  if average is greater than or equal to 80 and less than 90
    grade = B
otherwise
  if average is greater than or equal to 70 and less than 80
    grade = C
otherwise
  if average is greater than or equal to 60 and less than 70
    grade = D
otherwise
    grade = F
```

You can use the solutions of these subproblems to design the main algorithm as follows: (Suppose **totalAverage** stands for the sum of the averages of each student's test average.)

1.   **totalAverage = 0;**

2.   *Repeat* the following steps for each student in the class:

    a.   Get student's name.

    b.   Use the algorithm as discussed above to find the average test score.

    c.   Use the algorithm as discussed above to find the grade

    d.   Update `totalAverage` by adding current student's average test score.

3.   Determine the class average as follows:

```
classAverage = totalAverage / 10
```

A programming exercise in Chapter 7 asks you to write a C++ program to determine the average test score and grade for each student in a class.

Programming Methodologies

Two popular approaches to programming design are the structured approach and the object-oriented approach, which are outlined below.

Structured Programming

Dividing a problem into smaller subproblems is called **structured design**. Each subproblem is then analyzed and a solution is obtained to solve the subproblem. The solutions to all the subproblems are then combined to solve the overall problem. This process of implementing a structured design is called **structured programming**. The structured-design approach is also known as **top-down design**, **stepwise refinement**, and **modular programming**.

Object-Oriented Programming

Object-oriented design (OOD) is a widely used programming methodology. In OOD, the first step in the problem-solving process is to identify the components called objects, which form the basis of the solution, and to determine how these objects interact with one another. For example, suppose you want to write a program that automates the video rental process for a local video store. The two main objects in this problem are the video and the customer.

After identifying the objects, the next step is to specify for each object the relevant data and possible operations to be performed on that data. For example, for a video object, the *data* might include:

- movie name
- starring actors
- producer
- production company
- number of copies in stock

Some of the *operations* on a video object might include:

- checking the name of the movie
- reducing the number of copies in stock by one after a copy is rented
- incrementing the number of copies in stock by one after a customer returns a particular video

This illustrates that each object consists of data and operations on that data. An object combines data and operations on the data into a single unit. In OOD, the final program is a collection of interacting objects. A programming language that implements OOD is called an **object-oriented programming (OOP)** language. You will learn about the many advantages of OOD in later chapters.

Because an object consists of data and operations on that data, before you can design and use objects, you need to learn how to represent data in computer memory, how to manipulate data, and how to implement operations. In Chapter 2, you will learn the basic data types of C++ and discover how to represent and manipulate data in computer memory. Chapter 3 discusses how to input data into a C++ program and output the results generated by a C++ program.

To create operations, you write algorithms and implement them in a programming language. Because a data element in a complex program usually has many operations, to separate operations from each other and to use them effectively and in a convenient manner, you use functions to implement algorithms. After a brief introduction in Chapters 2 and 3, you will learn the details of functions in Chapters 6 and 7. Certain algorithms require that a program make decisions, a process called selection. Other algorithms might require certain statements to be repeated until certain conditions are met, a process called repetition. Still other algorithms might require both selection and repetition. You will learn about selection and repetition mechanisms, called control structures, in Chapters 4 and 5. Also, in Chapter 9, using a mechanism called an array, you will learn how to manipulate data when data items are of the same type, such as items in a list of sales figures.

Finally, to work with objects, you need to know how to combine data and operations on the data into a single unit. In C++, the mechanism that allows you to combine data and operations on the data into a single unit is called a class. You will learn how classes work, how to work with classes, and how to create classes in the chapter Classes and Data Abstraction (later in this book).

As you can see, you need to learn quite a few things before working with the OOD methodology. To make this learning easier and more effective, this book purposely divides control structures into two chapters (4 and 5) and user-defined functions into two chapters (6 and 7).

For some problems, the structured approach to program design will be very effective. Other problems will be better addressed by OOD. For example, if a problem requires manipulating sets of numbers with mathematical functions, you might use the structured design approach and outline the steps required to obtain the solution. The C++ library supplies a wealth of functions that you can use effectively to manipulate numbers. On the other hand, if you want to write a program that would make a candy machine operational, the OOD approach is more effective. C++ was designed especially to implement OOD. Furthermore, *OOD works well and is used in conjunction with structured design.*

Both the structured design and OOD approaches require that you master the basic components of a programming language to be an effective programmer. In Chapters 2 to 9, you will learn the basic components of C++, such as data types, input/output, control structures, user-defined functions, and array, required by either type of programming. We illustrate how these concepts work using the structured programming approach. Starting with the chapter Classes and Data Abstraction, we use the OOD approach.

ANSI/ISO Standard C++

The programming language C++ evolved from C and was designed by Bjarne Stroustrup at Bell Laboratories in the early 1980s. From the early 1980s through the early 1990s, several C++ compilers were available. Even though the fundamental features of C++ in all compilers were mostly the same, the C++ language, referred to in this book as Standard C++, was evolving in slightly different ways in different compilers. As a consequence, C++ programs were not always portable from one compiler to another.

To address this problem, in the early 1990s a joint committee of the American National Standard Institution (ANSI) and International Standard Organization (ISO) was established to standardize the syntax of C++. In mid-1998, ANSI/ISO C++ language standards were approved. Most of today's compilers comply with this new standard.

This book focuses on the syntax of C++ as approved by ANSI/ISO, referred to as ANSI/ISO Standard C++.

QUICK REVIEW

1. A computer is an electronic device capable of performing arithmetic and logical operations.

2. A computer system has two components: hardware and software.

3. The central processing unit (CPU) and the main memory are examples of hardware components.

4. The control unit (CU) controls a program's overall execution. It is one of several components of the CPU.

5. The arithmetic logic unit (ALU) is the component of the CPU that performs arithmetic and logical operations.

6. The instructor register (IR) holds the instruction currently being executed.

7. The program counter (PC) points to the next instruction to be executed.

8. All programs must be brought into main memory before they can be executed.

9. When the power is switched off, everything in main memory is lost.

10. Secondary storage provides permanent storage for information. Hard disks, flash drives, floppy disks, ZIP disks, CD-ROMs, and tapes are examples of secondary storage.

11. Input to the computer is done via an input device. Two common input devices are the keyboard and the mouse.

12. The computer sends its output to an output device, such as the computer screen.

13. Software are programs run by the computer.

14. The operating system monitors the overall activity of the computer and provides services.

15. The most basic language of a computer is a sequence of 0s and 1s called machine language. Every computer directly understands its own machine language.

16. A bit is a binary digit, 0 or 1.

17. A byte is a sequence of eight bits.

18. A sequence of 0s and 1s is referred to as a binarycode or a binary number.

19. One kilobyte (KB) is 2^{10} bytes = 1,024 bytes; one megabyte (MB) is 2^{20} bytes = 1,048,576 bytes; one gigabyte (GB) is 2^{30} bytes = 1,073,741,824 bytes; and one terabyte (TB) is 2^{40} bytes = 1,099,511,627,776 bytes.

20. Assembly language uses easy-to-remember instructions called mnemonics.

21. Assemblers are programs that translate a program written in assembly language into machine language.

22. Compilers are programs that translate a program written in a high-level language into machine code, called object code.

23. A linker links the object code with other programs provided by the software development kit (SDK) and used in the program to produce executable code.

24. Typically, six steps are needed to execute a C++ program: edit, preprocessor, compile, link, load, and execute.

25. A loader transfers executable code into main memory.

26. An algorithm is a step-by-step problem-solving process in which a solution is arrived at in a finite amount of time.

27. The problem-solving process has three steps: analyze the problem and design an algorithm, implement the algorithm in a programming language, and maintain the program.

28. Programs written using the structured design approach are easier to understand, easier to test and debug, and easier to modify.

29. In structured design, a problem is divided into smaller subproblems. Each subproblem is solved, and the solutions to all the subproblems are then combined to solve the problem.

30. In object-oriented design (OOD), a program is a collection of interacting objects.

31. An object consists of data and operations on those data.

32. The ANSI/ISO Standard C++ syntax was approved in mid-1998.

EXERCISES

1. Mark the following statements as true or false.

   a. Assembly language uses mnemonics for its instructions.

   b. A compiler translates an assembly language program into machine code.

   c. The arithmetic logic unit performs arithmetic operations and, if an error is found, it outputs the logical errors.

   d. A loader loads the object code from main memory into the CPU for execution.

   e. Processing a C++ program includes six steps.

   f. The CPU functions under the control of the control unit.

   g. RAM stands for readily available memory.

   h. A program written in a high-level programming language is called a source program.

   i. The operating system is the first program loaded into the computer when the power is turned on.

   j. The first step in the problem-solving process is to analyze the problem.

2. Name some components of the central processing unit.

3. What is the function of the control unit?

4. Name two input devices.

5. Name two output devices.

6. Why is secondary storage needed?

7. Why do you need to translate a program written in a high-level language into machine language?

8. Why would you prefer to write a program in a high-level language rather than a machine language?

9. What are the advantages of problem analysis and algorithm design over directly writing a program in a high-level language?

10. What is the output of the following C++ program?

```cpp
#include <iostream>
using namespace std;

int main()
{
    cout << "This is Exercise 10." << endl;
    cout << "In C++, the multiplication symbol is *."
         << endl;
    cout << "2 + 3 * 5 = " << 2 + 3 * 5 << endl;

    return 0;
}
```

11. Design an algorithm to find the weighted average of four test scores. The four test scores and their respective weights are given in the following format:

```
testscore1 weight1
...
```

For example, a sample data is as follows:

```
75 0.20
95 0.35
85 0.15
65 0.30
```

12. A salesperson leaves his home every Monday and returns every Friday. He travels by company car. Each day on the road, the salesperson records the amount of gasoline put in the car. Given the starting odometer reading (that is, the odometer reading before he leaves on Monday) and the ending odometer reading (the odometer reading after he returns home on Friday), design an algorithm to find the average miles per gallon. Sample data is as follows:

```
68723 71289 15.75 16.30 10.95 20.65 30.00
```

13. To make a profit, the prices of the items sold in a furniture store are marked up by 60%. Design an algorithm to find the selling price of an item sold at the furniture store. What information do you need to find the selling price?

14. Suppose a, b, and c denote the lengths of the sides of a triangle. Then the area of the triangle can be calculated using the formula:

$$\sqrt{s(s-a)(s-b)(s-c)},$$

where $s = (1/2)(a + b + c)$. Design an algorithm that uses this formula to find the area of a triangle. What information do you need to find the area?

15. A triangle ABC is inscribed in a circle, that is, the vertices of the triangle are on the circumference of the circle. Suppose the triangle ABC divides the circumference into lengths of a, b, and c inches. Design an algorithm that asks the user to specify the values of a, b, and c and then calculates the radius of the circle. Note that if r is the radius of the circle, then $2\pi r = a + b + c$.

16. The cost of an international call from New York to New Delhi is calculated as follows: Connection fee, \$1.99; \$2.00 for the first three minutes; and \$0.45 for each additional minute. Design an algorithm that asks the user to enter the number of minutes the call lasted. The algorithm then uses the number of minutes to calculate the amount due.

17. You are given a list of students' names and their test scores. Design an algorithm that does the following:

    a. Calculates the average test scores.

    b. Determines and prints the names of all the students whose test score is below the average test score.

    c.   Determines the highest test score.

    d.   Prints the names of all the students whose test score is the same as the highest test score.

(You must divide this problem into subproblems as follows: The first subproblem determines the average test score. The second subproblem determines and prints the names of all the students whose test score is below the average test score. The third subproblem determines the highest test score. The fourth subproblem prints the names of all the students whose test score is the same as the highest test score. The main algorithm combines the solutions of the subproblems.)

BASIC ELEMENTS OF C++

- Become familiar with the basic components of a C++ program, including functions, special symbols, and identifiers
- Explore simple data types
- Discover how to use arithmetic operators
- Examine how a program evaluates arithmetic expressions
- Learn what an assignment statement is and what it does
- Become familiar with the `string` data type
- Discover how to input data into memory using input statements
- Become familiar with the use of increment and decrement operators
- Examine ways to output results using output statements
- Learn how to use preprocessor directives and why they are necessary
- Explore how to properly structure a program, including using comments to document a program
- Learn how to write a C++ program

In this chapter, you will learn the basics of C++. As your objective is to learn the C++ programming language, two questions naturally arise. First, what is a computer program? Second, what is programming? A **computer program** or a program is a sequence of statements whose objective is to accomplish a task. **Programming** is a process of planning and creating a program. These two definitions tell the truth, but not the whole truth, about programming. It may very well take an entire book to give a good and satisfactory definition of programming. You might gain a better grasp of the nature of programming from an analogy, so let us turn to a topic about which almost everyone has some knowledge—cooking. A recipe is also a program, and everyone with some cooking experience can agree on the following:

1. It is usually easier to follow a recipe than to create one.
2. There are good recipes and there are bad recipes.
3. Some recipes are easy to follow and some are not easy to follow.
4. Some recipes produce reliable results and some do not.
5. You must have some knowledge of how to use cooking tools to follow a recipe to completion.
6. To create good new recipes, you must have much knowledge and understanding of cooking.

These same six points are also true about programming. Let us take the cooking analogy one step further. Suppose you need to teach someone how to become a chef. How would you go about it? Would you first introduce the person to good food, hoping that a taste for good food develops? Would you have the person follow recipe after recipe in the hope that some of it rubs off? Or would you first teach the use of tools and the nature of ingredients, the foods and spices, and explain how they fit together? Just as there is disagreement about how to teach cooking, there is disagreement about how to teach programming.

Learning a programming language is like learning to become a chef or learning to play a musical instrument. All three require direct interaction with the tools. You cannot become a good chef or even a poor chef just by reading recipes. Similarly, you cannot become a player by reading books about musical instruments. The same is true of programming. You must have a fundamental knowledge of the language, and you must test your programs on the computer to make sure that each program does what it is supposed to do.

The Basics of a C++ Program

A C++ program is a collection of one or more subprograms, called functions. Roughly speaking, a **subprogram** or a **function** is a collection of statements, and when it is activated, or executed, it accomplishes something. Some functions, called **predefined** or **standard** functions, are already written and are provided as part of the system. But to accomplish most tasks, programmers must learn to write their own functions.

Every C++ program has a function called `main`. Thus, if a C++ program has only one function, it must be the function `main`. Until Chapter 6, other than using some of the predefined functions, you will mainly deal with the function `main`. By the end of this chapter, you shall have learned how to write the function `main`.

The following is an example of a C++ program. At this point, you should not be concerned with the details of the program.

EXAMPLE 2-1

The following is a sample C++ program.

```cpp
#include <iostream>

using namespace std;

int main()
{
    cout << "Welcome to C++ Programming." << endl;

    return 0;
}
```

If you execute this program, it will print the following line on the screen:

```
Welcome to C++ Programming.
```

If you have never seen a program written in a programming language, the C++ program in Example 2-1 may look like a foreign language. To make meaningful sentences in a foreign language, you must learn its alphabet, words, and grammar. The same is true of a programming language. To write meaningful programs, you must learn the programming language's special symbols, words, and syntax rules. The **syntax rules** tell you which statements (instructions) are legal, or accepted by the programming language, and which are not. You must also learn **semantic rules**, which determine the meaning of the instructions. The programming language's rules, symbols, and special words enable you to write programs to solve problems. The syntax rules determine which instructions are valid.

Programming language: A set of rules, symbols, and special words.

In the remainder of this section, you will learn about some of the special symbols of a C++ program. Additional special symbols are introduced as other concepts are encountered in later chapters. Similarly, syntax and semantic rules are introduced and discussed throughout the book.

The smallest individual unit of a program written in any language is called a **token**. C++'s tokens are divided into special symbols, word symbols, and identifiers, and are described in the following sections.

Special Symbols

Following are some of the special symbols:

```
+      -      *      /
.      ;      ?      ,
<=     !=     ==     >=
```

The first row includes mathematical symbols for addition, subtraction, multiplication, and division. The second row consists of punctuation marks taken from English grammar. Note that the comma is also a special symbol. In C++, commas are used to separate items in a list. Semicolons are used to end a C++ statement. Note that a blank, which is not shown above, is also a special symbol. You create a blank symbol by pressing the space bar (only once) on the keyboard. The third row consists of tokens made up of two characters, but which are regarded as a single symbol. No character can come between the two characters in the token, not even a blank.

Word Symbols

A second category of tokens is word symbols. Some of the word symbols include the following:

```
int, float, double, char, const, void, return
```

Word symbols are also called **reserved words**, or **keywords**. The letters that make up a reserved word are always lowercase. Like the special symbols, each is considered to be a single symbol. Furthermore, word symbols cannot be redefined within any program; that is, they cannot be used for anything other than their intended use. For a complete list of reserved words, see Appendix A.

NOTE Throughout this book, reserved words are shown in blue.

Identifiers

A third category of tokens is identifiers. Identifiers are names of things that appear in programs, such as variables, constants, and functions. Some identifiers are predefined; others are defined by the user. All identifiers must obey C++'s rules for identifiers.

Identifier: A C++ identifier consists of letters, digits, and the underscore character (_) and must begin with a letter or underscore.

Identifiers can be made of only letters, digits, and the underscore character; no other symbols are permitted to form an identifier.

NOTE C++ is case sensitive—uppercase and lowercase letters are considered different. Thus, the identifier **NUMBER** is not the same as the identifier `number`. Similarly, the identifiers **X** and `x` are different.

In C++, identifiers can be of any length. In actuality, however, some compilers may not distinguish between identifiers that differ only beyond that system's maximum significant number of characters. (Check your system's documentation for restrictions on the length of identifiers.) For example, if only the first seven characters of the following two identifiers were distinguishable, they would be regarded as the same:

```
program1
program2
```

Two predefined identifiers that you will encounter frequently are `cout`, which is used when generating output, and `cin`, which is used to input data. Unlike reserved words, predefined identifiers can be redefined, but it would not be wise to do so.

EXAMPLE 2-2

The following are legal identifiers in C++:

```
first
conversion
payRate
counter1
```

Table 2-1 shows some illegal identifiers and explains why they are illegal.

TABLE 2-1   Examples of Illegal Identifiers

Illegal Identifier	Description
`employee Salary`	There can be no space between `employee` and `Salary`.
`Hello!`	The exclamation mark cannot be used in an identifier.
`one + two`	The symbol + cannot be used in an identifier.
`2nd`	An identifier cannot begin with a digit.

NOTE Compiler vendors usually begin certain identifiers with an underscore (_). When the linker links the object program with the system resources provided by the software development kit (SDK), certain errors could occur. Therefore, it is advisable that you should not begin identifiers in your program with an underscore (_).

Data Types

The objective of a C++ program is to manipulate data. Different programs manipulate different data. A program designed to calculate an employee's paycheck will add, subtract, multiply, and divide numbers, and some of the numbers might represent hours worked and pay rate. Similarly, a program designed to alphabetize a class list will manipulate names. You wouldn't expect a cherry pie recipe to help you bake cookies. Similarly, you wouldn't use a program designed to perform arithmetic calculations to manipulate alphabetic characters. Furthermore, you wouldn't multiply or subtract names. Reflecting these kinds of underlying differences, C++ categorizes data into different types, and only certain operations can be performed on particular types of data. Although at first it may seem confusing, by being so type conscious, C++ has built-in checks to guard against errors.

Data type: A set of values together with a set of operations.

C++ data types fall into the following three categories and are illustrated in Figure 2-1:

1.   Simple data type

2.   Structured data type

3.   Pointers

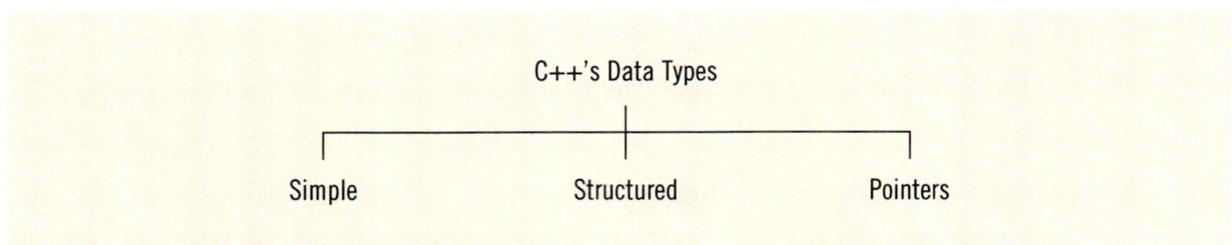

FIGURE 2-1   C++ data types

For the next few chapters, you will be concerned only with simple data types.

Simple Data Types

The simple data type is the fundamental data type in C++ because it becomes a building block for the structured data type, which you start learning about in Chapter 9. There are three categories of simple data:

1.   **Integral**, which is a data type that deals with integers, or numbers without a decimal part

2.   **Floating-point**, which is a data type that deals with decimal numbers

3.   **Enumeration type**, which is a user-defined data type

Figure 2-2 illustrates these three data types.

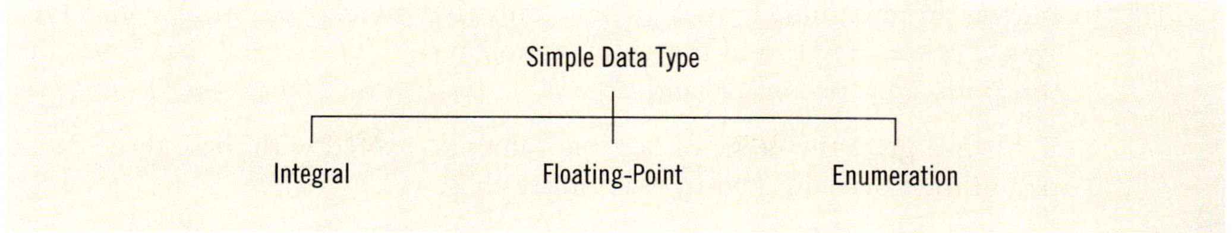

FIGURE 2-2 Simple data types

NOTE The enumeration type is C++'s method for allowing programmers to create their own simple data types. This data type will be discussed in Chapter 8.

Integral data types are further classified into nine categories, as shown in Figure 2-3.

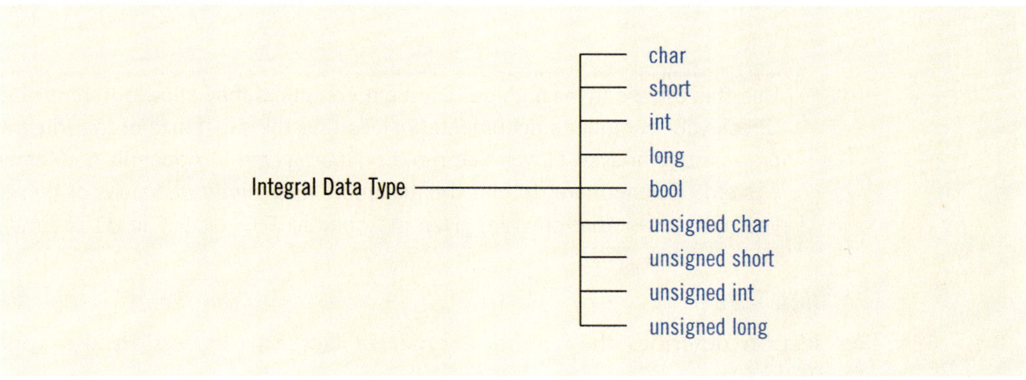

FIGURE 2-3 Integral data types

Why are there so many categories of the same data type? Every data type has a different set of values associated with it. For example, the **char** data type is used to represent integers between −128 and 127. The **int** data type is used to represent integers between −2147483648 and 2147483647, and the data type **short** is used to represent integers between −32768 and 32767.

Which data type you use depends on how big a number your program needs to deal with. In the early days of programming, computers and main memory were very expensive. Only a small amount of memory was available to execute programs and manipulate the data. As a result, programmers had to optimize the use of memory. Because writing a program and making it work is already a complicated process, not having to worry about the size of the memory makes for one less thing to think about. Thus, to effectively use memory, a programmer can look at the type of data used in a program and figure out which data type to use.

Newer programming languages have only five categories of simple data types: `integer`, `real`, `char`, `bool`, and the enumeration type. The integral data types that are used in this book are `int`, `bool`, and `char`.

Table 2-2 gives the range of possible values associated with these three data types and the size of memory allocated to manipulate these values.

TABLE 2-2   Values and Memory Allocation for Three Simple Data Types

Data Type	Values	Storage (in bytes)
int	−2147483648 to 2147483647	4
bool	**true** and **false**	1
char	−128 to 127	1

NOTE   Use this table only as a guide. Different compilers may allow different ranges of values. Check your compiler's documentation. To find the exact size of the integral data types on a particular system, you can run a program given in Appendix G (Memory Size of a System). Furthermore, to find the maximum and minimum values of these data types, you can run another program given in Appendix F (Header File `climits`).

`int` DATA TYPE

This section describes the `int` data type. In fact, this discussion also applies to other integral data types.

Integers in C++, as in mathematics, are numbers such as the following:

```
-6728, -67, 0, 78, 36782, +763
```

Note the following two rules from these examples:

1. Positive integers do not need a + sign in front of them.
2. No commas are used within an integer. Recall that in C++, commas are used to separate items in a list. So `36,782` would be interpreted as two integers: `36` and `782`.

`bool` DATA TYPE

The data type **bool** has only two values: **true** and **false**. Also, **true** and **false** are called the *logical (Boolean) values*. The central purpose of this data type is to manipulate logical (Boolean) expressions. Logical (Boolean) expressions will be formally defined and discussed in detail in Chapter 4. In C++, **bool**, **true**, and **false** are reserved words.

`char` DATA TYPE

The data type `char` is the smallest integral data type. In addition to dealing with small numbers (−128 to 127), the `char` data type is used to represent characters—that is, letters, digits, and special symbols. Thus, the `char` data type can represent every key on your keyboard. When using the `char` data type, you enclose each character represented within single quotation marks. Examples of values belonging to the `char` data type include the following:

```
'A', 'a', '0', '*', '+', '$', '&', ' '
```

Note that a blank space is a character and is written as `' '`, with a space between the single quotation marks.

The data type `char` allows only one symbol to be placed between the single quotation marks. Thus, the value `'abc'` is not of the type `char`. Furthermore, even though `'!='`and similar special symbols are considered to be one symbol, they are not regarded as possible values of the data type `char`. All the individual symbols located on the keyboard that are printable may be considered as possible values of the `char` data type.

Several different character data sets are currently in use. The most common are the American Standard Code for Information Interchange (ASCII) and Extended Binary-Coded Decimal Interchange Code (EBCDIC). The ASCII character set has 128 values. The EBCDIC character set has 256 values and was created by IBM. Both character sets are described in Appendix C.

Each of the 128 values of the ASCII character set represents a different character. For example, the value `65` represents `'A'`, and the value `43` represents `'+'`. Thus, each character has a predefined ordering, which is called a **collating sequence**, in the set. The collating sequence is used when you compare characters. For example, the value representing `'B'` is `66`, so `'A'` is smaller than `'B'`. Similarly, `'+'` is smaller than `'A'` because `43` is smaller than `65`.

The 14th character in the ASCII character set is called the newline character and is represented as `'\n'`. (Note that the position of the newline character in the ASCII character set is `13` because the position of the first character is 0.) Even though the newline character is a combination of two characters, it is treated as one character. Similarly, the horizontal tab character is represented in C++ as `'\t'` and the null character is represented as `'\0'` (backslash followed by zero). Furthermore, the first 32 characters in the ASCII character set are nonprintable. (See Appendix C for a description of these characters.)

Floating-Point Data Types

To deal with decimal numbers, C++ provides the floating-point data type, which we discuss in this section. To facilitate the discussion, let us review a concept from a high school or college algebra course.

You may be familiar with scientific notation. For example:

$$43872918 = 4.3872918 * 10^7 \qquad \{10 \text{ to the power of seven}\}$$
$$.0000265 = 2.65 * 10^{-5} \qquad \{10 \text{ to the power of minus five}\}$$
$$47.9832 = 4.79832 * 10^1 \qquad \{10 \text{ to the power of one}\}$$

To represent real numbers, C++ uses a form of scientific notation called **floating-point notation**. Table 2-3 shows how C++ might print a set of real numbers using one machine's interpretation of floating-point notation. In the C++ floating-point notation, the letter E stands for the exponent.

TABLE 2-3   Examples of Real Numbers Printed in C++ Floating-Point Notation

Real Number	C++ Floating-Point Notation
75.924	7.592400E1
0.18	1.800000E-1
0.0000453	4.530000E-5
-1.482	-1.482000E0
7800.0	7.800000E3

C++ provides three data types to manipulate decimal numbers: `float`, `double`, and `long double`. As in the case of integral data types, the data types `float`, `double`, and `long double` differ in the set of values. Figure 2-4 defines these data types.

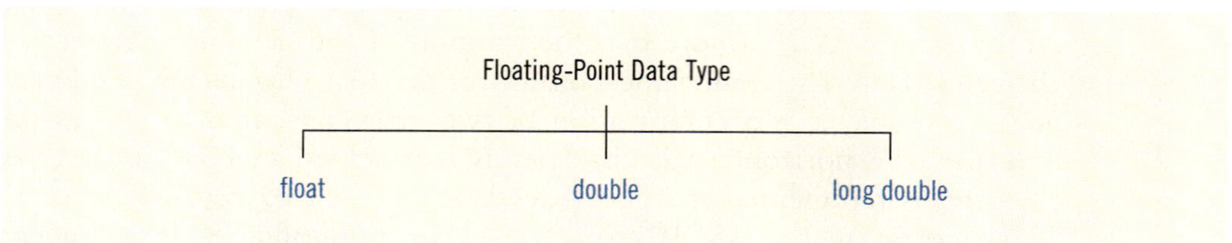

FIGURE 2-4   Floating-point data types

NOTE   On most newer compilers, the data types `double` and `long double` are the same. Therefore, only the data types `float` and `double` are described here.

float: The data type `float` is used in C++ to represent any real number between −3.4E+38 and 3.4E+38. The memory allocated for a value of the `float` data type is four bytes.

double: The data type `double` is used in C++ to represent any real number between −1.7E+308 and 1.7E+308. The memory allocated for a value of the `double` data type is eight bytes.

The maximum and minimum values of the data types `float` and `double` are system dependent. To find these values on a particular system, you can check your compiler's documentation or, alternatively, you can run a program given in Appendix F (Header File `cfloat`).

Other than the set of values, there is one more difference between the data types `float` and `double`. The maximum number of significant digits—that is, the number of decimal places—in `float` values is 6 or 7. The maximum number of significant digits in values belonging to the `double` type is 15.

NOTE For values of the `double` type, for better precision, some compilers might give more than 15 significant digits. Check your compiler's documentation.

The maximum number of significant digits is called the **precision**. Sometimes `float` values are called **single precision**, and values of type `double` are called **double precision**. If you are dealing with decimal numbers, for the most part you need only the `float` type; if you need accuracy to more than six or seven decimal places, you can use the `double` type.

NOTE In C++, by default, floating-point numbers are considered of type `double`. Therefore, if you use the data type `float` to manipulate floating-point numbers in a program, certain compilers might give you a warning message, such as "truncation from double to float". To avoid such warning messages, you should use the `double` data type. For illustration purposes and to avoid such warning messages in programming examples, this book mostly uses the data type `double` to manipulate floating-point numbers.

Arithmetic Operators and Operator Precedence

One of the most important uses of a computer is its ability to calculate. You can use the standard arithmetic operators to manipulate integral and floating-point data types. There are five arithmetic operators:

- \+ addition
- − subtraction
- * multiplication

- / division
- % modulus operator

You can use the operators +, −, *, and / with both integral and floating-point data types. You use % with only the integral data type to find the remainder in ordinary division. When you use / with the integral data type, it gives the quotient in ordinary division. That is, integral division truncates any fractional part; there is no rounding.

Since high school, you have been accustomed to working with arithmetic expressions such as the following:

    i.   −5
   ii.   8 − 7
  iii.   3 + 4
  iv.   2 + 3 * 5
   v.   5.6 + 6.2 * 3
  vi.   x + 2 * 5 + 6 / y

In expression (vi), x and y are unknown numbers. Formally, an **arithmetic expression** is constructed by using arithmetic operators and numbers. The numbers appearing in the expression are called **operands**. The numbers that are used to evaluate an operator are called the operands for that operator.

In expression (i), the symbol − specifies that the number 5 is negative. In this expression, − has only one operand. Operators that have only one operand are called **unary operators**.

In expression (ii), the symbol − is used to subtract 7 from 8. In this expression, − has two operands, 8 and 7. Operators that have two operands are called **binary operators**.

Unary operator: An operator that has only one operand.

Binary operator: An operator that has two operands.

In expression (iii), that is, 3 + 4, 3 and 4 are the operands for the operator +. In this expression, the operator + has two operands and is a binary operator. Now consider the following expression:

+27

In this expression, the operator + indicates that the number 27 is positive. Here, + has only one operand and so acts as a unary operator.

From the preceding discussion, it follows that − and + are both unary and binary arithmetic operators. However, as arithmetic operators, *, /, and % are binary and so must have two operands.

The following examples show how arithmetic operators—especially / and %—work with integral data types. As you can see from these examples, the operator / represents the quotient in ordinary division when used with integral data types.

EXAMPLE 2-3

Arithmetic Expression	Result	Description
2 + 5	7	
13 + 89	102	
34 - 20	14	
45 - 90	-45	
2 * 7	14	
5 / 2	2	In the division 5 / 2, the quotient is 2 and the remainder is 1. Therefore, 5 / 2 with the integral operands evaluates to the quotient, which is 2.
14 / 7	2	
34 % 5	4	In the division 34 / 5, the quotient is 6 and the remainder is 4. Therefore, 34 % 5 evaluates to the remainder, which is 4.
-34 % 5	-4	In the division -34 / 5, the quotient is -6 and the remainder is -4. Therefore, -34 % 5 evaluates to the remainder, which is -4.
34 % -5	4	In the division 34 / -5, the quotient is -6 and the remainder is 4. Therefore, 34 % -5 evaluates to the remainder, which is 4.
-34 % -5	-4	In the division -34 / -5, the quotient is 6 and the remainder is -4. Therefore, -34 % -5 evaluates to the remainder, which is -4.
4 % 6	4	In the division 4 / 6, the quotient is 0 and the remainder is 4. Therefore, 4 % 6 evaluates to the remainder, which is 4.

Note that in the divisions 34 / 5 and -34 / -5, the quotients, which are 6, are the same, but the remainders are different. In the division 34 / 5, the remainder is 4; in the division -34 /-5, the remainder is -4.

The following C++ program evaluates the preceding expressions:

```
#include <iostream>

using namespace std;

int main()
{
    cout << "2 + 5 = " << 2 + 5 << endl;
    cout << "13 + 89 = " << 13 + 89 << endl;
    cout << "34 - 20 = " << 34 - 20 << endl;
    cout << "45 - 90 = " << 45 - 90 << endl;
    cout << "2 * 7 = " << 2 * 7 << endl;
    cout << "5 / 2 = " << 5 / 2 << endl;
```

```cpp
    cout << "14 / 7 = " << 14 / 7 << endl;
    cout << "34 % 5 = " << 34 % 5 << endl;
    cout << "-34 % 5 = " << -34 % 5 << endl;
    cout << "34 % -5 = " << 34 % -5 << endl;
    cout << "-34 % -5 = " << -34 % -5 << endl;
    cout << "4 % 6 = " << 4 % 6 << endl;

    return 0;
}
```

Sample Run:

```
2 + 5 = 7
13 + 89 = 102
34 - 20 = 14
45 - 90 = -45
2 * 7 = 14
5 / 2 = 2
14 / 7 = 2
34 % 5 = 4
-34 % 5 = -4
34 % -5 = 4
-34 % -5 = -4
4 % 6 = 4
```

The following example shows how arithmetic operators work with floating-point numbers.

EXAMPLE 2-4

The following C++ program evaluates various floating-point expressions. (The details, of how the expressions are evaluated, are left as an exercise for you.)

```cpp
#include <iostream>

using namespace std;

int main()
{
    cout << "5.0 + 3.5 = " << 5.0 + 3.5 << endl;
    cout << "3.0 + 9.4 = " << 3.0 + 9.4 << endl;
    cout << "16.3 - 5.2 = " << 16.3 - 5.2 << endl;
    cout << "4.2 * 2.5 = " << 4.2 * 2.5 << endl;
    cout << "5.0 / 2.0 = " << 5.0 / 2.0 << endl;
```

```
cout << "34.5 / 6.0 = " << 34.5 / 6.0 << endl;
cout << "34.5 / 6.5 = " << 34.5 / 6.5 << endl;

    return 0;
}
```

Sample Run:

```
5.0 + 3.5 = 8.5
3.0 + 9.4 = 12.4
16.3 - 5.2 = 11.1
4.2 * 2.5 = 10.5
5.0 / 2.0 = 2.5
34.5 / 6.0 = 5.75
34.5 / 6.5 = 5.30769
```

Order of Precedence

When more than one arithmetic operator is used in an expression, C++ uses the operator precedence rules to evaluate the expression. According to the order of precedence rules for arithmetic operators,

```
*,  /,  %
```

are at a higher level of precedence than:

```
+,  -
```

Note that the operators `*`, `/`, and `%` have the same level of precedence. Similarly, the operators `+` and `-` have the same level of precedence.

When operators have the same level of precedence, the operations are performed from left to right. To avoid confusion, you can use parentheses to group arithmetic expressions. For example, using the order of precedence rules,

```
3 * 7 - 6 + 2 * 5 / 4 + 6
```

means the following:

```
  (((3 * 7)  - 6)  + ((2 * 5)  / 4 ))  + 6
= ((21 - 6)  + (10 / 4)) + 6       (Evaluate *)
= ((21 - 6)  + 2) + 6              (Evaluate /.   Note that this is an integer division.)
= (15 + 2)  + 6                    (Evaluate -)
= 17 + 6                           (Evaluate first +)
= 23                              (Evaluate +)
```

Note that the use of parentheses in the second example clarifies the order of precedence. You can also use parentheses to override the order of precedence rules (see Example 2-5).

EXAMPLE 2-5

In the expression:

```
3 + 4 * 5
```

* is evaluated before +. Therefore, the result of this expression is 23. On the other hand, in the expression:

```
(3 + 4) * 5
```

+ is evaluated before * and the result of this expression is 35.

Because arithmetic operators are evaluated from left to right, unless parentheses are present, the **associativity** of the arithmetic operators is said to be from left to right.

NOTE (**Character Arithmetic**) Because the `char` data type is also an integral data type, C++ allows you to perform arithmetic operations on `char` data. However, you should use this ability carefully. There is a difference between the character `'8'` and the integer 8. The integer value of 8 is 8. The integer value of `'8'` is 56, which is the ASCII collating sequence of the character `'8'`.

When evaluating arithmetic expressions, 8 + 7 = 15; `'8'` + `'7'` = 56 + 55, which yields 111; and `'8'` + 7 = 56 + 7, which yields 63. Furthermore, because `'8'` * `'7'` = 56 * 55 = 3080 and the ASCII character set has only 128 values, `'8'` * `'7'` is undefined in the ASCII character data set.

These examples illustrate that many things can go wrong when you are performing character arithmetic. If you must employ them, use arithmetic operations on the `char` data type with caution.

Expressions

To this point, we have discussed only arithmetic operators. In this section, we now discuss arithmetic expressions in detail. Arithmetic expressions were introduced in the last section.

If all operands (that is, numbers) in an expression are integers, the expression is called an **integral expression**. If all operands in an expression are floating-point numbers, the expression is called a **floating-point** or **decimal expression**. An integral expression yields an integral result; a floating-point expression yields a floating-point result. Looking at some examples will help clarify these definitions.

EXAMPLE 2-6

Consider the following C++ integral expressions:

```
2 + 3 * 5
3 + x - y / 7
x + 2 * (y - z) + 18
```

In these expressions, **x**, **y**, and **z** represent variables of the integer type; that is, they can hold integer values. Variables are discussed later in this chapter.

EXAMPLE 2-7

Consider the following C++ floating-point expressions:

```
12.8 * 17.5 - 34.50
x * 10.5 + y - 16.2
```

Here, **x** and **y** represent variables of the floating-point type; that is, they can hold floating-point values. Variables are discussed later in this chapter.

Evaluating an integral or a floating-point expression is straightforward. As before, when operators have the same precedence, the expression is evaluated from left to right. You can always use parentheses to group operands and operators to avoid confusion.

Mixed Expressions

An expression that has operands of different data types is called a **mixed expression**. A mixed expression contains both integers and floating-point numbers. The following expressions are examples of mixed expressions:

```
2 + 3.5
6 / 4 + 3.9
5.4 * 2 - 13.6 + 18 / 2
```

In the first expression, the operand + has one integer operand and one floating-point operand. In the second expression, both operands for the operator / are integers, the first operand of + is the result of 6 / 4, and the second operand of + is a floating-point number. The third example is an even more complicated mix of integers and floating-point numbers. The obvious question is: How does C++ evaluate mixed expressions?

Two rules apply when evaluating a mixed expression:

1. When evaluating an operator in a mixed expression:

    a. If the operator has the same types of operands (that is, either both integers or both floating-point numbers), the operator is evaluated according to the type of the operands. Integer operands thus yield an integer result; floating-point numbers yield a floating-point number.

b.   If the operator has both types of operands (that is, one is an integer and the other is a floating-point number), then during calculation the integer is changed to a floating-point number with the decimal part of zero and the operator is evaluated. The result is a floating-point number.

2.   The entire expression is evaluated according to the precedence rules; the multiplication, division, and modulus operators are evaluated before the addition and subtraction operators. Operators having the same level of precedence are evaluated from left to right. Grouping is allowed for clarity.

From these rules, it follows that when evaluating a mixed expression, you concentrate on one operator at a time, using the rules of precedence. If the operator to be evaluated has operands of the same data type, evaluate the operator using Rule 1(a). That is, an operator with integer operands will yield an integer result, and an operator with floating-point operands will yield a floating-point result. If the operator to be evaluated has one integer operand and one floating-point operand, before evaluating this operator convert the integer operand to a floating-point number with the decimal part of 0. The following examples show how to evaluate mixed expressions.

EXAMPLE 2-8

Mixed Expression	Evaluation	Rule Applied

`3 / 2 + 5.5`	`= 1 + 5.5`
	`= 6.5`
		`3/2 = 1` (integer division; Rule 1(a))
		`(1 + 5.5`
		`= 1.0 + 5.5` (Rule 1(b))
		`= 6.5)`

`15.6 / 2 + 5`	`= 7.8 + 5`
	
	`= 12.8`
		`15.6 / 2`
		`= 15.6 / 2.0` (Rule 1(b))
		`= 7.8`
		`7.8 + 5`
		`= 7.8 + 5.0` (Rule 1(b))
		`= 12.8`

`4 + 5 / 2.0`	`= 4 + 2.5`
	
	`= 6.5`
		`5 / 2.0 = 5.0 / 2.0` (Rule 1(b))
		`= 2.5`
		`4 + 2.5 = 4.0 + 2.5` (Rule 1(b))
		`= 6.5`

`4 * 3 + 7 / 5 - 25.5`	`= 12 + 7 / 5 - 25.5`
	`= 12 + 1 - 25.5`
	`= 13 - 25.5`
	`= -12.5`
		`4 * 3 = 12;` (Rule 1(a))
		`7 / 5 = 1` (integer division; Rule 1(a))
		`12 + 1 = 13;` (Rule 1(a))
		`13 - 25.5 = 13.0 - 25.5` (Rule 1(b))
		`= -12.5`

The following C++ program evaluates the preceding expressions:

```cpp
#include <iostream>

using namespace std;

int main()
{
    cout << "3 / 2 + 5.5 = " << 3 / 2 + 5.5 << endl;
    cout << "15.6 / 2 + 5 = " << 15.6 / 2 + 5 << endl;
    cout << "4 + 5 / 2.0 = " << 4 + 5 / 2.0 << endl;
    cout << "4 * 3 + 7 / 5 - 25.5 = "
         << 4 * 3 + 7 / 5 - 25.5
         << endl;

    return 0;
}
```

Sample Run:

```
3 / 2 + 5.5 = 6.5
15.6 / 2 + 5 = 12.8
4 + 5 / 2.0 = 6.5
4 * 3 + 7 / 5 - 25.5 = -12.5
```

These examples illustrate that an integer is not converted to a floating-point number unless the operator to be evaluated has one integer and one floating-point operand.

Type Conversion (Casting)

In the previous section, you learned that when evaluating an arithmetic expression if the operator has mixed operands, the integer value is changed to a floating-point value with the zero decimal part. When a value of one data type is automatically changed to another data type, an **implicit type coercion** is said to have occurred. As the examples in the preceding section illustrate, if you are not careful about data types, implicit type coercion can generate unexpected results.

To avoid implicit type coercion, C++ provides for explicit type conversion through the use of a cast operator. The **cast operator**, also called **type conversion** or **type casting**, takes the following form:

```cpp
static_cast<dataTypeName>(expression)
```

First, the expression is evaluated. Its value is then converted to a value of the type specified by `dataTypeName`. In C++, `static_cast` is a reserved word.

When converting a floating-point (decimal) number to an integer using the cast operator, you simply drop the decimal part of the floating-point number. That is, the floating-point number is truncated. Example 2-9 shows how cast operators work. Be sure you understand why the last two expressions evaluate as they do.

EXAMPLE 2-9

Expression	Evaluates to

```
static_cast<int>(7.9)          7
static_cast<int>(3.3)          3
static_cast<double>(25)        25.0
static_cast<double>(5+3)       = static_cast<double>(8) = 8.0
static_cast<double>(15) / 2    = 15.0 / 2
                               (because static_cast<double>(15) = 15.0)
                               = 15.0 / 2.0 = 7.5
static_cast<double>(15 / 2)    = static_cast<double>(7) (because 15 / 2 = 7)
                               = 7.0

static_cast<int>(7.8 +
static_cast<double>(15) / 2)   = static_cast<int>(7.8 + 7.5)
                               = static_cast<int>(15.3)
                               = 15

static_cast<int>(7.8 +
static_cast<double>(15 / 2))   = static_cast<int>(7.8 + 7.0)
                               = static_cast<int>(14.8)
                               = 14
```

The following C++ program evaluates the preceding expressions:

```cpp
#include <iostream>

using namespace std;

int main()
{
    cout << "static_cast<int>(7.9) = "
         << static_cast<int>(7.9)
         << endl;
    cout << "static_cast<int>(3.3) = "
         << static_cast<int>(3.3)
         << endl;
    cout << "static_cast<double>(25) = "
         << static_cast<double>(25)
         << endl;
    cout << "static_cast<double>(5 + 3) = "
         << static_cast<double>(5 + 3)
         << endl;
    cout << "static_cast<double>(15) / 2 = "
         << static_cast<double>(15) / 2
         << endl;
    cout << "static_cast<double>(15 / 2) = "
         << static_cast<double>(15 / 2)
         << endl;
    cout << "static_cast<int>(7.8 + static_cast<double>(15) / 2) = "
         << static_cast<int>(7.8 + static_cast<double>(15) / 2)
         << endl;
```

```cpp
    cout << "static_cast<int>(7.8 + static_cast<double>(15 / 2)) = "
         << static_cast<int>(7.8 + static_cast<double>(15 / 2))
         << endl;

    return 0;
}
```

Sample Run:

```
static_cast<int>(7.9) = 7
static_cast<int>(3.3) = 3
static_cast<double>(25) = 25
static_cast<double>(5 + 3) = 8
static_cast<double>(15) / 2 = 7.5
static_cast<double>(15 / 2) = 7
static_cast<int>(7.8 + static_cast<double>(15) / 2) = 15
static_cast<int>(7.8 + static_cast<double>(15 / 2)) = 14
```

Note that the value of the expression `static_cast<double>(25)` is `25.0`. However, it is output as `25` rather than `25.0`. This is because we have not yet discussed how to output decimal numbers with 0 decimal parts to show the decimal point and the trailing zeros. Chapter 3 explains how to output decimal numbers in a desired format. Similarly, the output of other decimal numbers with zero decimal parts is without the decimal point and the 0 decimal part.

Consider another series of examples. For these examples, `x = 15`, `y = 23`, and `z = 3.75`. A C++ program, similar to the preceding one, generated the output of the following expressions. (The Web site accompanying this book contains this program. It is named `Example2_9B.cpp`.)

Expression	Value
`static_cast<int>(7.9 + 6.7)`	14
`static_cast<int>(7.9) + static_cast<int>(6.7)`	13
`static_cast<double>(y / x) + z`	4.75
`static_cast<double>(y) / x + z`	5.28333

NOTE In C++, the cast operator can also take the form `dataType(expression)`. This form is called C-like casting. For example, `double(5) = 5.0` and `int(17.6) = 17`. However, `static_cast` is more stable than C-like casting.

You can also use cast operators to explicitly convert **char** data values into **int** data values, and **int** data values into **char** data values. To convert **char** data values into **int** data values, you use a collating sequence. For example, in the ASCII character set, `static_cast<int>('A')` is 65 and `static_cast<int>('8')` is 56. Similarly, `static_cast<char>(65)` is `'A'` and `static_cast<char>(56)` is `'8'`.

Earlier in this chapter, you learned how arithmetic expressions are formed and evaluated in C++. If you want to use the value of one expression in another expression, first you must save the value of the expression. There are many reasons to save the value of an expression. Some expressions are complex and may require a considerable amount of computer time to evaluate. By calculating the values once and saving them for further use, you not only save computer time and create a program that executes more quickly, you also avoid possible typographical errors. In C++, expressions are evaluated and if the value is not saved, it is lost. That is, unless it is saved, the value of an expression cannot be used in later calculations. In the next section, you will learn how to save the value of an expression and use it in subsequent calculations.

Before leaving the discussion of data types, let us discuss one more data type—`string`.

`string` Type

The data type `string` is a programmer-defined data type. It is not directly available for use in a program like the simple data types discussed earlier. To use this data type, you need to access program components from the library, which will be discussed later in this chapter. The data type `string` is a feature of ANSI/ISO Standard C++.

NOTE Prior to the ANSI/ISO C++ language standard, the standard C++ library did not provide a `string` data type. Compiler vendors often supplied their own programmer-defined `string` type, and the syntax and semantics of string operations often varied from vendor to vendor.

A **string** is a sequence of zero or more characters. Strings in C++ are enclosed in double quotation marks. A string containing no characters is called a **null** or **empty** string. The following are examples of strings. Note that `""` is the empty string.

```
"William Jacob"
"Mickey"
""
```

Every character in a string has a relative position in the string. The position of the first character is 0, the position of the second character is 1, and so on. The length of a string is the number of characters in it.

EXAMPLE 2-10

String	Position of a Character in the String	Length of the String
`"William Jacob"`	Position of `'W'` is 0. Position of the first `'i'` is 1. Position of `' '` (the space) is 7. Position of `'J'` is 8. Position of `'b'` is 12.	13

String	Position of a Character in the String	Length of the String
`"Mickey"`	Position of `'M'` is 0. Position of `'i'` is 1. Position of `'c'` is 2. Position of `'k'` is 3. Position of `'e'` is 4. Position of `'y'` is 5.	6

When determining the length of a string, you must also count any spaces in the string. For example, the length of the following string is 22.

`"It is a beautiful day."`

Input

As noted earlier, the main objective of a C++ program is to perform calculations and manipulate data. Recall that data must be loaded into main memory before it can be manipulated. In this section, you will learn how to put data into the computer's memory. Storing data in the computer's memory is a two-step process:

1. Instruct the computer to allocate memory.

2. Include statements in the program to put data into the allocated memory.

Allocating Memory with Constants and Variables

When you instruct the computer to allocate memory, you tell it not only what names to use for each memory location, but also what type of data to store in those memory locations. Knowing the location of data is essential, because data stored in one memory location might be needed at several places in the program. As you saw earlier, knowing what data type you have is crucial for performing accurate calculations. It is also critical to know whether your data needs to remain fixed throughout program execution or whether it should change.

Some data must stay the same throughout a program. For example, the pay rate is usually the same for all part-time employees. A conversion formula that converts inches into centimeters is fixed, because 1 inch is always equal to `2.54` centimeters. When stored in memory, this type of data needs to be protected from accidental changes during program execution. In C++, you can use a **named constant** to instruct a program to mark those memory locations in which data is fixed throughout program execution.

Named constant: A memory location whose content is not allowed to change during program execution.

To allocate memory, we use C++'s declaration statements. The syntax to declare a named constant is:

```
const dataType identifier = value;
```

In C++, `const` is a reserved word.

EXAMPLE 2-11

Consider the following C++ statements:

```
const double CONVERSION = 2.54;
const int NO_OF_STUDENTS = 20;
const char BLANK = ' ';
const double PAY_RATE = 15.75;
```

The first statement tells the compiler to allocate memory, (eight bytes), to store a value of type `double`, call this memory space `CONVERSION`, and store the value `2.54` in it. Throughout a program that uses this statement, whenever the conversion formula is needed, the memory space `CONVERSION` can be accessed. The meaning of the other statements is similar.

Note that the identifier for a named constant is in uppercase letters. Even though there are no written rules, C++ programmers typically prefer to use uppercase letters to name a named constant. Moreover, if the name of a named constant is a combination of more than one word, called a *run-together word*, then the words are separated using an underscore. For example, in the preceding example, `PAY_RATE` is a run-together word.

NOTE As noted earlier, the default type of floating-point numbers is `double`. Therefore, if you declare a named constant of type `float`, then you must specify that the value is of type `float` as follows:

```
const float PAY_RATE = 15.75f;
```

otherwise, the compiler will generate an error message. Notice that `15.75f` says that it is a `float` value. Recall that the memory size for `float` values is four bytes; for `double` values, eight bytes. Because these days memory size is of little concern, as indicated earlier, we will mostly use the type `double` to work with floating-point values.

Using a named constant to store fixed data, rather than using the data value itself, has one major advantage. If the fixed data changes, you do not need to edit the entire program and change the old value to the new value wherever the old value is used. Instead, you can make the change at just one place, recompile the program, and execute it using the new value throughout. In addition, by storing a value and referring to that memory location whenever the value is needed, you avoid typing the same value again and again and prevent accidental typos. If you misspell the name of the constant value's location, the computer will warn you through an error message, but it will not warn you if the value is mistyped.

In some programs, data needs to be modified during program execution. For example, after each test, the average test score and the number of tests taken changes. Similarly, after each pay increase, the employee's salary changes. This type of data must be stored in those memory cells whose contents can be modified during program execution. In C++, memory cells whose contents can be modified during program execution are called variables.

Variable: A memory location whose content may change during program execution.

The syntax for declaring one variable or multiple variables is:

```
dataType identifier, identifier, . . .;
```

EXAMPLE 2-12

Consider the following statements:

```
double amountDue;
int counter;
char ch;
int x, y;
string name;
```

The first statement tells the compiler to allocate enough memory to store a value of the type `double` and call it `amountDue`. The second and third statements have similar conventions. The fourth statement tells the compiler to allocate two different memory spaces, each large enough to store a value of the type `int`; name the first memory space `x`; and name the second memory space `y`. The fifth statement tells the compiler to allocate memory space to store a string and call it `name`.

As in the case of naming named constants, there are no written rules for naming variables. However, C++ programmers typically use lowercase letters to declare variables. If a variable name is a combination of more than one word, then the first letter of each word, except the first word, is uppercase. (For example, see the variable `amountDue` in the preceding example.)

From now on, when we say "variable," we mean a variable memory location.

NOTE In C++, you must declare all identifiers before you can use them. If you refer to an identifier without declaring it, the compiler will generate an error message, (syntax error), indicating that the identifier is not declared. Therefore, to use either a named constant or a variable, you must first declare it.

Now that data types, variables, and constants have been defined and discussed, it is possible to offer a formal definition of simple data types. A data type is called

simple if the variable or named constant of that type can store only one value at a time. For example, if **x** is an **int** variable, at a given time only one value can be stored in **x**.

Putting Data into Variables

Now that you know how to declare variables, the next question is: How do you put data into those variables? In C++, you can place data into a variable in two ways:

1. Use C++'s assignment statement.
2. Use input (read) statements.

Assignment Statement

The assignment statement takes the following form:

```
variable = expression;
```

In an assignment statement, the value of the **expression** should match the data type of the **variable**. The expression on the right side is evaluated, and its value is assigned to the variable (and thus to a memory location) on the left side.

A variable is said to be **initialized** the first time a value is placed in the variable.

In C++, = is called the **assignment operator**.

EXAMPLE 2-13

Suppose you have the following variable declarations:

```
int i, j;
double sale;
char first;
string str;
```

Now consider the following assignment statements:

```
i = 4;
j = 4 * 5 - 11;
sale = 0.02 * 1000;
first = 'D';
str = "It is a sunny day.";
```

For each of these statements, the computer first evaluates the expression on the right and then stores that value in a memory location named by the identifier on the left. The first statement stores the value 4 in i, the second statement stores 9 in j, the third statement stores 20.00 in **sale**, and the fourth statement stores the character D in `first`. The fifth statement stores the string `"It is a sunny day."` in the variable `str`.

The following C++ program shows the effect of the preceding statements:

```cpp
#include <iostream>
#include <string>

using namespace std;

int main()
{
    int i, j;
    double sale;
    char first;
    string str;

    i = 4;
    cout << "i = " << i << endl;

    j = 4 * 5 - 11;
    cout << "j = " << j << endl;
    sale = 0.02 * 1000;
    cout << "sale = " << sale << endl;

    first = 'D';
    cout << "first = " << first << endl;

    str = "It is a sunny day.";
    cout << "str = " << str << endl;

    return 0;
}
```

Sample Run:

```
i = 4
j = 9
sale = 20
first = D
str = It is a sunny day.
```

For the most part, the preceding program is straightforward. Let us take a look at the output statement:

```cpp
cout << "i = " << i << endl;
```

This output statement consists of the string `"i = "`, the operator `<<`, and the variable `i`. Here the first value of the string `"i = "` is output, then the value of the variable `i` is output. The meaning of the other output statements is similar.

A C++ statement such as:

```
i = i + 2;
```

means "evaluate whatever is in `i`, add 2 to it, and assign the new value to the memory location `i`." The expression on the right side must be evaluated first; that value is then assigned to the memory location specified by the variable on the left side. Thus, the sequence of C++ statements:

```
i = 6;
i = i + 2;
```

and the statement:

```
i = 8;
```

both assign 8 to `i`. Note that the statement `i = i + 2` is meaningless if `i` has not been initialized.

You read the statement `i = 5;` as "`i` becomes 5" or "`i` gets 5" or "`i` is assigned the value 5." Each time a new value is assigned to `i`, the old value is erased.

Suppose that `i`, `j`, and `k` are **int** variables. The sequence of statements:

```
i = 12;
i = i + 6;
j = i;
k = j / 2;
k = k / 3;
```

results in `k` having the value 3 stored in it. Tracing values through a sequence, called a **walk-through**, is a valuable tool to learn and practice. Try it in the sequence above. You will learn more about how to walk through a sequence of C++ statements later in this chapter.

Suppose that **x**, **y**, and **z** are **int** variables. The following is a legal statement in C++:

```
x = y = z;
```

NOTE In this statement, first the value of **z** is assigned to **y**, and then the new value of **y** is assigned to **x**. Because the assignment operator, =, is evaluated from right to left, the **associativity** of the **assignment operator** is said to be from right to left.

Saving and Using the Value of an Expression

Now that you know how to declare variables and put data into them, you can learn how to save the value of an expression. You can then use this value in a later expression without using the expression itself, thereby answering the question raised earlier in this chapter. To save the value of an expression and use it in a later expression, do the following:

1. Declare a variable of the appropriate data type. For example, if the result of the expression is an integer, declare an `int` variable.

2. Assign the value of the expression to the variable that was declared, using the assignment statement. This action saves the value of the expression into the variable.

3. Wherever the value of the expression is needed, use the variable holding the value. The following example further illustrates this concept.

EXAMPLE 2-14

Suppose that you have the following declaration:

```
int a, b, c, d;
int x, y;
```

Further suppose that you want to evaluate the expressions $-b + (b^2 - 4ac)$ and $-b - (b^2 - 4ac)$, and assign the values of these expressions to x and y, respectively. Because the expression $b^2 - 4ac$ appears in both expressions, you can first calculate the value of this expression and save its value in d. You can then use the value of d to evaluate the expressions, as shown by the following statements:

```
d = b * b - 4 * a * c;
x = -b + d;
y = -b - d;
```

Earlier, you learned that if a variable is used in an expression, the expression would yield a meaningful value only if the variable has first been initialized. You also learned that after declaring a variable, you can use an assignment statement to initialize it. It is possible to initialize and declare variables at the same time. Before we discuss how to use an input (read) statement, we address this important issue.

Declaring and Initializing Variables

When a variable is declared, C++ may not automatically put a meaningful value in it. In other words, C++ may not automatically initialize variables. For example, the `int` and `double` variables may not be initialized to 0, as happens in some programming languages. This does not mean, however, that there is no value in a variable after its declaration. When a variable is declared, memory is allocated for it.

Recall from Chapter 1 that main memory is an ordered sequence of cells, and each cell is capable of storing a value. Also, recall that the machine language is a sequence of 0s and 1s, or bits. Therefore, data in a memory cell is a sequence of bits. These bits are nothing but electrical signals, so when the computer is turned on, some of the bits are 1 and some are 0. The state of these bits depends on how the system functions. However, when you instruct the computer to store a particular value in a memory cell, the bits are set according to the data being stored.

During data manipulation, the computer takes the value stored in particular cells and performs a calculation. If you declare a variable and do not store a value in it, the memory cell still has a value—usually the value of the setting of the bits from their last use—and you have no way to know what this value is.

If you only declare a variable and do not instruct the computer to put data into the variable, the value of that variable is garbage. However, the computer does not warn us, regards whatever values are in memory as legitimate, and performs calculations using those values in memory. Using a variable in an expression without initializing it produces erroneous results. To avoid these pitfalls, C++ allows you to initialize variables while they are being declared. For example, consider the following C++ statements in which variables are first declared and then initialized:

```
int first, second;
char ch;
double x, y;

first = 13;
second = 10;
ch = ' ';
x = 12.6;
y = 123.456;
```

You can declare and initialize these variables at the same time using the following C++ statements:

```
int first = 13, second = 10;
char ch = ' ';
double x = 12.6, y = 123.456;
```

The first C++ statement declares two `int` variables, `first` and `second`, and stores 13 in `first` and 10 in `second`. The meaning of the other statements is similar.

In reality, not all variables are initialized during declaration. It is the nature of the program or the programmer's choice that dictates which variables should be initialized during declaration. The key point is that all variables must be initialized before they are used.

Input (Read) Statement

Previously, you learned how to put data into variables using the assignment statement. In this section, you will learn how to put data into variables from the *standard input device*, using C++'s input (or read) statements.

NOTE In most cases, the standard input device is the keyboard.

When the computer gets the data from the keyboard, the user is said to be acting interactively.

Putting data into variables from the standard input device is accomplished via the use of `cin` and the operator `>>`. The syntax of `cin` together with `>>` is:

```
cin >> variable >> variable ...;
```

This is called an **input (read)** statement. In C++, `>>` is called the **stream extraction operator**.

NOTE In a syntax, the shading indicates the part of the definition that is optional. Furthermore, throughout this book, the syntax is enclosed in yellow boxes.

EXAMPLE 2-15

Suppose that `miles` is a variable of the data type `double`. Further suppose that the input is `73.65`. Consider the following statements:

```
cin >> miles;
```

This statement causes the computer to get the input, which is `73.65`, from the standard input device, and stores it in the variable `miles`. That is, after this statement executes, the value of the variable `miles` is `73.65`.

Example 2-16 further explains how to input numeric data into a program.

EXAMPLE 2-16

Suppose we have the following statements:

```
int feet;
int inches;
```

Suppose the input is:

```
23 7
```

Next, consider the following statement:

```
cin >> feet >> inches;
```

This statement first stores the number 23 into the variable `feet` and then the number 7 into the variable `inches`. Notice that when these numbers are entered via the keyboard, they are separated with a blank. In fact, they can be separated with one or more blanks or lines or even the tab character.

The following C++ program shows the effect of the preceding input statements:

```cpp
#include <iostream>

using namespace std;

int main()
{
    int feet;
    int inches;

    cout << "Enter two integers separated by spaces: ";
    cin >> feet >> inches;
    cout << endl;

    cout << "Feet = " << feet << endl;
    cout << "Inches = " << inches << endl;

    return 0;
}
```

Sample Run: In this sample run, the user input is shaded.

```
Enter two integers separated by spaces: 23 7

Feet = 23
Inches = 7
```

The C++ program in Example 2-17 illustrates how to read strings and numeric data.

EXAMPLE 2-17

```cpp
#include <iostream>
#include <string>

using namespace std;

int main()
{
    string firstName;                          //Line 1
    string lastName;                           //Line 2
    int age;                                   //Line 3
    double weight;                             //Line 4
```

```cpp
    cout << "Enter first name, last name, age, "
         << "and weight, separated by spaces."
         << endl;                                   //Line  5

    cin >> firstName >> lastName;                   //Line  6
    cin >> age >> weight;                           //Line  7

    cout << "Name: " << firstName << " "
         << lastName << endl;                       //Line  8

    cout << "Age: " << age << endl;                 //Line  9
    cout << "Weight: " << weight << endl;           //Line 10

    return 0;                                        //Line 11
}
```

Sample Run: In this sample run, the user input is shaded.

```
Enter first name, last name, age, and weight, separated by spaces.
Sheila Mann 23 120.5
Name: Sheila Mann
Age: 23
Weight: 120.5
```

Before explaining how the preceding program works, let us note the following. Each statement in the body of the function `main` contains `//Line` and a number. These are called *single line comments*. All single line comments in C++ begin with `//`. Comments are typically used to document a program. Here we use them so that we can easily refer to a specific statement in the program and explain what the statement does. When a C++ program is compiled, the compiler ignores the comments. Moreover, notice that the comments are shown in green. Various SDKs show the comments in green.

The preceding program works as follows: The statements in Lines 1 to 4 declare the variables `firstName` and `lastName` of type `string`, `age` of type `int`, and `weight` of type `double`. The statement in Line 5 is an output statement and tells the user what to do. (Such output statements are called prompt lines.) As shown in the sample run, the input to the program is:

```
Sheila Mann 23 120.5
```

The statement in Line 6 first reads and stores the string `Sheila` into the variable `firstName` and then skips the space after `Sheila` and reads and stores the string `Mann` into the variable `lastName`. Next, the statement in Line 7 first skips the blank after `Mann` and reads and stores `23` into the variable `age` and then skips the blank after `23` and reads and stores `120.5` into the variable `weight`.

The statements in Lines 8, 9, and 10 produce the third, fourth, and fifth lines of the sample run.

During programming execution, if more than one value is entered in a line, these values must be separated by at least one blank or tab. Alternately, one value per line can be entered.

Variable Initialization

Remember, there are two ways to initialize a variable: by using the assignment statement and by using a read statement. Consider the following declaration:

```
int feet;
```

You can initialize the variable **feet** to a value of 35 either by using the assignment statement:

```
feet = 35;
```

or by executing the following statement and entering 35 during program execution:

```
cin >> feet;
```

If you use the assignment statement to initialize **feet**, then you are stuck with the same value each time the program runs unless you edit the source code, change the value, recompile, and run. By using an input statement each time the program runs, you are prompted to enter a value, and the value entered is stored into **feet**. Therefore, a read statement is much more versatile than an assignment statement.

Sometimes it is necessary to initialize a variable by using an assignment statement. This is especially true if the variable is used only for internal calculation and not for reading and storing data.

Recall that C++ does not automatically initialize variables when they are declared. Some variables can be initialized when they are declared, whereas others must be initialized using either an assignment statement or a read statement.

When the program is compiled, some of the newer SDKs might give warning messages if the program uses the value of a variable without first properly initializing that variable. In this case, if you ignore the warning and execute the program, the program might terminate abnormally with an error message.

Suppose you want to store a character into a **char** variable using an input statement. During program execution, when you enter the character, you do not include the single quotes. For example, suppose that **ch** is a **char** variable. Consider the following input statement:

```
cin >> ch;
```

If you want to store K into **ch** using this statement, during program execution, you only enter K. Similarly, if you want to store a string into a **string** variable using an input statement, during program execution, you enter only the string without the double quotes.

EXAMPLE 2-18

This example further illustrates how assignment statements and input statements manipulate variables. Consider the following declarations:

```
int firstNum, secondNum;
double z;
char ch;
string name;
```

Also, suppose that the following statements execute in the order given:

```
1.   firstNum = 4;

2.   secondNum = 2 * firstNum + 6;

3.   z = (firstNum + 1) / 2.0;

4.   ch = 'A';

5.   cin >> secondNum;

6.   cin >> z;

7.   firstNum = 2 * secondNum + static_cast<int>(z);

8.   cin >> name;

9.   secondNum = secondNum + 1;

10.  cin >> ch;

11.  firstNum = firstNum + static_cast<int>(ch);

12.  z = firstNum - z;
```

In addition, suppose the input is

```
8 16.3 Jenny D
```

This line has four values, 8, 16.3, Jenny, and D, and each value is separated from the others by a blank.

Let's now determine the values of the declared variables after the last statement executes. To explicitly show how a particular statement changes the value of a variable, the values of the variables after each statement executes are shown. (In Figures 2-5 through 2-17, a question mark [?] in a box indicates that the value in the box is unknown.)

Before statement 1 executes, all variables are uninitialized, as shown in Figure 2-5.

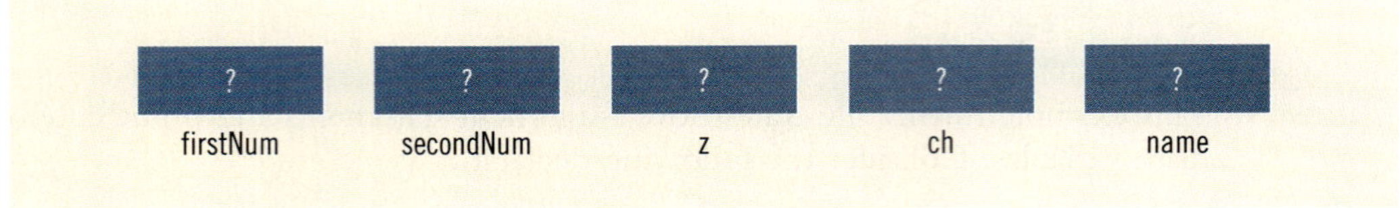

FIGURE 2-5 Variables before statement 1 executes

Statement 1 stores **4** into the variable named `firstNum`. After statement 1 executes, the values of the variables are as shown in Figure 2-6.

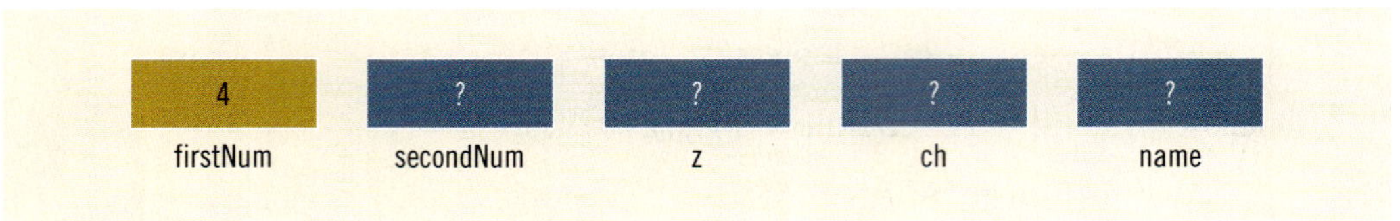

FIGURE 2-6 Values of `firstNum`, `secondNum`, `z`, `ch`, and `name` after statement 1 executes

Statement 2 first evaluates the expression `2 * firstNum + 6` (which evaluates to **14**) and then stores the value of the expression into `secondNum`. After statement 2 executes, the values of the variables are as shown in Figure 2-7.

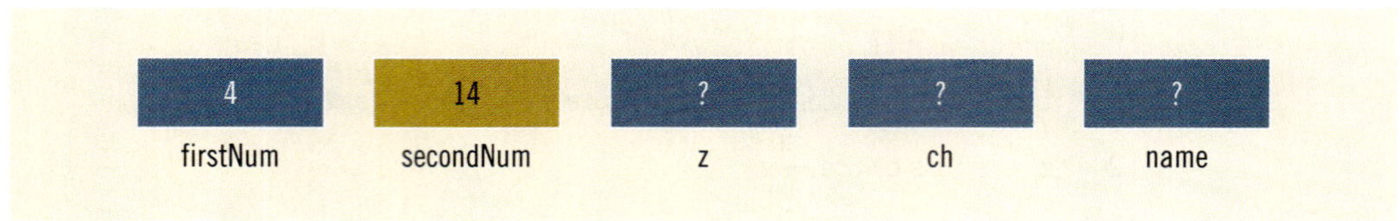

FIGURE 2-7 Values of `firstNum`, `secondNum`, `z`, `ch`, and `name` after statement 2 executes

Statement 3 first evaluates the expression `(firstNum + 1) / 2.0` (which evaluates to **2.5**) and then stores the value of the expression into `z`. After statement 3 executes, the values of the variables are as shown in Figure 2-8.

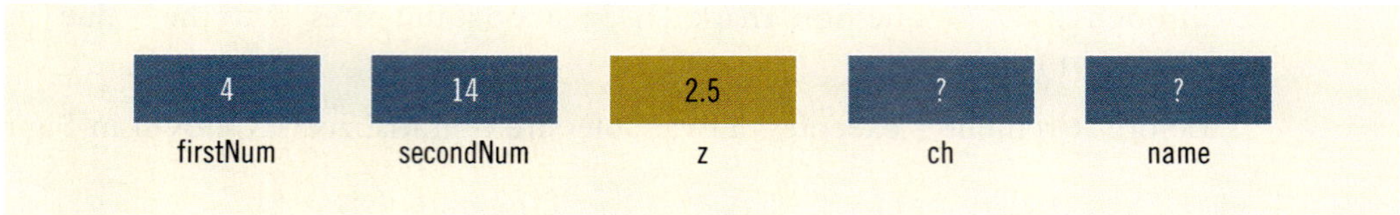

FIGURE 2-8 Values of `firstNum`, `secondNum`, `z`, `ch`, and `name` after statement 3 executes

Statement 4 stores the character **'A'** into **ch**. After statement 4 executes, the values of the variables are as shown in Figure 2-9.

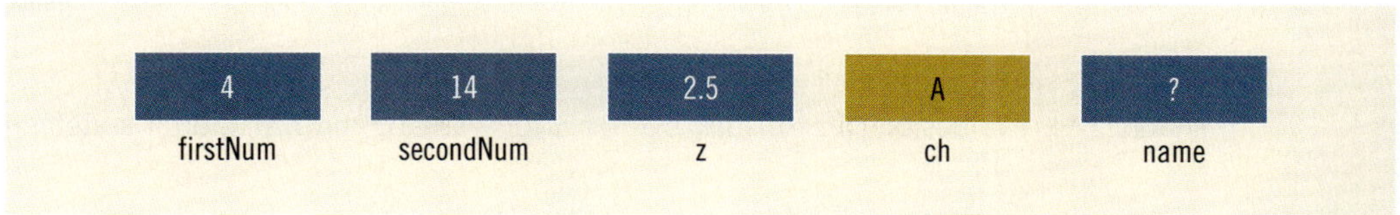

FIGURE 2-9 Values of `firstNum`, `secondNum`, `z`, `ch`, and `name` after statement 4 executes

Statement 5 reads a number from the keyboard (which is 8) and stores the number 8 into **secondNum**. This statement replaces the old value of **secondNum** with this new value. After statement 5 executes, the values of the variables are as shown in Figure 2-10.

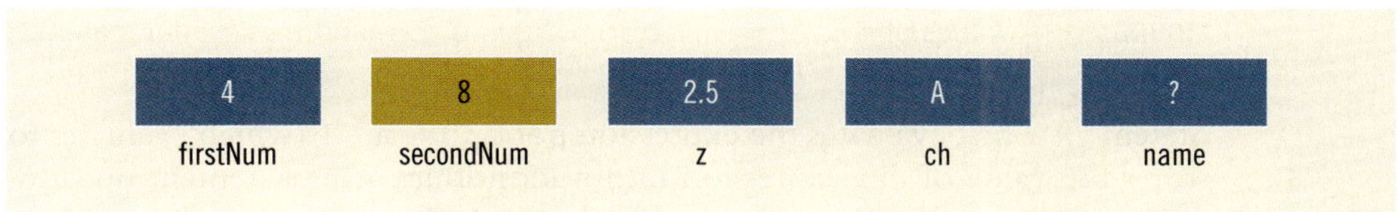

FIGURE 2-10 Values of `firstNum`, `secondNum`, `z`, `ch`, and `name` after statement 5 executes

Statement 6 reads a number from the keyboard (which is **16.3**) and stores the number into **z**. This statement replaces the old value of **z** with this new value. After statement 6 executes, the values of the variables are as shown in Figure 2-11.

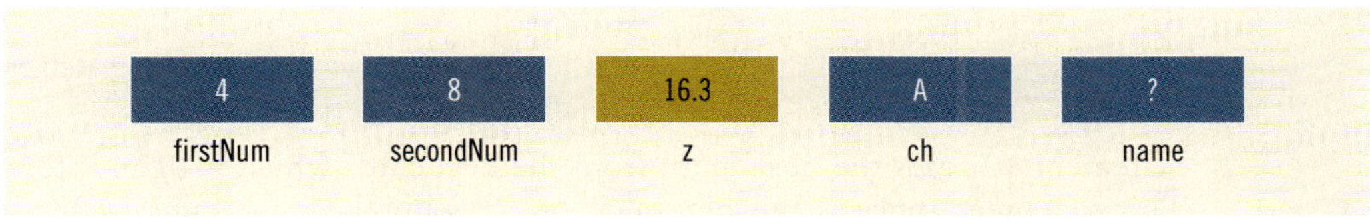

FIGURE 2-11 Values of `firstNum`, `secondNum`, `z`, `ch`, and `name` after statement 6 executes

Note that the variable **name** is still undefined. Statement 7 first evaluates the expression

```
2 * secondNum + static_cast<int>(z)
```

(which evaluates to **32**) and then stores the value of the expression into **firstNum**. This statement replaces the old value of **firstNum** with the new value. After statement 7 executes, the values of the variables are as shown in Figure 2-12.

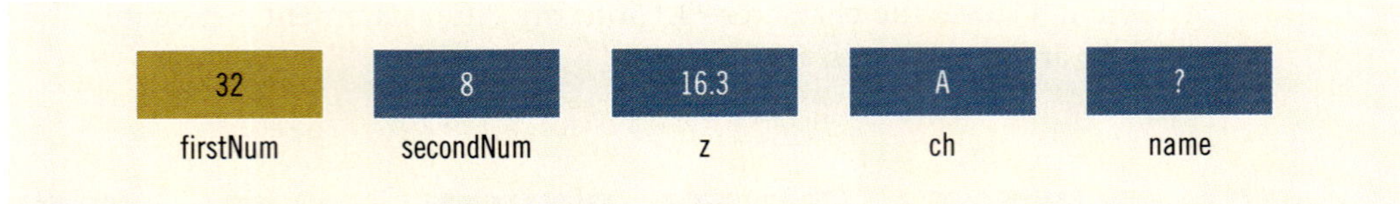

FIGURE 2-12 Values of `firstNum`, `secondNum`, `z`, `ch`, and `name` after statement 7 executes

Statement 8 gets the next input, **Jenny**, from the keyboard and stores it into **name**. After statement 8 executes, the values of the variables are as shown in Figure 2-13.

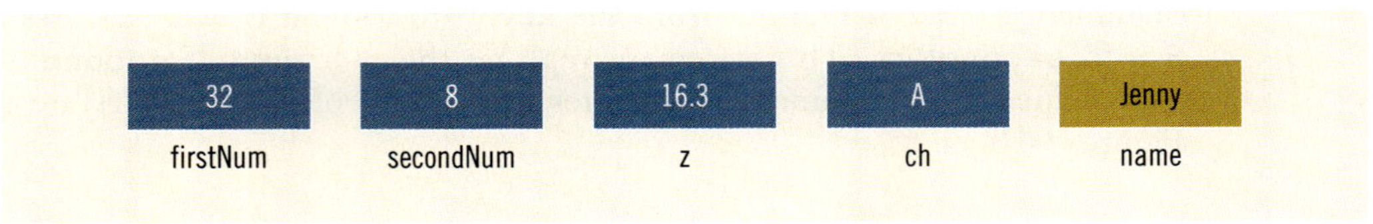

FIGURE 2-13 Values of `firstNum`, `secondNum`, `z`, `ch`, and `name` after statement 8 executes

Statement 9 first evaluates the expression **secondNum + 1** (which evaluates to 9) and then stores the value of this expression into **secondNum**. This statement updates the value of **secondNum** by incrementing the old value by 1. After statement 9 executes, the values of the variables are as shown in Figure 2-14.

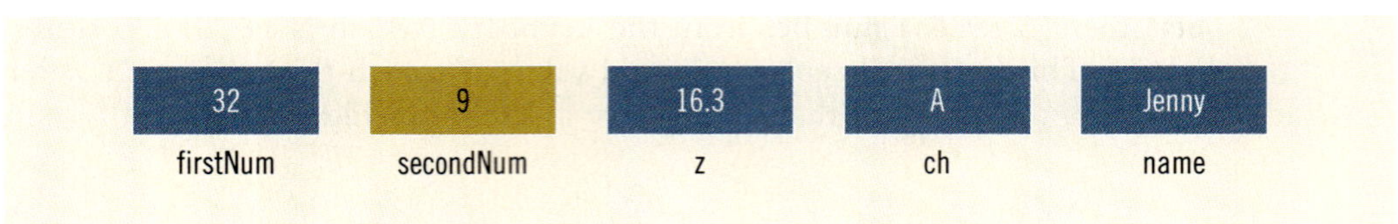

FIGURE 2-14 Values of `firstNum`, `secondNum`, `z`, `ch`, and `name` after statement 9 executes

Statement 10 reads the next input from the keyboard (which is **D**) and stores it into **ch**. This statement replaces the old value of **ch** with the new value. After statement 10 executes, the values of the variables are as shown in Figure 2-15.

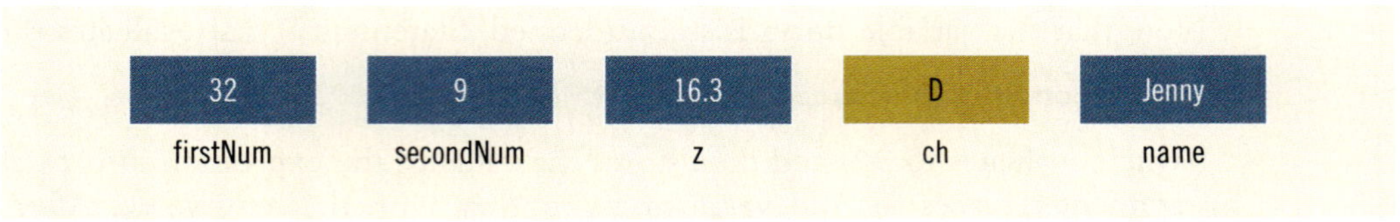

FIGURE 2-15 Values of `firstNum`, `secondNum`, `z`, `ch`, and `name` after statement 10 executes

Statement 11 first evaluates the expression

```
firstNum + static_cast<int>(ch)
```

which is

```
32 + static_cast<int>('D')
```

which equals 32 + 68 = 100. Here `static_cast<int>('D')` gives the collating sequence of the character D in the ASCII character data set, which is 68. Statement 11 then stores the value of this expression into `firstNum`. This statement replaces the old value of `firstNum` with the new value. After statement 11 executes, the values of the variables are as shown in Figure 2-16.

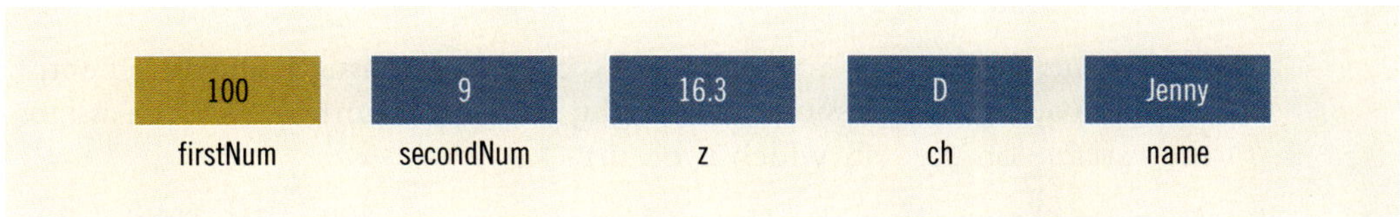

FIGURE 2-16   Values of `firstNum`, `secondNum`, z, ch, and name after statement 11 executes

Finally, statement 12 first evaluates the expression `firstNum - z` (which equals 100 – 16.3 = 100.0 – 16.3 = 83.7) and then stores the value of this expression into z. The values of the variables after the last statement executes are shown in Figure 2-17.

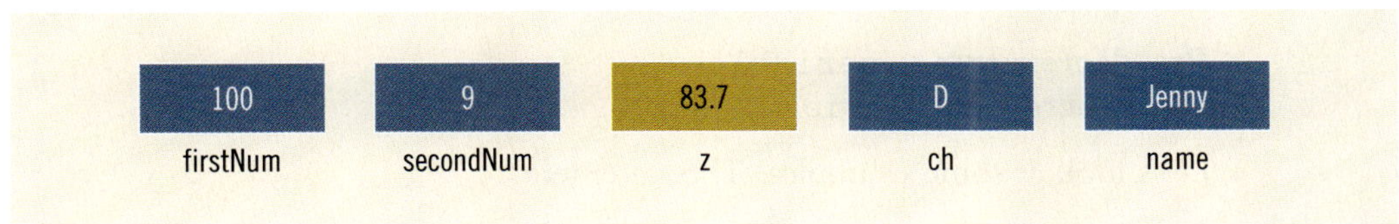

FIGURE 2-17   Values of `firstNum`, `secondNum`, z, ch, and name after statement 12 executes

NOTE When something goes wrong in a program and the results it generates are not what you expected, you should do a walk-through of the statements that assign values to your variables. Example 2-18 illustrates how to do a walk-through of your program. This is a very effective debugging technique. The Web site accompanying this book contains a C++ program that shows the effect of the 12 statements listed at the beginning of Example 2-18. The program is named `Example 2_18.cpp`.

NOTE If you assign the value of an expression that evaluates to a floating-point value—without using the cast operator—to a variable of type `int`, the fractional part is dropped. In this case, the compiler most likely will issue a warning message about the implicit type conversion.

Increment and Decrement Operators

Now that you know how to declare a variable and enter data into a variable, in this section you will learn about two more operators: the **increment** and **decrement operators**. These operators are used frequently by C++ programmers and are useful programming tools.

Suppose `count` is an `int` variable. The statement:

```
count = count + 1;
```

increments the value of `count` by 1. To execute this assignment statement, the computer first evaluates the expression on the right, which is `count + 1`. It then assigns this value to the variable on the left, which is `count`.

As you will see in later chapters, such statements are frequently used to keep track of how many times certain things have happened. To expedite the execution of such statements, C++ provides the **increment operator**, `++`, which increases the value of a variable by 1, and the **decrement operator**, `--`, which decreases the value of a variable by 1. Increment and decrement operators each have two forms, pre and post. The syntax of the increment operator is:

Pre-increment: `++variable`
Post-increment: `variable++`

The syntax of the decrement operator is:

Pre-decrement: `--variable`
Post-decrement: `variable--`

Let's look at some examples. The statement:

```
++count;
```

or:

```
count++;
```

increments the value of `count` by 1. Similarly, the statement:

```
--count;
```

or:

```
count--;
```

decrements the value of `count` by 1.

Because both the increment and decrement operators are built into C++, the value of the variable is quickly incremented or decremented without having to use the form of an assignment statement.

As you can see from these examples, both the pre- and post-increment operators increment the value of the variable by 1. Similarly, the pre- and post-decrement operators decrement the value of the variable by 1. What is the difference between the pre and post forms of these operators? The difference becomes apparent when the variable using these operators is employed in an expression.

Suppose that x is an int variable. If ++x is used in an expression, first the value of x is incremented by 1, and then the new value of x is used to evaluate the expression. On the other hand, if x++ is used in an expression, first the current value of x is used in the expression, and then the value of x is incremented by 1. The following example clarifies the difference between the pre- and post-increment operators.

Suppose that x and y are int variables. Consider the following statements:

```
x = 5;
y = ++x;
```

The first statement assigns the value 5 to x. To evaluate the second statement, which uses the pre-increment operator, first the value of x is incremented to 6, and then this value, 6, is assigned to y. After the second statement executes, both x and y have the value 6.

Now consider the following statements:

```
x = 5;
y = x++;
```

As before, the first statement assigns 5 to x. In the second statement, the post-increment operator is applied to x. To execute the second statement, first the value of x, which is 5, is used to evaluate the expression, and then the value of x is incremented to 6. Finally, the value of the expression, which is 5, is stored in y. After the second statement executes, the value of x is 6, and the value of y is 5.

The following example further illustrates how the pre and post forms of the increment operator work.

EXAMPLE 2-19

Suppose a and b are int variables and:

```
a = 5;
b = 2 + (++a);
```

The first statement assigns 5 to a. To execute the second statement, first the expression 2 + (++a) is evaluated. Because the pre-increment operator is applied to a, first the value of a is incremented to 6. Then 2 is added to 6 to get 8, which is then assigned to b. Therefore, after the second statement executes, a is 6 and b is 8.

On the other hand, after the execution of the following statements:

```
a = 5;
b = 2 + (a++);
```

the value of a is 6 while the value of b is 7.

This book will most often use the increment and decrement operators with a variable in a stand-alone statement. That is, the variable using the increment or decrement operator will not be part of any expression.

Output

In the preceding sections, you have seen how to put data into the computer's memory and how to manipulate that data. We also used certain output statements to show the results on the *standard output device*. This section explains in some detail how to further use output statements to generate the desired results.

NOTE The standard output device is usually the screen.

In C++, output on the standard output device is accomplished via the use of cout and the operator <<. The general syntax of cout together with << is:

```
cout << expression or manipulator << expression or manipulator...;
```

This is called an **output statement**. In C++, << is called the **stream insertion operator**. Generating output with cout follows two rules:

1. The expression is evaluated and its value is printed at the current insertion point on the output device.

2. A manipulator is used to format the output. The simplest manipulator is endl (the last character is the letter el), which causes the insertion point to move to the beginning of the next line.

NOTE On the screen, the insertion point is where the cursor is.

The next example illustrates how an output statement works. In an output statement, a string or an expression involving only one variable or a single value evaluates to itself.

NOTE When an output statement outputs **char** values, it outputs only the character without the single quotes (unless the single quotes are part of the output statement).

For example, suppose ch is a **char** variable and ch = 'A';. The statement:

```
cout << ch;
```

or:

```
cout << 'A';
```

outputs:

```
A
```

Similarly, when an output statement outputs the value of a string, it outputs only the string without the double quotes (unless you include double quotes as part of the output).

EXAMPLE 2-20

Consider the following statements. The output is shown to the right of each statement.

	Statement	**Output**
1	`cout << 29 / 4 << endl;`	7
2	`cout << "Hello there." << endl;`	Hello there.
3	`cout << 12 << endl;`	12
4	`cout << "4 + 7" << endl;`	4 + 7
5	`cout << 4 + 7 << endl;`	11
6	`cout << 'A' << endl;`	A
7	`cout << "4 + 7 = " << 4 + 7 << endl;`	4 + 7 = 11
8	`cout << 2 + 3 * 5 << endl;`	17
9	`cout << "Hello \nthere." << endl;`	Hello there.

Look at the output of statement 9. Recall that in C++, the newline character is '\n'; it causes the insertion point to move to the beginning of the next line before printing there. Therefore, when \n appears in a string in an output statement, it causes the insertion point to move to the beginning of the next line on the output device. This fact explains why Hello and there. are printed on separate lines.

NOTE In C++, \ is called the escape character and \n is called newline escape sequence.

Recall that all variables must be properly initialized; otherwise, the value stored in them may not make much sense. Also recall that C++ does not automatically initialize variables. The output of the C++ statement:

```
cout << a << endl;
```

is meaningful provided that the variable a has been given a value. For example, the sequence of C++ statements:

```
a = 45;
cout << a << endl;
```

will produce the output 45.

EXAMPLE 2-21

Consider the following C++ program.

```
#include <iostream>

using namespace std;

int main()
{
    int a, b;

    a = 65;                          //Line  1
    b = 78;                          //Line  2

    cout << 29 / 4 << endl;          //Line  3
    cout << 3.0 / 2 << endl;         //Line  4
    cout << "Hello there.\n";        //Line  5
    cout << 7 << endl;               //Line  6
    cout << 3 + 5 << endl;           //Line  7
    cout << "3 + 5";                 //Line  8
    cout << endl;                    //Line  9
    cout << 2 + 3 * 6 << endl;       //Line 10
    cout << "a" << endl;             //Line 11
    cout << a << endl;               //Line 12
    cout << b << endl;               //Line 13

    return 0;
}
```

In the following output, the column marked "Output of Statement at" and the line numbers are not part of the output. The line numbers are shown in this column to make it easy to see which output corresponds to which statement.

	Output of Statement at
7	Line 3
1.5	Line 4
Hello there.	Line 5
7	Line 6
8	Line 7
3 + 5	Line 8
20	Line 10
a	Line 11
65	Line 12
78	Line 13

For the most part, the output is straightforward. Look at the output of the statements in Lines 7, 8, 9, and 10. The statement in Line 7 outputs the result of 3 + 5, which is 8, and moves the insertion point to the beginning of the next line. The statement in Line 8 outputs the string 3 + 5. Note that the statement in Line 8 consists only of the string 3 + 5. Therefore, after printing 3 + 5, the insertion point stays positioned after 5; it does not move to the beginning of the next line.

The output statement in Line 9 contains only the manipulator `endl`, which moves the insertion point to the beginning of the next line. Therefore, when the statement in Line 10 executes, the output starts at the beginning of the line. Note that in this output, the column "Output of Statement at" does not contain Line 9. This is due to the fact that the statement in Line 9 does not produce any printable output. It simply moves the insertion point to the beginning of the next line. Next, the statement in Line 10 outputs the result of the expression 2 + 3 * 6, which is 20. The manipulator `endl` then moves the insertion point to the beginning of the next line.

NOTE   Outputting or accessing the value of a variable in an expression does not destroy or modify the contents of the variable.

Let us now take a close look at the newline character, `'\n'`. Consider the following C++ statements:

```
cout << "Hello there.";
cout << "My name is James.";
```

If these statements are executed in sequence, the output is:

```
Hello there.My name is James.
```

Now consider the following C++ statements:

```
cout << "Hello there.\n";
cout << "My name is James.";
```

The output of these C++ statements is:

```
Hello there.
My name is James.
```

When \n is encountered in the string, the insertion point is positioned at the beginning of the next line. Note also that \n may appear anywhere in the string. For example, the output of the statement:

```
cout << "Hello \nthere. \nMy name is James.";
```

is:

```
Hello
there.
My name is James.
```

Also, note that the output of the statement:

```
cout << '\n';
```

is the same as the output of the statement:

```
cout << "\n";
```

which is equivalent to the output of the statement:

```
cout << endl;
```

Thus, the output of the sequence of statements:

```
cout << "Hello there.\n";
cout << "My name is James.";
```

is equivalent to the output of the sequence of statements:

```
cout << "Hello there." << endl;
cout << "My name is James.";
```

EXAMPLE 2-22

Consider the following C++ statements:

```
cout << "Hello there.\nMy name is James.";
```

or:

```
cout << "Hello there.";
cout << "\nMy name is James.";
```

or:

```
cout << "Hello there.";
cout << endl << "My name is James.";
```

In each case, the output of the statements is:

```
Hello there.
My name is James.
```

EXAMPLE 2-23

The output of the C++ statements:

```
cout << "Count...\n....1\n.....2\n......3";
```

or:

```
cout << "Count..." << endl << "....1" << endl
     << ".....2" << endl << "......3";
```

is:

```
Count...
....1
.....2
......3
```

EXAMPLE 2-24

Suppose that you want to output the following sentence in one line as part of a message:

```
It is sunny, warm, and not a windy day. We can go golfing.
```

Obviously, you will use an output statement to produce this output. However, in the programming code, this statement may not fit in one line as part of the output statement. Of course, you can use multiple output statements as follows:

```
cout << "It is sunny, warm, and not a windy day. ";
cout << "We can go golfing." << endl;
```

Note the semicolon at the end of the first statement and the identifier cout at the beginning of the second statement. Also, note that there is no manipulator endl at the end of the first statement. Here two output statements are used to output the sentence in one line. Equivalently, you can use the following output statement to output this sentence:

```
cout << "It is sunny, warm, and not a windy day. "
     << "We can go golfing." << endl;
```

In this statement, note that there is no semicolon at the end of the first line and the identifier cout does not appear at the beginning of the second line. Because there is no semicolon at the end of the first line, this output statement continues at the second line. Also, note the double quotation marks at the beginning and end of the sentences on each line. The string is broken into two strings, but both strings are part of the same output statement.

If a string appearing in an output statement is long and you want to output the string in one line, you can break the string by using either of the previous two methods. However, the following statement would be incorrect:

```
cout << "It is sunny, warm, and not a windy day.
          We can go golfing." << endl;                              //illegal
```

In other words, the return (or Enter) key on your keyboard cannot be part of the string. That is, in programming code, a string *cannot* be broken into more than one line by using the return (Enter) key on your keyboard.

Recall that the newline character is \n, which causes the insertion point to move to the beginning of the next line. There are many escape sequences in C++, which allow you to control the output. Table 2-4 lists some of the commonly used escape sequences.

TABLE 2-4 Commonly Used Escape Sequences

	Escape Sequence	Description
\n	Newline	Cursor moves to the beginning of the next line
\t	Tab	Cursor moves to the next tab stop
\b	Backspace	Cursor moves one space to the left
\r	Return	Cursor moves to the beginning of the current line (not the next line)
\\	Backslash	Backslash is printed
\'	Single quotation	Single quotation mark is printed
\"	Double quotation	Double quotation mark is printed

The following example shows the effect of some of these escape sequences.

EXAMPLE 2-25

The output of the statement:

```
cout << "The newline escape sequence is \\n" << endl;
```

is:

```
The newline escape sequence is \n
```

The output of the statement:

```
cout << "The tab character is represented as \'\\t\'" << endl;
```

is:

```
The tab character is represented as '\t'
```

Note that the single quote can also be printed without using the escape sequence. Therefore, the preceding statement is equivalent to the following output statement:

```
cout << "The tab character is represented as '\\t'" << endl;
```

The output of the statement:

```
cout << "The string \"Sunny\" contains five characters." << endl;
```

is:

```
The string "Sunny" contains five characters.
```

NOTE The Web site accompanying this text contains the C++ program that shows the effect of the statements in Example 2-25. The program is named `Example2_25.cpp`.

To use `cin` and `cout` in a program, you must include a certain header file. The next section explains what this header file is, how to include a header file in a program, and why you need header files in a program. Chapter 3 will provide a full explanation of `cin` and `cout`.

Preprocessor Directives

Only a small number of operations, such as arithmetic and assignment operations, are explicitly defined in C++. Many of the functions and symbols needed to run a C++ program are provided as a collection of libraries. Every library has a name and is referred to by a header file. For example, the descriptions of the functions needed to perform input/output (I/O) are contained in the header file **iostream**. Similarly, the descriptions of some very useful mathematical functions, such as power, absolute, and sine, are contained in the header file **cmath**. If you want to use I/O or math functions, you need to tell the computer where to find the necessary code. You use preprocessor directives and the names of header files to tell the computer the locations of the code provided in libraries. Preprocessor directives are processed by a program called a **preprocessor**.

Preprocessor directives are commands supplied to the preprocessor that cause the preprocessor to modify the text of a C++ program before it is compiled. All preprocessor commands begin with **#**. There are no semicolons at the end of preprocessor commands because they are not C++ statements. To use a header file in a C++ program, use the preprocessor directive **include**.

The general syntax to include a header file (provided by the SDK) in a C++ program is:

```
#include <headerFileName>
```

For example, the following statement includes the header file **iostream** in a C++ program:

```
#include <iostream>
```

Preprocessor directives to include header files are placed as the first line of a program so that the identifiers declared in those header files can be used throughout the program. (Recall that in C++, identifiers must be declared before they can be used.)

Certain header files are required to be provided as part of C++. Appendix F describes some of the commonly used header files. Individual programmers can also create their own header files, which is discussed in the chapter Classes and Data Abstraction, later in this book.

Note that the preprocessor commands are processed by the preprocessor before the program goes through the compiler.

From Figure 1-3 (Chapter 1), we can conclude that a C++ system has three basic components: the program development environment, the C++ language, and the C++ library. All three components are integral parts of the C++ system. The program development environment consists of the six steps shown in Figure 1-3. As you learn the C++ language throughout the book, we will discuss components of the C++ library as we need them.

namespace and Using `cin` and `cout` in a Program

Earlier, you learned that both `cin` and `cout` are predefined identifiers. In ANSI/ISO Standard C++, these identifiers are declared in the header file `iostream`, but within a `namespace`. The name of this `namespace` is `std`. (The `namespace` mechanism will be formally defined and discussed in detail in Chapter 8. For now, you need to know only how to use `cin` and `cout`, and, in fact, any other identifier from the header file `iostream`.)

There are several ways you can use an identifier declared in the namespace `std`. One way to use `cin` and `cout` is to refer to them as `std::cin` and `std::cout` throughout the program.

Another option is to include the following statement in your program:

```
using namespace std;
```

This statement appears after the statement `#include <iostream>`. You can then refer to `cin` and `cout` without using the prefix `std::`. To simplify the use of `cin` and `cout`, this book uses the second form. That is, to use `cin` and `cout` in a program, the programs will contain the following two statements:

```
#include <iostream>
```

```
using namespace std;
```

In C++, `namespace` and `using` are reserved words.

The `namespace` mechanism is a feature of ANSI/ISO Standard C++. As you learn more C++ programming, you will become aware of other header files. For example, the header file `cmath` contains the specifications of many useful mathematical functions. Similarly, the header file `iomanip` contains the specifications of many useful functions and manipulators that help you format your output in a specific manner. However, just like the identifiers in the header file `iostream`, the identifiers in ANSI/ISO Standard C++ header files are declared within a `namespace`.

The name of the `namespace` in each of these header files is `std`. Therefore, whenever certain features of a header file in ANSI/ISO Standard C++ are discussed, this book will refer to the identifiers without the prefix `std::`. Moreover, to simplify the accessing of identifiers in programs, the statement `using namespace std;` will be included. Also, if a program uses multiple header files, only one `using` statement is needed. This `using` statement typically appears after all the header files.

Using the `string` Data Type in a Program

Recall that the `string` data type is a programmer-defined data type and is not directly available for use in a program. To use the `string` data type, you need to access its definition from the header file `string`. Therefore, to use the `string` data type in a program, you must include the following preprocessor directive:

```
#include <string>
```

Creating a C++ Program

In previous sections, you learned enough C++ concepts to write meaningful programs. You are now ready to create a complete C++ program.

A C++ program is a collection of functions, one of which is the function `main`. Therefore, if a C++ program consists of only one function, then it must be the function `main`. Moreover, a function is a set of instructions designed to accomplish a specific task. Until Chapter 6, you will deal mainly with the function `main`.

The statements to declare variables, the statements to manipulate data (such as assignments), and the statements to input and output data are placed within the function `main`. The statements to declare named constants are usually placed outside of the function `main`.

The syntax of the function `main` used throughout this book has the following form:

```
int main()
{
    statement1
        .
        .
        .
    statementn

    return 0;
}
```

In the syntax of the function `main`, each statement (`statement1, ..., statementn`) is usually either a declarative statement or an executable statement. The statement `return 0;` must be included in the function `main` and must be the last statement. If the statement `return 0;` is misplaced in the body of the function `main`, the results generated by the program may not be to your liking. The meaning of the statement `return 0;` will be discussed in Chapter 6. In C++, `return` is a reserved word.

A C++ program might use the resources provided by the SDK, such as the necessary code to input the data, which would require your program to include certain header files. You can, therefore, divide a C++ program into two parts: preprocessor directives and the program. The preprocessor directives tell the compiler which header files to include in the program. The program contains statements that accomplish meaningful results. Taken together, the preprocessor directives and the program statements constitute the C++ **source code**. Recall that to be useful, source code must be saved in a file with the file extension **.cpp**. For example, if the source code is saved in the file **firstProgram**, then the complete name of this file is **firstProgram.cpp**. The file containing the source code is called the **source code file** or **source file**.

When the program is compiled, the compiler generates the object code, which is saved in a file with the file extension `.obj`. When the object code is linked with the system resources, the executable code is produced and saved in a file with the file extension `.exe`. Typically, the name of the file containing the object code and the name of the file containing the executable code are the same as the name of the file containing the source code. For example, if the source code is located in a file named `firstProg.cpp`, the name of the file containing the object code is `firstProg.obj`, and the name of the file containing the executable code is `firstProg.exe`.

The extensions as given in the preceding paragraph—that is, `.cpp`, `.obj`, and `.exe`—are system dependent. Moreover, some SDKs maintain programs in the form of projects. The name of the project and the name of the source file need not be the same. It is possible that the name of the executable file is the name of the project, with the extension `.exe`. To be certain, check your system or SDK documentation. The Web site accompanying this book illustrates how to use some of the SDKs, such as Microsoft Visual C++ 6.0 and Microsoft Visual Studio .NET.

Because the programming instructions are placed in the function `main`, let us elaborate on this function.

The basic parts of the function `main` are the heading and the body. The first line of the function `main`, that is:

```
int main()
```

is called the heading of the function `main`.

The statements enclosed between the curly braces ({ and }) form the body of the function `main`. The body of the function `main` contains two types of statements:

- Declaration statements
- Executable statements

Declaration statements are used to declare things, such as variables.

In C++, variables or identifiers can be declared anywhere in the program, but they must be declared before they can be used.

EXAMPLE 2-26

The following statements are examples of variable declarations:

```
int a, b, c;
double x, y;
```

Executable statements perform calculations, manipulate data, create output, accept input, and so on.

Some executable statements that you have encountered so far are the assignment, input, and output statements.

EXAMPLE 2-27

The following statements are examples of executable statements:

```
a = 4;                           //assignment statement
cin >> b;                        //input statement
cout << a << " " << b << endl;   //output statement
```

In skeleton form, a C++ program looks like the following:

```
preprocessor directives to include header files

using statement

declare named constants, if necessary

int main()
{
    statement1
        .
        .
        .
    statementn

    return 0;
}
```

The C++ program in Example 2-28 shows where include statements, declaration statements, executable statements, and so on typically appear in the program.

EXAMPLE 2-28

```
#include <iostream>              //Line 1

using namespace std;             //Line 2

const int NUMBER = 12;           //Line 3

int main()                       //Line 4
{                                //Line 5
    int firstNum;                //Line 6
    int secondNum;               //Line 7
```

```cpp
    firstNum = 18;                                      //Line 8
    cout << "Line 9: firstNum = " << firstNum
         << endl;                                       //Line 9

    cout << "Line 10: Enter an integer: ";              //Line 10
    cin >> secondNum;                                   //Line 11
    cout << endl;                                       //Line 12

    cout << "Line 13: secondNum = " << secondNum
         << endl;                                       //Line 13

    firstNum = firstNum + NUMBER + 2 * secondNum;       //Line 14

    cout << "Line 15: The new value of "
         << "firstNum = " << firstNum << endl;          //Line 15

    return 0;                                           //Line 16
}                                                       //Line 17
```

Sample Run: In this sample run, the user input is shaded.

```
Line 9: firstNum = 18
Line 10: Enter an integer: 15

Line 13: secondNum = 15
Line 15: The new value of firstNum = 60
```

The preceding program works as follows: The statement in Line 1 includes the header file `iostream` so that program can perform input/output. The statement in Line 2 uses the **using namespace** statement so that identifiers declared in the header file `iostream`, such as `cin`, `cout`, and `endl`, can be used without using the prefix `std::`. The statement in Line 3 declares the named constant `NUMBER` and sets its value to `12`. The statement in Line 4 contains the heading of the function `main`, and the left brace in Line 5 marks the beginning of the function `main`. The statements in Lines 6 and 7 declare the variables `firstNum` and `secondNum`.

The statement in Line 8 sets the value of `firstNum` to `18` and the statement in Line 9 outputs the value of `firstNum`. Next, the statement in Line 10 prompts the user to enter an integer. The statement in Line 11 reads and stores the integer into the variable `secondNum`, which is `15` in the sample run. The statement in Line 12 positions the cursor on the screen at the beginning of the next line. The statement in Line 13 outputs the value of `secondNum`. The statement in Line 14 evaluates the expression:

```
firstNum + NUMBER + 2 * secondNum
```

and assigns the value of this expression to the variable `firstNum`, which is `60` in the sample run. The statement in Line 15 outputs the new value of `firstNum`. The statement in Line 16 contains the **return** statement. The right brace in Line 17 marks the end of the function `main`.

Program Style and Form

In previous sections, you learned enough C++ concepts to write meaningful programs. Before beginning to write programs, however, you need to learn their proper structure, among other things. Using the proper structure for a C++ program makes it easier to understand and subsequently modify the program. There is nothing more frustrating than trying to follow, and perhaps modify, a program that is syntactically correct but has no structure.

In addition, every C++ program must satisfy certain rules of the language. A C++ program must contain the function `main`. It must also follow the syntax rules, which, like grammar rules, tell what is right and what is wrong, and what is legal and what is illegal in the language. Other rules serve the purpose of giving precise meaning to the language; that is, they support the language's semantics.

The following sections are designed to help you learn how to use the C++ programming elements you have learned so far to create a functioning program. These sections cover the syntax; the use of blanks; the use of semicolons, brackets, and commas; semantics; naming identifiers; prompt lines; documentation, including comments; and form and style.

Syntax

The syntax rules of a language tell what is legal and what is not legal. Errors in syntax are detected during compilation. For example, consider the following C++ statements:

```cpp
int x;          //Line 1
int y           //Line 2
double z;       //Line 3

y = w + x;      //Line 4
```

When these statements are compiled, a compilation error will occur at Line 2 because the semicolon is missing after the declaration of the variable `y`. A second compilation error will occur at Line 4 because the identifier `w` is used but has not been declared.

As discussed in Chapter 1, you enter a program into the computer by using a text editor. When the program is typed, errors are almost unavoidable. Therefore, when the program is compiled, you are most likely to see syntax errors. It is quite possible that a syntax error at a particular place might lead to syntax errors in several subsequent statements. It is very common for the omission of a single character to cause four or five error messages. However, when the first syntax error is removed and the program is recompiled, subsequent syntax errors caused by this syntax error may disappear. Therefore, you should correct syntax errors in the order in which the compiler lists them. As you become more familiar and experienced with C++, you will learn how to quickly spot and fix syntax errors. Also, compilers not only discover syntax errors, but also hint and sometimes tell the user where the syntax errors are and how to fix them.

Use of Blanks

In C++, you use one or more blanks to separate numbers when data is input. Blanks are also used to separate reserved words and identifiers from each other and from other symbols. Blanks must never appear within a reserved word or identifier.

Use of Semicolons, Brackets, and Commas

All C++ statements must end with a semicolon. The semicolon is also called a **statement terminator**.

Note that brackets, { and }, are not C++ statements in and of themselves, even though they often appear on a line with no other code. You might regard brackets as delimiters, because they enclose the body of a function and set it off from other parts of the program. Brackets have other uses, which will be explained later.

Recall that commas are used to separate items in a list. For example, you use commas when you declare more than one variable following a data type.

Semantics

The set of rules that gives meaning to a language is called **semantics**. For example, the order-of-precedence rules for arithmetic operators are semantic rules.

If a program contains syntax errors, the compiler will warn you. What happens when a program contains semantic errors? It is quite possible to eradicate all syntax errors in a program and still not have it run. And if it runs, it may not do what you meant it to do. For example, the following two lines of code are both syntactically correct expressions, but they have different meanings:

```
2 + 3 * 5
```

and:

```
(2 + 3) * 5
```

If you substitute one of these lines of code for the other in a program, you will not get the same results—even though the numbers are the same, the semantics are different. You will learn about semantics throughout this book.

Naming Identifiers

Consider the following two sets of statements:

```
const double A = 2.54;      //conversion constant
double x;                   //variable to hold centimeters
double y;                   //variable to hold inches

x = y * a;
```

and:

```
const double CENTIMETERS_PER_INCH = 2.54;
double centimeters;
double inches;

centimeters = inches * CENTIMETERS_PER_INCH;
```

The identifiers in the second set of statements, such as `CENTIMETERS_PER_INCH`, are usually called **self-documenting** identifiers. As you can see, self-documenting identifiers can make comments less necessary.

Consider the self-documenting identifier `annualsale`. This identifier is called a **run-together word**. In using self-documenting identifiers, you may inadvertently include run-together words, which may lessen the clarity of your documentation. You can make run-together words easier to understand by either capitalizing the beginning of each new word or by inserting an underscore just before a new word. For example, you could use either `annualSale` or `annual_sale` to create an identifier that is more clear.

Recall that earlier in this chapter we specified the general rules for naming named constants and variables. For example, an identifier used to name a named constant is all uppercase. If this identifier is a run-together word, then the words are separated with the underscore character.

Prompt Lines

Part of good documentation is the use of clearly written prompts so that users will know what to do when they interact with a program. There is nothing more frustrating than sitting in front of a running program and not having the foggiest notion of whether to enter something or what to enter. **Prompt lines** are executable statements that inform the user what to do. For example, consider the following C++ statements, in which `num` is an `int` variable:

```
cout << "Please enter a number between 1 and 10 and "
     << "press the return key" << endl;
cin >> num;
```

When these two statements execute in the order given, first the output statement causes the following line of text to appear on the screen:

```
Please enter a number between 1 and 10 and press the return key
```

After seeing this line, users know that they must enter a number and press the return key. If the program contained only the second statement, users would have no idea that they must enter a number, and the computer would wait forever for the input. The preceding output statement is an example of a prompt line.

In a program, whenever input is needed from users, you must include the necessary prompt lines. Furthermore, these prompt lines should include as much information as possible about what input is acceptable. For example, the preceding prompt line not only tells the user to input a number, but also informs the user that the number should be between 1 and 10.

Documentation

The programs that you write should be clear not only to you, but also to anyone else. Therefore, you must properly document your programs. A well-documented program is easier to understand and modify, even a long time after you originally wrote it. You use comments to document programs. Comments should appear in a program to explain the purpose of the program, identify who wrote it, and explain the purpose of particular statements.

Comments

C++ has two types of comments: single line comments and multiple line comments. **Single line comments** begin with // anywhere in the line. Everything encountered on that line after // is ignored by the compiler. **Multiple line comments** are enclosed between /* and */. The compiler ignores anything that appears between /* and */.

You can insert comments at the top of a program to give a brief explanation of the program and information about the programmer. You can also include comments before each key step to give a brief description of what that step accomplishes.

Recall that in this book, in the programming code, the comments are shown in green color.

Form and Style

You might be thinking that C++ has too many rules. However, in practice, the rules give C++ a great degree of freedom. For example, consider the following two ways of declaring variables:

```
int feet, inch;
double x, y;
```

and:

```
int feet,inches;double x,y;
```

The computer would have no difficulty understanding either of these formats, but the first form is easier to read and follow. Of course, the omission of a single comma or semicolon in either format may lead to all sorts of strange error messages.

What about blank spaces? Where are they significant and where are they meaningless? Consider the following two statements:

```
int a,b,c;
```

and:

```
int    a,    b,    c;
```

Both of these declarations mean the same thing. Here the blanks between the identifiers in the second statement are meaningless. On the other hand, consider the following statement:

```
inta,b,c;
```

This statement contains a syntax error. The lack of a blank between `int` and the identifier a changes the reserved word `int` and the identifier `a` into a new identifier, `inta`.

The clarity of the rules of syntax and semantics frees you to adopt formats that are pleasing to you and easier to understand.

The following example further elaborates on this.

EXAMPLE 2-29

Consider the following C++ program:

```
//An improperly formatted C++ program.

#include <iostream>
#include <string>
using namespace std;

int main()
{
int num; double height;
string name;
cout << "Enter an integer: "; cin >> num; cout << endl;
    cout<<"num: "<<num<<endl;
cout<<"Enter the first name: "; cin>>name;
    cout<<endl; cout <<"Enter the height: ";
cin>>height; cout<<endl;

cout<<"Name: "<<name<<endl;cout<<"Height: "
<<height; cout <<endl;return 0;
}
```

This program is syntactically correct; the C++ compiler would have no difficulty reading and compiling this program. However, this program is very hard to read. The program that you write should be properly indented and formatted. Note the difference when the program is reformatted:

```
//A properly formatted C++ program.

#include <iostream>
#include <string>

using namespace std;
```

```cpp
int main()
{
    int num;
    double height;
    string name;

    cout << "Enter an integer: ";
    cin >> num;
    cout << endl;

    cout << "num: " << num << endl;

    cout << "Enter the first name: ";
    cin >> name;
    cout << endl;

    cout << "Enter the height: ";
    cin >> height;
    cout << endl;

    cout << "Name: " << name << endl;
    cout << "Height: " << height << endl;

    return 0;
}
```

As you can see, this program is easier to read. Your programs should be properly indented and formatted. To document the variables, programmers typically declare one variable per line. Also, always put a space before and after an operator.

More on Assignment Statements

The assignment statements you have seen so far are called **simple assignment statements**. In certain cases, you can use special assignment statements called **compound assignment statements** to write simple assignment statements in a more concise notation.

Corresponding to the five arithmetic operators +, −, *, /, and %, C++ provides five compound operators +=, −=, *=, /=, and %=, respectively. Consider the following simple assignment statement, where **x** and **y** are `int` variables:

```cpp
x = x * y;
```

Using the compound operator *=, this statement can be written as:

```cpp
x *= y;
```

In general, using the compound operator *=, you can rewrite the simple assignment statement:

```
variable = variable * (expression);
```

as:

```
variable *= expression;
```

The other arithmetic compound operators have similar conventions. For example, using the compound operator +=, you can rewrite the simple assignment statement:

```
variable = variable + (expression);
```

as:

```
variable += expression;
```

The compound assignment statement allows you to write simple assignment statements in a concise fashion by combining an arithmetic operator with the assignment operator.

EXAMPLE 2-30

This example shows several compound assignment statements that are equivalent to simple assignment statements.

Simple Assignment Statement	**Compound Assignment Statement**
`i = i + 5;`	`i += 5;`
`counter = counter + 1;`	`counter += 1;`
`sum = sum + number;`	`sum += number;`
`amount = amount * (interest + 1);`	`amount *= interest + 1;`
`x = x / ( y + 5);`	`x /= y + 5;`

NOTE Any compound assignment statement can be converted into a simple assignment statement. However, a simple assignment statement may not be (easily) converted to a compound assignment statement. For example, consider the following simple assignment statement:

```
x = x * y + z - 5;
```

To write this statement as a compound assignment statement, the variable **x** must be a common factor in the right side, which is not the case. Therefore, you cannot immediately convert this statement into a compound assignment statement. In fact, the equivalent compound assignment statement is:

```
x *=  y + (z - 5)/x;
```

which is more complicated than the simple assignment statement. Furthermore, in the preceding compound statement **x** cannot be 0. We recommend avoiding such compound expressions.

NOTE   In programming code, this book typically uses only the compound operator +=. So statements such as a = a + b; are written as a += b;.

PROGRAMMING EXAMPLE: Convert Length

Write a program that takes as input given lengths expressed in feet and inches. The program should then convert and output the lengths in centimeters. Assume that the given lengths in feet and inches are integers.

Input   Length in feet and inches.

Output   Equivalent length in centimeters.

PROBLEM ANALYSIS AND ALGORITHM DESIGN   The lengths are given in feet and inches, and you need to find the equivalent length in centimeters. One inch is equal to 2.54 centimeters. The first thing the program needs to do is convert the length given in feet and inches to all inches. Then you can use the conversion formula, 1 inch = 2.54 centimeters, to find the equivalent length in centimeters. To convert the length from feet and inches to inches, you multiply the number of feet by 12, as 1 foot is equal to 12 inches, and add the given inches.

For example, suppose the input is 5 feet and 7 inches. You then find the total inches as follows:

```
totalInches = (12 * feet) + inches
            = 12 * 5 + 7
            = 67
```

You can then apply the conversion formula, 1 inch = 2.54 centimeters, to find the length in centimeters.

```
centimeters = totalInches * 2.54
            = 67 * 2.54
            = 170.18
```

Based on this analysis of the problem, you can design an algorithm as follows:

1. Get the length in feet and inches.
2. Convert the length into total inches.
3. Convert total inches into centimeters.
4. Output centimeters.

Variables   The input for the program is two numbers: one for feet and one for inches. Thus, you need two variables: one to store feet and the other to store inches. Because the program will first convert the given length into inches, you need another variable to store the total inches. You also need a variable to store the equivalent length in centimeters. In summary, you need the following variables:

```
int feet;                //variable to hold given feet
int inches;              //variable to hold given inches
int totalInches;         //variable to hold total inches
double centimeters;      //variable to hold length in centimeters
```

Named Constants To calculate the equivalent length in centimeters, you need to multiply the total inches by `2.54`. Instead of using the value `2.54` directly in the program, you will declare this value as a named constant. Similarly, to find the total inches, you need to multiply the feet by `12` and add the inches. Instead of using `12` directly in the program, you will also declare this value as a named constant. Using a named constant makes it easier to modify the program later.

```
const double CENTIMETERS_PER_INCH = 2.54;
const int INCHES_PER_FOOT = 12;
```

MAIN ALGORITHM In the preceding sections, we analyzed the problem and determined the formulas to do the calculations. We also determined the necessary variables and named constants. We can now expand the algorithm given in the section, Problem Analysis and Algorithm Design, to solve the problem given at the beginning of this programming example.

1. Prompt the user for the input. (Without a prompt line, the user will be staring at a blank screen and will not know what to do.)

2. Get the data.

3. Echo the input—that is, output what the program read as input. (Without this step, after the program has executed, you will not know what the input was.)

4. Find the length in inches.

5. Output the length in inches.

6. Convert the length to centimeters.

7. Output the length in centimeters.

Putting It Together Now that the problem has been analyzed and the algorithm has been designed, the next step is to translate the algorithm into C++ code. Because this is the first complete C++ program you are writing, let's review the necessary steps in sequence.

The program will begin with comments that document its purpose and functionality. As there is both input to this program (the length in feet and inches) and output (the equivalent length in centimeters), you will be using system resources for input/output. In other words, the program will use input statements to get data into the program and output statements to print the results. Because the data will be entered from the keyboard and the output will be displayed on the screen, the program must include the header file `iostream`. Thus, the first statement of the program, after the comments as described above, will be the preprocessor directive to include this header file.

This program requires two types of memory locations for data manipulation: named constants and variables. Typically, named constants hold special data, such as `CENTIMETERS_PER_INCH`. Depending on the nature of a named constant, it can be placed before the function `main` or within the function `main`. If a named constant is to be used throughout the program, then it is typically placed before the function `main`. We will comment further on where to put named constants within a program in Chapter 7, when we discuss user-defined functions in general. Until then, usually, we will place named constants before the function `main` so that they can be used throughout the program.

This program has only one function, the function `main`, which will contain all of the programming instructions in its body. In addition, the program needs variables to manipulate data, and these variables will be declared in the body of the function `main`. The reasons for declaring variables in the body of the function `main` are explained in Chapter 7. The body of the function `main` will also contain the C++ statements that implement the algorithm. Therefore, the body of the function `main` has the following form:

```cpp
int main()
{
    declare variables

    statements

    return 0;
}
```

To write the complete length conversion program, follow these steps:

1. Begin the program with comments for documentation.
2. Include header files, if any are used in the program.
3. Declare named constants, if any.
4. Write the definition of the function `main`.

COMPLETE PROGRAM LISTING

```cpp
//****************************************************************
// Program Convert Measurements: This program converts
// measurements in feet and inches into centimeters using
// the formula that 1 inch is equal to 2.54 centimeters.
//****************************************************************
```

```cpp
    //Header file
#include <iostream>

using namespace std;

    //Named constants
const double CENTIMETERS_PER_INCH = 2.54;
const int INCHES_PER_FOOT = 12;

int main ()
{
        //Declare variables
    int feet, inches;
    int totalInches;
    double centimeter;

        //Statements: Step 1 - Step 7
    cout << "Enter two integers, one for feet and "
         << "one for inches: ";                        //Step 1
    cin >> feet >> inches;                             //Step 2
    cout << endl;
    cout << "The numbers you entered are " << feet
         << " for feet and " << inches
         << " for inches. " << endl;                   //Step 3

    totalInches = INCHES_PER_FOOT * feet + inches;     //Step 4

    cout << "The total number of inches = "
         << totalInches << endl;                       //Step 5

    centimeter = CENTIMETERS_PER_INCH * totalInches;   //Step 6

    cout << "The number of centimeters = "
         << centimeter << endl;                        //Step 7

    return 0;
}
```

Sample Run: In this sample run, the user input is shaded.

```
Enter two integers, one for feet, one for inches: 15 7

The numbers you entered are 15 for feet and 7 for inches.
The total number of inches = 187
The number of centimeters = 474.98
```

PROGRAMMING EXAMPLE: Make Change

Write a program that takes as input any change expressed in cents. It should then compute the number of half-dollars, quarters, dimes, nickels, and pennies to be returned, returning as many half-dollars as possible, then quarters, dimes, nickels, and pennies, in that order. For example, 483 cents should be returned as 9 half-dollars, 1 quarter, 1 nickel, and 3 pennies.

Input   Change in cents.

Output   Equivalent change in half-dollars, quarters, dimes, nickels, and pennies.

PROBLEM
ANALYSIS
AND
ALGORITHM
DESIGN

Suppose the given change is 646 cents. To find the number of half-dollars, you divide 646 by 50, the value of a half-dollar, and find the quotient, which is 12, and the remainder, which is 46. The quotient, 12, is the number of half-dollars, and the remainder, 46, is the remaining change.

Next, divide the remaining change by 25, to find the number of quarters. Since the remaining change is 46, division by 25 gives the quotient 1, which is the number of quarters, and a remainder of 21, which is the remaining change. This process continues for dimes and nickels. To calculate the remainder in an integer division, you use the mod operator, %.

Applying this discussion to 646 cents yields the following calculations:

1. Change = 646
2. Number of half-dollars = 646 / 50 = 12
3. Remaining change = 646 % 50 = 46
4. Number of quarters = 46 / 25 = 1
5. Remaining change = 46 % 25 = 21
6. Number of dimes = 21 / 10 = 2
7. Remaining change = 21 % 10 = 1
8. Number of nickels = 1 / 5 = 0
9. Number of pennies = remaining change = 1 % 5 = 1

This discussion translates into the following algorithm:

1. Get the change in cents.
2. Find the number of half-dollars.
3. Calculate the remaining change.
4. Find the number of quarters.
5. Calculate the remaining change.
6. Find the number of dimes.

7. Calculate the remaining change.

8. Find the number of nickels.

9. Calculate the remaining change.

10. The remaining change is the number of pennies.

Variables From the previous discussion and algorithm, it appears that the program will need variables to hold the number of half-dollars, quarters, and so on. However, the numbers of half-dollars, quarters, and so on are not used in later calculations, so the program can simply output these values without saving each of them in a variable. The only thing that keeps changing is the change, so the program actually needs only one variable:

```
int change;
```

Named Constants To calculate the equivalent change, the program performs calculations using the values of a half-dollar, which is 50; a quarter, which is 25; a dime, which is 10; and a nickel, which is 5. Because these data are special and the program uses these values more than once, it makes sense to declare them as named constants. Using named constants also simplifies later modification of the program:

```
const int HALFDOLLAR = 50;
const int QUARTER   = 25;
const int DIME = 10;
const int NICKEL = 5;
```

MAIN ALGORITHM

1. Prompt the user for input.

2. Get input.

3. Echo the input by displaying the entered change on the screen.

4. Compute and print the number of half-dollars.

5. Calculate the remaining change.

6. Compute and print the number of quarters.

7. Calculate the remaining change.

8. Compute and print the number of dimes.

9. Calculate the remaining change.

10. Compute and print the number of nickels.

11. Calculate the remaining change.

12. Print the remaining change.

COMPLETE PROGRAM LISTING

```cpp
//**************************************************************
// Program Make Change: Given any amount of change expressed
// in cents, this program computes the number of half-dollars,
// quarters, dimes, nickels, and pennies to be returned,
// returning as many half-dollars as possible, then quarters,
// dimes, nickels, and pennies in that order.
//**************************************************************

    //Header file
#include <iostream>

using namespace std;

    //Named constants
const int HALFDOLLAR = 50;
const int QUARTER  = 25;
const int DIME = 10;
const int NICKEL = 5;

int main()
{
        //Declare variable
    int change;

        //Statements: Step 1 - Step 12
    cout << "Enter change in cents: ";                   //Step 1
    cin >> change;                                       //Step 2
    cout << endl;

    cout << "The change you entered is " << change
         << endl;                                        //Step 3

    cout << "The number of half-dollars to be returned "
         << "is " << change / HALFDOLLAR
         << endl;                                        //Step 4

    change = change % HALFDOLLAR;                        //Step 5

    cout << "The number of quarters to be returned is "
         << change / QUARTER << endl;                    //Step 6

    change = change % QUARTER;                           //Step 7

    cout << "The number of dimes to be returned is "
         << change / DIME << endl;                       //Step 8

    change = change % DIME;                              //Step 9
```

```cpp
    cout << "The number of nickels to be returned is "
         << change / NICKEL << endl;                        //Step 10

    change = change % NICKEL;                               //Step 11

    cout << "The number of pennies to be returned is "
         << change << endl;                                 //Step 12

    return 0;
}
```

Sample Run: In this sample run, the user input is shaded.

```
Enter change in cents: 583

The change you entered is 583
The number of half-dollars to be returned is 11
The number of quarters to be returned is 1
The number of dimes to be returned is 0
The number of nickels to be returned is 1
The number of pennies to be returned is 3
```

QUICK REVIEW

1. A C++ program is a collection of functions.

2. Every C++ program has a function called `main`.

3. In C++, identifiers are names of things.

4. A C++ identifier consists of letters, digits, and underscores, and must begin with a letter or underscore.

5. Reserved words cannot be used as identifiers in a program.

6. All reserved words in C++ consist of lowercase letters (see Appendix A).

7. The most common character sets are ASCII, which has 128 values, and EBCDIC, which has 256 values.

8. The collating sequence of a character is its preset number in the character data set.

9. The arithmetic operators in C++ are addition (+), subtraction (−), multiplication (*), division (/), and modulus (%).

10. The modulus operator, %, takes only integer operands.

11. Arithmetic expressions are evaluated using the precedence rules and the associativity of the arithmetic operators.

2

12. All operands in an integral expression, or integer expression, are integers, and all operands in a floating-point expression are decimal numbers.

13. A mixed expression is an expression that consists of both integers and decimal numbers.

14. When evaluating an operator in an expression, an integer is converted to a floating–point number, with a decimal part of 0, only if the operator has mixed operands.

15. You can use the cast operator to explicitly convert values from one data type to another.

16. During program execution, the contents of a named constant cannot be changed.

17. A named constant is declared by using the reserved word `const`.

18. A named constant is initialized when it is declared.

19. All variables must be declared before they can be used.

20. C++ does not automatically initialize variables.

21. Every variable has a name, a value, a data type, and a size.

22. When a new value is assigned to a variable, the old value is destroyed.

23. Only an assignment statement or an input (read) statement can change the value of a variable.

24. In C++, >> is called the stream extraction operator.

25. Input from the standard input device is accomplished by using `cin` and the stream extraction operator >>.

26. When data is input in a program, the data items, such as numbers, are usually separated by blanks, lines, or tabs.

27. In C++, << is called the stream insertion operator.

28. Output of the program to the standard output device is accomplished by using `cout` and the stream insertion operator <<.

29. Outputting or accessing the value of a variable in an expression does not destroy or modify the contents of the variable.

30. To use `cin` and `cout`, the program must include the header file `iostream` and either include the statement `using namespace std;` or refer to these identifiers as `std::cin` and `std::cout`.

31. The manipulator `endl` positions the insertion point at the beginning of the next line on an output device.

32. The character \ is called the escape character.

33. The sequence \n is called the newline escape sequence.

34. All preprocessor commands start with the symbol #.

35. The preprocessor commands are processed by the preprocessor before the program goes through the compiler.

36. The preprocessor command **#include** <iostream> instructs the preprocessor to include the header file **iostream** in the program.

37. All C++ statements end with a semicolon. The semicolon in C++ is called the statement terminator.

38. A C++ system has three components: environment, language, and the standard libraries.

39. Standard libraries are not part of the C++ language. They contain functions to perform operations, such as mathematical operations.

40. A file containing a C++ program usually ends with the extension **.cpp**.

41. A single line comment starts with the pair of symbols **//** anywhere in the line.

42. Multiline comments are enclosed between **/*** and ***/**.

43. The compiler skips comments.

44. Prompt lines are executable statements that tell the user what to do.

45. Corresponding to the five arithmetic operators **+, −, *, /,** and **%,** C++ provides five compound operators **+=, −=, *=, /=,** and **%=,** respectively.

46. Using the compound operator ***=**, you can rewrite the simple assignment statement:

```
variable = variable * (expression);
```

as:

```
variable *= expression;
```

The other arithmetic compound operators have similar conventions.

EXERCISES

1. Mark the following statements as true or false.

    a. An identifier can be any sequence of digits and letters.

    b. In C++, there is no difference between a reserved word and a predefined identifier.

    c. A C++ identifier can start with a digit.

    d. The operands of the modulus operator must be integers.

    e. If a = 4; and b = 3;, then after the statement a = b; the value of b is still 3.

    f. In the statement cin >> y; y can only be an **int** or a **double** variable.

    g. In an output statement, the newline character may be a part of the string.

h. The following is a legal C++ program:

```cpp
int main()
{
    return 0;
}
```

i. In a mixed expression, all the operands are converted to floating-point numbers.

j. Suppose `x = 5`. After the statement `y = x++;` executes, `y` is 5 and `x` is 6.

k. Suppose `a = 5`. After the statement `++a;` executes, the value of `a` is still 5 because the value of the expression is not saved in another variable.

2. Which of the following are valid C++ identifiers?

    a. `RS6S6`

    b. `MIX-UP`

    c. `STOP!`

    d. `exam1`

    e. `September1Lecture`

    f. `2May`

    g. `Mike's`

    h. `First Exam`

    i. `J`

    j. `Three`

3. Which of the following is a reserved word in C++?

    a. `int`

    b. `long`

    c. `Char`

    d. `CHAR`

    e. `Float`

    f. `Double`

4. Circle the best answer.

    a. The value of `15 / 2` is:
       (i) `7`   (ii) `7.5`   (iii) `7 1/2`   (iv) `0.75`   (v) none of these

    b. The value of `18 / 3` is:
       (i) `6`   (ii) `0.167`   (iii) `6.0`   (iv) none of these

    c. The value of `22 % 7` is:
       (i) `3`   (ii) `1`   (iii) `3.142`   (iv) `22/7`

d. The value of `5 % 7` is:
   (i) 0   (ii) 2   (iii) 5   (iv) undefined

e. The value of `17.0 / 4` is:
   (i) 4   (ii) `4.25`   (iii) 4 1/4   (iv) undefined

f. The value of `5 - 3.0 + 2` is:
   (i) 0   (ii) `0.0`   (iii) 4   (iv) `4.0`

g. The value of `7 - 5 * 2 + 1` is:
   (i) -2   (ii) 5   (iii) 6   (iv) none of these

h. The value of `15.0 / 3.0 + 2.0` is:
   (i) 3   (ii) `3.0`   (iii) 5   (iv) none of these

5. If `x = 5`, `y = 6`, `z = 4`, and `w = 3.5`, evaluate each of the following statements, if possible. If it is not possible, state the reason.

   a. `(x + z) % y`

   b. `(x + y) % w`

   c. `(y + w) % x`

   d. `(x + y) * w`

   e. `(x % y) % z`

   f. `(y % z) % x`

   g. `(x * z) % y`

   h. `((x * y) * w) * z`

6. Given:

```
int n, m, l;
double x, y;
```

   Which of the following assignments are valid? If an assignment is not valid, state the reason. When not given, assume that each variable is declared.

   a. `n = m = 5;`

   b. `m = l = 2 * n;`

   c. `n = 5; m = 2 + 6; n = 6 / 3;`

   d. `m + n = l;`

   e. `x = 2 * n + 5.3;`

   f. `l + 1 = n;`

   g. `x / y = x * y;`

   h. `m = n % l;`

   i. `n = x % 5;`

   j. `x = x + 5;`

   k. `n = 3 + 4.6`

7. Do a walk-through to find the value assigned to e. Assume that all variables are properly declared.

```
a = 3;
b = 4;
c = (a % b) * 6;
d = c / b;
e = (a + b + c + d) / 4;
```

8. Which of the following variable declarations are correct? If a variable declaration is not correct, give the reason(s) and provide the correct variable declaration.

```
n = 12;                    //Line 1
char letter = ;            //Line 2
int one = 5, two;          //Line 3
double x, y, z;            //Line 4
```

9. Which of the following are valid C++ assignment statements? Assume that i, x, and percent are double variables.

   a. `i = i + 5;`

   b. `x + 2 = x;`

   c. `x = 2.5 * x;`

   d. `percent = 10%;`

10. Write C++ statements that accomplish the following:

   a. Declares int variables x and y.

   b. Initializes an int variable x to 10 and a char variable ch to 'B'.

   c. Updates the value of an int variable x by adding 5 to it.

   d. Sets the value of a double variable z to 25.3.

   e. Copies the content of an int variable y into an int variable z.

   f. Swaps the contents of the int variables x and y. (Declare additional variables, if necessary.)

   g. Outputs the content of a variable x and an expression 2 * x + 5 − y, where x and y are double variables.

   h. Declares a char variable grade and sets the value of grade to 'A'.

   i. Declares int variables to store four integers.

   j. Copies the value of a double variable z to the nearest integer into an int variable x.

11. Write each of the following as a C++ expression.

   a. −10 times a

   b. The character that represents 8

   c. $(b^2 - 4ac)$ / 2a

   d. $(-b + (b^2 - 4ac))$ / 2a

12. Suppose **x**, **y**, **z**, and **w** are **int** variables. What value is assigned to each of these variables after the last statement executes?

```
x = 5; z = 3;
y = x - z;
z = 2 * y + 3;
w = x - 2 * y + z;
z = w - x;
w++;
```

13. Suppose **x**, **y**, and **z** are **int** variables and **w** and **t** are **double** variables. What value is assigned to each of these variables after the last statement executes?

```
x = 17;
y = 15;
x = x + y / 4;
z = x % 3 + 4;
w = 17 / 3 + 6.5;
t = x / 4.0 + 15 % 4 - 3.5;
```

14. Suppose **x**, **y**, and **z** are **int** variables and x = 2, y = 5, and z = 6. What is the output of each of the following statements?

   a.   `cout << "x = " << x << ", y = " << y << ", z = " << z << endl;`

   b.   `cout << "x + y = " << x + y << endl;`

   c.   `cout << "Sum of " << x << " and " << z << " is " << x + z << endl;`

   d.   `cout << "z / x = " << z / x << endl;`

   e.   `cout << "2 times " << x << " = " << 2 * x << endl;`

15. What is the output of the following statements? Suppose a and b are **int** variables, c is a **double** variable, and a = 13, b = 5, and c = 17.5.

   a.   `cout << a + b - c << endl;`

   b.   `cout << 15 / 2 + c << endl;`

   c.   `cout << a / static_cast<double>(b) + 2 * c`
       `<< endl;`

   d.   `cout << 14 % 3 + 6.3 + b / a << endl;`

   e.   `cout << static_cast<int>(c) % 5 + a - b`
       `<< endl;`

   f.   `cout << 13.5 / 2 + 4.0 * 3.5 + 18 << endl;`

16. How do you print the carriage return?

17. Which of the following are correct C++ statements?

   a.   `cout << "Hello There!" << endl;`

   b.   `cout << "Hello";`
       `<< " There!" << endl;`

c.
```
cout << "Hello"
        << " There!" << endl;
```

d.
```
cout << 'Hello There!' << endl;
```

18. The following two programs have syntax mistakes. Correct them. On each successive line, assume that any preceding error has been corrected.

a.
```
#include <iostream>

const int  PRIME = 11,213;
const RATE = 15.6

int main ()
{
    int i, x, y, w;
    x = 7;
    y = 3;
    x = x + w;
    PRIME = x + PRIME;
    cout << PRIME << endl;
    wages = RATE * 36.75;
    cout << "Wages = " << wages << endl;
    return 0;
}
```

b.
```
const char = BLANK = ' ';
const int  ONE 5;

int main (
{
    int a, b, cc;

    a = ONE + 5;
    b = a + BLANK;
    cc := a + ONE * 2;
    a + cc = b;
    one = b + c;
    cout << "a = " << a << ", b = " << b << ", cc = "
            << cc << endl;

    return 0;
}
```

19. Write equivalent compound statements if possible.

a. `x = 2 * x`

b. `x = x + y - 2;`

c. `sum = sum + num;`

d. `z = z * x + 2 * z;`

e. `y = y / (x + 5);`

20. Write the following compound statements as equivalent simple statements.

    a. `x += 5 - z;`

    b. `y *=2 * x + 5 - z;`

    c. `w += 2 * z + 4;`

    d. `x -= z + y - t;`

    e. `sum += num;`

21. Suppose a, b, and c are **int** variables and a = 5 and b = 6. What value is assigned to each variable after each statement executes? If a variable is undefined at a particular statement, report UND (`undefined`).

```
                              a      b      c
a = (b++) + 3;               ___    ___    ___
c = 2 * a + (++b);           ___    ___    ___
b = 2 * (++c) - (a++);       ___    ___    ___
```

22. Suppose a, b, and sum are **int** variables and c is a **double** variable. What value is assigned to each variable after each statement executes? Suppose a = 3, b = 5, and c = 14.1.

```
                        a      b      c      sum
sum = a + b + c;       ___    ___    ___    ___
c /= a;                ___    ___    ___    ___
b += c - a;            ___    ___    ___    ___
a *= 2 * b + c;        ___    ___    ___    ___
```

23. What is printed by the following program? Suppose the input is:

    `20 15`

```cpp
#include <iostream>

using namespace std;

const int NUM = 10;
const double X = 20.5;

int main()
{
    int a, b;
    double z;
    char grade;

    a = 25;

    cout << "a = " << a << endl;
```

```cpp
    cout << "Enter two integers : ";
    cin >> a >> b;
    cout << endl;

    cout << "The numbers you entered are "
         << a << " and " << b << endl;

    z = X + 2 * a - b;
    cout << "z = " << z << endl;

    grade = 'A';
    cout << "Your grade is " << grade << endl;

    a = 2 * NUM + z;
    cout << "The value of a = " << a << endl;

    return 0;
}
```

24. What is printed by the following program? Suppose the input is:

```
Miller
34
340
```

```cpp
#include <iostream>
#include <string>

using namespace std;

const int PRIME_NUM = 11;

int main()
{
    const int SECRET = 17;

    string name;
    int id;
    int num;
    int mysteryNum;

    cout << "Enter last name: ";
    cin >> name;
    cout << endl;

    cout << "Enter a two digit number: ";
    cin >> num;
    cout << endl;

    id = 100 * num + SECRET;

    cout << "Enter a positive integer less than 1000: ";
    cin >> num;
    cout << endl;
```

```
        mysteryNum = num * PRIME_NUM - 3 * SECRET;

        cout << "Name: " << name << endl;
        cout << "Id: " << id << endl;
        cout << "Mystery number: " << mysteryNum << endl;

        return 0;
    }
```

25. Rewrite the following program so that it is properly formatted.

```cpp
#include <iostream>
#include <string>
using namespace std;
const double X = 13.45; const int Y=34;
const char BLANK= ' ';
int main()
{ string firstName,lastName;int num;
double salary;
cout<<"Enter first name: "; cin>> firstName; cout<<endl;
cout<<"Enter last name: "; cin
>>lastName;cout<<endl;
      cout<<"Enter a positive integer less than 70:";
cin>>num;cout<<endl; salary=num*X;
 cout<<"Name: "<<firstName<<BLANK<<lastName<<endl;cout
<<"Wages: $"<<salary<<endl; cout<<"X = "<<X<<endl;
 cout<<"X+Y = " << X+Y << endl; return 0;
}
```

26. What type of input does the following program require, and in what order does the input need to be provided?

```cpp
#include <iostream>

using namespace std;

int main()
{
    int x, y;
    char ch;

    cin >> x;
    cin >> ch >> y;

    return 0;
}
```

PROGRAMMING EXERCISES

1. Write a program that produces the following output:

```
**********************************
*     Programming Assignment 1    *
*       Computer Programming I     *
*             Author: ???          *
*     Due Date: Thursday, Jan. 24  *
**********************************
```

In your program, substitute **???** with your own name. If necessary, adjust the positions and the number of the stars to produce a rectangle.

2. Write a program that produces the following output:

```
CCCCCCCCC                  ++                      ++
CC                         ++                      ++
CC              ++++++++++++++      ++++++++++++++
CC              ++++++++++++++      ++++++++++++++
CC                         ++                      ++
CCCCCCCCC                  ++                      ++
```

3. Write a program that prompts the user to input a decimal number and outputs the number rounded to the nearest integer.

4. Consider the following program segment:

```cpp
//include statement(s)
//using namespace statement

int main()
{
    //variable declaration

    //executable statements

    //return statement
}
```

a. Write C++ statements that include the header files `iostream` and `string`.

b. Write a C++ statement that allows you to use `cin`, `cout`, and `endl` without the prefix `std::`.

c. Write C++ statements that declare and initialize the following named constants: **SECRET** of type `int` initialized to `11`, and **RATE** of type `double` initialized to `12.50`.

d. Write C++ statements that declare the following variables: `num1`, `num2`, and `newNum` of type `int`; `name` of type `string`; and `hoursWorked` and `wages` of type `double`.

e. Write C++ statements that prompt the user to input two integers and stores the first number in `num1` and the second number in `num2`.

f. Write a C++ statement(s) that outputs the values of `num1` and `num2`, indicating which is `num1` and which is `num2`. For example, if `num1` is 8 and `num2` is 5, then the output is:

```
The value of num1 = 8 and the value of num2 = 5.
```

g. Write a C++ statement that multiplies the value of `num1` by 2, adds the value of `num2` to it, and then stores the result in `newNum`. Then write a C++ statement that outputs the value of `newNum`.

h. Write a C++ statement that updates the value of `newNum` by adding the value of the named constant `SECRET`. Then write a C++ statement that outputs the value of `newNum` with an appropriate message.

i. Write C++ statements that prompt the user to enter a person's last name and then store the last name into the variable `name`.

j. Write C++ statements that prompt the user to enter a decimal number between 0 and 70 and then store the number entered into `hoursWorked`.

k. Write a C++ statement that multiplies the value of the named constant `RATE` with the value of `hoursWorked`, and then stores the result into the variable `wages`.

l. Write C++ statements that produce the following output:

```
Name:               //output the value of the variable name
Pay Rate: $         //output the value of the variable rate
Hours Worked:       //output the value of the variable
                    //hoursWorked
Salary: $           //output the value of the variable wages
```

For example, if the value of name is `"Rainbow"` and `hoursWorked` is `45.50`, then the output is:

```
Name: Rainbow
Pay Rate: $12.50
Hours Worked: 45.50
Salary: $568.75
```

m. Write a C++ program that tests each of the C++ statements that you wrote in parts a through l. Place the statements at the appropriate place in the previous C++ program segment. Test run your program (twice) on the following input data:

    a. `num1 = 13, num2 = 28; name = "Jacobson"; hoursWorked = 48.30.`

    b. `num1 = 32, num2 = 15; name = "Crawford"; hoursWorked = 58.45.`

5. Write a program that prompts the user to input the length and width of a rectangle and then prints the rectangle's area and perimeter. (Assume that the length and the width are decimal numbers.)

6. Write a program that prompts the user to enter five test scores and then prints the average test score. (Assume that the test scores are decimal numbers.)

7. Write a program that prints the following pattern:

8. Write a program that prints the following banner:

```
*************************
*************************
********* WELCOME ********
=========================
=========================
*********   HOME   ********
*************************
*************************
```

9. Write a program that prompts the user to input five decimal numbers. The program should then add the five decimal numbers, convert the sum to the nearest integer, and print the result.

10. Write a program that does the following:

    a. Prompts the user to input five decimal numbers.

    b. Prints the five decimal numbers.

    c. Converts each decimal number to the nearest integer.

    d. Adds the five integers.

    e. Prints the sum and average of the five integers.

11. Write a program that prompts the user to input a four-digit positive integer. The program then outputs the digits of the number, one digit per line. For example, if the input is 3245, the output is:

```
3
2
4
5
```

12. Write a C++ program that prompts the user to input the elapsed time for an event in seconds. The program then outputs the elapsed time in hours, minutes, and seconds. (For example, if the elapsed time is 9630 seconds, then the output is 2:40:30.)

13. Write a C++ program that prompts the user to input the elapsed time for an event in hours, minutes, and seconds. The program then outputs the elapsed time in seconds.

14. To make a profit, a local store marks up the prices of its items by a certain percentage. Write a C++ program that reads the original price of the item sold, the percentage of the marked-up price, and the sales tax rate. The program then outputs the original price of the item, the percentage of the mark-up, the store's selling price of the item, the sales tax rate, the sales tax, and the final price of the item. (The final price of the item is the selling price plus the sales tax.)

15. Write a program that prompts the user to input a length expressed in centimeters. The program should then convert the length to inches (to the nearest inch) and output the length expressed in yards, feet, and inches, in that order. For example, suppose the input for centimeters is 312. To the nearest inch, 312 centimeters is equal to 123 inches. 123 inches would thus be output as:

```
3 yard(s), 1 feet (foot), and 3 inch(es).
```

It should not be output as:

```
2 yard(s) 4 feet (foot) 3 inch(es),
```

or:

```
10 feet (foot) 3 inch(es),
```

or:

```
10.25 feet (foot).
```

16. Write a program to implement and test the algorithm that you designed for Exercise 15 of Chapter 1. (You may assume that the value of π = 3.141593. In your program, declare a named constant PI to store this value.)

17. A milk carton can hold 3.78 liters of milk. Each morning, a dairy farm ships cartons of milk to a local grocery store. The cost of producing one liter of milk is $0.38 and the profit of each carton of milk is $0.27. Write a program that does the following:

   a. Prompts the user to enter the total amount of milk produced in the morning.

   b. Outputs the number of milk cartons needed to hold milk. (Round your answer to the nearest integer.)

   c. Outputs the cost of producing milk.

   d. Outputs the profit for producing milk.

18. Redo Programming Exercise 17 so that the user can also input the cost of producing one liter of milk and the profit on each carton of milk.

19. You found an exciting summer job for five weeks. It pays, say, $15.50 per hour. Suppose that the total tax you pay on your summer job income is 14%. After paying the taxes, you spend 10% of your net income to buy new clothes and other accessories for the next school year and 1% to buy school supplies. After buying clothes and school

supplies, you use 25% of the remaining money to buy savings bonds. For each dollar you spend to by savings bonds, your parents spend $0.50 to buy additional savings bonds for you. Write a program that prompts the user to enter the pay rate for an hour and the number of hours you worked each week. The program then outputs the following:

a. Your income before and after taxes from your summer job.

b. The money you spend on clothes and other accessories.

c. The money you spend on school supplies.

d. The money you spend to buy savings bonds.

e. The money your parents spend to buy additional savings bonds for you.

20. A permutation of three objects, *a*, *b*, and *c*, is any arrangement of these objects in a row. For example, some of the permutations of these objects are *abc*, *bca*, and *cab*. The number of permutations of three objects is 6. Suppose that these three objects are strings. Write a program that prompts the user to enter three strings. The program then outputs the six permutations of those strings.

INPUT/OUTPUT

IN THIS CHAPTER, YOU WILL:

- Learn what a stream is and examine input and output streams
- Explore how to read data from the standard input device
- Learn how to use predefined functions in a program
- Explore how to use the input stream functions `get`, `ignore`, `putback`, and `peek`
- Become familiar with input failure
- Learn how to write data to the standard output device
- Discover how to use manipulators in a program to format output
- Learn how to perform input and output operations with the `string` data type
- Become familiar with file input and output

In Chapter 2, you were introduced to some of C++'s input/output (I/O) instructions, which get data into a program and print the results on the screen. You used `cin` and the extraction operator `>>` to get data from the keyboard, and `cout` and the insertion operator `<<` to send output to the screen. Because I/O operations are fundamental to any programming language, in this chapter, you will learn about C++'s I/O operations in more detail. First, you will learn about statements that extract input from the standard input device and send output to the standard output device. You will then learn how to format output using manipulators. In addition, you will learn about the limitations of the I/O operations associated with the standard input/output devices and learn how to extend these operations to other devices.

I/O Streams and Standard I/O Devices

A program performs three basic operations: it gets data, it manipulates the data, and it outputs the results. In Chapter 2, you learned how to manipulate numeric data using arithmetic operations. In later chapters, you will learn how to manipulate non-numeric data. Because writing programs for I/O is quite complex, C++ offers extensive support for I/O operations by providing substantial prewritten I/O operations, some of which you encountered in Chapter 2. In this chapter, you will learn about various I/O operations that can greatly enhance the flexibility of your programs.

In C++, I/O is a sequence of bytes, called a stream, from the source to the destination. The bytes are usually characters, unless the program requires other types of information, such as a graphic image or digital speech. Therefore, a **stream** is a sequence of characters from the source to the destination. There are two types of streams:

Input stream: A sequence of characters from an input device to the computer.

Output stream: A sequence of characters from the computer to an output device.

Recall that the standard input device is usually the keyboard, and the standard output device is usually the screen. To receive data from the keyboard and send output to the screen, every C++ program must use the header file `iostream`. This header file contains, among other things, the definitions of two data types, `istream` (input stream) and `ostream` (output stream). The header file also contains two variable declarations, one for `cin` (pronounced "see-in"), which stands for **common input**, and one for `cout` (pronounced "see-out"), which stands for **common output**.

These variable declarations are similar to the following C++ statements:

```
istream cin;
ostream cout;
```

To use `cin` and `cout`, every C++ program must use the preprocessor directive:

```
#include <iostream>
```

NOTE From Chapter 2, recall that you have been using the statement `using namespace std;` in addition to including the header file `iostream` to use `cin` and `cout`. Without the statement `using namespace std;`, you refer to these identifiers as `std::cin` and `std::cout`. In Chapter 8, you will learn about the meaning of the statement `using namespace std;` in detail.

3

Variables of type `istream` are called **input stream variables**; variables of type `ostream` are called **output stream variables**. A **stream variable** is either an input stream variable or an output stream variable.

Because `cin` and `cout` are already defined and have specific meanings, to avoid confusion you should never redefine them in programs.

The variable `cin` has access to operators and functions that can be used to extract data from the standard input device. You have briefly used the extraction operator `>>` to input data from the standard input device. The next section describes in detail how the extraction operator `>>` works. In the following sections, you will learn how to use the functions `get`, `ignore`, `peek`, and `putback` to input data in a specific manner.

`cin` **and the Extraction Operator** `>>`

In Chapter 2, you saw how to input data from the standard input device by using `cin` and the extraction operator `>>`. Suppose `payRate` is `double` variable. Consider the following C++ statement:

```
cin >> payRate;
```

When the computer executes this statement, it inputs the next number typed on the keyboard and stores this number in the variable `payRate`. Therefore, if the user types `15.50`, the value stored in `payRate` after this statement executes is `15.50`.

The extraction operator `>>` is binary and thus takes two operands. The left-side operand must be an input stream variable, such as `cin`. Because the purpose of an input statement is to read and store values in a memory location, and because only variables refer to memory locations, the right-side operand is a variable.

NOTE The extraction operator `>>` is defined only for putting data into variables of simple data types. Therefore, the right-side operand of the extraction operator `>>` is a variable of the simple data type. However, C++ allows the programmer to extend the definition of the extraction operator `>>` so that data can also be put into other types of variables by using an input statement. You will learn this mechanism in the chapter entitled Overloading and Templates, later in this book.

The syntax of an input statement using `cin` and the extraction operator `>>` is:

```
cin >> variable >> variable...;
```

As you can see in the preceding syntax, a single input statement can read more than one data item by using the operator `>>` several times. Every occurrence of `>>` extracts the next data item from the input stream. For example, you can read both `payRate` and `hoursWorked` via a single input statement by using the following code:

```
cin >> payRate >> hoursWorked;
```

There is no difference between the preceding input statement and the following two input statements. Which form you use is a matter of convenience and style:

```
cin >> payRate;
cin >> hoursWorked;
```

How does the extraction operator `>>` work? When scanning for the next input, `>>` skips all whitespace characters. **Whitespace characters** consist of blanks and certain nonprintable characters, such as tabs and the newline character. Thus, whether you separate the input data by lines or blanks, the extraction operator `>>` simply finds the next input data in the input stream. For example, suppose that `payRate` and `hoursWorked` are **double** variables. Consider the following input statement:

```
cin >> payRate >> hoursWorked;
```

Whether the input is:

```
15.50 48.30
```

or:

```
15.50    48.30
```

or:

```
15.50
48.30
```

the preceding input statement would store `15.50` in `payRate` and `48.30` in `hoursWorked`. Note that the first input is separated by a blank, the second input is separated by a tab, and the third input is separated by a line.

Now suppose that the input is 2. How does the extraction operator `>>` distinguish between the character 2 and the number 2? The right-side operand of the extraction operator `>>` makes this distinction. If the right-side operand is a variable of the data type **char**, the input 2 is treated as the character 2 and, in this case, the ASCII value of 2 is stored. If the right-side operand is a variable of the data type **int** or **double**, the input 2 is treated as the number 2.

Next, consider the input 25 and the statement:

```
cin >> a;
```

where a is a variable of some simple data type. If a is of the data type **char**, only the single character 2 is stored in a. If a is of the data type **int**, 25 is stored in a. If a is of the data type **double**, the input 25 is converted to the decimal number 25.0. Table 3–1 summarizes this discussion by showing the valid input for a variable of the simple data type.

TABLE 3-1 Valid Input for a Variable of the Simple Data Type

Data Type of a	Valid Input for a
char	One printable character except the blank
int	An integer, possibly preceded by a + or − sign
double	A decimal number, possibly preceded by a + or − sign. If the actual data input is an integer, the input is converted to a decimal number with the zero decimal part.

When reading data into a **char** variable, after skipping any leading whitespace characters, the extraction operator >> finds and stores only the next character; reading stops after a single character. To read data into an **int** or **double** variable, after skipping all leading whitespace characters and reading the plus or minus sign (if any), the extraction operator >> reads the digits of the number, including the decimal point for floating-point variables, and stops when it finds a whitespace character or a character other than a digit.

EXAMPLE 3-1

Suppose you have the following variable declarations:

```
int a, b;
double z;
char ch, ch1, ch2;
```

The following statements show how the extraction operator >> works.

	Statement	Input	Value Stored in Memory
1	cin >> ch;	A	ch = 'A'
2	cin >> ch;	AB	ch = 'A', 'B' is held for later input
3	cin >> a;	48	a = 48

Statement	Input	Value Stored in Memory
4 `cin >> a;`	46.35	a = 46, .35 is held for later input
5 `cin >> z;`	74.35	z = 74.35
6 `cin >> z;`	39	z = 39.0
7 `cin >> z >> a;`	65.78 38	z = 65.78, a = 38
8 `cin >> a >> b;`	4 60	a = 4, b = 60
9 `cin >> a >> ch >> z;`	57 A 26.9	a = 57, ch = 'A', z = 26.9
10 `cin >> a >> ch >> z;`	57 A 26.9	a = 57, ch = 'A', z = 26.9
11 `cin >> a >> ch >> z;`	57 A 26.9	a = 57, ch = 'A', z = 26.9
12 `cin >> a >> ch >> z;`	57A26.9	a = 57, ch = 'A', z = 26.9
13 `cin >> z >> ch >> a;`	36.78B34	z = 36.78, ch = 'B', a = 34
14 `cin >> z >> ch >> a;`	36.78 B34	z = 36.78, ch = 'B', a = 34
15 `cin >> a >> b >> z;`	11 34	a = 11, b = 34, computer waits for the next number
16 `cin >> a >> z;`	46 32.4 68	a = 46, z = 32.4, 68 is held for later input
17 `cin >> a >> z;`	78.49	a = 78, z = 0.49
18 `cin >> ch >> a;`	256	ch = '2', a = 56
19 `cin >> a >> ch;`	256	a = 256, computer waits for the input value for ch
20 `cin >> ch1 >> ch2;`	A B	ch1 = 'A', ch2 = 'B'

In statement 1, the extraction operator >> extracts the character 'A' from the input stream and stores it in the variable ch. In statement 2, the extraction operator >> extracts the character 'A' from the input stream and stores it in the variable ch, and the value 'B' is held in the input stream for later input, if necessary.

Similarly, in statement 16, the value 68 is held for later input. In statement 15, 11 is stored in a, and 34 is stored in b, but the input stream does not have enough input data to fill each variable. In this case, the computer waits (and waits, and waits,. . .) for the next input to be entered. The computer does not continue to execute until the next value is entered.

In statement 4, the extraction operator >> extracts 46 from the input stream and stores this value in a. Note that because a is an `int` variable and the character after 46 is . (which is non-numeric), only 46 is extracted from the input stream; as a result, reading stops at `.` and `.35` is held for later input. In statement 5, the extraction operator `>>` extracts `74.35` from the input stream and stores this value in z. In statement 6, z is a variable of the **double** data type and the input `39` is an integer. Therefore, `39` is converted to the decimal number `39.0`, and the value stored in z is `39.0`.

In statement 7, the first right-side operand of the extraction operator `>>` is a **double** variable and the second right-side operand is an **int** variable. Therefore, in statement 7, first the value `65.78` is extracted from the input stream and stored in z. The extraction operator then skips the blank after `65.78`, and the value `38` is extracted and stored in a. Statement 8 works similarly.

Note that for statements 9 through 12, the input statement is the same; however, the data is entered differently. For statement 9, data is entered on the same line separated by blanks. For statement 10, data is entered on two lines; the first two input values are separated by two blank spaces, and the third input is on the next line. For statement 11, all three input values are separated by lines and for statement 12, all three input values are on the same line, but there is no space between them. Note that the second input is a non-numeric character. These statements work as follows.

In statement 9, first the extraction operator `>>` extracts `57` from the input stream and stores it in a. The extraction operator `>>` then skips the blank after `57`, and extracts and stores the character `'A'` in ch. Next, the extraction operator `>>` skips the blank after `'A'` and extracts and stores the value `26.9` in z from the input stream.

In statement 10, first the extraction operator `>>` extracts `57` from the input stream and stores this value in a. The extraction operator `>>` then skips the two blank spaces after `57`, extracts the character `'A'` from the input stream, and stores it in ch. Next, the extraction operator `>>` skips the newline character `'\n'` after `'A'`, extracts `26.9` from the input stream, and stores it in z.

In statement 11, first the extraction operator `>>` extracts `57` from the input stream, and stores it in a. The extraction operator `>>` then skips the newline character `'\n'` after `57`, extracts the character `'A'` from the input stream, and stores it in ch. Next, the extraction operator `>>` skips the newline character `'\n'` after `'A'`, extracts `26.9` from the input stream, and stores it in z.

Statements 9, 10, and 11 illustrate that regardless of whether the input is separated by blanks or by lines, the extraction operator `>>` always finds the next input.

In statement 12, first the extraction operator `>>` extracts `57` from the input stream and stores it in a. Then the extraction operator `>>` extracts the character `'A'` from the input stream and stores it in ch. Next, `26.9` is extracted and stored in z.

In statement 13, because the first right-side operand of `>>` is z, which is a **double** variable, `36.78` is extracted from the input stream and the value `36.78` is stored in z. Next, `'B'` is extracted and stored in ch. Finally, `34` is extracted and stored in a. Statement 14 works similarly.

In statement 17, the first right-side operand of the extraction operator >> is an `int` variable and the input is `78.49`. Now for `int` variables, after inputting the digits of the number, the reading stops at the first whitespace character or a character other than a digit. Therefore, the operator >> stores `78` into `a`. The next right-side operand of >> is the variable z, which is of type `double`. Therefore, the operator >> stores the value `.49` as `0.49` into z.

In statement 18, the first right-side operand of the extraction operator >> is a `char` variable, so the first nonwhitespace character, `'2'`, is extracted from the input stream. The character `'2'` is stored in the variable ch. The next right-side operand of the extraction operator >> is an `int` variable, so the next input value, `56`, is extracted and stored in `a`.

In statement 19, the first right-side operator of the extraction operator >> is an `int` variable, so the first data item, `256`, is extracted from the input stream and stored in `a`. Now the computer waits for the next data item for the variable ch.

In statement 20, `'A'` is stored into `ch1`. The extraction operator >> then skips the blank, and `'B'` is stored in `ch2`.

NOTE　Recall that, during program execution, when entering character data such as letters, you do not enter the single quotes around the character.

What happens if the input stream has more data items than required by the program? After the program terminates, any values left in the input stream are discarded. When you enter data for processing, the data values should correspond to the data types of the variables in the input statement. Recall that when entering a number for a `double` variable, it is not necessary for the input number to have a decimal part. If the input number is an integer and has no decimal part, it is converted to a decimal value. The computer, however, does not tolerate any other kind of mismatch. For example, entering a `char` value into an `int` or `double` variable causes serious errors, called **input failure**. Input failure is discussed later in this chapter.

What happens when you try to read a non-numeric character into an `int` variable? Example 3-6 (given later in this chapter) illustrates this situation.

The extraction operator, when scanning for the next input in the input stream, skips whitespace such as blanks and the newline character. However, there are situations when these characters must also be stored and processed. For example, if you are processing text in a line-by-line fashion, you must know where in the input stream the newline character is located. Without identifying the position of the newline character, the program would not know where one line ends and another begins. The next few sections teach you how to input data into a program using the input functions, such as `get`, `ignore`, `putback`, and `peek`. These functions are associated with the data type `istream` and are called **istream member functions**. I/O functions, such as `get`, are typically called **stream member functions** or **stream functions.**

Before you can learn about the input functions `get`, `ignore`, `putback`, `peek`, and other I/O functions that are used in this chapter, you need to first understand what a function is and how it works. You will study functions in detail, and learn how to write your own, in Chapters 6 and 7.

Using Predefined Functions in a Program

As noted in Chapter 2, a function, also called a subprogram, is a set of instructions. When a function executes, it accomplishes something. The function `main`, as you saw in Chapter 2, executes automatically when you run a program. Other functions execute only when they are activated—that is, called. C++ comes with a wealth of functions, called **predefined functions**, that are already written. In this section, you will learn how to use some predefined functions that are provided as part of the C++ system. Later, in this chapter, you will learn how to use stream functions to perform a specific I/O operation.

Recall from Chapter 2 that predefined functions are organized as a collection of libraries, called header files. A particular header file may contain several functions. Therefore, to use a particular function, you need to know the name of the function and a few other things, which are described shortly.

A very useful function, `pow`, called the power function, can be used to calculate x^y in a program. That is, `pow(x, y)` $= x^y$. For example, `pow(2, 3)` $= 2^3 = 8$ and `pow(4, 0.5)` $= 4^{0.5} = \sqrt{4} = 2$. The numbers `x` and `y` that you use in the function `pow` are called the **arguments** or **parameters** of the function `pow`. For example, in `pow(2, 3)`, the parameters are 2 and 3.

An expression such as `pow(2, 3)` is called a **function call**, which causes the code attached to the predefined function `pow` to execute and, in this case, computes 2^3. The header file `cmath` contains the specification of the function `pow`.

To use a predefined function in a program, you need to know the name of the header file containing the specification of the function and include that header file in the program. In addition, you need to know the name of the function, the number of parameters the function takes, and the type of each parameter. You must also be aware of what the function is going to do. For example, to use the function `pow`, you must include the header file `cmath`. The function `pow` has two parameters, both of which are numbers. The function calculates the first parameter to the power of the second parameter.

The program in the following example illustrates how to use predefined functions in a program. More specifically, we use some math functions, from the header file `cmath`, and the `string` function `length`, from the header file `string`. Note that the function `length` determines the length of a `string`.

EXAMPLE 3-2

```cpp
// How to use predefined functions.
#include <iostream>
#include <cmath>
#include <string>

using namespace std;

int main()
{
    double u, v;
    string str;

    cout << "Line 1: 2 to the power of 6 = "
         << pow(2, 6) << endl;                           //Line 1

    u = 12.5;                                            //Line 2
    v = 3.0;                                             //Line 3
    cout << "Line 4: " << u << " to the power of "
         << v << " = " << pow(u, v) << endl;             //Line 4

    cout << "Line 5: Square root of 24 = "
         << sqrt(24.0) << endl;                          //Line 5

    u = pow(8.0, 2.5);                                   //Line 6
    cout << "Line 7: u = " << u << endl;                 //Line 7

    str = "Programming with C++";                        //Line 8

    cout << "Line 9: Length of str = "
         << str.length() << endl;                        //Line 9

    return 0;
}
```

Sample Run:

```
Line 1: 2 to the power of 6 = 64
Line 4: 12.5 to the power of 3 = 1953.13
Line 5: Square root of 24 = 4.89898
Line 7: u = 181.019
Line 9: Length of str = 20
```

The preceding program works as follows. The statement in Line 1 uses the function
pow to determine and output 2^6. The statement in Line 2 sets u to 12.5 and
the statement in Line 3 sets v to 3.0. The statement in Line 4 determines and
outputs u^v. The statement in Line 5 uses the function sqrt, of the header
file cmath, to determine and output the square root of 24.0. The statement

in Line 6 determines and assigns $8.0^{2.5}$ to u. The statement in Line 7 outputs the value of u.

The statement in Line 8 stores the string **"Programming with C++"** in **str**. The statement in Line 9 uses the string function **length** to determine and output the length of **str**. Note how the function **length** is used. Later in this chapter, we explain the meaning of expressions such as **str.length()**.

Because I/O is fundamental to any programming language, and because writing instructions to perform a specific I/O operation is not a job for everyone, every programming language provides a set of useful functions to perform specific I/O operations. In the remainder of this chapter, you will learn how to use some of these functions in a program. As a programmer, you must pay close attention to how these functions are used so that you can get the most out of them. The first function you will learn about here is the function **get**.

`cin` **and the** `get` **Function**

As you have seen, the extraction operator skips all leading whitespace characters when scanning for the next input value. Consider the variable declarations:

```
char ch1, ch2;
int num;
```

and the input:

```
A 25
```

Now consider the following statement:

```
cin >> ch1 >> ch2 >> num;
```

When the computer executes this statement, **'A'** is stored in **ch1**, the blank is skipped by the extraction operator **>>**, the character **'2'** is stored in **ch2**, and 5 is stored in **num**. However, what if you intended to store **'A'** in **ch1**, the blank in **ch2**, and 25 in **num**? It is clear that you cannot use the extraction operator **>>** to input this data.

As stated earlier, sometimes you need to process the entire input, including whitespace characters, such as blanks and the newline character. For example, suppose you want to process the entered data on a line-by-line basis. Because the extraction operator **>>** skips the newline character, and unless the program captures the newline character, the computer does not know where one line ends and the next begins.

The variable **cin** can access the stream function **get**, which is used to read character data. The **get** function inputs the very next character, including whitespace characters, from the input stream and stores it in the memory location indicated by its argument. The function `get` comes in many forms. Next, we discuss the one that is used to read a character.

The syntax of `cin`, together with the `get` function to read a character, follows:

```
cin.get(varChar);
```

In the `cin.get` statement, `varChar` is a `char` variable. `varChar`, which appears in parentheses following the function name, is called the **argument** or **parameter** of the function. The effect of the preceding statement would be to store the next input character in the variable `varChar`.

Now consider the following input again:

```
A 25
```

To store `'A'` in `ch1`, the blank in `ch2`, and `25` in `num`, you can effectively use the `get` function as follows:

```
cin.get(ch1);
cin.get(ch2);
cin >> num;
```

Because this form of the `get` function has only one argument and reads only one character, and you need to read two characters from the input stream, you need to call this function twice. Notice that you cannot use the `get` function to read data into the variable `num` because `num` is an `int` variable. The preceding form of the `get` function reads values of only the `char` data type.

The preceding set of `cin.get` statements is equivalent to the following statements:

```
cin >> ch1;
cin.get(ch2);
cin >> num;
```

NOTE The function `get` has other forms, one of which you will study in Chapter 9. For the next few chapters, you need only the form of the function `get` introduced here.

`cin` **and the** `ignore` **Function**

When you want to process only partial data (say, within a line), you can use the stream function `ignore` to discard a portion of the input. The syntax to use the function `ignore` is:

```
cin.ignore(intExp, chExp);
```

Here `intExp` is an integer expression yielding an integer value, and `chExp` is a `char` expression yielding a `char` value. In fact, the value of the expression `intExp` specifies the maximum number of characters to be ignored in a line.

Suppose `intExp` yields a value, say 100. This statement says to ignore the next 100 characters or ignore the input until it encounters the character specified by `chExp`, whichever comes first. To be specific, consider the following statement:

```
cin.ignore(100, '\n');
```

When this statement executes, it ignores either the next 100 characters or all characters until the newline character is found, whichever comes first. For example, if the next 120 characters do not contain the newline character, then only the first 100 characters are discarded and the next input data is the character 101. However, if the 75th character is the newline character, then the first 75 characters are discarded and the next input data is the 76th character. Similarly, the execution of the statement:

```
cin.ignore(100, 'A');
```

results in ignoring the first 100 characters or all characters until the character `'A'` is found, whichever comes first.

EXAMPLE 3-3

Consider the declaration:

```
int a, b;
```

and the input:

```
25 67 89 43 72
12 78 34
```

Now consider the following statements:

```
cin >> a;
cin.ignore(100, '\n');
cin >> b;
```

The first statement, `cin >> a;`, stores 25 in a. The second statement, `cin.ignore(100, '\n');`, discards all of the remaining numbers in the first line. The third statement, `cin >> b;`, stores 12 (from the next line) in b.

EXAMPLE 3-4

Consider the declaration:

```
char ch1, ch2;
```

and the input:

```
Hello there. My name is Mickey.
```

Now consider the following statements:

```
cin >> ch1;
cin.ignore(100, '.');
cin >> ch2;
```

The first statement, `cin >> ch1;`, stores `'H'` in `ch1`. The second statement, `cin.ignore(100,'.' );`, results in discarding all characters until . (period). The third statement, `cin >> ch2;`, stores the character `'M'` (from the same line) in `ch2`. (Remember that the extraction operator `>>` skips all leading whitespace characters. Thus, the extraction operator skips the space after . (period) and stores `'M'` in `ch2`.)

The `putback` and `peek` Functions

Suppose you are processing data that is a mixture of numbers and characters. Moreover, the numbers must be read and processed as numbers. You have also looked at many sets of sample data and cannot determine whether the next input is a character or a number. You could read the entire data set character-by-character and check whether a certain character is a digit. If a digit is found, you could then read the remaining digits of the number and somehow convert these characters into numbers. This programming code would be somewhat complex. Fortunately, C++ provides two very useful stream functions that can be used effectively in these types of situations.

The stream function **putback** lets you put the last character extracted from the input stream by the **get** function back into the input stream. The stream function **peek** looks into the input stream and tells you what the next character is without removing it from the input stream. By using these functions, after determining that the next input is a number, you can read it as a number. You do not have to read the digits of the number as characters and then convert these characters to that number.

The syntax to use the function **putback** is:

```
istreamVar.putback(ch);
```

Here `istreamVar` is an input stream variable, such as `cin`, and `ch` is a **char** variable.

The **peek** function returns the next character from the input stream but does not remove the character from that stream. In other words, the function **peek** looks into the input stream and checks the identity of the next input character. Moreover, after checking the next input character in the input stream, it can store this character in a designated memory location without removing it from the input stream. That is, when you use the **peek** function, the next input character stays the same, even though you now know what it is.

The syntax to use the function **peek** is:

```
ch = istreamVar.peek();
```

Here `istreamVar` is an input stream variable, such as `cin`, and `ch` is a **char** variable.

Notice how the function `peek` is used. First, the function `peek` is used in an assignment statement. It is not a stand-alone statement like `get`, `ignore`, and `putback`. Second, the function `peek` has empty parentheses. Until you become comfortable with using a function and learn how to write one, pay close attention to how to use a predefined function.

The following example illustrates how to use the `peek` and `putback` functions.

EXAMPLE 3-5

```cpp
//Functions peek and putback

#include <iostream>

using namespace std;

int main()
{
    char ch;

    cout << "Line 1: Enter a string: ";                    //Line 1
    cin.get(ch);                                           //Line 2
    cout << endl;                                          //Line 3
    cout << "Line 4: After first cin.get(ch); "
         << "ch = " << ch << endl;                         //Line 4

    cin.get(ch);                                           //Line 5
    cout << "Line 6: After second cin.get(ch); "
         << "ch = " << ch << endl;                         //Line 6

    cin.putback(ch);                                       //Line 7
    cin.get(ch);                                           //Line 8
    cout << "Line 9: After putback and then "
         << "cin.get(ch); ch = " << ch << endl;            //Line 9

    ch = cin.peek();                                       //Line 10
    cout << "Line 11: After cin.peek(); ch = "
         << ch << endl;                                    //Line 11

    cin.get(ch);                                           //Line 12
    cout << "Line 13: After cin.get(ch); ch = "
         << ch << endl;                                    //Line 13

    return 0;
}
```

Sample Run: In this sample run, the user input is shaded.

```
Line 1: Enter a string: abcd

Line 4: After first cin.get(ch); ch = a
Line 6: After second cin.get(ch); ch = b
Line 9: After putback and then cin.get(ch); ch = b
Line 11: After cin.peek(); ch = c
Line 13: After cin.get(ch); ch = c
```

The user input, `abcd`, allows you to see the effect of the functions `get`, `putback`, and `peek` in the preceding program. The statement in Line 1 prompts the user to enter a string. In Line 2, the statement `cin.get(ch);` extracts the first character from the input stream and stores it in the variable `ch`. So after Line 2 executes, the value of `ch` is `'a'`.

The `cout` statement in Line 4 outputs the value of `ch`. The statement `cin.get(ch);` in Line 5 extracts the next character from the input stream, which is `'b'`, and stores it in `ch`. At this point, the value of `ch` is `'b'`.

The `cout` statement in Line 6 outputs the value of `ch`. The `cin.putback(ch);` statement in Line 7 puts the previous character extracted by the `get` function, which is `'b'`, back into the input stream. Therefore, the next character to be extracted from the input stream is `'b'`.

The `cin.get(ch);` statement in Line 8 extracts the next character from the input stream, which is still `'b'`, and stores it in `ch`. Now the value of `ch` is `'b'`. The `cout` statement in Line 9 outputs the value of `ch` as `'b'`.

In Line 10, the statement `ch = cin.peek();` checks the next character in the input stream, which is `'c'`, and stores it in `ch`. The value of `ch` is now `'c'`. The `cout` statement in Line 11 outputs the value of `ch`. The `cin.get(ch);` statement in Line 12 extracts the next character from the input stream and stores it in `ch`. The `cout` statement in Line 13 outputs the value of `ch`, which is still `'c'`.

Note that the statement `ch = cin.peek();` in Line 10 did not remove the character `'c'` from the input stream; it only peeked into the input stream. The output of Lines 11 and 13 demonstrate this functionality.

The Dot Notation Between I/O Stream Variables and I/O Functions: A Precaution

In the preceding sections, you learned how to manipulate an input stream to get data into a program. You also learned how to use the functions `get`, `ignore`, `peek`, and `putback`. It is important that you use these functions exactly as shown. For example, to use the `get` function, the text showed statements such as the following:

```
cin.get(ch);
```

Omitting the dot—that is, the period between the variable `cin` and the function name `get`—results in a syntax error. For example, in the statement:

```
cin.get(ch);
```

`cin` and `get` are two separate identifiers separated by a dot. In the statement:

```
cinget(ch);
```

`cinget` becomes a new identifier. If you used `cinget(ch);` in a program, the compiler would try to resolve an undeclared identifier, which would generate an error. Similarly, missing parentheses, as in `cin.getch;`, result in a syntax error. Also, remember that you must use the input functions together with an input stream variable. If you try to use any of the input functions alone—that is, without the input stream variable—the compiler might generate an error message such as "undeclared identifier." For example, the statement `get(ch);` could result in a syntax error.

As you can see, several functions are associated with an `istream` variable, each doing a specific job. Recall that the functions `get`, `ignore`, and so on are *members* of the data type `istream`. Called the **dot notation,** the dot separates the input stream variable name from the member, or function, name. In fact, in C++, the dot is an operator called the **member access operator**.

NOTE   C++ has a special name for the data types `istream` and `ostream`. The data types `istream` and `ostream` are called classes. The variables `cin` and `cout` also have special names, called objects. Therefore, `cin` is called an `istream` object, and `cout` is called an `ostream` object. In fact, stream variables are called stream objects. You will learn these concepts in the chapter entitled Inheritance and Composition later in this book.

Input Failure

Many things can go wrong during program execution. A program that is syntactically correct might produce incorrect results. For example, suppose that a part-time employee's paycheck is calculated by using the following formula:

```
wages = payRate * hoursWorked;
```

If you accidentally type + in place of *, the calculated wages would be incorrect, even though the statement containing a + is syntactically correct.

What about an attempt to read invalid data? For example, what would happen if you tried to input a letter into an `int` variable? If the input data did not match the corresponding variables, the program would run into problems. For example, trying to read a letter into an `int` or `double` variable would result in an **input failure**. Consider the following statements:

```
int a, b, c;
double x;
```

If the input is:

```
W 54
```

then the statement:

```
cin >> a >> b;
```

would result in an input failure, because you are trying to input the character **'W'** into the **int** variable a. If the input were:

```
35 67.93 48
```

then the input statement:

```
cin >> a >> x > >b;
```

would result in storing 35 in a, 67.93 in x, and 48 in b.

Now consider the following read statement with the previous input (the input with three values):

```
cin >> a >> b >> c;
```

This statement stores 35 in a and 67 in b. The reading stops at . (the decimal point). Because the next variable c is of the data type **int**, the computer tries to read . into c, which is an error. The input stream then enters a state called the **fail state**.

What actually happens when the input stream enters the fail state? Once an input stream enters a fail state, all further I/O statements using that stream are ignored. Unfortunately, the program quietly continues to execute with whatever values are stored in variables and produces incorrect results. The program in Example 3-6 illustrates an input failure. This program on your system may produce different results.

EXAMPLE 3-6

```cpp
//Input Failure program

#include <iostream>

using namespace std;

int main()
{
    int a = 10;                                 //Line 1
    int b = 20;                                 //Line 2
    int c = 30;                                 //Line 3
    int d = 40;                                 //Line 4

    cout << "Line 5: Enter four integers: ";    //Line 5
    cin >> a >> b >> c >> d;                     //Line 6
    cout << endl;                                //Line 7
```

```
    cout << "Line 8: The numbers you entered are:"
         << endl;                                        //Line 8
    cout << "Line 9: a = " << a << ", b = " << b
         << ", c = " << c << ", d = " << d << endl;   //Line 9

    return 0;
}
```

Sample Runs: In these sample runs, the user input is shaded.

Sample Run 1

```
Line 5: Enter four integers: 34 K 67 28

Line 8: The numbers you entered are:
Line 9: a = 34, b = 20, c = 30, d = 40
```

The statements in Lines 1, 2, 3, and 4 declare and initialize the variables a, b, c, and d to 10, 20, 30, and 40, respectively. The statement in Line 5 prompts the user to enter four integers; the statement in Line 6 inputs these four integers into variables a, b, c, and d.

In this sample run, the second input value is the character 'K'. The cin statement tries to input this character into the variable b. However, because b is an **int** variable, the input stream enters the fail state. Note that the values of b, c, and d are unchanged, as shown by the output of the statement in Line 9.

Sample Run 2

```
Line 5: Enter four integers: 37 653.89 23 76

Line 8: The numbers you entered are:
Line 9: a = 37, b = 653, c = 30, d = 40
```

In this sample run, the cin statement in Line 6 inputs 37 into a, and 653 into b, and then tries to input the decimal point into c. Because c is an **int** variable, the decimal point is regarded as a character, so the input stream enters the fail state. In this sample run, the values of c and d are unchanged, as shown by the output of the statement in Line 9.

The clear **Function**

When an input stream enters the fail state, the system ignores all further I/O using that stream. You can use the stream function clear to restore the input stream to a working state.

The syntax to use the function clear is:

```
istreamVar.clear();
```

Here istreamVar is an input stream variable, such as cin.

After using the function `clear` to return the input stream to a working state, you still need to clear the rest of the garbage from the input stream. This can be accomplished by using the function `ignore`. Example 3-7 illustrates this situation.

EXAMPLE 3-7

```cpp
//Input failure and the clear function

#include <iostream>

using namespace std;

int main()
{
    int a = 23;                                 //Line 1
    int b = 34;                                 //Line 2

    cout << "Line 3: Enter a number followed"
        << " by a character: ";                 //Line 3
    cin >> a >> b;                              //Line 4
    cout << endl << "Line 5: a = " << a
        << ", b = " << b << endl;               //Line 5

    cin.clear();                 //Restore input stream; Line 6

    cin.ignore(200,'\n');            //Clear the buffer; Line 7

    cout << "Line 8: Enter two numbers: ";      //Line 8
    cin >> a >> b;                              //Line 9
    cout << endl << "Line 10: a = " << a
        << ", b = " << b << endl;               //Line 10

    return 0;
}
```

Sample Run: In this sample run, the user input is shaded.

```
Line 3: Enter a number followed by a character: 78 d

Line 5: a = 78, b = 34
Line 8: Enter two numbers: 65 88

Line 10: a = 65, b = 88
```

The statements in Lines 1 and 2 declare and initialize the variables a and b to 23 and 34, respectively. The statement in Line 3 prompts the user to enter a number followed by a character; the statement in Line 4 inputs this number into the variable a and then tries to input the character into the variable b. Because b is an `int` variable, an attempt to input a character into b causes the input stream to enter the fail state. The value of b is unchanged, as shown by the output of the statement in Line 5.

The statement in Line 6 restores the input stream by using the function `clear`, and the statement in Line 7 ignores the rest of the input. The statement in Line 8 again prompts the user to input two numbers; the statement in Line 9 stores these two numbers into `a` and `b`. Next, the statement in Line 10 outputs the values of `a` and `b`.

Output and Formatting Output

Other than writing efficient programs, generating the desired output is one of a programmer's highest priorities. Chapter 2 briefly introduced the process involved in generating output on the standard output device. More precisely, you learned how to use the insertion operator << and the manipulator `endl` to display results on the standard output device.

However, there is a lot more to output than just displaying results. Sometimes floating-point numbers must be output in a specific way. For example, a paycheck must be printed to two decimal places, whereas the results of a scientific experiment might require the output of floating-point numbers to six, seven, or perhaps even ten decimal places. Also, you might like to align the numbers in specific columns or fill the empty space between strings and numbers with a character other than the blank. For example, in preparing the table of contents, the space between the section heading and the page number might need to be filled with dots or dashes. In this section, you will learn about various output functions and manipulators that allow you to format your output in a desired way.

Recall that the syntax of `cout` when used together with the insertion operator << is:

```
cout << expression or manipulator << expression or manipulator...;
```

Here `expression` is evaluated, its value is printed, and `manipulator` is used to format the output. The simplest manipulator that you have used so far is `endl`, which is used to move the insertion point to the beginning of the next line.

Other output manipulators that are of our interest include: `setprecision`, `fixed`, `showpoint`, `setw`, and `flush`. The next few sections describe these manipulators.

setprecision Manipulator

You use the manipulator `setprecision` to control the output of floating-point numbers. The default output of floating-point numbers is scientific notation. Some software development kits (SDKs) might use a maximum of six decimal places for the default output of floating-point numbers. However, when an employee's paycheck is printed, the desired output is a maximum of two decimal places. To print floating-point output to two decimal places, you use the `setprecision` manipulator to set the precision to 2.

The general syntax of the `setprecision` manipulator is:

```
setprecision(n)
```

where n is the number of decimal places.

You use the `setprecision` manipulator with `cout` and the insertion operator. For example, the statement:

```
cout << setprecision(2);
```

formats the output of decimal numbers to two decimal places, until a similar subsequent statement changes the precision. Notice that the number of decimal places, or the precision value, is passed as an argument to `setprecision`.

To use the manipulator `setprecision`, the program must include the header file `iomanip`. Thus, the following include statement is required:

```
#include <iomanip>
```

`fixed` Manipulator

To further control the output of floating-point numbers, you can use other manipulators. To output floating-point numbers in a fixed decimal format, you use the manipulator `fixed`. The following statement sets the output of floating-point numbers in a fixed decimal format on the standard output device:

```
cout << fixed;
```

After the preceding statement executes, all floating-point numbers are displayed in the fixed decimal format until the manipulator `fixed` is disabled. You can disable the manipulator `fixed` by using the stream member function `unsetf`. For example, to disable the manipulator `fixed` on the standard output device, you use the following statement:

```
cout.unsetf(ios::fixed);
```

After the manipulator `fixed` is disabled, the output of the floating-point numbers return to their default settings. The manipulator `scientific` is used to output floating-point numbers in scientific format.

`showpoint` Manipulator

Suppose that the decimal part of a decimal number is zero. In this case, when you instruct the computer to output the decimal number in a fixed decimal format, the output may not show the decimal point and the decimal part. To force the output to show the decimal point and trailing zeros, you use the manipulator `showpoint`. The following statement sets the output of decimal numbers with a decimal point and trailing zeros on the standard input device:

```
cout << showpoint;
```

Of course, the following statement sets the output of a floating-point number in a fixed decimal format with the decimal point and trailing zeros on the standard output device:

```
cout << fixed << showpoint;
```

The program in Example 3-8 illustrates how to use the manipulators `setprecision`, `fixed`, and `showpoint`.

EXAMPLE 3-8

```cpp
//Example: setprecision, fixed, showpoint

#include <iostream>
#include <iomanip>

using namespace std;

int main()
{
    double x, y, z;

    x = 15.674;                                     //Line 1
    y = 235.73;                                      //Line 2
    z = 9525.9864;                                   //Line 3

    cout << fixed << showpoint;                      //Line 4

    cout << setprecision(2)
         << "Line 5: setprecision(2)" << endl;       //Line 5
    cout << "Line 6: x = " << x << endl;             //Line 6
    cout << "Line 7: y = " << y << endl;             //Line 7
    cout << "Line 8: z = " << z << endl;             //Line 8

    cout << setprecision(3)
         << "Line 9: setprecision(3)" << endl;       //Line 9
    cout << "Line 10: x = " << x << endl;            //Line 10
    cout << "Line 11: y = " << y << endl;            //Line 11
    cout << "Line 12: z = " << z << endl;            //Line 12

    cout << setprecision(4)
         << "Line 13: setprecision(4)" << endl;      //Line 13
    cout << "Line 14: x = " << x << endl;            //Line 14
    cout << "Line 15: y = " << y << endl;            //Line 15
    cout << "Line 16: z = " << z << endl;            //Line 16

    cout << "Line 17: "
         << setprecision(3) << x << "  "
         << setprecision(2) << y << "  "
         << setprecision(4) << z << endl;            //Line 17

    return 0;
}
```

Sample Run:

```
Line 5: setprecision(2)
Line 6: x = 15.67
Line 7: y = 235.73
Line 8: z = 9525.99
Line 9: setprecision(3)
Line 10: x = 15.674
Line 11: y = 235.730
Line 12: z = 9525.986
Line 13: setprecision(4)
Line 14: x = 15.6740
Line 15: y = 235.7300
Line 16: z = 9525.9864
Line 17: 15.674   235.73   9525.9864
```

The statements in Lines 1, 2, and 3 initialize **x**, **y**, and **z** to 15.674, 235.73, and 9525.9864, respectively. The statement in Line 4 sets the output of floating-point numbers in a fixed decimal format with a decimal point and trailing zeros. The statement in Line 5 sets the output of floating-point numbers to two decimal places.

The statements in Lines 6, 7, and 8 output the values of **x**, **y**, and **z** to two decimal places. Note that the printed value of **z** in Line 8 is rounded. The statement in Line 9 sets the output of floating-point numbers to three decimal places; the statements in Lines 10, 11, and 12 output the values of **x**, **y**, and **z** to three decimal places. Note that the value of **y**, in Line 11, is output to three decimal places. Because the number stored in **y** has only two decimal places, a 0 is printed as the third decimal place.

The statement in Line 13 sets the output of floating-point numbers to four decimal places; the statements in Lines 14, 15, and 16 output the values of **x**, **y**, and **z** to four decimal places. Note that in Line 14, the printed value of **x** contains a 0 in the fourth decimal place. The printed value of **y**, in Line 15, contains a 0 in the third and fourth decimal places.

The statement in Line 17 first sets the output of floating-point numbers to three decimal places and then outputs the value of **x** to three decimal places. After printing the value of **x**, the statement in Line 17 sets the output of floating-point numbers to two decimal places and then outputs the value of **y** to two decimal places. Next, it sets the output of floating-point numbers to four decimal places and then outputs the value of **z** to four decimal places.

---

setw

The manipulator **setw** is used to output the value of an expression in a specific number of columns. The value of the expression can be either a string or a number. The expression **setw(n)** outputs the value of the next expression in n columns. The output is right-justified. Thus, if you specify the number of columns to be 8, for example, and the output requires only 4 columns, the first four columns are left blank. Furthermore, if the number of columns specified is less than the number of columns required by the output, the output automatically expands to the required number of columns; the output is not truncated. For example, if **x** is an **int** variable, the following statement outputs the value of **x** in five columns on the standard output device:

```
cout << setw(5) << x << endl;
```

To use the manipulator **setw**, the program must include the header file **iomanip**. Thus, the following include statement is required:

```
#include <iomanip>
```

Unlike **setprecision**, which controls the output of all floating-point numbers until it is reset, **setw** controls the output of only the next expression.

EXAMPLE 3-9

```cpp
//Example: setw

#include <iostream>
#include <iomanip>

using namespace std;

int main()
{
    int x = 19;                                        //Line 1
    int a = 345;                                       //Line 2
    double y = 76.384;                                 //Line 3

    cout << fixed << showpoint;                        //Line 4

    cout << "12345678901234567890" << endl;            //Line 5

    cout << setw(5) << x << endl;                      //Line 6
    cout << setw(5) << a << setw(5) << "Hi"
         << setw(5) << x << endl << endl;              //Line 7

    cout << setprecision(2);                           //Line 8
    cout << setw(6) << a << setw(6) << y
         << setw(6) << x << endl;                      //Line 9
    cout << setw(6) << x << setw(6) << a
         << setw(6) << y << endl << endl;              //Line 10

    cout << setw(5) << a << x << endl;                 //Line 11
    cout << setw(2) << a << setw(4) << x << endl;      //Line 12

    return 0;
}
```

Sample Run:

```
12345678901234567890
   19
   345    Hi    19

    345 76.38     19
     19    345 76.38

   34519
345   19
```

The statements in Lines 1, 2, and 3 declare the variables **x**, **a**, and **y** and initialize these variables to `19`, `345`, and `76.384`, respectively. The statement in Line 4 sets the output of floating-point numbers in a fixed decimal format with a decimal point and trailing zeros. The output of the statement in Line 5 shows the column positions when the specific values are printed; it is the first line of output.

The statement in Line 6 outputs the value of **x** in five columns. Because **x** has only two digits, only two columns are needed to output its value. Therefore, the first three columns are left blank in the second line of output. The statement in Line 7 outputs the value of **a** in the first five columns, the string **"Hi"** in the next five columns, and then the value of **x** in the following five columns. Because the string **"Hi"** contains only two characters, and five columns are set to output these two characters, the first three columns are left blank. See the third line of output. The fourth line of output is blank because the manipulator **endl** appears twice in the statement in Line 7.

The statement in Line 8 sets the output of floating-point numbers to two decimal places. The statement in Line 9 outputs the values of **a** in the first six columns, **y** in the next six columns, and **x** in the following six columns, creating the fifth line of output. The output of the statement in Line 10 (which is the sixth line of output) is similar to the output of the statement in Line 9. Notice how the numbers are nicely aligned in the outputs of the statements in Lines 9 and 10. The seventh line of output is blank because the manipulator **endl** appears twice in the statement in Line 10.

The statement in Line 11 outputs first the value of **a** in five columns and then the value of **x**. Note that the manipulator **setw** in the statement in Line 11 controls only the output of **a**. Thus, after the value of **a** is printed, the value of **x** is printed at the current cursor position (see the eighth line of output).

In the **cout** statement in Line 12, only two columns are assigned to output the value of **a**. However, the value of **a** has three digits, so the output is expanded to three columns. The value of **x** is then printed in four columns. Because the value of **x** contains only two digits, only two columns are required to output the value of **x**. Therefore, because four columns are allocated to output the value of **x**, the first two columns are left blank (see the ninth line of output).

`flush` **Manipulator**

Both the manipulator `endl` and the newline escape sequence `'\n'` position the insertion point at the beginning of the next line on the output device. However, the manipulator `endl` also has another use.

When a program sends output to an output device, the output first goes to the buffer in the computer. Whenever the buffer becomes full, the output is sent to the output device. However, as soon as the manipulator `endl` is encountered, the output from the buffer is sent to the output device immediately, even if the buffer is not full. Therefore, the manipulator `endl` positions the insertion point at the beginning of the next line on an output device and helps clear the buffer.

In C++, you can use the manipulator `flush` to clear the buffer even if the buffer is not full. In contrast to the manipulator `endl`, the manipulator `flush` does not move the insertion point to the beginning of the next line.

The syntax to use the `flush` manipulator is:

```
ostreamVar << flush;
```

where `ostreamVar` is an output stream variable, such as `cout`. For example, the following statement sends the output from the buffer to the standard output device:

```
cout << flush;
```

EXAMPLE 3-10

The output of the following statement goes to the buffer:

```
cout << "Enter an integer: ";
```

However, the output of the following statement immediately goes to the standard output device, which typically is the screen:

```
cout << "Enter an integer: " << flush;
```

Additional Output Formatting Tools

In the previous section, you learned how to use the manipulators `setprecision`, `fixed`, and `showpoint` to control the output of floating-point numbers, and how to use the manipulator `setw` to display the output in specific columns. Even though these manipulators are adequate to produce an elegant report, in some situations you may want to do more. In this section, you will learn additional formatting tools that give you more control over your output.

`setfill` Manipulator

Recall that, in the manipulator `setw`, if the number of columns specified exceeds the number of columns required by the expression, the output of the expression is right-justified and the unused columns to the left are filled with spaces. The output stream variables can use the manipulator `setfill` to fill the unused columns with a character other than a space.

The syntax to use the manipulator `setfill` is:

```
ostreamVar << setfill(ch);
```

where `ostreamVar` is an output stream variable and `ch` is a character. For example, the statement:

```
cout << setfill('#');
```

sets the fill character to `'#'` on the standard output device.

To use the manipulator `setfill`, the program must include the header file `iomanip`.

The program in Example 3-11 illustrates the effect of using `setfill` in a program.

EXAMPLE 3-11

```cpp
//Example: setfill

#include <iostream>
#include <iomanip>

using namespace std;

int main()
{
    int x = 15;                                         //Line 1
    int y = 7634;                                       //Line 2

    cout << "12345678901234567890" << endl;            //Line 3
    cout << setw(5) << x << setw(7) << y
         << setw(8) << "Warm" << endl;                  //Line 4

    cout << setfill('*');                               //Line 5
    cout << setw(5) << x << setw(7) << y
         << setw(8) << "Warm" << endl;                  //Line 6

    cout << setw(5) << x << setw(7) << setfill('#')
         << y << setw(8) << "Warm" << endl;             //Line 7

    cout << setw(5) << setfill('@') << x
         << setw(7) << setfill('#') << y
         << setw(8) << setfill('^') << "Warm"
         << endl;                                       //Line 8
```

```cpp
    cout << setfill(' ');                        //Line 9
    cout << setw(5) << x << setw(7) << y
         << setw(8) << "Warm" << endl;           //Line 10

    return 0;
}
```

Sample Run:

```
12345678901234567890
   15   7634    Warm
***15***7634****Warm
***15###7634####Warm
@@@15###7634^^^^Warm
   15   7634    Warm
```

The statements in Lines 1 and 2 declare and initialize the variables **x** and **y** to **15** and
7634, respectively. The output of the statement in Line 3—the first line of output—
shows the column position when the subsequent statements output the values of the
variables. The statement in Line 4 outputs the value of **x** in five columns, the value of **y**
in seven columns, and the string **"Warm"** in eight columns. In this statement, the filling
character is the blank character, as shown in the second line of output.

The statement in Line 5 sets the filling character to *. The statement in Line 6 outputs the
value of **x** in five columns, the value of **y** in seven columns, and the string **"Warm"** in
eight columns. Because **x** is a two-digit number and five columns are assigned to output
its value, the first three columns are unused by **x** and are, therefore, filled by the filling
character *. To print the value of **y**, seven columns are assigned; **y** is a four-digit number,
however, so the filling character fills the first three columns. Similarly, to print the value
of the string **"Warm"**, eight columns are assigned; the string **"Warm"** has only four
characters, so the filling character fills the first four columns. See the third line of output.

The output of the statement in Line 7—the fourth line of output—is similar to the output
of the statement in Line 6, except that the filling character for **y** and the string **"Warm"** is
#. In the output of the statement in Line 8 (the fifth line of output), the filling character
for **x** is @, the filling character for **y** is #, and the filling character for the string **"Warm"** is
^. The manipulator **setfill** sets these filling characters.

The statement in Line 9 sets the filling character to blank. The statement in Line 10
outputs the values of **x**, **y**, and the string **"Warm"** using the filling character blank, as
shown in the sixth line of output.

`left` **and** `right` **Manipulators**

Recall that if the number of columns specified in the **setw** manipulator exceeds the
number of columns required by the next expression, the default output is right-justified.
Sometimes you might want the output to be left-justified. To left-justify the output, you
use the manipulator **left**.

The syntax to set the manipulator `left` is:

```
ostreamVar << left;
```

where `ostreamVar` is an output stream variable. For example, the following statement sets the output to be left-justified on the standard output device:

```
cout << left;
```

You can disable the manipulator `left` by using the stream function `unsetf`. The syntax to disable the manipulator `left` is:

```
ostreamVar.unsetf(ios::left);
```

where `ostreamVar` is an output stream variable. Disabling the manipulator `left` returns the output to the settings of the default output format. For example, the following statement disables the manipulator `left` on the standard output device:

```
cout.unsetf(ios::left);
```

The syntax to set the manipulator `right` is:

```
ostreamVar << right;
```

where `ostreamVar` is an output stream variable. For example, the following statement sets the output to be right-justified on the standard output device:

```
cout << right;
```

The program in Example 3-12 illustrates the effect of the manipulators `left` and `right`.

EXAMPLE 3-12

```cpp
//Example: left justification

#include <iostream>
#include <iomanip>

using namespace std;

int main()
{
    int x = 15;                                        //Line 1
    int y = 7634;                                      //Line 2

    cout << left;                                      //Line 3

    cout << "12345678901234567890" << endl;            //Line 4
    cout << setw(5) << x << setw(7) << y
         << setw(8) << "Warm" << endl;                 //Line 5
```

```cpp
    cout << setfill('*');                                   //Line 6

    cout << setw(5) << x << setw(7) << y
         << setw(8) << "Warm" << endl;                      //Line 7

    cout << setw(5) << x << setw(7) << setfill('#')
         << y << setw(8) << "Warm" << endl;                 //Line 8

    cout << setw(5) << setfill('@') << x
         << setw(7) << setfill('#') << y
         << setw(8) << setfill('^') << "Warm"
         << endl;                                           //Line 9

    cout << right;                                          //Line 10
    cout << setfill(' ');                                   //Line 11

    cout << setw(5) << x << setw(7) << y
         << setw(8) << "Warm" << endl;                      //Line 12

    return 0;
}
```

Sample Run:

```
12345678901234567890
15    7634    Warm
15***7634***Warm****
15***7634###Warm####
15@@@7634###Warm^^^^
   15    7634    Warm
```

The output of this program is the same as the output of Example 3-11. The only difference here is that for the statements in Lines 4 through 9, the output is left-justified. You are encouraged to do a walk-through of this program.

NOTE This chapter discusses several stream functions and stream manipulators. To use stream functions such as `get`, `ignore`, `fill`, and `clear` in a program, the program must include the header file `iostream`.

There are two types of manipulators: those with parameters and those without parameters. Manipulators with parameters are called **parameterized stream manipulators**. For example, manipulators such as `setprecision`, `setw`, and `setfill` are parameterized. On the other hand, manipulators such as `endl`, `fixed`, `scientific`, `showpoint`, `flush`, and `left` do not have parameters.

To use a parameterized stream manipulator in a program, you must include the header file `iomanip`. Manipulators without parameters are part of the `iostream` header file and, therefore, do not require inclusion of the header file `iomanip`.

Input/Output and the `string` Type

You can use an input stream variable, such as `cin`, and the extraction operator `>>` to read a string into a variable of the data type `string`. For example, if the input is the string `"Shelly"`, the following code stores this input into the `string` variable `name`:

```
string name;      //variable declaration
cin >> name;      //input statement
```

Recall that the extraction operator skips any leading whitespace characters and that reading stops at a whitespace character. As a consequence, you cannot use the extraction operator to read strings that contain blanks. For example, suppose that the variable `name` is defined as noted above. If the input is:

```
Alice Wonderland
```

then after the statement:

```
cin >> name;
```

executes, the value of the variable `name` is `"Alice"`.

To read a string containing blanks, you can use the function `getline`.

The syntax to use the function `getline` is:

```
getline(istreamVar, strVar);
```

where `istreamVar` is an input stream variable and `strVar` is a `string` variable. The reading is delimited by the newline character `'\n'`.

The function `getline` reads until it reaches the end of the current line. The newline character is also read but not stored in the `string` variable.

Consider the following statement:

```
string myString;
```

If the input is 29 characters:

```
bbbbHello there. How are you?
```

where b represents a blank, after the statement:

```
getline(cin, myString);
```

the value of `myString` is:

```
myString = "    Hello there. How are you?"
```

All 29 characters, including the first four blanks, are stored into `myString`.

Similarly, you can use an output stream variable, such as `cout`, and the insertion operator `<<` to output the contents of a variable of the data type `string`.

File Input/Output

The previous sections discussed in some detail how to get input from the keyboard (standard input device) and send output to the screen (standard output device). However, getting input from the keyboard and sending output to the screen have several limitations. Inputting data in a program from the keyboard is comfortable as long as the amount of input is very small. Sending output to the screen works well if the amount of data is small (no larger than the size of the screen), and you do not want to distribute the output in a printed format to others.

If the amount of input data is large, however, it is inefficient to type it at the keyboard each time you run a program. In addition to the inconvenience of typing large amounts of data, typing can generate errors, and unintentional typos cause erroneous results. You must have some way to get data into the program from other sources. By using alternative sources of data, you can prepare the data before running a program, and the program can access the data each time it runs.

Suppose you want to present the output of a program in a meeting. Distributing printed copies of the program output is a better approach than showing the output on a screen. For example, you might give a printed report to each member of a committee before an important meeting. Furthermore, output must sometimes be saved so that the output produced by one program can be used as an input to other programs.

This section discusses how to obtain data from other input devices, such as a disk (that is, secondary storage), and how to save the output to a disk. C++ allows a program to get data directly from, and save output directly to, secondary storage. A program can use the file I/O and read data from, or write data to, a file. Formally, a file is defined as follows:

File: An area in secondary storage used to hold information.

The standard I/O header file, `iostream`, contains data types and variables that are used only for input from the standard input device and output to the standard output device. In addition, C++ provides a header file called `fstream`, which is used for file I/O. Among other things, the `fstream` header file contains the definitions of two data types: `ifstream`, which means input file stream and is similar to `istream`, and `ofstream`, which means output file stream and is similar to `ostream`.

The variables `cin` and `cout` are already defined and associated with the standard input/output devices. In addition, `>>`, `get`, `ignore`, `putback`, `peek`, and so on can be used with `cin`, while `<<`, `setfill`, and so on can be used with `cout`. These same operators and functions are also available for file I/O, but the header file `fstream` does not declare variables to use them. You must declare variables called **file stream variables**, which include `ifstream` variables for input and `ofstream` variables for output. You then use these variables together with `>>`, `<<`, or other functions for I/O. Remember that C++ does not automatically initialize user-defined variables. Once you declare the `fstream` variables, you must associate these file variables with the input/output sources.

File I/O is a five-step process:

1. Include the header file `fstream` in the program.
2. Declare file stream variables.
3. Associate the file stream variables with the input/output sources.
4. Use the file stream variables with >>, <<, or other input/output functions.
5. Close the files.

We will now describe these five steps in detail. A skeleton program then shows how the steps might appear in a program.

Step 1 requires that the header file `fstream` be included in the program. The following statement accomplishes this task:

```
#include <fstream>
```

Step 2 requires you to declare file stream variables. Consider the following statements:

```
ifstream inData;
ofstream outData;
```

The first statement declares `inData` to be an input file stream variable. The second statement declares `outData` to be an output file stream variable.

Step 3 requires you to associate file stream variables with the input/output sources. This step is called **opening the files**. The stream member function `open` is used to open files. The syntax for opening a file is:

```
fileStreamVariable.open(sourceName);
```

Here `fileStreamVariable` is a file stream variable and `sourceName` is the name of the input/output file.

Suppose you include the declaration from Step 2 in a program. Further suppose that the input data is stored in a file called `prog.dat` on a floppy disk in drive `A:`, and you want to save the output in a file called `prog.out` on a floppy disk in drive `A:`. The following statements associate `inData` with `prog.dat` and `outData` with `prog.out`. That is, the file `prog.dat` is opened for inputting data and the file `prog.out` is opened for outputting data.

```
inData.open("a:\\prog.dat");   //open the input file
outData.open("a:\\prog.out"); //open the output file
```

NOTE

1. Notice that there are two \s after `a:`. In C++, \ is the escape character. Therefore, to produce a \ within a string, you need \\.

2. Some SDKs maintain programs in the form of projects. If your C++ project and the input file reside in the same directory, you do not need to include `a:\\` before the name of the file. Similarly, if you want the output file to be stored in the same directory as the C++ program, you can omit `a:\\` before the file name. These options are SDK-dependent. To be absolutely sure, check your SDK's documentation.

Step 4 typically works as follows. You use the file stream variables with >>, <<, or other input/output functions. The syntax for using >> or << with file stream variables is exactly the same as the syntax for using `cin` and `cout`. Instead of using `cin` and `cout`, however, you use the file stream variable names that were declared. For example, the statement

```
inData >> payRate;
```

reads the data from the file `prog.dat` and stores it in the variable `payRate`. The statement:

```
outData << "The paycheck is: $" << pay << endl;
```

stores the output—`The paycheck is: $565.78`—in the file `prog.out`. This statement assumes that the pay was calculated as `565.78`.

Once the I/O is complete, Step 5 requires closing the files. Closing a file means that the file stream variables are disassociated from the storage area and are freed. Once these variables are freed, they can be reused for other file I/O. Moreover, closing an output file ensures that the entire output is sent to the file; that is, the buffer is emptied. You close files by using the stream function `close`. For example, assuming the program includes the declarations listed in Steps 2 and 3, the statements for closing the files are:

```
inData.close();
outData.close();
```

NOTE On some systems, it is not necessary to close the files. When the program terminates, the files are closed automatically. Nevertheless, it is a good practice to close the files yourself. Also, if you want to use the same file stream variable to open another file, you must close the first file opened with that file stream variable.

In skeleton form, a program that uses file I/O usually takes the following form:

```
#include <fstream>

//Add additional header files you use

using namespace std;

int main()
{
        //Declare file stream variables such as the following
    ifstream inData;
    ofstream outData;
    .
    .
    .

        //Open the files
    inData.open("a:\\prog.dat");   //open the input file
    outData.open("a:\\prog.out"); //open the output file
```

```cpp
    //Code for data manipulation

    //Close files
inData.close();
outData.close();

return 0;
}
```

Recall that Step 3 requires the file to be opened for file I/O. Opening a file associates a file stream variable declared in the program with a physical file at the source, such as a disk. In the case of an input file, the file must exist before the **open** statement executes. If the file does not exist, the **open** statement fails and the input stream enters the fail state. An output file does not have to exist before it is opened; if the output file does not exist, the computer prepares an empty file for output. If the designated output file already exists, by default the old contents are erased when the file is opened.

NOTE To add the output at the end of an existing file, you can use the option `ios::app` as follows. Suppose that `outData` is declared as before and you want to add the output at the end of the existing file, say, `firstProg.out` on drive `A:`. The statement to open this file is:

```cpp
outData.open("a:\\firstProg.out", ios::app);
```

If the file `firstProg.out` does not exist, then the system creates an empty file.

NOTE Appendix E discusses binary and random access files.

Movie Ticket Sale and Donation to Charity

A movie in a local theater is in great demand. To help a local charity, the theater owner has decided to donate to the charity a portion of the gross amount generated from the movie. This example designs and implements a program that prompts the user to input the movie name, adult ticket price, child ticket price, number of adult tickets sold, number of child tickets sold, and percentage of the gross amount to be donated to the charity. The output of the program is as follows.

Variables The program needs to read a student's first and last name and five test scores. Therefore, you need two variables to store the student name and five variables to store the five test scores.

To find the average, you must add the five test scores and then divide the sum by 5. Thus, you need a variable to store the average test score. Furthermore, because the input data is in a file, you need an `ifstream` variable to open the input file. Because the program output will be stored in a file, you need an `ofstream` variable to open the output file. The program, therefore, needs at least the following variables:

```
ifstream inFile;     //input file stream variable
ofstream outFile;    //output file stream variable

double test1, test2, test3, test4, test5; //variables to
                             //read the five test scores
double average;      //variable to store the average test score
string firstName;    //variable to store the first name
string lastName;     //variable to store the last name
```

MAIN ALGORITHM In the preceding sections, we analyzed the problem and determined the formulas to perform the calculations. We also determined the necessary variables and named constants. We can now expand the previous algorithm to solve the problem given at the beginning of this programming example:

1. Declare the variables.
2. Open the input file.
3. Open the output file.
4. To output the floating-point numbers in a fixed decimal format with a decimal point and trailing zeros, set the manipulators `fixed` and `showpoint`. Also, to output the floating-point numbers with two decimal places, set the precision to two decimal places.
5. Read the student name.
6. Output the student name.
7. Read the five test scores.
8. Output the five test scores.
9. Find the average test score.
10. Output the average test score.
11. Close the input and output files.

Because this program reads data from a file and outputs data to a file, it must include the header file `fstream`. Because the program outputs the average test score to two decimal places, you need to set the precision to two decimal places. Therefore, the program uses the manipulator `setprecision`, which requires you to include the header file `iomanip`. Because `firstName` and `lastName` are `string` variables, we must include the header file `string`. The program also includes the header file iostream to print a message on the screen so that you will not stare at a blank screen while the program executes.

COMPLETE PROGRAM LISTING

```cpp
//Program to calculate the average test score.

#include <iostream>
#include <fstream>
#include <iomanip>
#include <string>

using namespace std;

int main()
{
        //Declare variables;  Step 1
    ifstream inFile;
    ofstream outFile;

    double test1, test2, test3, test4, test5;
    double average;

    string firstName;
    string lastName;

    inFile.open("a:\\test.txt");                        //Step 2
    outFile.open("a:\\testavg.out");                    //Step 3

    outFile << fixed << showpoint;                      //Step 4
    outFile << setprecision(2);                         //Step 4

    cout << "Processing data" << endl;

    inFile >> firstName >> lastName;                    //Step 5
    outFile << "Student name: " << firstName
            << " " << lastName << endl;                 //Step 6

    inFile >> test1 >> test2 >> test3
           >> test4 >> test5;                           //Step 7
    outFile << "Test scores: " << setw(6) << test1
            << setw(6) << test2 << setw(6) << test3
            << setw(6) << test4 << setw(6) << test5
            << endl;                                    //Step 8

    average = (test1 + test2 + test3 + test4
            + test5) / 5.0;                             //Step 9

    outFile << "Average test score: " << setw(6)
            << average << endl;                         //Step 10
```

```
    inFile.close();                                           //Step 11
    outFile.close();                                          //Step 11

    return 0;
}
```

Sample Run

Input File (contents of the file `test.txt`):

```
Andrew Miller 87.50 89 65.75 37 98.50
```

Output File (contents of the file `testavg.out`):

```
Student name: Andrew Miller
Test scores:  87.50 89.00 65.75 37.00 98.50
Average test score:  75.55
```

NOTE The preceding program uses five variables—`test1`, `test2`, `test3`, `test4`, and `test5`—to read the five test scores and then find the average test score. The Web site accompanying this book contains a modified version of this program that uses only one variable, `testScore`, to read the test scores and another variable, `sum`, to find the sum of the test scores. The program is named `Ch3_AverageTestScoreVersion2.cpp`.

QUICK REVIEW

1. A stream in C++ is an infinite sequence of characters from a source to a destination.

2. An input stream is a stream from a source to a computer.

3. An output stream is a stream from a computer to a destination.

4. cin, which stands for common input, is an input stream object, typically initialized to the standard input device, which is the keyboard.

5. cout, which stands for common output, is an output stream object, typically initialized to the standard output device, which is the screen.

6. When the binary operator >> is used with an input stream object, such as cin, it is called the stream extraction operator. The left-side operand of >> must be an input stream variable, such as cin; the right-side operand must be a variable.

7. When the binary operator << is used with an output stream object, such as cout, it is called the stream insertion operator. The left-side operand of << must be an output stream variable, such as cout; the right-side operand of << must be an expression or a manipulator.

8. When inputting data into a variable, the operator `>>` skips all leading whitespace characters.

9. To use `cin` and `cout`, the program must include the header file `iostream`.

10. The function `get` is used to read data on a character-by-character basis and does not skip any whitespace characters.

11. The function `ignore` is used to skip data in a line.

12. The function `putback` puts the last character retrieved by the function `get` back into the input stream.

13. The function `peek` returns the next character from the input stream but does not remove the character from the input stream.

14. Attempting to read invalid data into a variable causes the input stream to enter the fail state.

15. Once an input failure has occurred, you use the function `clear` to restore the input stream to a working state.

16. The manipulator `setprecision` formats the output of floating-point numbers to a specified number of decimal places.

17. The manipulator `fixed` outputs floating-point numbers in the fixed decimal format.

18. The manipulator `showpoint` outputs floating-point numbers with a decimal point and trailing zeros.

19. The manipulator `setw` formats the output of an expression in a specific number of columns; the default output is right-justified.

20. If the number of columns specified in the argument of `setw` is less than the number of columns needed to print the value of the expression, the output is not truncated and the output of the expression expands to the required number of columns.

21. The manipulator `flush` clears the buffer even if the buffer is not full. In contrast to the manipulator `endl`, the manipulator `flush` does not move the insertion point to the beginning of the next line.

22. The manipulator `setfill` is used to fill the unused columns on an output device with a character other than a space.

23. If the number of columns specified in the `setw` manipulator exceeds the number of columns required by the next expression, the output is right-justified. To left-justify the output, you use the manipulator `left`.

24. To use the stream functions `get`, `ignore`, `putback`, `peek`, `clear`, and `unsetf` for standard I/O, the program must include the header file `iostream`.

25. To use the manipulators `setprecision`, `setw`, and `setfill`, the program must include the header file `iomanip`.

26. The header file `fstream` contains the definitions of `ifstream` and `ofstream`.

27. For file I/O, you must use the statement `#include <fstream>` to include the header file `fstream` in the program. You must also do the following: declare variables of type `ifstream` for file input and of type `ofstream` for file output; use open statements to open input and output files; and use `<<`, `>>`, `get`, `ignore`, `peek`, `putback`, or `clear` with file stream variables.

28. To close a file as indicated by the `ifstream` variable `inFile`, you use the statement `inFile.close();`. To close a file as indicated by the `ofstream` variable `outFile`, you use the statement `outFile.close();`.

EXERCISES

1. Mark the following statements as true or false.

    a. The extraction operator `>>` skips all leading whitespace characters when searching for the next data in the input stream.

    b. In the statement `cin >> x;`, `x` must be a variable.

    c. The statement `cin >> x >> y;` requires the input values for `x` and `y` to appear on the same line.

    d. The statement `cin >> num;` is equivalent to the statement `num >> cin;`.

    e. You generate the newline character by pressing the Enter (return) key on the keyboard.

    f. The function `ignore` is used to skip certain input in a line.

2. Suppose `x` and `y` are `int` variables and `ch` is a `char` variable. Consider the following input:

   `5 28 36`

   What value (if any) is assigned to `x`, `y`, and `ch` after each of the following statements executes? (Use the same input for each statement.)

    a. `cin >> x >> y >> ch;`

    b. `cin >> ch >> x >> y;`

    c. `cin >> x >> ch >> y;`

    d. `cin >> x >> y;`
       `cin.get(ch);`

3. Suppose `x` and `y` are `int` variables and `z` is a `double` variable. Assume the following input data:

   `37 86.56 32`

What value (if any) is assigned to **x**, **y**, and **z** after each of the following statements executes? (Use the same input for each statement.)

a. `cin >> x >> y >> z;`

b. `cin >> x >> z >> y;`

c. `cin >> z >> x >> y;`

4. Suppose **x** and **y** are **int** variables and **ch** is a **char** variable. Assume the following input data:

```
13 28 D
14 E 98
A B 56
```

What value (if any) is assigned to **x**, **y**, and **ch** after each of the following statements executes? (Use the same input for each statement.)

a.
```
cin >> x >> y;
cin.ignore(50, '\n');
cin >> ch;
```

b.
```
cin >> x;
cin.ignore(50, '\n');
cin >> y;
cin.ignore(50, '\n');
cin.get(ch);
```

c.
```
cin >> y;
cin.ignore(50, '\n');
cin >> x >> ch;
```

d.
```
cin.get(ch);
cin.ignore(50, '\n');
cin >> x;
cin.ignore(50, 'E');
cin >> y;
```

5. Given the input:

```
46 A 49
```

and the C++ code:

```cpp
int x = 10, y = 18;
char z = 'A';
cin >> x >> y >> z;
cout << x << " " << y << " " << z;
```

What is the output?

6. Write a C++ statement that uses the manipulator **setfill** to output a line containing 35 stars, as in the following line:

```
***********************************
```

7. Suppose that `age` is an `int` variable and `name` is a `string` variable. What are the values of `age` and `name` after the following input statements execute?

```
cin >> age;
getline(cin, name);
```

if the input is:

a.   `35 Mickey Balto`

b.   `35`
     `Mickey Balto`

8. Suppose that `age` is an `int` variable, `ch` is a `char` variable, and `name` is a `string` variable. What are the values of `age` and `name` after the following input statements execute?

```
cin >> age;
cin.get(ch);
getline(cin, name);
```

if the input is:

a.   `35 Mickey Balto`

b.   `35`
     `Mickey Balto`

9. The following program is supposed to read two numbers from a file named `input.dat`, and write the sum of the numbers to a file named `output.dat`. However, it fails to do so. Rewrite the program so that it accomplishes what it is intended to do. (Also, include statements to close the files.)

```cpp
#include <iostream>
#include <fstream>
using namespace std;

int main()
{
    int num1, num2;
    ifstream infile;

    outfile.open("output.dat");
    infile >> num1 >> num2;
    outfile << "Sum = " << num1 + num2 << endl;
    return 0;
}
```

10. What may cause an input stream to enter the fail state? What happens when an input stream enters the fail state?

11. A program reads data from a file called `inputFile.dat` and, after doing some calculations, writes the results to a file called `outFile.dat`. Answer the following questions:

   a. After the program executes, what are the contents of the file `inputFile.dat`?

   b. After the program executes, what are the contents of the file `outFile.dat` if this file was empty before the program executed?

   c. After the program executes, what are the contents of the file `outFile.dat` if this file contained 100 numbers before the program executed?

   d. What would happen if the file `outFile.dat` did not exist before the program executed?

PROGRAMMING EXERCISES

1. Consider the following incomplete C++ program:

```cpp
#include <iostream>

int main()
{
    ...
}
```

   a. Write a statement that includes the header file `fstream` in this program.

   b. Write statements that declare `inFile` to be an `ifstream` variable and `outFile` to be an `ofstream` variable.

   c. The program will read data from the file `inData.txt` and write output to the file `outData.txt`. Write statements to open both these files, associate `inFile` with `inData.txt`, and associate `outFile` with `outData.txt`.

   d. Suppose that the file `inData.txt` contains the following data:

```
56 38
A
7 8
```

   Write statements so that after the program executes, the contents of the file `outData.txt` are as shown below. If necessary, declare additional variables. Your statements should be general enough so that if the content of the input file changes and the program is run again (without editing and recompiling), it outputs the appropriate results:

```
Sum of 56 and 38 = 94.
The character that comes after A in the ASCII set is B.
The product of 7 and 8 = 56.
```

e. Write statements that close the input and output files.

f. Write a C++ program that tests the statements in parts a through e.

2. Write a program that prompts the user to enter a decimal number and then outputs this number rounded to two decimal places.

3. The manager of a football stadium wants you to write a program that calculates the total ticket sales after each game. There are four types of tickets—box, sideline, premium, and general admission. After each game, data is stored in a file in the following form:

```
ticketPrice    numberOfTicketsSold
...
```

Sample data are shown below:

```
250 5750
100 28000
 50 35750
 25 18750
```

The first line indicates that the ticket price is $250 and that 5750 tickets were sold at that price. Output the number of tickets sold and the total sale amount. Format your output with two decimal places.

4. Write a program to calculate the property tax. Property tax is calculated on 92% of the assessed value of the property. For example, if the assessed value is $200,000, the property tax is on $184,000. Assume that the property tax rate is $1.05 for each $100 of the assessed value. Your program should prompt the user to enter the assessed value of the property. Store the output in a file in the following format. (Here is a sample output.)

```
Assessed Value:              200000.00
Taxable Amount:              184000.00
Tax Rate for each $100.00:        1.05
Property Tax:                  1932.00
```

Format your output to have two decimal places. (Note that the left column is left-justified and the right column is right-justified.)

5. Write a program that converts a temperature from degrees Fahrenheit to degrees Celsius. The formula for converting the temperature from degrees Fahrenheit to degrees Celsius is:

```
C = (5/9) (F - 32)
```

Your program should prompt the user to enter a temperature given in degrees Fahrenheit as an integer. The program should output the temperature both in degrees Fahrenheit and degrees Celsius.

6. Write a program that calculates and prints the monthly paycheck for an employee. The net pay is calculated after taking the following deductions:

```
Federal Income Tax: 15%
State Tax: 3.5%
Social Security Tax: 5.75%
Medicare/Medicaid Tax: 2.75%
Pension Plan: 5%
Health Insurance: $75.00
```

Your program should prompt the user to input the gross amount and the employee name. The output will be stored in a file. Format your output to have two decimal places. A sample output follows:

```
Bill Robinson
Gross Amount:      ............ $3575.00
Federal Tax:       ............ $ 536.25
State Tax:         ............ $ 125.13
Social Security Tax: ..... $ 205.56
Medicare/Medicaid Tax: ... $   98.31
Pension Plan:      ............ $ 178.75
Health Insurance:  ........ $   75.00
Net Pay:           ............ $2356.00
```

Note that the first column is left-justified, and the right column is right-justified.

7. Redo Programming Exercise 20, in Chapter 2, so that each string can store a line of text.

8. Three employees in a company are up for a special pay increase. You are given a file, say `Ch3_Ex8Data.txt`, with the following data:

```
Miller Andrew 65789.87 5
Green Sheila 75892.56 6
Sethi Amit 74900.50 6.1
```

Each input line consists of an employee's last name, first name, current salary, and percent pay increase. For example, in the first input line, the last name of the employee is `Miller`, the first name is `Andrew`, the current salary is `65789.87`, and pay increase is `5%`. Write a program that reads data from the specified file and stores the output in the file `Ch3_Ex8Output.dat`. For each employee, the data must be output in the following form: `firstName lastName updatedSalary`. Format the output of decimal numbers to two decimal places.

CONTROL STRUCTURES I (SELECTION)

IN THIS CHAPTER, YOU WILL:

- Learn about control structures
- Examine relational and logical operators
- Explore how to form and evaluate logical (Boolean) expressions
- Discover how to use the selection control structures `if`, `if...else`, and `switch` in a program
- Learn to use the `assert` function to terminate a program

Chapter 2 defined a program as a sequence of statements whose objective is to accomplish some task. The programs you have examined so far were simple and straightforward. To process a program, the computer begins at the first executable statement and executes the statements in order until it comes to the end. In this chapter and Chapter 5, you will learn how to tell a computer that it does not have to follow a simple sequential order of statements; it can also make decisions and repeat certain statements over and over until certain conditions are met.

Control Structures

A computer can process a program in one of three ways: in sequence; selectively, by making a choice, which is also called a branch; or repetitively, by executing a statement over and over, using a structure called a loop (as shown in Figure 4-1). The programming examples in Chapters 2 and 3 included simple sequential programs. With such a program, the computer starts at the beginning and follows the statements in order. No choices are made; there is no repetition. Control structures provide alternatives to sequential program execution and are used to alter the sequential flow of execution. The two most common control structures are selection and repetition. In selection, the program executes particular statements depending on some condition(s). In repetition, the program repeats particular statements a certain number of times based on some condition(s).

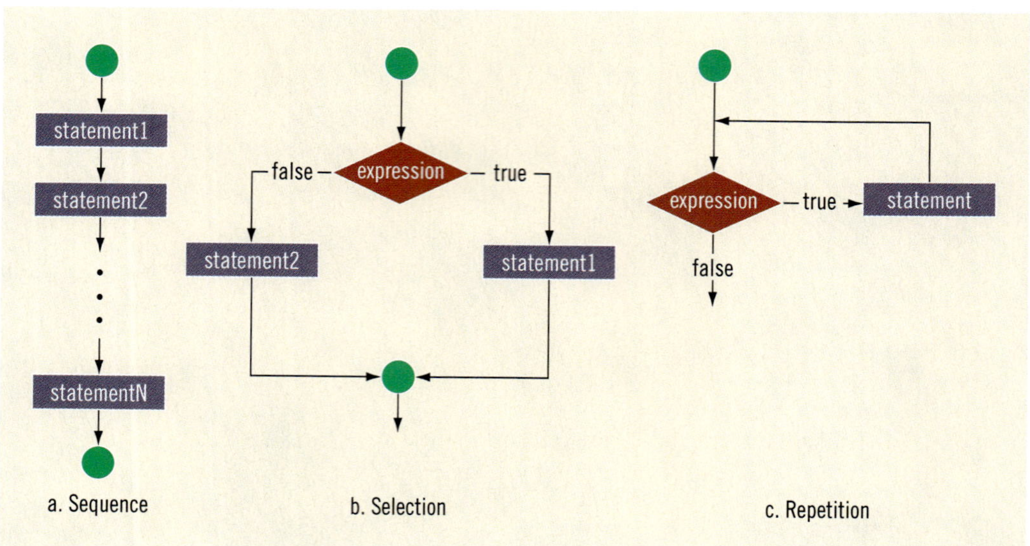

FIGURE 4-1 Flow of execution

Before you can learn about selection and repetition, you must understand the nature of conditional statements and how to use them. Consider the following three statements:

1. `if (score is greater than or equal to 90)`
   `grade is A`

2. `if (hours worked are less than or equal to 40)`
   `wages = rate * hours`
   `otherwise`
   `wages = (rate * 40) + 1.5 * (rate * (hours - 40))`

3. `if (temperature is greater than 70 degrees and it is not raining)`
   `recommended activity is golfing`

These statements are examples of conditional statements. You can see that certain statements are to be executed only if certain conditions are met. A condition is met if it evaluates to `true`. For example, in statement 1:

`score is greater than or equal to 90`

is `true` if the value of `score` is greater than or equal to 90; it is `false` otherwise. For example, if the value of `score` is 95, the statement evaluates to `true`. Similarly, if the value of `score` is 86, the statement evaluates to `false`.

It would be useful if the computer could recognize these types of statements to be true for appropriate values. Furthermore, in certain situations, the truth or falsity of a statement could depend on more than one condition. For example, in statement 3, both `temperature is greater than 70 degrees` and `it is not raining` must be true for the recommended activity to be `golfing`.

As you can see, for the computer to make decisions and repeat statements, it must be able to react to conditions that exist when the program executes. The next few sections discuss how to represent and evaluate conditional statements in C++.

Relational Operators

To make decisions, you must be able to express conditions and make comparisons. For example, the interest rate and service charges on a checking account might depend on the balance at the end of the month. If the balance is less than some minimum balance, not only is the interest rate lower, but there is also usually a service charge. Therefore, to determine the interest rate, you must be able to state the minimum balance (a condition) and compare the account balance with the minimum balance. The premium on an insurance policy is also determined by stating conditions and making comparisons. For example, to determine an insurance premium, you must be able to check the smoking status of the policyholder. Nonsmokers (the condition) receive lower premiums than smokers. Both of these examples involve comparing items. Certain items are compared for equality against a particular condition; others are compared for inequality (greater than or less than) against a particular condition.

In C++, a condition is represented by a logical (Boolean) expression. An expression that has a value of either **true** or **false** is called **a logical (Boolean) expression**. Moreover, **true** and **false** are **logical (Boolean) values**. Suppose i and j are integers. Consider the expression:

```
i > j
```

If this expression is a logical expression, it will have the value **true** if the value of i is greater than the value of j; otherwise, it will have the value **false**. You can think of the symbol > as an operator that (in this case) takes integer operands and yields a logical result. Here, the symbol > is similar to the operators + and − that yield integer or real results. In fact, the symbol > is called a relational operator because the value of i > j is **true** only when the relationship "greater than" holds between i and j. A **relational operator** allows you to make comparisons in a program.

C++ includes six relational operators that allow you to state conditions and make comparisons. Table 4-1 lists the relational operators.

TABLE 4-1   Relational Operators in C++

Operator	Description
==	equal to
!=	not equal to
<	less than
<=	less than or equal to
>	greater than
>=	greater than or equal to

NOTE   In C++, the symbol ==, which consists of two equal signs, is called the equality operator. Recall that the symbol = is called the assignment operator. Remember that the equality operator, ==, determines whether two expressions are equal, whereas the assignment operator, =, assigns the value of an expression to a variable.

Each of the relational operators is a binary operator; that is, it requires two operands. Because the result of a comparison is **true** or **false**, expressions using these operators evaluate to **true** or **false**.

Relational Operators and Simple Data Types

You can use the relational operators with all three simple data types. For example, the following expressions use both integers and real numbers:

Expression	Meaning	Value
8 < 15	8 is less than 15	true
6 != 6	6 is not equal to 6	false
2.5 > 5.8	2.5 is greater than 5.8	false
5.9 <= 7.5	5.9 is less than or equal to 7.5	true

NOTE   It is important to remember that the comparison of real numbers for equality may not behave as you would expect; see Example 4-1.

EXAMPLE 4-1

```cpp
#include <iostream>
#include <iomanip>

using namespace std;

int main()
{
    cout << fixed << showpoint << setprecision(17);

    cout << "3.0 / 7.0 = " << (3.0 / 7.0) << endl;
    cout << "2.0 / 7.0 = " << (2.0 / 7.0) << endl;
    cout << "3.0 / 7.0 + 2.0 / 7.0 + 2.0 / 7.0 = "
         << (3.0 / 7.0 + 2.0 / 7.0 + 2.0 / 7.0) << endl;

    return 0;
}
```

Sample Run:

```
3.0 / 7.0 = 0.42857142857142855
2.0 / 7.0 = 0.28571428571428570
3.0 / 7.0 + 2.0 / 7.0 + 2.0 / 7.0 = 0.99999999999999989
```

From the output, it follows that the following equality would evaluate to **false**.

```
1.0 == 3.0 / 7.0 + 2.0 / 7.0 + 2.0 / 7.0
```

NOTE   The preceding program and its output show that you should be careful when comparing floating-point numbers for equality. One way to check whether two floating-point numbers are equal is to check whether the absolute value of their difference is less than a certain tolerance.

For example, suppose **x** and **y** are floating-point numbers and the tolerance is 0.000001. Then **x** and **y** are equal if the absolute value of (**x** − **y**) is less than 0.000001. To find the absolute value, you can use the function **fabs** of the header file **cmath**. For example, the expression **fabs(x − y)** gives the absolute value of **x** − **y**. Therefore, the expression **fabs(x − y) < 0.000001** determines whether the absolute value of (**x** − **y**) is less than 0.000001. See the program **Example 4-1A.cpp** at the Web site accompanying this book.

For **char** values, whether an expression using relational operators evaluates to **true** or **false** depends on a machine's collating sequence. Table 4-2 shows how expressions using the ASCII data set are evaluated.

TABLE 4-2   Evaluating Expressions Using Relational Operators and the ASCII Collating Sequence

Expression	Value of Expression	Explanation
' ' < 'a'	true	The ASCII value of ' ' is 32, and the ASCII value of 'a' is 97. Because 32 < 97 is true, it follows that ' ' < 'a' is true.
'R' > 'T'	false	The ASCII value of 'R' is 82, and the ASCII value of 'T' is 84. Because 82 > 84 is false, it follows that 'R' > 'T' is false.
'+' < '*'	false	The ASCII value of '+' is 43, and the ASCII value of '*' is 42. Because 43 < 42 is false, it follows that '+' < '*' is false.
'6' <= '>'	true	The ASCII value of '6' is 54, and the ASCII value of '>' is 62. Because 54 <= 62 is true, it follows that '6' <= '>' is true.

Comparing values of different data types may produce unpredictable results. For example, the following expression compares an integer and a character:

8 < '5'

In this expression, on a particular machine, 8 would be compared with the collating sequence of '5', which is 53. That is, 8 is compared with 53, which makes this particular expression evaluate to **true**.

Expressions such as 4 < 6 and 'R' > 'T' are examples of **logical (Boolean) expressions**. When C++ evaluates a logical expression, it returns an integer value of 1 if the logical expression evaluates to **true**; it returns an integer value of 0 otherwise. In C++, any nonzero value is treated as **true**.

> **NOTE** Chapter 2 introduced the data type **bool**. Recall that the data type **bool** has two values, **true** and **false**. In C++, **true** and **false** are reserved words. The identifier **true** is set to 1, and the identifier **false** is set to 0. For readability, whenever logical expressions are used, the identifiers **true** and **false** will be used here as the value of the logical expression.

Relational Operators and the `string` Type

The relational operators can be applied to variables of type **string**. Variables of type **string** are compared character-by-character, starting with the first character and using the ASCII collating sequence. The character-by-character comparison continues until either a mismatch is found or the last characters have been compared and are equal. Consider the following declarations:

```
string str1 = "Hello";
string str2 = "Hi";
string str3 = "Air";
string str4 = "Bill";
string str5 = "Big";
```

Using these variable declarations, Table 4–3 shows how various logical expressions are evaluated.

TABLE 4-3 Evaluating Logical Expressions with `string` Variables

Expression	Value	Explanation
`str1 < str2`	`true`	`str1 = "Hello"` and `str2 = "Hi"`. The first character of `str1` and `str2` are the same, but the second character `'e'` of `str1` is less than the second character `'i'` of `str2`. Therefore, `str1 < str2` is `true`.
`str1 > "Hen"`	`false`	`str1 = "Hello"`. The first two characters of `str1` and `"Hen"` are the same, but the third character `'l'` of `str1` is less than the third character `'n'` of `"Hen"`. Therefore, `str1 > "Hen"` is `false`.
`str3 < "An"`	`true`	`str3 = "Air"`. The first characters of `str3` and `"An"` are the same, but the second character `'i'` of `"Air"` is less than the second character `'n'` of `"An"`. Therefore, `str3 < "An"` is `true`.

TABLE 4-3 Evaluating Logical Expressions with `string` Variables (continued)

Expression	Value	Explanation
str1 == "hello"	false	str1 = "Hello". The first character 'H' of str1 is less than the first character 'h' of "hello" because the ASCII value of 'H' is 72, and the ASCII value of 'h' is 104. Therefore, str1 == "hello" is **false**.
str3 <= str4	true	str3 = "Air" and str4 = "Bill". The first character 'A' of str3 is less than the first character 'B' of str4. Therefore, str3 <= str4 is **true**.
str2 > str4	true	str2 = "Hi" and str4 = "Bill". The first character 'H' of str2 is greater than the first character 'B' of str4. Therefore, str2 > str4 is **true**.

If two strings of different lengths are compared and the character-by-character comparison is equal until it reaches the last character of the shorter string, the shorter string is evaluated as less than the larger string. For example:

TABLE 4-4 Evaluating Logical Expressions with `string` Variables

Expression	Value	Explanation
str4 >= "Billy"	false	str4 = "Bill". It has four characters and "Billy" has five characters. Therefore, str4 is the shorter string. All four characters of str4 are the same as the corresponding first four characters of "Billy", and "Billy" is the larger string. Therefore, str4 >= "Billy" is **false**.
str5 <= "Bigger"	true	str5 = "Big". It has three characters and "Bigger" has six characters. Therefore, str5 is the shorter string. All three characters of str5 are the same as the corresponding first three characters of "Bigger", and "Bigger" is the larger string. Therefore, str5 <= "Bigger" is **true**.

Logical (Boolean) Operators and Logical Expressions

This section describes how to form and evaluate logical expressions that are combinations of other logical expressions. **Logical (Boolean) operators** enable you to combine logical expressions. C++ has three logical (Boolean) operators, as shown in Table 4-5.

TABLE 4-5   Logical (Boolean) Operators in C++

Operator	Description
!	not
&&	and
||	or

Logical operators take only logical values as operands and yield only logical values as results. The operator ! is unary, so it has only one operand. The operators && and || are binary operators. Table 4-6, 4-7, and 4-8 define these operators.

Table 4-6 defines the operator ! (not). When you use the ! operator, !**true** is **false** and !**false** is **true**. Putting ! in front of a logical expression reverses the value of that logical expression.

TABLE 4-6   The ! (Not) Operator

Expression	!(Expression)
true (nonzero)	false (0)
false (0)	true (1)

EXAMPLE 4-2

Expression	Value	Explanation
!('A' > 'B')	true	Because 'A' > 'B' is false, !('A' > 'B') is true.
!(6 <= 7)	false	Because 6 <= 7 is true, !(6 <= 7) is false.

Table 4-7 defines the operator `&&` (and). From this table, it follows that `Expression1 && Expression2` is **true** if and only if both `Expression1` and `Expression2` are **true**; otherwise, `Expression1 && Expression2` evaluates to **false**.

TABLE 4-7 The `&&` (And) Operator

Expression1	Expression2	Expression1 `&&` Expression2
true (nonzero)	**true** (nonzero)	**true** (1)
true (nonzero)	**false** (0)	**false** (0)
false (0)	**true** (nonzero)	**false** (0)
false (0)	**false** (0)	**false** (0)

EXAMPLE 4-3

Expression	Value	Explanation
`(14 >= 5) && ('A' < 'B')`	true	Because `(14 >= 5)` is **true**, `('A' < 'B')` is **true**, and **true** `&&` **true** is **true**, the expression evaluates to **true**.
`(24 >= 35) && ('A' < 'B')`	false	Because `(24 >= 35)` is **false**, `('A' < 'B')` is **true**, and **false** `&&` **true** is **false**, the expression evaluates to **false**.

Table 4-8 defines the operator `||` (or). From this table, it follows that `Expression1 || Expression2` is **true** if and only if at least one of the expressions, `Expression1` or `Expression2`, is **true**; otherwise, `Expression1 || Expression2` evaluates to **false**.

TABLE 4-8 The `||` (Or) Operator

Expression1	Expression2	Expression1 `||` Expression2
true (nonzero)	**true** (nonzero)	**true** (1)
true (nonzero)	**false** (0)	**true** (1)

TABLE 4-8 The | | (Or) Operator (continued)

Expression1	Expression2	Expression1		Expression2
false (0)	true (nonzero)	true (1)
false (0)	false (0)	false (0)

EXAMPLE 4-4

Expression	Value	Explanation
(14 >= 5) || ('A' > 'B')	true	Because (14 >= 5) is **true**, ('A' > 'B') is **false**, and **true** || **false** is **true**, the expression evaluates to **true**.
(24 >= 35) || ('A' > 'B')	false	Because (24 >= 35) is **false**, ('A' > 'B') is **false**, and **false** || **false** is **false**, the expression evaluates to **false**.
('A' <= 'a') || (7 != 7)	true	Because ('A' <= 'a') is **true**, (7 != 7) is **false**, and **true** || **false** is **true**, the expression evaluates to **true**.

Order of Precedence

Complex logical expressions can be difficult to evaluate. Consider the following logical expression:

```
11 > 5 || 6 < 15 && 7 >= 8
```

This logical expression yields different results, depending on whether || or && is evaluated first. If || is evaluated first, the expression evaluates to **false**. If && is evaluated first, the expression evaluates to **true**.

An expression might contain arithmetic, relational, and logical operators, as in the expression:

```
5 + 3 <= 9 && 2 > 3.
```

To work with complex logical expressions, there must be some priority scheme for evaluating operators. Table 4-9 shows the order of precedence of some C++ operators, including the arithmetic, relational, and logical operators. (See Appendix B for the precedence of all C++ operators.)

TABLE 4-9 Precedence of Operators

Operators	Precedence
!, +, − (unary operators)	first
*, /, %	second
+, −	third
<, <=, >=, >	fourth
==, !=	fifth
&&	sixth
||	seventh
= (assignment operator)	last

NOTE In C++, & and | are also operators. The meaning of these operators is different from the meaning of && and ||. Using & in place of && or | in place of ||—as might result from a typographical error—would produce very strange results.

Using the precedence rules in an expression, relational and logical operators are evaluated from left to right. Because relational and logical operators are evaluated from left to right, the **associativity** of these operators is said to be from left to right.

Example 4-5 illustrates how logical expressions consisting of variables are evaluated.

EXAMPLE 4-5

Suppose you have the following declarations:

```
bool found = true;
bool flag = false;
int num = 1;
double x = 5.2;
double y = 3.4;
int a = 5, b = 8;
int n = 20;
char ch = 'B';
```

Consider the following expressions:

Expression	Value	Explanation
`!found`	false	Because `found` is `true`, `!found` is `false`.
`x > 4.0`	true	Because `x` is `5.2` and `5.2 > 4.0` is `true`, the expression `x > 4.0` evaluates to `true`.
`!num`	false	Because `num` is `1`, which is nonzero, `num` is `true` and so `!num` is `false`.
`!found && (x >= 0)`	false	In this expression, `!found` is `false`. Also, because `x` is `5.2` and `5.2 >= 0` is `true`, `x >= 0` is `true`. Therefore, the value of the expression `!found && (x >= 0)` is `false && true`, which evaluates to `false`.
`!(found && (x >= 0))`	false	In this expression, `found && (x >= 0)` is `true && true`, which evaluates to `true`. Therefore, the value of the expression `!(found && (x >= 0))` is `!true`, which evaluates to `false`.
`x + y <= 20.5`	true	Because `x + y = 5.2 + 3.4 = 8.6` and `8.6 <= 20.5`, it follows that `x + y <= 20.5` evaluates to `true`.
`(n >= 0) && (n <= 100)`	true	Here `n` is `20`. Because `20 >= 0` is `true`, `n >= 0` is `true`. Also, because `20 <= 100` is `true`, `n <= 100` is `true`. Therefore, the value of the expression `(n >= 0) && (n <= 100)` is `true && true`, which evaluates to `true`.
`('A' <= ch && ch <= 'Z')`	true	In this expression, the value of `ch` is `'B'`. Because `'A' <= 'B'` is `true`, `'A' <= ch` evaluates to `true`. Also, because `'B' <= 'Z'` is `true`, `ch <= 'Z'` evaluates to `true`. Therefore, the value of the expression `('A' <= ch && ch <= 'Z')` is `true && true`, which evaluates to `true`.
`(a + 2 <= b) && !flag`	true	Now `a + 2 = 5 + 2 = 7` and `b` is `8`. Because `7 <= 8` is `true`, the expression `a + 2 <= b` evaluates to `true`. Also, because `flag` is `false`, `!flag` is `true`. Therefore, the value of the expression `(a + 2 <= b) && !flag` is `true && true`, which evaluates to `true`.

You can also write a C++ program to evaluate the logical expressions given in Example 4-5, as shown in Example 4-6.

EXAMPLE 4-6

The following program evaluates and outputs the values of the logical expressions given in
Example 4-5. Note that if a logical expression evaluates to **true**, the corresponding output
is 1; if the logical expression evaluates to **false**, the corresponding output is 0, as shown in
the output at the end of the program. (Recall that if the value of a logical expression is **true**,
it evaluates to 1, and if the value of the logical expression is **false**, it evaluates to 0.)

```cpp
//Chapter 4 Logical operators

#include <iostream>

using namespace std;

int main()
{
    bool found = true ;
    bool flag = false ;
    int num = 1;
    double x = 5.2;
    double y = 3.4;
    int a = 5, b = 8;
    int n = 20;
    char ch = 'B';

    cout << "Line 1: !found evaluates to "
         << !found << endl;                                    //Line 1
    cout << "Line 2: x > 4.0 evaluates to "
         << (x > 4.0) << endl;                                 //Line 2
    cout << "Line 3: !num evaluates to "
         << !num << endl;                                      //Line 3
    cout << "Line 4: !found && (x >= 0) evaluates to "
         << (!found && (x >= 0)) << endl;                      //Line 4
    cout << "Line 5: !(found && (x >= 0)) evaluates to "
         << (!(found && (x >= 0))) << endl;                    //Line 5
    cout << "Line 6: x + y <= 20.5 evaluates to "
         << (x + y <= 20.5) << endl;                           //Line 6
    cout << "Line 7: (n >= 0) && (n <= 100) evaluates to "
         << ((n >= 0) && (n <= 100)) << endl;                  //Line 7
    cout << "Line 8: ('A' <= ch && ch <= 'Z') evaluates to "
         << ('A' <= ch && ch <= 'Z') << endl;                  //Line 8
    cout << "Line 9: (a + 2 <= b) && !flag evaluates to "
         << ((a + 2 <= b) && !flag) << endl;                   //Line 9

    return 0;
}
```

Sample Run:

```
Line 1: !found evaluates to 0
Line 2: x > 4.0 evaluates to 1
```

```
Line 3: !num evaluates to 0
Line 4: !found && (x >= 0) evaluates to 0
Line 5: !(found && (x >= 0)) evaluates to 0
Line 6: x + y <= 20.5 evaluates to 1
Line 7: (n >= 0) && (n <= 100) evaluates to 1
Line 8: ('A' <= ch && ch <= 'Z') evaluates to 1
Line 9: (a + 2 <= b) && !flag evaluates to 1
```

You can insert parentheses into an expression to clarify its meaning. You can also use parentheses to override the precedence of operators. Using the standard order of precedence, the expression:

```
11 > 5 || 6 < 15 && 7 >= 8
```

is equivalent to:

```
11 > 5 || (6 < 15 && 7 >= 8)
```

In this expression, 11 > 5 is **true**, 6 < 15 is **true**, and 7 >= 8 is **false**. Substitute these values in the expression 11 > 5 || (6 < 15 && 7 >= 8) to get **true** || (**true** && **false**) = **true** || **false** = **true**. Therefore, the expression 11 > 5 || (6 < 15 && 7 >= 8) evaluates to **true**.

EXAMPLE 4-7

Evaluate the following expression:

```
(17 < 4 * 3 + 5) || (8 * 2 == 4 * 4) && !(3 + 3 == 6)
```

Now,

```
    (17 < 4 * 3 + 5) || (8 * 2 == 4 * 4) && !(3 + 3 == 6)
=   (17 < 12 + 5) || (16 == 16) && !(6 == 6)
=   (17 < 17) || true && !(true)
=   false || true && false
=   false || false   (Because true && false is false)
=   false
```

Therefore, the value of the original logical expression is **false**—that is, 0.

Short-Circuit Evaluation

Logical expressions in C++ are evaluated using a highly efficient algorithm. This algorithm is illustrated with the help of the following statements:

```
(x > y) || (x == 5)        //Line 1
(a == b) && (x >= 7)       //Line 2
```

In the statement in Line 1, the two operands of the operator || are the expressions (x > y) and (x == 5). This expression evaluates to **true** if either the operand (x > y) is **true** or the operand (x == 5) is **true**. With short-circuit evaluation, the computer evaluates the logical expression from left to right. As soon as the value of the entire logical expression is known, the evaluation stops. For example, in statement 1, if the operand (x > y) evaluates to **true**, then the entire expression evaluates to **true** because **true** || **true** is **true** and **true** || **false** is **true**. Therefore, the value of the operand (x == 5) has no bearing on the final outcome.

Similarly, in the statement in Line 2, the two operands of the operator && are (a == b) and (x >= 7). If the operand (a == b) evaluates to **false**, then the entire expression evaluates to **false** because **false** && **true** is **false** and **false** && **false** is **false**.

Short-circuit evaluation (of a logical expression): A process in which the computer evaluates a logical expression from left to right and stops as soon as the value of the expression is known.

EXAMPLE 4-8

Consider the following expressions:

```
(age >= 21) || ( x == 5)          //Line 1
(grade == 'A') && (x >= 7)        //Line 2
```

For the expression in Line 1, suppose that the value of age is 25. Because (25 >= 21) is **true** and the logical operator used in the expression is ||, the expression evaluates to **true**. Due to short-circuit evaluation, the computer does not evaluate the expression (x == 5). Similarly, for the expression in Line 2, suppose that the value of grade is 'B'. Because ('B' == 'A') is **false** and the logical operator used in the expression is &&, the expression evaluates to **false**. The computer does not evaluate (x >= 7).

In C++, logical (Boolean) expressions can be manipulated or processed in either of two ways: by using **int** variables or by using **bool** variables. The following sections describe these methods.

int **Data Type and Logical (Boolean) Expressions**

Earlier versions of C++ did not provide built-in data types that had logical (or Boolean) values **true** and **false**. Because logical expressions evaluate to either 1 or 0, the value of a logical expression was stored in a variable of the data type **int**. Therefore, you can use the **int** data type to manipulate logical (Boolean) expressions.

Recall that nonzero values are treated as **true**. Now, consider the declarations:

```
int legalAge;
int age;
```

and the assignment statement:

```
legalAge = 21;
```

If you regard `legalAge` as a logical variable, the value of `legalAge` assigned by this statement is `true`.

The assignment statement:

```
legalAge = (age >= 21);
```

assigns the value 1 to `legalAge` if the value of `age` is greater than or equal to 21. The statement assigns the value 0 if the value of `age` is less than 21.

`bool` Data Type and Logical (Boolean) Expressions

More recent versions of C++ contain a built-in data type, `bool`, that has the logical (Boolean) values `true` and `false`. Therefore, you can manipulate logical (Boolean) expressions using the `bool` data type. Recall that in C++, `bool`, `true`, and `false` are reserved words. In addition, the identifier `true` has the value 1, and the identifier `false` has the value 0. Now consider the following declaration:

```
bool legalAge;
int age;
```

The statement:

```
legalAge = true;
```

sets the value of the variable `legalAge` to `true`. The statement:

```
legalAge = (age >= 21);
```

assigns the value `true` to `legalAge` if the value of `age` is greater than or equal to 21. This statement assigns the value `false` to `legalAge` if the value of `age` is less than 21. For example, if the value of `age` is 25, the value assigned to `legalAge` is `true`—that is, 1. Similarly, if the value of `age` is 16, the value assigned to `legalAge` is `false`—that is, 0.

NOTE   You can use either an `int` variable or a `bool` variable to store the value of a logical expression. For the purpose of clarity, this book uses `bool` variables to store the values of logical expressions.

Sometimes logical expressions do not behave as you might expect. Suppose, for example, that num is an `int` variable. Further suppose that you want to write a logical expression that evaluates to `true` if the value of num is between 0 and 10, including 0 and 10, and that evaluates to `false` otherwise. The following expression appears to represent a comparison of 0, num, and 10 that will yield the desired result:

```
0 <= num <= 10
```

Although this statement is a legal C++ expression, you will not get the result you might expect. Does this expression evaluate to **true** if the value of num is between 0 and 10? What happens if the value of num is greater than 10? Suppose that num = 5. Then:

```
    0 <= num <= 10

= 0 <= 5 <= 10

= (0 <= 5) <= 10        (Because relational operators are evaluated from
                         left to right)

= 1 <= 10               (Because 0 <= 5 is true, 0 <= 5 evaluates to 1)

= 1 (true)
```

Now suppose that num = 20. Then:

```
    0 <= num <= 10

= 0 <= 20 <= 10

= (0 <= 20) <= 10       (Because relational operators are evaluated from left to right)

= 1 <= 10               (Because 0 <= 20 is true, 0 <= 20 evaluates to 1)

= 1 (true)
```

Clearly, this answer is incorrect. Because num is 20, it is not between 0 and 10, and 0 <= 20 <= 10 should not evaluate to **true**. Note that this expression will always evaluate to **true**, no matter what num is. This is due to the fact that the expression 0 <= num evaluates to either 0 or 1, and 0 <= 10 is **true** and 1 <= 10 is **true**. So what is wrong with the expression 0 <= num <= 10? It is missing the logical operator **&&**. A correct way to write this expression in C++ is:

```
0 <= num && num <= 10
```

or:

```
num >= 0 && num <= 10
```

You must take care when formulating logical expressions. When creating a complex logical expression, you must use the proper logical operators.

Selection: `if` and `if...else`

Although there are only two logical values, **true** and **false**, they turn out to be extremely useful because they permit programs to incorporate decision making that alters the processing flow. The remainder of this chapter discusses ways to incorporate decisions into a program. In C++, there are two selections, or branch control structures: `if` statements and the **switch** structure. This section discusses how `if` and `if...else` statements can be used to create one-way selection, two-way selection, and multiple selections. The **switch** structure is discussed later in this chapter.

One-Way Selection

A bank would like to send a notice to a customer if her or his checking account balance falls below the required minimum balance. That is, if the account balance is below the required minimum balance, it should send a notice to the customer; otherwise, it should do nothing. Similarly, if the policyholder of an insurance policy is a nonsmoker, the company would like to apply a 10% discount to the policy premium. Both of these examples involve one-way selection. In C++, one-way selections are incorporated using the `if` statement. The syntax of one-way selection is:

```
if (expression)
    statement
```

Note the elements of this syntax. It begins with the reserved word `if`, followed by an **expression** contained within parentheses, followed by a **statement**. Note that the parentheses around the **expression** are part of the syntax. The **expression** is sometimes called a **decision maker** because it decides whether to execute the **statement** that follows it. The **expression** is usually a logical expression. If the value of the **expression** is **true**, the **statement** executes. If the value is **false**, the **statement** does not execute and the computer goes on to the next statement in the program. The **statement** following the **expression** is sometimes called the **action statement**. Figure 4-2 shows the flow of execution of the `if` statement (one-way selection).

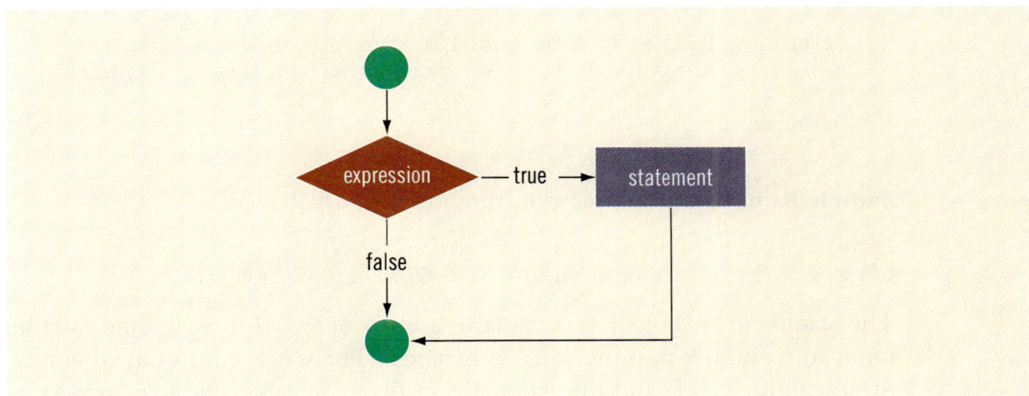

FIGURE 4-2   One-way selection

EXAMPLE 4-9

```cpp
if (score >= 90)
    grade = 'A';
```

In this code, if the expression (`score >= 90`) evaluates to **true**, the assignment statement, `grade = 'A';`, executes. If the expression evaluates to **false**, the statements (if any) following the **if** structure execute. For example, if the value of `score` is 95, the value assigned to the variable `grade` is `'A'`.

EXAMPLE 4-10

The following C++ program finds the absolute value of an integer:

```cpp
//Program: Absolute value of an integer

#include <iostream>

using namespace std;

int main()
{
    int number, temp;

    cout << "Line 1: Please enter an integer: ";   //Line 1
    cin >> number;                                  //Line 2
    cout << endl;                                   //Line 3

    temp = number;                                  //Line 4

    if (number < 0)                                 //Line 5
        number = -number;                           //Line 6

    cout << "Line 7: The absolute value of "
         << temp << " is " << number << endl;       //Line 7

    return 0;
}
```

Sample Run: In this sample run, the user input is shaded.

```
Line 1: Please enter an integer: -6734
Line 7: The absolute value of -6734 is 6734
```

The statement in Line 1 prompts the user to enter an integer; the statement in Line 2 inputs the number into the variable `number`. The statement in Line 4 copies the value of `number` into `temp`, and the statement in sin Line 5 checks whether `number` is negative. If `number` is negative, the statement in Line 6 changes `number` to a positive number. The statement in Line 7 outputs the number and its absolute value.

EXAMPLE 4-11

Consider the following statement:

```
if score >= 90        //syntax error
    grade = 'A';
```

This statement illustrates an incorrect version of an `if` statement. The parentheses around the logical expression are missing, which is a syntax error.

Putting a semicolon after the parentheses following the **expression** in an `if` statement (that is, before the **statement**) is a semantic error. If the semicolon immediately follows the closing parenthesis, the `if` statement will operate on the empty statement.

EXAMPLE 4-12

Consider the following C++ statements:

```
if (score >= 90);           //Line 1
    grade = 'A';            //Line 2
```

Because there is a semicolon at the end of the expression (see Line 1), the `if` statement in Line 1 terminates. The action of this `if` statement is null, and the statement in Line 2 is not part of the `if` statement in Line 1. Hence, the statement in Line 2 executes regardless of how the `if` statement evaluates.

Two-Way Selection

There are many programming situations in which you must choose between two alternatives. For example, if a part-time employee works overtime, the paycheck is calculated using the overtime payment formula; otherwise, the paycheck is calculated using the regular formula. This is an example of two-way selection. To choose between two alternatives—that is, to implement two-way selections—C++ provides the `if...else` statement. Two-way selection uses the following syntax:

```
if (expression)
    statement1
else
    statement2
```

Take a moment to examine this syntax. It begins with the reserved word `if`, followed by a logical expression contained within parentheses, followed by a statement, followed by the reserved word `else`, followed by a second statement. Statements 1 and 2 are any valid C++ statements. In a two-way selection, if the value of the `expression` is `true`, `statement1` executes. If the value of the `expression` is `false`, `statement2` executes. Figure 4-3 shows the flow of execution of the `if...else` statement (two-way selection).

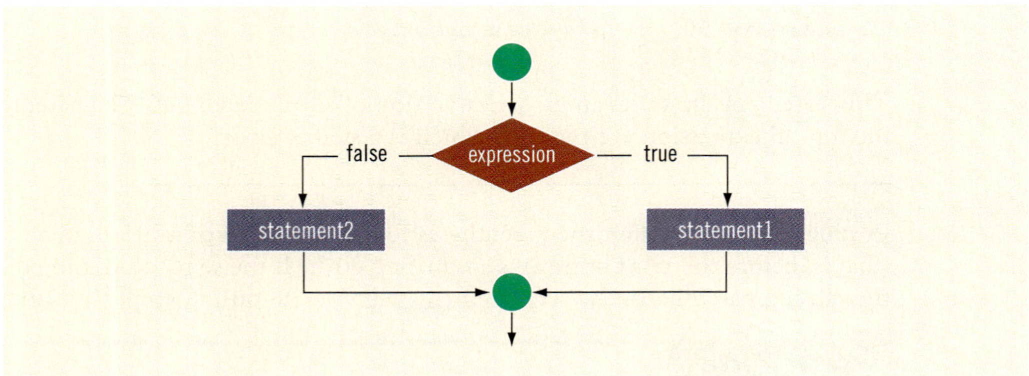

FIGURE 4-3   Two-way selection

EXAMPLE 4-13

Consider the following statements:

```
if (hours > 40.0)                          //Line 1
    wages = 40.0 * rate +
            1.5 * rate * (hours - 40.0);    //Line 2
else                                        //Line 3
    wages = hours * rate;                   //Line 4
```

if the value of the variable `hours` is greater than `40.0`, then the `wages` include overtime payment. Suppose that `hours` is `50`. The expression in the `if` statement, in Line 1, evaluates to `true`, so the statement in Line 2 executes. On the other hand, if `hours` is 30, or any number less than or equal to `40`, the expression in the `if` statement, in Line 1, evaluates to `false`. In this case, the program skips the statement in Line 2 and executes the statement in Line 4—that is, the statement following the reserved word `else` executes.

In a two-way selection statement, putting a semicolon after the `expression` and before `statement1` creates a syntax error. If the `if` statement ends with a semicolon, `statement1` is no longer part of the `if` statement, and the `else` part of the `if...else` statement stands all by itself. There is no stand-alone `else` statement in C++. That is, it cannot be separated from the `if` statement.

EXAMPLE 4-14

The following statements show an example of a syntax error:

```cpp
if (hours > 40.0);                                    //Line 1
    wages = 40.0 * rate +
            1.5 * rate * (hours - 40.0);  //Line 2
else                                      //Line 3
    wages = hours * rate;                 //Line 4
```

The semicolon at the end of the `if` statement (see Line 1) ends the `if` statement, so the statement in Line 2 separates the `else` clause from the `if` statement. That is, `else` is all by itself. Because there is no standalone `else` statement in C++, this code generates a syntax error.

EXAMPLE 4-15

The following program determines an employee's weekly wages. If the hours worked exceed 40, wages include overtime payment:

```cpp
//Program: Weekly wages

#include <iostream>
#include <iomanip>

using namespace std;

int main()
{
    double wages, rate, hours;

    cout << fixed << showpoint << setprecision(2);      //Line 1
    cout << "Line 2: Enter working hours and rate: "; //Line 2
    cin >> hours >> rate;                               //Line 3

    if (hours > 40.0)                                   //Line 4
        wages = 40.0 * rate +
                1.5 * rate * (hours - 40.0);            //Line 5
    else                                                //Line 6
        wages = hours * rate;                           //Line 7

    cout << endl;                                       //Line 8
    cout << "Line 9: The wages are $" << wages
         << endl;                                       //Line 9

    return 0;
}
```

Sample Run: In this sample run, the user input is shaded.

```
Line 2: Enter working hours and rate: 56.45 12.50

Line 9: The wages are $808.44
```

The statement in Line 1 sets the output of the floating-point numbers in a fixed decimal format, with a decimal point, trailing zeros, and two decimal places. The statement in Line 2 prompts the user to input the number of hours worked and the pay rate. The statement in Line 3 inputs these values into the variables `hours` and `rate`, respectively. The statement in Line 4 checks whether the value of the variable `hours` is greater than `40.0`. If `hours` is greater than `40.0`, then the wages are calculated by the statement in Line 5, which includes overtime payment. Otherwise, the wages are calculated by the statement in Line 7. The statement in Line 9 outputs the wages.

Let us now consider more examples of `if` statements and examine some of the semantic errors that can occur.

EXAMPLE 4-16

Consider the following statements:

```
if (score >= 90)
    grade = 'A';
    cout << "The grade is " << grade << endl;
```

These statements contain a semantic error. The `if` statement acts on only one statement, which is `grade = 'A';`. The `cout` statement executes regardless of whether (`score >= 90`) is `true` or `false`.

Example 4-17 illustrates another common mistake.

EXAMPLE 4-17

Consider the following statements:

```
if (score >= 60)                    //Line 1
    cout << "Passing" << endl;      //Line 2
    cout << "Failing" << endl;      //Line 3
```

If the expression (`score >= 60`) evaluates to `false`, the output statement in Line 2 does not execute. So the output would be `Failing`. That is, this set of statements performs the same action as an `if...else` statement. It will execute the output statement in Line 3 rather than the output statement in Line 2. For example, if the value of `score` is 50, these statements will output the following line:

```
Failing
```

However, if the expression (`score >= 60`) evaluates to **true**, the program will execute both the output statements, giving a very unsatisfactory result. For example, if the value of `score` is 70, these statements will output the following lines:

```
Passing
Failing
```

The `if` statement controls the execution of only the statement in Line 2. The statement in Line 3 always executes.

The correct code to print `Passing` or `Failing`, depending on the value of `score`, is:

```
if (score >= 60)
    cout << "Passing" << endl;
else
    cout << "Failing" << endl;
```

Compound (Block of) Statements

The `if` and `if...else` structures control only one statement at a time. Suppose, however, that you want to execute more than one statement if the **expression** in an `if` or `if...else` statement evaluates to **true**. To permit more complex statements, C++ provides a structure called a **compound statement** or a **block of statements**. A compound statement takes the following form:

```
{
    statement1
    statement2
       .
       .
       .
    statementn
}
```

That is, a compound statement consists of a sequence of statements enclosed in curly braces, { and }. In an `if` or `if ...else` structure, a compound statement functions as if it were a single statement. Thus, instead of having a simple two-way selection similar to the following code:

```
if (age >= 18)
    cout << "Eligible to vote." << endl;
else
    cout << "Not eligible to vote." << endl;
```

you could include compound statements, similar to the following code:

```cpp
if (age >= 18)
{
    cout << "Eligible to vote." << endl;
    cout << "No longer a minor." << endl;
}
else
{
    cout << "Not eligible to vote." << endl;
    cout << "Still a minor." << endl;
}
```

The compound statement is very useful and will be used in most of the structured statements in this chapter.

Multiple Selections: Nested `if`

In the previous sections, you learned how to implement one-way and two-way selections in a program. Some problems require the implementation of more than two alternatives. For example, suppose that if the checking account balance is more than $50,000, the interest rate is 7%; if the balance is between $25,000 and $49,999.99, the interest rate is 5%; if the balance is between $1,000 and $24,999.99, the interest rate is 3%; otherwise, the interest rate is 0%. This particular problem has four alternatives—that is, multiple selection paths. You can include multiple selection paths in a program by using an `if...else` structure, if the action statement itself is an `if` or `if...else` statement. When one control statement is located within another, it is said to be **nested**.

Example 4-18 illustrate how to incorporate multiple selections using a nested `if...else` structure.

EXAMPLE 4-18

Suppose that `balance` and `interestRate` are variables of type `double`. The following statements determine the `interestRate` depending on the value of the `balance`:

```cpp
if (balance > 50000.00)                     //Line 1
    interestRate = 0.07;                    //Line 2
else                                        //Line 3
    if (balance >= 25000.00)                //Line 4
        interestRate = 0.05;                //Line 5
    else                                    //Line 6
        if (balance >= 1000.00)             //Line 7
            interestRate = 0.03;            //Line 8
        else                                //Line 9
            interestRate = 0.00;            //Line 10
```

A nested `if...else` structure demands the answer to an important question: How do you know which `else` is paired with which `if`? Recall that in C++ there is no stand-alone

else statement. Every **else** must be paired with an **if**. The rule to pair an **else** with an **if** is as follows:

Pairing an `else` with an `if`: In a nested **if** statement, C++ associates an **else** with the most recent incomplete **if**—that is, the most recent **if** that has not been paired with an **else**.

Using this rule, in Example 4-18, the **else** in Line 3 is paired with the **if** in Line 1. The **else** in Line 6 is paired with the **if** in Line 4, and the **else** in Line 9 is paired with the **if** in Line 7.

To avoid excessive indentation, the code in Example 4-18 can be rewritten as follows:

```cpp
if (balance > 50000.00)                    //Line 1
    interestRate = 0.07;                   //Line 2
else if (balance >= 25000.00)              //Line 3
    interestRate = 0.05;                   //Line 4
else if (balance >= 1000.00)               //Line 5
    interestRate = 0.03;                   //Line 6
else                                       //Line 7
    interestRate = 0.00;                   //Line 8
```

The following examples will help you to see the various ways in which you can use nested **if** structures to implement multiple selection.

EXAMPLE 4-19

Assume that **score** is a variable of type **int**. Based on the value of **score**, the following code outputs the grade:

```cpp
if (score >= 90)
    cout << "The grade is A." << endl;
else if (score >= 80)
    cout << "The grade is B." << endl;
else if (score >= 70)
    cout << "The grade is C." << endl;
else if (score >= 60)
    cout << "The grade is D." << endl;
else
    cout << "The grade is F." << endl;
```

EXAMPLE 4-20

Assume that all variables are properly declared, and consider the following statements:

```cpp
if (temperature >= 50)                                      //Line 1
    if (temperature >= 80)                                  //Line 2
        cout << "Good day for swimming." << endl;           //Line 3
    else                                                    //Line 4
        cout << "Good day for golfing." << endl;            //Line 5
else                                                        //Line 6
    cout << "Good day to play tennis." << endl;             //Line 7
```

In this C++ code, the **else** in Line 4 is paired with the **if** in Line 2, and the **else** in Line 6 is paired with the **if** in Line 1. Note that the **else** in Line 4 cannot be paired with the **if** in Line 1. If you pair the **else** in Line 4 with the **if** in Line 1, the **if** in Line 2 becomes the action statement part of the **if** in Line 1, leaving the **else** in Line 6 dangling. Also, the statements in Lines 2 though 5 form the statement part of the **if** in Line 1.

EXAMPLE 4-21

Assume that all variables are properly declared, and consider the following statements:

```cpp
if (temperature >= 70)                              //Line 1
    if (temperature >= 80)                          //Line 2
        cout << "Good day for swimming." << endl;   //Line 3
    else                                            //Line 4
        cout << "Good day for golfing." << endl;    //Line 5
```

In this code, the **else** in Line 4 is paired with the **if** in Line 2. Note that for the **else** in Line 4, the most recent incomplete **if** is in Line 2. In this code, the **if** in Line 1 has no **else** and is a one-way selection.

EXAMPLE 4-22

Assume that all variables are properly declared, and consider the following statements:

```cpp
if (GPA >= 2.0)                                     //Line 1
    if (GPA >= 3.9)                                 //Line 2
        cout << "Dean\'s Honor List." << endl;      //Line 3
else                                                //Line 4
        cout << "Current GPA below graduation requirement. "
             << "\nSee your academic advisor." << endl;    //Line 5
```

This code is awkward. Following the rule of pairing an **else** with an **if**, the **else** in Line 4 is paired with the **if** in Line 2. However, this pairing produces an unsatisfactory result. Suppose that **GPA** is **3.8**. The **expression** in the **if** in Line 1 evaluates to **true**, and the statement part of the **if**, which is an **if...else** structure, executes. Because **GPA** is **3.8**, the **expression** in the **if** in Line 2 evaluates to **false**, and the **else** associated with this **if** executes, producing the following output:

```
Current GPA below graduation requirement.
See your academic advisor.
```

However, a student with a GPA of 3.8 would graduate with some type of honor. In fact, the code intended to print the message:

```
Current GPA below graduation requirement.
See your academic advisor.
```

only if the GPA is less than 2.0, and the message:

```
Dean's Honor List.
```

if the GPA is greater than or equal to 3.9. To achieve that result, the `else` in Line 4 needs to be paired with the `if` in Line 1. To pair the `else` in Line 4 with the `if` in Line 1, you need to use a compound statement as follows:

```
if (GPA >= 2.0)                                            //Line 1
{
    if (GPA >= 3.9)                                        //Line 2
        cout << "Dean\'s Honor List." << endl;             //Line 3
}
else                                                       //Line 4
    cout << "Current GPA below graduation requirement. "
         << "\nSee your academic advisor." << endl;        //Line 5
```

In cases such as this one, the general rule is that you cannot look inside a block (that is, inside the braces) to pair an `else` with an `if`. The `else` in Line 4 cannot be paired with the `if` in Line 2 because the `if` statement in Line 2 is enclosed within braces, and the `else` in Line 4 cannot look inside those braces. Therefore, the `else` in Line 4 is paired with the `if` in Line 1.

Comparing `if...else` Statements with a Series of `if` Statements

Consider the following C++ program segments, all of which accomplish the same task:

```
a.  if (month == 1)                          //Line 1
        cout << "January" << endl;           //Line 2
    else if (month == 2)                     //Line 3
        cout << "February" << endl;          //Line 4
    else if (month == 3)                     //Line 5
        cout << "March" << endl;             //Line 6
    else if (month == 4)                     //Line 7
        cout << "April" << endl;             //Line 8
    else if (month == 5)                     //Line 9
        cout << "May" << endl;               //Line 10
    else if (month == 6)                     //Line 11
        cout << "June" << endl;              //Line 12

b.  if (month == 1)
        cout << "January" << endl;
    if (month == 2)
        cout << "February" << endl;
```

```
if (month == 3)
    cout << "March" << endl;
if (month == 4)
    cout << "April" << endl;
if (month == 5)
    cout << "May" << endl;
if (month == 6)
    cout << "June" << endl;
```

Program segment (a) is written as a sequence of `if...else` statements; program segment (b) is written as a series of `if` statements. Both program segments accomplish the same thing. If `month` is 3, then both program segments output `March`. If `month` is 1, then in program segment (a), the expression in the `if` statement in Line 1 evaluates to `true`. The statement (in Line 2) associated with this `if` then executes; the rest of the structure, which is the `else` of this `if` statement, is skipped; and the remaining `if` statements are not evaluated. In program segment (b), the computer has to evaluate the expression in each `if` statement because there is no `else` statement. As a consequence, program segment (b) executes more slowly than does program segment (a).

Using Pseudocode to Develop, Test, and Debug a Program

There are several ways to develop a program. One method involves using an informal mixture of C++ and ordinary language, called **pseudocode** or just **pseudo**. Sometimes pseudo provides a useful means to outline and refine a program before putting it into formal C++ code. When you are constructing programs that involve complex nested control structures, pseudo can help you quickly develop the correct structure of the program and avoid making common errors.

One useful program segment determines the larger of two integers. If `x` and `y` are integers, using pseudo you can quickly write the following:

a.
```
if (x > y) then
     x is larger
```

b.
```
if (y > x) then
     y is larger
```

If the statement in (a) is `true`, then `x` is larger. If the statement in (b) is `true`, then `y` is larger. However, for this code to work in concert to determine the larger of two integers, the computer needs to evaluate both expressions:

```
(x > y)      and      (y > x)
```

even if the first statement is `true`. Evaluating both expressions is a waste of computer time.

Let's rewrite this pseudo as follows:

```
if (x > y) then
     x is larger
else
     y is larger
```

Here, only one condition needs to be evaluated. This code looks okay, so let's put it into C++.

```cpp
#include <iostream>

using namespace std;

int main()
{
    if (x > y)
```

Wait...once you begin translating the pseudo into a C++ program, you should immediately notice that there is no place to store the value of **x** or **y**. The variables were not declared, which is a very common oversight, especially for new programmers. If you examine the pseudo, you will see that the program needs three variables, and you might as well make them self-documenting. Let's start the program code again:

```cpp
#include <iostream>

using namespace std;

int main()
{
    int num1, num2, larger;     //Line 1

    if (num1 > num2);           //Line 2; error
        larger = num1;          //Line 3
    else                        //Line 4
        larger = num2;          //Line 5

    return 0;
}
```

Compiling this program will result in the identification of a common syntax error (in Line 2). Recall that a semicolon cannot appear after the **expression** in the **if...else** statement. However, even if you corrected this syntax error, the program still would not give satisfactory results because it tries to use identifiers that have no values. The variables have not been initialized, which is another common error. In addition, because there are no output statements, you would not be able to see the results of the program.

Because there are so many mistakes in the program, you should try a walk-through to see whether it works at all. You should always use a wide range of values in a walk-through to evaluate the program under as many different circumstances as possible. For example, does this program work if one number is zero, if one number is negative and the other number is positive, if both numbers are negative, or if both numbers are the same? Examining the program, you can see that it does not check whether the two numbers are equal. Taking all of these points into account, you can rewrite the program as follows:

```cpp
//Program: Compare Numbers
//This program compares two integers and finds the largest.

#include <iostream>

using namespace std;

int main()
{
    int num1, num2, larger;

    cout << "Enter any two integers: ";
    cin >> num1 >> num2;
    cout << endl;

    cout << "The two integers entered are " << num1
         << " and " << num2 << endl;

    if (num1 > num2)
    {
        larger = num1;
        cout << "The larger number is " << larger << endl;
    }
    else if (num2 > num1)
    {
        larger = num2;
        cout << "The larger number is " << larger << endl;
    }
    else
        cout << "Both numbers are equal." << endl;

    return 0;
}
```

Sample Run: In this sample run, the user input is shaded.

```
Enter any two integers: 78 90
The two integers entered are 78 and 90
The larger number is 90
```

One thing you can learn from the preceding program is that you must first develop a program using paper and pencil. Although a program that is first written on a piece of paper is not guaranteed to run successfully on the first try, this step is still a good starting point. On paper, it is easier to spot errors and improve the program, especially with large programs.

Input Failure and the `if` Statement

In Chapter 3, you saw that an attempt to read invalid data causes the input stream to enter a fail state. Once an input stream enters a fail state, all subsequent input statements associated with that input stream are ignored, and the computer continues to execute the program, which produces erroneous results. You can use `if` statements to check the status of an input stream variable and, if the input stream enters the fail state, include instructions that stop program execution.

In addition to reading invalid data, other events can cause an input stream to enter the fail state. Two additional common causes of input failure are the following:

- Attempting to open an input file that does not exist
- Attempting to read beyond the end of an input file

One way to address these causes of input failure is to check the status of the input stream variable. You can check the status by using the input stream variable as the logical expression in an `if` statement. If the last input succeeded, the input stream variable evaluates to `true`, if the last input failed, it evaluates to `false`.

The statement:

```
if (cin)
    cout << "Input is OK." << endl;
```

prints:

```
Input is OK.
```

if the last input from the standard input device succeeded. Similarly, if `infile` is an `ifstream` variable, the statement:

```
if (!infile)
    cout << "Input failed." << endl;
```

prints:

```
Input failed.
```

if the last input associated with the stream variable `infile` failed.

Suppose an input stream variable tries to open a file for inputting data into a program. If the input file does not exist, you can use the value of the input stream variable, in conjunction with the `return` statement, to terminate the program.

Recall that the last statement included in the function `main` is:

```
return 0;
```

This statement returns a value of 0 to the operating system when the program terminates. A value of 0 indicates that the program terminated normally and that no error occurred during program execution. Values of type `int` other than 0 can also be returned to the operating system via the `return` statement. The return of any value other than 0, however, indicates that something went wrong during program execution.

The `return` statement can appear anywhere in the program. Whenever a `return` statement executes, it immediately exits the function in which it appears. In the case of the function `main`, the program terminates when the `return` statement executes. You can use these properties of the `return` statement to terminate the function `main` whenever the input stream fails. This technique is especially useful when a program tries to open an input file. Consider the following statements:

```cpp
ifstream infile;

infile.open("a:\\inputdat.dat");   //open inputdat.dat

if (!infile)
{
    cout << "Cannot open the input file. "
         << "The program terminates." << endl;
    return 1;
}
```

Suppose that the file `inputdat.dat` does not exist. The operation to open this file fails, causing the input stream to enter the fail state. As a logical expression, the file stream variable `infile` then evaluates to `false`. Because `infile` evaluates to `false`, the expression `!infile` (in the `if` statement) evaluates to `true`, and the body of the `if` statement executes. The message:

```
Cannot open the input file. The program terminates.
```

is printed on the screen, and the `return` statement terminates the program by returning a value of 1 to the operating system.

Let's now use the code that responds to input failure by including these features in the Programming Example: Student Grade from Chapter 3. Recall that this program calculates the average test score based on data from an input file and then outputs the results to another file. The following programming code is the same as the code from Chapter 3, except that it includes statements to exit the program if the input file does not exist:

```cpp
//Program to calculate the average test score.

#include <iostream>
#include <fstream>
#include <iomanip>
#include <string>
```

```cpp
using namespace std;

int main()
{
    ifstream inFile;     //input file stream variable
    ofstream outFile;    //output file stream variable

    double test1, test2, test3, test4, test5;
    double average;

    string firstName;
    string lastName;

    inFile.open("a:\\test.txt"); //open the input file

    if (!inFile)
    {
        cout << "Cannot open the input file. "
             << "The program terminates." << endl;
        return  1;
    }

    outFile.open("a:\\testavg.out");   //open the output file

    outFile << fixed << showpoint;
    outFile << setprecision(2);

    cout << "Processing data" << endl;

    inFile >> firstName >> lastName;
    outFile << "Student name: " << firstName
            << " " << lastName << endl;

    inFile >> test1 >> test2 >> test3
           >> test4 >> test5;
    outFile << "Test scores: " << setw(4) << test1
            << setw(4) << test2 << setw(4) << test3
            << setw(4) << test4 << setw(4) << test5
            << endl;

    average = (test1 + test2 + test3 + test4 + test5) / 5.0;

    outFile << "Average test score: " << setw(6)
            << average << endl;

    inFile.close();
    outFile.close();

    return 0;
}
```

Confusion Between the Equality Operator (==) and the Assignment Operator (=)

Recall that if the decision-making expression in the `if` statement evaluates to `true`, the `statement` part of the `if` statement executes. In addition, the `expression` is usually a logical expression. However, C++ allows you to use *any* expression that can be evaluated to either `true` or `false` as an `expression` in the `if` statement. Consider the following statement:

```
if (x = 5)
    cout << "The value is five." << endl;
```

The `expression`—that is, the decision maker—in the `if` statement is `x = 5`. The expression `x = 5` is called an assignment expression because the operator `=` appears in the expression and there is no semicolon at the end.

This expression is evaluated as follows. First, the right side of the operator `=` is evaluated, which evaluates to 5. The value 5 is then assigned to `x`. Moreover, the value 5—that is, the new value of `x`—also becomes the value of the expression in the `if` statement—that is, the value of the assignment expression. Because 5 is nonzero, the expression in the `if` statement evaluates to `true`, so the statement part of the `if` statement outputs: `The value is five.`

No matter how experienced a programmer is, almost everyone makes the mistake of using `=` in place of `==` at one time or another. One reason why these two operators are often confused is that most programming languages use `=` as an equality operator. Thus, experience with other programming languages can create confusion. Sometimes the error is merely typographical, another reason to be careful when typing code.

Despite the fact that an assignment expression can be used as an expression, using the assignment operator in place of the equality operator can cause serious problems in a program. For example, suppose that the discount on a car insurance policy is based on the insured's driving record. A driving record of 1 means that the driver is accident-free and receives a 25% discount on the policy. The statement:

```
if (drivingCode == 1)
    cout << "The discount on the policy is 25%." << endl;
```

outputs:

```
The discount on the policy is 25%.
```

only if the value of `drivingCode` is 1. However, the statement:

```
if (drivingCode = 1)
    cout << "The discount on the policy is 25%." << endl;
```

always outputs:

```
The discount on the policy is 25%.
```

because the right side of the assignment expression evaluates to 1, which is nonzero and so evaluates to `true`. Therefore, the expression in the `if` statement evaluates to `true`, outputting the following line of text: `The discount on the policy is 25%`. Also, the value 1 is assigned to the variable `drivingCode`. Suppose that before the `if` statement executes, the value of the variable `drivingCode` is 4. After the `if` statement executes, not only is the output wrong, but the new value also replaces the old driving code.

The appearance of = in place of == resembles a *silent killer*. It is not a syntax error, so the compiler does not warn you of an error. Rather, it is a logical error.

NOTE Using = in place of == can cause serious problems, especially if it happens in a looping statement. Chapter 5 discusses looping structures.

The appearance of the equality operator in place of the assignment operator can also cause errors in a program. For example, suppose `x`, `y`, and `z` are `int` variables. The statement:

```
x = y + z;
```

assigns the value of the expression `y + z` to `x`. The statement:

```
x == y + z;
```

compares the value of the expression `y + z` with the value of `x`; the value of `x` remains the same, however. If somewhere else in the program you are counting on the value of `x` being `y + z`, a logic error will occur, the program output will be incorrect, and you will receive no warning of this situation from the compiler. The compiler provides feedback only about syntax errors, not logic errors. For this reason, you must use extra care when working with the equality operator and the assignment operator.

Conditional Operator (?:)

NOTE The reader can skip this section without any discontinuation.

Certain `if...else` statements can be written in a more concise way by using C++'s conditional operator. The **conditional operator**, written as **?:**, is a **ternary operator**, which means that it takes three arguments. The syntax for using the conditional operator is:

```
expression1 ? expression2 : expression3
```

This type of statement is called a **conditional expression**. The conditional expression is evaluated as follows: If `expression1` evaluates to a nonzero integer (that is, to `true`), the result of the conditional expression is `expression2`. Otherwise, the result of the conditional expression is `expression3`.

Consider the following statements:

```cpp
if (a >= b)
    max = a;
else
    max = b;
```

You can use the conditional operator to simplify the writing of this **if...else** statement as follows:

```cpp
max = (a >= b) ? a : b;
```

switch Structures

Recall that there are two selection, or branch, structures in C++. The first selection structure, which is implemented with **if** and **if...else** statements, usually requires the evaluation of a (logical) expression. The second selection structure, which does not require the evaluation of a logical expression, is called the **switch structure**. C++'s **switch** structure gives the computer the power to choose from among many alternatives.

A general syntax of the **switch** statement is:

```cpp
switch (expression)
{
case value1:
    statements1
    break;
case value2:
    statements2
    break;
    .
    .
    .
case valuen:
    statementsn
    break;
default:
    statements
}
```

In C++, **switch**, **case**, **break**, and **default** are reserved words. In a **switch** structure, first the **expression** is evaluated. The value of the **expression** is then used to perform the actions specified in the statements that follow the reserved word **case**. Recall that, in a syntax, shading indicates an optional part of the definition.

Although it need not be, the **expression** is usually an identifier. Whether it is an identifier or an expression, the value can be only integral. The **expression** is sometimes called the **selector**. Its value determines which statement is selected for execution. A particular **case** value should appear only once. One or more statements may follow a **case** label, so you do not need to use braces to turn multiple statements into a single compound statement. The **break** statement may or may not appear after each statement. Figure 4-4 shows the flow of execution of the **switch** statement.

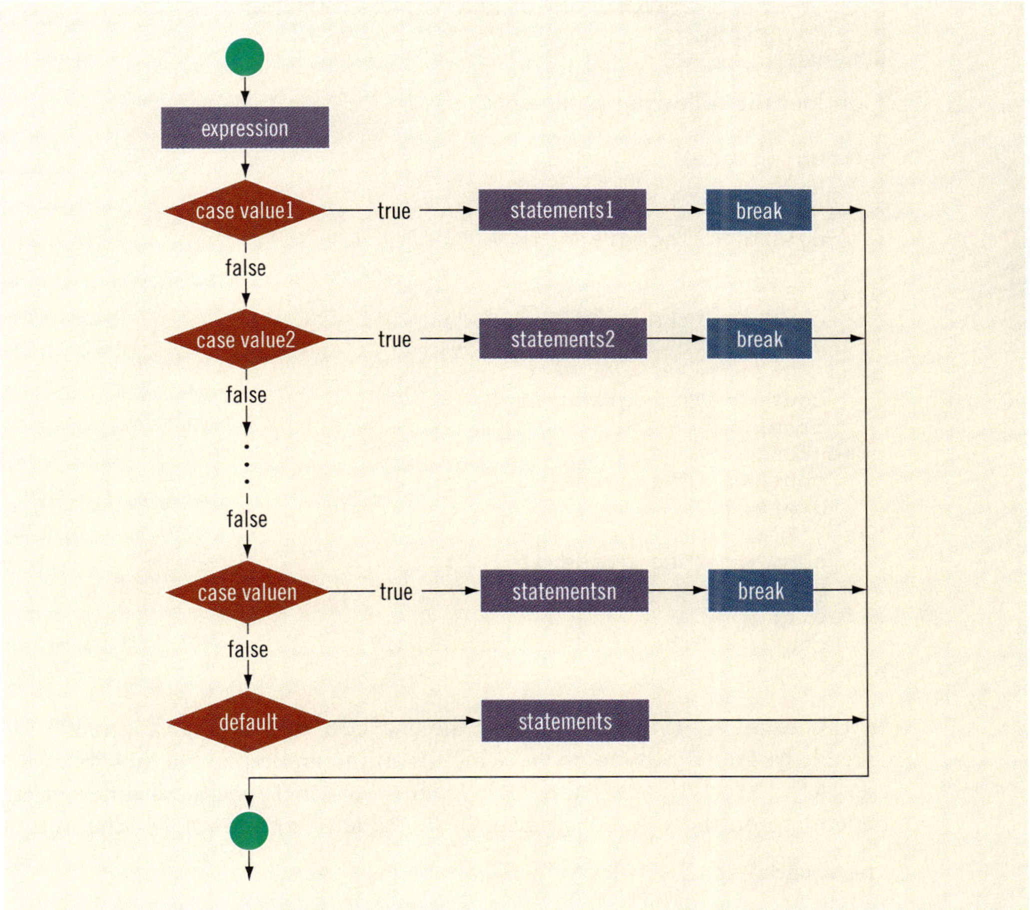

FIGURE 4-4 **switch** statement

The **switch** statement executes according to the following rules:

1. When the value of the **expression** is matched against a **case** value (also called a label), the statements execute until either a **break** statement is found or the end of the **switch** structure is reached.

2. If the value of the **expression** does not match any of the **case** values, the statements following the **default** label execute. If the **switch** structure has no **default** label, and if the value of the **expression**

does not match any of the `case` values, the entire `switch` statement is skipped.

3. A `break` statement causes an immediate *exit* from the `switch` structure.

EXAMPLE 4-23

Consider the following statements:

```cpp
switch (grade)
{
case 'A':
    cout << "The grade is A.";
    break;
case 'B':
    cout << "The grade is B.";
    break;
case 'C':
    cout << "The grade is C.";
    break;
case 'D':
    cout << "The grade is D.";
    break;
case 'F':
    cout << "The grade is F.";
    break;
default:
    cout << "The grade is invalid.";
}
```

In this example, the expression in the `switch` statement is a variable identifier. The variable `grade` is of type `char`, which is an integral type. The possible values of `grade` are `'A'`, `'B'`, `'C'`, `'D'`, and `'F'`. Each `case` label specifies a different action to take, depending on the value of `grade`. If the value of `grade` is `'A'`, the output is:

```cpp
The grade is A.
```

EXAMPLE 4-24

The following program illustrates the effect of the `break` statement. It asks the user to input a number between 0 and 10:

```cpp
//Program: Effect of break statements in a switch structure

#include <iostream>

using namespace std;
```

```cpp
int main()
{
    int num;

    cout << "Enter an integer between 0 and 10: "; //Line 1
    cin >> num;                                    //Line 2

    cout << "\nThe number you entered is " << num
         << endl;                                  //Line 3

    switch (num)                                   //Line 4
    {
    case 0:                                        //Line 5
    case 1:                                        //Line 6
        cout << "Hello ";                          //Line 7
    case 2:                                        //Line 8
        cout << "there. ";                         //Line 9
    case 3:                                        //Line 10
        cout << "I am ";                           //Line 11
    case 4:                                        //Line 12
        cout << "Mickey." << endl;                 //Line 13
        break;                                     //Line 14
    case 5:                                        //Line 15
        cout << "How ";                            //Line 16
    case 6:                                        //Line 17
    case 7:                                        //Line 18
    case 8:                                        //Line 19
        cout << "are you?" << endl;                //Line 20
        break;                                     //Line 21
    case 9:                                        //Line 22
        break;                                     //Line 23
    case 10:                                       //Line 24
        cout << "Have a nice day." << endl;        //Line 25
        break;                                     //Line 26
    default:                                       //Line 27
        cout << "Sorry, the number is out of "
             << "range." << endl;                  //Line 28
    }

    cout << "Out of the switch structure."
         << endl;                                  //Line 29

    return 0;
}
```

Sample Runs

These outputs were obtained by executing the preceding program several times. In each of these outputs, the user input is shaded.

Sample Run 1:

Enter an integer between 0 and 10: `0`

The number you entered is 0
Hello there. I am Mickey.
Out of the switch structure.

Sample Run 2:

Enter an integer between 0 and 10: `1`

The number you entered is 1
Hello there. I am Mickey.
Out of the switch structure.

Sample Run 3:

Enter an integer between 0 and 10: `3`

The number you entered is 3
I am Mickey.
Out of the switch structure.

Sample Run 4:

Enter an integer between 0 and 10: `4`

The number you entered is 4
Mickey.
Out of the switch structure.

Sample Run 5:

Enter an integer between 0 and 10: `5`

The number you entered is 5
How are you?
Out of the switch structure.

Sample Run 6:

Enter an integer between 0 and 10: `7`

The number you entered is 7
are you?
Out of the switch structure.

Sample Run 7:

Enter an integer between 0 and 10: `9`

The number you entered is 9
Out of the switch structure.

Sample Run 8:

```
Enter an integer between 0 and 10: 10

The number you entered is 10
Have a nice day.
Out of the switch structure.
```

Sample Run 9:

```
Enter an integer between 0 and 10: 11

The number you entered is 11
Sorry, the number is out of range.
Out of the switch structure.
```

A walk-through of this program, using certain values of the switch expression, num, can help you understand how the break statement functions. If the value of num is 0, the value of the switch expression matches the case value 0. All statements following case 0: execute until a break statement appears.

The first break statement appears in Line 14, just before the case value of 5. Even though the value of the switch expression does not match any of the case values (that is, 1, 2, 3, or 4), the statements following these values execute.

When the value of the switch expression matches a case value, *all* statements execute until a break is encountered, and the program skips all case labels in between. Similarly, if the value of num is 3, it matches the case value of 3 and the statements following this label execute until the break statement is encountered in Line 14. If the value of num is 9, it matches the case value of 9. In this situation, the action is empty because only the break statement, in Line 23, follows the case value of 9.

EXAMPLE 4-25

Although a switch structure's case values (labels) are limited, the switch statement expression can be as complex as necessary. For example, consider the following switch statement:

```
switch (score / 10)
{
case 0:
case 1:
case 2:
case 3:
case 4:
case 5:
    grade = 'F';
    break;
```

```cpp
case 6:
    grade = 'D';
    break;
case 7:
    grade = 'C';
    break;
case 8:
    grade = 'B';
    break;
case 9:
case 10:
    grade = 'A';
    break;
default:
    cout << "Invalid test score." << endl;
}
```

Assume that `score` is an `int` variable with values between 0 and 100. If `score` is 75, then `score / 10 = 75 / 10 = 7` and the grade assigned is `'C'`. If the value of `score` is between 0 and 59, then the grade is `'F'`. If `score` is between 0 and 59, `score / 10` is 0, 1, 2, 3, 4, or 5. Each of these values corresponds to the grade `'F'`.

Therefore, in this `switch` structure, the action statements of `case` 0, `case` 1, `case` 2, `case` 3, `case` 4, and `case` 5 are all the same. Rather than write the statement `grade = 'F';` followed by the `break` statement for each of the `case` values of 0, 1, 2, 3, 4, and 5, you can simplify the programming code by first specifying all of the case values (as shown in the preceding code) and then specifying the desired action statement. The `case` values of 9 and 10 follow similar conventions.

In addition to being a variable identifier or a complex expression, the `switch` expression can evaluate to a logical value. Consider the following statements:

```cpp
switch (age >= 18)
{
case 1:
    cout << "Old enough to be drafted." << endl;
    cout << "Old enough to vote." << endl;
    break;
case 0:
    cout << "Not old enough to be drafted." << endl;
    cout << "Not old enough to vote." << endl;
}
```

If the value of `age` is 25, the expression `age >= 18` evaluates to 1—that is, `true`. If the `expression` evaluates to 1, the statements following the `case` label 1 execute. If the value of `age` is 14, the expression `age >= 18` evaluates to 0—that is, `false`—and the statements following the `case` label 0 execute.

You can use **true** and **false**, instead of 1 and 0, respectively, in the case labels, and rewrite the preceding **switch** statement as follows:

```
switch (age >= 18)
{
case true:
    cout << "Old enough to be drafted." << endl;
    cout << "Old enough to vote." << endl;
    break;
case false:
    cout << "Not old enough to be drafted." << endl;
    cout << "Not old enough to vote." << endl;
}
```

As you can see from the preceding examples, the **switch** statement is an elegant way to implement multiple selections. You will see the use of a **switch** statement in the programming example at the end of this chapter. Even though no fixed rules exist that can be applied to decide whether to use an **if...else** structure or a **switch** structure to implement multiple selections, the following considerations should be remembered. If multiple selections involve a range of values, you should use either an **if...else** structure or a **switch** structure, wherein you convert each range to a finite set of values.

For instance, in Example 4-25, the value of **grade** depends on the value of **score**. If **score** is between 0 and 59, **grade** is **'F'**. Because **score** is an **int** variable, 60 values correspond to the grade of **'F'**. If you list all 60 values as **case** values, the **switch** statement could be very long. However, dividing by 10 reduces these 60 values to only 6 values: 0, 1, 2, 3, 4, and 5.

If the range of values consists of infinitely many values and you cannot reduce them to a set containing a finite number of values, you must use the **if...else** structure. For example, if **score** happens to be a **double** variable, the number of values between 0 and 60 is infinite. However, you can use the expression **static_cast<int>(score) / 10** and still reduce this infinite number of values to just six values.

Terminating a Program with the `assert` Function

Certain types of errors that are very difficult to catch can occur in a program. For example, division by zero can be difficult to catch using any of the programming techniques you have examined so far. C++ includes a predefined function, **assert**, that is useful in stopping program execution when certain elusive errors occur. In the case of division by zero, you can use the **assert** function to ensure that a program terminates with an appropriate error message indicating the type of error and the program location where the error occurred.

Consider the following statements:

```
int numerator;
int denominator;
int quotient;
```

```
double hours;
double rate;
double wages;
char ch;
```

```
1.  quotient = numerator / denominator;
2.  if (hours > 0 && (0 < rate && rate <= 15.50))
        wages = rate * hours;
3.  if ('A' <= ch && ch <= 'Z')
```

In the first statement, if the **denominator** is 0, logically you should not perform the division. During execution, however, the computer would try to perform the division. If the **denominator** is 0, the program would terminate with an error message stating that an illegal operation has occurred.

The second statement is designed to compute **wages** only if **hours** is greater than 0 and **rate** is positive and less than or equal to **15.50**. The third statement is designed to execute certain statements only if **ch** is an uppercase letter.

For all of these statements (for that matter, in any situation in which certain conditions must be met), if conditions are not met, it would be useful to halt program execution with a message indicating where in the program an error occurred. You could handle these types of situations by including output and return statements in your program. However, C++ provides an effective method to halt a program if required conditions are not met through the **assert** function.

The syntax to use the **assert** function is:

```
assert(expression);
```

Here **expression** is any logical expression. If **expression** evaluates to **true**, the next statement executes. If expression evaluates to **false**, the program terminates and indicates where in the program the error occurred.

The specification of the **assert** function is found in the header file **cassert**. Therefore, for a program to use the **assert** function, it must include the following statement:

```
#include <cassert>
```

NOTE The name of the header file containing the specification of the function **assert** in Standard C++ is **assert.h**.

A statement using the **assert** function is sometimes called an **assert** statement.

Returning to the preceding statements, you can rewrite statement 1 (**quotient = numerator / denominator;**) using the **assert** function. Because **quotient** should be calculated only if `denominator` is nonzero, you include an `assert` statement before the assignment statement as follows:

```
assert(denominator);
quotient = numerator / denominator;
```

Now, if `denominator` is 0, the `assert` statement halts the execution of the program with an error message similar to the following:

```
Assertion failed: denominator, file c:\temp\assert
function\assertfunction.cpp, line 20
```

This error message indicates that the assertion of `denominator` failed. The error message also gives the name of the file containing the source code and the line number where the assertion failed.

You can also rewrite statement 2 using an assertion statement as follows:

```
assert(hours > 0 && (0 < rate && rate <= 15.50));
if (hours > 0 && (0 < rate && rate <= 15.50))
    wages = rate * hours;
```

If the `expression` in the `assert` statement fails, the program terminates with an error message similar to the following:

```
Assertion failed: hours > 0 && (0 < rate && rate <= 15.50), file
c:\temp\assertfunction\assertfunction.cpp, line 26
```

During program development and testing, the `assert` statement is very useful for enforcing programming constraints. As you can see, the `assert` statement not only halts the program, but also identifies the expression where the assertion failed, the name of the file containing the source code, and the line number where the assertion failed.

Although `assert` statements are useful during program development, after a program has been developed and put into use, if an `assert` statement fails for some reason, an end user would have no idea what the error means. Therefore, after you have developed and tested a program, you might want to remove or disable the `assert` statements. In a very large program, it could be tedious, and perhaps impossible, to remove all of the `assert` statements you used during development. In addition, if you plan to modify a program in the future, you might like to keep the `assert` statements. Therefore, the logical choice is to keep these statements, but to disable them. You can disable `assert` statements by using the following preprocessor directive:

```
#define NDEBUG
```

This preprocessor directive `#define NDEBUG` must be placed *before* the directive `#include <cassert>`.

PROGRAMMING EXAMPLE: Cable Company Billing

This programming example demonstrates a program that calculates a customer's bill for a local cable company. There are two types of customers: residential and business. There are two rates for calculating a cable bill: one for residential customers and one for business customers. For residential customers, the following rates apply:

- Bill processing fee: $4.50
- Basic service fee: $20.50
- Premium channels: $7.50 per channel.

For business customers, the following rates apply:

- Bill processing fee: $15.00
- Basic service fee: $75.00 for first 10 connections, $5.00 for each additional connection
- Premium channels: $50.00 per channel for any number of connections.

The program should ask the user for an account number (an integer) and a customer code. Assume that R or r stands for a residential customer, and B or b stands for a business customer.

Input The customer's account number, customer code, number of premium channels to which the user subscribes, and, in the case of business customers, number of basic service connections.

Output Customer's account number and the billing amount.

PROBLEM ANALYSIS AND ALGORITHM DESIGN

The purpose of this program is to calculate and print the billing amount. To calculate the billing amount, you need to know the customer for whom the billing amount is calculated (whether the customer is residential or business) and the number of premium channels to which the customer subscribes. In the case of a business customer, you also need to know the number of basic service connections and the number of premium channels. Other data needed to calculate the bill, such as the bill processing fees and the cost of a premium channel, are known quantities. The program should print the billing amount to two decimal places, which is standard for monetary amounts. This problem analysis translates into the following algorithm:

1. Set the precision to two decimal places.
2. Prompt the user for the account number and customer type.

3. Based on the customer type, determine the number of premium channels and basic service connections, compute the bill, and print the bill:

   a. If the customer type is R or r,

      i. Prompt the user for the number of premium channels.

      ii. Compute the bill.

      iii. Print the bill.

   b. If the customer type is B or b,

      i. Prompt the user for the number of basic service connections and number of premium channels.

      ii. Compute the bill.

      iii. Print the bill.

Variables Because the program will ask the user to input the customer account number, customer code, number of premium channels, and number of basic service connections, you need variables to store all of this information. Also, because the program will calculate the billing amount, you need a variable to store the billing amount. Thus, the program needs at least the following variables to compute and print the bill:

```
int accountNumber;     //variable to store the customer's
                       //account number
char customerType;       //variable to store the customer code
int numOfPremChannels; //variable to store the number
                       //of premium channels to which the
                       //customer subscribes
int numOfBasicServConn; //variable to store the
                        //number of basic service connections
                        //to which the customer subscribes
double amountDue;     //variable to store the billing amount
```

Named Constants As you can see, the bill processing fees, the cost of a basic service connection, and the cost of a premium channel are fixed, and these values are needed to compute the bill. Although these values are constants in the program, the cable company can change them with little warning. To simplify the process of modifying the program later, instead of using these values directly in the program, you should declare them as named constants. Based on the problem analysis, you need to declare the following named constants:

```
      //Named constants - residential customers
const double RES_BILL_PROC_FEES = 4.50;
const double RES_BASIC_SERV_COST = 20.50;
const double RES_COST_PREM_CHANNEL = 7.50;
```

```
//Named constants - business customers
const double BUS_BILL_PROC_FEES = 15.00;
const double BUS_BASIC_SERV_COST = 75.00;
const double BUS_BASIC_CONN_COST = 5.00;
const double BUS_COST_PREM_CHANNEL = 50.00;
```

Formulas   The program uses a number of formulas to compute the billing amount. To compute the residential bill, you need to know only the number of premium channels to which the user subscribes. The following statement calculates the billing amount for a residential customer:

```
amountDue = RES_BILL_PROC_FEES + RES_BASIC_SERV_COST
            + numOfPremChannels * RES_COST_PREM_CHANNEL;
```

To compute the business bill, you need to know the number of basic service connections and the number of premium channels to which the user subscribes. If the number of basic service connections is less than or equal to 10, the cost of the basic service connections is fixed. If the number of basic service connections exceeds 10, you must add the cost for each connection over 10. The following statement calculates the business billing amount:

```
if (numOfBasicServConn <= 10)
    amountDue = BUS_BILL_PROC_FEES + BUS_BASIC_SERV_COST
                + numOfPremChannels * BUS_COST_PREM_CHANNEL;
else
    amountDue = BUS_BILL_PROC_FEES + BUS_BASIC_SERV_COST
                + (numOfBasicServConn - 10)
                  * BUS_BASIC_CONN_COST
                + numOfPremChannels * BUS_COST_PREM_CHANNEL;
```

MAIN ALGORITHM   Based on the preceding discussion, you can now write the main algorithm.

1. To output floating-point numbers in a fixed decimal format with a decimal point and trailing zeros, set the manipulators `fixed` and `showpoint`. Also, to output floating-point numbers with two decimal places, set the precision to two decimal places. Recall that to use these manipulators, the program must include the header file `iomanip`.

2. Prompt the user to enter the account number.

3. Get the customer account number.

4. Prompt the user to enter the customer code.

5. Get the customer code.

6. If the customer code is `r` or R,

   a. Prompt the user to enter the number of premium channels.

   b. Get the number of premium channels.

   c. Calculate the billing amount.

   d. Print the account number and the billing amount.

7. If the customer code is **b** or **B**,

    a. Prompt the user to enter the number of basic service connections.

    b. Get the number of basic service connections.

    c. Prompt the user to enter the number of premium channels.

    d. Get the number of premium channels.

    e. Calculate the billing amount.

    f. Print the account number and the billing amount.

8. If the customer code is something other than **r**, **R**, **b**, or **B**, output an error message.

For Steps 6 and 7, the program uses a `switch` statement to calculate the bill for the desired customer.

COMPLETE PROGRAM LISTING

```cpp
#include <iostream>
#include <iomanip>

using namespace std;

    //Named constants - residential customers
const double RES_BILL_PROC_FEES = 4.50;
const double RES_BASIC_SERV_COST = 20.50;
const double RES_COST_PREM_CHANNEL = 7.50;

    //Named constants - business customers
const double BUS_BILL_PROC_FEES = 15.00;
const double BUS_BASIC_SERV_COST = 75.00;
const double BUS_BASIC_CONN_COST = 5.00;
const double BUS_COST_PREM_CHANNEL = 50.00;

int main()
{
    //Variable declaration
    int accountNumber;
    char customerType;
    int numOfPremChannels;
    int numOfBasicServConn;
    double amountDue;

    cout << fixed << showpoint;                 //Step 1
    cout << setprecision(2);                    //Step 1

    cout << "This program computes a cable "
         << "bill." << endl;
```

```cpp
    cout << "Enter account number (an integer): ";   //Step 2
    cin >> accountNumber;                             //Step 3
    cout << endl;

    cout << "Enter customer type: "
         << "R or r (Residential), "
         << "B or b (Business):   ";                  //Step 4
    cin >>  customerType;                             //Step 5
    cout << endl;

switch (customerType)
{
case 'r':                                             //Step 6
case 'R':
    cout << "Enter the number"
         << " of premium channels: ";                //Step 6a
    cin >> numOfPremChannels;                         //Step 6b
    cout << endl;

    amountDue = RES_BILL_PROC_FEES                    //Step 6c
              + RES_BASIC_SERV_COST
              + numOfPremChannels *
                RES_COST_PREM_CHANNEL;

    cout << "Account number: "
         << accountNumber
         << endl;                                     //Step 6d
    cout << "Amount due: $"
         << amountDue
         << endl;                                     //Step 6d
    break;

case 'b':                                             //Step 7
case 'B':
    cout << "Enter the number of basic "
         << "service connections: ";                  //Step 7a
    cin >> numOfBasicServConn;                        //Step 7b
    cout << endl;

    cout << "Enter the number"
         << " of premium channels: ";                 //Step 7c
    cin >> numOfPremChannels;                         //Step 7d
    cout << endl;

    if (numOfBasicServConn<= 10)                      //Step 7e
        amountDue = BUS_BILL_PROC_FEES
                  + BUS_BASIC_SERV_COST
                  + numOfPremChannels *
                    BUS_COST_PREM_CHANNEL;
```

```
        else
            amountDue = BUS_BILL_PROC_FEES
                    + BUS_BASIC_SERV_COST
                    + (numOfBasicServConn - 10) *
                        BUS_BASIC_CONN_COST
                    + numOfPremChannels *
                        BUS_COST_PREM_CHANNEL;

        cout << "Account number: "
                << accountNumber << endl;            //Step 7f
        cout << "Amount due: $" << amountDue
                << endl;                             //Step 7f
        break;

    default:
        cout << "Invalid customer type." << endl;    //Step 8
    } //end switch

    return 0;
}
```

Sample Run: In this sample run, the user input is shaded.

```
This program computes a cable bill.
Enter account number (an integer): 12345

Enter customer type: R or r (Residential), B or b (Business): b

Enter the number of basic service connections: 16

Enter the number of premium channels: 8

Account number: 12345
Amount due: $520.00
```

QUICK REVIEW

1. Control structures alter the normal flow of control.

2. The two most common control structures are selection and repetition.

3. Selection structures incorporate decisions in a program.

4. The relational operators are == (equality), < (less than), <= (less than or equal to), > (greater than), >= (greater than or equal to), and != (not equal to).

5. Including a space between the relational operators ==, <=, >=, and ! = creates a syntax error.

6. Characters are compared using a machine's collating sequence.

7. Logical expressions evaluate to 1 (or a nonzero value) or 0. The logical value 1 (or any nonzero value) is treated as **true**; the logical value 0 is treated as **false**.

8. In C++, **int** variables can be used to store the value of a logical expression.

9. In C++, **bool** variables can be used to store the value of a logical expression.

10. In C++, the logical operators are ! (not), && (and), and || (or).

11. There are two selection structures in C++.

12. One-way selection takes the following form:

```
if (expression)
    statement
```

If **expression** is **true**, the **statement** executes; otherwise, the computer executes the **statement** following the **if** statement.

13. Two-way selection takes the following form:

```
if (expression)
    statement1
else
    statement2
```

If **expression** is **true**, then **statement1** executes; otherwise, **statement2** executes.

14. The expression in an **if** or **if...else** structure is usually a logical expression.

15. Including a semicolon before the **statement** in a one-way selection creates a semantic error. In this case, the action of the **if** statement is empty.

16. Including a semicolon before **statement1** in a two-way selection creates a syntax error.

17. There is no stand-alone **else** statement in C++. Every **else** has a related **if**.

18. An **else** is paired with the most recent **if** that has not been paired with any other **else**.

19. A sequence of statements enclosed between curly braces, { and }, is called a compound statement or block of statements. A compound statement is treated as a single statement.

20. You can use the input stream variable in an **if** statement to determine the state of the input stream.

21. Using the assignment operator in place of the equality operator creates a semantic error. This can cause serious errors in the program.

22. The **switch** structure is used to handle multiway selection.

23. The execution of a **break** statement in a **switch** statement immediately exits the **switch** structure.

24. If certain conditions are not met in a program, the program can be terminated using the **assert** function.

EXERCISES

1. Mark the following statements as true or false.

   a. The result of a logical expression cannot be assigned to an `int` variable.

   b. In a one-way selection, if a semicolon is placed after the expression in an `if` statement, the expression in the `if` statement is always `true`.

   c. Every `if` statement must have a corresponding `else`.

   d. The expression in the `if` statement:

   ```
   if (score = 30)
       grade = 'A';
   ```

   always evaluates to `true`.

   e. The expression:

   ```
   (ch >= 'A' && ch <= 'Z')
   ```

   evaluates to `false` if either ch < 'A' or ch >= 'Z'.

   f. Suppose the input is 5. The output of the code:

   ```
   cin >> num;
   if (num > 5)
       cout << num;
       num = 0;
   else
       cout << "Num is zero" << endl;
   is:  Num is zero
   ```

   g. The expression in a `switch` statement should evaluate to a value of the simple data type.

   h. The expression ! (x > 0) is `true` only if x is a negative number.

   i. In C++, both ! and != are logical operators.

   j. The order in which statements execute in a program is called the flow of control.

2. Circle the best answer.

   a.
   ```
   if (6 < 2 * 5)
       cout << "Hello";
       cout << " There";
   ```

   outputs the following:

   (i) Hello There   (ii) Hello   (iii) Hello   (iv) There
                                         There

b.
```
if ('a' > 'b' || 66 > static_cast<int>('A'))
        cout << "#*#" << endl;
```

outputs the following:

(i) #*#   (ii) #   (iii) *   (iv) none of these

```
            *
            #
```

c.
```
if (7 <= 7)
        cout << 6 - 9 * 2 / 6 << endl;
```

outputs the following:

(i) -1   (ii) 3   (iii) 3.0   (iv) none of these

d.
```
if (7 < 8)
{
    cout << "2 4 6 8" << endl;
    cout << "1 3 5 7" << endl;
}
```

outputs the following:

(i) 2 4 6 8   (ii) 1 3 5 7   (iii) none of these
    1 3 5 7

e.
```
if (5 < 3)
        cout << "*";
else
    if (7 == 8)
        cout << "&";
    else
        cout << "$";
```

outputs the following:

(i) *   (ii) &   (iii) $ (v) none of these

3. What is the output of the following C++ code?
```
x = 100;
y = 200;
if (x > 100 && y <= 200)
    cout << x << " " << y << " " << x + y << endl;
else
    cout << x << " " << y << " " << 2 * x - y << endl;
```

4. Write C++ statements that output Male if the gender is 'M', Female if the gender is 'F', and invalid gender otherwise.

5. Correct the following code so that it prints the correct message.

```cpp
if (score >= 60)
    cout << "You pass." << endl;
else;
    cout << "You fail." << endl;
```

6. State whether the following are valid **switch** statements. If not, explain why. Assume that n and **digit** are **int** variables.

a.
```cpp
switch (n <= 2)
{
case 0:
    cout << "Draw." << endl;
    break;
case 1:
    cout << "Win." << endl;
    break;
case 2:
    cout << "Lose." << endl;
    break;
}
```

b.
```cpp
switch (digit / 4)
{
case 0,
case 1:
    cout << "low." << endl;
    break;
case 1,
case 2:
    cout << "middle." << endl;
    break;
case 3:
    cout << "high." << endl;
}
```

c.
```cpp
switch (n % 6)
{
case 1:
case 2:
case 3:
case 4:
case 5:
    cout << n;
    break;
case 0:
    cout << endl;
    break;
}
```

d.
```
switch (n % 10)
{
case 2:
case 4:
case 6:
case 8:
    cout << "Even";
    break;
case 1:
case 3:
case 5:
case 7:
    cout << "Odd";
    break;
}
```

7. Suppose the input is 5. What is the value of `alpha` after the following C++ code executes?

```
cin >> alpha;
switch (alpha)
{
case 1:
case 2:
    alpha = alpha + 2;
    break;
case 4:
    alpha++;
case 5:
    alpha = 2 * alpha;
case 6:
    alpha = alpha + 5;
    break;
default:
    alpha--;
}
```

8. Suppose the input is 3. What is the value of `beta` after the following C++ code executes?

```
cin >> beta;
switch (beta)
{
case 3:
    beta = beta + 3;
case 1:
    beta++;
    break;
case 5:
    beta = beta + 5;
```

```
case 4:
    beta = beta + 4;
}
```

9. Suppose the input is 6. What is the value of `a` after the following C++ code executes?

```
cin >> a;
if (a > 0)
    switch (a)
    {
    case 1:
        a = a + 3;
    case 3:
        a++;
        break;
    case 6:
        a = a + 6;
    case 8:
        a = a * 8;
        break;
    default:
        a--;
    }
else
    a = a + 2;
```

10. In the following code, correct any errors that would prevent the program from compiling or running:

```
include <iostream>

main ()
{
    int a, b;
    bool found;
    cout << "Enter two integers: ;
    cin >> a >> b;

    if  a > a*b  &&  10 < b
        found = 2 * a > b;
    else
    {
        found = 2 * a < b;
        if found
            a = 3;
            c = 15;
            if b
            {
                b = 0;
                a = 1;
            }
}
```

11. The following program contains errors. Correct them so that the program will run and output w = 21.

```cpp
#include <iostream>

using namespace std;

const int ONE = 5

main ()
{
    int x, y, w, z;
    z = 9;

    if z > 10
        x = 12; y = 5, w = x + y + ONE;
    else
        x = 12; y = 4, w = x + y + ONE;

    cout << "w = " << w << endl;
}
```

PROGRAMMING EXERCISES

1. Write a program that prompts the user to input a number. The program should then output the number and a message saying whether the number is positive, negative, or zero.

2. Write a program that prompts the user to input three numbers. The program should then output the numbers in ascending order.

3. Write a program that prompts the user to input an integer between 0 and 35. If the number is less than or equal to 9, the program should output the number; otherwise, it should output A for 10, B for 11, C for 12, . . ., and Z for 35. (*Hint:* Use the cast operator, `static_cast<char>( )`, for numbers >= 10.)

4. The cost of an international call from New York to New Delhi is calculated as follows: Connection fee, $1.99; $2.00 for the first three minutes; and $0.45 for each additional minute. Write a program that prompts the user to enter the number of minutes the call lasted and outputs the amount due. Format your output with two decimal places.

5. In a right triangle, the square of the length of one side is equal to the sum of the squares of the lengths of the other two sides. Write a program that prompts the user to enter the lengths of three sides of a triangle and then outputs a message indicating whether the triangle is a right triangle.

6. A box of cookies can hold 24 cookies and a container can hold 75 boxes of cookies. Write a program that prompts the user to enter the total number of cookies, the number of cookies in a box, and the number of cookie

boxes in a container. The program then outputs the number of boxes and the number of containers to ship the cookies. Note that each box must contain the specified number of cookies and each container must contain the specified number of boxes. If the last box of cookies contains less than the number of specified cookies, you can discard it, and output the number of leftover cookies. Similarly, if the last container contains less than the number of specified boxes, you can discard it, and output the number of leftover boxes.

7. The roots of the quadratic equation $ax^2 + bx + c = 0$, $a \neq 0$ are given by the following formula:

$$\frac{-b \pm \sqrt{b^2 - 4ac}}{2a}$$

In this formula, the term $b^2 - 4ac$ is called the **discriminant**. If $b^2 - 4ac = 0$, then the equation has a single (repeated) root. If $b^2 - 4ac > 0$, the equation has two real roots. If $b^2 - 4ac < 0$, the equation has two complex roots. Write a program that prompts the user to input the value of a (the coefficient of x^2), b (the coefficient of x), and c (the constant term), and outputs the type of roots of the equation. Furthermore, if $b^2 - 4ac \geq 0$, the program should output the roots of the quadratic equation. (*Hint:* Use the function `pow` from the header file `cmath` to calculate the square root. Chapter 3 explains how the function `pow` is used.)

8. Write a program that prompts the user to input the *x-y* coordinate of a point in a Cartesian plane. The program should then output a message indicating whether the point is the origin, is located on the *x-* (or *y-*) axis, or appears in a particular quadrant. For example:

```
(0, 0) is the origin
(4, 0) is on the x-axis
(0, -3) is on the y-axis
(-2, 3) is in the second quadrant
```

9. Write a program that mimics a calculator. The program should take as input two integers and the operation to be performed. It should then output the numbers, the operator, and the result. (For division, if the denominator is zero, output an appropriate message.) Some sample outputs follow:

```
3 + 4 = 7
13 * 5 = 65
```

10. Redo Exercise 9 to handle floating-point numbers. (Format your output to two decimal places.)

11. Redo Programming Exercise 19 of Chapter 2, taking into account that your parents buy additional savings bonds for you as follows:

   a. If you do not spend any money to buy savings bonds, then because you had a summer job, your parents buy savings bonds for you in an amount equal to 1% of the money you save after paying taxes, buying clothes and other accessories, and school supplies.

   b. If you spend up to 25% of your net income to buy savings bonds, your parents spend $0.25 for each dollar you spend to buy savings bonds, plus money equal to 1% of the money you save after paying taxes, buying clothes and other accessories, and school supplies.

   c. If you spend more than 25% of your net income to buy savings bonds, your parents spend $0.40 for each dollar you spend to buy savings bonds, plus money equal to 2% of the money you save after paying taxes, buying clothes and other accessories, and school supplies.

12. A bank in your town updates its customers' accounts at the end of each month. The bank offers two types of accounts: savings and checking. Every customer must maintain a minimum balance. If a customer's balance falls below the minimum balance, there is a service charge of $10.00 for savings accounts and $25.00 for checking accounts. If the balance at the end of the month is at least the minimum balance, the account receives interest as follows:

   a. Savings accounts receive 4% interest.

   b. Checking accounts with balances of up to $5,000 more than the minimum balance receive 3% interest; otherwise, the interest is 5%.

   Write a program that reads a customer's account number (`int` type), account type (`char`; s for savings, c for checking), minimum balance that the account should maintain, and current balance. The program should then output the account number, account type, current balance, and an appropriate message. Test your program by running it five times, using the following data:

```
46728 S 1000 2700
87324 C 1500 7689
79873 S 1000 800
89832 C 2000 3000
98322 C 1000 750
```

13. Write a program that implements the algorithm given in Example 1-2 (Chapter 1), which determines the monthly wages of a salesperson.

14. The number of lines that can be printed on a paper depends on the paper size, the point size of each character in a line, whether lines are double-spaced or single-spaced, the top and bottom margin, and the left and right margins of the paper. Assume that all characters are of the same point size, and all lines are either single-spaced or double-spaced. Note that 1 inch = 72 points. Moreover, assume that the lines are printed along the width of the paper. For example, if the length of the paper is 11 inches and width is 8.5 inches, then the maximum length of a line is 8.5 inches. Write a program that calculates the number of characters in a line and the number of lines that can be printed on a paper based on the following input from the user:

    a. The length and width, in inches, of the paper.

    b. The top, bottom, left, and right margins.

    c. The point size of a line.

    d. If the lines are double-spaced, then double the point size of each character.

15. Write a program that calculates and prints the bill for a cellular telephone company. The company offers two types of service: regular and premium. Its rates vary, depending on the type of service. The rates are computed as follows:

Regular service:	$10.00 plus first 50 minutes are free. Charges for over 50 minutes are $0.20 per minute.
Premium service:	$25.00 plus:

    a. For calls made from 6:00 a.m. to 6:00 p.m., the first 75 minutes are free; charges for over 75 minutes are $0.10 per minute

    b. For calls made from 6:00 p.m. to 6:00 a.m., the first 100 minutes are free; charges for over 100 minutes are $0.05 per minute.

    Your program should prompt the user to enter an account number, a service code (type **char**), and the number of minutes the service was used. A service code of **r** or **R** means regular service; a service code of **p** or **P** means premium service. Treat any other character as an error. Your program should output the account number, type of service, number of minutes the telephone service was used, and the amount due from the user.

    For the premium service, the customer may be using the service during the day and the night. Therefore, to calculate the bill, you must ask the user to input the number of minutes the service was used during the day and the number of minutes the service was used during the night.

16. You have several pictures of different sizes that you would like to frame. A local picture-framing store offers two types of frames—regular and fancy. The frames are available in white and can be ordered in any color the

customer desires. Suppose that each frame is 1 inch wide. The cost of coloring the frame is $0.10 per inch. The cost of a regular frame is $0.15 per inch and the cost of a fancy frame is $0.25 per inch. The cost of putting a cardboard paper behind the picture is $0.02 per square inch, and the cost of putting glass on top of the picture is $0.07 per square inch. The customer can also choose to put crowns on the corners, which costs $0.35 per crown. Write a program that prompts the user to input the following information and then output the cost of framing the picture:

a. The length and width, in inches, of the picture.

b. The type of the frame.

c. Customer's choice of color to color the frame.

d. If the user wants to put the crowns, then the number of crowns.

CONTROL STRUCTURES II (REPETITION)

IN THIS CHAPTER, YOU WILL:

- Learn about repetition (looping) control structures
- Explore how to construct and use count-controlled, sentinel-controlled, flag-controlled, and EOF-controlled repetition structures
- Examine `break` and `continue` statements
- Discover how to form and use nested control structures

In Chapter 4, you saw how decisions are incorporated in programs. In this chapter, you learn how repetitions are incorporated in programs.

Why Is Repetition Needed?

Suppose you want to add five numbers to find their average. From what you have learned so far, you could proceed as follows (assume that all variables are properly declared):

```
cin >> num1 >> num2 >> num3 >> num4 >> num5;    //read five numbers
sum = num1 + num2 + num3 + num4 + num5;         //add the numbers
average = sum / 5;                              //find the average
```

But suppose you want to add and average 100, or 1,000, or more numbers. You would have to declare that many variables, and list them again in `cin` statements and, perhaps, again in the output statements. This takes an exorbitant amount of space and time. Also, if you want to run this program again with different values, or with a different number of values, you have to rewrite the program.

Suppose you want to add the following numbers:

5 3 7 9 4

Consider the following statements, in which `sum` and `num` are variables of type `int`:

1. `sum = 0;`

2. `cin >> num;`

3. `sum = sum + num;`

The first statement initializes `sum` to 0. Let us execute statements 2 and 3. Statement 2 stores 5 in `num`; statement 3 updates the value of `sum` by adding `num` to it. After statement 3, the value of `sum` is 5.

Let us repeat statements 2 and 3. After statement 2 (after the programming code reads the next number):

num = 3

After statement 3:

sum = sum + num = 5 + 3 = 8

At this point, `sum` contains the sum of the first two numbers. Let us again repeat statements 2 and 3 (third time). After statement 2 (after the code reads the next number):

num = 7

After statement 3:

sum = sum + num = 8 + 7 = 15

Now `sum` contains the sum of the first three numbers. If you repeat statements 2 and 3 two more times, `sum` will contain the sum of all five numbers.

If you want to add 10 numbers, you can repeat statements 2 and 3 ten times. And if you want to add 100 numbers, you can repeat statements 2 and 3 one hundred times. In either case, you do not have to declare any additional variables, as you did in the first code. You can use this C++ code to add any set of numbers, whereas the earlier code requires you to drastically change the code.

There are many other situations where it is necessary to repeat a set of statements. For example, for each student in a class, the formula for determining the course grade is the same. C++ has three repetition, or looping, structures that let you repeat statements over and over until certain conditions are met. This chapter introduces all three looping (repetition) structures. The next section discusses the first repetition structure, called the `while` loop.

`while` Looping (Repetition) Structure

In the previous section, you saw that sometimes it is necessary to repeat a set of statements several times. One way to repeat a set of statements is to type the set of statements in the program over and over. For example, if you want to repeat a set of statements 100 times, you type the set of statements 100 times in the program. However, this solution of repeating a set of statements is impractical, if not impossible. Fortunately, there is a better way to repeat a set of statements. As noted earlier, C++ has three repetition, or looping, structures that allow you to repeat a set of statements until certain conditions are met. This section discusses the first looping structure, called a `while` **loop**.

The general form of the `while` statement is:

```
while (expression)
    statement
```

In C++, `while` is a reserved word. Of course, the `statement` can be either a simple or compound statement. The `expression` acts as a **decision maker** and is usually a logical expression. The `statement` is called the body of the loop. Note that the parentheses around the `expression` are part of the syntax. Figure 5-1 shows the flow of execution of a `while` loop.

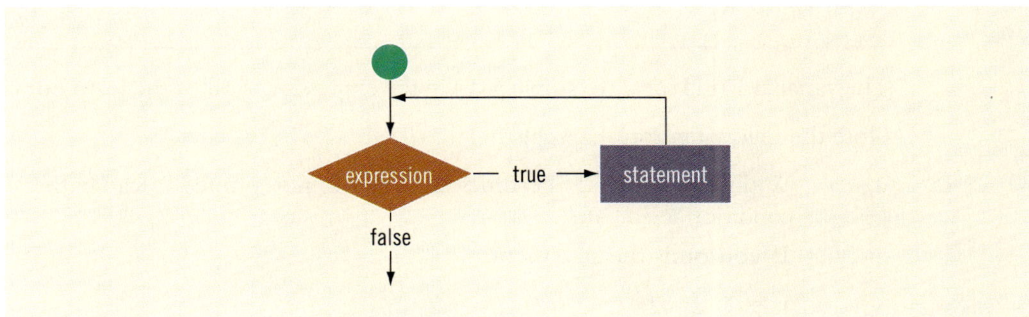

FIGURE 5-1 `while` loop

The **expression** provides an entry condition. If it initially evaluates to **true**, the **statement** executes. The loop condition—the **expression**—is then re-evaluated. If it again evaluates to **true**, the **statement** executes again. The **statement** (body of the loop) continues to execute until the **expression** is no longer **true**. A loop that continues to execute endlessly is called an **infinite loop**. To avoid an infinite loop, make sure that the loop's body contains statement(s) that assure that the exit condition—the expression in the **while** statement—will eventually be **false**.

EXAMPLE 5-1

Consider the following C++ program segment:

```
i = 0;                          //Line 1

while (i <= 20)                 //Line 2
{
    cout << i << " ";           //Line 3
    i = i + 5;                  //Line 4
}

cout << endl;
```

Sample Run:

```
0 5 10 15 20
```

In Line 1, the variable i is set to 0. The **expression** in the **while** statement (in Line 2), i <= 20, is evaluated. Because the expression i <= 20 evaluates to **true**, the body of the **while** loop executes next. The body of the **while** loop consists of the statements in Lines 3 and 4. The statement in Line 3 outputs the value of i, which is 0. The statement in Line 4 changes the value of i to 5. After executing the statements in Lines 3 and 4, the **expression** in the **while** loop (Line 2) is evaluated again. Because i is 5, the expression i <= 20 evaluates to **true** and the body of the **while** loop executes again. This process of evaluating the **expression** and executing the body of the **while** loop continues until the **expression**, i <= 20 (in Line 2), no longer evaluates to **true**.

The variable i (in Line 2, Example 5-1) in the expression is called the **loop control variable**.

Note the following from Example 5-1:

a. Within the loop i becomes 25, but is not printed because the entry condition is **false**.

b. If you omit the statement:

```
i = i + 5;
```

from the body of the loop, you will have an infinite loop, continually printing rows of zeros.

c. You must initialize the loop control variable i before you execute the loop. If the statement:

```
i = 0;
```

(in Line 1) is omitted, the loop may not execute at all. (Recall that variables in C++ are not automatically initialized.)

d. In Example 5-1, if the two statements in the body of the loop are interchanged, it may drastically alter the result. For example, consider the following statements:

```
i = 0;

while (i <= 20)
{
    i = i + 5;
    cout << i << " ";
}

cout << endl;
```

Here the output is:

```
5 10 15 20 25
```

Typically, this would be a semantic error because you rarely want a condition to be true for i <= 20, and yet produce results for i > 20.

NOTE (**Designing while loops**) As in Example 5-1, the body of a **while** executes only when the expression, in the **while** statement, evaluates to **true**. Typically, the expression checks whether a variable(s), called the loop control variable (**LCV**), satisfies certain conditions. For example, in Example 5-1, the expression in the **while** statement checks whether i <= 20. The LCV must be properly initialized before the **while** loop, and it should eventually make the expression evaluate to **false**. We do this by updating or reinitializing the LCV in the body of the **while** loop. Therefore, typically, **while** loops are written in the following form:

```
//initialize the loop control variable(s)

while (expression)   //expression tests the LCV
{
    .
    .
    .
    //update the loop control variable(s)
    .
    .
    .
}
```

For instance, in Example 5-1, the statement in Line 1 initializes the LCV i to 0. The expression, i <= 20, in Line 2, checks whether i is less than or equal to 20, and the statement in Line 4 updates the value of i.

EXAMPLE 5-2

Consider the following C++ program segment:

```
i = 20;                     //Line 1
while (i < 20)              //Line 2
{
    cout << i << " ";      //Line 3
    i = i + 5;             //Line 4
}
cout << endl;              //Line 5
```

It is easy to overlook the difference between this example and Example 5-1. In this example, in Line 1, i is set to 20. Because i is 20, the expression i < 20 in the **while** statement (Line 2) evaluates to **false**. Because initially the loop entry condition, i < 20, is **false**, the body of the **while** loop never executes. Hence, no values are output and the value of i remains 20.

The next few sections describe the various forms of **while** loops.

Case 1: Counter-Controlled `while` Loops

Suppose you know exactly how many times certain statements need to be executed. For example, suppose you know exactly how many pieces of data (or entries) need to be read. In such cases, the **while** loop assumes the form of a **counter-controlled while loop**. Suppose that a set of statements needs to be executed N times. You can set up a counter (initialized to 0 before the **while** statement) to track how many items have been read. Before executing the body of the **while** statement, the counter is compared with N. If counter < N, the body of the **while** statement executes. The body of the loop continues to execute until the value of counter >= N. Thus, inside the body of the **while** statement, the value of counter increments after it reads a new item. In this case, the **while** loop might look like the following:

```
counter = 0;        //initialize the loop control variable

while (counter < N) //test the loop control variable
{
    .
    .
    .

    counter++;          //update the loop control variable
    .
    .
    .
}
```

If N represents the number of data items in a file, then the value of N can be determined several ways. The program can prompt you to specify the number of items in the file; an input statement can read the value; or you can specify the first item in the file as the number of items in the file, so that you need not remember the number of input values (items). This is useful if someone other than the programmer enters the data. Consider Example 5-3.

EXAMPLE 5-3

Suppose the input is:

12 8 9 2 3 90 38 56 8 23 89 7 2 8 3 8

The first number, 12, specifies the number of values in the data set. Suppose you want to add these numbers and find their average. Note that only 12 values are read; the others are discarded. The complete program is as follows:

```cpp
//Program: AVG1

#include <iostream>

using namespace std;

int main()
{
    int limit;         //variable to store the number of items
                       //in the list
    int number;        //variable to store the number
    int sum;           //variable to store the sum
    int counter;       //loop control variable

    cout << "Line 1: Enter data for processing"
         << endl;                                        //Line 1
    cin >> limit;                                        //Line 2

    sum = 0;                                             //Line 3
    counter = 0;                                         //Line 4

    while (counter < limit)                              //Line 5
    {
        cin >> number;                                  //Line 6
        sum = sum + number;                             //Line 7
        counter++;                                      //Line 8
    }

    cout << "Line 9: The sum of the " << limit
         << " numbers = " << sum << endl;               //Line 9

    if (counter != 0)                                    //Line 10
        cout << "Line 11: The average = "
             << sum / counter << endl;                  //Line 11
```

```
    else                                                    //Line 12
        cout << "Line 13: No input." << endl;               //Line 13

    return 0;
}
```

Sample Run: In this sample run, the user input is shaded.

```
Line 1: Enter data for processing
12 8 9 2 3 90 38 56 8 23 89 7 2 8 3 8
Line 9: The sum of the 12 numbers = 335
Line 11: The average = 27
```

This program works as follows. The statement in Line 1 prompts the user to input data for processing. The statement in Line 2 reads the first item from the input data and stores it in the variable `limit`. The value of `limit` indicates the number of items in the list. The statements in Lines 3 and 4 initialize the variables `sum` and `counter` to 0. (The variable `counter` is the loop control variable.) The `while` statement in Line 5 checks the value of `counter` to determine how many items have been read. If `counter` is less than `limit`, the `while` loop proceeds for the next iteration. The statement in Line 6 reads the next number and stores it in the variable `number`. The statement in Line 7 updates the value of `sum` by adding the value of `number` to the previous value, and the statement in Line 8 increments the value of `counter` by 1. The statement in Line 9 outputs the sum of the numbers; the statements in Lines 10 through 13 output the average.

Note that `sum` is initialized to 0 in Line 3 in this program. In Line 7, after reading a number in Line 6, the program adds it to the sum of all the numbers scanned before the current number. The first number read will be added to zero (because `sum` is initialized to 0), giving the correct sum of the first number. To find the average, divide `sum` by `counter`. If `counter` is 0, then dividing by zero will terminate the program and you get an error message. Therefore, before dividing `sum` by `counter`, you must check whether `counter` is 0.

Notice that in this program, the statement in Line 4 initializes the LCV `counter` to 0. The expression `counter < limit` in Line 5 evaluates whether `counter` is less than `limit`. The statement in Line 8 updates the value of `counter`.

Case 2: Sentinel-Controlled `while` Loops

You do not always know how many pieces of data (or entries) need to be read, but you may know that the last entry is a special value, called a **sentinel**. In this case, you read the first item before the `while` statement. If this item does not equal the sentinel, the body of the `while` statement executes. The `while` loop continues to execute as long as the program has not read the sentinel. Such a **while** loop is called a **sentinel-controlled while loop**. In this case, a **while** loop might look like the following:

```cpp
cin >> variable;                 //initialize the loop control variable

while (variable != sentinel)  //test the loop control variable
{
    .
    .
    .
    cin >> variable;        //update the loop control variable
    .
    .
    .
}
```

EXAMPLE 5-4

Suppose you want to read some positive integers and average them, but you do not have a preset number of data items in mind. Suppose the number −999 marks the end of the data. You can proceed as follows.

```cpp
//Program:   AVG2

#include <iostream>

using namespace std;

const int SENTINEL = -999;

int main()
{
    int number;        //variable to store the number
    int sum = 0;       //variable to store the sum
    int count = 0;     //variable to store the total
                       //numbers read

    cout << "Line 1: Enter integers ending with "
         << SENTINEL << endl;                           //Line 1
    cin >> number;                                      //Line 2

    while (number != SENTINEL)                          //Line 3
    {
        sum = sum + number;                             //Line 4
        count++;                                        //Line 5
        cin >> number;                                  //Line 6
    }
```

```
    cout << "Line 7: The sum of the " << count
         << " numbers is " << sum << endl;              //Line 7

    if (count != 0)                                      //Line 8
        cout << "Line 9: The average is "
             <<   sum / count << endl;                   //Line 9
    else                                                 //Line 10
        cout << "Line 11: No input." << endl;            //Line 11

    return 0;
}
```

Sample Run: In this sample run, the user input is shaded.

```
Line 1: Enter integers ending with -999
34 23 9 45 78 0 77 8 3 5 -999
Line 7: The sum of the 10 numbers is 282
Line 9: The average is 28
```

This program works as follows. The statement in Line 1 prompts the user to enter numbers ending with -999. The statement in Line 2 reads the first number and stores it in number. The **while** statement in Line 3 checks whether number is not equal to SENTINEL. (The variable number is the loop control variable.) If number is not equal to SENTINEL, the body of the **while** loop executes. The statement in Line 4 updates the value of sum by adding number to it. The statement in Line 5 increments the value of count by 1; the statement in Line 6 reads and stores the next number into number. The statements in Lines 4 through 6 repeat until the program reads the SENTINEL. The statement in Line 7 outputs the sum of the numbers, and the statements in Lines 8 through 10 output the average of the numbers.

Notice that the statement in Line 2 initializes the LCV number. The expression number != SENTINEL in Line 3 checks whether the value of number is not equal to SENTINEL. The statement in Line 6 reinitializes the LCV number.

Next, consider another example of a sentinel-controlled **while** loop. In this example, the user is prompted to enter the value to be processed. If the user wants to stop the program, he or she can enter the sentinel.

EXAMPLE 5-5

Telephone Digits

The following program reads the letter codes A to Z and prints the corresponding telephone digit. This program uses a sentinel-controlled **while** loop. To stop the program, the user is prompted for the sentinel, which is #. This is also an example of a nested control structure, where if...else, switch, and the **while** loop are nested.

```cpp
//*************************************************************
// Program: Telephone Digits
// This is an example of a sentinel-controlled loop. This
// program converts uppercase letters to their corresponding
// telephone digits.
//*************************************************************

#include <iostream>

using namespace std;

int main()
{
    char letter;                              //Line 1

    cout << "Program to convert uppercase "
         << "letters to their corresponding "
         << "telephone digits." << endl;      //Line 2

    cout << "To stop the program enter #."
         << endl;                             //Line 3

    cout << "Enter a letter: ";               //Line 4
    cin >> letter;                            //Line 5
    cout << endl;                             //Line 6

    while (letter != '#')                     //Line 7
    {
        cout << "The letter you entered is: "
             << letter << endl;               //Line 8
        cout << "The corresponding telephone "
             << "digit is: ";                 //Line 9

        if (letter >= 'A' && letter <= 'Z')   //Line 10
            switch (letter)                   //Line 11
            {
            case 'A':
            case 'B':
            case 'C':
                cout << "2" <<endl;           //Line 12
                break;                        //Line 13
            case 'D':
            case 'E':
            case 'F':
                cout << "3" << endl;          //Line 14
                break;                        //Line 15
            case 'G':
            case 'H':
            case 'I':
                cout << "4" << endl;          //Line 16
                break;                        //Line 17
```

```cpp
        case 'J':
        case 'K':
        case 'L':
            cout << "5" << endl;                    //Line 18
            break;                                  //Line 19
        case 'M':
        case 'N':
        case 'O':
            cout << "6" << endl;                    //Line 20
            break;                                  //Line 21
        case 'P':
        case 'Q':
        case 'R':
        case 'S':
            cout << "7" << endl;                    //Line 22
            break;                                  //Line 23
        case 'T':
        case 'U':
        case 'V':
            cout << "8" << endl;                    //Line 24
            break;                                  //Line 25
        case 'W':
        case 'X':
        case 'Y':
        case 'Z':
            cout << "9" << endl;                    //Line 26
        }
    else                                            //Line 27
        cout << "Invalid input." << endl;           //Line 28

    cout << "\nEnter another uppercase "
         << "letter to find its "
         << "corresponding telephone digit."
         << endl;                                   //Line 29
    cout << "To stop the program enter #."
         << endl;                                   //Line 30

    cout << "Enter a letter: ";                     //Line 31
    cin >> letter;                                  //Line 32
    cout << endl;                                   //Line 33
    }//end while

    return 0;
}
```

Sample Run: In this sample run, the user input is shaded.

```
Program to convert uppercase letters to their corresponding telephone
digits.
To stop the program enter #.
```

```
Enter a letter: A
The letter you entered is: A
The corresponding telephone digit is: 2

Enter another uppercase letter to find its corresponding telephone digit.
To stop the program enter #.
Enter a letter: D
The letter you entered is: D
The corresponding telephone digit is: 3

Enter another uppercase letter to find its corresponding telephone digit.
To stop the program enter #.
Enter a letter: #
```

This program works as follows. The statements in Lines 2 and 3 tell the user what to do. The statement in Line 4 prompts the user to input a letter; the statement in Line 5 reads and stores that letter into the variable `letter`. The **while** loop in Line 7 checks that the letter is #. If the letter entered by the user is not #, the body of the **while** loop executes. The statement in Line 8 outputs the letter entered by the user. The **if** statement in Line 10 checks whether the letter entered by the user is uppercase. The statement part of the **if** statement is the **switch** statement (Line 11). If the letter entered by the user is uppercase, the **expression** in the **if** statement (in Line 10) evaluates to **true** and the **switch** statement executes; if the letter entered by the user is not uppercase, the **else** (Line 27) executes. The statements in Lines 12 through 26 determine the corresponding telephone digit.

Once the current letter is processed, the statements in Lines 29 and 30 again inform the user what to do next. The statement in Line 31 prompts the user to enter a letter; the statement in Line 32 reads and stores that letter into the variable `letter`. (Note that the statement in Line 29 is similar to the statement in Line 2 and that the statements in Lines 30 through 33 are the same as the statements in Lines 3 through 6.) After the statement in Line 33 (at the end of the **while** loop) executes, the control goes back to the top of the **while** loop and the same process begins again. When the user enters #, the program terminates.

Notice that in this program, the variable `letter` is the loop control variable. First, it is initialized in Line 5, by the input statement, and then updated in Line 32. The expression in Line 7 checks whether `letter` is #.

NOTE   In the program in Example 5-5, you can write the statements between Lines 10 and 28 using a **switch** structure. (See Programming Exercise 3 at the end of this chapter.)

Case 3: Flag-Controlled while Loops

A **flag-controlled while loop** uses a **bool** variable to control the loop. Suppose **found** is a **bool** variable. The flag-controlled **while** loop takes the following form:

```cpp
found = false;          //initialize the loop control variable

while (!found)          //test the loop control variable
{
    .
    .
    .
    if (expression)
        found = true;  //update the loop control variable
    .
    .
    .
}
```

The variable `found`, which is used to control the execution of the `while` loop, is called a **flag variable**.

Example 5-6 further illustrates the use of a flag-controlled `while` loop.

EXAMPLE 5-6

Number Guessing Game

The following program randomly generates an integer greater than or equal to 0 and less than 100. The program then prompts the user to guess the number. If the user guesses the number correctly, the program outputs an appropriate message. Otherwise, the program checks whether the guessed number is less than the random number. If the guessed number is less than the random number generated by the program, the program outputs the message "Your guess is lower than the number. Guess again!"; otherwise, the program outputs the message "Your guess is higher than the number. Guess again!". The program then prompts the user to enter another number. The user is prompted to guess the random number until the user enters the correct number.

The program uses the function `rand` of the header file `cstdlib` to generate a random number. To be specific, the expression:

```cpp
rand()
```

returns an `int` value between 0 and 32767. To convert it to an integer greater than or equal to 0 and less than 100, we use the following expression:

```cpp
rand() % 100
```

It is possible that every time you run your program, the function `rand` gives the same random number. In this case, you can use the function `time`, of the header file `ctime`, to include the time. The function `time` returns time as a `long` value. The following expression uses both the functions `rand` and `time` to generate a random integer greater than or equal to 0 and less than 100:

```cpp
(rand() + time(0)) % 100;
```

(Note how the function `time` is used. It is used with an argument, that is, a parameter, which is 0.)

Furthermore, the program uses the **bool** variable done to control the loop. The **bool** variable done is initialized to **false**. It is set to **true** when the user guesses the correct number.

```cpp
//Flag-controlled while loop.
//Number guessing game.

#include <iostream>
#include <cstdlib>
#include <ctime>

using namespace std;

int main()
{
        //declare the variables
    int num;      //variable to store the random
                  //number
    int guess;    //variable to store the number
                  //guessed by the user
    bool done;    //boolean variable to control
                  //the loop

    num = (rand() + time(0)) % 100;           //Line 1

    done = false;                             //Line 2

    while (!done)                             //Line 3
    {                                         //Line 4
        cout << "Enter an integer greater"
            << " than or equal to 0 and "
            << "less than 100: ";             //Line 5

        cin >> guess;                         //Line 6
        cout << endl;                         //Line 7

        if (guess == num)                     //Line 8
        {                                     //Line 9
            cout << "You guessed the correct "
                << "number." << endl;         //Line 10
            done = true;                      //Line 11
        }                                     //Line 12
        else                                  //Line 13
            if (guess < num)                  //Line 14
                cout << "Your guess is lower "
                    << "than the number.\n"
                    << "Guess again!" << endl; //Line 15
            else                              //Line 16
                cout << "Your guess is higher "
                    << "than the number.\n"
                    << "Guess again!" << endl; //Line 17
    } //end while                             //Line 18

    return 0;
}
```

Sample Run: In this sample run, the user input is shaded.

```
Enter an integer greater than or equal to 0 and less than 100: 25

Your guess is higher than the number.
Guess again!
Enter an integer greater than or equal to 0 and less than 100: 5

Your guess is lower than the number.
Guess again!
Enter an integer greater than or equal to 0 and less than 100: 10

Your guess is higher than the number.
Guess again!
Enter an integer greater than or equal to 0 and less than 100: 8

Your guess is higher than the number.
Guess again!
Enter an integer greater than or equal to 0 and less than 100: 6

Your guess is lower than the number.
Guess again!
Enter an integer greater than or equal to 0 and less than 100: 7

You guessed the correct number.
```

The preceding program works as follows: The statement in Line 1 creates an integer greater than or equal to 0 and less than 100 and stores this number in the variable num. The statement in Line 2 sets the `bool` variable done to `false`. The `while` loop starts at Line 3 and ends at Line 18. The expression in the `while` loop at Line 3 evaluates the expression !done. If done is `false`, then !done is `true` and the body of the `while` loop executes; if done is `true`, then !done is `false`, so the `while` loop terminates.

The statement in Line 5 prompts the user to enter an integer greater than or equal to 0 and less than 100. The statement in Line 6 stores the number entered by the user in the variable guess. The expression in the `if` statement in Line 8 determines whether the value of guess is the same as num; that is, if the user guessed the number correctly. If the value of guess is the same as num, then the statements in Lines 10 and 11 execute. The statement in Line 10 outputs the message:

```
You guessed the correct number.
```

The statement in Line 11 sets the variable done to `true`. The control then goes back to Line 3. Because done is `true`, !done is `false` and the `while` loop terminates.

If the expression in Line 8 evaluates to `false`, then the `else` statement in Line 13 executes. The statement part of this `else` is an `if...else` statement, starting at Line 14 and ending at Line 17. The `if` statement in Line 14 determines whether the value of guess is less than num. In this case, the statement in Line 15 outputs the message:

```
Your guess is lower than the number.
Guess again!
```

If the expression in the **if** statement in Line 14 evaluates to **false**, then the statement in Line 17 executes, which outputs the message:

```
Your guess is higher than the number.
Guess again!
```

The program then prompts the user to enter an integer greater than or equal to 0 and less than 100.

Case 4: EOF-Controlled while Loops

If the data file is frequently altered (for example, if data is frequently added or deleted), it's best not to read the data with a sentinel value. Someone might accidentally erase the sentinel value or add data past the sentinel, especially if the programmer and the data entry person are different people. Also, the programmer sometimes does not know what the sentinel is. In such situations, you can use an **EOF (End Of File)–controlled while loop**.

Until now, we have used an input stream variable, such as **cin**, and the extraction operator, **>>**, to read and store data into variables. However, the input stream variable can also return a value after reading data, as follows:

1. If the program has reached the end of the input data, the input stream variable returns the logical value **false**.

2. If the program reads any faulty data (such as a **char** value into an **int** variable), the input stream enters the fail state. Once a stream enters the fail state, any further I/O operations using that stream are considered to be null operations; that is, they have no effect. Unfortunately, the computer does not halt the program or give any error messages. It just continues executing the program, silently ignoring each additional attempt to use that stream. In this case, the input stream variable returns the value **false**.

3. In cases other than (1) and (2), the input stream variable returns the logical value **true**.

You can use the value returned by the input stream variable to determine whether the program has reached the end of the input data. Because the input stream variable returns the logical value **true** or **false**, in a **while** loop, it can be considered a logical expression.

The following is an example of an EOF-controlled **while** loop:

```
cin >> variable;        //initialize the loop control variable

while (cin)             //test the loop control variable
{
    .
    .
    .
```

```
    cin >> variable;  //update the loop control variable
          .
          .
          .
}
```

Notice that here the variable `cin` acts as the loop control variable.

eof **Function**

In addition to checking the value of an input stream variable, such as `cin`, to determine whether the end of the file has been reached, C++ provides a function that you can use with an input stream variable to determine the end-of-file status. This function is called `eof`. Like the I/O functions—such as `get`, `ignore`, and `peek`, discussed in Chapter 3— the function `eof` is a member of the data type `istream`.

The syntax to use the function `eof` is:

```
istreamVar.eof()
```

where `istreamVar` is an input stream variable, such as `cin`.

Suppose you have the declaration:

```
ifstream infile;
```

Further suppose that you opened a file using the variable `infile`. Consider the expression:

```
infile.eof()
```

This is a logical (Boolean) expression. The value of this expression is **true** if the program has read past the end of the input file, `infile`; otherwise, the value of this expression is **false**.

This method of determining the end-of-file status (that is, using the function `eof`) works best if the input is text. The earlier method of determining the end-of-file status works best if the input consists of numeric data.

Suppose you have the declaration:

```
ifstream infile;
char ch;
```

```
infile.open("inputDat.dat");
```

The following **while** loop continues to execute as long as the program has not reached the end of the file.

```
infile.get(ch);
```

```
while (!infile.eof())
{
    cout << ch;
    infile.get(ch);
}
```

As long as the program has not reached the end of the input file, the expression:

```
infile.eof()
```

is `false` and so the expression:

```
!infile.eof()
```

in the `while` statement is `true`. When the program reads past the end of the input file, the expression:

```
infile.eof()
```

becomes `true` and so the expression:

```
!infile.eof()
```

in the `while` statement becomes `false` and the loop terminates.

NOTE In the Windows console environment, the end-of-file marker is entered using `Ctrl+z` (hold the `Ctrl` key and press `z`). In the UNIX environment, the end-of-file marker is entered using `Ctr+d` (hold the `Ctrl` key and press `d`).

The Programming Example Checking Account Balance, of this chapter, further illustrates how to use an EOF–controlled `while` loop in a program.

More on Expressions in `while` Statements

In the examples of the previous sections, the expression in the `while` statement is quite simple. In other words, the `while` loop is controlled by a single variable. However, there are situations when the expression in the `while` statement may be more complex.

For example, the program in Example 5-6 uses a flag-controlled `while` loop to implement the Number Guessing Game. However, the program gives as many tries as the user needs to guess the number. Suppose you want to give the user no more than five tries to guess the number. If the user does not guess the number correctly within five tries, then the program outputs the random number generated by the program as well as a message that you have lost the game. In this case, you can write the `while` loop as follows (assume that `noOfGuesses` is an `int` variable initialized to 0):

```
while ((noOfGuesses < 5) && (!done))
{
    cout << "Enter an integer greater than or equal to 0 and "
         << "less than 100: ";
    cin >> guess;
    cout << endl;
    noOfGuesses++;
```

```cpp
        if (guess == num)
        {
            cout << "Winner!. You guessed the correct number."
                << endl;
            done = true;
        }
        else if (guess < num)
            cout << "Your guess is lower than the number.\n"
                << "Guess again!" << endl;
        else
            cout << "Your guess is higher than the number.\n"
                << "Guess again!" << endl;
}//end while
```

You also need the following code, to be included after the `while` loop, in case the user cannot guess the correct number in five tries.

```cpp
if (!done)
    cout << "You lose! The correct number is " << num << endl;
```

Programming Exercise 14 at the end of this chapter asks you to write a complete C++ program to implement the Number Guessing Game in which the user has, at most, five tries to guess the number.

As you can see from the preceding `while` loop, the expression in a `while` statement can be complex. The main objective of a `while` loop is to repeat certain statement(s) until certain conditions are met.

PROGRAMMING EXAMPLE: Checking Account Balance

A local bank in your town is looking for someone to write a program that calculates a customer's checking account balance at the end of each month. The data is stored in a file in the following form:

```
467343 23750.40
W 250.00
D 1200.00
W 75.00
I 120.74
   .
   .
   .
```

The first line of data shows the account number followed by the account balance at the beginning of the month. Thereafter, each line has two entries: the transaction code and the transaction amount. The transaction code `W` or `w` means withdrawal, `D` or `d` means deposit, and `I` or `i` means interest paid by the bank. The program updates the balance after each transaction. During the month, if at any time the balance goes below

$1000.00, a $25.00 service fee is charged. The program prints the following information: account number, balance at the beginning of the month, balance at the end of the month, interest paid by the bank, total amount of deposits, number of deposits, total amount of withdrawals, number of withdrawals, and service charge, if any.

Input   A file consisting of data in the above format.

Output   The output is of the following form:

```
Account Number: 467343
Beginning Balance: $23750.40
Ending Balance: $24611.49

Interest Paid: $366.24

Amount Deposited: $2230.50
Number of Deposits:   3

Amount Withdrawn: $1735.65
Number of Withdrawals: 6
```

The output is to be stored in a file.

PROBLEM ANALYSIS AND ALGORITHM DESIGN

The first entry in the input file is the account number and the beginning balance, so the program first reads the account number and beginning balance. Thereafter, each entry in the file is of the following form:

```
transactionCode transactionAmount
```

To determine the account balance at the end of the month, you need to process each entry that contains the transaction code and transaction amount. Begin with the starting balance and then update the account balance after processing each entry. If the transaction code is D, d, I, or i, the transaction amount is added to the account balance. If the transaction code is W or w, the transaction amount is subtracted from the balance. Because the program also outputs the number of withdrawals and deposits, you need to keep separate counts of withdrawals and deposits. This discussion translates into the following algorithm:

1. Declare the variables.
2. Initialize the variables.
3. Get the account number and beginning balance.
4. Get the transaction code and transaction amount.
5. Analyze the transaction code and update the appropriate variables.
6. Repeat Steps 4 and 5 until there is no more data.
7. Print the result.

Variables The program outputs the account number, beginning balance, balance at the end of the month, interest paid, amount deposited, number of deposits, amount withdrawn, number of withdrawals, and service charge, if any. You need variables to store all this information. So far, you need the following variables:

```
acctNumber               //variable to store the account number
beginningBalance         //variable to store the beginning balance
accountBalance           //variable to store the account balance at the
                         //end of the month
amountDeposited          //variable to store the total amount deposited
numberOfDeposits         //variable to store the number of deposits
amountWithdrawn          //variable to store the total amount withdrawn
numberOfWithdrawals //variable to store the number of withdrawals
interestPaid             //variable to store the interest paid
```

Because the program reads the data from a file and the output is stored in a file, the program needs both input and output stream variables. After the first line, the data in each line is the transaction code and the transaction amount; the program needs a variable to store this information.

Whenever the account balance goes below the minimum balance, a service charge for that month is applied. After each withdrawal, you need to check the account balance. If the balance goes below the minimum after a withdrawal, a service charge is applied. You can potentially have several withdrawals in a month; once the account balance goes below the minimum, a subsequent deposit might bring the balance above the minimum, and another withdrawal might again reduce it below the minimum. However, the service charge is applied only once.

To implement this idea, the program uses a `bool` variable, `isServiceCharged`, which is initialized to `false` and set to `true` whenever the account balance goes below the minimum. Before applying a service charge, the program checks the value of the variable `isServiceCharged`. If the account balance is less than the minimum and `isServiceCharged` is `false`, a service charge is applied. The program needs the following variables:

```
int acctNumber;
double beginningBalance;
double accountBalance;

double amountDeposited;
int numberOfDeposits;
double amountWithdrawn;
int numberOfWithdrawals;

double interestPaid;

char transactionCode;
double transactionAmount;
```

```
bool isServiceCharged;

ifstream infile;   //input file stream variable
ofstream outfile;  //output file stream variable
```

Named Constants Because the minimum account balance and the service charge amount are fixed, the program uses two named constants to store them:

```
const double MINIMUM_BALANCE = 1000.00;
const double SERVICE_CHARGE = 25.00;
```

PROBLEM ANALYSIS AND ALGORITHM DESIGN (CONTINUED) Because this program is more complex than previous ones, before writing the main algorithm, the above seven steps are described more fully here.

1. **Declare the variables.** Declare variables as discussed previously.

2. **Initialize the variables.** After each deposit, the total amount deposited is updated and the number of deposits is incremented by 1. Before the first deposit, the total amount deposited is 0, and the number of withdrawals is 0. Therefore, the variables `amountDeposited` and `numberOfDeposits` must be initialized to 0. Similarly, the variables `amountWithdrawn`, `numberOfWithdrawals`, and `interestPaid` must be initialized to 0. Also, as discussed previously, the variable `isServiceCharged` is initialized to `false`. Of course, you can initialize these variables when you declare them.

   Before the first deposit, withdrawal, or interest paid, the account balance is the same as the beginning balance. Therefore, after reading the beginning balance in the variable `beginningBalance` from the file, you need to initialize the variable `accountBalance` to the value of the variable `beginningBalance`.

   Because the data will be read from a file, you need to open the input file. If the input file does not exist, output an appropriate message and terminate the program. Because the output will be stored in a file, you need to open the output file. Suppose the input data is in the file `Ch5_money.txt` on a floppy disk in drive `A:`. Also suppose that the output will be stored in the file `Ch5_money.out` on a floppy disk in drive `A:`. The following code opens the files:

```
infile.open("a:\\Ch5_money.txt"); //open the input file

if (!infile)
{
    cout << "Cannot open the input file." << endl;
    cout << "Program terminates!!!" << endl;
    return 1;
}
```

```cpp
outfile.open("a:\\Ch5_money.out");  //open the output file
```

3. **Get the account number and starting balance.** This is accomplished by the following input statement:

```cpp
infile >> acctNumber >> beginningBalance;
```

4. **Get the transaction code and transaction amount.** This is accomplished by the following input statement:

```cpp
infile >> transactionCode >> transactionAmount;
```

5. **Analyze the transaction code and update the appropriate variables:** If the `transactionCode` is `'D'` or `'d'`, update `accountBalance` by adding `transactionAmount`, update `amountDeposited` by adding `transactionAmount`, and increment `numberOfDeposits`. If the `transactionCode` is `'I'` or `'i'`, update `accountBalance` by adding `transactionAmount` and update `interestPaid` by adding `transactionAmount`. If the `transactionCode` is `'W'` or `'w'`, update `accountBalance` by subtracting `transactionAmount`, update `amountWithdrawn` by adding `transactionAmount`, increment `numberOfWithdrawals`, and—if the account balance is below the minimum and service charges have not been applied—subtract the service charge from the account balance and mark the service charges as having been applied. The following `switch` statement accomplishes this task.

```cpp
switch (transactionCode)
{
case 'D':
case 'd':
    accountBalance = accountBalance  + transactionAmount;
    amountDeposited = amountDeposited + transactionAmount;
    numberOfDeposits++;
    break;
case 'I':
case 'i':
    accountBalance = accountBalance + transactionAmount;
    interestPaid = interestPaid + transactionAmount;
    break;
case 'W':
case 'w':
    accountBalance = accountBalance - transactionAmount;
    amountWithdrawn = amountWithdrawn + transactionAmount;
    numberOfWithdrawals++;

    if ((accountBalance < MINIMUM_BALANCE)
               && (!isServiceCharged))
```

```
        {
            accountBalance = accountBalance - SERVICE_CHARGE;
            isServiceCharged = true;
        }
        break;

    default:
        cout << "Invalid transaction code." << endl;
    } //end switch
```

6. **Repeat Steps 4 and 5 until there is no more data.** Because the number of entries in the input file is not known, the program needs an EOF-controlled `while` loop.

7. **Print the result.** This is accomplished by using output statements.

Based on the above discussion, the main algorithm is as follows:

Main Algorithm

1. Declare and initialize the variables.

2. Open the input file.

3. If the input file does not exist, exit the program.

4. Open the output file.

5. To output floating-point numbers in a fixed decimal format with the decimal point and trailing zero, set the manipulators `fixed` and `showpoint`. To output floating-point numbers to two decimal places, set the precision to two decimal places.

6. Read `accountNumber` and `beginningBalance`.

7. Set `accountBalance` to `beginningBalance`.

8. Read `transactionCode` and `transactionAmount`.

9. `while` (not end of input file)

   a. If `transactionCode` is `'D'`

      i.   Add `transactionAmount` to `accountBalance`

      ii. Add `transactionAmount` to `amountDeposited`

      iii. Increment `numberOfDeposits`

   b. If `transactionCode` is `'I'`

      i. Add `transactionAmount` to `accountBalance`

      ii. Add `transactionAmount` to `interestPaid`

   c. If `transactionCode` is `'W'`

      i. Subtract `transactionAmount` from `accountBalance`

      ii. Add `transactionAmount` to `amountWithdrawn`

      iii.   Increment `numberOfWithDrawals`

      iv.   If `(accountBalance < MINIMUM_BALANCE`
                   `&& !isServiceCharged)`

         1.   Subtract `SERVICE_CHARGE` from `accountBalance`

         2.   Set `isServiceCharged` to `true`

    d.   If `transactionCode` is other than `'D'`, `'d'`, `'I'`, `'i'`, `'W'`,
        or `'w'`, output an error message.

  10.   Output the results.

Because the data will be read from an input file, you must include the header file `fstream`. Because you will use the manipulator `setprecision`, you must also include the header file `iomanip`. If the input file does not exist, an appropriate message on the screen will be displayed, so the header file `iostream` is also included.

COMPLETE PROGRAM LISTING

```cpp
//****************************************************************
// Program -- Checking Account Balance.
// This program calculates a customer's checking account
// balance at the end of the month.
//****************************************************************

#include <iostream>
#include <fstream>
#include <iomanip>

using namespace std;

const double MINIMUM_BALANCE = 1000.00;
const double SERVICE_CHARGE = 25.00;

int main()
{
        //Declare and initialize variables          //Step 1
    int acctNumber;
    double beginningBalance;
    double accountBalance;

    double amountDeposited = 0.0;
    int numberOfDeposits = 0;

    double amountWithdrawn = 0.0;
    int numberOfWithdrawals = 0;
    double interestPaid = 0.0;
```

```cpp
char transactionCode;
double transactionAmount;

bool isServiceCharged = false;

ifstream infile;
ofstream outfile;

infile.open("a:\\Ch5_money.txt");                   //Step 2

if (!infile)                                         //Step 3
{
    cout << "Cannot open the input file." << endl;
    cout << "Program terminates!!!" << endl;
    return 1;
}

outfile.open("a:\\Ch5_money.out");                   //Step 4

outfile << fixed << showpoint;                        //Step 5
outfile << setprecision(2);                          //Step 5

cout << "Processing data" << endl;

infile >> acctNumber >> beginningBalance;           //Step 6

accountBalance = beginningBalance;                   //Step 7

infile >> transactionCode >> transactionAmount; //Step 8

while (infile)                                       //Step 9
{
    switch (transactionCode)
    {
    case 'D':                                        //Step 9.a
    case 'd':
        accountBalance = accountBalance
                        + transactionAmount;
        amountDeposited = amountDeposited
                        + transactionAmount;
        numberOfDeposits++;
        break;
    case 'I':                                        //Step 9.b
    case 'i':
        accountBalance = accountBalance
                        + transactionAmount;
        interestPaid = interestPaid
                        + transactionAmount;
        break;
```

```cpp
        case 'W':                                       //Step 9.c
        case 'w':
            accountBalance = accountBalance
                            - transactionAmount;
            amountWithdrawn = amountWithdrawn
                            + transactionAmount;
            numberOfWithdrawals++;

            if ((accountBalance < MINIMUM_BALANCE)
                        && (!isServiceCharged))
            {
                accountBalance = accountBalance
                                - SERVICE_CHARGE;
                isServiceCharged = true;
            }
            break;

        default:
            cout << "Invalid transaction code" << endl;
        } //end switch

        infile >>  transactionCode >> transactionAmount;
    }//end while

        //Output Results                                //Step 10
    outfile << "Account Number: " << acctNumber << endl;
    outfile << "Beginning Balance: $" << beginningBalance
            << endl;
    outfile << "Ending Balance: $" << accountBalance
            << endl << endl;
    outfile << "Interest Paid: $" << interestPaid << endl
            << endl;
    outfile << "Amount Deposited: $" << amountDeposited
            << endl;
    outfile << "Number of Deposits: " << numberOfDeposits
            << endl << endl;
    outfile << "Amount Withdrawn: $" << amountWithdrawn
            << endl;
    outfile << "Number of Withdrawals: "
            << numberOfWithdrawals << endl << endl;

    if (isServiceCharged)
        outfile << "Service Charge: $" << SERVICE_CHARGE
                << endl;
    return 0;
}
```

Sample Run: (Contents of the output file `Ch5_money.out`)

```
Account Number: 467343
Beginning Balance: $23750.40
Ending Balance: $24490.75

Interest Paid: $245.50

Amount Deposited: $2230.50
Number of Deposits: 3

Amount Withdrawn: $1735.65
Number of Withdrawals: 6
```

Input File: (`Ch5_money.txt`)

```
467343 23750.40
W 250.00
D 1200.00
W 75.00
W 375.00
D 580.00
I 245.50
W 400.00
W 600.00
D 450.50
W 35.65
```

PROGRAMMING EXAMPLE: Fibonacci Number

So far, you have seen several examples of loops. Recall that in C++, `while` loops are used when a certain statement(s) must be executed repeatedly until certain conditions are met. Following is a C++ program that uses a `while` loop to find a **Fibonacci number**.

Consider the following sequence of numbers:

```
1, 1, 2, 3, 5, 8, 13, 21, 34, ....
```

Given the first two numbers of the sequence (say, a_1 and a_2), the nth number a_n, $n >= 3$, of this sequence is given by:

$$a_n = a_{n-1} + a_{n-2}$$

Thus:

$$a_3 = a_2 + a_1 = 1 + 1 = 2,$$
$$a_4 = a_3 + a_2 = 2 + 1 = 3,$$

and so on.

Such a sequence is called a **Fibonacci sequence**. In the preceding sequence, $a_2 = 1$ and $a_1 = 1$. However, given any first two numbers, using this process, you can determine the nth number, $a_n, n >= 3$, of the sequence. The number determined this way is called the **nth Fibonacci number**. Suppose $a_2 = 6$ and $a_1 = 3$.

Then:

$$a_3 = a_2 + a_1 = 6 + 3 = 9; \quad a_4 = a_3 + a_2 = 9 + 6 = 15$$

Next, we write a program that determines the nth Fibonacci number given the first two numbers.

Input   The first two Fibonacci numbers and the desired Fibonacci number.

Output   The nth Fibonacci number.

PROBLEM ANALYSIS AND ALGORITHM DESIGN

To find, say, the tenth Fibonacci number of a sequence, you must first find a_9 and a_8, which requires you to find a_7 and a_6, and so on. Therefore, to find a_{10}, you must first find $a_3, a_4, a_5, \ldots, a_9$. This discussion translates into the following algorithm:

1. Get the first two Fibonacci numbers.
2. Get the desired Fibonacci number. That is, get the position, n, of the Fibonacci number in the sequence.
3. Calculate the next Fibonacci number by adding the previous two elements of the Fibonacci sequence.
4. Repeat Step 2 until the nth Fibonacci number is found.
5. Output the nth Fibonacci number.

Note that the program assumes that the first number of the Fibonacci sequence is less than or equal to the second number of the Fibonacci sequence, and both numbers are non-negative. Moreover, the program also assumes that the user enters a valid value for the position of the desired number in the Fibonacci sequence; that is, it is a positive integer. (See Programming Exercise 12 at the end of this chapter.)

Variables   Because the last two numbers must be known in order to find the current Fibonacci number, you need the following variables: two variables—say, `previous1` and `previous2` to hold the previous two numbers of the Fibonacci sequence; and one variable—say, `current`—to hold the current Fibonacci number. The number of times that Step 2 of the algorithm repeats depends on the position of the Fibonacci number you are calculating. For example, if you want to calculate the tenth

Fibonacci number, you must execute Step 3 eight times. (Remember—the user gives the first two numbers of the Fibonacci sequence.) Therefore, you need a variable to store the number of times that Step 3 should execute. You also need a variable to track the number of times that Step 3 has executed the loop control variable. You therefore need five variables for the data manipulation:

```cpp
int previous1;    //variable to store the first Fibonacci number
int previous2;    //variable to store the second Fibonacci number
int current;      //variable to store the current
                  //Fibonacci number
int counter;      //loop control variable
int nthFibonacci; //variable to store the desired
                  //Fibonacci number
```

To calculate the third Fibonacci number, add the values of `previous1` and `previous2` and store the result in `current`. To calculate the fourth Fibonacci number, add the value of the second Fibonacci number (that is, `previous2`) and the value of the third Fibonacci number (that is, `current`). Thus, when the fourth Fibonacci number is calculated, you no longer need the first Fibonacci number. Instead of declaring additional variables, which could be too many, after calculating a Fibonacci number to determine the next Fibonacci number, `current` becomes `previous2` and `previous2` becomes `previous1`. Therefore, you can again use the variable `current` to store the next Fibonacci number. This process is repeated until the desired Fibonacci number is calculated. Initially, `previous1` and `previous2` are the first two elements of the sequence, supplied by the user. From the preceding discussion, it follows that you need five variables.

MAIN ALGORITHM

1. Prompt the user for the first two numbers—that is, `previous1` and `previous2`.

2. Read (input) the first two numbers into `previous1` and `previous2`.

3. Output the first two Fibonacci numbers. (Echo input.)

4. Prompt the user for the position of the desired Fibonacci number.

5. Read the position of the desired Fibonacci number into `nthFibonacci`.

6. a. `if` (`nthFibonacci == 1`)
      the desired Fibonacci number is the first Fibonacci number.
      Copy the value of `previous1` into `current`.

   b. `else if` (`nthFibonacci == 2`)
      the desired Fibonacci number is the second Fibonacci number.
      Copy the value of `previous2` into `current`.

   c. `else` calculate the desired Fibonacci number as follows:

      Because you already know the first two Fibonacci numbers of the sequence, start by determining the third Fibonacci number.

    c.1. Initialize `counter` to 3, to keep track of the calculated Fibonacci numbers.

    c.2. Calculate the next Fibonacci number, as follows:

```cpp
current = previous2 + previous1;
```

    c.3. Assign the value of `previous2` to `previous1`.

    c.4. Assign the value of `current` to `previous2`.

    c.5. Increment `counter`.

Repeat Steps c.2 through c.5 until the Fibonacci number you want is calculated.

The following `while` loop executes Steps c.2 through c.5 and determines the *n*th Fibonacci number.

```cpp
while (counter <= nthFibonacci)
{
    current = previous2 + previous1;
    previous1 = previous2;
    previous2 = current;
    counter++;
}
```

7. Output the `nthFibonacci` number, which is current.

COMPLETE PROGRAM LISTING

```cpp
//Program: nth Fibonacci number

#include <iostream>

using namespace std;

int main()
{
        //Declare variables
    int previous1;
    int previous2;
    int current;
    int counter;
    int nthFibonacci;

    cout << "Enter the first two Fibonacci "
         << "numbers: ";                                //Step 1
    cin >> previous1 >> previous2;                      //Step 2
    cout << endl;
    cout << "The first two Fibonacci numbers are "
         << previous1 << " and " << previous2
         << endl;                                       //Step 3
```

```cpp
    cout << "Enter the position of the desired "
         << "Fibonacci number: ";                      //Step 4
    cin >> nthFibonacci;                               //Step 5
    cout << endl;

    if (nthFibonacci == 1)                             //Step 6.a
        current = previous1;
    else if (nthFibonacci == 2)                        //Step 6.b
            current = previous2;
    else                                               //Step 6.c
    {
        counter = 3;                                   //Step 6.c.1

                //Steps 6.c.2 - 6.c.5
        while (counter <= nthFibonacci)
        {
            current = previous2 + previous1;           //Step 6.c.2
            previous1 = previous2;                     //Step 6.c.3
            previous2 = current;                       //Step 6.c.4
            counter++;                                 //Step 6.c.5
        }//end while
    }//end else

    cout << "The Fibonacci number at position "
         << nthFibonacci << " is " << current
         << endl;                                      //Step 7

    return 0;
}//end main
```

Sample Runs: In these sample runs, the user input is shaded. This program was executed three times.

Sample Run 1:

```
Enter the first two Fibonacci numbers: 12 16

The first two Fibonacci numbers are 12 and 16
Enter the position of the desired Fibonacci number: 10

The Fibonacci number at position 10 is 796
```

Sample Run 2:

```
Enter the first two Fibonacci numbers: 1 1

The first two Fibonacci numbers are 1 and 1
Enter the position of the desired Fibonacci number: 15

The Fibonacci number at position 15 is 610
```

Sample Run 3:

```
Enter the first two Fibonacci numbers:  20 25

The first two Fibonacci numbers are 20 and 25
Enter the position of the desired Fibonacci number:  10

The Fibonacci number at position 10 is 1270
```

for Looping (Repetition) Structure

The **while** loop discussed in the previous section is general enough to implement most forms of repetitions. The C++ **for** looping structure discussed here is a specialized form of the **while** loop. Its primary purpose is to simplify the writing of count-controlled loops. For this reason, the **for** loop is typically called a counted or indexed **for** loop.

The general form of the **for** statement is:

```
for (initial statement; loop condition; update statement)
    statement
```

The **initial statement**, **loop condition**, and **update statement** (called **for** loop control statements) enclosed within the parentheses control the body (**statement**) of the **for** statement. Figure 5-2 shows the flow of execution of a **for** loop.

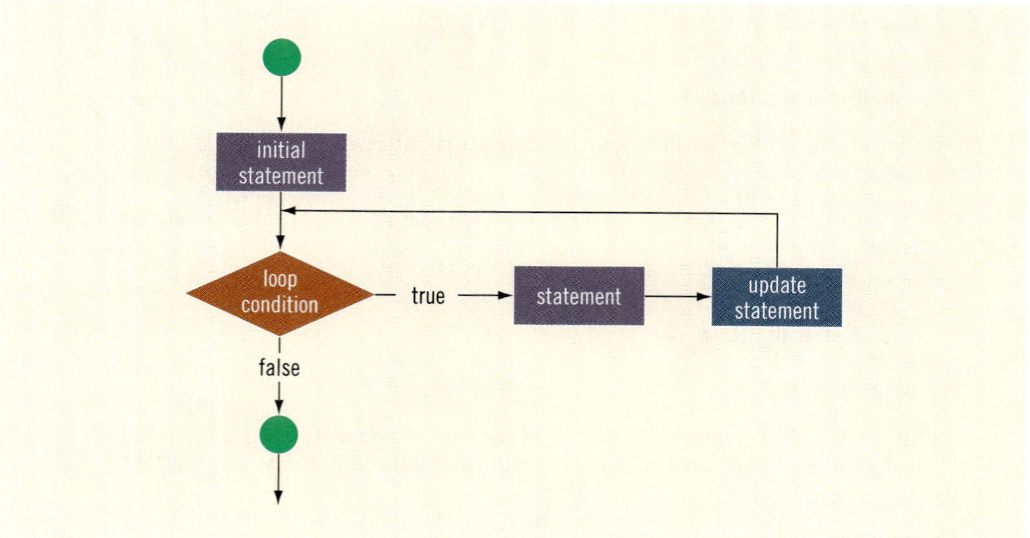

FIGURE 5-2 **for** loop

The **for** loop executes as follows:

1. The `initial statement` executes.
2. The `loop condition` is evaluated. If the `loop condition` evaluates to **true**
   i. Execute the **for** loop `statement`.
   ii. Execute the `update statement` (the third expression in the parentheses).
3. Repeat Step 2 until the `loop condition` evaluates to **false**.

The `initial statement` usually initializes a variable (called the **for** **loop control**, or **for** **indexed, variable**).

In C++, **for** is a reserved word.

NOTE As the name implies, the initial statement in the **for** loop is the first statement to execute; it executes only once.

EXAMPLE 5-7

The following **for** loop prints the first 10 non-negative integers:

```
for (i = 0; i < 10; i++)
    cout << i << " ";
cout << endl;
```

The `initial statement`, i = 0;, initializes the **int** variable i to 0. Next, the loop condition, i < 10, is evaluated. Because 0 < 10 is **true**, the print statement executes and outputs 0. The `update statement`, i++, then executes, which sets the value of i to 1. Once again, the `loop condition` is evaluated, which is still **true**, and so on. When i becomes 10, the `loop condition` evaluates to **false**, the **for** loop terminates, and the statement following the **for** loop executes.

A **for** loop can have either a simple or compound statement.

The following examples further illustrate how a **for** loop executes.

EXAMPLE 5-8

1. The following **for** loop outputs `Hello!` and a star (on separate lines) five times:

```
for (i = 1; i <= 5; i++)
{
    cout << "Hello!" << endl;
    cout << "*" << endl;
}
```

2. Consider the following **for** loop:

```cpp
for (i = 1; i <= 5; i++)
    cout << "Hello!" << endl;
    cout << "*" << endl;
```

This loop outputs `Hello!` five times and the star only once. Note that the **for** loop controls only the first output statement because the two output statements are not made into a compound statement. Therefore, the first output statement executes five times because the **for** loop body executes five times. After the **for** loop executes, the second output statement executes only once.

EXAMPLE 5-9

The following **for** loop executes five empty statements:

```cpp
for (i = 0; i < 5; i++);      //Line 1
    cout << "*" << endl;      //Line 2
```

The semicolon at the end of the **for** statement (before the output statement, Line 1) terminates the **for** loop. The action of this **for** loop is empty, that is, null.

The preceding examples show that care is required in getting a **for** loop to perform the desired action.

The following are some comments on **for** loops:

- If the **loop condition** is initially **false**, the loop body does not execute.

- The **update expression**, when executed, changes the value of the loop control variable (initialized by the initial expression), which eventually sets the value of the **loop condition** to **false**. The **for** loop body executes indefinitely if the **loop condition** is always **true**.

- C++ allows you to use fractional values for loop control variables of the **double** type (or any real data type). Because different computers can give these loop control variables different results, you should avoid using such variables.

- A semicolon at the end of the **for** statement (just before the body of the loop) is a semantic error. In this case, the action of the **for** loop is empty.

- In the **for** statement, if the **loop condition** is omitted, it is assumed to be **true**.

- In a **for** statement, you can omit all three statements—initial statement, **loop condition**, and **update statement**. The following is a legal **for** loop:

```
for (;;)
    cout << "Hello" << endl;
```

This is an infinite **for** loop, continuously printing the word Hello.

Following are more examples of **for** loops.

EXAMPLE 5-10

You can count backward using a **for** loop if the **for** loop control expressions are set correctly.

For example, consider the following **for** loop:

```
for (i = 10; i >= 1; i--)
    cout << " " << i;
cout << endl;
```

The output is:

```
10 9 8 7 6 5 4 3 2 1
```

In this **for** loop, the variable i is initialized to 10. After each iteration of the loop, i is decremented by 1. The loop continues to execute as long as i >= 1.

EXAMPLE 5-11

You can increment (or decrement) the loop control variable by any fixed number. In the following **for** loop, the variable is initialized to 1; at the end of the **for** loop, i is incremented by 2. This **for** loop outputs the first 10 positive odd integers.

```
for (i = 1; i <= 20; i = i + 2)
    cout << " " << i;
cout << endl;
```

EXAMPLE 5-12

Suppose that i is an **int** variable.

1. Consider the following **for** loop:

```
for (i = 10; i <= 9; i++)
    cout << i << " ";
cout << endl;
```

In this **for** loop, the initial statement sets i to 10. Because initially the loop condition (i <= 9) is **false**, nothing happens.

2. Consider the following **for** loop:

```
for (i = 9; i >= 10; i--)
    cout << i << " ";
cout << endl;
```

In this **for** loop, the initial statement sets i to 9. Because initially the loop condition (i >= 10) is **false**, nothing happens.

3. Consider the following **for** loop:

```
for (i = 10; i <= 10; i++)          //Line 1
    cout << i << " ";               //Line 2
cout << endl;                       //Line 3
```

In this **for** loop, the initial statement sets i to 10. The loop condition (i <= 10) evaluate to **true**, so the output statement in Line 2 executes, which outputs 10. Next, the update statement increments the value of i by 1, so the value of i becomes 11. Now the loop condition evaluates to **false** and the **for** loop terminates. Note that the output statement in Line 2 executes only once.

4. Consider the following **for** loop:

```
for (i = 1; i <= 10; i++);          //Line 1
    cout << i << " ";               //Line 2
cout << endl;                       //Line 3
```

This **for** loop has no effect on the output statement in Line 2. The semicolon at the end of the **for** statement terminates the **for** loop; the action of the **for** loop is thus empty. The output statement is all by itself and executes only once.

5. Consider the following **for** loop:

```
for (i = 1;  ; i++)
    cout << i << " ";
cout << endl;
```

In this **for** loop, because the `loop condition` is omitted from the **for** statement, the `loop condition` is always **true**. This is an infinite loop.

EXAMPLE 5-13

In this example, a **for** loop reads five numbers and finds their sum and average. Consider the following program code, in which i, newNum, sum, and **average** are **int** variables.

```
sum = 0;

for (i = 1; i <= 5; i++)
{
    cin >> newNum;
    sum = sum + newNum;
}

average = sum / 5;
cout << "The sum is " << sum << endl;
cout << "The average is " << average << endl;
```

In the preceding **for** loop, after reading a newNum, this value is added to the previously calculated (partial) sum of all the numbers read before the current number. The variable sum is initialized to 0 before the **for** loop. Thus, after the program reads the first number and adds it to the value of sum, the variable sum holds the correct sum of the first number.

In the following C++ program, we recommend that you walk through each step.

EXAMPLE 5-14

The following C++ program finds the sum of the first n positive integers.

```
//Program to determine the sum of the first n positive numbers.

#include <iostream>

using namespace std;

int main()
{
    int counter;       //loop control variable
    int sum;           //variable to store the sum of numbers
    int N;             //variable to store the number of
                       //first positive integers to be added

    cout << "Line 1: Enter the number of positive "
         << "integers to be added: ";                    //Line 1
    cin >> N;                                             //Line 2
    sum = 0;                                              //Line 3
    cout << endl;                                         //Line 4

    for (counter = 1; counter <= N; counter++)           //Line 5
        sum = sum + counter;                             //Line 6

    cout << "Line 7: The sum of the first " << N
         << " positive integers is " << sum
         << endl;                                         //Line 7

    return 0;
}
```

Sample Run: In this sample run, the user input is shaded.

```
Line 1: Enter the number of positive integers to be added:  100

Line 7: The sum of the first 100 positive integers is 5050
```

The statement in Line 1 prompts the user to enter the number of first positive integers to be added. The statement in Line 2 stores the number entered by the user in N, and the statement in Line 3 initializes sum to 0. The `for` loop in Line 5 executes N times. In the `for` loop, counter is initialized to 1 and is incremented by 1 after each iteration of the loop. Therefore, counter ranges from 1 to N. Each time through the loop, the value of counter is added to sum. The variable sum was initialized to 0, counter ranges from 1 to N, and the current value of counter is added to the value of sum. Therefore, after the `for` loop executes, sum contains the sum of the first N values, which in the sample run is 100 positive integers.

Recall that putting one control structure statement inside another is called **nesting**. The following programming example demonstrates a simple instance of nesting. It also nicely demonstrates counting.

PROGRAMMING EXAMPLE: Classifying Numbers

This program reads a given set of integers and then prints the number of odd and even integers. It also outputs the number of zeros.

The program reads 20 integers, but you can easily modify it to read any set of numbers. In fact, you can modify the program so that it first prompts the user to specify how many integers are to be read.

Input   20 integers—positive, negative, or zeros.

Output   The number of zeros, even numbers, and odd numbers.

PROBLEM
ANALYSIS
AND
ALGORITHM
DESIGN

After reading a number, you need to check whether it is even or odd. Suppose the value is stored in number. Divide number by 2 and check the remainder. If the remainder is 0, number is even. Increment the even count and then check whether number is 0. If it is, increment the zero count. If the remainder is not 0, increment the odd count.

The program uses a `switch` statement to decide whether number is odd or even. Suppose that number is odd. Dividing by 2 gives the remainder 1 if number is positive and the remainder -1 if it is negative. If number is even, dividing by 2 gives the remainder 0 whether `number` is positive or negative. You can use the mod operator, `%`, to find the remainder. For example:

```
6 % 2 = 0; -4 % 2 = 0; -7 % 2 = -1; 15 % 2 = 1.
```

Repeat the preceding process of analyzing a number for each number in the list.

This discussion translates into the following algorithm:

1. For each number in the list

    a. Get the number.
    b. Analyze the number.
    c. Increment the appropriate count.

2. Print the results.

Variables Because you want to count the number of zeros, even numbers, and odd numbers, you need three variables of type `int`—say, `zeros`, `evens`, and `odds`—to track the counts. You also need a variable—say, `number`—to read and store the number to be analyzed and another variable—say, `counter`—to count the numbers analyzed. Therefore, you need the following variables in the program:

```
int counter;    //loop control variable
int number;     //variable to store the number read
int zeros;      //variable to store the zero count
int evens;      //variable to store the even count
int odds;       //variable to store the odd count
```

Clearly, you must initialize the variables `zeros`, `evens`, and `odds` to zero. You can initialize these variables when you declare them.

MAIN ALGORITHM

1. Initialize the variables.
2. Prompt the user to enter 20 numbers.
3. For each number in the list:

    a. Read the number.
    b. Output the number (echo input).
    c. If the number is even
        ```
        {
        ```
        i.   Increment the even count.
        ii. If the number is zero, increment the zero count.
        ```
        }
        otherwise
            Increment the odd count.
        ```

4. Print the results.

Before writing the C++ program, let us describe Steps 1–4 in more detail. It will be much easier for you to then write the instructions in C++.

1. Initialize the variables. You can initialize the variables `zeros`, `evens`, and `odds` when you declare them.

2. Use an output statement to prompt the user to enter 20 numbers.

3. For Step 3, you can use a `for` loop to process and analyze the 20 numbers. In pseudocode, this step is written as follows:

```
for (counter = 1; counter <= 20; counter++)
{
    read the number;
    output number;

    switch (number % 2)    // check the remainder
    {
    case 0:
        increment even count;
        if (number == 0)
            increment zero count;
        break;
    case 1:
    case -1:
        increment odd count;
    }//end switch
}//end for
```

4. Print the result. Output the value of the variables `zeros`, `evens`, and `odds`.

COMPLETE PROGRAM LISTING

```cpp
//************************************************************
// Program: Counts zeros, odds, and evens
// This program counts the number of odd and even numbers.
// The program also counts the number of zeros.
//************************************************************

#include <iostream>
#include <iomanip>

using namespace std;

const int N = 20;

int main()
{
        //Declare variables
    int counter;    //loop control variable
    int number;     //variable to store the new number
```

```cpp
    int zeros = 0;                                          //Step 1
    int odds = 0;                                           //Step 1
    int evens = 0;                                          //Step 1

    cout << "Please enter " << N << " integers, "
         << "positive, negative, or zeros."
         << endl;                                           //Step 2

    cout << "The numbers you entered are:" << endl;

    for (counter = 1; counter <= N; counter++)             //Step 3
    {
        cin >> number;                                     //Step 3a
        cout << number << " ";                             //Step 3b

            //Step 3c
        switch (number % 2)
        {
        case 0:
            evens++;
            if (number == 0)
                zeros++;
            break;
        case 1:
        case -1:
            odds++;
        } //end switch
    } //end for loop

    cout << endl;
                    //Step 4
    cout << "There are " << evens << " evens, "
         << "which includes " << zeros << " zeros."
         << endl;
    cout << "The number of odd numbers is: " << odds
         << endl;

    return 0;
}
```

Sample Run: In this sample run, the user input is shaded.

```
Please enter 20 integers, positive, negative, or zeros.
The numbers you entered are:
0 0 -2 -3 -5 6 7 8 0 3 0 -23 -8 0 2 9 0 12 67 54
0 0 -2 -3 -5 6 7 8 0 3 0 -23 -8 0 2 9 0 12 67 54
There are 13 evens, which includes 6 zeros.
The number of odd numbers is: 7
```

We recommend that you do a walk-through of this program using the above sample input.

do...while Looping (Repetition) Structure

This section describes the third type of looping or repetition structure, called a do...while loop. The general form of a do...while statement is as follows:

```
do
    statement
while (expression);
```

Of course, `statement` can be either a simple or compound statement. If it is a compound statement, enclose it between braces. Figure 5-3 shows the flow of execution of a do...while loop.

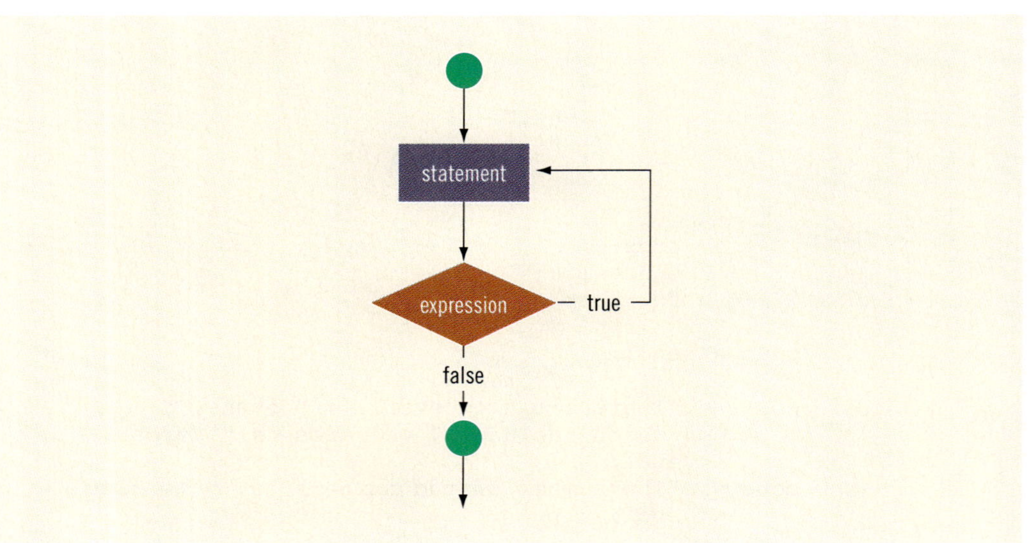

FIGURE 5-3 do...while loop

In C++, do is a reserved word.

The **statement** executes first, and then the **expression** is evaluated. If the **expression** evaluates to **true**, the **statement** executes again. As long as the **expression** in a **do...while** statement is **true**, the **statement** executes. To avoid an infinite loop, you must, once again, make sure that the loop body contains a statement that ultimately makes the **expression false** and assures that it exits properly.

EXAMPLE 5-15

```
i = 0;

do
{
    cout << i << " ";
    i = i + 5;
}
while (i <= 20);
```

The output of this code is:

```
0 5 10 15 20
```

After 20 is output, the statement:

```
i = i + 5;
```

changes the value of i to 25 and so i <= 20 becomes **false**, which halts the loop.

In a **while** and **for** loop, the loop condition is evaluated before executing the body of the loop. Therefore, **while** and **for** loops are called **pretest loops**. On the other hand, the loop condition in a **do...while** loop is evaluated after executing the body of the loop. Therefore, **do...while** loops are called **posttest loops**.

Because the **while** and **for** loops both have entry conditions, these loops may never activate. The **do...while** loop, on the other hand, has an exit condition and therefore always executes the statement at least once.

EXAMPLE 5-16

Consider the following two loops:

```
a.  i = 11;
    while (i <= 10)
    {
        cout << i << " ";
        i = i + 5;
    }
    cout << endl;
```

```
b.  i = 11;
    do
    {
        cout << i << " ";
        i = i + 5;
    }
    while (i <= 10);

    cout << endl;
```

In (a), the `while` loop produces nothing. In (b) the `do...while` loop outputs the number 11 and also changes the value of i to 16.

Divisibility Test by 3 and 9

Suppose that m and n are integers and m is nonzero. Then m is called a **divisor** of n if $n = mt$ for some integer t; that is, when m divides n, the remainder is 0.

Let $n = a_k a_{k-1} a_{k-2} \ldots a_1 a_0$ be an integer. Let $s = a_k + a_{k-1} + a_{k-2} + \cdots + a_1 + a_0$ be the sum of the digits of n. It is known that n is divisible by 3 and 9 if s is divisible by 3 and 9. In other words, an integer is divisible by 3 and 9 if and only if the sum of its digits is divisible by 3 and 9.

For example, suppose $n = 27193257$. Then $s = 2 + 7 + 1 + 9 + 3 + 2 + 5 + 7 = 36$. Because 36 is divisible by both 3 and 9, it follows that 27193257 is divisible by both 3 and 9.

Next, we write a program that determines whether a positive integer is divisible by 3 and 9 by first finding the sum of its digits and then checking whether the sum is divisible by 3 and 9.

To find the sum of the digits of a positive integer, we need to extract each digit of the number. Consider the number 951372. Note that 951372 % 10 = 2, which is the last digit of 951372. Also note that 951372 / 10 = 95137; that is, when the number is divided by 10, it removes the last digit. Next, we repeat this process on the number 95137. Of course, we need to add the extracted digits.

Suppose that `sum` and `num` are `int` variables and the positive integer is stored in `num`. We thus have the following algorithm to find the sum of the digits:

break and continue Statements

The **break** statement, when executed in a **switch** structure, provides an immediate exit from the **switch** structure. Similarly, you can use the **break** statement in **while**, **for**, and **do...while** loops. When the **break** statement executes in a repetition structure, it immediately exits from the structure. The **break** statement is typically used for two purposes:

- To exit early from a loop
- To skip the remainder of the **switch** structure

After the **break** statement executes, the program continues to execute with the first statement after the structure.

The use of a **break** statement in a loop can eliminate the use of certain (flag) variables. The following C++ code segment helps illustrate this idea. (Assume that all variables are properly declared.)

```cpp
sum = 0;
isNegative = false;

cin >> num;

while (cin && !isNegative)
{
    if (num < 0)    //if num is negative, terminate the loop
                    //after this iteration
    {
        cout << "Negative number found in the data." << endl;
        isNegative = true;
    }
    else
    {
        sum = sum + num;
        cin >> num;
    }
}
```

This **while** loop is supposed to find the sum of a set of positive numbers. If the data set contains a negative number, the loop terminates with an appropriate error message. This **while** loop uses the flag variable **isNegative** to accomplish the desired result. The variable **isNegative** is initialized to **false** before the **while** loop. Before adding **num** to **sum**, check whether **num** is negative. If **num** is negative, an error message appears on the screen and **isNegative** is set to **true**. In the next iteration, when the expression in the **while** statement is evaluated, it evaluates to **false** because **!isNegative** is **false**. (Note that because **isNegative** is **true**, **!isNegative** is **false**.)

The following **while** loop is written without using the variable **isNegative**:

```cpp
sum = 0;
cin >> num;

while (cin)
{
    if (num < 0)     //if num is negative, terminate the loop
    {
        cout << "Negative number found in the data." << endl;
        break;
    }

    sum = sum + num;
    cin >> num;
}
```

In this form of the **while** loop, when a negative number is found, the expression in the **if** statement evaluates to **true**; after printing an appropriate message, the **break** statement terminates the loop. (After executing the **break** statement in a loop, the remaining statements in the loop are discarded.)

The **continue** statement is used in **while**, **for**, and **do...while** structures. When the **continue** statement is executed in a loop, it skips the remaining statements in the loop and proceeds with the next iteration of the loop. In a **while** and **do...while** structure, the **expression** (that is, the loop-continue test) is evaluated immediately after the **continue** statement. In a **for** structure, the **update statement** is executed after the **continue** statement, and then the **loop condition** (that is, the loop-continue test) executes.

If the previous program segment encounters a negative number, the **while** loop terminates. If you want to discard the negative number and read the next number rather than terminate the loop, replace the **break** statement with the **continue** statement, as shown in the following example:

```cpp
sum = 0;
cin >> num;

while (cin)
{
    if (num < 0)
    {
        cout << "Negative number found in the data." << endl;
        cin >> num;
        continue;
    }

    sum = sum + num;
    cin >> num;
}
```

It was stated earlier that all three loops have their place in C++ and that one loop can often replace another. The execution of a **continue** statement, however, is where the **while** and **do...while** structures differ from the **for** structure. When the **continue** statement is executed in a **while** or a **do...while** loop, the update statement may not execute. In a **for** structure, the update statement *always* executes.

Nested Control Structures

This section briefly reviews the control structures discussed so far in this chapter and in Chapter 4. You have seen that by putting one control structure within another, you can achieve dramatic and productive results. Nesting of control structures takes on new power, subtlety, and complexity. Consider the following program:

```cpp
#include <iostream>

using namespace std;

int main()
{
    int studentID, testScore, count = 0;

    cout << "Enter student ID and the test score." << endl;
    cout << "To terminate the program enter -1 for student ID."
         << endl;
    cin >> studentID;
    while (studentID != -1)
    {
        count++;
        cin >> testScore;
        cout << "Student ID = " << studentID << ", test score = "
             << testScore << ", and grade = ";

        if (testScore >= 90)
            cout << "A." << endl;
        else if (testScore >= 80)
            cout << "B." << endl;
        else if (testScore >= 70)
            cout << "C." << endl;
        else if (testScore >= 60)
            cout << "D." << endl;
        else
            cout << "F." << endl;
        cin >> studentID;
    }//end while

    cout << "The number of students in class = "
         << count << endl;

    return 0;
}
```

How would this program work if you wrote it as a sequence of **if**... statements (with no **else** or as a **switch** structure) within the **while** loop?

The remainder of this section gives examples that illustrate how to use nested loops to process data and achieve impressive results.

EXAMPLE 5-18

Suppose you want to create the following pattern:

```
*
**
***
****
*****
```

Clearly, you want to print five lines of stars. In the first line, you want to print one star, in the second line, two stars, and so on. Because five lines will be printed, start with the following **for** statement:

```
for (i = 1; i <= 5; i++)
```

The value of i in the first iteration is 1, in the second iteration it is 2, and so on. You can use the value of i as the limiting condition in another **for** loop nested within this loop to control the number of stars in a line. A little more thought produces the following code:

```
for (i = 1; i <= 5; i++)                    //Line 1
{                                           //Line 2
    for (j = 1; j <= i; j++)                //Line 3
        cout << "*";                        //Line 4
    cout << endl;                           //Line 5
}                                           //Line 6
```

A walk-through of this code shows that the **for** loop, in Line 1, starts with i = 1. When i is 1, the inner **for** loop, in Line 3, outputs one star and the insertion point moves to the next line. Then i becomes 2, the inner **for** loop outputs two stars, and the output statement in Line 5 moves the insertion point to the next line, and so on. This process continues until i becomes 6 and the loop stops.

What pattern does this code produce if you replace the **for** statement, in Line 1, with the following?

```
for (i = 5; i >= 1; i--)
```

EXAMPLE 5-19

Suppose you want to create the following grid of numbers:

```
1 2 3 4 5
2 3 4 5 6
3 4 5 6 7
4 5 6 7 8
5 6 7 8 9
```

There are five lines in this grid. Therefore, as in Example 5-18, we use a **for** statement to output these lines as follows:

```
for (i = 1; i <= 5; i++)
    //output a line of numbers
```

In the first line, we want to print the numbers 1 through 5, in the second line we want to print the numbers 2 through 6, and so on. Notice that the first line starts with 1 and when this line is printed, i is 1. Similarly, the second line starts with 2 and when this line is printed, the value of i is 2, and so on. If i is 1, i + 4 is 5; if i is 2, i + 4 is 6; and so on. Therefore, to print a line of numbers we can use the value of i as the starting number and the value of i + 4 as the limiting value. That is, consider the following **for** loop:

```
for (j = i; j <= i + 4; j++)
    cout << j << " ";
```

Let us take a look at this **for** loop. Suppose i is 1. Then we are printing the first line of the grid. Also, j goes from 1 to 5 and so this **for** loop outputs the numbers 1 through 5, which is the first line of the grid. Similarly, if i is 2, we are printing the second line of the grid. Also, j goes from 2 to 6, and so this **for** loop outputs the numbers 2 through 6, which is the second line of the grid, and so on.

A little more thought produces the following nested loops to output the desired grid:

```
for (i = 1; i <= 5; i++)                    //Line 1
{                                           //Line 2
    for (j = i; j <= i + 4; j++)            //Line 3
        cout << j << " ";                   //Line 4
    cout << endl;                           //Line 5
}                                           //Line 6
```

EXAMPLE 5-20

Consider the following data:

```
65 78 65 89 25 98 -999
87 34 89 99 26 78 64 34 -999
23 99 98 97 26 78 100 63 87 23 -999
62 35 78 99 12 93 19 -999
```

The number -999 at the end of each line acts as a sentinel and therefore is not part of the data. Our objective is to find the sum of the numbers in each line and output the sum. Moreover, assume that this data is to be read from a file, say, `Exp_5_20.txt`. We assume that the input file has been opened using the input file stream variable `infile`.

This particular data set has four lines of input. So we can use a **for** loop or a counter-controlled **while** loop to process each line of data. Let us use a **while** loop to process these four lines. It follows that the **while** loop takes the following form:

```
counter = 0;                    //Line 1
while (counter < 4)             //Line 2
{                               //Line 3
        //process the line      //Line 4

        //output the sum
    counter++;
}
```

Let us now concentrate on processing a line. Each line has a varying number of data items. For example, the first line has 6 numbers, the second line has 8 numbers, and so on. Because each line ends with -999, we can use a sentinel-controlled **while** loop to find the sum of the numbers in each line. (Remember how a sentinel-controlled loop works.) Consider the following **while** loop:

```
sum = 0;                    //Line 4
infile >> num;              //Line 5
while (num != -999)         //Line 6
{                           //Line 7
    sum = sum + num;        //Line 8
    infile >> num;          //Line 9
}                           //Line 10
```

The statement in Line 4 initializes **sum** to 0, and the statement in Line 5 reads and stores the first number of the line into **num**. The Boolean expression, **num** != -999, in Line 6, checks whether the number is -999. If **num** is not -999, the statements in Lines 8 and 9 execute. The statement in Line 8 updates the value of **sum**; the statement in Line 9 reads and stores the next number into **num**. The loop continues to execute as long as **num** is not -999.

It now follows that the nested loop to process the data is as follows. (Assume that all variables are properly declared.)

```cpp
counter = 0;                                      //Line 1
while (counter < 4)                               //Line 2
{                                                 //Line 3
    sum = 0;                                      //Line 4
    infile >> num;                                //Line 5
    while (num != -999)                           //Line 6
    {                                             //Line 7
        sum = sum + num;                          //Line 8
        infile >> num;                            //Line 9
    }                                             //Line 10

    cout << "Line " << counter + 1
         << ": Sum = " << sum << endl;   //Line 11
    counter++;                                     //Line 12
}                                                 //Line 13
```

EXAMPLE 5-21

Suppose that we want to process data similar to the data in Example 5-20, but the input file is of an unspecified length. That is, each line contains the same data as the data in each line in Example 5-20, but we do not know the number of input lines.

Because we do not know the number of input lines, we must use an EOF-controlled `while` loop to process the data. In this case, the required code is as follows. (Assume that all variables are properly declared and the input file has been opened using the input file stream variable `infile`.)

```cpp
counter = 0;                                      //Line 1
infile >> num;                                    //Line 2
while (infile)                                    //Line 3
{                                                 //Line 4
    sum = 0;                                      //Line 5
    while (num != -999)                           //Line 6
    {                                             //Line 7
        sum = sum + num;                          //Line 8
        infile >> num;                            //Line 9
    }                                             //Line 10

    cout << "Line " << counter + 1
         << ": Sum = " << sum << endl;   //Line 11
    counter++;                                     //Line 12
    infile >> num;                                //Line 13
}                                                 //Line 14
```

Notice that we have again used the variable `counter`. The only reason to do so is because we want to print the line number with the sum of each line.

EXAMPLE 5-22

Consider the following data:

```
John 65 78 65 89 25 98 -999
Peter 87 34 89 99 26 78 64 34 -999
Buddy 23 99 98 97 26 78 100 63 87 23 -999
Doctor 62 35 78 99 12 93 19 -999
...
```

The number -999 at the end of each line acts as a sentinel and therefore is not part of the data. The objective is to find the sum of the numbers in each line and output the sum and average of the numbers. Moreover, assume that this data is to be read from a file, `Exp_5_22.txt`, of unknown size. We assume that the input file has been opened using the input file stream variable `infile`.

As in Example 5-21, because the input file is of an unspecified length, we use an EOF-controlled `while` loop. The first data item in each line is a string, and the remaining data items are numbers. Therefore, for each line, first we read and store the name in a `string` variable, say, `name`. Then we process the numbers in each line. The necessary `while` loop takes the following form:

```cpp
infile >> name;                                   //Line 1
while (infile)                                     //Line 2
{                                                  //Line 3
    //process the numbers in each line    //Line 4
    //output the name and average
    infile >> name;       //begin processing the next line
}
```

In this example, for the numbers in each line, we want to find the average. Therefore, we must add the numbers as well as count them. The required `while` loop is:

```cpp
sum = 0;                    //Line 4
count = 0;                  //Line 5
infile >> num;             //Line 6; read the first number
while (num != -999)         //Line 7
{                           //Line 8
    sum = sum + num;        //Line 9; update sum
    count++;                //Line 10; update count
    infile >> num;          //Line 11; read the next number
}                           //Line 12
```

We can now write the following nested loop to process the data as follows:

```cpp
infile >> name;                         //Line 1
while (infile)                          //Line 2
{                                       //Line 3
    sum = 0;                            //Line 4
    count = 0;                          //Line 5
    infile >> num;                      //Line 6; read the first number
    while (num != -999)                 //Line 7
    {                                   //Line 8
        sum = sum + num;                //Line 9; update sum
        count++;                        //Line 10; update count
        infile >> num;                  //Line 11; read the next number
    }

        //find the average
    if (count != 0)                     //Line 12
        average = sum / count;          //Line 13
    else                                //Line 14
        average = 0;                    //Line 15

    cout << name << " "
        << average << endl;             //Line 16

    infile >> name; //Line 17; begin processing the next line
}
```

EXAMPLE 5-23

Consider the following data:

```
101
John Smith
65 78 65 89 25 98 -999
102
Peter Gupta
87 34 89 99 26 78 64 34 -999
103
Buddy Friend
23 99 98 97 26 78 100 63 87 23 -999
104
Doctor Miller
62 35 78 99 12 93 19 -999
...
```

The number -999 at the end of a line acts as a sentinel and therefore is not part of
the data.

Assume that this is the data of certain candidates seeking the student council's presidential seat.

For each candidate, the data is in the following form:

```
ID
Name
Votes
```

The objective is to find the total number of votes received by the candidate. We assume that the data is input from the file, `Exp_5_23.txt`, of unknown size. We also assume that the input file has been opened using the input file stream variable `infile`.

As in Example 5-22, because the input file is of an unspecified length we use an EOF-controlled `while` loop. For each candidate, the first data item is the `ID` of type `int` on a line by itself; the second data item is the name, which may consist of more than one word; and the third line contains the votes received from the various departments.

To read the `ID`, we use the extraction operator `>>`; to read the name, we use the stream function `getline`. Notice that after reading the `ID`, the reading marker is after the `ID` and the character after the `ID` is the newline character. Therefore, after reading the `ID`, the reading marker is after the `ID` and before the newline character (of the line containing the `ID`).

The function `getline` reads until the end of the line. Therefore, if we read the name immediately after reading the `ID`, then what is stored in the variable name is the newline character (after the `ID`). It follows that to read the name, we must read and discard the newline character after the `ID`, which we can accomplish using the stream function `get`. Therefore, the statements to read the `ID` and name are as follows:

```
infile >> ID;              //read the ID
infile.get(ch);            //read the newline character after the ID
getline(infile, name);     //read the name
```

(Assume that `ch` is a variable of type `char`.) The general loop to process the data is:

```
infile >> ID;                                  //Line 1
while (infile)                                 //Line 2
{                                              //Line 3
    infile.get(ch);                            //Line 4
    getline(infile, name);                     //Line 5

    //process the numbers in each line    //Line 6
    //output the name and total votes
    infile >> ID;    //begin processing the next line
}
```

The code to read and sum up the voting data is the same as in Example 5-21. That is, the required `while` loop is:

```
sum = 0;                           //Line 6
infile >> num;                     //Line 7; read the first number
while (num != -999)                //Line 8
{                                  //Line 9
    sum = sum + num;               //Line 10; update sum
    infile >> num;                 //Line 11; read the next number
}                                  //Line 12
```

We can now write the following nested loop to process data as follows:

```
infile >> ID;                         //Line 1
while (infile)                        //Line 2
{                                     //Line 3
    infile.get(ch);                   //Line 4
    getline(infile, name);            //Line 5
    sum = 0;                          //Line 6
    infile >> num;                    //Line 7; read the first number
    while (num != -999)               //Line 8
    {                                 //Line 9
        sum = sum + num;              //Line 10; update sum
        infile >> num;               //Line 11; read the next number
    }

    cout << "Name: " << name
         << ", Votes: " << sum
         << endl;                     //Line 12

    infile >> ID;         //Line 13; begin processing the next line
}
```

QUICK REVIEW

1. C++ has three looping (repetition) structures: **while**, **for**, and **do...while**.

2. The syntax of the **while** statement is:

   ```
   while (expression)
        statement
   ```

3. In C++, **while** is a reserved word.

4. In the **while** statement, the parentheses around the **expression** (the decision maker) are important; they mark the beginning and end of the expression.

5. The **statement** is called the body of the loop.

6. The body of the **while** loop must contain a statement that eventually sets the expression to **false**.

7. A counter-controlled **while** loop uses a counter to control the loop.

8. In a counter-controlled `while` loop, you must initialize the counter before the loop, and the body of the loop must contain a statement that changes the value of the counter variable.

9. A sentinel is a special value that marks the end of the input data. The sentinel must be similar to, yet differ from, all the data items.

10. A sentinel-controlled `while` loop uses a sentinel to control the `while` loop. The `while` loop continues to execute until the sentinel is read.

11. An EOF-controlled `while` loop continues to execute until the program detects the end-of-file marker.

12. In the Windows console environment, the end-of-file marker is entered using `Ctrl+z` (hold the `Ctrl` key and press `z`). In the UNIX environment, the end-of-file marker is entered using `Ctrl+d` (hold the `Ctrl` key and press `d`).

13. A `for` loop simplifies the writing of a count-controlled `while` loop.

14. In C++, `for` is a reserved word.

15. The syntax of the `for` loop is:

```
for (initialize statement; loop condition; update statement)
    statement
```

statement is called the body of the `for` loop.

16. Putting a semicolon at the end of the `for` loop (before the body of the `for` loop) is a semantic error. In this case, the action of the `for` loop is empty.

17. The syntax of the `do...while` statement is:

```
do
    statement
while (expression);
```

statement is called the body of the `do...while` loop.

18. Both `while` and `for` loops are called pretest loops. A `do...while` loop is called a posttest loop.

19. The `while` and `for` loops may not execute at all, but the `do...while` loop always executes at least once.

20. Executing a `break` statement in the body of a loop immediately terminates the loop.

21. Executing a `continue` statement in the body of a loop skips the loop's remaining statements and proceeds with the next iteration.

22. When a `continue` statement executes in a `while` or `do...while` loop, the expression update statement in the body of the loop may not execute.

23. After a `continue` statement executes in a `for` loop, the update statement is the next statement executed.

EXERCISES

1. Mark the following statements as true or false.

   a. In a counter-controlled `while` loop, it is not necessary to initialize the loop control variable.

   b. It is possible that the body of a `while` loop may not execute at all.

   c. In an infinite `while` loop, the `while` expression (the decision maker) is initially false, but after the first iteration it is always true.

   d. The `while` loop:

   ```
   j = 0;
   while (j <= 10)
       j++;
   ```

   terminates if `j > 10`.

   e. A sentinel-controlled `while` loop is an event-controlled `while` loop whose termination depends on a special value.

   f. A loop is a control structure that causes certain statements to execute over and over.

   g. To read data from a file of an unspecified length, an EOF-controlled loop is a good choice.

   h. When a `while` loop terminates, the control first goes back to the statement just before the `while` statement, and then the control goes to the statement immediately following the `while` loop.

2. What is the output of the following C++ code?

   ```cpp
   count = 1;
   y = 100;
   while (count < 100)
   {
       y = y - 1;
       count++;
   }
   cout << " y = " << y << " and count = " << count << endl;
   ```

3. What is the output of the following C++ code?

   ```cpp
   num = 5;
   while (num > 5)
       num = num + 2;
   cout << num << endl;
   ```

4. What is the output of the following C++ code?

   ```cpp
   num = 1;
   while (num < 10)
   {
   ```

```
        cout << num << " ";
        num = num + 2;
    }
    cout << endl;
```

5. When does the following `while` loop terminate?

```
ch = 'D';
while ('A' <= ch && ch <= 'Z')
    ch = static_cast<char>(static_cast<int>(ch) + 1);
```

6. Suppose that the input is 38   45   71   4   -1. What is the output of the following code? Assume all variables are properly declared.

```
cin >> sum;
cin >> num;

for (j = 1; j <= 3; j++)
{
    cin >> num;
    sum = sum + num;
}
cout << "Sum = " << sum << endl;
```

7. Suppose that the input is 38   45   71   4   -1. What is the output of the following code? Assume all variables are properly declared.

```
cin >> sum;
cin >> num;

while (num != -1)
{
    sum = sum + num;
    cin >> num;
}
cout << "Sum = " << sum << endl;
```

8. Suppose that the input is 38   45   71   4   -1. What is the output of the following code? Assume all variables are properly declared.

```
cin >> num;
sum = num;

while (num != -1)
{
    cin >> num;
    sum = sum + num;
}
cout << "Sum = " << sum << endl;
```

9. Suppose that the input is 38   45   71   4   -1. What is the output of the following code? Assume all variables are properly declared.

```
sum = 0;
cin >> num;
```

```
    while (num != -1)
    {
        sum = sum + num;
        cin >> num;
    }
    cout << "Sum = " << sum << endl;
```

10. Correct the following code so that it finds the sum of 10 numbers.

```
sum = 0;

while (count < 10)
    cin >> num;
    sum = sum + num;
    count++;
```

11. What is the output of the following program?

```cpp
#include <iostream>

using namespace std;

int main()
{
    int  x, y, z;

    x = 4;    y = 5;
    z = y + 6;

    while(((z - x) % 4) != 0)
    {
        cout << z << " ";
        z = z + 7;
    }
    cout << endl;

    return 0;
}
```

12. Suppose that the input is:

```
58   23   46   75   98   150   12   176   145 -999
```

What is the output of the following program?

```cpp
#include <iostream>

using namespace std;

int main()
{
    int num;

    cin >> num;
```

```cpp
        while (num != -999)
        {
            cout << num % 25 << "   ";
            cin >> num;
        }

        cout << endl;

        return 0;
    }
```

13. Given:

```cpp
for (i = 12; i <= 25; i++)
    cout << i;
```

   a. The seventh integer printed is ________________________.

   b. The statement produces ____________________ lines of output.

   c. If i++ were changed to i--, a compilation error would result. True or false?

14. Given that the following code is correctly inserted into a program, state its entire output as to content and form.

```cpp
num = 0;
for (i = 1; i <= 4; i++)
{
    num = num + 10 * (i - 1);
    cout << num << " ";
}
cout << endl;
```

15. Given that the following code is correctly inserted into a program, state its entire output as to content and form.

```cpp
j = 2;
for (i = 0; i <= 5; i++)
{
    cout << j << " ";
    j = 2 * j + 3;
}
cout << j << " " << endl;
```

16. Assume that the following code is correctly inserted into a program:

```cpp
int s = 0;

for (i = 0; i < 5; i++)
{
    s = 2 * s + i;
    cout << s << " ";
}
cout << endl;
```

a. What is the final value of s?
    (i) 11   (ii) 4   (iii) 26   (iv) none of these

b. If a semicolon is inserted after the right parentheses in the **for** loop statement, what is the final value of s?
    (i) 0   (ii) 1   (iii) 2   (iv) 5   (v) none of these

c. If the 5 is replaced with a 0 in the **for** loop control expression, what is the final value of s?
    (i) 0   (ii) 1   (iii) 2   (iv) none of these

17. State what output, if any, results from each of the following statements:

a.
```
for (i = 1; i <= 1; i++)
    cout << "*";
cout << endl;
```

b.
```
for (i = 2; i >= 1; i++)
    cout << "*";
cout << endl;
```

c.
```
for (i = 1; i <= 1; i--)
    cout << "*";
cout << endl;
```

d.
```
for (i = 12; i >= 9; i--)
    cout << "*";
cout << endl;
```

e.
```
for (i = 0; i <= 5; i++)
    cout << "*";
cout << endl;
```

f.
```
for (i = 1; i <= 5; i++)
{
    cout << "*";
    i = i + 1;
}
cout << endl;
```

18. Write a **for** statement to add all the multiples of 3 between 1 and 100.

19. What is the exact output of the following program?

```cpp
#include <iostream>

using namespace std;

int main()
{
    int counter;
    for (counter = 7; counter <= 16; counter++)
        switch (counter % 10)
        {
        case 0:
            cout << ", ";
            break;
        case 1:
            cout << "OFTEN ";
            break;
        case 2:
        case 8:
            cout << "IS ";
            break;
        case 3:
            cout << "NOT ";
            break;
        case 4:
        case 9:
            cout << "DONE ";
            break;
        case 5:
            cout << "WELL";
            break;
        case 6:
            cout << ".";
            break;
        case 7:
            cout << "WHAT ";
             break;
        default:
            cout << "Bad number. ";
        }
    cout << endl;

    return 0;
}
```

20. Suppose that the input is 5 3 8. What is the output of the following code? Assume all variables are properly declared.

```cpp
cin >> a >> b >> c;
for (j = 1; j < a; j++)
{
    d = b + c;
    b = c;
    c = d;
    cout << c << " ";
}
cout << endl;
```

21. What is the output of the following C++ program segment? Assume all variables are properly declared.

```cpp
for (j = 0; j < 8; j++)
{
    cout << j * 25 << " - ";

    if (j != 7)
        cout << (j + 1) * 25 - 1 << endl;
    else
        cout << (j + 1) * 25 << endl;
}
```

22. The following program has more than five mistakes that prevent it from compiling and/or running. Correct all such mistakes:

```cpp
#include <iostream>

using namespace std;
const int N = 2,137;

main ()
{
    int a, b, c, d:

    a := 3;
    b = 5;
    c = c + d;
    N = a + n;
    for (i = 3; i <= N; i++)
    {
        cout << setw(5) << i;
        i = i + 1;
    }
    return 0;
}
```

23. Which of the following apply to the **while** loop only? To the **do...while** loop only? To both?

a. It is considered a conditional loop.

b. The body of the loop executes at least once.

c. The logical expression controlling the loop is evaluated before the loop is entered.

d. The body of the loop may not execute at all.

24. How many times will each of the following loops execute? What is the output in each case?

a.
```
x = 5;   y = 50;
do
     x = x + 10;
while (x < y);
cout << x << " " << y << endl;
```

b.
```
x = 5;   y = 80;
do
     x = x * 2;
while (x < y);
cout << x << " " << y << endl;
```

c.
```
x = 5;   y = 20;
do
     x = x + 2;
while (x >= y);
cout << x << " " << y << endl;
```

d.
```
x = 5;   y = 35;
while (x < y)
     x = x + 10;
cout << x << " " << y << endl;
```

e.
```
x = 5;   y = 30;
while (x <= y)
     x = x * 2;
cout << x << " " << y << endl;
```

f.
```
x = 5;   y = 30;
while (x > y)
     x = x + 2;
cout << x << " " << y << endl;
```

25. The do...while loop in the following program is supposed to read some numbers until it reaches a sentinel (in this case, −1). It is supposed to add all of the numbers except for the sentinel. If the data looks like:

```
12     5    30    48    −1
```

the program does not add the numbers correctly. Correct the program so that it adds the numbers correctly.

```cpp
#include <iostream>

using namespace std;
int main()
{
    int total = 0,
        count = 0,
        number;
    do
    {
        cin >> number;
        total = total + number;
        count++;
    }
    while (number != -1);

    cout << "The number of data read is " << count << endl;
    cout << "The sum of the numbers entered is  " << total
        << endl;

    return 0;
}
```

26. Using the same data as in Exercise 25, the following two loops also fail. Correct them.

    a.

    ```cpp
    cin >> number;

    while (number != -1)
        total =  total + number;
        cin >> number;
        cout << endl;
        cout << total << endl;
    ```

    b.

    ```cpp
    cin >> number;
    while (number != -1)
    {
        cin >> number;
        total = total + number;
    }
    cout << endl;
    cout << total << endl;
    ```

27. Given the following program segment:

    ```cpp
    for (number = 1; number <= 10; number++)
        cout << setw(3) << number;
    ```

    write a **while** loop and a **do...while** loop that have the same output.

28. Given the following program segment:

```
j = 2;
for (i = 1; i <= 5; i++);
{
    cout << setw(4) << j;
    j = j + 5;
}
cout << endl;
```

write a **while** loop and a **do...while** loop that have the same output.

29. What is the output of the following program?

```
#include <iostream>

using namespace std;

int main()
{
    int x, y, z;
    x = 4;   y = 5;
    z = y + 6;
    do
    {
            cout << z << " ";
            z = z + 7;
    }
    while (((z - x) % 4) != 0);

    cout << endl;

    return 0;
}
```

30. To learn how nested **for** loops work, do a walk-through of the following program segments and determine, in each case, the exact output.

    a.

```
int i, j;
for (i = 1; i <= 5; i++)
{
    for (j = 1; j <= 5; j++)
        cout << setw(3) << i * j;
    cout << endl;
}
```

b.

```cpp
int i, j;

for (i = 1; i <= 5; i++)
{
    for (j = 1; j <= 5; j++)
        cout << setw(3) << i;
    cout << endl;
}
```

c.

```cpp
int i, j;
for (i = 1; i <= 5; i++)
{
    for (j = (i + 1); j <= 5; j++)
        cout << setw(5) << j;
    cout << endl;
}
```

d.

```cpp
int i, j;
for (i = 1; i <= 5; i++)
{
    for (j = 1; j <= i; j++)
        cout << setw(3) << j;
    cout << endl;
}
```

e.

```cpp
const int M = 10;
const int N = 10;
int i, j;

for (i = 1; i <= M; i++)
{
    for (j = 1; j <= N; j++)
        cout << setw(3) << M * (i - 1) + j;
    cout << endl;
}
```

f.

```cpp
int i, j;

for (i = 1; i <= 9; i++)
{
    for (j = 1; j <= (9 - i); j++)
        cout << " ";
    for (j = 1; j <= i; j++)
        cout << setw(1) << j;
    for (j = (i - 1); j >= 1; j--)
        cout << setw(1) << j;
    cout << endl;
}
```

PROGRAMMING EXERCISES

1. Write a program that prompts the user to input an integer and then outputs both the individual digits of the number and the sum of the digits. For example, it should output the individual digits of 3456 as 3 4 5 6, output the individual digits of 8030 as 8 0 3 0, output the individual digits of 2345526 as 2 3 4 5 5 2 6, output the individual digits of 4000 as 4 0 0 0, and output the individual digits of −2345 as 2 3 4 5.

2. Write a program that prompts the user to input an integer and then outputs the number with the digits reversed. For example, if the input is 12345, the output should be 54321. Your program must also output 5000 as 0005 and 980 as 089.

3. Rewrite the program of Example 5-5, Telephone Digits. Replace the statements from Line 10 to Line 28 so that it uses only a `switch` structure to find the digit that corresponds to an uppercase letter.

4. The program Telephone Digits outputs only telephone digits that correspond to uppercase letters. Rewrite the program so that it processes both uppercase and lowercase letters and outputs the corresponding telephone digit. If the input is other than an uppercase or lowercase letter, the program must output an appropriate error message.

5. To make telephone numbers easier to remember, some companies use letters to show their telephone number. For example, using letters, the telephone number 438−5626 can be shown as GET LOAN. In some cases, to make a telephone number meaningful, companies might use more than seven letters. For example, 225−5466 can be displayed as CALL HOME, which uses eight letters. Write a program that prompts the user to enter a telephone number expressed in letters and outputs the corresponding telephone number in digits. If the user enters more than 7 letters, then process only the first seven letters. Also output the − (hyphen) after the third digit. Allow the user to use both uppercase and lowercase letters as well as spaces between words. Moreover, your program should process as many telephone numbers as the user wants.

6. Write a program that reads a set of integers, and then finds and prints the sum of the even and odd integers.

7. Write a program that prompts the user to input a positive integer. It should then output a message indicating whether the number is a prime number. (*Note:* An even number is prime if it is 2. An odd integer is prime if it is not divisible by any odd integer less than or equal to the square root of the number.)

8. Let $n = a_k a_{k-1} a_{k-2} \ldots a_1 a_0$ be an integer and $t = a_0 - a_1 + a_2 - \cdots + (-1)^k a_k$. It is known that n is divisible by 11 if and only if t is divisible by 11. For example, suppose that $n = 8784204$. Then $t = 4 - 0 + 2 - 4 + 8 - 7 + 8 = 11$. Because 11 is divisible by 11, it follows that 8784204 is divisible by 11.

If $n = 54063297$, then $t = 7 - 9 + 2 - 3 + 6 - 0 + 4 - 5 = 2$. Because 2 is not divisible by 11, 54063297 is not divisible by 11. Write a program that prompts the user to enter a positive integer and then uses this criterion to determine whether the number is divisible by 11.

9. Write a program that uses `while` loops to perform the following steps:

   a. Prompt the user to input two integers: `firstNum` and `secondNum` (`firstNum` must be less than `secondNum`).

   b. Output all odd numbers between `firstNum` and `secondNum`.

   c. Output the sum of all even numbers between `firstNum` and `secondNum`.

   d. Output the numbers and their squares between 1 and 10.

   e. Output the sum of the square of the odd numbers between `firstNum` and `secondNum`.

   f. Output all uppercase letters.

10. Redo Exercise 8 using `for` loops.

11. Redo Exercise 8 using `do...while` loops.

12. The program in the Programming Example Fibonacci Number does not check whether the first number entered by the user is less than or equal to the second number and whether both the numbers are non-negative. Also, the program does not check whether the user entered a valid value for the position of the desired number in the Fibonacci sequence. Rewrite that program so that it checks for these things.

13. Suppose that m and n are integers and m is nonzero. Recall that m is called a *divisor* of n if $n = mt$ for some integer t; that is, when m divides n, the remainder is 0. Moreover, m is called a **proper divisor** of n if $m < n$ and m divides n. A positive integer is called **perfect** if it is the sum of its positive proper divisors. For example, the positive proper divisors of 28 are 1, 2, 4, 7, and 14 and $1 + 2 + 4 + 7 + 14 = 28$. Therefore, 28 is perfect. Write a program that does the following:

   a. Outputs the first four perfect integers.

   b. Takes as input a positive integer and then outputs whether the integer is perfect.

14. The program in Example 5-6 implements the Number Guessing Game. However, in that program the user is given as many tries as needed to guess the correct number. Rewrite the program so that the user has no more than five tries to guess the correct number. Your program should print an appropriate message, such as "You win!" or "You lose!".

15. Example 5-6 implements the Number Guessing Game program. If the guessed number is not correct, the program outputs a message indicating whether the guess is low or high. Modify the program as follows: Suppose

that the variables `num` and `guess` are as declared in Example 5-6 and `diff` is an `int` variable. Let `diff` = the absolute value of (num − guess). If `diff` is 0, then `guess` is correct and the program outputs a message indicating that the user guessed the correct number. Suppose `diff` is not 0. Then the program outputs the message as follows:

a. If `diff` is greater than or equal to 50, the program outputs the message indicating that the guess is very high (if `guess` is greater than `num`) or very low (if `guess` is less than `num`).

b. If `diff` is greater than or equal to 30 and less than 50, the program outputs the message indicating that the guess is high (if `guess` is greater than `num`) or low (if `guess` is less than `num`).

c. If `diff` is greater than or equal to 15 and less than 30, the program outputs the message indicating that the guess is moderately high (if `guess` is greater than `num`) or moderately low (if `guess` is less than `num`).

d. if `diff` is greater than 0 and less than 15, the program outputs the message indicating that the guess is somewhat high (if `guess` is greater than `num`) or somewhat low (if `guess` is less than `num`).

As in Programming Exercise 14, give the user no more than five tries to guess the number. (To find the absolute value of num − guess, use the expression `abs(num - guess)`. The function `abs` is from the header file `cstdlib`.

16. A high school has 1000 students and 1000 lockers, one locker for each student. On the first day of school, the principal plays the following game: She asks the first student to go and open all the lockers. She then asks the second student to go and close all the even-numbered lockers. The third student is asked to check every third locker. If it is open, the student closes it; if it is closed, the student opens it. The fourth student is asked to check every fourth locker. If it is open, the student closes it; if it is closed, the student opens it. The remaining students continue this game. In general, the *n*th student checks every *n*th locker. If the locker is open, the student closes it; if it is closed, the student opens it. After all the students have taken their turn, some of the lockers are open and some are closed. Write a program that prompts the user to enter the number of lockers in a school. After the game is over, the program outputs the number of lockers that are opened. Test run your program for the following inputs: 1000, 5000, 10000. Do you see any pattern developing?

(*Hint*: Consider locker number 100. This locker is visited by student numbers 1, 2, 4, 5, 10, 20, 25, 50, and 100. These are the positive divisors of 100. Similarly, locker number 30 is visited by student numbers 1, 2, 3, 5, 6, 10, 15, and 30. Notice that if the number of positive divisors of a locker number is odd, then at the end of the game the locker is opened. If the number of positive divisors of a locker number is even, then at the end of the game the locker is closed.)

17. For research purposes and to better help students, the admissions office of your local university wants to know how well female and male students perform in certain courses. You receive a file that contains female and male student GPAs for certain courses. Due to confidentiality, the letter code f is used for female students and m for male students. Every file entry consists of a letter code followed by a GPA. Each line has one entry. The number of entries in the file is unknown. Write a program that computes and outputs the average GPA for both female and male students. Format your results to two decimal places.

18. If interest is compounded annually, it grows as follows. Suppose P0 is the initial amount and INT is the interest rate per year. If P1, P2, and P3 is the balance at the end of the first, second, and third year, respectively, then:

```
P1 = P0 + P0*INT = P0*(1+INT)
P2 = P1 + P1*INT = P1*(1+INT)  = P0*(1+INT)*(1+INT)
   = P0*(1+INT) 2
P3 = P2 + P2*INT = P2*(1+INT)  = P0*(1+INT)*(1+INT)*(1+INT)
   = P0*(1+INT) 3
```

and so on.

When money is deposited in an IRA account, it is usually sheltered from taxes until the money is withdrawn after the age of 59. Suppose that someone dear to you opened such an account for you on your sixteenth birthday at 10% interest and that he or she forgot about it (so no money was added or withdrawn). On your sixtieth birthday, you are notified about this account by some fortune hunters. The money has been compounded annually at the 10% rate. Write a program that reads an initial amount and computes the total in the account on your sixtieth birthday.

You decide to leave the money in for another year. Starting from your sixty-first birthday, you decide to withdraw each year's interest income. In other words, you withdraw the interest and leave the rest of the money untouched. How much income per month for the rest of your life would you have?

Design your program to accept any integer input. Test it with initial investments of: $1700, $3600, and $8500.

(*Note*: Use a loop to compute the amount at your sixtieth birthday. Do not use the predefined function **pow**.)

The program should do all the computing needed, and output all the relevant data as follows:

The initial investment was $____. The total amount accumulated after ____ years, if $____ is allowed to compound with an interest of 10.00%, comes to $____.
The total amount accumulated after ____ (years + 1) years, if $____ is allowed to compound with an interest of 10%, comes to $____.
The interest earned during this year is $____. If interest is withdrawn each year thereafter, my income is $____ per month.

19. Write a complete program to test the code in Example 5-18.

20. Write a complete program to test the code in Example 5-19.

21. Write a complete program to test the code in Example 5-20.

22. Write a complete program to test the code in Example 5-21.

23. Write a complete program to test the code in Example 5-22.

24. Write a complete program to test the code in Example 5-23.

25. **(The conical paper cup problem)** You have been given the contract for making little conical cups that come with bottled water. These cups are to be made from a circular waxed paper die of 4 inches in radius, by removing a sector of length x, see Figure 5-4. By closing the remaining part of the circle, a conical cup is made. Your objective is to remove the sector so that the cup is of maximum volume.

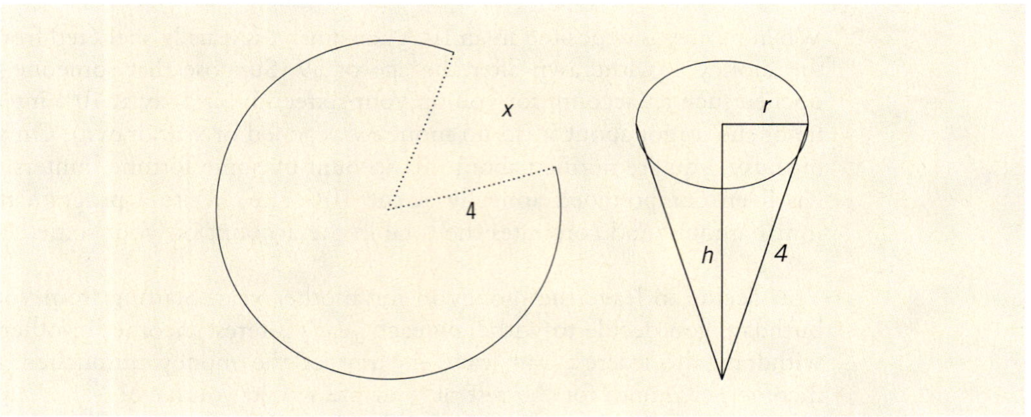

FIGURE 5-4 Conical paper cup

Write a program that prompts the user to enter the radius of the circular waxed paper. The program should then output the length of the removed sector so that the resulting cup is of maximum volume. Calculate your answer to two decimal places.

26. **(Apartment problem)** A real estate office handles, say, 50 apartment units. When the rent is, say, $600 per month, all the units are occupied. However,

for each, say, \$40 increase in rent, one unit becomes vacant. Moreover, each occupied unit requires an average of \$27 per month for maintenance. How many units should be rented to maximize the profit?

Write a program that prompts the user to enter:

a. The rent to occupy all the units

b. The increase in rent that results in a vacant unit

c. Amount to maintain a rented unit

The program then outputs the number of units to be rented to maximize the profit.

USER-DEFINED FUNCTIONS I

IN THIS CHAPTER, YOU WILL:

- Learn about standard (predefined) functions and discover how to use them in a program
- Learn about user-defined functions
- Examine value-returning functions, including actual and formal parameters
- Explore how to construct and use a value-returning, user-defined function in a program

In Chapter 2, you learned that a C++ program is a collection of functions. One such function is `main`. The programs in Chapters 1 through 5 use only the function `main`; the programming instructions are packed into one function. This technique, however, is good only for short programs. For large programs, it is not practical (although it is possible) to put the entire programming instructions into one function, as you will soon discover. You must learn to break the problem into manageable pieces. This chapter first discusses the functions previously defined and then discusses user-defined functions.

Let us imagine an automobile factory. When an automobile is manufactured, it is not made from basic raw materials; it is put together from previously manufactured parts. Some parts are made by the company itself, others by different companies.

Functions are like building blocks. They let you divide complicated programs into manageable pieces. They have other advantages, too:

- While working on one function, you can focus on just that part of the program and construct it, debug it, and perfect it.
- Different people can work on different functions simultaneously.
- If a function is needed in more than one place in a program, or in different programs, you can write it once and use it many times.
- Using functions greatly enhances the program's readability because it reduces the complexity of the function `main`.

Functions are often called **modules**. They are like miniature programs; you can put them together to form a larger program. When user-defined functions are discussed, you will see that this is the case. This ability is less apparent with predefined functions because their programming code is not available to us. However, because predefined functions are already written for us, you will learn these first so that you can use them when needed. To use a predefined function in your programs, you need to know only how to use it.

Predefined Functions

Before formally discussing predefined functions in C++, let us review a concept from a college algebra course. In algebra, a function can be considered a rule or correspondence between values, called the function's arguments, and the unique value of the function associated with the arguments. Thus, if `f(x) = 2x + 5`, then `f(1) = 7`, `f(2) = 9`, and `f(3) = 11`, where 1, 2, and 3 are the arguments of `f`, and 7, 9, and 11 are the corresponding values of the function `f`.

In C++, the concept of a function, either predefined or user-defined, is similar to that of a function in algebra. For example, every function has a name and, depending on the values specified by the user, it does some computation. This section discusses various predefined functions.

Some of the predefined mathematical functions are `pow(x, y)`, `sqrt(x)`, and `floor(x)`.

The *power* function, `pow(x, y)`, calculates x^y; that is, the value of `pow(x, y)` $= x^y$. For example, `pow(2, 3)` $= 2^3 = 8.0$ and `pow(2.5, 3)` $= 2.5^3 = 15.625$. Because the value of `pow(x, y)` is of type `double`, we say that the function `pow` is of type `double` or that the function `pow` returns a value of type `double`. Moreover, `x` and `y` are called the parameters (or arguments) of the function `pow`. Function `pow` has two parameters.

The *square root* function, `sqrt(x)`, calculates the non-negative square root of `x` for `x >= 0.0`. For example, `sqrt(2.25)` is `1.5`. The function `sqrt` is of type `double` and has only one parameter.

The *floor* function, `floor(x)`, calculates the largest whole number that is less than or equal to `x`. For example, `floor(48.79)` is `48.0`. The function `floor` is of type `double` and has only one parameter.

In C++, predefined functions are organized into separate libraries. For example, the header file `iostream` contains I/O functions, and the header file `cmath` contains math functions. Table 6-1 lists some of the predefined functions, the name of the header file in which each function's specification can be found, the data type of the parameters, and the function type. The function type is the data type of the final value returned by the function. (For a list of additional predefined functions, see Appendix F.)

TABLE 6-1 Predefined Functions

Function	Header File	Purpose	Parameter(s) Type	Result
`abs(x)`	`<cstdlib>`	Returns the absolute value of its argument: `abs(-7) = 7`	`int`	`int`
`ceil(x)`	`<cmath>`	Returns the smallest whole number that is not less than x: `ceil(56.34) = 57.0`	`double`	`double`
`cos(x)`	`<cmath>`	Returns the cosine of angle x: `cos(0.0) = 1.0`	`double` (radians)	`double`
`exp(x)`	`<cmath>`	Returns e^x, where e = `2.718`: `exp(1.0) = 2.71828`	`double`	`double`
`fabs(x)`	`<cmath>`	Returns the absolute value of its argument: `fabs(-5.67) = 5.67`	`double`	`double`

TABLE 6-1 Predefined Functions (continued)

Function	Header File	Purpose	Parameter(s) Type	Result
`floor(x)`	`<cmath>`	Returns the largest whole number that is not greater than x: `floor(45.67) = 45.00`	`double`	`double`
`pow(x, y)`	`<cmath>`	Returns x^y; If x is negative, y must be a whole number: `pow(0.16, 0.5) = 0.4`	`double`	`double`
`tolower(x)`	`<cctype>`	Returns the lowercase value of x if x is uppercase; otherwise, returns x	`int`	`int`
`toupper(x)`	`<cctype>`	Returns the uppercase value of x if x is lowercase; otherwise, returns x	`int`	`int`

To use predefined functions in a program, you must include the header file that contains the function's specification via the include statement. For example, to use the function pow, the program must include:

```
#include <cmath>
```

Example 6-1 shows you how to use some of the predefined functions.

EXAMPLE 6-1

```cpp
//How to use predefined functions.

#include <iostream>
#include <cmath>
#include <cctype>
#include <cstdlib>

using namespace std;

int main()
{
    int    x;
    double u, v;
```

```cpp
    cout << "Line 1: Uppercase a is "
         << static_cast<char>(toupper('a'))
         << endl;                                    //Line 1

    u = 4.2;                                         //Line 2
    v = 3.0;                                         //Line 3
    cout << "Line 4: " << u << " to the power of "
         << v << " = " << pow(u, v) << endl;         //Line 4

    cout << "Line 5: 5 to the power of 4 = "
         << pow(5, 4) << endl;                       //Line 5

    u = u + pow(3, 3);                               //Line 6
    cout << "Line 7: u = " << u << endl;             //Line 7

    x = -15;                                         //Line 8
    cout << "Line 9: Absolute value of " << x
         << " = " << abs(x) << endl;                 //Line 9

    return 0;
}
```

Sample Run:

```
Line 1: Uppercase a is A
Line 4: 4.2 to the power of 3 = 74.088
Line 5: 5 to the power of 4 = 625
Line 7: u = 31.2
Line 9: Absolute value of -15 = 15
```

This program works as follows. The statement in Line 1 outputs the uppercase letter that corresponds to `'a'`, which is A. Note that the function `toupper` returns an `int` value. Therefore, the value of the expression `toupper('a')` is 65, which is the ASCII value of `'A'`. To print A rather than 65, you need to apply the `cast` operator, as shown in the statement in Line 1. In the statement in Line 4, the function `pow` is used to output u^v. In C++ terminology, it is said that the function `pow` is called with the parameters u and v. In this case, the values of u and v are passed to the function `pow`. The other statements have similar meanings.

User-Defined Functions

As Example 6-1 illustrates, using functions in a program greatly enhances the program's readability because it reduces the complexity of the function `main`. Also, once you write and properly debug a function, you can use it in the program (or different programs) again and again without having to rewrite the same code repeatedly. For instance, in Example 6-1, the function `pow` is used more than once.

Because C++ does not provide every function that you will ever need, and designers cannot possibly know a user's specific needs, you must learn to write your own functions.

User-defined functions in C++ are classified into two categories:

- **Value-returning functions**—functions that have a return type.
- **Void functions**—functions that do not have a return type.

The remainder of this chapter discusses value-returning functions. Many of the concepts discussed in regard to value-returning functions also apply to void functions. Chapter 7 describes void functions.

Value-Returning Functions

The previous section introduced some predefined C++ functions such as `pow`, `abs`, `islower`, and `toupper`. These are examples of value-returning functions. To use these functions in your programs, you must know the name of the header file that contains the functions' specification. You need to include this header file in your program using the include statement and know the following items:

1. The name of the function

2. The number of **parameters**, if any

3. The data type of each parameter

4. The data type of the value computed (that is, the value returned) by the function, called the type of the function

Because the value returned by a value-returning function is unique, the natural thing for you to do is to use the value in one of three ways:

- Save the value for further calculation.
- Use the value in some calculation.
- Print the value.

This suggests that a value-returning function is used:

- In an assignment statement.
- In an output statement.
- As a parameter in a function call.

That is, a value-returning function is used (called) in an expression.

Before we look at the syntax of a user-defined, value-returning function, let us consider the things associated with such functions. In addition to the four properties described previously, one more thing is associated with functions (both value-returning and void):

5. The code required to accomplish the task

The first four properties form what is called the **heading** of the function (also called the **function header**); the fifth property is called the **body** of the function. Together, these five properties form what is called the **definition** of the function. For example, for the function abs, the heading might look like:

```
int abs(int number)
```

Similarly, the function abs might have the following definition:

```
int abs(int number)
{
    if (number < 0)
        number = -number;

    return number;
}
```

The variable declared in the heading of the function abs is called the **formal parameter** of the function abs. Thus, the formal parameter of abs is number.

The program in Example 6-1 contains several statements that use the function pow. That is, in C++ terminology, the function pow is called several times. Later in this chapter, we discuss what happens when a function is called.

Suppose that the heading of the function pow is:

```
double pow(double base, double exponent)
```

From the heading of the function pow, it follows that the formal parameters of pow are base and exponent. Consider the following statements:

```
double u = 2.5;
double v = 3.0;
double x, y, w;

x = pow(u, v);              //Line 1
y = pow(2.0, 3.2);         //Line 2
w = pow(u, 7);             //Line 3
```

In Line 1, the function pow is called with the parameters u and v. In this case, the values of u and v are passed to the function pow. In fact, the value of u is copied into base and the value of v is copied into exponent. The variables u and v that appear in the call to the function pow in Line 1 are called the actual parameters of that call. In Line 2, the function pow is called with the parameters 2.0 and 3.2. In this call, the value 2.0 is copied into base and 3.2 is copied into exponent. Moreover, in this call of the function pow, the actual parameters are 2.0 and 3.2, respectively. Similarly, in Line 3, the actual parameters of the function pow are u and 7, the value of u is copied into base, and 7.0 is copied into exponent.

We can now formally present two definitions:

Formal Parameter: A variable declared in the function heading.

Actual Parameter: A variable or expression listed in a call to a function.

For predefined functions, you need to be concerned only with the first four properties. Software companies do not give out the actual source code, which is the body of the function. Otherwise, software costs would be exorbitant.

Syntax: Value-Returning function

The syntax of a value-returning function is:

```
functionType functionName(formal parameter list)
{
    statements
}
```

where statements are usually declaration statements and/or executable statements. In this syntax, `functionType` is the type of the value that the function returns. The `functionType` is also called the **data type** or the **return type** of the value-returning function. Moreover, statements enclosed between curly braces form the body of the function.

Syntax: Formal Parameter List

The syntax of the formal parameter list is:

```
dataType identifier, dataType identifier, ...
```

Function Call

The syntax to call a value-returning function is:

```
functionName(actual parameter list)
```

Syntax: Actual Parameter List

The syntax of the actual parameter list is:

```
expression or variable, expression or variable, ...
```

(In this syntax, `expression` can be a single constant value.) Thus, to call a value-returning function, you use its name, with the actual parameters (if any) in parentheses.

A function's formal parameter list *can* be empty. However, if the formal parameter list is empty, the parentheses are still needed. The function heading of the value-returning function thus takes, if the formal parameter list is empty, the following form:

```
functionType functionName()
```

If the formal parameter list of a value-returning function is empty, in a function call the actual parameter is also empty. In this case (that is, an empty formal parameter list), in a function call the empty parentheses are still needed. Thus, a call to a value-returning function with an empty formal parameter list is:

```
functionName()
```

In a function call, the number of actual parameters, together with their data types, must match with the formal parameters in the order given. That is, actual and formal parameters have a one-to-one correspondence. (Chapter 7 discusses functions with default parameters.)

As stated previously, a value-returning function is called in an expression. The expression can be part of either an assignment statement or an output statement, or a parameter in a function call. A function call in a program causes the body of the called function to execute.

`return` Statement

Once a value-returning function computes the value, the function returns this value via the **`return`** statement. In other words, it passes this value outside the function via the **`return`** statement.

Syntax: `return` Statement

The **`return`** statement has the following syntax:

```
return expr;
```

where **`expr`** is a variable, constant value, or expression. The **`expr`** is evaluated and its value is returned. The data type of the value that **`expr`** computes must match the function type.

In C++, **`return`** is a reserved word.

When a **`return`** statement executes in a function, the function immediately terminates and the control goes back to the caller. Moreover, the function call statement is replaced by the value returned by the **`return`** statement. When a **`return`** statement executes in the function **`main`**, the program terminates.

To put the ideas in this discussion to work, let us write a function that determines the larger of two numbers. Because the function compares two numbers, it follows that this function has two parameters and that both parameters are numbers. Let us assume that the data type of these numbers is floating-point (decimal)—say, **`double`**. Because the larger number is of type `double`, the function's data type is also `double`. Let us name this function `larger`. The only thing you need to complete this function is the body of the function. Thus, following the syntax of a function, you can write this function as follows:

```
double larger(double x, double y)
{
    double max;

    if (x >= y)
        max = x;
    else
        max = y;

    return max;
}
```

You can also write this function as follows:

```
double larger(double x, double y)
{
    if (x >= y)
        return x;
    else
        return y;
}
```

Because the execution of a `return` statement in a function terminates the function, the preceding function `larger` can also be written (without the word `else`) as:

```
double larger(double x, double y)
{
    if (x >= y)
        return x;

    return y;
}
```

The first form of the function `larger` requires that you use an additional variable `max` (called a **local declaration**, where `max` is a variable local to the function `larger`); the second form does not.

NOTE

1. In the definition of the function `larger`, `x` and `y` are formal parameters.

2. The `return` statement can appear anywhere in the function. Recall that once a `return` statement executes, all subsequent statements are skipped. Thus, it's a good idea to return the value as soon as it is computed.

EXAMPLE 6-2

Now that the function `larger` is written, the following C++ code illustrates how to use it in the function `main`.

```cpp
int main()
{
    double one, two, maxNum;                          //Line 1

    cout << "The larger of 5 and 6 is "
         << larger(5, 6) << endl;                     //Line 2

    cout << "Enter two numbers: ";                    //Line 3
    cin >> one >> two;                                //Line 4
    cout << endl;                                     //Line 5

    cout << "The larger of " << one << " and " << two
         << " is " << larger(one, two) << endl;       //Line 6

    cout << "The larger of " << one << " and 29 is "
         << larger(one, 29) << endl;                  //Line 7

    maxNum = larger(38.45, 56.78);                    //Line 8
    cout << "maxNum = " << maxNum << endl;            //Line 9

    return 0;
}
```

Note that in Example 6-2:

1. The expression `larger(5, 6)`, in Line 2, is a function call, and 5 and 6 are actual parameters.

2. The expression `larger(one, two)`, in Line 6, is a function call. Here, `one` and `two` are actual parameters.

3. The expression `larger(one, 29)`, in Line 7, is also a function call. Here, `one` and 29 are actual parameters.

4. The expression `larger(38.45, 56.78)`, in Line 8, is a function call. In this call, the actual parameters are `38.45` and `56.78`. In this statement, the value returned by the function `larger` is assigned to the variable `maxNum`.

In a function call, you specify only the actual parameter, not its data type. For example, in the preceding function `main`, the statements in Lines 2, 6, 7, and 8 show how to call the function `larger` with the actual parameters. However, the following statements contain incorrect calls to the function `larger` and would result in syntax errors. (Assume that all variables are properly declared.)

```
x = larger(int one, 29);             //illegal
y = larger(int one, int 29);         //illegal
cout << larger(int one, int two);    //illegal
```

Once a function is written, you can use it anywhere in the program. The function `larger` compares two numbers and returns the larger of the two. Let us now write another function that uses this function to determine the largest of three numbers. We call this function `compareThree`.

```
double compareThree(double x, double y, double z)
{
    return larger(x, larger(y, z));
}
```

In the function heading, `x`, `y`, and `z` are formal parameters.

Let us take a look at the expression:

```
larger(x, larger(y, z))
```

In the definition of the function `compareThree`. This expression has two calls to the function `larger`. The actual parameters to the outer call are `x` and `larger(y, z)`; the actual parameters to the inner call are `y` and `z`. It follows that first the expression `larger(y, z)` is evaluated, that is, the inner call executes first, which gives the larger of `y` and `z`. Suppose that `larger(y, z)` evaluates to, say, `t`. (Notice that `t` is either `y` or `z`.) Next, the outer call determines the larger of `x` and `t`. Finally, the `return` statement returns the largest number. It thus follows that to execute a function call, the parameters are evaluated first. For example, the actual parameter `larger(y, z)` of the outer call evaluates first.

Function Prototype

Now that you have some idea of how to write and use functions in a program, the next question relates to the order in which user-defined functions should appear in a program. For example, do you place the function `larger` before or after the function `main`? Should `larger` be placed before `compareThree` or after it? Following the rule that you must declare an identifier before you can use it, and knowing that the function `main` uses the identifier `larger`, logically you must place `larger` before `main`.

In reality, C++ programmers customarily place the function `main` before all other user-defined functions. However, this organization could produce a compilation error because functions are compiled in the order in which they appear in the program. For example, if the function `main` is placed before the function `larger`, the identifier `larger` is undefined when the function `main` is compiled. To work around this problem of undeclared identifiers, we place **function prototypes** before any function definition (including the definition of `main`).

Function Prototype: The function heading without the body of the function.

Syntax: Function Prototype

The general syntax of the function prototype of a value-returning function is:

```
functionType functionName(parameter list);
```

(Note that the function prototype ends with a semicolon.)

For the function `larger`, the prototype is:

```
double larger(double x, double y);
```

NOTE When writing the function prototype, you do not have to specify the variable name in the parameter list. However, you must specify the data type of each parameter.

You can rewrite the function prototype of the function `larger` as follows:

```
double larger(double, double);
```

FINAL PROGRAM

You now know enough to write the entire program, compile it, and run it. The following program uses the functions `larger`, `compareThree`, and `main` to determine the larger/largest of two or three numbers.

```cpp
//Program: Largest of three numbers

#include <iostream>

using namespace std;

double larger(double x, double y);
double compareThree(double x, double y, double z);

int main()
{
    double one, two;                                    //Line 1

    cout << "Line 2: The larger of 5 and 10 is "
         << larger(5, 10) << endl;                      //Line 2

    cout << "Line 3: Enter two numbers: ";              //Line 3
    cin >> one >> two;                                  //Line 4
    cout << endl;                                       //Line 5

    cout << "Line 6: The larger of " << one
         << " and " << two << " is "
         << larger(one, two) << endl;                   //Line 6
```

```cpp
    cout << "Line 7: The largest of 23, 34, and "
         << "12 is " << compareThree(23, 34, 12)
         << endl;                                            //Line 7

    return 0;
}

double larger(double x, double y)
{
    if (x >= y)
        return x;
    else
        return y;
}

double compareThree (double x, double y, double z)
{
    return larger(x, larger(y, z));
}
```

Sample Run: In this sample run, the user input is shaded.

```
Line 2: The larger of 5 and 10 is 10
Line 3: Enter two numbers: 25 73

Line 6: The larger of 25 and 73 is 73
Line 7: The largest of 23, 34, and 12 is 34
```

 **NOTE** In the previous program, the function prototypes of the functions `larger` and `compareThree` appear before their function definitions. Therefore, the definition of the functions `larger` and `compareThree` can appear in any order.

 **NOTE** A value-returning function must return a value. Consider the following function, `secret`, that takes as a parameter an `int` value. If the value of the parameter, `x`, is greater than 5, it returns twice the value of `x`; otherwise, the value of `x` remains unchanged.

```cpp
int secret(int x)
{
    if (x > 5)              //Line 1
        return 2 * x;       //Line 2
}
```

Because this is a value-returning function of type `int`, it must return a value of type `int`. Suppose the value of `x` is 10. Then the expression, `x > 5`, in Line 1, evaluates to `true`. So the `return` statement in Line 2 returns the value 20. Now suppose that `x` is 3. The expression, `x > 5`, in Line 1, now evaluates to `false`. The `if` statement, therefore, fails, and the `return` statement in Line 2 *does not* execute. However, there are no more statements to be executed in the body of the function. In this case, the function returns a strange value. It thus follows that if the value of **x** is less than or equal to 5, the function does not contain any valid **return** statements to return the value of **x**.

The correct definition of the function **secret** is:

```
int secret(int x)
{
    if (x > 5)                  //Line 1
            return 2 * x;       //Line 2

    return x;                   //Line 3
}
```

Here, if the value of **x** is less than or equal to 5, the **return** statement in Line 3 executes, which returns the value of **x**. On the other hand, if the value of **x** is, say, 10, the **return** statement in Line 2 executes, which returns the value 20 and also terminates the function.

NOTE   Recall that in a value-returning function, the **return** statement returns the value. Consider the following **return** statement:

```
return x, y;   //only the value of y will be returned
```

This is a legal **return** statement. You might think that this **return** statement is returning the values of **x** and **y**. However, this is not the case. Remember, a **return** statement returns only one value, even if the **return** statement contains more than one expression. If a **return** statement contains more than one expression, *only the value of the last expression is returned*. Therefore, in the case of the above **return** statement, the value of **y** is returned. The following program further illustrates this concept:

```
//A value returned by a return statement
//This program illustrates that a value-returning function
//returns only one value, even if the return statement
//contains more than one expression.

#include <iostream>

using namespace std;

int funcRet1();
int funcRet2();
int funcRet3();
int funcRet4(int z);

int main()
{
    int num = 4;

    cout << "Line 1: The value returned by funcRet1: "
         << funcRet1() << endl;                              // Line 1
    cout << "Line 2: The value returned by funcRet2: "
         << funcRet2() << endl;                              // Line 2
```

```cpp
        cout << "Line 3: The value returned by funcRet3: "
             << funcRet3() << endl;                            // Line 3
        cout << "Line 4: The value returned by funcRet4: "
             << funcRet4(num) << endl;                         // Line 4
    return 0;
}

int funcRet1()
{
    return 23, 45;   //only 45 is returned
}

int funcRet2()
{
    int x = 5;
    int y = 6;

    return x, y; //only the value of y is returned
}

int funcRet3()
{
    int x = 5;
    int y = 6;

    return 37, y, 2 * x;   //only the value of 2 * x is returned
}

int funcRet4(int z)
{
    int a = 2;
    int b = 3;

    return 2 * a + b, z + b; //only the value of z + b is returned
}
```

Sample Run:

```
Line 1: The value returned by funcRet1: 45
Line 2: The value returned by funcRet2: 6
Line 3: The value returned by funcRet3: 10
Line 4: The value returned by funcRet4: 7
```

EXAMPLE 6-3

In this example, we write the definition of function `courseGrade`. This function takes as
a parameter an **int** value specifying the score for a course and returns the grade, a value of
type **char**, for the course. (We assume that the test score is a value between 0 and 100
inclusive.)

```
char courseGrade(int score)
{
    switch (score / 10)
    {
    case 0:
    case 1:
    case 2:
    case 3:
    case 4:
    case 5:
        return 'F';
    case 6:
        return 'D';
    case 7:
        return 'C';
    case 8:
        return 'B';
    case 9:
    case 10:
        return 'A';
    }
}
```

You can also write an equivalent definition of the function `courseGrade` that uses an `if...else` structure to determine the course grade.

Following is an example of a function that returns a Boolean value.

EXAMPLE 6-4

Palindrome Number

In this example, a function, `isNumPalindrome`, is designed that returns `true` if a non-negative integer is a palindrome and `false` otherwise. A non-negative integer is a palindrome if it reads forward and backward in the same way. For example, the integers 5, 44, 434, 1881, and 789656987 are all palindromes.

Suppose `num` is a non-negative integer. If `num < 10`, it is a palindrome and so the function should return `true`. Suppose `num >= 10`. To determine whether `num` is a palindrome, first compare the first and the last digits of `num`. If the first and the last digits of `num` are not the same, it is not a palindrome and so the function should return `false`. If the first and the last digits of `num` are the same, remove the first and last digits of `num` and repeat this process on the new number, which is obtained from `num` after removing the first and last digits of `num`. Repeat this process as long as the number is `>= 10`.

For example, suppose that the input is 18281. Because the first and last digits of 18281 are the same, remove the first and last digits to get the number 828. Repeat this process of comparing the first and last digits on 828. Once again, the first and last digits are the same. After removing the first and last digits of 828, the resulting number is 2, which is less than 10. Thus, 18281 is a palindrome.

To remove the first and last digits of num, you first need to find the highest power of 10 that divides num, call it pwr. The highest power of 10 that divides 18281 is 4, that is, pwr = 4. Now 18281 % 10^{pwr} = 8281, and so the first digit is removed. Also, because 8281 / 10 = 828, the last digit is removed. Therefore, to remove the first digit, you can use the mod operator, where the divisor is 10^{pwr}. To remove the last digit, divide the number by 10. You then decrement pwr by 2 for the next iteration. The following algorithm implements this discussion:

1. If num < 10, it is a palindrome and so the function should return true.

2. Suppose num is an integer and num >= 10. To see if num is a palindrome:

   a. Find the highest power of 10 that divides num and call it pwr. For example, the highest power of 10 that divides 434 is 2; the highest power of 10 that divides 789656987 is 8.

   b. While num is greater than or equal to 10, compare the first and last digits of num.

      b.1. If the first and last digits of num are not the same, num is not a palindrome. Return false.

      b.2. If the first and the last digits of num are the same:

         b.2.1. Remove the first and last digits of num.

         b.2.2. Decrement pwr by 2.

   c. Return true.

The following function implements this algorithm:

```cpp
bool isNumPalindrome(int num)
{
    int pwr = 0;

    if (num < 10)                                       //Step 1
        return true;
    else                                                //Step 2
    {
                                                        //Step 2.a
        while (num / static_cast<int>(pow(10, pwr)) >= 10)
            pwr++;
```

```cpp
    while (num >= 10)                              //Step 2.b
    {
        int tenTopwr = static_cast<int>(pow(10, pwr));

        if ((num / tenTopwr) != (num % 10))
            return false;                          //Step 2.b.1
        else                                       //Step 2.b.2
        {
            num = num % tenTopwr;                  //Step 2.b.2.1
            num = num / 10;                        //Step 2.b.2.1
            pwr = pwr - 2;                         //Step 2.b.2.2
        }
    }//end while

    return true;
    }//end else
}
```

NOTE   In the definition of the function `isNumPalindrome`, the function `pow` from the header file `cmath` is used to find the highest power of 10 that divides the number. Therefore, make sure to include the header file `cmath` in your program.

Flow of Execution

As stated earlier, a C++ program is a collection of functions. Recall that functions can appear in any order. The only thing that you have to remember is that you must declare an identifier before you can use it. The program is compiled by the compiler sequentially from beginning to end. Thus, if the function `main` appears before any other user-defined functions, it is compiled first. However, if `main` appears at the end (or middle) of the program, all functions whose definitions (not prototypes) appear before the function `main` are compiled before the function `main`, in the order they are placed.

Function prototypes appear before any function definition, so the compiler translates these first. The compiler can then correctly translate a function call. However, when the program executes, the first statement in the function `main` always executes first, regardless of where in the program the function `main` is placed. Other functions execute only when they are called.

A function call statement transfers control to the first statement in the body of the function. In general, after the last statement of the called function executes, control is passed back to the point immediately following the function call. A value-returning function returns a value. Therefore, after executing the value-returning function, when the control goes back to the caller, the value that the function returns replaces the function call statement. The execution continues at the point immediately following the function call.

PROGRAMMING EXAMPLE: Largest Number

In this programming example, the function `larger` is used to determine the largest number from a set of numbers. For the purpose of illustration, this program determines the largest number from a set of 10 numbers. You can easily enhance this program to accommodate any set of numbers.

Input   A set of 10 numbers.

Output   The largest of 10 numbers.

PROBLEM
ANALYSIS
AND
ALGORITHM
DESIGN

Suppose that the input data is:

```
15 20 7 8 28 21 43 12 35 3
```

Read the first number of the data set. Because this is the only number read to this point, you may assume that it is the largest number so far and call it `max`. Read the second number and call it `num`. Now compare `max` and `num`, and store the larger number into `max`. Now `max` contains the larger of the first two numbers. Read the third number. Compare it with `max` and store the larger number into `max`. At this point, `max` contains the largest of the first three numbers. Read the next number, compare it with `max`, and store the larger into `max`. Repeat this process for each remaining number in the data set. Eventually, `max` will contain the largest number in the data set. This discussion translates into the following algorithm:

1. Read the first number. Because this is the only number that you have read so far, it is the largest number so far. Save it in a variable called `max`.

2. For each remaining number in the list:

   a. Read the next number. Store it in a variable called `num`.

   b. Compare `num` and `max`. If `max < num`, then `num` is the new largest number and so update the value of `max` by copying `num` into `max`. If `max >= num`, discard `num`; that is, do nothing.

3. Because `max` now contains the largest number, print it.

To find the larger of two numbers, the program uses the function `larger`.

COMPLETE PROGRAM LISTING

```cpp
// Program: Largest

#include <iostream>

using namespace std;

double larger(double x, double y);
```

```
        bAmount = RES_BILL_PROC_FEES +
                  RES_BASIC_SERV_COST +
                  noOfPChannels * RES_COST_PREM_CHANNEL;

        return bAmount;
}
```

Function business

To compute the business bill, you need to know the number of both the basic service connections and the premium channels to which the customer subscribes. Then, based on these numbers, you can calculate the billing amount. The billing amount is then returned using the `return` statement. The following six steps describe this function:

    a.   Prompt the user for the number of basic service connections.

    b.   Read the number of basic service connections.

    c.   Prompt the user for the number of premium channels.

    d.   Read the number of premium channels.

    e.   Calculate the bill.

    f.   Return the amount due.

This function contains the statements to prompt the user to enter the number of basic service connections and premium channels (Steps a and c). The function also contains statements to input the number of basic service connections and premium channels (Steps b and d). Other items needed to calculate the billing amount, such as the cost of basic service connections and bill-processing fees, are defined as named constants (before the definition of the function `main`). It follows that to calculate the billing amount, this function does not need to get any values from the function `main`. Therefore, it has no parameters.

Local Variables (Function business)

From the preceding discussion, it follows that the function `business` requires variables to store the number of basic service connections and of premium channels, as well as the billing amount. In fact, this function needs only three local variables to calculate the billing amount:

```
int noOfBasicServiceConnections;
int noOfPChannels;      //number of premium channels
double bAmount;         //billing amount
```

The definition of the function `business` can now be written as follows:

```
double business()
{
    int noOfBasicServiceConnections;
    int noOfPChannels;      //number of premium channels
    double bAmount;         //billing amount
```

```cpp
    cout << "Enter the number of basic "
         << "service connections: ";
    cin >> noOfBasicServiceConnections;
    cout << endl;

    cout << "Enter the number of premium "
         << "channels used: ";
    cin >> noOfPChannels;
    cout << endl;

    if (noOfBasicServiceConnections <= 10)
        bAmount = BUS_BILL_PROC_FEES + BUS_BASIC_SERV_COST +
                    noOfPChannels * BUS_COST_PREM_CHANNEL;
    else
        bAmount = BUS_BILL_PROC_FEES + BUS_BASIC_SERV_COST +
                    (noOfBasicServiceConnections - 10) *
                    BUS_BASIC_CONN_COST +
                    noOfPChannels * BUS_COST_PREM_CHANNEL;

    return bAmount;
}
```

MAIN ALGORITHM (Function main)

1. To output floating-point numbers in a fixed decimal format with the decimal point and trailing zeros, set the manipulators `fixed` and `showpoint`.

2. To output floating-point numbers to two decimal places, set the precision to two decimal places.

3. Prompt the user for the account number.

4. Get the account number.

5. Prompt the user to enter the customer type.

6. Get the customer type.

7. a. If the customer type is R or r,

    i. Call the function `residential` to calculate the bill.

    ii. Print the bill.

   b. If the customer type is B or b,

    i. Call the function `business` to calculate the bill.

    ii. Print the bill.

   c. If the customer type is other than R, r, B, or b, it is an invalid customer type.

COMPLETE PROGRAM LISTING

```cpp
//Cable company billing program

#include <iostream>
#include <iomanip>
using namespace std;

    //Named constants - residential customers
const double RES_BILL_PROC_FEES = 4.50;
const double RES_BASIC_SERV_COST = 20.50;
const double RES_COST_PREM_CHANNEL = 7.50;

    //Named constants - business customers
const double BUS_BILL_PROC_FEES = 15.00;
const double BUS_BASIC_SERV_COST = 75.00;
const double BUS_BASIC_CONN_COST = 5.00;
const double BUS_COST_PREM_CHANNEL = 50.00;

double residential();       //Function prototype
double business();          //Function prototype

int main()
{
        //declare variables
    int accountNumber;
    char customerType;
    double amountDue;

    cout << fixed << showpoint;                         //Step 1
    cout << setprecision(2);                            //Step 2

    cout << "This program computes a cable bill."
         << endl;
    cout << "Enter account number: ";                   //Step 3
    cin >> accountNumber;                               //Step 4
    cout << endl;

    cout << "Enter customer type: R, r "
         << "(Residential), B, b (Business): ";         //Step 5
    cin >> customerType;                                //Step 6
    cout << endl;

    switch (customerType)                               //Step 7
    {
    case 'r':                                           //Step 7a
    case 'R':
```

```cpp
            amountDue = residential();                      //Step 7a.i
            cout << "Account number = "
                 << accountNumber << endl;                  //Step 7a.ii
            cout << "Amount due = $"
                 << amountDue << endl;                      //Step 7a.ii
            break;
        case 'b':                                           //Step 7b
        case 'B':
            amountDue = business();                         //Step 7b.i
            cout << "Account number = "
                 << accountNumber << endl;                  //Step 7b.ii
            cout << "Amount due = $"
                 << amountDue << endl;                      //Step 7b.ii
            break;
        default:
            cout << "Invalid customer type."
                 << endl;                                   //Step 7c
    }

    return 0;
}

double residential()
{
    int noOfPChannels;      //number of premium channels
    double bAmount;         //billing amount

    cout << "Enter the number of premium "
         << "channels used: ";
    cin >>  noOfPChannels;
    cout << endl;

    bAmount = RES_BILL_PROC_FEES +
              RES_BASIC_SERV_COST +
              noOfPChannels * RES_COST_PREM_CHANNEL;

    return bAmount;
}

double business()
{
    int noOfBasicServiceConnections;
    int  noOfPChannels;     //number of premium channels
    double bAmount;         //billing amount

    cout << "Enter the number of basic "
         << "service connections: ";
    cin >> noOfBasicServiceConnections;
    cout << endl;
```

```cpp
    cout << "Enter the number of premium "
         << "channels used: ";
    cin >> noOfPChannels;
    cout << endl;

    if (noOfBasicServiceConnections <= 10)
        bAmount = BUS_BILL_PROC_FEES + BUS_BASIC_SERV_COST +
                noOfPChannels * BUS_COST_PREM_CHANNEL;
    else
        bAmount = BUS_BILL_PROC_FEES + BUS_BASIC_SERV_COST +
                (noOfBasicServiceConnections - 10) *
                BUS_BASIC_CONN_COST +
                noOfPChannels * BUS_COST_PREM_CHANNEL;

    return bAmount;
}
```

Sample Run: In this sample run, the user input is shaded.

```
This program computes a cable bill.
Enter account number: 21341

Enter customer type: R, r (Residential), B, b (Business): B

Enter the number of basic service connections: 25

Enter the number of premium channels used: 9

Account number = 21341
Amount due = $615.00
```

QUICK REVIEW

1. Functions are like miniature programs and are called modules.

2. Functions enable you to divide a program into manageable tasks.

3. The C++ system provides the standard (predefined) functions.

4. To use a standard function, you must:

    i.   know the name of the header file that contains the function's specification,

    ii. include that header file in the program, and

    iii. know the name and type of the function, and number and types of the parameters (arguments).

5. There are two types of user-defined functions: value-returning functions and void functions.

6. Variables defined in a function heading are called formal parameters.

7. Expressions, variables, or constant values used in a function call are called actual parameters.

8. In a function call, the number of actual parameters and their types must match with the formal parameters in the order given.

9. To call a function, use its name together with the actual parameter list.

10. A value-returning function returns a value. Therefore, a value-returning function is used (called) in either an expression or an output statement, or as a parameter in a function call.

11. The general syntax of a user-defined function is:

```
functionType   functionName(formal parameter list)
{
     statements
}
```

12. The line `functionType functionName(formal parameter list)` is called the function heading (or function header). Statements enclosed between braces { and } are called the body of the function.

13. The function heading and the body of the function are called the definition of the function.

14. If a function has no parameters, you still need the empty parentheses in both the function heading and the function call.

15. A value-returning function returns its value via the **return** statement.

16. A function can have more than one **return** statement. However, whenever a **return** statement executes in a function, the remaining statements are skipped and the function exits.

17. A **return** statement returns only one value.

18. A function prototype is the function heading without the body of the function; the function prototype ends with the semicolon.

19. A function prototype announces the function type, as well as the type and number of parameters, used in the function.

20. In a function prototype, the names of the variables in the formal parameter list are optional.

21. Function prototypes help the compiler correctly translate each function call.

22. In a program, function prototypes are placed before every function definition, including the definition of the function `main`.

23. When you use function prototypes, user-defined functions can appear in any order in the program.

24. When the program executes, the execution always begins with the first statement in the function `main`.

25. User-defined functions execute only when they are called.

26. A call to a function transfers control from the caller to the called function.

27. In a function call statement, you specify only the actual parameters, not their data type or the function type.

28. When a function exits, the control goes back to the caller.

EXERCISES

1. Mark the following statements as true or false.

   a. To use a predefined function in a program, you need to know only the name of the function and how to use it.

   b. A value-returning function returns only one value.

   c. Parameters allow you to use different values each time the function is called.

   d. When a `return` statement executes in a user-defined function, the function immediately exits.

   e. A value-returning function returns only integer values.

2. Which of the following function headings are valid? If they are invalid, explain why.

   a. `one (int a, int b)`

   b. `int thisone(char x)`

   c. `char another(int a, b)`

   d. `double yetanother`

3. Consider the following statements:

```
double num1, num2, num3;
int int1, int2, int3;
int value;

num1 = 5.0; num2 = 6.0; num3 = 3.0;
int1 = 4; int2 = 7; int3 = 8;
```

and the function prototype:

```
double cube(double a, double b, double c);
```

Which of the following statements are valid? If they are invalid, explain why.

   a. `value = cube (num1, 15.0, num3);`

   b. `cout << cube(num1, num3, num2) << endl;`

   c. `cout << cube(6.0, 8.0, 10.5) << endl;`

   d. `cout << cube(num1, num3) << endl;`

   e. `value = cube(num1, int2, num3);`

```
f.   value = cube(7, 8, 9);

g.   value = cube(int1, int2, int3);
```

4. Consider the following functions:

```cpp
int secret(int x)
{
    int i, j;

    i = 2 * x;

    if (i > 10)
        j = x / 2;
    else
        j = x / 3;

    return j - 1;
}

int another(int a, int b)
{
    int i, j;

    j = 0;

    for (i = a; i <= b; i++)
        j = j + i;

    return j;
}
```

What is the output of each of the following program segments? Assume that x, y, and k are **int** variables.

```cpp
a.  x = 10;
    cout << secret(x) << endl;

b.  x = 5; y = 8;
    cout << another(x, y) << endl;

c.  x = 10; k = secret(x);
    cout << x << " " << k << " " << another(x, k) << endl;

d.  x = 5; y = 8;
    cout << another(y, x) << endl;
```

5. Consider the following function prototypes:

```cpp
int test(int, char, double, int);
double two(double, double);
char three(int, int, char, double);
```

Answer the following questions.

a. How many parameters does the function `test` have? What is the type of the function `test` ?

b. How many parameters does function `two` have? What is the type of function `two`?

c. How many parameters does function `three` have? What is the type of function `three` ?

d. How many actual parameters are needed to call the function `test`? What is the type of each actual parameter, and in what order should you use these parameters in a call to the function `test`?

e. Write a C++ statement that prints the value returned by the function `test` with the actual parameters 5, 5, 7.3, and `'z'`.

f. Write a C++ statement that prints the value returned by function `two` with the actual parameters `17.5` and `18.3`, respectively.

g. Write a C++ statement that prints the next character returned by function `three`. (Use your own actual parameters.)

6. Consider the following function:

```cpp
int mystery(int x, double y, char ch)
{
    int u;
    if ('A' <= ch && ch <= 'R')
        return (2 * x + static_cast<int>(y));
    else
        return (static_cast<int>(2 * y) - x);
}
```

What is the output of the following C++ statements?

a. `cout << mystery(5, 4.3, 'B') << endl;`

b. `cout << mystery(4, 9.7, 'v') << endl;`

c. `cout << 2 * mystery(6, 3.9, 'D') << endl;`

7. Consider the following function:

```cpp
int secret(int one)
{
    int i;
    int prod = 1;

    for (i = 1; i <= 3; i++)
        prod = prod * one;
    return prod;
}
```

    a.   What is the output of the following C++ statements?

```
    i.   cout << secret(5) << endl;
    ii.  cout << 2 * secret(6) << endl;
```

    b.   What does the function `secret` do?

8. What is the output of the following C++ program? (Recall that the function `sqrt` returns the square root of its argument. For example, `sqrt(16.0) = 4.0`. The specification of the function `sqrt` is in the header file `cmath`.)

```cpp
#include <iostream>
#include <cmath>

using namespace std;

int main()
{
    int counter;

    for (counter = 1; counter <= 100; counter++)
        if (pow(floor(sqrt(counter + 0.0)), 2) == counter)
            cout << counter << " ";

    cout << endl;

    return 0;
}
```

9. Show the output of the following program:

```cpp
#include <iostream>

using namespace std;

int mystery(int);

int main()
{
    int n;

    for (n = 1; n <= 5; n++)
        cout << mystery(n) << endl;

    return 0;
}
```

```cpp
int mystery(int k)
{
    int x, y;

    y = k;

    for (x = 1; x <= (k - 1); x++)
        y = y * (k - x);

    return y;
}
```

10. Show the output of the following program:

```cpp
#include <iostream>

using namespace std;

bool strange(int);

int main()
{
    int num = 0;

    while (num <= 29)
    {
        if (strange(num))
            cout << "True" << endl;
        else
            cout << "False" << endl;

        num = num + 4;
    }

    return 0;
}

bool strange(int n)
{
    if (n % 2 == 0 && n % 3 == 0)
        return true;
    else
        return false;
}
```

PROGRAMMING EXERCISES

1. Write a program that uses the function `isNumPalindrome` given in Example 6-3 (Palindrome Number). Test your program on the following numbers: 10, 34, 22, 333, 678, 67876, 44444, and 123454321.

2. Write a value-returning function, `isVowel`, that returns the value **true** if a given character is a vowel and otherwise returns **false**.

3. Write a program that prompts the user to input a sequence of characters and outputs the number of vowels. (Use the function `isVowel` written in Programming Exercise 2.)

4. Consider the following program:

```cpp
#include <iostream>

using namespace std;

int one(int x, int y);
double two(int x, double a);

int main()
{
    int num;
    double dec;
        .
        .
        .
    return 0;
}

int one(int x, int y)
{
        .
        .
        .
}

double two(int x, double a)
{
    int first;
    double z;
        .
        .
        .
}
```

a. Write the definition of function `one` so that it returns the sum of `x` and `y` if `x` is greater than `y`; otherwise, it should return `x` minus 2 times `y`.

b. Write the definition of function `two` as follows:

    i. Read a number and store it in `z`.

    ii. Update the value of `z` by adding the value of `a` to its previous value.

    iii.   Assign the variable `first` the value returned by function `one` with parameters 6 and 8.

    iv.   Update the value of `first` by adding the value of `x` to its previous value.

    v.   If the value of `z` is more than twice the value of `first`, return `z`; otherwise, return 2 times `first` minus `z`.

  c. Write a C++ program that tests parts a and b. (Declare additional variables in the function `main`, if necessary.)

5. Write a function, `reverseDigit`, that takes an integer as a parameter and returns the number with its digits reversed. For example, the value of `reverseDigit(12345)` is 54321; the value of `reverseDigit(5600)` is 65; the value of `reverseDigit(7008)` is 8007; and the value of `reverseDigit(-532)` is -235.

6. The following formula gives the distance between two points (x_1, y_1) and (x_2, y_2) in the Cartesian plane:

$$\sqrt{(x_2 - x_1)^2 + (y_2 - y_1)^2}$$

Given the center and a point on the circle, you can use this formula to find the radius of the circle. Write a program that prompts the user to enter the center and a point on the circle. The program should then output the circle's radius, diameter, circumference, and area. Your program must have at least the following functions:

  a. `distance`: This function takes as its parameters four numbers that represent two points in the plane and returns the distance between them.

  b. `radius`: This function takes as its parameters four numbers that represent the center and a point on the circle, calls the function `distance` to find the radius of the circle, and returns the circle's radius.

  c. `circumference`: This function takes as its parameter a number that represents the radius of the circle and returns the circle's circumference. (If r is the radius, the circumference is $2\pi r$.)

  d. `area`: This function takes as its parameter a number that represents the radius of the circle and returns the circle's area. (If r is the radius, the area is πr^2.)

    Assume that $\pi = 3.1416$.

7. If P is the population on the first day of the year, B is the birth rate, and D is the death rate, the estimated population at the end of the year is given by the formula:

$$P + \frac{B * P}{100} - \frac{D * P}{100}.$$

The population growth rate is given by the formula:

$$B - D$$

Write a program that prompts the user to enter the starting population, birth and death rates, and n, the number of years. The program should then calculate and print the estimated population after n years. Your program must consist of the following functions:

a. `growthRate`: This function takes as its parameters the birth and death rates, and it returns the population growth rate.

b. `estimatedPopulation`: This function takes as its parameters the current population, population growth rate, and n, the number of years. It returns the estimated population after n years.

Your program should not accept a negative birth rate, negative death rate, or a population less than 2.

8. Rewrite the program in Programming Exercise 12 of Chapter 4 (cell phone company) so that it uses the following functions to calculate the billing amount. (In this programming exercise, do not output the number of minutes during which the service is used.)

a. `regularBill`: This function calculates and returns the billing amount for regular service.

b. `premiumBill`: This function calculates and returns the billing amount for premium service.

USER-DEFINED FUNCTIONS II

IN THIS CHAPTER, YOU WILL:

- Learn how to construct and use void functions in a program
- Discover the difference between value and reference parameters
- Explore reference parameters and value-returning functions
- Learn about the scope of an identifier
- Examine the difference between local and global identifiers
- Discover static variables
- Learn function overloading
- Explore functions with default parameters

In Chapter 6, you learned how to use value-returning functions. In this chapter, you will explore user-defined functions in general and, in particular, those C++ functions that do not have a data type, called **void functions**.

Void Functions

Void functions and value-returning functions have similar structures. Both have a heading and a body. You can place user-defined void functions either before or after the function `main`. However, the program execution always begins with the first statement in the function `main`. If you place user-defined void functions after the function `main`, you should place the function prototype before the function `main`. A void function does not have a data type. Therefore, `functionType`, that is, the return type, in the heading part and the return statement in the body of the void functions are meaningless. However, in a void function, you can use the return statement without any value; it is typically used to exit the function early. Like value-returning functions, void functions may or may not have formal parameters.

Because void functions do not have a data type, they are not used (called) in an expression. A call to a void function is a stand-alone statement. Thus, to call a void function, you use the function name together with the actual parameters (if any) in a stand-alone statement.

Void Functions Without Parameters

This section discusses void functions that do not have formal parameters.

FUNCTION DEFINITION

The general form (syntax) of the void function without formal parameters is as follows:

```
void functionName()
{
    statements
}
```

where `statements` are usually declaration and/or executable statements. In C++, `void` is a reserved word.

NOTE Like a variable name, a function name should be descriptive, so be sure to use meaningful names when naming functions.

FUNCTION CALL

The function call has the following syntax:

```
functionName();
```

Because these void functions do not have parameters, no value can be passed to them (unless you use global variables, defined later in this chapter). Such functions are thus usually good only for displaying information about the program or for printing statements. Consider the following program.

EXAMPLE 7-1

Suppose you want to print the following banner to announce the annual spring sale. (Programming Exercise 7 in Chapter 2 shows a similar output.)

```
* * * * * * * * * * * * * * * * * * * * * * * * * *
* * * * * * * * * * * * * * * * * * * * * * * * * * *
* * * * * * * * * *  Annual  * * * * * * * * * *
* * * * * * * * * * * * * * * * * * * * * * * * * * *
* * * * * * * * * * * * * * * * * * * * * * * * * * *
* * * * * * *  Spring Sale * * * * * * * * * *
* * * * * * * * * * * * * * * * * * * * * * * * * * *
* * * * * * * * * * * * * * * * * * * * * * * * * *
```

The banner starts with two lines of stars. After printing the line containing the text Annual, you need to print another two lines of stars. After printing the line containing the text Spring Sale, you need to print two more lines of stars. You can write a function that prints two lines of stars and call it whenever you need it. The complete program looks like this:

```cpp
#include <iostream>

using namespace std;

void printStars();

int main()
{
    printStars();                                          //Line 1
    cout << "********** Annual  **********" << endl;       //Line 2
    printStars();                                          //Line 3
    cout << "******* Spring Sale **********" << endl;      //Line 4
    printStars();                                          //Line 5

    return 0;
}

void printStars()
{
    cout << "*****************************" << endl;
    cout << "*****************************" << endl;
}
```

Sample Run:

```
******************************
******************************
*********** Annual  **********
******************************
******************************
******* Spring Sale *********
******************************
******************************
```

In Line 1, the function `printStars` is called and it outputs the first two lines of the output. The statement in Line 2 outputs the line of stars containing the text `Annual`, which is the third line of the output. In Line 3, the function `printStars` is called again and it outputs the next two lines of the output. The statement in Line 4 then outputs the line of stars containing the text `Spring Sale`, which is the sixth line of the output. In Line 5, the function `printStars` is called again and it outputs the last two lines of the output.

NOTE   The statement `printStars();` in the function `main` is a function call.

In the previous program, you can replace the function `printStars` with the following function:

```cpp
void printStars()
{
    int stars, lines;

    for (lines = 1; lines <= 2; lines++)              //Line 6
    {
        for (stars = 1; stars <= 30; stars++)         //Line 7
            cout << ' * ';                            //Line 8
        cout << endl;                                 //Line 9
    }
}
```

In this function definition, the outer **for** loop (Line 6) has two iterations. For each iteration of the outer **for** loop, the body of the inner **for** loop (Line 7) executes 30 times, each time printing a star. The statement in Line 8 prints each star. The output statement in Line 9 positions the cursor at the beginning of the next line on the standard output device. Because the outer **for** loop has two iterations, this function outputs two lines of stars with 30 stars in each line.

You would agree that the definition of the function `printStars` using **for** loops to output two lines of stars with 30 stars in each line is much easier to modify than the definition of `printStars` given earlier. If you need to output five lines of stars instead of two lines, for instance, you can replace the number 2 (in the first **for** loop, Line 6) with the number 5. Similarly, if you need to output 40 stars instead of 30 stars in each line, you can replace the number 30 (in the second **for** loop, Line 7) with the number 40. Furthermore, as you will soon discover, the definition of the function `printStars` using **for** loops is much easier to modify in order to establish the communication links with the calling function (such as the function `main`) and to do different things each time the function `printStars` is called.

In the previous program, the function `printStars` always prints two lines of stars, with 30 stars in each line. Now suppose that you want to print the following pattern (a triangle of stars):

```
   *
  *  *
 *  *  *
*  *  *  *
```

You could write a function similar to the function `printStars`. However, if you need to extend this pattern to 20 lines, the function `printStars` will have 20 lines. Every time you call the function `printStars`, it prints the same number of lines; the function `printStars` is inflexible. However, if you can somehow tell the function `printStars` how many lines to print, you can enhance its flexibility considerably. A communication link must exist between the calling function and the called function.

Void Functions with Parameters

The previous section discussed void functions without parameters and pointed out the limitations of such functions. In particular, you learned that no information can be passed in and out of void functions without parameters. The communication link between the calling function and the called function is established by using parameters. This section discusses void functions with parameters.

FUNCTION DEFINITION

The function definition of void functions with parameters has the following syntax:

```
void functionName(formal parameter list)
{
    statements
}
```

where `statements` are usually declaration and/or executable statements.

FORMAL PARAMETER LIST

The formal parameter list has the following syntax:

```
dataType& variable, dataType& variable, ...
```

You must specify both the data type and the variable name in the formal parameter list. The symbol & after `dataType` has a special meaning; it is used only for certain formal parameters and is discussed later in this chapter.

FUNCTION CALL

The function call has the following syntax:

```
functionName(actual parameter list);
```

ACTUAL PARAMETER LIST

The actual parameter list has the following syntax:

```
expression or variable, expression or variable, ...
```

where `expression` can consist of a single constant value. As with value-returning functions, in a function call the number of actual parameters together with their data types must match the formal parameters in the order given. Actual and formal parameters have a one-to-one correspondence. A function call results in the execution of the body of the called function. (Functions with default parameters are discussed at the end of this chapter.)

Example 7-2 shows a void function with parameters.

EXAMPLE 7-2

```
void funexp(int a, double b, char c, int x)
{
    .
    .
    .
}
```

The function `funexp` has four parameters.

Parameters provide a communication link between the calling function (such as `main`) and the called function. They enable functions to manipulate different data each time they are called. In general, there are two types of formal parameters: **value parameters** and **reference parameters**.

Value parameter: A formal parameter that receives a copy of the content of the corresponding actual parameter.

Reference parameter: A formal parameter that receives the location (memory address) of the corresponding actual parameter.

When you attach & after the `dataType` in the formal parameter list of a function, the variable following that `dataType` becomes a reference parameter.

Example 7-3 shows a void function with value and reference parameters.

EXAMPLE 7-3

```cpp
void expfun(int one, int& two, char three, double& four)
{
    .
    .
    .
}
```

The function `expfun` has four parameters: (1) one, a value parameter of type `int`; (2) two, a reference parameter of type `int`; (3) three, a value parameter of type `char`, and (4) four, a reference parameter of type `double`.

7

Let us now write the C++ program to print the pattern (triangle of stars) shown in the previous section.

EXAMPLE 7-4

The following C++ program prints a triangle of stars:

```cpp
//Program: Print a triangle of stars

#include <iostream>

using namespace std;

void printStars(int blanks, int starsInLine);

int main()
{
    int noOfLines;  //variable to store the number of lines
    int counter;    //for loop control variable
    int noOfBlanks; //variable to store the number of blanks
    cout << "Enter the number of star lines (1 to 20) "
         << "to be printed: ";                              //Line 1
```

```cpp
    cin >> noOfLines;                                      //Line 2

    while (noOfLines < 0 || noOfLines > 20)                //Line 3
    {
        cout << "Number of star lines should be "
             << "between 1 and 20" << endl;                //Line 4
        cout << "Enter the number of star lines "
             << "(1 to 20) to be printed: ";               //Line 5
        cin >> noOfLines;                                  //Line 6
    }

    cout << endl << endl;                                  //Line 7
    noOfBlanks = 30;                                       //Line 8

    for (counter = 1; counter <= noOfLines; counter++)     //Line 9
    {
        printStars(noOfBlanks, counter);                   //Line 10
        noOfBlanks--;                                      //Line 11
    }

    return 0;                                              //Line 12
}

void printStars(int blanks, int starsInLine)
{
    int count;

    for (count = 1; count <= blanks; count++)              //Line 13
        cout << ' ';                                       //Line 14
    for (count = 1; count <= starsInLine; count++)         //Line 15
        cout << " * ";                                     //Line 16
    cout << endl;
}
```

Sample Run: In this sample run, the user input is shaded.

```
Enter the number of star lines (1 to 20) to be printed: 15
```

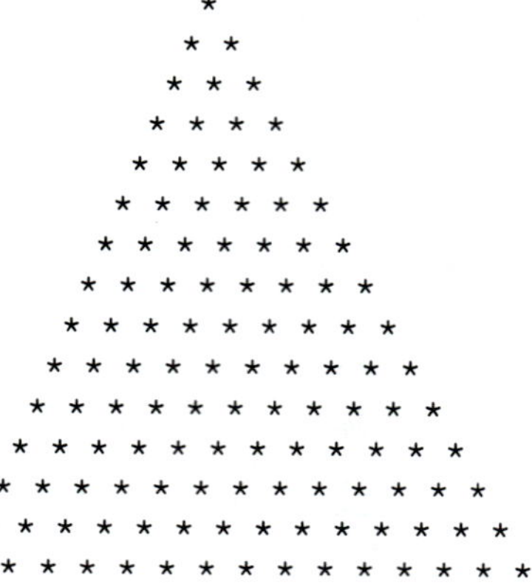

In this program, the statement (see Line 10):

```
printStars(noOfBlanks, counter);
```

in the function `main` is a function call. The identifier `noOfBlanks` and `counter` are actual parameters.

The function `printStars` works as follows. The function `printStars` has two parameters. Whenever this function executes, it outputs a line of stars with a certain number of blanks before the stars. The number of blanks and the number of stars in a line are passed as parameters to the function `printStars`. The first parameter, `blanks`, tells how many blanks to print; the second parameter, `starsInLine`, tells how many stars to print in a line. If the value of the parameter `blanks` is 30, for instance, then the first **for** loop (Line 13) in the function `printStars` has 30 iterations and prints 30 blanks. Also, because you want to print spaces between the stars, every iteration of the second **for** loop (Line 15) in the function `printStars` prints "*" (Line 16)—that is, a blank followed by a star.

In the function `main`, the user is first asked to specify how many lines of stars to print (Line 1). (In this program, the user is restricted to 20 lines because a triangular grid of up to 20 lines fits nicely on the screen.) Because the program is restricted to only 20 lines, the **while** loop at Lines 3 through 6 ensures that the program prints only the triangular grid of stars if the number of lines is between 1 and 20.

The **for** loop (Line 9) in the function `main` calls the function `printStars` (Line 10). Every iteration of this **for** loop specifies the number of blanks followed by the number of stars to print in a line, using the variables `noOfBlanks` and `counter`. Every call of the function `printStars` receives one fewer blank and one more star than the previous call. For example, the first iteration of the **for** loop in the function `main` specifies 30 blanks and 1 star (which are passed as parameters, `noOfBlanks` and `counter`, to the function `printStars`). The **for** loop then:

- Decrements the number of blanks by 1. This is done by executing the following statement in Line 11:

  ```
  noOfBlanks--;
  ```

- At the end of the **for** loop, the number of stars is incremented by 1 for the next iteration. This is done by executing the update statement, `counter++` (Line 9), in the **for** statement, which increments the value of the variable `counter` by 1.

In other words, the second call of the function `printStars` receives 29 blanks and 2 stars as parameters.

Value Parameters

The previous section defined two types of parameters—value parameters and reference parameters. Example 7-4 shows a program that uses a function with parameters. Before considering more examples of void functions with parameters, let us make the following observation about value and reference parameters. When a function is called, the value of the actual parameter is copied into the corresponding formal parameter. If the formal parameter is a value parameter, then after copying the value of the actual parameter, there is no connection between the formal parameter and actual parameter; that is, the formal parameter has its own copy of the data. Therefore, during program execution, the formal parameter manipulates the data stored in its own memory space. The program in Example 7-5 further illustrates how a value parameter works.

EXAMPLE 7-5

The following program shows how a formal parameter of a primitive data type works.

```cpp
//Example 7-5
//Program illustrating how a value parameter works.

#include <iostream>

using namespace std;

void funcValueParam(int num);

int main()
{
    int number = 6;                                     //Line 1

    cout << "Line 2: Before calling the function "
         << "funcValueParam, number = " << number
         << endl;                                       //Line 2

    funcValueParam(number);                             //Line 3

    cout << "Line 4: After calling the function "
         << "funcValueParam, number = " << number
         << endl;                                       //Line 4

    return 0;
}

void funcValueParam(int num)
{
    cout << "Line 5: In the function funcValueParam, "
         << "before changing, num = " << num
         << endl;                                       //Line 5
```

```cpp
    num = 15;                                                   //Line 6

    cout << "Line 7: In the function funcValueParam, "
         << "after changing, num = " << num
         << endl;                                               //Line 7
}
```

Sample Run:

```
Line 2: Before calling the function funcValueParam, number = 6
Line 5: In the function funcValueParam, before changing, num = 6
Line 7: In the function funcValueParam, after changing, num = 15
Line 4: After calling the function funcValueParam, number = 6
```

This program works as follows. The execution begins at the function `main`. The statement in Line 1 declares and initializes the **int** variable `number`. The statement in Line 2 outputs the value of `number` before calling the function `funcValueParam`; the statement in Line 3 calls the function `funcValueParam`. The value of the variable `number` is then passed to the formal parameter `num`. Control now transfers to the function `funcValueParam`.

The statement in Line 5 outputs the value of `num` before changing its value. The statement in Line 6 changes the value of `num` to `15`; the statement in Line 7 outputs the value of `num`. After this statement executes, the function `funcValueParam` exits and control goes back to the function `main`.

The statement in Line 4 outputs the value of `number` after calling the function `funcValueParam`. The Sample Run shows that the value of `number` (Lines 2 and 4) remains the same even though the value of its corresponding formal parameter `num` was changed within the function `funcValueParam`.

The output shows the sequence in which the statements execute.

After copying data, a value parameter has no connection with the actual parameter, so a value parameter cannot pass any result back to the calling function. When the function executes, any changes made to the formal parameters do not in any way affect the actual parameters. The actual parameters have no knowledge of what is happening to the formal parameters. Thus, value parameters cannot pass information outside the function. Value parameters provide only a one-way link between actual parameters and formal parameters. Hence, functions with only value parameters have limitations.

Reference Variables as Parameters

The program in Example 7-5 illustrates how a value parameter works. On the other hand, suppose that a formal parameter is a reference parameter. Because a reference parameter receives the address (memory location) of the actual parameter, reference parameters can pass one or more values from a function and can change the value of the actual parameter.

Reference parameters are useful in three situations:

- When you want to return more than one value from a function
- When the value of the actual parameter needs to be changed
- When passing the address would save memory space and time relative to copying a large amount of data

The first two situations are illustrated throughout this book. Chapters 9 and 11 discuss the third situation, when arrays and classes are introduced.

Recall that, when you attach `&` after the `dataType` in the formal parameter list of a function, the variable following that `dataType` becomes a reference parameter.

NOTE You can declare a reference (formal) parameter as a constant by using the keyword `const`. Chapters 10 and 11 discuss constant reference parameters. Until then, the reference parameters that you use will be nonconstant as defined in this chapter. From the definition of a reference parameter, it follows that a constant value or an expression cannot be passed to a nonconstant reference parameter. If a formal parameter is a nonconstant reference parameter, during a function call its corresponding actual parameter must be a variable.

EXAMPLE 7-6

Calculate Grade

The following program takes a course score (a value between 0 and 100) and determines a student's course grade. This program has three functions: `main`, `getScore`, and `printGrade`, as follows:

1. `main`

   a. Get the course score.

   b. Print the course grade.

2. `getScore`

   a. Prompt the user for the input.

   b. Get the input.

   c. Print the course score.

3. `printGrade`

   a. Calculate the course grade.

   b. Print the course grade.

The complete program is as follows:

```cpp
//This program reads a course score and prints the
//associated course grade.

#include <iostream>
using namespace std;

void getScore(int& score);
void printGrade(int score);

int main()
{
    int courseScore;

    cout << "Line 1: Based on the course score, \n"
         << "    this program computes the "
         << "course grade." << endl;                    //Line 1

    getScore(courseScore);                              //Line 2

    printGrade(courseScore);                            //Line 3

    return 0;
}

void getScore(int& score)
{
    cout << "Line 4: Enter course score: ";            //Line 4
    cin >> score;                                       //Line 5
    cout << endl << "Line 6: Course score is "
         << score << endl;                              //Line 6
}

void printGrade(int cScore)
{
    cout << "Line 7: Your grade for the course is ";   //Line 7

    if (cScore >= 90)                                   //Line 8
        cout << "A." << endl;
    else if (cScore >= 80)
        cout << "B." << endl;
    else if(cScore >= 70)
        cout << "C." << endl;
    else if (cScore >= 60)
        cout << "D." << endl;
    else
        cout << "F." << endl;
}
```

Sample Run: In this sample run, the user input is shaded.

```
Line 1: Based on the course score,
        this program computes the course grade.
Line 4: Enter course score: 85

Line 6: Course score is 85
Line 7: Your grade for the course is B.
```

This program works as follows. The program starts to execute at Line 1, which prints the first line of the output (see the Sample Run). The statement in Line 2 calls the function `getScore` with the actual parameter `courseScore` (a variable declared in `main`). Because the formal parameter `score` of the function `getScore` is a reference parameter, the address (that is, the memory location of the variable `courseScore`) passes to `score`. Thus, both `score` and `courseScore` refer to the same memory location, which is `courseScore` (see Figure 7-1).

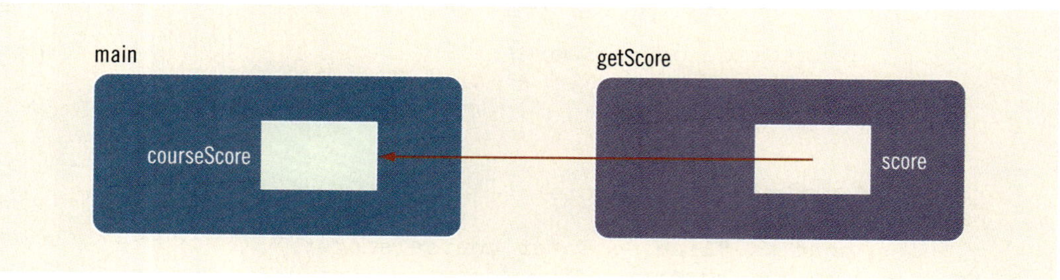

FIGURE 7-1 Variable `courseScore` and the parameter `score`

Any changes made to `score` immediately change the value of `courseScore`.

Control is then transferred to the function `getScore`, and the statement in Line 4 executes, printing the second line of output. This statement prompts the user to enter the course score. The statement in Line 5 reads and stores the value entered by the user (85 in the Sample Run) in `score`, which is actually `courseScore` (because `score` is a reference parameter). Thus, at this point, the value of the variables `score` and `courseScore` is 85 (see Figure 7-2).

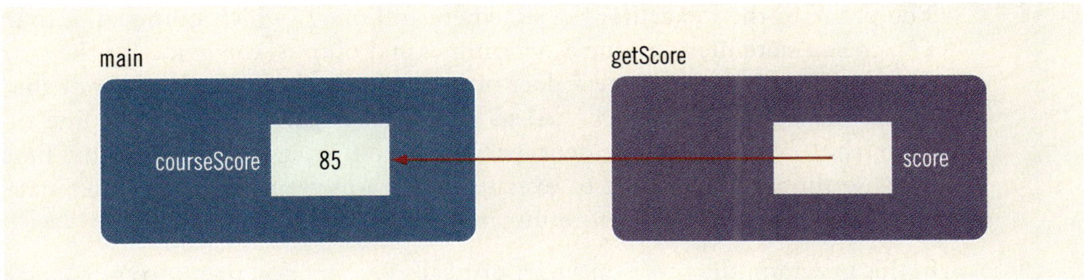

FIGURE 7-2 Variable `courseScore` and the parameter `score` after the statement in Line 5 executes

Next, the statement in Line 6 outputs the value of **score** as shown by the third line of the Sample Run. After Line 6 executes, control goes back to the function **main** (see Figure 7-3).

FIGURE 7-3 Variable `courseScore` after the statement in Line 6 is executed and control goes back to `main`

The statement in Line 3 executes next. It is a function call to the function **printGrade** with the actual parameter **courseScore**. Because the formal parameter **cScore** of the function **printScore** is a value parameter, the parameter **cScore** receives the value of the corresponding actual parameter **courseScore**. Thus, the value of **cScore** is 85. After copying the value of **courseScore** into **cScore**, no communication exists between **cScore** and **courseScore** (see Figure 7-4).

FIGURE 7-4 Variable `courseScore` and the parameter `cScore`

The program then executes the statement in Line 7, which outputs the fourth line. The `if...else` statement in Line 8 determines and outputs the grade for the course. Because the output statement in Line 7 does not contain the newline character or the manipulator `endl`, the output of the `if...else` statement is part of the fourth line of the output. After the `if...else` statement executes, control goes back to the function `main`. Because the next statement to execute in the function `main` is the last statement of the function `main`, the program terminates.

In this program, the function `main` first calls the function `getScore` to obtain the course score from the user. The function `main` then calls the function `printGrade` to calculate and print the grade based on this course score. The course score is retrieved by the function `getScore`; later, this course score is used by the function `printGrade`. Because the value retrieved by the `getScore` function is used later in the program, the function `getScore` must pass this value outside. Thus, the formal parameter that holds this value must be a reference parameter.

Value and Reference Parameters and Memory Allocation

When a function is called, memory for its formal parameters and variables declared in the body of the function (called **local variables**) is allocated in the function data area. Recall that, in the case of a value parameter, the value of the actual parameter is copied into the memory cell of its corresponding formal parameter. In the case of a reference parameter, the address of the actual parameter passes to the formal parameter. That is, the content of the formal parameter is an address. During data manipulation, the content of the formal parameter directs the computer to manipulate the data of the memory cell indicated by its content. Thus, in the case of a reference parameter, both the actual and formal parameters refer to the same memory location. Consequently, during program execution, changes made by the formal parameter permanently change the value of the actual parameter.

NOTE Stream variables (for example, `ifstream` and `ofstream`) should be passed by reference to a function. After opening the input/output file or after reading and/or outputting data, the state of the input and/or output stream can then be passed outside the function.

Because parameter passing is fundamental to any programming language, Examples 7-7 through 7-9 further illustrate this concept. Each covers a different scenario.

EXAMPLE 7-7

The following program shows how reference and value parameters work.

```cpp
//Example 7-7: Reference and value parameters

#include <iostream>

using namespace std;

void funOne(int a, int& b, char v);
void funTwo(int& x, int y, char& w);

int main()
{
    int num1, num2;
    char ch;

    num1 = 10;                                          //Line 1
    num2 = 15;                                          //Line 2
    ch = 'A';                                           //Line 3

    cout << "Line 4: Inside main: num1 = " << num1
         << ", num2 = " << num2 << ", and ch = "
         << ch << endl;                                 //Line 4

    funOne(num1, num2, ch);                             //Line 5

    cout << "Line 6: After funOne: num1 = " << num1
         << ", num2 = " << num2 << ", and ch = "
         << ch << endl;                                 //Line 6

    funTwo(num2, 25, ch);                               //Line 7

    cout << "Line 8: After funTwo: num1 = " << num1
         << ", num2 = " << num2 << ", and ch = "
         << ch << endl;                                 //Line 8

    return 0;
}

void funOne(int a, int& b, char v)
{
    int one;

    one = a;                                            //Line 9
    a++;                                                //Line 10
    b = b * 2;                                          //Line 11
    v = 'B';                                            //Line 12
```

```
    cout << "Line 13: Inside funOne: a = " << a
         << ", b = " << b << ", v = " << v
         << ", and one = " << one << endl;              //Line 13
}

void funTwo(int& x, int y, char& w)
{
    x++;                                                //Line 14
    y = y * 2;                                          //Line 15
    w = 'G';                                            //Line 16

    cout << "Line 17: Inside funTwo: x = " << x
         << ", y = " << y << ", and w = " << w
         << endl;                                       //Line 17
}
```

Sample Run:

```
Line 4: Inside main: num1 = 10, num2 = 15, and ch = A
Line 13: Inside funOne: a = 11, b = 30, v = B, and one = 10
Line 6: After funOne: num1 = 10, num2 = 30, and ch = A
Line 17: Inside funTwo: x = 31, y = 50, and w = G
Line 8: After funTwo: num1 = 10, num2 = 31, and ch = G
```

Let us walk through this program. The values of the variables are shown before and/or after each statement executes.

Just before the statement in Line 1 executes, memory is allocated only for the variables of the function **main**; this memory is not initialized. After the statement in Line 3 executes, the variables are as shown in Figure 7-5.

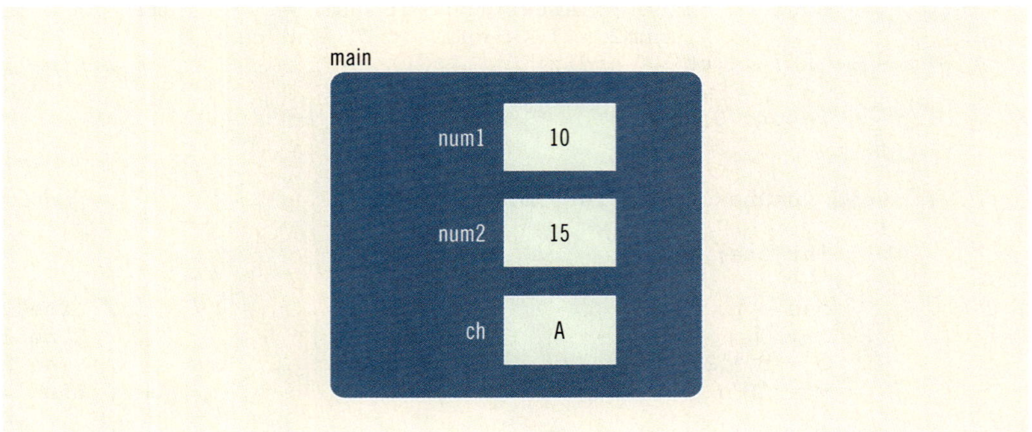

FIGURE 7-5 Values of the variables after the statement in Line 3 executes

The statement in Line 4 produces the following output:

```
Line 4: Inside main: num1 = 10, num2 = 15, and ch = A
```

The statement in Line 5 is a function call to the function `funOne`. Now function `funOne` has three parameters and one local variable. Memory for the parameters and the local variable of function `funOne` is allocated. Because the formal parameter b is a reference parameter, it receives the address (memory location) of the corresponding actual parameter, which is num2. The other two formal parameters are value parameters, so they copy the values of their corresponding actual parameters. Just before the statement in Line 9 executes, the variables are as shown in Figure 7-6.

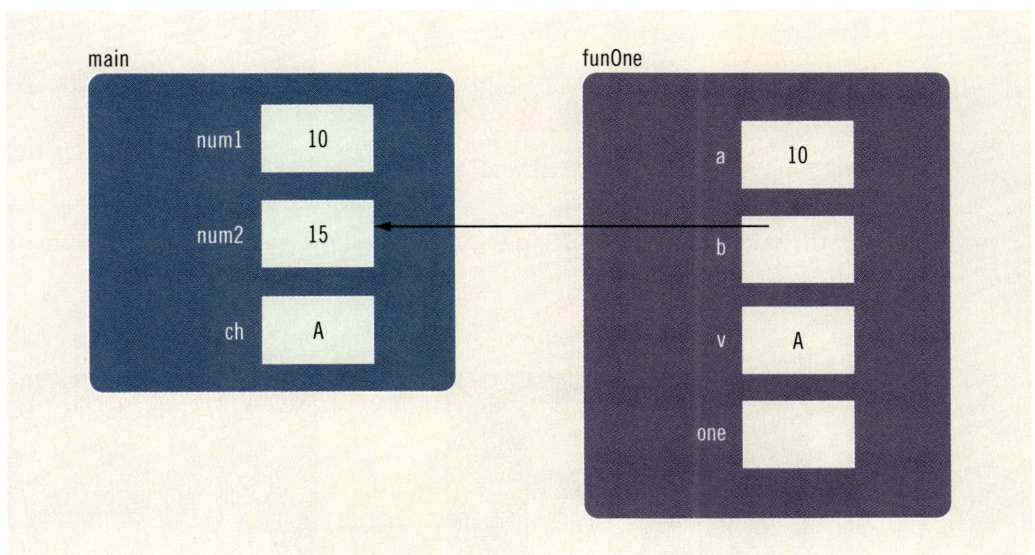

FIGURE 7-6 Values of the variables just before the statement in Line 9 executes

After the statement in Line 9, `one = a;`, executes, the variables are as shown in Figure 7-7.

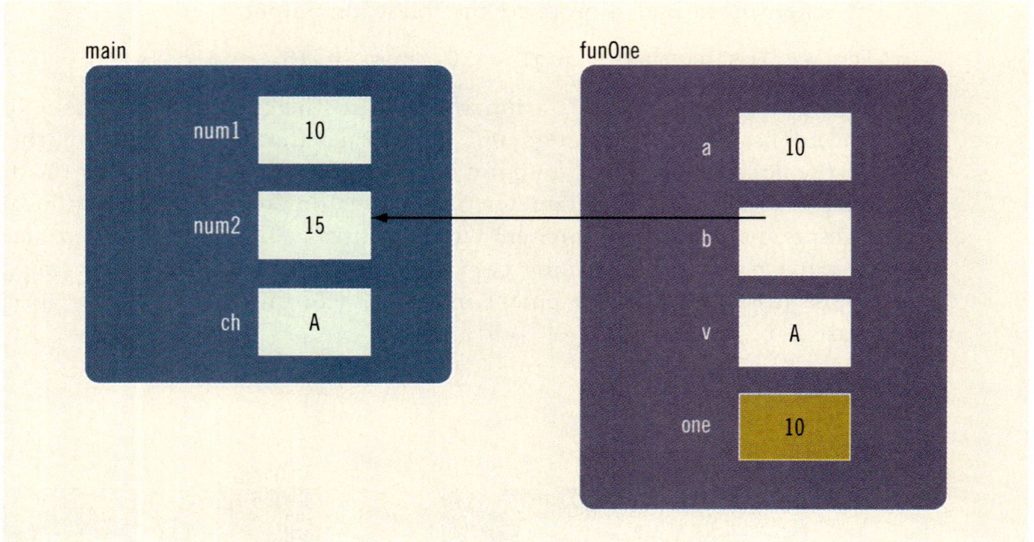

FIGURE 7-7 Values of the variables after the statement in Line 9 executes

After the statement in Line 10, `a++;`, executes, the variables are as shown in Figure 7–8.

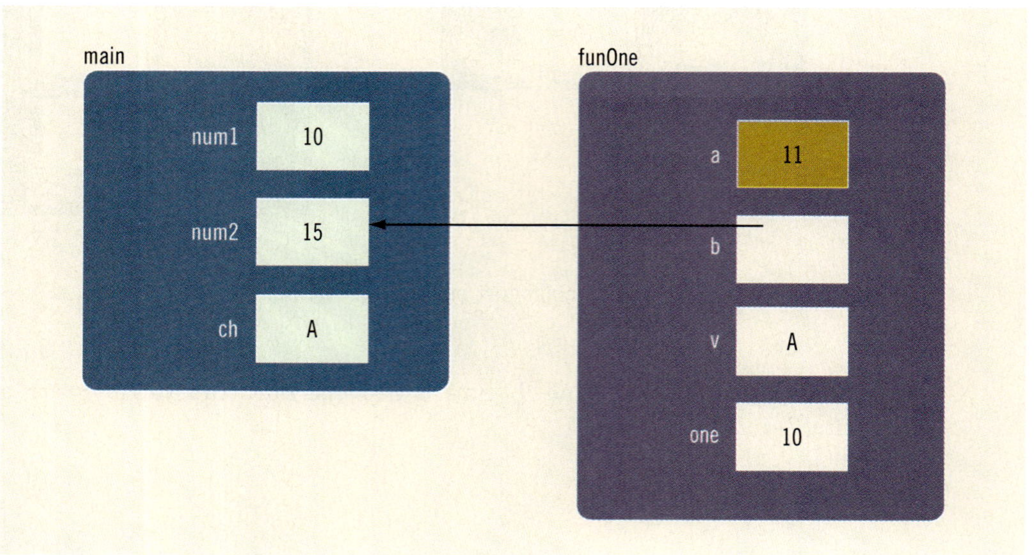

FIGURE 7-8 Values of the variables after the statement in Line 10 executes

After the statement in Line 11, `b = b * 2;`, executes, the variables are as shown in Figure 7–9. (Note that the variable b changed the value of num2.)

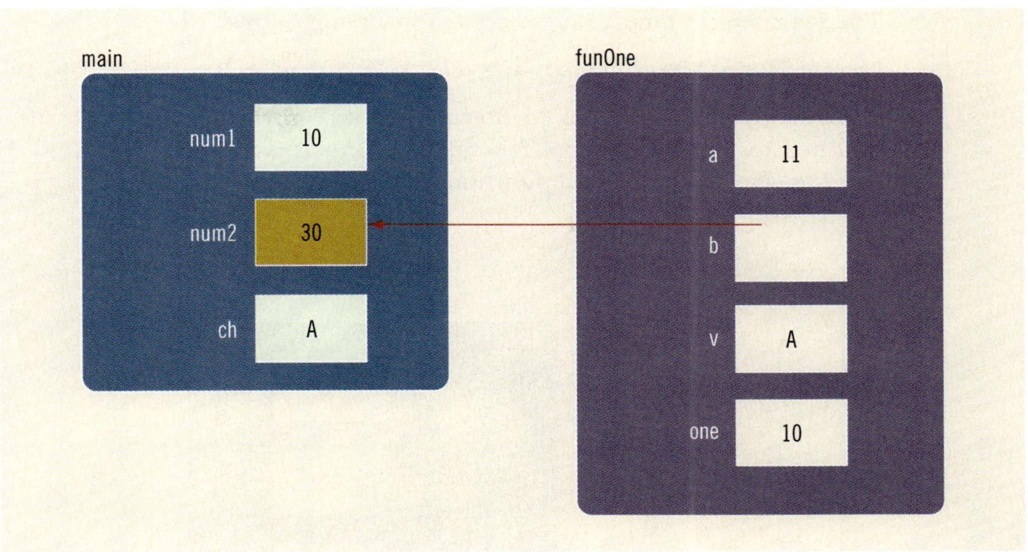

FIGURE 7-9 Values of the variables after the statement in Line 11 executes

After the statement in Line 12, `v = 'B';`, executes, the variables are as shown in Figure 7-10.

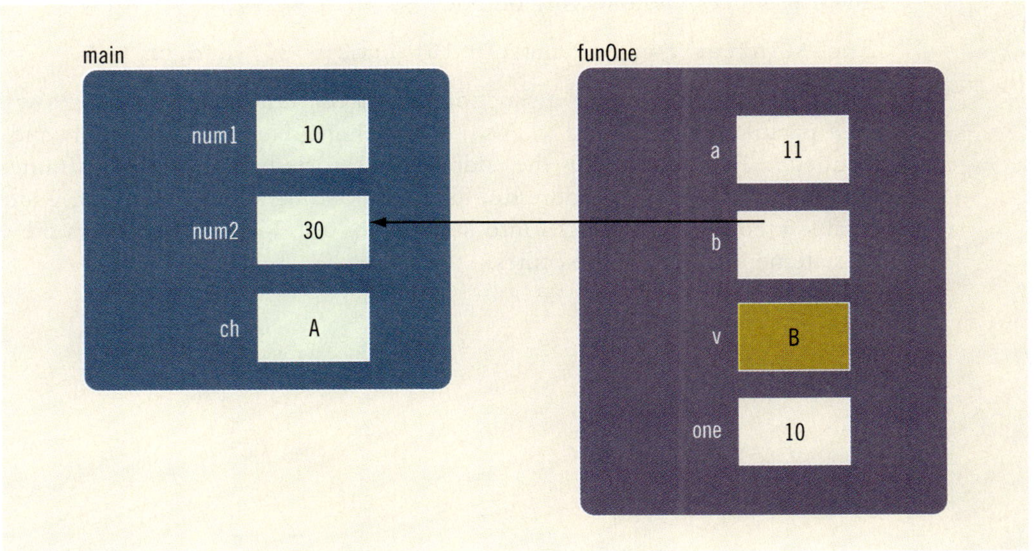

FIGURE 7-10 Values of the variables after the statement in Line 12 executes

The statement in Line 13 produces the following output:

```
Line 13: Inside funOne: a = 11, b = 30, v = B, and one = 10
```

After the statement in Line 13 executes, control goes back to Line 6 and the memory allocated for the variables of function `funOne` is deallocated. Figure 7-11 shows the values of the variables of the function `main`.

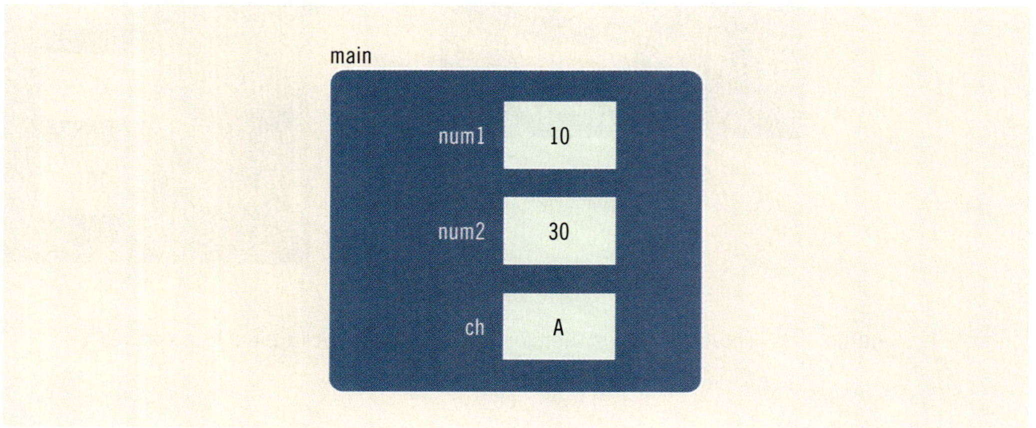

FIGURE 7-11 Values of the variables when control goes back to Line 6

Line 6 produces the following output:

```
Line 6: After funOne: num1 = 10, num2 = 30, and ch = A
```

The statement in Line 7 is a function call to the function `funTwo`. Now `funTwo` has three parameters: `x`, `y`, and `w`. Also, `x` and `w` are reference parameters and `y` is a value parameter. Thus, `x` receives the address of its corresponding actual parameter, which is `num2`, and `w` receives the address of its corresponding actual parameter, which is `ch`. The variable `y` copies the value 25 into its memory cell. Figure 7-12 shows the values before the statement in Line 14 executes.

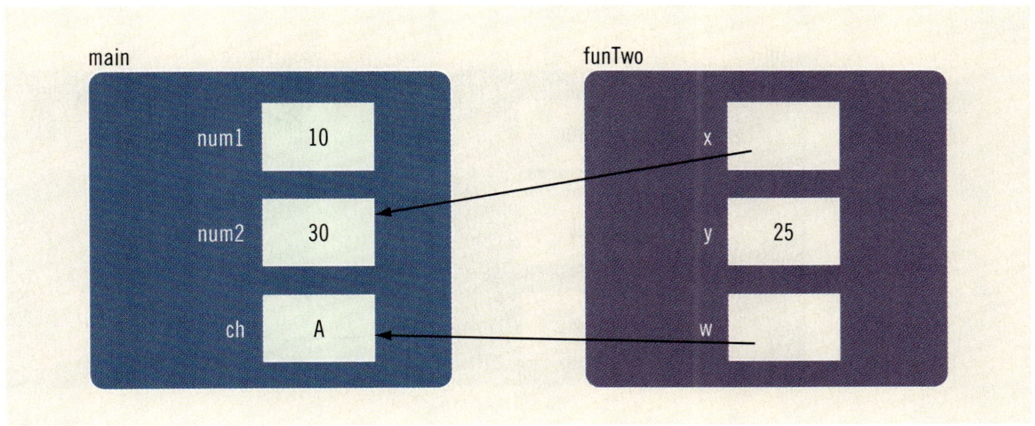

FIGURE 7-12 Values of the variables before the statement in Line 14 executes

After the statement in Line 14, **x++;**, executes, the variables are as shown in Figure 7-13. (Note that the variable **x** changed the value of **num2**.)

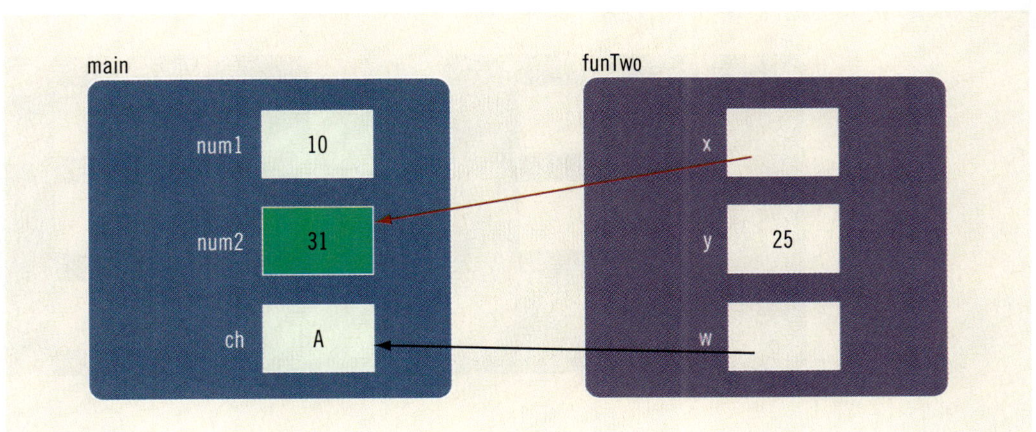

FIGURE 7-13 Values of the variables after the statement in Line 14 executes

After the statement in Line 15, **y = y * 2;**, executes, the variables are as shown in Figure 7-14.

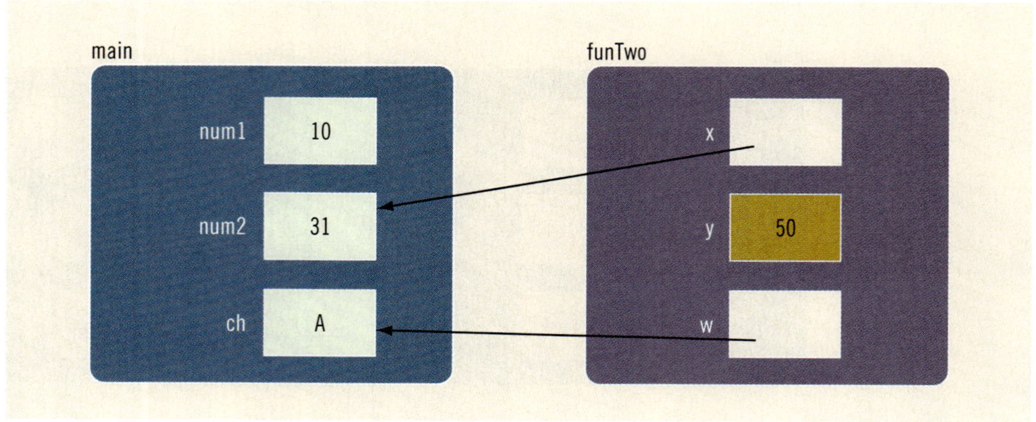

FIGURE 7-14 Values of the variables after the statement in Line 15 executes

After the statement in Line 16, `w = 'G';`, executes, the variables are as shown in Figure 7–15. (Note that the variable w changed the value of ch.)

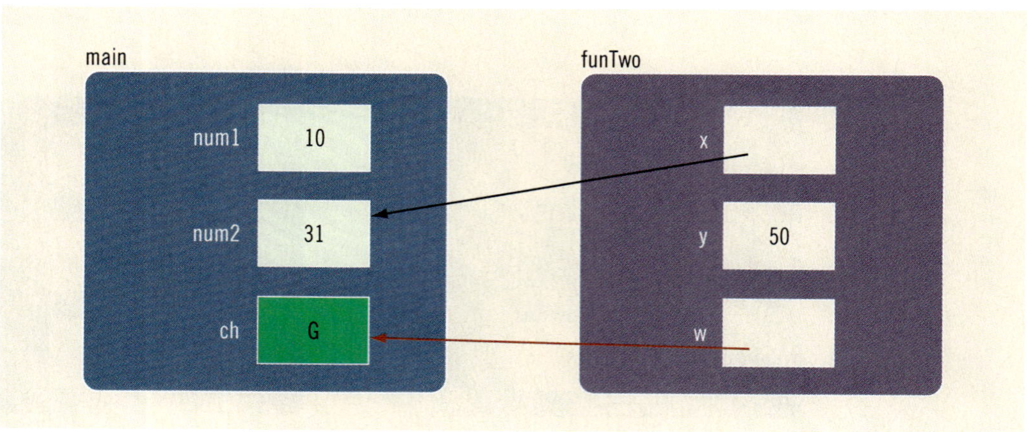

FIGURE 7-15 Values of the variables after the statement in Line 16 executes

Line 17 produces the following output:

```
Line 17: Inside funTwo: x = 31, y = 50, and w = G
```

After the statement in Line 17 executes, control goes to Line 8. The memory allocated for the variables of function `funTwo` is deallocated. The values of the variables of the function `main` are as shown in Figure 7–16.

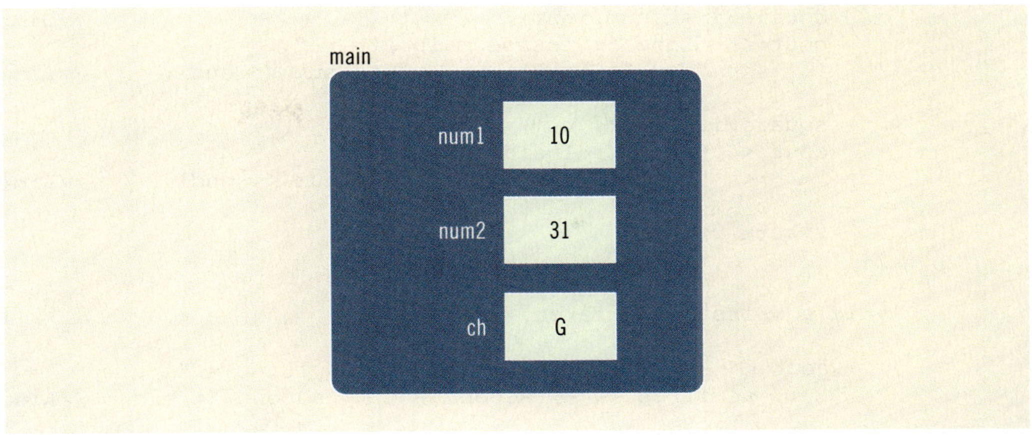

FIGURE 7-16 Values of the variables when control goes to Line 8

The statement in Line 8 produces the following output:

```
Line 8: After funTwo: num1 = 10, num2 = 31, and ch = G
```

After the statement in Line 8 executes, the program terminates.

EXAMPLE 7-8

This example also shows how reference parameters manipulate actual parameters.

```cpp
//Example 7-8: Reference and value parameters.
//Program: Makes You Think.

#include <iostream>

using namespace std;

void addFirst(int& first, int& second);
void doubleFirst(int one, int two);
void squareFirst(int& ref, int val);

int main()
{
    int num = 5;

    cout << "Line 1: Inside main: num = " << num
        << endl;                                          //Line 1

    addFirst(num, num);                                   //Line 2
    cout << "Line 3: Inside main after addFirst:"
        << " num = " << num << endl;                      //Line 3
```

```cpp
    doubleFirst(num, num);                                //Line 4
    cout << "Line 5: Inside main after "
         << "doubleFirst: num = " << num << endl;     //Line 5

    squareFirst(num, num);                                //Line 6
    cout << "Line 7: Inside main after "
         << "squareFirst: num = " << num << endl;     //Line 7

    return 0;
}

void addFirst(int& first, int& second)
{
    cout << "Line 8: Inside addFirst:  first = "
         << first << ", second = " << second << endl; //Line 8

    first = first + 2;                                    //Line 9

    cout << "Line 10: Inside addFirst:  first = "
         << first << ", second = " << second << endl; //Line 10

    second = second * 2;                                  //Line 11

    cout << "Line 12: Inside addFirst:  first = "
         << first << ", second = " << second << endl; //Line 12
}

void doubleFirst(int one, int two)
{
    cout << "Line 13: Inside doubleFirst:  one = "
         << one << ", two = " << two << endl;          //Line 13

    one = one * 2;                                        //Line 14

    cout << "Line 15: Inside doubleFirst:  one = "
         << one << ", two = " << two << endl;          //Line 15

    two = two + 2;                                        //Line 16

    cout << "Line 17: Inside doubleFirst:  one = "
         << one << ", two = " << two << endl;          //Line 17
}

void squareFirst(int& ref, int val)
{
    cout << "Line 18: Inside squareFirst: ref = "
         << ref << ", val = " << val << endl;          //Line 18

    ref = ref * ref;                                      //Line 19
```

```cpp
    cout << "Line 20: Inside squareFirst: ref = "
         << ref << ", val = " << val << endl;        //Line 20

    val = val + 2;                                    //Line 21

    cout << "Line 22: Inside squareFirst: ref = "
         << ref << ", val = " << val << endl;        //Line 22
}
```

Sample Run:

```
Line 1: Inside main:   num = 5
Line 8: Inside addFirst:   first = 5, second = 5
Line 10: Inside addFirst:   first = 7, second = 7
Line 12: Inside addFirst:   first = 14, second = 14
Line 3: Inside main after addFirst:   num = 14
Line 13: Inside doubleFirst:   one = 14, two = 14
Line 15: Inside doubleFirst:   one = 28, two = 14
Line 17: Inside doubleFirst:   one = 28, two = 16
Line 5: Inside main after doubleFirst:   num = 14
Line 18: Inside squareFirst: ref = 14, val = 14
Line 20: Inside squareFirst: ref = 196, val = 14
Line 22: Inside squareFirst: ref = 196, val = 16
Line 7: Inside main after squareFirst:   num = 196
```

Both parameters of the function `addFirst` are reference parameters, and both parameters of the function `doubleFirst` are value parameters. The statement:

```cpp
addFirst(num, num);
```

in the function `main` (Line 2) passes the reference of `num` to both formal parameters `first` and `second` of the function `addFirst`, because the corresponding actual parameters for both formal parameters are the same. That is, the variables `first` and `second` refer to the same memory location, which is `num`. Figure 7-17 illustrates this situation.

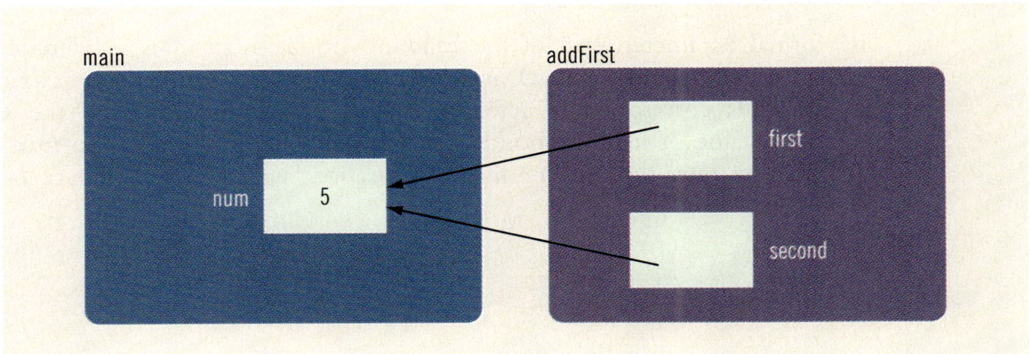

FIGURE 7-17 Parameters of the function `addFirst`

Any changes that `first` makes to its value immediately change the value of `second` and `num`. Similarly, any changes that `second` makes to its value immediately change `first` and `num`, because all three variables refer to the same memory location. (Note that `num` was initialized to 5.)

The formal parameters of the function `doubleFirst` are value parameters. So the statement:

```
doubleFirst(num, num);
```

in the function `main` (Line 4) copies the value of `num` into `one` and `two` because the corresponding actual parameters for both formal parameters are the same. Figure 7-18 illustrates this scenario.

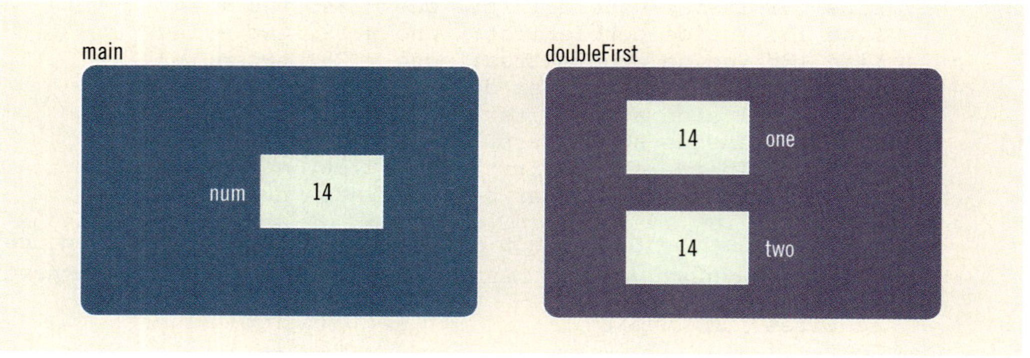

FIGURE 7-18   Parameters of the function `doubleFirst`

Because both `one` and `two` are value parameters, any changes that `one` makes to its value do not affect the values of `two` and `num`. Similarly, any changes that `two` makes to its value do not affect `one` and `num`. (Note that the value of `num` before the function `doubleFirst` executes is 14.)

The formal parameter `ref` of the function `squareFirst` is a reference parameter, and the formal parameter `val` is a value parameter. The variable `ref` receives the address of its corresponding actual parameter, which is `num`, and the variable `val` copies the value of its corresponding actual parameter, which is also `num`. Thus, both `num` and `ref` refer to the same memory location, which is `num`. Figure 7-19 illustrates this situation.

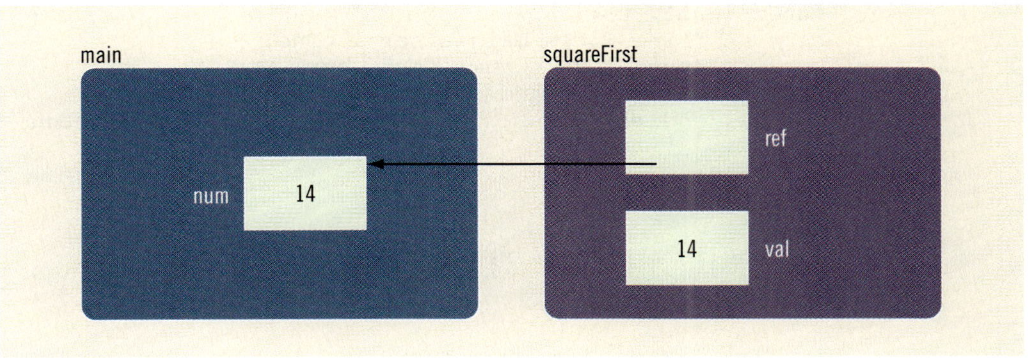

FIGURE 7-19 Parameters of the function `squareFirst`

Any changes that `ref` makes immediately change `num`. Any changes made by `val` do not affect `num`. (Note that the value of `num` before the function `squareFirst` executes is 14.)

We recommend that you walk through the program in Example 7-8. The output shows the order in which the statements execute.

EXAMPLE 7-9

This example shows how a variable declared outside of any function (or block) behaves.

```cpp
//Example 7-9: Reference and value parameters

#include <iostream>

using namespace std;

int t;

void funOne(int& a, int& x);

int main()
{
    int num1, num2;

    num1 = 10;                                          //Line 1
    num2 = 20;                                          //Line 2
    t = 15;                                             //Line 3

    cout << "Line 4: In main: num1 = " << num1
         << ", num2 = " << num2 << ", and t = "
         << t << endl;                                  //Line 4
```

```cpp
    funOne(num1, t);                                      //Line 5
    cout << "Line 6: In main after funOne: "
         << "num1 = " << num1 << ", num2 = "
         << num2 << ", and t = " << t
         << endl;                                         //Line 6

    return 0;                                             //Line 7
}

void funOne(int& a, int& x)
{
    int z;

    z = a + x;                                            //Line 8

    cout << "Line 9: In funOne: a = " << a
         << ", x = " << x << ", z = " << z
         << ", and t = " << t << endl;                    //Line 9

    x = x + 5;                                            //Line 10
    cout << "Line 11: In funOne: a = " << a
         << ", x = " << x << ", z = " << z
         << ", and t = " << t << endl;                    //Line 11

    a = a + 12;                                           //Line 12
    cout << "Line 13: In funOne: a = " << a
         << ", x = " << x << ", z = " << z
         << ", and t = " << t << endl;                    //Line 13

    t = t + 13;                                           //Line 14

    cout << "Line 15: In funOne: a = " << a
         << ", x = " << x << ", z = " << z
         << ", and t = " << t << endl;                    //Line 15
}
```

Sample Run:

```
Line 4: In main: num1 = 10, num2 = 20, and t = 15
Line 9: In funOne: a = 10, x = 15, z = 25, and t = 15
Line 11: In funOne: a = 10, x = 20, z = 25, and t = 20
Line 13: In funOne: a = 22, x = 20, z = 25, and t = 20
Line 15: In funOne: a = 22, x = 33, z = 25, and t = 33
Line 6: In main after funOne: num1 = 22, num2 = 20, and t = 33
```

This program has a variable t that is declared before the definition of any function. Because none of the functions has an identifier t, the variable t is accessible anywhere in the program. Also, the program consists of a void function: funOne, which has two formal parameters, both of which are reference parameters.

In Line 5, the function `main` calls the function `funOne`, and the actual parameters passed to `funOne` are `num1` and `t`. Thus, `a`, the formal parameter of `funOne`, receives the address of `num1`, and `x` receives the address of `t`. Any changes that `a` makes to its value immediately change `num1`, and any changes that `x` makes immediately change `t`. Because `t` can be directly accessed anywhere in the program, in Line 14 the function `funOne` changes the value of `t` by using `t` itself (see the output of Line 15). Thus, you can manipulate the value of `t` by using either a reference parameter or `t` itself.

Once again, the output shows the order in which the statements are executed.

Reference Parameters and Value-Returning Functions

In Chapter 6, in the discussion of value-returning functions, you learned how to use value parameters only. You can also use reference parameters in a value-returning function, although this approach is not recommended. By definition, a value-returning function returns a single value; this value is returned via the return statement. If a function needs to return more than one value, you should change it to a void function and use the appropriate reference parameters to return the values.

Scope of an Identifier

The previous sections and Chapter 6 presented several examples of programs with user-defined functions. Identifiers are declared in a function heading, within a block, or outside a block. A question naturally arises: Are you allowed to access any identifier anywhere in the program? The answer is no. You must follow certain rules to access an identifier. The **scope** of an identifier refers to where in the program an identifier is accessible (visible). Recall that an identifier is the name of something in C++, such as a variable or function name.

This section examines the scope of an identifier. First, we define the following two terms:

Local identifier: Identifiers declared within a function (or block).

Local identifiers are not accessible outside of the function (block).

Global identifier: Identifiers declared outside of every function definition.

Also, C++ does not allow the nesting of functions. That is, you cannot include the definition of one function in the body of another function.

In general, the following rules apply when an identifier is accessed:

1. Global identifiers (such as variables) are accessible by a function or a block if:

    a. The identifier is declared before the function definition (block),

    b. The function name is different from the identifier,

   c.   All parameters of the function have names different than the name of the identifier, and

   d.   All local identifiers (such as local variables) have names different than the name of the identifier.

2.   **(Nested Block)** An identifier declared within a block is accessible:

   a.   Only within the block from the point at which it is declared until the end of the block, and

   b.   By those blocks that are nested within that block if the nested block does not have an identifier with the same name as that of the outside block (the block that encloses the nested block).

3.   The scope of a function name is similar to the scope of an identifier declared outside any block. That is, the scope of a function name is the same as the scope of a global variable.

Before considering an example to explain these scope rules, first note the scope of the identifier declared in the **for** statement. C++ allows the programmer to declare a variable in the initialization statement of the **for** statement. For example, the following **for** statement:

```cpp
for (int count = 1; count < 10; count++)
    cout << count << endl;
```

declares the variable count and initializes it to 1. The scope of the variable count is limited to only the body of the **for** loop.

NOTE   This scope rule for the variable declared in a **for** statement may not apply to Standard C++. In Standard C++, the scope of the variable declared in the `initialize` statement may extend from the point at which it is declared until the end of the block that immediately surrounds the **for** statement. (To be absolutely sure, check your compiler's documentation.)

The following C++ program helps illustrate the scope rules:

```cpp
#include <iostream>

using namespace std;

const double rate = 10.50;
int z;
double t;

void one(int x, char y);
void two(int a, int b, char x);
void three(int one, double y, int z);
```

```
int main()
{
    int num, first;
    double x, y, z;
    char name, last;
        .
        .
        .
    return 0;
}

void one(int x, char y)
{
        .
        .
        .
}

int w;

void two(int a, int b, char x)
{
    int count;
        .
        .
        .
}

void three(int one, double y, int z)
{
    char ch;
    int a;
        .
        .
        .
    //Block four
    {
        int x;
        char a;
            .
            .
    }//end Block four
        .
        .
        .
}
```

Table 7–1 summarizes the scope (visibility) of the identifiers.

TABLE 7-1 Scope (Visibility) of the Identifiers

Identifier	Visibility in `one`	Visibility in `two`	Visibility in `three`	Visibility in Block `four`	Visibility in `main`
`rate` (before `main`)	Y	Y	Y	Y	Y
`z` (before `main`)	Y	Y	N	N	N
`t` (before `main`)	Y	Y	Y	Y	Y
`main`	Y	Y	Y	Y	Y
local variables of `main`	N	N	N	N	Y
`one` (function name)	Y	Y	N	N	Y
`x` (one's formal parameter)	Y	N	N	N	N
`y` (one's formal parameter)	Y	N	N	N	N
`w` (before function `two`)	N	Y	Y	Y	N
`two` (function name)	Y	Y	Y	Y	Y
`a` (two's formal parameter)	N	Y	N	N	N
`b` (two's formal parameter)	N	Y	N	N	N
`x` (two's formal parameter)	N	Y	N	N	N
local variables of `two`	N	Y	N	N	N
`three` (function name)	Y	Y	Y	Y	Y
`one` (three's formal parameter)	N	N	Y	Y	N
`y` (three's formal parameter)	N	N	Y	Y	N
`z` (three's formal parameter)	N	N	Y	Y	N
`ch` (three's local variable)	N	N	Y	Y	N
`a` (three's local variable)	N	N	Y	N	N
`x` (Block `four`'s local variable)	N	N	N	Y	N
`a` (Block `four`'s local variable)	N	N	N	Y	N

Note that function `three` cannot call function `one`, because function `three` has a formal parameter named one. Similarly, the block marked `four` in function `three` cannot use the `int` variable a, which is declared in function `three`, because block `four` has an identifier named a.

Before closing this section, let us note the following about global varaibles:

1. Chapter 2 stated that C++ does not automatically initialize variables. However, some compilers initialize global variables to their default values. For example, if a global variable is of type `int`, `char`, or `double`, it is initialized to zero.

2. In C++, `::` is called the **scope resolution operator**. By using the scope resolution operator, a global variable declared before the definition of a function (block) can be accessed by the function (or block) even if the function (or block) has an identifier with the same name as the variable. In the preceding program, by using the scope resolution operator, the function `main` can refer to the global variable z as `::z`. Similarly, suppose that a global variable t is declared before the definition of the function—say, `funExample`. Then `funExample` can access the variable t using the scope resolution operator even if `funExample` has an identifier t. Using the scope resolution operator, `funExample` refers to the variable t as `::t`. Also, in the preceding program, using the scope resolution operator, function `three` can call function `one`.

3. C++ provides a way to access a global variable declared after the definition of a function. In this case, the function must not contain any identifier with the same name as the global variable. In the preceding program, the global variable w is declared after the definition of function one. The function `one` does not contain any identifier named w; therefore, w can be accessed by function `one` only if you declare w as an **external variable** inside one. To declare w as an external variable inside function one, the function `one` must contain the following statement:

```
extern int w;
```

In C++, `extern` is a reserved word. The word `extern` in the above statement announces that w is a global variable declared elsewhere. Thus, when function `one` is called, no memory for w, as declared inside one, is allocated. In C++, external declaration also has another use, but it is not discussed in this book.

Global Variables, Named Constants, and Side Effects

A C++ program can contain global variables. Using global variables, however, has side effects. If more than one function uses the same global variable and something goes wrong, it is difficult to discover what went wrong and where. Problems caused by global variables in one area of a program might be misunderstood as problems caused in another area. We strongly recommend that you do not use global variables; instead, use the appropriate parameters.

In the programs given in this book, we typically placed named constants before the function `main`, outside of every function definition. That is, the named constants we used are *global named constants*. Unlike global variables, global named constants have no side effects because during program execution their values cannot be changed. Moreover, placing a named constant in the beginning of the program can increase readability, even if it is used only in one function. If you need to later modify the program and change the value of a named constant, it will be easier to find if it is placed in the beginning of the program.

Static and Automatic Variables

The variables discussed so far have followed two simple rules:

1. Memory for global variables remains allocated as long as the program executes.

2. Memory for a variable declared within a block is allocated at block entry and deallocated at block exit. For example, memory for the formal parameters and local variables of a function is allocated when the function is called and deallocated when the function exits.

A variable for which memory is allocated at block entry and deallocated at block exit is called an **automatic variable**. A variable for which memory remains allocated as long as the program executes is called a **static variable**. Global variables are static variables and, by default, variables declared within a block are automatic variables. You can declare a static variable within a block by using the reserved word **static**. The syntax for declaring a static variable is:

```
static dataType identifier;
```

The statement:

```
static int x;
```

declares `x` to be a static variable of type `int`.

Static variables declared within a block are local to the block, and their scope is the same as that of any other local identifier of that block.

Most compilers initialize **static** variables to their default values. For example, **static int** variables are initialized to 0. However, it is a good practice to initialize **static** variables yourself, especially if the initial value is not the default value. In this case, **static** variables are initialized when they are declared. The statement:

```
static int x = 0;
```

declares `x` to be a static variable of type `int` and initializes `x` to 0.

EXAMPLE 7-10

The following program shows how static and automatic variables behave.

```cpp
//Program: Static and automatic variables

#include <iostream>

using namespace std;

void test();

int main()
{
    int count;

    for (count = 1; count <= 5; count++)
        test();

    return 0;
}

void test()
{
    static int x = 0;
    int y = 10;

    x = x + 2;
    y = y + 1;

    cout << "Inside test x = " << x << " and y = "
        << y << endl;
}
```

Sample Run:

```
Inside test x = 2 and y = 11
Inside test x = 4 and y = 11
Inside test x = 6 and y = 11
Inside test x = 8 and y = 11
Inside test x = 10 and y = 11
```

In the function `test`, `x` is a **static** variable initialized to 0, and `y` is an automatic variable initialized to 10. The function `main` calls the function `test` five times. Memory for the variable `y` is allocated every time the function `test` is called and deallocated when the function exits. Thus, every time the function `test` is called, it prints the same value for `y`. However, because `x` is a static variable, memory for `x` remains allocated as long as the program executes. The variable `x` is initialized once to 0. The subsequent calls of the function `test` use the current value of `x`.

Because memory for static variables remains allocated between function calls, static variables allow you to use the value of a variable from one function call to another function call. Even though you can use global variables if you want to use certain values from one function call to another, the local scope of a static variable prevents other functions from manipulating its value.

Before we look at some programming examples, another concept about functions is worth mentioning: function overloading.

Function Overloading: An Introduction

In a C++ program, several functions can have the same name. This is called **function overloading** or **overloading a function name**. Before we state the rules to overloading a function, let us define the following:

Two functions are said to have **different formal parameter lists** if both functions have:

- A different number of formal parameters, or
- If the number of formal parameters is the same, then the data type of the formal parameters, in the order you list them, must differ in at least one position.

For example, consider the following function headings:

```
void functionOne(int x)
void functionTwo(int x, double y)
void functionThree(double y, int x)
int functionFour(char ch, int x, double y)
int functionFive(char ch, int x, string name)
```

These functions all have different formal parameter lists.

Now consider the following function headings:

```
void functionSix(int x, double y, char ch)
void functionSeven(int one, double u, char firstCh)
```

The functions `functionSix` and `functionSeven` both have three formal parameters, and the data type of the corresponding parameters is the same. Therefore, these functions have the same formal parameter list.

To overload a function name, any two definitions of the function must have different formal parameter lists.

Function overloading: Creating several functions with the same name.

The **signature** of a function consists of the function name and its formal parameter list. Two functions have different signatures if they have either different names or different formal parameter lists. (Note that the signature of a function does not include the return type of the function.)

If a function's name is overloaded, then all the functions in the set have the same name. Therefore, all the functions in the set have different signatures if they have different formal parameter lists. Thus, the following function headings correctly overload the function `functionXYZ`:

```
void functionXYZ()
void functionXYZ(int x, double y)
void functionXYZ(double one, int y)
void functionXYZ(int x, double y, char ch)
```

Consider the following function headings to overload the function `functionABC`:

```
void functionABC(int x, double y)
int functionABC(int x, double y)
```

Both of these function headings have the same name and same formal parameter list. Therefore, these function headings to overload the function `functionABC` are incorrect. In this case, the compiler will generate a syntax error. (Notice that the return types of these function headings are different.)

If a function is overloaded, then in a call to that function the signature—that is, the formal parameter list of the function—determines which function to execute.

NOTE   Some authors define the signature of a function as the formal parameter list and some consider the entire heading of the function as its signature. However, in this book, the signature of a function consists of the function's heading and its formal parameter list. If the function's names are different, then, of course, the compiler would have no problem in identifying which function is called and it will correctly translate the code. However, if a function's name is overloaded, then, as noted, the function's formal parameter list determines which function's body executes.

Suppose you need to write a function that determines the larger of two items. Both items can be integers, floating-point numbers, characters, or strings. You could write several functions as follows:

```
int largerInt(int x, int y);
char largerChar(char first, char second);
double largerDouble(double u, double v);
string largerString(string first, string second);
```

The function `largerInt` determines the larger of two integers; the function `largerChar` determines the larger of two characters, and so on. All of these functions perform similar operations. Instead of giving different names to these functions, you can use the same name—say, `larger`—for each function; that is, you can overload the function `larger`. Thus, you can write the previous function prototypes simply as:

```
int larger(int x, int y);
char larger(char first, char second);
```

```
double larger(double u, double v);
string larger(string first, string second);
```

If the call is `larger(5, 3)`, for example, the first function is executed. If the call is `larger('A', '9')`, the second function is executed, and so on.

Function overloading is used when you have the same action for different sets of data. Of course, for function overloading to work, you must give the definition of each function.

Functions with Default Parameters

NOTE   This section is not needed until Chapter 11.

This section discusses functions with default parameters. Recall that when a function is called, the number of actual and formal parameters must be the same. C++ relaxes this condition for functions with default parameters. You specify the value of a default parameter when the function name appears for the first time, such as in the prototype. In general, the following rules apply for functions with default parameters:

- If you do not specify the value of a default parameter, the default value is used for that parameter.

- All of the default parameters must be the rightmost parameters of the function.

- Suppose a function has more than one default parameter. In a function call, if a value to a default parameter is not specified, then you must omit all of the arguments to its right.

- Default values can be constants, global variables, or function calls.

- The caller has the option of specifying a value other than the default for any default parameter.

- You cannot assign a constant value as a default value to a reference parameter.

Consider the following function prototype:

```
void funcExp(int x, int y, double t, char z = 'A', int u = 67,
             char v = 'G', double w = 78.34);
```

The function `funcExp` has seven parameters. The parameters z, u, v, and w are default parameters. If no values are specified for z, u, v, and w in a call to the function `funcExp`, their default values are used.

Suppose you have the following statements:

```
int a, b;
char ch;
double d;
```

The following function calls are legal:

1. `funcExp(a, b, d);`
2. `funcExp(a, 15, 34.6, 'B', 87, ch);`
3. `funcExp(b, a, 14.56, 'D');`

In statement 1, the default values of z, u, v, and w are used. In statement 2, the default value of z is replaced by `'B'`, the default value of u is replaced by 87, the default value of v is replaced by the value of ch, and the default value of w is used. In statement 3, the default value of z is replaced by `'D'`, and the default values of u, v, and w are used.

The following function calls are illegal:

1. `funcExp(a, 15, 34.6, 46.7);`
2. `funcExp(b, 25, 48.76, 'D', 4567, 78.34);`

In statement 1, because the value of z is omitted, all other default values must be omitted. In statement 2, because the value of v is omitted, the value of w should be omitted, too.

The following are illegal function prototypes with default parameters:

1. `void funcOne(int x, double z = 23.45, char ch, int u = 45);`
2. `int funcTwo(int length = 1, int width, int height = 1);`
3. `void funcThree(int x, int& y = 16, double z = 34);`

In statement 1, because the second parameter z is a default parameter, all other parameters after z must be default parameters. In statement 2, because the first parameter is a default parameter, all parameters must be the default parameters. In statement 3, a constant value cannot be assigned to y because y is a reference parameter.

Example 7-11 further illustrates functions with default parameters.

EXAMPLE 7-11

```cpp
#include <iostream>
#include <iomanip>

using namespace std;

int volume(int l = 1, int w = 1, int h = 1);
void funcOne(int& x, double y = 12.34, char z = 'B');

int main()
{
    int a = 23;
    double b = 48.78;
    char ch = 'M';

    cout << fixed << showpoint;
    cout << setprecision(2);
```

```cpp
    cout << "Line 1: a = " << a << ", b = "
         << b  << ", ch = " << ch << endl;           //Line 1
    cout << "Line 2: Volume = " << volume()
         << endl;                                     //Line 2
    cout << "Line 3: Volume = " << volume(5, 4)
         << endl;                                     //Line 3
    cout << "Line 4: Volume = " << volume(34)
         << endl;                                     //Line 4
    cout << "Line 5: Volume = "
         << volume(6, 4, 5) << endl;                  //Line 5

    funcOne(a);                                       //Line 6
    funcOne(a, 42.68);                                //Line 7
    funcOne(a, 34.65, 'Q');                           //Line 8

    cout << "Line 9: a = " << a << ", b = "
         << b << ", ch = " << ch << endl;             //Line 9

    return 0;
}

int volume(int l, int w, int h)
{
    return l * w * h;                                 //Line 10
}

void funcOne(int& x, double y, char z)
{
    x = 2 * x;                                        //Line 11
    cout << "Line 12: x = " << x << ", y = "
         << y << ", z = " << z << endl;               //Line 12
}
```

Sample Run:

```
Line 1: a = 23, b = 48.78, ch = M
Line 2: Volume = 1
Line 3: Volume = 20
Line 4: Volume = 34
Line 5: Volume = 120
Line 12: x = 46, y = 12.34, z = B
Line 12: x = 92, y = 42.68, z = B
Line 12: x = 184, y = 34.65, z = Q
Line 9: a = 184, b = 48.78, ch = M
```

NOTE In programs in this book, the definition of the function `main` is placed before the definition of any user-defined functions. You must, therefore, specify the default value for a parameter in the function prototype, and in the function prototype only, *not* in the function definition.

PROGRAMMING EXAMPLE: Classify Numbers

In this example, we use functions to rewrite the program that determines the number of odds and evens from a given list of integers. This program was first written in Chapter 5.

The main algorithm remains the same:

1. Initialize the variables, `zeros`, `odds`, and `evens` to 0.
2. Read a number.
3. If the number is even, increment the even count, and if the number is also zero, increment the zero count; else increment the odd count.
4. Repeat Steps 2 and 3 for each number in the list.

The main parts of the program are: initialize the variables, read and classify the numbers, and then output the results. To simplify the function `main` and further illustrate parameter passing, the program includes:

- A function, `initialize`, to initialize the variables, such as `zeros`, `odds`, and `evens`.
- A function, `getNumber`, to get the number.
- A function, `classifyNumber`, to determine whether the number is odd or even (and whether it is also zero). This function also increments the appropriate count.
- A function, `printResults`, to print the results.

Let us now describe each of these functions.

initialize   The function `initialize` initializes variables to their initial values. The variables that we need to initialize are `zeros`, `odds`, and `evens`. As before, their initial values are all zero. Clearly, this function has three parameters. Because the values of the formal parameters initializing these variables must be passed outside the function, these formal parameters must be reference parameters. Essentially this function is:

```cpp
void initialize(int& zeroCount, int& oddCount, int& evenCount)
{
    zeroCount = 0;
    oddCount = 0;
    evenCount = 0;
}
```

getNumber   The function `getNumber` reads a number and then passes this number to the function `main`. Because you need to pass only one number, this function has only one parameter. The formal parameter of this function must be a reference parameter because the number read is passed outside the function. Essentially, this function is:

```cpp
void getNumber(int& num)
{
    cin >> num;
}
```

You can also write the function `getNumber` as a value-returning function. See the note at the end of this programming example.

classifyNumber The function `classifyNumber` determines whether the number is odd or even, and, if the number is even, it also checks whether the number is zero. It also updates the values of some of the variables, `zeros`, `odds`, and `evens`. This function needs to know the number to be analyzed; therefore, the number must be passed as a parameter. Because this function also increments the appropriate count, the variables (that is, `zeros`, `odds`, and `evens` declared in `main`) holding the counts must be passed as parameters to this function. Thus, this function has four parameters.

Because the number will only be analyzed, you need to pass only its value. Thus, the formal parameter corresponding to this variable is a value parameter. After analyzing the number, this function increments the values of some of the variables, `zeros`, `odds`, and `evens`. Therefore, the formal parameters corresponding to these variables must be reference parameters. The algorithm to analyze the number and increment the appropriate count is the same as before. The definition of this function is:

```cpp
void classifyNumber(int num, int& zeroCount, int& oddCount,
                    int& evenCount)
{
    switch (num % 2)
    {
    case 0:
        evenCount++;
        if (num == 0)
            zeroCount++;
        break;
    case 1:
    case -1:
        oddCount++;
    } //end switch
} //end classifyNumbers
```

printResults The function `printResults` prints the final results. To print the results (that is, the number of zeros, odds, and evens), this function must have access to the values of the variables, `zeros`, `odds`, and `evens`, declared in the function `main`. Therefore, this function has three parameters. Because this function prints only the values of the variables, the formal parameters are value parameters. The definition of this function is:

```cpp
void printResults(int zeroCount, int oddCount, int evenCount)
{
    cout << "There are " << evenCount << " evens, "
         << "which includes " << zeroCount << " zeros"
         << endl;

    cout << "The number of odd numbers is: " << oddCount
         << endl;
} //end printResults
```

We now give the main algorithm and show how the function `main` calls these functions.

MAIN
ALGORITHM

1. Call the function `initialize` to initialize the variables.
2. Prompt the user to enter 20 numbers.
3. For each number in the list,

    a. Call the function `getNumber` to read a number.
    b. Output the number.
    c. Call the function `classifyNumber` to classify the number and increment the appropriate count.

4. Call the function `printResults` to print the final results.

COMPLETE PROGRAM LISTING

```cpp
//Program: Classify Numbers
//This program counts the number of zeros, odd, and even numbers

#include <iostream>
#include <iomanip>

using namespace std;

const int N = 20;

    //Function prototypes
void initialize(int& zeroCount, int& oddCount, int& evenCount);
void getNumber(int& num);
void classifyNumber(int num, int& zeroCount, int& oddCount,
                    int& evenCount);
void printResults(int zeroCount, int oddCount, int evenCount);
```

```cpp
int main()
{
        //Variable declaration
    int counter; //loop control variable
    int number;  //variable to store the new number
    int zeros;   //variable to store the number of zeros
    int odds;    //variable to store the number of odd integers
    int evens;   //variable to store the number of even integers

    initialize(zeros, odds, evens);                     //Step 1

    cout << "Please enter " << N << " integers."
         << endl;                                       //Step 2
    cout << "The numbers you entered are: "
         << endl;

    for (counter = 1; counter <= N; counter++)          //Step 3
    {
        getNumber(number);                              //Step 3a
        cout << number << " ";                          //Step 3b
        classifyNumber(number, zeros, odds, evens); //Step 3c
    } // end for loop

    cout << endl;

    printResults(zeros, odds, evens);                   //Step 4

    return 0;
}

void initialize(int& zeroCount, int& oddCount, int& evenCount)
{
    zeroCount = 0;
    oddCount = 0;
    evenCount = 0;
}

void getNumber(int& num)
{
    cin >> num;
}

void classifyNumber(int num, int& zeroCount, int& oddCount,
                    int& evenCount)
{
    switch (num % 2)
    {
    case 0:
        evenCount++;
```

```cpp
        if (num == 0)
            zeroCount++;
        break;
    case 1:
    case -1:
        oddCount++;
    } //end switch
} //end classifyNumbers

void printResults(int zeroCount, int oddCount, int evenCount)
{
    cout << "There are " << evenCount << " evens, "
         << "which includes " << zeroCount << " zeros"
         << endl;

    cout << "The number of odd numbers is: " << oddCount
         << endl;
} //end printResults
```

Sample Run: In this sample run, the user input is shaded.

```
Please enter 20 integers.
The numbers you entered are:
0 0 12 23 45 7 -2 -8 -3 -9 4 0 1 0 -7 23 -24 0 0 12
0 0 12 23 45 7 -2 -8 -3 -9 4 0 1 0 -7 23 -24 0 0 12
There are 12 evens, which includes 6 zeros
The number of odd numbers is: 8
```

NOTE   In the previous program, because the data is assumed to be input from the standard input device (the keyboard) and the function `getNumber` returns only one value, you can also write the function `getNumber` as a value-returning function. If written as a value-returning function, the definition of the function `getNumber` is:

```cpp
int getNumber()
{
    int num;

    cin >> num;

    return num;
}
```

In this case, the statement (function call):

```cpp
getNumber(number);
```

in the function `main` should be replaced by the statement:

```cpp
number = getNumber();
```

Of course, you also need to change the function prototype.

PROGRAMMING EXAMPLE: Data Comparison

This programming example illustrates:

- How to read data from more than one file in the same program.
- How to send output to a file.
- How to generate bar graphs.
- With the help of functions and parameter passing, how to use the same program segment on different (but similar) sets of data.
- How to use structured design to solve a problem and how to perform parameter passing.

This program is broken into two parts. First, you learn how to read data from more than one file. Second, you learn how to generate bar graphs.

Two groups of students at a local university are enrolled in certain special courses during the summer semester. The courses are offered for the first time and are taught by different teachers. At the end of the semester, both groups are given the same tests for the same courses and their scores are recorded in separate files. The data in each file is in the following form:

```
courseNo   score1, score2, ..., scoreN -999
courseNo   score1, score2, ..., scoreM -999
   .
   .
   .
```

Let us write a program that finds the average course score for each course for each group. The output is of the following form:

```
Course No   Group No    Course Average
   CSC          1           83.71
                2           80.82

   ENG          1           82.00
                2           78.20


     .
     .
     .


Avg for group 1: 82.04
Avg for group 2: 82.01
```

Input   Because the data for the two groups are recorded in separate files, the input data appears in two separate files.

Output   As shown above.

<table>
<tr><td valign="top"></td><td>

Reading input data from both files is straightforward. Suppose the data is stored in the file `group1.txt` for group 1 and file `group2.txt` for group 2, and these files are on drive A. After processing the data for one group, we can process the data for the second group for the same course, and continue until we run out of data. Processing data for each course is similar and is a two-step process:

</td></tr>
</table>

1. a. Sum the scores for the course.

   b. Count the number of students in the course.

   c. Divide the total score by the number of students to find the course average.

2. Output the results.

We are comparing only the averages of the corresponding courses in each group, and the data in each file is ordered according to course ID. To ensure that only the averages of the corresponding courses are compared, we compare the course IDs for each group. If the corresponding course IDs are not the same, we output an error message and terminate the program.

This discussion suggests that we should write a function, `calculateAverage`, to find the course average. We should also write another function, `printResult`, to output the data in the form given. By passing the appropriate parameters, we can use the same functions, `calculateAverage` and `printResult`, to process each course's data for both groups. (In the second part of the program, we modify the function `printResult`.)

The preceding discussion translates into the following algorithm:

1. Initialize the variables.
2. Get the course IDs for group 1 and group 2.
3. If the course IDs are different, print an error message and exit the program.
4. Calculate the course averages for group 1 and group 2.
5. Print the results in the form given above.
6. Repeat Steps 2 through 5 for each course.
7. Print the final results.

Variables (Function main)

The preceding discussion suggests that the program needs the following variables for data manipulation in the function `main`:

```
string courseId1;        //course ID for group 1
string courseId2;        //course ID for group 2
int numberOfCourses;
double avg1;             //average for a course in group 1
double avg2;             //average for a course in group 2
```

```
double avgGroup1;       //average group 1
double avgGroup2;       //average group 2
ifstream group1;        //input stream variable for group 1
ifstream group2;        //input stream variable for group 2

ofstream outfile;       //output stream variable
```

Next, we discuss the functions `calculateAverage` and `printResult`. Then we will put the function `main` together.

calculateAverage This function calculates the average for a course. Because the input is stored in a file and the input file is opened in the function `main`, we must pass the `ifstream` variable associated with the input file to this function. Furthermore, after calculating the course average, this function must pass the course average to the function `main`. Therefore, this function has two parameters, and both parameters must be reference parameters.

To find the course average, we must first find the sum of all scores for the course and the number of students who took the course, and then divide the sum by the number of students. Thus, we need a variable to find the sum of the scores, a variable to count the number of students, and a variable to read and store a score. Of course, we must initialize the variable to find the sum and the variable to count the number of students to zero.

Local Variables (Function calculateAverage) In the previous discussion of data manipulation, we identified three variables for the function `calculateAverage`:

```
double totalScore = 0.0;
int numberOfStudents = 0;
int score;
```

The above discussion translates into the following algorithm for the function `calculateAverage`:

1.   Declare and initialize variables.

2.   Get the (next) course score, `score`.

3.   `while` the `score` is not -999

   a.   Update `totalScore` by adding the course score.

   b.   Increment `numberOfStudents` by 1.

   c.   Get the (next) course score, `score`.

4.   `courseAvg = totalScore / numberOfStudents;`

We are now ready to write the definition of the function `calculateAverage`.

```cpp
void calculateAverage(ifstream& inp, double& courseAvg)
{
    double totalScore = 0.0;
    int numberOfStudents = 0;
    int score;

    inp >> score;
    while (score != -999)
    {
        totalScore = totalScore + score;
        numberOfStudents++;
        inp >> score;
    } //end while

    courseAvg = totalScore / numberOfStudents;
} //end calculate Average
```

`printResult` The function `printResult` prints the group's course ID, group number, and course average. The output is stored in a file. So we must pass four parameters to this function: the `ofstream` variable associated with the output file, the group number, the course ID, and the course average for the group. The `ofstream` variable must be passed by reference. Because the function uses only the values of the other variables, the remaining three parameters should be value parameters. Also, from the output, it is clear that we print the course ID only before group

1. In pseudocode, the algorithm is:

```
if (group number == 1)
    print course ID
else
    print a blank

print group number and course average
```

The definition of the function `printResult` follows:

```cpp
void printResult(ofstream& outp, string courseID, int groupNo,
                 double avg)
{
    if (groupNo == 1)
        outp << "  " << courseID << "    ";
    else
        outp << "           ";

    outp << setw(8) << groupNo << setw(17) << avg << endl;
} //end printResult
```

Now that we have designed and defined the functions `calculateAverage` and `printResult`, we can describe the algorithm for the function `main`. Before outlining the algorithm, however, we note the following: It is quite possible that in both input files the data is ordered according to the course IDs, but one file might have fewer courses than the other. We do not discover this error until after we have processed both files and discover that one file has unprocessed data. Make sure to check for this error before printing the final answer—that is, the averages for group 1 and group 2.

MAIN ALGORITHM: Function `main`

1. Declare the variables (local declaration).

2. Open the input files.

3. Print a message if you are unable to open a file and terminate the program.

4. Open the output file.

5. To output floating-point numbers in a fixed decimal format with the decimal point and trailing zeros, set the manipulators `fixed` and `showpoint`. Also, to output floating-point numbers to two decimal places, set the precision to two decimal places.

6. Initialize the course average for group 1 to `0.0`.

7. Initialize the course average for group 2 to `0.0`.

8. Initialize the number of courses to `0`.

9. Print the heading.

10. Get the course ID, `courseId1`, for group 1.

11. Get the course ID, `courseId2`, for group 2.

12. For each course in group 1 and group 2,

    a. ```
        if (courseId1 != courseId2)
        {
            cout << "Data error: Course IDs do not match.\n";
            return 1;
        }
        ```

    b.  ```
        else
        {
        ```

        i.   Calculate the course average for group 1 (call the function `calculateAverage` and pass the appropriate parameters).

        ii. Calculate the course average for group 2 (call the function `calculateAverage` and pass the appropriate parameters).

        iii. Print the results for group 1 (call the function `printResult` and pass the appropriate parameters).

    iv. Print the results for group 2 (call the function `printResult` and pass the appropriate parameters).

    v. Update the average for group 1.

    vi. Update the average for group 2.

    vii. Increment the number of courses.

    }

  c. Get the course ID, `courseId1`, for group 1.

  d. Get the course ID, `courseId2`, for group 2.

13. a. if not_end_of_file on group 1 and end_of_file on group 2 print "Ran out of data for group 2 before group 1"

    b. else if end_of_file on group 1 and not_end_of_file on group 2 print "Ran out of data for group 1 before group 2"

    c. else print the average of group 1 and group 2.

14. Close the input and output files.

COMPLETE PROGRAM LISTING

```cpp
//Program: Comparison of Class Averages

#include <iostream>
#include <iomanip>
#include <fstream>
#include <string>
using namespace std;

    //Function prototypes
void calculateAverage(ifstream& inp, double& courseAvg);
void printResult(ofstream& outp, string courseId,
                 int groupNo, double avg);

int main()
{
        //Step 1
    string courseId1;       //course ID for group 1
    string courseId2;       //course ID for group 2
    int numberOfCourses;
    double avg1;            //average for a course in group 1
    double avg2;            //average for a course in group 2
    double avgGroup1;       //average group 1
    double avgGroup2;       //average group 2
    ifstream group1;        //input stream variable for group 1
    ifstream group2;        //input stream variable for group 2
    ofstream outfile;       //output stream variable
```

```cpp
    group1.open("a:\\group1.txt");                    //Step 2
    group2.open("a:\\group2.txt");                    //Step 2

    if (!group1 || !group2)                           //Step 3
    {
        cout << "Unable to open files." << endl;
        cout << "Program terminates." << endl;
        return 1;
    }

    outfile.open("a:\\student.out");                  //Step 4
    outfile << fixed << showpoint;                     //Step 5
    outfile << setprecision(2);                        //Step 5

    avgGroup1 = 0.0;                                   //Step 6
    avgGroup2 = 0.0;                                   //Step 7

    numberOfCourses = 0;                              //Step 8

    outfile << "Course No      Group No     "
            << "Course Average" << endl;               //Step 9


    group1 >> courseId1;                              //Step 10
    group2 >> courseId2;                              //Step 11
    while (group1 && group2)                          //Step 12
    {
        if (courseId1 != courseId2)                  //Step 12a
        {
            cout << "Data error: Course IDs "
                 << "do not match." << endl;
            cout << "Program terminates." << endl;
            return 1;
        }
        else                                          //Step 12b
        {
            calculateAverage(group1, avg1);           //Step 12b.i
            calculateAverage(group2, avg2);           //Step 12b.ii
            printResult(outfile, courseId1,
                        1, avg1);                     //Step 12b.iii
            printResult(outfile, courseId2,
                        2, avg2);                     //Step 12b.iv
            avgGroup1 = avgGroup1 + avg1;             //Step 12b.v
            avgGroup2 = avgGroup2 + avg2;             //Step 12b.vi
            outfile << endl;
            numberOfCourses++;                        //Step 12b.vii
        }

        group1 >> courseId1;                          //Step 12c
        group2 >> courseId2;                          //Step 12d
    } //end while
```

```cpp
        if (group1 && !group2)                          //Step 13a
            cout << "Ran out of data for group 2 "
                 << "before group 1." << endl;
        else if (!group1 && group2)                      //Step 13b
            cout << "Ran out of data for group 1 "
                 << "before group 2." << endl;
        else                                             //Step 13c
        {
            outfile << "Avg for group 1: "
                    << avgGroup1 / numberOfCourses
                    << endl;
            outfile << "Avg for group 2: "
                    << avgGroup2 / numberOfCourses
                    << endl;
        }

        group1.close();                                  //Step 14
        group2.close();                                  //Step 14
        outfile.close();                                 //Step 14

        return 0;
}

void calculateAverage(ifstream& inp, double& courseAvg)
{
        double totalScore = 0.0;
        int numberOfStudents = 0;
        int score;

        inp >> score;
        while (score != -999)
        {
            totalScore = totalScore + score;
            numberOfStudents++;
            inp >> score;
        }//end while

        courseAvg = totalScore / numberOfStudents;
} //end calculate Average

void printResult(ofstream& outp, string courseID, int groupNo,
                 double avg)
{
        if (groupNo == 1)
            outp << "  " << courseID << "    ";
        else
            outp << "            ";
        outp << setw(8) << groupNo << setw(17) << avg << endl;
} //end printResult
```

Sample Run:

```
Course No    Group No     Course Average
   CSC          1            83.71
                2            80.82

   ENG          1            82.00
                2            78.20

   HIS          1            77.69
                2            84.15

   MTH          1            83.57
                2            84.29

   PHY          1            83.22
                2            82.60

Avg for group 1: 82.04
Avg for group 2: 82.01
```

Input Data Group 1

```
CSC 80 100 70 80 72 90 89 100 83 70 90 73 85 90 -999
ENG 80 90 80 94 90 74 78 63 83 80 90 -999
HIS 90 70 80 70 90 50 89 83 90 68 90 60 80 -999
MTH 74 80 75 89 90 73 90 82 74 90 84 100 90 79 -999
PHY 100 83 93 80 63 78 88 89 75 -999
```

Input Data Group 2

```
CSC 90 75 90 75 80 89 100 60 80 70 80 -999
ENG 80 80 70 68 70 78 80 90 90 76 -999
HIS 100 80 80 70 90 76 88 90 90 75 90 85 80 -999
MTH 80 85 85 92 90 90 74 90 83 65 72 90 84 100 -999
PHY 90 93 73 85 68 75 67 100 87 88 -999
```

BAR GRAPH

In the business world, company executives often like to see results in some visual form, such as bar graphs. Many currently available software packages can analyze data in several forms and then display the results in a visual form, such as bar graphs or pie charts. The second part of this program aims to display the results found earlier in the form of bar graphs, as shown below:

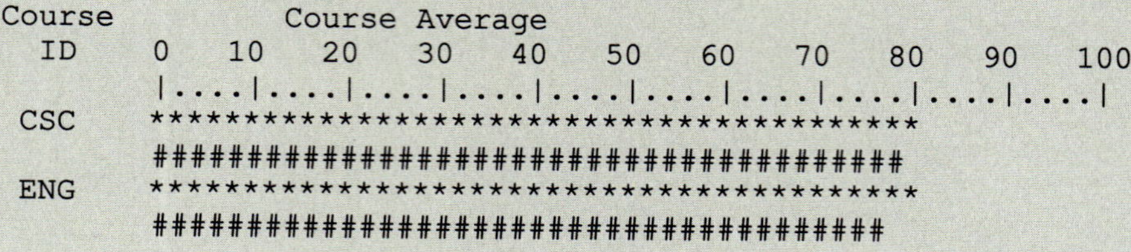

```
    .
    .
    .
Group 1 -- ****
Group 2 -- ####

Avg for group 1: 82.04
Avg for group 2: 82.01
```

Each symbol (* or #) in the bar graph represents 2 points. If a course average is less than 2, no symbol is printed.

Because the output is in the form of a bar graph, we need to modify the function `printResult`.

Print Bars The function `printResult` prints the course ID and the bar graph representing the average for a course. The output is stored in a file. So we must pass four parameters to this function: the `ofstream` variable associated with the output file, the group number (to print * or #), the course ID, and the course average for the department. To print the bar graph, we can use a loop to print a symbol for each two points. If the average is `78.45`, for example, we must print 39 symbols to represent this average. To find the number of symbols to print, we can use integer division as follows:

```
numberOfSymbols = static_cast<int>(average) / 2;
```

For example, `static_cast<int>(78.45) / 2 = 78 / 2 = 39.`

Following this discussion, the definition of the function `printResult` is:

```cpp
void printResult(ofstream& outp, string courseID,
                 int groupNo, double avg)
{
    int noOfSymbols;
    int count;

    if (groupNo == 1)
        outp << setw(4) << courseID << "      ";
    else
        outp << "          ";

    noOfSymbols = static_cast<int>(avg)/2;

    if (groupNo == 1)
        for (count = 1; count <= noOfSymbols; count++)
            outp << '*';
    else
        for (count = 1; count <= noOfSymbols; count++)
            outp << '#';
    outp << endl;
}//end printResults
```

We also include a function, `printHeading`, to print the first two lines of the output. The definition of this function is:

```cpp
void printHeading(ofstream& outp)
{
    outp << "Course              Course Average" << endl;
    outp << "  ID    0    10    20    30    40    50    60    70"
         << "    80    90    100" << endl;
    outp << "              |....|....|....|....|....|....|....|"
         << "....|....|....|" << endl;
}//end printHeading
```

If you replace the function `printResult` in the preceding program, include the function `printHeading`, include the statements to output — Group 1 -- **** and Group 2 -- #### — , and rerun the program. The output for the previous data is as follows:

Sample Run:

```
Course              Course Average
  ID    0    10    20    30    40    50    60    70    80    90    100
        |....|....|....|....|....|....|....|....|....|....|....|
CSC     ******************************************
        ########################################

ENG     ********************************************
        #######################################

HIS     *****************************************
        ###########################################

MTH     *********************************************
        ############################################

PHY     *********************************************
        ###########################################

Group 1 -- ****
Group 2 -- ####
Avg for group 1: 82.04
Avg for group 2: 82.01
```

Compare both outputs. Which one do you think is better?

QUICK REVIEW

1. A function that does not have a data type is called a void function.

2. A return statement without any value can be used in a void function. If a return statement is used in a void function, it is typically used to exit the function early.

3. The heading of a void function starts with the word **void**.

4. In C++, **void** is a reserved word.

5. A void function may or may not have parameters.

6. A call to a void function is a stand-alone statement.

7. To call a void function, you use the function name together with the actual parameters in a stand-alone statement.

8. There are two types of formal parameters: value parameters and reference parameters.

9. A value parameter receives a copy of its corresponding actual parameter.

10. A reference parameter receives the address (memory location) of its corresponding actual parameter.

11. The corresponding actual parameter of a value parameter is an expression, a variable, or a constant value.

12. A constant value cannot be passed to a reference parameter.

13. The corresponding actual parameter of a reference parameter must be a variable.

14. When you include & after the data type of a formal parameter, the formal parameter becomes a reference parameter.

15. The stream variables should be passed by reference to a function.

16. If a formal parameter needs to change the value of an actual parameter, in the function heading you must declare this formal parameter as a reference parameter.

17. The scope of an identifier refers to those parts of the program where it is accessible.

18. Variables declared within a function (or block) are called local variables.

19. Variables declared outside of every function definition (and block) are called global variables.

20. The scope of a function name is the same as the scope of an identifier declared outside of any block.

21. See the scope rules in this chapter (section, Scope of an Identifier).

22. C++ does not allow the nesting of function definitions.

23. An automatic variable is a variable for which memory is allocated on function (or block) entry and deallocated on function (or block) exit.

24. A static variable is a variable for which memory remains allocated throughout the execution of the program.

25. By default, global variables are static variables.

26. In C++, a function can be overloaded.

27. Two functions are said to have different formal parameter lists if both functions have:

    - A different number of formal parameters, or
    - If the number of formal parameters is the same, then the data type of the formal parameters, in the order you list them, must differ in at least one position.

28. The signature of a function consists of the function name and its formal parameter list. Two functions have different signatures if they have either different names or different formal parameter lists.

29. If a function is overloaded, then in a call to that function the signature, that is, the formal parameter list of the function, determines which function to execute.

30. C++ allows functions to have default parameters.

31. If you do not specify the value of a default parameter, the default value is used for that parameter.

32. All of the default parameters must be the rightmost parameters of the function.

33. Suppose a function has more than one default parameter. In a function call, if a value to a default parameter is not specified, then you must omit all arguments to its right.

34. Default values can be constants, global variables, or function calls.

35. The calling function has the option of specifying a value other than the default for any default parameter.

36. You cannot assign a constant value as a default value to a reference parameter.

EXERCISES

1. Mark the following statements as true or false.

    a. A function that changes the value of a reference parameter also changes the value of the actual parameter.

    b. A variable name cannot be passed to a value parameter.

    c. If a C++ function does not use parameters, parentheses around the empty parameter list are still required.

    d. In C++, the names of the corresponding formal and actual parameters must be the same.

    e. Whenever the value of a reference parameter changes, the value of the actual parameter changes.

    f. In C++, function definitions can be nested; that is, the definition of one function can be enclosed in the body of another function.

g. Using global variables in a program is a better programming style than using local variables, because extra variables can be avoided.

h. In a program, global constants are as dangerous as global variables.

i. The memory for a static variable remains allocated between function calls.

2. Identify the following items in the programming code shown below:

a. Function prototype, function heading, function body, and function definitions.

b. Function call statements, formal parameters, and actual parameters.

c. Value parameters and reference parameters.

d. Local variables and global variables.

```cpp
#include <iostream>                                //Line 1

using namespace std;                               //Line 2

int one;                                           //Line 3

void hello(int&, double, char);                    //Line 4

int main()                                         //Line 5
{                                                  //Line 6
    int x;                                         //Line 7
    double y;                                      //Line 8
    char z;                                        //Line 9
       .
       .
       .
    hello(x, y, z);                                //Line 10
       .
       .
       .
    hello(x, y - 3.5, 'S');                        //Line 11
       .
       .
       .
}                                                  //Line 12

void hello(int& first, double second, char ch)    //Line 13
{                                                  //Line 14
    int num;                                       //Line 15
    double y;                                      //Line 16
    int u ;                                        //Line 17
       .
       .
       .
}                                                  //Line 18
```

3. a. Explain the difference between an actual and a formal parameter.

   b. Explain the difference between a value and a reference parameter.

   c. Explain the difference between a local and a global variable.

4. What is the output of the following program?

```cpp
#include <iostream>
#include <iomanip>

using namespace std;

void test(int first, int& second);

int main()
{
    int num;
    num = 5;

    test(24, num);
    cout << num << endl;

    test(num, num);
    cout << num << endl;

    test(num * num, num);
    cout << num << endl;

    test(num + num, num);
    cout << num << endl;

    return 0;
}

void test(int first, int& second)
{
    int third;

    third = first + second * second + 2;
    first = second - first;
    second = 2 * second;

    cout << first << "   " << second << "   "
         << third << endl;
}
```

5. Assume the following input values:

```
7 3 6 4
2 6 3 5
```

Show the output of the following program:

```cpp
#include <iostream>

using namespace std;

void goofy(int&, int&, int, int&);

int main()
{
    int first, second, third, fourth;

    first = 3; second = 4; third = 20; fourth = 78;
    cout << first << "   " << second << "   " << third << "   "
         << fourth << endl;

    goofy(first, second, third, fourth);
    cout << first << "   " << second << "   " << third << "   "
         << fourth << endl;

    fourth = first * second + third - fourth;
    goofy(fourth, third, first, second);

    cout << first << "   " << second << "   " << third << "   "
         << fourth << endl;

    return 0;
}

void goofy(int& a, int& b, int c, int& d)
{
    cin >> a >> b >> c >> d;
    c = a * b + d - c;
    c = 2 * c;
}
```

6. What is the output of the following program?

```cpp
#include <iostream>
using namespace std;

int x;

void mickey(int&, int);
void minnie(int, int&);

int main()
{
    int first;
    int second = 5;
    x = 6;
```

```
    mickey(first, second);
    cout << first << " " << second << " " << x << endl;

    minnie(first, second);
    cout << first << " " << second << " " << x << endl;
    return 0;
}

void mickey(int& a, int b)
{
    int first;
    first = b + 12;
    a = 2 * b;
    b = first + 4;
}

void minnie(int u, int& v)
{
    int second;
    second = x;
    v = second + 4;
    x = u + v;
}
```

7. In the following program, number the marked statements to show the order in which they will execute (the logical order of execution).

```
#include <iostream>

using namespace std;

void func(int val1, int val2);

int main()
{
    int num1, num2;
____    cout << "Please enter two integers." << endl;
____    cin >> num1 >> num2;
____    func (num1, num2);
____    cout << " The two integers are " << num1
            << ", " << num2 << endl;
____    return 0;
}
void func(int val1, int val2)
{
    int val3, val4;
____    val3 = val1 + val2;
____    val4 = val1 * val2;
____    cout << "The sum and product are " << val3
            << " and " << val4 << endl;
}
```

8. What is the output of the following code fragment? (*Note:* `alpha` and `beta` are **int** variables.)

```cpp
alpha = 5;
beta = 10;

if (beta >= 10)
{
    int alpha = 10;
    beta = beta + alpha;
    cout << alpha << ' ' << beta << endl;
}
cout << alpha << ' ' << beta << endl;
```

9. Show the output of the program in Example 7-9 if you replace Line 5 with the following line:

```cpp
funOne(t, num1);
```

Show the values of the variables after each statement executes.

10. Consider the following program. What is its exact output? Show the values of the variables after each line executes, as in Example 7-7.

```cpp
#include <iostream>

using namespace std;

void funOne(int& a);

int main()
{
    int num1, num2;

    num1 = 10;                                              //Line 1

    num2 = 20;                                              //Line 2

    cout << "Line 3: In main: num1 = " << num1
         << ", num2 = " << num2 << endl;                   //Line 3

    funOne(num1);                                          //Line 4
    cout << "Line 5: In main after funOne: num1 = "
         << num1 << ", num2 = " << num2 << endl;           //Line 5

    return 0;                                              //Line 6
}

void funOne(int& a)
{
    int x = 12;
    int z;
```

```cpp
    z = a + x;                                          //Line 7

    cout << "Line 8: In funOne: a = " << a
         << ", x = " << x
         << ", and z = " << z << endl;                 //Line 8

    x = x + 5;                                          //Line 9

    cout << "Line 10: In funOne: a = " << a
         << ", x = " << x
         << ", and z = " << z << endl;                 //Line 10

    a = a + 8;                                          //Line 11

    cout << "Line 12: In funOne: a = " << a
         << ", x = " << x
         << ", and z = " << z << endl;                 //Line 12
}
```

11. Consider the following function prototype:

```cpp
void testDefaultParam(int a, int b = 7, char z = '*');
```

Which of the following function calls is correct?

a. `testDefaultParam(5);`

b. `testDefaultParam(5, 8);`

c. `testDefaultParam(6, '#');`

d. `testDefaultParam(0, 0, '*');`

12. Consider the following function definition:

```cpp
void defaultParam(int u, int v = 5, double z = 3.2)
{
    int a;
    u = u + static_cast<int>(2 * v + z);
    a = u + v * z;
    cout << "a = " << a << endl;
}
```

What is the output of the following function calls?

a. `defaultParam(6);`

b. `defaultParam(3, 4);`

c. `defaultParam(3, 0, 2.8);`

PROGRAMMING EXERCISES

1. Consider the definition of the function `main`:

```
int main()
{
    int x, y;
    char z;
    double rate, hours;
    double amount;
    .
    .
    .
}
```

The variables `x`, `y`, `z`, `rate`, and `hours` referred to in items a through f below are the variables of the function `main`. Each of the functions described must have the appropriate parameters to access these variables. Write the following definitions:

a. Write the definition of the function `initialize` that initializes `x` and `y` to 0, and `z` to the blank character.

b. Write the definition of the function `getHoursRate` that prompts the user to input the hours worked and rate per hour to initialize the variables `hours` and `rate` of the function `main`.

c. Write the definition of the value-returning function `payCheck` that calculates and returns the amount to be paid to an employee based on the hours worked and rate per hour. The hours worked and rate per hour are stored in the variables `hours` and `rate`, respectively, of the function `main`. The formula for calculating the amount to be paid is as follows: For the first 40 hours, the rate is the given rate; for hours over 40, the rate is 1.5 times the given rate.

d. Write the definition of the function `printCheck` that prints the hours worked, rate per hour, and the amount due.

e. Write the definition of the function `funcOne` that prompts the user to input a number. The function then changes the value of `x` by assigning the value of the expression 2 times the (old) value of `x` plus the value of `y` minus the value entered by the user.

f. Write the definition of the function `nextChar` that sets the value of `z` to the next character stored in `z`.

g. Write the definition of a function `main` that tests each of these functions.

2. The function `printGrade` in Example 7-6 is written as a **void** function to compute and output the course grade. The course score is passed as a parameter to the function `printGrade`. Rewrite the function `printGrade` as a value-returning function so that it computes and returns

the course grade. (The course grade must be output in the function `main`.) Also, change the name of the function to `calculateGrade`.

3. In this exercise, you are to modify the Classify Numbers programming example in this chapter. As written, the program inputs the data from the standard input device (keyboard) and outputs the results on the standard output device (screen). The program can process only 20 numbers. Rewrite the program to incorporate the following requirements:

    a. Data to the program is input from a file of an unspecified length; that is, the program does not know in advance how many numbers are in the file.

    b. Save the output of the program in a file.

    c. Modify the function `getNumber` so that it reads a number from the input file (opened in the function `main`), outputs the number to the output file (opened in the function `main`), and sends the number read to the function `main`. Print only 10 numbers per line.

    d. Have the program find the sum and average of the numbers.

    e. Modify the function `printResult` so that it outputs the final results to the output file (opened in the function `main`). Other than outputting the appropriate counts, this new definition of the function `printResult` should also output the sum and average of the numbers.

4. Rewrite the program developed in Programming Exercise 11 in Chapter 5, so that the function `main`, in addition to the variable declarations, is merely a collection of function calls. Your program should use the following functions:

    a. Function `openFiles`: This function opens the input and output files, and sets the output of the floating-point numbers to two decimal places in a fixed decimal format with a decimal point and trailing zeros.

    b. Function `initialize`: This function initializes variables such as `countFemale`, `countMale`, `sumFemaleGPA`, and `sumMaleGPA`.

    c. Function `sumGrades`: This function finds the sum of the female and male students' GPAs.

    d. Function `averageGrade`: This function finds the average GPA for female and male students.

    e. Function `printResults`: This function outputs the relevant results.

    f. There can be no global variables. Use the appropriate parameters to pass information in and out of functions.

5. Write a program that prints the day number of the year, given the date in the form month–day–year. For example, if the input is 1-1-2006, the day number is 1; if the input is 12-25-2006, the day number is 359. The program should check for a leap year. A year is a leap year if it is divisible by 4 but not divisible by 100. For example, 1992 and 2008 are divisible by 4, but not

by 100. A year that is divisible by 100 is a leap year if it is also divisible by 400. For example, 1600 and 2000 are divisible by 400. However, 1800 is not a leap year because 1800 is not divisible by 400.

6. Write a program that reads a student's name together with his or her test scores. The program should then compute the average test score for each student and assign the appropriate grade. The grade scale is as follows: 90-100, A; 80-89, B; 70-79, C; 60-69, D; 0-59, F. Your program must use the following functions:

a. A void function, `calculateAverage`, to determine the average of the five test scores for each student. Use a loop to read and sum the five test scores. (This function does not output the average test score. That task must be done in the function `main`.)

b. A value-returning function, `calculateGrade`, to determine and return each student's grade. (This function does not output the grade. That task must be done in the function `main`.)

Test your program on the following data. Read the data from a file and send the output to a file. Do not use any global variables. Use the appropriate parameters to pass values in and out of functions.

```
Johnson 85 83 77 91 76
Aniston 80 90 95 93 48
Cooper 78 81 11 90 73
Gupta 92 83 30 69 87
Blair 23 45 96 38 59
Clark 60 85 45 39 67
Kennedy 77 31 52 74 83
Bronson 93 94 89 77 97
Sunny 79 85 28 93 82
Smith 85 72 49 75 63
```

Sample Output:
The output should be of the following form: (Fill the last two columns and the last line showing the class average.)

Student	Test1	Test2	Test3	Test4	Test5	Average	Grade
Johnson	85	83	77	91	76		
Aniston	80	90	95	93	48		
Cooper	78	81	11	90	73		
Gupta	92	83	30	69	87		
Blair	23	45	96	38	59		
Clark	60	85	45	39	67		
Kennedy	77	31	52	74	83		
Bronson	93	94	89	77	97		
Sunny	79	85	28	93	82		
Smith	85	72	49	75	63		

Class Average =

7. Write a program to process text files. The program should read a text file and output the data in the file as is. The program should also output the number of words, number of lines, and number of paragraphs. (When you create the input file, insert a blank line between paragraphs, see part d.)

You must write and use the following functions.

a. `initialize`: This function initializes all the variables of the function `main`.

b. `processBlank`: This function reads and writes blanks. Whenever it hits a nonblank (except whitespace characters), it increments the number of words in a line. The number of words in a line is set back to zero in the function `updateCount`. The function exits after processing the blanks.

c. `copyText`: This function reads and writes the nonblank characters. Whenever it hits a blank, it exits.

d. `updateCount`: This function takes place at the end of each line. It updates the total word count, increments the number of lines, and sets the number of words on a line back to zero. If there are no words in a line, it increments the number of paragraphs. One blank line (between paragraphs) is used to distinguish paragraphs and should not be counted with the number of lines.

e. `printTotal`: This function outputs the number of words, number of lines, and number of paragraphs.

Your program should read data from a file and send output to a file. Do not use any global variables. Use the appropriate parameters to pass values in and out of the functions described above. Test your program using the function `main` as shown below.

```
int main()
{
    variables declaration
    open files

    read a character
    while (not end of file)
    {
        while (not end of line)
        {
            processBlank(parameters);
            copyText(parameters);
        }
        updateCount(parameters);
        read a character;
        .
        .
        .
    }
```

```
    printTotal(parameters);
    close files;

    return 0;
}
```

8. **(The box problem)** You have been given a flat cardboard of area, say, 70 square inches, to make an open box by cutting a square from each corner and folding the sides (see Figure 7-20). Your objective is to determine the dimension, that is, the length and width, and the side of the square to be cut from the corners so that the resulting box is of maximum length.

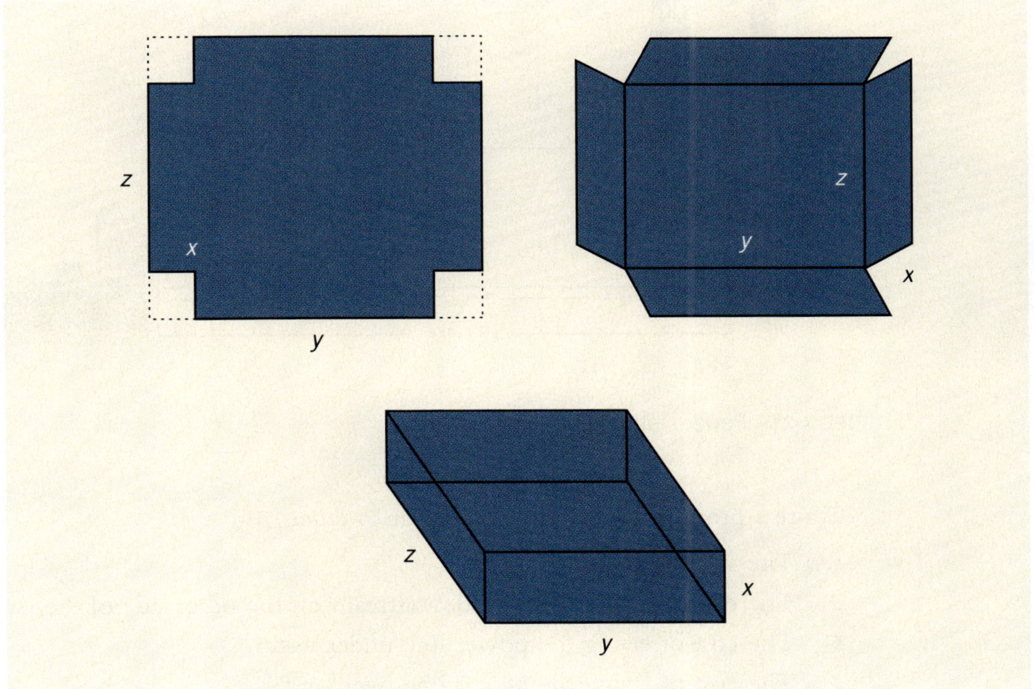

FIGURE 7-20 Cardboard box

Write a program that prompts the user to enter the area of the flat cardboard. The program then outputs the length and width of the cardboard and the length of the side of the square to be cut from the corner so that the resulting box is of maximum volume. Calculate your answer to three decimal places. Your program must contain a function that takes as input the length and width of the cardboard and returns the side of the square that should be cut to maximize the volume. The function also returns the maximum volume.

9. (**The Power Station Problem**) A power station is on one side of a river that is one-half mile wide, and a factory is 8 miles downstream on the other side of the river (see Figure 7-21). It costs $7 per foot to run power lines overland and $9 per foot to run them under water. Your objective is to determine the most economical path to lay the power line. That is, determine how long the power line should run under water and how long should it run over land, to achieve the minimum total cost of laying the power line.

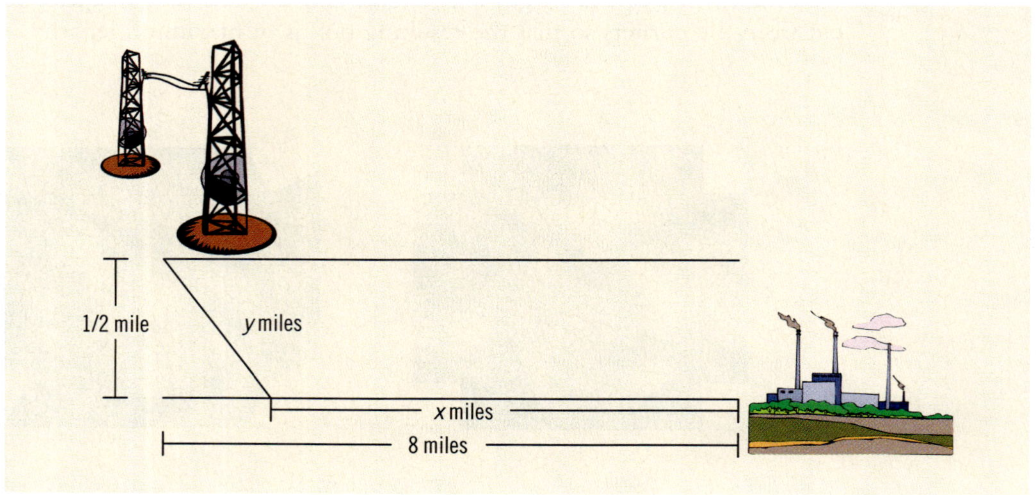

FIGURE 7-21   Power station, river, and factory

Write a program that prompts the user to enter:

a. The width of the river.

b. The distance of the factory downstream on the other side of the river.

c. The cost of laying the power line under water.

d. The cost of laying the power line over land.

The program then outputs the length of the power line that should run under water and the length that should run over land, so the cost of constructing the power line is at the minimum. The program should also output the total cost of constructing the power line.

10. (**Pipe Problem, requires trigonometry**) A pipe is to be carried around the right-angled corner of two intersecting corridors. Suppose that the widths of the two intersecting corridors are 5 feet and 8 feet (see Figure 7-22). Your objective is to find the length of the longest pipe, rounded to the nearest foot, that can be carried level around the right-angled corner.

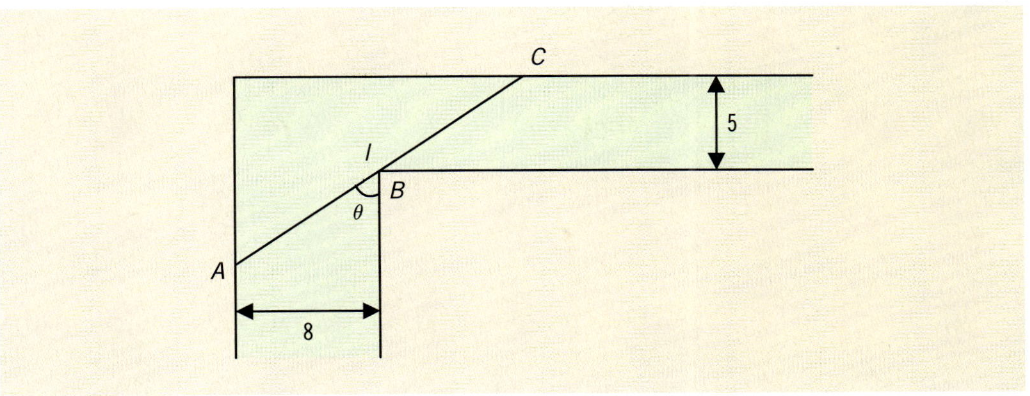

FIGURE 7-22 Pipe problem

Write a program that prompts the user to input the widths of both the hallways. The program then outputs the length of the longest pipe, rounded to the nearest foot, that can be carried level around the right-angled corner. (Note that the length of the pipe is given by $l = AB + BC = 8 / \sin \theta + 5 / \cos \theta$, where $0 < \theta < \pi/2$.)

USER-DEFINED SIMPLE DATA TYPES, NAMESPACES, AND THE string TYPE

IN THIS CHAPTER, YOU WILL:

- Learn how to create and manipulate your own simple data type—called the enumeration type
- Become familiar with the `typedef` statement
- Learn about the `namespace` mechanism
- Explore the `string` data type, and learn how to use the various `string` functions to manipulate strings

In Chapter 2, you learned that C++'s simple data type is divided into three categories: integral, floating-point, and **enum**. In subsequent chapters, you worked mainly with integral and floating-point data types. In this chapter, you will learn about the **enum** type. Moreover, the statement **using namespace** std; (discussed in Chapter 2) is used in every C++ program that uses ANSI/ISO Standard C++ style header files. The second half of this chapter examines the purpose of this statement. In fact, you will learn what the **namespace** mechanism is. You will also learn about the **string** type and many useful functions that you can use to effectively manipulate strings.

Enumeration Type

NOTE   This section may be skipped without any loss of continuity.

Chapter 2 defined a data type as a set of values together with a set of operations on them. For example, the **int** data type consists of integers from –2,147,483,648 to 2,147,483,647 and the set of operations on these numbers—namely, the arithmetic operations (+, –, *, /, and %). Because the main objective of a program is to manipulate data, the concept of a data type becomes fundamental to any programming language. By providing data types, you specify what values are legal and tell the user what kinds of operations are allowed on those values. The system thus provides you with built-in checks against errors.

The data types that you have worked with until now were mostly **int**, **bool**, **char**, and **double**. Even though these data types are sufficient to solve just about any problem, situations occur when these data types are not adequate to solve a particular problem. C++ provides a mechanism for users to create their own data types, which greatly enhances the flexibility of the programming language.

In this section, you will learn how to create your own simple data types, known as the enumeration type. In ensuing chapters, you will learn more advanced techniques to create complex data types.

To define an **enumeration type**, you need the following items:

- A name for the data type
- A set of values for the data type
- A set of operations on the values

C++ lets you define a new simple data type wherein you specify its name and values, but not the operations. Preventing users from creating their own operations avoids potential system failures.

The values that you specify for the data type must be identifiers.

The syntax for enumeration type is:

```
enum typeName {value1, value2, ...};
```

where `value1`, `value2`, . . . are identifiers called **enumerators**. In C++, `enum` is a reserved word.

By listing all of the values between the braces, you also specify an ordering between the values. That is, `value1 < value2 < value3 <. . ..` Thus, the enumeration type is an ordered set of values. Moreover, the default value assigned to these enumerators starts at 0. That is, the default value assigned to `value1` is 0, the default value assigned to `value2` is 1, and so on. (You can assign different values—other than the default values—for the enumerators when you define the enumeration type.) Also notice that the enumerators `value1`, `value2`, . . . are *not* variables.

EXAMPLE 8-1

The statement:

```
enum colors {BROWN, BLUE, RED, GREEN, YELLOW};
```

defines a new data type, called `colors`, and the values belonging to this data type are `BROWN`, `BLUE`, `RED`, `GREEN`, and `YELLOW`.

EXAMPLE 8-2

The statement:

```
enum standing {FRESHMAN, SOPHOMORE, JUNIOR, SENIOR};
```

defines `standing` to be an enumeration type. The values belonging to `standing` are `FRESHMAN`, `SOPHOMORE`, `JUNIOR`, and `SENIOR`.

EXAMPLE 8-3

Consider the following statements:

```
enum grades {'A', 'B', 'C', 'D', 'F'}; //illegal enumeration type
enum places {1ST, 2ND, 3RD, 4TH};  //illegal enumeration type
```

These are illegal enumeration types because none of the values is an identifier. The following, however, are legal enumeration types:

```
enum grades {A, B, C, D, F};
enum places {FIRST, SECOND, THIRD, FOURTH};
```

If a value has already been used in one enumeration type, it cannot be used by any other enumeration type in the same block. The same rules apply to enumeration types declared outside of any blocks. Example 8-4 illustrates this concept.

EXAMPLE 8-4

Consider the following statements:

```
enum mathStudent {JOHN, BILL, CINDY, LISA, RON};
enum compStudent {SUSAN, CATHY, JOHN, WILLIAM}; //illegal
```

Suppose that these statements are in the same program in the same block. The second enumeration type, `compStudent`, is not allowed because the value JOHN was used in the previous enumeration type `mathStudent`.

Declaring Variables

Once a data type is defined, you can declare variables of that type. The syntax for declaring variables of an **enum** type is the same as before:

```
dataType identifier, identifier,...;
```

The statement:

```
enum sports {BASKETBALL, FOOTBALL, HOCKEY, BASEBALL, SOCCER,
             VOLLEYBALL};
```

defines an enumeration type, called **sports**. The statement:

```
sports popularSport, mySport;
```

declares `popularSport` and `mySport` to be variables of type `sports`.

Assignment

Once a variable is declared, you can store values in it. Assuming the previous declaration, the statement:

```
popularSport = FOOTBALL;
```

stores FOOTBALL in `popularSport`. The statement:

```
mySport = popularSport;
```

copies the value of `popularSport` into `mySport`.

Operations on Enumeration Types

No arithmetic operations are allowed on the enumeration type. So the following state-ments are illegal:

```
mySport = popularSport + 2;              //illegal
popularSport = FOOTBALL + SOCCER;        //illegal
popularSport = popularSport * 2;         //illegal
```

Also, the increment and decrement operations are not allowed on enumeration types. So the following statements are illegal:

```
popularSport++; //illegal
popularSport--; //illegal
```

Suppose you want to increment the value of `popularSport` by 1. You can use the cast operator as follows:

```
popularSport = static_cast<sports>(popularSport + 1);
```

When the type name is used, the compiler assumes that the user understands what he or she is doing. Thus, the preceding statement is compiled, and during execution it advances the value of `popularSport` to the next value in the list. Consider the following statements:

```
popularSport = FOOTBALL;
popularSport = static_cast<sports>(popularSport + 1);
```

After the second statement, the value of `popularSport` is HOCKEY. Similarly, the statements:

```
popularSport = FOOTBALL;
popularSport = static_cast<sports>(popularSport - 1);
```

result in storing BASKETBALL in `popularSport`.

Relational Operators

Because an enumeration is an ordered set of values, the relational operators can be used with the enumeration type. Once again, suppose you have the enumeration type `sports` and the variables `popularSport` and `mySport` as defined earlier. Then,

```
FOOTBALL <= SOCCER is true
HOCKEY > BASKETBALL is true
BASEBALL < FOOTBALL is false
```

Suppose that:

```
popularSport = SOCCER;
mySport = VOLLEYBALL;
```

Then,

```
popularSport < mySport is true
```

ENUMERATION TYPES AND LOOPS

Recall that the enumeration type is an integral type and that, using the cast operator (that is, type name), you can increment, decrement, and compare the values of the enumeration type. Therefore, you can use these enumeration types in loops. Suppose `mySport` is a variable as declared earlier. Consider the following `for` loop:

```
for (mySport = BASKETBALL; mySport <= SOCCER;
                        mySport = static_cast<sports>(mySport + 1))
    .
    .
    .
```

This `for` loop has 5 iterations.

Using enumeration types in loops increases the readability of the program.

Input/Output of Enumeration Types

Because input and output are defined only for built-in data types such as `int`, `char`, `double`, and so on, the enumeration type can be neither input nor output (directly). However, you can input and output enumeration indirectly. Example 8-5 illustrates this concept.

EXAMPLE 8-5

Suppose you have the following statements:

```
enum courses {ALGEBRA, BASIC, PASCAL, CPP, PHILOSOPHY, ANALYSIS,
                CHEMISTRY, HISTORY};
courses registered;
```

The first statement defines an enumeration type, `courses`; the second declares a variable `registered` of type `courses`. You can read (that is, input) the enumeration type with the help of the `char` data type. Note that you can distinguish between some of the values in the enumeration type `courses` just by reading the first character and others by reading the first two characters. For example, you can distinguish between ALGEBRA and BASIC just by reading the first character; you can distinguish between ALGEBRA and ANALYSIS by reading the first two characters. To read these values from, say, the keyboard, you read two characters and then use a selection structure to assign the value to the variable `registered`. Thus, you need to declare two variables of type `char`.

```cpp
char ch1, ch2;
cin >> ch1 >> ch2; //Read two characters
```

The following **switch** statement assigns the appropriate value to the variable `registered`:

```cpp
switch (ch1)
{
case 'a':
case 'A':
    if (ch2 == 'l' || ch2 == 'L')
        registered = ALGEBRA;
    else
        registered = ANALYSIS;
    break;
case 'b':
case 'B':
    registered = BASIC;
    break;
case 'c':
case 'C':
    if (ch2 == 'h' || ch2 == 'H')
        registered = CHEMISTRY;
    else
        registered = CPP;
    break;
case 'h':
case 'H':
    registered = HISTORY;
    break;
case 'p':
case 'P':
    if (ch2 == 'a' || ch2 == 'A')
        registered = PASCAL;
    else
        registered = PHILOSOPHY;
    break;
default:
    cout << "Illegal input." << endl;
}
```

Similarly, you can output the enumeration type indirectly:

```cpp
switch (registered)
{
case ALGEBRA:
    cout << "Algebra";
    break;
case analysis:
    cout << "Analysis";
    break;
case BASIC:
    cout << "Basic";
    break;
```

```cpp
case CHEMISTRY:
    cout << "Chemistry";
    break;
case CPP:
    cout << "CPP";
    break;
case HISTORY:
    cout << "History";
    break;
case PASCAL:
    cout << "Pascal";
    break;
case PHILOSOPHY:
    cout << "Philosophy";
}
```

NOTE If you try to output the value of an enumerator directly, the computer will output the value assigned to the enumerator. For example, suppose that `registered = ALGEBRA;`. The following statement will output the value 0 because the (default) value assigned to `ALGEBRA` is 0:

```cpp
cout << registered << endl;
```

Similarly, the following statement will output 4:

```cpp
cout << PHILOSOPHY << endl;
```

Functions and Enumeration Types

You can pass the enumeration type as a parameter to functions just like any other simple data type—that is, by either value or reference. Also, just like any other simple data type, a function can return a value of the enumeration type. Using this facility, you can use functions to input and output enumeration types.

The following function inputs data from the keyboard and returns a value of the enumeration type. Assume that the enumeration type `courses` is defined as before:

```cpp
courses readCourses()
{
    courses registered;
    char ch1, ch2;

    cout << "Enter the first two letters of the course: "
         << endl;
    cin >> ch1 >> ch2;
```

```cpp
    switch (ch1)
    {
    case 'a':
    case 'A':
        if (ch2 == 'l' || ch2 == 'L')
            registered = ALGEBRA;
        else
            registered = ANALYSIS;
        break;
    case 'b':
    case 'B':
        registered = BASIC;
        break;
    case 'c':
    case 'C':
        if (ch2 == 'h' || ch2 == 'H')
            registered = CHEMISTRY;
        else
            registered = CPP;
        break;
    case 'h':
    case 'H':
        registered = HISTORY;
        break;
    case 'p':
    case 'P':
        if (ch2 == 'a' || ch2 == 'A')
            registered = PASCAL;
        else
            registered = PHILOSOPHY;
        break;
    default:
        cout << "Illegal input." << endl;
    }
    return registered;
}  //end readCourse
```

The following function outputs an enumeration type value:

```cpp
void printEnum(courses registered)
{
    switch (registered)
    {
    case ALGEBRA:
        cout << "Algebra";
        break;
    case ANALYSIS:
        cout << "Analysis";
        break;
    case BASIC:
        cout << "Basic";
        break;
```

```
     case CHEMISTRY:
          cout << "Chemistry";
          break;
     case CPP:
          cout << "CPP";
          break;
     case HISTORY:
          cout << "History";
          break;
     case PASCAL:
          cout << "Pascal";
          break;
     case PHILOSOPHY:
          cout << "Philosophy";
     }//end switch
}//end printEnum
```

Declaring Variables When Defining the Enumeration Type

In previous sections, you first defined an enumeration type and then declared variables of that type. C++ allows you to combine these two steps into one. That is, you can declare variables of an enumeration type when you define an enumeration type. For example, the statement:

```
enum grades {A, B, C, D, F} courseGrade;
```

defines an enumeration type, grades, and declares a variable courseGrade of type grades.

Similarly, the statement:

```
enum coins {PENNY, NICKEL, DIME, HALFDOLLAR, DOLLAR} change, usCoins;
```

defines an enumeration type, coins, and declares two variables, change and usCoins, of type coins.

Anonymous Data Types

A data type wherein you directly specify values in the variable declaration with no type name is called an **anonymous type**. The following statement creates an anonymous type:

```
enum {BASKETBALL, FOOTBALL, BASEBALL, HOCKEY} mySport;
```

This statement specifies the values and declares a variable mySport, but no name is given to the data type.

Creating an anonymous type, however, has drawbacks. First, because there is no name for the type, you cannot pass an anonymous type as a parameter to a function and a function cannot return an anonymous type value. Second, values used in one anonymous type can be used in another anonymous type, but variables of those types are treated differently. Consider the following statements:

```
enum {ENGLISH, FRENCH, SPANISH, GERMAN, RUSSIAN} languages;
enum {ENGLISH, FRENCH, SPANISH, GERMAN, RUSSIAN} foreignLanguages;
```

Even though the variables `languages` and `foreignLanguages` have the same values, the compiler treats them as variables of different types. The following statement is, therefore, illegal:

```
languages = foreignLanguages; //illegal
```

Even though these facilities are available, use them with care. To avoid confusion, first define an enumeration type and then declare the variables.

We now describe the `typedef` statement in C++.

typedef Statement

In C++, you can create synonyms or aliases to a previously defined data type by using the `typedef` statement. The general syntax of the `typedef` statement is:

```
typedef existingTypeName newTypeName;
```

In C++, `typedef` is a reserved word. Note that the `typedef` statement does not create any new data type; it creates only an alias to an existing data type.

EXAMPLE 8-6

The statement:

```
typedef int integer;
```

creates an alias, `integer`, for the data type `int`. Similarly, the statement:

```
typedef double real;
```

creates an alias, `real`, for the data type `double`. The statement:

```
typedef double decimal;
```

creates an alias, `decimal`, for the data type `double`.

Using the `typedef` statement, you can create your own Boolean data type, as shown in Example 8-7.

EXAMPLE 8-7

From Chapter 4, recall that logical (Boolean) expressions in C++ evaluate to 1 or 0, which are, in fact, `int` values. As a logical value, 1 represents `true` and 0 represents `false`. Consider the following statements:

```
typedef int Boolean;        //Line 1
const Boolean TRUE = 1;      //Line 2
const Boolean FALSE = 0;     //Line 3
Boolean flag;                //Line 4
```

The statement at Line 1 creates an alias, `Boolean`, for the data type `int`. The statements at Lines 2 and 3 declare the named constants `TRUE` and `FALSE` and initialize them to `1` and `0`, respectively. The statement at Line 4 declares `flag` to be a variable of type `Boolean`. Because `flag` is a variable of type `Boolean`, the following statement is legal:

```
flag = TRUE;
```

PROGRAMMING EXAMPLE: The Game of Rock, Paper, and Scissors

Children often play the game of rock, paper, and scissors. This game has two players, each of whom chooses one of the three objects: rock, paper, or scissors. If player 1 chooses rock and player 2 chooses paper, player 2 wins the game because paper covers the rock. The game is played according to the following rules:

- If both players choose the same object, this play is a tie.

- If one player chooses rock and the other chooses scissors, the player choosing the rock wins this play because the rock breaks the scissors.

- If one player chooses rock and the other chooses paper, the player choosing the paper wins this play because the paper covers the rock.

- If one player chooses scissors and the other chooses paper, the player choosing the scissors wins this play because the scissors cut the paper.

Write an interactive program that allows two people to play this game.

Input   This program has two types of input:

- The users' responses when asked to play the game

- The players' choices

Output   The players' choices and the winner of each play. After the game is over, the total number of plays, and the number of times that each player won, should be output as well.

PROBLEM ANALYSIS AND ALGORITHM DESIGN   Two players play this game. Players enter their choices via the keyboard. Each player enters R or r for Rock, P or p for Paper, or S or s for Scissors. While the first player enters a choice, the second player looks elsewhere. Once both entries are in, if the entries are valid, the program outputs the players' choices and declares the winner of the play. The game continues until one of the players decides to quit the game. After the game ends, the program outputs the total number of plays and the number of times that each player won. This discussion translates into the following algorithm:

1. Provide a brief explanation of the game and how it is played.

2. Ask the users if they want to play the game.

3. Get plays for both players.

4. If the plays are valid, output the plays and the winner.

5. Update the total game count and winner count.

6. Repeat Steps 2 through 5, while the users agree to play the game.

7. Output the number of plays and times that each player won.

We will use the enumeration type to describe the objects.

```cpp
enum objectType {ROCK, PAPER, SCISSORS};
```

Variables (Function main) It is clear that you need the following variables in the function `main`:

```cpp
int gameCount;   //variable to store the number of
                 //games played
int winCount1;   //variable to store the number of games
                 //won by player 1
int winCount2;   //variable to store the number of games
                 //won by player 2
int gamewinner;
char response;   //variable to get the user's response to
                 //play the game
char selection1;
char selection2;
objectType play1;   //player1's selection
objectType play2;   //player2's selection
```

This program is divided into the following functions, which the ensuing sections describe in detail.

- **displayRules**: This function displays some brief information about the game and its rules.

- **validSelection**: This function checks whether a player's selection is valid. The only valid selections are R, r, P, p, S, and s.

- **retrievePlay**: Because enumeration types cannot be read directly, this function converts the entered choice (R, r, P, p, S, or s) and returns the appropriate object type.

- **gameResult**: This function outputs the players' choices and the winner of the game.

- **convertEnum**: This function is called by the function `gameResult` to output the enumeration type values.

- **winningObject**: This function determines and returns the winning object.

- **displayResults**: After the game is over, this function displays the final results.

Function `displayRules`
This function has no parameters. It consists only of output statements to explain the game and rules of play. Essentially, this function's definition is:

```cpp
void displayRules()
{
    cout << "  Welcome to the game of Rock, Paper, "
         << "and Scissors." << endl;
    cout << "   This is a game for two players. For each "
         << "game, each" << endl;
    cout << " player selects one of the objects, Rock, "
         << "Paper or Scissors." << endl;
    cout << " The rules for winning the game are: " << endl;
    cout << "1. If both player selects the same object, it "
         << "is a tie." << endl;
    cout << "2. Rock breaks Scissors: So player who selects "
         << "Rock wins." << endl;
    cout << "3. Paper covers Rock: So player who selects "
         << "Paper wins." << endl;
    cout << "4. Scissors cuts Paper: So player who selects "
         << "Scissors wins." << endl << endl;
    cout << "Enter R or r to select Rock, P or p to select "
         << "Paper, and S or s to select Scissors." << endl;
}
```

Function `validSelection`
This function checks whether a player's selection is valid.

```
if selection is 'R' or 'r' or 'S' or 's' or 'P' or 'p', then
   it is a valid selection;
otherwise the selection is invalid.
```

Let's use a `switch` statement to check for the valid selection. The definition of this function is:

```cpp
bool validSelection(char selection)
{
    switch (selection)
    {
    case 'R':
    case 'r':
    case 'P':
    case 'p':
    case 'S':
```

```
        case 's':
            return true;
        default:
            return false;
        }
}
```

Function retrievePlay

Because the enumeration type cannot be read directly, this function converts the entered choice (R, r, P, p, S, or s) and returns the appropriate object type. This function thus has one parameter, of type `char`. It is a value-returning function, and it returns a value of type `objectType`. In pseudocode, the algorithm of this function is:

```
if selection is 'R' or 'r'
    return ROCK;

if selection is 'P' or 'p'
    return PAPER;

if selection is 'S' or 's'
    return   SCISSORS;
```

The definition of the function `retrievePlay` is:

```
objectType retrievePlay(char selection)
{
    objectType object;

    switch (selection)
    {
    case 'R':
    case 'r':
        object = ROCK;
        break;
    case 'P':
    case 'p':
        object = PAPER;
        break;
    case 'S':
    case 's':
        object = SCISSORS;
    }

    return object;
}
```

Function gameResult

This function decides whether a game is a tie or which player is the winner. It outputs the players' selections and the winner of the game. Clearly, this function has three parameters: player 1's choice, player 2's choice, and a parameter to return the winner. In pseudocode, this function is:

```
a. if player1 and player2 have the same selection, then
   this is a tie game.
```

b. `else`
```
   {
```
1. Determine the winning object. (Call function winningObject)
2. Output each player's choice.
3. Determine the winning player.
4. Return the winning player via a reference parameter to the function main so that the function main can update the winning player's win count.
```
   }
```

The definition of this function is:

```cpp
void gameResult(objectType play1, objectType play2,
                int& winner)
{
    objectType winnerObject;

    if (play1 == play2)
    {
        winner = 0;
        cout << "Both players selected ";
        convertEnum(play1);
        cout << ". This game is a tie." << endl;
    }
    else
    {
        winnerObject = winningObject(play1, play2);

            //Output each player's choice
        cout << "Player 1 selected ";
        convertEnum(play1);
        cout << " and player 2 selected ";
        convertEnum(play2);
        cout << ". ";

            //Decide the winner
        if (play1 == winnerObject)
            winner = 1;
        else if (play2 == winnerObject)
            winner = 2;

            //Output the winner
        cout << "Player " << winner << " wins this game."
             << endl;
    }
}
```

Function convertEnum Because enumeration types cannot be output directly, let's write the function convertEnum to output objects of the **enum** type objectType. This function has one parameter, of type objectType. It outputs the string that corresponds to the objectType. In pseudocode, this function is:

```
if object is ROCK
   output "Rock"

if object is PAPER
   output "Paper"

if object is SCISSORS
   output "Scissors"
```

The definition of the function `convertNum` is:

```
void convertEnum(objectType object)
{
    switch (object)
    {
    case ROCK:
        cout << "Rock";
        break;
    case PAPER:
        cout << "Paper";
        break;
    case SCISSORS:
        cout << "Scissors";
    }
}
```

Function winningObject

To decide the winner of the game, you look at the players' selections and then at the rules of the game. For example, if one player chooses ROCK and another chooses PAPER, the player who chose PAPER wins. In other words, the winning object is PAPER. The function `winningObject`, given two objects, decides and returns the winning object. Clearly, this function has two parameters of type `objectType`, and the value returned by this function is also of type `objectType`. The definition of this function is:

```
objectType winningObject(objectType play1, objectType play2)
{
    if ((play1 == ROCK && play2 == SCISSORS)
            || (play2 == ROCK && play1 == SCISSORS))
        return ROCK;
    else if ((play1 == ROCK && play2 == PAPER)
            || (play2 == ROCK && play1 == PAPER))
        return PAPER;
    else
        return SCISSORS;
}
```

Function displayResults

After the game is over, this function outputs the final results—that is, the total number of plays and the number of plays won by each player. The total number of plays is stored in the variable `gameCount`, the number of plays won by player 1 is stored in the variable `winCount1`, and the number of plays won by player 2 is stored in the variable `winCount2`. This function has three parameters corresponding to these three variables. Essentially, the definition of this function is:

```
void displayResults(int gCount, int wCount1, int wCount2)
{
    cout << "The total number of plays: " << gCount
         << endl;
    cout << "The number of plays won by player 1: "
         << wCount1 << endl;
    cout << "The number of plays won by player 2: "
         << wCount2 << endl;
}
```

We are now ready to write the algorithm for the function `main`.

MAIN ALGORITHM

1. Declare the variables.
2. Initialize the variables.
3. Display the rules.
4. Prompt the users to play the game.
5. Get the users' responses to play the game.
6. `while` (response is yes)

   {

   a. Prompt player 1 to make a selection.
   b. Get the play for player 1.
   c. Prompt player 2 to make a selection.
   d. Get the play for player 2.
   e. If both plays are legal

      {

      i. Increment the total game count.
      ii. Declare the winner of the game.
      iii. Increment the winner's game win count by 1.

      }

   f. Prompt the users to determine whether they want to play again.
   g. Get the players' responses.

   }

7. Output the game results.

COMPLETE PROGRAM LISTING

```cpp
#include <iostream>

using namespace std;

enum objectType {ROCK, PAPER, SCISSORS};

    //Function prototypes
void displayRules();
objectType retrievePlay(char selection);
bool validSelection(char selection);
void convertEnum(objectType object);
objectType winningObject(objectType play1, objectType play2);
void gameResult(objectType play1, objectType play2, int& winner);
void displayResults(int gCount, int wCount1, int wCount2);

int main()
{
        //Step 1
    int gameCount;  //variable to store the number of
                    //games played
    int winCount1;  //variable to store the number of games
                    //won by player 1
    int winCount2;  //variable to store the number of games
                    //won by player 2
    int gamewinner;
    char response;   //variable to get the user's response to
                     //play the game
    char selection1;
    char selection2;
    objectType play1;   //player1's selection
    objectType play2;   //player2's selection

        //Initialize variables; Step 2
    gameCount = 0;
    winCount1 = 0;
    winCount2 = 0;

    displayRules();                                          //Step 3

    cout << "Enter Y/y to play the game: ";                  //Step 4
    cin >> response;                                         //Step 5
    cout << endl;

    while (response == 'Y' ||  response == 'y')    //Step 6
    {
        cout << "Player 1 enter your choice: ";    //Step 6a
```

```cpp
        cin >> selection1;                              //Step 6b
        cout << endl;

        cout << "Player 2 enter your choice: ";     //Step 6c
        cin >> selection2;                              //Step 6d
        cout << endl;

            //Step 6e
        if (validSelection(selection1)
              && validSelection(selection2))
        {
            play1 = retrievePlay(selection1);
            play2 = retrievePlay(selection2);
            gameCount++;                                //Step 6e.i
            gameResult(play1, play2, gamewinner); //Step 6e.ii

            if (gamewinner == 1)                        //Step 6e.iii
                winCount1++;
            else if (gamewinner == 2)
                winCount2++;
        }//end if

        cout << "Enter Y/y to play the game: ";     //Step 6f
        cin >> response;                                //Step 6g
        cout << endl;
    }//end while

    displayResults(gameCount, winCount1,
                winCount2);                             //Step 7


    return 0;
}//end main

void displayRules()
{
    cout << "  Welcome to the game of Rock, Paper, "
         << "and Scissors." << endl;
    cout << "  This is a game for two players. For each "
         << "game, each" << endl;
    cout << " player selects one of the objects, Rock, "
         << "Paper or Scissors." << endl;
    cout << " The rules for winning the game are: " << endl;
    cout << "1. If both player selects the same object, it "
         << "is a tie." << endl;
    cout << "2. Rock breaks Scissors: So player who selects "
         << "Rock wins." << endl;
    cout << "3. Paper covers Rock: So player who selects "
         << "Paper wins." << endl;
    cout << "4. Scissors cuts Paper: So player who selects "
         << "Scissors wins." << endl << endl;
```

```cpp
    cout << "Enter R or r to select Rock, P or p to select "
         << "Paper, and S or s to select Scissors." << endl;
}

bool validSelection(char selection)
{
    switch (selection)
    {
    case 'R':
    case 'r':
    case 'P':
    case 'p':
    case 'S':
    case 's':
        return true;
    default:
        return false;
    }
}

objectType retrievePlay(char selection)
{
    objectType object;

    switch (selection)
    {
    case 'R':
    case 'r':
        object = ROCK;
        break;
    case 'P':
    case 'p':
        object = PAPER;
        break;
    case 'S':
    case 's':
        object = SCISSORS;
    }

    return object;
}

void convertEnum(objectType object)
{
    switch (object)
    {
    case ROCK:
        cout << "Rock";
        break;
```

```cpp
    case PAPER:
        cout << "Paper";
        break;
    case SCISSORS:
        cout << "Scissors";
    }
}

objectType winningObject(objectType play1, objectType play2)
{
    if ((play1 == ROCK && play2 == SCISSORS)
            || (play2 == ROCK && play1 == SCISSORS))
        return ROCK;
    else if ((play1 == ROCK && play2 == PAPER)
            || (play2 == ROCK && play1 == PAPER))
        return PAPER;
    else
        return SCISSORS;
}

void gameResult(objectType play1, objectType play2,
                int& winner)
{
    objectType winnerObject;

    if (play1 == play2)
    {
        winner = 0;
        cout << "Both players selected ";
        convertEnum(play1);
        cout << ". This game is a tie." << endl;
    }
    else
    {
        winnerObject = winningObject(play1, play2);

            //Output each player's choice
        cout << "Player 1 selected ";
        convertEnum(play1);
        cout << " and player 2 selected ";
        convertEnum(play2);
        cout << ". ";

            //Decide the winner
        if (play1 == winnerObject)
            winner = 1;
        else if (play2 == winnerObject)
            winner = 2;
```

```cpp
                //Output the winner
        cout << "Player " << winner << " wins this game."
             << endl;
    }
}


void displayResults(int gCount, int wCount1, int wCount2)
{
    cout << "The total number of plays: " << gCount
         << endl;
    cout << "The number of plays won by player 1: "
         << wCount1 << endl;
    cout << "The number of plays won by player 2: "
         << wCount2 << endl;
}
```

Namespaces

In July 1998, ANSI/ISO Standard C++ was officially approved. Most recent compilers are also compatible with ANSI/ISO Standard C++. (To be absolutely sure, check your compiler's documentation.) The two standards, Standard C++ and ANSI/ISO Standard C++, are virtually the same. The ANSI/ISO Standard C++ language has some features that are not available in Standard C++, which the remainder of this chapter addresses. In subsequent chapters, unless specified otherwise, the C++ syntax applies to both standards. First, we discuss the **namespace** mechanism of the ANSI/ISO Standard C++, which was introduced in Chapter 2.

When a header file, such as `iostream`, is included in a program, the global identifiers in the header file also become the global identifiers in the program. Therefore, if a global identifier in a program has the same name as one of the global identifiers in the header file, the compiler generates a syntax error (such as "identifier redefined"). The same problem can occur if a program uses third-party libraries. To overcome this problem, third-party vendors begin their global identifiers with a special symbol. In Chapter 2, you learned that because compiler vendors begin their global identifier names with an underscore (_), to avoid linking errors you should not begin identifier names in your program with an underscore (_).

ANSI/ISO Standard C++ tries to solve this problem of overlapping global identifier names with the **namespace** mechanism.

The general syntax of the statement **namespace** is:

```cpp
namespace namespace_name
{
    members
}
```

where a **member** is usually a named constant, variable declaration, function, or another **namespace**. Note that `namespace_name` is a C++ identifier.

In C++, **namespace** is a reserved word.

EXAMPLE 8-8

The statement:

```
namespace globalType
{
    const int N = 10;
    const double RATE = 7.50;
    int count = 0;
    void printResult();
}
```

defines `globalType` to be a **namespace** with four members: named constants `N` and `RATE`, the variable `count`, and the function `printResult`.

The scope of a **namespace** member is local to the **namespace**. You can usually access a **namespace** member outside the **namespace** in one of two ways, as described below.

The general syntax for accessing a **namespace** member is:

> `namespace_name::identifier`

Recall that, in C++, `::` is called the scope resolution operator.

To access the member `RATE` of the **namespace** `globalType`, the following statement is required:

```
globalType::RATE
```

To access the member `printResult` (which is a function), the following statement is required:

```
globalType::printResult();
```

Thus, to access a member of a **namespace**, you use the `namespace_name`, followed by the scope resolution operator, followed by the member name.

To simplify the accessing of a **namespace** member, ANSI/ISO Standard C++ provides the use of the statement **using**. The syntax to use the statement **using** is as follows:

a. To simplify the accessing of all **namespace** members:

> `using namespace namespace_name;`

b. To simplify the accessing of a specific **namespace** member:

```
using namespace_name::identifier;
```

For example, the **using** statement:

```
using namespace globalType;
```

simplifies the accessing of all members of the **namespace** `globalType`. The statement:

```
using globalType::RATE;
```

simplifies the accessing of the member `RATE` of the **namespace** `globalType`.

In C++, **using** is a reserved word.

You typically put the **using** statement after the **namespace** declaration. For the **namespace** `globalType`, for example, you usually write the code as follows:

```
namespace globalType
{
    const int N = 10;
    const double RATE = 7.50;
    int count = 0;
    void printResult();
}
using namespace globalType;
```

After the **using** statement, to access a **namespace** member you do not have to put the namespace_name and the scope resolution operator before the **namespace** member. However, if a **namespace** member and a global identifier in a program have the same name, to access this **namespace** member in the program, the namespace_name and the scope resolution operator must precede the **namespace** member. Similarly, if a **namespace** member and an identifier in a block have the same name, to access this **namespace** member in the block, the namespace_name and the scope resolution operator must precede the **namespace** member.

Examples 8-9 through 8-12 help clarify the use of the **namespace** mechanism.

EXAMPLE 8-9

Consider the following C++ code:

```
#include <iostream>

using namespace std;
    .
    .
    .
int main()
```

```
{
    .
    .
    .
}
.
.
.
```

In this example, you can refer to the global identifiers of the header file `iostream`, such as `cin`, `cout`, and `endl`, without using the prefix `std::` before the identifier name. The obvious restriction is that the block (or function) that refers to the global identifier (of the header file `iostream`) must not contain any identifier with the same name as this global identifier.

EXAMPLE 8-10

Consider the following C++ code:

```
#include <cmath>

int main()
{
    double x = 15.3;
    double y;

    y = std::pow(x, 2);
    .
    .
    .
}
```

This example accesses the function `pow` of the header file `cmath`.

EXAMPLE 8-11

Consider the following C++ code:

```
#include <iostream>
    .
    .
    .
int main()
```

```
{
    using namespace std;
        .
        .
        .
}
    .
    .
    .
```

In this example, the function `main` can refer to the global identifiers of the header file `iostream` without using the prefix `std::` before the identifier name. The **using** statement appears inside the function `main`. Therefore, other functions (if any) should use the prefix `std::` before the name of the global identifier of the header file `iostream` unless the function has a similar **using** statement.

Consider the following C++ code:

```
#include <iostream>

using namespace std;           //Line 1

int t;                         //Line 2
double u;                      //Line 3

namespace expN
{
    int x;                     //Line 4
    char t;                    //Line 5
    double u;                  //Line 6
    void printResult();        //Line 7
}

using namespace expN;

int main()
{
    int one;                   //Line 8
    double t;                  //Line 9
    double three;              //Line 10

        .
        .
        .
}
```

```
void expN::printResult()  //Definition of the function printResult
{
      .
      .
      .
}
```

In this C++ program:

1. To refer to the variable t at Line 2 in main, use the *scope resolution operator*, which is :: (that is, refer to t as ::t), because the function main has a variable named t (declared at Line 9). For example, to copy the value of x into t, you can use the statement ::t = x;.

2. To refer to the member t (declared at Line 5) of the **namespace** expN in main, use the prefix expN:: with t (that is, refer to t as expN::t) because there is a global variable named t (declared at Line 2) and a variable named t in main.

3. To refer to the member u (declared at Line 6) of the **namespace** expN in main, use the prefix expN:: with u (that is, refer to u as expN::u) because there is a global variable named u (declared at Line 3).

4. You can reference the member x (declared at Line 4) of the **namespace** expN in main as either x or expN::x because there is no global identifier named x and the function main does not contain any identifier named x.

5. The definition of a function that is a member of a **namespace**, such as printResult, is usually written outside the **namespace** as in the preceding program. To write the definition of the function printResult, the name of the function in the function heading can be either printResult or expN::printResult (because no other global identifier is named printResult).

NOTE The identifiers in the system-provided header files, such as iostream, cmath, and iomanip, are defined in the **namespace** std. For this reason, to simplify the accessing of identifiers from these header files, we have been using the following statement in the programs that we write:

```
using namespace std;
```

string Type

In Chapter 2, you were introduced to the data type string. Recall that, prior to the ANSI/ISO C++ language standard, the Standard C++ library did not provide a string data type. Compiler vendors often supplied their own programmer-defined string type, and the syntax and semantics of string operations often varied from vendor to vendor.

The data type `string` is a programmer-defined type and is not part of the C++ language; the C++ standard library supplies it. Before using the data type `string`, the program must include the header file `string`, as follows:

```
#include <string>
```

Recall that, in C++, a string is a sequence of zero or more characters, and strings are enclosed in double quotation marks.

The statement:

```
string name = "William Jacob";
```

declares `name` to be a `string` variable and initializes `name` to `"William Jacob"`. The position of the first character, `W`, in `name` is 0; the position of the second character, `i`, is 1; and so on. That is, the position of the first character in a `string` variable starts with 0, not 1.

The variable `name` can store (just about) any size string.

Chapter 3 discussed I/O operations on the `string` type; Chapter 4 explained relational operations on the `string` type. We recommend that you revisit Chapters 3 and 4 and review the I/O and relational operations on the `string` type.

Other operators, such as the binary operator + (to allow the string concatenation operation) and the array index (subscript) operator [], have also been defined for the data type `string`. Let's see how these operators work on the `string` data type.

Suppose you have the following declarations:

```
string str1, str2, str3;
```

The statement:

```
str1 = "Hello There";
```

stores the string `"Hello There"` in `str1`. The statement:

```
str2 = str1;
```

copies the value of `str1` into `str2`.

if `str1 = "Sunny"`, the statement:

```
str2 = str1 + " Day";
```

stores the string `"Sunny Day"` into `str2`.

Suppose `str1 = "Hello"` and `str2 = "There"`. The statement:

```
str3 = str1 + " " + str2;
```

stores `"Hello There"` into `str3`. This statement is equivalent to the statement:

```
str3 = str1 + ' ' + str2;
```

Also, the statement:

```
str1 = str1 + " Mickey";
```

updates the value of `str1` by appending the string `" Mickey"` to its old value. Therefore, the new value of `str1` is `"Hello Mickey"`.

NOTE For the operator + to work with the `string` data type, one of the operands of + must be a `string` variable. For example, the following statements will not work:

```
str1 = "Hello " + "there!"; //illegal
str2 = "Sunny Day" + '!';    //illegal
```

If `str1 = "Hello there"`, the statement:

```
str1[6] = 'T';
```

replaces the character t with the character T. Recall that the position of the first character in a `string` variable is 0. Therefore, because t is the seventh character in `str1`, its position is 6.

In C++, `[]` is called the **array subscript operator**.

As illustrated previously, using the array subscript operator together with the position of the character, you can access an individual character within a string.

EXAMPLE 8-13

The following program shows the effect of the preceding statements.

```
//Example string operations

#include <iostream>
#include <string>

using namespace std;

int main()
{
    string name = "William Jacob";                    //Line 1
    string str1, str2, str3, str4;                    //Line 2

    cout << "Line 3: Name = " << name << endl;        //Line 3

    str1 = "Hello There";                             //Line 4
    cout << "Line 5: str1 = " << str1 << endl;        //Line 5
```

```cpp
    str2 = str1;                                        //Line 6
    cout << "Line 7: str2 = " << str2 << endl;          //Line 7

    str1 = "Sunny";                                     //Line 8
    str2 = str1 + " Day";                               //Line 9
    cout << "Line 10: str2 = " << str2 << endl;         //Line 10

    str1 = "Hello";                                     //Line 11
    str2 = "There";                                     //Line 12
    str3 = str1 + " " + str2;                           //Line 13
    cout << "Line 14: str3 = " << str3 << endl;         //Line 14

    str3 = str1 + ' ' + str2;                           //Line 15
    cout << "Line 16: str3 = " << str3 << endl;         //Line 16

    str1 = str1 + " Mickey";                            //Line 17
    cout << "Line 18: str1 = " << str1 << endl;         //Line 18

    str1 = "Hello there";                               //Line 19
    cout << "Line 20: str1[6] = " << str1[6]
         << endl;                                       //Line 20

    str1[6] = 'T';                                      //Line 21
    cout << "Line 22: str1 = " << str1 << endl;         //Line 22

        //String input operations
    cout << "Line 23: Enter a string with "
         << "no blanks: ";                              //Line 23
    cin >> str1;                                        //Line 24

    char ch;                                            //Line 25
    cin.get(ch);              //Read the newline character; Line 26
    cout << endl;                                       //Line 27

    cout << "Line 28: The string you entered = "
         << str1 << endl;                               //Line 28

    cout << "Line 29: Enter a sentence: ";              //Line 29
    getline(cin, str2);                                 //Line 30
    cout << endl;                                       //Line 31

    cout << "Line 32: The sentence is: " << str2
         << endl;                                       //Line 32

    return 0;
}
```

Sample Run: In the following sample run, the user input is shaded.

```
Line 3: Name = William Jacob
Line 5: str1 = Hello There
Line 7: str2 = Hello There
Line 10: str2 = Sunny Day
```

```
Line 14: str3 = Hello There
Line 16: str3 = Hello There
Line 18: str1 = Hello Mickey
Line 20: str1[6] = t
Line 22: str1 = Hello There
Line 23: Enter a string with no blanks: Programming

Line 28: The string you entered = Programming
Line 29: Enter a sentence: Testing string operations

Line 32: The sentence is: Testing string operations
```

The preceding output is self-explanatory, and its unraveling is left as an exercise for you.

Additional string Operations

The data type string contains several other functions for string manipulation. The five in which we are interested—length, size, find, substr, and swap—are described in the next five sections.

The data type string has a data type, string::size_type, and a named constant, string::npos, associated with it.

string::size_type	An unsigned integer (data) type
string::npos	The maximum value of the (data) type string::size_type, a number such as 4294967295 on many machines

length Function

The length function returns the number of characters currently in the string. The value returned is an unsigned integer. The syntax to call the length function is:

```
strVar.length()
```

where strVar is a variable of type string. The length function has no arguments.

Be careful with the syntax of the length function. The dot (period) between the strVar and length is crucial; it separates the name of the string variable and the word length. Moreover, because length is a function with no arguments, you still need the empty parentheses. Also, because length is a value-returning function, the function call should appear in an expression.

Consider the following statements:

```
string firstName;
string name;
string str;
```

```
firstName = "Elizabeth";
name = firstName + " Jones";
str = "It is sunny.";
```

Statement	Effect
`cout << firstName.length() << endl;`	Outputs 9
`cout << name.length() << endl;`	Outputs 15
`cout << str.length() << endl;`	Outputs 12

Because the function `length` returns an unsigned integer, the value returned can be stored in an integer variable. Also, because the data type `string` has the data type `string::size_type` associated with it, the variable to hold the value returned by the `length` function is usually of this type. This prevents you from guessing whether the value returned is of type **unsigned int** or **unsigned long**.

Suppose you have the previous declaration and the statement:

```
string::size_type len;
```

Statement	Effect
`len = firstName.length();`	The value of `len` is 9
`len = name.length();`	The value of `len` is 15
`len = str.length();`	The value of `len` is 12

EXAMPLE 8-14

The following program illustrates the use of the `length` function:

```
//Example length function

#include <iostream>
#include <string>

using namespace std;

int main()
{
    string name, firstName;                  //Line 1
    string str;                              //Line 2
    string::size_type len;                   //Line 3

    firstName = "Elizabeth";                 //Line 4
    name = firstName + " Jones";             //Line 5
    str = "It is sunny and warm.";           //Line 6
```

```cpp
    cout << "Line 7: Length of \"" << firstName << "\" = "
         << static_cast<unsigned int> (firstName.length())
         << endl;                                          //Line 7
    cout << "Line 8: Length of \"" << name << "\" = "
         << static_cast<unsigned int> (name.length())
         << endl;                                          //Line 8
    cout << "Line 9: Length of \"" << str << "\" = "
         << static_cast<unsigned int> (str.length())
         << endl;                                          //Line 9

    len = firstName.length();                              //Line 10
    cout << "Line 11: len = "
         << static_cast<unsigned int> (len)
         << endl;                                          //Line 11

    len = name.length();                                  //Line 12
    cout << "Line 13: len = "
         << static_cast<unsigned int> (len) << endl;      //Line 13

    len = str.length();                                   //Line 14
    cout << "Line 15: len = "
         << static_cast<unsigned int> (len) << endl;      //Line 15

    return 0;
}
```

Sample Run:

```
Line 7: Length of "Elizabeth" = 9
Line 8: Length of "Elizabeth Jones" = 15
Line 9: Length of "It is sunny and warm." = 21
Line 11: len = 9
Line 13: len = 15
Line 15: len = 21
```

The output of this program is self-explanatory. The details are left as an exercise for you. Notice that this program uses the static cast operator to output the value returned by the function length. This is because the function length returns a value of type string::size_type. Without the cast operator, some compilers might give the following warning message:

```
conversion from 'size_t' to 'unsigned int', possible loss of data
```

size Function

Some people prefer to use the word size instead of the word length. Thus, to accommodate both terms, the string type provides a function named size that returns the same value as does the function length. The syntax to call the function size is:

```
strVar.size()
```

where `strVar` is a variable of type `string`. Like the function `length`, the function `size` has no arguments.

`find` Function

The `find` function searches a string to find the first occurrence of a particular substring and returns an unsigned integer value (of type `string::size_type`), giving the result of the search. The syntax to call the function `find` is:

```
strVar.find(strExp)
```

or:

```
strVar.find(strExp, pos)
```

where `strVar` is a string variable and `strExp` is a string expression evaluating to a string. The string expression, `strExp`, can also be a character. If the search is successful, the function `find` returns the position in `strVar` where the match begins. For the search to be successful, the match must be exact. If the search is unsuccessful, the function returns the special value `string::npos` ("not a position within the string"). (This value is suitable for "not a valid position" because the string operations do not let any string become this long.) Because the function `find` returns an unsigned integer, the returned value can be stored in an integer variable (usually of type `string::size_type`). In the second form of the function `find`, `pos` specifies the position in the string where to begin the search.

Suppose `str1` and `str2` are of type `string`. The following are valid calls to the function `find`:

```
str1.find(str2)
str1.find("the")
str1.find('a')
str1.find(str2 + "xyz")
str1.find(str2 + 'b')
```

Consider the following statements:

```
string sentence;
string str;
string::size_type position;

sentence = "Outside it is cloudy and warm.";
str = "cloudy";
```

Statement	Effect
`cout << sentence.find("is") << endl;`	Outputs 11
`cout << sentence.find("and") << endl;`	Outputs 21
`cout << sentence.find('s') << endl;`	Outputs 3
`cout << sentence.find('o') << endl;`	Outputs 16
`cout << sentence.find(str) << endl;`	Outputs 14
`cout << sentence.find("the") << endl;`	Outputs the value of `string::nops`
`cout << sentence.find('i', 6) << endl;`	Outputs 8
`position = sentence.find("warm");`	Assigns 25 to `position`

Note that the search is case-sensitive. Therefore, the position of o (lowercase o) in the string `sentence` is 16.

EXAMPLE 8-15

The following program illustrates how to use the `string` function `find`.

```cpp
//Example find function

#include <iostream>
#include <string>

using namespace std;

int main()
{
    string sentence, str;                        //Line 1
    string::size_type position;                  //Line 2

    sentence = "Outside it is cloudy and warm."; //Line 3
    str = "cloudy";                              //Line 4

    cout << "Line 5: sentence = \"" << sentence
         << "\"" << endl;                        //Line 5

    cout << "Line 6: The position of \"is\" in sentence = "
         << static_cast<unsigned int> (sentence.find("is"))
         << endl;                                //Line 6

    cout << "Line 7: The position of \"and\" in sentence = "
         << static_cast<unsigned int> (sentence.find("and"))
         << endl;                                //Line 7

    cout << "Line 8: The position of 's' in sentence = "
         << static_cast<unsigned int> (sentence.find('s'))
         << endl;                                //Line 8
```

```cpp
    cout << "Line 9: The position of 'o' in sentence = "
         << static_cast<unsigned int> (sentence.find('o'))
         << endl;                                              //Line 9

    cout << "Line 10: The position of \"" << str
         << "\" in sentence = "
         << static_cast<unsigned int> (sentence.find(str))
         << endl;                                              //Line 10

    cout << "Line 11: The position of \"the\" in sentence = "
         << static_cast<unsigned int> (sentence.find("the"))
         << endl;                                              //Line 11

    cout << "Line 12: The first occurrence of \'i\' in "
         << "sentence \n            after position 6 = "
         << static_cast<unsigned int> (sentence.find('i', 6))
         << endl;                                              //Line 12

    position = sentence.find("warm");                          //Line 13
    cout << "Line 14: " << "Position = "
         << static_cast<unsigned int> (position)
         << endl;                                              //Line 14

    return 0;
}
```

Sample Run:

```
Line 5: sentence = "Outside it is cloudy and warm."
Line 6: The position of "is" in sentence = 11
Line 7: The position of "and" in sentence = 21
Line 8: The position of 's' in sentence = 3
Line 9: The position of 'o' in sentence = 16
Line 10: The position of "cloudy" in sentence = 14
Line 11: The position of "the" in sentence = 4294967295
Line 12: The first occurrence of 'i' in sentence
         after position 6 = 8
Line 14: Position = 25
```

The output of this program is self-explanatory. The details are left as an exercise for you. Notice that this program uses the static cast operator to output the value returned by the function `find`. This is because the function `find` returns a value of the type `string::size_type`. Without the cast operator, some compilers might give the following warning message:

```
conversion from 'size_t' to 'unsigned int', possible loss of data
```

The output of this program is self-explanatory. The details are left as an exercise for you.

substr Function

The substr function returns a particular substring of a string. The syntax to call the function substr is:

```
strVar.substr(expr1, expr2)
```

where expr1 and expr2 are expressions evaluating to unsigned integers. The expression expr1 specifies a position within the string (the starting position of the substring); the expression expr2 specifies the length of the substring to be returned. If, starting at expr1, the number of characters (that is, the length of the substring) specified by expr2 exceeds the length of the string, characters until the end of the string are returned. (For example, see the fourth output statement, below, in which sentence is a string of length 22, and starting at position 17 we try to extract a substring of length 10. However, starting at position 17, sentence has only five characters and so only warm. is output.)

Consider the following statements:

```
string sentence;
string str;

sentence = "It is cloudy and warm.";
```

Statement	Effect
cout << sentence.substr(0, 5) << endl;	Outputs: It is
cout << sentence.substr(6, 6) << endl;	Outputs: cloudy
cout << sentence.substr(6, 16) << endl;	Outputs: cloudy and warm.
cout << sentence.substr(17, 10) << endl;	Outputs: warm.
cout << sentence.substr(3, 6) << endl;	Outputs: is clo
str = sentence.substr(0, 8);	str = "It is cl"
str = sentence.substr(2, 10);	str = " is cloudy"

EXAMPLE 8-16

The following program illustrates how to use the string function substr:

```
//Example substr function

#include <iostream>
#include <string>

using namespace std;
```

```cpp
int main()
{
    string sentence;                                        //Line 1
    string str;                                             //Line 2

    sentence = "It is cloudy and warm.";                    //Line 3

    cout << "Line 4: substr(0, 5) in \""
         << sentence << "\" = \""
         << sentence.substr(0, 5) << "\""
         << endl;                                           //Line 4

    cout << "Line 5: substr(6, 6) in \""
         << sentence << "\" = \""
         << sentence.substr(6, 6) << "\""
         << endl;                                           //Line 5

    cout << "Line 6: substr(6, 16) in \""
         << sentence << "\" = " << endl
         << "            \"" << sentence.substr(6, 16)
         << "\"" << endl;                                   //Line 6

    cout << "Line 7: substr(17, 10) in \""
         << sentence << "\" = \""
         << sentence.substr(17, 10) << "\""
         << endl;                                           //Line 7

    cout << "Line 8: substr(3, 6) in \""
         << sentence << "\" = \""
         << sentence.substr(3, 6) << "\""
         << endl;                                           //Line 8

    str = sentence.substr(0, 8);                            //Line 9
    cout << "Line 10: " << "str = \"" << str
         << "\"" << endl;                                   //Line 10

    str = sentence.substr(2, 10);                           //Line 11
    cout << "Line 12: " << "str = \"" << str
         << "\"" << endl;                                   //Line 12

    return 0;
}
```

Sample Run:

```
Line 4: substr(0, 5) in "It is cloudy and warm." = "It is"
Line 5: substr(6, 6) in "It is cloudy and warm." = "cloudy"
Line 6: substr(6, 16) in "It is cloudy and warm." =
        "cloudy and warm."
Line 7: substr(17, 10) in "It is cloudy and warm." = "warm."
Line 8: substr(3, 6) in "It is cloudy and warm." = "is clo"
```

```
Line 10: str = "It is cl"
Line 12: str = " is cloudy"
```

The output of this program is self-explanatory. The details are left as an exercise for you.

`swap` Function

The `swap` function is used to swap—that is, interchange—the contents of two string variables. The syntax to use the `swap` function is:

```
strVar1.swap(strVar2);
```

where `strVar1` and `strVar2` are `string` variables. After this statement executes, the contents of `strVar1` and `strVar2` are swapped.

Suppose you have the following statements:

```
string str1 = "Warm";
string str2 = "Cold";
```

After the following statement executes, the value of `str1` is `"Cold"` and the value of `str2` is `"Warm"`.

```
str1.swap(str2);
```

Additional `string` functions, such as `empty`, `clear`, `erase`, `insert`, and `replace`, are provided in Appendix F (Header File `string`).

PROGRAMMING EXAMPLE: Pig Latin Strings

In this programming example, we write a program that prompts the user to input a string and then outputs the string in the pig Latin form. The rules for converting a string into pig Latin form are as follows:

1. If the string begins with a vowel, add the string `"-way"` at the end of the string. For example, the pig Latin form of the string `"eye"` is `"eye-way"`.

2. If the string does not begin with a vowel, first add `"-"` at the end of the string. Then rotate the string one character at a time; that is, move the first character of the string to the end of the string until the first character of the string becomes a vowel. Then add the string `"ay"` at the end. For example, the pig Latin form of the string `"There"` is `"ere-Thay"`.

3. Strings such as `"by"` contain no vowels. In cases like this, the letter `y` can be considered a vowel. So, for this program the vowels are `a`,

e, i, o, u, y, A, E, I, O, U, and Y. Therefore, the pig Latin form of `"by"` is `"y-bay"`.

4. Strings such as `"1234"` contain no vowels. The pig Latin form of the string `"1234"` is `"1234-way"`. That is, the pig Latin form of a string that has no vowels in it is the string followed by the string `"-way"`.

Input   Input to the program is a string.

Output   Output of the program is the string in the pig Latin form.

PROBLEM ANALYSIS AND ALGORITHM DESIGN

Suppose that `str` denotes a string. To convert `str` into pig Latin, check the first character, `str[0]`, of `str`. If `str[0]` is a vowel, add `"-way"` at the end of `str`— that is, `str = str + "-way"`.

Suppose that the first character of `str`, `str[0]`, is not a vowel. First add `"-"` at the end of the string. Then remove the first character of `str` from `str` and put it at end of `str`. Now the second character of `str` becomes the first character of `str`. This process of checking the first character of `str` and moving it to the end of `str` if the first character of `str` is not a vowel is repeated until either the first character of `str` is a vowel or all the characters of `str` are processed, in which case `str` does not contain any vowels.

In this program, we write a function `isVowel`, to determine whether a character is a vowel; a function `rotate`, to move the first character of `str` to the end of `str`; and a function `pigLatinString`, to find the pig Latin form of `str`. The previous discussion translates into the following algorithm:

1. Get `str`.
2. Find the pig Latin form of `str` by using the function `pigLatinString`.
3. Output the pig Latin form of `str`.

Before writing the main algorithm, each of these functions is described in detail.

Function isVowel

This function takes a character as a parameter and returns **true** if the character is a vowel, and **false** otherwise. The definition of the function `isVowel` is:

```cpp
bool isVowel(char ch)
{
    switch (ch)
    {
    case 'A':
    case 'E':
    case 'I':
    case 'O':
    case 'U':
    case 'Y':
    case 'a':
    case 'e':
    case 'i':
```

```
case 'o':
case 'u':
case 'y':
    return true;
default:
    return false;
}
}
```

Function rotate This function takes a string as a parameter, removes the first character of the string, and places it at the end of the string. This is done by extracting the substring starting at position 1 (which is the second character) until the end of the string, and then adding the first character of the string. The new string is returned as the value of this function. Essentially, the definition of the function `rotate` is:

```
string rotate(string pStr)
{
    string::size_type len = pStr.length();

    string rStr;

    rStr = pStr.substr(1, len - 1) + pStr[0];

    return rStr;
}
```

Function pigLatinString This function takes a string, `pStr`, as a parameter and returns the pig Latin form of `pStr`. Suppose `pStr` denotes the string to be converted to its pig Latin form. There are three possible cases: `pStr[0]` is a vowel; `pStr` contains a vowel and the first character of `pStr` is not a vowel; or `pStr` contains no vowels. Suppose that `pStr[0]M` is not a vowel. Move the first character of `pStr` to the end of `pStr`. This process is repeated until either the first character of `pStr` has become a vowel or all the characters of `pStr` are checked, in which case `pStr` does not contain any vowels. This discussion translates into the following algorithm:

1. If `pStr[0]` is a vowel, add `"-way"` at the end of `pStr`.

2. Suppose `pStr[0]` is not a vowel.

3. ove the first character of `pStr` to the end of `pStr`. The second character of `pStr` becomes the first character of `pStr`. Now `pStr` may or may not contain a vowel. We use a **bool** variable, `foundVowel`, which is set to **true** if `pStr` contains a vowel and **false** otherwise.

   a. Suppose that `len` denotes the length of `pStr`.

   b. Initialize `foundVowel` to **false**.

   c. If `pStr[0]` is not a vowel, move `pStr[0]` to the end of `pStr` by calling the function `rotate`.

    d.   Repeat Step b until either the first character of pStr becomes a vowel or all the characters of pStr have been checked.

4.   Convert pStr into the pig Latin form.

5.   Return pStr.

The definition of the function pigLatinString is:

```cpp
string pigLatinString(string pStr)
{
    string::size_type len;

    bool foundVowel;

    string::size_type counter;

    if (isVowel(pStr[0]))                           //Step 1
        pStr = pStr + "-way";
    else                                            //Step 2
    {
        pStr = pStr + '-';
        pStr = rotate(pStr);                        //Step 3

        len = pStr.length();                        //Step 3.a
        foundVowel = false;                         //Step 3.b

        for (counter = 1; counter < len - 1;
                          counter++)                //Step 3.d
            if (isVowel(pStr[0]))
            {
                foundVowel = true;
                break;
            }
            else                                    //Step 3.c
                pStr = rotate(pStr);

        if (!foundVowel)                            //Step 4
            pStr = pStr.substr(1, len) + "-way";
        else
            pStr = pStr + "ay";
    }

    return pStr;                                    //Step 5
}
```

<table>
<tr><td></td><td>

1.   Get the string.

2.   Call the function pigLatinString to find the pig Latin form of the string.

3.   Output the pig Latin form of the string.

</td></tr>
</table>

COMPLETE PROGRAM LISTING

```cpp
#include <iostream>
#include <string>

using namespace std;

bool isVowel(char ch);
string rotate(string pStr);
string pigLatinString(string pStr);

int main()
{
    string str;

    cout << "Enter a string: ";
    cin >> str;
    cout << endl;

    cout << "The pig Latin form of " << str << " is: "
         << pigLatinString(str) << endl;

    return 0;
}

bool isVowel(char ch)
{
    switch (ch)
    {
    case 'A':
    case 'E':
    case 'I':
    case 'O':
    case 'U':
    case 'Y':
    case 'a':
    case 'e':
    case 'i':
    case 'o':
    case 'u':
    case 'y':
        return true;
    default:
        return false;
    }
}
```

```cpp
string rotate(string pStr)
{
    string::size_type len = pStr.length();

    string rStr;

    rStr = pStr.substr(1, len - 1) + pStr[0];

    return rStr;
}

string pigLatinString(string pStr)
{
    string::size_type len;

    bool foundVowel;

    string::size_type counter;

    if (isVowel(pStr[0]))                           //Step 1
        pStr = pStr + "-way";
    else                                            //Step 2
    {
        pStr = pStr + '-';
        pStr = rotate(pStr);                        //Step 3

        len = pStr.length();                        //Step 3.a
        foundVowel = false;                         //Step 3.b

        for (counter = 1; counter < len - 1;
                        counter++)                  //Step 3.d
            if (isVowel(pStr[0]))
            {
                foundVowel = true;
                break;
            }
            else                                    //Step 3.c
                pStr = rotate(pStr);

        if (!foundVowel)                            //Step 4
            pStr = pStr.substr(1, len) + "-way";
        else
            pStr = pStr + "ay";
    }

    return pStr;                                     //Step 5
}
```

Sample Runs: In these sample runs, the user input is shaded.

Sample Run 1:

```
Enter a string: eye

The pig Latin form of eye is: eye-way
```

Sample Run 2:

```
Enter a string: There

The pig Latin form of There is: ere-Thay
```

Sample Run 3:

```
Enter a string: why

The pig Latin form of why is: y-whay
```

Sample Run 4:

```
Enter a string: 123456

The pig Latin form of 123456 is: 123456-way
```

QUICK REVIEW

1. An enumeration type is a set of ordered values.
2. C++'s reserved word **enum** is used to create an enumeration type.
3. The syntax of **enum** is:

   ```
   enum typeName {value1, value2,...};
   ```

   where `value1, value2,...` are identifiers, and `value1 < value2 < ....`
4. No arithmetic operations are allowed on the enumeration type.
5. Relational operators can be used with **enum** values.
6. Enumeration type values cannot be input or output directly.
7. Enumeration types can be passed as parameters to functions either by value or by reference.
8. A function can return a value of the enumeration type.
9. An anonymous type is one where a variable's values are specified without any type name.

10. C++'s reserved word `typedef` is used to create synonyms or aliases to previously defined data types.

11. Anonymous types cannot be passed as parameters to functions.

12. The `namespace` mechanism is a feature of ANSI/ISO Standard C++.

13. A `namespace` member is usually a named constant, variable, function, or another `namespace`.

14. The scope of a `namespace` member is local to the `namespace`.

15. One way to access a `namespace` member outside the `namespace` is to precede the `namespace` member name with the `namespace` name and scope resolution operator.

16. In C++, `namespace` is a reserved word.

17. To use the `namespace` mechanism, the program must include the ANSI/ISO Standard C++ header files—that is, the header files without the extension h.

18. The `using` statement simplifies the accessing of `namespace` members.

19. In C++, `using` is a reserved word.

20. The keyword `namespace` must appear in the `using` statement.

21. When accessing a `namespace` member without the `using` statement, the `namespace` name and the scope resolution operator must precede the name of the `namespace` member.

22. To use an identifier declared in the standard header files without the `namespace` name, after including all the necessary header files, the following statement must appear in the program:

```
using namespace std;
```

23. A string is a sequence of zero or more characters.

24. Strings in C++ are enclosed in double quotation marks.

25. To use the type `string`, the program must include the header file `string`. The other header files used in the program should be ANSI/ISO Standard C++ style header files.

26. The assignment operator can be used with the `string` type.

27. The operator + can be used to concatenate two values of the type `string`. For the operator + to work with the `string` data type, one of the operands of + must be a `string` variable.

28. Relational operators, discussed in Chapter 4, can be applied to the `string` type.

29. In a string, the position of the first character is 0, the position of the second character is 1, and so on.

30. The length of a string is the number of characters in the string.

31. In C++, [] is called the array subscript operator.

32. To access an individual character within a string, use the array subscript operator together with the position of the character.

33. The function `length` returns the number of characters currently in the string. The syntax to call the function `length` is:

```
strVar.length()
```

where `strVar` is a variable of the type `string`.

34. The function `size` returns the number of characters currently in the string. The syntax to call the function `size` is:

```
strVar.size()
```

where `strVar` is a variable of the type `string`. The function `size` works in the same way as the `length` function does.

35. The function `find` searches a string to locate the first occurrence of a particular substring and returns an unsigned integer value (of the type `string::size_type`) giving the result of the search. The syntax to call the function `find` is:

```
strVar.find(strExp)
```

or:

```
strVar.find(strExp, pos)
```

where `strVar` is a string variable and `strExp` is a string expression evaluating to a string. In the second form of the function `find`, `pos` specifies the position in the string where the search should begin.

36. The argument of the function `find` (that is, `strExp`) can also be a character.

37. If the search is successful, the function `find` returns the position in `strVar` where the match begins. If the search is unsuccessful, the function `find` returns the `npos` value.

38. The function `substr` returns a particular substring of a string. The syntax to call the function `substr` is:

```
strVar.substr(expr1, expr2)
```

where `expr1` and `expr2` are expressions evaluating to unsigned integers. The expression `expr1` specifies a position within the string (the starting position of the substring). The expression `expr2` specifies the length of the substring to be returned.

39. The function `swap` is used to swap the contents of two string variables. The syntax to use the function `swap` is:

```
strVar1.swap(strVar2);
```

where `strVar1` and `strVar2` are string variables. This statement swaps the values of `strVar1` and `strVar2`.

EXERCISES

1. Mark the following statements as true or false.

   a. The following is a valid C++ enumeration type:

   ```cpp
   enum romanNumerals {I, V, X, L, C, D, M};
   ```

   b. Given the declaration:

   ```cpp
   enum cars {FORD, GM, TOYOTA, HONDA};
   cars domesticCars = FORD;
   ```

   the statement:

   ```cpp
   domesticCars = domesticCars + 1;
   ```

   sets the value of `domesticCars` to GM.

   c. A function can return a value of an enumeration type.

   d. You can input the value of an enumeration type directly from a standard input device.

   e. The only arithmetic operations allowed on the enumeration type are increment and decrement.

   f. The values in the domain of an enumeration type are called enumerators.

   g. The following are legal C++ statements in the same block of a C++ program:

   ```cpp
   enum mathStudent {BILL, JOHN, LISA, RON, CINDY, SHELLY};
   enum historyStudent {AMANDA, BOB, JACK, TOM, SUSAN};
   ```

   h. The following statement creates an anonymous type:

   ```cpp
   enum {A, B, C, D, F} studentGrade;
   ```

   i. You can use the `namespace` mechanism with header files with the extension h.

   j. Suppose `str = "ABCD";`. After the statement `str[1] = 'a';`, the value of `str` is `"aBCD"`.

   k. Suppose `str = "abcd"`. After the statement:

   ```cpp
   str = str + "ABCD";
   ```

   the value of `str` is `"ABCD"`.

2. Write C++ statements that do the following:

   a. Define an `enum` type, `bookType`, with the values MATH, CSC, ENGLISH, HISTORY, PHYSICS, and PHILOSOPHY.

   b. Declare a variable `book` of type `bookType`.

   c. Assign MATH to the variable `book`.

   d. Advance `book` to the next value in the list.

   e. Output the value of the variable `book`.

3. Given:

```
enum currencyType {DOLLAR, POUND, FRANK, LIRA, MARK};
currencyType currency;
```

which of the following statements are valid?

a. `currency = DOLLAR;`

b. `cin >> currency;`

c. `currency = static_cast<currencyType>(currency + 1);`

d. `for (currency = DOLLAR; currency <= MARK; currency++)`
   `    cout << "*";`

4. Given:

```
enum cropType {WHEAT, CORN, RYE, BARLEY, OATS};
cropType   crop;
```

circle the correct answer.

a. `static_cast<int>(WHEAT) is 0`
   (i) true   (ii) false

b. `static_cast<cropType>(static_cast<int>(WHEAT) - 1) is`
   `WHEAT`
   (i) true   (ii) false

c. `Rye > WHEAT`
   (i) true   (ii) false

d. `for (crop = wheat; crop <= oats; ++crop)`
   `    cout << "*";`
   `cout << endl;`

   outputs: *****
   (i) true   (ii) false

5. What is wrong with the following program?

```
#include <iostream>                        //Line 1

int main()                                 //Line 2
{
    cout << "Hello World! " << endl;       //Line 3

    return 0;                              //Line 4
}
```

6. What is wrong with the following program?

```
#include <iostream.h>                       //Line 1

using namespace std;                        //Line 2
```

```cpp
int main()                                        //Line 3
{
    int x = 0;                                    //Line 4
    cout << "x = " << x << endl;                  //Line 5
    return 0;                                      //Line 6
}
```

7. What is wrong with the following program?

```cpp
#include <iostream>                               //Line 1

namespace aaa                                      //Line 2
{
    const int X = 0;                               //Line 3
    double y;                                       //Line 4
}

using namespace std;                               //Line 5

int main()                                          //Line 6
{
    y = 34.50;                                       //Line 7
    cout << "X = " << X << ", y = " << y
         << endl;                                    //Line 8
    return 0;                                         //Line 9
}
```

8. What is wrong with the following program?

```cpp
#include <iostream>   //Line 1
#include <cmath>      //Line 2

using std;            //Line 3

int main()            //Line 4
{
    return 0;          //Line 5
}
```

9. What is the output of the following program?

```cpp
#include <iostream>
#include <string>

using namespace std;

int main()
{
    string str1 = "Amusement Park";
    string str2 = "Going to";
    string str3 = "the";
    string str;
```

```cpp
    cout << str2 + ' '+  str3 + ' ' + str1 << endl;
    cout << str1.length() << endl;
    cout << str1.find('P') << endl;
    cout << str1.substr(1, 5) << endl;

    str = "ABCDEFGHIJK";
    cout << str << endl;
    cout << str.length() << endl;

    str[0] = 'a';
    str[2] = 'd';

    cout << str << endl;

    return 0;
}
```

PROGRAMMING EXERCISES

1. a. Define an enumeration type, `triangleType`, that has the values `scalene`, `isosceles`, `equilateral`, and `noTriangle`.

   b. Write a function, `triangleShape`, that takes as parameters three numbers, each of which represents the length of a side of the triangle. The function should return the shape of the triangle. (*Note:* In a triangle, the sum of the lengths of any two sides is greater than the length of the third side.)

   c. Write a program that prompts the user to input the length of the sides of a triangle and outputs the shape of the triangle.

2. Redo Programming Exercise 12 of Chapter 4 (cell phone company) so that all of the named constants are defined in a `namespace`.

3. The Programming Example: Pig Latin Strings converts a string into the pig Latin form, but it processes only one word. Rewrite the program so that it can be used to process a text of an unspecified length. If a word ends with a punctuation mark, in the pig Latin form put the punctuation at the end of the string. For example, the pig Latin form of `Hello!` is `ello-Hay!`. Assume that the text contains the following punctuation marks: , (comma), . (period), ? (question mark), ; (semicolon), and : (colon). (Your program may store the output in a file.)

4. Write a program that can be used to calculate the federal tax. The tax is calculated as follows: For single people, the standard exemption is $4,000; for married people, the standard exemption is $7,000. A person can also put up to 6% of his or her gross income in a pension plan. The tax rates are as follows: If the taxable income is:

   - Between $0 and $15,000, the tax rate is 15%
   - Between $15,001 and $40,000, the tax is $2,250 plus 25% of the taxable income over $15,000

- Over \$40,000, the tax is \$8,460 plus 35% of the taxable income over \$40,000

Prompt the user to enter the following information:

- Marital status
- If the martial status is "married," ask for the number of children under the age of 14
- Gross salary (If the marital status is "married" and both spouses have income, enter the combined salary.)
- Percentage of gross income contributed to a pension fund

Your program must consist of at least the following functions:

a. Function `getData`: This function asks the user to enter the relevant data.

b. Function `taxAmount`: This function computes and returns the tax owed.

   To calculate the taxable income, subtract the sum of the standard exemption, the amount contributed to a pension plan, and the personal exemption, which is \$1,500 per person.

5. A set of integers a, b, and c is called a **Pythagorean triple** if $a^2 + b^2 = c^2$. For example, the integers 3, 4, and 5 form a Pythagorean triple because $3^2 + 4^2 = 5^2$. To find Pythagorean triples, use the following formula. Let m and n be integers. If $a = m^2 - n^2$, $b = 2mn$, and $c = m^2 + n^2$, then a, b, and c are a Pythagorean triple. Write a program that prompts the user to enter values for m and n and then outputs the Pythagorean triple corresponding to m and n.

6. (**Fraction Calculator**) Write a program that lets the user perform arithmetic operations on fractions. Fractions are of the form a/b, where a and b are integers and $b \neq 0$. Your program must be menu driven, allowing the user to select the operation (+, -, *, or /) and input the numerator and denominator of each fraction. Furthermore, your program must consist of at least the following functions:

a. Function `menu`: This function informs the user about the program's purpose, explains how to enter data, and allows the user to select the operation.

b. Function `addFractions`: This function takes as input four integers representing the numerators and denominators of two fractions, adds the fractions, and returns the numerator and denominator of the result. (Notice that this function has a total of six parameters.)

c. Function `subtractFractions`: This function takes as input four integers representing the numerators and denominators of two fractions, subtracts the fractions, and returns the numerator and denominator of the result. (Notice that this function has a total of six parameters.)

d. Function `multiplyFractions`: This function takes as input four integers representing the numerators and denominators of two fractions, multiplies the fractions, and returns the numerators and denominators of the result. (Notice that this function has a total of six parameters.)

e. Function `divideFractions`: This function takes as input four integers representing the numerators and denominators of two fractions, divides the fractions, and returns the numerator and denominator of the result. (Notice that this function has a total of six parameters.)

Some sample outputs are:

```
3 / 4 + 2 / 5 = 23 / 20
2 / 3 * 3 / 5 = 6 / 15
```

Your answer need not be in the lowest terms.

ARRAYS AND STRINGS

IN THIS CHAPTER, YOU WILL:

- Learn about arrays
- Explore how to declare and manipulate data into arrays
- Understand the meaning of "array index out of bounds"
- Become familiar with the restrictions on array processing
- Discover how to pass an array as a parameter to a function
- Learn about C-strings
- Examine the use of string functions to process C-strings
- Discover how to input data into—and output data from—a C-string
- Learn about parallel arrays
- Discover how to manipulate data in a two-dimensional array
- Learn about multidimensional arrays

In previous chapters, you worked with simple data types. In Chapter 2, you learned that C++ data types fall into three categories. One of these categories is the structured data type. This chapter and the next few chapters focus on structured data types.

Recall that a data type is called **simple** if variables of that type can store only one value at a time. In contrast, in a **structured data type** each data item is a collection of other data items. Simple data types are building blocks of structured data types. The first structured data type that we will discuss is an array. In Chapters 10 and 11, we will discuss other structured data types.

Before formally defining an array, let us consider the following problem. We want to write a C++ program that reads five numbers, finds their sum, and prints the numbers in reverse order.

In Chapter 5, you learned how to read numbers, print them, and find the sum. The difference here is that we want to print the numbers in reverse order. This means we cannot print the first four numbers until we have printed the fifth, and so on. To do this, we need to store all the numbers before we start printing them in reverse order. From what we have learned so far, the following program accomplishes this task.

```cpp
//Program to read five numbers, find their sum, and print the
//numbers in reverse order.

#include <iostream>

using namespace std;

int main()
{
    int item0, item1, item2, item3, item4;
    int sum;

    cout << "Enter five integers: ";
    cin >> item0 >> item1 >> item2 >> item3 >> item4;
    cout << endl;

    sum = item0 + item1 + item2 + item3 + item4;

    cout << "The sum of the numbers = " << sum << endl;
    cout << "The numbers in the reverse order are: ";
    cout << item4 << " " << item3 << " " << item2 << " "
         << item1 << " " << item0 << endl;

    return 0;
}
```

This program works fine. However, if you need to read 100 (or more) numbers and print them in reverse order, you would have to declare 100 variables and write many `cin` and `cout` statements. Thus, for large amounts of data, this type of program is not desirable.

Note the following in the previous program:

1. Five variables must be declared because the numbers are to be printed in reverse order.

2. All variables are of type `int`—that is, of the same data type.

3. The way in which these variables are declared indicates that the variables to store these numbers all have the same name—except the last character, which is a number.

Statement 1 tells you that you have to declare five variables. Statement 3 tells you that it would be convenient if you could somehow put the last character, which is a number, into a counter variable and use one `for` loop to count from 0 to 4 for reading and another `for` loop to count from 4 to 0 for printing. Finally, because all variables are of the same type, you should be able to specify how many variables must be declared—and their data type—with a simpler statement than the one we used earlier.

The data structure that lets you do all of these things in C++ is called an array.

Arrays

An **array** is a collection of a fixed number of components all of the same data type. A **one-dimensional array** is an array in which the components are arranged in a list form. This section discusses only one-dimensional arrays. Arrays of two dimensions or more are discussed later in this chapter.

The general form for declaring a one-dimensional array is:

```
dataType arrayName[intExp];
```

where `intExp` is any constant expression that evaluates to a positive integer. Also, `intExp` specifies the number of components in the array.

EXAMPLE 9-1

The statement:

```
int num[5];
```

declares an array num of 5 components. Each component is of type `int`. The components are `num[0]`, `num[1]`, `num[2]`, `num[3]`, and `num[4]`. Figure 9-1 illustrates the array num.

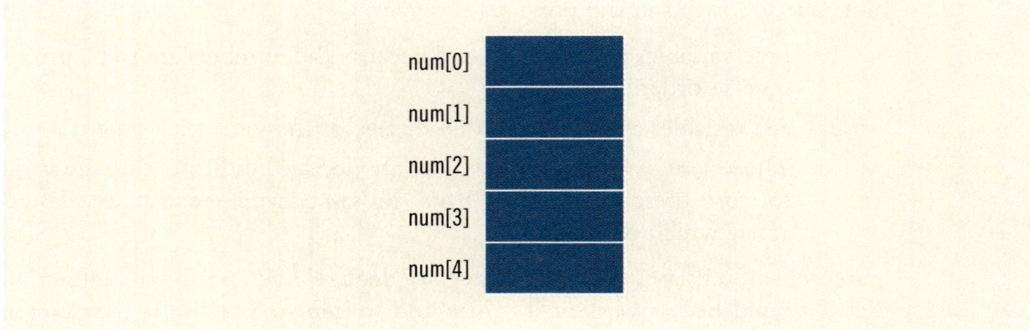

FIGURE 9-1 Array num

Accessing Array Components

The general form (syntax) used for accessing an array component is:

```
arrayName[indexExp]
```

where `indexExp`, called the **index**, is any expression whose value is a non-negative integer. The index value specifies the position of the component in the array.

In C++, `[]` is an operator, called the **array subscripting operator**. Moreover, in C++, the array index starts at `0`.

Consider the following statement:

```
int list[10];
```

This statement declares an array `list` of 10 components. The components are `list[0]`, `list[1]`, `. . .`, `list[9]`. In other words, we have declared 10 variables (see Figure 9-2).

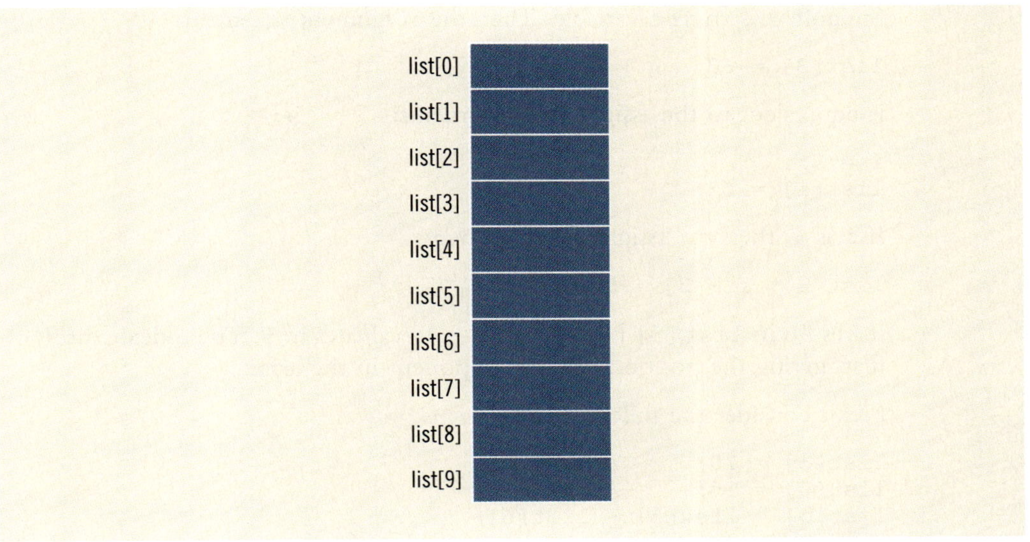

FIGURE 9-2 Array `list`

The assignment statement:

```
list[5] = 34;
```

stores 34 in `list[5]`, which is the sixth component of the array `list` (see Figure 9-3).

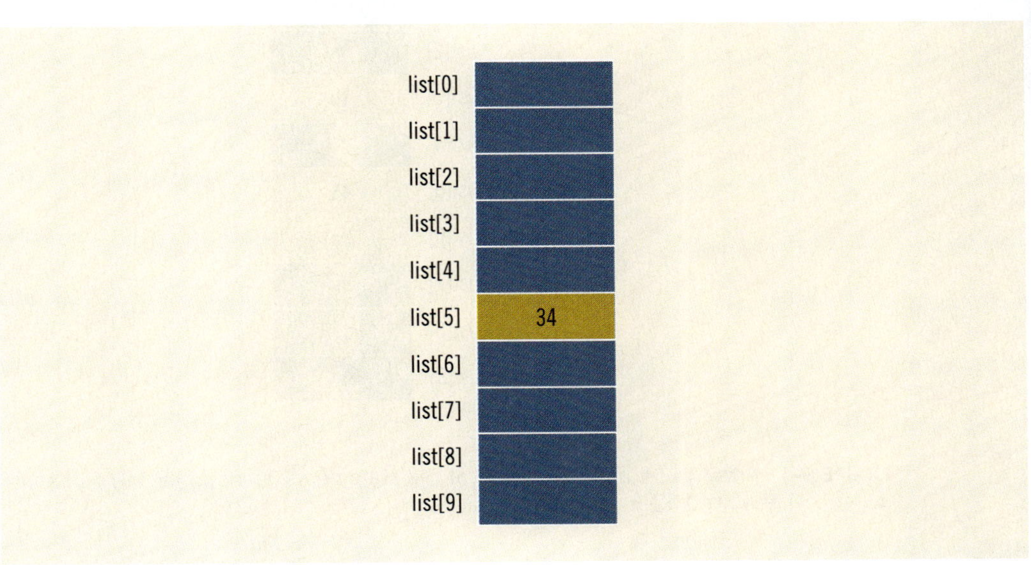

FIGURE 9-3 Array `list` after execution of the statement `list[5]= 34;`

Suppose i is an **int** variable. Then the assignment statement:

```
list[3] = 63;
```

is equivalent to the assignment statements:

```
i = 3;
list[i] = 63;
```

If i is 4, then the assignment statement:

```
list[2 * i - 3] = 58;
```

stores 58 in list[5] because 2 * i – 3 evaluates to 5. The index expression is evaluated first, giving the position of the component in the array.

Next, consider the following statements:

```
list[3] = 10;
list[6] = 35;
list[5] = list[3] + list[6];
```

The first statement stores 10 in list[3], the second statement stores 35 in list[6], and the third statement adds the contents of list[3] and list[6] and stores the result in list[5] (see Figure 9-4).

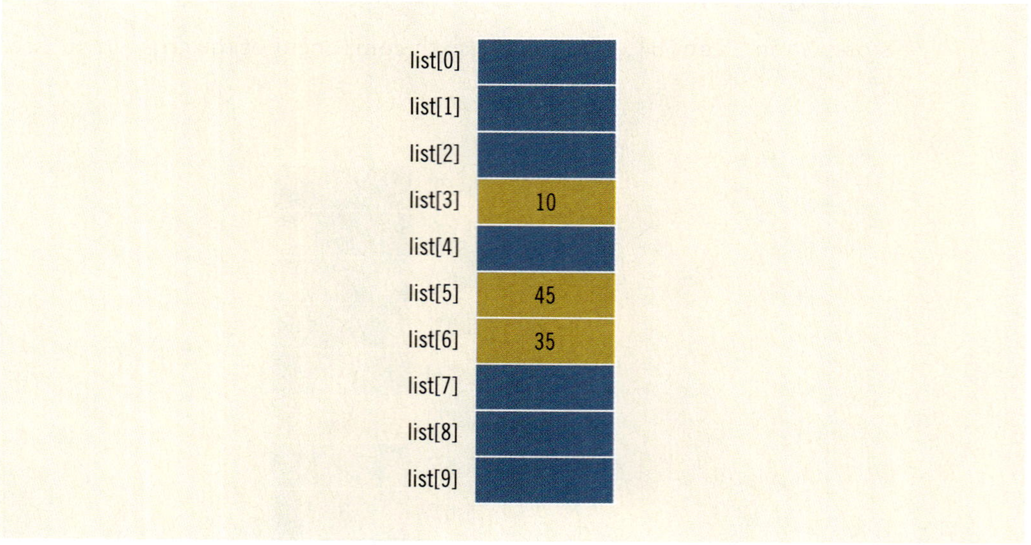

FIGURE 9-4 Array list after execution of the statements list[3]= 10;, list[6]= 35;, and list[5] = list[3] + list[6];

EXAMPLE 9-2

You can also declare arrays as follows:

```
const int ARRAY_SIZE = 10;
int list[ARRAY_SIZE];
```

That is, you can first declare a named constant and then use the value of the named constant to declare an array and specify its size.

NOTE　When you declare an array, its size must be known. For example, you cannot do the following:

```
int arraySize;                              //Line 1

cout << "Enter the size of the array: ";    //Line 2
cin >> arraySize;                           //Line 3
cout << endl;                               //Line 4

int list[arraySize];                        //Line 5; not allowed
```

The statement in Line 2 asks the user to enter the size of the array when the program executes. The statement in Line 3 inputs the size of the array into `arraySize`. When the compiler compiles Line 1, the value of the variable `arraySize` is unknown. Thus, when the compiler compiles Line 5, the size of the array is unknown and the compiler will not know how much memory space to allocate for the array. In Chapter 13, you will learn how to specify the size of an array during program execution and then declare an array of that size using pointers. Arrays that are created by using pointers during program execution are called **dynamic arrays**. For now, whenever you declare an array, its size must be known.

Processing One-Dimensional Arrays

Some of the basic operations performed on a one-dimensional array are initializing, inputting data, outputting data stored in an array, and finding the largest and/or smallest element. Moreover, if the data is numeric, some other basic operations are finding the sum and average of the elements of the array. Each of these operations requires the ability to step through the elements of the array. This is easily accomplished using a loop. For example, suppose that we have the following statements:

```
int list[100];    //list is an array of size 100
int i;
```

The following **for** loop steps through each element of the array **list**, starting at the first element of **list**:

```cpp
for (i = 0; i < 100; i++)        //Line 1
    //process list[i]            //Line 2
```

If processing the list requires inputting data into **list**, the statement in Line 2 takes the form of an input statement, such as the **cin** statement. For example, the following statements read 100 numbers from the keyboard and store the numbers in **list**:

```cpp
for (i = 0; i < 100; i++)        //Line 1
    cin >> list[i];              //Line 2
```

Similarly, if processing **list** requires outputting the data, then the statement in Line 2 takes the form of an output statement. Example 9-3 further illustrates how to process one-dimensional arrays.

EXAMPLE 9-3

This example shows how loops are used to process arrays. The following declaration is used throughout this example:

```cpp
double sales[10];
int index;
double largestSale, sum, average;
```

The first statement declares an array **sales** of 10 components, with each component being of type **double**. The meaning of the other statements is clear.

a. **Initializing an array:** The following loop initializes every component of the array **sales** to **0.0**.

```cpp
for (index = 0; index < 10; index++)
    sales[index] = 0.0;
```

b. **Reading data into an array:** The following loop inputs the data into the array **sales**. For simplicity, we assume that the data is entered at the keyboard:

```cpp
for (index = 0; index < 10; index++)
    cin >> sales[index];
```

c. **Printing an array:** The following loop outputs the array **sales**. For simplicity, we assume that the output goes to the screen:

```cpp
for (index = 0; index < 10; index++)
    cout << sales[index] << " ";
```

d. **Finding the sum and average of an array:** Because the array **sales**, as its name implies, represents certain sales data, it is natural to find the total sale and average sale amounts. The following C++

code finds the sum of the elements of the array `sales` and the average sale amount:

```
sum = 0;
for (index = 0; index < 10; index++)
    sum = sum + sales[index];

average = sum / 10;
```

e. **Largest element in the array:** We now discuss the algorithm to find the largest element in an array—that is, the array component with the largest value. However, in general, the user is more interested in determining the location of the largest element in the array. Of course, if you know the location (that is, the index of the largest element in the array), you can easily determine the value of the largest element in the array. So let us describe the algorithm to determine the index of the largest element in an array—in particular, the index of the largest sale amount in the array `sales`. We will use the index of the largest element in the array to find the largest sale.

We assume that `maxIndex` will contain the index of the first occurence of the largest element in the array `sales`. The general algorithm is straightforward. Initially, we assume that the first element in the list is the largest element and so `maxIndex` is initialized to 0. We then compare the element pointed to by `maxIndex` with every subsequent element in the list. Whenever we find an element in the array larger than the element pointed to by `maxIndex`, we update `maxIndex` so that it points to the new larger element. The algorithm is as follows:

```
maxIndex = 0;
for (index = 1; index < 10; index++)
    if (sales[maxIndex] < sales[index])
        maxIndex = index;
largestSale = sales[maxIndex];
```

Let us demonstrate how this algorithm works with an example. Suppose the array `sales` is as given in Figure 9-5.

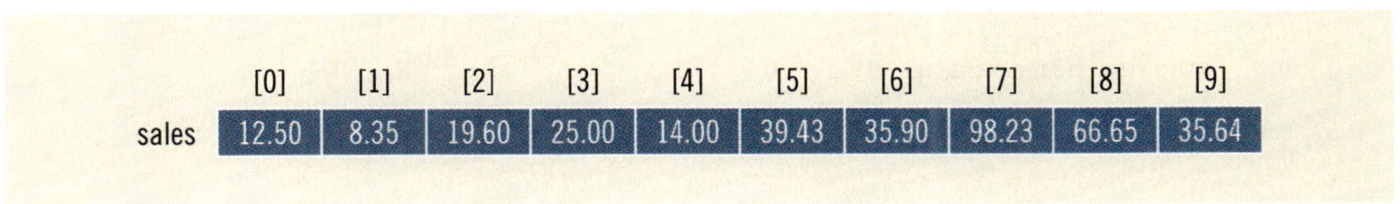

FIGURE 9-5 Array `sales`

Here we determine the largest element in the array `sales`. Before the **for** loop begins, `maxIndex` is initialized to 0 and the **for** loop initializes `index` to 1. In the following, we show the values of `maxIndex`, `index`, and certain array elements during each iteration of the **for** loop:

index	maxIndex	sales [maxIndex]	sales [index]	sales[maxIndex] < sales[index]
1	0	12.50	8.35	12.50 < 8.35 is **false**
2	0	12.50	19.60	12.50 < 19.60 is **true**; maxIndex = 2
3	2	19.60	25.00	19.60 < 25.00 is **true**; maxIndex = 3
4	3	25.00	14.00	25.00 < 14.00 is **false**
5	3	25.00	39.43	25.00 < 39.43 is **true**; maxIndex = 5
6	5	39.43	35.90	39.43 < 35.90 is **false**
7	5	39.43	98.23	39.43 < 98.23 is **true**; maxIndex = 7
8	7	98.23	66.65	98.23 < 66.65 is **false**
9	7	98.23	35.64	98.23 < 35.64 is **false**

After the **for** loop executes, `maxIndex = 7`, giving the index of the largest element in the array `sales`. Thus, `largestSale = sales[maxIndex] = 98.23`.

NOTE You can write an algorithm to find the smallest element in the array that is similar to the algorithm for finding the largest element in an array. (See Programming Exercise 2 at the end of this chapter.)

Now that we know how to declare and process arrays, let us rewrite the program that we discussed in the beginning of this chapter. Recall that this program reads five numbers, finds the sum, and prints the numbers in reverse order.

EXAMPLE 9-4

```cpp
//Program to read five numbers, find their sum, and
//print the numbers in reverse order.

#include <iostream>

using namespace std;

int main()
{
    int item[5];   //Declare an array item of five components
    int sum;
    int counter;
```

```cpp
cout << "Enter five numbers: ";

sum = 0;

for (counter = 0; counter < 5; counter++)
{
    cin >> item[counter];
    sum = sum + item[counter];
}

cout << endl;

cout << "The sum of the numbers is: " << sum << endl;
cout << "The numbers in reverse order are: ";

    //Print the numbers in reverse order.
for (counter = 4; counter >= 0; counter--)
    cout << item[counter] << " ";

cout << endl;

    return 0;
}
```

Sample Run: In this sample run, the user input is shaded.

```
Enter five numbers: 12 76 34 52 89

The sum of the numbers is: 263
The numbers in reverse order are: 89 52 34 76 12
```

Array Index Out of Bounds

Consider the following declaration:

```cpp
double num[10];
int i;
```

The component `num[i]` is valid, that is, `i` is a valid index if i = 0, 1, 2, 3, 4, 5, 6, 7, 8, or 9.

The index—say, `index`—of an array is **in bounds** if `index >= 0` and `index <= ARRAY_SIZE − 1`. If either `index < 0` or `index > ARRAY_SIZE − 1`, then we say that the index is **out of bounds**.

Unfortunately, in C++, there is no guard against out-of-bound indices. Thus, C++ does not check whether the index value is within range—that is, between 0 and `ARRAY_SIZE − 1`. If the index goes out of bounds and the program tries to access the component specified by the index, then whatever memory location is indicated by the index is accessed. This situation can result in altering or accessing the data of a memory location that you never intended. Consequently, if during execution the index goes out of bounds, several strange things can happen. It is solely the programmer's responsibility to make sure that the index is within bounds.

A loop such as the following can set the index out of bounds:

```
for (i = 0; i <= 10; i++)
    list[i] = 0;
```

Here we assume that `list` is an array of 10 components. When `i` becomes 10, the loop test condition `i <= 10` evaluates to **true** and the body of the loop executes, which results in storing 0 in `list[10]`. Logically, `list[10]` does not exist.

NOTE On some new compilers, if an array index goes out of bounds in a progam, it is possible that the program terminates with an error message. For example, see the programs `Example_ArrayIndexOutOfBoundsA.cpp` and `Example_ArrayIndexOutOfBoundsB.cpp` at the Web site accompanying this book.

Array Initialization During Declaration

Like any other simple variable, an array can also be initialized while it is being declared. For example, the following C++ statement declares an array, `sales`, of five components and initializes these components:

```
double sales[5] = {12.25, 32.50, 16.90, 23, 45.68};
```

The values are placed between curly braces and separated by commas—here `sales[0] = 12.25`, `sales[1] = 32.50`, `sales[2] = 16.90`, `sales[3] = 23.00`, and `sales[4] = 45.68`.

When initializing arrays as they are declared, it is not necessary to specify the size of the array. The size is determined by the number of initial values in the braces. However, you must include the brackets following the array name. The previous statement is, therefore, equivalent to:

```
double sales[] = {12.25, 32.50, 16.90, 23, 45.68};
```

Although it is not necessary to specify the size of the array if it is initialized during declaration, it is a good practice to do so.

Partial Initialization of Arrays During Declaration

When you declare and initialize an array simultaneously, you do not need to initialize all components of the array. This procedure is called **partial initialization of an array during declaration**. However, if you partially initialize an array during declaration, you must exercise some caution. The following examples help explain what happens when you declare and partially initialize an array.

The statement:

```
int list[10] = {0};
```

declares `list` to be an array of 10 components and initializes all the components to 0. The statement:

```
int list[10] = {8, 5, 12};
```

declares `list` to be an array of 10 components, initializes `list[0]` to 8, `list[1]` to 5, `list[2]` to 12, and all other components to 0. Thus, if all the values are not specified in the initialization statement, the array components for which the values are not specified are initialized to 0. Note that here the size of the array in the declaration statement does matter. For example, the statement:

```
int list[] = {5, 6, 3};
```

declares `list` to be an array of 3 components and initializes `list[0]` to 5, `list[1]` to 6, and `list[2]` to 3. In contrast, the statement:

```
int list[25] = {4, 7};
```

declares `list` to be an array of 25 components. The first two components are initialized to 4 and 7, respectively, and all other components are initialized to 0.

Some Restrictions on Array Processing

Consider the following statements:

```
int myList[5] = {0, 4, 8, 12, 16};   //Line 1
int yourList[5];   //Line 2
```

The statement in Line 1 declares and initializes the array `myList` and the statement in Line 2 declares the array `yourList`. Note that these arrays are of the same type and have the same number of components. Suppose that you want to copy the elements of `myList` into the corresponding elements of `yourList`. The following statement is illegal:

```
yourList = myList;   //illegal
```

In fact, this statement will generate a syntax error. C++ does not allow aggregate operations on an array. An **aggregate operation** on an array is any operation that manipulates the entire array as a single unit.

To copy one array into another array, you must copy it component-wise—that is, one component at a time. This can be done using a loop, such as the following:

```
for (int index = 0; index < 5; index ++)
    yourList[index] = myList[index];
```

Next, suppose that you want to read data into the array `yourList`. The following statement is illegal and, in fact, would generate a syntax error.

```
cin >> yourList; //illegal
```

To read data into `yourList`, you must read one component at a time, using a loop such as the following:

```
for (int index = 0; index < 5; index ++)
    cin >> yourList[index];
```

Similarly, determining whether two arrays have the same elements and printing the contents of an array must be done component-wise. Note that the following statements are illegal in the sense that they do not generate a syntax error; however, they do not give the desired results:

```
cout << yourList;

if (myList <= yourList)
```
.
.
.

We will comment on these statements in the section, Base Address of an Array and Array in Computer Memory, later in this chapter.

Arrays as Parameters to Functions

Now that you have seen how to work with arrays, a question naturally arises: How are arrays passed as parameters to functions?

By reference only: In C++, arrays are passed by reference only.

Because arrays are passed by reference only, you *do not* use the symbol & when declaring an array as a formal parameter.

When declaring a one-dimensional array as a formal parameter, the size of the array is usually omitted. If you specify the size of a one-dimensional array when it is declared as a formal parameter, the size is ignored by the compiler.

EXAMPLE 9-5

Consider the following function:

```
void funcArrayAsParam(int listOne[], double listTwo[])
{
       .
       .
       .
}
```

The function `funcArrayAsParam` has two formal parameters: (1) `listOne`, a one-dimensional array of type `int` (that is, the component type is `int`); (2) `listTwo`, a one-dimensional array of type `double`. In this declaration, the size of both arrays is unspecified.

Sometimes, the number of elements in the array might be less than the size of the array. For example, the number of elements in an array storing student data might increase or decrease as students drop or add courses. In such situations, we want to process only the components of the array that hold actual data. To write a function to process such arrays, in addition to declaring an array as a formal parameter, we declare another formal parameter specifying the number of elements in the array, as in the following function:

```cpp
void initialize(int list[], int listSize)
{
    int count;

    for (count = 0; count < listSize; count++)
        list[count] = 0;
}
```

The first parameter of the function `initialize` is an `int` array of any size. When the function `initialize` is called, the size of the actual array is passed as the second parameter of the function `initialize`.

Constant Arrays as Formal Parameters

Recall that when a formal parameter is a reference parameter, then whenever the formal parameter changes, the actual parameter changes as well. However, even though an array is always passed by reference, you can still prevent the function from changing the actual parameter. You do so by using the reserved word `const` in the declaration of the formal parameter. Consider the following function:

```cpp
void example(int x[], const int y[], int sizeX, int sizeY)
{
       .
       .
       .
}
```

Here the function `example` can modify the array `x`, but not the array `y`. Any attempt to change `y` results in a compile-time error. It is a good programming practice to declare an array to be constant as a formal parameter if you do not want the function to modify the array.

EXAMPLE 9-6

This example shows how to write functions for array processing and declare an array as a formal parameter.

```cpp
    //Function to initialize an int array to 0.
    //The array to be initialized and its size are passed
    //as parameters. The parameter listSize specifies the
    //number of elements to be initialized.
void initializeArray(int list[], int listSize)
{
    int index;

    for (index = 0; index < listSize; index++)
        list[index] = 0;
}


    //Function to read and store the data into an int array.
    //The array to store the data and its size are passed as
    //parameters. The parameter listSize specifies the number
    //of elements to be read.
void fillArray(int list[], int listSize)
{
    int index;

    for (index = 0; index < listSize; index++)
        cin >> list[index];
}


    //Function to print the elements of an int array.
    //The array to be printed and the number of elements
    //are passed as parameters. The parameter listSize
    //specifies the number of elements to be printed.
void printArray(const int list[], int listSize)
{
    int index;

    for (index = 0; index < listSize; index++)
        cout << list[index] << " ";
}
    //Function to find and return the sum of the
    //elements of an int array. The parameter listSize
    //specifies the number of elements to be added.
int sumArray(const int list[], int listSize)
{
    int index;
    int sum = 0;

    for (index = 0; index < listSize; index++)
        sum = sum + list[index];
```

```cpp
        return sum;
}


    //Function to find and return the index of the first
    //largest element in an int array. The parameter listSize
    //specifies the number of elements in the array.
int indexLargestElement(const int list[], int listSize)
{
    int index;
    int maxIndex = 0; //assume the first element is the largest

    for (index = 1; index < listSize; index++)
        if (list[maxIndex] < list[index])
            maxIndex = index;

    return maxIndex;
}


    //Function to copy one array into another array.
    //The elements of listOne are copied into listTwo.
    //The array listTwo must be at least as large as the
    //number of elements to be copied. The parameter
    //listOneSize specifies the number of elements of
    //listOne to be copied into listTwo.
void copyArray(const int listOne[], int listTwo[],
               int listOneSize)
{
    int index;

    for (index = 0; index < listOneSize; index++)
        listTwo[index] = listOne[index];
}
```

Note that for the function `copyArray` to work correctly, the array `listTwo` must be at least as large as the array `listOne`.

Base Address of an Array and Array in Computer Memory

The **base address** of an array is the address (that is, memory location) of the first array component. For example, if `list` is a one-dimensional array, then the base address of `list` is the address of the component `list[0]`.

Consider the following statements:

```cpp
int myList[5];          //Line 1
```

This statement declares `myList` to be an array of five components of type `int`. The components are `myList[0]`, `myList[1]`, `myList[2]`, `myList[3]`, and `myList[4]`. The computer allocates five memory spaces, each large enough to store an `int` value, for these components. Moreover, the five memory spaces are contiguous.

The base address of the array `myList` is the address of the component `myList[0]`. Suppose that the base address of the array `myList` is 1000. Then the address of the component `myList[0]` is 1000. Typically, the memory allocated for an `int` variable is four bytes. Recall from Chapter 1 that main memory is an ordered sequence of cells and each cell has a unique address. Typically, each cell is one byte. Therefore, to store a value into `myList[0]`, starting at the address 1000 the next four bytes are allocated for `myList[0]`. It follows that the starting address of `myList[1]` is 1004, starting address of `myList[2]` is 1008, and so on (see Figure 9-6).

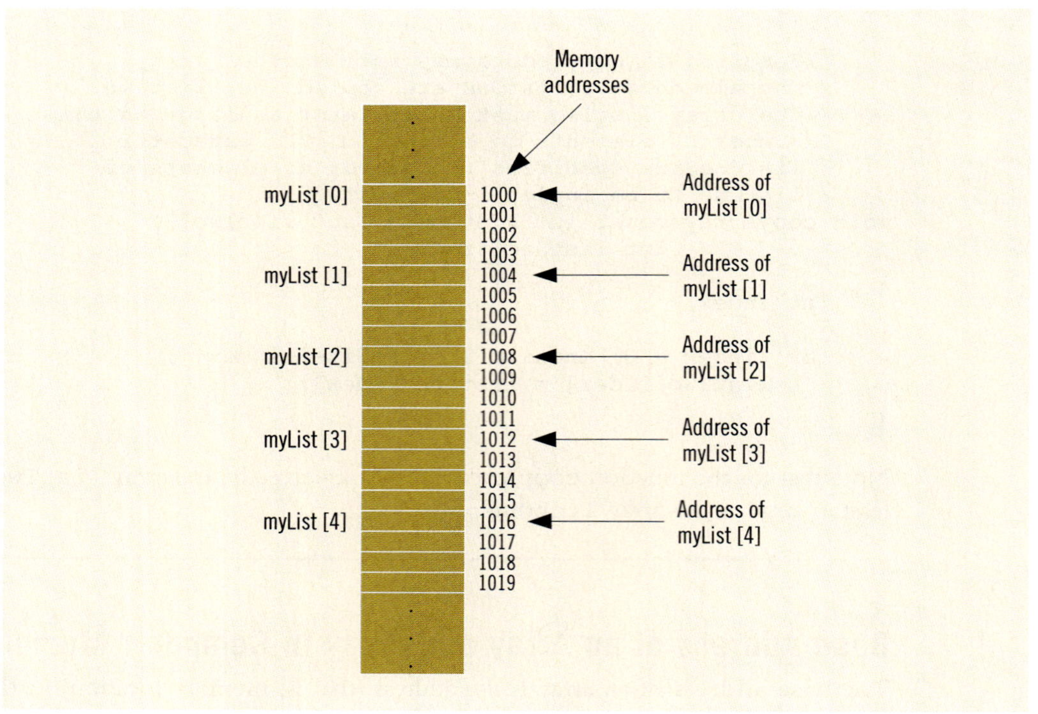

FIGURE 9-6 Array `myList` and the addresses of its components

Now `myList` is the name of an array. There is also a memory space associated with the identifier `myList`, and the base address of the array is stored in that memory space. Consider the following statement:

```
cout << myList << endl;                 //Line 2
```

Earlier, we said that this statement won't give the desired result. That is, this statement will not output the values of the *components* of `myList`. In fact, the statement outputs the value of `myList`, which is the base address of the array. This is why the statement will not generate a syntax error.

Suppose that you also have the following statement:

```
int yourList[5];
```

Then, in the statement:

```
if (myList <= yourList)          //Line 3
     .
     .
     .
```

the expression `myList <= yourList` evaluates to **true** if the base address of the array `myList` is less than the base address of the array `yourList`; and evaluates to **false** otherwise. It *does not* determine whether the elements of `myList` are less than or equal to the corresponding elements of `yourList`.

NOTE The Web site accompanying this book contains the program `BaseAddressOfAnArray.cpp`, that clarifies statements such as those in Lines 2 and 3.

You might be wondering why the base address of an array is so important. The reason is that when you declare an array, the only things about the array that the computer remembers are the name of the array, its base address, the data type of each component, and (possibly) the number of components. Using the base address of the array and the index of an array component, the computer determines the address of a particular component. For example, suppose you want to access the value of `myList[3]`. Now, the base address of `myList` is 1000. Each component of `myList` is of type **int**, so it uses four bytes to store a value, and the index is 3. To access the value of `myList[3]`, the computer calculates the address $1000 + 4 * 3 = 1000 + 12 = 1012$. That is, this is the starting address of `myList[3]`. So starting at 1012, the computer accesses the next four bytes.

When you pass an array as a parameter, the base address of the actual array is passed to the formal parameter. For example, suppose that you have the following function:

```
void arrayAsParameter(int list[], int size)
{
     .
     .
     .

     list[2] = 28;          //Line 4

     .
     .
     .
}
```

Also, suppose that you have the following call to this function:

```
arrayAsParameter(myList, 5);   //Line 5
```

In this statement, the base address of `myList` is passed to the formal parameter `list`. Therefore, the base address of `list` is 1000. The definition of the function contains the statement `list[2] = 28;`. This statement stores 28 into `list[2]`. To access `list[2]`, the computer calculates the address as follows: 1000 + 4 * 2 = 1008. So starting at the address 1008, the computer accesses the next four bytes and stores 28. Note that, in fact, 1008 is the address of `myList[2]` (see Figure 9-6). It follows that during the execution of the statement in Line 5, the statement in Line 4 stores the value 28 into `myList[2]`. It also follows that during the execution of the function call statement in Line 5, `list[index]` and `myList[index]` refer to the same memory space, where 0 <= `index` and `index` < 5.

NOTE If you allow arrays to be passed by value, the computer has to allocate memory for the components of the formal parameter and copy the contents of the actual array into the corresponding formal parameter. If the array size is large, this process wastes memory as well as computer time in copying the data.

Functions Cannot Return a Value of the Type array

C++ does not allow functions to return a value of the type array. Note that the functions `sumArray` and `indexLargestElement` described earlier return values of type `int`.

EXAMPLE 9-7

The following program illustrates how arrays are passed as actual parameters in a function call.

```
//Arrays as parameters to functions

#include <iostream>

using namespace std;

const int ARRAY_SIZE = 10;

void initializeArray(int x[],int sizeX);
void fillArray(int x[],int sizeX);
void printArray(const int x[],int sizeX);
int sumArray(const int x[],int sizeX);
int indexLargestElement(const int x[],int sizeX);
void copyArray(const int x[], int y[], int length);
```

```cpp
int main()
{
    int listA[ARRAY_SIZE] = {0};    //Declare the array listA
                                    //of 10 components and
                                    //initialize each component
                                    //to 0.
    int listB[ARRAY_SIZE];          //Declare the array listB
                                    //of 10 components.

    cout << "Line 1: listA elements: ";             //Line 1

        //Output the elements of listA using
        //the function printArray
    printArray(listA, ARRAY_SIZE);                  //Line 2
    cout << endl;                                   //Line 3

        //Initialize listB using the function
        //initialize
    initializeArray(listB, ARRAY_SIZE);             //Line 4

    cout << "Line 5: listB elements: ";             //Line 5

        //Output the elements of listB
    printArray(listB, ARRAY_SIZE);                  //Line 6
    cout << endl << endl;                           //Line 7

    cout << "Line 8: Enter " << ARRAY_SIZE
         << " integers: ";                          //Line 8

        //Input data into listA using the
        //function fillArray
    fillArray(listA, ARRAY_SIZE);                   //Line 9
    cout << endl;                                   //Line 10

    cout << "Line 11: After filling listA, "
         << "the elements are:" << endl;            //Line 11

        //Output the elements of listA
    printArray(listA, ARRAY_SIZE);                  //Line 12
    cout << endl << endl;                           //Line 13

        //Find and output the sum of the elements
        //of listA
    cout << "Line 14: The sum of the elements of "
         << "listA is: "
         << sumArray(listA, ARRAY_SIZE) << endl
         << endl;                                   //Line 14

        //Find and output the position of the largest
        //element in listA
    cout << "Line 15: The position of the largest "
         << "element in listA is: "
```

```cpp
                << indexLargestElement(listA, ARRAY_SIZE)
                << endl;                                    //Line 15

            //Find and output the largest element
            //in listA
        cout << "Line 16: The largest element in "
             << "listA is: "
             << listA[indexLargestElement(listA, ARRAY_SIZE)]
             << endl << endl;                               //Line 16

            //Copy the elements of listA into listB using the
            //function copyArray
        copyArray(listA, listB, ARRAY_SIZE);               //Line 17

        cout << "Line 18: After copying the elements "
             << "of listA into listB," << endl
             << "          listB elements are: ";           //Line 18

            //Output the elements of listB
        printArray(listB, ARRAY_SIZE);                     //Line 19
        cout << endl;                                      //Line 20

        return 0;
}

//Place the definitions of the functions initializeArray,
//fillArray, and so on here. Example 9-6 gives the definitions
//of these functions.
```

Sample Run: In this sample run, the user input is shaded.

```
Line 1: listA elements: 0 0 0 0 0 0 0 0 0 0
Line 5: ListB elements: 0 0 0 0 0 0 0 0 0 0

Line 8: Enter 10 integers: 33 77 25 63 56 48 98 39 5 12

Line 11: After filling listA, the elements are:
33 77 25 63 56 48 98 39 5 12

Line 14: The sum of the elements of listA is: 456

Line 15: The position of the largest element in listA is: 6
Line 16: The largest element in listA is: 98

Line 18: After copying the elements of listA into listB,
         listB elements are: 33 77 25 63 56 48 98 39 5 12
```

The output of this program is straightforward. First, we declare the array `listA` of 10 components and initialize each component of `listA` to 0. Then we declare the array `listB` of 10 components. The statement in Line 2 calls the function `printArray` and outputs the values stored in `listA`. The statement in Line 9 calls the function `fillArray` to input the data into `listA`. The statement in Line 14 calls the function `sumArray` and outputs the sum of all the elements of `listA`. Similarly, the statement in Line 16 outputs the value of the largest element in `listA`.

Integral Data Type and Array Indices

NOTE The sections "Enumeration Type" and "`typedef` Statement" in Chapter 8 are required to understand this section.

Other than integers, C++ allows any integral type to be used as an array index. This flexibility can greatly enhance a program's readability. Consider the following statements:

```
enum paintType {GREEN, RED, BLUE, BROWN, WHITE, ORANGE, YELLOW};
double paintSale[7];
paintType paint;
```

The following loop initializes each component of the array `paintSale` to 0:

```
for (paint = GREEN; paint <= YELLOW;
                    paint = static_cast<paintType>(paint + 1))
      paintSale[paint] = 0.0;
```

The following statement updates the sale amount of `RED` paint:

```
paintSale[RED] = paintSale[RED] + 75.69;
```

As you can see, the above code is much easier to follow than the code that used integers for the index. For this reason, you should use the enumeration type for the array index or other integral data types wherever possible.

Other Ways to Declare Arrays

Suppose that a class has 20 students and you need to keep track of their scores. Because the number of students can change from semester to semester, instead of specifying the size of the array while declaring it, you can declare the array as follows:

```
const int NO_OF_STUDENTS = 20;
int testScores[NO_OF_STUDENTS];
```

Other forms used to declare arrays are:

```
const int SIZE = 50;            //Line 1
typedef double list[SIZE];      //Line 2

list yourList;                  //Line 3
list myList;                    //Line 4
```

The statement in Line 2 defines a data type `list`, which is an array of 50 components of type `double`. The statements in Lines 3 and 4 declare two variables, `yourList` and `myList`. Both are arrays of 50 components of type `double`. Of course, these statements are equivalent to:

```
double yourList[50];
double myList[50];
```

C-strings (Character Arrays)

Until now, we have avoided discussing character arrays for a simple reason: Character arrays are of special interest, and you process them differently than you process other arrays. C++ provides many (predefined) functions that you can use with character arrays.

Character array: An array whose components are of type `char`.

Recall that the most widely used character sets are ASCII and EBCDIC. The first character in the ASCII character set is the null character, which is nonprintable. Also, recall that in C++, the null character is represented as `'\0'`, a backslash followed by a zero.

The statement:

```
ch = '\0';
```

stores the null character in `ch`, where `ch` is a `char` variable.

As you will see, the null character plays an important role in processing character arrays. Because the collating sequence of the null character is 0, the null character is less than any other character in the `char` data set.

The most commonly used term for character arrays is C-strings. However, there is a subtle difference between character arrays and C-strings. Recall that a string is a sequence of zero or more characters, and strings are enclosed in double quotation marks. In C++, C-strings are null terminated; that is, the last character in a C-string is always the null character. A character array might not contain the null character, but the last character in a C-string is always the null character. As you will see, the null character should not appear anywhere in the C-string except the last position. Also, C-strings are stored in (one-dimensional) character arrays.

The following are examples of C-strings:

```
"John L. Johnson"
"Hello there."
```

From the definition of C-strings, it is clear that there is a difference between `'A'` and `"A"`. The first one is character A; the second is C-string A. Because C-strings are null terminated, `"A"` represents two characters: `'A'` and `'\0'`. Similarly, the C-string `"Hello"` represents six characters: `'H'`, `'e'`, `'l'`, `'l'`, `'o'`, and `'\0'`. To store `'A'`, we need only one memory cell of type `char`; to store `"A"`, we need two memory cells of type `char`—one for `'A'` and one for `'\0'`. Similarly, to store the C-string `"Hello"` in computer memory, we need six memory cells of type `char`.

Consider the following statement:

```
char name[16];
```

This statement declares an array `name` of 16 components of type `char`. Because C-strings are null terminated and `name` has 16 components, the largest string that can be stored in `name` is of length 15. If you store a C-string of length 10 in `name`, the first 11 components of `name` are used and the last 5 are left unused.

The statement:

```
char name[16] = {'J', 'o', 'h', 'n', '\0'};
```

declares an array `name` containing 16 components of type `char` and stores the C-string `"John"` in it. During `char` array variable declaration, C++ allows the C-string notation to be used in the initialization statement. The above statement is, therefore, equivalent to:

```
char name[16] = "John";          //Line A
```

Recall that the size of an array can be omitted if the array is initialized during the declaration.

The statement:

```
char name[] = "John";            //Line B
```

declares a C-string variable `name` of a length large enough—in this case, 5—and stores `"John"` in it. There is a difference between the last two statements: Both statements store `"John"` in name, but the size of `name` in the statement in Line A is 16, and the size of `name` in the statement in Line B is 5.

Most rules that apply to other arrays also apply to character arrays. Consider the following statement:

```
char studentName[26];
```

Suppose you want to store `"Lisa L. Johnson"` in `studentName`. Because aggregate operations, such as assignment and comparison, are not allowed on arrays, the following statement is not legal:

```
studentName = "Lisa L. Johnson"; //illegal
```

C++ provides a set of functions that can be used for C-string manipulation. The header file `cstring` describes these functions. We often use three of these functions: `strcpy` (string copy, to copy a C-string into a C-string variable—that is, assignment); `strcmp` (string comparison, to compare C-strings); and `strlen` (string length, to find the length of a C-string). Table 9-1 summarizes these functions.

TABLE 9-1 `strcpy`, `strcmp`, and `strlen` functions

Function	Effect
`strcpy(s1, s2)`	Copies the string s2 into the string variable s1 The length of s1 should be at least as large as s2
`strcmp(s1, s2)`	Returns a value < 0 if s1 is less than s2 Returns 0 if s1 and s2 are the same Returns a value > 0 if s1 is greater than s2
`strlen(s)`	Returns the length of the string s, excluding the null character

To use these functions, the program must include the header file `cstring` via the `include` statement. That is, the following statement must be included in the program:

```
#include <cstring>
```

String Comparison

In C++, C-strings are compared character-by-character using the system's collating sequence. Let us assume that you use the ASCII character set.

1. The C-string `"Air"` is less than the C-string `"Boat"` because the first character of `"Air"` is less than the first character of `"Boat"`.

2. The C-string `"Air"` is less than the C-string `"An"` because the first character of both strings are the same, but the second character `'i'` of `"Air"` is less than the second character `'n'` of `"An"`.

3. The C-string `"Bill"` is less than the C-string `"Billy"` because the first four characters of `"Bill"` and `"Billy"` are the same, but the fifth character of `"Bill"`, which is `'\0'` (the null character), is less than the fifth character of `"Billy"`, which is `'y'`. (Recall that C-strings in C++ are null terminated.)

4. The C-string `"Hello"` is less than `"hello"` because the first character `'H'` of the C-string `"Hello"` is less than the first character `'h'` of the C-string `"hello"`.

As you can see, the function `strcmp` compares its first C-string argument with its second C-string argument character-by-character.

EXAMPLE 9-8

Suppose you have the following statements:

```
char studentName[21];
char myname[16];
char yourname[16];
```

The following statements show how string functions work:

Statement	Effect
`strcpy(myname, "John Robinson");`	Myname = "John Robinson"
`strlen("John Robinson");`	Returns 13, the length of the string "John Robinson"
`int len;` `len = strlen("Sunny Day");`	Stores 9 into `len`
`strcpy(yourname, "Lisa Miller");` `strcpy(studentName, yourname);`	yourname = "Lisa Miller" studentName = "Lisa Miller"
`strcmp("Bill", "Lisa");`	Returns a value < 0

`strcpy(yourname, "Kathy Brown");`
`strcpy(myname, "Mark G. Clark");`
`strcmp(myname, yourname);`
	yourname = "Kathy Brown"
	myname = "Mark G. Clark"
	Returns a value > 0

NOTE In this chapter, we defined a C-string to be a sequence of zero or more characters. C-strings are enclosed in double quotation marks. We also said that C-strings are null terminated, so the C-string `"Hello"` has six characters even though only five are enclosed in double quotation marks. Therefore, to store the C-string `"Hello"` in computer memory, you must use a character array of size 6. The length of a C-string is the number of actual characters enclosed in double quotation marks; for example, the length of the C-string `"Hello"` is 5. Thus, in a logical sense, a C-string is a sequence of zero or more characters, but in the physical sense (that is, to store the C-string in computer memory), a C-string has at least one character. Because the length of the C-string is the actual number of characters enclosed in double quotation marks, we defined a C-string to be a sequence of zero or more characters. However, you must remember that the null character stored in computer memory at the end of the C-string plays a key role when we compare C-strings, especially C-strings such as `"Bill"` and `"Billy"`.

Reading and Writing Strings

As mentioned earlier, most rules that apply to arrays apply to C-strings as well. Aggregate operations, such as assignment and comparison, are not allowed on arrays. Even the input/output of arrays is done component-wise. However, the one place where C++ allows aggregate operations on arrays is the input and output of C-strings (that is, character arrays).

We will use the following declaration for our discussion:

```
char name[31];
```

String Input

Because aggregate operations are allowed for C-string input, the statement:

```
cin >> name;
```

stores the next input C-string into `name`. The length of the input C-string must be less than or equal to 30. If the length of the input string is 4, the computer stores the four characters that are input and the null character `'\0'`. If the length of the input C-string is more than 30, then because there is no check on the array index bounds, the computer continues storing the string in whatever memory cells follow `name`. This process can cause serious problems, because data in the adjacent memory cells will be corrupted.

NOTE When you input a C-string using an input device, such as the keyboard, you do not include the double quotes around it, unless the double quotes are part of the string. For example, the C-string `"Hello"` is entered as `Hello`.

Recall that the extraction operator, `>>`, skips all leading whitespace characters and stops reading data into the current variable as soon as it finds the first whitespace character or invalid data. As a result, C-strings that contain blanks cannot be read using the extraction operator, `>>`. For example, if a first name and last name are separated by blanks, they cannot be read into `name`.

How do you input C-strings with blanks into a character array? Once again, the function `get` comes to our rescue. Recall that the function `get` is used to read character data. Until now, the form of the function `get` that you have used (Chapter 3) read only a single character. However, the function `get` can also be used to read strings. To read C-strings, you use the form of the function `get` that has two parameters. The first parameter is a C-string variable; the second parameter specifies how many characters to read into the string variable.

To read C-strings, the general form (syntax) of the `get` function, together with an input stream variable such as `cin`, is:

```
cin.get(str, m + 1);
```

This statement stores the next `m` characters, or all characters until the newline character `'\n'` is found, into `str`. The newline character is not stored in `str`. If the input C-string has fewer than `m` characters, then the reading stops at the newline character.

Consider the following statements:

```
char str[31];
cin.get(str, 31);
```

If the input is:

```
William T. Johnson
```

then `"William T. Johnson"` is stored in `str`. Suppose that the input is:

```
Hello there. My name is Mickey Blair.
```

Then, because `str` can store at most 30 characters, the C-string `"Hello there. My name is Mickey"` is stored in `str`.

Now suppose that we have the statements:

```
char str1[26];
char str2[26];
char discard;
```

and the two lines of input:

```
Summer is warm.
Winter will be cold.
```

Further suppose that we want to store the first C-string in `str1` and the second C-string in `str2`. Both `str1` and `str2` can store C-strings that are up to 25 characters in length. Because the number of characters in the first line is 15, the reading stops at `'\n'`. You must read and discard the newline character at the end of the first line to store the second line into `str2`. The following sequence of statements stores the first line into `str1` and the second line into `str2`:

```
cin.get(str1, 26);
cin.get(discard);
cin.get(str2, 26);
```

String Output

The output of C-strings is another place where aggregate operations on arrays are allowed. You can output C-strings by using an output stream variable, such as `cout`, together with the insertion operator, `<<`. For example, the statement:

```
cout << name;
```

outputs the contents of `name` on the screen. The insertion operator, `<<`, continues to write the contents of `name` until it finds the null character. Thus, if the length of `name` is 4, the above statement outputs only four characters. If `name` does not contain the null character, then you will see strange output because the insertion operator continues to output data from memory adjacent to `name` until `'\0'` is found.

Specifying Input/Output Files at Execution Time

In Chapter 3, you learned how to read data from a file. In subsequent chapters, the name of the input file was included in the open statement. By doing so, the program always received data from the same input file. In real-world applications, the data may actually be collected at several locations and stored in separate files. Also, for comparison purposes, someone might want to process each file separately and then store the output in separate files. To accomplish this task efficiently, the user would prefer to specify the name of the input and/or output file at execution time rather than in the programming code. C++ allows the user to do so.

Consider the following statements:

```
ifstream infile;
ofstream outfile;

char fileName[51];      //assume that the file name is at most
                        //50 characters long
```

The following statements prompt and allow the user to specify the input and output files at execution time:

```
cout << "Enter the input file name: ";
cin >> fileName;

infile.open(fileName);    //open the input file
 .
 .
 .

cout << "Enter the output file name: ";
cin >> fileName;

outfile.open(fileName);   //open the output file
```

Programming Example: Code Detection further illustrates how to specify the names of input and output files during program execution.

string Type and Input/Output Files

In Chapter 8, we discussed the data type string. We now want to point out that values (that is, strings) of type string are not null terminated. Variables of type string can also be used to read and store the names of input/output files. However, the argument to the function open must be a null-terminated string—that is, a C-string. Therefore, if we use a variable of type string to read the name of an input/output file and then use this variable to open a file, the value of the variable must (first) be converted to a C-string (that is, a null-terminated string). The header file string contains the function c_str, which converts a value of type string to a null-terminated character array (that is, C-string). The syntax to use the function c_str is:

```
strVar.c_str()
```

where strVar is a variable of type string.

The following statements illustrate how to use variables of type `string` to read the names of the input/output files during program execution and to open those files:

```
ifstream infile;
string fileName;

cout << "Enter the input file name: ";
cin >> fileName;

infile.open(fileName.c_str());    //open the input file
```

Of course, you must also include the header file `string` in the program. The output file has similar conventions.

Parallel Arrays

Two (or more) arrays are called **parallel** if their corresponding components hold related information.

Suppose you need to keep track of students' course grades, together with their ID numbers, so that their grades can be posted at the end of the semester. Further suppose that there is a maximum of 50 students in a class and their IDs are 5 digits long. Because there may be 50 students, you need 50 variables to store the students' IDs and 50 variables to store their grades. You can declare two arrays: `studentId` of type `int` and `courseGrade` of type `char`. Each array has 50 components. Furthermore, `studentId[0]` and `courseGrade[0]` will store the ID and course grade of the first student, `studentId[1]` and `courseGrade[1]` will store the ID and course grade of the second student, and so on.

The statements:

```
int studentId[50];
char courseGrade[50];
```

declare these two arrays.

Suppose you need to input data into these arrays, and the data is provided in a file in the following form:

```
studentId courseGrade
```

For example, a sample data set is:

```
23456 A
86723 B
22356 C
92733 B
11892 D
 .
 .
 .
```

Suppose that the input file is opened using the `ifstream` variable `infile`. Because the size of each array is 50, a maximum of 50 elements can be stored into each array. Moreover, it is possible that there may be fewer than 50 students in the class. Therefore, while reading the data, we also count the number of students and ensure that the array indices do not go out of bounds. The following loop reads the data into the parallel arrays `studentId` and `courseGrade`:

```
int noOfStudents = 0;

infile >> studentId[noOfStudents] >> courseGrade[noOfStudents];

while (infile && noOfStudents < 50)
{
    noOfStudents++;
    infile >> studentId[noOfStudents]
           >> courseGrade[noOfStudents];
}
```

Two- and Multidimensional Arrays

The remainder of this chapter discusses two-dimensional arrays and ways to work with multidimensional arrays.

In the previous section, you learned how to use one-dimensional arrays to manipulate data. If the data is provided in a list form, you can use one-dimensional arrays. However, sometimes data is provided in a table form. For example, suppose that you want to track the number of cars in a particular color that are in stock at a local dealership. The dealership sells six types of cars in five different colors. Figure 9-7 shows sample data.

inStock	[RED]	[BROWN]	[BLACK]	[WHITE]	[GRAY]
[GM]	10	7	12	10	4
[FORD]	18	11	15	17	10
[TOYOTA]	12	10	9	5	12
[BMW]	16	6	13	8	3
[NISSAN]	10	7	12	6	4
[VOLVO]	9	4	7	12	11

FIGURE 9-7 Table `inStock`

You can see that the data is in a table format. The table has 30 entries, and every entry is an integer. Because the table entries are all of the same type, you can declare a one-dimensional array of 30 components of type `int`. The first five components of the one-dimensional array can store the data of the first row of the table, the next five components of the one-dimensional array can store the data of the second row of the table, and so on. In other words, you can simulate the data given in a table format in a one-dimensional array.

If you do so, the algorithms to manipulate the data in the one-dimensional array will be somewhat complicated, because you must know where one row ends and another begins. You must also correctly compute the index of a particular element. C++ simplifies the processing of manipulating data in a table form with the use of two-dimensional arrays. This section first discusses how to declare two-dimensional arrays and then looks at ways to manipulate data in a two-dimensional array.

Two-dimensional array: A collection of a fixed number of components arranged in rows and columns (that is, in two dimensions), wherein all components are of the same type.

The syntax for declaring a two-dimensional array is:

```
dataType   arrayName[intExp1][intExp2];
```

where `intExp1` and `intExp2` are constant expressions yielding positive integer values. The two expressions, `intExp1` and `intExp2`, specify the number of rows and the number of columns, respectively, in the array.

The statement:

```
double sales[10][5];
```

declares a two-dimensional array `sales` of 10 rows and 5 columns, where every component is of type `double`. As in the case of a one-dimensional array, the rows are numbered 0...9 and the columns are numbered 0...4 (see Figure 9-8).

9

FIGURE 9-8 Two-dimensional array `sales`

Accessing Array Components

To access the components of a two-dimensional array, you need a pair of indices: one for the row position and one for the column position.

The syntax to access a component of a two-dimensional array is:

```
arrayName[indexExp1][indexExp2]
```

where `indexExp1` and `indexExp2` are expressions yielding non-negative integer values. `indexExp1` specifies the row position; `indexExp2` specifies the column position.

The statement:

```
sales[5][3] = 25.75;
```

stores `25.75` into row number 5 and column number 3 (that is, the sixth row and the fourth column) of the array `sales` (see Figure 9-9).

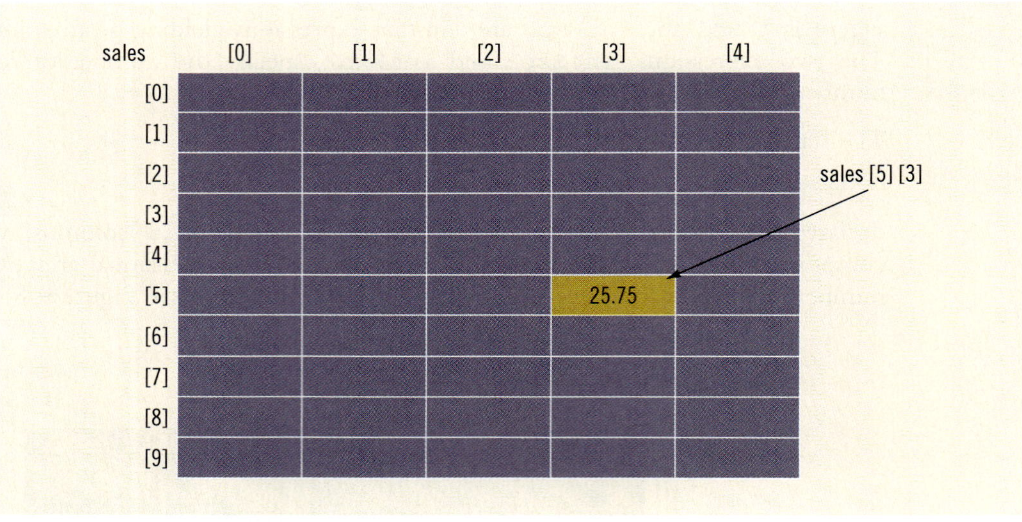

FIGURE 9-9 `sales[5][3]`

Suppose that:

```
int i = 5;
int j = 3;
```

Then, the previous statement:

```
sales[5][3] = 25.75;
```

is equivalent to:

```
sales[i][j] = 25.75;
```

So the indices can also be variables.

Two-Dimensional Array Initialization During Declaration

Like one-dimensional arrays, two-dimensional arrays can be initialized when they are declared. The following example helps illustrate this concept. Consider the following statement:

```
int board[4][3] = {{2, 3, 1},
                    {15, 25, 13},
                    {20, 4, 7},
                    {11, 18, 14}};
```

This statement declares `board` to be a two-dimensional array of 4 rows and 3 columns. The components of the first row are 2, 3, and 1; the components of the second row are 15, 25, and 13; the components of the third row are 20, 4, and 7; and the components of the fourth row are 11, 18, and 14, respectively. Figure 9-10 shows the array `board`.

board	[0]	[1]	[2]
[0]	2	3	1
[1]	15	25	13
[2]	20	4	7
[3]	11	18	14

FIGURE 9-10 Two-dimensional array `board`

To initialize a two-dimensional array when it is declared:

1. The elements of each row are enclosed within curly braces and separated by commas.

2. All rows are enclosed within curly braces.

3. For number arrays, if all components of a row are not specified, the unspecified components are initialized to 0. In this case, at least one of the values must be given to initialize all the components of a row.

Two-Dimensional Arrays and Enumeration Types

NOTE   The section "Enumeration Types" in Chapter 8 is required to understand this section.

You can also use the enumeration type for array indices. Consider the following statements:

```
const int NUMBER_OF_ROWS = 6;
const int NUMBER_OF_COLUMNS = 5;
```

```
enum carType {GM, FORD, TOYOTA, BMW, NISSAN, VOLVO};
enum colorType {RED, BROWN, BLACK, WHITE, GRAY};

int inStock[NUMBER_OF_ROWS][NUMBER_OF_COLUMNS];
```

These statements define the `carType` and `colorType` enumeration types and define `inStock` as a two-dimensional array of 6 rows and 5 columns. Suppose that each row in `inStock` corresponds to a car type, and each column in `inStock` corresponds to a color type. That is, the first row corresponds to the car type GM, the second row corresponds to the car type FORD, and so on. Similarly, the first column corresponds to the color type RED, the second column corresponds to the color type BROWN, and so on. Suppose further that each entry in `inStock` represents the number of cars of a particular type and color (see Figure 9-11).

inStock	[RED]	[BROWN]	[BLACK]	[WHITE]	[GRAY]
[GM]					
[FORD]					
[TOYOTA]					
[BMW]					
[NISSAN]					
[VOLVO]					

FIGURE 9-11 Two-dimensional array `inStock`

The statement:

```
inStock[1][3] = 15;
```

is equivalent to the following statement (see Figure 9-12):

```
inStock[FORD][WHITE] = 15;
```

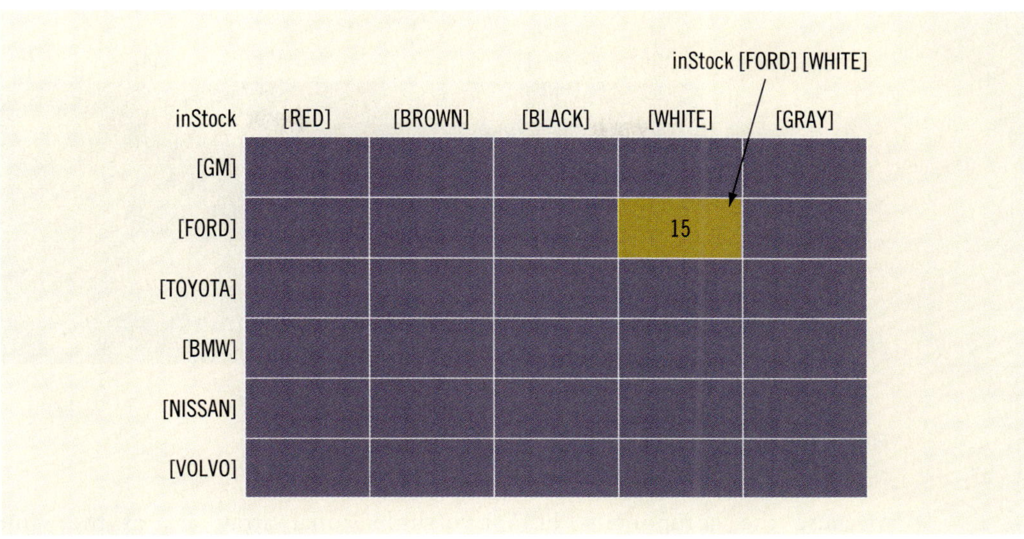

FIGURE 9-12 `inStock[FORD][WHITE]`

The second statement easily conveys the message—that is, set the number of WHITE FORD cars to 15. This example illustrates that enumeration types can be used effectively to make the program readable and easy to manage.

PROCESSING TWO-DIMENSIONAL ARRAYS

A two-dimensional array can be processed in three ways:

1. Process the entire array.
2. Process a particular row of the array, called **row processing**.
3. Process a particular column of the array, called **column processing**.

Initializing and printing the array are examples of processing the entire two-dimensional array. Finding the largest element in a row (column) or finding the sum of a row (column) are examples of row (column) processing. We will use the following declaration for our discussion:

```cpp
const int NUMBER_OF_ROWS = 7;     //This can be set to any number.
const int NUMBER_OF_COLUMNS = 6; //This can be set to any number.

int matrix[NUMBER_OF_ROWS][NUMBER_OF_COLUMNS];
int row;
int col;
int sum;
int largest;
int temp;
```

Figure 9-13 shows the array `matrix`.

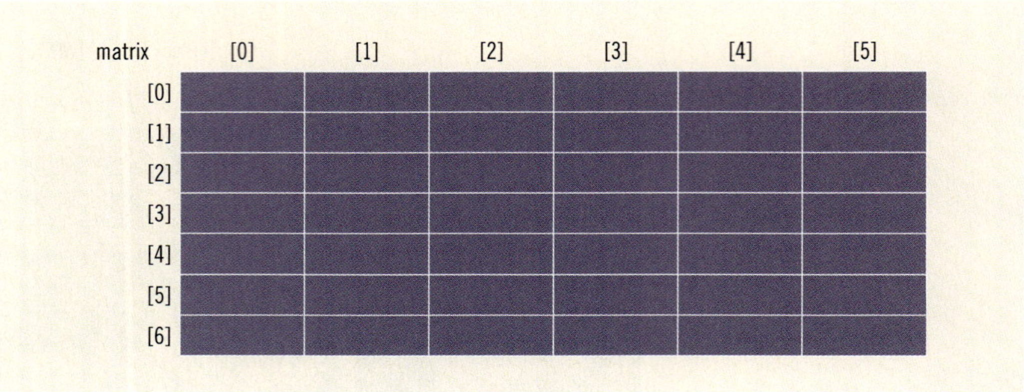

FIGURE 9-13 Two-dimensional array `matrix`

Because the components of a two-dimensional array are of the same type, the components of any row or column are of the same type. This means that each row and each column of a two-dimensional array is a one-dimensional array. Therefore, when processing a particular row or column of a two-dimensional array, we use algorithms similar to those that process one-dimensional arrays. We further explain this concept with the help of the two-dimensional array **matrix**, as declared previously.

Suppose that we want to process row number 5 of `matrix` (that is, the sixth row of `matrix`). The components of row number 5 of `matrix` are:

```
matrix[5][0], matrix[5][1], matrix[5][2], matrix[5][3], matrix[5][4],
matrix[5][5]
```

We see that in these components the first index (the row position) is fixed at 5. The second index (the column position) ranges from 0 to 5. Therefore, we can use the following **for** loop to process row number 5:

```
for (col = 0; col < NUMBER_OF_COLUMNS; col++)
    process matrix[5][col]
```

Clearly, this **for** loop is equivalent to the following **for** loop:

```
row = 5;
for (col = 0; col < NUMBER_OF_COLUMNS; col++)
    process matrix[row][col]
```

Similarly, suppose that we want to process column number 2 of `matrix`, that is, the third column of `matrix`. The components of this column are:

```
matrix[0][2], matrix[1][2], matrix[2][2], matrix[3][2], matrix[4][2],
matrix[5][2], matrix[6][2]
```

Here the second index (that is, the column position) is fixed at 2. The first index (that is, the row position) ranges from 0 to 6. In this case, we can use the following `for` loop to process column 2 of `matrix`:

```
for (row = 0; row < NUMBER_OF_ROWS; row++)
    process matrix[row][2]
```

Clearly, this `for` loop is equivalent to the following `for` loop:

```
col = 2;
for (row = 0; row < NUMBER_OF_ROWS; row++)
    process matrix[row][col]
```

Next, we discuss specific processing algorithms.

Initialization

Suppose that you want to initialize row number 4, that is, the fifth row, to 0. As explained earlier, the following `for` loop does this:

```
row = 4;
for (col = 0; col < NUMBER_OF_COLUMNS; col++)
    matrix[row][col] = 0;
```

If you want to initialize the entire `matrix` to 0, you can also put the first index (that is, the row position) in a loop. By using the following nested `for` loops, we can initialize each component of `matrix` to 0:

```
for (row = 0; row < NUMBER_OF_ROWS; row++)
    for (col = 0; col < NUMBER_OF_COLUMNS; col++)
        matrix[row][col] = 0;
```

Print

By using a nested `for` loop, you can output the components of `matrix`. The following nested `for` loops print the components of `matrix`, one row per line:

```
for (row = 0; row < NUMBER_OF_ROWS; row++)
{
    for (col = 0; col < NUMBER_OF_COLUMNS; col++)
        cout << setw(5) << matrix[row][col] << " ";

    cout << endl;
}
```

Input

The following `for` loop inputs the data into row number 4, that is, the fifth row of `matrix`:

```
row = 4;

for (col = 0; col < NUMBER_OF_COLUMNS; col++)
    cin >> matrix[row][col];
```

As before, by putting the row number in a loop, you can input data into each component of `matrix`. The following `for` loop inputs data into each component of `matrix`:

```cpp
for (row = 0; row < NUMBER_OF_ROWS; row++)
    for (col = 0; col < NUMBER_OF_COLUMNS; col++)
        cin >> matrix[row][col];
```

Sum by Row

The following `for` loop finds the sum of row number 4 of `matrix`; that is, it adds the components of row number 4:

```cpp
sum = 0;
row = 4;
for (col = 0; col < NUMBER_OF_COLUMNS; col++)
    sum = sum + matrix[row][col];
```

Once again, by putting the row number in a loop, we can find the sum of each row separately. Following is the C++ code to find the sum of each individual row:

```cpp
    //Sum of each individual row
for (row = 0; row < NUMBER_OF_ROWS; row++)
{
    sum = 0;
    for (col = 0; col < NUMBER_OF_COLUMNS; col++)
        sum = sum + matrix[row][col];

    cout << "Sum of row " << row + 1 << " = " << sum << endl;
}
```

Sum by Column

As in the case of sum by row, the following nested `for` loop finds the sum of each individual column:

```cpp
    //Sum of each individual column
for (col = 0; col < NUMBER_OF_COLUMNS; col++)
{
    sum = 0;
    for (row = 0; row < NUMBER_OF_ROWS; row++)
        sum = sum + matrix[row][col];

    cout << "Sum of column " << col + 1 << " = " << sum
         << endl;
}
```

Largest Element in Each Row and Each Column

As stated earlier, two other operations on a two-dimensional array are finding the largest element in each row and each column, and finding the sum of both diagonals. Next, we give the C++ code to perform these operations.

The following **for** loop determines the largest element in row number 4:

```cpp
row = 4;
largest = matrix[row][0]; //Assume that the first element of
                          //the row is the largest.
for (col = 1; col < NUMBER_OF_COLUMNS; col++)
    if (largest < matrix[row][col])
        largest = matrix[row][col];
```

The following C++ code determines the largest element in each row and each column:

```cpp
    //Largest element in each row
for (row = 0; row < NUMBER_OF_ROWS; row++)
{
    largest = matrix[row][0]; //Assume that the first element
                              //of the row is the largest.
    for (col = 1; col < NUMBER_OF_COLUMNS; col++)
        if (largest < matrix[row][col])
            largest = matrix[row][col];

    cout << "The largest element in row " << row + 1 << " = "
         << largest << endl;
}

    //Largest element in each column
for (col = 0; col < NUMBER_OF_COLUMNS; col++)
{
    largest = matrix[0][col]; //Assume that the first element
                              //of the column is the largest.
    for (row = 1; row < NUMBER_OF_ROWS; row++)
        if (largest < matrix[row][col])
            largest = matrix[row][col];

    cout << "The largest element in column " << col + 1
         << " = " << largest << endl;
}
```

Reversing Diagonal

Suppose that **matrix** is a square array, that is, the number of rows and the number of columns are the same. Then, **matrix** has a main diagonal and an opposite diagonal. To be specific, suppose that we have the following:

```cpp
const int NUMBER_OF_ROWS = 4;
const int NUMBER_OF_COLUMNS = 4;
```

The components of the main diagonal of **matrix** are **matrix[0][0]**, **matrix[1][1]**, **matrix[2][2]**, and **matrix[3][3]**. The components of the opposite diagonal are **matrix[0][3]**, **matrix[1][2]**, **matrix[2][1]**, and **matrix[3][0]**.

We want to write a C++ code to reverse both the diagonals of **matrix**.

Assume that the array **matrix** is as shown in Figure 9-14.

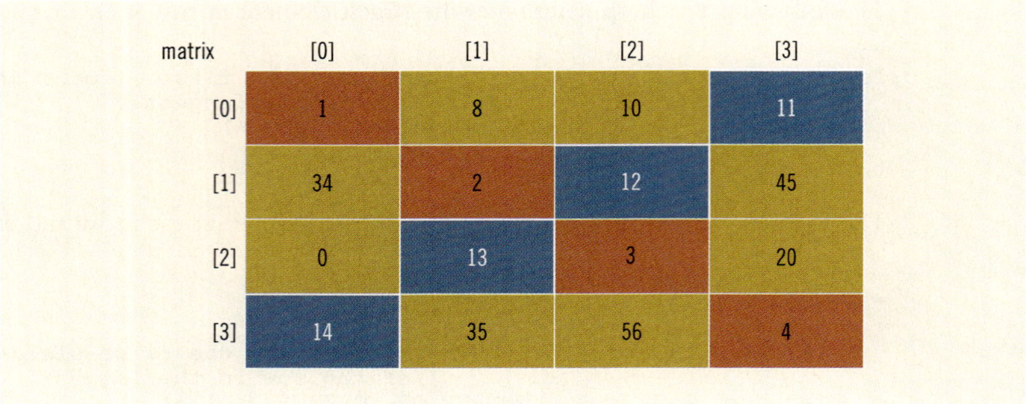

matrix	[0]	[1]	[2]	[3]
[0]	1	8	10	11
[1]	34	2	12	45
[2]	0	13	3	20
[3]	14	35	56	4

FIGURE 9-14 Two-dimensional array `matrix`

After reversing both the diagonals, the array **matrix** is as shown in Figure 9-15.

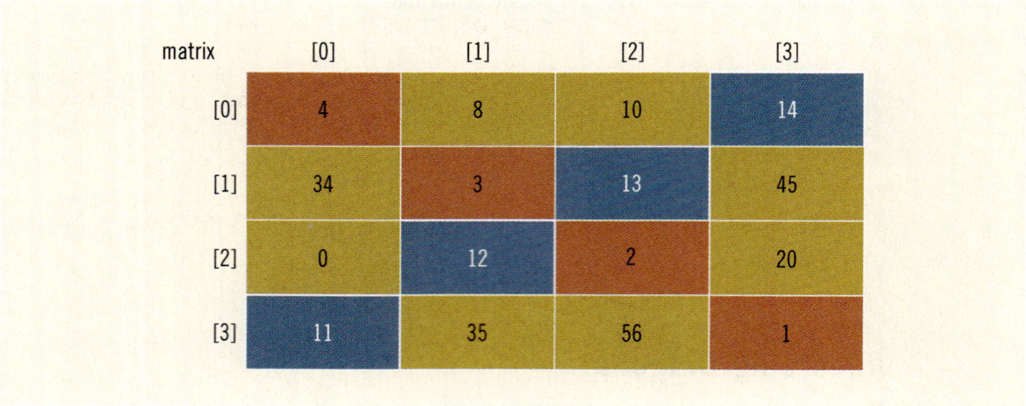

matrix	[0]	[1]	[2]	[3]
[0]	4	8	10	14
[1]	34	3	13	45
[2]	0	12	2	20
[3]	11	35	56	1

FIGURE 9-15 The array `matrix` after reversing diagonals

It is clear that, to reverse the main diagonal, we do the following:

1. Swap `matrix[0][0]` with `matrix[3][3]`.
2. Swap `matrix[1][1]` with `matrix[2][2]`.

To reverse the opposite diagonal, we do the following:

1. Swap `matrix[0][3]` with `matrix[3][0]`.
2. Swap `matrix[1][2]` with `matrix[2][1]`.

The following `for` loops reverse the diagonals:

```cpp
    //Reverse the main diagonal
for (row = 0; row < NUMBER_OF_ROWS / 2; row++)
{
    temp = matrix[row][row];
    matrix[row][row] =
       matrix[NUMBER_OF_ROWS - 1 - row][NUMBER_OF_ROWS - 1 - row];
    matrix[NUMBER_OF_ROWS - 1 - row][NUMBER_OF_ROWS - 1 - row]
          = temp;
}

    //Reverse the opposite diagonal
for (row = 0; row < NUMBER_OF_ROWS / 2; row++)
{
    temp = matrix[row][NUMBER_OF_ROWS - 1 - row];
    matrix[row][NUMBER_OF_ROWS - 1 - row] =
                 matrix[NUMBER_OF_ROWS - 1 - row][row];
    matrix[NUMBER_OF_ROWS - 1 - row][row] = temp;
}
```

This C++ code to reverse the diagonals of a square, two-dimensional array works for an array of any size.

Passing Two-Dimensional Arrays as Parameters to Functions

Two-dimensional arrays can be passed as parameters to a function, and they are passed by reference. The base address (that is, the address of the first component of the actual parameter) is passed to the formal parameter. If `matrix` is the name of a two-dimensional array, then `matrix[0][0]` is the first component of `matrix`.

When storing a two-dimensional array in the computer's memory, C++ uses the **row order form**. That is, the first row is stored first, followed by the second row, followed by the third row, and so on.

In the case of a one-dimensional array, when declaring it as a formal parameter, we usually omit the size of the array. Because C++ stores two-dimensional arrays in row order form, to compute the address of a component correctly, the compiler must know where one row ends and the next row begins. Thus, when declaring a two-dimensional array as a formal parameter, you can omit the size of the first dimension, but not the second; that is, you must specify the number of columns.

Suppose we have the following declaration:

```cpp
const int NUMBER_OF_ROWS = 6;
const int NUMBER_OF_COLUMNS = 5;
```

Consider the following definition of the function `printMatrix`:

```cpp
void printMatrix(int matrix[][NUMBER_OF_COLUMNS],
                 int noOfRows)
{
    int row, col;
```

```cpp
for (row = 0; row < noOfRows; row++)
{
    for (col = 0; col < NUMBER_OF_COLUMNS; col++)
        cout << setw(5) << matrix[row][col] << " ";

    cout << endl;
}
}
```

This function takes as a parameter a two-dimensional array of an unspecified number of rows, and 5 columns, and outputs the content of the two-dimensional array. During the function call, the number of columns of the actual parameter must match the number of columns of the formal parameter.

Similarly, the following function outputs the sum of the elements of each row of a two-dimensional array whose elements are of type `int`.

```cpp
void sumRows(int matrix[][NUMBER_OF_COLUMNS], int noOfRows)
{
    int row, col;
    int sum;

        //Sum of each individual row
    for (row = 0; row < noOfRows; row++)
    {
        sum = 0;

        for (col = 0; col < NUMBER_OF_COLUMNS; col++)
            sum = sum + matrix[row][col];

        cout << "Sum of row " << (row + 1) << " = " << sum
            << endl;
    }
}
```

The following function determines the largest element in each row:

```cpp
void largestInRows(int matrix[][NUMBER_OF_COLUMNS],
                   int noOfRows)
{
    int row, col;
    int largest;

        //Largest element in each row
    for (row = 0; row < noOfRows; row++)
    {
        largest = matrix[row][0]; //Assume that the first element
                                  //of the row is the largest.
        for (col = 1; col < NUMBER_OF_COLUMNS; col++)
            if (largest < matrix[row][col])
                largest = matrix[row][col];

        cout << "The largest element of row " << (row + 1)
            << " = " << largest << endl;
    }
}
```

Likewise, you can write a function to find the sum of the elements of each column, read the data into a two-dimensional array, find the largest and/or smallest element in each row or column, and so on.

Example 9-9 shows how the functions `printMatrix`, `sumRows`, and `largestInRows` are used in a program.

EXAMPLE 9-9

The following program illustrates how two-dimensional arrays are passed as parameters to methods.

```cpp
#include <iostream>
#include <iomanip>

using namespace std;

const int NUMBER_OF_ROWS = 6;
const int NUMBER_OF_COLUMNS = 5;

void printMatrix(int matrix[][NUMBER_OF_COLUMNS],
                 int NUMBER_OF_ROWS);
void sumRows(int matrix[][NUMBER_OF_COLUMNS],
             int NUMBER_OF_ROWS);
void largestInRows(int matrix[][NUMBER_OF_COLUMNS],
                   int NUMBER_OF_ROWS);

int main()
{
    int board[NUMBER_OF_ROWS][NUMBER_OF_COLUMNS]
              = {{23, 5, 6, 15, 18},
                 {4, 16, 24, 67, 10},
                 {12, 54, 23, 76, 11},
                 {1, 12, 34, 22, 8},
                 {81, 54, 32, 67, 33},
                 {12, 34, 76, 78, 9}};        //Line 1

    printMatrix(board, NUMBER_OF_ROWS);        //Line 2
    cout << endl;                              //Line 3
    sumRows(board, NUMBER_OF_ROWS);            //Line 4
    cout << endl;                              //Line 5
    largestInRows(board, NUMBER_OF_ROWS);      //Line 6

    return 0;
}

//Place the definitions of the functions printMatrix,
//sumRows, and largestInRows as described previously here.
```

Sample Run:

```
23     5     6    15    18
 4    16    24    67    10
12    54    23    76    11
 1    12    34    22     8
81    54    32    67    33
12    34    76    78     9

Sum of row 1 = 67
Sum of row 2 = 121
Sum of row 3 = 176
Sum of row 4 = 77
Sum of row 5 = 267
Sum of row 6 = 209


The largest element in row 1 = 23
The largest element in row 2 = 67
The largest element in row 3 = 76
The largest element in row 4 = 34
The largest element in row 5 = 81
The largest element in row 6 = 78
```

In this program, the statement in Line 1 declares and initializes `board` to be a two-dimensional array of 6 rows and 5 columns. The statement in Line 2 uses the function `printMatrix` to output the elements of `board` (see the first six lines of the Sample Run). The statement in Line 4 uses the function `sumRows` to calculate and print the sum of each row. The statement in Line 6 uses the function `largestInRows` to find and print the largest element in each row.

Arrays of Strings

Suppose that you need to perform an operation, such as alphabetizing a list of names. Because every name is a string, a convenient way to store the list of names is to use an array. Strings in C++ can be manipulated using either the data type `string` or character arrays (C-strings). Also, on some compilers, the data type `string` may not be available in Standard C++ (that is, non-ANSI/ISO Standard C++). This section illustrates both ways to manipulate a list of strings.

Arrays of Strings and the `string` Type

Processing a list of strings using the data type `string` is straightforward. Suppose that the list consists of a maximum of 100 names. You can declare an array of 100 components of type `string` as follows:

```
string list[100];
```

Basic operations, such as assignment, comparison, and input/output, can be performed on values of the `string` type. Therefore, the data in `list` can be processed just like any one-dimensional array discussed in the first part of this chapter.

Arrays of Strings and C-Strings (Character Arrays)

Suppose that the largest string (for example, name) in your list is 15 characters long and your list has 100 strings. You can declare a two-dimensional array of characters of 100 rows and 16 columns as follows (see Figure 9-16):

```
char list[100][16];
```

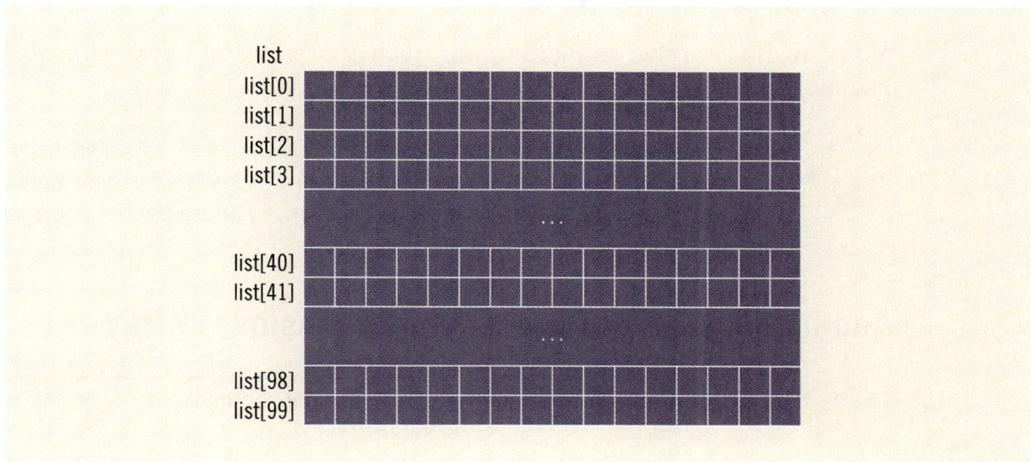

FIGURE 9-16 Array `list` of strings

Now `list[j]` for each j, 0 <= j <= 99, is a string of at most 15 characters in length. The following statement stores `"Snow White"` in `list[1]` (see Figure 9-17):

```
strcpy(list[1], "Snow White");
```

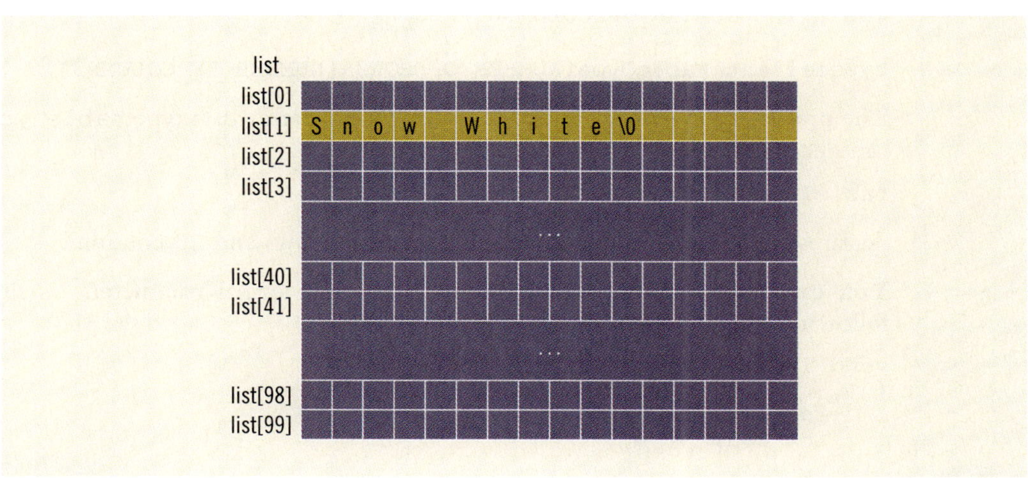

FIGURE 9-17 Array `list`, showing `list[1]`

Suppose that you want to read and store data in `list` and that there is one entry per line. The following **for** loop accomplishes this task:

```
for (j = 0; j < 100; j++)
    cin.get(list[j], 16);
```

The following **for** loop outputs the string in each row:

```
for (j = 0; j < 100; j++)
    cout << list[j] << endl;
```

You can also use other string functions (such as `strcmp` and `strlen`) and **for** loops to manipulate `list`.

NOTE The data type `string` has operations such as assignment, concatenation, and relational operations defined for it. If you use Standard C++ header files and the data type `string` is available on your compiler, we recommend that you use the data type `string` to manipulate lists of strings.

Another Way to Declare a Two-Dimensional Array

NOTE This section may be skipped without any loss of continuity.

If you know the size of the tables with which the program will be working, then you can use **typedef** to first define a two-dimensional array data type and then declare variables of that type.

For example, consider the following:

```
const int NUMBER_OF_ROWS = 20;
const int NUMBER_OF_COLUMNS = 10;

typedef int tableType[NUMBER_OF_ROWS][NUMBER_OF_COLUMNS];
```

The previous statement defines a two-dimensional array data type `tableType`. Now we can declare variables of this type. So:

```
tableType matrix;
```

declares a two-dimensional array `matrix` of 20 rows and 10 columns.

You can also use this data type when declaring formal parameters, as shown in the following code:

```
void initialize(tableType table)
{
    int row;
    int col;

    for (row = 0; row < NUMBER_OF_ROWS; row++)
```

```
    for (col = 0; col < NUMBER_OF_COLUMNS; col++)
        table[row][col] = 0;
}
```

This function takes as an argument any variable of type `tableType`, which is a two-dimensional array, and initializes the array to 0.

By first defining a data type, you do not need to keep checking the exact number of columns when you declare a two-dimensional array as a variable or formal parameter, or when you pass an array as a parameter during a function call.

Multidimensional Arrays

In this chapter, we defined an array as a collection of a fixed number of elements (called components) of the same type. A one-dimensional array is an array in which the elements are arranged in a list form; in a two-dimensional array, the elements are arranged in a table form. We can also define three-dimensional or larger arrays. In C++, there is no limit on the dimension of arrays. Following is the general definition of an array.

Array: A collection of a fixed number of elements (called components) arranged in n dimensions ($n >= 1$), called an n-**dimensional array**.

The general syntax for declaring an n-dimensional array is:

```
dataType arrayName[intExp1][intExp2] ... [intExpn];
```

where `intExp1`, `intExp2`, . . . , and `intExpn` are constant expressions yielding positive integer values.

The syntax to access a component of an n-dimensional array is:

```
arrayName[indexExp1][indexExp2] ... [indexExpn]
```

where `indexExp1`,`indexExp2`, . . ., and `indexExpn` are expressions yielding non-negative integer values. `indexExpi` gives the position of the array component in the `ith` dimension.

For example, the statement:

```
double carDealers[10][5][7];
```

declares `carDealers` to be three-dimensional array. The size of the first dimension is 10, the size of the second dimension is 5, and the size of the third dimension is 7. The first dimension ranges from 0 to 9, the second dimension ranges from 0 to 4, and the third dimension ranges from 0 to 6. The base address of the array `carDealers` is the address of the first array component—that is, the address of `carDealers[0][0][0]`. The total number of components in the array `carDealers` is 10 * 5 * 7 = 350.

The statement:

```
carDealers[5][3][2] = 15564.75;
```

sets the value of the component `carDealers[5][3][2]` to `15564.75`.

You can use loops to process multidimensional arrays. For example, the nested `for` loops:

```
for (i = 0; i < 10; i++)
    for (j = 0; j < 5; j++)
        for (k = 0; k < 7; k++)
            carDealers[i][j][k] = 0.0;
```

initialize the entire array to `0.0`.

When declaring a multidimensional array as a formal parameter in a function, you can omit the size of the first dimension but not the other dimensions. As parameters, multi-dimensional arrays are passed by reference only, and a function cannot return a value of the array type. There is no check to determine whether the array indices are within bounds.

PROGRAMMING EXAMPLE: Code Detection

When a message is transmitted in secret code over a transmission channel, it is usually sent as a sequence of bits, that is, 0s and 1s. Due to noise in the transmission channel, the transmitted message may become corrupted. That is, the message received at the destination is not the same as the message transmitted; some of the bits may have been changed. There are several techniques to check the validity of the transmitted message at the destination. One technique is to transmit the same message twice. At the destination, both copies of the message are compared bit by bit. If the corresponding bits are the same, the message received is error-free.

Let's write a program to check whether the message received at the destination is error-free. For simplicity, assume that the secret code representing the message is a sequence of digits (0 to 9) and the maximum length of the message is 250 digits. Also, the first number in the message is the length of the message. For example, if the secret code is:

7 9 2 7 8 3 5 6

then the actual message is 7 digits long, and it is transmitted twice.

The above message is transmitted as:

7 9 2 7 8 3 5 6 7 9 2 7 8 3 5 6

Input A file containing the secret code and its copy.

Output The secret code, its copy, and a message—if the received code is error-free—in the following form:

```
Code Digit       Code Digit Copy
   9                    9
   2                    2
   7                    7
   8                    8
   3                    3
   5                    5
   6                    6
Message transmitted OK.
```

PROBLEM ANALYSIS AND ALGORITHM DESIGN

Because we have to compare the corresponding digits of the secret code and its copy, we first read the secret code and store it in an array. Then we read the first digit of the copy and compare it with the first digit of the secret code, and so on. If any corresponding digits are not the same, we indicate this fact by printing a message next to the digits. Because the maximum length of the message is 250, we use an array of 250 components. The first number in the secret code, and in the copy of the secret code, indicates the length of the code. This discussion translates into the following algorithm:

1. Open the input and output files.

2. If the input file does not exist, exit the program.

3. Read the length of the secret code.

4. If the length of the secret code is greater than 250, terminate the program because the maximum length of the code in this program is 250.

5. Read and store the secret code into an array.

6. Read the length of the copy.

7. If the length of the secret code and its copy are the same, compare the codes. Otherwise, print an error message.

To simplify the function `main`, let us write a function, `readCode`, to read the secret code and another function, `compareCode`, to compare the codes.

readCode This function first reads the length of the secret code. If the length of the secret code is greater than 250, a `bool` variable `lenCodeOk`, which is a reference parameter, is set to `false` and the function terminates. The value of `lenCodeOk` is passed to the calling function to indicate whether the secret code was read successfully. If the length of the code is less than 250, the `readCode` function reads and stores the secret code into an array. Because the input is stored into a file and the file was opened in the function `main`, the input stream variable corresponding to the input file must be passed as a parameter to this function.

Furthermore, after reading the length of the secret code and the code itself, the `readCode` function must pass these values to the function `main`. Therefore, this function has four parameters: an input file stream variable, an array to store the secret code, the length of the code, and the `bool` parameter `lenCodeOk`. The definition of the function `readCode` is as follows:

```cpp
void readCode(ifstream& infile, int list[], int& length,
              bool& lenCodeOk)
{
    int count;

    lenCodeOk = true;

    infile >> length;   //get the length of the secret code

    if (length > MAX_CODE_SIZE)
    {
        lenCodeOk = false;
        return;
    }

        //Get the secret code.
    for (count = 0; count < length; count++)
        infile >> list[count];
}
```

compareCode This function compares the secret code with its copy. Therefore, it must have access to the array containing the secret code and the length of the secret code. The copy of the secret code and its length are stored in the input file. Thus, the input stream variable corresponding to the input file must be passed as a parameter to this function. Also, the `compareCode` function compares the secret code with the copy and prints an appropriate message. Because the output will be stored in a file, the output stream variable corresponding to the output file must also be passed as a parameter to this function. Therefore, the function has four parameters: an input file stream variable, an output file stream variable, the array containing the secret code, and the length of the secret code. This discussion translates into the following algorithm for the function `compareCode`:

    a.   Declare the variables.

    b.   Set a `bool` variable `codeOk` to `true`.

    c.   Read the length of the copy of the secret code.

    d.   If the length of the secret code and its copy are not the same, output an appropriate error message and terminate the function.

    e.   For each digit in the input file:

        e.1.   Read the next digit of the copy of the secret code.

        e.2.   Output the corresponding digits from the secret code and its copy.

e.3.   If the corresponding digits are not the same, output an error message and set the `bool` variable `codeOk` to `false`.

   f.   If the `bool` variable `codeOk` is `true`

Output a message indicating that the secret code was transmitted correctly.

else

Output an error message.

Following this algorithm, the definition of the function `compareCode` is:

```cpp
void compareCode(ifstream& infile, ofstream& outfile,
                 int list[], int length)
{
        //Step a
    int length2;
    int digit;
    bool codeOk;
    int count;

    codeOk = true;                                      //Step b

    infile >> length2;                                  //Step c

    if (length != length2)                              //Step d
    {
        cout << "The original code and its copy "
             << "are not of the same length."
             << endl;
        return;
    }

    outfile << "Code Digit    Code Digit Copy"
            << endl;

    for (count = 0; count < length; count++)            //Step e
    {
        infile >> digit;                                //Step e.1
        outfile << setw(5) << list[count]
                << setw(17) << digit;                   //Step e.2

        if (digit != list[count])                       //Step e.3
        {
            outfile << "  code digits are not the same"
                    << endl;
            codeOk = false;
        }
        else
            outfile << endl;
    }
```

```cpp
        if (codeOk)                                      //Step f
            outfile << "Message transmitted OK."
                    << endl;
        else
            outfile << "Error in transmission. "
                    << "Retransmit!!" << endl;
}
```

Following is the algorithm for the function `main`.

Main
Algorithm

1. Declare the variables.
2. Open the files.
3. Call the function `readCode` to read the secret code.
4. `if` (length of the secret code <= 250)

    Call the function `compareCode` to compare the codes.

    `else`

    Output an appropriate error message.

COMPLETE PROGRAM LISTING

```cpp
//Program: Check Code

#include <iostream>
#include <fstream>
#include <iomanip>

using namespace std;

const int MAX_CODE_SIZE = 250;

void readCode(ifstream& infile, int list[],
              int& length, bool& lenCodeOk);
void compareCode(ifstream& infile, ofstream& outfile,
                 int list[], int length);

int main()
{
        //Step 1
    int codeArray[MAX_CODE_SIZE]; //array to store the secret
                                  //code
    int codeLength;               //variable to store the
                                  //length of the secret code
    bool lengthCodeOk;  //variable to indicate if the length
                        //of the secret code is less than or
                        //equal to 250
```

```cpp
    ifstream incode;      //input file stream variable
    ofstream outcode;     //output file stream variable

    char inputFile[51];  //variable to store the name of the
                         //input file
    char outputFile[51];    //variable to store the name of
                            //the output file

    cout << "Enter the input file name: ";
    cin >> inputFile;
    cout << endl;

        //Step 2
    incode.open(inputFile);
    if (!incode)
    {
        cout << "Cannot open the input file." << endl;
        return 1;
    }

    cout << "Enter the output file name: ";
    cin >> outputFile;
    cout << endl;

    outcode.open(outputFile);

    readCode(incode, codeArray, codeLength,
            lengthCodeOk);                              //Step 3

    if (lengthCodeOk)                                   //Step 4
        compareCode(incode, outcode, codeArray,
                    codeLength);
    else
        cout << "Length of the secret code "
            << "must be <= " << MAX_CODE_SIZE
            << endl;                                    //Step 5

    incode.close();
    outcode.close();

    return 0;
}

void readCode(ifstream& infile, int list[], int& length,
            bool& lenCodeOk)
{
    int count;

    lenCodeOk = true;

    infile >> length;  //get the length of the secret code
```

```cpp
    if (length > MAX_CODE_SIZE)
    {
        lenCodeOk = false;
        return;
    }

        //Get the secret code.
    for (count = 0; count < length; count++)
        infile >> list[count];
}

void compareCode(ifstream& infile, ofstream& outfile,
                 int list[], int length)
{
        //Step a
    int length2;
    int digit;
    bool codeOk;
    int count;

    codeOk = true;                                          //Step b

    infile >> length2;                                      //Step c

    if (length != length2)                                  //Step d
    {
        cout << "The original code and its copy "
             << "are not of the same length."
             << endl;
        return;
    }

    outfile << "Code Digit    Code Digit Copy"
            << endl;

    for (count = 0; count < length; count++)               //Step e
    {
        infile >> digit;                                   //Step e.1
        outfile << setw(5) << list[count]
                << setw(17) << digit;                      //Step e.2

        if (digit != list[count])                          //Step e.3
        {
            outfile << "  code digits are not the same"
                    << endl;
            codeOk = false;
        }
        else
            outfile << endl;
    }
```

```cpp
        if (codeOk)                                    //Step f
            outfile << "Message transmitted OK."
                    << endl;
        else
            outfile << "Error in transmission. "
                    << "Retransmit!!" << endl;
}
```

Sample Run: In this sample run, the user input is shaded.

```
Enter the input file name: a:\Ch9_SecretCodeData.txt

Enter the output file name: a:\Ch9_SecretCodeOut.txt
```

Input File Data: (a:\Ch9_SecretCodeData.txt)

```
7 9 2 7 8 3 5 6 7 9 2 7 8 3 5 6
```

Output File Data: (a:\Ch9_SecretCodeOut.txt)

```
 Code Digit    Code Digit Copy
     9              9

     2              2

     7              7

     8              8

     3              3

     5              5

     6              6
Message transmitted OK.
```

9

PROGRAMMING EXAMPLE: Text Processing

(Line and letter count) Let us now write a program that reads a given text, outputs the text as is, and also prints the number of lines and the number of times each letter appears in the text. An uppercase letter and a lowercase letter are treated as being the same; that is, they are tallied together.

Because there are 26 letters, we use an array of 26 components to perform the letter count. We also need a variable to store the line count.

The text is stored in a file, which we will call `textin.txt` (and is on a floppy drive, which we will assume is A:). The output will be stored in a file, which we will call `textout.out`.

Input   A file containing the text to be processed.

Output   A file containing the text, number of lines, and the number of times a letter appears in the text.

PROBLEM
ANALYSIS
AND
ALGORITHM
DESIGN

Based on the desired output, it is clear that we must output the text as is. That is, if the text contains any whitespace characters, they must be output as well. Furthermore, we must count the number of lines in the text. Therefore, we must know where the line ends, which means that we must trap the newline character. This requirement suggests that we cannot use the extraction operator to process the input file. Because we also need to perform the letter count, we use the `get` function to read the text.

Let us first describe the variables that are necessary to develop the program. This will simplify the discussion that follows.

Variables

We need to store the line count and the letter count. Therefore, we need a variable to store the line count and 26 variables to perform the letter count. We will use an array of 26 components to perform the letter count. We also need a variable to read and store each character in turn, because the input file is to be read character-by-character. Because data is to be read from an input file and output is to be saved in a file, we need an input stream variable to open the input file and an output stream variable to open the output file. These statements indicate that the function `main` needs (at least) the following variables:

```cpp
int lineCount;          //variable to store the line count
int letterCount[26];    //array to store the letter count
char ch;                //variable to store a character
ifstream infile;        //input file stream variable
ofstream outfile;       //output file stream variable
```

In this declaration, `letterCount[0]` stores the A count, `letterCount[1]` stores the B count, and so on. Clearly, the variable `lineCount` and the array `letterCount` must be initialized to 0.

The algorithm for the program is:

1. Declare the variables.
2. Open the input and output files.
3. Initialize the variables.
4. While there is more data in the input file:
    4.1. For each character in a line:
        4.1.1. Read and write the character.
        4.1.2. Increment the appropriate letter count.

     4.2.   Increment the line count.

5.   Output the line count and letter counts.

6.   Close the files.

To simplify the function `main`, we divide it into four functions:

- Function `initialize`
- Function `copyText`
- Function `characterCount`
- Function `writeTotal`

The following sections describe each of these functions in detail. Then, with the help of these functions, we describe the algorithm for the function `main`.

initialize This function initializes the variable `lineCount` and the array `letterCount` to 0. It, therefore, has two parameters: one corresponding to the variable `lineCount` and one corresponding to the array `letterCount`. Clearly, the parameter corresponding to `lineCount` must be a reference parameter. The definition of this function is:

```cpp
void initialize(int& lc, int list[])
{
    int j;
    lc = 0;

    for (j = 0; j < 26; j++)
        list[j] = 0;
} //end initialize
```

copyText This function reads a line and outputs the line. After reading a character, it calls the function `characterCount` to update the letter count. Clearly, this function has four parameters: an input file stream variable, an output file stream variable, a `char` variable, and the array to update the letter count.

Note that the `copyText` function does not perform the `letter count`, but we still pass the array `letterCount` to it. We take this step because this function calls the function `characterCount`, which needs the array `letterCount` to update the appropriate `letter count`. Therefore, we must pass the array `letterCount` to the `copyText` function so that it can pass the array to the function `characterCount`.

```cpp
void copyText(ifstream& intext, ofstream& outtext, char& ch,
              int list[])
{
    while (ch != '\n')            //process the entire line
    {
        outtext << ch;            //output the character
        characterCount(ch, list); //call the function
                                  //character count
```

```
        intext.get(ch);           //read the next character
    }
    outtext << ch;                //output the newline character
} //end copyText
```

characterCount This function increments the letter count. To increment the appropriate letter count, it must know what the letter is. Therefore, the `characterCount` function has two parameters: a `char` variable and the array to update the letter count. In pseudocode, this function is:

    a.   Convert the letter to uppercase.

    b.   Find the index of the array corresponding to this letter.

    c.   If the index is valid, increment the appropriate count. At this step, we must ensure that the character is a letter. We are counting only letters, so other characters—such as commas, hyphens, and periods—are ignored.

Following this algorithm, the definition of this function is:

```
void characterCount(char ch, int list[])
{
    int index;

    ch = toupper(ch);                         //Step a

    index = static_cast<int>(ch)
            - static_cast<int>('A');          //Step b

    if (0 <= index && index < 26)             //Step c
        list[index]++;
} //end characterCount
```

writeTotal This function outputs the line count and the letter count. It has three parameters: the output file stream variable, the line count, and the array to output the letter count. The definition of this function is:

```
void writeTotal(ofstream& outtext, int lc, int list[])
{
    int index;

    outtext << endl << endl;
    outtext << "The number of lines = " << lc << endl;

    for (index = 0; index < 26; index++)
        outtext << static_cast<char>(index
                            + static_cast<int>('A'))
                << " count = " << list[index] << endl;
} //end writeTotal
```

We now describe the algorithm for the function `main`.

1. Declare the variables.
2. Open the input file.
3. If the input file does not exist, exit the program.
4. Open the output file.
5. Initialize the variables, such as `lineCount` and the array `letterCount`.
6. Read the first character.
7. while (not end of input file):

   7.1. Process the next line; call the function `copyText`.

   7.2. Increment the line count. (Increment the variable `lineCount`.)

   7.3. Read the next character.
8. Output the line count and letter counts. Call the function `writeTotal`.
9. Close the files.

COMPLETE PROGRAM LISTING

```cpp
//Program: Line and letter count

#include <iostream>
#include <fstream>
#include <cctype>

using namespace std;

void initialize(int& lc, int list[]);
void copyText(ifstream& intext, ofstream& outtext, char& ch,
              int list[]);
void characterCount(char ch, int list[]);
void writeTotal(ofstream& outtext, int lc, int list[]);

int main()
{
        //Step 1; Declare variables
    int lineCount;
    int letterCount[26];
    char ch;
    ifstream infile;
    ofstream outfile;
```

```cpp
    infile.open("a:\\textin.txt");                          //Step 2

    if (!infile)                                            //Step 3
    {
        cout << "Cannot open the input file."
             << endl;
        return 1;
    }

    outfile.open("a:\\textout.out");                        //Step 4

    initialize(lineCount, letterCount);                     //Step 5

    infile.get(ch);                                         //Step 6

    while (infile)                                          //Step 7
    {
        copyText(infile, outfile, ch, letterCount); //Step 7.1
        lineCount++;                                        //Step 7.2
        infile.get(ch);                                     //Step 7.3
    }

    writeTotal(outfile, lineCount, letterCount);     //Step 8

    infile.close();                                        //Step 9
    outfile.close();                                       //Step 9

    return 0;
}

void initialize(int& lc, int list[])
{
    int j;
    lc = 0;

    for (j = 0; j < 26; j++)
        list[j] = 0;
} //end initialize

void copyText(ifstream& intext, ofstream& outtext, char& ch,
              int list[])
{
    while (ch != '\n')            //process the entire line
    {
        outtext << ch;            //output the character

        characterCount(ch, list);   //call the function
                                    //character count
        intext.get(ch);           //read the next character
    }
```

```cpp
    outtext << ch;            //output the newline character
} //end copyText

void characterCount(char ch, int list[])
{
    int index;

    ch = toupper(ch);                              //Step a

    index = static_cast<int>(ch)
            - static_cast<int>('A');               //Step b

    if (0 <= index & index < 26)                   //Step c
        list[index]++;
} //end characterCount

void writeTotal(ofstream& outtext, int lc, int list[])
{
    int index;

    outtext << endl << endl;
    outtext << "The number of lines = " << lc << endl;

    for (index = 0; index < 26; index++)
        outtext << static_cast<char>(index
                                + static_cast<int>('A'))
                << " count = " << list[index] << endl;
} //end writeTotal
```

Sample Run (a:\textout.out):

Today we live in an era where information is processed almost at the
speed of light. Through computers, the technological revolution is
drastically changing the way we live and communicate with one
another. Terms such as "the Internet," which was unfamiliar just a
few years ago, are very common today. With the help of computers you
can send letters to, and receive letters from, loved ones within
seconds. You no longer need to send a résumé by mail to apply for a
job; in many cases you can simply submit your job application via
the Internet. You can watch how stocks perform in real time, and
instantly buy and sell them. Students regularly "surf" the Internet
and use computers to design their classroom projects. They also use
powerful word processing software to complete their term papers.
Many people maintain and balance their checkbooks on computers.

The number of lines = 15
A count = 53
B count = 7

```
C count = 30
D count = 19
E count = 81
F count = 11
G count = 10
H count = 29
I count = 41
J count = 4
K count = 3
L count = 31
M count = 26
N count = 50
O count = 59
P count = 21
Q count = 0
R count = 45
S count = 48
T count = 62
U count = 24
V count = 7
W count = 15
X count = 0
Y count = 20
Z count = 0
```

QUICK REVIEW

1. A data type is simple if variables of that type can hold only one value at a time.

2. In a structured data type, each data item is a collection of other data items.

3. An array is a structured data type with a fixed number of components. Every component is of the same type, and components are accessed using their relative positions in the array.

4. Elements of a one-dimensional array are arranged in the form of a list.

5. There is no check on an array index out of bounds.

6. In C++, an array index starts with 0.

7. An array index can be any expression that evaluates to a non-negative integer. The value of the index must always be less than the size of the array.

8. There are no aggregate operations on arrays, except for the input/output of character arrays (C-strings).

9. Arrays can be initialized during their declaration. If there are fewer initial values than the array size, the excess elements are initialized to 0.

10. The base address of an array is the address of the first array component. For example, if `list` is a one-dimensional array, the base address of `list` is the address of `list[0]`.

11. When declaring a one-dimensional array as a formal parameter, you usually omit the array size. If you specify the size of a one-dimensional array in the formal parameter declaration, the compiler will ignore the size.

12. In a function call statement, when passing an array as an actual parameter, you use only its name.

13. As parameters to functions, arrays are passed by reference only.

14. Because, as parameters, arrays are passed by reference only, when declaring an array as a formal parameter you do not use the symbol & after the data type.

15. A function cannot return a value of type array.

16. Although, as parameters, arrays are passed by reference, when declaring an array as a formal parameter, using the reserved word `const` before the data type prevents the function from modifying the array.

17. Individual array components can be passed as parameters to functions.

18. In C++, a string is any sequence of characters enclosed between double quotation marks.

19. In C++, C-strings are null terminated.

20. In C++, the null character is represented as `'\0'`.

21. In the ASCII character set, the collating sequence of the null character is 0.

22. C-strings are stored in character arrays.

23. Character arrays can be initialized during declaration using string notation.

24. Input and output of C-strings is the only place where C++ allows aggregate operations.

25. The header file `cstring` contains the specifications of the functions that can be used for C-string manipulation.

26. Commonly used C-string manipulation functions include `strcpy` (string copy), `strcmp` (string comparison), and `strlen` (string length).

27. C-strings are compared character-by-character.

28. Because C-strings are stored in arrays, individual characters in the C-string can be accessed using the array component access notation.

29. Parallel arrays are used to hold related information.

30. In a two-dimensional array, the elements are arranged in a table form.

31. To access an element of a two-dimensional array, you need a pair of indices: one for the row position and one for the column position.

32. In a two-dimensional array, the rows are numbered 0 to ROW_SIZE − 1 and the columns are numbered 0 to COLUMN_SIZE − 1.

33. If `matrix` is a two-dimensional array, then the base address of `matrix` is the address of the array component `matrix[0][0]`.

34. In row processing, a two-dimensional array is processed one row at a time.

35. In column processing, a two-dimensional array is processed one column at a time.

36. When declaring a two-dimensional array as a formal parameter, you can omit the size of the first dimension but not the second.

37. When a two-dimensional array is passed as an actual parameter, the number of columns of the actual and formal arrays must match.

38. C++ stores, in computer memory, two-dimensional arrays in a row order form.

EXERCISES

1. Mark the following statements as true or false.

   a. A `double` type is an example of a simple data type.

   b. A one-dimensional array is an example of a structured data type.

   c. Arrays can be passed as parameters to a function either by value or by reference.

   d. A function can return a value of type array.

   e. The size of an array is determined at compile time.

   f. The only aggregate operations allowable on `int` arrays are the increment and decrement operations.

   g. Given the declaration:

      ```
      int list[10];
      ```

      the statement:

      ```
      list[5] = list[3] + list[2];
      ```

      updates the content of the fifth component of the array `list`.

   h. If an array index goes out of bounds, the program always terminates in an error.

   i. In C++, some aggregate operations are allowed for strings.

   j. The declaration:

      ```
      char name[16] = "John K. Miller";
      ```

      declares `name` to be an array of 15 characters because the string `"John K. Miller"` has only 14 characters.

   k. The declaration:

      ```
      char str = "Sunny Day";
      ```

      declares `str` to be a string of an unspecified length.

   l. As parameters, two-dimensional arrays are passed either by value or by reference.

2. Write C++ statements to do the following:

   a. Declare an array `alpha` of 15 components of type `int`.

   b. Output the value of the tenth component of the array `alpha`.

   c. Set the value of the fifth component of the array `alpha` to 35.

   d. Set the value of the ninth component of the array `alpha` to the sum of the sixth and thirteenth components of the array `alpha`.

   e. Set the value of the fourth component of the array `alpha` to three times the value of the eighth component minus 57.

   f. Output `alpha` so that five components per line are printed.

3. Consider the function headings:

```
void funcOne(int alpha[], int size);
int funcSum(int x, int y);
void funcTwo(const int alpha[], int beta[]);
```

   and the declarations:

```
int list[50];
int aList[60];
int num;
```

   Write C++ statements that do the following:

   a. Call the function `funcOne` with the actual parameters, `list` and 50, respectively.

   b. Print the value returned by the function `funcSum` with the actual parameters, 50 and the fourth component of `list`, respectively.

   c. Print the value returned by the function `funcSum` with the actual parameters, the thirtieth and tenth components of `list`, respectively.

   d. Call the function `funcTwo` with the actual parameters, `list` and `aList`, respectively.

4. Suppose `list` is an array of five components of type `int`. What is stored in `list` after the following C++ code executes?

```
for (i = 0; i < 5; i++)
{
    list[i] = 2 * i + 5;
    if (i % 2 == 0)
        list[i] = list[i] - 3;
}
```

5. Suppose `list` is an array of six components of type `int`. What is stored in `list` after the following C++ code executes?

```
list[0] = 5;
for (i = 1; i < 6; i++)
{
    list[i] = i * i + 5;
```

```
        if (i > 2)
            list[i] = 2 * list[i] - list[i - 1];
    }
```

6. Given the declaration:

```
char string15[16];
```

mark the following statements as valid or invalid. If a statement is invalid, explain why.

a. `strcpy(string15, "Hello there");`

b. `strlen(string15);`

c. `string15 = "Jacksonville";`

d. `cin >> string15;`

e. `cout << string15;`

f. ```
    if (string15 >= "Nice day")
        cout << string15;
    ```

g.  `string15[6] = 't';`

7.  Given the declaration:

```
char str1[15];
char str2[15] = "Good day";
```

mark the following statements as valid or invalid. If a statement is invalid, explain why.

a. `str1 = str2;`

b. ```
    if (str1 == str2)
        cout << " Both strings are of the same length." << endl;
    ```

c. ```
    if (strlen(str1) >= strlen(str2))
        str1 = str2;
    ```

d.  ```
    if (strcmp(str1, str2) < 0)
        cout << "str1 is less that str2." << endl;
    ```

8. Given the declaration:

```
char name[8] = "Shelly";
```

mark the following statements as "Yes" if they output Shelly. Otherwise, mark the statement as "No" and explain why it does not output Shelly.

a. `cout << name;`

b. ```
    for (int j = 0; j < 6; j++)
        cout << name[j];
    ```

c.  ```
    int j = 0;
    while (name[j] != '\0')
        cout << name[j++];
    ```

d. ```
    int j = 0;
    while (j < 8)
        cout << name[j++];
    ```
    ```

9. Given the declaration:

```cpp
char str1[21];
char str2[21];
```

   a. Write a C++ statement that stores "Sunny Day" in str1.

   b. Write a C++ statement that stores the length of str1 into the **int** variable length.

   c. Write a C++ statement that copies the value of name into str2.

   d. Write C++ code that outputs str1 if str1 is less than or equal to str2, and otherwise outputs str2.

10. Assume the following declarations:

```cpp
char name[21];
char yourName[21];
char studentName[31];
```

Mark the following statements as valid or invalid. If a statement is invalid, explain why.

   a.
```cpp
cin >> name;
```

   b.
```cpp
cout << studentName;
```

   c.
```cpp
yourName[0] = '\0';
```

   d.
```cpp
yourName = studentName;
```

   e.
```cpp
if (yourName == name)
    studentName = name;
```

   f.
```cpp
int x = strcmp(yourName, studentName);
```

   g.
```cpp
strcpy(studentName, Name);
```

   h.
```cpp
for (int j = 0; j < 21; j++)
    cout << name[j];
```

11. What is the output of the following program?

```cpp
#include <iostream>

using namespace std;

int main()
{
    int count;
    int alpha[5];

    alpha[0] = 5;
    for (count = 1; count < 5; count++)
    {
        alpha[count] = 5 * count + 10;
        alpha[count - 1] = alpha[count] - 4;
    }
```

```cpp
        cout << "List elements: ";
        for (count = 0; count < 5; count++)
            cout << alpha[count] << " ";
        cout << endl;

        return 0;
    }
```

12. What is the output of the following program?

```cpp
#include <iostream>

using namespace std;

int main()
{
    int j;
    int one[5];
    int two[10];

    for (j = 0; j < 5; j++)
        one[j] = 5 * j + 3;

    cout << "One contains: ";
    for (j = 0; j < 5; j++)
        cout << one[j] << " ";
    cout << endl;
    for (j = 0; j < 5; j++)
    {
        two[j] = 2 * one[j] - 1;
        two[j + 5] = one[4 - j] + two [j];
    }

    cout << "Two contains: ";
    for (j = 0; j < 10; j++)
        cout << two[j] << " ";
    cout << endl;

    return 0;
}
```

13. Consider the following declarations:

```cpp
const int CAR_TYPES = 5;
const int COLOR_TYPES = 6;

double sales[CAR_TYPES][COLOR_TYPES];
```

   a. How many components does the array sales have?

   b. What is the number of rows in the array sales?

   c. What is the number of columns in the array sales?

   d. To sum the sales by CAR_TYPES, what kind of processing is required?

   e. To sum the sales by COLOR_TYPES, what kind of processing is required?

14. Write C++ statements that do the following:

    a. Declare an array `alpha` of 10 rows and 20 columns of type `int`.

    b. Initialize the array `alpha` to 0.

    c. Store 1 in the first row and 2 in the remaining rows.

    d. Store 5 in the first column, and make sure that the value in each subsequent column is twice the value in the previous column.

    e. Print the array `alpha` one row per line.

    f. Print the array `alpha` one column per line.

15. Consider the following declaration:

```cpp
int beta[3][3];
```

What is stored in `beta` after each of the following statements executes?

    a.
```cpp
for (i = 0; i < 3; i++)
    for (j = 0; j < 3; j++)
        beta[i][j] = 0;
```

    b.
```cpp
for (i = 0; i < 3; i++)
    for (j = 0; j < 3; j++)
        beta[i][j] = i + j;
```

    c.
```cpp
for (i = 0; i < 3; i++)
    for (j = 0; j < 3; j++)
        beta[i][j] = i * j;
```

    d.
```cpp
for (i = 0; i < 3; i++)
    for (j = 0; j < 3; j++)
        beta[i][j] =  2 * (i + j) % 4;
```

PROGRAMMING EXERCISES

1. Write a C++ program that declares an array `alpha` of 50 components of type `double`. Initialize the array so that the first 25 components are equal to the square of the index variable, and the last 25 components are equal to three times the index variable. Output the array so that 10 elements per line are printed.

2. Write a C++ function, `smallestIndex`, that takes as parameters an `int` array and its size, and returns the index of the smallest element in the array. Also, write a program to test your function.

3. Write a program that reads a file consisting of students' test scores in the range 0–200. It should then determine the number of students having scores in each of the following ranges: 0–24, 25–49, 50–74, 75–99, 100–124, 125–149, 150–174, and 175–200. Output the score ranges and the number of students. (Run your program with the following input data: 76, 89, 150, 135, 200, 76, 12, 100, 150, 28, 178, 189, 167, 200, 175, 150, 87, 99, 129, 149, 176, 200, 87, 35, 157, 189.)

4. In a gymnastics or diving competition, each contestant's score is calculated by dropping the lowest and highest scores and then adding the remaining scores. Write a program that allows the user to enter eight judges' scores and outputs the points received by the contestant. Format your output with two decimal places. (A judge awards points between 1 and 10, with 1 being the lowest and 10 being the highest.) For example, if the scores are 9.2, 9.3, 9.0, 9.9, 9.5, 9.5, 9.6, and 9.8, the contestant receives a total of 56.90 points.

5. Write a program that prompts the user to input a string and outputs the string in uppercase letters. (Use a character array to store the string.)

6. The history teacher at your school needs help in grading a True/False test. The students' IDs and test answers are stored in a file. The first entry in the file contains answers to the test in the form:

```
TFFTFFTTTTFFTFTFTFT
```

Every other entry in the file is the student ID, followed by a blank, followed by the student's responses. For example, the entry:

```
ABC54301 TFTFTFTT TFTFTFFFTTFT
```

indicates that the student ID is ABC54301 and the answer to question 1 is True, the answer to question 2 is False, and so on. This student did not answer question 9. The exam has 20 questions, and the class has more than 150 students. Each correct answer is awarded two points, each wrong answer gets −1 point, and no answer gets 0 points. Write a program that processes the test data. The output should be the student's ID, followed by the answers, followed by the test score, followed by the test grade. Assume the following grade scale: 90%–100%, A; 80%–89.99%, B; 70%–79.99%, C; 60%–69.99%, D; and 0%–59.99%, F.

7. Write a program that allows the user to enter the last names of five candidates in a local election and the number of votes received by each candidate. The program should then output each candidate's name, the number of votes received, and the percentage of the total votes received by the candidate. Your program should also output the winner of the election. A sample output is:

```
Candidate        Votes Received        % of Total Votes

Johnson              5000                   25.91
Miller               4000                   20.73
Duffy                6000                   31.09
Robinson             2500                   12.95
Ashtony              1800                    9.33
Total               19300


The Winner of the Election is Duffy.
```

8. Assume that the maximum number of students in a class is 50. Write a program that reads students' names followed by their test score from a file and outputs the following:

    a. Class average

    b. Names of all the students whose test scores are below the class average, with an appropriate message

    c. Highest test score and the names of all the students having the highest score

9. Consider the following function `main`:

```
int main()
{
    int inStock[10][4];
    int alpha[20];
    int beta[20];
    int gamma[4] = {11, 13, 15, 17};
    int delta[10] = {3, 5, 2, 6, 10, 9, 7, 11, 1, 8};



        .
        .
        .


}
```

    a. Write the definition of the function `setZero` that initializes any one-dimensional array of type `int` to 0.

    b. Write the definition of the function `inputArray` that prompts the user to input 20 numbers and stores the numbers into `alpha`.

    c. Write the definition of the function `doubleArray` that initializes the elements of `beta` to two times the corresponding elements in `alpha`. Make sure that you prevent the function from modifying the elements of `alpha`.

    d. Write the definition of the function `copyGamma` that sets the elements of the first row of `inStock` to `gamma` and the remaining rows of `inStock` to three times the previous row of `inStock`. Make sure that you prevent the function from modifying the elements of `gamma`.

    e. Write the definition of the function `copyAlphaBeta` that stores `alpha` into the first five rows of `inStock` and `beta` into the last five rows of `inStock`. Make sure that you prevent the function from modifying the elements of `alpha` and `beta`.

    f. Write the definition of the function `printArray` that prints any one-dimensional array of type `int`. Print 15 elements per line.

    g. Write the definition of the function `setInStock` that prompts the user to input the elements for the first column of `inStock`. The function should then set the elements in the remaining columns to two times the corresponding element in the previous column, minus the corresponding element in `delta`.

h. Write C++ statements that call each of the functions in parts a through g.

i. Write a C++ program that tests the function main and the functions discussed in parts a through g. (Add additional functions, such as printing a two-dimensional array, as needed.)

10. Write a program that uses a two-dimensional array to store the highest and lowest temperatures for each month of the year. The program should output the average high, average low, and the highest and lowest temperatures for the year. Your program must consist of the following functions:

a. Function `getData`: This function reads and stores data in the two-dimensional array.

b. Function `averageHigh`: This function calculates and returns the average high temperature for the year.

c. Function `averageLow`: This function calculates and returns the average low temperature for the year.

d. Function `indexHighTemp`: This function returns the index of the highest high temperature in the array.

e. Function `indexLowTemp`: This function returns the index of the lowest low temperature in the array.

(These functions must all have the appropriate parameters.)

11. Write a program that reads in a set of positive integers and outputs how many times a particular number appears in the list. You may assume that the data set has at most 100 numbers and –999 marks the end of the input data. The numbers must be output in increasing order. For example, for the data:

```
15 40 28 62 95 15 28 13 62 65 48 95 65 62 65 95 95
```

the output is:

```
Number        Count
13            1
15            2
28            2
40            1
48            1
62            3
65            3
95            4
```

12. (**Airplane Seating Assignment**) Write a program that can be used to assign seats for a commercial airplane. The airplane has 13 rows, with 6 seats in each row. Rows 1 and 2 are first class; the remaining rows are economy class. Also, rows 1 through 7 are nonsmoking. Your program must prompt the user to enter the following information:

a. Ticket type (first class or economy class)

b. For economy class, the smoking or nonsmoking section

c. Desired seat

Output the seating plan in the following form:

	A	B	C	D	E	F
Row 1	*	*	X	*	X	X
Row 2	*	X	*	X	*	X
Row 3	*	*	X	X	*	X
Row 4	X	*	X	*	X	X
Row 5	*	X	*	X	*	*
Row 6	*	X	*	*	*	X
Row 7	X	*	*	*	X	X
Row 8	*	X	*	X	X	*
Row 9	X	*	X	X	*	X
Row 10	*	X	*	X	X	X
Row 11	*	*	X	*	X	*
Row 12	*	*	X	X	*	X
Row 13	*	*	*	*	X	*

Here, * indicates that the seat is available; X indicates that the seat is occupied. Make this a menu-driven program; show the user's choices and allow the user to make the appropriate choices.

13. (**Magic Square**) For this exercise, the functions written in parts a through e should be general enough to apply to an array of any size. (That is, the work should be done by using loops.)

a. Write a function `createArithmeticSeq` that prompts the user to input two numbers, `first` and `diff`. The function then creates a one-dimensional array of 16 elements ordered in an arithmetic sequence. It also outputs the arithmetic sequence. For example, if `first` = 21 and `diff` = 5, the arithmetic sequence is: 21 26 31 36 41 46 51 56 61 66 71 76 81 86 91 96.

b. Write a function `matricize` that takes a one-dimensional array of 16 elements and a two-dimensional array of 4 rows and 4 columns as parameters. (Other values, such as the sizes of the arrays, must also be passed as parameters.) It puts the elements of the one-dimensional array into the two-dimensional array. For example, if A is the one-dimensional array created in part a and B is a two-dimensional array, then after putting the elements of A into B, the array B is:

```
21 26 31 36
41 46 51 56
61 66 71 76
81 86 91 96
```

c. Write a function `reverseDiagonal` that reverses both the diagonals of a two-dimensional array. For example, if the two-dimensional array is as in part b, after reversing the diagonals, the two-dimensional array is:

```
96 26 31 81
41 71 66 56
61 51 46 76
36 86 91 21
```

d. Write a function `magicCheck` that takes a one-dimensional array of size 16, a two-dimensional array of 4 rows and 4 columns, and the sizes of the arrays as parameters. By adding all the elements of the one-dimensional array and dividing by 4, this function determines the `magicNumber`. The function then adds each row, each column, and each diagonal of the two-dimensional array and compares each sum with the magic number. If the sum of each row, each column, and each diagonal is equal to the `magicNumber`, the function outputs "It is a magic square". Otherwise, it outputs "It is not a magic number". Do not print the sum of each row, each column, and the diagonals.

e. Write a function `printMatrix` that outputs the elements of a two-dimensional array, one row per line. This output should be as close to a square form as possible.

f. Test the functions you wrote for parts a through e using the following function `main`:

```cpp
const int ROWS = 4;
const int COLUMNS = 4;

const int LIST_SIZE = 16;
...
```

```c
int main()
{
    int list[LIST_SIZE];
    int matrix[ROWS][COLUMNS];

    createArithmeticSeq(list, LIST_SIZE);
    matricize(list, matrix, ROWS);
    printMatrix(matrix, ROWS);
    reverseDiagonal(matrix, ROWS);
    printMatrix(matrix, ROWS);
    magicCheck(list, matrix, LIST_SIZE, ROWS);

    return 0;
}
```

9

RECORDS (structs)

IN THIS CHAPTER, YOU WILL:

- Learn about records (structs)
- Examine various operations on a struct
- Explore ways to manipulate data using a struct
- Learn about the relationship between a struct and functions
- Discover how arrays are used in a struct
- Learn how to create an array of struct items

In Chapter 9, you learned how to group values of the same type by using arrays. You also learned how to process data stored in an array and how to perform list operations, such as searching and sorting.

NOTE This chapter may be skipped without experiencing any discontinuation.

In this chapter, you will learn how to group related values that are of different types. C++ provides another structured data type, called a **struct** (some languages use the term "record") to group related items of different types. An array is a homogeneous data structure; a **struct** is typically a heterogeneous data structure. The treatment of a **struct** in this chapter is similar to the treatment of a **struct** in C. A **struct** in this chapter, therefore, is a C-like **struct**. Chapter 11 introduces and discusses another structured data type, called a class.

Records (**structs**)

Suppose that you want to write a program to process student data. A student record consists of, among other things, the student's name, student ID, GPA, courses taken, and course grades. Thus, various components are associated with a student. However, these components are all of different types. For example, the student's name is a string and the GPA is a floating-point number. Because these components are of different types, you cannot use an array to group all of the items associated with a student. C++ provides a structured data type called **struct** to group items of different types. Grouping components that are related, but of different types, offers several advantages. For example, a single variable can pass all the components as parameters to a function.

struct: A collection of a fixed number of components in which the components are accessed by name. The components may be of different types.

The components of a **struct** are called the members of the **struct**. The general syntax of a **struct** in C++ is:

```
struct structName
{
    dataType1 identifier1;
    dataType2 identifier2;
        .
        .
        .
    dataTypen identifiern;
};
```

In C++, **struct** is a reserved word. The members of a **struct**, even though enclosed in braces (that is, they form a block), are not considered to form a compound statement. Thus, a semicolon (after the right brace) is essential to end the **struct** statement. A semicolon at the end of the **struct** definition is, therefore, a part of the syntax.

The statement:

```
struct employeeType
{
    string firstName;
    string lastName;
    string address1;
    string address2;
    double salary;
    string deptID;
};
```

defines a **struct** employeeType with 6 members. The members firstName, lastName, address1, address2, and deptID are of type string, and the member salary is of type **double**.

Like any type definition, a **struct** is a definition, not a declaration. That is, it defines only a data type; no memory is allocated.

Once a data type is defined, you can declare variables of that type. Let us first define a **struct** type, studentType, and then declare variables of that type:

```
struct studentType
{
    string firstName;
    string lastName;
    char courseGrade;
    int testScore;
    int programmingScore;
    double GPA;
};

    //variable declaration
studentType newStudent;
studentType student;
```

These statements declare two **struct** variables, newStudent and student, of type studentType. The memory allocated is large enough to store firstName, lastName, courseGrade, testScore, programmingScore, and GPA (see Figure 10-1).

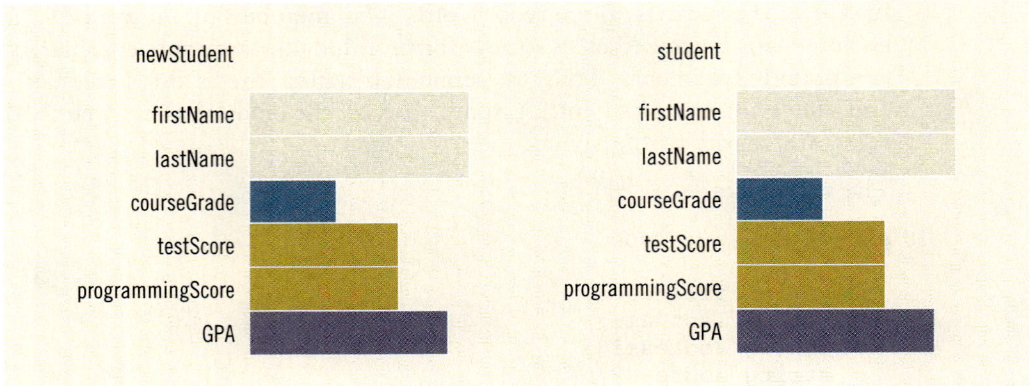

FIGURE 10-1   struct newStudent and student

> **NOTE**   You can also declare **struct** variables when you define the **struct**. For example, consider the following statements:

```
struct studentType
{
    string firstName;
    string lastName;
    char courseGrade;
    int testScore;
    int programmingScore;
    double GPA;
} tempStudent;
```

These statements define the **struct** studentType and also declare tempStudent to be a variable of type studentType.

Typically, in a program, a **struct** is defined before the definitions of all the functions in the program, so that the **struct** can be used throughout the program. Therefore, if you define a **struct** and also simultaneously declare a **struct** variable (as in the preceding statements), then that **struct** variable becomes a global variable and thus can be accessed anywhere in the program. Keeping in mind the side effects of global variables, you first should only define a **struct** and then declare the **struct** variables.

Accessing struct Members

In arrays, you access a component by using the array name together with the relative position (index) of the component. The array name and index are separated using square brackets. To access a structure member (component), you use the **struct** variable name together with the member name; these names are separated by a dot (period). The syntax for accessing a **struct** member is:

```
structVariableName.memberName
```

The `structVariableName.memberName` is just like any other variable. For example, `newStudent.courseGrade` is a variable of type **char**, `newStudent.firstName` is a string variable, and so on. As a result, you can do just about anything with **struct** members that you normally do with variables. You can, for example, use them in assignment statements or input/output (where permitted) statements.

In C++, the dot, (.), is an operator, called the **member access operator**.

Suppose you want to initialize the member GPA of `newStudent` to 0.0. The following statement accomplishes this task:

```cpp
newStudent.GPA = 0.0;
```

Similarly, the statements:

```cpp
newStudent.firstName = "John";
newStudent.lastName = "Brown";
```

store `"John"` in the member `firstName` and `"Brown"` in the member `lastName` of `newStudent`.

After the preceding three assignment statements execute, `newStudent` is as shown in Figure 10-2.

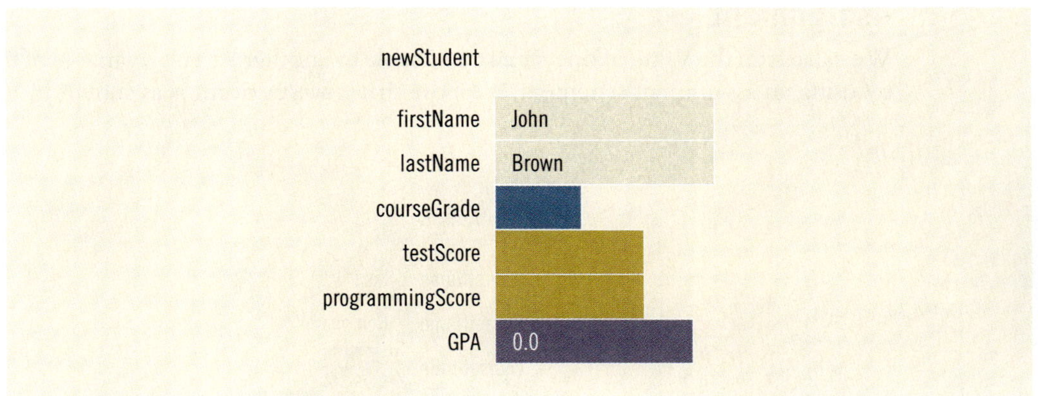

FIGURE 10-2 **struct** `newStudent`

The statement:

```cpp
cin >> newStudent.firstName;
```

reads the next string from the standard input device and stores it in:

```cpp
newStudent.firstName
```

The statement:

```cpp
cin >> newStudent.testScore >> newStudent.programmingScore;
```

reads two integer values from the keyboard and stores them in newStudent.testScore and newStudent.programmingScore, respectively.

Suppose that score is a variable of type int. The statement:

```
score = (newStudent.testScore + newStudent.programmingScore) / 2;
```

assigns the average of newStudent.testScore and newStudent.programmingScore to score.

The following statement determines the course grade and stores it in newStudent.courseGrade:

```
if (score >= 90)
    newStudent.courseGrade = 'A';
else if (score >= 80)
    newStudent.courseGrade = 'B';
else if (score >= 70)
    newStudent.courseGrade = 'C';
else if (score >= 60)
    newStudent.courseGrade = 'D';
else
    newStudent.courseGrade = 'F';
```

Assignment

We can assign the value of one **struct** variable to another **struct** variable of the same type by using an assignment statement. Suppose that newStudent is as shown in Figure 10-3.

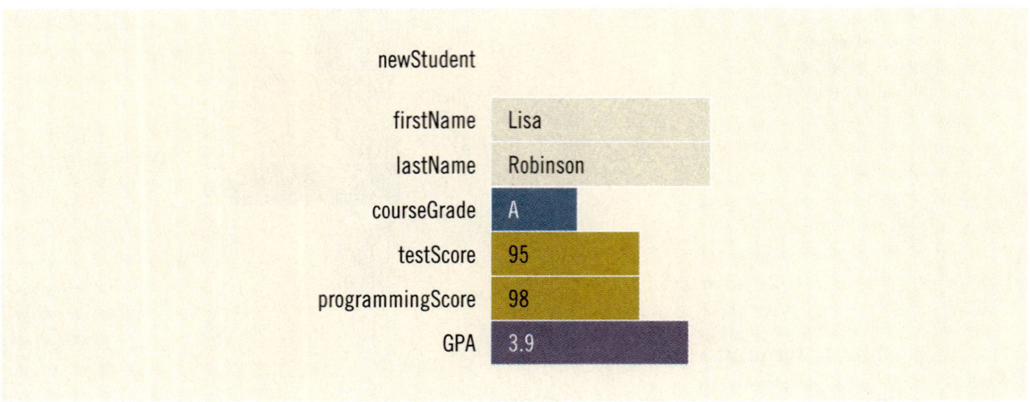

FIGURE 10-3 **struct** newStudent

The statement:

```
student = newStudent;
```

copies the contents of newStudent into student. After this assignment statement executes, the values of student are as shown in Figure 10-4.

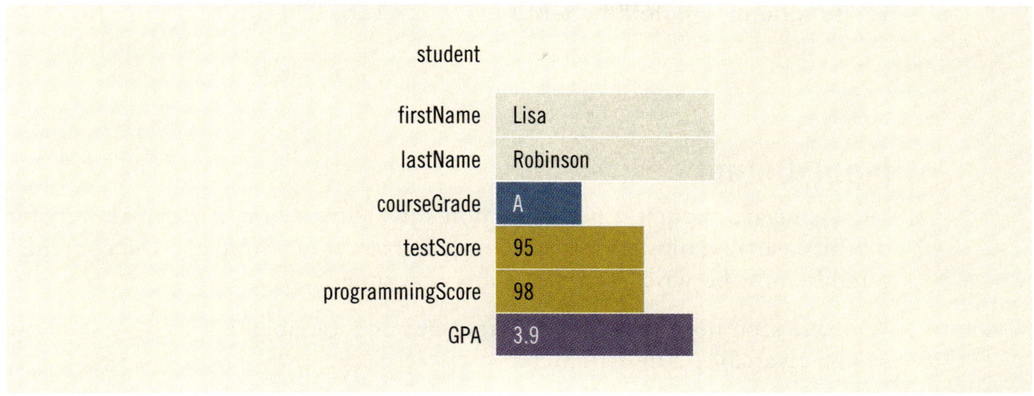

FIGURE 10-4 student after student = newStudent

In fact, the assignment statement:

```
student = newStudent;
```

is equivalent to the following statements:

```
student.firstName = newStudent.firstName;
student.lastName = newStudent.lastName;
student.courseGrade = newStudent.courseGrade;
student.testScore = newStudent.testScore;
student.programmingScore = newStudent.programmingScore;
student.GPA = newStudent.GPA;
```

Comparison (Relational Operators)

To compare **struct** variables, you compare them member-wise. As with an array, no aggregate relational operations are performed on a **struct**. For example, suppose that newStudent and student are declared as shown earlier. Furthermore, suppose that you want to see whether student and newStudent refer to the same student. Now newStudent and student refer to the same student if they have the same first name and the same last name. To compare the values of student and newStudent, you must compare them member-wise, as follows:

```
if (student.firstName == newStudent.firstName &&
    student.lastName == newStudent.lastName)
```

.
.
.

Although you can use an assignment statement to copy the contents of one **struct** into another **struct** of the same type, you cannot use relational operators on **struct** variables. Therefore, the following would be illegal:

```cpp
if (student == newStudent)      //illegal
   .
   .
   .
```

Input/Output

No aggregate input/output operations are allowed on a **struct** variable. Data in a **struct** variable must be read one member at a time. Similarly, the contents of a **struct** variable must be written one member at a time.

We have seen how to read data into a **struct** variable. Let us now see how to output a **struct** variable. The statement:

```cpp
cout << newStudent.firstName << " " << newStudent.lastName
     << " " << newStudent.courseGrade
     << " " << newStudent.testScore
     << " " << newStudent.programmingScore
     << " " << newStudent.GPA << endl;
```

outputs the contents of the **struct** variable newStudent.

struct Variables and Functions

Recall that arrays are passed by reference only, and a function cannot return a value of type `array`. However,

- A **struct** variable can be passed as a parameter either by value or by reference, and
- A function can return a value of type **struct**.

The following function reads and stores a student's first name, last name, test score, programming score, and GPA. It also determines the student's course grade and stores it in the member courseGrade.

```cpp
void readIn(studentType& student)
{
    int score;

    cin >> student.firstName >> student.lastName;
    cin >> student.testScore >> student.programmingScore;
    cin >> student.GPA;

    score = (newStudent.testScore + newStudent.programmingScore) / 2;

    if (score >= 90)
        student.courseGrade = 'A';
```

```
    else if (score >= 80)
        student.courseGrade = 'B';
    else if (score >= 70)
        student.courseGrade = 'C';
    else if (score >= 60)
        student.courseGrade = 'D';
    else
        student.courseGrade = 'F';
}
```

The statement:

```
readIn(newStudent);
```

calls the function `readIn`. The function `readIn` stores the appropriate information in the variable `newStudent`.

Similarly, we can write a function that will print the contents of a **struct** variable. For example, the following function outputs the contents of a **struct** variable of type `studentType` on the screen:

```
void printStudent(studentType student)
{
    cout << student.firstName << " " << student.lastName
         << " " << student.courseGrade
         << " " << student.testScore
         << " " << student.programmingScore
         << " " << student.GPA << endl;
}
```

Arrays versus structs

The previous discussion shows us that a **struct** and an array have similarities as well as differences. Table 10-1 summarizes this discussion.

TABLE 10-1 Arrays vs. **struct**s

Aggregate Operation	Array	struct
Arithmetic	No	No
Assignment	No	Yes
Input/output	No (except strings)	No
Comparison	No	No
Parameter passing	By reference only	By value or by reference
Function returning a value	No	Yes

Arrays in structs

A list is a set of elements of the same type. Thus, a list has two things associated with it: the values (that is, elements), and the length. Because the values and the length are both related to a list, we can define a **struct** containing both items.

```
const int ARRAY_SIZE = 1000;

struct listType
{
    int listElem[ARRAY_SIZE];      //array containing the list
    int listLength;                //length of the list
};
```

The following statement declares `intList` to be a **struct** variable of type `listType` (see Figure 10-5):

```
listType intList;
```

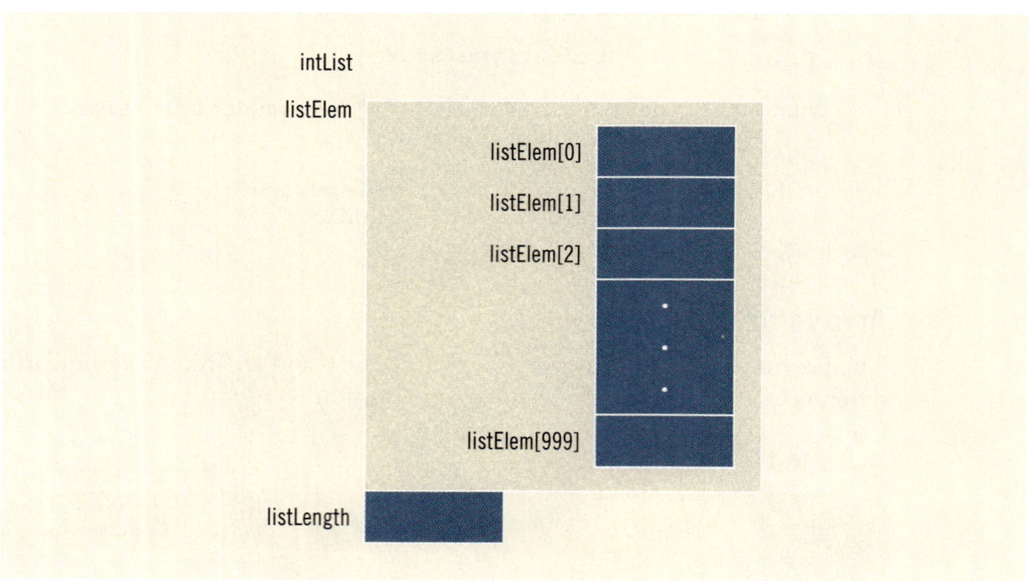

FIGURE 10-5 **struct** variable `intList`

The variable `intList` has two members: `listElem`, an array of 1000 components of type **int**; and `listLength`, of type **int**. Moreover, `intList.listElem` accesses the member `listElem` and `intList.listLength` accesses the member `listLength`.

Consider the following statements:

```
intList.listLength = 0;          //Line 1
intList.listElem[0] = 12;        //Line 2
intList.listLength++;            //Line 3
```

```
intList.listElem[1] = 37;        //Line 4
intList.listLength++;            //Line 5
```

The statement in Line 1 sets the value of the member `listLength` to 0. The statement in Line 2 stores 12 in the first component of the array `listElem`. The statement in Line 3 increments the value of `listLength` by 1. The meaning of the other statements is similar. After these statements execute, `intList` is as shown in Figure 10-6.

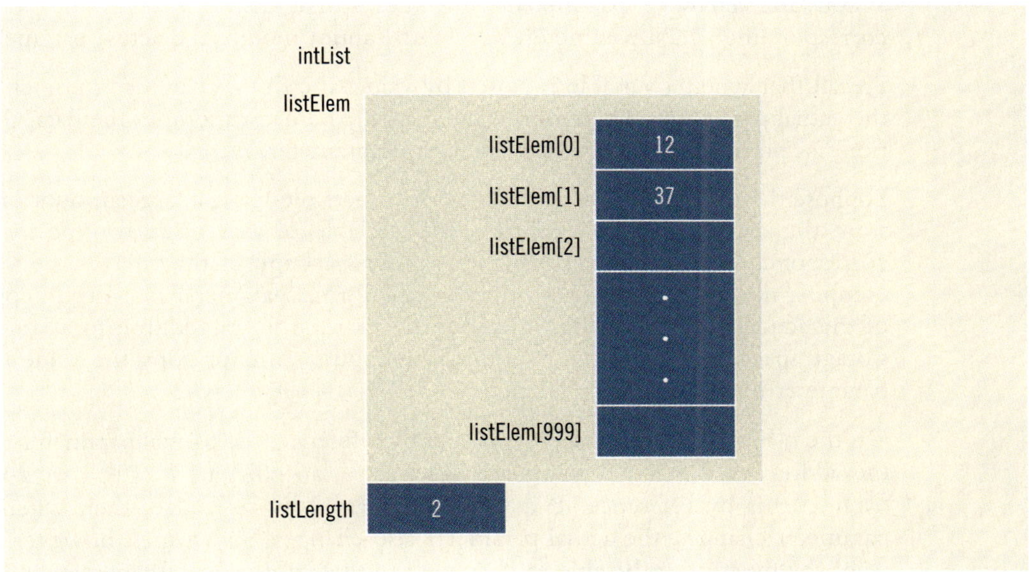

FIGURE 10-6 `intList` after the statements in Lines 1 through 5 execute

Next, we write the sequential search algorithm to determine whether a given item is in the list. If `searchItem` is found in the list, then the function returns its location in the list; otherwise, the function returns –1.

```cpp
int seqSearch(const listType& list, int searchItem)
{
    int loc;

    bool found = false;

    for (loc = 0; loc < list.listLength; loc++)
        if (list.listElem[loc] == searchItem)
        {
            found = true;
            break;
        }

    if (found)
        return loc;
```

```
    else
        return -1;
}
```

In this function, because `listLength` is a member of `list`, we access this by `list.listLength`. Similarly, we can access an element of `list` via `list.listElem[loc]`.

Notice that the formal parameter `list` of the function `seqSearch` is declared as a constant reference parameter. This means that `list` receives the address of the corresponding actual parameter, but `list` cannot modify the actual parameter.

Recall that when a variable is passed by value, the formal parameter copies the value of the actual parameter. Therefore, if the formal parameter modifies the data, the modification has no effect on the data of the actual parameter.

Suppose that a **struct** has several data members requiring a large amount of memory to store the data, and you need to pass a variable of that **struct** type by value. The corresponding formal parameter then receives a copy of the data of the variable. The compiler must then allocate memory for the formal parameter in order to copy the value of the actual parameter. This operation might require, in addition to a large amount of storage space, a considerable amount of computer time to copy the value of the actual parameter into the formal parameter.

On the other hand, if a variable is passed by reference, the formal parameter receives only the address of the actual parameter. Therefore, an efficient way to pass a variable as a parameter is by reference. If a variable is passed by reference, then when the formal parameter changes, the actual parameter also changes. Sometimes, however, you do not want the function to be able to change the values of the actual parameter. In C++, you can pass a variable by reference and still prevent the function from changing its value. This is done by using the keyword **const** in the formal parameter declaration, as shown in the definition of the function `seqSearch`.

Likewise, we can also rewrite the sorting, binary search, and other list-processing functions.

structs in Arrays

Suppose a company has 50 full-time employees. We need to print their monthly paychecks and keep track of how much money has been paid to each employee in the year-to-date. First, let's define an employee's record:

```
struct employeeType
{
    string firstName;
    string lastName;
    int    personID;
    string deptID;
    double yearlySalary;
```

```
    double monthlySalary
    double yearToDatePaid;
    double monthlyBonus;
};
```

Each employee has the following members (components): first name, last name, personal ID, department ID, yearly salary, monthly salary, year-to-date paid, and monthly bonus.

Because we have 50 employees, and the data type of each employee is the same, we can use an array of 50 components to process the employees' data.

```
employeeType employees[50];
```

This statement declares an array `employees` of 50 components of type `employeeType` (see Figure 10-7). Every element of `employees` is a **struct** . For example, Figure 10-7 also shows `employees[2]`.

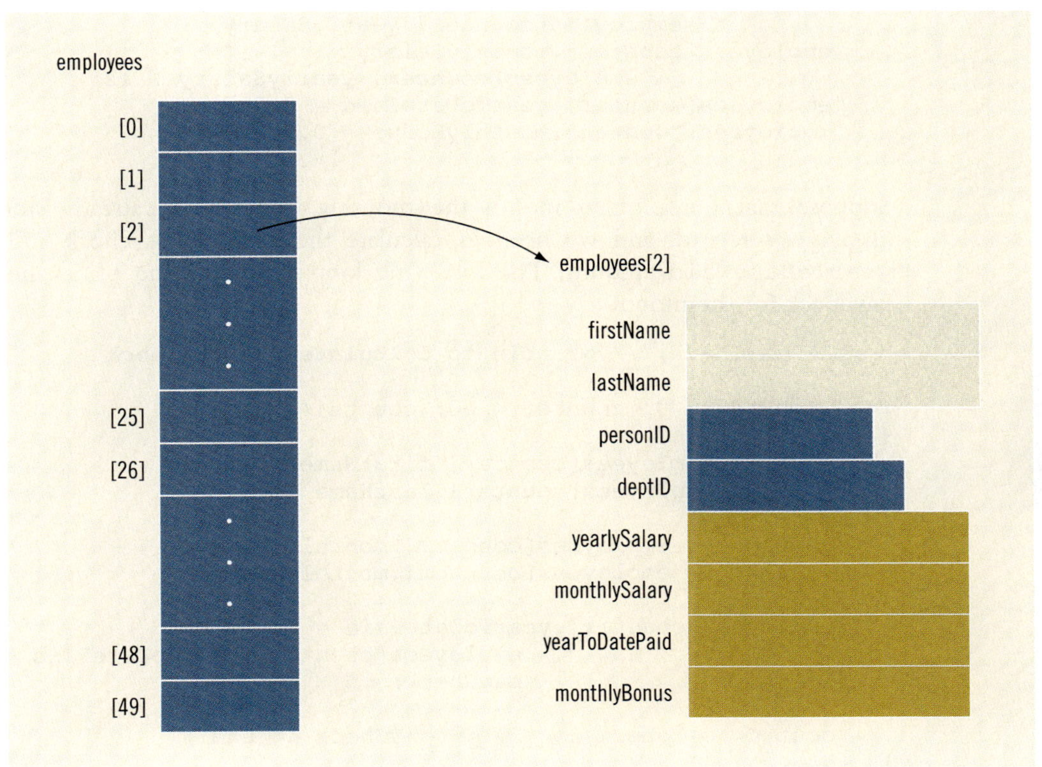

FIGURE 10-7 Array of `employees`

Suppose we also have the following declaration:

```
int   counter;
```

Further suppose that every employee's initial data—first name, last name, personal ID, department ID, and yearly salary—are provided in a file. For our discussion, we assume that each employee's data is stored in a file, say, employee.dat. The following C++ code loads the data into the employees' array. We assume that, initially, yearToDatePaid is 0 and that the monthly bonus is determined each month based on performance:

```
ifstream infile; //input stream variable
                 //assume that the file employee.dat has been opened
for (counter = 0; counter < 50; counter++)
{
    infile >> employees[counter].firstName
           >> employees[counter].lastName
           >> employees[counter].personID
           >> employees[counter].deptID
           >> employees[counter].yearlySalary;
    employees[counter].monthlySalary =
                employees[counter].yearlySalary / 12;
    employees[counter].yearToDatePaid = 0.0;
    employees[counter].monthlyBonus = 0.0;
}
```

Suppose that for a given month the monthly bonuses are already stored in each employee's record, and we need to calculate the monthly paycheck and update the yearToDatePaid amount. The following loop computes and prints the employee's paycheck for the month:

```
double payCheck; //variable to calculate the paycheck

for (counter = 0; counter < 50; counter++)
{
    cout << employees[counter].firstName << " "
         << employees[counter].lastName << " ";

    payCheck = employees[counter].monthlySalary +
                employees[counter].monthlyBonus;

    employees[counter].yearToDatePaid =
                        employees[counter].yearToDatePaid +
                        payCheck;

    cout << setprecision(2) << payCheck << endl;
}
```

structs within a struct

You have seen how the struct and array data structures can be combined to organize information. You also saw examples wherein a member of a struct is an array, and the array type is a struct. In this section, you will learn about situations where it is beneficial to organize data in a struct by using another struct.

Let us consider the following employee record:

```
struct   employeeType
{
    string firstname;
    string middlename;
    string lastname;
    string empID;
    string address1;
    string address2;
    string city;
    string state;
    string zip;
    int hiremonth;
    int hireday;
    int hireyear;
    int quitmonth;
    int quitday;
    int quityear;
    string phone;
    string cellphone;
    string fax;
    string pager;
    string email;
    string deptID;
    double salary;
};
```

As you can see, a lot of information is packed into one struct. This struct has 22 members. Some members of this struct will be accessed more frequently than others, and some members are more closely related than others. Moreover, some members will have the same underlying structure. For example, the hire date and the quit date are of the date type int. Let us reorganize this struct as follows:

```
struct nameType
{
    string first;
    string middle;
    string last;
};
```

```
struct addressType
{
    string address1;
    string address2;
    string city;
    string state;
    string zip;
};

struct dateType
{
    int month;
    int day;
    int year;
};

struct contactType
{
    string phone;
    string cellphone;
    string fax;
    string pager;
    string email;
};
```

We have separated the employee's name, address, and contact type into subcategories. Furthermore, we have defined a **struct** dateType. Let us rebuild the employee's record as follows:

```
struct employeeType
{
    nameType name;
    string empID;
    addressType address;
    dateType hireDate;
    dateType quitDate;
    contactType contact;
    string deptID;
    double salary;
};
```

The information in this employee's **struct** is easier to manage than the previous one. Some of this **struct** can be reused to build another **struct**. For example, suppose that you want to define a customer's record. Every customer has a first name, last name, and middle name, as well as an address and a way to be contacted. You can, therefore, quickly put together a customer's record by using the **struct**s nameType, addressType, contactType, and the members specific to the customer.

Next, let us declare a variable of type `employeeType` and discuss how to access its members.

Consider the following statement:

```
employeeType newEmployee;
```

This statement declares `newEmployee` to be a **struct** variable of type `employeeType` (see Figure 10-8).

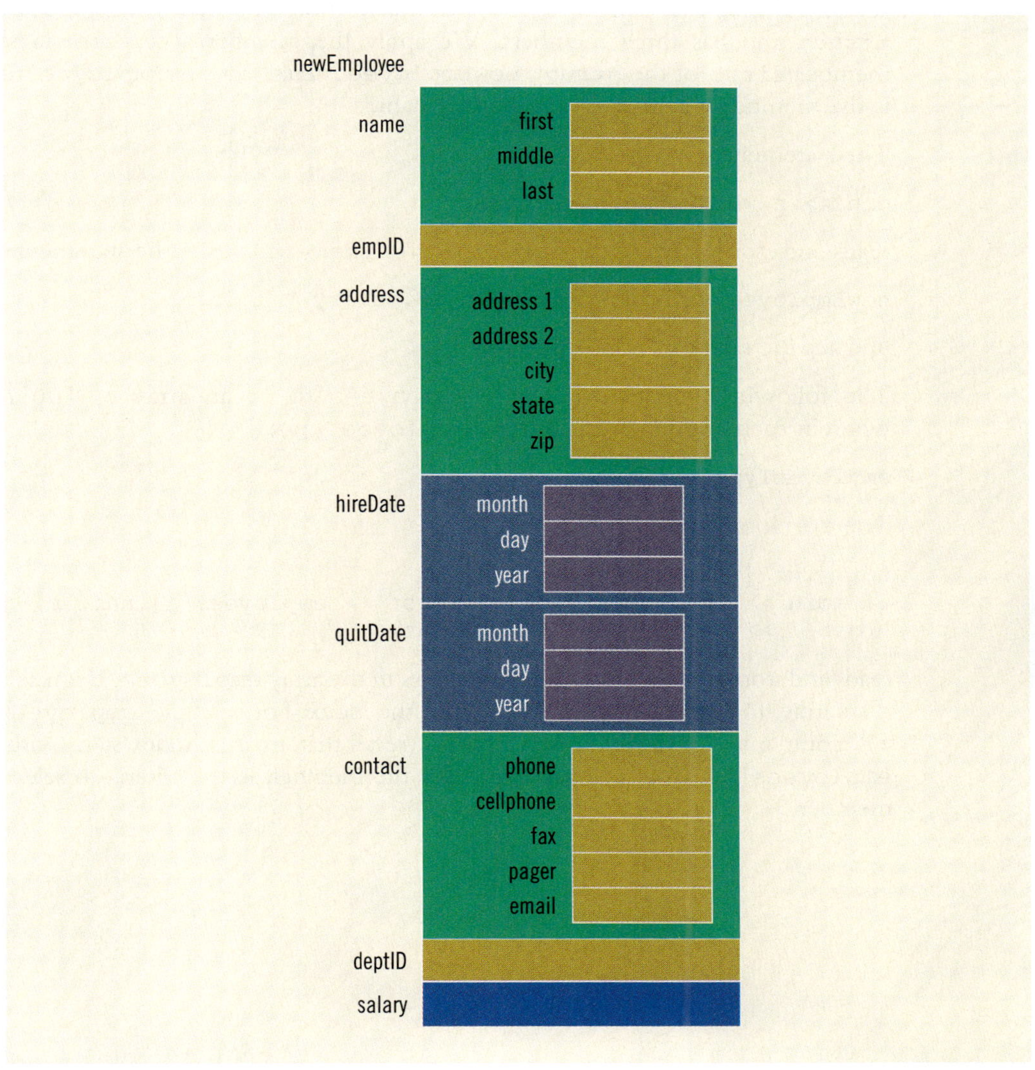

FIGURE 10-8 `struct` variable `newEmployee`

The statement:

```
newEmployee.salary = 45678.00;
```

sets the salary of newEmployee to 45678.00. The statements:

```
newEmployee.name.first = "Mary";
newEmployee.name.middle = "Beth";
newEmployee.name.last = "Simmons";
```

set the first, middle, and last name of newEmployee to "Mary", "Beth", and "Simmons", respectively. Note that newEmployee has a member called name. We access this member via newEmployee.name. Note also that newEmployee.name is a struct and has three members. We apply the member access criteria to access the member first of the struct newEmployee.name. So newEmployee.name.first is the member where we store the first name.

The statement:

```
cin >> newEmployee.name.first;
```

reads and stores a string into newEmployee.name.first. The statement:

```
newEmployee.salary = newEmployee.salary * 1.05;
```

updates the salary of newEmployee.

The following statement declares employees to be an array of 100 components, wherein each component is of type employeeType:

```
employeeType employees[100];
```

The for loop:

```
for (int j = 0; j < 100; j++)
    cin >> employees[j].name.first >> employees[j].name.middle
        >> employees[j].name.last;
```

reads and stores the names of 100 employees in the array employees. Because employees is an array, to access a component, we use the index. For example, employees[50] is the 51st component of the array employees (recall that an array index starts with 0). Because employees[50] is a struct, we apply the member access criteria to select a particular member.

PROGRAMMING EXAMPLE: Sales Data Analysis

A company has six salespeople. Every month they go on road trips to sell the company's product. At the end of each month, the total sales for each salesperson, together with that salesperson's ID and the month, is recorded in a file. At the end of each year, the manager of the company wants to see this report in this following tabular format:

```
-----------    Annual Sales Report  -----------

   ID          QT1          QT2          QT3          QT4          Total

   12345      1892.00         0.00       494.00       322.00       2708.00
   32214       343.00       892.00      9023.00         0.00      10258.00
   23422      1395.00      1901.00         0.00         0.00       3296.00
   57373       893.00       892.00      8834.00         0.00      10619.00
   35864      2882.00      1221.00         0.00      1223.00       5326.00
   54654       893.00         0.00       392.00      3420.00       4705.00
   Total      8298.00      4906.00     18743.00      4965.00


Max Sale by SalesPerson: ID = 57373, Amount = $10619.00
Max Sale by Quarter: Quarter = 3, Amount = $18743.00
```

In this report, QT1 stands for quarter 1 (months 1 to 3), QT2 for quarter 2 (months 4 to 6), QT3 for quarter 3 (months 7 to 9), and QT4 for quarter 4 (months 10 to 12).

The salespeople's IDs are stored in one file; the sales data is stored in another file. The sales data is in the following form:

```
salesPersonID   month   saleAmount
.
.
.
```

Furthermore, the sales data is in no particular order; it is not ordered by ID.

A sample sales data is:

```
12345 1 893
32214 1 343
23422 3 903
57373 2 893
.
.
.
```

10

Let us write a program that produces the output in the specified format.

Input   One file containing each salesperson's ID, and a second file containing the sales data.

Output   A file containing the annual sales report in the above format.

PROBLEM
ANALYSIS
AND
ALGORITHM
DESIGN

Based on the problem's requirements, it is clear that the main components for each salesperson are the salesperson's ID, quarterly sales amount, and total annual sales amount. Because the components are of different types, we can group them with the help of a `struct`, defined as follows:

```cpp
struct salesPersonRec
{
    string ID;          //salesperson's ID
    double saleByQuarter[4];    //array to store the total
                                //sales for each quarter
    double totalSale;   //salesperson's yearly sales amount
};
```

Because there are six salespeople, we use an array of 6 components, wherein each component is of type `salesPersonRec`, defined as follows:

```cpp
salesPersonRec salesPersonList[noOfSalesPersons];
```

where the value of `noOfSalesPersons` is 6.

Because the program requires us to find the company's total sales for each quarter, we need an array of four components to store the data. Note that this data will be used to determine the quarter in which the maximum sales were made. Therefore, the program also needs the following array:

```cpp
double totalSaleByQuarter[4];
```

Recall that in C++, the array index starts with 0. Therefore, `totalSaleByQuarter[0]` stores data for quarter 1, `totalSaleByQuarter[1]` stores data for quarter 2, and so on.

We will refer to these variables throughout the discussion.

The array `salesPersonList` is as shown in Figure 10-9.

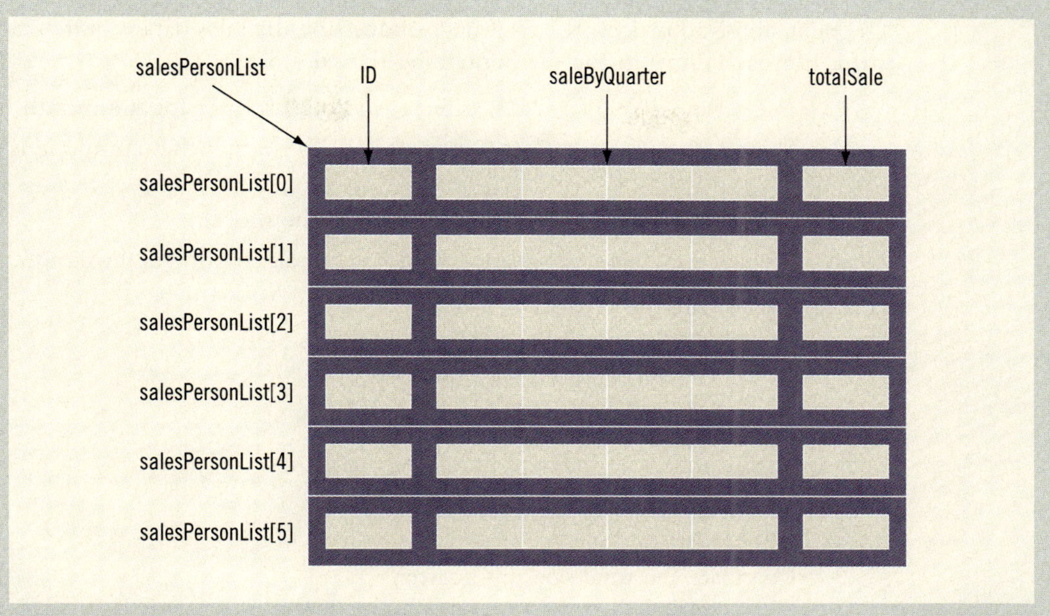

FIGURE 10-9 Array `salesPersonList`

The first step of the program is to read the salespeople's IDs into the array `salesPersonList` and initialize the quarterly sales and total sales for each salesperson to 0. After this step, the array `salesPersonList` is as shown in Figure 10-10.

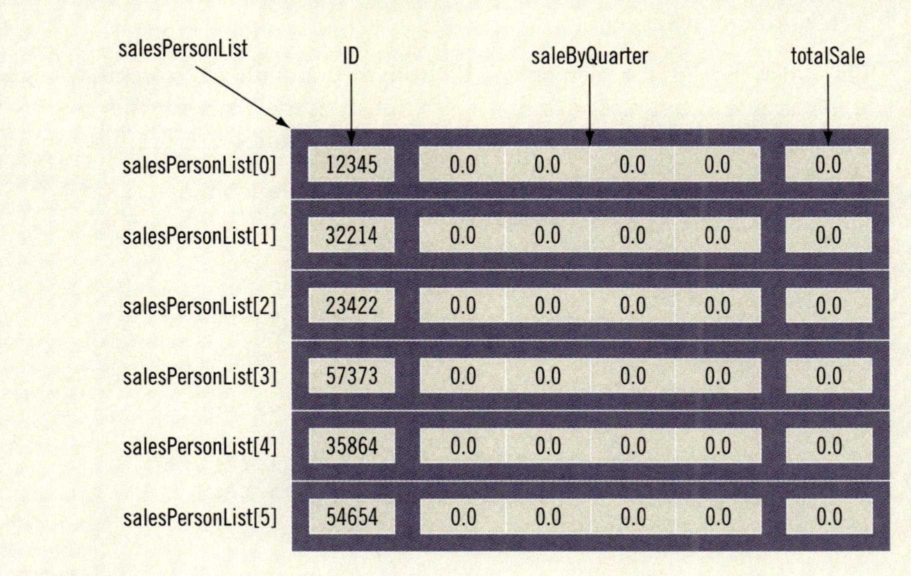

FIGURE 10-10 Array `salesPersonList` after initialization

The next step is to process the sales data. Processing the sales data is quite straightforward. For each entry in the file containing the sales data,

1. Read the salesperson's ID, month, and sale amount for the month.

2. Search the array salesPersonList to locate the component corresponding to this salesperson.

3. Determine the quarter corresponding to the month.

4. Update the sales for the quarter by adding the sale amount for the month.

Once the sales data file is processed,

a. Calculate the total sales by salesperson.

b. Calculate the total sales by quarter.

c. Print the report.

This discussion translates into the following algorithm:

1. Initialize the array salesPersonList.

2. Process the sales data.

3. Calculate the total sales by quarter.

4. Calculate the total sales by salesperson.

5. Print the report.

6. Calculate and print the maximum sales by salesperson.

7. Calculate and print the maximum sales by quarter.

To reduce the complexity of the main program, let us write a separate function for each of these seven steps.

Function initialize This function reads the salesperson's ID from the input file and stores the salesperson's ID in the array salesPersonList. It also initializes the quarterly sales amount and the total sales amount for each salesperson to 0. The definition of this function is:

```cpp
void initialize(ifstream& indata, salesPersonRec list[],
                int listSize)
{
    int index;
    int quarter;

    for (index = 0; index < listSize; index++)
    {
        indata >> list[index].ID; //get salesperson's ID

        for (quarter = 0; quarter < 4; quarter++)
            list[index].saleByQuarter[quarter] = 0.0;

        list[index].totalSale = 0.0;
    }
} //end initialize
```

Function getData This function reads the sales data from the input file and stores the appropriate information in the array **salesPersonList**. The algorithm for this function is:

1. Read the salesperson's ID, month, and sales amount for the month.
2. Search the array **salesPersonList** to locate the component corresponding to the salesperson. (Because the salespeople's IDs are not sorted, we will use a sequential search to search the array.)
3. Determine the quarter corresponding to the month.
4. Update the sales for the quarter by adding the sales amount for the month.

Suppose that the entry read is:

```
57373 2 350
```

Here the salesperson's ID is 57373, the month is 2, and the sale amount is 350. Suppose that the array **salesPersonList** is as shown in Figure 10-11.

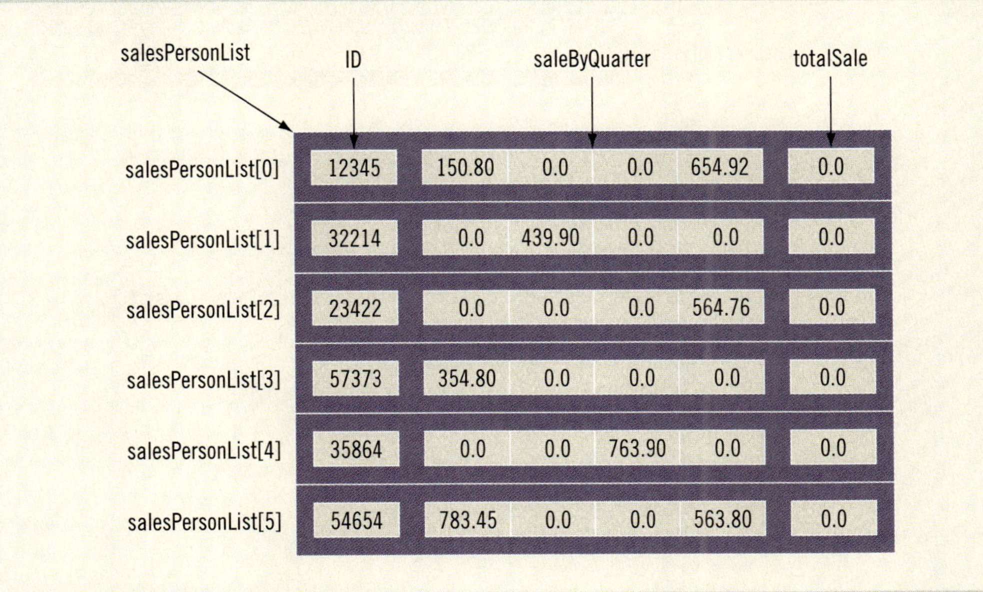

FIGURE 10-11 Array salesPersonList

Now ID 57373 corresponds to the array component **salesPersonList[3]**, and month 2 corresponds to quarter 1. Therefore, you add 350 to 354.80 to get the new amount, **704.80**. After processing this entry, the array **salesPersonList** is as shown in Figure 10-12.

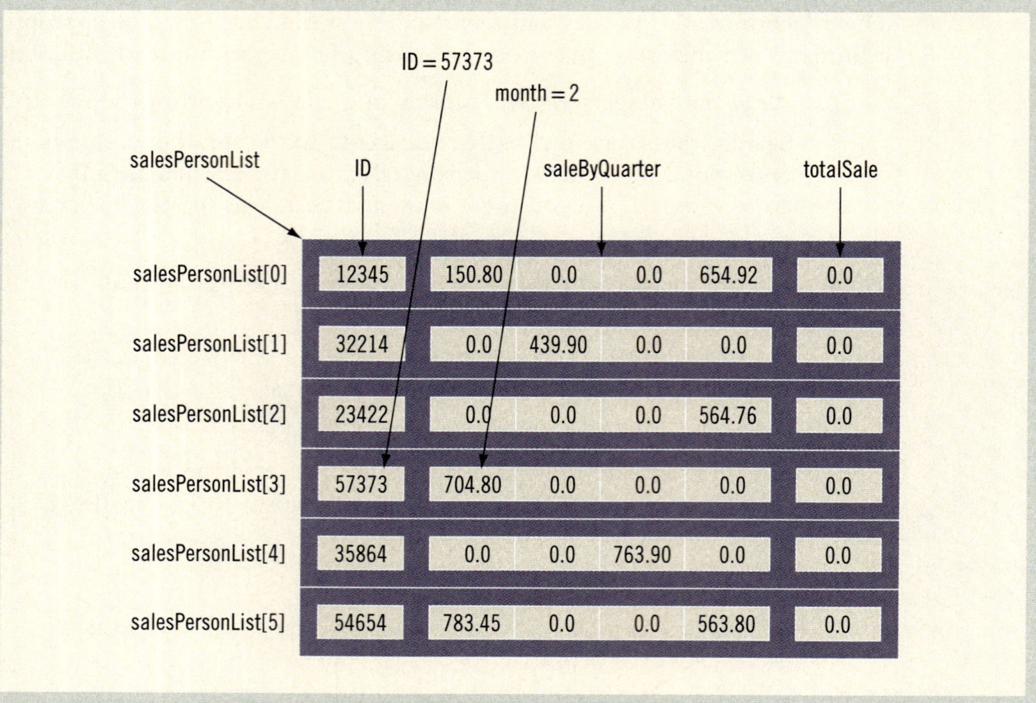

FIGURE 10-12 Array `salesPersonList` after processing entry 57373 2 350

The definition of the function `getData` is:

```cpp
void getData(ifstream& infile, salesPersonRec list[],
             int listSize)
{
    int index;
    int quarter;
    string sID;
    int month;
    double amount;

    infile >> sID;          //get salesperson's ID

    while (infile)
    {
        infile >> month >> amount;   //get the sale month and
                                     //the sale amount

        for (index = 0; index < listSize; index++)
            if (sID == list[index].ID)
                break;
```

```
        if (1 <= month && month <= 3)
            quarter = 0;
        else if (4 <= month && month <= 6)
            quarter = 1;
        else if (7 <= month && month <= 9)
            quarter = 2;
        else
            quarter = 3;

        if (index < listSize)
            list[index].saleByQuarter[quarter] += amount;
        else
            cout << "Invalid salesperson's ID." << endl;

        infile >> sID;
    } //end while
} //end getData
```

Function
saleByQuarter

This function finds the company's total sales for each quarter. To find the total sales for each quarter, we add the sales amount of each salesperson for that quarter. Clearly, this function must have access to the array `salesPersonList` and the array `totalSaleByQuarter`. This function also needs to know the number of rows in each array. Thus, this function has three parameters. The definition of this function is:

```
void saleByQuarter(salesPersonRec list[], int listSize,
                   double totalByQuarter[])
{
    int quarter;
    int index;

    for (quarter = 0; quarter < 4; quarter++)
        totalByQuarter[quarter] = 0.0;

    for (quarter = 0; quarter < 4; quarter++)
        for (index = 0; index < listSize; index++)
            totalByQuarter[quarter] +=
                        list[index].saleByQuarter[quarter];
} //end saleByQuarter
```

Function
totalSaleByPerson

This function finds each salesperson's yearly sales amount. To find an employee's yearly sales amount, we add that employee's sales amount for the four quarters. Clearly, this function must have access to the array `salesPersonList`. This function also needs to know the size of the array. Thus, this function has two parameters.

The definition of this function is:

```
void totalSaleByPerson(salesPersonRec list[], int listSize)
{
    int index;
    int quarter;
```

```
        for (index = 0; index < listSize; index++)
            for (quarter = 0; quarter < 4; quarter++)
                list[index].totalSale +=
                            list[index].saleByQuarter[quarter];
} //end totalSaleByPerson
```

Function printReport This function prints the annual report in the specified format. The algorithm in pseudocode is:

    a.   Print the heading—that is, the first three lines of output.

    b.   Print the data for each salesperson.

    c.   Print the last line of the table.

Note that the next two functions will produce the final two lines of output.

Clearly, the `printReport` function must have access to the array `salesPersonList` and the array `totalSaleByQuarter`. Also, because the output will be stored in a file, this function must have access to the `ofstream` variable associated with the output file. Thus, this function has four parameters: a parameter corresponding to the array `salesPersonList`, a parameter corresponding to the array `totalSaleByQuarter`, a parameter specifying the size of the array, and a parameter corresponding to the `ofstream` variable. The definition of this function is:

```
void printReport(ofstream& outfile, salesPersonRec list[],
                 int listSize, double saleByQuarter[])
{
    int index;
    int quarter;

    outfile << "----------- Annual Sales Report ----------"
            << "----" << endl;
    outfile << endl;
    outfile << "   ID            QT1           QT2          QT3          "
            << "QT4         Total" << endl;
    outfile << "____________________________________________________"
            << "__________________" << endl;

    for (index = 0; index < listSize; index++)
    {
        outfile << list[index].ID << "    ";

        for (quarter = 0; quarter < 4; quarter++)
            outfile << setw(10)
                    << list[index].saleByQuarter[quarter];

        outfile << setw(10) << list[index].totalSale << endl;
    }

    outfile << "Total    ";
```

```
        for (quarter = 0; quarter < 4; quarter++)
            outfile << setw(10)<< saleByQuarter[quarter];

        outfile << endl << endl;
} //end printReport
```

Function maxSaleByPerson

This function prints the name of the salesperson who produces the maximum sales amount. To identify this salesperson, we look at the sales total for each salesperson and find the largest sales amount. Because each employee's sales total is maintained in the array `salesPersonList`, this function must have access to the array `salesPersonList`. Also, because the output will be stored in a file, this function must have access to the `ofstream` variable associated with the output file. Therefore, this function has three parameters: a parameter corresponding to the array `salesPersonList`, a parameter specifying the size of this array, and a parameter corresponding to the output file.

The algorithm to find the largest sales amount is similar to the algorithm to find the largest element in an array (discussed in Chapter 9). The definition of this function is:

```
void maxSaleByPerson(ofstream& outData, salesPersonRec list[],
                     int listSize)
{
    int maxIndex = 0;
    int index;

    for (index = 1; index <listSize; index++)
        if (list[maxIndex].totalSale <list[index].totalSale)
            maxIndex = index;

    outData << "Max Sale by SalesPerson: ID = "
            << list[maxIndex].ID
            << ", Amount = $" << list[maxIndex].totalSale
            << endl;
} //end maxSaleByPerson
```

Function maxSaleByQuarter

This function prints the quarter in which the maximum sales were made. To identify this quarter, we look at the total sales for each quarter and find the largest sales amount. Because the sales total for each quarter is in the array `totalSaleByQuarter`, this function must have access to the array `totalSaleByQuarter`. Also, because the output will be stored in a file, this function must have access to the `ofstream` variable associated with the output file. Therefore, this function has two parameters: a parameter corresponding to the array `totalSaleByQuarter`, and a parameter corresponding to the output file.

The algorithm to find the largest sales amount is the same as the algorithm to find the largest element in an array (discussed in Chapter 9). The definition of this function is:

```
void maxSaleByQuarter(ofstream& outData,
                      double saleByQuarter[])
```

```cpp
{
    int quarter;
    int maxIndex = 0;

    for (quarter = 0; quarter < 4; quarter++)
        if (saleByQuarter[maxIndex] < saleByQuarter[quarter])
            maxIndex = quarter;

    outData << "Max Sale by Quarter: Quarter = "
            << maxIndex + 1
            << ", Amount = $" << saleByQuarter[maxIndex]
            << endl;
} //end maxSaleByQuarter
```

To make the program more flexible, we will prompt the user to specify the input and output files during its execution.

We are now ready to write the algorithm for the function main.

Main
Algorithm

1. Declare the variables.

2. Prompt the user to enter the name of the file containing the salesperson's ID data.

3. Read the name of the input file.

4. Open the input file.

5. If the input file does not exist, exit the program.

6. Initialize the array `salesPersonList`. Call the function `initialize`.

7. Close the input file containing the salesperson's ID data and clear the input stream.

8. Prompt the user to enter the name of the file containing the sales data.

9. Read the name of the input file.

10. Open the input file.

11. If the input file does not exist, exit the program.

12. Prompt the user to enter the name of the output file.

13. Read the name of the output file.

14. Open the output file.

15. To output floating-point numbers in a fixed decimal format with the decimal point and trailing zeroes, set the manipulators `fixed` and `showpoint`. Also, to output floating-point numbers to two decimal places, set the precision to two decimal places.

16. Process the sales data. Call the function `getData`.

17. Calculate the total sales by quarter. Call the function `saleByQuarter`.

18. Calculate the total sales for each salesperson. Call the function `totalSaleByPerson`.

19. Print the report in a tabular format. Call the function `printReport`.

20. Find and print the salesperson who produces the maximum sales for the year. Call the function `maxSaleByPerson`.

21. Find and print the quarter that produces the maximum sales for the year. Call the function `maxSaleByQuarter`.

22. Close the files.

PROGRAM LISTING

```cpp
//Program: Sales data analysis
#include <iostream>
#include <fstream>
#include <iomanip>
#include <string>

using namespace std;

const int NO_OF_SALES_PERSON = 6;

struct salesPersonRec
{
    string ID;          //salesperson's ID
    double saleByQuarter[ 4] ;   //array to store the total
                                 //sales for each quarter
    double totalSale;    //salesperson's yearly sales amount
};

void initialize(ifstream& indata, salesPersonRec list[],
              int listSize);
void getData(ifstream& infile, salesPersonRec list[],
              int listSize);
void saleByQuarter(salesPersonRec list[], int listSize,
                  double totalByQuarter[]);
void totalSaleByPerson(salesPersonRec list[], int  listSize);
void printReport(ofstream& outfile, salesPersonRec list[],
                 int listSize, double saleByQuarter[]);
void maxSaleByPerson(ofstream& outData, salesPersonRec list[],
                    int listSize);
void maxSaleByQuarter(ofstream& outData, double saleByQuarter[]);
```

```cpp
int main()
{
        //Step 1
    ifstream infile;      //input file stream variable
    ofstream outfile;     //output file stream variable

    string inputFile;     //variable to hold the input file name
    string outputFile;    //variable to hold the output file name

    double totalSaleByQuarter[4];    //array to hold the
                                     //sale by quarter

    salesPersonRec salesPersonList[NO_OF_SALES_PERSON]; //array
                               //to hold the salesperson's data

    cout << "Enter the salesPerson ID file name: "; //Step 2
    cin >> inputFile;                               //Step 3
    cout << endl;

    infile.open(inputFile.c_str());                    //Step 4

    if (!infile)                                       //Step 5
    {
        cout << "Cannot open the input file."
             << endl;
        return 1;
    }

    initialize(infile, salesPersonList,
            NO_OF_SALES_PERSON);                       //Step 6

    infile.close();                                    //Step 7
    infile.clear();                                    //Step 7

    cout << "Enter the sales data file name: ";        //Step 8
    cin >> inputFile;                                  //Step 9
    cout << endl;

    infile.open(inputFile.c_str());                    //Step 10

    if (!infile)                                       //Step 11
    {
        cout << "Cannot open the input file."
             << endl;
        return 1;
    }

    cout << "Enter the output file name: ";            //Step 12
    cin >> outputFile;                                 //Step 13
    cout << endl;
```

```cpp
    outfile.open(outputFile.c_str());                   //Step 14
    outfile << fixed << showpoint
            << setprecision(2);                         //Step 15

    getData(infile, salesPersonList,
            NO_OF_SALES_PERSON);                        //Step 16
    saleByQuarter(salesPersonList,
                  NO_OF_SALES_PERSON,
                  totalSaleByQuarter);                  //Step 17
    totalSaleByPerson(salesPersonList,
                  NO_OF_SALES_PERSON);                  //Step 18

    printReport(outfile, salesPersonList,
                NO_OF_SALES_PERSON,
                totalSaleByQuarter);                    //Step 19
    maxSaleByPerson(outfile, salesPersonList,
                    NO_OF_SALES_PERSON);                //Step 20
    maxSaleByQuarter(outfile, totalSaleByQuarter);  //Step 21

    infile.close();                                     //Step 22
    outfile.close();                                    //Step 22

    return  0;
}

void initialize(ifstream& indata, salesPersonRec list[],
                int listSize)
{
    int index;
    int quarter;

    for (index = 0; index < listSize; index++)
    {
        indata >> list[index].ID; //get salesperson's ID

        for (quarter = 0; quarter < 4; quarter++)
            list[index].saleByQuarter[quarter] = 0.0;

        list[index].totalSale = 0.0;
    }
} //end initialize

void getData(ifstream& infile, salesPersonRec list[],
             int listSize)
{
    int index;
    int quarter;
    string sID;
    int month;
    double amount;
    infile >> sID;          //get salesperson's ID
```

```cpp
    while (infile)
    {
        infile >> month >> amount;   //get the sale month and
                                     //the sale amount

        for (index = 0; index < listSize; index++)
            if (sID == list[index].ID)
                break;
        if (1 <= month && month <= 3)
            quarter = 0;
        else if (4 <= month && month <= 6)
            quarter = 1;
        else if (7 <= month && month <= 9)
            quarter = 2;
        else
            quarter = 3;

        if (index <listSize)
            list[index].saleByQuarter[quarter] += amount;
        else
            cout << "Invalid salesperson's ID." << endl;

        infile >> sID;
    } //end while
} //end getData

void saleByQuarter(salesPersonRec list[], int listSize,
                   double totalByQuarter[])
{
    int quarter;
    int index;

    for (quarter = 0; quarter < 4; quarter++)
        totalByQuarter[quarter] = 0.0;

    for (quarter = 0; quarter < 4; quarter++)
        for (index = 0; index < listSize; index++)
            totalByQuarter[quarter] +=
                    list[index].saleByQuarter[quarter];
} //end saleByQuarter

void totalSaleByPerson(salesPersonRec list[], int listSize)
{
    int index;
    int quarter;

    for (index = 0; index < listSize; index++)
        for (quarter = 0; quarter < 4; quarter++)
            list[index].totalSale +=
                    list[index].saleByQuarter[quarter];
} //end totalSaleByPerson
```

```cpp
void printReport(ofstream& outfile, salesPersonRec list[],
                 int listSize, double saleByQuarter[])
{
    int index;
    int quarter;

    outfile << "----------- Annual Sales Report ----------"
            << "----" << endl;
    outfile << endl;
    outfile << "  ID          QT1         QT2         QT3        "
            << "QT4          Total" << endl;
    outfile << "_____________________________________________"
            << "________________" << endl;

    for (index = 0; index < listSize; index++)
    {
        outfile << list[index].ID << "    ";

        for (quarter = 0; quarter < 4; quarter++)
            outfile << setw(10)
                    << list[index].saleByQuarter[quarter];

        outfile << setw(10) << list[index].totalSale << endl;
    }

    outfile << "Total    ";

    for (quarter = 0; quarter < 4; quarter++)
        outfile << setw(10) << saleByQuarter[quarter];

    outfile << endl << endl;
} //end printReport

void maxSaleByPerson(ofstream& outData, salesPersonRec list[],
                     int listSize)
{
    int maxIndex = 0;
    int index;

    for (index = 1; index < listSize; index++)
        if (list[maxIndex].totalSale < list[index].totalSale)
            maxIndex = index;

    outData << "Max Sale by SalesPerson: ID = "
            << list[maxIndex].ID
            << ", Amount = $" << list[maxIndex].totalSale
            << endl;
} //end maxSaleByPerson
```

```cpp
void maxSaleByQuarter(ofstream& outData,
                      double saleByQuarter[])
{
    int quarter;
    int maxIndex = 0;

    for (quarter = 0; quarter < 4; quarter++)
        if (saleByQuarter[maxIndex] < saleByQuarter[quarter])
            maxIndex = quarter;

    outData << "Max Sale by Quarter: Quarter = "
            << maxIndex + 1
            << ", Amount = $" << saleByQuarter[maxIndex]
            << endl;
} //end maxSaleByQuarter
```

Sample Run: In this sample run, the user input is shaded.

Enter the salesPerson ID file name: a:\Ch10_SalesManID.txt

Enter the sales data file name: a:\Ch10_SalesData.txt

Enter the output file name: a:\Ch10_SalesDataAnalysis.txt

Input File: Salespeople's IDs

```
12345
32214
23422
57373
35864
54654
```

Input File: Salespeople's Data

```
12345  1  893
32214  1  343
23422  3  903
57373  2  893
35864  5  329
54654  9  392
12345  2  999
32214  4  892
23422  4  895
23422  2  492
57373  6  892
35864  10 1223
54654  11 3420
12345  12 322
35864   5  892
```

```
54654  3 893
12345  8 494
32214  8 9023
23422  6 223
23422  4 783
57373  8 8834
35864  3 2882
```

Sample Run:

```
------------- Annual Sales Report -------------

     ID         QT1         QT2         QT3         QT4         Total

     ------------------------------------------------------------------------
     12345      1892.00        0.00      494.00      322.00      2708.00
     32214       343.00      892.00     9023.00        0.00     10258.00
     23422      1395.00     1901.00        0.00        0.00      3296.00
     57373       893.00      892.00     8834.00        0.00     10619.00
     35864      2882.00     1221.00        0.00     1223.00      5326.00
     54654       893.00        0.00      392.00     3420.00      4705.00
     Total      8298.00     4906.00    18743.00     4965.00

Max Sale by SalesPerson: ID = 57373, Amount = $10619.00
Max Sale by Quarter: Quarter = 3, Amount = $18743.00
```

QUICK REVIEW

1. A `struct` is a collection of a fixed number of components.

2. Components of a `struct` can be of different types.

3. The syntax to define a `struct` is:

```
struct structName
{
    dataType1 identifier1;
    dataType2 identifier2;
        .
        .
        .
    dataTypen identifiern;
};
```

4. In C++, `struct` is a reserved word.

5. In C++, `struct` is a definition; no memory is allocated. Memory is allocated for the `struct` variables only when you declare them.

6. Components of a `struct` are called members of the `struct`.

7. Components of a **struct** are accessed by name.

8. In C++, the dot (.) operator is called the member access operator.

9. Members of a **struct** are accessed by using the dot (.) operator. For example, if `employeeType` is a **struct**, `employee` is a variable of type `employeeType`, and `name` is a member of `employee`, then the expression `employee.name` accesses the member `name`. That is, `employee.name` is a variable and can be manipulated like other variables.

10. The only built-in operations on a **struct** are the assignment and member access operations.

11. Neither arithmetic nor relational operations are allowed on **struct**(s).

12. As a parameter to a function, a **struct** can be passed either by value or by reference.

13. A function can return a value of type **struct**.

14. A **struct** can be a member of another **struct**.

EXERCISES

1. Mark the following statements as true or false.

    a. All members of a **struct** must be of different types.

    b. A function cannot return a value of type **struct**.

    c. A member of a **struct** can be another **struct**.

    d. The only allowable operations on a **struct** are assignment and member selection.

    e. An array can be a member of a **struct**.

    f. In C++, some aggregate operations are allowed on a **struct**.

    g. Because a **struct** has a finite number of components, relational operations are allowed on a **struct**.

2. Consider the following statements:

```cpp
struct nameType
{
    string first;
    string last;
};
struct dateType
{
    int month;
    int day;
    int year;
};
```

```
struct personalInfoType
{
    nameType name;
    int pID;
    dateType dob;
};
personalInfoType person;
personalInfoType classList[100];
nameType student;
```

Mark the following statements as valid or invalid. If a statement is invalid, explain why.

a.   `person.name.first = "William";`

b.   `cout << person.name << endl;`

c.   `classList[1] = person;`

d.   `classList[20].pID = 000011100;`

e.   `person = classList[20];`

f.   `student = person.name;`

g.   `cin >> student;`

h.   `for (int j = 0; j < 100; j++)`
     `    classList[j].pID = 00000000;`

i.   `classList.dob.day = 1;`

j.   `student = name;`

3.   Consider the following statements (`nameType` is as defined in Exercise 2):

```
struct employeeType
{
    nameType name;
    int performanceRating;
    int pID;
    string dept;
    double salary;
};
employeeType employees[100];
employeeType newEmployee;
```

Mark the following statements as valid or invalid. If a statement is invalid, explain why.

a.   `newEmployee.name = "John Smith";`

b.   `cout << newEmployee.name;`

c.   `employees[35] = newEmployee;`

d.   `if (employees[45].pID == 555334444)`
     `    employees[45].performanceRating = 1;`

e.   `employees.salary = 0;`

4. Assume the declarations of Exercises 2 and 3. Write C++ statements that do the following:

    a. Store the following information in `newEmployee`:

        ```
        name: Mickey Doe
        pID:  111111111
        performanceRating: 2
        dept: ACCT
        salary: 34567.78
        ```

    b. In the array `employees`, initialize each `performanceRating` to 0.

    c. Copy the information of the 20th component of the array `employees` into `newEmployee`.

    d. Update the salary of the 50th employee in the array `employees` by adding `5735.87` to its previous value.

PROGRAMMING EXERCISES

1. Write a program that reads students' names followed by their test scores. The program should output each student's name followed by the test scores and the relevant grade. It should also find and print the highest test score and the name of the students having the highest test score.

    Student data should be stored in a **struct** variable of type `studentType`, which has four components: `studentFName` and `studentLName` of type `string`, `testScore` of type **int** (`testScore` is between 0 and 100), and `grade` of type **char**. Suppose that the class has 20 students. Use an array of 20 components of type `studentType`.

    Your program must contain at least the following functions:

    a. A function to read the students' data into the array.

    b. A function to assign the relevant grade to each student.

    c. A function to find the highest test score.

    d. A function to print the names of the students having the highest test score.

    Your program must output each student's name in this form: last name followed by a comma, followed by a space, followed by the first name, and the name must be left-justified. Moreover, other than declaring the variables and opening the input and output files, the function main should only be a collection of function calls.

2. Define a **struct**, `menuItemType`, with two components: `menuItem` of type `string`, and `menuPrice` of type **double**.

3. Write a program to help a local restaurant automate its breakfast billing system. The program should do the following:

   a. Show the customer the different breakfast items offered by the restaurant.

   b. Allow the customer to select more than one item from the menu.

   c. Calculate and print the bill.
      Assume that the restaurant offers the following breakfast items (the price of each item is shown to the right of the item):

```
Plain Egg                          $1.45
Bacon and Egg                      $2.45
Muffin                             $0.99
French Toast                       $1.99
Fruit Basket                       $2.49
Cereal                             $0.69
Coffee                             $0.50
Tea                                $0.75
```

   Use an array, menuList, of the **struct** menuItemType, as defined in Programming Exercise 2. Your program must contain at least the following functions:

   - Function getData: This function loads the data into the array menuList.

   - Function showMenu: This function shows the different items offered by the restaurant and tells the user how to select the items.

   - Function printCheck: This function calculates and prints the check. (Note that the billing amount should include a 5% tax.)
     A sample output is:

```
Welcome to Johnny's Restaurant
Bacon and Egg      $2.45
Muffin             $0.99
Coffee             $0.50
Tax                $0.20
Amount Due         $4.14
```

   Format your output with two decimal places. The name of each item in the output must be left-justified. You may assume that the user selects only one item of a particular type.

4. Redo Exercise 3 so that the customer can select multiple items of a particular type. A sample output in this case is:

```
Welcome to Johnny's Restaurant
1 Bacon and Egg      $2.45
2 Muffin             $1.98
1 Coffee             $0.50
   Tax               $0.25
   Amount Due        $5.18
```

5. Write a program whose main function is merely a collection of variable declarations and function calls. This program reads a text and outputs the letters, together with their counts, as explained below in the function printResult. (There can be no global variables! All information must be passed in and out of the functions. Use a structure to store the information.) Your program must consist of at least the following functions:

- Function openFile: Opens the input and output files. You must pass the file streams as parameters (by reference, of course). If the file does not exist, the program should print an appropriate message and exit. The program must ask the user for the names of the input and output files.

- Function count: Counts every occurrence of capital letters A-Z and small letters a-z in the text file opened in the function openFile. This information must go into an array of structures. The array must be passed as a parameter, and the file identifier must also be passed as a parameter.

- Function printResult: Prints the number of capital letters and small letters, as well as the percentage of capital letters for every letter A-Z and the percentage of small letters for every letter a-z. The percentages should look like this: "25%". This information must come from an array of structures, and this array must be passed as a parameter.

CLASSES AND DATA ABSTRACTION

- Learn about classes
- Learn about `private`, `protected`, and `public` members of a class
- Explore how classes are implemented
- Examine constructors and destructors
- Learn about the abstract data type (ADT)
- Explore how classes are used to implement ADTs
- Learn about information hiding
- Explore how information hiding is implemented in C++
- Learn about the `static` members of a class

In Chapter 10, you learned how to group data items that are of different types by using a `struct`. The definition of a `struct` given in Chapter 10 is similar to the definition of a C-`struct`. However, the members of a C++ `struct` can be data items as well as functions. C++ provides another structured data type, called a **class**, which is specifically designed to group data and functions. This chapter first introduces classes and explains how to use them, and then discusses the similarities and differences between a `struct` and a `class`.

NOTE Chapter 10 is not a prerequisite for this chapter. In fact, a `struct` and a `class` have similar capabilities, as discussed in the section "A `struct` versus a `class`" in this chapter.

Classes

Chapter 1 introduced the problem-solving methodology called **object-oriented design (OOD)**. In OOD, the first step is to identify the components, called **objects**. An object combines data and the operations on that data in a single unit. In C++, the mechanism that allows you to combine data and the operations on that data in a single unit is called a class. Now that you know how to store and manipulate data in computer memory and how to construct your own functions, you are ready to learn how objects are constructed. This and subsequent chapters develop and implement programs using OOD. This chapter first explains how to define a class and use it in a program.

A **class** is a collection of a fixed number of components. The components of a class are called the **members** of the class.

The general syntax for defining a class is:

```
class classIdentifier
{
    classMembersList
};
```

where `classMembersList` consists of variable declarations and/or functions. That is, a member of a class can be either a variable (to store data) or a function.

- If a member of a class is a variable, you declare it just like any other variable. Also, in the definition of the class, you cannot initialize a variable when you declare it.

- If a member of a class is a function, you typically use the function prototype to declare that member.

- If a member of a class is a function, it can (directly) access any member of the class—member variables and member functions. That is, when you write the definition of a member function, you can directly access any member variable of the class without passing it as a parameter. The only obvious condition is that you must declare an identifier before you can use it.

In C++, `class` is a reserved word, and it defines only a data type; no memory is allocated. It announces the declaration of a class. Moreover, note the semicolon (`;`) after the right brace. The semicolon is part of the syntax. A missing semicolon, therefore, will result in a syntax error.

The members of a `class` are classified into three categories: `private`, `public`, and `protected`. This chapter mainly discusses the first two types, `private` and `public`.

In C++, `private`, `protected`, and `public` are reserved words and are called member access specifiers.

Following are some facts about `public` and `private` members of a class:

- By default, all members of a class are `private`.
- If a member of a class is `private`, you cannot access it outside the class. (Example 11-1 illustrates this concept.)
- A `public` member is accessible outside the `class`. (Example 11-1 illustrates this concept.)
- To make a member of a class `public`, you use the member access specifier `public` with a colon, :.

Suppose that we want to define a class to implement the time of day in a program. Because a clock gives the time of day, let us call this `class clockType`. Furthermore, to represent time in computer memory, we use three `int` variables: one to represent the hours, one to represent the minutes, and one to represent the seconds.

Suppose these three variables are:

```
int hr;
int min;
int sec;
```

We also want to perform the following operations on the time:

1. Set the time.
2. Retrieve the time.
3. Print the time.
4. Increment the time by one second.
5. Increment the time by one minute.
6. Increment the time by one hour.
7. Compare the two times for equality.

To implement these seven operations, we will write seven functions—`setTime`, `getTime`, `printTime`, `incrementSeconds`, `incrementMinutes`, `incrementHours`, and `equalTime`.

From this discussion, it is clear that the `class clockType` has 10 members: three member variables and seven member functions.

Some members of the **class clockType** will be **private**; others will be **public**. Deciding which member to make **public** and which to make **private** depends on the nature of the member. The general rule is that any member that needs to be accessed outside the class is declared **public**; any member that should not be accessed directly by the user should be declared **private**. For example, the user should be able to set the time and print the time. Therefore, the members that set the time and print the time should be declared **public**.

Similarly, the members to increment the time, and compare the time for equality, should be declared **public**. On the other hand, to prevent the *direct* manipulation of the member variables **hr**, **min**, and **sec**, we will declare them **private**. Furthermore, note that if the user has direct access to the member variables, member functions such as **setTime** are not needed. The second part of this chapter (beginning with the section "Information Hiding") explains why some members need to be **public** and others should be **private**.

The following statements define the **class clockType**:

```
class clockType
{
public:
    void setTime(int, int, int);
    void getTime(int&, int&, int&) const;
    void printTime() const;
    void incrementSeconds();
    void incrementMinutes();
    void incrementHours();
    bool equalTime(const clockType&) const;

private:
    int hr;
    int min;
    int sec;
};
```

In this definition:

- The **class clockType** has seven member functions: **setTime**, **getTime**, **printTime**, **incrementSeconds**, **incrementMinutes**, **incrementHours**, and **equalTime**. It has three member variables: **hr**, **min**, and **sec**.

- The three member variables—**hr**, **min**, and **sec**—are **private** to the class and cannot be accessed outside the class. (Example 11-1 illustrates this concept.)

- The seven member functions—**setTime**, **getTime**, **printTime**, **incrementSeconds**, **incrementMinutes**, **incrementHours**, and **equalTime**—can directly access the member variables (**hr**, **min**, and **sec**). In other words, when we write the definitions of these functions, we do not pass these member variables as parameters to the member functions.

- In the function `equalTime`, the formal parameter is a constant reference parameter. That is, in a call to the function `equalTime`, the formal parameter receives the address of the actual parameter, but the formal parameter cannot modify the value of the actual parameter. You could have declared the formal parameter as a value parameter, but that would require the formal parameter to copy the value of the actual parameter, which could result in poor performance. (See the section "Reference Parameters and Class Objects (Variables)" in this chapter for an explanation.)

- The word `const` at the end of the member functions `getTime`, `printTime`, and `equalTime` specifies that these functions cannot modify the member variables of a variable of type `clockType`.

NOTE The `private` and `public` members can appear in any order. If you want, you can declare the `private` members first and then declare the `public` ones. The section "Order of `public` and `private` Members of a Class" in this chapter discusses this issue.

NOTE In the definition of the `class` `clockType`, all member variables are `private` and all member functions are `public`. However, a member function can also be `private`. For example, if a member function is used only to implement other member functions of the class, and the user does not need to access this function, you make it `private`. Similarly, a member variable of a class can also be `public`.

Note that we have not yet written the definitions of the member functions of the class. You will learn how to write them shortly.

The function `setTime` sets the three member variables—`hr`, `min`, and `sec`—to a given value. The given values are passed as parameters to the function `setTime`. The function `printTime` prints the time, that is, the values of `hr`, `min`, and `sec`. The function `incrementSeconds` increments the time by one second, the function `incrementMinutes` increments the time by one minute, the function `incrementHours` increments the time by one hour, and the function `equalTime` compares two times for equality.

Note that the function `equalTime` has only one parameter, although you need two things to make a comparison. We will explain this point with the help of an example in the section "Implementation of Member Functions," later in this chapter.

Unified Modeling Language Class Diagrams

A class and its members can be described graphically using a notation known as the **Unified Modeling Language** (UML) notation. For example, Figure 11-1 shows the UML class diagram of the `class` `clockType`.

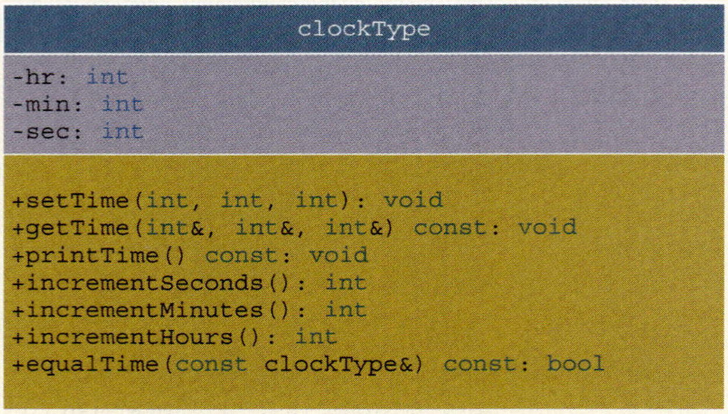

FIGURE 11-1 UML class diagram of the **class** clockType

The top box contains the name of the class. The middle box contains the member variables and their data types. The last box contains the member function name, parameter list, and the return type of the function. A + (plus) sign in front of a member name indicates that this member is a **public** member; a – (minus) sign indicates that this is a **private** member. The symbol # before the member name indicates that the member is a **protected** member.

Variable (Object) Declaration

Once a class is defined, you can declare variables of that type. In C++ terminology, a class variable is called a **class object** or **class instance**. To help you become familiar with this terminology, from now on we will use the term class object, or simply **object**, for a class variable.

The syntax for declaring a class object is the same as that for declaring any other variable. The following statements declare two objects of type clockType:

```
clockType myClock;
clockType yourClock;
```

Each object has 10 members: seven member functions and three member variables. Each object has separate memory allocated for hr, min, and sec.

In actuality, memory is allocated only for the member variables of each class object. The C++ compiler generates only one physical copy of a member function of a class, and each class object executes the same copy of the member function. Therefore, whenever we draw the figure of a class object, we will show only the member variables. As an example, Figure 11-2 shows the objects myClock and yourClock with values in their member variables.

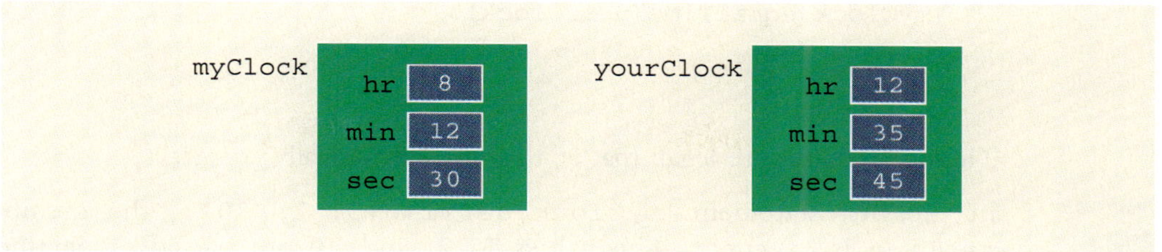

FIGURE 11-2 Objects `myClock` and `yourClock`

Accessing Class Members

Once an object of a class is declared, it can access the members of the class. The general syntax for an object to access a member of a class is:

```
classObjectName.memberName
```

The class members that a class object can access depend on where the object is declared.

- If the object is declared in the definition of a member function of the class, then the object can access both the **public** and **private** members. (We will elaborate on this when we write the definition of the member function `equalTime` of the **class** `clockType` in the section "Implementation of Member Functions," later in this chapter.)

- If the object is declared elsewhere (for example, in a user's program), then the object can access *only* the **public** members of the class.

Recall that in C++, the dot, . (period), is an operator called the member access operator.

Example 11-1 illustrates how to access the members of a class.

EXAMPLE 11-1

Suppose we have the following declaration (say, in a user's program):

```
clockType myClock;
clockType yourClock;
```

Consider the following statements:

```
myClock.setTime(5, 2, 30);
myClock.printTime();
yourClock.setTime(x, y, z);     //assume x, y, and z are
                                //variables of type int
```

```
if (myClock.equalTime(yourClock))
    .
    .
    .
```

These statements are legal; that is, they are syntactically correct.

In the first statement, `myClock.setTime(5, 2, 30);`, the member function `setTime` is executed. The values `5`, `2`, and `30` are passed as parameters to the function `setTime`, and the function uses these values to set the values of the three member variables `hr`, `min`, and `sec` of `myClock` to `5`, `2`, and `30`, respectively. Similarly, the second statement executes the member function `printTime` and outputs the contents of the three member variables of `myClock`. In the third statement, the values of the variables `x`, `y`, and `z` are used to set the values of the three member variables of `yourClock`.

In the fourth statement, the member function `equalTime` executes and compares the three member variables of `myClock` to the corresponding member variables of `yourClock`. Because in this statement `equalTime` is a member of the object `myClock`, it has direct access to the three member variables of `myClock`. So it needs one more object, which in this case is `yourClock`, to compare. This explains why the function `equalTime` has only one parameter.

The objects `myClock` and `yourClock` can access only **public** members of the class. Thus, the following statements are illegal because `hr` and `min` are declared as **private** members of the **class** `clockType` and, therefore, cannot be accessed by the objects `myClock` and `yourClock`:

```
myClock.hr = 10;                    //illegal
myClock.min = yourClock.min;   //illegal
```

Built-in Operations on Classes

Most of C++'s built-in operations do not apply to classes. You cannot use arithmetic operators to perform arithmetic operations on class objects (unless they are overloaded; see Chapter 14). For example, you cannot use the operator + to add two class objects of, say, type `clockType`. Also, you cannot use relational operators to compare two class objects for equality (unless they are overloaded; see Chapter 14).

The two built-in operations that are valid for class objects are member access (`.`) and assignment (`=`). You have seen how to access an individual member of a class by using the name of the class object, then a dot, and then the member name.

We now show how an assignment statement works with the help of an example.

Assignment Operator and Classes

Suppose that `myClock` and `yourClock` are variables of type `clockType`, as defined previously. Furthermore, suppose that the values of `myClock` and `yourClock` are as shown in Figure 11-3.

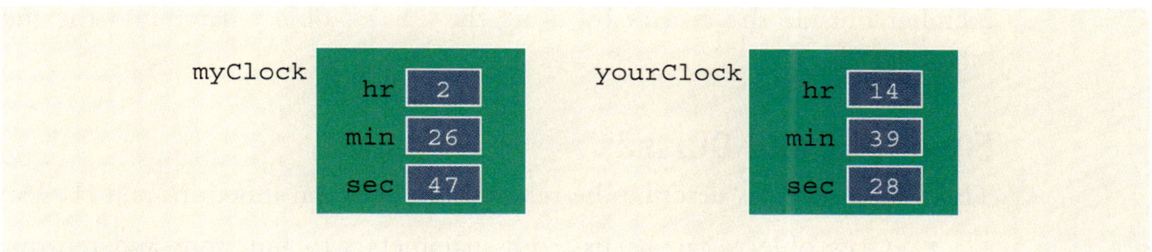

FIGURE 11-3 Objects `myClock` and `yourClock`

The statement:

```
myClock = yourClock;              //Line 1
```

copies the value of `yourClock` into `myClock`. That is,

- the value of `yourClock.hr` is copied into `myClock.hr`,
- the value of `yourClock.min` is copied into `myClock.min`, and
- the value of `yourClock.sec` is copied into `myClock.sec`.

In other words, the values of the three member variables of `yourClock` are copied into the corresponding member variables of `myClock`. Therefore, an assignment statement performs a member-wise copy. After the statement in Line 1 executes, the values of `myClock` and `yourClock` are as shown in Figure 11-4.

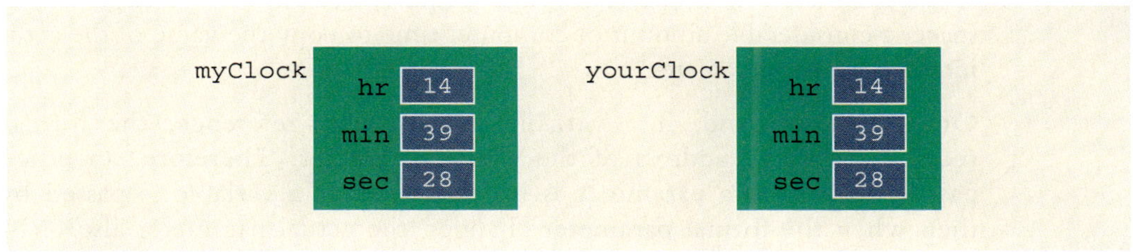

FIGURE 11-4 Objects `myClock` and `yourClock` after the assignment statement `myClock = yourClock;` executes

Class Scope

A `class` object can be either automatic (that is, created each time the control reaches its declaration, and destroyed when the control exits the surrounding block) or static (that is, created once, when the control reaches its declaration, and destroyed when the program terminates). Also, you can declare an array of `class` objects. A `class` object has the same scope as other variables. A member of a `class` has the same scope as a member of a `struct`. That is, a member of a `class` is local to the `class`. You access a `class` member outside the `class` by using the `class` object name and the member access operator (`.`).

Functions and Classes

The following rules describe the relationship between functions and classes:

- Class objects can be passed as parameters to functions and returned as function values.

- As parameters to functions, classes can be passed either by value or by reference.

- If a class object is passed by value, the contents of the member variables of the actual parameter are copied into the corresponding member variables of the formal parameter.

Reference Parameters and Class Objects (Variables)

Recall that when a variable is passed by value, the formal parameter copies the value of the actual parameter. That is, memory to copy the value of the actual parameter is allocated for the formal parameter. As a parameter, a class object can be passed by value.

Suppose that a class has several member variables requiring a large amount of memory to store data, and you need to pass a variable by value. The corresponding formal parameter then receives a copy of the data of the variable. That is, the compiler must allocate memory for the formal parameter, so as to copy the value of the member variables of the actual parameter. This operation might require, in addition to a large amount of storage space, a considerable amount of computer time to copy the value of the actual parameter into the formal parameter.

On the other hand, if a variable is passed by reference, the formal parameter receives only the address of the actual parameter. Therefore, an efficient way to pass a variable as a parameter is by reference. If a variable is passed by reference, then when the formal parameter changes, the actual parameter also changes. Sometimes, however, you do not want the function to be able to change the values of the member variables. In C++, you can pass a variable by reference and still prevent the function from changing its value by using the keyword `const` in the formal parameter declaration. As an example, consider the following function definition:

```
void testTime(const clockType& otherClock)
{
    clockType dClock;
        .
        .
        .
}
```

The function `testTime` contains a reference parameter, `otherClock`. The parameter `otherClock` is declared using the keyword `const`. Thus, in a call to the function `testTime`, the formal parameter `otherClock` receives the address of the actual parameter, but `otherClock` cannot modify the contents of the actual parameter. For example, after the following statement executes, the value of `myClock` will not be altered:

```
testTime(myClock);
```

Generally, if you want to declare a class object as a value parameter, you declare it as a reference parameter using the keyword `const`, as described previously.

Recall that if a formal parameter is a value parameter, within the function definition you can change the value of the formal parameter. That is, you can use an assignment statement to change the value of the formal parameter (which, of course, would have no effect on the actual parameter). However, if a formal parameter is a constant reference parameter, you cannot use an assignment statement to change its value within the function, nor can you use any other function to change its value. Therefore, within the definition of the function `testTime`, you cannot alter the value of `otherClock`. For example, the following would be illegal in the definition of the function `testTime`:

```
otherClock.setTime(5, 34, 56);  //illegal
otherClock = dClock;            //illegal
```

Implementation of Member Functions

When we defined the `class clockType`, we included only the function prototype for the member functions. For these functions to work properly, we must write the related algorithms. One way to implement these functions is to provide the function definition rather than the function prototype in the class itself. Unfortunately, the class definition would then be very long and difficult to comprehend. Another reason for providing function prototypes instead of function definitions relates to information hiding; that is, we want to hide the details of the operations on the data. We will discuss this issue later in this chapter, in the section "Information Hiding."

Next, let us write the definitions of the member functions of the `class clockType`. That is, we will write the definitions of the functions `setTime`, `getTime`, `printTime`, `incrementSeconds`, `equalTime`, and so on. Because the identifiers `setTime`, `printTime`, and so forth are local to the class, we cannot reference them (directly) outside the class. In order to reference these identifiers, we use the **scope resolution operator**, : : (double colon). In the function definition's heading, the name of the function is the name of the class, followed by the scope resolution operator, followed by the function name. For example, the definition of the function setTime is as follows:

```
void clockType::setTime(int hours, int minutes, int seconds)
{
    if (0 <= hours && hours < 24)
        hr = hours;
    else
        hr = 0;

    if (0 <= minutes && minutes < 60)
        min = minutes;
    else
        min = 0;

    if (0 <= seconds && seconds < 60)
        sec = seconds;
    else
        sec = 0;
}
```

Note that the definition of the function setTime checks for the valid values of hours, minutes, and seconds. If these values are out of range, the member variables hr, min, and sec are initialized to 0. Let us now explain how the member function setTime works when accessed by an object of type clockType.

The member function setTime is a **void** function and has three parameters. Therefore,

- A call to this function is a stand-alone statement.
- We must use three parameters in a call to this function.

Furthermore, recall that, because setTime is a member of the **class** clockType, it can directly access the member variables hr, min, and sec, as shown in the definition of setTime.

Suppose that myClock is an object of type clockType (as declared previously). The object myClock has three member variables, as shown in Figure 11-5.

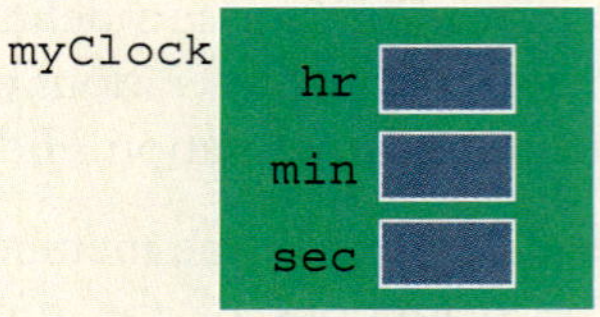

FIGURE 11-5 Object myClock

Consider the following statement:

```
myClock.setTime(3, 48, 52);
```

In the statement `myClock.setTime(3, 48, 52);`, `setTime` is accessed by the object `myClock`. Therefore, the three variables—`hr`, `min`, and `sec`—referred to in the body of the function `setTime` are the three member variables of `myClock`. Thus, the values, 3, 48, and 52, which are passed as parameters in the preceding statement, are assigned to the three member variables of `myClock` by the function `setTime` (see the body of the function `setTime`). After the previous statement executes, the object `myClock` is as shown in Figure 11-6.

FIGURE 11-6 Object `myClock` after the statement `myClock.setTime(3, 48, 52);` executes

Next, let us give the definitions of the other member functions of the **class** `clockType`. The definitions of these functions are simple and easy to follow:

```cpp
void clockType::getTime(int& hours, int& minutes,
                        int& seconds) const
{
    hours = hr;
    minutes = min;
    seconds = sec;
}

void clockType::printTime() const
{
    if (hr < 10)
        cout << "0";
    cout << hr << ":";

    if (min < 10)
        cout << "0";
    cout << min << ":";

    if (sec < 10)
        cout << "0";
    cout << sec;
}
```

```cpp
void clockType::incrementHours()
{
    hr++;
    if (hr > 23)
        hr = 0;
}

void clockType::incrementMinutes()
{
    min++;
    if (min > 59)
    {
        min = 0;
        incrementHours(); //increment hours
    }
}

void clockType::incrementSeconds()
{
    sec++;

    if (sec > 59)
    {
        sec = 0;
        incrementMinutes(); //increment minutes
    }
}
```

From the definitions of the functions `incrementMinutes` and `incrementSeconds`, it is clear that a member function of a class can call other member functions of the class.

The function `equalTime` has the following definition:

```cpp
bool clockType::equalTime(const clockType& otherClock) const
{
    return (hr == otherClock.hr
            && min == otherClock.min
            && sec == otherClock.sec);
}
```

Let us see how the member function `equalTime` works.

Suppose that `myClock` and `yourClock` are objects of type `clockType`, as declared previously. Further suppose that we have `myClock` and `yourClock`, as shown in Figure 11-7.

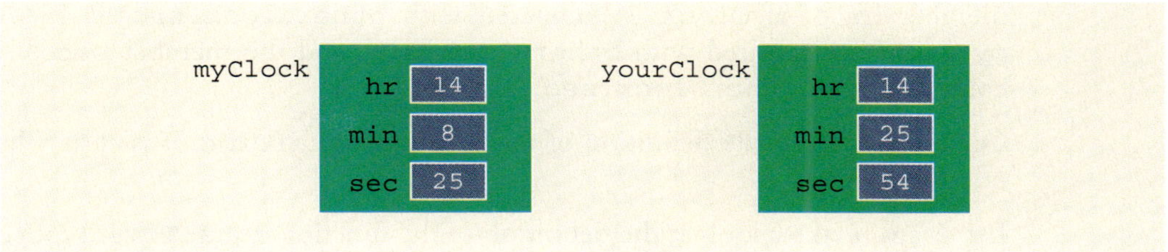

FIGURE 11-7 Objects `myClock` and `yourClock`

Consider the following statement:

```
if (myClock.equalTime(yourClock))
    .
    .
    .
```

In the expression:

```
myClock.equalTime(yourClock)
```

the object `myClock` accesses the member function `equalTime`. Because `otherClock` is a reference parameter, the address of the actual parameter `yourClock` is passed to the formal parameter `otherClock`, as shown in Figure 11-8.

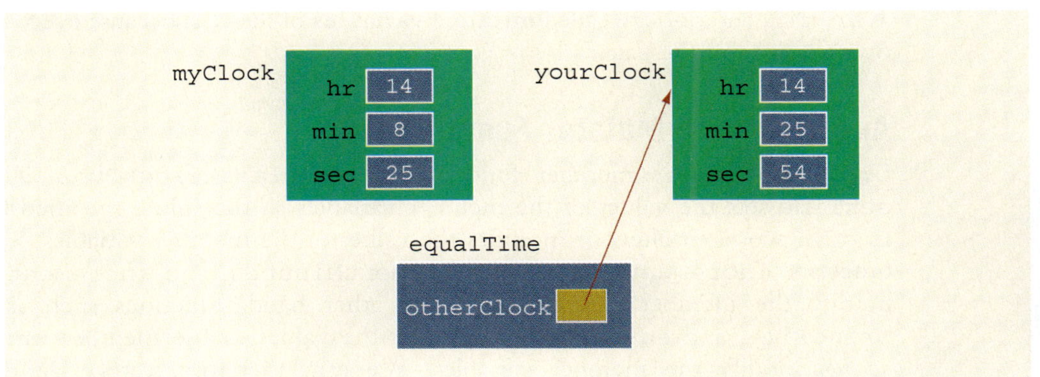

FIGURE 11-8 Object `myClock` and parameter `otherClock`

The member variables `hr`, `min`, and `sec` of `otherClock` have the values 14, 25, and 54, respectively. In other words, when the body of the function `equalTime` executes, the value of `otherClock.hr` is 14, the value of `otherClock.min` is 25, and the value of `otherClock.sec` is 54. The function `equalTime` is a member of `myClock`. When the function `equalTime` executes, the variables `hr`, `min`, and `sec` in the body of the function `equalTime` are the member variables of the object `myClock`. Therefore, the member `hr` of `myClock` is compared with `otherClock.hr`, the member `min` of `myClock` is compared with `otherClock.min`, and the member `sec` of `myClock` is compared with `otherClock.sec`.

Once again, from the definition of the function `equalTime`, it is clear why it has only one parameter.

Let us again take a look at the definition of the function `equalTime`. Notice that within the definition of this function, the object `otherClock` accesses the member variables `hr`, `min`, and `sec`. However, these member variables are **private**. So is there any violation? The answer is no. The function `equalTime` is a member of the **class** `clockType` and `hr`, `min`, and `sec` are the member variables. Moreover, `otherClock` is an object of type `clockType`. Therefore, the object `otherClock` can access its **private** member variables within the definition of the function `equalTime`.

The same is true for any member function of a class. In general, when you write the definition of a member function, say, `dummyFunction`, of a **class**, say, `dummyClass`, and the function uses an object, `dummyObject` of the **class** `dummyClass`, then within the definition of `dummyFunction`, the object `dummyObject` can access its **private** member variables (in fact, any **private** member of the class).

Once a class is properly defined and implemented, it can be used in a program. A program or software that uses and manipulates the objects of a class is called a **client** of that class.

When you declare objects of the **class** `clockType`, every object has its own copy of the member variables `hr`, `min`, and `sec`. In object-oriented terminology, variables such as `hr`, `min`, and `sec` are called **instance variables** of the class because every object has its own instance of the data.

Accessor and Mutator Functions

Let us look at the member functions of the **class** `clockType`. The function `setTime` sets the values of the member variables to the values specified by the user. In other words, it alters or modifies the values of the member variables. Similarly, the functions `incrementSeconds`, `incrementMinutes`, and `incrementHours` also modify the member variables. On the other hand, functions such as `getTime`, `printTime`, and `equalTime` only *access* the values of the member variables. They *do not* modify the member variables. We can, therefore, categorize the member functions of the **class** `clockType` into two categories: member functions that modify the member variables, and member functions that only access, and do not modify, the member variables.

This is typically true for any class. That is, every class has member functions that only access and do not modify the member variables, called accessor functions, and member functions that modify the member variables, called mutator functions.

Accessor function: A member function of a class that only accesses (that is, does not modify) the value(s) of the member variable(s).

Mutator function: A member function of a class that modifies the value(s) of the member variable(s).

Because an accessor function only accesses the values of the member variables, as a safeguard, we typically include the reserved word `const` at the end of the headings of these functions. Moreover, a constant member function of a class cannot modify the member variables of that class. For example, see the headings of the member functions `getTime`, `printTime`, and `equalTime` of the `class clockType`.

A member function of a class is called a constant function if its heading contains the reserved word `const` at the end. For example, the member functions `getTime`, `printTime`, and `equalTime` of the `class clockType` are constant functions. A constant member function of a class cannot modify the member variables of that class, and so these are accessor functions. One thing that should be remembered about constant member functions is that a constant member function of a class can *only* call other constant member functions of that class. Therefore, you should be careful when you make a member function constant.

Now that you have seen how to define a class, how to access the members of a class, and how to implement the member functions, let us write a simple program that uses a class. We will write a simple function that uses the `class clockType`.

```cpp
//Program that uses the class clockType

int main()
{
    clockType myClock;
    clockType yourClock;

    int hours;
    int minutes;
    int seconds;

        //Set the time of myClock
    myClock.setTime(5, 4, 30);                          //Line 1

    cout << "Line 2: myClock: ";                        //Line 2
    myClock.printTime();    //print the time of myClock //Line 3
    cout << endl;                                       //Line 4

    cout << "Line 5: yourClock: ";                      //Line 5
    yourClock.printTime(); //print the time of yourClock Line 6
    cout << endl;                                       //Line 7

        //Set the time of yourClock
    yourClock.setTime(5, 45, 16);                       //Line 8

    cout << "Line 9: After setting, yourClock: ";       //Line 9
    yourClock.printTime(); //print the time of yourClock Line 10
    cout << endl;                                       //Line 11
```

```cpp
        //Compare myClock and yourClock
    if (myClock.equalTime(yourClock))                    //Line 12
        cout << "Line 13: Both times are equal."
            << endl;                                     //Line 13
    else                                                 //Line 14
        cout << "Line 15: The two times are not equal."
            << endl;                                     //Line 15

    cout << "Line 16: Enter the hours, minutes, and "
        << "seconds: ";                                  //Line 16
    cin >> hours >> minutes >> seconds;                  //Line 17
    cout << endl;                                        //Line 18

        //Set the time of myClock using the value of the
        //variables hours, minutes, and seconds
    myClock.setTime(hours, minutes, seconds);            //Line 19

    cout << "Line 20: New myClock: ";                    //Line 20
    myClock.printTime();    //print the time of myClock  //Line 21
    cout << endl;                                        //Line 22

        //Increment the time of myClock by one second
    myClock.incrementSeconds();                          //Line 23

    cout << "Line 24: After incrementing myClock by "
        << "one second, myClock: ";                      //Line 24
    myClock.printTime();    //print the time of myClock  //Line 25
    cout << endl;                                        //Line 26

        //Retrieve the hours, minutes, and seconds of the
        //object myClock
    myClock.getTime(hours, minutes, seconds);            //Line 27

        //Output the value of hours, minutes, and seconds
    cout << "Line 28: hours = " << hours
        << ", minutes = " << minutes
        << ", seconds = " << seconds << endl;            //Line 28

    return 0;
}//end main
```

This function requires the user to input three numbers: the number of hours, minutes, and seconds.

Example 11-2 combines the definition of the class, the definition of the member functions, and the function main to create a complete program.

EXAMPLE 11-2

```cpp
//The complete program listing of the program that defines
//and uses the class clockType

#include <iostream>
using namespace std;

class clockType
{
public:
    void setTime(int, int, int);
    void getTime(int&, int&, int&) const;
    void printTime() const;
    void incrementSeconds();
    void incrementMinutes();
    void incrementHours();
    bool equalTime(const clockType&) const;

private:
    int hr;
    int min;
    int sec;
};


int main()
{
    clockType myClock;
    clockType yourClock;

    int hours;
    int minutes;
    int seconds;

        //Set the time of myClock
    myClock.setTime(5, 4, 30);                          //Line 1

    cout << "Line 2: myClock: ";                        //Line 2
    myClock.printTime();  //print the time of myClock     Line 3
    cout << endl;                                       //Line 4

    cout << "Line 5: yourClock: ";                      //Line 5
    yourClock.printTime(); //print the time of yourClock Line 6
    cout << endl;                                       //Line 7

        //Set the time of yourClock
    yourClock.setTime(5, 45, 16);                       //Line 8

    cout << "Line 9: After setting, yourClock: ";       //Line 9
    yourClock.printTime(); //print the time of yourClock Line 10
    cout << endl;                                       //Line 11
```

```cpp
        //Compare myClock and yourClock
    if (myClock.equalTime(yourClock))                   //Line 12
        cout << "Line 13: Both times are equal."
            << endl;                                     //Line 13
    else                                                 //Line 14
        cout << "Line 15: The two times are not equal."
            << endl;                                     //Line 15

    cout << "Line 16: Enter the hours, minutes, and "
        << "seconds: ";                                  //Line 16
    cin >> hours >> minutes >> seconds;                  //Line 17
    cout << endl;                                        //Line 18

        //Set the time of myClock using the value of the
        //variables hours, minutes, and seconds
    myClock.setTime(hours, minutes, seconds);            //Line 19

    cout << "Line 20: New myClock: ";                    //Line 20
    myClock.printTime();    //print the time of myClock     Line 21
    cout << endl;                                        //Line 22

        //Increment the time of myClock by one second
    myClock.incrementSeconds();                          //Line 23

    cout << "Line 24: After incrementing myClock by "
        << "one second, myClock: ";                      //Line 24
    myClock.printTime();    //print the time of myClock     Line 25
    cout << endl;                                        //Line 26

        //Retrieve the hours, minutes, and seconds of the
        //object myClock
    myClock.getTime(hours, minutes, seconds);            //Line 27

        //Output the value of hours, minutes, and seconds
    cout << "Line 28: hours = " << hours
        << ", minutes = " << minutes
        << ", seconds = " << seconds << endl;            //Line 28

    return  0;
}//end main

void clockType::setTime(int hours, int minutes, int seconds)
{
    if (0 <= hours && hours < 24)
        hr = hours;
    else
        hr = 0;

    if (0 <= minutes && minutes < 60)
        min = minutes;
```

```cpp
    else
        min = 0;

    if (0 <= seconds && seconds < 60)
        sec = seconds;
    else
        sec = 0;
}

void clockType::getTime(int& hours, int& minutes,
                        int& seconds) const
{
    hours = hr;
    minutes = min;
    seconds = sec;
}

void clockType::incrementHours()
{
    hr++;
    if (hr > 23)
        hr = 0;
}

void clockType::incrementMinutes()
{
    min++;
    if (min > 59)
    {
        min = 0;
        incrementHours(); //increment hours
    }
}

void clockType::incrementSeconds()
{
    sec++;

    if (sec > 59)
    {
        sec = 0;
        incrementMinutes(); //increment minutes
    }
}

void clockType::printTime() const
{
    if (hr < 10)
        cout << "0";
    cout << hr << ":";
```

```cpp
    if (min < 10)
        cout << "0";
    cout << min << ":";

    if (sec < 10)
        cout << "0";
    cout << sec;
}

bool clockType::equalTime(const clockType& otherClock) const
{
    return (hr == otherClock.hr
            && min == otherClock.min
            && sec == otherClock.sec);
}
```

Sample Run: In this sample run, the user input is shaded.

```
Line 2: myClock: 05:04:30
Line 5: yourClock: 0-858993460:0-858993460:0-858993460
Line 9: After setting, yourClock: 05:45:16
Line 15: The two times are not equal.
Line 16: Enter the hours, minutes, and seconds: 5 23 59

Line 20: New myClock: 05:23:59
Line 24: After incrementing myClock by one second, myClock: 05:24:00
Line 28: hours = 5, minutes = 24, seconds = 0
```

The value of `yourClock`, as printed in the second line of the output (Line 5), is machine-dependent; you might get different values.

Order of `public` and `private` Members of a Class

C++ has no fixed order in which you declare `public` and `private` members; you can declare them in any order. The only thing you need to remember is that, by default, all members of a class are `private`. You must use the member access specifier `public` to make a member available for `public` access. If you decide to declare the `private` members after the `public` members (as is done in the case of `clockType`), you must use the member access specifier `private` to begin the declaration of the `private` members.

We can declare the `class` clockType in one of three ways, as shown in Examples 11-3 through 11-5.

EXAMPLE 11-3

This declaration is the same as before. For the sake of completeness, we include the class definition:

```cpp
class clockType
{
public:
    void setTime(int, int, int);
    void getTime(int&, int&, int&) const;
    void printTime() const;
    void incrementSeconds();
    void incrementMinutes();
    void incrementHours();
    bool equalTime(const clockType&) const;

private:
    int hr;
    int min;
    int sec;
};
```

EXAMPLE 11-4

```cpp
class clockType
{
private:
    int hr;
    int min;
    int sec;

public:
    void setTime(int, int, int);
    void getTime(int&, int&, int&) const;
    void printTime() const;
    void incrementSeconds();
    void incrementMinutes();
    void incrementHours();
    bool equalTime(const clockType&) const;
};
```

EXAMPLE 11-5

```
class clockType
{
    int hr;
    int min;
    int sec;

public:
    void setTime(int, int, int);
    void getTime(int&, int&, int&) const;
    void printTime() const;
    void incrementSeconds();
    void incrementMinutes();
    void incrementHours();
    bool equalTime(const clockType&) const;
};
```

In Example 11-5, because the identifiers `hr`, `min`, and `sec` do not follow any member access specifier, they are `private`.

It is a common practice to list all of the `public` members first, and then the `private` members. This way, you can focus your attention on the `public` members.

Constructors

In the program in Example 11-2, when we printed the value of `yourClock` without calling the function `setTime`, the output was some strange numbers (see the output of Line 5 in the sample run). This is due to the fact that C++ does not automatically initialize the variables. Because the `private` members of a class cannot be accessed outside the class (in our case, the member variables), if the user forgets to initialize these variables by calling the function `setTime`, the program will produce erroneous results.

To guarantee that the member variables of a class are initialized, you use constructors. There are two types of constructors: with parameters and without parameters. The constructor without parameters is called the **default constructor**.

Constructors have the following properties:

- The name of a constructor is the same as the name of the class.
- A constructor, even though it is a function, has no type. That is, it is neither a value-returning function nor a `void` function.
- A class can have more than one constructor. However, all constructors of a class have the same name.
- If a class has more than one constructor, the constructors must have different formal parameter lists. That is, either they have a different

number of formal parameters or, if the number of formal parameters is the same, then the data type of the formal parameters, in the order you list, must differ in at least one position.

- Constructors execute automatically when a class object enters its scope. Because they have no types, they cannot be called like other functions.

- Which constructor executes depends on the types of values passed to the class object when the class object is declared.

Let us extend the definition of the **class** clockType by including two constructors:

```cpp
class clockType
{
public:
    void setTime(int, int, int);
    void getTime(int&, int&, int&) const;
    void printTime() const;
    void incrementSeconds();
    void incrementMinutes();
    void incrementHours();
    bool equalTime(const clockType&) const;
    clockType(int, int, int);   //constructor with parameters
    clockType();   //default constructor

private:
    int hr;
    int min;
    int sec;
};
```

This definition of the **class** clockType includes two constructors: one with three parameters and one without any parameters. Let us now write the definitions of these constructors:

```cpp
clockType::clockType(int hours, int minutes, int seconds)
{
    if (0 <= hours && hours < 24)
        hr = hours;
    else
        hr = 0;

    if (0 <= minutes && minutes < 60)
        min = minutes;
    else
        min = 0;

    if (0 <= seconds && seconds < 60)
        sec = seconds;
    else
        sec = 0;
}
```

```
clockType::clockType()    //default constructor
{
    hr = 0;
    min = 0;
    sec = 0;
}
```

From the definitions of these constructors, it follows that the default constructor sets the three member variables—`hr`, `min`, and `sec`—to 0. Also, the constructor with parameters sets the member variables to whatever values are assigned to the formal parameters. Moreover, we can write the definition of the constructor with parameters by calling the function `setTime`, as follows:

```
clockType::clockType(int hours, int minutes, int seconds)
{
    setTime(hours, minutes, seconds);
}
```

Invoking a Constructor

Recall that, when a class object is declared, a constructor is automatically executed. Because a class might have more than one constructor, including the default constructor, next we discuss how to invoke a specific constructor.

Invoking the Default Constructor

Suppose that a class contains the default constructor. The syntax to invoke the default constructor is:

```
className classObjectName;
```

For example, the statement:

```
clockType yourClock;
```

declares `yourClock` to be an object of type `clockType`. In this case, the default constructor executes and the member variables of `yourClock` are initialized to 0.

NOTE If you declare an object and want the default constructor to be executed, the empty parentheses after the object name are not required in the object declaration statement. In fact, if you accidentally include the empty parentheses, the compiler generates a syntax error message. For example, the following statement to declare the object `yourClock` is illegal:

```
clockType yourClock();   //illegal object declaration
```

Invoking a Constructor with Parameters

Suppose a class contains constructors with parameters. The syntax to invoke a constructor with a parameter is:

```
className classObjectName(argument1, argument2, ...);
```

where `argument1`, `argument2`, and so on, is either a variable or an expression.

Note the following:

- The number of arguments and their type should match the formal parameters (in the order given) of one of the constructors.

- If the type of the arguments does not match the formal parameters of any constructor (in the order given), C++ uses type conversion and looks for the best match. For example, an integer value might be converted to a floating-point value with a zero decimal part. Any ambiguity will result in a compile-time error.

Consider the statement:

```
clockType myClock(5, 12, 40);
```

This statement declares an object `myClock` of type `clockType`. Here we are passing three values of type `int`, which matches the type of the formal parameters of the constructor with a parameter. Therefore, the constructor with parameters of the **class** `clockType` executes and the three member variables of the object `myClock` are set to 5, 12, and 40.

Example 11-6 further illustrates how constructors are executed.

EXAMPLE 11-6

Consider the following class definition:

```
class testClass
{
public:
    void print() const;             //Line a

    testClass();                    //Line b
    testClass(int, int);            //Line c
    testClass(int, int, double);    //Line d
    testClass(double, char);        //Line e

private:
    int x;
    int y;
    double z;
    char ch;
};
```

This class has five member functions, including four constructors. It also has four member variables. Suppose that the definitions of the member functions of the **class** testClass are as follows:

```cpp
void testClass::print() const
{
    cout << "x = " << x << ", y = " << y << ", z = " << z
         << ", ch = " << ch << endl;
}

testClass::testClass() //default constructor
{
    x = 0;
    y = 0;
    z = 0;
    ch = '*';
}

testClass::testClass(int tX, int tY)
{
    x = tX;
    y = tY;
    z = 0;
    ch = '*';
}

testClass::testClass(int tX, int tY, double tZ)
{
    x = tX;
    y = tY;
    z = tZ;
    ch = '*';
}

testClass::testClass(double tZ, char tCh)
{
    x = 0;
    y = 0;
    z = tZ;
    ch = tCh;
}
```

Consider the following declarations:

```cpp
testClass one;                  //Line 1
testClass two(5, 6);            //Line 2
testClass three(5, 7, 4.5);     //Line 3
testClass four(4, 9, 12);       //Line 4
testClass five(3.4, 'D');       //Line 5
```

For object **one** (declared in Line 1), the default constructor (in Line b) executes because no value is passed to this variable. Therefore, the member variables **x**, **y**, **z**, and **ch** of **one** are initialized to 0, 0, 0, and `'*'`, respectively. For object `two` (declared in Line 2), the constructor with `int` parameters in Line c executes because the arguments passed to object `two` are 5 and 6, which are of type `int`. Therefore, the member variables `x`, `y`, `z`, and `ch` of `two` are initialized to 5, 6, 0, and `'*'`, respectively (see the definition of the constructor in Line c).

The arguments passed to object `three` (declared in Line 3) are 5, 7, and 4.5. These arguments match the parameters of the constructor in Line d. Therefore, to initialize the member variables of object `three`, the constructor in Line d executes. From the definition of the constructor in Line d, it follows that the member variables `x`, `y`, `z`, and `ch` of `three` are initialized to 5, 7, 4.5, and `'*'`, respectively.

The arguments passed to object `four` are 4, 9, and 12. The **class** `testClass` does not contain any constructor with three `int` parameters. However, it does contain a constructor with three parameters in the order `int`, `int`, and **double** (see the constructor in Line d). Because an `int` value can be converted to a **double** value with a zero decimal value, in the case of object `four`, the constructor in Line d executes. Thus, the member variables `x`, `y`, `z`, and `ch` of `four` are initialized to 4, 9, 12.0, and `'*'`, respectively (see the definition of the constructor in Line d).

The arguments passed to object `five` are 3.4 and `'D'`. These values match the parameters of the constructor in Line e. Therefore, to initialize the member variables of object `five`, the constructor in Line e executes. From the definition of the constructor in Line e, it follows that the member variables `x`, `y`, `z`, and `ch` of `five` are initialized to 0, 0, 3.4, and `'D'`, respectively (see the definition of the constructor in Line e).

> **NOTE** If the values passed to a class object do not match the parameters of any constructor, and if no type conversion is possible, a compile-time error will be generated.

The following program tests the previous class objects.

```cpp
int main()
{
    testClass one;                  //Line 1
    testClass two(5, 6);            //Line 2
    testClass three(5, 7, 4.5);     //Line 3
    testClass four(4, 9, 12);       //Line 4
    testClass five(3.4, 'D');       //Line 5

    one.print();                    //Line 6; output one
    two.print();                    //Line 7; output two
    three.print();                  //Line 8; output three
    four.print();                   //Line 9; output four
    five.print();                   //Line 10; output five

    return 0;
}
```

Sample Run:

```
x = 0, y = 0, z = 0, ch = *
x = 5, y = 6, z = 0, ch = *
x = 5, y = 7, z = 4.5, ch = *
x = 4, y = 9, z = 12, ch = *
x = 0, y = 0, z = 3.4, ch = D
```

As explained previously, the statements in Lines 1 through 5 declare and initialize objects one, two, three, four, and five. The statements in Lines 6 through 10 output the values of these objects—that is, the values of the member variables of these objects.

Constructors and Default Parameters

A constructor can also have default parameters. In such cases, the rules for declaring formal parameters are the same as those for declaring default formal parameters in a function. Moreover, actual parameters to a constructor with default parameters are passed according to the rules for functions with default parameters. (Chapter 7 discusses functions with default parameters.) Using the rules for defining default parameters, in the definition of the **class** clockType, you can replace both constructors using the following statement. (Recall that in the function prototype, the name of a formal parameter is optional.)

```
clockType clockType(int = 0, int = 0, int = 0);    //Line 1
```

In the implementation file, the definition of this constructor is the same as the definition of the constructor with parameters.

If you replace the constructors of the **class** clockType with the constructor in Line 1 (the constructor with the default parameters), then you can declare clockType objects with zero, one, two, or three arguments, as follows:

```
clockType clock1;              //Line 2
clockType clock2(5);           //Line 3
clockType clock3(12, 30);      //Line 4
clockType clock4(7, 34, 18);   //Line 5
```

The member variables of clock1 are initialized to 0. The member variable hr of clock2 is initialized to 5, and the member variables min and sec of clock2 are initialized to 0. The member variable hr of clock3 is initialized to 12, the member variable min of clock3 is initialized to 30, and the member variable sec of clock3 is initialized to 0. The member variable hr of clock4 is initialized to 7, the member variable min of clock4 is initialized to 34, and the member variable sec of clock4 is initialized to 18.

Using these conventions, we can say that a constructor that has no parameters, or has all default parameters, is called the **default constructor**.

EXAMPLE 11-7

Using default constructors, you can write the definition of the **class** testClass (defined previously) as follows:

```cpp
class testClass
{
public:
    void print() const ;

    testClass(int = 0, int = 0, double = 0.0, char = '*');

private:
    int x;
    int y;
    double z;
    char ch;
};
```

The definition of the constructor is as follows:

```cpp
testClass::testClass(int tX, int  tY, double tZ, char tCh)
{
    x = tX;
    y = tY;
    z = tZ;
    ch = tCh;
}
```

Notice that the formal parameters tX, tY, tZ, and tCh are default parameters. (See the prototype of the constructor in the definition of the **class** testClass.)

You can now declare objects one, two, three, four, and five as follows:

```cpp
testClass one;
testClass two(5, 6);
testClass three(5, 7, 4.5);
testClass four(4, 9, 12);
testClass five(0, 0, 3.4, 'D');
```

For object one, we want to initialize its member variables to their default values. Therefore, no values are specified in the object declaration. When the constructor executes, the formal parameters assume their default values and initialize the member variables of one.

For object two, we want to initialize its member variables x to 5, y to 6, and z and ch to their default values. Therefore, in the declaration of object two, only two values are specified. When the constructor executes, the value of the formal parameter tX is 5, the value of tY is 6, and the values of tZ and tCh are their default values. Objects three and four have similar conventions.

For object `five`, we want to initialize its member variables `x` and `y` to their default values, the member variable `z` to `3.4`, and the member variable `ch` to `'D'`. Also, in the heading of the constructor, both formal parameters `tX` and `tY` occur before the formal parameters `tZ` and `tCh`. Therefore, in the declaration of object `five`, we must specify the default values for the parameters `tX` and `tY` as shown in the declaration.

As you can see, by using the default parameters, several constructors can be combined into one constructor. Wherever possible (and when no confusion arises), we will effectively make use of constructors with default parameters.

Classes and Constructors: A Precaution

As discussed in the preceding section, constructors provide guaranteed initialization of the object's member variables. Typically, the default constructor is used to initialize the member variables to some default values, and this constructor has no parameters. A constructor with parameters is used to initialize the member variables to some specific values.

We have seen that if a class has no constructor(s), then the object created is uninitialized because C++ does not automatically initialize variables when they are declared. In reality, if a class has no constructor(s), then C++ automatically provides the default constructor. However, this default constructor does not do anything. The object declared is still uninitialized.

The important things to remember about classes and constructors are the following:

- If a class has no constructor(s), C++ *automatically provides* the default constructor. However, the object declared is still uninitialized.
- On the other hand, suppose a `class`, say, `dummyClass`, includes constructor(s) with parameter(s) and does not include the default constructor. In this case, C++ *does not* provide the default constructor for the `class` `dummyClass`. Therefore, when an object of the `class` `dummyClass` is declared, we must include the appropriate arguments in its declaration.

The following code further explains this. Consider the definition of the following class:

```cpp
class dummyClass
{
public:
    void print() const;

    dummyClass(int dX, int dY);

private:
    int x;
    int y;
};
```

The **class** dummyClass *does not* have the default constructor. It has a constructor with parameters. Given this definition of the **class** dummyClass, the following object declaration is legal:

```cpp
dummyClass myObject(10, 25);   //object declaration is legal
```

However, because the **class** dummyClass does not contain the default constructor, the following declaration is incorrect and would generate a syntax error:

```cpp
dummyClass dummyObject;   //incorrect object declaration
```

Therefore, to avoid such pitfalls, if a class has constructor(s), the class should also include the default constructor.

Arrays of Class Objects (Variables) and Constructors

If a class has constructors and you declare an array of that class's objects, the class should have the default constructor. The default constructor is typically used to initialize each (array) class object.

For example, if you declare an array of 100 class objects, then it is impractical (if not impossible), to specify different constructors for each component. (We will further clarify this at the end of this section.)

Suppose that you have 100 employees who are paid on an hourly basis and you need to keep track of their arrival and departure times. You can declare two arrays—arrivalTimeEmp and departureTimeEmp—of 100 components each, wherein each component is an object of type clockType.

Consider the following statement:

```cpp
clockType arrivalTimeEmp[100];                    //Line 1
```

The statement in Line 1 creates the array of objects arrivalTimeEmp[0], arrivalTimeEmp[1], ..., arrivalTimeEmp[99], as shown in Figure 11-9.

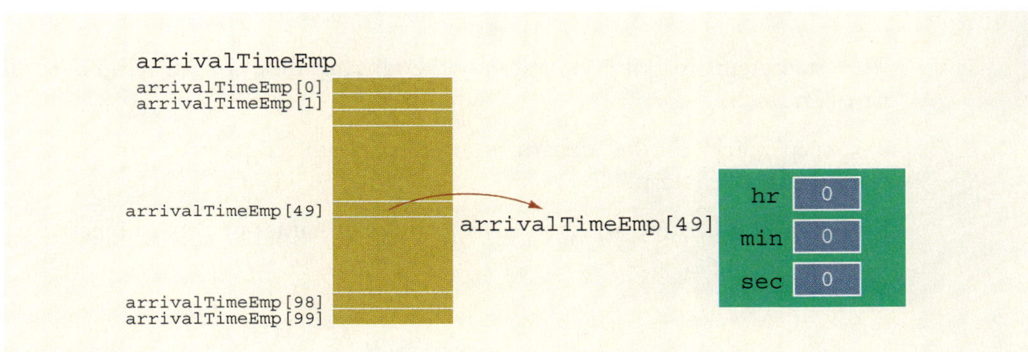

FIGURE 11-9 Array arrivalTimeEmp

You can now use the functions of the **class** clockType to manipulate the time for each employee. For example, the following statement sets the arrival time, that is, hr, min, and sec, of employee 49 to 8, 5, and 10, respectively (see Figure 11-10).

```
arrivalTimeEmp[49].setTime(8, 5, 10);            //Line 2
```

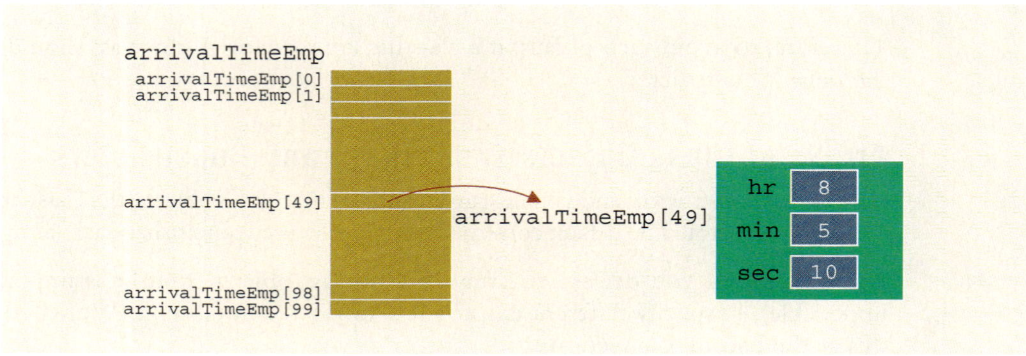

FIGURE 11-10 Array arrivalTimeEmp after setting the time of employee 49

To output the arrival time of each employee, you can use a loop, such as the following:

```
for (int j = 0; j < 100; j++)                    //Line 3
{
    cout << "Employee " << (j + 1)
        << " arrival time: ";
    arrivalTimeEmp[j].printTime();               //Line 4
    cout << endl;
}
```

The statement in Line 4 outputs the arrival time of an employee in the form hr:min:sec.

To keep track of the departure time of each employee, you can use the array departureTimeEmp.

Similarly, you can use arrays to manage a list of names or other objects.

NOTE Before leaving our discussion of arrays of class objects, we would like to point out the following: The beginning of this section stated that if you declare an array of class objects and the class has constructor(s), then the class should have the default constructor. The compiler uses the default constructor to initialize the array of objects. If the array size is large, then it is impractical to specify a different constructor with parameters for each object. For a small-sized array, we can manage to specify a different constructor with parameters.

For example, the following statement declares `clocks` to be an array of two components. The member variables of the first component are initialized to 8, 35, and 42, respectively. The member variables of the second component are initialized to 6, 52, and 39, respectively.

```
clockType clocks[2] = {clockType(8, 35, 42), clockType(6, 52, 39)};
```

In fact, the expression `clockType(8, 35, 42)` creates an anonymous object of the **class** `clockType`; initializes its member variables to 8, 35, and 42, respectively; and then uses a member-wise copy to initialize the object `clock[0]`.

Consider the following statement, which creates the object `myClock` and initializes its member variables to 10, 45, and 38, respectively. This is how we have been creating and initializing objects. In fact, the statement:

```
clockType myClock(10, 45, 38);
```

is equivalent to the statement:

```
clockType myClock = clockType(10, 45, 38);
```

However, the first statement is more efficient. It does not first require that an anonymous object be created and then member-wise copied in order to initialize `myClock`.

The main point that we are stressing here, as well as discussed in the preceding section, is the following: To avoid any pitfalls, if a class has constructor(s), it should also have the default constructor.

Destructors

Like constructors, destructors are also functions. Moreover, like constructors, a destructor does not have a type. That is, it is neither a value-returning function nor a void function. However, a class can have only one destructor, and the destructor has no parameters. The name of a destructor is the *tilde* character (~), followed by the name of the class. For example, the name of the destructor for the **class** `clockType` is:

```
~clockType();
```

The destructor automatically executes when the class object goes out of scope. The use of destructors is discussed in subsequent chapters.

Data Abstraction, Classes, and Abstract Data Types

For the car that we drive, most of us want to know how to start the car and drive it. Most people are not concerned with the complexity of how the engine works. By separating the design details of a car's engine from its use, the manufacturer helps the driver focus on how to drive the car. Our daily life has other similar examples. For the most part, we are concerned only with how to use certain items, rather than with how they work.

Separating the design details (that is, how the car's engine works) from its use is called **abstraction**. In other words, abstraction focuses on what the engine does and not on how it works. Thus, abstraction is the process of separating the logical properties from the implementation details. Driving the car is a logical property; the construction of the engine constitutes the implementation details. We have an abstract view of what the engine does, but are not interested in the engine's actual implementation.

Abstraction can also be applied to data. Earlier sections of this chapter defined a data type `clockType`. The data type `clockType` has three member variables and the following basic operations:

1. Set the time.
2. Return the time.
3. Print the time.
4. Increment the time by one second.
5. Increment the time by one minute.
6. Increment the time by one hour.
7. Compare two times to see whether they are equal.

The actual implementation of the operations on, that is, the definitions of the member functions of the class, `clockType` was postponed.

Data abstraction is defined as a process of separating the logical properties of the data from its implementation. The definition of `clockType` and its basic operations are the logical properties; the storing of `clockType` objects in the computer, and the algorithms to perform these operations, are the implementation details of `clockType`.

Abstract data type (ADT): A data type that separates the logical properties from the implementation details.

Like any other data type, an ADT has three things associated with it: the name of the ADT, called the **type name**; the set of values belonging to the ADT, called the **domain**; and the set of **operations** on the data. Following these conventions, we can define the `clockType` ADT as follows:

```
dataTypeName
    clockType
domain
    Each clockType value is a time of day in the form of hours,
    minutes, and seconds.
operations
    Set the time.
    Return the time.
    Print the time.
    Increment the time by one second.
    Increment the time by one minute.
    Increment the time by one hour.
    Compare the two times to see whether they are equal.
```

EXAMPLE 11-8

A list is defined as a set of values of the same type. Because all values in a list are of the same type, a convenient way to represent and process a list is to use an array. You can define a list as an ADT as follows:

```
dataTypeName
    listType
domain
    Every listType value is an array of, say, 1000 numbers
operations
    Check to see whether the list is empty.
    Check to see whether the list is full.
    Search the list for a given item.
    Delete an item from the list.
    Insert an item in the list.
    Sort the list.
    Destroy the list.
    Print the list.
```

The next obvious question is how to implement an ADT in a program. To implement an ADT, you must represent the data and write algorithms to perform the operations.

The previous section used classes to group data and functions together. Furthermore, our definition of a class consisted only of the specifications of the operations; functions to implement the operations were written separately. Thus, we see that classes are a convenient way to implement an ADT. In fact, in C++, classes were specifically designed to handle ADTs.

Next, we define the **class** listType to implement a list as an ADT. Typically in a list, not only do we store the elements, we also keep track of the number of elements in the list. Therefore, our **class** listType has two member variables: one to store the elements and another to keep track of the number of elements in the list. The following **class**, listType, defines the list as an ADT.

```cpp
class listType
{
public:
    bool isEmptyList() const;
    bool isFullList() const;
    int search(int searchItem) const;
    void insert(int newElement);
    void remove(int removeElement);
    void destroyList();
    void printList() const;
    listType(); //constructor

private:
    int list[1000];
    int length;
};
```

Figure 11-11 shows the UML class diagram of the **class listType**.

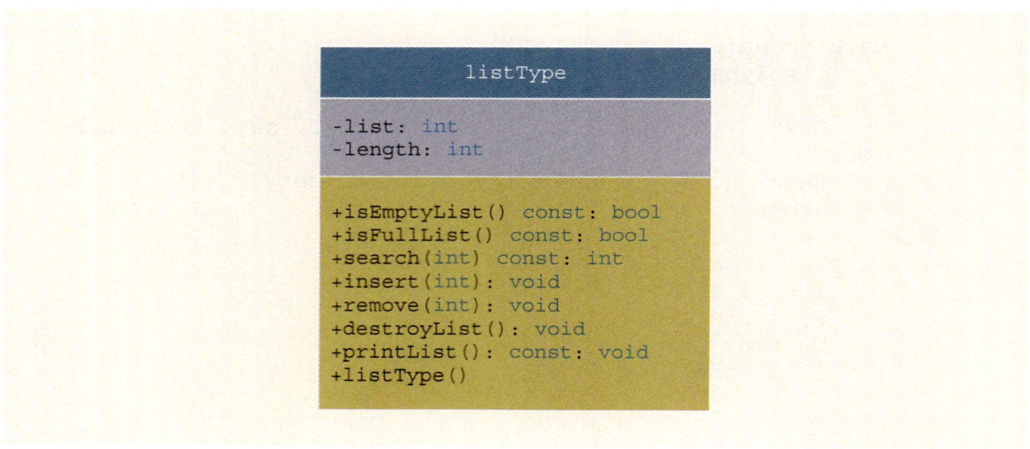

FIGURE 11-11   UML class diagram of the **class** listType

A **struct** Versus a **class**

Chapter 10 defined a **struct** as a fixed collection of components, wherein the components can be of different types. This definition of components in a **struct** included only member variables. However, a C++ **struct** is very similar to a C++ **class**. As with a **class**, members of a **struct** can also be functions, including constructors and a destructor. The only difference between a **struct** and a **class** is that, by default, all members of a **struct** are **public**, and all members of a **class** are **private**. You can use the member access specifier **private** in a **struct** to make a member **private**.

In C, the definition of a **struct** is similar to the definition of a **struct** in C++, as given in Chapter 10. Because C++ evolved from C, the standard **C-struct**s are perfectly acceptable in C++. However, the definition of a **struct** in C++ was expanded to include member functions and constructors and destructors. In the future, because a **class** is a syntactically separate entity, specially designed to handle an ADT, the definition of a **class** may evolve in a completely different way than the definition of a C-like **struct**.

Both C++ **class**es and **struct**s have the same capabilities. However, most programmers restrict their use of structures to adhere to their C-like structure form, and so do not use them to include member functions. In other words, if all of the member variables of a **class** are **public** and the **class** has no member functions, you typically use a **struct** to group these members. This is, in fact, how it is done in this book.

Information Hiding

The previous section defined the **class** clockType to implement the time in a program. We then wrote a program that used the **class** clockType. In fact, we combined the **class** clockType with the function definitions to implement the operations and the function main so as to complete the program. That is, the specification and implementation details of the **class** clockType were directly incorporated into the program.

Is it a good practice to include the specification and implementation details of a class in the program? Definitely not. There are several reasons for not doing so. Suppose the definition of the class and the definitions of the member functions are directly included in the user's program. The user then has direct access to the definition of the class and the definitions of the member functions. Therefore, the user can modify the operations in any way the user pleases. The user can also modify the member variables of an object in any way the user pleases. Thus, in this sense, the **private** member variables of an object are no longer **private** to the object.

If several programmers use the same object in a project, and if they have direct access to the internal parts of the object, there is no guarantee that every programmer will use the same object in exactly the same way. Thus, we must hide the implementation details. The user should know only what the object does, not how it does it. Hiding the implementation details frees the user from having to fit this extra piece of code in the program. Also, by hiding the details, we can ensure that an object will be used in exactly the same way throughout the project. Furthermore, once an object has been written, debugged, and tested properly, it becomes (and remains) error-free.

This section discusses how to hide the implementation details of an object. For illustration purposes, we will use the **class** clockType.

To implement clockType in a program, the user must declare objects of type clockType, and know which operations are allowed and what the operations do.

So the user must have access to the specification details. Because the user is not concerned with the implementation details, we must put those details in a separate file, called an **implementation file**. Also, because the specification details can be too long, we must free the user from having to include them directly in the program. However, the user must be able to look at the specification details so that he or she can correctly call the functions, and so forth. We must, therefore, put the specification details in a separate file. The file that contains the specification details is called the **header file** (or **interface file**).

The implementation file contains the definitions of the functions to implement the operations of an object. This file contains, among other things (such as the preprocessor directives), the C++ statements. Because a C++ program can have only one function, `main`, the implementation file does not contain the function `main`. Only the user program contains the function `main`. Because the implementation file does not contain the function `main`, we cannot produce the executable code from this file. In fact, we produce what is called the object code from the implementation file. The user then links the object code produced by the implementation file with the object code of the program that uses the class to create the final executable code.

Finally, the header file has an extension h, whereas the implementation file has an extension cpp. Suppose that the specification details of the `class` `clockType` are in a file called `clockType`. The complete name of this file should then be `clockType.h`. If the implementation details of the `class` `clockType` are in a file—say, `clockTypeImp`— the name of this file must be `clockTypeImp.cpp`.

The file `clockTypeImp.cpp` contains only the definitions of the functions, not the definition of the class. Thus, to resolve the problem of an undeclared identifier (such as the function names and variable names), we include the header file `clockType.h` in the file `clockTypeImp.cpp` with the help of the `include` statement. The following `include` statement is required by any program that uses the `class` `clockType`, as well as by the implementation file that defines the operations for the `class` `clockType`:

```
#include "clockType.h"
```

Note that the header file `clockType.h` is enclosed in double quotation marks, not angular brackets. The header file `clockType.h` is called the user-defined header file. Typically, all user-defined header files are enclosed in double quotation marks, whereas the system-provided header files (such as `iostream`) are enclosed between angular brackets.

The implementation contains the definitions of the functions, and these definitions are hidden from the user because the user is typically provided *only* the object code. However, the user of the class should be aware of what a particular function does and how to use it. Therefore, in the specification file with the function prototypes, we include comments that briefly describe the function and specify any preconditions and/or postconditions.

Precondition: A statement specifying the condition(s) that must be true before the function is called.

Postcondition: A statement specifying what is true after the function call is completed.

Following are the specification and implementation files for the **class** clockType:

```cpp
//clockType.h, the specification file for the class clockType

class clockType
{
public:
    void  setTime(int  hours, int  minutes, int seconds);
      //Function to set the time.
      //The time is set according to the parameters.
      //Postcondition: hr = hours; min = minutes;
      //               sec = seconds;
      //               The function checks whether the
      //               values of hours, minutes, and seconds
      //               are valid. If a value is invalid, the
      //               default value 0 is assigned.

    void getTime(int& hours, int& minutes, int& seconds) const;
      //Function to return the time.
      //Postcondition: hours = hr; minutes = min;
      //               seconds = sec;

    void printTime() const;
      //Function to print the time.
      //Postcondition: The time is printed in the form
      //               hh:mm:ss.

    void incrementSeconds();
      //Function to increment the time by one second.
      //Postcondition: The time is incremented by one second.
      //               If the before-increment time is
      //               23:59:59, the time is reset to 00:00:00.

    void incrementMinutes();
      //Function to increment the time by one minute.
      //Postcondition: The time is incremented by one minute.
      //               If the before-increment time is
      //               23:59:53, the time is reset to 00:00:53.

    void incrementHours();
      //Function to increment the time by one hour.
      //Postcondition: The time is incremented by one hour.
      //               If the before-increment time is
      //               23:45:53, the time is reset to 00:45:53.

    bool equalTime(const clockType& otherClock) const;
      //Function to compare the two times.
      //Postcondition: Returns true if this time is equal to
      //               otherClock; otherwise, returns false.
```

```cpp
    clockType(int hours, int minutes, int seconds);
      //Constructor with parameters.
      //The time is set according to the parameters.
      //Postcondition: hr = hours; min = minutes;
      //               sec = seconds;
      //               The constructor checks whether the
      //               values of hours, minutes, and seconds
      //               are valid. If a value is invalid, the
      //               default value 0 is assigned.

    clockType();
      //Default constructor
      //The time is set to 00:00:00.
      //Postcondition: hr = 0; min = 0; sec = 0;

private:
    int hr;   //variable to store the hours
    int min;  //variable to store the minutes
    int sec;  //variable to store the seconds
};

//clockTypeImp.cpp, the implementation file

#include  <iostream>
#include  "clockType.h"

using namespace  std;
     .
     .
     .
//Place the definitions of the member functions of the class
//clockType here.
     .
     .
     .
```

Next, we describe the user file containing the program that uses the **class** clockType.

```cpp
//The user program that uses the class clockType

#include  <iostream>
#include  "clockType.h"

using namespace  std;
     .
     .
     .
//Place the definitions of the function main and the other
//user-defined functions here
     .
     .
     .
```

NOTE To save space, we have not provided the complete details of the implementation file and the file that contains the user program. However, you can find these files and the specification (header) file at the Web site accompanying this book.

Executable Code

The previous section discussed how to hide the implementation details of a class. To use an object in a program, during execution the program must be able to access the implementation details of the object (that is, the algorithms to implement the operations on the object). This section discusses how a client's program obtains access to the implementation details of an object. For illustration purposes, we will use the **class** clockType.

As explained previously, to use the **class** clockType, the program must include the header file clockType.h via the **include** statement. For example, the following program segment includes the header file clockType.h:

```
//Program test.cpp

#include "clockType.h"
  .
  .
  .
int main()
{
    .
    .
    .
}
```

The program test.cpp must include only the header file, not the implementation file. To create the executable code to run the program test.cpp, the following steps are required:

1. We separately compile the file clockTypeImp.cpp and create the object code file clockTypeImp.obj. The object code file contains the machine language code, but the code is not in an executable form. Suppose that the command cc invokes the C++ compiler or linker, or both, on the computer's system command line. The command:

    ```
    cc -c clockTypeImp.cpp
    ```

    creates the object code file clockTypeImp.obj.

2. To create the executable code for the source code file test.cpp, we compile the source code file test.cpp, create the object code file test.obj, and then link the files test.obj and clockTypeImp.obj to create the executable file test.exe. The following command on the system command line creates the executable file test.exe:

    ```
    cc test.cpp clockTypeImp.obj
    ```

NOTE

1. To create the object code file for any source code file, we use the command line option `-c` on the system command line. For example, to create the object code file for the source code file, called `exercise.cpp`, we use the following command on the system command line:

   ```
   cc -c exercise.cpp
   ```

2. To link more than one object code file with a source code file, we list all of the object code files on the system command line. For example, to link `A.obj` and `B.obj` with the source code file `test.cpp`, we use the command:

   ```
   cc test.cpp A.obj B.obj
   ```

3. If a source code file is modified, it must be recompiled.

4. If modifications in one source file affect other files, the other files must be recompiled and relinked.

5. The user must have access to the header file and the object code file. Access to the header file is needed to see what the objects do and how to use them. Access to the object code file is needed so that the user can link the program with the object code to produce an executable code. The user does not need access to the source code file containing the implementation details.

As stated in Chapter 1, SDK's Visual C++, Visual Studio .NET, C++ Builder, and CodeWarrior put the editor, compiler, and linker all into one package. With one command, the program is compiled and linked with the other necessary files. These systems also manage multiple-file programs in the form of a project. Thus, a project consists of several files, called the project files. These systems usually have a command, called **build, rebuild,** or **make**. (Check your system's documentation.) When the build, rebuild, or make command is applied to a project, the system automatically compiles and links all the files required to create the executable code. When one or more files in the project change, you can use these commands to recompile and relink the files.

Example 11-9 further illustrates how classes are designed and implemented. The **class personType** that is designed in Example 11-9 is very useful; we will use this class in subsequent chapters.

EXAMPLE 11-9

The most common attributes of a person are the person's first name and last name. The typical operations on a person's name are to set the name and print the name. The following statements define a class with these properties:

```cpp
#include <string>

using namespace std;

class personType
{
public:
    void print() const;
      //Function to output the first name and last name
      //in the form firstName lastName.

    void setName(string first, string last);
      //Function to set firstName and lastName according
      //to the parameters.
      //Postcondition: firstName = first; lastName = last;

    string getFirstName() const;
      //Function to return the first name.
      //Postcondition: The value of firstName is returned.

    string getLastName() const;
      //Function to return the last name.
      //Postcondition: The value of lastName is returned.

    personType(string first = "", string last = "");
      //Constructor
      //Sets firstName and lastName according to the parameters.
      //The default values of the parameters are null strings.
      //Postcondition: firstName = first; lastName = last;

private:
    string firstName; //variable to store the first name
    string lastName;  //variable to store the last name
};
```

Figure 11-12 shows the UML class diagram of the **class** personType.

```
                      personType
-firstName: string
-lastName: string

+print(): void
+setName(string, string): void
+getFirstName() const: string
+getLastName() const: string
+personType(string = "", string = "")
```

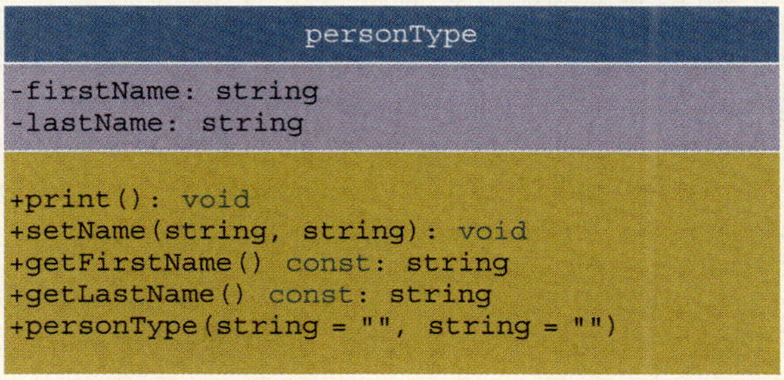

FIGURE 11-12   UML class diagram of the **class** personType

We now give the definitions of the member functions of the **class** personType:

```cpp
void personType::print() const
{
    cout << firstName << " " << lastName;
}

void personType::setName(string first, string last)
{
    firstName = first;
    lastName = last;
}

string personType::getFirstName() const
{
    return firstName;
}

string personType::getLastName() const
{
    return lastName;
}

    //constructor
personType::personType(string first, string last)

{
    firstName = first;
    lastName = last;
}
```

Static Members of a Class

NOTE   This section may be skipped without any loss of continuation.

In Chapter 7, we described two types of variables, automatic and **static**. Recall that if a local variable of a function is **static**, it exists between function calls. Similar to **static** variables, a class can have **static** members, functions, or variables. Let us note the following about the **static** members of a class:

- If a function of a class is **static**, in the class definition it is declared using the keyword **static** in its heading.

- If a member variable of a class is **static**, it is declared using the keyword **static**, as discussed in Chapter 7 and also illustrated in Example 11-10.

- A **public static** member, function, or variable of a class can be accessed using the class name and the scope resolution operator.

Example 11-10 clarifies the effect of the keyword **static**.

EXAMPLE 11-10

Consider the following definition of the **class illustrate**:

```cpp
class illustrate
{
public:
    static int count;     //public static variable

    void print() const;
      //Function to output x, y, and count.

    void setX(int a);
      //Function to set x.
      //Postcondition: x = a;

    static void incrementY();
      //static function
      //Function to increment y by 1.
      //Postcondition: y = y + 1

    illustrate(int a = 0);
      //constructor
      //Postcondition: x = a;
      //                  If no value is specified for a, x = 0;

private:
    int x;
    static int y;   //private static variable
};
```

Suppose that the **static** member variables, and the definitions of the member functions of the **class** illustrate, are as follows. (These statements are all placed in the implementation file. Also, notice that all **static** member variables are initialized, as shown below.)

```cpp
int illustrate::count = 0;
int illustrate::y = 0;

void illustrate::print() const
{
    cout << "x = " << x << ", y = " << y
         << ", count = " << count << endl;
}
```

```cpp
void illustrate::setX(int a)
{
    x = a;
}

void illustrate::incrementY()
{
    y++;
}

illustrate::illustrate(int a)
{
    x = a;
}
```

Because the function `incrementY` is **static** and **public**, the following statement is legal:

```cpp
illustrate::incrementY();
```

Similarly, because the member variable `count` is **static** and **public**, the following statement is legal:

```cpp
illustrate::count++;
```

Next, we elaborate on **static** member variables a bit more. Suppose that you have a **class**, say, `myClass`, with member variables (**static** as well as non-**static**). When you create objects of type `myClass`, only non-**static** member variables of the **class** `myClass` become the member variables of each object. For each **static** member variable of a **class**, C++ allocates only one memory space. All `myClass` objects refer to the same memory space. In fact, **static** member variables of a **class** *exist* even when no object of that **class** type exists. You can access the **public static** member variables outside the **class**, as explained in the previous section.

Example 11-11 further clarifies how memory space is allocated for **static** and non-**static** member variables of a class.

Suppose that you have the **class** `illustrate`, as given in Example 11-10. Memory space then exists for the **static** member variables `y` and `count`.

Consider the following statements:

```cpp
illustrate illusObject1(3);     //Line 1
illustrate illusObject2(5);     //Line 2
```

The statements in Line 1 and Line 2 declare `illusObject1` and `illusObject2` to be `illustrate` type objects (see Figure 11-13).

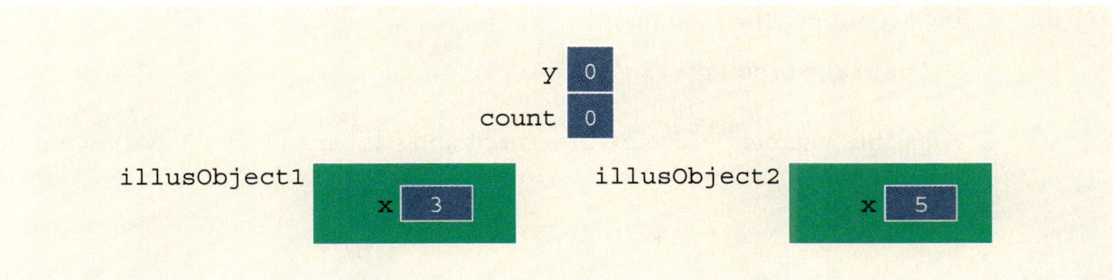

FIGURE 11-13 `illusObject1` and `illusObject2`

Now consider the following statements:

```
illustrate::incrementY();
illustrate::count++;
```

After these statements execute, the objects and static members are as shown in Figure 11-14.

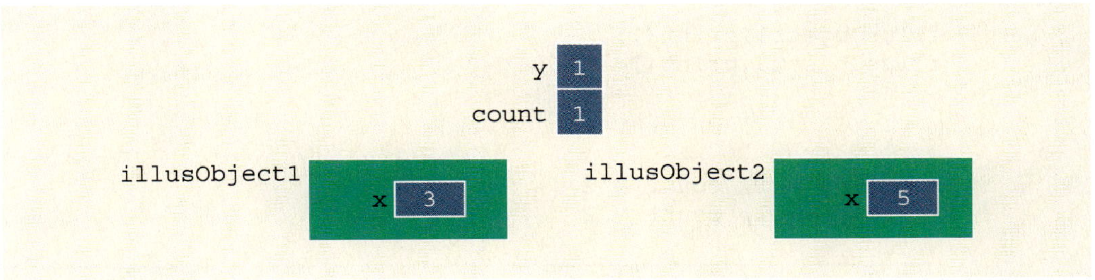

FIGURE 11-14 `illusObject1` and `illusObject2` after the statements `illustrate::incrementY();` and `illustrate::count++;` execute

The output of the statement:

```
illusObject1.print();
```

is:

```
x = 3, y = 1, count = 1
```

Similarly, the output of the statement:

```
illusObject2.print();
```

is:

```
x = 5, y = 1, count = 1
```

Now consider the statement:

```
illustrate::count++;
```

After this statement executes, the objects and static members are as shown in Figure 11-15.

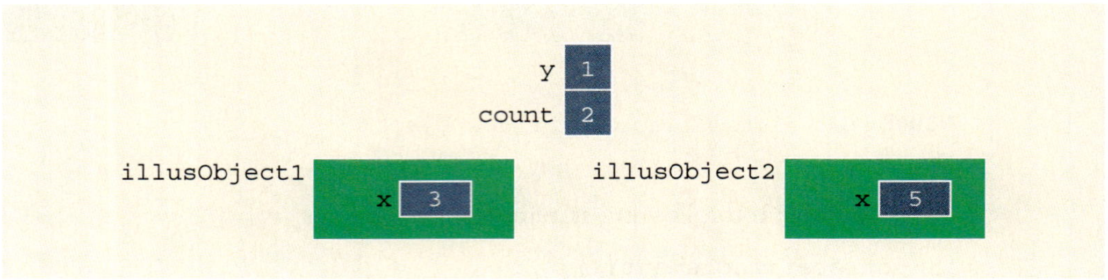

FIGURE 11-15 `illusObject1` and `illusObject2` after the statement `illustrate::count++;` executes

The output of the statements:

```
illusObject1.print();
illusObject2.print();
```

is:

```
x = 3, y = 1, count = 2
x = 5, y = 1, count = 2
```

The program in Example 11-11 further illustrates how **static** members of a class work.

EXAMPLE 11-11

```cpp
#include <iostream>

#include "illustrate.h"

using namespace std;

int main()
{
    illustrate illusObject1(3);                  //Line 1
    illustrate illusObject2(5);                  //Line 2

    illustrate::incrementY();                    //Line 3
    illustrate::count++;                         //Line 4
    illusObject1.print();                        //Line 5
    illusObject2.print();                        //Line 6
```

```cpp
    cout << "Line 7: ***Increment y using "
         << "illusObject1***" << endl;                  //Line 7

    illusObject1.incrementY();                          //Line 8
    illusObject1.setX(8);                               //Line 9
    illusObject1.print();                               //Line 10
    illusObject2.print();                               //Line 11

    cout << "Line 12: ***Increment y using "
         << "illusObject2***" << endl;                  //Line 12

    illusObject2.incrementY();                          //Line 13
    illusObject2.setX(23);                              //Line 14
    illusObject1.print();                               //Line 15
    illusObject2.print();                               //Line 16

    return 0;
}
```

Sample Run:

```
x = 3, y = 1, count = 1
x = 5, y = 1, count = 1
Line 7: ***Increment y using illusObject1***
x = 8, y = 2, count = 1
x = 5, y = 2, count = 1
Line 12: ***Increment y using illusObject2***
x = 8, y = 3, count = 1
x = 23, y = 3, count = 1
```

The preceding program works as follows. The **static** member variables y and count are initialized to 0. The statement in Line 1 declares illusObject1 to be an object of the **class** illustrate and initializes its member variable x to 3. The statement in Line 2 declares illusObject2 to be an object of the **class** illustrate and initializes its member variable x to 5.

The statement in Line 3 uses the name of the **class** illustrate and the function incrementY to increment y. Now count is a **public static** member of the **class** illustrate. So the statement in Line 4 uses the name of the **class** illustrate to directly access count, and increments it by 1. The statements in Lines 5 and 6 output the data stored in the objects illusObject1 and illusObject2. Notice that the value of y for both objects is the same. Similarly, the value of count for both objects is the same.

The statement in Line 7 is an output statement. The statement in Line 8 uses the object illusObject1 and the function incrementY to increment y. The statement in Line 9 sets the value of the member variable x of illusObject1 to 8. Lines 10 and 11 output the data stored in the objects illusObject1 and illusObject2. Notice that the value of y for both objects is the same. Similarly, the value of count for both objects is the same. Moreover, notice that the statement in Line 9 changes only the value of the member variable x of illusObject1 because x is *not* a **static** member of the **class** illustrate.

The statement in Line 13 uses the object `illusObject2` and the function `incrementY` to increment `y`. The statement in Line 14 sets the value of the member variable `x` of `illusObject2` to 23. Lines 15 and 16 output the data stored in the objects `illusObject1` and `illusObject2`. Notice that the value of `y` for both objects is the same. Similarly, the value of `count` for both objects is the same. Moreover, notice that the statement in Line 14 changes only the value of the member variable `x` of `illusObject2`, because `x` is *not* a `static` member of the `class` illustrate.

NOTE Here are some additional comments on `static` members of a class. As you have seen in this section, a `static` member function of a class does not need any object to be invoked. It can be called using the name of the class and the scope resolution operator, as illustrated. Therefore, a `static` member function cannot use anything that depends on a calling object. In other words, in the definition of a `static` member function you cannot use a non-`static` member variable or a non-`static` function, unless there is an object declared locally that accesses the non-`static` member variable or the non-`static` member function.

Let us again consider the `class` illustrate, as defined in Example 11-10. This class contains both `static` and non-`static` member variables. When we declare objects of this class, each object has its own copy of the member variable `x`, which is non-`static`, and all objects share the member variables `y` and `count`, which are `static`. Earlier in this chapter, we defined the terminology instance variables of a class using the `class` clockType. However, at that point, we did not discuss `static` member variables of a class. A class can have `static` as well as non-`static` member variables. We can, therefore, make the general statement that non-`static` member variables of a class are called the instance variables of the class.

PROGRAMMING EXAMPLE: Candy Machine

A common place to buy candy is from a machine. A new candy machine has been purchased for the gym, but it is not working properly. The machine sells candies, chips, gum, and cookies. You have been asked to write a program for this candy machine so that it can be put into operation.

The program should do the following:

1. Show the customer the different products sold by the candy machine.
2. Let the customer make the selection.

3. Show the customer the cost of the item selected.

4. Accept money from the customer.

5. Release the item.

Input The item selection and the cost of the item.

Output The selected item.

PROBLEM
ANALYSIS
AND
ALGORITHM
DESIGN

A candy machine has two main components: a built-in cash register and several dispensers to hold and release the products.

Cash Register

Let us first discuss the properties of a cash register. The register has some cash on hand, it accepts the amount from the customer, and if the amount deposited is more than the cost of the item, then—if possible—it returns the change. For simplicity, we assume that the user deposits the exact amount of money for the product. The cash register should also be able to show to the candy machine's owner the amount of money in the register at any given time. The following class defines the properties of a cash register:

```cpp
class cashRegister
{
public:
    int getCurrentBalance() const;
      //Function to show the current amount in the cash
      //register.
      //Postcondition: The value of cashOnHand is returned.

    void acceptAmount(int amountIn);
      //Function to receive the amount deposited by
      //the customer and update the amount in the register.
      //Postcondition: cashOnHand = cashOnHand + amountIn;

    cashRegister(int cashIn = 500);
      //Constructor
      //Sets the cash in the register to a specific amount.
      //Postcondition: cashOnHand = cashIn;
      //               If no value is specified when the
      //               object is declared, the default value
      //               assigned to cashOnHand is 500.

private:
    int cashOnHand;   //variable to store the cash
                      //in the register
};
```

Figure 11-16 shows the UML class diagram of the **class** cashRegister.

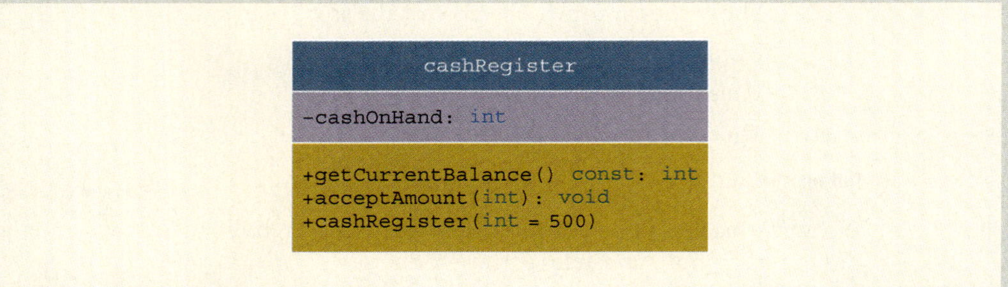

FIGURE 11-16 UML class diagram of the `class` `cashRegister`

Next, we give the definitions of the functions to implement the operations of the `class` `cashRegister`. The definitions of these functions are very simple and easy to follow.

The function `getCurrentBalance` shows the current amount in the cash register. It returns the value of the `private` member variable `cashOnHand`. So its definition is:

```
int cashRegister::getCurrentBalance() const
{
    return cashOnHand;
}
```

The function `acceptAmount` accepts the amount of money deposited by the customer. It updates the cash in the register by adding the amount deposited by the customer to the previous amount in the cash register. Essentially, the definition of this function is:

```
void cashRegister::acceptAmount(int amountIn)
{
    cashOnHand = cashOnHand + amountIn;
}
```

In the definition of the `class` `cashRegister`, the constructor is declared with a default value. Therefore, if the user does not specify any value when the object is declared, the default value is used to initialize the member variable `cashOnHand`. Recall that, because we have specified the default value for the constructor's parameter in the definition of the class, in the heading of the definition of the constructor we do not specify the default value. The definition of the constructor is as follows:

```
cashRegister::cashRegister(int cashIn)
{
    if (cashIn >= 0)
        cashOnHand = cashIn;
    else
        cashOnHand = 500;
}
```

Note that the definition of the constructor checks for valid values of the parameter `cashIn`. If the value of `cashIn` is less than 0, the value assigned to the member variable `cashOnHand` is 500.

Dispenser The dispenser releases the selected item if it is not empty. It should show the number of items in the dispenser and the cost of the item. The following class defines the properties of a dispenser. Let us call this `class dispenserType`:

```cpp
class dispenserType
{
public:
    int getNoOfItems() const;
        //Function to show the number of items in the machine.
        //Postcondition: The value of numberOfItems is returned.

    int getCost() const;
        //Function to show the cost of the item.
        //Postcondition: The value of cost is returned.

    void makeSale();
        //Function to reduce the number of items by 1.
        //Postcondition: numberOfItems--;

    dispenserType(int setNoOfItems = 50, int setCost = 50);
        //Constructor
        //Sets the cost and number of items in the dispenser
        //to the values specified by the user.
        //Postcondition: numberOfItems = setNoOfItems;
        //               cost = setCost;
        //               If no value is specified for a
        //               parameter, then its default value is
        //               assigned to the corresponding member
        //               variable.

private:
    int numberOfItems;   //variable to store the number of
                         //items in the dispenser
    int cost;  //variable to store the cost of an item
};
```

Figure 11-17 shows the UML class diagram of the `class dispenserType`.

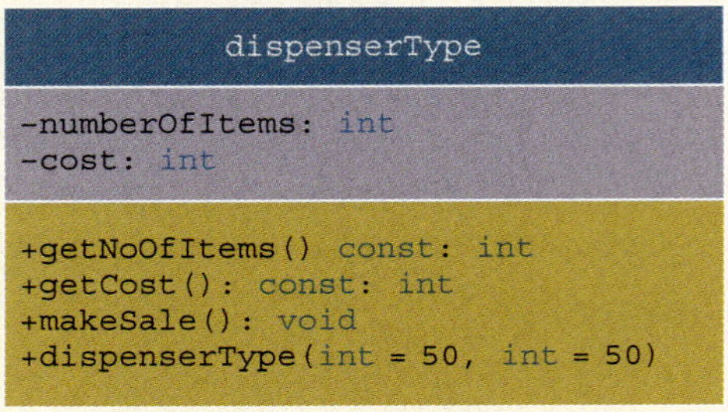

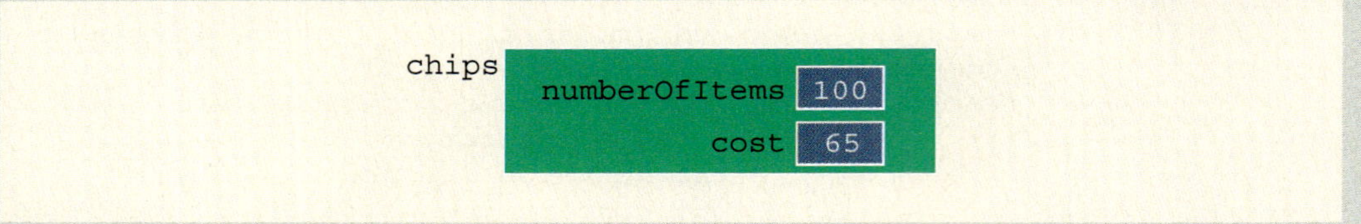

FIGURE 11-17 UML class diagram of the **class** dispenserType

Because the candy machine sells four types of items, we shall declare four objects of type `dispenserType`. For example, the statement:

```
dispenserType chips(100, 65);
```

declares `chips` to be an object of type `dispenserType`, and sets the number of chip bags in the dispenser to 100 and the cost of each chip bag to 65 cents (see Figure 11-18).

FIGURE 11-18 Object chips

Next, we discuss the definitions of the functions to implement the operations of the **class** `dispenserType`.

The function `getNoOfItems` returns the number of items of a particular product. Because the number of items currently in the dispenser is stored in the **private** member variable `numberOfItems`, the function returns the value of `numberOfItems`. The definition of this function is:

```
int dispenserType::getNoOfItems() const
{
    return numberOfItems;
}
```

The function `getCost` returns the cost of a product. Because the cost of a product is stored in the **private** member variable `cost`, the function returns the value of `cost`. The definition of this function is:

```cpp
int dispenserType::getCost() const
{
    return cost;
}
```

When a product is sold, the number of items in that dispenser is reduced by 1. Therefore, the function `makeSale` reduces the number of items in the dispenser by 1. That is, it decrements the value of the **private** member variable `numberOfItems` by 1. The definition of this function is:

```cpp
void dispenserType::makeSale()
{
    numberOfItems--;
}
```

The definition of the constructor checks for valid values of the parameters. If these values are less than 0, the default values are assigned to the member variables. The definition of the constructor is:

```cpp
    //constructor
dispenserType::dispenserType(int setNoOfItems, int setCost)
{
    if (setNoOfItems >= 0)
        numberOfItems = setNoOfItems;
    else
        numberOfItems = 50;

    if (setCost >= 0)
        cost = setCost;
    else
        cost = 50;
}
```

MAIN PROGRAM

When the program executes, it must do the following:

1. Show the different products sold by the candy machine.
2. Show how to select a particular product.
3. Show how to terminate the program.

Furthermore, these instructions must be displayed after processing each selection (except exiting the program), so that the user need not remember what to do if he or she wants to buy two or more items. Once the user has made the appropriate selection, the candy machine must act accordingly. If the user has opted to buy a product and if that product is available, the candy machine should show the cost of the product and ask the user to deposit the money. If the amount deposited is at least the cost of the item, the candy machine should sell the item and display an appropriate message.

This discussion translates into the following algorithm:

1. Show the selection to the customer.
2. Get the selection.
3. If the selection is valid and the dispenser corresponding to the selection is not empty, sell the product.

We divide this program into three functions—showSelection, sellProduct, and main.

showSelection This function displays the information necessary to help the user select and buy a product. Essentially, it contains the following output statements. (We assume that the candy machine sells four types of products.)

a. *** Welcome to Shelly's Candy Shop ***"
b. To select an item, enter
c. 1 for Candy
d. 2 for Chips
e. 3 for Gum
f. 4 for Cookies
g. 9 to exit

This definition of the function showSelection is:

```cpp
void showSelection()
{
    cout << "*** Welcome to Shelly's Candy Shop ***" << endl;
    cout << "To select an item, enter " << endl;
    cout << "1 for Candy" << endl;
    cout << "2 for Chips" << endl;
    cout << "3 for Gum" << endl;
    cout << "4 for Cookies" << endl;
    cout << "9 to exit" << endl;
}//end showSelection
```

sellProduct This function attempts to sell the product selected by the customer. Therefore, it must have access to the dispenser holding the product. The first thing that this function does is check whether the dispenser holding the product is empty. If the dispenser is empty, the function informs the customer that this product is sold out. If the dispenser is not empty, it tells the user to deposit the necessary amount to buy the product.

If the user does not deposit enough money to buy the product, sellProduct tells the user how much additional money must be deposited. If the user fails to deposit enough money, in two tries, to buy the product, the function simply returns the money. (Programming Exercise 8, at the end of this chapter, asks you to revise the definition of the method sellProduct so that it keeps asking the user to enter the additional amount as long as the user has not entered enough money to buy the product.) If the amount deposited by the user is sufficient, it accepts the money and sells the product. Selling the product means to decrement the number of items in the dispenser by 1, and to update the money in the cash register by adding the cost of the product. (Because this program does not return the extra money deposited by the customer, the cash register is updated by adding the money entered by the user.)

From this discussion, it is clear that the function `sellProduct` must have access to the dispenser holding the product (to decrement the number of items in the dispenser by 1 and to show the cost of the item) as well as the cash register (to update the cash). Therefore, this function has two parameters: one corresponding to the dispenser and the other corresponding to the cash register. Furthermore, both parameters must be referenced.

In pseudocode, the algorithm for this function is:

1. If the dispenser is not empty,

    a. Show and prompt the customer to enter the cost of the item.

    b. Get the amount entered by the customer.

    c. If the amount entered by the customer is less than the cost of the product,

        i. Show and prompt the customer to enter the additional amount.

        ii. Calculate the total amount entered by the customer.

    d. If the amount entered by the customer is at least the cost of the product,

        i. Update the amount in the cash register.

        ii. Sell the product—that is, decrement the number of items in the dispenser by 1.

        iii. Display an appropriate message.

    e. If the amount entered by the user is less than the cost of the item, return the amount.

2. If the dispenser is empty, tell the user that this product is sold out.

This definition of the function `sellProduct` is:

```
void sellProduct(dispenserType& product,
                 cashRegister& pCounter)
{
    int amount;   //variable to hold the amount entered
    int amount2;  //variable to hold the extra amount needed

    if (product.getNoOfItems() > 0) //if the dispenser is not
                                    //empty
```

```cpp
    {
        cout << "Please deposit " << product.getCost()
            << " cents" << endl;
        cin >> amount;

        if (amount < product.getCost())
        {
            cout << "Please deposit another "
                << product.getCost()- amount
                << " cents" << endl;
            cin >> amount2;
            amount = amount + amount2;
        }

        if (amount >= product.getCost())
        {

            pCounter.acceptAmount(amount);
            product.makeSale();
            cout << "Collect your item at the bottom and "
                << "enjoy." << endl;
        }
        else
            cout << "The amount is not enough. "
                << "Collect what you deposited." << endl;

        cout << "*-*-*-*-*-*-*-*-*-*-*-*-*-*-*-*-*-*-*"
            << endl << endl;
    }
    else
        cout << "Sorry, this item is sold out." << endl;
}//end sellProduct
```

Now that we have described the functions `showSelection` and `sellProduct`, the function **main** is described next.

<table>
<tr><td><code>main</code></td><td>

The algorithm for the function **main** is as follows:

1. Create the cash register—that is, declare an object of type `cashRegister`.

2. Create four dispensers—that is, declare four objects of type `dispenserType` and initialize these objects. For example, the statement:

```cpp
dispenserType candy(100, 50);
```

creates a dispenser object, `candy`, to hold the candies. The number of items in the dispenser is 100, and the cost of an item is 50 cents.

3. Declare additional variables as necessary.

4. Show the selection; call the function `showSelection`.
</td></tr>
</table>

5.   Get the selection.

6.   While not done (a selection of 9 exits the program),

    a.   Sell the product; call the function `sellProduct`.

    b.   Show the selection; call the function `showSelection`.

    c.   Get the selection.

The definition of the function `main` is as follows:

```cpp
int main()
{
    cashRegister counter;
    dispenserType candy(100, 50);
    dispenserType chips(100, 65);
    dispenserType gum(75, 45);
    dispenserType cookies(100, 85);

    int choice;   //variable to hold the selection

    showSelection();
    cin >> choice;

    while (choice != 9)
    {
        switch (choice)
        {
        case 1:
            sellProduct(candy, counter);
            break;
        case 2:
            sellProduct(chips, counter);
            break;
        case 3:
            sellProduct(gum, counter);
            break;
        case 4:
            sellProduct(cookies, counter);
            break;
        default :
            cout << "Invalid selection." << endl;
        }//end switch

        showSelection();
        cin >> choice;
    }//end while

    return 0;

}//end main
```

COMPLETE PROGRAM LISTING

```cpp
//Candy Machine Header File

class cashRegister
{
public:
    int getCurrentBalance() const;
        //Function to show the current amount in the cash
        //register.
        //Postcondition: The value of cashOnHand is returned.

    void acceptAmount(int amountIn);
        //Function to receive the amount deposited by
        //the customer and update the amount in the register.
        //Postcondition: cashOnHand = cashOnHand + amountIn;

    cashRegister(int cashIn = 500);
        //Constructor
        //Sets the cash in the register to a specific amount.
        //Postcondition: cashOnHand = cashIn;
        //               If no value is specified when the
        //               object is declared, the default value
        //               assigned to cashOnHand is 500.

private:
    int cashOnHand;     //variable to store the cash
                        //in the register
};



//*********** class dispenserType

class dispenserType
{
public:
    int getNoOfItems() const;
        //Function to show the number of items in the machine.
        //Postcondition: The value of numberOfItems is returned.

    int getCost() const;
        //Function to show the cost of the item.
        //Postcondition: The value of cost is returned.

    void makeSale();
        //Function to reduce the number of items by 1.
        //Postcondition: numberOfItems--;

    dispenserType(int setNoOfItems = 50, int setCost = 50);
        //Constructor
        //Sets the cost and number of items in the dispenser
        //to the values specified by the user.
```

```cpp
        //Postcondition: numberOfItems = setNoOfItems;
        //                cost = setCost;
        //                If no value is specified for a
        //                parameter, then its default value is
        //                assigned to the corresponding member
        //                variable.

private:
    int numberOfItems;        //variable to store the number of
                              //items in the dispenser
    int cost;  //variable to store the cost of an item
};


//Implementation file candyMachineImp.cpp
//This file contains the definitions of the functions to
//implement the operations of the classes cashRegister and
//dispenserType

#include <iostream>
#include "candyMachine.h"

using namespace std;

int cashRegister::getCurrentBalance() const
{
    return cashOnHand;
}

void cashRegister::acceptAmount(int amountIn)
{
    cashOnHand = cashOnHand + amountIn;
}

cashRegister::cashRegister(int cashIn)
{
    if (cashIn >= 0)
        cashOnHand = cashIn;
    else
        cashOnHand = 500;
}

int dispenserType::getNoOfItems() const
{
    return numberOfItems;
}

int dispenserType::getCost() const
{
    return cost;
}

void dispenserType::makeSale()
{
    numberOfItems--;
}
```

```cpp
dispenserType::dispenserType(int setNoOfItems, int setCost)
{
    if (setNoOfItems >= 0)
        numberOfItems = setNoOfItems;
    else
        numberOfItems = 50;

    if (setCost >= 0)
        cost = setCost;
    else
        cost = 50;
}


// Main Program
#include <iostream>
#include "candyMachine.h"

using namespace std;

void showSelection();
void sellProduct(dispenserType& product,
                 cashRegister& pCounter);

int main()
{
    cashRegister counter;
    dispenserType candy(100, 50);
    dispenserType chips(100, 65);
    dispenserType gum(75, 45);
    dispenserType cookies(100, 85);

    int choice;   //variable to hold the selection

    showSelection();
    cin >> choice;

    while (choice != 9)
    {
        switch (choice)
        {
        case 1:
            sellProduct(candy, counter);
            break;
        case 2:
            sellProduct(chips, counter);
            break;
        case 3:
            sellProduct(gum, counter);
            break;
        case 4:
            sellProduct(cookies, counter);
            break;
        default:
            cout << "Invalid selection." << endl;
        }//end switch
```

```cpp
        showSelection();
        cin >> choice;
    }//end while

    return 0;
}//end main

void showSelection()
{
    cout << "*** Welcome to Shelly's Candy Shop ***" << endl;
    cout << "To select an item, enter " << endl;
    cout << "1 for Candy" << endl;
    cout << "2 for Chips" << endl;
    cout << "3 for Gum" << endl;
    cout << "4 for Cookies" << endl;
    cout << "9 to exit" << endl;
}//end showSelection

void sellProduct(dispenserType& product,
                 cashRegister& pCounter)
{
    int amount;   //variable to hold the amount entered
    int amount2;  //variable to hold the extra amount needed

    if (product.getNoOfItems() > 0) //if the dispenser is not
                                    //empty
    {
        cout << "Please deposit " << product.getCost()
             << " cents" << endl;
        cin >> amount;

        if (amount < product.getCost())
        {
            cout << "Please deposit another "
                 << product.getCost()- amount
                 << " cents" << endl;
            cin >> amount2;
            amount = amount + amount2;
        }

        if (amount >= product.getCost())
        {
            pCounter.acceptAmount(amount);
            product.makeSale();
            cout << "Collect your item at the bottom and "
                 << "enjoy." << endl;
        }
        else
            cout << "The amount is not enough. "
                 << "Collect what you deposited." << endl;

        cout << "*-*-*-*-*-*-*-*-*-*-*-*-*-*-*-*-*-*-*-*"
             << endl << endl;
    }
```

```
        else
            cout << "Sorry, this item is sold out." << endl;
}//end sellProduct
```

Sample Run: In this sample run, the user input is shaded.

```
*** Welcome to Shelly's Candy Shop ***
To select an item, enter
1 for Candy
2 for Chips
3 for Gum
4 for Cookies
9 to exit
1
Please deposit 50 cents
50
Collect your item at the bottom and enjoy.
* -* -* -* -* -* -* -* -* -* -* -* -* -* -* -* -* -* -*

*** Welcome to Shelly's Candy Shop ***
To select an item, enter
1 for Candy
2 for Chips
3 for Gum
4 for Cookies
9 to exit
3
Please deposit 45 cents
45
Collect your item at the bottom and enjoy.
* -* -* -* -* -* -* -* -* -* -* -* -* -* -* -* -* -* -*

*** Welcome to Shelly's Candy Shop ***
To select an item, enter
1 for Candy
2 for Chips
3 for Gum
4 for Cookies
9 to exit
9
```

NOTE We placed the definitions of the **class**es cashRegister and dispenserType in the same header file candyMachine.h. However, you can also place the definitions of these classes in separate header files and include those header files in the files that use these classes, such as the implementation file of these classes and the file that contains the main program. Similarly, you can also create separate implementation files for these classes. The Web site accompanying this book contains these header and implementation files.

QUICK REVIEW

1. A `class` is a collection of a fixed number of components.

2. Components of a `class` are called the members of the class.

3. Members of a `class` are accessed by name.

4. In C++, `class` is a reserved word.

5. Members of a class are classified into one of three categories: `private`, `protected`, and `public`.

6. The `private` members of a class are not accessible outside the class.

7. The `public` members of a class are accessible outside the class.

8. By default, all members of a class are `private`.

9. The `public` members are declared using the member access specifier `public` and the colon, :.

10. The `private` members are declared using the member access specifier `private` and the colon, :.

11. A member of a class can be a function or a variable.

12. If any member of a class is a function, you usually use the function prototype to declare it.

13. If any member of a class is a variable, it is declared like any other variable.

14. In the definition of a class, you cannot initialize a variable when you declare it.

15. In the Unified Modeling Language (UML) diagram of a class, the top box contains the name of the class. The middle box contains the member variables and their data types. The last box contains the member function name, parameter list, and the return type of the function. A + (plus) sign in front of a member indicates that this member is a `public` member. A – (minus) sign preceding a member indicates that this is a `private` member. The symbol # before the member name indicates that the member is a `protected` member.

16. In C++, a `class` is a definition. No memory is allocated for the `class` itself; memory is allocated for the class variables when you declare them.

17. In C++, class variables are called class objects or class instances, or, simply, objects.

18. A class member is accessed using the class variable name, followed by the dot operator (.), followed by the member name.

19. The only built-in operations on classes are the assignment and member selection.

20. As parameters to functions, classes can be passed either by value or by reference.

21. A function can return a value of type `class`.

22. Any program (or software) that uses a class is called a client of the class.

23. A member function of a class that only accesses (that is, does not modify) the value(s) of the member variable(s) is called an accessor function.

24. A member function of a class that modifies the value(s) of the member variable(s) is called a mutator function.

25. A member function of a class is called a constant function if its heading contains the reserved word `const` at the end. Moreover, a constant member function of a class cannot modify the member variables of the class.

26. A constant member function of a class can only call the other constant member functions of the class.

27. Constructors guarantee that the member variables are initialized when an object is declared.

28. The name of a constructor is the same as the name of the class.

29. A class can have more than one constructor.

30. A constructor without parameters is called the default constructor.

31. Constructors automatically execute when a class object enters its scope.

32. Destructors automatically execute when a class object goes out of scope.

33. A class can have only one destructor, and the destructor has no parameters.

34. The name of a destructor is the tilde (~), followed by the class name (no spaces in between).

35. Constructors and destructors are functions without any type; that is, they are neither value-returning nor void. As a result, they cannot be called like other functions.

36. A data type that separates the logical properties from the implementation details is called an abstract data type (ADT).

37. Classes were specifically designed in C++ to handle ADTs.

38. To implement an ADT, you must represent the data and write related algorithms to implement the operations.

39. A precondition is a statement specifying the condition(s) that must be true before the function is called.

40. A postcondition is a statement specifying what is true after the function call is completed.

41. A `public static` member, function or variable, of a class can be accessed using the class name and the scope resolution operator.

42. For each `static` variable of a class, C++ allocates only one memory space. All objects of the class refer to the same memory space.

43. `static` member variables of a class exist even when no object of the `class` type exists.

44. Non-`static` member variables of a class are called the instance variables of the class.

EXERCISES

1. Mark the following statements as true or false.

    a. The member variables of a class must be of the same type.

    b. The member functions of a class must be `public`.

    c. A class can have more than one constructor.

    d. A class can have more than one destructor.

    e. Both constructors and destructors can have parameters.

2. Find the syntax errors in the definitions of the following classes.

    a.
    ```cpp
    class AA
    {
    public:
        void print() const;
        int sum();
        AA();
        int AA(int, int);
    private:
        int x;
        int y;
    };
    ```

    b.
    ```cpp
    class BB
    {
        int one;
        int two;
    public:
        bool equal() const;
        print();
        BB(int, int);
    }
    ```

    c.
    ```cpp
    class CC
    {
    public;
        void set(int, int);
        void print() const;
        CC();
        CC(int, int);
        bool CC(int, int);
    private:
        int u;
        int v;
    };
    ```

3. Consider the following declarations:
    ```cpp
    class xClass
    {
    public:
        void func();
        void print() const ;
    ```

```
    xClass ();
    xClass (int, double);
private:
    int u;
    double w;
};
```

and assume that the following statement is in a user program:

```
xClass x;
```

a. How many members does **class** **xClass** have?

b. How many **private** members does **class** **xClass** have?

c. How many constructors does **class** **xClass** have?

d. Write the definition of the member function `func` so that u is set to `10` and w is set to `15.3`.

e. Write the definition of the member function `print` that prints the contents of u and w.

f. Write the definition of the default constructor of the **class** **xClass** so that the **private** member variables are initialized to 0.

g. Write a C++ statement that prints the values of the member variables of the object **x**.

h. Write a C++ statement that declares an object t of type **xClass**, and initializes the member variables of t to `20` and `35.0`, respectively.

4. Consider the definition of the following class:

```
class CC
{
public :
    CC();              //Line 1
    CC(int);           //Line 2
    CC(int, int);      //Line 3
    CC(double, int);   //Line 4
        .
        .
        .
private:
    int   u;
    double  v;
};
```

a. Give the line number containing the constructor that is executed in each of the following declarations.

    i.   CC one;

    ii.   CC two(5, 6);

    iii.   CC three(3.5, 8);

b. Write the definition of the constructor in Line 1 so that the **private** member variables are initialized to 0.

c. Write the definition of the constructor in Line 2 so that the **private** member variable u is initialized according to the value of the parameter, and the **private** member variable v is initialized to 0.

d. Write the definition of the constructors in Lines 3 and 4 so that the **private** member variables are initialized according to the values of the parameters.

5. Consider the definition of the following **class**:

```cpp
class testClass
{
public:
    int sum();
        //Returns the sum of the private member variables
    void print() const;
        //Prints the values of the private member variables
    testClass();
        //Default constructor
        //Initializes the private member variables to 0
    testClass(int a, int b);
        //Constructors with parameters
        //initializes the private member variables to the values
        //specified by the parameters
        //Postcondition: x = a; y = b;
private:
    int x;
    int y;
};
```

a. Write the definitions of the member functions as described in the definition of the **class** testClass.

b. Write a test program to test the various operations of the **class** testClass.

6. Given the definition of the **class** clockType with constructors (as described in this chapter), what is the output of the following C++ code?

```cpp
clockType clock1;
clockType clock2(23, 13, 75);

clock1.printTime();
cout << endl;
clock2.printTime();
cout << endl;

clock1.setTime(6, 59, 39);
clock1.printTime();
cout << endl;
```

```
clock1.incrementMinutes();
clock1.printTime();
cout << endl;

clock1.setTime(0, 13, 0);

if (clock1.equalTime(clock2))
    cout << "Clock1 time is the same as clock2 time."
        << endl;
else
    cout << "The two times are different." << endl;
```

7. Assume the definition of the **class** `personType` as given in this chapter.

    a. Write a C++ statement that declares `student` to be a `personType` object, and initialize its first name to `"Buddy"` and last name to `"Arora"`.

    b. Write a C++ statement that outputs the data stored in the object `student`.

    c. Write C++ statements that change the first name of `student` to `"Susan"` and the last name to `"Gilbert"`.

8. Write the definition of a class that has the following properties:

    a. The name of the **class** is `secretType`.

    b. The **class** `secretType` has four member variables: `name` of type `string`, `age` and `weight` of type **int**, and `height` of type **double**.

    c. The **class** `secretType` has the following member functions. (Make each accessor function constant.)

    `print`—outputs the data stored in the member variables with the appropriate titles

    `setName`—function to set the name

    `setAge`—function to set the age

    `setWeight`—function to set the weight

    `setHeight`—function to set the height

    `getName`—value-returning function to return the name

    `getAge`—value-returning function to return the age

    `getWeight`—value-returning function to return the weight

    `getHeight`—value-returning function to return the height

    constructor—with default parameters: The default value of `name` is the empty string `" "`, and the default values of `age`, `weight`, and `height` are 0.

    d. Write the definition of the member functions of the **class** `secretType`, as described in Part c.

9. Consider the following definition of the **class** `myClass`:

```
class myClass
{
public:
    void setX(int a);
     //Function to set the value of x.
     //Postcondition: x := a;
    void printX() const ;
     //Function to output x.
    static void printCount();
     //Function to output count.
    static void incrementCount();
     //Function to increment count.
     //Postcondition: count++;
    myClass(int a = 0);
     //constructor with default parameters
     //Postcondition x = a;
     //If no value is specified for a, x = 0;

private:
    int x;
    static int count;
};
```

a. Write a C++ statement that initializes the member variable count to 0.

b. Write a C++ statement that increments the value of count by 1.

c. Write a C++ statement that outputs the value of count.

d. Write the definitions of the functions of the **class** `myClass` as described in its definition.

e. Write a C++ statement that declares `myObject1` to be a `myClass` object and initializes its member variable `x` to 5.

f. Write a C++ statement that declares `myObject2` to be a `myClass` object and initializes its member variable `x` to 7.

g. Which of the following statements are valid? (Assume that `myObject1` and `myObject2` are as declared in Parts e and f.)

```
myObject1.printCount();        //Line 1
myObject1.printX();            //Line 2
myClass.printCount();          //Line 3
myClass.printX();              //Line 4
myClass::count++;              //Line 5
```

h. Assume that `myObject1` and `myObject2` are as declared in Parts e and f. What is the output of the following C++ code?

```
myObject1.printX();
cout << endl;
myObject1.incrementCount();
myClass::incrementCount();
myObject1.printCount();
```

```
cout << endl;
myObject2.printCount();
cout << endl;
myObject2.printX();
cout << endl;
myObject1.setX(14);
myObject1.incrementCount();
myObject1.printX();
cout << endl;
myObject1.printCount();
cout << endl;
myObject2.printCount();
cout << endl;
```

PROGRAMMING EXERCISES

1. Write a program that converts a number entered in Roman numerals to decimal. Your program should consist of a **class**, say, `romanType`. An object of type `romanType` should do the following:

    a. Store the number as a Roman numeral.

    b. Convert and store the number into decimal form.

    c. Print the number as a Roman numeral or decimal number as requested by the user.

        The decimal values of the Roman numerals are:

M	1000
D	500
C	100
L	50
X	10
V	5
I	1

    d. Test your program using the following Roman numerals: MCXIV, CCCLIX, MDCLXVI.

2. Design and implement a **class** `dayType` that implements the day of the week in a program. The **class** `dayType` should store the day, such as `Sun` for Sunday. The program should be able to perform the following operations on an object of type `dayType`:

    a. Set the day.

    b. Print the day.

    c. Return the day.

   d. Return the next day.

   e. Return the previous day.

   f. Calculate and return the day by adding certain days to the current day. For example, if the current day is Monday and we add 4 days, the day to be returned is Friday. Similarly, if today is Tuesday and we add 13 days, the day to be returned is Monday.

   g. Add the appropriate constructors.

3. Write the definitions of the functions to implement the operations for the `class dayType` as defined in Programming Exercise 2. Also, write a program to test various operations on this class.

4. Example 11-9 defined a `class personType` to store the name of a person. The member functions that we included merely print the name and set the name of a person. Redefine the `class personType` so that, in addition to what the existing `class` does, you can:

   a. Set the first name only.

   b. Set the last name only.

   c. Store and set the middle name.

   d. Check whether a given first name is the same as the first name of this person.

   e. Check whether a given last name is the same as the last name of this person.

   Write the definitions of the member functions to implement the operations for this class. Also, write a program to test various operations on this class.

5. **a.** Some of the characteristics of a book are the title, author(s), publisher, ISBN, price, and year of publication. Design a `class bookType` that defines the book as an ADT.

     i. Each object of the `class bookType` can hold the following information about a book: title, up to four authors, publisher, ISBN, price, and number of copies in stock. To keep track of the number of authors, add another member variable.

     ii. Include the member functions to perform the various operations on objects of type `bookType`. For example, the usual operations that can be performed on the title are to show the title, set the title, and check whether a title is the same as the actual title of the book. Similarly, the typical operations that can be performed on the number of copies in stock are to show the number of copies in stock, set the number of copies in stock, update the number of copies in stock, and return the number of copies in stock. Add similar operations for the publisher, ISBN, book price, and authors. Add the appropriate constructors and a destructor (if one is needed).

    b. Write the definitions of the member functions of the **class** bookType.

    c. Write a program that uses the **class** bookType and tests various operations on the objects of the **class** bookType. Declare an array of 100 components of type bookType. Some of the operations that you should perform are to search for a book by its title, search by ISBN, and update the number of copies of a book.

6. In this exercise, you will design a **class** memberType.

    a. Each object of memberType can hold the name of a person, member ID, number of books bought, and amount spent.

    b. Include the member functions to perform the various operations on the objects of memberType—for example, modify, set, and show a person's name. Similarly, update, modify, and show the number of books bought and the amount spent.

    c. Add the appropriate constructors.

    d. Write the definitions of the member functions of memberType.

    e. Write a program to test various operations of your **class** memberType.

7. Using the classes designed in Programming Exercises 5 and 6, write a program to simulate a bookstore. The bookstore has two types of customers: those who are members of the bookstore, and those who buy books from the bookstore only occasionally. Each member has to pay a $10 yearly membership fee and receives a 5% discount on each book purchased.

   For each member, the bookstore keeps track of the number of books purchased and the total amount spent. For every eleventh book that a member buys, the bookstore takes the average of the total amount of the last 10 books purchased, applies this amount as a discount, and then resets the total amount spent to 0.

   Write a program that can process up to 1000 book titles and 500 members. Your program should contain a menu that gives the user different choices to effectively run the program; in other words, your program should be user-driven.

8. The function sellProduct of the Candy Machine programming example gives the user only two chances to enter enough money to buy the product. Rewrite the definition of the function sellProduct so that it keeps prompting the user to enter more money as long as the user has not entered enough money to buy the product. Also, write a program to test your function.

9. (Tic-Tac-Toe) Write a program that allows two players to play the tic-tac-toe game. Your program must contain the **class** ticTacToe to implement a ticTacToe object. Include a 3-by-3 two-dimensional array, as a **private** member variable, to create the board. If needed, include additional member variables. Some of the operations on a ticTacToe object are printing the current board, getting a move, checking if a move is valid, and determining the winner after each move. Add additional operations as needed.

INHERITANCE AND COMPOSITION

IN THIS CHAPTER, YOU WILL:

- Learn about inheritance
- Learn about derived and base classes
- Explore how to redefine the member functions of a base class
- Examine how the constructors of base and derived classes work
- Learn how to construct the header file of a derived class
- Explore three types of inheritance: `public`, `protected`, and `private`
- Learn about composition
- Become familiar with the three basic principles of object-oriented design

Chapter 11 introduced classes, abstract data types (ADT), and ways to implement ADT in C++. By using classes, you can combine data and operations in a single unit. An object, therefore, becomes a self-contained entity. Operations can directly access the data, but the internal state of an object cannot be manipulated directly.

In addition to implementing ADT, classes have other features. For instance, classes can create new classes from existing classes. This important feature encourages code reuse. In C++, you can relate two or more classes in more than one way. Two common ways to relate classes in a meaningful way are:

- **Inheritance** ("is-a" relationship), and
- **Composition** ("has-a" relationship).

Inheritance

Suppose that you want to design a `class`, `partTimeEmployee`, to implement and process the characteristics of a part-time employee. The main features associated with a part-time employee are the name, pay rate, and number of hours worked. In Example 11-9 (in Chapter 11), we designed a class to implement a person's name. Every part-time employee is a person. Therefore, rather than design the `class` `partTimeEmployee` from scratch, we want to be able to extend the definition of the `class personType` (from Example 11-9) by adding additional members (data and/or functions).

Of course, we do not want to make the necessary changes directly to the `class` `personType`—that is, edit the `class personType`, and add and/or delete members. In fact, we want to create the `class partTimeEmployee` without making any physical changes to the `class personType`, by adding only the members that are necessary. For example, because the `class personType` already has members to store the first name and last name, we will not include any such members in the `class partTimeEmployee`. In fact, these member variables will be inherited from the `class personType`. (We will design such a `class` in Example 12-1.)

In Chapter 11, we extensively studied and designed the `class clockType` to implement the time of day in a program. The `class clockType` has three member variables, to store the hours, minutes, and seconds. Certain applications, in addition to the hours, minutes, and seconds, might also require us to store the time zone. In this case, we would like to extend the definition of the `class clockType` and create a `class`, `extClockType`, to accommodate this new information. That is, we want to derive the `class extClockType` by adding a member variable—say, `timeZone`—and the necessary member functions to manipulate the time (see Programming Exercise 1 at the end of this chapter). In C++, the mechanism that allows us to accomplish this task is the principle of inheritance. Inheritance is an "is-a" relationship; for instance, "every employee is a person."

Inheritance lets us create new classes from existing classes. The new classes that we create from the existing classes are called the **derived classes**; the existing classes are called the

base classes. The derived classes inherit the properties of the base classes. So rather than create completely new classes from scratch, we can take advantage of inheritance and reduce software complexity.

Each derived class, in turn, becomes a base class for a future derived class. Inheritance can be either single inheritance or multiple inheritance. In **single inheritance**, the derived class is derived from a single base class; in **multiple inheritance**, the derived class is derived from more than one base class. This chapter concentrates on single inheritance.

Inheritance can be viewed as a tree–like, or hierarchical, structure wherein a base class is shown with its derived classes. Consider the tree diagram shown in Figure 12-1.

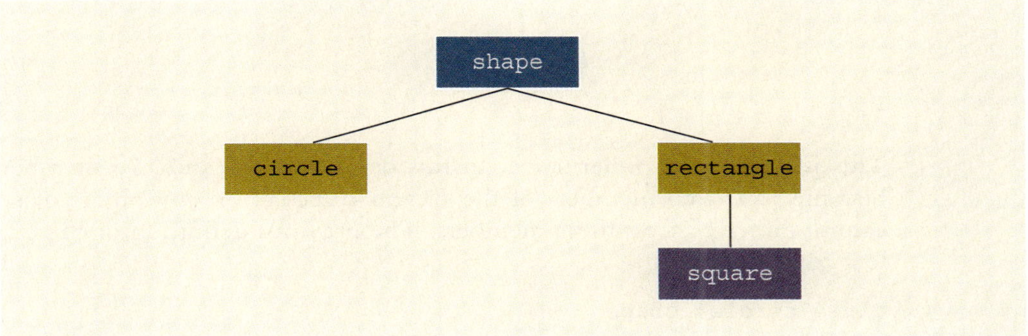

FIGURE 12-1 Inheritance hierarchy

In this diagram, `shape` is the base class. The `class`es `circle` and `rectangle` are derived from `shape`, and the `class` `square` is derived from `rectangle`. Every `circle` and every `rectangle` is a `shape`. Every `square` is a `rectangle`.

The general syntax of a derived class is:

```
class className: memberAccessSpecifier baseClassName
{
    member list
};
```

where `memberAccessSpecifier` is **public**, **protected**, or **private**. When no `memberAccessSpecifier` is specified, it is assumed to be a **private** inheritance. (We discuss **protected** inheritance later in this chapter.)

EXAMPLE 12-1

Suppose that we have defined a class called `shape`. The following statements specify that the `class circle` is derived from `shape`, and it is a `public` inheritance.

```
class circle: public shape
{
        .
        .
        .
};
```

On the other hand, consider the following definition of the `class circle`:

```
class circle: private shape
{
        .
        .
        .
};
```

This is a `private` inheritance. In this definition, the `public` members of `shape` become `private` members of the `class circle`. So any object of type `circle` cannot directly access these members. The previous definition of `circle` is equivalent to:

```
class circle: shape
{
        .
        .
        .
};
```

That is, if we do not use either the `memberAccessSpecifier public` or `private`, the `public` members of a base class are inherited as `private` members.

The following facts about the base and the derived classes should be kept in mind.

1. The `private` members of a base class are `private` to the base class; hence, the members of the derived class cannot directly access them. In other words, when you write the definitions of the member functions of the derived class, you cannot directly access the `private` members of the base class.

2. The `public` members of a base class can be inherited either as `public` members or as `private` members by the derived class. That is, the `public` members of the base class can become either `public` or `private` members of the derived class.

3. The derived class can include additional members—data and/or functions.

4. The derived class can redefine the **public** member functions of the base class. That is, in the derived class, you can have a member function with the same name, number, and types of parameters as a function in the base class. However, this redefinition applies only to the objects of the derived class, not to the objects of the base class.

5. All member variables of the base class are also member variables of the derived class. Similarly, the member functions of the base class (unless redefined) are also member functions of the derived class. (Remember Rule 1 when accessing a member of the base class in the derived class.)

The next sections describe two important issues related to inheritance. The first issue is the redefinition of the member functions of the base class in the derived class. While discussing this issue, we will also address how to access the **private** (data) members of the base class in the derived class. The second key inheritance issue is related to the constructor. The constructor of a derived class cannot *directly* access the **private** member variables of the base class. Thus, we need to ensure that the **private** member variables that are inherited from the base class are initialized when a constructor of the derived class executes.

Redefining (Overriding) Member Functions of the Base Class

Suppose that a **class** derivedClass is derived from the **class** baseClass. Further assume that both derivedClass and baseClass have some member variables. It then follows that the member variables of the **class** derivedClass are its own member variables, together with the member variables of baseClass. Suppose that baseClass contains a function, print, that prints the values of the member variables of baseClass. Now derivedClass contains member variables in addition to the member variables inherited from baseClass. Suppose that you want to include a function that prints the values of the member variables of derivedClass. You can give any name to this function. However, in the **class** derivedClass, you can also name this function as print (the same name used by baseClass). This is called redefining (or overriding) the member function of the base class. Next, we illustrate how to redefine the member functions of a base class with the help of an example.

NOTE To redefine a **public** member function of a base class in the derived class, the corresponding function in the derived class must have the same name, number, and types of parameters. In other words, the name of the function being redefined in the derived class must have the same name and the same set of parameters. If the corresponding functions in the base class and the derived class have the same name but different sets of parameters, then this is function overloading in the derived class, which is also allowed.

Consider the definition of the following class:

```cpp
class rectangleType
{
public:
    void setDimension(double l, double w);
      //Function to set the length and width of the rectangle.
      //Postcondition: length = l; width = w;

    double getLength() const;
      //Function to return the length of the rectangle.
      //Postcondition: The value of length is returned.

    double getWidth() const;
      //Function to return the width of the rectangle.
      //Postcondition: The value of width is returned.

    double area() const;
      //Function to return the area of the rectangle.
      //Postcondition: The area of the rectangle is
      //               calculated and returned.

    double perimeter() const;
      //Function to return the perimeter of the rectangle.
      //Postcondition: The perimeter of the rectangle is
      //               calculated and returned.

    void print() const;
      //Function to output the length and width of
      //the rectangle.

    rectangleType();
      //Default constructor
      //Postcondition: length = 0; width = 0;

    rectangleType(double l, double w);
      //Constructor with parameters
      //Postcondition: length = l; width = w;

private:
    double length;
    double width;
};
```

Figure 12-2 shows the UML class diagram of the **class** `rectangleType` and the inheritance hierarchy.

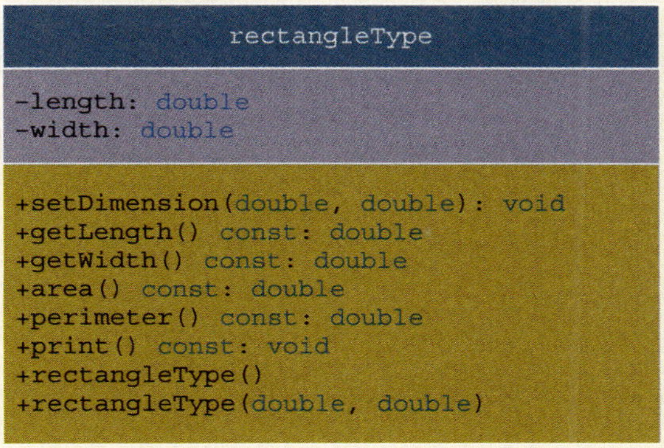

FIGURE 12-2   UML class diagram of the **class** rectangleType

The **class** rectangleType has ten members.

Suppose that the definitions of the member functions of the **class** rectangleType are as follows:

```cpp
void rectangleType::setDimension(double l, double w)
{
    if (l >= 0)
        length = l;
    else
        length = 0;

    if (w >= 0)
        width = w;
    else
        width = 0;
}

double rectangleType::getLength() const
{
    return length;
}

double rectangleType::getWidth() const
{
    return width;
}

double rectangleType::area() const
{
    return length * width;
}
```

```cpp
double rectangleType::perimeter() const
{
    return 2 * (length + width);
}

void rectangleType::print() const
{
    cout << "Length = "  << length
         << "; Width = " << width;
}

rectangleType::rectangleType(double l, double w)
{
    setDimension(l, w);
}

rectangleType::rectangleType()
{
    length = 0;
    width = 0;
}
```

Now consider the definition of the following **class** boxType, derived from the
class rectangleType:

```cpp
class boxType: public rectangleType
{
public:
    void setDimension(double l, double w, double h);
      //Function to set the length, width, and height
      //of the box.
      //Postcondition: length = l; width = w; height = h;

    double getHeight() const;
      //Function to return the height of the box.
      //Postcondition: The value of height is returned.

    double area() const;
      //Function to return the surface area of the box.
      //Postcondition: The surface area of the box is
      //               calculated and returned.

    double volume() const;
      //Function to return the volume of the box.
      //Postcondition: The volume of the box is
      //               calculated and returned.

    void print() const;
      //Function to output the length and width of a rectangle.

    boxType();
      //Default constructor
      //Postcondition: length = 0; width = 0; height = 0;
```

```
boxType(double l, double w, double h);
   //Constructor with parameters
   //Postcondition: length = l; width = w; height = h;

private:
   double height;
};
```

Figure 12-3 shows the UML class diagram of the **class** boxType and the inheritance hierarchy.

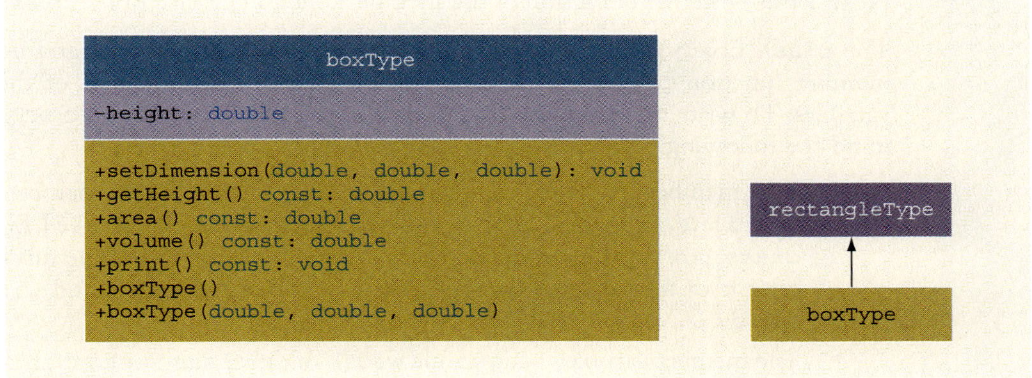

FIGURE 12-3 UML class diagram of the **class** boxType and the inheritance hierarchy

From the definition of the **class** boxType, it is clear that the **class** boxType is derived from the **class** rectangleType, and it is a **public** inheritance. Therefore, all **public** members of the **class** rectangleType are **public** members of the **class** boxType. The **class** boxType also overrides (redefines) the functions print and area.

In general, while writing the definitions of the member functions of a derived class to specify a call to a **public** member function of the base class, we do the following:

- If the derived class overrides a **public** member function of the base class, then to specify a call to that **public** member function of the base class you use the name of the base class, followed by the scope resolution operator, ::, followed by the function name with the appropriate parameter list.

- If the derived class does not override a **public** member function of the base class, you may specify a call to that **public** member function by using the name of the function and the appropriate parameter list. (See the following note for member functions of the base class that are overloaded in the derived class.)

NOTE

If a derived class *overloads* a `public` member function of the base class, then while writing the definition of a member function of the derived class, to specify a call to that (overloaded) member function of the base class you might need (depending on the compiler) to use the name of the base class followed by the scope resolution operator, `::`, followed by the function name with the appropriate parameter list. For example, the `class` `boxType` overloads the member function `setDimension` of the `class` `rectangleType`. (See the definition of the function `setDimension` (of the `class` `boxType`), given later in this section.)

Next, let us write the definition of the member function `print` of the `class` `boxType`.

The `class` `boxType` has three member variables: `length`, `width`, and `height`. The member function `print` of the `class` `boxType` prints the values of these member variables. To write the definition of the function `print` of the `class` `boxType`, keep in mind the following:

- The member variables `length` and `width` are `private` members of the `class` `rectangleType`, and so cannot be directly accessed in the `class` `boxType`. Therefore, when writing the definition of the function `print` of the `class` `boxType`, we cannot access `length` and `width` directly.

- The member variables `length` and `width` of the `class` `rectangleType` are accessible in the `class` `boxType` through the `public` member functions of the `class` `rectangleType`. Therefore, when writing the definition of the member function `print` of the `class` `boxType`, we first call the member function `print` of the `class` `rectangleType` to print the values of `length` and `width`. After printing the values of `length` and `width`, we output the values of `height`.

To call the member function `print` of `rectangleType` in the definition of the member function `print` of `boxType`, we must use the following statement:

```
rectangleType::print();
```

This statement ensures that we call the member function `print` of the base `class` `rectangleType`, not of the `class` `boxType`.

The definition of the member function `print` of the `class` `boxType` is:

```
void boxType::print() const
{
    rectangleType::print();
    cout << "; Height = " << height;
}
```

Let us write the definitions of the remaining member functions of the `class` `boxType`.

The definition of the function `setDimension` is:

```cpp
void boxType::setDimension(double l, double w, double h)
{
    rectangleType::setDimension(l, w);

    if (h >= 0)
        height = h;
    else
        height = 0;
}
```

Notice that in the preceding definition of the function `setDimension`, a call to the member function `setDimension` of the **class** `rectangleType` is preceded by the name of the class and the scope resolution operator, even though the **class** `boxType` overloads—not overrides—the function `setDimension`.

The definition of the function `getHeight` is:

```cpp
double boxType::getHeight() const
{
    return height;
}
```

The member function `area` of the **class** `boxType` determines the surface area of a box. To determine the surface area of a box, we need to access the length and width of the box, which are declared as **private** members of the **class** `rectangleType`. Therefore, we use the member functions `getLength` and `getWidth` of the **class** `rectangleType` to retrieve the length and width, respectively. Because the **class** `boxType` does not contain any member functions that have the names `getLength` or `getWidth`, we call these member functions of the **class** `rectangleType` without using the name of the base class.

```cpp
double boxType::area() const
{
    return  2 * (getLength() * getWidth()
              + getLength() * height
              + getWidth() * height);
}
```

The member function `volume` of the **class** `boxType` determines the volume of a box. To determine the volume of a box, you multiply the length, width, and height of the box, or multiply the area of the base of the box by its height. Let us write the definition of the member function `volume` by using the second alternative. To do this, you can use the member function `area` of the **class** `rectangleType` to determine the area of the base. Because the **class** `boxType` overrides the member function `area`, to specify a call to the member function `area` of the **class** `rectangleType`, we use the name of the base class and the scope resolution operator, as shown in the following definition:

```cpp
double boxType::volume() const
{
    return rectangleType::area() * height;
}
```

In the next section, we discuss how to specify a call to the constructor of the base class when writing the definition of a constructor of the derived class.

Constructors of Derived and Base Classes

A derived class can have its own `private` member variables, and so a derived class can explicitly include its own constructors. A constructor typically serves to initialize the member variables. When we declare a derived class object, this object inherits the members of the base class, but the derived class object cannot directly access the `private` (data) members of the base class. The same is true for the member functions of a derived class. That is, the member functions of a derived class cannot directly access the `private` members of the base class.

As a consequence, the constructors of a derived class can (directly) initialize only the (`public` data) members inherited from the base class of the derived class. Thus, when a derived class object is declared, it must also automatically execute one of the constructors of the base class. Because constructors cannot be called like other functions, the execution of a derived class's constructor must trigger the execution of one of the base class's constructors. This is, in fact, what happens. Furthermore, a call to the base class's constructor is specified in the *heading of the definition* of a derived class constructor.

In the preceding section, we defined the `class rectangleType` and derived the `class boxType` from it. Moreover, we illustrated how to override a member function of the `class rectangleType`. Let us now discuss how to write the definitions of the constructors of the `class boxType`.

The `class rectangleType` has two constructors and two member variables. The `class boxType` has three member variables: `length`, `width`, and `height`. The member variables `length` and `width` are inherited from the `class rectangleType`.

First, let us write the definition of the default constructor of the `class boxType`. Recall that, if a class contains the default constructor and no values are specified when the object is declared, the default constructor executes and initializes the object. Because the `class rectangleType` contains the default constructor, when writing the definition of the default constructor of the `class boxType`, we do not specify any constructor of the base class.

```
boxType::boxType()
{
    height = 0.0;
}
```

Next, we discuss how to write the definitions of constructors with parameters. To trigger the execution of a constructor (with parameters) of the base class, you specify the name of a constructor of the base class with the parameters in the heading of the definition of the constructor of the derived class.

Consider the following definition of the constructor with parameters of the **class** boxType:

```
boxType::boxType(double l, double w, double h)
        : rectangleType(l, w)
{
    if (h >= 0)
        height = h;
    else
        height = 0;
}
```

In this definition, we specify the constructor of rectangleType with two parameters. When this constructor of boxType executes, it triggers the execution of the constructor with two parameters of type **double** of the **class** rectangleType.

Consider the following statements:

```
rectangleType myRectangle(5.0, 3.0);   //Line 1
boxType myBox(6.0, 5.0, 4.0);          //Line 2
```

The statement in Line 1 creates the rectangleType object myRectangle. Thus, the object myRectangle has two member variables: length and width. The statement in Line 2 creates the boxType object myBox. Thus, the object myBox has three member variables: length, width, and height (see Figure 12-4).

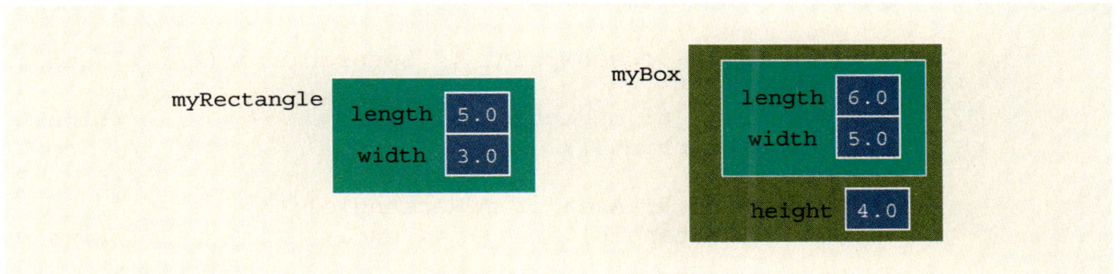

FIGURE 12-4 Objects myRectangle and myBox

Consider the following statements:

```
myRectangle.print();     //Line 3
cout << endl;            //Line 4
myBox.print();           //Line 5
cout << endl;            //Line 6
```

In the statement in Line 3, the member function print of the **class** rectangleType is executed. In the statement in Line 5, the function print associated with the **class** boxType is executed. Recall that, if a derived class overrides a member function of the base class, the redefinition applies only to the objects of the derived class. Thus, the output of the statement in Line 3 is:

```
Length = 5.0; Width = 3.0
```

The output of the statement in Line 5 is:

```
Length = 6.0; Width = 5.0; Height = 4.0
```

The program in Example 12-2 shows how the objects of a base class and a derived class behave.

EXAMPLE 12-2

Consider the following C++ program:

```cpp
#include <iostream>
#include <iomanip>
#include "rectangleType.h"
#include "boxType.h"

using namespace std;

int main()
{
    rectangleType myRectangle1;                        //Line 1
    rectangleType myRectangle2(8, 6);                  //Line 2

    boxType myBox1;                                     //Line 3
    boxType myBox2(10, 7, 3);                           //Line 4

    cout << fixed << showpoint << setprecision(2);      //Line 5

    cout << "Line 6: myRectangle1: ";                  //Line 6
    myRectangle1.print();                              //Line 7
    cout << endl;                                       //Line 8
    cout << "Line 9: Area of myRectangle1: "
         << myRectangle1.area() << endl;                //Line 9

    cout << "Line 10: myRectangle2: ";                 //Line 10
    myRectangle2.print();                              //Line 11
    cout << endl;                                       //Line 12
    cout << "Line 13: Area of myRectangle2: "
         << myRectangle2.area() << endl;                //Line 13

    cout << "Line 14: myBox1: ";                       //Line 14
    myBox1.print();                                     //Line 15
    cout << endl;                                       //Line 16
    cout << "Line 17: Surface Area of myBox1: "
         << myBox1.area() << endl;                      //Line 17
    cout << "Line 18: Volume of myBox1: "
         << myBox1.volume() << endl;                    //Line 18

    cout << "Line 19: myBox2: ";                       //Line 19
    myBox2.print();                                     //Line 20
    cout << endl;                                       //Line 21
```

```
    cout << "Line 22: Surface Area of myBox2: "
         << myBox2.area() << endl;                    //Line 22
    cout << "Line 23: Volume of myBox2: "
         << myBox2.volume() << endl;                  //Line 23

    return 0;                                         //line 24
}
```

Sample Run:

```
Line 6: myRectangle1: Length = 0.00; Width = 0.00
Line 9: Area of myRectangle1: 0.00
Line 10: myRectangle2: Length = 8.00; Width = 6.00
Line 13: Area of myRectangle2: 48.00
Line 14: myBox1: Length = 0.00; Width = 0.00; Height = 0.00
Line 17: Surface Area of myBox1: 0.00
Line 18: Volume of myBox1: 0.00
Line 19: myBox2: Length = 10.00; Width = 7.00; Height = 3.00
Line 22: Surface Area of myBox2: 242.00
Line 23: Volume of myBox2: 210.00
```

The preceding program works as follows: The statement in Line 1 creates the `rectangleType` object `myRectangle1` and initializes its member variables to 0. The statement in Line 2 creates the `rectangleType` object `myRectangle2` and initializes its member variables `length` and `width` to `8.0` and `6.0`, respectively.

The statement in Line 3 creates the `boxType` object `myBox1` and initializes its member variables to 0. The statement in Line 4 creates the `boxType` object `myBox2` and initializes its member variables `length`, `width`, and `height` to `10.0`, `7.0`, and `3.0`, respectively.

The statement in Line 5 sets the output of the decimal number to two decimal places in a fixed decimal format with the decimal point and trailing zeros.

The statements in Lines 6 through 9 output the length, width, and area of `myRectangle1`. Because the member variables of `myRectangle1` are initialized to 0 by the default constructor, the area of the rectangle is 0 square units. See Line 9 in the sample run.

The statements in Lines 10 through 13 output the length, width, and area of `myRectangle2`. Because the member variables `length` and `width` of `myRectangle2` are initialized to 8.0 and 6.0, respectively, by the constructor with parameters, the area of this rectangle is `48.0` square units. See Line 13 in the sample run.

The statements in Lines 14 through 18 output the length, width, height, surface area, and volume of `myBox1`. Because the member variables of `myBox1` are initialized to 0 by the default constructor, the surface area of this box is `0.0` square units, and the volume is `0.0` cubic units. See Lines 17 and 18 in the sample run.

The statements in Lines 19 through 23 output the length, width, height, surface area, and volume of `myBox2`. Because the member variables `length`, `width`, and `height` of `myBox2` are initialized to `10.0`, `7.0`, and `3.0`, respectively, by the constructor with parameters, the surface area of this box is `242.0` square units, and the volume is `210.0` cubic units. See Lines 22 and 23 in the sample run.

From the output of this program, it follows that the redefinition of the functions `print` and `area` in the **class** `boxType` applies only to an object of type `boxType`.

NOTE **(Constructors with default parameters and the inheritance hierarchy)** Recall that a class can have a constructor with default parameters. Therefore, a derived class can also have a constructor with default parameters. For example, suppose that the definition of the **class** `rectangleType` is as shown below. (To save space, these definitions have no documentation.)

```cpp
class rectangleType
{
public:
    void setDimension(double l, double w);
    double getLength() const;
    double getWidth() const;
    double area() const;
    double perimeter()const;
    void print() const;
    rectangleType(double l = 0, double w = 0);
       //Constructor with default parameters

private:
    double length;
    double width;
};
```

Suppose the definition of the constructor is:

```cpp
rectangleType::rectangleType(double l, double w)
{
    setDimension(l, w);
}
```

Now suppose that the definition of the **class** `boxType` is:

```cpp
class boxType: public rectangleType
{
public:
    void setDimension(double l, double w, double h);
    double getHeight()const;
    double area() const;
    double volume() const;
    void print() const;
    boxType(double l = 0, double w = 0, double h = 0);
       //Constructor with default parameters

private:
    double height;
};
```

You can write the definition of the constructor of the `class` `boxType` as follows:

```
boxType::boxType(double l, double w, double h)
       : rectangleType(l, w)
{
    if (h >= 0)
        height = h;
    else
        height = 0;
}
```

Notice that this definition also takes care of the default constructor of the `class` `boxType`.

NOTE   Suppose that a base `class`, baseClass, has *private* member variables and constructors. Further suppose that the `class` derivedClass is derived from baseClass, and derivedClass has no member variables. Therefore, the member variables of derivedClass are the ones inherited from baseClass. A constructor cannot be called like other functions, and the member variables of baseClass cannot be directly accessed by the member functions of derivedClass. To guarantee the initialization of the inherited member variables of an object of type derivedClass, even though derivedClass has no member variables, it must have the appropriate constructors. A constructor (with parameters) of derivedClass merely issues a call to a constructor (with parameters) of baseClass. Therefore, when you write the definition of the constructor (with parameters) of derivedClass, the heading of the definition of the constructor contains a call to an appropriate constructor (with parameters) of baseClass, and the body of the constructor is empty—that is, it contains only the opening and closing braces.

EXAMPLE 12-3

Suppose that you want to define a class to group the attributes of an employee. There are both full-time employees and part-time employees. Part-time employees are paid based on the number of hours worked and an hourly rate. Suppose that you want to define a class to keep track of a part-time employee's information, such as `name`, `pay rate`, and `hours worked`. You can then print the employee's name together with his or her wages. Because every employee is a person, and Example 11-9 (Chapter 11) defined the `class` `personType` to store the first name and the last name together with the necessary operations on name, we can define a `class` `partTimeEmployee` based on the `class` `personType`. You can also redefine the `print` function to print the appropriate information.

```cpp
class partTimeEmployee: public personType
{
public:
    void print() const;
        //Function to output the first name, last name, and
        //the wages.
        //Postcondition: Outputs
        //          firstName lastName wages are $$$$.$$

    double calculatePay() const;
        //Function to calculate and return the wages.
        //Postcondition: Pay is calculated and returned

    void setNameRateHours(string first, string last,
                          double rate, double hours);
        //Function to set the first name, last name, payRate,
        //and hoursWorked according to the parameters.
        //Postcondition: firstName = first; lastName = last;
        //               payRate = rate; hoursWorked = hours

    partTimeEmployee(string first = "", string last = "",
                     double rate = 0, double hours = 0);
        //Constructor with parameters
        //Sets the first name, last name, payRate, and hoursWorked
        //according to the parameters. If no value is specified,
        //the default values are assumed.
        //Postcondition: firstName = first; lastName = last;
        //               payRate = rate; hoursWorked = hours

private:
    double payRate;     //variable to store the pay rate
    double hoursWorked; //variable to store the hours worked
};
```

Figure 12-5 shows the UML class diagram of the **class** partTimeEmployee and the
inheritance hierarchy.

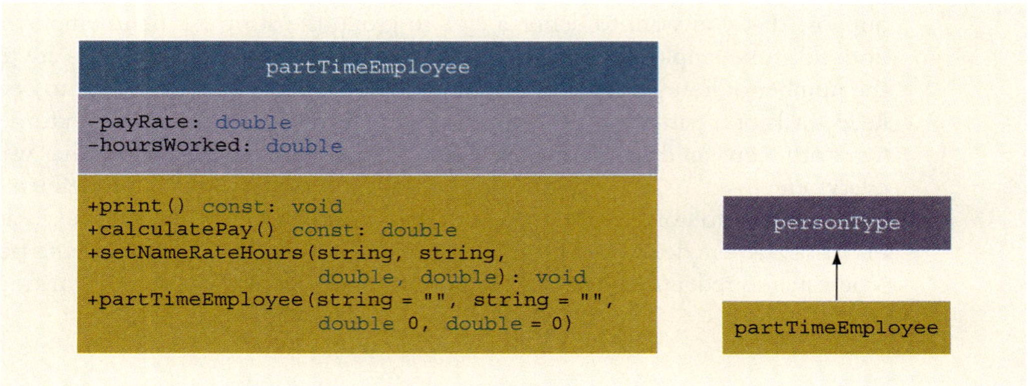

FIGURE 12-5 UML class diagram of the **class** partTimeEmployee and inheritance hierarchy

The definitions of the member functions of the **class** `partTimeEmployee` are as follows:

```cpp
void partTimeEmployee::print() const
{
    personType::print();   //print the name of the employee
    cout << "'s wages are: $" << calculatePay() << endl;
}


double partTimeEmployee::calculatePay() const
{
    return (payRate * hoursWorked);
}


void partTimeEmployee::setNameRateHours(string first,
                        string last, double rate, double hours)
{
    personType::setName(first, last);
    payRate = rate;
    hoursWorked = hours;
}


    //Constructor
partTimeEmployee::partTimeEmployee(string first, string last,
                                double rate, double hours)
        : personType(first, last)
{
    payRate = rate;
    hoursWorked = hours;
}
```

HEADER FILE OF A DERIVED CLASS

The previous section explained how to derive new classes from previously defined classes. To define new classes, you create new header files. The base classes are already defined, and header files contain their definitions. Thus, to create new classes based on the previously defined classes, the header files of the new classes contain commands that tell the computer where to look for the definitions of the base classes.

Suppose that the definition of the **class** `personType` is placed in the header file `personType.h`. To create the definition of the **class** `partTimeEmployee`, the header file—say, `partTimeEmployee.h`—must contain the preprocessor directive:

```cpp
#include "personType.h"
```

before the definition of the **class** `partTimeEmployee`. To be specific, the header file `partTimeEmployee.h` is as shown below.

```
//Header file partTimeEmployee

#include "personType.h"

class partTimeEmployee: public personType
{
public:
    void print() const;
      //Function to output the first name, last name, and
      //the wages.
      //Postcondition: Outputs
      //            firstName lastName wages are $$$$.$$

    double calculatePay() const;
      //Function to calculate and return the wages.
      //Postcondition: Pay is calculated and returned

    void setNameRateHours(string first, string last,
                          double rate, double hours);
      //Function to set the first name, last name, payRate,
      //and hoursWorked according to the parameters.
      //Postcondition: firstName = first; lastName = last;
      //               payRate = rate; hoursWorked = hours

    partTimeEmployee(string first = "", string last = "",
                     double rate = 0, double hours = 0);
      //Constructor with parameters
      //Sets the first name, last name, payRate, and hoursWorked
      //according to the parameters. If no value is specified,
      //the default values are assumed.
      //Postcondition: firstName = first; lastName = last;
      //               payRate = rate; hoursWorked = hours

private:
    double payRate;      //variable to store the pay rate
    double hoursWorked;  //variable to store the hours worked
};
```

The definitions of the member functions can be placed in a separate file. Recall that to include a system-provided header file, such as `iostream`, in a user program, you enclose the header file between angular brackets; to include a user-defined header file in a program, you enclose the header file between double quotation marks.

Multiple Inclusions of a Header File

The previous section discussed how to create the header file of a derived class. To include a header file in a program, you use the preprocessor command. Recall that before a program is compiled, the preprocessor first processes the program. Consider the following header file:

```
//Header file test.h

const int ONE = 1;
const int TWO = 2;
```

Suppose that the header file `testA.h` includes the file `test.h` in order to use the identifiers ONE and TWO. To be specific, suppose that the header file `testA.h` looks like:

```
//Header file testA.h

#include "test.h"
 .
 .
 .
```

Now consider the following program code:

```
//Program headerTest.cpp

#include "test.h"
#include "testA.h"
 .
 .
 .
```

When the program `headerTest.cpp` is compiled, it is first processed by the preprocessor. The preprocessor includes first the header file `test.h` and then the header file `testA.h`. When the header file `testA.h` is included, because it contains the preprocessor directive `#include "test.h"`, the header file `test.h` is included twice in the program. The second inclusion of the header file `test.h` results in compile-time errors, such as the identifier ONE already being declared. This problem occurs because the first inclusion of the header file `test.h` has already defined the variables ONE and TWO. To avoid multiple inclusion of a file in a program, we use certain preprocessor commands in the header file. Let us first rewrite the header file `test.h` using these preprocessor commands, and then explain the meaning of these commands.

```
//Header file test.h

#ifndef H_test
#define H_test
const int ONE = 1;
const int TWO = 2;
#endif
```

   a. `#ifndef H_test` means "if not defined H_test"

   b. `#define H_test` means "define H_test"

   c. `#endif` means "end if"

Here `H_test` is a preprocessor identifier.

The effect of these commands is as follows: If the identifier `H_test` is not defined, we must define the identifier `H_test` and let the remaining statements between `#define` and `#endif` pass through the compiler. If the header file `test.h` is included the second time in the program, the statement `#ifndef` fails and all the statements until `#endif` are skipped. In fact, all header files are written using similar preprocessor commands.

C++ Stream Classes

Chapter 3 described in detail how to perform input/output (I/O) using standard I/O devices and file I/O. In particular, you used the object `cin`, the extraction operator `>>`, and functions such as `get` and `ignore` to read data from the standard input device. You also used the object `cout` and the insertion operator `<<` to send output to the standard output device. To use `cin` and `cout`, the programs included the header file `iostream`, which includes the definitions of the classes `istream` and `ostream`. Moreover, for file I/O, the programs included the header file `ifstream`, and they used objects of type `ifstream` for file input, and objects of type `ofstream` for file output. This section briefly describes how stream classes are related and implemented in C++.

In C++, stream classes are implemented using the inheritance mechanism, as shown in Figure 12-6.

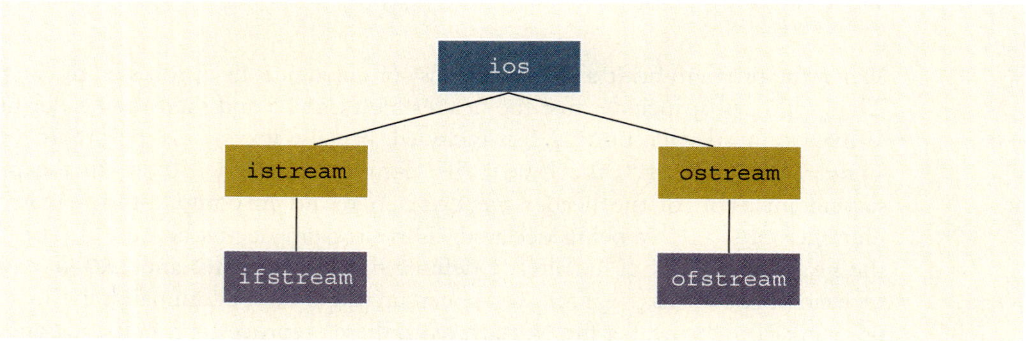

FIGURE 12-6 C++ stream classes hierarchy

Figure 12-6 shows the stream classes that we have encountered in previous chapters. From this figure, it follows that the **class** `ios` is the base class for all stream classes. Classes `istream` and `ostream` are directly derived from the **class** `ios`. The **class** `ifstream` is derived from the **class** `istream`, and the **class** `ofstream` is derived from the **class** `ostream`. Moreover, using the mechanism of multiple inheritance, the **class** `iostream` (not to be confused with the *header* file `iostream`—these are separate things) and the **class** `fstream` are derived from the **class** `iostream`. (The classes `iostream` and `fstream` are not discussed in this book.)

The **class** `ios` contains formatting flags and member functions to access and/or modify the setting of these flags. To identify the I/O status, the **class** `ios` contains an integer status word. This integer status word provides a continuous update reporting the status of the stream.

The **classes** `istream` and `ostream` are responsible for providing the operations for the data transfer between memory and devices. The **class** `istream` defines the extraction operator, `>>`, and functions such as `get` and `ignore`. The **class** `ostream` defines the insertion operator, `<<`, which is used by the object `cout`.

The `class ifstream` is derived from the `class istream` to provide the file input operations. Similarly, the `class ofstream` is derived from the `class ostream` to provide the file output operations. Objects of type `ifstream` are used for file input; objects of type `ofstream` are used for file output. The header file `fstream` contains the definitions of the `classes ifstream` and `ofstream`.

Protected Members of a Class

The `private` members of a class are `private` to the class and cannot be directly accessed outside the class. Only member functions of that class can access the `private` members. As discussed previously, the derived class cannot directly access the `private` members of a base class. However, it is sometimes necessary (say, for efficiency and/or to simplify the code) for a derived class to directly access a `private` member of a base class. If you make a `private` member become `public`, then anyone can access that member. Recall that the members of a class are classified into three categories: `public`, `private`, and `protected`. So, for a base class to give access to a member to its derived class and still prevent its direct access outside the class, you must declare that member under the `memberAccessSpecifier protected`. Thus, the accessibility of a `protected` member of a class is in between `public` and `private`. A derived class can directly access the `protected` members of a base class.

To summarize, if a member of a base class needs to be accessed by a derived class, that member is declared under the `memberAccessSpecifier protected`.

Inheritance as `public`, `protected`, or `private`

Suppose `class B` is derived from `class A`. Then `B` cannot directly access the `private` members of A. That is, the `private` members of A are hidden in B. What about the `public` and `protected` members of A? This section gives the rules that generally apply when accessing the members of a base class.

Consider the following statement:

```
class B: memberAccessSpecifier A
{
        .
        .
        .
};
```

In this statement, `memberAccessSpecifier` is either `public`, `protected`, or `private`.

1. If `memberAccessSpecifier` is `public`—that is, the inheritance is `public`—then:

    a. The `public` members of A are `public` members of B. They can be directly accessed in `class B`.

    b. The `protected` members of A are `protected` members of B. They can be directly accessed by the member functions (and `friend` functions) of B.

    c.   The **private** members of A are hidden in B. They can be accessed by the member functions (and **friend** functions) of B through the **public** or **protected** members of A.

2.   If **memberAccessSpecifier** is **protected**—that is, the inheritance is **protected**—then:

    a.   The **public** members of A are **protected** members of B. They can be accessed by the member functions (and **friend** functions) of B.

    b.   The **protected** members of A are **protected** members of B. They can be accessed by the member functions (and **friend** functions) of B.

    c.   The **private** members of A are hidden in B. They can be accessed by the member functions (and **friend** functions) of B through the **public** or **protected** members of A.

3.   If **memberAccessSpecifier** is **private**—that is, the inheritance is **private**—then:

    a.   The **public** members of A are **private** members of B. They can be accessed by the member functions (and **friend** functions) of B.

    b.   The **protected** members of A are **private** members of B. They can be accessed by the member functions (and **friend** functions) of B.

    c.   The **private** members of A are hidden in B. They can be accessed by the member functions (and **friend** functions) of B through the **public** or **protected** members of A.

NOTE   Chapter 14 describes the **friend** functions.

Example 12-4 illustrates how the member functions of a derived class can directly access a **protected** member of the base class.

EXAMPLE 12-4 (ACCESSING protected MEMBERS IN THE DERIVED CLASS)

Consider the following definition of the **class** bClass:

```
class bClass
{
public:
    void setData(double);
    void setData(char, double);
    void print() const;

    bClass(char = '*', double = 0.0);

protected:
```

```
    char bCh;

private:
    double bX;
};
```

The definition of the **class** bClass contains a **protected** member variable bCh of type **char**, and a **private** member variable bX of type **double**. It also contains an overloaded member function setData. One version is used to set both member variables; the other version is used to set only the **private** member variable. The class also has a constructor with default parameters. Suppose that the definitions of the member functions and the constructor are as follows:

```
void bClass::setData(double u)
{
    bX = u;
}
void bClass::setData(char ch, double u)
{
    bCh = ch;
    bX = u;
}

void bClass::print() const
{
    cout << "Base class: bCh = " << bCh << ", bX = " << bX
         << endl;
}

bClass::bClass(char ch, double u)
{
    bCh = ch;
    bX = u;
}
```

Next, we derive a **class** dClass from the **class** bClass using **public** inheritance as follows:

```
class dClass: public bClass
{
public:
    void setData(char, double, int);
    void print() const;

private:
    int dA;
};
```

The **class** dClass contains a **private** member variable dA of type **int**. It also contains a member function setData, with three parameters, and the function print.

Let us now write the definition of the function `setData`. Because bCh is a **protected** member variable of the **class** bClass, it can be directly accessed in the definition of the function `setData`. However, because bX is a **private** member variable of the **class** bClass, the function `setData` cannot directly access it. Thus, the function `setData` must set bX by using the function `setData` of the **class** bClass. The definition of the function `setData` of the **class** dClass can be written as follows:

```cpp
void dClass::setData(char ch, double v, int a)
{
    bClass::setData(v);

    bCh = ch; //initialize bCh using the assignment statement
    dA = a;
}
```

Note that the definition of the function `setData` calls the function `bClass::setData`, with one parameter to set the member variable bX, and then directly sets the value of bCh. Next, let us write the definition of the function `print` (of the **class** dClass).

We now write the definition of the function `print` of the **class** dClass. Notice that in the definition of the **class** bClass, the member function `print` is not overloaded as in the member function `setData`. It prints the values of both member variables, bCh and bX. The member variable bX is a **private** member variable, and so it cannot be directly accessed in the **class** dClass. Even though bCh is a **protected** member variable and it can be directly accessed in the **class** dClass, we must print its value using the function `print` of the **class** bClass, because this function outputs the values of both bCh and dX. For this reason, we first call the function `print` (of the **class** bClass) and then output only the value of dA. The definition of the function `print` is:

```cpp
void dClass::print() const
{
    bClass::print();

    cout << "Derived class dA = " << dA << endl;
}
```

The following program illustrates how the objects of bClass and dClass work. We assume that the definition of the **class** bClass is in the header file protectMembClass.h, and the definition of the **class** dClass is in the header file protectMembInDerivedCl.h.

```cpp
//Accessing protected members of a base class in the derived
//class.

#include <iostream>
#include "protectMembClass.h"
#include "protectMembInDerivedCl.h"

using namespace std;

int main()
{
    bClass bObject;                                    //Line 1
```

```cpp
    dClass dObject;                                  //Line 2

    bObject.print();                                 //Line 3
    cout << endl;                                    //Line 4

    cout << "*** Derived class object ***" << endl;  //Line 5

    dObject.setData('&', 2.5, 7);                    //Line 6

    dObject.print();                                 //Line 7

    return 0;
}
```

Sample Run:

```
Base class: bCh = *, bX = 0

*** Derived class object ***
Base class: bCh = &, bX = 2.5
Derived class dA = 7
```

When you write the definitions of the member functions of the **class** dClass, the **protected** member variable bCh can be accessed directly. However, dClass objects cannot directly access bCh. That is, the following statement is illegal (it is, in fact, a syntax error):

```cpp
dObject.bCh = '&';      //illegal
```

Composition

Composition is another way to relate two classes. In composition, one or more members of a class are objects of another class type. Composition is a "has-a" relation; for example, "every person has a date of birth."

Example 11-9, in Chapter 11, defined a class called personType. The **class** personType stores a person's first name and last name. Suppose we want to keep track of additional information for a person, such as a personal ID (e.g., a Social Security number) and a date of birth. Because every person has a personal ID and a date of birth, we can define a new class, called personalInfo, in which one of the members is an object of type personType. We can declare additional members to store the personal ID and date of birth for the **class** personalInfo.

First, we define another **class**, dateType, to store only a person's date of birth. Then, we construct the **class** personalInfo from the **class**es personType and dateType. This way, we can demonstrate how to define a new class using two classes.

To define the **class** `dateType`, we need three member variables—to store the month, day number, and year. Some of the operations that need to performed on a date are to set the date and to print the date. The following statements define the **class** `dateType`:

```
class dateType
{
public:
    void setDate(int month, int day, int year);
      //Function to set the date.
      //The member variables dMonth, dDay, and dYear are set
      //according to the parameters.
      //Postcondition: dMonth = month; dDay = day;
      //               dYear = year

    int getDay() const;
      //Function to return the day.
      //Postcondition: The value of dDay is returned.

    int getMonth() const;
      //Function to return the month.
      //Postcondition: The value of dMonth is returned.

    int getYear() const;
      //Function to return the year.
      //Postcondition: The value of dYear is returned.

    void printDate() const;
      //Function to output the date in the form mm-dd-yyyy.

    dateType(int month = 1, int day = 1, int year = 1900);
      //Constructor to set the date
      //The member variables dMonth, dDay, and dYear are set
      //according to the parameters.
      //Postcondition: dMonth = month; dDay = day; dYear = year;
      //               If no values are specified, the default
      //               values are used to initialize the member
      //               variables.

private:
    int dMonth; //variable to store the month
    int dDay;   //variable to store the day
    int dYear;  //variable to store the year
};
```

Figure 12-7 shows the UML class diagram of the **class** `dateType`.

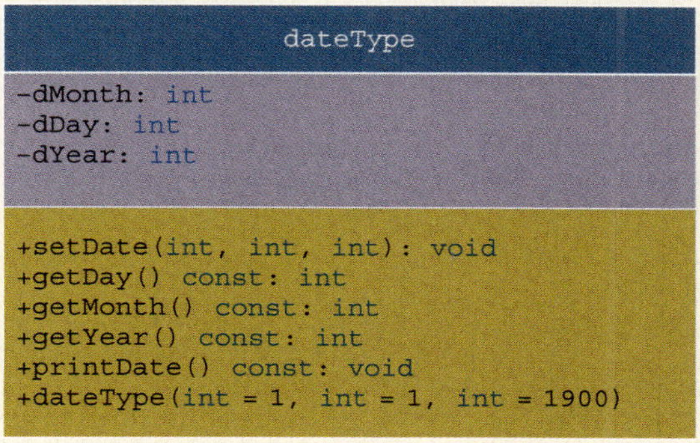

FIGURE 12-7 UML class diagram of the **class** dateType

The definitions of the member functions of the **class** dateType are as follows:

```cpp
void dateType::setDate(int month, int day, int year)
{
    dMonth = month;
    dDay = day;
    dYear = year;
}
```

The definition of the function setDate, before storing the date into the member variables, does not check whether the date is valid. That is, it does not confirm whether month is between 1 and 12, year is greater than 0, and day is valid (for example, for January, day should be between 1 and 31). In Programming Exercise 2 at the end of this chapter, you are asked to rewrite the definition of the function setDate so that the date is validated before storing it in the member variables. The definitions of the remaining member functions are as follows:

```cpp
int dateType::getDay() const
{
    return dDay;
}

int dateType::getMonth() const
{
    return dMonth;
}

int dateType::getYear() const
{
    return dYear;
}
```

```
void dateType::printDate() const
{
    cout << dMonth << "-" << dDay << "-" << dYear;
}


    //Constructor with parameters
dateType::dateType(int month, int day, int year)
{
    dMonth = month;
    dDay = day;
    dYear = year;
}
```

Just as in the case of setDate, in Programming Exercise 2, you are asked to rewrite the definition of the constructor so that it checks for the valid values of month, day, and year before storing the date into the member variables.

Next, we give the definition of the class personalInfo:

```
class personalInfo
{
public:
    void setpersonalInfo(string first, string last, int month,
                         int day, int year, int ID);
    //Function to set the personal information.
    //The member variables are set according to the
    //parameters.
    //Postcondition: firstName = first; lastName = last;
    //               dMonth = month; dDay = day;
    //               dYear = year; personID = ID;

    void printpersonalInfo () const;
    //Function to print the personal information.

    personalInfo(string first = "", string last = "",
                 int month = 1, int day = 1, int year = 1900,
                 int ID = 0);
    //Constructor
    //The member variables are set according to the
    //parameters.
    //Postcondition: firstName = first; lastName = last;
    //               dMonth = month; dDay = day;
    //               dYear = year; personID = ID;
    //               If no values are specified, the default
    //               values are used to initialize the member
    //               variables.

private:
    personType name;
    dateType bDay;
    int personID;
};
```

Figure 12-8 shows the UML class diagram of the **class** `personalInfo`.

```
                    personalInfo
─────────────────────────────────────────────
-name: personType
-bDay: dateType
-personID: int
─────────────────────────────────────────────
+setpersonalInfo(string, string, int, int,
                 int, int): void
+printpersonalInfo() const: void
+personalInfo(string = "", string = "",
              int = 1, int = 1,
              int = 1900, int = 0)
```

FIGURE 12-8 UML class diagram of the **class** `personalInfo`

Before we give the definition of the member functions of the **class** `personalInfo`, let us discuss how the constructors of the objects `bDay` and `name` are invoked.

Recall that a class constructor is automatically executed when a class object enters its scope. Suppose that we have the following statement:

```
personalInfo student;
```

When the object `student` enters its scope, the objects `bDay` and `name`, which are members of `student`, also enter their scopes. As a result, one of their constructors is executed. We, therefore, need to know how to pass arguments to the constructors of the member objects (that is, `bDay` and `name`), which occurs when we give the definitions of the constructors of the class. Recall that constructors do not have a type and so cannot be called like other functions. The arguments to the constructor of a member-object (such as `bDay`) are specified in the heading part of the definition of the constructor of the class. Furthermore, member-objects of a class are constructed (that is, initialized) in the order they are declared (not in the order they are listed in the constructor's member initialization list) and before the containing class objects are constructed. Thus, in our case, the object `name` is initialized first, then `bDay`, and finally `student`.

The following statements illustrate how to pass arguments to the constructors of the member objects `name` and `bDay`:

```
personalInfo::personalInfo(string first, string last, int month,
                           int day, int year, int ID)
        : name(first, last), bDay(month, day, year)
{
    .
    .
    .
}
```

The definitions of the member functions of the **class** personalInfo are as follows:

```
void personalInfo::setpersonalInfo(string first, string last,
                         int month, int day, int year, int ID)
{
    name.setName(first,last);
    bDay.setDate(month,day,year);
    personID = ID;
}

void personalInfo::printpersonalInfo() const
{
    name.print();
    cout << "'s date of birth is ";
    bDay.printDate();
    cout << endl;
    cout << "and personal ID is " << personID;
}

personalInfo::personalInfo(string first, string last, int month,
                         int day, int year, int ID)
        : name(first, last), bDay(month, day, year)
{
    personID = ID;

}
```

NOTE In the case of inheritance, use the class name to invoke the base class's constructor. In the case of composition, use the member-object name to invoke its own constructor.

Object-Oriented Design (OOD) and Object-Oriented Programming (OOP)

The first eleven chapters of this book used the top-down approach to programming, also called structured programming, to write programs. Problems were broken down into modules, and each module solved a particular part of the problem. Data requirements were identified, and functions were written to manipulate the data. The functions and the data were kept separate, and the functions acted on the data in a passive way. Structured programming, therefore, has certain limitations. In structured programming, functions are dependent on the data, and functions are designed specifically to solve a particular problem. It is quite difficult, if not impossible, to reuse a function written for one program in another program. For some of these reasons, structured programming is not very efficient for large software development.

Chapter 11 began with the introduction of classes. We learned how classes are defined and used. Later in that chapter, we concentrated on the data requirements of a problem and the logical operations on that data. With the help of classes, we combined the data—and the operations on that data—in a single unit. That is, the data and operations were encapsulated in a single unit. Also, with the help of classes, we were able to separate the data and the algorithms to manipulate that data. However, the functions to implement the operations on the data had direct access to the data. This chapter explains how to create new classes from existing classes through inheritance (and also using composition). Furthermore, an object has the capability to hide the information details. These are some of the features of object-oriented design (OOD).

The three basic principles of OOD are as follows:

- **Encapsulation**—The ability to combine data, and operations on that data, in a single unit.
- **Inheritance**—The ability to create new objects from existing objects.
- **Polymorphism**—The ability to use the same expression to denote different operations.

In OOD, an object is a fundamental entity; in structured programming, a function is a fundamental entity. In OOD, we debug objects; in structured programming, we debug functions. In OOD, a program is a collection of interacting objects; in structured programming, a program is a collection of interacting functions. Also, OOD encourages code reuse. Once an object becomes error-free, it can be reused in many programs because it is a self-contained entity. Object-oriented programming (OOP) implements OOD.

To create objects, we must know how to represent the data and write functions to manipulate that data. Thus, we must know everything that we have learned in Chapters 2 through 9. The first nine chapters are essential for any type of programming, whether structured or object-oriented.

C++ supports OOP through the use of classes. We have already examined the first two features of OOP, encapsulation and inheritance, in this chapter and Chapter 11. Chapter 14 discusses the third feature of OOD: polymorphism. A polymorphic function or operator has many forms.

In C++, a function name and the operators can be overloaded. An example of function overloading occurs when the function is called, and the operator is evaluated according to the arguments used. For instance, if both operands are integers, the division operator yields an integer result; otherwise, the division operator yields a decimal result. Suppose a class has constructors. If no arguments are passed to an object when it is declared, the default constructor is executed; otherwise, one of the constructors with parameters is executed. However, all constructors have the same name.

C++ also provides parametric polymorphism. In parametric polymorphism, the (data) type is left unspecified and then later instantiated. Templates (discussed in Chapter 14) provide parametric polymorphism. Also, C++ provides virtual functions as a means to implement polymorphism in an inheritance hierarchy, which allows the run-time selection of appropriate member functions. (Chapter 13 discusses virtual functions.)

There are several OOP languages in existence today, including Ada, Modula-2, Object Pascal, Turbo Pascal, Eiffel, C++, Java, and Smalltalk. The earliest OOP language was Simula, developed in 1967. The OOP terminology is influenced by the vocabulary of Smalltalk, the OOP language largely developed at a Xerox research center during the 1970s. An OOP language uses many "fancy" words, such as methods, message passing, and so forth.

OOP is a natural and intuitive way to view the programming process. When we view an object, we immediately think of what it can do. For example, when we think about a car, we also think about the operations on the car, such as starting the car and driving the car. When programmers think about a list, they also think about the operations on the list, such as searching, sorting, and inserting. OOP allows ADT to be created and used. In C++, we implement ADT through the use of classes.

Objects are created when class variables are declared. Objects interact with each other via function calls. Every object has an internal state and an external state. The `private` members form the internal state; the `public` members form the external state. Only the object can manipulate its internal state.

Identifying Classes, Objects, and Operations

In this book's first eleven chapters, in the problem analysis phase we analyzed the problem, identified the data, and outlined the algorithm. To reduce the complexity of the function `main`, we wrote functions to manipulate the data. In Chapter 11, we used the OOD technique and first identified the objects that made up the overall problem. The objects were designed and implemented independent of the main program. The hardest part in OOD is to identify the classes and objects. In this section, we describe a common and simple technique to identify classes and objects.

We begin with a description of the problem and then identify all of the nouns and verbs. From the list of nouns we choose our classes, and from the list of verbs we choose our operations.

For example, suppose that we want to write a program that calculates and prints the volume and surface area of a cylinder. We can state this problem as follows:

Write a **program** to *input* the **dimensions** of a **cylinder** and *calculate* and *print* the **surface area** and **volume**.

In this statement, the nouns are bold and the verbs are italic. From the list of nouns—**program**, **dimensions**, **cylinder**, **surface area**, and **volume**—we can easily visualize **cylinder** to be a class—say, `cylinderType`—from which we can create many cylinder objects of various dimensions. The nouns, **dimensions**, **surface area**, and **volume** are characteristics of a **cylinder** and thus can hardly be considered classes.

After we identify a class, the next step is to determine three pieces of information:

- Operations that an object of that class type can perform
- Operations that can be performed on an object of that class type
- Information that an object of that class type must maintain

From the list of verbs identified in the problem description, we choose a list of possible operations that an object of that class can perform, or has performed, on itself. For example, from the list of verbs for the cylinder problem description—*write, input, calculate, and print*—the possible operations for a cylinder object are *input, calculate,* and *print*.

For the **class** cylinderType, the dimensions represent the data. The center of the base, radius of the base, and height of the cylinder are the characteristics of the dimensions. You can input data to the object either by a constructor or by a mutator function.

The verb *calculate* applies to determining the volume and the surface area. From this, you can deduce the operations: cylinderVolume and cylinderSurfaceArea. Similarly, the verb *print* applies to the display of the volume and the surface area on an output device. In Programming Exercise 5 at the end of this chapter, you are asked to design a class to implement the characteristics of a cylinder.

Identifying classes via the nouns and verbs from the descriptions of the problem is not the only technique possible. There are several other OOD techniques in the literature. However, this technique is sufficient for the programming exercises in this book.

PROGRAMMING EXAMPLE: Grade Report

This programming example further illustrates the concepts of inheritance and composition.

The mid-semester point at your local university is approaching. The registrar's office wants to prepare the grade reports as soon as the students' grades are recorded. However, some of the students enrolled have not yet paid their tuition.

1. If a student has paid the tuition, the grades are shown on the grade report together with the grade-point average (GPA).

2. If a student has not paid the tuition, the grades are not printed. For these students, the grade report contains a message indicating that the grades have been held for nonpayment of the tuition. The grade report also shows the billing amount.

The registrar's office and the business office want your help in writing a program that can analyze the students' data and print the appropriate grade reports. The data is stored in a file in the following form:

```
15000 345
studentName studentID isTuitionPaid numberOfCourses
courseName courseNumber creditHours grade
courseName courseNumber creditHours grade
    .
    .
    .
```

```
studentName studentID isTuitionPaid numberOfCourses
courseName courseNumber creditHours grade
courseName courseNumber creditHours grade
    .
    .
    .
```

The first line indicates the number of students enrolled and the tuition rate per credit hour. The students' data is given thereafter.

A sample input file is as follows:

```
3 345
Lisa Miller 890238 Y 4
Mathematics MTH345 4 A
Physics PHY357 3 B
ComputerSci CSC478 3 B
History HIS356 3 A
    .
    .
    .
```

The first line indicates that the input file contains 3 students' data and the tuition rate is $345 per credit hour. Next, the course data for student Lisa Miller is given: Lisa Miller's ID is 890238, she has paid the tuition, and is taking 4 courses. The course number for the mathematics class she is taking is MTH345, the course has 4 credit hours, her mid-semester grade is A, and so on.

The desired output for each student is in the following form:

```
Student Name: Lisa Miller
Student ID: 890238
Number of courses enrolled: 4

Course No    Course Name        Credits    Grade
CSC478       ComputerSci           3         B
HIS356       History               3         A
MTH345       Mathematics           4         A
PHY357       Physics               3         B

Total number of credits: 13
Mid-Semester GPA: 3.54
```

It is clear from this output that the courses must be ordered according to the course number. To calculate the GPA, we assume that the grade A is equivalent to 4 points, B is equivalent to 3 points, C is equivalent to 2 points, D is equivalent to 1 point, and F is equivalent to 0 points.

Input   A file containing the data in the form given previously. For easy reference, let us assume that the name of the input file is `stData.txt`.

Output   A file containing the output in the form given previously.

PROBLEM
ANALYSIS
AND
ALGORITHM
DESIGN

We must first identify the main components of the program. The university has students, and every student takes courses. Thus, the two main components are the student and the course.

Let us first describe the course component.

Course   The main characteristics of a course are the course name, course number, and number of credit hours.

Some of the basic operations that need to be performed on an object of the course type are:

1.   Set the course information.

2.   Print the course information.

3.   Show the credit hours.

4.   Show the course number.

The following class defines the course as an ADT:

```cpp
class courseType
{
public:
    void setCourseInfo(string cName, string cNo, int credits);
      //Function to set the course information.
      //The course information is set according to the
      //parameters.
      //Postcondition: courseName = cName; courseNo = cNo;
      //               courseCredits = credits;

    void print(ostream& outF);
      //Function to print the course information.
      //This function sends the course information to the
      //output device specified by the parameter outF. If the
      //actual parameter to this function is the object cout,
      //then the output is shown on the standard output device.
      //If the actual parameter is an ofstream variable, say,
      //outFile, then the output goes to the file specified by
      //outFile.

    int getCredits();
      //Function to return the credit hours.
      //Postcondition: The value of courseCredits is returned.
```

```cpp
    string getCourseNumber();
      //Function to return the course number.
      //Postcondition: The value of courseNo is returned.

    string getCourseName();
      //Function to return the course name.
      //Postcondition: The value of courseName is returned.

    courseType(string cName = "", string cNo = "",
              int credits = 0);
      //Constructor
      //The object is initialized according to the parameters.
      //Postcondition: courseName = cName; courseNo = cNo;
      //                courseCredits = credits;

private:
    string courseName;   //variable to store the course name
    string courseNo;     //variable to store the course number
    int courseCredits;   //variable to store the credit hours
};
```

Figure 12-9 shows the UML class diagram of the **class** courseType.

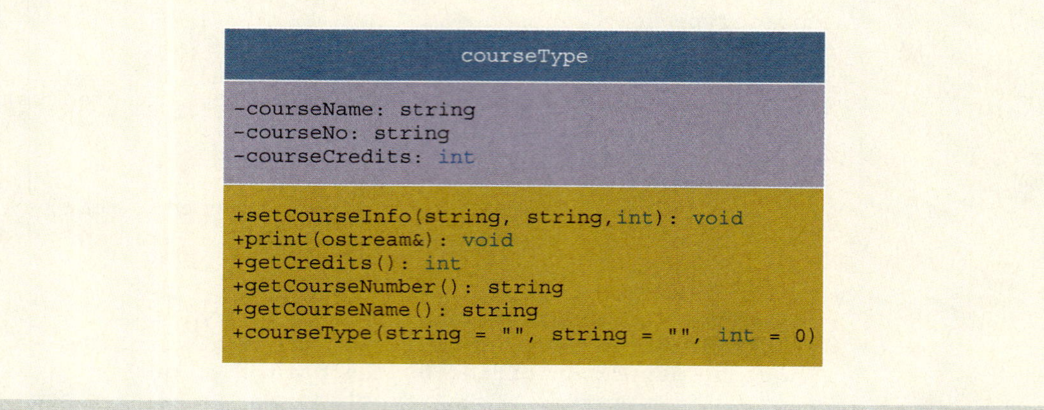

FIGURE 12-9 UML class diagram of the **class** courseType

Next, we discuss the definitions of the functions to implement the operations of the **class** courseType. These definitions are quite straightforward and easy to follow.

The function setCourseInfo sets the values of the **private** member variables according to the values of the parameters. Its definition is:

```
void courseType::setCourseInfo(string cName, string cNo,
                               int credits)
{
    courseName = cName;
    courseNo = cNo;
    courseCredits = credits;
} //end setCourseInfo
```

The function `print` prints the course information. The parameter `outF` specifies the output device. Also, we print the course name and course number left-justified rather than right-justified (the default). Thus, we need to set the `left` manipulator. Before printing the credit hours, the manipulator is set to be right-justified. The following steps describe this function:

1. Set the `left` manipulator.

2. Print the course number.

3. Print the course name.

4. Set the `right` manipulator.

5. Print the credit hours.

The definition of the function `print` is:

```
void courseType::print(ostream& outF)
{
    outF << left;                                //Step 1
    outF << setw(8) << courseNo << "    ";       //Step 2
    outF << setw(15) << courseName;              //Step 3
    outF << right;                               //Step 4
    outF << setw(3) << courseCredits << "    ";  //Step 5
} //end print
```

The constructor is declared with the default values. If no values are specified when a `courseType` object is declared, the constructor uses the default to initialize the object. Using the default values, the object's member variables are initialized as follows: `courseNo` to blank, `courseName` to blank, and `courseCredits` to 0. Otherwise, the values specified in the object declaration are used to initialize the object. Its definition is:

```
courseType::courseType(string cName, string cNo, int credits)
{
    courseName = cName;
    courseNo =   cNo;
    courseCredits = credits;
} //end default constructor
```

The definitions of the remaining functions are as follows:

```cpp
int courseType::getCredits()
{
    return courseCredits;
} //end getCredits

string courseType::getCourseNumber()
{
    return courseNo;
}//end getCourseNumber

string courseType::getCourseName()
{
    return courseName;
} //end getCourseName
```

Next, we discuss the student component.

NOTE Notice that in the definition of the `class` courseType, the member functions, such as `print` and `getCredits`, are accessor functions. This class also has other accessor functions. As noted in Chapter 11, we typically define the accessor functions with the keyword `const` at the end of their headings. We leave it as an exercise for you to redefine this class so that the accessor functions are declared as constant functions. (See Programming Exercise 12 at the end of this chapter.)

Student The main characteristics of a student are the student name, student ID, number of courses in which enrolled, courses in which enrolled, and grade for each course. Because every student has to pay tuition, we also include a member to indicate whether the student has paid the tuition.

Every student is a person, and every student takes courses. We have already designed a `class` personType to process a person's first name and last name. We have also designed a class to process the information for a course. Thus, we see that we can derive the `class` studentType to keep track of a student's information from the `class` personType, and one member of this class is of type courseType. We can add more members as needed.

The basic operations to be performed on an object of type studentType are as follows:

1. Set the student information.
2. Print the student information.
3. Calculate the number of credit hours taken.

4. Calculate the GPA.

5. Calculate the billing amount.

6. Because the grade report will print the courses in ascending order, sort the courses according to the course number.

The following class defines studentType as an ADT. We assume that a student takes no more than six courses per semester:

```cpp
class studentType: public personType
{
public:
    void setInfo(string fname, string lName, int ID,
                 int nOfCourses, bool isTPaid,
                 courseType courses[], char courseGrades[]);
    //Function to set the student's information.
    //Postcondition: The member variables are set
    //               according to the parameters.

    void print(ostream& outF, double tuitionRate);
    //Function to print the student's grade report.
    //If the member variable isTuitionPaid is true, the grades
    //are shown, otherwise three stars are printed. If the
    //actual parameter corresponding to outF is the object
    //cout, then the output is shown on the standard output
    //device. If the actual parameter corresponding to outF
    //is an ofstream object, say outFile, then the output
    //goes to the file specified by outFile.

    studentType();
    //Default constructor
    //The member variables are initialized.

    int getHoursEnrolled();
    //Function to return the credit hours a student is
    //enrolled in.
    //Postcondition: The number of credit hours are
    //               calculated and returned.

    double getGpa();
    //Function to return the grade point average.
    //Postcondition: The gpa is calculated and returned.

    double billingAmount(double tuitionRate);
    //Function to return the tuition fees.
    //Postcondition: The billing amount is calculated
    //and returned.
```

```
private:
    void sortCourses();
        //Function to sort the courses.
        //Postcondition: The array coursesEnrolled is sorted.
        //                For each course, its grade is stored in
        //                the array coursesGrade. Therefore, when
        //                the array coursesEnrolled is sorted, the
        //                corresponding entries in the array
        //                coursesGrade are adjusted.

    int sId;                //variable to store the student ID
    int numberOfCourses;    //variable to store the number
                            //of courses
    bool isTuitionPaid;     //variable to indicate whether the
                            //tuition is paid
    courseType coursesEnrolled[6]; //array to store the courses
    char coursesGrade[6];   //array to store the course grades
};
```

Figure 12-10 shows the UML class diagram of the **class** studentType and the inheritance hierarchy.

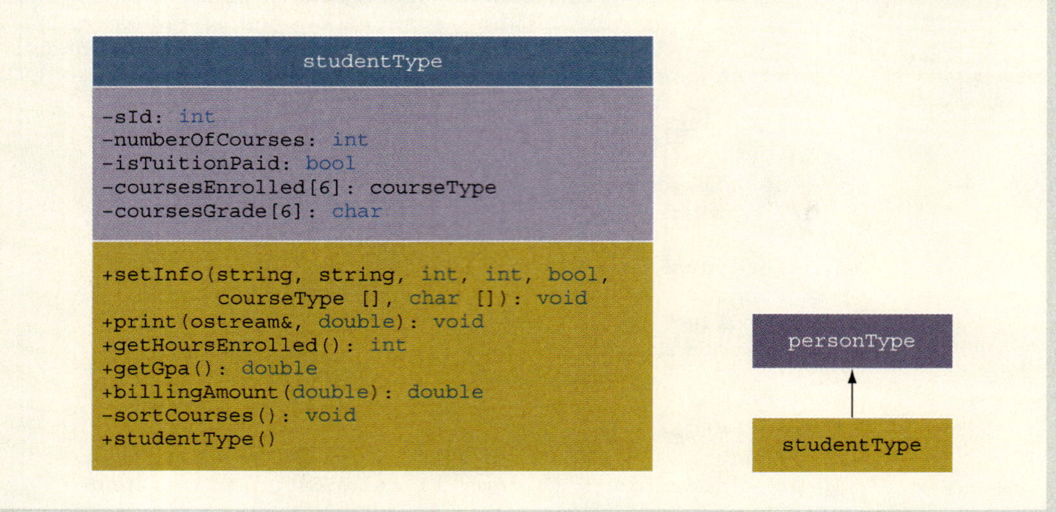

FIGURE 12-10 UML class diagram of the **class** studentType and the inheritance hierarchy

Before writing the definitions of the member functions of the **class** studentType, we make the following note.

NOTE Notice that in the definition of the `class` `studentType`, the member functions, such as `print` and `getGpa`, are accessor functions. This class also has other accessor functions. As noted in Chapter 11, we typically define the accessor functions with the keyword `const` at the end of their headings. We leave it as an exercise for you to redefine this class so that the accessor functions are declared as constant functions. (See Programming Exercise 12 at the end of this chapter.)

Note that the member function `sortCourses` to sort the array `coursesEnrolled` is a `private` member of the `class` `studentType`. This is due to the fact that this function is needed for internal data manipulation, and the user of the class does not need to access this member.

Next, we discuss the definitions of the functions to implement the operations of the `class` `studentType`.

The function `setInfo` first initializes the `private` member variables according to the incoming parameters. This function then calls the function `sortCourses` to sort the array `coursesEnrolled` by course number. The `class` `studentType` is derived from the `class` `personType`, and the variables to store the first name and last name are `private` member variables of that class. Therefore, we call the member function `setName` of the `class` `personType`, and pass the appropriate variables to set the first and last names. The definition of the function `setInfo` is as follows:

```cpp
void studentType::setInfo(string fName, string lName, int ID,
                          int nOfCourses, bool isTPaid,
                          courseType courses[], char cGrades[])
{
    int i;

    setName(fName, lName);               //set the name

    sId = ID;                            //set the student ID
    isTuitionPaid = isTPaid;             //set isTuitionPaid
    numberOfCourses = nOfCourses;        //set the number of courses

        //set the course information
    for (i = 0; i < numberOfCourses; i++)
    {
        coursesEnrolled[i] = courses[i];
        coursesGrade[i] = cGrades[i];
    }

    sortCourses();      //sort the array coursesEnrolled
} //end setInfo
```

The default constructor initializes the **private** member variables to the default values. Note that because the **private** member variable `coursesEnrolled` is of type `courseType` and is an array, the default constructor of the **class** `courseType` executes automatically, and the entire array is initialized.

```
studentType::studentType()
{
    numberOfCourses = 0;
    sId = 0;
    isTuitionPaid = false;

    for (int i = 0; i < 6; i++)
        coursesGrade[i] = '*';
} //end default constructor
```

The function `print` prints the grade report. The parameter `outF` specifies the output device. If the student has paid his or her tuition, the grades and the GPA are shown. Otherwise, three stars are printed in place of each grade, the GPA is not shown, a message indicates that the grades are being held for nonpayment of the tuition, and the amount due is shown. This function has the following steps:

1. Output the student's name.
2. Output the student's ID.
3. Output the number of courses in which the student is enrolled.
4. Output the heading:
    `Course No   Course Name    Credits    Grade`
5. Print each course's information.

    For each course, print:

    a. `Course No, Course Name, Credits`

    b. **if** `isTuitionPaid` is **true**

        Output the grade

    else

        Output three stars.
6. Print the total credit hours.
7. To output the GPA and billing amount in a fixed decimal format with the decimal point and trailing zeros, set the necessary flag. Also, set the precision to two decimal places.
8. **if** `isTuitionPaid` is **true**

    Output the GPA

    else

    Output the billing amount and a message about withholding the grades.

The definition of the function print is as follows:

```cpp
void studentType::print(ostream& outF, double tuitionRate)
{
    int i;

    outF << "Student Name: " << getFirstName()
         << " " << getLastName() << endl;            //Step 1

    outF << "Student ID: " << sId << endl;           //Step 2

    outF << "Number of courses enrolled: "
         << numberOfCourses << endl;                 //Step 3
    outF << endl;

    outF << left;
    outF << "Course No" << setw(15) << "  Course Name"
         << setw(8) << "Credits"
         << setw(6) << "Grade" << endl;              //Step 4

    outF << right;
    for (i = 0; i < numberOfCourses; i++)            //Step 5
    {
        coursesEnrolled[i].print(outF);              //Step 5a

        if (isTuitionPaid)                           //Step 5b
            outF <<setw(4) << coursesGrade[i] << endl;
        else
            outF << setw(4) << "***" << endl;
    }
    outF << endl;

    outF << "Total number of credit hours: "
         << getHoursEnrolled() << endl;              //Step 6

    outF << fixed << showpoint << setprecision(2);   //Step 7

    if (isTuitionPaid)                               //Step 8
        outF << "Mid-Semester GPA: " << getGpa()
             << endl;
    else
    {
        outF << "*** Grades are being held for not paying "
             << "the tuition. ***" << endl;
        outF << "Amount Due: $" << billingAmount(tuitionRate)
             << endl;
    }

    outF << "-*-*-*-*-*-*-*-*-*-*-*-*-*-*-*-*-*-*-*"
         << "-*-*-*-*-" << endl << endl;
} //end print
```

NOTE   Let us take a look at the formal parameter of the function `print`. The formal parameter `outF` is an object of the **class** `ostream`. We can use this function to send the output to the standard output device, the screen, or to a file. As indicated in the definition of the class, if the actual parameter is, say, `cout`, then the output is displayed on the screen. If the actual parameter is, say, `outfile`, an object of the **class** `ofstream`, then the output is sent to the device indicated by `outfile`. As mentioned in the section, "C++ Stream Hierarchy," the **class** `ofstream` is derived from the **class** `ostream`. Therefore, the **class** `ostream` is the base class. In C++, if a formal reference parameter is of the type `ostream`, it can refer to an object of the **class** `ofstream`.

In general, C++ allows a formal reference parameter of the base class type to refer to an object of the derived class. Of course, for user-defined classes, for this mechanism to work properly some other things need to be taken into account, which we will discuss in Chapter 13 (in the section, "Inheritance, Pointers, and Virtual Functions").

The function `getHoursEnrolled` calculates and returns the total credit hours that a student is taking. These credit hours are needed to calculate both the GPA and the billing amount. The total credit hours are calculated by adding the credit hours of each course in which the student is enrolled. Because the credit hours for a course are in the **private** member variable of an object of type `courseType`, we use the member function `getCredits` of the **class** `courseType` to retrieve the credit hours. The definition of this function is:

```cpp
int studentType::getHoursEnrolled()
{
    int totalCredits = 0;
    int i;

    for (i = 0; i < numberOfCourses; i++)
        totalCredits += coursesEnrolled[i].getCredits();

    return totalCredits;
} //end getHoursEnrolled
```

If a student has not paid the tuition, the function `billingAmount` calculates and returns the amount due, based on the number of credit hours enrolled. The definition of this function is:

```cpp
double studentType::billingAmount(double tuitionRate)
{
    return tuitionRate * getHoursEnrolled();
} //end billingAmount
```

We now discuss the function `getGpa`. This function calculates a student's GPA. To find the GPA, we find the equivalent points for each grade, add the points, and then divide the sum by the total credit hours the student is taking. The definition of this function is:

```cpp
double studentType::getGpa()
{
    int i;
    double sum = 0.0;

    for (i = 0; i < numberOfCourses; i++)
    {
        switch (coursesGrade[i])
        {
        case 'A':
            sum += coursesEnrolled[i].getCredits() * 4;
            break;
        case 'B':
            sum += coursesEnrolled[i].getCredits() * 3;
            break;
        case 'C':
            sum += coursesEnrolled[i].getCredits() * 2;
            break;
        case 'D':
            sum += coursesEnrolled[i].getCredits() * 1;
            break;
        case 'F':
            sum += coursesEnrolled[i].getCredits() * 0;
            break;
        default:
            cout << "Invalid Course Grade." << endl;
        }
    }

    return sum / getHoursEnrolled();
} //end getGpa
```

The function `sortCourses` sorts the array `coursesEnrolled` by course number. To sort the array, we use a selection sort algorithm. Because we will compare the course numbers, which are strings and **private** member variables of the **class** `courseType`, we first retrieve and store the course numbers in local variables.

```cpp
void studentType::sortCourses()
{
    int i, j;
    int minIndex;
    courseType temp;        //variable to swap the data
    char tempGrade;         //variable to swap the grades
    string course1;
    string course2;
```

```cpp
    for (i = 0; i < numberOfCourses - 1; i++)
    {
        minIndex = i;

        for (j = i + 1; j < numberOfCourses; j++)
        {
                //get the course numbers
            course1 =
                coursesEnrolled[minIndex].getCourseNumber();
            course2 = coursesEnrolled[j].getCourseNumber();

            if (course1 > course2)
                minIndex = j;
        }//end for

        temp = coursesEnrolled[minIndex];
        coursesEnrolled[minIndex] = coursesEnrolled[i];
        coursesEnrolled[i] = temp;

        tempGrade = coursesGrade[minIndex];
        coursesGrade[minIndex] = coursesGrade[i];
        coursesGrade[i] = tempGrade;
    } //end for
} //end sortCourses
```

MAIN PROGRAM

Now that we have designed the classes `courseType` and `studentType`, we will use these classes to complete the program.

We will restrict our program to process a maximum of 10 students. Note that this program can easily be enhanced to process any number of students.

Because the `print` function of the class does the necessary computations to print the final grade report, the main program has very little work to do. In fact, all that is left for the main program is to declare the objects to hold the students' data, load the data into these objects, and then print the grade reports. Because the input is in a file and the output will be sent to a file, we declare stream variables to access the input and output files. Essentially, the main algorithm for the program is:

1. Declare the variables.
2. Open the input file.
3. If the input file does not exist, exit the program.
4. Open the output file.
5. Get the number of students registered and the tuition rate.
6. Load the students' data.
7. Print the grade reports.

VARIABLES

This program processes a maximum of 10 students. Therefore, we must declare an array of 10 components of type `studentType` to hold the students' data. We also need to store the number of students registered and the tuition rate. Because the data will be read from a file, and because the output is sent to a file, we need two stream variables to access the input and output files. Thus, we need the following variables:

```cpp
studentType studentList[MAX_NO_OF_STUDENTS]; //array to store
                                             //the students' data

int noOfStudents;       //variable to store the number of students
double tuitionRate;     //variable to store the tuition rate

ifstream infile;        //input stream variable
ofstream outfile;       //output stream variable
```

Function
getStudentData

This function has three parameters: a parameter to access the input file, a parameter to access the array `studentList`, and a parameter to know the number of students registered. In pseudocode, the definition of this function is as follows:

For each student in the university,

1. Get the first name, last name, student ID, and `isPaid`.

2. `if` `isPaid` is 'Y'
        set `isTuitionPaid` to `true`
   `else`
        set `isTuitionPaid` to `false`

3. Get the number of courses the student is taking.

4. For each course,
   Get the course name, course number, credit hours, and grade.
   Load the course information into a `courseType` object.

5. Load the data into a `studentType` object.

We need to declare several local variables to read and store the data. The definition of the function `getStudentData` is:

```cpp
void getStudentData(ifstream& infile,
                    studentType studentList[],
                    int numberOfStudents)
{
        //local variables
    string fName;       //variable to store the first name
    string lName;       //variable to store the last name
    int ID;             //variable to store the student ID
    int noOfCourses;    //variable to store the number of courses
```

1
2

```cpp
    char isPaid;        //variable to store Y/N, that is,
                        //is tuition paid
    bool isTuitionPaid; //variable to store true/false

    string cName;       //variable to store the course name
    string cNo;         //variable to store the course number
    int credits;        //variable to store the course credit hours

    int count;          //loop control variable
    int i;              //loop control variable

    courseType courses[6]; //array of objects to store the
                        //course information
    char cGrades[6];        //array to hold the course grades

    for (count = 0; count < numberOfStudents; count++)
    {
        infile >> fName >> lName >> ID >> isPaid;   //Step 1

        if (isPaid == 'Y')                          //Step 2
            isTuitionPaid = true;
        else
            isTuitionPaid = false;

        infile >> noOfCourses;                      //Step 3

        for (i = 0; i < noOfCourses; i++)           //Step 4
        {
            infile >> cName >> cNo >> credits
                   >> cGrades[i];                   //Step 4.a
            courses[i].setCourseInfo(cName, cNo,
                                credits);           //Step 4.b
        }
        studentList[count].setInfo(fName, lName, ID,
                            noOfCourses,
                            isTuitionPaid,
                            courses, cGrades); //Step 5
    }//end for
} //end getStudentData
```

Function printGradeReports

This function prints the grade reports. For each student, it calls the function `print` of the **class** `studentType` to print the grade report. The definition of the function `printGradeReports` is:

```cpp
void printGradeReports(ofstream& outfile,
                       studentType studentList[],
                       int numberOfStudents,
                       double tuitionRate)
```

```cpp
{
    int count;
    for (count = 0; count < numberOfStudents; count++)
        studentList[count].print(outfile, tuitionRate);
} //end printGradeReports
```

PROGRAMMING LISTING

```cpp
//Header file courseType.h
#ifndef H_courseType
#define H_courseType

#include <fstream>
#include <string>

using namespace std;

//The definition of the class courseType goes here.
    .
    .
    .
#endif
```

```cpp
//Implementation file courseTypeImp.cpp
#include <iostream>
#include <fstream>
#include <string>
#include <iomanip>
#include "courseType.h"

using namespace std;

//The definitions of the member functions of the class
//courseType go here.
    .
    .
    .
```

```cpp
//Header file personType.h
#ifndef H_personType
#define H_personType

#include <string>

using namespace std;
```

```cpp
    //The definition of the class personType goes here.
        .
        .
        .
    #endif


    //Implementation file personTypeImp.cpp

    #include <iostream>
    #include <string>
    #include "personType.h"

    using namespace std;

    //The definitions of the member functions of the class
    //personType go here.
        .
        .
        .


    //Header file studentType.h
    #ifndef H_studentType
    #define H_studentType

    #include <fstream>
    #include <string>
    #include "personType.h"
    #include "courseType.h"

    using namespace std;

    //The definition of the class studentType goes here.
        .
        .
        .

    #endif


    //Implementation file studentTypeImp.cpp

    #include <iostream>
    #include <iomanip>
    #include <fstream>
    #include <string>
    #include "personType.h"
    #include "courseType.h"
    #include "studentType.h"
```

```cpp
using namespace std;

//The definitions of the member functions of the class
//studentType go here.
    .
    .
    .

//Main Program
#include <iostream>
#include <fstream>
#include <string>
#include "studentType.h"

using namespace std;

const int MAX_NO_OF_STUDENTS = 10;

void getStudentData(ifstream& infile,
                    studentType studentList[],
                    int numberOfStudents);

void printGradeReports(ofstream& outfile,
                       studentType studentList[],
                       int numberOfStudents,
                       double tuitionRate);

int main()
{
    studentType studentList[MAX_NO_OF_STUDENTS];

    int noOfStudents;
    double tuitionRate;
    ifstream infile;
    ofstream outfile;

    infile.open("a:\\stData.txt");

    if (!infile)
    {
        cout << "The input file does not exist. "
             << "Program terminates." << endl;
        return 1;
    }

    outfile.open("a:\\sDataOut.txt");

    infile >> noOfStudents; //get the number of students
    infile >> tuitionRate;  //get the tuition rate
```

```
        getStudentData(infile, studentList, noOfStudents);
        printGradeReports(outfile, studentList,
                          noOfStudents, tuitionRate);

    return 0;
}

//Place the definitions of the functions getStudentData and
//printGradeReports here.
```

Sample Run:

```
Student Name: Lisa Miller
Student ID: 890238
Number of courses enrolled: 4

Course No   Course Name   Credits Grade
CSC478      ComputerSci      3      B
HIS356      History          3      A
MTH345      Mathematics      4      A
PHY357      Physics          3      B

Total number of credit hours: 13
Mid-Semester GPA: 3.54
-*-*-*-*-*-*-*-*-*-*-*-*-*-*-*-*-*-*-*-*-*-*-*-

Student Name: Bill Wilton
Student ID: 798324
Number of courses enrolled: 5

Course No   Course Name   Credits Grade
BIO234      Biology          4      ***
CHM256      Chemistry        4      ***
ENG378      English          3      ***
MTH346      Mathematics      3      ***
PHL534      Philosophy       3      ***

Total number of credit hours: 17
*** Grades are being held for not paying the tuition. ***
Amount Due: $5865.00
-*-*-*-*-*-*-*-*-*-*-*-*-*-*-*-*-*-*-*-*-*-*-*-

Student Name: Dandy Goat
Student ID: 746333
Number of courses enrolled: 6

Course No   Course Name   Credits Grade
BUS128      Business         3      C
CHM348      Chemistry        4      B
CSC201      ComputerSci      3      B
ENG328      English          3      B
```

```
HIS101      History           3      A
MTH137      Mathematics       3      A

Total number of credit hours: 19
Mid-Semester GPA: 3.16
_*_*_*_*_*_*_*_*_*_*_*_*_*_*_*_*_*_*_*_*_*_
```

Input File:

```
3 345
Lisa Miller 890238 Y 4
Mathematics MTH345 4 A
Physics PHY357 3 B
ComputerSci CSC478 3 B
History HIS356 3 A

Bill Wilton 798324 N 5
English ENG378 3 B
Philosophy PHL534 3 A
Chemistry CHM256 4 C
Biology BIO234 4 A
Mathematics MTH346 3 C

Dandy Goat 746333 Y 6
History HIS101 3 A
English ENG328 3 B
Mathematics MTH137 3 A
Chemistry CHM348 4 B
ComputerSci CSC201 3 B
Business BUS128 3 C
```

QUICK REVIEW

1. Inheritance and composition are meaningful ways to relate two or more classes.

2. Inheritance is an "is–a" relation.

3. Composition is a "has–a" relation.

4. In a single inheritance, the derived class is derived from only one existing class, called the base class.

5. In a multiple inheritance, a derived class is derived from more than one base class.

6. The `private` members of a base class are `private` to the base class. The derived class cannot directly access them.

7. The **public** members of a base class can be inherited either as **public** or **private** by the derived class.

8. A derived class can redefine the member functions of a base class, but this redefinition applies only to the objects of the derived class.

9. A call to a base class's constructor (with parameters) is specified in the heading of the definition of the derived class's constructor.

10. If in the heading of the definition of a derived class's constructor, no call to a constructor (with parameters) of a base class is specified, then during the derived class's object declaration and initialization the default constructor (if any) of the base class executes.

11. When initializing the object of a derived class, the constructor of the base class is executed first.

12. Review the inheritance rules given in this chapter.

13. In composition, a member of a class is an object of another class.

14. In composition, a call to the constructor of the member objects is specified in the heading of the definition of the class's constructor.

15. The three basic principles of OOD are encapsulation, inheritance, and polymorphism.

16. An easy way to identify classes, objects, and operations is to describe the problem in English and then identify all of the nouns and verbs. Choose your classes (objects) from the list of nouns and operations from the list of verbs.

EXERCISES

1. Mark the following statements as true or false.

    a. The constructor of a derived class can specify a call to the constructor of the base class in the heading of the function definition.

    b. The constructor of a derived class can specify a call to the constructor of the base class using the name of the class.

    c. Suppose that **x** and **y** are classes, one of the member variables of **x** is an object of type **y**, and both classes have constructors. The constructor of **x** specifies a call to the constructor of **y** by using the object name of type **y**.

2. Draw a class hierarchy in which several classes are derived from a single base class.

3. Suppose that a **class** employeeType is derived from the **class** personType (see Example 11-9, in Chapter 11). Give examples of members—data and functions—that can be added to the **class** employeeType.

4. Explain the difference between the **private** and **protected** members of a class.

5. Consider the following class definition:

```cpp
class aClass
{
public:
    void print() const;
    void set(int, int);
    aClass();
    aClass(int, int);

private:
    int u;
    int v;
};
```

What is wrong with the following class definitions?

a.

```cpp
class bClass public aClass
{
public:
    void print();
    void set(int, int, int);

private:
    int z;
}
```

b.

```cpp
class cClass: public aClass
{
public:
    void print();
    int sum();
    cClass();
    cClass(int)
}
```

6. Consider the following statements:

```cpp
class yClass
{
public:
    void one();
    void two(int, int);
    yClass();

private:
    int a;
    int b;
};
```

```cpp
class xClass: public yClass
{
public:
    void one();
    xClass();

private:
    int z;
};
```

Suppose the following statements are in a user program (client code):

```cpp
yClass y;
xClass x;
```

a. The **private** members of yClass are **public** members of xClass. True or False?

b. Mark the following statements as valid or invalid. If a statement is invalid, explain why.

   i. ```cpp
       void yClass::one()
       {
           cout << a + b << endl;
       }
       ```

   ii. ```cpp
       y.a = 15;
       x.b = 30;
       ```

   iii. ```cpp
        void xClass::one()
        {
            a = 10;
            b = 15;
            z = 30;
            cout << a + b + z << endl;
        }
        ```

   iv. ```cpp
       cout << y.a << " " << y.b << " " << x.z << endl;
       ```

7. Assume the declaration of Exercise 6.

   a. Write the definition of the default constructor of yClass so that the **private** member variables of yClass are initialized to 0.

   b. Write the definition of the default constructor of xClass so that the **private** member variables of xClass are initialized to 0.

   c. Write the definition of the member function two of yClass so that the **private** member variable a is initialized to the value of the first parameter of two, and the **private** member variable b is initialized to the value of the second parameter of two.

8. What is wrong with the following code?

```cpp
class classA
{
protected:
    void setX(int a);              //Line 1
        //Postcondition: x = a;    //Line 2

private:                           //Line 3
    int x;                         //Line 4
};
    .
    .
    .
int main()
{
    classA aObject;                //Line 5

    aObject.setX(4);               //Line 6
    return 0;                      //Line 7
}
```

9. Consider the following code:

```cpp
class one
{
public:
    void print() const;
        //Output the values of x and y
protected:
    void setData(int u, int v);
        //Postcondition: x = u; y = v;
private:
    int x;
    int y;
};

class two: public one
{
public:
    void setData(int a, int b, int c);
        //Postcondition: x = a; y = b; z = c;
      void print() const;
        //Output the values of x, y, and z
  private:
        int z;
 };
```

   a. Write the definition of the function `setData` of the **class** two.

   b. Write the definition of the function `print` of the **class** two.

10. What is the output of the following C++ program?

```cpp
#include <iostream>
#include <string>

using namespace std;

class baseClass
{
public:
    void print() const;

    baseClass(string s = " ", int a = 0);
      //Postcondition: str = s; x = a;

protected:
    int x;

private:
    string str;
};

class derivedClass: public baseClass
{
public:
    void print() const;

    derivedClass(string s = "", int a = 0, int b = 0);
      //Postcondition: str = s; x = a; y = b;

private:
    int y;
};

int main()
{
    baseClass baseObject("This is the base class", 2);
    derivedClass derivedObject("DDDDDD", 3, 7);

    baseObject.print();
    derivedObject.print();

    return 0;
}
void baseClass::print() const
{
    cout << x << " " << str << endl;
}

baseClass::baseClass(string s, int a)
{
    str = s;
    x = a;
}
```

```cpp
void derivedClass::print() const
{
    cout << "Derived class: " << y << endl;
    baseClass::print();
}

derivedClass::derivedClass(string s, int a, int b)
            :baseClass("Hello Base", a + b)
{
    y = b;
}
```

11. Consider the following class definitions:

```cpp
class baseClass
{
public:
    void print() const;
    int getX() const;
    baseClass(int a = 0);

protected:
    int x;
};

class derivedClass: public baseClass
{
public:
    void print() const;
    int getResult() const;
    derivedClass(int a = 0, int b = 0);

private:
    int y;
};
```

Suppose the definitions of the member functions of these classes are as follows:

```cpp
void baseClass::print() const
{
    cout << "In base: x = " << x << endl;
}

baseClass::baseClass(int a)
{
    x = a;
}

int baseClass::getX() const
{
    return x;
}
```

```cpp
void derivedClass::print() const
{
    cout << "In derived: x = " << x << ", y = " << y
         << "; x + y = " << x + y << endl;
}

int derivedClass::getResult() const
{
    return x + y;
}

derivedClass::derivedClass(int a, int b)
            : baseClass(a)
{
    y = b;
}
```

What is the output of the following function `main`?

```cpp
int main()
{
    baseClass baseObject(7);
    derivedClass derivedObject(3, 8);

    baseObject.print();
    derivedObject.print();

    cout << "****" << baseObject.getX() << endl;
    cout << "####" << derivedObject.getResult() << endl;

    return 0;
}
```

PROGRAMMING EXERCISES

1. In Chapter 11, the **class** `clockType` was designed to implement the time of day in a program. Certain applications, in addition to hours, minutes, and seconds, might require you to store the time zone. Derive the **class** `extClockType` from the **class** `clockType` by adding a member variable to store the time zone. Add the necessary member functions and constructors to make the class functional. Also, write the definitions of the member functions and the constructors. Finally, write a test program to test your **class**.

2. In this chapter, the **class** `dateType` was designed to implement the date in a program, but the member function `setDate` and the constructor do not check whether the date is valid before storing the date in the member variables. Rewrite the definitions of the function `setDate` and the constructor so that the values for the month, day, and year are checked before

storing the date into the member variables. Add a member function, `isLeapYear`, to check whether a year is a leap year. Moreover, write a test program to test your class.

3. A point in the x-y plane is represented by its x-coordinate and y-coordinate. Design a **class**, `pointType`, that can store and process a point in the x-y plane. You should then perform operations on the point, such as setting the coordinates of the point, printing the coordinates of the point, returning the x-coordinate, and returning the y-coordinate. Also, write a program to test various operations on the point.

4. Every circle has a center and a radius. Given the radius, we can determine the circle's area and circumference. Given the center, we can determine its position in the x-y plane. The center of the circle is a point in the x-y plane. Design a **class**, `circleType`, that can store the radius and center of the circle. Because the center is a point in the x-y plane, and you designed the class to capture the properties of a point in Programming Exercise 3, you must derive the **class** `circleType` from the **class** `pointType`. You should be able to perform the usual operations on the circle, such as setting the radius, printing the radius, calculating and printing the area and circumference, and carrying out the usual operations on the center. Also, write a program to test various operations on a circle.

5. Every cylinder has a base and height, where the base is a circle. Design a **class**, `cylinderType`, that can capture the properties of a cylinder and perform the usual operations on the cylinder. Derive this class from the **class** `circleType` designed in Programming Exercise 4. Some of the operations that can be performed on a cylinder are as follows: calculate and print the volume, calculate and print the surface area, set the height, set the radius of the base, and set the center of the base. Also, write a program to test various operations on a cylinder.

6. Using classes, design an online address book to keep track of the names, addresses, phone numbers, and dates of birth of family members, close friends, and certain business associates. Your program should be able to handle a maximum of 500 entries.

   a. Define a **class**, `addressType`, that can store a street address, city, state, and ZIP code. Use the appropriate functions to print and store the address. Also, use constructors to automatically initialize the member variables.

   b. Define a **class** `extPersonType` using the **class** `personType` (as defined in Example 11-9, Chapter 11), the **class** `dateType` (as designed in this chapter's Programming Exercise 2), and the **class** `addressType`. Add a member variable to this class to classify the person as a family member, friend, or business associate. Also, add a member variable to store the phone number. Add (or override) the functions to print and store the appropriate information. Use constructors to automatically initialize the member variables.

c. Define the **class** `addressBookType` using the previously defined classes. An object of the type `addressBookType` should be able to process a maximum of 500 entries.

The program should perform the following operations:

i. Load the data into the address book from a disk.

ii. Sort the address book by last name.

iii. Search for a person by last name.

iv. Print the address, phone number, and date of birth (if it exists) of a given person.

v. Print the names of the people whose birthdays are in a given month.

vi. Print the names of all the people between two last names.

vii. Depending on the user's request, print the names of all family members, friends, or business associates.

7. In Programming Exercise 2, the **class** `dateType` was designed and implemented to keep track of a date, but it has very limited operations. Redefine the **class** `dateType` so that it can perform the following operations on a date, in addition to the operations already defined:

a. Set the month.

b. Set the day.

c. Set the year.

d. Return the month.

e. Return the day.

f. Return the year.

g. Test whether the year is a leap year.

h. Return the number of days in the month. For example, if the date is 3-12-2006, the number of days to be returned is 31 because there are 31 days in March.

i. Return the number of days passed in the year. For example, if the date is 3-18-2006, the number of days passed in the year is 77. Note that the number of days returned also includes the current day.

j. Return the number of days remaining in the year. For example, if the date is 3-18-2006, the number of days remaining in the year is 288.

k. Calculate the new date by adding a fixed number of days to the date. For example, if the date is 3-18-2006 and the days to be added are 25, the new date is 4-12-2006.

8. Write the definitions of the functions to implement the operations defined for the **class dateType** in Programming Exercise 7.

9. The **class dateType** defined in Programming Exercise 7 prints the date in numerical form. Some applications might require the date to be printed in another form, such as March 24, 2006. Derive the **class extDateType** so that the date can be printed in either form.

   Add a member variable to the **class extDateType** so that the month can also be stored in string form. Add a member function to output the month in the string format, followed by the year—for example, in the form March 2006.

   Write the definitions of the functions to implement the operations for the **class extDateType**.

10. Using the **class**es **extDateType** (Programming Exercise 9) and **dayType** (Chapter 11, Programming Exercise 2), design the **class calendarType** so that, given the month and the year, we can print the calendar for that month. To print a monthly calendar, you must know the first day of the month and the number of days in that month. Thus, you must store the first day of the month, which is of the form **dayType**, and the month and the year of the calendar. Clearly, the month and the year can be stored in an object of the form **extDateType** by setting the day component of the date to 1, and the month and year as specified by the user. Thus, the **class calendarType** has two member variables: an object of the type **dayType**, and an object of the type **extDateType**.

    Design the **class calendarType** so that the program can print a calendar for any month starting January 1, 1500. Note that the day for January 1 of the year 1500 is a Monday. To calculate the first day of a month, you can add the appropriate days to Monday of January 1, 1500.

    For the **class calendarType**, include the following operations:

    a. Determine the first day of the month for which the calendar will be printed. Call this operation **firstDayOfMonth**.

    b. Set the month.

    c. Set the year.

    d. Return the month.

    e. Return the year.

    f. Print the calendar for the particular month.

    g. Add the appropriate constructors to initialize the member variables.

11. a. Write the definitions of the member functions of the **class calendarType** (designed in Programming Exercise 10) to implement the operations of the **class calendarType**.

b. Write a test program to print the calendar for either a particular month or a particular year. For example, the calendar for September 2006 is:

```
                      September 2006

    Sun     Mon     Tue     Wed     Thu     Fri     Sat
                                             1       2
     3       4       5       6       7       8       9
    10      11      12      13      14      15      16
    17      18      19      20      21      22      23
    24      25      26      27      28      29      30
```

12. In the Programming Example Grade Report, in the definitions of the classes `courseType` and `studentType`, the accessor functions are not made constants; that is, they are not defined with the reserved word `const` at the end of their headings. Redefine these classes so that all the accessor functions are constant functions. Accordingly, modify the definitions of the accessor functions and rerun the program.

POINTERS, CLASSES, VIRTUAL FUNCTIONS, ABSTRACT CLASSES, AND LISTS

IN THIS CHAPTER, YOU WILL:

- Learn about the pointer data type and pointer variables
- Explore how to declare and manipulate pointer variables
- Learn about the address of operator and the dereferencing operator
- Discover dynamic variables
- Explore how to use the `new` and `delete` operators to manipulate dynamic variables
- Learn about pointer arithmetic
- Discover dynamic arrays
- Become aware of the shallow and deep copies of data
- Discover the peculiarities of classes with pointer member variables
- Learn about virtual functions
- Examine the relationship between the address of operator and classes
- Become aware of abstract classes

In Chapter 2, you learned that C++'s data types are classified into three categories: simple, structured, and pointers. Until now, you have studied only the first two data types. This chapter discusses the third data type, called the pointer data type. You will first learn how to declare pointer variables (or pointers, for short) and manipulate the data to which they point. Later, you will use these concepts when you study dynamic arrays and linked lists. Linked lists are discussed in Chapter 17.

Pointer Data Type and Pointer Variables

Chapter 2 defined a data type as a set of values together with a set of operations. Recall that the set of values is called the domain of the data type. In addition to these two properties, until now all the data types you have encountered have one more thing associated with them: the name of the data type. For example, there is a data type called `int`. The set of values belonging to this data type are integers that range between −2147483648 and 2147483647, and the operations allowed on these values are the arithmetic operators described in Chapter 2. To manipulate numeric integer data in the range −2147483648 and 2147483647, you can declare variables using the word `int`. The name of the data type allows you to declare a variable. Next, we describe the pointer data type.

The values belonging to pointer data types are the memory addresses of your computer. As in many other languages, there is no name associated with the pointer data type in C++. Because the domain—that is, the values of a pointer data type—are the addresses (memory locations), a pointer variable is a variable whose content is an address, that is, a memory location.

Pointer variable: A variable whose content is an address (that is, a memory address).

Declaring Pointer Variables

As remarked previously, there is no name associated with pointer data types. Moreover, pointer variables store memory addresses. So the obvious question is: If no name is associated with a pointer data type, how do you declare pointer variables?

The value of a pointer variable is an address. That is, the value refers to another memory space. The data is typically stored in this memory space. Therefore, when you declare a pointer variable, you also specify the data type of the value to be stored in the memory location pointed to by the pointer variable.

In C++, you declare a pointer variable by using the asterisk symbol (*) between the data type and the variable name. The general syntax to declare a pointer variable is:

```
dataType *identifier;
```

As an example, consider the following statements:

```
int *p;
char *ch;
```

In these statements, both `p` and `ch` are pointer variables. The content of `p` (when properly assigned) points to a memory location of type `int`, and the content of `ch` points to a memory location of type `char`. Usually, `p` is called a pointer variable of type `int`, and `ch` is called a pointer variable of type `char`.

Before discussing how pointers work, let us make the following observations. The statement:

```
int *p;
```

is equivalent to the statement:

```
int*   p;
```

which is equivalent to the statement:

```
int *  p;
```

Thus, the character `*` can appear anywhere between the data type name and the variable name.

Now consider the following statement:

```
int*  p, q;
```

In this statement, only `p` is the pointer variable, not `q`. Here, `q` is an `int` variable. To avoid confusion, we prefer to attach the character `*` to the variable name. So the preceding statement is written as:

```
int *p, q;
```

Of course, the statement:

```
int *p, *q;
```

declares both `p` and `q` to be pointer variables of type `int`.

Now that you know how to declare pointers, next we will discuss how to make a pointer point to a memory space and how to manipulate the data stored in these memory locations.

Because the value of a pointer is a memory address, a pointer can store the address of a memory space of the designated type. For example, if `p` is a pointer of type `int`, `p` can store the address of any memory space of type `int`. C++ provides two operators—the address of operator (&) and the dereferencing operator (*)—to work with pointers. The next two sections describe these operators.

Address of Operator (&)

In C++, the ampersand, &, called the **address of operator**, is a unary operator that returns the address of its operand. For example, given the statements:

```
int x;
int *p;
```

the statement:

```
p = &x;
```

assigns the address of **x** to **p**. That is, **x** and the value of **p** refer to the same memory location.

Dereferencing Operator (*)

Every chapter until now has used the asterisk character, *****, as the binary multiplication operator. C++ also uses ***** as a unary operator. When used as a unary operator, *****, commonly referred to as the **dereferencing operator** or **indirection operator**, refers to the object to which its operand (that is, the pointer) points. For example, given the statements:

```
int x = 25;
int *p;
p = &x;    //store the address of x in p
```

the statement:

```
cout << *p << endl;
```

prints the value stored in the memory space pointed to by **p**, which is the value of **x**. Also, the statement:

```
*p = 55;
```

stores 55 in the memory location pointed to by **p**—that is, in **x**.

Let us consider the following statements:

```
int *p;
int num;
```

In these statements, **p** is a pointer variable of type **int** and num is a variable of type **int** (see Figure 13-1).

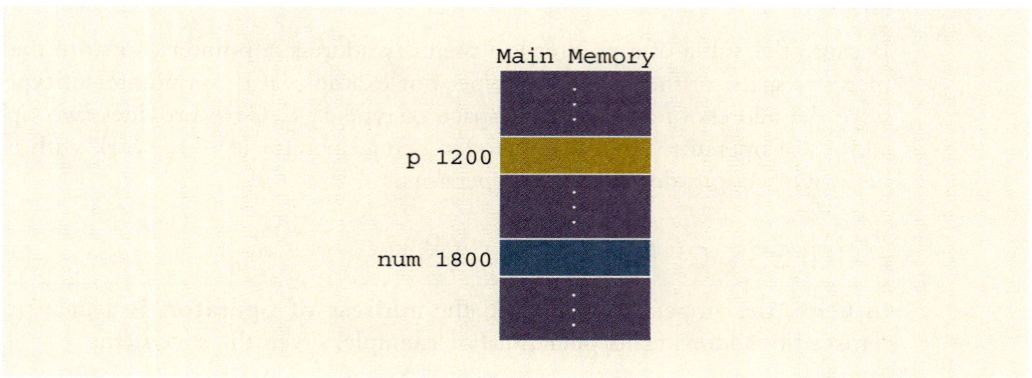

FIGURE 13-1   Main memory, p, and num

Let us assume that memory location 1200 is allocated for p and memory location 1800 is allocated for num. The statement:

num = 78;

stores 78 in num—that is, in memory location 1800 (see Figure 13-2).

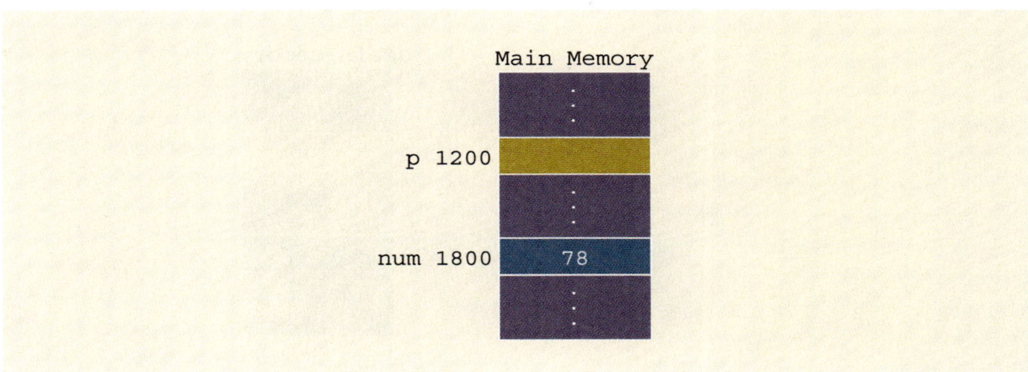

FIGURE 13-2 num after the statement num = 78; executes

The statement:

p = #

stores the address—that is, 1800—into p. After this statement executes, both *p and num refer to the content of memory location 1800—that is, num (see Figure 13-3).

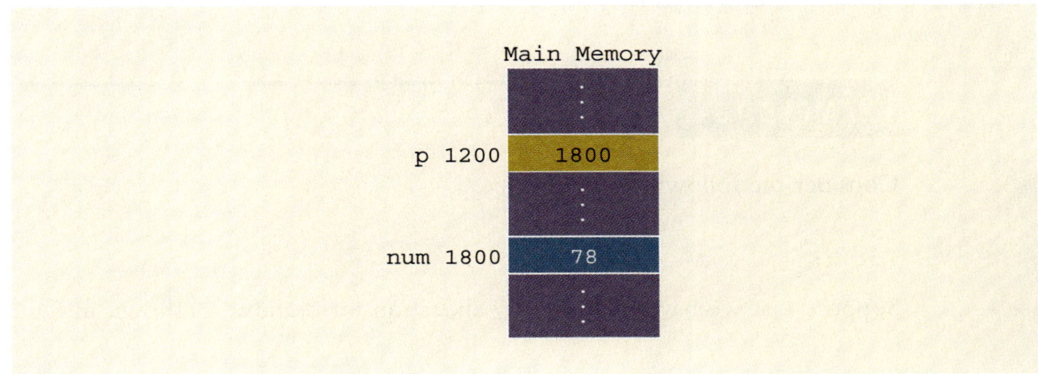

FIGURE 13-3 p after the statement p = # executes

The assignment statement:

```
*p = 24;
```

changes the content of memory location 1800 and thus also changes the content of num (see Figure 13-4).

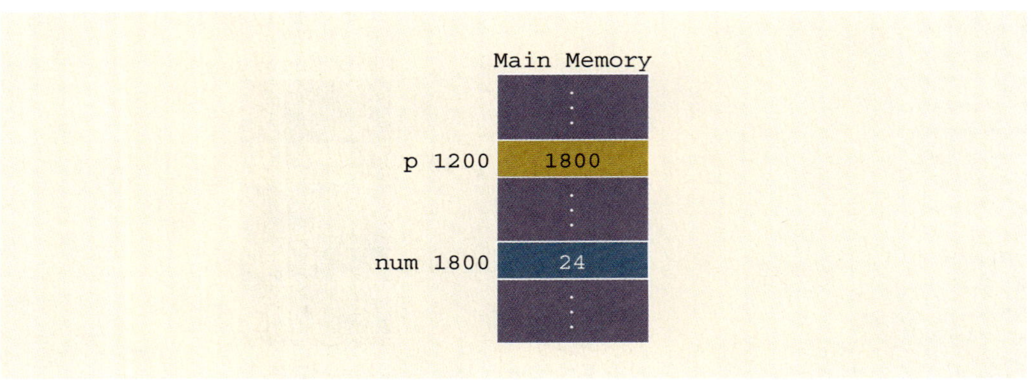

FIGURE 13-4 *p and num after the statement *p = 24; executes

Let us summarize the preceding discussion.

1. &p, p, and *p all have different meanings.
2. &p means the address of p—that is, 1200 (in Figure 13-4).
3. p means the content of p (1800 in Figure 13-4).
4. *p means the content (24 in Figure 13-4) of the memory location (1800 in Figure 13-4) pointed to by p (that is, pointed to by the content of memory location 1200).

EXAMPLE 13-1

Consider the following statements:

```
int *p;
int x;
```

Suppose that we have the memory allocation for p and x, as shown in Figure 13-5.

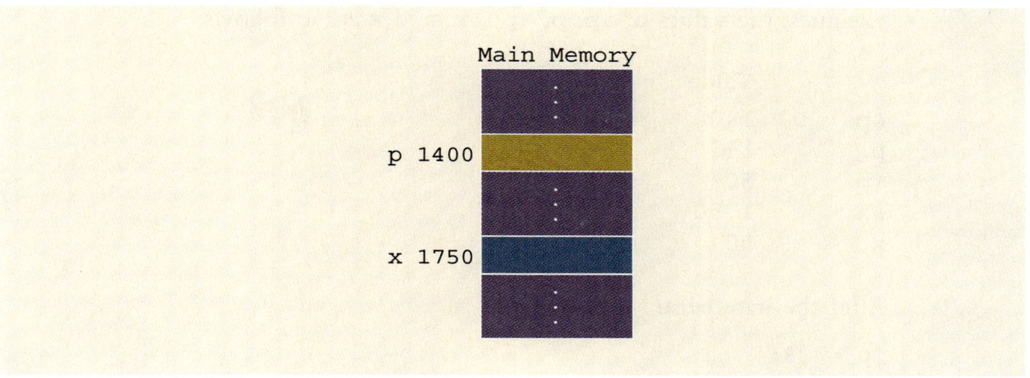

FIGURE 13-5 Main memory, p, and x

The values of &p, p, *p, &x, and x are as follows:

	Value
&p	1400
p	??? (unknown)
*p	Does not exist (undefined)
&x	1750
x	??? (unknown)

Suppose that the following statements are executed in the order given:

```
x = 50;
p = &x;
*p = 38;
```

The values of &p, p, *p, &x, and x are shown after each of these statements executes. After the statement:

```
x = 50;
```

executes, the values of &p, p, *p, &x, and x are as follows:

	Value
&p	1400
p	??? (unknown)
*p	Does not exist (undefined)
&x	1750
x	50

After the statement:

```
p = &x;
```

executes, the values of &p, p, *p, &x, and x are as follows:

	Value
&p	1400
p	1750
*p	50
&x	1750
x	50

After the statement:

```
*p = 38;
```

executes, the values of &p, p, *p, &x, and x are as follows. (Because *p and x refer to the same memory space, the value of x is also changed to 38.)

	Value
&p	1400
p	1750
*p	38
&x	1750
x	38

Let us note the following from Example 13-1:

1. A declaration such as:

   ```
   int *p;
   ```

   allocates memory for p only, not for *p. Later, you will learn how to allocate memory for *p.

2. Assume the following:

   ```
   int *p;
   ```

   ```
   int x;
   ```

   Then,

   a. p is a pointer variable.

   b. The content of p points only to a memory location of type `int`.

   c. Memory location x exists and is of type `int`. Therefore, the assignment statement:

      ```
      p = &x;
      ```

      is legal. After this assignment statement executes, *p is valid and meaningful.

EXAMPLE 13-2

The following program illustrates how pointer variables work:

```cpp
//Chapter 13: Example 13-2

#include <iostream>

using namespace std;

int main()
{
    int *p;
    int x = 37;

    cout << "Line 1: x = " << x << endl;                        //Line 1

    p = &x;                                                     //Line 2

    cout << "Line 3: *p = " << *p
         << ", x = " << x << endl;                             //Line 3

    *p = 58;                                                    //Line 4

    cout << "Line 5: *p = " << *p
         << ", x = " << x << endl;                             //Line 5

    cout << "Line 6: Address of p = " << &p << endl;           //Line 6

    cout << "Line 7: Value of p = " << p << endl;              //Line 7

    cout << "Line 8: Value of the memory location "
         << "pointed to by *p = " << *p << endl;               //Line 8
    cout << "Line 9: Address of x = " << &x << endl;           //Line 9
    cout << "Line 10: Value of x = " << x << endl;             //Line 10

    return 0;
}
```

Sample Run:

```
Line 1: x = 37
Line 3: *p = 37, x = 37
Line 5: *p = 58, x = 58
Line 6: Address of p = 006BFDF4
Line 7: Value of p = 006BFDF0
Line 8: Value of the memory location pointed to by *p = 58
Line 9: Address of x = 006BFDF0
Line 10: Value of x = 58
```

The preceding program works as follows. The statement in Line 1 outputs the value of x, and
the statement in Line 2 stores the address of x into p. The statement in Line 3 outputs the

values of `*p` and `x`. Because p contains the address of p, the values of `*p` and `x` are the same, as shown by the output of Line 3. The statement in Line 4 changes the value of `*p` to 58, and the statement in Line 5 outputs the values of `*p` and `x`, which are again the same. The statements in Lines 6 through 10 output the address of p, the value of p, the value of `*p`, the address of `x`, and the value of `x`. Note that the value of p and the address of `x` are the same because the address of `x` is stored in p by the statement in Line 2. (Note that the address of p, the value of p, and the address of `x`, as shown by the outputs of Lines 6, 7, and 9, respectively, are machine dependent. When you run this program on your machine, you are likely to get different values.)

Classes, Structs, and Pointer Variables

In the previous section, you learned how to declare and manipulate pointers of simple data types, such as `int` and `char`. You can also declare pointers to other data types, such as classes. You will now learn how to declare and manipulate pointers to classes and structs. (Recall that both classes and structs have the same capabilities. The only difference between classes and structs is that, by default, all members of a class are `private`, and, by default, all members of a struct are `public`. Therefore, the following discussion applies to both.)

Consider the following declaration of a `struct`:

```
struct studentType
{
    char name[26];
    double gpa;
    int sID;
    char grade;
};


studentType   student;
studentType *studentPtr;
```

In the preceding declaration, `student` is an object of type `studentType`, and `studentPtr` is a pointer variable of type `studentType`. The following statement stores the address of `student` in `studentPtr`:

```
studentPtr = &student;
```

The following statement stores `3.9` in the component `gpa` of the object `student`:

```
(*studentPtr).gpa = 3.9;
```

The expression `(*studentPtr).gpa` is a mixture of pointer dereferencing and the class component selection. In C++, the dot operator, `.`, has a higher precedence than the dereferencing operator.

Let us elaborate on this a bit. In the expression `(*studentPtr).gpa`, the operator `*` evaluates first and so the expression `*studentPtr` evaluates first. Because `studentPtr` is a pointer variable of type `studentType`, `*studentPtr` refers to a memory space of type `studentType`, which is a **struct**. Therefore, `(*studentPtr).gpa` refers to the component `gpa` of that **struct**.

Consider the expression `*studentPtr.gpa`. Let us see how this expression gets evaluated. Because `.` (dot) has a higher precedence than `*`, the expression `studentPtr.gpa` evaluates first. The expression `studentPtr.gpa` would result in syntax error as `studentPtr` is *not* a **struct** variable, and so it has no such component as `gpa`.

As you can see, in the expression `(*studentPtr).gpa`, the parentheses are important. However, typos can be problematic. Therefore, to simplify the accessing of class or **struct** components via a pointer, C++ provides another operator, called the **member access operator arrow**, `->`. The operator `->` consists of two consecutive symbols: a hyphen and the "greater than" sign.

The syntax for accessing a **class** (**struct**) member using the operator `->` is:

```
pointerVariableName->classMemberName
```

Thus, the statement:

```
(*studentPtr).gpa = 3.9;
```

is equivalent to the statement:

```
studentPtr->gpa = 3.9;
```

Accessing **class** (**struct**) components via pointers using the operator `->` thus eliminates the use of both parentheses and the dereferencing operator. Because typos are unavoidable and missing parentheses can result in either an abnormal program termination or erroneous results, when accessing **class** (**struct**) components via pointers, this book uses the arrow notation.

Example 13-3 illustrates how pointers work with class member functions.

EXAMPLE 13-3

Consider the following class:

```
class classExample
{
public:
    void setX(int a);
      //Function to set the value of x
      //Postcondition: x = a;
    void print() const;
      //Function to output the value of x

private:
    int x;
};
```

The definition of the member function is as follows:

```
void classExample::setX(int a)
{
    x = a;
}

void classExample::print() const
{
    cout << "x = " << x << endl;
}
```

Consider the following function `main`:

```
int main()
{
    classExample *cExpPtr;          //Line 1
    classExample cExpObject;        //Line 2

    cExpPtr = &cExpObject;          //Line 3

    cExpPtr->setX(5);               //Line 4
    cExpPtr->print();               //Line 5

    return 0;
}
```

Sample Run:

```
x = 5
```

In the function `main`, the statement in Line 1 declares `cExpPtr` to be a pointer of type `classExample`, and the statement in Line 2 declares `cExpObject` to be an object of type `classExample`. The statement in Line 3 stores the address of `cExpObject` into `cExpPtr` (see Figure 13-6).

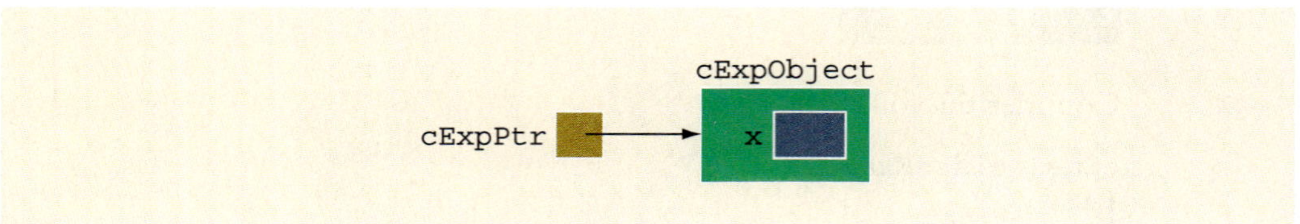

FIGURE 13-6 `cExpObject` and `cExpPtr` after the statement `cExpPtr = &cExpObject;` executes

In the statement in Line 4, the pointer `cExpPtr` accesses the member function `setX` to set the value of the member variable `x` (see Figure 13-7).

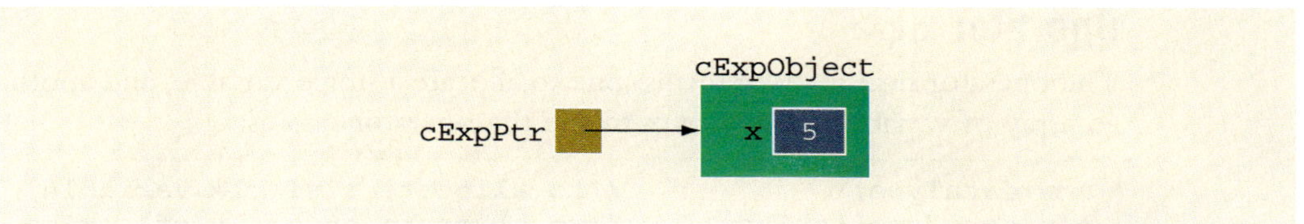

FIGURE 13-7 `cExpObject` and `cExpPtr` after the statement `cExpPtr->setX(5);` executes

In the statement in Line 5, the pointer **cExpPtr** accesses the member function `print` to print the value of **x**, as shown above.

Initializing Pointer Variables

Because C++ does not automatically initialize variables, pointer variables must be initialized if you do not want them to point to anything. Pointer variables are initialized using the constant value 0, called the **null pointer**. Thus, the statement **p = 0;** stores the null pointer in **p**; that is, **p** points to nothing. Some programmers use the named constant **NULL** to initialize pointer variables. The following two statements are equivalent:

```
p = NULL;
p = 0;
```

The number 0 is the only number that can be directly assigned to a pointer variable.

Dynamic Variables

In the previous sections, you learned how to declare pointer variables, how to store the address of a variable into a pointer variable of the same type as the variable, and how to manipulate data using pointers. However, you learned how to use pointers to manipulate data only into memory spaces that were created using other variables. In other words, the pointers manipulated data into existing memory spaces. So what is the benefit to using pointers? You can access these memory spaces by working with the variables that were used to create them. In this section, you will learn about the power behind pointers. In particular, you will learn how to allocate and deallocate memory during program execution using pointers.

Variables that are created during program execution are called **dynamic variables**. With the help of pointers, C++ creates dynamic variables. C++ provides two operators, **new** and **delete**, to create and destroy dynamic variables, respectively. When a program requires a new variable, the operator **new** is used. When a program no longer needs a dynamic variable, the operator **delete** is used.

In C++, **new** and **delete** are reserved words.

Operator `new`

The operator **new** has two forms: one to allocate a single variable, and another to allocate an array of variables. The syntax to use the operator **new** is:

```
new dataType;              //to allocate a single variable
new dataType[intExp];      //to allocate an array of variables
```

where `intExp` is any expression evaluating to a positive integer.

The operator **new** allocates memory (a variable) of the designated type and returns a pointer to it—that is, the address of this allocated memory. Moreover, the allocated memory is uninitialized.

Consider the following declaration:

```
int *p;
char *q;
int x;
```

The statement:

```
p = &x;
```

stores the address of **x** in p. However, no new memory is allocated. On the other hand, consider the following statement:

```
p = new int;
```

This statement creates a variable during program execution somewhere in memory and stores the address of the allocated memory in p. The allocated memory is accessed via pointer dereferencing—namely, ***p**. Similarly, the statement:

```
q = new char[16];
```

creates an array of 16 components of type **char** and stores the base address of the array in q.

Because a dynamic variable is unnamed, it cannot be accessed directly. It is accessed indirectly by the pointer returned by **new**. The following statements illustrate this concept:

```
int *p;            //p is a pointer of type int
char *name;        //name is a pointer of type char
string *str;       //str is a pointer of type string

p = new int;       //allocates memory of type int
                   //and stores the address of the
                   //allocated memory in p
*p = 28;           //stores 28 in the allocated memory

name = new char[5];    //allocates memory for an array of
                       //five components of type char and
                       //stores the base address of the array
```

```
                    //in name
strcpy(name, "John");   //stores John in name

str = new string;   //allocates memory of type string
                    //and stores the address of the
                    //allocated memory in str
*str = "Sunny Day";     //stores the string "Sunny Day" in
                    //the memory pointed to by str
```

NOTE Recall that the operator **new** allocates memory space of a specific type and returns the address of the allocated memory space. However, if the operator **new** is unable to allocate the required memory space (for example, there is not enough memory space), then it throws bad_alloc exception and if this exception is not handled, it terminates the program with an error message. Exceptions are covered in detail in Chapter 15. This chapter also discusses bad_alloc exception.

Operator `delete`

Suppose you have the following declaration:

```
int *p;
```

This statement declares p to be a pointer variable of type `int`. Next, consider the following statements:

```
p = new int;        //Line 1
*p = 54;            //Line 2
p = new int;        //Line 3
*p = 73;            //Line 4
```

Let us see the effect of these statements. The statement in Line 1 allocates memory space of type `int` and stores the address of the allocated memory space into p. Suppose that the address of allocated memory space is 1500. Then the value of p after the execution of this statement is 1500 (see Figure 13–8).

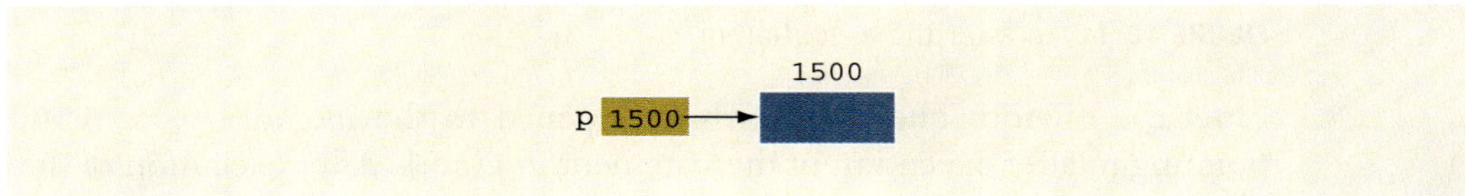

FIGURE 13-8 p after the execution of p = **new int**;

(In Figure 13-8, the number 1500 on top of the box indicates the address of the memory space.) The statement in Line 2 stores 54 into the memory space that p points to, which is 1500. In other words, after execution of the statement in Line 2, the value stored into memory space at location 1500 is 54 (see Figure 13-9).

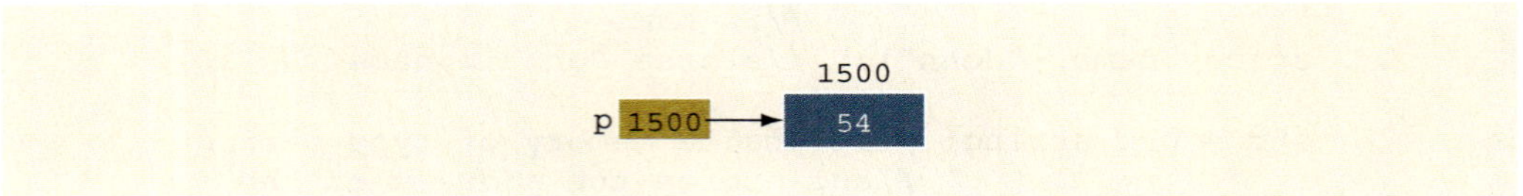

FIGURE 13-9 p and *p after the execution of *p = 54;

Next, the statement in Line 3 executes, which allocates a memory space of type **int** and stores the address of the allocated memory space into p. Suppose the address of this allocated memory space is 1800. It follows that the value of p is now 1800 (see Figure 13–10).

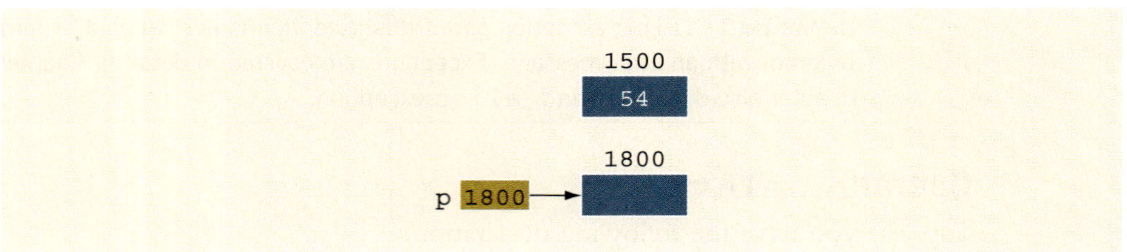

FIGURE 13-10 p after the execution of p = **new int**;

The statement in Line 4 stores 73 into the memory space that p points to, which is 1800. In other words, after execution of the statement in Line 4, the value stored into memory space at location 1800 is 73 (see Figure 13–11).

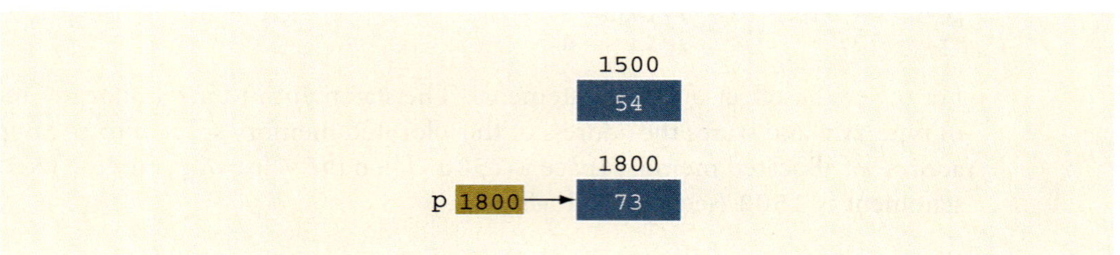

FIGURE 13-11 p after the execution of *p = 73;

Now the obvious question is what happened to the memory space 1500 that p was pointing to after execution of the statement in Line 1. After execution of the statement in Line 3, p points to the new memory space at location 1800. The previous memory space at location 1500 is now inaccessible. In addition, the memory space 1500 remains as marked allocated. In other words, it cannot be reallocated. This is called **memory leak**. That is, there is an unused memory space that cannot be allocated.

Imagine what would happen if you execute statements, such as Line 1, a few thousand times or a few million times. There will be a good amount of memory leak. The program might then run out of memory spaces for data manipulation and eventually result in an abnormal termination of the program.

The question at hand is how to *avoid* memory leak. When a dynamic variable is no longer needed, it can be destroyed; that is, its memory can be deallocated. The C++ operator `delete` is used to destroy dynamic variables. The syntax to use the operator `delete` has two forms:

```
delete pointerVariable;     //to deallocate a single
                            //dynamic variable
delete [] pointerVariable;  //to deallocate a dynamically
                            //created array
```

Thus, given the declarations of the previous section, the statements:

```
delete p;
delete [] name;
delete str;
```

deallocate the memory spaces that the pointers p, `name`, and `str` point to.

Suppose p and `name` are pointer variables, as declared previously. Notice that an expression such as:

```
delete p;
```

or

```
delete [] name;
```

only marks the memory spaces that these pointer variables point to as deallocated. Depending on a particular system, after these statements execute, these pointer variables may still contain the addresses of the deallocated memory spaces. In this case, we say that these pointers are **dangling**. Therefore, if later you access the memory spaces via these pointers without properly initializing them, depending on a particular system, either the program will access a wrong memory space, which may result in corrupting data, or the program will terminate with an error message. One way to avoid this pitfall is to set these pointers to NULL after the `delete` operation.

Operations on Pointer Variables

The operations that are allowed on pointer variables are the assignment and relational operations and some limited arithmetic operations. The value of one pointer variable can be assigned to another pointer variable of the same type. Two pointer variables of the same type can be compared for equality, and so on. Integer values can be added and subtracted from a pointer variable. The value of one pointer variable can be subtracted from another pointer variable.

For example, suppose that we have the following statements:

```
int *p, *q;
```

The statement:

```
p = q;
```

copies the value of q into p. After this statement executes, both p and q point to the same memory location. Any changes made to *p automatically change the value of *q, and vice versa.

The expression:

```
p == q
```

evaluates to **true** if p and q have the same value—that is, if they point to the same memory location. Similarly, the expression:

```
p != q
```

evaluates to **true** if p and q point to different memory locations.

The arithmetic operations that are allowed differ from the arithmetic operations on numbers. First, let us use the following statements to explain the increment and decrement operations on pointer variables:

```
int *p;
double *q;
char *chPtr;
studentType *stdPtr;   //studentType is as defined before
```

Recall that the size of the memory allocated for an **int** variable is 4 bytes, a **double** variable is 8 bytes, and a **char** variable is 1 byte. The memory allocated for a variable of type studentType is then 40 bytes.

The statement:

```
p++;    or    p = p + 1;
```

increments the value of p by 4 bytes because p is a pointer of type **int**. Similarly, the statements:

```
q++;
chPtr++;
```

increment the value of q by 8 bytes and the value of chPtr by 1 byte, respectively. The statement:

```
stdPtr++;
```

increments the value of stdPtr by 40 bytes.

The increment operator increments the value of a pointer variable by the size of the memory to which it is pointing. Similarly, the decrement operator decrements the value of a pointer variable by the size of the memory to which it is pointing.

Moreover, the statement:

```
p = p + 2;
```

increments the value of p by 8 bytes.

Thus, when an integer is added to a pointer variable, the value of the pointer variable is incremented by the integer times the size of the memory that the pointer is pointing to. Similarly, when an integer is subtracted from a pointer variable, the value of the pointer variable is decremented by the integer times the size of the memory to which the pointer is pointing.

NOTE Pointer arithmetic can be very dangerous. Using pointer arithmetic, the program can accidentally access the memory locations of other variables and change their content without warning, leaving the programmer trying to find out what went wrong. If a pointer variable tries to access either the memory spaces of other variables or an illegal memory space, some systems might terminate the program with an appropriate error message. Always exercise extra care when doing pointer arithmetic.

Dynamic Arrays

In Chapter 9, you learned how to declare and process arrays. The arrays discussed in Chapter 9 are called static arrays because their size was fixed at compile time. One of the limitations of a static array is that every time you execute the program, the size of the array is fixed, so it might not be possible to use the same array to process different data sets of the same type. One way to handle this limitation is to declare an array that is large enough to process a variety of data sets. However, if the array is very big and the data set is small, such a declaration would result in memory waste. On the other hand, it would be helpful if, during program execution, you could prompt the user to enter the size of the array and then create an array of the appropriate size. This approach is especially helpful if you cannot even guess the array size. In this section, you will learn how to create arrays during program execution and process such arrays.

An array created during the execution of a program is called a **dynamic array**. To create a dynamic array, we use the second form of the `new` operator.

The statement:

```
int *p;
```

declares p to be a pointer variable of type `int`. The statement:

```
p = new int[10];
```

allocates 10 contiguous memory locations, each of type `int`, and stores the address of the first memory location into p. In other words, the operator `new` creates an array of 10 components of type `int`, it returns the base address of the array, and the assignment operator stores the base address of the array into p. Thus, the statement:

```
*p = 25;
```

stores 25 into the first memory location, and the statements:

```
p++;           //p points to the next array component
*p = 35;
```

store 35 into the second memory location. Thus, by using the increment and decrement operations, you can access the components of the array. Of course, after performing a few increment operations, it is possible to lose track of the first array component. C++ allows us to use array notation to access these memory locations. For example, the statements:

```
p[0] = 25;
p[1] = 35;
```

store 25 and 35 into the first and second array components, respectively. That is, `p[0]` refers to the first array component, `p[1]` refers to the second array component, and so on. In general, `p[i]` refers to the (i + 1)th array component. After the preceding statements execute, p still points to the first array component. Moreover, the following `for` loop initializes each array component to 0:

```
for (j = 0; j < 10; j++)
    p[j] = 0;
```

where j is an `int` variable.

When the array notation is used to process the array pointed to by p, p stays fixed at the first memory location. Moreover, p is a dynamic array, created during program execution.

NOTE The statement:

```
int list[5];
```

declares `list` to be an array of 5 components. Recall from Chapter 9 that `list` itself is a variable and the value stored in `list` is the base address of the array—that is, the address of the first array component. Suppose the address of the first array component is 1000. Figure 13-12 shows `list` and the array `list`.

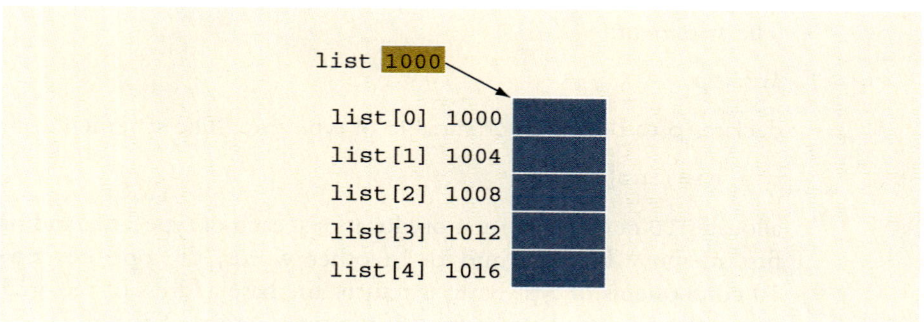

FIGURE 13-12 `list` and array `list`

Because the value of `list`, which is 1000, is a memory address, `list` is a pointer variable. However, the value stored in `list`, which is 1000, *cannot be altered during program execution.* That is, the value of `list` is *constant*. Therefore, the increment and decrement operations cannot be applied to `list`. In fact, any attempt to use the increment or decrement operations on `list` results in a compile-time error.

Notice that here we are *only* saying that the value of `list` cannot be changed. However, the data into the array list can be manipulated as before. For example, the statement `list[0] = 25;` stores 25 into the first array component. Similarly, the statement `list[3] = 78;` stores 78 into the fourth component of `list` (see Figure 13-13).

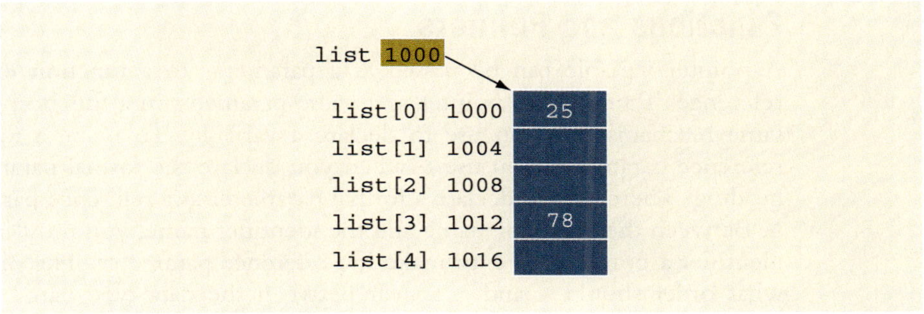

FIGURE 13-13 Array `list` after the execution of the statements `list[0] = 25;` and `list[3] = 78;`

If `p` is a pointer variable of type `int`, then the statement:

```
p = list;
```

copies the value of `list`, which is `1000`, the base address of the array, into `p`. We are allowed to perform increment and decrement operations on `p`.

An *array name* is a *constant pointer.*

EXAMPLE 13-4

The following program segment illustrates how to obtain a user's response to get the array size and create a dynamic array during program execution. Consider the following statements:

```
int *intList;                        //Line 1
int arraySize;                       //Line 2

cout << "Enter array size: ";        //Line 3
cin >> arraySize;                    //Line 4
cout << endl;                        //Line 5

intList = new int[arraySize];        //Line 6
```

The statement in Line 1 declares `intList` to be a pointer of type `int`, and the statement in Line 2 declares `arraySize` to be an `int` variable. The statement in Line 3 prompts the user to enter the size of the array, and the statement in Line 4 inputs the array size into the variable `arraySize`. The statement in Line 6 creates an array of the size specified by `arraySize`, and the base address of the array is stored in `intList`. From this point on, you can treat `intList` just like any other array. For example, you can use the array notation to process the elements of `intList` and pass `intList` as a parameter to the function.

Functions and Pointers

A pointer variable can be passed as a parameter to a function either by value or by reference. To declare a pointer as a value parameter in a function heading, you use the same mechanism as you use to declare a variable. To make a formal parameter be a reference parameter, you use `&` when you declare the formal parameter in the function heading. Therefore, to declare a formal parameter as a reference parameter, you must use `&`. Between the data type name and the identifier name, you must include `*` to make the identifier a pointer and `&` to make it a reference parameter. The obvious question is: In what order should `&` and `*` appear between the data type name and the identifier to declare a pointer as a reference parameter? In C++, to make a pointer a reference parameter in a function heading, `*` appears before the `&` between the data type name and the identifier. The following example illustrates this concept:

```
void example(int* &p, double *q)
{
    .
    .
    .
}
```

In this example, both `p` and `q` are pointers. The parameter `p` is a reference parameter; the parameter `q` is a value parameter.

Pointers and Function Return Values

In C++, the return type of a function can be a pointer. For example, the return type of the function:

```
int* testExp(...)
{
    .
    .
    .
}
```

is a pointer type `int`.

Dynamic Two-Dimensional Arrays

The beginning of this section discussed how to create dynamic one-dimensional arrays. You can also create dynamic multidimensional arrays. In this section, we discuss how to create dynamic two-dimensional arrays. Dynamic multidimensional arrays are created similarly.

There are various ways you can create dynamic dimensional arrays. One way is as follows. Consider the statement:

```
int *board[4];
```

This statement declares `board` to be an array of four pointers wherein each pointer is of type `int`. Because `board[0]`, `board[1]`, `board[2]`, and `board[3]` are pointers, you can now use these pointers to create the rows of `board`. Suppose that each row of `board` has six columns. Then, the following `for` loop creates the rows of board:

```
for (int row = 0; row < 4; row++)
    board[row] = new int[6];
```

Note that the exression `new int[6]` creates an array of 6 components of type `int` and returns the base address of the array. The assignment statement then stores the returned address into `board[row]`. It follows that after the execution of the previous `for` loop, `board` is a two-dimensional array of 4 rows and 6 columns.

In the previous `for` loop, if you replace the number 6 with the number 10, then the loop will create a two-dimensional array of 4 rows and 10 columns. In other words, the number of columns of `board` can be specified during execution. However, the way `board` is declared, the number of rows is fixed. So in reality, `board` is not a true dynamic two-dimensional array.

Next, consider the following statement:

```
int **board;
```

This statement declares `board` to be a pointer to a pointer. In other words, `board` and `*board` are pointers. Now `board` can store the address of a pointer or an array of pointers of type `int`, and `*board` can store the address of an `int` memory space or an array of `int` values.

Suppose that you want `board` to be an array of 10 rows and 15 columns. To accomplish this, first we create an array of 10 pointers of type `int` and assign the address of that array to `board`. The following statement accomplishes this:

```
board = new int* [10];
```

Next, we create the columns of `board`. The following `for` loop accomplishes this:

```
for (int row = 0; row < 10; row++)
    board[row] = new int[15];
```

To access the components of `board`, you can use the array subscripting notation discussed in Chapter 9.

Note that the number of rows and the number of columns of `board` can be specified during program execution. The following program further explains how to create two-dimensional arrays.

EXAMPLE 13-5

```cpp
#include <iostream>
#include <iomanip>

using namespace std;

void fill(int **p, int rowSize, int columnSize);
void print(int **p, int rowSize, int columnSize);

int main()
{
    int **board;                                    //Line 1

    int rows;                                       //Line 2
    int columns;                                    //Line 3

    cout << "Line 4: Enter the number of rows "
         <<"and columns: ";                         //Line 4
    cin >> rows >> columns;                         //Line 5
    cout << endl;                                   //Line 6

        //Create the rows of board
    board = new int* [rows];                        //Line 7

        //Create the columns of board
    for (int row = 0; row < rows; row++)            //Line 8
        board[row] = new int[columns];              //Line 9

        //Insert elements into board
    fill(board, rows, columns);                     //Line 10

    cout << "Line 11: Board:" << endl;              //Line 11

        //Output the elements of board
    print(board, rows, columns);                    //Line 12

    return 0;
}
```

```cpp
void fill(int **p, int rowSize, int columnSize)
{
    for (int row = 0; row < rowSize; row++)
    {
        cout << "Enter " << columnSize << " number(s) for row "
            << "number " << row << ": ";
        for (int col = 0; col < columnSize; col++)
            cin >> p[row][col];
        cout << endl;
    }
}

void print(int **p, int rowSize, int columnSize)
{
    for (int row = 0; row < rowSize; row++)
    {
        for (int col = 0; col < columnSize; col++)
            cout << setw(5) << p[row][col];
        cout << endl;
    }
}
```

Sample Run: In this sample run, the user input is shaded.

```
Line 4: Enter the number of rows and columns: 3 4

Enter 4 number(s) for row number 0: 1 2 3 4

Enter 4 number(s) for row number 1: 5 6 7 8

Enter 4 number(s) for row number 2: 9 10 11 12

Line 11: Board:
    1     2     3     4
    5     6     7     8
    9    10    11    12
```

The preceding program contains the functions `fill` and `print`. The function `fill` prompts the user to enter the elements of a two-dimensional array of type `int`. The function `print` outputs the elements of a two-dimensional array of type `int`.

For the most part, the preceding output is self-explanatory. Let us look at the statements in the function `main`. The statement in Line 1 declares `board` to be a pointer to a pointer of type `int`. The statements in Lines 2 and 3 declare `int` variables `rows` and `columns`. The statement in Line 4 prompts the user to input the number of rows and number of columns. The statement in Line 5 stores the number of rows in the variable `rows` and the number of columns in the variable `columns`. The statement in Line 7 creates the rows of `board`, and the `for` loop in Lines 8 and 9 creates the columns of `board`. The statement in Line 10 used the function `fill` to fill the array `board`, and the statement in Line 12 uses the function `print` to output the elements of `board`.

Shallow versus Deep Copy and Pointers

In an earlier section, we discussed pointer arithmetic and explained that if we are not careful, one pointer might access the data of another (completely unrelated) pointer. This event might result in unsuspected or erroneous results. Here, we discuss another peculiarity of pointers. To facilitate the discussion, we will use diagrams to show pointers and their related memory.

Consider the following statements:

```
int *p;

p = new int;
```

The first statement declares p to be a pointer variable of type `int`. The second statement allocates memory of type `int`, and the address of the allocated memory is stored in p. Figure 13-14 illustrates this situation.

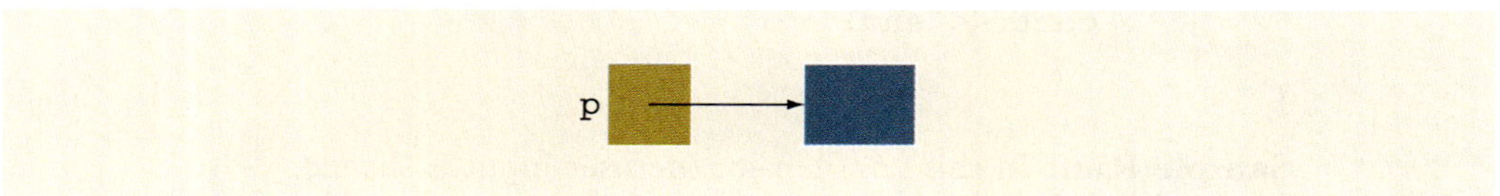

FIGURE 13-14   Pointer p and the memory to which it points

The box indicates the allocated memory (in this case, of type `int`), and p together with the arrow indicates that p points to the allocated memory. Now consider the following statement:

```
*p = 87;
```

This statement stores 87 in the memory pointed to by p. Figure 13-15 illustrates this situation.

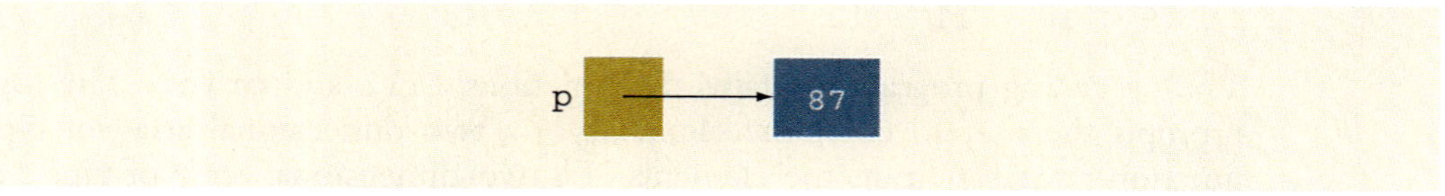

FIGURE 13-15   Pointer p with 87 in the memory to which it points

Consider the following statements:

```
int *first;
int *second;

first = new int[10];
```

The first two statements declare `first` and `second` pointer variables of type `int`. The third statement creates an array of 10 components, and the base address of the array is stored into `first` (see Figure 13-16).

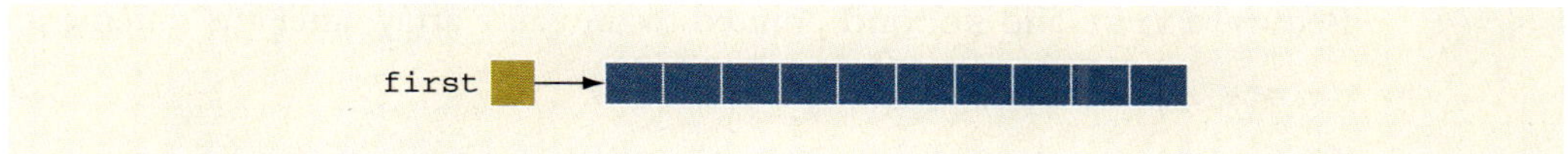

FIGURE 13-16 Pointer `first` and the array to which it points

Suppose that some meaningful data is stored in the array pointed to by `first`. To be specific, suppose that this array is as shown in Figure 13-17.

FIGURE 13-17 Pointer `first` and its array

Next, consider the following statement:

```
second = first;              //Line A
```

This statement copies the value of `first` into `second`. After this statement executes, both `first` and `second` point to the same array, as shown in Figure 13-18.

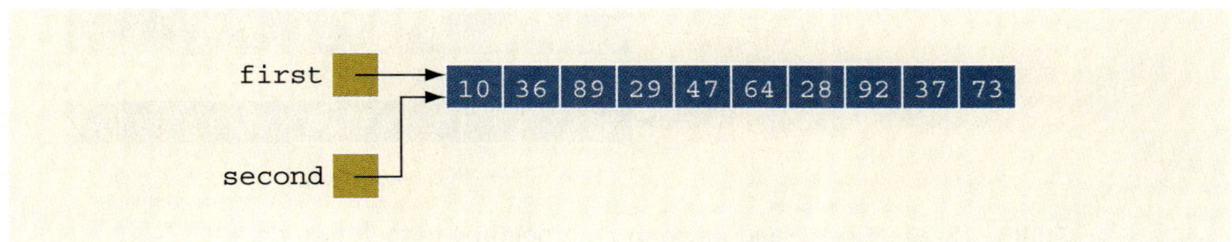

FIGURE 13-18 `first` and `second` after the statement `second = first;` executes

Let us next execute the following statement:

```
delete [] second;
```

After this statement executes, the array pointed to by `second` is deleted. This action results in Figure 13-19.

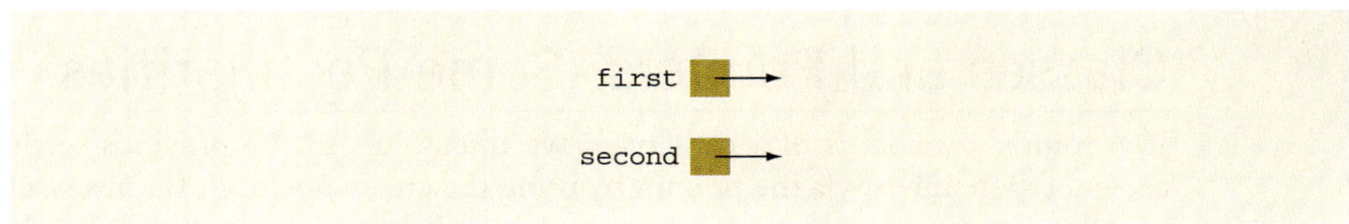

FIGURE 13-19 `first` and `second` after the statement **delete** [] second; executes

Because `first` and `second` pointed to the same array, after the statement:

```
delete [] second;
```

executes, `first` becomes invalid, that is, `first` (as well as `second`) are now dangling pointers. Therefore, if the program later tries to access the memory pointed to by `first`, either the program will access the wrong memory or it will terminate in an error. This case is an example of a shallow copy. More formally, in a **shallow copy**, two or more pointers of the same type point to the same memory; that is, they point to the same data.

On the other hand, suppose that instead of the earlier statement, `second = first;`, (in Line A), we have the following statements:

```
second = new int[10];

for (int j = 0; j < 10; j++)
    second[j] = first[j];
```

The first statement creates an array of 10 components of type `int`, and the base address of the array is stored in `second`. The second statement copies the array pointed to by `first` into the array pointed to by `second` (see Figure 13-20).

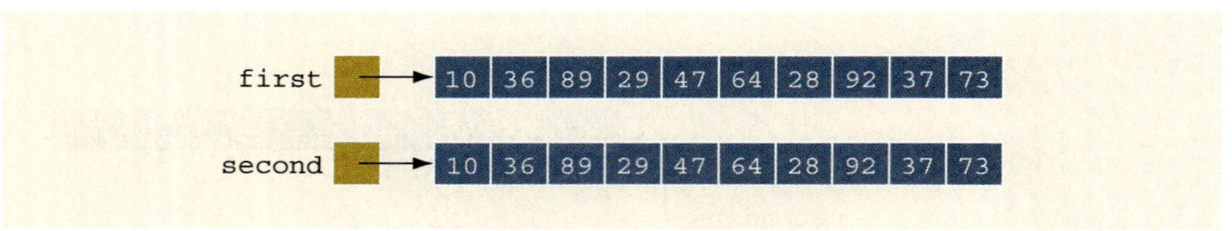

FIGURE 13-20 `first` and `second` both pointing to their own data

Both `first` and `second` now point to their own data. If `second` deletes its memory, there is no effect on `first`. This case is an example of a deep copy. More formally, in a **deep copy**, two or more pointers have their own data.

From the preceding discussion, it follows that you must know when to use a shallow copy and when to use a deep copy.

Classes and Pointers: Some Peculiarities

If a pointer variable is of a class type, we discussed—in the previous section—how to access class members via the pointer by using the arrow notation. Because a class can have pointer member variables, this section discusses some peculiarities of such classes. To facilitate the discussion, we will use the following class:

```
class pointerDataClass
{
public:
    .
    .
    .
private:
    int x;
    int lenP;
    int *p;
};
```

Also, consider the following statements (see Figure 13-21):

```
pointerDataClass objectOne;
pointerDataClass objectTwo;
```

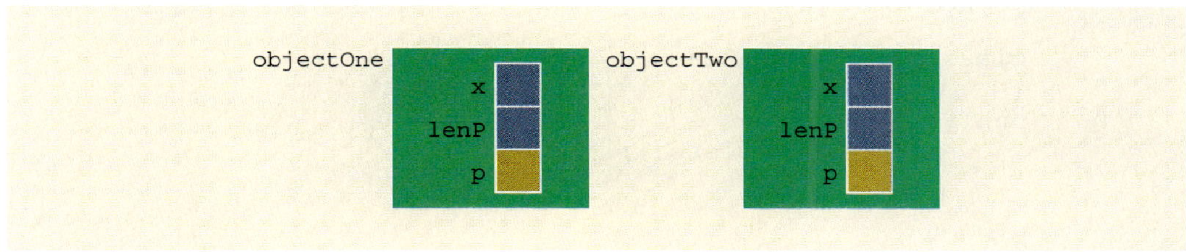

FIGURE 13-21   Objects `objectOne` and `objectTwo`

Destructor

The object `objectOne` has a pointer member variable p. Suppose that during program execution the pointer p creates a dynamic array. When `objectOne` goes out of scope, all the member variables of `objectOne` are destroyed. However, p created a dynamic array, and dynamic memory must be deallocated using the operator **delete**. Thus, if the pointer p does not use the **delete** operator to deallocate the dynamic array, the memory space of the dynamic array would stay marked as allocated, even though it cannot be accessed. How do we ensure that when p is destroyed, the dynamic memory created by p is also destroyed? Suppose that `objectOne` is as shown in Figure 13-22.

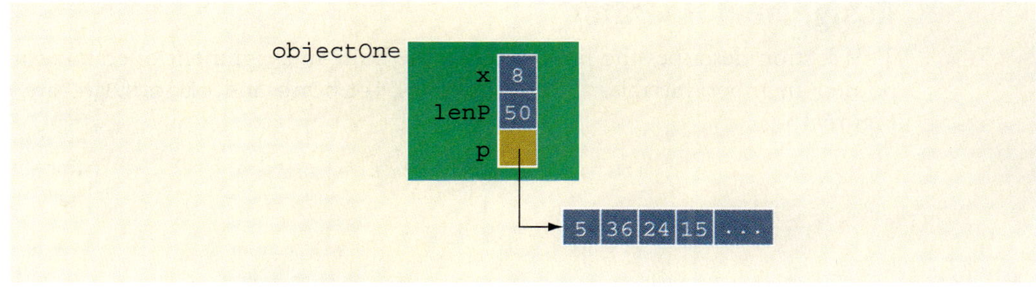

FIGURE 13-22   Object `objectOne` and its data

Recall that if a class has a destructor, the destructor automatically executes whenever a class object goes out of scope (see Chapter 11). Therefore, we can put the necessary code in the destructor to ensure that when `objectOne` goes out of scope, the memory created by the pointer p is deallocated. For example, the definition of the destructor for the `class pointerDataClass` is:

```
pointerDataClass::~pointerDataClass()
{
    delete [] p;
}
```

Of course, you must include the destructor as a member of the class in its definition. Let us extend the definition of the `class pointerDataClass` by including the destructor. Moreover, the remainder of this section assumes that the definition of the destructor is as given previously—that is, the destructor deallocates the memory space pointed to by p:

```
class pointerDataClass
{
public:
    ~pointerDataClass();
         .
         .
         .

private:
    int x;
    int lenP;
    int *p;
};
```

NOTE For the destructor to work properly, the pointer p must have a valid value. If p is not properly initialized (that is, if the value of p is garbage) and the destructor executes, either the program terminates with an error message or the destructor deallocates an unrelated memory space. For this reason, you should exercise extra caution while working with pointers.

Assignment Operator

This section describes the limitations of the built-in assignment operators for classes with pointer member variables. Suppose that `objectOne` and `objectTwo` are as shown in Figure 13-23.

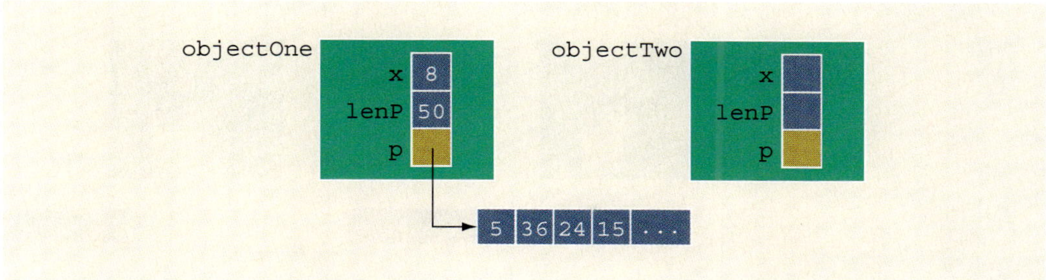

FIGURE 13-23 Objects `objectOne` and `objectTwo`

Recall that one of the built-in operations on classes is the assignment operator. For example, the statement:

```
objectTwo = objectOne;
```

copies the member variables of `objectOne` into `objectTwo`. That is, the value of `objectOne.x` is copied into `objectTwo.x`, and the value of `objectOne.p` is copied into `objectTwo.p`. Because `p` is a pointer, this member-wise copying of the data would lead to a shallow copying of the data. That is, both `objectTwo.p` and `objectOne.p` would point to the same memory space, as shown in Figure 13-24.

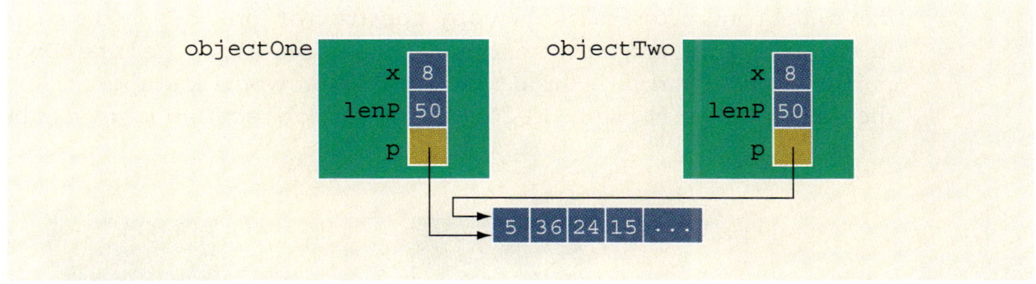

FIGURE 13-24 Objects `objectOne` and `objectTwo` after the statement `objectTwo = objectOne;` executes

Now if `objectTwo.p` deallocates the memory space to which it points, `objectOne.p` would become invalid. This situation could very well happen, if the **class** `pointerDataClass` has a destructor that deallocates the memory space pointed to by `p` when an object of type `pointerDataClass` goes out of scope. It suggests that there must be a way to avoid this pitfall. To avoid this shallow copying of data for classes with a pointer member variable, C++ allows the programmer to extend the definition of the assignment operator. This process is called overloading the assignment operator. Chapter 14 explains how to accomplish this task by using operator overloading. Once the assignment operator is properly overloaded, both `objectOne` and `objectTwo` have their own data, as shown in Figure 13-25.

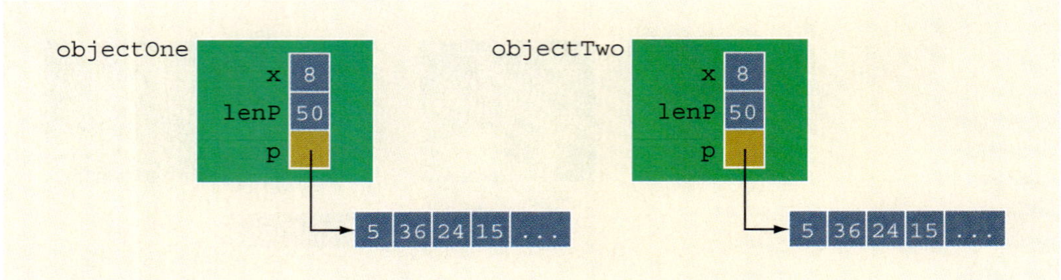

FIGURE 13-25 Objects `objectOne` and `objectTwo`

Copy Constructor

When declaring a class object, you can initialize it by using the value of an existing object of the same type. For example, consider the following statement:

```
pointerDataClass objectThree(objectOne);
```

The object `objectThree` is being declared and is also being initialized by using the value of `objectOne`. That is, the values of the member variables of `objectOne` are copied into the corresponding member variables of `objectThree`. This initialization is called the default member-wise initialization. The default member-wise initialization is due to the constructor, called the **copy constructor** (provided by the compiler). Just as in the case of the assignment operator, because the **class** `pointerDataClass` has pointer member variables, this default initialization would lead to a shallow copying of the data, as shown in Figure 13-26. (Assume that `objectOne` is given as before.)

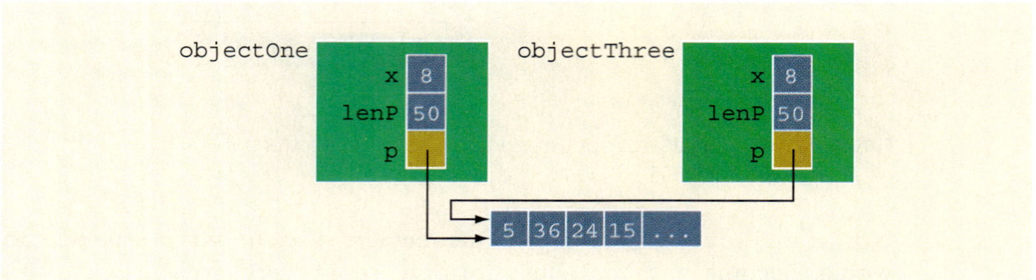

FIGURE 13-26 Objects `objectOne` and `objectThree`

Before describing how to overcome this deficiency, let us describe one more situation that could also lead to a shallow copying of the data. The solution to both these problems is the same.

Recall that, as parameters to a function, class objects can be passed either by reference or by value. Remember that the **class** `pointerDataClass` has the destructor, which deallocates the memory space pointed to by p. Suppose that `objectOne` is as shown in Figure 13-27.

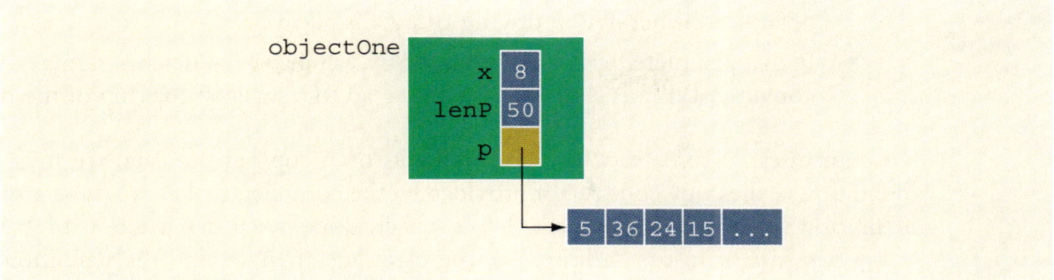

FIGURE 13-27 Object `objectOne`

Let us consider the following function prototype:

```
void destroyList(pointerDataClass paramObject);
```

The function `pointerDataClass` has a formal value parameter, `paramObject`. Now consider the following statement:

```
destroyList(objectOne);
```

In this statement, `objectOne` is passed as a parameter to the function `destroyList`. Because `paramObject` is a value parameter, the copy constructor copies the member variables of `objectOne` into the corresponding member variables of `paramObject`. Just as in the previous case, `paramObject.p` and `objectOne.p` would point to the same memory space, as shown in Figure 13-28.

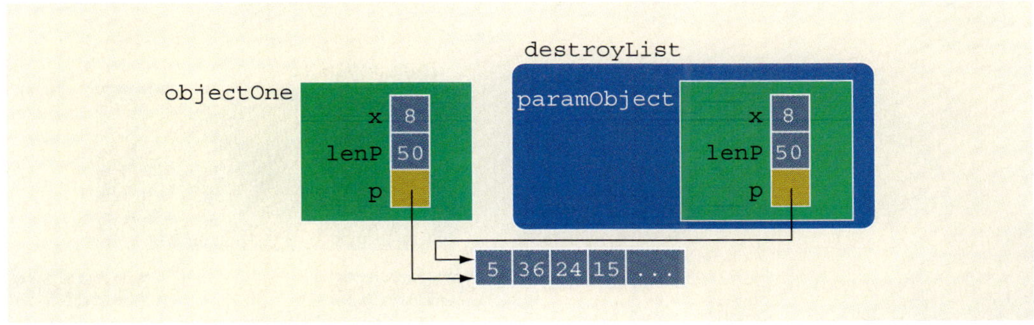

FIGURE 13-28 Pointer member variables of objects `objectOne` and `paramObject` pointing to the same array

Because `objectOne` is passed by value, the member variables of `paramObject` should have their own copy of the data. In particular, `paramObject.p` should have its own memory space. How do we ensure that this is, in fact, the case?

If a class has pointer member variables:

- During object declaration, the initialization of one object using the value of another object would lead to a shallow copying of the data, if the default member-wise copying of data is allowed.
- If, as a parameter, an object is passed by value and the default member-wise copying of data is allowed, it would lead to a shallow copying of the data.

In both cases, to force each object to have its own copy of the data, we must override the definition of the copy constructor provided by the compiler; that is, we must provide our own definition of the copy constructor. This is usually done by putting a statement that includes the copy constructor in the definition of the class, and then writing the definition of the copy constructor. Then, whenever the copy constructor needs to be executed, the system would execute the definition provided by us, not the one provided by the compiler. Therefore, for the **class** pointerDataClass, we can overcome this shallow copying problem by including the copy constructor in the **class** pointerDataClass. Example 13-6 illustrates this.

The copy constructor automatically executes in three situations (the first two are described previously):

- When an object is declared and initialized by using the value of another object
- When, as a parameter, an object is passed by value
- When the return value of a function is an object

Therefore, once the copy constructor is properly defined for the **class** pointerDataClass, both objectOne.p and objectThree.p will have their own copies of the data. Similarly, objectOne.p and paramObject.p will have their own copies of the data, as shown in Figure 13-29.

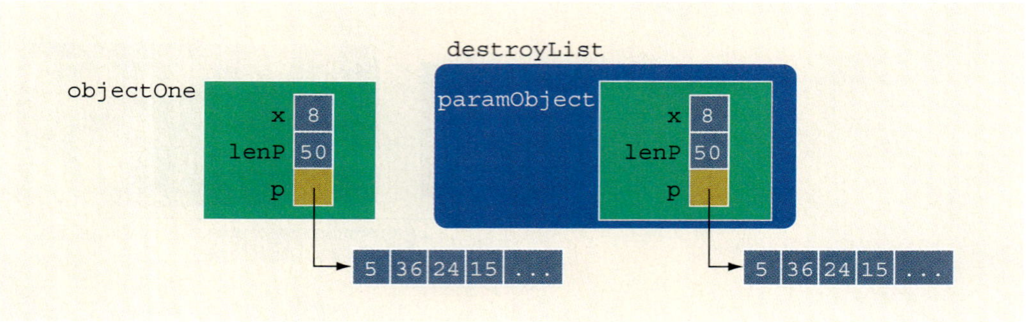

FIGURE 13-29   Pointer member variables of objects objectOne and paramObject with their own data

When the function destroyList exits, the formal parameter paramObject goes out of scope, and the destructor for the object paramObject deallocates the memory space pointed to by paramObject.p. However, this deallocation has no effect on objectOne.

The general syntax to include the copy constructor in the definition of a class is:

```cpp
className(const className& otherObject);
```

Notice that the formal parameter of the copy constructor is a constant reference parameter.

Example 13-6 illustrates how to include the copy constructor in a class and how it works.

EXAMPLE 13-6

Consider the following class:

```cpp
class pointerDataClass
{
public:
    void print() const;
      //Function to output the data stored in the array p.

    void insertAt(int index, int num);
      //Function to insert num into the array p at the
      //position specified by index.
      //If index is out of bounds, the program is terminated.
      //If index is within bounds, but greater than the index
      //of the last item in the list, num is added at the end
      //of the list.

    pointerDataClass(int size = 10);
      //Constructor
      //Creates an array of the size specified by the
      //parameter size; the default array size is 10.

    ~pointerDataClass();
      //Destructor
      //deallocates the memory space occupied by the array p.

    pointerDataClass (const pointerDataClass& otherObject);
      //Copy constructor

private:
    int maxSize; //variable to store the maximum size of p
    int length;  //variable to store the number elements in p
    int *p;      //pointer to an int array
};
```

Suppose that the definitions of the members of the **class** `pointerDataClass` are as follows:

```cpp
#include <iostream>
#include <cassert>

#include "ptrDataClass.h"
```

```cpp
using namespace std;

void pointerDataClass::print() const
{
    for (int i = 0; i < length; i++)
        cout << p[i] << " ";
}

void pointerDataClass::insertAt(int index,  int num)
{
        //if index is out of bounds, terminate the program
    assert(index >= 0 && index < maxSize);

    if (index < length)
        p[index] = num;
    else
    {
        p[length] = num;
        length++;
    }
}

pointerDataClass::pointerDataClass(int size)
{
    if (size <= 0)
    {
        cout << "The array size must be positive." << endl;
        cout << "Creating an array of the size 10." << endl;

        maxSize = 10;
    }
    else
        maxSize = size;

    length = 0;

    p = new int[maxSize];
}

pointerDataClass::~pointerDataClass()
{
    delete [] p;
}

        //copy constructor
pointerDataClass::pointerDataClass
                (const pointerDataClass& otherObject)
{
    maxSize = otherObject.maxSize;
    length = otherObject.length;
```

```cpp
    p = new int[maxSize];

    for (int i = 0; i < length; i++)
        p[i] = otherObject.p[i];
}
```

Consider the following function main. (We assume that the definition of the **class** pointerDataClass is in the header file ptrDataClass.h.)

```cpp
void testCopyConst(pointerDataClass temp);

#include <iostream>
#include "ptrDataClass.h"

using namespace std;

void testCopyConst(pointerDataClass temp);

int main()
{
    pointerDataClass listOne;                           //Line 1

    int num;                                            //Line 2
    int index;                                          //Line 3

    cout << "Line 4: Enter 5 integers." << endl;        //Line 4

    for (index = 0; index < 5; index++)                 //Line 5
    {
        cin >> num;                                     //Line 6
        listOne.insertAt(index, num);                   //Line 7
    }

    cout << "Line 8: listOne: ";                        //Line 8
    listOne.print();                                    //Line 9
    cout << endl;                                       //Line 10

        //Declare listTwo and initialize it using listOne
    pointerDataClass listTwo(listOne);                  //Line 11

    cout << "Line 12: listTwo: ";                       //Line 12
    listTwo.print();                                    //Line 13
    cout << endl;                                       //Line 14

    listTwo.insertAt(5, 34);                            //Line 15
    listTwo.insertAt(2, -76);                           //Line 16

    cout << "Line 17: After modifying listTwo: ";       //Line 17
    listTwo.print();                                    //Line 18
    cout << endl;                                       //Line 19
```

```cpp
    cout << "Line 20: After modifying listTwo, "
         << "listOne: ";                            //Line 20
    listOne.print();                                //Line 21
    cout << endl;                                   //Line 22

    cout << "Line 23: Calling the function testCopyConst"
         << endl;                                   //Line 23

        //Call function testCopyConst
    testCopyConst(listOne);                         //Line 24

    cout << "Line 25: After a call to the function "
         << "testCopyConst, " << endl
         << "             listOne is: ";            //Line 25

    listOne.print();                                //Line 26
    cout << endl;                                   //Line 27

    return 0;                                       //Line 28
}

void testCopyConst(pointerDataClass temp)
{
    cout << "Line 29: *** Inside the function "
         << "testCopyConst ***" << endl;            //Line 29

    cout << "Line 30: Object temp data: ";          //Line 30
    temp.print();                                   //Line 31
    cout << endl;                                   //Line 32

    temp.insertAt(3, -100);                         //Line 33
    cout << "Line 34: After changing temp: ";       //Line 34
    temp.print();                                   //Line 35
    cout << endl;                                   //Line 36

    cout << "Line 37: *** Exiting the function "
         << "testCopyConst ***" << endl;            //Line 37
}
```

Sample Run: In this sample run, the user input is shaded.

```
Line 4: Enter 5 integers.
14 8 34 2 58
Line 8: listOne: 14 8 34 2 58
Line 12: listTwo: 14 8 34 2 58
Line 17: After modifying listTwo: 14 8 -76 2 58 34
Line 20: After modifying listTwo, listOne: 14 8 34 2 58
Line 23: Calling the function testCopyConst
Line 29: *** Inside the function testCopyConst ***
Line 30: Object temp data: 14 8 34 2 58
Line 34: After changing temp: 14 8 34 -100 58
```

```
Line 37: *** Exiting the function testCopyConst ***
Line 25: After a call to the function testCopyConst,
         listOne is: 14 8 34 2 58
```

In the preceding program, the statement in Line 1 declares listOne to be an object of type pointerDataClass. The member variable p of listOne is an array of size 10, which is the default array size. The for loop in Line 5 reads and stores five integers in listOne.p. The statement in Line 9 outputs the numbers stored in listOne, that is, the five numbers stored in p. (See the output of the line marked Line 8 in the sample run.)

The statement in Line 11 declares listTwo to be an object of type pointerDataClass and also initializes listTwo using the values of listOne. The statement in Line 13 outputs the numbers stored in listTwo. (See the output of the line marked Line 12 in the sample run.)

The statements in Lines 15 and 16 modify listTwo, and the statement in Line 18 outputs the modified data of listTwo. (See the output of the line marked Line 17 in the sample run.) The statement in Line 21 outputs the data stored in listOne. Notice that the data stored in listOne is unchanged, even though listTwo modified its data. It follows that the copy constructor used to initialize listTwo using listOne (at Line 11) provides listTwo its own copy of the data.

The statements in Lines 23 through 28 show that when listOne is passed as a parameter by value to the function testCopyConst (see Line 24), the corresponding formal parameter temp has its own copy of data. Notice that the function testCopyConst modifies the object temp; however, the object listOne remains unchanged. See the outputs of the lines marked Line 23 (before the function testCopyConst is called) and Line 25 (after the function testCopyConst terminates) in the sample run. Also notice that when the function testCopyConst terminates, the destructor of the class pointerDataClass deallocates the memory space occupied by temp.p, which has no effect on listOne.p.

For classes with pointer member variables, three things are normally done:

1. Include the destructor in the class.
2. Overload the assignment operator for the class.
3. Include the copy constructor.

Chapter 14 discusses overloading the assignment operator. Until then, whenever we discuss classes with pointer member variables, out of the three items in the previous list, we will implement only the destructor and the copy constructor.

Inheritance, Pointers, and Virtual Functions

Recall that, as a parameter, a class object can be passed either by value or by reference. Earlier chapters also said that the types of the actual and formal parameters must match. However, in the case of classes, C++ *allows the user to pass an object of a derived class to a formal parameter of the base class type.*

First, let us discuss the case when the formal parameter is either a reference parameter or a pointer. To be specific, let us consider the following classes:

```cpp
class baseClass
{
public:
    void print();
    baseClass(int u = 0);

private:
    int x;
};

class derivedClass: public baseClass
{
public:
    void print();
    derivedClass(int u = 0, int v = 0);

private:
    int a;
};
```

The `class` `baseClass` has three members. The `class` `derivedClass` is derived from the `class` `baseClass` and has three members of its own. Both classes have a member function `print`. Suppose that the definitions of the member functions of both classes are as follows:

```cpp
void baseClass::print()
{
    cout << "In baseClass x = " << x << endl;
}

baseClass::baseClass(int u)
{
    x = u;
}

void derivedClass::print()
{
    cout << "In derivedClass ***: ";
    baseClass::print();
    cout << "In derivedClass a = " << a << endl;
}

derivedClass::derivedClass(int u, int v)
                : baseClass(u)
{
    a = v;
}
```

Consider the following function in a user program (client code):

```cpp
void callPrint(baseClass& p)
{
    p.print();
}
```

The function `callPrint` has a formal reference parameter p of type `baseClass`. You can call the function `callPrint` by using an object of either type `baseClass` or type `derivedClass` as a parameter. Moreover, the body of the function `callPrint` calls the member function `print`. Consider the following function `main`:

```cpp
int main()
{
    baseClass one(5);                        //Line 1
    derivedClass two(3, 15);                 //Line 2

    one.print();                             //Line 3
    two.print();                             //Line 4

    cout << "*** Calling the function "
         << "callPrint  ***" << endl;        //Line 5

    callPrint(one);                          //Line 6
    callPrint(two);                          //Line 7

    return 0;
}
```

Sample Run:

```
In baseClass x = 5
In derivedClass ***: In baseClass x = 3
In derivedClass a = 15
*** Calling the function callPrint  ***
In baseClass x = 5
In baseClass x = 3
```

The statements in Lines 1 through 5 are quite straightforward. Let us look at the statements in Lines 6 and 7. The statement in Line 6 calls the function `callPrint` and passes the object one as the parameter; it generates the fifth line of the output. The statement in Line 7 also calls the function `callPrint`, but passes the object two as the parameter; it generates the sixth line of the output. The output generated by the statements in Lines 6 and 7 shows only the value of x, even though in these statements a different class object is passed as a parameter. (Because in Line 7 object two is passed as a parameter to the function `callPrint`, one would expect that the output generated by the statement in Line 7 should be similar as the second and third lines of the output.) What actually occurred is that for both statements (Lines 6 and 7), the member function `print` of the **class** baseClass is executed. This is due to the fact that the binding of the member function `print`, in the body of the function `callPrint`, occurred at compile time. Because the formal parameter p of the function `callPrint` is of type `baseClass`, for the statement `p.print();`, the compiler associates the function `print` of the **class** `baseClass`. More specifically, in **compile-time binding**, the necessary code to call a specific function is generated by the compiler. (Compile-time binding is also known as **static binding**.)

For the statement in Line 7, the actual parameter is of type `derivedClass`. Thus, when the body of the function `callPrint` executes, logically the `print` function of object `two` should execute, which is not the case. So, during program execution, how does C++ correct this problem of making the call to the appropriate function? C++ corrects this problem by providing the mechanism of **virtual functions**. The binding of virtual functions occurs at program execution time, not at compile time. This kind of binding is called **run-time binding**. More formally, in run-time binding, the compiler does not generate the code to call a specific function. Instead, it generates enough information to enable the run-time system to generate the specific code for the appropriate function call. Run-time binding is also known as **dynamic binding**.

In C++, virtual functions are declared using the reserved word **virtual**. Let us redefine the previous classes using this feature:

```cpp
class baseClass
{
public:
    virtual void print();          //virtual function
    baseClass(int u = 0);

private:
    int x;
};

class derivedClass: public baseClass
{
public:
    void print();
    derivedClass(int u = 0, int v = 0);

private:
    int a;
};
```

Note that we need to declare a **virtual** function only in the base **class**.

The definition of the member function `print` is the same as before. If we execute the previous program with these modifications, the output is as follows:

Sample Run:

```
In baseClass x = 5
In derivedClass ***: In baseClass x = 3
In derivedClass a = 15
*** Calling the function callPrint  ***
In baseClass x = 5
```

```
In derivedClass ***: In baseClass x = 3
In derivedClass a = 15
```

This output shows that for the statement in Line 7, the `print` function of `derivedClass` is executed (see the last two lines of the output).

The previous discussion also applies when a formal parameter is a pointer to a class, and a pointer of the derived class is passed as an actual parameter. To illustrate this feature, suppose we have the preceding classes. (We assume that the definition of the **class** `baseClass` is in the header file `baseClass.h`, and the definition of the **class** `derivedClass` is in the header file `derivedClass.h`.) Consider the following program:

```cpp
//Chapter 13: Virtual Functions

#include <iostream>

#include "derivedClass.h"

using namespace std;

void callPrint(baseClass *p);

int main()
{
    baseClass *q;                           //Line 1
    derivedClass *r;                        //Line 2

    q = new baseClass(5);                   //Line 3
    r = new derivedClass(3, 15);            //Line 4

    q->print();                             //Line 5
    r->print();                             //Line 6

    cout << "*** Calling the function "
         << "callPrint  ***" << endl;       //Line 7

    callPrint(q);                           //Line 8
    callPrint(r);                           //Line 9

    return 0;
}

void callPrint(baseClass *p)
{
    p->print();
}
```

Sample Run:

```
In baseClass x = 5
In derivedClass ***: In baseClass x = 3
```

```
In derivedClass a = 15
*** Calling the function callPrint  ***
In baseClass x = 5
In derivedClass ***: In baseClass x = 3
In derivedClass a = 15
```

The preceding examples show that if a formal parameter, say, p of a class type, is either a reference parameter or a pointer and p uses a virtual function of the base class, we can effectively pass a derived class object as an actual parameter to p.

However, if p is a *value parameter*, then this mechanism of passing a derived class object as an actual parameter to p does not work, even if p uses a virtual function. Recall that, if a formal parameter is a value parameter, the value of the actual parameter is copied into the formal parameter. Therefore, if a formal parameter is of a **class** type, the member variables of the actual object are copied into the corresponding member variables of the formal parameter.

Suppose that we have the classes defined above—that is, baseClass and derivedClass. Consider the following function definition:

```
void callPrint(baseClass p)   //p is a value parameter
{
    p.print();
}
```

Further suppose that we have the following declaration:

```
derivedClass two;
```

The object two has two member variables, x and a. The member variable x is inherited from the base class. Consider the following function call:

```
callPrint(two);
```

In this statement, because the formal parameter p is a value parameter, the member variables of two are copied into the member variables of p. However, because p is an object of type baseClass, it has only one member variable. Consequently, only the member variable x of two will be copied into the member variable x of p. Also, the statement:

```
p.print();
```

in the body of the function will result in executing the member function print of the **class** baseClass.

The output of the following program further illustrates this concept. (As before, we assume that the definition of the **class** baseClass is in the header file baseClass.h, and the definition of the **class** derivedClass is in the header file derivedClass.h.)

```cpp
//Chapter 13: Virtual Functions and value parameters

#include <iostream>

#include "derivedClass.h"

using namespace std;

void callPrint(baseClass p);

int main()
{
    baseClass one(5);                                   //Line 1
    derivedClass two(3, 15);                            //Line 2

    one.print();                                        //Line 3
    two.print();                                        //Line 4

    cout << "*** Calling the function "
         << "callPrint  ***" << endl;                   //Line 5

    callPrint(one);                                     //Line 6
    callPrint(two);                                     //Line 7

    return 0;
}

void callPrint(baseClass p)   //p is a value parameter
{
    p.print();
}
```

Sample Run:

```
In baseClass x = 5
In derivedClass ***: In baseClass x = 3
In derivedClass a = 15
*** Calling the function callPrint  ***
In baseClass x = 5
In baseClass x = 3
```

Look closely at the output of the statements in Lines 6 and 7 (the last two lines of output). In Line 7, because the formal parameter p is a value parameter, the member variables of two are copied into the corresponding member variables of p. However, because p is an object of type baseClass, it has only one member variable. Consequently, only the member variable x of two is copied into the member variable x of p. Moreover, the statement p.print(); in the function callPrint executes the function print of the **class** baseClass, not the **class** derivedClass. Therefore, the last line of the output shows only the value of x (the member variable of two).

NOTE | An object of the base class type cannot be passed to a formal parameter of the derived class type.

Classes and Virtual Destructors

One thing recommended for classes with pointer member variables is that these classes should have the destructor. The destructor is automatically executed when the class object goes out of scope. Thus, if the object creates dynamic objects, the destructor can be designed to deallocate the storage for them. If a derived class object is passed to a formal parameter of the base class type, the destructor of the base class executes regardless of whether the derived class object is passed by reference or by value. Logically, however, the destructor of the derived class should be executed when the derived class object goes out of scope.

To correct this problem, the destructor of the base class must be virtual. The **virtual destructor** of a base class automatically makes the destructor of a derived class virtual. When a derived class object is passed to a formal parameter of the base class type, then when the object goes out of scope, the destructor of the derived class executes. After executing the destructor of the derived class, the destructor of the base class executes. Therefore, when the derived class object is destroyed, the base class part (that is, the members inherited from the base class) of the derived class object is also destroyed.

If a base class contains virtual functions, make the destructor of the base class virtual.

Abstract Classes and Pure Virtual Functions

The preceding sections discussed virtual functions. Other than enforcing run-time binding of functions, virtual functions also have another use, which is discussed in this section. Chapter 12 discussed the second principal of OOD—inheritance. Through inheritance we can derive new classes without designing them from scratch. The derived classes, in addition to inheriting the existing members of the base class, can add their own members and also redefine or override public and protected member functions of the base class. The base class can contain functions that you would want each derived class to implement. There are many scenarios when a class is desired to be served as a base class for a number of derived classes; however, the base class may contain certain functions that may not have meaningful definitions in the base class.

Let us consider the `class` shape given in Chapter 12. As noted in that chapter, from the `class` shape you can derive other `class`es, such as `rectangle`, `circle`, `ellipse`, and so on. Some of the things common to every shape are its center, using the center to move a shape to a different location, and drawing the shape. Among others, we can include these in the `class` shape. For example, you could have the definition of the `class` shape similar to the following:

```
class shape
{
public:
    virtual void draw();
      //Function to draw the shape.

    virtual void move(double x, double y);
      //Function to move the shape at the position
      //(x, y).

        .
        .
        .

};
```

Because the definitions of the functions `draw` and `move` are specific to a particular shape, each derived class can provide an appropriate definition of these functions. Note that we have made the functions `draw` and `move` **virtual** to enforce run-time binding of these functions.

The way the definition of the **class** shape is written when you write the definition of the functions of the **class** shape, you must also write the definitions of the functions `draw` and `move`. However, at this point, there is no shape to draw or move. Therefore, these function bodies have no code. One way to handle this is to make the body of these functions empty. This solution would work, but it has another drawback. Once we write the definitions of the functions of the **class** shape, then we could create an object of this class. Because there is no shape to work with, we would like to prevent the user from creating objects of the **class** shape. It follows that we would like to do the following two things—to not include the definitions of the functions `draw` and `move`, and to prevent the user from creating objects of the **class** shape.

Because we do not want to include the definitions of the functions `draw` and `move` of the **class** shape, we must convert these functions to **pure virtual functions**. In this case, the prototypes of these functions are:

```
virtual void draw() = 0;
virtual void move(double x, double y) = 0;
```

Note the expression = 0 before the semicolon. Once you make these functions pure **virtual** functions in the **class** shape, you no longer need to provide the definitions of these functions for the **class** shape.

Once a class contains one or more pure virtual functions, then that class is called an **abstract class**. Thus, the abstract definition of the **class** shape is similar to the following:

```
class shape
{
public:
    virtual void draw() = 0;
      //Function to draw the shape. Note that this is a
      //pure virtual function.
```

```
virtual void move(double x, double y) = 0;
   //Function to move the shape at the position
   //(x, y). Note that this is a pure virtual
   //function.

         .
         .
         .

};
```

Because an abstract class is *not* a complete class, as it (or its implementation file) does not contain the definitions of certain functions, you cannot create objects of that class.

Now suppose that we derive the **class** rectangle from the **class** shape. To make rectangle a nonabstract class, so that we can create objects of this class, the class (or its implementation file) must provide the definitions of the pure **virtual** functions of its base class, which is the **class** shape.

Note that in addition to the pure virtual functions, an abstract class can contain instance variables, constructors, and functions that are not pure virtual. However, the abstract class must provide the definitions of constructors and functions that are not pure virtual. The following example further illustrates how abstract classes work.

EXAMPLE 13-7

In Chapter 12 we defined the **class** partTimeEmployee, which was derived from the **class** personType, to illustrate inheritance. We also noted that there are two types of employees—full-time and part-time. The base salary of a full-time employee is, usually, fixed for a year. In addition, a full-time employee may receive a bonus. On the other hand, usually, the salary of a part-time employee is calculated according to the pay rate, per hour, and the number of hours worked. In this example, we first define the **class** employeeType, derived from the **class** personType, to store an employee's name and ID. We include functions to set the ID and retrieve the ID. We also include pure **virtual** functions print and calculatePay to print an employee's data, which includes the employee's ID, name, and wages.

From the **class** employeeType, we derive the **class**es fullTimeEmployee and partTimeEmployee and provide the definitions of the pure **virtual** functions of the **class** employeeType.

The definition of the **class** employeeType is:

```
#include "personType.h"

class employeeType: public personType
{
public:
    virtual void print() const = 0;
      //Function to output employee's data.
```

```cpp
    virtual double calculatePay() const = 0;
      //Function to calculate and return the wages.
      //Postcondition: Pay is calculated and returned

    void setId(long id);
      //Function to set the salary.
      //Postcondition: personId = id;

    long getId() const;
      //Function to retrieve the id.
      //Postcondition: returns personId

    employeeType(string first = "", string last = "",
                 long id = 0);
      //Constructor with parameters
      //Sets the first name, last name, payRate, and
      //hoursWorked according to the parameters. If
      //no value is specified, the default values are
      //assumed.
      //Postcondition: firstName = first;
      //                 lastName = last; personId = id;

private:
    long personId;        //stores the id
};
```

The definitions of the constructor and functions of the **class** `employeeType` that are not pure **virtual** are:

```cpp
void employeeType::setId(long id)
{
    personId = id;
}

long employeeType::getId() const
{
    return personId;
}

employeeType::employeeType(string first, string last, long id)
            : personType(first, last)
{
    personId = id;
}
```

The definition of the **class** `fullTimeEmployee` is:

```cpp
#include "employeeType.h"

class fullTimeEmployee: public employeeType
{
public:
    void set(string first, string last, long id,
```

```cpp
                double salary, double bonus);
      //Function to set the first name, last name,
      //id, and salary according to the parameters.
      //Postcondition: firstName = first; lastName = last;
      //                personId = id; empSalary = salary;
      //                empBonus = bonus;

    void setSalary(double salary);
      //Function to set the salary.
      //Postcondition: empSalary = salary;

    double getSalary();
      //Function to retrieve the salary.
      //Postcondition: returns empSalary

    void setBonus(double bonus);
      //Function to set the bonus.
      //Postcondition: empBonus = bonus;

    double getBonus();
      //Function to retrieve the bonus.
      //Postcondition: returns empBonus;

    void print() const;
      //Function to output the first name, last name,
      //and the wages.
      //Postcondition: Outputs
      //         Id:
      //         Name: firstName lastName
      //         Wages: $$$$.$$

    double calculatePay() const;
      //Function to calculate and return the wages.
      //Postcondition: Pay is calculated and returned

    fullTimeEmployee(string first = "", string last = "",
                     long id = 0, double salary = 0,
                     double bonus = 0);
      //Constructor with default parameters.
      //Sets the first name, last name, id, salary, and
      //bonus according to the parameters. If
      //no value is specified, the default values are
      //assumed.
      //Postcondition: firstName = first; lastName = last;
      //                personId = id; empSalary = salary;
      //                empBonus = bonus;

private:
    double empSalary;
    double empBonus;
};
```

The definitions of the constructor and functions of the **class** `fullTimeEmployee` are:

```cpp
void fullTimeEmployee::set(string first, string last,
                           long id,
                           double salary, double bonus)
{
    setName(first, last);
    setId(id);
    empSalary = salary;
    empBonus = bonus;
}

void fullTimeEmployee::setSalary(double salary)
{
    empSalary = salary;
}

double fullTimeEmployee::getSalary()
{
    return empSalary;
}

void fullTimeEmployee::setBonus(double bonus)
{
    empBonus = bonus;
}

double fullTimeEmployee::getBonus()
{
    return empBonus;
}

void fullTimeEmployee::print() const
{
    cout << "Id: " << getId() << endl;
    cout << "Name: ";
    personType::print();
    cout << endl;
    cout << "Wages: $" << calculatePay() << endl;
}

double fullTimeEmployee::calculatePay() const
{
    return empSalary + empBonus;
}

fullTimeEmployee::fullTimeEmployee(string first, string last,
                                   long id, double salary,
                                   double bonus)
                 : employeeType(first, last, id)
```

```cpp
{
    empSalary = salary;
    empBonus = bonus;
}
```

The definition of the **class** partTimeEmployee is:

```cpp
#include "employeeType.h"

class partTimeEmployee: public employeeType
{
public:
    void set(string first, string last, long id, double rate,
             double hours);
      //Function to set the first name, last name, id,
      //payRate, and hoursWorked according to the
      //parameters.
      //Postcondition: firstName = first; lastName = last;
      //                  personId = id;
      //                  payRate = rate; hoursWorked = hours

    double calculatePay() const;
      //Function to calculate and return the wages.
      //Postcondition: Pay is calculated and returned.

    void setPayRate(double rate);
      //Function to set the salary.
      //Postcondition: payRate = rate;

    double getPayRate();
      //Function to retrieve the salary.
      //Postcondition: returns payRate;

    void setHoursWorked(double hours);
      //Function to set the bonus.
      //Postcondition: hoursWorked = hours

    double getHoursWorked();
      //Function to retrieve the bonus.
      //Postcondition: returns empBonus;

    void print() const;
      //Function to output the Id, first name, last name,
      //and the wages.
      //Postcondition: Outputs
      //          Id:
      //          Name: firstName lastName
      //          Wages: $$$$.$$

    partTimeEmployee(string first = "", string last = "",
                     long id = 0,
                     double rate = 0, double hours = 0);
```

```cpp
    //Constructor with parameters
    //Sets the first name, last name, payRate, and
    //hoursWorked according to the parameters. If
    //no value is specified, the default values are
    //assumed.
    //Postcondition: firstName = first; lastName = last;
    //               personId = id, payRate = rate;
    //               hoursWorked = hours;

private:
    double payRate;      //stores the pay rate
    double hoursWorked;  //stores the hours worked
};
```

The definitions of the constructor and functions of the **class** partTimeEmployee are:

```cpp
void partTimeEmployee::set(string first, string last, long id,
                           double rate, double hours)
{
    setName(first, last);
    setId(id);
    payRate = rate;
    hoursWorked = hours;
}


void partTimeEmployee::setPayRate(double rate)
{
    payRate = rate;
}


double partTimeEmployee::getPayRate()
{
    return payRate;
}


void partTimeEmployee::setHoursWorked(double hours)
{
    hoursWorked = hours;
}


double partTimeEmployee::getHoursWorked()
{
    return hoursWorked;
}


void partTimeEmployee::print() const
{
    cout << "Id: " << getId() << endl;
    cout << "Name: ";
    personType::print();
    cout << endl;
    cout << "Wages: $" << calculatePay() << endl;
}
```

```cpp
double partTimeEmployee::calculatePay() const
{
    return (payRate * hoursWorked);
}

        //constructor
partTimeEmployee::partTimeEmployee(string first, string last,
                                   long id,
                                   double rate, double hours)
                : employeeType(first, last, id)
{
    payRate = rate;
    hoursWorked = hours;
}
```

The following function `main` tests these classes:

```cpp
#include <iostream>
#include "partTimeEmployee.h"
#include "fullTimeEmployee.h"

int main()
{
    fullTimeEmployee newEmp("John", "Smith", 75, 56000, 5700);
    partTimeEmployee tempEmp("Bill", "Nielson", 275, 15.50, 57);

    newEmp.print();
    cout << endl;
    tempEmp.print();

    return 0;
}
```

Sample Run:

```
Id: 75
Name: John Smith
Wages: $61700

Id: 275
Name: Bill Nielson
Wages: $883.5
```

The preceding output is self-explanatory. We leave the details as an exercise.

Array-Based Lists

A previous section of this chapter discussed how to use pointers to create dynamic arrays. Chapter 9 briefly explained how loops can be used to process elements stored in an array. Moreover, the previous sections of this chapter discussed abstract classes. Using these features, this section discusses how to use arrays to manipulate lists. Let us first make the following definition.

List: A collection of elements of the same type.

The **length** of a list is the number of elements in the list. Some of the operations performed on a list are as follows:

1. Create the list. The list is initialized to an empty state.
2. Determine whether the list is empty.
3. Determine whether the list is full.
4. Find the size of the list.
5. Destroy, or clear, the list.
6. Determine whether an item is the same as a given list element.
7. Insert an item in the list at the specified location.
8. Remove an item from the list at the specified location.
9. Replace an item at the specified location with another item.
10. Retrieve an item from the list at the specified location.
11. Search the list for a given item.

The list we create can be sorted or unsorted. However, the algorithms to implement certain operations are the same whether the list is sorted or unsorted. For example, a list, sorted or unsorted, is empty if the length of the list is 0. However, the search algorithms for sorted and unsorted lists are typically different. Therefore, next we create the abstract class that implements some of these operations. We will separately describe the classes to create sorted and unsorted lists. However, we must first decide how to store the list in the computer's memory.

Because all the elements of a list are of the same type, an effective, convenient, and a common way to process a list is to store it in an array. Initially, the size of the array holding the list elements is usually larger than the number of elements in the list so that, at a later stage, the list can grow to a specific size. Thus, we must know how full the array is, that is, we must keep track of the number of list elements stored in the array. Now, C++ allows the programmer to create dynamic arrays. Therefore, we will leave it for the user to specify the size of the array. The size of the array can be specified when a list object is declared. It follows that, in order to maintain and process the list in an array, we need the following three variables:

1. The array, `list`, holding the list elements.
2. A variable, `length`, to store the length of the list (that is, the number of list elements currently in the array).
3. A variable, `maxSize`, to store the size of the array (that is, the maximum number of elements that can be stored in the array).

Now that you know the operations to be performed on a list and ways to store the list into computer memory, we can define the class implementing the list as an ADT (abstract data type). For illustration purposes, we assume that the elements of the list are of type `int`. We will remove this restriction when we discuss class templates in Chapter 14; there, we will develop a generic class that can be used to process a variety of lists.

The following class defines array-based `int` lists as an ADT:

```cpp
class arrayListType
{
public:
    bool isEmpty() const;
      //Function to determine whether the list is empty
      //Postcondition: Returns true if the list is empty;
      //               otherwise, returns false.

    bool isFull() const;
      //Function to determine whether the list is full
      //Postcondition: Returns true if the list is full;
      //               otherwise, returns false.

    int listSize() const;
      //Function to determine the number of elements in
      //the list.
      //Postcondition: Returns the value of length.

    int maxListSize() const;
      //Function to determine the maximum size of the list
      //Postcondition: Returns the value of maxSize.

    void print() const;
      //Function to output the elements of the list
      //Postcondition: Elements of the list are output on the
      //               standard output device.

    bool isItemAtEqual(int location, int item) const;
      //Function to determine whether item is the same as
      //the item in the list at the position specified
      //by location.
      //Postcondition: Returns true if list[location]
      //               is the same as item; otherwise,
      //               returns false.
      //               If location is out of range, an
      //               appropriate message is displayed.

    virtual void insertAt(int location, int insertItem) = 0;
      //Function to insert insertItem in the list at the
      //position specified by location.
      //Note that this is an abstract function.
      //Postcondition: Starting at location, the elements of
      //               the list are shifted down,
      //               list[location] = insertItem; length++;
      //               If the list is full or location is out of
      //               range, an appropriate message is displayed.
```

```cpp
virtual void insertEnd(int insertItem) = 0;
  //Function to insert insertItem an item at the end of
  //the list. Note that this is an abstract function.
  //Postcondition: list[length] = insertItem; and length++;
  //               If the list is full, an appropriate
  //               message is displayed.

void removeAt(int location);
  //Function to remove the item from the list at the
  //position specified by location
  //Postcondition: The list element at list[location] is
  //               removed and length is decremented by 1.
  //               If location is out of range, an
  //               appropriate message is displayed.

void retrieveAt(int location, int& retItem) const;
  //Function to retrieve the element from the list at the
  //position specified by location
  //Postcondition: retItem = list[location]
  //               If location is out of range, an
  //               appropriate message is displayed.

virtual void replaceAt(int location, int repItem) = 0;
  //Function to replace the element in the list
  //at the position specified by location.
  //Note that this is an abstract function.
  //Postcondition: list[location] = repItem
  //               If location is out of range, an
  //               appropriate message is displayed.

void clearList();
  //Function to remove all the elements from the list
  //After this operation, the size of the list is zero.
  //Postcondition: length = 0;

virtual int seqSearch(int searchItem) const = 0;
  //Function to search the list for searchItem.
  //Note that this is an abstract function.
  //Postcondition: If the item is found, returns the
  //               location in the array where the item is
  //               found; otherwise, returns -1.

virtual void remove(int removeItem) = 0;
  //Function to remove removeItem from the list.
  //Note that this is an abstract function.
  //Postcondition: If removeItem is found in the list,
  //               it is removed from the list and length
  //               is decremented by one.

arrayListType(int size = 100);
  //Constructor
  //Creates an array of the size specified by the
  //parameter size. The default array size is 100.
  //Postcondition: The list points to the array, length = 0,
  //               and maxSize = size;
```

```
arrayListType (const arrayListType& otherList);
   //Copy constructor

virtual ~arrayListType();
   //Destructor
   //Deallocate the memory occupied by the array.

protected:
    int *list;       //array to hold the list elements
    int length;      //variable to store the length of the list
    int maxSize;     //variable to store the maximum
                     //size of the list
};
```

Figure 13-30 shows the UML class diagram of the **class arrayListType**. Note that in the UML class diagram, the name of an abstract class and abstract function is shown in italics.

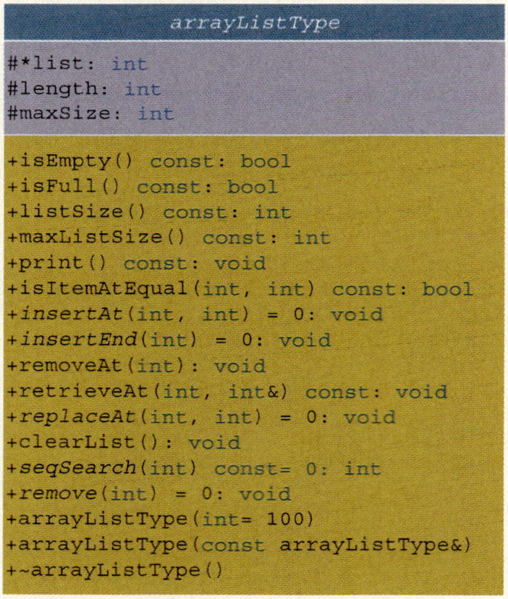

FIGURE 13-30   UML diagram of the **class arrayListType**

Notice that the member variables of the **class arrayListType** are declared as **protected**. Moreover, notice that the functions **insertAt**, **insertEnd**, **replaceAt**, **seqSearch**, **insert**, and **remove** are declared as abstract. This is because, as noted earlier, typically we deal with two types of lists—lists whose elements are arranged according to some criteria, such as sorted lists, and lists whose elements are in no particular order, such as unsorted lists. The algorithms to implement the operations, search, insert, and remove slightly differs for sorted and unsorted lists. Therefore, by using the principal of inheritance, from the **class** `arrayListType`, we, in fact, will derive two **class**es `orderedArrayListType` and `unorderedArrayListType`.

Objects of the **class** `unorderedArrayListType` would arrange list elements in no particular order, that is, these lists are unsorted. On the other hand, objects of the **class** `orderedArrayListType` would arrange elements according to some comparison criteria, usually, greater than or equal to. That is, these lists will be in ascending order. Moreover, after inserting an element into or remove an element from an ordered list, the resulting list will be ordered. We will, therefore, separately describe the algorithm to implement the operations search, insert, and remove for unsorted and sorted lists. Because each of the classes `orderedArrayListType` and `unorderedArrayListType` will provide separate definitions of the functions `insertAt`, `insertEnd`, `replaceAt`, `seqSearch`, `insert`, and `remove`, and because these methods would access the instance variable, to provide direct access to the instance variables, the instance variables are declared as protected.

Next, we write the definitions of the nonabstract functions.

The list is empty if `length` is 0; it is full if `length` is equal to `maxSize`. Therefore, the definitions of the functions `isEmpty` and `isFull` are:

```cpp
bool arrayListType::isEmpty() const
{
    return (length == 0);
} //end isEmpty

bool arrayListType::isFull() const
{
    return (length == maxSize);
} //end isFull
```

The member variable `length` of the **class** `arrayListType` stores the number of elements currently in the list. Similarly, because the size of the array holding the list elements is stored in the member variable `maxSize`, `maxSize` specifies the maximum size of the list. Therefore, the definitions of the functions `listSize` and `maxListSize` are:

```cpp
int arrayListType::listSize() const
{
    return length;
} //end listSize

int arrayListType::maxListSize() const
{
    return maxSize;
} //end maxListSize
```

The member function `print` outputs the elements of the list. We assume that the output is sent to the standard output device:

```cpp
void arrayListType::print() const
{
    for (int i = 0; i < length; i++)
        cout << list[i] << " ";
    cout << endl;
} //end print
```

The definition of the function `isItemAtEqual` is straightforward. If element at the position `location` is the same as `item`, it returns `true`. If either `location` is out of range or `item` is not in the list, it returns `false`. The definition of this function is:

```cpp
bool arrayListType::isItemAtEqual(int location, int item) const
{
    if (location < 0 || location >= length)
    {
        cout << "The location of the item to be removed "
             << "is out of range." << endl;

        return false;
    }
    else
        return (list[location] == item);
} //end isItemAtEqual
```

The function `removeAt` removes an item from a specific location in the list. The location of the item to be removed is passed as a parameter to this function. After removing the item from the list, the length of the list is reduced by 1. If the item to be removed is somewhere in the middle of the list, after removing the item we must move certain elements up one array slot because we cannot leave holes in the portion of the array containing the list. Figure 13–31 illustrates this concept.

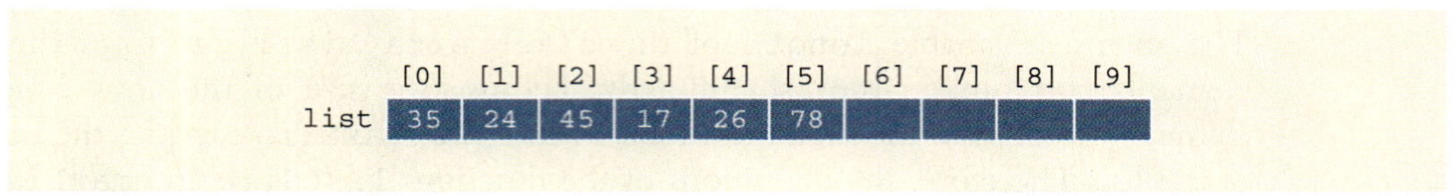

FIGURE 13-31 Array `list`

The number of elements currently in the list is 6, and so `length` is 6. Thus, after removing an element, the length of the list is 5. Suppose that the item to be removed is at, say, location 3. Clearly, we must move `list[4]` into `list[3]` and `list[5]` into `list[4]`, in this order.

The definition of the function `removeAt` is:

```cpp
void arrayListType::removeAt(int location)
{
    if (location < 0 || location >= length)
        cout << "The location of the item to be removed "
             << "is out of range." << endl;
```

```
        else
        {
            for (int i = location; i < length - 1; i++)
                list[i] = list[i + 1];

            length--;
        }
} //end removeAt
```

The definition of the function `retrieveAt` is straightforward. The index of the item to be retrieved, and the location where to retrieve the item, are passed as parameters to this function. The definition of this function is:

```
void arrayListType::retrieveAt(int location, int& retItem) const
{
    if (location < 0 || location >= length)
        cout << "The location of the item to be retrieved is "
             << "out of range" << endl;
    else
        retItem = list[location];
} //end retrieveAt
```

The function `clearList` removes the elements from the list, leaving it empty. Because the member variable `length` indicates the number of elements in the list, the elements are removed by simply setting `length` to 0. Therefore, the definition of this function is:

```
void arrayListType::clearList()
{
    length = 0;
} //end clearList
```

We now discuss the definition of the constructors and destructor. The constructor creates an array of the size specified by the user and initializes the `length` of the list to zero and the `maxSize` to the size of the array specified by the user. The size of the array is passed as a parameter to the constructor. The default array size is 100. The destructor deallocates the memory occupied by the array holding the list elements. The definitions of the constructor and the destructor are as follows:

```
arrayListType::arrayListType(int size)
{
    if (size <= 0)
    {
        cout << "The array size must be positive. Creating "
             << "an array of the size 100." << endl;

        maxSize = 100;
    }
    else
        maxSize = size;

    length = 0;
    list = new int[maxSize];
} //end constructor
```

```
arrayListType::~arrayListType()
{
    delete [] list;
} //end destructor
```

Next, we describe copy constructor. Recall that the copy constructor is called when an object is passed as a (value) parameter to a function, and when an object is declared and initialized using the value of another object of the same type. It copies the values of the member variables of the actual object into the corresponding member variables of the formal parameter and the object being created. Its definition is:

```
arrayListType::arrayListType(const arrayListType& otherList)
{
    maxSize = otherList.maxSize;
    length = otherList.length;

    list = new int[maxSize];  //create the array

    for (int j = 0; j < length; j++)   //copy otherList
        list [j] = otherList.list[j];
}//end copy constructor
```

Unordered Lists

As described in the preceding section, we derive the **class** unorderedArrayListType from the abstract **class** arrayListType and implement the operations insertAt, insertEnd, replaceAt, seqSearch, insert, and remove.

The definition of the **class** unorderedArrayListType is: (To save space, we list the member functions without documentation. The descriptions of these functions are the same as the descriptions of the functions of the **class** arrayListType.)

```
class unorderedArrayListType: public arrayListType
{
public:
    void insertAt(int location, int insertItem);
    void insertEnd(int insertItem);
    void replaceAt(int location, int repItem);
    int seqSearch(int searchItem) const;
    void remove(int removeItem);

    unorderedArrayListType(int size = 100);
      //Constructor.
};
```

We leave the UML class diagram and its inheritance hierarchy of the **class** unorderedArrayListType as an exercise for you.

The function **insertAt** inserts an item at a specific location in the list. The item to be inserted and the insert location in the array are passed as parameters to this function. In order to insert the item somewhere in the middle of the list, we must first make room for the new item. That is, we need to move certain elements down one array slot. Consider the list in Figure 13-32.

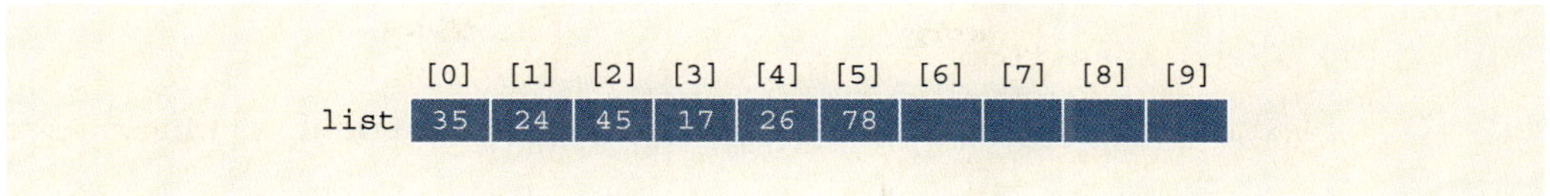

FIGURE 13-32 Array `list`

The number of elements currently in the list is 6, and so `length` is 6. Thus, after inserting a new element, the `length` of the list is 7. If the item is to be inserted at, say, location 6, we can easily accomplish this by copying the item in `list[6]`. On the other hand, if the item is to be inserted at, say, location 3, we first need to move elements `list[3]`, `list[4]`, and `list[5]` one array slot right to make room for the new item. Thus, we must first copy `list[5]` into `list[6]`, `list[4]` into `list[5]`, and `list[3]` into `list[4]`, in this order. Then, we can copy the new item into `list[3]`.

Of course, special cases, such as trying to insert in a full list, must be handled separately. Some of these cases can be accomplished by other member functions.

The definition of the function `insertAt` is as follows:

```cpp
void unorderedArrayListType::insertAt(int location,
                                      int insertItem)
{
    if (location < 0 || location >= maxSize)
        cout << "The position of the item to be inserted "
             << "is out of range." << endl;
    else if (length >= maxSize)  //list is full
        cout << "Cannot insert in a full list" << endl;
    else
    {
        for (int i = length; i > location; i--)
            list[i] = list[i - 1];  //move the elements down

        list[location] = insertItem; //insert the item at
                                     //the specified position

        length++; //increment the length
    }
} //end insertAt
```

The function `insertEnd` can be implemented by using the function `insertAt`. However, the function `insertEnd` does not require the shifting of elements. Therefore, we give its definition directly:

```cpp
void unorderedArrayListType::insertEnd(int insertItem)
{
    if (length >= maxSize)  //the list is full
        cout << "Cannot insert in a full list." << endl;
```

```
    else
    {
        list[length] = insertItem; //insert the item at the end
        length++; //increment the length
    }
} //end insertEnd
```

Next, we describe the search algorithm called a **sequential**, or **linear**, search.

Consider the list of seven elements shown in Figure 13-33.

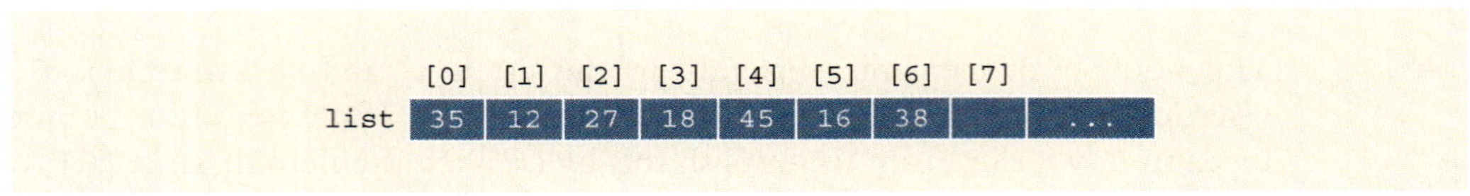

FIGURE 13-33 List of seven elements

Suppose that you want to determine whether 27 is in the list. The sequential search works as follows: First, you compare 27 with `list[0]`—that is, compare 27 with 35. Because `list[0]` ≠ 27, you then compare 27 with `list[1]` (that is, with 12, the second item in the list). Because `list[1]` ≠ 27, you compare 27 with the next element in the list—that is, compare 27 with `list[2]`. Because `list[2]` = 27, the search stops. This is a successful search.

Let us now search for 10. As before, the search starts with the first element in the list— that is, at `list[0]`. This time the search item, which is 10, is compared with every item in the list. Eventually, no more data is left in the list to compare with the search item. This is an unsuccessful search.

It now follows that, as soon as you find an element in the list that is equal to the search item, you must stop the search and report "success." (In this case, you usually also tell the location in the list where the search item was found.) Otherwise, after the search item is compared with every element in the list, you must stop the search and report "failure."

The previous discussion translates into the following algorithm for the sequential search:

```
found is set to false;

for (loc = 0; loc < length; loc++)
    if (list[loc] is equal to searchItem)
    {
        found is set to true
        exit loop
    }
if (found)
    return loc;
else
    return -1;
```

The following function performs a sequential search on a list:

```cpp
int unorderedArrayListType::seqSearch(int searchItem) const
{
    int loc;
    bool found = false;

    for (loc = 0; loc < length; loc++)
        if (list[loc] == searchItem)
        {
            found = true;
            break;
        }

    if (found)
        return loc;
    else
        return -1;
} //end seqSearch
```

The function **remove** deletes an item from the list. The item to be deleted is passed as a parameter to this function. In order to delete the item, the function calls the member function **seqSearch** to determine whether or not the item to be deleted is in the list. If the item to be deleted is found in the list, the item is removed from the list and the length of the list is decremented by 1. If the item to be removed is found in the list, the function **seqSearch** returns the **index** of the item in the list to be deleted. We can now use the **index** returned by the function **seqSearch**, and use the function **removeAt** to remove the item from the list. Therefore, the definition of the function **remove** is:

```cpp
void unorderedArrayListType::remove(int removeItem)
{
    int loc;

    if (length == 0)
        cout << "Cannot delete from an empty list." << endl;
    else
    {
        loc = seqSearch(removeItem);
        if (loc != -1)
            removeAt(loc);
        else
            cout << "The item to be deleted is not in the list."
                 << endl;
    }
} //end remove
```

The definition of the function **replaceAt** is:

```cpp
void unorderedArrayListType::replaceAt(int location, int repItem)
{
    if (location < 0 || location >= length)
        cout << "The location of the item to be "
             << "replaced is out of range." << endl;
```

```
    else
        list[location] = repItem;
} //end replaceAt
```

The definition of the constructor is:

```
unorderedArrayListType::unorderedArrayListType(int size)
                    : arrayListType(size)
{
} //end constructor
```

The following program tests the various operations on an unordered list.

EXAMPLE 13-8

```
#include <iostream>
#include "unorderedArrayListType.h"

using namespace std;

int main()
{
    unorderedArrayListType intList(25);             //Line 1

    int number;                                     //Line 2

    cout << "List 3: Enter 8 integers: ";           //Line 3

    for (int count = 0; count < 8; count++)         //Line 4
    {
        cin >> number;                              //Line 5
        intList.insertEnd(number);                  //Line 6
    }

    cout << endl;                                   //Line 7
    cout << "Line 8: intList: ";                    //Line 8
    intList.print();                                //Line 9
    cout << endl;                                   //Line 10

    cout << "Line 11: Enter the number to be "
         << "deleted: ";                            //Line 11
    cin >> number;                                  //Line 12
    cout << endl;                                   //Line 13

    intList.remove(number);                         //Line 14

    cout << "Line 15: After removing " << number
         << " intList: ";                           //Line 15
    intList.print();                                //Line 16
    cout << endl;                                   //Line 17

    cout << "Line 18: Enter the search item: ";     //Line 18
```

```cpp
    cin >> number;                                  //Line 19
    cout << endl;                                   //Line 20

    if (intList.seqSearch(number) != -1)            //Line 21
        cout << "Line 22: " << number
             << " found in intList." << endl;       //Line 22
    else                                            //Line 23
        cout << "Line 24: " << number
             << " is not in intList." << endl;      //Line 24
    return 0;
}
```

Sample Run: In this sample run, the user input is shaded.

```
List 3: Enter 8 integers: 23 89 54 32 56 11 88 39

Line 8: intList: 23 89 54 32 56 11 88 39

Line 11: Enter the number to be deleted: 23

Line 15: After removing 23 intList: 89 54 32 56 11 88 39

Line 18: Enter the search item: 11

Line 22: 11 found in intList.
```

The preceding program is self-explanatory. We leave the details as an exercise.

NOTE The Web site accompanying this book contains the program `testProgUnorderedList_II.cpp`, which illustrates how the copy constructor on an `unorderedArrayListType` object works.

NOTE **(Unordered Set)** Recall that a list is a collection of elements of the same type. However, in a list, an element may repeat. That is, the elements of the list need not be distinct. On the other hand, a **set** is also a collection of elements of the same type. However, the elements of a set are distinct. It follows that a set is a list with distinct elements. In this section, we deigned the **class** `unorderedArrayListType` to process unordered lists. Note that the functions `insertAt` and `insertEnd` do not check whether the item to be inserted is already in the list. Similarly, the function `replaceAt` also does not check if the item to be replaced is already in the list. Just as you can design a class to manipulate lists, you can also design a class to manipulate sets. Programming Exercise 10 at the end of this chapter asks you to design the **class** `unorderedSetType`, derived from the **class** `unorderedArrayListType`, to manipulate sets.

Ordered Lists

As described earlier, we derive two classes from the abstract **class** `arrayListType`, which are: `unorderedArrayListType` and `orderedArrayListType`. Elements of an `unorderedArrayListType` object are in no particular order. However, elements of an object `orderedArrayListType` are in ascending order. The preceding section described the operation of the **class** `unorderedArrayListType`. This section describes the **class** `orderedArrayListType`.

The **class** `orderedArrayListType` also contains the function `insert` to insert an item at the proper place in the list. The following class defines ordered array-based **int** lists as an ADT. (To save space, we list the member function without any documentation, which is left as an exercise for you.)

```cpp
class orderedArrayListType: public arrayListType
{
public:
    void insertAt(int location, int insertItem);
    void insertEnd(int insertItem);
    void replaceAt(int location, int repItem);
    int seqSearch(int searchItem) const;
    void insert(int insertItem);
    void remove(int removeItem);

    orderedArrayListType(int size = 100);
        //Constructor
};
```

We leave the UML class diagram and its inheritance hierarchy of the **class** `orderedArrayListType` as an exercise for you.

We give only the definition of the function `insert` and leave others as an exercise for you.

The function `insert` inserts a new item at the proper place in the list, and the length of the list is increased by 1. The definition of this function is:

```cpp
void orderedArrayListType::insert(int insertItem)
{
    if (length == 0)                 //list is empty
        list[length++] = insertItem;   //insert insertItem
                                        //and increment length
    else if (length == maxSize)
        cout << "Cannot insert in a full list." << endl;
    else
    {
            //Find the location in the list where to insert
            //insertItem.
        int loc;

        bool found = false;
```

```
    for (loc = 0; loc < length; loc++)
    {
        if (list[loc] >= insertItem)
        {
            found = true;
            break;
        }
    }

    for (int i = length; i > loc; i--)
        list[i] = list[i - 1];   //move the elements down

    list[loc] = insertItem;   //insert insertItem
    length++;   //increment the length
    }
} //end insert
```

NOTE **(Ordered Set)** An ordered set is a collection of distinct elements of the same type. Programming Exercise 11 at the end of this chapter asks you to design the **class** `orderedSetType`, derived from the **class** `orderdArrayListType`, to manipulate ordered sets.

Address of Operator and Classes

This chapter has used the address of operator, &, to store the address of a variable into a pointer variable. The address of operator is also used to create aliases to an object. Consider the following statements:

```
int x;
int &y = x;
```

The first statement declares **x** to be an **int** variable, and the second statement declares **y** to be an alias of **x**. That is, both **x** and **y** refer to the same memory location. Thus, **y** is like a constant pointer variable. The statement:

```
y = 25;
```

sets the value of **y**, and hence the value of **x**, to 25. Similarly, the statement:

```
x = 2 * x + 30;
```

updates the value of **x** and hence the value of **y**.

The address of operator can also be used to return the address of a **private** member variable of a class. However, if you are not careful, this operation can result in serious errors in the program. The following example helps illustrate this idea.

Consider the following class definition:

```cpp
//header file testadd.h

#ifndef H_testAdd
#define H_testAdd

class testAddress
{
public:
    void setX(int);
    void printX() const;
    int& addressOfX();    //this function returns the address
                          //of the x
private:
    int x;
};

#endif
```

The definitions of the functions to implement the member functions are as follows:

```cpp
//Implementation file testAdd.cpp

#include <iostream>
#include "testAdd.h"

using namespace std;

void testAddress::setX(int inX)
{
    x = inX;
}

void testAddress::printX() const
{
    cout << x;
}

int& testAddress::addressOfX()
{
    return x;
}
```

Because the return type of the function `addressOfX`, which is `int&`, is an address of an `int` memory location, the effect of the statement:

```cpp
return x;
```

is that the address of `x` is returned.

Next, let us write a simple program that uses the `class` `testAddress` and illustrates what can go wrong. Later, we will show how to fix the problem.

```cpp
//Test program.
#include <iostream>
#include "testAdd.h"

using namespace std;

int main()
{
    testAddress a;
    int &y = a.addressOfX();

    a.setX(50);
    cout << "x in class testAddress = ";
    a.printX();
    cout << endl;

    y = 25;
    cout << "After y = 25, x in class testAddress = ";
    a.printX();
    cout << endl;

    return 0;
}
```

Sample Run:

```
x in class testAddress = 50
After y = 25, x in class testAddress = 25
```

In the preceding program, after the statement:

```cpp
int &y = a.addressOfX();
```

executes, y becomes an alias of the **private** member variable **x** of the object a. Thus, the statement:

```cpp
y = 25;
```

changes the value of **x**.

Chapter 11 said that **private** member variables are not accessible outside the class. However, by returning their addresses, the programmer can manipulate them. One way to resolve this problem is to never provide the user of the class with the addresses of the **private** member variables. Sometimes, however, it is necessary to return the address of a **private** member variable, as we will see in the next chapter. How can we prevent the program from directly manipulating the **private** member variables? To fix this problem, we use the word **const** before the return type of the function. This way, we can still return the addresses of the **private** member variables, but at the same time prevent the programmer from directly manipulating the **private** member variables. Let us rewrite the **class** testAddress using this feature:

```cpp
#ifndef H_testAdd
#define H_testAdd

class testAddress
{
public:
    void setX(int);
    void printX() const;
    const int& addressOfX(); //this function returns the
                             //address of the private data
                             //member
private:
    int x;
};

#endif
```

The definition of the function `addressOfX` in the implementation file is:

```cpp
const int& testAddress::addressOfX()
{
    return x;
}
```

The same program will now generate a compile-time error.

QUICK REVIEW

1. Pointer variables contain the addresses of other variables as their values.

2. In C++, no name is associated with the pointer data type.

3. A pointer variable is declared using an asterisk, `*`, between the data type and the variable. For example, the statements:

   ```cpp
   int *p;
   char *ch;
   ```

   declare `p` and `ch` to be pointer variables. The value of `p` points to a memory space of type `int`, and the value of `ch` points to a memory space of type `char`. Usually, `p` is called a pointer variable of type `int`, and `ch` is called a pointer variable of type `char`.

4. In C++, `&` is called the address of operator.

5. The address of operator returns the address of its operand. For example, if `p` is a pointer variable of type `int` and `num` is an `int` variable, the statement:

   ```cpp
   p = &num;
   ```

   sets the value of `p` to the address of `num`.

6. When used as a unary operator, `*` is called the dereferencing operator.

7. The memory location indicated by the value of a pointer variable is accessed by using the dereferencing operator, `*`. For example, if `p` is a pointer variable of type `int`, the statement:

```
*p = 25;
```

sets the value of the memory location indicated by the value of p to 25.

8. You can use the member access operator arrow, ->, to access the component of an object pointed to by a pointer.

9. Pointer variables are initialized using either 0 (the integer zero), NULL, or the address of a variable of the same type.

10. The only number that can be directly assigned to a pointer variable is 0.

11. The only arithmetic operations allowed on pointer variables are increment (++), decrement (--), addition of an integer to a pointer variable, subtraction of an integer from a pointer variable, and subtraction of a pointer from another pointer.

12. Pointer arithmetic is different from ordinary arithmetic. When an integer is added to a pointer, the value added to the value of the pointer variable is the integer times the size of the object to which the pointer is pointing. Similarly, when an integer is subtracted from a pointer, the value subtracted from the value of the pointer variable is the integer times the size of the object to which the pointer is pointing.

13. Pointer variables can be compared using relational operators. (It makes sense to compare pointers of the same type.)

14. The value of one pointer variable can be assigned to another pointer variable of the same type.

15. A variable created during program execution is called a dynamic variable.

16. The operator **new** is used to create a dynamic variable.

17. The operator **delete** is used to deallocate the memory occupied by a dynamic variable.

18. In C++, both **new** and **delete** are reserved words.

19. The operator **new** has two forms: one to create a single dynamic variable, and another to create an array of dynamic variables.

20. If p is a pointer of type **int**, the statement:

```
p = new int;
```

allocates storage of type **int** somewhere in memory and stores the address of the allocated storage in p.

21. The operator **delete** has two forms: one to deallocate the memory occupied by a single dynamic variable, and another to deallocate the memory occupied by an array of dynamic variables.

22. If p is a pointer of type **int**, the statement:

```
delete p;
```

deallocates the memory pointed to by p.

23. The array name is a constant pointer. It always points to the same memory location, which is the location of the first array component.

24. To create a dynamic array, the form of the **new** operator that creates an array of dynamic variables is used. For example, if `p` is a pointer of type `int`, the statement:

```
p = new int[10];
```

creates an array of 10 components of type `int`. The base address of the array is stored in `p`. We call `p` a dynamic array.

25. Array notation can be used to access the components of a dynamic array. For example, suppose `p` is a dynamic array of 10 components. Then, `p[0]` refers to the first array component, `p[1]` refers to the second array component, and so on. In particular, `p[i]` refers to the `(i + 1)`th component of the array.

26. An array created during program execution is called a dynamic array.

27. If `p` is a dynamic array, then the statement:

```
delete [] p;
```

deallocates the memory occupied by `p`—that is, the components of `p`.

28. C++ allows a program to create dynamic multidimensional arrays.

29. In the statement `int **board;`, the variable `board` is a pointer to a pointer.

30. In a shallow copy, two or more pointers of the same type point to the same memory space; that is, they point to the same data.

31. In a deep copy, two or more pointers of the same type have their own copies of the data.

32. If a class has a destructor, the destructor is automatically executed whenever a class object goes out of scope.

33. If a class has pointer member variables, the built-in assignment operators provide a shallow copy of the data.

34. A copy constructor executes when an object is declared and initialized by using the value of another object, and when an object is passed by value as a parameter.

35. C++ allows a user to pass an object of a derived class to a formal parameter of the base class type.

36. The binding of virtual functions occurs at execution time, not at compile time, and is called dynamic or run-time binding.

37. In C++, virtual functions are declared using the reserved word **virtual**.

38. A class is called an abstract class if it contains one or more pure virtual functions.

39. Because an abstract class is *not* a complete class—as it (or its implementation file) does not contain the definitions of certain functions—you cannot create objects of that class.

40. In addition to the pure virtual functions, an abstract class can contain instance variables, constructors, and functions that are not pure virtual. However, the abstract class must provide the definitions of constructors and functions that are not pure virtual.

41. The address of operator can be used to return the address of a **private** member variable of a class.

42. A list is a collection of elements of the same type.

43. The commonly performed operations on a list are create the list, determine whether the list is empty, determine whether the list is full, find the size of the list, destroy or clear the list, determine whether an item is the same as a given list element, insert an item in the list at the specified location, remove an item from the list at the specified location, replace an item at the specified location with another item, retrieve an item from the list from the specified location, and search the list for a given item.

44. C++ allows a user to pass an object of a derived class to a formal parameter of the base class type.

EXERCISES

1. Mark the following statements as true or false.

    a. In C++, pointer is a reserved word.

    b. In C++, pointer variables are declared using the word pointer.

    c. The statement **delete** p; deallocates the variable pointer p.

    d. The statement **delete** p; deallocates the dynamic variable that is pointed to by p.

    e. Given the declaration:

    ```
    int list[10];
    int *p;
    ```

    the statement:

    ```
    p = list;
    ```

    is valid in C++.

    f. Given the declaration:

    ```
    int *p;
    ```

    the statement:

    ```
    p = new int[50];
    ```

dynamically allocates an array of 50 components of type `int`, and p contains the base address of the array.

   g.   The address of operator returns the address and value of its operand.

   h.   If p is a pointer variable, then the statement p = p * 2; is valid in C++.

2. Given the declaration:

```
int x;
int *p;
int *q;
```

mark the following statements as valid or invalid. If a statement is invalid, explain why.

   a.   p = q;

   b.   *p = 56;

   c.   p = x;

   d.   *p = *q;

   e.   q = &x;

   f.   *p = q;

3. What is the output of the following C++ code?

```
int x;
int y;
int *p = &x;
int *q = &y;
*p = 35;
*q = 98;
*p = *q;
cout << x << "   " << y << endl;
cout << *p << "   " << *q << endl;
```

4. What is the output of the following C++ code?

```
int x;
int y;
int *p = &x;
int *q = &y;
x = 35;
y = 46;
p = q;
*p = 78;
cout << x << "   " << y << endl;
cout << *p << "   " << *q << endl;
```

5. Given the declaration:

```
int num = 6;
int *p = &num;
```

which of the following statements increment(s) the value of num?

   a.   p++;

   b.   (*p)++;

   c. `num++;`

   d. `(*num)++;`

6. What is the output of the following code?

```
int *p;
int *q;
p = new int;
q = p;
*p = 46;
*q = 39;
cout << *p << " " << *q << endl;
```

7. What is the output of the following code?

```
int *p;
int *q;
p = new int;
*p = 43;
q = p;
*q = 52;
p = new int;
*p = 78;
q = new int;
*q = *p;
cout << *p << " " << *q << endl;
```

8. What is wrong with the following code?

```
int *p;                              //Line 1
int *q;                              //Line 2

p = new int;                         //Line 3
*p = 43;                             //Line 4

q = p;                               //Line 5
*q = 52;                             //Line 6

delete q;                            //Line 7

cout << *p << " " << *q << endl;     //Line 8
```

9. What is the output of the following code?

```
int x;
int *p;
int *q;
p = new int[10];
q = p;
*p = 4;
for (int j = 0; j < 10; j++)
{
    x = *p;
    p++;
    *p = x + j;
}
```

```cpp
for (int k = 0; k < 10; k++)
{
    cout << *q << " ";
    q++;
}
cout << endl;
```

10. What is the output of the following code?

```cpp
int *secret;
int j;

secret = new int[10];
secret[0] = 10;
for (j = 1; j < 10; j++)
    secret[j] = secret[j - 1] + 5;
for (j = 0; j < 10; j++)
    cout << secret[j] << " ";
cout << endl;
```

11. Explain the difference between a shallow copy and a deep copy of data.

12. What is wrong with the following code?

```cpp
int *p;                             //Line 1
int *q;                             //Line 2

p = new int[5];                     //Line 3
*p = 2;                             //Line 4

for (int i = 1; i < 5; i++)         //Line 5
    p[i] = p[i - 1] + i;            //Line 6

q = p;                              //Line 7

delete [] p;                        //Line 8

for (int j = 0; j < 5; j++)         //Line 9
    cout << q[j] << " ";           //Line 10

cout << endl;                       //Line 11
```

13. What is the output of the following code?

```cpp
int *p;
int *q;
int i;

p = new int[5];
p[0] = 5;
for (i = 1; i < 5; i++)
    p[i] = p[i - 1] + 2 * i;

cout << "Array p: ";
for (i = 0; i < 5; i++)
    cout << p[i] << " ";
cout << endl;
```

```
q = new int[5];

for (i = 0; i < 5; i++)
    q[i] = p[4 - i];

cout << "Array q: ";
for (i = 0; i < 5; i++)
    cout << q[i] << " ";

cout << endl;
```

14. a. Write a statement that declares `table` to be a pointer to a pointer of type `double`.

   b. Write C++ statements that create `table` to be a two-dimensional array of 5 rows and 7 columns.

15. What is the purpose of a copy constructor?

16. Name two situations when a copy constructor executes.

17. Name three things that you should do for classes with pointer member variables.

18. Suppose that you have the following classes, `classA` and `classB`:

```
class classA
{
public:
    virtual void print() const;
    void doubleNum();
    classA(int a = 0);

private:
    int x;
};

void classA::print() const
{
    cout << "ClassA x: " << x << endl;
}

void classA::doubleNum()
{
    x = 2 * x;
}
classA::classA(int a)
{
    x = a;
}

class classB: public classA
{
public:
```

```cpp
    void print() const;
    void doubleNum();
    classB(int a = 0, int b = 0);

private:
    int y;
};

void classB::print() const
{
    classA::print();
    cout << "ClassB y: " << y << endl;
}

void classB::doubleNum()
{
    classA::doubleNum();

    y = 2 * y;
}

classB::classB(int a, int b)
       : classA(a)
{
    y = b;
}
```

What is the output of the following function main?

```cpp
int main()
{
    classA *ptrA;
    classA objectA(2);

    classB objectB(3, 5);

    ptrA = &objectA;
    ptrA->doubleNum();
    ptrA->print();
    cout << endl;

    ptrA = &objectB;

    ptrA->doubleNum();
    ptrA->print();
    cout << endl;

    return 0;
}
```

19. What is the output of the function `main` of Exercise 18, if the definition of `classA` is replaced by the following definition?

```
class classA
{
public:
    virtual void print() const;
    virtual void doubleNum();
    classA(int a = 0);

private:
    int x;
};
```

20. What is the difference between compile-time binding and run-time binding?

21. Is it legal to have an abstract class with all member functions pure virtual?

22. Consider the following definition of the `class studentType`:

```
public studentType: public personType
{
public:
    void print();
    void calculateGPA();
    void setID(long id);
    void setCourses(const string c[], int noOfC);
    void setGrades(const char cG[], int noOfC);

    void getID();
    void getCourses(string c[], int noOfC);
    void getGrades(char cG[], int noOfC);
    void studentType(string fName = "", string lastName = "",
                     long id, string c[] = NULL,
                     char cG[] = NULL, int noOfC = 0);

private:
    long studentId;
    string courses[6];
    char coursesGrade[6];
    int noOfCourses;
};
```

Rewrite the definition of the `class studentType` so that the functions `print` and `calculateGPA` are pure `virtual` functions.

23. Suppose that the definitions of the `classes employeeType`, `fullTimeEmployee`, and `partTimeEmployee` are as given in Example 13-7 of this chapter. Which of the following statements is legal?

   a. `employeeType tempEmp;`

   b. `fullTimeEmployee newEmp();`

   c. `partTimeEmployee pEmp("Molly", "Burton", 101, 0.0, 0);`

24. What is the effect of the following statements?

    a.   `unorderedArrayListType intList1(100);`

    b.   `unorderedArrayListType intList2(1000);`

    c.   `unorderedArrayListType intList3(-10);`

PROGRAMMING EXERCISES

1. Redo Programming Exercise 5 of Chapter 9 using dynamic arrays.

2. Redo Programming Exercise 6 of Chapter 9 using dynamic arrays.

3. Redo Programming Exercise 7 of Chapter 9 using dynamic arrays. You must ask the user for the number of candidates, and then create the appropriate arrays to hold the data.

4. The function `retrieveAt` of the **class** `arrayListType` is written as a **void** function. Rewrite this function so that it is written as a value returning function, returning the required item. If location of the item to be returned is out of range, use the assert function to terminate the program. Also, write a program to test your function. Use the **class** `unorderedArrayListType` to test your function.

5. The function `removeAt` of the **class** `arrayListType` removes an element from the list by shifting the elements of the list. However, if the element to be removed is at the beginning of the list and the list is fairly large, it could take a lot of computer time. Because the list elements are in no particular order, you could simply remove the element by swapping the last element of the list with the item to be removed and reducing the length of the list. Rewrite the definition of the function `removeAt` using this technique. Use the **class** `unorderedArrayListType` to test your function.

6. The function `remove` of the **class** `arrayListType` removes only the first occurrence of an element. Add the function `removeAll`, as an abstract function, to the **class** `arrayListType` that would remove all occurrences of a given element. Also, write the definition of the function `removeAll`, in the **class** `unorderedArrayListType`, and a program to test this function.

7. Add the function `min`, as an abstract function, to the **class** `arrayListType` to return the smallest element of the list. Also, write the definition of the function `min`, in the **class** `unorderedArrayListType`, and a program to test this function.

8. Add the function `max`, as an abstract function, to the **class** `arrayListType` to return the largest element of the list. Also, write the definition of the function `max`, in the **class** `unorderedArrayListType`, and a program to test this function.

9. Write the definitions of the functions of the **class** orderedArrayListType, that are not given in this chapter. Also, write a program to test various operations of this class.

10. (**Unordered Sets**) As explained in this chapter, a set is a collection of distinct elements of the same type. Design the **class** unorderedSetType, derived from the **class** unorderedArrayListType, to manipulate sets. Note that you need to redefine only the functions insertAt, insertEnd, and replaceAt. If the item to be inserted is already in the list, the functions insertAt and insertEnd output an appropriate message. Similarly, if the item to be replaced is already in the list, the function replaceAt outputs an appropriate message. Also, write a program to test your class.

11. (**Ordered Sets**) Programming Exercise 10 asks you to define the **class** unorderedSetType to manipulate sets. The elements of an unorderedSetType object are distinct, but in no particular order. Design the **class** orderedSetType, derived from the **class** orderedArrayListType, to manipulate ordered sets. The elements of an orderedSetType object are distinct and in ascending order. Note that you need to redefine only the functions insert and replaceAt. If the item to be inserted is already in the list, the function insert outputs an appropriate message. Similarly, if the item to be replaced is already in the list, the function replaceAt outputs an appropriate message. Also, write a program to test your class.

OVERLOADING AND TEMPLATES

IN THIS CHAPTER, YOU WILL:

- Learn about overloading
- Become aware of the restrictions on operator overloading
- Examine the pointer `this`
- Learn about `friend` functions
- Explore the members and nonmembers of a class
- Discover how to overload various operators
- Learn about templates
- Explore how to construct function templates and class templates

In Chapter 11, you learned how classes in C++ are used to combine data, and operations on that data, in a single entity. The ability to combine data and operations on the data is called encapsulation. It is the first principle of object-oriented design (OOD). Chapter 11 defined the abstract data type (ADT) and described how classes in C++ implement ADT. Chapter 12 discussed how new classes can be derived from existing classes through the mechanism of inheritance. Inheritance, the second principle of OOD, encourages code reuse.

This chapter covers **operator overloading** and **templates**. Templates enable the programmer to write generic code for related functions and classes. We will also simplify function overloading (introduced in Chapter 7) through the use of templates, called **function templates**.

Why Operator Overloading Is Needed

Chapter 11 defined and implemented the `class` `clockType`. It also showed how you can use the `class` `clockType` to represent the time of day in a program. Let us review some of the characteristics of the `class` `clockType`.

Consider the following statements:

```
clockType myClock(8, 23, 34);
clockType yourClock(4, 5, 30);
```

The first statement declares `myClock` to be an object of type `clockType` and initializes the member variables `hr`, `min`, and `sec` of `myClock` to 8, 23, and 34, respectively. The second statement declares `yourClock` to be an object of type `clockType` and initializes the member variables `hr`, `min`, and `sec` of `yourClock` to 4, 5, and 30, respectively.

Now consider the following statements:

```
myClock.printTime();

myClock.incrementSeconds();

if (myClock.equalTime(yourClock))
    .
    .
    .
```

The first statement prints the value of `myClock` in the form `hr:min:sec`. The second statement increments the value of `myClock` by one second. The third statement checks whether the value of `myClock` is the same as the value of `yourClock`.

These statements do their job. However, if we can use the insertion operator `<<` to output the value of `myClock`, the increment operator `++` to increment the value of `myClock` by one second, and relational operators for comparison, we can enhance the flexibility of C++ considerably. More specifically, we prefer to use the following statements instead of the previous statements:

```
cout << myClock;

myClock++;

if (myClock == yourClock)
    .
    .
    .
```

Recall that the only built-in operations on classes are the assignment operator and the member selection operator. Therefore, other operators cannot be directly applied to class objects. However, C++ allows the programmer to extend the definitions of most of the operators so that operators—such as relational operators, arithmetic operators, the insertion operator for data output, and the extraction operator for data input—can be applied to classes. In C++ terminology, this is called **operator overloading**.

Operator Overloading

Recall how the arithmetic operator / works. If both operands of / are integers, the result is an integer; otherwise, the result is a floating-point number. Similarly, the stream insertion operator, <<, and the stream extraction operator, >>, are overloaded. The operator >> is used as both a stream extraction operator and a right shift operator. The operator << is used as both a stream insertion operator and a left shift operator. These are examples of operator overloading.

Other examples of overloaded operators are + and −. The results of + and − are different for integer arithmetic, floating-point arithmetic, and pointer arithmetic.

C++ allows the user to overload most of the operators so that the operators can work effectively in a specific application. It does not allow the user to create new operators. Most of the existing operators can be overloaded to manipulate class objects.

In order to overload operators, you must write functions (that is, the header and body). The name of the function that overloads an operator is the reserved word `operator` followed by the operator to be overloaded. For example, the name of the function to overload the operator >= is:

```
operator>=
```

Operator function: The function that overloads an operator.

Syntax for Operator Functions

The result of an operation is a value. Therefore, the operator function is a value-returning function.

The syntax of the heading for an operator function is:

```
returnType operator operatorSymbol(formal parameter list)
```

In C++, `operator` is a reserved word.

Recall that the only built-in operations on classes are assignment (=) and member selection. To use other operators on class objects, they must be explicitly overloaded. Operator overloading provides the same concise expressions for user-defined data types as it does for built-in data types.

To overload an operator for a class:

1. Include the statement to declare the function to overload the operator (that is, the operator function) prototype in the definition of the class.

2. Write the definition of the operator function.

Certain rules must be followed when you include an operator function in a class definition. These rules are described in the section, "Operator Functions as Member Functions and Nonmember Functions" later in this chapter.

Overloading an Operator: Some Restrictions

When overloading an operator, keep the following in mind:

1. You cannot change the precedence of an operator.

2. The associativity cannot be changed. (For example, the associativity of the arithmetic operator addition is from left to right, and it cannot be changed.)

3. Default parameters cannot be used with an overloaded operator.

4. You cannot change the number of parameters an operator takes.

5. You cannot create new operators. Only existing operators can be overloaded.

6. The operators that cannot be overloaded are:

   ```
   .    .*    ::    ?:    sizeof
   ```

7. The meaning of how an operator works with built-in types, such as `int`, remains the same.

8. Operators can be overloaded either for objects of the user-defined types, or for a combination of objects of the user-defined type and objects of the built-in type.

Pointer `this`

A member function of a class can (directly) access the member variables of that class for a given object. Sometimes, it is necessary for a member function to refer to the object as a whole, rather than the object's individual member variables. How do you refer to the object as a whole (that is, as a single unit) in the definition of the member function, especially when the object is not passed as a parameter? Every object of a class maintains a (hidden) pointer to itself, and the name of this pointer is `this`. In C++, `this` is a reserved word. The pointer `this` (in a member function) is available for you to use. When an object invokes a member function, the member function references the pointer `this` of the object. For example, suppose that `test` is a class and has a member function called `one`. Further suppose that the definition of `one` looks like the following:

```
test test::one()
{
    .
    .
    .
    return *this;
}
```

If `x` and `y` are objects of type `test`, then the statement:

```
y = x.one();
```

copies the value of object `x` into object `y`. That is, the member variables of `x` are copied into the corresponding member variables of `y`. When object `x` invokes function `one`, the pointer `this` in the definition of member function `one` refers to object `x`, and so `this` means the address of `x` and `*this` means the value of `x`.

The following example illustrates how the pointer `this` works.

EXAMPLE 14-1

Consider the following class:

```
class thisPointerClass
{
public:
    void set(int a, int b, int c);
    void print() const;

    thisPointerClass updateXYZ();
      // Postcondition: x = 2 * x; y = y + 2;
      //                z = z * z;

    thisPointerClass(int a = 0, int b = 0, int c = 0);
```

```
private:
    int x;
    int y;
    int z;
};
```

Suppose that the definitions of the member functions of the **class** thisPointerClass are as follows:

```
void thisPointerClass::set(int a, int b, int c)
{
    x = a;
    y = b;
    z = c;
}

void thisPointerClass::print() const
{
    cout << "x = " << x
         << ", y = " << y
         << ", z = " << z << endl;
}

thisPointerClass thisPointerClass::updateXYZ()
{
    x = 2 * x;
    y = y + 2;
    z = z * z;

    return *this;
}
```

The definition of the function **updateXYZ** updates the values of **x**, **y**, and **z**. Using the pointer **this** returns the value of the entire object. That is, the values of the member variables **x**, **y**, and **z** are returned.

```
thisPointerClass::thisPointerClass(int a, int b, int c)
{
    x = a;
    y = b;
    z = c;
}
```

Consider the following function **main**:

```
//Chapter 14: this pointer illustration

#include <iostream>
#include "thisPointerIllus.h"

using namespace std;
```

```cpp
int main()
{
    thisPointerClass object1(3, 5, 7);          //Line 1
    thisPointerClass object2;                    //Line 2

    cout << "Object 1: ";                        //Line 3
    object1.print();                             //Line 4

    object2 = object1.updateXYZ();               //Line 5

    cout << "After updating object1: ";          //Line 6
    object1.print();                             //Line 7

    cout << "Object 2: ";                        //Line 8
    object2.print();                             //Line 9

    return 0;
}
```

Sample Run:

```
Object 1: x = 3, y = 5, z = 7
After updating object1: x = 6, y = 7, z = 49
Object 2: x = 6, y = 7, z = 49
```

For the most part, the output is self-explanatory. The statement in Line 5 evaluates the expression `object1.updateXYZ()`, which updates the values of the member variables of `object1`. The value of `object1` is then returned by the pointer **this**, as shown in the definition of the function `updateXYZ`. The assignment operator then copies the value into `object2`.

The following example also shows how the pointer **this** works.

EXAMPLE 14-2

In Example 11-9 in (Chapter 11), we designed a class to implement a person's name in a program. Here, we extend the definition of the **class** `personType` to individually set a person's first name and last name, and then return the entire object. The extended definition of the **class** `personType` is:

```cpp
class personType
{
public:
    void print() const;
        //Function to output the first name and last name
        //the form firstName lastName

    void setName(string first, string last);
        //Function to set firstName and lastName according
        //to the parameters.
        //Postcondition: firstName = first; lastName = last
```

```cpp
    personType& setFirstName(string first);
      //Function to set the first name.
      //Postcondition: firstName = first
      //      After setting the first name, a reference
      //      to the object, that is, the address of the
      //      object, is returned.

    personType& setLastName(string last);
      //Function to set the last name.
      //Postcondition: lastName = last
      //      After setting the last name, a reference
      //      to the object, that is, the address of the
      //      object, is returned.

    string getFirstName() const;
      //Function to return the first name.
      //Postcondition: The value of firstName is returned.

    string getLastName() const;
      //Function to return the last name.
      //Postcondition: The value of lastName is returned.

    personType(string first = "", string last = "");
      //Constructor
      //Sets firstName and lastName according to the parameters.
      //Postcondition: firstName = first; lastName = last

private:
    string firstName;  //variable to store the first name
    string lastName;   //variable to store the last name
};
```

Notice that in this definition of the **class** `personType`, we replace the default const-ructor and the constructor with parameters by one constructor with default parameters.

The definitions of the functions `print`, `setTime`, `getFirstName`, `getLastName`, and the constructor is the same as before (see Example 11-9). The definitions of the functions `setFirstName` and `setLastName` are as follows:

```cpp
personType& personType::setLastName(string last)
{
    lastName = last;

    return *this;
}


personType& personType::setFirstName(string first)
{
    firstName = first;

    return *this;
}
```

Consider the following function `main`:

```cpp
int main()
{
    personType student1("Angela", "Clodfelter");            //Line 1

    personType student2;                                     //Line 2

    personType student3;                                     //Line 3

    cout << "Line 4 -- Student 1: ";                         //Line 4
    student1.print();                                        //Line 5
    cout << endl;                                            //Line 6

    student2.setFirstName("Shelly").setLastName("Malik");    //Line 7

    cout << "Line 8 -- Student 2: ";                         //Line 8
    student2.print();                                        //Line 9
    cout << endl;                                            //Line 10

    student3.setFirstName("Chelsea");                        //Line 11

    cout << "Line 12 -- Student 3: ";                        //Line 12
    student3.print();                                        //Line 13
    cout << endl;                                            //Line 14

    student3.setLastName("Tomek");                           //Line 15

    cout << "Line 16 -- Student 3: ";                        //Line 16
    student3.print();                                        //Line 17
    cout << endl;                                            //Line 18

    return 0;
}
```

Sample Run:

```
Line 4 -- Student 1: Angela Clodfelter
Line 8 -- Student 2: Shelly Malik
Line 12 -- Student 3: Chelsea
Line 16 -- Student 3: Chelsea Tomek
```

The statements in Lines 1, 2, and 3 declare and initialize the objects `student1`, `student2`, and `student3`, respectively. The objects `student2` and `student3` are initialized to empty strings. The statement in Line 5 outputs the value of `student1` (see Line 4 in the sample run, which contains the output of Lines 4, 5, and 6). The statement in Line 7 works as follows. In the statement:

```cpp
student2.setFirstName("Shelly").setLastName("Malik");
```

first the expression:

```
student2.setFirstName("Shelly")
```

is executed because the associativity of the dot operator is from left to right. This expression sets the first name to `"Shelly"` and returns a reference of the object, which is `student2`. Thus, the next expression executed is:

```
student2.setLastName("Malik")
```

which sets the last name of `student2` to `"Malik"`. The statement in Line 9 outputs the value of `student2`. The statement in Line 11 sets the first name of the object `student3` to `"Chelsea"` and ignores the value returned. The statement in Line 13 outputs the value of `student3`. Notice the output in Line 12. The output shows only the first name, not the last name, because we have not yet set the last name of `student3`. The last name of `student3` is still empty, which was set by the statement in Line 3 when `student3` was declared. Next, the statement in Line 15 sets the last name of `student3`, and the statement in Line 17 outputs the value of `student3`.

Friend Functions of Classes

A **friend function** of a class is a nonmember function of the class, but has access to all the members (`public` or non-`public`) of the class. To make a function be a friend to a class, the reserved word `friend` precedes the function prototype (in the class definition). The word `friend` appears only in the function prototype in the class definition, not in the definition of the friend function.

Consider the following statements:

```
class classIllusFriend
{
    friend void two(/*parameters*/);
       .
       .
       .
};
```

In the definition of the `class classIllusFriend`, `two` is declared as a `friend` of the `class classIllusFriend`. That is, it is a nonmember function of the `class classIllusFriend`. When you write the definition of the function `two`, any object of type `classIllusFriend`—which is either a local variable of `two` or a formal parameter of `two`—can access its `private` members within the definition of the function `two`. (Example 14-3 illustrates this concept.) Moreover, because a `friend` function is not a member of a class, its declaration can be placed within the `private`, `protected`, or `public` part of the class. However, they are typically placed before any member function declaration.

DEFINITION OF A `friend` FUNCTION

When writing the definition of a **friend** function, the name of the class and the scope resolution operator do not precede the name of the **friend** function in the function heading. Also, recall that the word **friend** does not appear in the heading of the **friend** function's definition. Thus, the definition of the function `two` in the previous **class** `classIllusFriend` is:

```
void two(/*parameters*/)
{
        .
        .
        .

}
```

Of course, we will place the definition of the **friend** function in the implementation file.

The next section illustrates the difference between a member function and a nonmember function (**friend** function) when we overload some of the operators for a specific class.

The following example shows how a **friend** function accesses the **private** members of a class.

EXAMPLE 14-3

Consider the following class:

```
class classIllusFriend
{
        friend void two(classIllusFriend cIFObject);

public:
        void print();
        void setx(int a);

private:
        int x;
};
```

In the definition of the **class** `classIllusFriend`, two is declared as a **friend** function. Suppose that the definitions of the member functions of the **class** `classIllusFriend` are as follows:

```
void classIllusFriend::print()
{
        cout << "In class classIllusFriend: x = " << x << endl;
}

void classIllusFriend::setx(int a)
{
        x = a;
}
```

Consider the following definition of the function `two`:

```cpp
void two(classIllusFriend cIFObject)                //Line 1
{
    classIllusFriend localTwoObject;                //Line 2

    localTwoObject.x = 45;                          //Line 3

    localTwoObject.print();                         //Line 4

    cout << "Line 5: In Friend Function two "
         << "accessing private member variable "
         << "x = " << localTwoObject.x
         << endl;                                   //Line 5

    cIFObject.x = 88;                               //Line 6

    cIFObject.print();                              //Line 7

    cout << "Line 8: In Friend Function two "
         << "accessing private member variable "
         << "x = " << cIFObject.x << endl;          //Line 8
}
```

The function `two` contains a formal parameter `cIFObject` and a local variable `localTwoObject`, both of type `classIllusFriend`. In the statement in Line 3, the object `localTwoObject` accesses its **private** member variable `x` and sets its value to 45. If `two` is not declared as a **friend** function of the **class** `classIllusFriend`, then this statement would result in a syntax error because an object cannot directly access its **private** members. Similarly, in the statement in Line 6, the formal parameter `cIFObject` accesses its **private** member variable `x` and sets its value to 88. Once again, this statement would result in a syntax error if `two` is not declared a **friend** function of the **class** `classIllusFriend`. The statement in Line 5 outputs the value of the **private** member variable `x` of `localTwoObject` by directly accessing `x`. Similarly, the statement in Line 8 outputs the value of `x` of `cIFObject` by directly accessing it. The function `two` also prints the value of `x` by using the function `print` (see the statements in Lines 4 and 7).

Now consider the definition of the following function `main`:

```cpp
int main()
{
    classIllusFriend aObject;                       //Line 9

    aObject.setx(32);                               //Line 10

    cout << "Line 11: aObject.x: ";                 //Line 11
    aObject.print();                                //Line 12
    cout << endl;                                   //Line 13
```

```
    cout << "*~*~*~*~*~*  Testing Friend Function "
         << "two *~*~*~*~*~*" << endl << endl;        //Line 14

    two(aObject);                                     //Line 15

    return 0;
}
```

Sample Run:

```
Line 11: aObject.x: In class classIllusFriend: x = 32

*~*~*~*~*~*  Testing Friend Function two *~*~*~*~*~*

In class classIllusFriend: x = 45
Line 5: In Friend Function two accessing private member variable x = 45
In class classIllusFriend: x = 88
Line 8: In Friend Function two accessing private member variable x = 88
```

For the most part, the output is self-explanatory. The statement in Line 15 calls the function two (a **friend** function of the **class** classIllusFriend) and passes the object aObject as an actual parameter. Notice that the function two generates the last four lines of the output.

Operator Functions as Member Functions and Nonmember Functions

The beginning of this chapter stated that certain rules must be followed when you include an operator function in the definition of a class. This section describes these rules.

Most operator functions can be either member functions or nonmember functions—that is, **friend** functions of a class. To make an operator function be a member or non-member function of a class, keep the following in mind:

1. The function that overloads any of the operators (), [], ->, or = for a class must be declared as a member of the class.

2. Suppose that an operator op is overloaded for a class—say, opOverClass. (Here, op stands for an operator that can be overloaded, such as + or >>.)

   a. If the leftmost operand of op is an object of a different type (that is, not of type opOverClass), the function that overloads the operator op for opOverClass must be a nonmember—that is, a friend of the **class** opOverClass.

   b. If the operator function that overloads the operator op for the **class** opOverClass is a member of the **class** opOverClass, then when applying op on objects of type opOverClass, the leftmost operand of op must be of type opOverClass.

You must follow these rules when including an operator function in a class definition.

You will see later in this chapter that functions that overload the insertion operator, <<, and the extraction operator, >>, for a class must be nonmembers—that is, **friend** functions of the class.

Except for certain operators noted previously, operators can be overloaded either as member functions or as nonmember functions. The following discussion shows the difference between these two types of functions.

To facilitate our discussion of operator overloading, we will use the **class rectangleType**, given next. (Although Chapter 12 defines this class, Chapter 12 is not a prerequisite for this chapter. For easy reference, we reproduce the definition of this class and the definitions of the member functions.)

```cpp
class rectangleType
{
public:
    void setDimension(double l, double w);
      //Function to set the length and width of the rectangle.
      //Postcondition: length = l; width = w;

    double getLength() const;
      //Function to return the length of the rectangle.
      //Postcondition: The value of length is returned.

    double getWidth() const;
      //Function to return the width of the rectangle.
      //Postcondition: The value of width is returned.

    double area() const;
      //Function to return the area of the rectangle.
      //Postcondition: The area of the rectangle is
      //               calculated and returned.

    double perimeter() const;
      //Function to return the perimeter of the rectangle.
      //Postcondition: The perimeter of the rectangle is
      //               calculated and returned.

    void print() const;
      //Function to output the length and width of
      //the rectangle.

    rectangleType();
      //Default constructor
      //Postcondition: length = 0; width = 0;

    rectangleType(double l, double w);
      //Constructor with parameters
      //Postcondition: length = l; width = w;
```

```cpp
private:
    double length;
    double width;
};
```

The definitions of the member functions of the **class** `rectangleType` are as follows:

```cpp
void rectangleType::setDimension(double l, double w)
{
    if (l >= 0)
        length = l;
    else
        length = 0;

    if (w >= 0)
        width = w;
    else
        width = 0;
}

double rectangleType::getLength() const
{
    return length;
}

double rectangleType::getWidth() const
{
    return width;
}

double rectangleType::area() const
{
    return length * width;
}

double rectangleType::perimeter() const
{
    return 2 * (length + width);
}

void rectangleType::print() const
{
    cout << "Length = "  << length
         << "; Width = " << width;
}

rectangleType::rectangleType(double l, double w)
{
    setDimension(l, w);
}
```

```
rectangleType::rectangleType()
{
    length = 0;
    width = 0;
}
```

The `class rectangleType` has two `private` member variables: `length` and `width`, both of type `double`. We will add operator functions to the `class rectangleType` as we overload the operators.

Also, suppose that you have the following statements:

```
rectangleType myRectangle;
rectangleType yourRectangle;
rectangleType tempRect;
```

That is, `myRectangle`, `yourRectangle`, and `tempRect` are objects of type `rectangleType`.

C++ consists of both binary and unary operators. It also has a ternary operator, which *cannot* be overloaded. The next few sections discuss how to overload various binary and unary operators.

Overloading Binary Operators

Suppose that `#` represents a binary operator (arithmetic, such as `+`; or relational, such as `==`) that is to be overloaded for the `class rectangleType`. This operator can be overloaded as either a member function of the class or as a `friend` function. We will describe both ways to overload this operator.

OVERLOADING THE BINARY OPERATORS AS MEMBER FUNCTIONS

Suppose that `#` is overloaded as a member function of the `class rectangleType`. The name of the function to overload `#` for the `class rectangleType` is:

`operator#`

Because `myRectangle` and `yourRectangle` are objects of type `rectangleType`, you can perform the operation:

`myRectangle # yourRectangle`

The compiler translates this expression into the following expression:

`myRectangle.operator#(yourRectangle)`

This expression clearly shows that the function `operator#` has only one parameter, which is `yourRectangle`.

Because `operator#` is a member of the `class rectangleType` and `myRectangle` is an object of type `rectangleType`, in the previous statement, `operator#` has direct access to the `private` members of the object `myRectangle`. Thus, the first parameter of `operator#` is the object that is invoking the function `operator#`, and the second parameter is passed as a parameter to this function.

GENERAL SYNTAX TO OVERLOAD THE BINARY (ARITHMETIC OR RELATIONAL) OPERATORS AS MEMBER FUNCTIONS

This section describes the general form of the functions to overload the binary operators as member functions of a class.

Function Prototype (to be included in the definition of the class):

```
returnType operator#(const className&) const;
```

where # stands for the binary operator, arithmetic or relational, to be overloaded; `returnType` is the type of value returned by the function; and `className` is the name of the class for which the operator is being overloaded.

Function Definition:

```
returnType className::operator#
                    (const className& otherObject) const
{
    //algorithm to perform the operation

    return value;
}
```

> **NOTE** The return type of the functions that overload relational operators is `bool`.

EXAMPLE 14-4

Let us overload +, *, ==, and != for the `class rectangleType`. These operators are overloaded as member functions:

```
class rectangleType
{
public:
    void setDimension(double l, double w);
    double getLength() const;
    double getWidth() const;
    double area() const;
    double perimeter() const;
    void print() const;

    rectangleType operator+(const rectangleType&) const;
        //Overload the operator +
    rectangleType operator*(const rectangleType&) const;
        //Overload the operator *
```

```cpp
    bool operator==(const rectangleType&) const;
      //Overload the operator ==
    bool operator!=(const rectangleType&) const;
      //Overload the operator !=

    rectangleType();
    rectangleType(double l, double w);

private:
    double length;
    double width;
};
```

The definition of the function **operator+** is as follows:

```cpp
rectangleType rectangleType::operator+
                      (const rectangleType& rectangle) const
{
    rectangleType tempRect;

    tempRect.length = length + rectangle.length;
    tempRect.width = width + rectangle.width;

    return tempRect;
}
```

Notice that **operator** + adds the corresponding lengths and widths of the two rectangles. The definition of the function **operator*** is as follows:

```cpp
rectangleType rectangleType::operator*
                      (const rectangleType& rectangle) const
{
    rectangleType tempRect;

    tempRect.length = length * rectangle.length;
    tempRect.width = width * rectangle.width;

    return tempRect;
}
```

Notice that **operator*** multiplies the corresponding lengths and widths of the two rectangles.

Two rectangles are equal if their lengths and widths are equal. Therefore, the definition of the function to overload the operator == is:

```cpp
bool rectangleType::operator==
                      (const rectangleType& rectangle) const
{
    return (length == rectangle.length &&
            width == rectangle.width);
}
```

Two rectangles are not equal if either their lengths are not equal or their widths are not equal. Therefore, the definition of the function to overload the operator `!=` is:

```cpp
bool rectangleType::operator!=
                        (const rectangleType& rectangle) const
{
    return (length != rectangle.length ||
            width != rectangle.width);
}
```

Consider the following program. (We assume that the definition of the `class` `rectangleType` is in the header file `rectangleType.h`.)

```cpp
#include <iostream>
#include "rectangleType.h"

using namespace std;

int main()
{
    rectangleType rectangle1(23, 45);               //Line 1
    rectangleType rectangle2(12, 10);               //Line 2
    rectangleType rectangle3;                       //Line 3
    rectangleType rectangle4;                       //Line 4

    cout << "Line 5: rectangle1: ";                 //Line 5
    rectangle1.print();                             //Line 6
    cout << endl;                                   //Line 7

    cout << "Line 8: rectangle2: ";                 //Line 8
    rectangle2.print();                             //Line 9
    cout << endl;                                   //Line 10

    rectangle3 = rectangle1 + rectangle2;           //Line 11

    cout << "Line 12: rectangle3: ";                //Line 12
    rectangle3.print();                             //Line 13
    cout << endl;                                   //Line 14

    rectangle4 = rectangle1 * rectangle2;           //Line 15

    cout << "Line 16: rectangle4: ";                //Line 16
    rectangle4.print();                             //Line 17
    cout << endl;                                   //Line 18

    if (rectangle1 == rectangle2)                   //Line 19
        cout << "Line 20: rectangle1 and "
             << "rectangle2 are equal." << endl;    //Line 20
    else                                            //Line 21
        cout << "Line 22: rectangle1 and "
             << "rectangle2 are not equal."
             << endl;                               //Line 22
```

```
    if (rectangle1 != rectangle3)                      //Line 23
        cout << "Line 24: rectangle1 and "
             << "rectangle3 are not equal."
             << endl;                                   //Line 24
    else                                                //Line 25
        cout << "Line 25: rectangle1 and "
             << "rectangle3 are equal." << endl;    //Line 26

    return 0;
}
```

Sample Run:

```
Line 5: rectangle1: Length = 23; Width = 45
Line 8: rectangle2: Length = 12; Width = 10
Line 12: rectangle3: Length = 35; Width = 55
Line 16: rectangle4: Length = 276; Width = 450
Line 22: rectangle1 and rectangle2 are not equal.
Line 24: rectangle1 and rectangle3 are not equal.
```

For the most part, the preceding output is self-explanatory. However, let us look at the statements in Lines 11, 15, 19, and 23. The statement in Line 11 uses the operator + to add the lengths and widths of `rectangle1` and `rectangle2` and stores the result in `rectangle3`. (That is, after the execution of this statement, the length of `rectangle3` is the sum of the lengths of `rectangle1` and `rectangle2`, and the width of `rectangle3` is the sum of the widths of `rectangle1` and `rectangle2`. The statement in Line 13 outputs the length and width of `rectangle3`.) Similarly, the statement in Line 15 uses the operator `*` to multiply the lengths and widths of `rectangle1` and `rectangle2` and stores the result in `rectangle4`. (The statement in Line 17 outputs the length and width of `rectangle4`.) The statement in Line 19 uses the relational operator `==` to determine whether the dimensions of `rectangle1` and `rectangle2` are the same. Similarly, the statement in Line 23 uses the relational operator `!=` to determine whether the dimensions of `rectangle1` and `rectangle3` are the same.

OVERLOADING THE BINARY OPERATORS (ARITHMETIC OR RELATIONAL) AS NONMEMBER FUNCTIONS

Suppose that `#` represents the binary operator (arithmetic or relational) that is to be overloaded as a *nonmember* function of the `class` rectangleType.

Further suppose that the following operation is to be performed:

```
myRectangle # yourRectangle
```

In this case, the expression is compiled as:

```
operator#(myRectangle, yourRectangle)
```

Here, we see that the function **operator#** has two parameters. This expression also clearly shows that the function **operator#** is neither a member of the object **myRectangle** nor a member of the object **yourRectangle**. Both the objects, **myRectangle** and **yourRectangle**, are passed as parameters to the function **operator#**.

To include the operator function **operator#** as a nonmember function of the class in the definition of the class, the reserved word **friend** must appear before the function heading. Also, the function **operator#** must have two parameters.

GENERAL SYNTAX TO OVERLOAD THE BINARY (ARITHMETIC OR RELATIONAL) OPERATORS AS NONMEMBER FUNCTIONS

This section describes the general form of the functions to overload the binary operators as nonmember functions of a class.

Function Prototype (to be included in the definition of the class):

```
friend returnType operator#(const className&,
                            const className&);
```

where # stands for the binary operator to be overloaded, **returnType** is the type of value returned by the function, and **className** is the name of the class for which the operator is being overloaded.

Function Definition:

```
returnType operator#(const className& firstObject,
                     const className& secondObject)
{
    //algorithm to perform the operation

    return value;
}
```

EXAMPLE 14-5

This example illustrates how to overload the operators + and == as nonmember functions of the **class rectangleType**.

To include the operator function **operator+** as a nonmember function of the **class rectangleType**, its prototype in the definition of **rectangleType** is:

```
friend rectangleType operator+(const rectangleType&,
                               const rectangleType&);
```

The definition of the function **operator+** is as follows:

```
rectangleType operator+(const rectangleType& firstRect,
                        const rectangleType& secondRect)
```

```
{
    rectangleType tempRect;

    tempRect.length = firstRect.length + secondRect.length;
    tempRect.width = firstRect.width + secondRect.width;

    return tempRect;
}
```

In the preceding definition, the corresponding member variables of `firstRect` and `secondRect` are added and the result is stored in `tempRect`. Recall that the `private` members of a class are local to the class, and, therefore, cannot be accessed outside the class. If we follow this rule, then because `operator+` is not a member of the `class` `rectangleType`, in its definition, expressions such as `firstRect.length` must be illegal because `length` is a `private` member of `firstRect`. However, because `operator+` was declared as a `friend` function of the `class` `rectangleType`, an object of type `rectangleType` can access its `private` members in the definition of `operator+`. Also, note that in the function heading, the name of the class—that is, `rectangleType`—and the scope resolution operator *are not included* before the name of the function `operator+`, because the function `operator+` is not a member of the class.

To include the operator function `operator==` as a nonmember function of the `class` `rectangleType`, its prototype in the definition of `rectangleType` is:

```
friend bool operator==(const rectangleType& ,
                       const rectangleType&);
```

The definition of the function `operator+` is as follows:

```
bool operator==(const rectangleType& firstRect,
                const rectangleType& secondRect)
{
    return (firstRect.length == secondRect.length &&
            firstRect.width == secondRect.width);
}
```

You can write a program similar to the one in Example 14-4 to test the overloading of the operators + and == as nonmembers.

Overloading the Stream Insertion (<<) and Extraction (>>) Operators

The operator function that overloads the insertion operator, <<, or the extraction operator, >>, for a class must be a nonmember function of that class for the following reason.

Consider the expression:

```
cout << myRectangle;
```

In this expression, the leftmost operand of << (that is, `cout`) is an `ostream` object, not an object of type `rectangleType`. Because the leftmost operand of << is not an object of type `rectangleType`, the operator function that overloads the insertion operator for `rectangleType` must be a *nonmember* function of the **class** `rectangleType`.

Similarly, the operator function that overloads the stream extraction operator for `rectangleType` must be a nonmember function of the **class** `rectangleType`.

OVERLOADING THE STREAM INSERTION OPERATOR (<<)

The general syntax to overload the stream insertion operator, <<, for a class is described next.

Function Prototype (to be included in the definition of the class):

```
friend ostream& operator<<(ostream&, const className&);
```

Function Definition:

```
ostream& operator<<(ostream& osObject, const className& cObject)
{
    //local declaration, if any
    //Output the members of cObject.
    //osObject << . . .

    //Return the stream object.
    return osObject;
}
```

In this function definition:

- Both parameters are reference parameters.
- The first parameter—that is, `osObject`— is a reference to an `ostream` object.
- The second parameter is usually a **const** reference to a particular class, because (recall from Chapter 11) the most effective way to pass an object as a parameter to a class is by reference. In this case, the formal parameter does not need to copy the member variables of the actual parameter. The word **const** appears before the class name because we want to print only the member variables of the object. That is, the function should not modify the member variables of the object.
- The function return type is a reference to an `ostream` object.

The return type of the function to overload the operator << must be a reference to an `ostream` object for the following reasons.

Suppose that the operator << is overloaded for the **class** `rectangleType`. The statement:

```
cout << myRectangle;
```

is equivalent to the statement:

```
operator<<(cout, myRectangle);
```

This is a perfectly legal statement because both of the actual parameters are objects, not the value of the objects. The first parameter, `cout`, is of type `ostream`; the second parameter, `myRectangle`, is of type `rectangleType`.

Now consider the following statement:

```
cout << myRectangle << yourRectangle;
```

This statement is equivalent to the statement:

```
operator<<(operator<<(cout, myRectangle), yourRectangle); //Line A
```

because the associativity of the operator `<<` is from left to right.

To execute the previous statement, you must first execute the expression:

```
cout << myRectangle
```

that is, the expression:

```
operator<<(cout, myRectangle)
```

After executing this expression, which outputs the value of `myRectangle`, whatever is returned by the function `operator` `<<` will become the left-side parameter of the operator `<<` (that is, the first parameter of the function `operator<<`) in order to output the value of object `yourRectangle` (see the statement in Line A). Because the left-side parameter of the operator `<<` must be an object of the `ostream` type, the expression:

```
cout << myRectangle
```

must return the object `cout` (not its value) in order to output the value of `yourRectangle`.

Therefore, the return type of the function `operator<<` must be a reference to an object of the `ostream` type.

OVERLOADING THE STREAM EXTRACTION OPERATOR (>>)

The general syntax to overload the stream extraction operator, >>, for a class is described next.

Function Prototype (to be included in the definition of the class):

```
friend istream& operator>>(istream&, className&);
```

Function Definition:

```
istream& operator>>(istream& isObject, className& cObject)
{
        //local declaration, if any
        //Read the data into cObject.
        //isObject >> . . .

        //Return the stream object.
    return isObject;
}
```

In this function definition:

- Both parameters are reference parameters.
- The first parameter—that is, `isObject`—is a reference to an `istream` object.
- The second parameter is usually a reference to a particular class. The data read will be stored in the object.
- The function return type is a reference to an `istream` object.

For the same reasons as explained previously (when we overloaded the insertion operator `<<`), the return type of the function `operator>>` must be a reference to an `istream` object. We can then successfully execute statements of the following type:

```
cin >> myRectangle >> yourRectangle;
```

Example 14-6 shows how the stream insertion and extraction operators are overloaded for the **class** `rectangleType`.

EXAMPLE 14-6

The definition of the **class** `rectangleType` and the definitions of the operator functions are:

```cpp
#include <iostream>

using namespace std;

class rectangleType
{
        //Overload the stream insertion and extraction operators
    friend ostream& operator<< (ostream&, const rectangleType &);
    friend istream& operator>> (istream&, rectangleType &);

public:
    void setDimension(double l, double w);
    double getLength() const;
    double getWidth() const;
    double area() const;
    double perimeter() const;
    void print() const;

    rectangleType operator+(const rectangleType&) const;
        //Overload the operator +
    rectangleType operator*(const rectangleType&) const;
        //Overload the operator *

    bool operator==(const rectangleType&) const;
        //Overload the operator ==
    bool operator!=(const rectangleType&) const;
        //Overload the operator !=
```

```
    rectangleType();
    rectangleType(double l, double w);

private:
    double length;
    double width;
};
```

Notice that we have removed the member function `print` because we are overloading the stream insertion operator <<:

```
//The definitions of the functions operator+, operator*,
//operator==, and operator!= are the same as in Example 14-5.
```

```
ostream& operator<< (ostream& osObject,
                     const rectangleType& rectangle)
{
    osObject << "Length = "  << rectangle.length
             << "; Width = " << rectangle.width;

    return osObject;
}

istream& operator>> (istream& isObject,
                     rectangleType& rectangle)
{
    isObject >> rectangle.length >> rectangle.width;

    return isObject;
}
```

Consider the following program. (We assume that the definition of the `class` `rectangleType` is in the header file `rectangleType.h`.)

```
#include <iostream>

#include "rectangleType.h"

using namespace std;

int main()
{
    rectangleType myRectangle(23, 45);              //Line 1
    rectangleType yourRectangle;                    //Line 2

    cout << "Line 3: myRectangle: " << myRectangle
         << endl;                                   //Line 3

    cout << "Line 4: Enter the length and width "
         <<"of a rectangle: ";                      //Line 4
    cin >> yourRectangle;                           //Line 5
    cout << endl;                                   //Line 6
```

```cpp
    cout << "Line 7: yourRectangle: "
         << yourRectangle << endl;                    //Line 7

    cout << "Line 8: myRectangle + yourRectangle: "
         << myRectangle + yourRectangle << endl;      //Line 8
    cout << "Line 9: myRectangle * yourRectangle: "
         << myRectangle * yourRectangle << endl;      //Line 9

    return 0;
}
```

Sample Run: In this sample run, the user input is shaded.

```
Line 3: myRectangle: Length = 23; Width = 45
Line 4: Enter the length and width of a rectangle: 32 15

Line 7: yourRectangle: Length = 32; Width = 15
Line 8: myRectangle + yourRectangle: Length = 55; Width = 60
Line 9: myRectangle * yourRectangle: Length = 736; Width = 675
```

The statements in Lines 1 and 2 declare and initialize `myRectangle` and `yourRectangle` to be objects of type `rectangleType`. The statement in Line 3 outputs the value of `myRectangle` using `cout` and the insertion operator. The statement in Line 5 inputs the data into `yourRectangle` using `cin` and the extraction operator. The statement in Line 7 outputs the value of `yourRectangle` using `cout` and the insertion operator. The `cout` statement in Line 8 adds the lengths and widths of `myRectangle` and `yourRectangle` and outputs the result. Similarly, the `cout` statement in Line 9 multiplies the lengths and widths of `myRectangle` and `yourRectangle` and outputs the result. The output shows that both the stream insertion and stream extraction operators were overloaded successfully.

Overloading the Assignment Operator (=)

One of the built-in operations on classes is the assignment operation. The assignment operator causes a member-wise copy of the member variables of the class. For example, the statement:

```cpp
myRectangle = yourRectangle;
```

is equivalent to the statements:

```cpp
myRectangle.length = yourRectangle.length;
myRectangle.width = yourRectangle.width;
```

From Chapter 13, recall that the built-in assignment operator works well for classes that do not have pointer member variables, but not for classes with pointer member variables. Therefore, to avoid the shallow copy of data for classes with pointer member variables, we must explicitly overload the assignment operator.

Recall that to overload the assignment operator = for a class, the operator function `operator=` must be a member of that class.

GENERAL SYNTAX TO OVERLOAD THE ASSIGNMENT OPERATOR = FOR A CLASS

The general syntax to overload the assignment operator = for a class is described next.

Function Prototype (to be included in the definition of the class):

```cpp
const className& operator=(const className&);
```

Function Definition:

```cpp
const className& className::operator=
                            (const className& rightObject)
{
    //local declaration, if any

    if (this != &rightObject)   //avoid self-assignment
    {
        //algorithm to copy rightObject into this object
    }

    //Return the object assigned.
    return *this;
}
```

In the definition of the function **operator=**:

- There is only one formal parameter.
- The formal parameter is usually a **const** reference to a particular class.
- The function return type is a constant reference to a particular class.

We now explain why the return type of the function **operator=** should be a reference of the class type.

Suppose that the assignment operator = is overloaded for the **class rectangleType**. The statement:

```cpp
myRectangle = yourRectangle;
```

is equivalent to the statement:

```cpp
myRectangle.operator=(yourRectangle);
```

That is, the object **yourRectangle** becomes the actual parameter to the function

operator=.

Now consider the statement:

```cpp
myRectangle = yourRectangle = tempRect;
```

Because the associativity of the operator = is from right to left, this statement is equivalent to the statement:

```cpp
myRectangle.operator=(yourRectangle.operator=(tempRect)); //Line A
```

Clearly, we must first execute the expression:

```
yourRectangle.operator=(tempRect)
```

that is, the expression:

```
yourRectangle = tempRect
```

The value returned by the expression:

```
yourRectangle.operator=(tempRect)
```

will become the parameter to the function `operator=` in order to assign a value to the object `myRectangle` (see the statement in Line A). Because the formal parameter of the function `operator=` is a reference parameter, the expression:

```
yourRectangle.operator=(tempRect)
```

must return a reference to the object, rather than its value. That is, it must return a reference to the object `yourRectangle`, not the value of `yourRectangle`. For this reason, the return type of the function to overload the assignment operator = for a class must be a reference to the class type.

Now consider the statement:

```
myRectangle = myRectangle;                    //Line B
```

Here, we are trying to copy the value of `myRectangle` into `myRectangle`; that is, this statement is a self-assignment. One reason why we must prevent such assignments is because they waste computer time. First, however, we explain how the body of the assignment operator prevents such assignments.

As noted above, the body of the function `operator=` does prevent assignments, such as the one given in Line B. Let us see how.

Consider the `if` statement in the body of the operator function `operator=`:

```
if (this != &rightObject)   //avoid self-assignment
{
    //algorithm to copy rightObject into this object
}
```

The statement:

```
myRectangle = myRectangle;
```

is compiled into the statement:

```
myRectangle.operator=(myRectangle);
```

Because the function `operator=` is invoked by the object `myRectangle`, the pointer `this` in the body of the function `operator=` refers to the object `myRectangle`. Furthermore, because `myRectangle` is also a parameter of the function `operator=`, the formal parameter `rightObject` also refers to the object `myRectangle`. Therefore, in the expression:

```
this != &rightObject
```

`this` and `&rightObject` both mean the address of `myRectangle`. Thus, the expression will evaluate to `false` and, therefore, the body of the `if` statement will be skipped.

NOTE This note illustrates another reason why the body of the operator function must prevent self-assignments. Let us consider the following class:

```cpp
class arrayClass
{
public:
    const arrayClass& operator= (const& arrayClass);
        .
        .
        .
private:
    int *list;
    int length;
    int maxSize;
};
```

The `class arrayClass` has a pointer member variable, `list`, which is used to create an array to store integers. Suppose that the definition of the function to overload the assignment operator for the `class arrayClass` is written without the `if` statement, as follows:

```cpp
const arrayClass & arrayClass::operator=
                (const arrayClass& otherList)
{
    delete [] list;                         //Line 1
    maxSize = otherList.maxSize;            //Line 2
    length = otherList.length;             //Line 3

    list = new int[maxSize];               //Line 4

    for (int i = 0; i < length; i++)       //Line 5
        list[i] = otherList.list[i];       //Line 6

    return *this;                          //Line 7
}
```

Suppose that we have the following declaration in a user program:

```cpp
arrayClass myList;
```

Consider the following statement:

```cpp
myList = myList;
```

This is a self-assignment. When this statement executes in the body of the function `operator=`:

1. `list` means `myList.list`, `maxSize` means `myList.maxSize`, and `length` means `myList.length`.

2. `otherList` is the same as `myList`.

The statement in Line 1 destroys `list`, that is, `myList.list`, and so the array holding the numbers no longer exists. That is, it is not valid. The problem is in Line 6. Here, the expression `list[i] = otherList.list[i]` is equivalent to the statement `myList.list[i] = myList.list[i]`. Because `myList.list[i]` has no valid data (it was destroyed in Line 1), the statement in Line 6 produces garbage.

It follows that the definition of the function `operator=` must prevent self-assignments. The correct definition of `operator=` for the `class arrayClass` is:

```cpp
const arrayClass& arrayClass::operator=
                      (const arrayClass& otherList)
{
    if (this != & otherList)                     //Line 1
    {
        delete [] list;                          //Line 2
        maxSize = otherList.maxSize;             //Line 3
        length = otherList.length;               //Line 4

        list = new int[maxSize];                 //Line 5

        for (int i = 0; i < length; i++)         //Line 6
            list[i] = otherList.list[i];         //Line 7
    }

    return *this;                                //Line 8
}
```

The following example illustrates how to overload the assignment operator.

EXAMPLE 14-7

Consider the following class:

```cpp
class cAssignmentOprOverload
{
public:
    const cAssignmentOprOverload&
            operator=(const cAssignmentOprOverload& otherList);
        //Overload assignment operator
```

```cpp
    void print() const;
      //Function to print the list
    void insertEnd(int item);
      //Function to insert an item at the end of the list
      //Postcondition: if the list is not full,
      //                     length++; list[length] = item;
      //                 if the list is full,
      //                     output an appropriate message
    void destroyList();
      //Function to destroy the list
      //Postcondition: length = 0; maxSize = 0; list = NULL;

    cAssignmentOprOverload(int size = 0);
      //Constructor
      //Postcondition: length = 0; maxSize = size;
      //                 list is an arry of size maxSize

private:
    int maxSize;
    int length;
    int *list;
};
```

The definitions of the member functions of the **class** `cAssignmentOprOverload` are:

```cpp
void cAssignmentOprOverload::print() const
{
    if (length == 0)
        cout << "The list is empty." << endl;
    else
    {
        for (int i = 0; i < length; i++)
            cout << list[i] << " ";
        cout << endl;
    }
}

void cAssignmentOprOverload::insertEnd(int item)
{
    if (length == maxSize)
        cout << "List is full" << endl;
    else
        list[length++] = item;
}

void cAssignmentOprOverload::destroyList()
{
    delete [] list;
    list = NULL;
    length = 0;
    maxSize = 0;
}
```

```cpp
cAssignmentOprOverload::cAssignmentOprOverload(int size)
{
    maxSize = size;
    length = 0;

    if (maxSize == 0)
        list = NULL;
    else
        list = new int[maxSize];
}

const cAssignmentOprOverload& cAssignmentOprOverload::operator=
                   (const cAssignmentOprOverload& otherList)
{
    if (this != &otherList)   //avoid self-assignment; Line 1
    {
        delete [] list;                             //Line 2
        maxSize = otherList.maxSize;                //Line 3
        length = otherList.length;                  //Line 4

        list = new int[maxSize];                    //Line 5

        for (int i = 0; i < length; i++)            //Line 6
            list[i] = otherList.list[i];            //Line 7
    }

    return *this;                                   //Line 8
}
```

The function to overload the assignment operator works as follows. The statement in Line 1 checks whether an object is copying itself. The statement in Line 2 destroys `list`. The statements in Lines 3 and 4 copy the values of the member variables `maxSize` and `length` of `otherList` into the member variables `maxSize` and `length` of `list`, respectively. The statement in Line 5 creates the array to store the numbers. The `for` loop in Line 6 copies `otherList` into `list`. The statement in Line 8 returns the address of this object, because the return type of the function `operator=` is a reference type.

The following function tests the `class cAssignmentOprOverload`:

```cpp
#include <iostream>

#include "classAssignmentOverload.h"

using namespace std;
int main()
{
    cAssignmentOprOverload intList1(10);            //Line 9
    cAssignmentOprOverload intList2;                //Line 10
    cAssignmentOprOverload intList3;                //Line 11
```

```cpp
    int i;                                      //Line 12
    int number;                                 //Line 13

    cout << "Line 14: Enter 5 integers: ";      //Line 14

    for (i = 0; i < 5; i++)                      //Line 15
    {
        cin >> number;                          //Line 16
        intList1.insertEnd(number);             //Line 17
    }

    cout << endl;                               //Line 18
    cout << "Line 19: intList1: ";              //Line 19
    intList1.print();                           //Line 20

    intList3 = intList2 = intList1;             //Line 21

    cout << "Line 22: intList2: ";              //Line 22
    intList2.print();                           //Line 23

    intList2.destroyList();                     //Line 24

    cout << endl;                               //Line 25
    cout << "Line 26: intList2: ";              //Line 26
    intList2.print();                           //Line 27

    cout << "Line 28: After destroying intList2, "
         << "intList1: ";                       //Line 28
    intList1.print();                           //Line 29

    cout << "Line 30: After destroying intList2, "
         << "intList3: ";                       //Line 30
    intList3.print();                           //Line 31
    cout << endl;                               //Line 32

    return 0;
}
```

Sample Run: In this sample run, the user input is shaded.

```
Line 14: Enter 5 integers: 8 5 3 7 2

Line 19: intList1: 8 5 3 7 2
Line 22: intList2: 8 5 3 7 2

Line 26: intList2: The list is empty.
Line 28: After destroying intList2, intList1: 8 5 3 7 2
Line 30: After destroying intList2, intList3: 8 5 3 7 2
```

The statement in Line 9 creates `intList1` of size 10; the statements in Lines 10 and 11 create `intList2` and `intList3` of (default) size 50. The statements in Lines 15 through 17 input the data into `intList1`, and the statement in Line 20 outputs `intList1`. The statement in Line 21 copies `intList1` into `intList2`, and then copies `intList2` into `intList3`. The statement in Line 23 outputs `intList2` (see Line 22 in the sample run, which contains the output of Lines 22 and 23). The statement in Line 24 destroys `intList2`. The statement in Line 27 outputs `intList2`, which is empty. (See Line 26 in the sample run, which contains the output of Lines 26 and 27.) After destroying `intList2`, the program outputs the contents of `intList1` and `intList3` (see Lines 28 and 30 in the sample run). The sample run clearly shows that the destruction of `intList2` affects neither `intList1` nor `intList3`, because `intList1` and `intList3` each have their own data.

Overloading Unary Operators

The process of overloading unary operators is similar to the process of overloading binary operators. The only difference is that in the case of binary operators, the operator has two operands. In the case of unary operators, the operator has only one parameter. Therefore, to overload a unary operator for a class:

1.   If the operator function is a member of the class, it has no parameters.

2.   If the operator function is a nonmember—that is, a **friend** function of the class—it has one parameter.

Next, we describe how to overload the increment and decrement operators.

OVERLOADING THE INCREMENT (++) AND DECREMENT (−−) OPERATORS

The increment operator has two forms: pre-increment (++u) and post-increment (u++), where u is a variable, say, of type **int**. In the case of pre-increment, ++u, the value of the variable, u, is incremented by 1 before the value of u is used in an expression. In the case of post-increment, the value of u is used in the expression before it is incremented by 1.

Overloading the Pre-Increment Operator. Overloading the pre-increment operator is quite straightforward. In the function definition, first we increment the value of the object and then use the pointer **this** to return the object's value.

For example, suppose that we overload the pre-increment operator for the **class** `rectangleType` to increment the length and width of a rectangle by 1. Also, suppose that the operator function **operator++** is a member of the **class** `rectangleType`. The operator function **operator++** then has no parameters. Because the operator function **operator++** has no parameters, we use the pointer **this** to return the incremented value of the object:

```
rectangleType rectangleType::operator++()
{
        //increment the length and width
    ++length;
    ++width;
```

```
    return *this; //return the incremented value of the object
}
```

Because `myRectangle` is an object of type `rectangleType`, the statement:

```
++myRectangle;
```

increments the values of the length and width of `myRectangle` by 1. Moreover, the pointer `this` associated with `myRectangle` returns the incremented value of `myRectangle`, which is ignored.

Now `yourRectangle` is also an object of type `rectangleType` and so the statement:

```
yourRectangle = ++myRectangle;
```

increments the length and width of `myRectangle` by 1, and the pointer `this` associated with `myRectangle` returns the incremented value of `myRectangle`, which is copied into `yourRectangle`.

GENERAL SYNTAX TO OVERLOAD THE PRE-INCREMENT OPERATOR ++ AS A MEMBER FUNCTION

The general syntax to overload the pre-increment operator ++ as a member function is described next.

Function Prototype (to be included in the definition of the class):

```
className operator++();
```

Function Definition:

```
className className::operator++()
{
    //increment the value of the object by 1
    return *this;
}
```

The operator function to overload the pre-increment operator can also be a nonmember of the **class** rectangleType, which we describe next.

Because the operator function **operator**++ is a nonmember function of the **class** rectangleType, it has one parameter, which is an object of type `rectangleType`. (As before, we assume that the increment operator increments the length and width of a rectangle by 1.)

```
rectangleType operator++(rectangleType& rectangle)
{
        //increment the length and width of the rectangle
    (rectangle.length)++;
    (rectangle.width)++;
    return rectangle; //return the incremented
                      //value of the object
}
```

GENERAL SYNTAX TO OVERLOAD THE PRE-INCREMENT OPERATOR ++ AS A NONMEMBER FUNCTION

The general syntax to overload the pre-increment operator ++ as a nonmember function is described next.

Function Prototype (to be included in the definition of the class):

```
friend className operator++(className&);
```

Function Definition:

```
className operator++(className& incObj)
{
        //increment incObj by 1
    return incObj;
}
```

OVERLOADING THE POST-INCREMENT OPERATOR

We now discuss how to overload the post-increment operator. As in the case of the pre-increment operator, we first describe the overloading of this operator as a member of a class.

Let us overload the post-increment operator for the **class rectangleType**. In both cases, pre- and post-increment, the name of the operator function is the same—**operator++**. To distinguish between pre- and post-increment operator overloading, we use a dummy parameter (of type **int**) in the function heading of the operator function. Thus, the function prototype for the post-increment operator of the **class rectangleType** is:

```
rectangleType operator++(int);
```

The statement:

```
myRectangle++;
```

is compiled by the compiler in the statement:

```
myRectangle.operator++(0);
```

and so the function **operator++** with a parameter executes. The parameter 0 is used merely to distinguish between the pre- and post-increment operator functions.

The post-increment operator first uses the value of the object in the expression and then increments the value of the object. So the steps required to implement this function are:

1. Save the value of the object—in, say, **temp**.
2. Increment the value of the object.
3. Return the value that was saved in **temp**.

The function definition of the post-increment operator for the **class rectangleType** is:

```
rectangleType rectangleType::operator++(int u)
{
```

```
    rectangleType temp = *this;   //use this pointer to copy
                                  //the value of the object

        //increment the length and width
    length++;
    width++;

    return temp;    //return the old value of the object
}
```

GENERAL SYNTAX TO OVERLOAD THE POST-INCREMENT OPERATOR ++ AS A MEMBER FUNCTION

The general syntax to overload the post-increment operator ++ as a member function is described next.

Function Prototype (to be included in the definition of the class):

```
className operator++(int);
```

Function Definition:

```
className className::operator++(int u)
{
    className temp = *this;      //use this pointer to copy
                                //the value of the object
        //increment the object

    return temp;   //return the old value of the object
}
```

The post-increment operator can also be overloaded as a nonmember function of the class. In this situation, the operator function `operator++` has two parameters. The definition of the function to overload the post-increment operator for the **class** `rectangleType` as a nonmember is:

```
rectangleType operator++(rectangleType& rectangle, int u)
{
    rectangleType temp = rectangle; //copy rectangle into temp

        //increment the length and width of rectangle
    (rectangle.length)++;
    (rectangle.width)++;

    return temp;    //return the old value of the object
}
```

GENERAL SYNTAX TO OVERLOAD THE POST-INCREMENT OPERATOR ++ AS A NONMEMBER FUNCTION

The general syntax to overload the post-increment operator ++ as a nonmember function is described next.

Function Prototype (to be included in the definition of the class):

```cpp
friend className operator++(className&, int);
```

Function Definition:

```cpp
className operator++(className& incObj, int u)
{
    className temp = incObj; //copy incObj into temp

        //increment incObj

    return temp;    //return the old value of the object
}
```

The decrement operators can be overloaded in a similar way, the details of which are left as an exercise for you.

Let us now write the definition of the **class** rectangleType and show how the operator functions appear in the class definition. Because certain operators can be overloaded as either member or nonmember functions, we give two equivalent definitions of the **class** rectangleType. In the first definition, the increment, decrement, arithmetic, and relational operators are overloaded as member functions. In the second definition, the increment, decrement, arithmetic, and relational operators are overloaded as nonmember functions.

The definition of the **class** rectangleType is as follows:

```cpp
//Definition of the class rectangleType
//The increment, decrement, arithmetic, and relational
//operator functions are members of the class.

#include <iostream>

using namespace std;

class rectangleType
{
        //Overload the stream insertion and extraction operators
    friend ostream& operator<<(ostream&, const rectangleType &);
    friend istream& operator>>(istream&, rectangleType &);

public:
    void setDimension(double l, double w);
    double getLength() const;
    double getWidth() const;
    double area() const;
    double perimeter() const;

        //Overload the arithmetic operators
    rectangleType operator+(const rectangleType &) const;
    rectangleType operator-(const rectangleType &) const;
```

```cpp
    rectangleType operator*(const rectangleType&) const;
    rectangleType operator/(const rectangleType&) const;

        //Overload the increment and decrement operators
    rectangleType operator++();            //pre-increment
    rectangleType operator++(int);         //post-increment
    rectangleType operator--();            //pre-decrement
    rectangleType operator--(int);         //post-decrement

        //Overload the relational operators
    bool operator==(const rectangleType&) const;
    bool operator!=(const rectangleType&) const;
    bool operator<=(const rectangleType&) const;
    bool operator<(const rectangleType&) const;
    bool operator>=(const rectangleType&) const;
    bool operator>(const rectangleType&) const;

        //Constructors
    rectangleType();
    rectangleType(double l, double w);

private:
    double length;
    double width;
};
```

Following is the definition of the **class** rectangleType, in which the increment, decrement, arithmetic, and relational operators are overloaded as nonmembers:

```cpp
//Definition of the class rectangleType
//The increment, decrement, arithmetic, and relational
//operator functions are nonmembers of the class.

#include <iostream>

using namespace std;

class rectangleType
{
        //Overload the stream insertion and extraction operators
    friend ostream& operator<<(ostream&, const rectangleType&);
    friend istream& operator>>(istream&, rectangleType&);

        //Overload the arithmetic operators
    friend rectangleType operator+(const rectangleType&,
                                   const rectangleType&);
    friend rectangleType operator-(const rectangleType&,
                                   const rectangleType&);
    friend rectangleType operator*(const rectangleType&,
                                   const rectangleType&);
    friend rectangleType operator/(const rectangleType&,
                                   const rectangleType&);
```

```
    //Overload the increment and decrement operators
friend rectangleType operator++(rectangleType&);
  //pre-increment
friend rectangleType operator++(rectangleType&, int);
  //post-increment
friend rectangleType operator--(rectangleType&);
  //pre-decrement
friend rectangleType operator--(rectangleType&, int);
  //post-decrement

    //Overload the relational operators
friend bool operator==(const rectangleType&,
                       const rectangleType&);
friend bool operator!=(const rectangleType&,
                       const rectangleType&);
friend bool operator<=(const rectangleType&,
                       const rectangleType&);
friend bool operator<(const rectangleType&,
                      const rectangleType&);
friend bool operator>=(const rectangleType&,
                       const rectangleType&);
friend bool operator>(const rectangleType&,
                      const rectangleType&);

public:
    void setDimension(double l, double w);
    double getLength() const;
    double getWidth() const;
    double area() const;
    double perimeter() const;

    //Constructors
    rectangleType();
    rectangleType(double l, double w);

private:
    double length;
    double width;
};
```

The definitions of the functions to overload the operators for the **class** `rectangleType` are left as an exercise for you. (See Programming Exercises 1 and 2 at the end of this chapter.)

Operator Overloading: Member versus Nonmember

The preceding sections discussed and illustrated how to overload operators. Certain operators must be overloaded as member functions of the class, and some must be overloaded as nonmember (**friend**) functions. What about the operators that can be overloaded as either member functions or nonmember functions? For example, the binary arithmetic operator + can be overloaded as a member function or a nonmember function. If you overload + as a member function, then the operator + has direct access to the member variables of one of the objects, and you need to pass only one object as a parameter. On the other hand, if you overload + as a nonmember function, then you must pass both objects as parameters. Therefore, overloading + as a nonmember could require additional memory and computer time to make a local copy of the data. Thus, for efficiency purposes, wherever possible, you should overload operators as member functions.

Classes and Pointer Member Variables (Revisited)

Chapter 13 described the peculiarities of classes with pointer member variables. Now that we have discussed how to overload various operators, let us review the peculiarities of classes with pointer member variables, for the sake of completeness, and how to avoid them.

Recall that the only built-in operations on classes are assignment and member selection. The assignment operator provides a member-wise copy of the data. That is, the member variables of an object are copied into the corresponding member variables of another object of the same type. We have seen that this member-wise copy does not work well for classes with pointer member variables. Other problems that may arise with classes with pointer member variables relate to deallocating dynamic memory when an object goes out of scope, and passing a class object as a parameter by value. To resolve these problems, classes with pointer member variables must:

1.   Explicitly overload the assignment operator
2.   Include the copy constructor
3.   Include the destructor

Operator Overloading: One Final Word

Next, we look at three examples that illustrate operator overloading. Before delving into these examples, you must remember the following: Suppose that an operator op is overloaded for a **class**—say, `rectangleType`. Whenever we use the operator op on objects of type `rectangleType`, the body of the function that overloads the operator op for the **class** `rectangleType` executes. Therefore, whatever code you put in the body of the function executes.

PROGRAMMING EXAMPLE: clockType

Chapter 11 defined a **class** `clockType` to implement the time of day in a program. We implemented the operations to print the time, increment the time, and compare the two times for equality using functions. This example redefines the **class** `clockType`. It also overloads the stream insertion and extraction operators for easy input and output, relational operators for comparisons, and the increment operator to increment the time by one second. The program that uses the **class** `clockType` requires the user to input the time in the form `hr:min:sec`.

The definition of the **class** clockType is as follows:

```cpp
//Header file newClock.h

#ifndef H_newClock
#define H_newClock

#include <iostream>

using namespace std;

class clockType
{
    friend ostream& operator<<(ostream&, const clockType&);
    friend istream& operator>>(istream&, clockType&);

public:
    void setTime(int hours, int minutes, int seconds);
    //Function to set the member variables hr, min, and sec.
    //Postcondition: hr = hours; min = minutes; sec = seconds;

    void getTime(int& hours, int& minutes, int& seconds) const;
    //Function to return the time.
    //Postcondition: hours = hr; minutes = min; seconds = sec;

    clockType operator++();
    //Overload the pre-increment operator.
    //Postcondition: The time is incremented by one second.

    bool operator==(const clockType& otherClock) const;
    //Overload the equality operator.
    //Postcondition: Returns true if the time of this clock
    //               is equal to the time of otherClock,
    //               otherwise it returns false.

    bool operator!=(const clockType& otherClock) const;
    //Overload the not equal operator.
    //Postcondition: Returns true if the time of this clock
    //               is not equal to the time of otherClock,
    //               otherwise it returns false.

    bool operator<=(const clockType& otherClock) const;
    //Overload the less than or equal to operator.
    //Postcondition: Returns true if the time of this clock
    //               is less than or equal to the time of
    //               otherClock, otherwise it returns false.

    bool operator<(const clockType& otherClock) const;
    //Overload the less than operator.
    //Postcondition: Returns true if the time of this clock
    //               is less than the time of otherClock,
    //               otherwise it returns false.
```

```cpp
    bool operator>=(const clockType& otherClock) const;
      //Overload the greater than or equal to operator.
      //Postcondition: Returns true if the time of this clock
      //               is greater than or equal to the time of
      //               otherClock, otherwise it returns false.

    bool operator>(const clockType& otherClock) const;
      //Overload the greater than operator.
      //Postcondition: Returns true if the time of this clock
      //               is greater than the time of otherClock,
      //               otherwise it returns false.

    clockType(int hours = 0, int minutes = 0, int seconds = 0);
      //Constructor to initialize the object with the values
      //specified by the user. If no values are specified,
      //the default values are assumed.
      //Postcondition: hr = hours; min = minutes;
      //               sec = seconds;


private:
    int hr;   //variable to store the hours
    int min;  //variable to store the minutes
    int sec;  //variable to store the seconds
};

#endif
```

Figure 14-1 shows a UML class diagram of the **class** clockType.

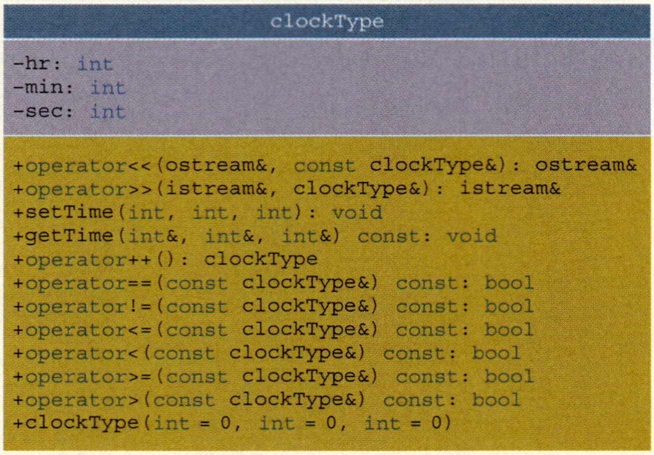

FIGURE 14-1 UML class diagram of the **class** clockType

Let us now write the definitions of the functions to implement the operations of the **class** clockType. Notice that the **class** clockType overloads only the pre-increment operator. For consistency, however, the class should also overload the post-increment operator. This step is left as an exercise for you. (See Programming Exercise 3 at the end of this chapter.)

First, we write the definition of the function operator++. The algorithm to increment the time by one second is as follows:

    a.   Increment the seconds by 1.

    b.   If seconds > 59,

        b.1.   Set the seconds to 0.

        b.2.   Increment the minutes by 1.

        b.3.   If minutes > 59,

            b.3.1.   Set the minutes to 0.

            b.3.2.   Increment the hours by 1.

            b.3.3.   If hours > 23,

                b.3.3.1.   Set the hours to 0.

    c.   Return the incremented value of the object.

The definition of the function operator++ is:

```cpp
    //Overload the pre-increment operator.
clockType clockType::operator++()
{
    sec++;                      //Step a

    if (sec > 59)               //Step b
    {
        sec = 0;                //Step b.1
        min++;                  //Step b.2

        if (min > 59)           //Step b.3
        {
            min = 0;            //Step b.3.1
            hr++;               //Step b.3.2

            if (hr > 23)        //Step b.3.3
                hr = 0;         //Step b.3.3.1
        }
    }

    return *this;               //Step c
}
```

The definition of the function `operator==` is quite simple. The two times are the same if they have the same hours, minutes, and seconds. Therefore, the definition of the function `operator==` is:

```cpp
    //Overload the equality operator.
bool clockType::operator==(const clockType& otherClock) const
{
    return (hr == otherClock.hr && min == otherClock.min
            && sec == otherClock.sec);
}
```

The definition of the function `operator<=` is given next. The first time is less than or equal to the second time if:

1. The hours of the first time are less than the hours of the second time, or

2. The hours of the first time and the second time are the same, but the minutes of the first time are less than the minutes of the second time, or

3. The hours and minutes of the first time and the second time are the same, but the seconds of the first time are less than or equal to the seconds of the second time.

The definition of the function `operator<=` is:

```cpp
    //Overload the less than or equal to operator.
bool clockType::operator<=(const clockType& otherClock) const
{
    return ((hr < otherClock.hr) ||
            (hr == otherClock.hr && min < otherClock.min) ||
            (hr == otherClock.hr && min == otherClock.min &&
             sec <= otherClock.sec));
}
```

In a similar manner, we can write the definitions of the other relational operator functions as follows:

```cpp
    //Overload the not equal operator.
bool clockType::operator!=(const clockType& otherClock) const
{
    return (hr != otherClock.hr || min != otherClock.min
            || sec != otherClock.sec);
}
```

```cpp
    //Overload the less than operator.
bool clockType::operator<(const clockType& otherClock) const
{
    return ((hr < otherClock.hr) ||
            (hr == otherClock.hr && min < otherClock.min) ||
            (hr == otherClock.hr && min == otherClock.min &&
             sec < otherClock.sec));
}
```

```cpp
    //Overload the greater than or equal to operator.
bool clockType::operator>=(const clockType& otherClock) const
{
    return ((hr > otherClock.hr) ||
            (hr == otherClock.hr && min > otherClock.min) ||
            (hr == otherClock.hr && min == otherClock.min &&
             sec >= otherClock.sec));
}

    //Overload the greater than or equal to operator.
bool clockType::operator>(const clockType& otherClock) const
{
    return ((hr > otherClock.hr) ||
            (hr == otherClock.hr && min > otherClock.min) ||
            (hr == otherClock.hr && min == otherClock.min &&
             sec > otherClock.sec));
}
```

The definitions of the functions `setTime` and `getTime` are the same as given in Chapter 11. They are included here for the sake of completeness. Moreover, we have modified the definition of the constructor so that it uses the function `setTime` to set the time. The definitions are as follows:

```cpp
void clockType::setTime(int hours, int minutes, int seconds)
{
    if (0 <= hours && hours < 24)
        hr = hours;
    else
        hr = 0;

    if (0 <= minutes && minutes < 60)
        min = minutes;
    else
        min = 0;

    if (0 <= seconds && seconds < 60)
        sec = seconds;
    else
        sec = 0;
}

void clockType::getTime(int& hours, int& minutes,
                        int& seconds) const
{
    hours = hr;
    minutes = min;
    seconds = sec;
}

    //Constructor
clockType::clockType(int hours, int minutes, int seconds)
```

```
{
    setTime(hours, minutes, seconds);
}
```

We now discuss the definition of the function **operator<<**. The time must be output in the form:

```
hh:mm:ss
```

The algorithm to output the time in this format is the same as the body of the `printTime` function of `clockType` given in Chapter 11. Here, after printing the time in the previous format, we must return the `ostream` object. Therefore, the definition of the function **operator<<** is:

```cpp
    //Overload the stream insertion operator.
ostream& operator<<(ostream& osObject, const clockType& timeOut)
{
    if (timeOut.hr < 10)
        osObject << '0';
    osObject << timeOut.hr << ':';

    if (timeOut.min < 10)
        osObject << '0';
    osObject << timeOut.min << ':';

    if (timeOut.sec < 10)
        osObject << '0';
    osObject << timeOut.sec;

    return osObject;   //return the ostream object
}
```

Let us now discuss the definition of the function **operator>>**. The input to the program is of the form:

```
hh:mm:ss
```

That is, the input is the hours followed by a colon, followed by the minutes, followed by a colon, followed by the seconds. Clearly, the algorithm to input the time is:

a. Get the input, which is a number, and store it in the member variable `hr`.

b. Get the next input, which is a colon, and discard it.

c. Get the next input, which is a number, and store it in the member variable `min`.

d. Get the next input, which is a colon, and discard it.

e. Get the next input, which is a number, and store it in the member variable `sec`.

f. Return the `istream` object.

Clearly, we need a local variable of type **char** to read the colon.

The definition of the function **operator>>** is:

```cpp
    //Overload the stream extraction operator.
istream& operator>>(istream& isObject, clockType& timeIn)
{
    char ch;

    isObject >> timeIn.hr;        //Step a
    isObject.get(ch);             //Step b; read and discard :
    isObject >> timeIn.min;       //Step c
    isObject.get(ch);             //Step d; read and discard :
    isObject >> timeIn.sec;       //Step e

    return isObject;              //Step f
}
```

The following test program uses the **class** clockType:

```cpp
//Program that uses the class clockType

#include <iostream>
#include "newClock.h"

using namespace std;

int main()
{
    clockType myClock(5, 6, 23);                      //Line 1
    clockType yourClock;                              //Line 2

    cout << "Line 3: myClock = " << myClock
         << endl;                                     //Line 3
    cout << "Line 4: yourClock = " << yourClock
         << endl;                                     //Line 4

    cout << "Line 5: Enter the time in the form "
         << "hr:min:sec ";                            //Line 5
    cin >> myClock;                                   //Line 6
    cout << endl;                                     //Line 7

    cout << "Line 8: The new time of myClock = "
         << myClock << endl;                          //Line 8

    ++myClock;                                        //Line 9

    cout << "Line 10: After incrementing the time, "
         << "myClock = " << myClock << endl;          //Line 10

    yourClock.setTime(13, 35, 38);                    //Line 11
```

```cpp
    cout << "Line 12: After setting the time, "
         << "yourClock = " << yourClock << endl;       //Line 12

    if (myClock == yourClock)                          //Line 13
        cout << "Line 14: The times of myClock and "
             << "yourClock are equal." << endl;         //Line 14
    else                                               //Line 15
        cout << "Line 16: The times of myClock and "
             << "yourClock are not equal." << endl;   //Line 16

    if (myClock <= yourClock)                          //Line 17
        cout << "Line 18: The time of myClock is "
             << "less than or equal to " << endl
             << "the time of yourClock." << endl;       //Line 18
    else                                               //Line 19
        cout << "Line 20: The time of myClock is "
             << "greater than the time of "
             << "yourClock." << endl;                   //Line 20

    return 0;
}
```

Sample Run: In this sample run, the user input is shaded.

```
Line 3: myClock = 05:06:23
Line 4: yourClock = 00:00:00
Line 5: Enter the time in the form hr:min:sec 4:50:59

Line 8: The new time of myClock = 04:50:59
Line 10: After incrementing the time, myClock = 04:51:00
Line 12: After setting the time, yourClock = 13:35:38
Line 16: The times of myClock and yourClock are not equal.
Line 18: The time of myClock is less than or equal to
the time of yourClock.
```

PROGRAMMING EXAMPLE: Complex Numbers

A number of the form $a + ib$, where $i^2 = -1$, and a and b are real numbers, is called a **complex number**. We call a the real part and b the imaginary part of $a + ib$. Complex numbers can also be represented as ordered pairs (a, b). The addition and multiplication of complex numbers is defined by the following rules:

$$(a + ib) + (c + id) = (a + c) + i(b + d)$$

$$(a + ib) \star (c + id) = (ac - bd) + i(ad + bc)$$

Using the ordered pair notation, these rules are written as:

$$(a, b) + (c, d) = ((a + c), (b + d))$$

$$(a, b) \star (c, d) = ((ac - bd), (ad + bc))$$

C++ has no built-in data type that allows us to manipulate complex numbers. In this example, we will construct a data type, `complexType`, that can be used to process complex numbers. We will overload the stream insertion and stream extraction operators for easy input and output. We will also overload the operators + and $\star$ to perform addition and multiplication of complex numbers. If x and y are complex numbers, we can evaluate expressions such as $x + y$ and $x \star y$:

```cpp
//Specification file complexType.h

#ifndef H_complexNumber
#define H_complexNumber

#include <iostream>
using namespace std;

class complexType
{
        //Overload the stream insertion and extraction operators
    friend ostream& operator<<(ostream&, const complexType&);
    friend istream& operator>>(istream&, complexType&);

public:
    void setComplex(const double& real, const double& imag);
        //Function to set the complex numbers according to
        //the parameters.
        //Postcondition: realPart = real; imaginaryPart = imag;

    void getComplex(double& real, double& imag) const;
        //Function to retrieve the complex number.
        //Postcondition: real = realPart; imag = imaginaryPart;

    complexType(double real = 0, double imag = 0);
        //Constructor
        //Initializes the complex number according to
        //the parameters.
        //Postcondition: realPart = real; imaginaryPart = imag;

    complexType operator+
                    (const complexType& otherComplex) const;
        //Overload the operator +

    complexType operator*
                    (const complexType& otherComplex) const;
        //Overload the operator *
```

```cpp
    bool operator== (const complexType& otherComplex) const;
        //Overload the operator ==
private:
    double realPart;         //variable to store the real part
    double imaginaryPart;    //variable to store the
                             //imaginary part

};

#endif
```

Figure 14-2 shows a UML class diagram of the **class** complexType.

```
complexType
-realPart: double
-imaginaryPart: double

+operator<<(ostream&, const complexType&): ostream&
+operator>>(istream&, complexType&): istream&
+setComplex(const double&, const double&): void
+getComplex(double&  double&) const: void
+operator+(const complexType&) const: complexType
+operator*(const complexType&) const: complexType
+operator==(const complexType&) const: bool
+complexType(double = 0, double = 0)
```

FIGURE 14-2 UML class diagram of the **class** complexType

Next, we write the definitions of the functions to implement various operations of the **class** complexType.

The definitions of most of these functions are straightforward. We will discuss only the definitions of the functions to overload the stream insertion operator, **<<**, and the stream extraction operator, **>>**.

To output a complex number in the form:

```
(a, b)
```

where **a** is the real part and **b** is the imaginary part, clearly the algorithm is:

    a.   Output the left parenthesis, **(**.

    b.   Output the real part.

    c.   Output the comma and a space.

    d.   Output the imaginary part.

    e.   Output the right parenthesis, **)**.

Therefore, the definition of the function `operator<<` is:

```
ostream& operator<<(ostream& osObject,
                    const complexType& complex)

{
    osObject << "(";                          //Step a
    osObject << complex.realPart;             //Step b
    osObject << ", ";                         //Step c
    osObject << complex.imaginaryPart;        //Step d
    osObject << ")";                          //Step e

    return osObject;      //return the ostream object
}
```

Next, we discuss the definition of the function to overload the stream extraction operator, >>.

The input is of the form:

`(3, 5)`

In this input, the real part of the complex number is 3 and the imaginary part is 5. Clearly, the algorithm to read this complex number is:

   a.   Read and discard the left parenthesis.

   b.   Read and store the real part.

   c.   Read and discard the comma.

   d.   Read and store the imaginary part.

   e.   Read and discard the right parenthesis.

Following these steps, the definition of the function `operator>>` is:

```
istream& operator>>(istream& isObject, complexType& complex)
{
    char ch;

    isObject >> ch;                           //Step a
    isObject >> complex.realPart;             //Step b
    isObject >> ch;                           //Step c
    isObject >> complex.imaginaryPart;        //Step d
    isObject >> ch;                           //Step e

    return isObject;      //return the istream object
}
```

The definitions of the other functions are as follows:

```
bool complexType::operator==
                (const complexType& otherComplex) const
```

```cpp
{
    return (realPart == otherComplex.realPart &&
            imaginaryPart == otherComplex.imaginaryPart);
}


    //Constructor
complexType::complexType(double real, double imag)
{
    realPart = real;
    imaginaryPart = imag;
}


    //Function to set the complex number after the object
    //has been declared.
void complexType::setComplex(const double& real,
                             const double& imag)
{
    realPart = real;
    imaginaryPart = imag;
}


void complexType::getComplex(double& real, double& imag) const
{
    real = realPart;
    imag = imaginaryPart;
}


    //overload the operator +
complexType complexType::operator+
                    (const complexType& otherComplex) const
{
    complexType temp;

    temp.realPart = realPart + otherComplex.realPart;
    temp.imaginaryPart = imaginaryPart
                    + otherComplex.imaginaryPart;

    return temp;
}


    //overload the operator *
complexType complexType::operator*
                    (const complexType& otherComplex) const
{
    complexType temp;
    temp.realPart = (realPart * otherComplex.realPart) -
                (imaginaryPart * otherComplex.imaginaryPart);
```

```cpp
        temp.imaginaryPart = (realPart * otherComplex.imaginaryPart)
                       + (imaginaryPart * otherComplex.realPart);
    return temp;
}
```

The following program illustrates the use of the **class** complexType:

```cpp
//Program that uses the class complexType

#include <iostream>
#include "complexType.h"

using namespace std;

int main()
{
    complexType num1(23, 34);                            //Line 1
    complexType num2;                                    //Line 2
    complexType num3;                                    //Line 3

    cout << "Line 4: Num1 = " << num1 << endl;           //Line 4
    cout << "Line 5: Num2 = " << num2 << endl;           //Line 5

    cout << "Line 6: Enter the complex number "
         << "in the form (a, b) ";                       //Line 6
    cin >> num2;                                         //Line 7
    cout << endl;                                        //Line 8

    cout << "Line 9: New value of num2 = "
         << num2 << endl;                                //Line 9

    num3 = num1 + num2;                                  //Line 10

    cout << "Line 11: Num3 = " << num3 << endl;          //Line 11

    cout << "Line 12: " << num1 << " + " << num2
         << " = " << num1 + num2 << endl;                //Line 12

    cout << "Line 13: " << num1 << " * " << num2
         << " = " << num1 * num2 << endl;                //Line 13

    return 0;
}
```

Sample Run: In this sample run, the user input is shaded.

```
Line 4: Num1 = (23, 34)
Line 5: Num2 = (0, 0)
Line 6: Enter the complex number in the form (a, b) (3, 4)
```

```
Line 9: New value of num2 = (3, 4)
Line 11: Num3 = (26, 38)
Line 12: (23, 34) + (3, 4) = (26, 38)
Line 13: (23, 34) * (3, 4) = (-67, 194)
```

You can extend this data type to perform subtraction and division on complex numbers.

Next, we will define a class, called `newString`, and overload the assignment and relational operators. That is, when we declare a variable of type `newString`, we will be able to use the assignment operator to copy one string into another, and relational operators to compare the two strings.

Before discussing the **class** `newString`, however, we examine the overloading of the operator `[]`. Recall that we have used the operator `[]` to access the components of an array. To access individual characters in a string of type `newString`, we have to overload the operator `[]` for the **class** `newString`.

Overloading the Array Index (Subscript) Operator ([])

Recall that the function to overload the operator `[]` for a class must be a member of the class. Furthermore, because an array can be declared as constant or nonconstant, we need to overload the operator `[]` to handle both the cases.

The syntax to declare the operator function `operator[]` as a member of a class for nonconstant arrays is:

```
Type& operator[](int index);
```

The syntax to declare the operator function `operator[]` as a member of a class for constant arrays is:

```
const Type& operator[](int index) const;
```

where `Type` is the data type of the array elements.

Suppose that `classTest` is a class that has an array member variable. The definition of `classTest` to overload the operator `[]` is:

```
class classTest
{
public:
    Type& operator[](int index);
        //Overload the operator for nonconstant arrays
```

```
    const Type& operator[](int index) const;
      //Overload the operator for constant arrays
      .
      .
      .
private:
    Type *list; //pointer to the array
    int arraySize;
};
```

where `Type` is the data type of the array elements.

The definitions of the functions to overload the operator `[]` for `classTest` are:

```
    //Overload the operator [] for nonconstant arrays
Type& classTest::operator[](int index)
{
    assert(0 <= index && index < arraySize);
    return list[index];    //return a pointer of the
                           //array component

}


    //Overload the operator [] for constant arrays
const Type& classTest::operator[](int index) const
{
    assert(0 <= index && index < arraySize);
    return list[index];   //return a pointer of the
                          //array component

}
```

NOTE The preceding function definitions use the `assert` statement. (For an explanation of the `assert` statement, see Chapter 4 or the Appendix.)

Consider the following statements:

```
classTest list1;
classTest list2;
const classTest list3;
```

In the case of the statement:

```
list1[2] = list2[3];
```

the body of the operator function **operator**`[]` for nonconstant arrays is executed. In the case of the statement:

```
list1[2] = list3[5];
```

first the body of the operator function **operator**`[]` for constant arrays is executed because `list3` is a constant array. Next, the body of the operator function **operator**`[]` for nonconstant arrays is executed to complete the execution of the assignment statement.

PROGRAMMING EXAMPLE: `newString`

Chapter 9 discussed C-strings. Recall that:

1. A C-string is a sequence of one or more characters.
2. C-strings are enclosed in double quotation marks.
3. C-strings are null terminated.
4. C-strings are stored in character arrays.

The only aggregate operations allowed on C-strings are input and output. To use other operations, the programmer needs to include the header file `cstring`, which contains the specifications of many functions for string manipulation.

Initially, C++ did not provide any built-in data types to handle C-strings. More recent versions of C++, however, provide a string class to handle C-strings and operations on C-strings.

Our objective in this example is to define our own class for C-string manipulation and, at the same time, to further illustrate operator overloading. More specifically, we overload the assignment operator, the relational operators, and the stream insertion and extraction operators for easy input and output. Let us call this **class** newString. First, we give the definition of the **class** newString:

```cpp
//Header file myString.h

#ifndef H_myString
#define H_myString

#include <iostream>

using namespace std;

class newString
{
        //Overload the stream insertion and extraction operators.
    friend ostream& operator << (ostream&, const newString&);
    friend istream& operator >> (istream&, newString&);

public:
    const newString& operator=(const newString&);
      //overload the assignment operator
    newString(const char *);
      //constructor; conversion from the char string
    newString();
      //Default constructor to initialize the string to null
    newString(const newString&);
      //Copy constructor
```

```cpp
    ~newString();
      //Destructor
    char &operator[] (int);
    const char &operator[](int) const;

      //overload the relational operators
    bool operator==(const newString&) const;
    bool operator!=(const newString&) const;
    bool operator<=(const newString&) const;
    bool operator<(const newString&) const;
    bool operator>=(const newString&) const;
    bool operator>(const newString&) const;

private:
    char *strPtr;      //pointer to the char array
                       //that holds the string
    int strLength;     //variable to store the length
                       //of the string
};

#endif
```

The **class** `newString` has two **private** member variables: one to store the C-string and one to store the length of the C-string.

Next, we give the definitions of the functions to implement the `newString` operations. The implementation file includes the header file `cassert` because we are using the function `assert`. (For an explanation of the function `assert`, see Chapter 4 or the header file `cassert` in the Appendix).

```cpp
//Implementation file myStringImp.cpp
#include <iostream>
#include <iomanip>
#include <cstring>
#include <cassert>
#include "myString.h"

using namespace std;

    //Constructor: conversion from the char string to newString
newString::newString(const char *str)
{
    strLength = strlen(str);
    strPtr = new char[strLength + 1]; //allocate memory to
                                      //store the char string
    strcpy(strPtr, str);  //copy string into strPtr
}
```

```cpp
        //Default constructor to store the null string
newString::newString()
{
    strLength = 0;
    strPtr = new char[1];
    strcpy(strPtr, "");
}

newString::newString(const newString& rightStr)  //copy constructor
{
    strLength = rightStr.strLength;
    strPtr = new char[strLength + 1];
    strcpy(strPtr, rightStr.strPtr);
}

newString::~newString()  //destructor
{
   delete [] strPtr;
}


  //overload the assignment operator
const newString& newString::operator=(const newString& rightStr)
{
    if (this != &rightStr) //avoid self-copy
    {
       delete [] strPtr;
       strLength = rightStr.strLength;
       strPtr = new char[strLength + 1];
       strcpy(strPtr, rightStr.strPtr);
    }

    return *this;
}

char& newString::operator[] (int index)
{
    assert(0 <= index && index < strLength);
    return strPtr[index];
}

const char& newString::operator[](int index) const
{
    assert(0 <= index && index < strLength);
    return strPtr[index];
}

  //Overload the relational operators.
bool newString::operator==(const newString& rightStr) const
{
    return (strcmp(strPtr, rightStr.strPtr) == 0);
}
```

```cpp
bool newString::operator<(const newString& rightStr) const
{
    return (strcmp(strPtr, rightStr.strPtr) < 0);
}

bool newString::operator<=(const newString& rightStr) const
{
    return (strcmp(strPtr, rightStr.strPtr) <= 0);
}

bool newString::operator>(const newString& rightStr) const
{
    return (strcmp(strPtr, rightStr.strPtr) > 0);
}

bool newString::operator>=(const newString& rightStr) const
{
    return (strcmp(strPtr, rightStr.strPtr) >= 0);
}

bool newString::operator!=(const newString& rightStr) const
{
    return (strcmp(strPtr, rightStr.strPtr) != 0);
}

    //Overload the stream insertion operator <<
ostream& operator << (ostream& osObject, const newString& str)
{
    osObject << str.strPtr;

    return osObject;
}

    //Overload the stream extraction operator >>
istream& operator >> (istream& isObject, newString& str)
{
    char temp[81];

    isObject >> setw(81) >> temp;
    str = temp;
    return isObject;
}
```

Consider the statement:

```cpp
is >> setw(81) >> temp;
```

in the definition of the function `operator>>`. Because `temp` is declared to be an array of size 81, the largest string that can be stored into `temp` is of length 80. The manipulator `setw` in this statement (that is, in the input statement) ensures that no more than 80 characters are read into `temp`.

Most of these functions are quite straightforward. Let us explain the functions that overload the conversion constructor, the assignment operator, and the copy constructor.

The **conversion constructor** is a single-parameter function that converts its argument to an object of the constructor's class. In our case, the conversion constructor converts a string to an object of the `newString` type.

Note that the assignment operator is explicitly overloaded only for objects of the `newString` type. However, the overloaded assignment operator also works if we want to store a C-string into a `newString` object. Consider the declaration:

```
newString str;
```

and the statement:

```
str = "Hello there";
```

The compiler translates this statement into:

```
str.operator=("Hello there");
```

1. First, the compiler automatically invokes the conversion constructor to create an object of the `newString` type to temporarily store the string `"Hello there"`.
2. Second, the compiler invokes the overloaded assignment operator to assign the temporary `newString` object to the object `str`.

Hence, it is not necessary to explicitly overload the assignment operator to store a C-string into an object of type `newString`.

Next, we write a C++ program that tests some of the operations of the `class` `newString`:

```cpp
//Test Program
#include <iostream>
#include "myString.h"

using namespace std;

int main()
{
    newString str1 = "Sunny";        //initialize str1 using
                                     //the assignment operator
    const newString str2("Warm");    //initialize str2 using the
                                     //conversion constructor
```

```cpp
    newString str3;  //initialize str3 to null
    newString str4;  //initialize str4 to null

    cout << "Line 1: " << str1 << "     " << str2
         << "  ***" << str3 << "###." << endl;        //Line 1

    if (str1 <= str2)            //compare str1 and str2; Line 2
        cout << "Line 3: " << str1 << " is less "
             << "than " << str2 << endl;              //Line 3
    else                                              //Line 4
        cout << "Line 5: " << str2 << " is less "
             << "than " << str1 << endl;              //Line 5

    cout << "Line 6: Enter a string with a length "
         << "of at least 7: ";                        //Line 6
    cin >> str1;          //input str1;                 Line 7
    cout << endl;                                     //Line 8

    cout << "Line 9: The new value of "
         << "str1 = " << str1 << endl;                //Line 9

    str4 = str3 = "Birth Day";                        //Line 10

    cout << "Line 11: str3 = " << str3
         << ", str4 = " << str4 << endl;              //Line 11

    str3 = str1;                                      //Line 12
    cout << "Line 13: The new value of str3 = "
         << str3 << endl;                             //Line 13

    str1 = "Bright Sky";                              //Line 14

    str3[1] = str1[5];                                //Line 15
    cout << "Line 16: After replacing the second "
         << "character of str3 = " << str3 << endl; //Line 16

    str3[2] = str2[0];                                //Line 17
    cout << "Line 18: After replacing the third "
         << "character of str3 = " << str3 << endl; //Line 18

    str3[5] = 'g';                                    //Line 19
    cout << "Line 20: After replacing the sixth "
         << "character of str3 = " << str3 << endl; //Line 20

    return 0;
}
```

Sample Run: In this sample run, the user input is shaded.

```
Line 1: Sunny     Warm  ***###.
Line 3: Sunny is less than Warm
```

```
Line  6: Enter a string with a length of at least 7: 123456789
Line  9: The new value of str1 = 123456789
Line 11: str3 = Birth Day, str4 = Birth Day
Line 13: The new value of str3 = 123456789
Line 16: After replacing the second character of str3 = 1t3456789
Line 18: After replacing the third character of str3 = 1tW456789
Line 20: After replacing the sixth character of str3 = 1tW45g789
```

The preceding program works as follows. The statement in Line 1 outputs the values of `str1`, `str2`, and `str3`. Notice that the value of `str3` is to be printed between ******* and **###**. Because `str3` is empty, nothing is printed between ******* and **###**; see Line 1 in the sample run. The statements in Lines 2 through 5 compare `str1` and `str2` and output the result. The statement in Line 7 inputs a string with a length of at least 7 into `str1`, and the statement in Line 9 outputs the new value of `str1`. Note that in the statement (see Line 10):

```
str4 = str3 = "Birth Day";
```

because the associativity of the assignment operator is from right to left, first the statement `str3 = "Birth Day";` executes and then the statement `str4 = str3;` executes. The statement in Line 11 outputs the values of `str3` and `str4`. The statements in Lines 15, 17, and 19 use the array subscripting operator `[ ]` to individually manipulate the characters of `str3`. The meanings of the remaining statements are straightforward.

Function Overloading

The previous section discussed operator overloading. Operator overloading provides the programmer with the same concise notation for user-defined data types as the operator has for built-in types. The types of parameters used with an operator determine the action to take. Similar to operator overloading, C++ allows the programmer to overload a function name. Chapter 7 introduced function overloading. For easy reference in the following discussion, let us review this concept.

Recall that a class can have more than one constructor, but all constructors of a class have the same name, which is the name of the class. This is an example of overloading a function. Further recall that overloading a function refers to having several functions with the same name but different parameter lists. The parameter list determines which function will execute.

For function overloading to work, we must give the definition of each function. The next section teaches you how to overload functions with a single code segment and leave the job of generating code for separate functions for the compiler.

Templates

Templates are a very powerful feature of C++. They allow you to write a single code segment for both a set of related functions, called a **function template**, and for a set of related classes, called a **class template**. The syntax we use for templates is:

```
template <class Type>
declaration;
```

where `Type` is the name of a data type, built-in or user-defined, and `declaration` is either a function declaration or a class declaration. In C++, `template` is a reserved word. The word `class` in the heading refers to any user-defined type or built-in type. `Type` is referred to as a formal parameter to the template.

Similar to variables being parameters to functions, types (that is, data types) are parameters to templates.

Function Templates

In Chapter 7, when we introduced function overloading, the function `larger` was overloaded to find the larger of two integers, characters, floating-point numbers, or strings. To implement the function `larger`, we need to write four function definitions for the data type: one for `int`, one for `char`, one for `double`, and one for `string`. However, the body of each function is similar. C++ simplifies the process of overloading functions by providing function templates.

The syntax of the function template is:

```
template <class Type>
function definition;
```

where `Type` is referred to as a formal parameter of the template. It is used to specify the type of parameters to the function and the return type of the function and to declare variables within the function.

The statements:

```
template <class Type>
Type larger(Type x, Type y)
{
    if (x >= y)
        return x;
    else
        return y;
}
```

define a function template `larger`, which returns the larger of two items. In the function heading, the type of the formal parameters `x` and `y` is `Type`, which will be specified by the type of the actual parameters when the function is called. The statement:

```
cout << larger(5, 6) << endl;
```

is a call to the function template `larger`. Because 5 and 6 are of type `int`, the data type `int` is substituted for `Type` and the compiler generates the appropriate code.

If we omit the body of the function in the function template definition, the function template, as usual, is the prototype.

The following example illustrates the use of function templates.

EXAMPLE 14-8

This example uses the function template `larger` to determine the larger of the two items:

```cpp
#include <iostream>
#include "myString.h"

using namespace std;

template <class Type>
Type larger(Type x, Type y);

int main()
{
    cout << "Line 1: Larger of 5 and 6 = "
         << larger(5, 6) << endl;                       //Line 1
    cout << "Line 2: Larger of A and B = "
         << larger('A', 'B') << endl;                   //Line 2
    cout << "Line 3: Larger of 5.6 and 3.2 = "
         << larger(5.6, 3.2) << endl;                   //Line 3

    newString str1 = "Hello";                           //Line 4
    newString str2 = "Happy";                           //Line 5

    cout << "Line 6: Larger of " << str1 << " and "
         << str2 << " = " << larger(str1, str2)
         << endl;                                       //Line 6

    return 0;
}

template <class Type>
Type larger(Type x, Type y)
{
    if (x >= y)
        return x;
    else
        return y;
}
```

Sample Run:

```
Line 1: Larger of 5 and 6 = 6
Line 2: Larger of A and B = B
Line 3: Larger of 5.6 and 3.2 = 5.6
Line 6: Larger of Hello and Happy = Hello
```

Class Templates

Like function templates, class templates are used to write a single code segment for a set of related classes. For example, in Chapter 11, we defined a list as an ADT; our list element type was `int`. If the list element type changes from `int` to, say, `char`, `double`, or `string`, we need to write separate classes for each element type. For the most part, the operations on the list and the algorithms to implement those operations remain the same. Using class templates, we can create a generic `class listType`, and the compiler can generate the appropriate source code for a specific implementation.

The syntax we use for a class template is:

```
template <class Type>
class declaration
```

Class templates are called **parameterized types** because, based on the parameter type, a specific class is generated.

The following statements define `listType` to be a class template:

```
template <class elemType>
class listType
{
public:
    bool isEmpty() const;
      //Function to determine whether the list is empty.
      //Postcondition: Returns true if the list is empty,
      //               otherwise it returns false.

    bool isFull() const;
      //Function to determine whether the list is full.
      //Postcondition: Returns true if the list is full,
      //               otherwise it returns false.

    bool search(const elemType& searchItem) const;
      //Function to search the list for searchItem.
      //Postcondition: Returns true if searchItem
      //               is found in the list, and
      //               false otherwise.

    void insert(const elemType& newElement);
      //Function to insert newElement in the list.
      //Precondition: Prior to insertion, the list must
```

```cpp
    //                 not be full.
    //Postcondition: The list is the old list plus
    //                 newElement.

   void remove(const elemType& removeElement);
     //Function to remove removeElement from the list.
     //Postcondition: If removeElement is found in the list,
     //                 it is deleted from the list, and the
     //                 list is the old list minus removeElement.
     //                 If the list is empty, output the message
     //                 "Cannot delete from the empty list."

   void destroyList();
     //Function to destroy the list.
     //Postcondition: length = 0;

   void printList();
     //Function to output the elements of the list.

   listType();
     //Default constructor
     //Sets the length of the list to 0.
     //Postcondition: length = 0;

protected:
    elemType list[100];    //array to hold the list elements
    int length;            //variable to store the number of
                           //elements in the list
};
```

This definition of the class template `listType` is a generic definition and includes only
the basic operations on a list. To derive a specific list from this list and to add or rewrite
the operations, we declare the array containing the list elements and the length of the list
as **protected**.

Next, we describe a specific list. Suppose that you want to create a list to process integer
data. The statement:

```cpp
listType<int> intList;                      //Line 1
```

declares `intList` to be an object of `listType`. The **protected** member `list` is an array
of 100 components, with each component being of type `int`. Similarly, the statement:

```cpp
listType<newString> stringList;             //Line 2
```

declares `stringList` to be an object of `listType`. The **protected** member `list` is
an array of 100 components, with each component being of type `newString`.

In the statements in Lines 1 and 2, `listType<int>` and `listType<newString>` are
referred to as *template instantiations* or *instantiations of the class template* `listType<elemType>`,
where `elemType` is the class parameter in the template header. A template instantiation can
be created with either a built-in or user-defined type.

The function members of a class template are considered function templates. Thus, when giving the definitions of the function members of a class template, we must follow the definition of the function template. For example, the definition of the member `insert` of the `class listType` is:

```
template <class elemType>
void listType<elemType>::insert(elemType newElement)
{
        .
        .
        .

}
```

In the heading of the member function's definition, the name of the class is specified with the parameter `elemType`.

The statement in Line 1 declares `intList` to be a list of 100 components. When the compiler generates the code for `intList`, it replaces the word `elemType` with `int` in the definition of the `class listType`. The template parameter in the definitions of the member functions (for example, `elemType` in the definition of `insert`) of the `class listType` is also replaced by `int`.

HEADER FILE AND IMPLEMENTATION FILE OF A CLASS TEMPLATE

Until now, we have placed the definition of the class (in the header file) and the definitions of the member functions (in the implementation file) in separate files. The object code was generated from the implementation file and linked with the user code. However, this mechanism of separating the class definition and the definitions of the member functions does not work with class templates. Passing parameters to a function has an effect at run time, whereas passing a parameter to a class template has an effect at compile time. Because the actual parameter to a class is specified in the user code, and because the compiler cannot instantiate a function template without the actual parameter to the template, we can no longer compile the implementation file independently of the user code.

This problem has several possible solutions. We could put the class definition and the definitions of the function templates directly in the client code, or we could put the class definition and the definitions of the function templates together in the same header file. Another alternative is to put the class definition and the definitions of the functions in separate files (as usual), but include a directive to the implementation file at the end of the header file. In either case, the function definitions and the client code are compiled together. For illustrative purposes, we will put the class definition and the function definitions in the same header file.

Array-Based Lists (Revisited)

In Chapter 13, we designed the `class`es `arrayListType`, `unorderedArrayListType`, and `orderedArrayListType` to process lists in an array. However, these classes, as designed in Chapter 13, processes only those lists whose elements are of type `int`. Now that we have discussed how to use class templates to create a generic code, in this section, we redesign these classes so that they can be used to process any type of list. Moreover, in this chapter, we discussed how to overload the assignment operator. Therefore, in addition to the operations discussed in Chapter 13, we also overload the assignment operator for the `class` `arrayListType` because it has a pointer member variable.

The following class template defines the abstract `class` `arrayListType` as an ADT. (To save space, we only list the functions. The documentation of these functions is similar to ones given in Chapter 13. The source code file at the Web site accompanying this book contains the documentation of these functions.)

```cpp
template <class elemType>
class arrayListType
{
public:
    const arrayListType<elemType>&
                operator=(const arrayListType<elemType>&);
      //Overloads the assignment operator

    bool isEmpty() const;
    bool isFull() const;
    int listSize() const;
    int maxListSize() const;
    void print() const;
    bool isItemAtEqual(int location, const elemType& item) const;
    virtual void insertAt(int location, const elemType& insertItem) = 0;
    virtual void insertEnd(const elemType& insertItem) = 0;
    void removeAt(int location);
    void retrieveAt(int location, elemType& retItem) const;
    virtual void replaceAt(int location, const elemType& repItem) = 0;
    void clearList();
    virtual int seqSearch(const elemType& searchItem) const = 0;
    virtual void remove(const elemType& removeItem) = 0;
    arrayListType(int size = 100);
    arrayListType (const arrayListType<elemType>& otherList);
    virtual ~arrayListType();

protected:
    elemType *list;  //array to hold the list elements
    int length;      //variable to store the length of the list
    int maxSize;     //variable to store the maximum
                     //size of the list
};
```

The definitions of the functions to implement the operations of the `class` `arrayListType` are similar to the ones given in Chapter 13. Here, the functions to implement these operations are function templates. For example, the definitions of the functions `print`, `isItemAtEqual`, `removeAt`, `retrieveAt`, the constructor, and the destructor are:

```cpp
template <class elemType>
void arrayListType<elemType>::print() const
{
    for (int i = 0; i < length; i++)
        cout << list[i] << " ";
    cout << endl;
}

template <class elemType>
bool arrayListType<elemType>::isItemAtEqual(int location,
                                    const elemType& item) const
{
    if (location < 0 || location >= length)
    {
        cout << "The location of the item to be removed "
            << "is out of range." << endl;

        return false;
    }
    else
        return (list[location] == item);
} //end isItemAtEqual

template <class elemType>
void arrayListType<elemType>::removeAt(int location)
{
    if (location < 0 || location >= length)
        cout << "The location of the item to be removed "
            << "is out of range." << endl;
    else
    {
        for (int i = location; i < length - 1; i++)
            list[i] = list[i + 1];
        length--;
    }
} //end removeAt

template <class elemType>
void arrayListType<elemType>::retrieveAt(int location,
                                    elemType& retItem) const
{
    if (location < 0 || location >= length)
        cout << "The location of the item to be retrieved is "
            << "out of range" << endl;
    else
        retItem = list[location];
} //end retrieveAt
```

```cpp
template <class elemType>
arrayListType<elemType>::arrayListType(int size)
{
    if (size <= 0)
    {
        cout << "The array size must be positive. Creating "
             << "an array of the size 100. " << endl;

        maxSize = 100;
    }
    else
        maxSize = size;

    length = 0;

    list = new elemType[maxSize];
}


template <class elemType>
arrayListType<elemType>::~arrayListType()
{
    delete [] list;
}
```

Next, because we are overloading the assignment for the **class** `arrayListType`, we give the definition of the function template to overload the assignment operator:

```cpp
template <class elemType>
const arrayListType<elemType>& arrayListType<elemType>::
            operator=(const arrayListType<elemType>& otherList)
{
    if (this != &otherList)     //avoid self-assignment
    {
        delete [] list;
        maxSize = otherList.maxSize;
        length = otherList.length;

        list = new elemType[maxSize];

        for (int i = 0; i < length; i++)
            list[i] = otherList.list[i];
    }
    return *this;
}
```

We leave it as an exercise for you to provide the definitions of the remaining function templates for the **class** `arrayListType`. (See Programming Exercise 14 at the end of this chapter.)

Recall that the **class** `arrayListType` is an abstract class. So its object cannot be instantiated. Next, we describe the nonabstract **class** `unorderedArrayListType` derived from the **class** `arrayListType`:

```cpp
template <class elemType>
class unorderedArrayListType: public arrayListType<elemType>
{
public:
    void insertAt(int location, const elemType& insertItem);
    void insertEnd(const elemType& insertItem);
    void replaceAt(int location, const elemType& repItem);
    int seqSearch(const elemType& searchItem) const;
    void remove(const elemType& removeItem);

    unorderedArrayListType(int size = 100);
      //Constructor
};
```

As in the case of the **class** `arrayListType`, the definitions of the member functions of the **class** `unorderedArrayListType` is simialr to ones given in Chapter 13. For example, the definitions of the functions `insertEnd`, `seqSearch`, `replaceAt`, and remove, and constructor are as follows:

```cpp
template <class elemType>
void unorderedArrayListType<elemType>::insertEnd
                                  (const elemType& insertItem)
{
    if (length >= maxSize)   //the list is full
        cout << "Cannot insert in a full list." << endl;
    else
    {
        list[length] = insertItem; //insert the item at the end
        length++; //increment the length
    }
} //end insertEnd

template <class elemType>
int unorderedArrayListType<elemType>::seqSearch
                          (const elemType& searchItem) const
{
    int loc;
    bool found = false;

    for (loc = 0; loc < length; loc++)
        if (list[loc] == searchItem)
        {
            found = true;
            break;
        }

    if (found)
        return loc;
    else
        return -1;
} //end seqSearch
```

```cpp
template <class elemType>
void unorderedArrayListType<elemType>::remove
                                    (const elemType& removeItem)
{
    int loc;

    if (length == 0)
        cout << "Cannot delete from an empty list." << endl;
    else
    {
        loc = seqSearch(removeItem);

        if (loc != -1)
            removeAt(loc);
        else
            cout << "The item to be deleted is not in the list."
                << endl;
    }
} //end remove

template <class elemType>
void unorderedArrayListType<elemType>::replaceAt(int location,
                                    const elemType& repItem)
{
    if (location < 0 || location >= length)
        cout << "The location of the item to be "
            << "replaced is out of range." << endl;
    else
        list[location] = repItem;
} //end replaceAt

template <class elemType>
unorderedArrayListType<elemType>::
                    unorderedArrayListType(int size)
                    : arrayListType<elemType>(size)
{
}
```

We leave it as an exercise for you to provide the definitions of the remaining function templates for the **class** unorderedArrayListType. (See Programming Exercise 14 at the end of this chapter.)

The following example illustrates how to use the **class** unorderedArrayListType to process a list of strings.

The following program tests the various operations on an array-based list:

```cpp
#include <iostream>
#include <string>
#include "unorderedArrayListType.h"
```

```cpp
using namespace std;

int main()
{
    unorderedArrayListType<string> stringList(25);   //Line 1

    string str;                                       //Line 2

    cout << "List 3: Enter 5 strings: ";              //Line 3

    for (int count = 0; count < 5; count++)           //Line 4
    {
        cin >> str;                                   //Line 5
        stringList.insertEnd(str);                    //Line 6
    }

    cout << endl;                                     //Line 7
    cout << "Line 8: stringList: ";                   //Line 8
    stringList.print();                               //Line 9
    cout << endl;                                     //Line 10

    cout << "Line 11: Enter the string to be "
         << "deleted: ";                              //Line 11
    cin >> str;                                       //Line 12
    cout << endl;                                     //Line 13

    stringList.remove(str);                           //Line 14
    cout << "Line 15: After removing " << str
         << " stringList: ";                          //Line 15
    stringList.print();                               //Line 16
    cout << endl;                                     //Line 17

    cout << "Line 18: Enter the search item: ";       //Line 18

    cin >> str;                                       //Line 19
    cout << endl;                                     //Line 20

    if (stringList.seqSearch(str) != -1)              //Line 21
        cout << "Line 22: " << str
             << " found in stringList." << endl;      //Line 22
    else                                              //Line 23
        cout << "Line 24: " << str
             << " is not in stringList." << endl;     //Line 24

    return 0;
}
```

1
4

Sample Run: In this sample run, the user input is shaded.

```
List 3: Enter 5 strings: hello sunny warm winter summer

Line 8: stringList: hello sunny warm winter summer

Line 11: Enter the string to be deleted: hello

Line 15: After removing hello stringList: sunny warm winter summer

Line 18: Enter the search item: winter

Line 22: winter found in stringList.
```

The preceding program works as follows. The statement in Line 1 declares `stringList` to be an object of the type `unorderedArrayListType`. The member variable `list` of `stringList` is an array of 25 components, and the component type is `string`. The statement in Line 2 declares the `string` variable `str`. The statement in Line 3 prompts the user to enter 5 strings. The statement in Line 5 gets the next string from the input stream. The statement in Line 6 uses the member function `insertEnd` of `stringList` to store the string into `stringList`. The statement in Line 9 uses the member function print of `stringList` to output the elements of `stringList`. The statement in Line 11 prompts the user to enter the string to be deleted from `stringList`, and the statement in Line 12 gets the string to be deleted from the input stream. The statement in Line 14 uses the member function `remove` of `stringList` to remove the string from `stringList`. The statement in Line 16 outputs the modified `stringList`.

The statements in Lines 18 through 24 tests the function `seqSearch`.

NOTE The Web site accompanying contains additional programs illustrating how to use the **class template** unorderedArrayListType to create lists of **double** elements and **clockType** objects.

Just as we can derive the **class template** unorderedArrayListType, from the abstact **class template** arrayListType, to manipulate unordered lists, we can also derive the **class template** orderedArrayListType to manipulate ordered lists. (See Programming Exercise 15 at the end of this chapter.)

QUICK REVIEW

1. An operator that has different meanings with different data types is said to be overloaded.

2. In C++, >> is used as a stream extraction operator and as a right shift operator. Similarly, << is used as a stream insertion operator and as a left shift operator. Both are examples of operator overloading.

3. Any function that overloads an operator is called an operator function.

4. The syntax of the heading of the operator function is:

```
returnType operator operatorSymbol(parameters)
```

5. In C++, `operator` is a reserved word.

6. Operator functions are value-returning functions.

7. Except for the assignment operator and the member selection operator, to use an operator on class objects, that operator must be overloaded. The assignment operator performs a default member-wise copy.

8. For classes with pointer member variables, the assignment operator must be explicitly overloaded.

9. Operator overloading provides the same concise notation for user-defined data types as is available for built-in data types.

10. When an operator is overloaded, its precedence cannot be changed, its associativity cannot be changed, default parameters cannot be used with an overloaded operator, the number of parameters that the operator takes cannot be changed, and the meaning of how an operator works with built-in data types remains the same.

11. It is not possible to create new operators. Only existing operators can be overloaded.

12. Most C++ operators can be overloaded.

13. The operators that cannot be overloaded are `.`, `.*`, `::`, `?:`, and `sizeof`.

14. The pointer `this` refers to the object as a whole.

15. The operator functions that overload the operators `()`, `[]`, `->`, or `=` for a class must be members of that class.

16. A friend function is a nonmember of a class.

17. The heading of the prototype of a friend function is preceded by the word `friend`.

18. In C++, `friend` is a reserved word.

19. If an operator function is a member of a class, the leftmost operand of the operator must be a class object (or a reference to a class object) of that operator's class.

20. The binary operator function as a member of a class has only one parameter; as a nonmember of a class, it has two parameters.

21. The operator functions that overload the stream insertion operator, `<<`, and the stream extraction operator, `>>`, for a class must be friend functions of that class.

22. To overload the pre-increment (++) operator for a class if the operator function is a member of that class, it must have no parameters. Similarly, to overload the pre-decrement (--) operator for a class if the operator function is a member of that class, it must have no parameters.

23. To overload the post-increment (++) operator for a class if the operator function is a member of that class, it must have one parameter, of type `int`. The user does not specify any value for the parameter. The dummy parameter in the function heading helps the compiler generate the correct code. The post-decrement operator has similar conventions.

24. A conversion constructor is a single-parameter function.

25. A conversion constructor converts its argument to an object of the constructor's class. The compiler implicitly calls such constructors.

26. Classes with pointer member variables must overload the assignment operator and include both the copy constructor and the destructor.

27. In C++, a function name can be overloaded.

28. Every instance of an overloaded function has different sets of parameters.

29. In C++, `template` is a reserved word.

30. Using templates, you can write a single code segment for a set of related functions—called the function template.

31. Using templates, you can write a single code segment for a set of related classes—called the class template.

32. The syntax of a template is:

```
template <class Type>
declaration;
```

where `Type` is a user-defined identifier, which is used to pass types (that is, data types) as parameters, and `declaration` is either a function or a class. The word `class` in the heading refers to any user-defined data type or built-in data type.

33. Class templates are called parameterized types.

34. In a class template, the parameter `Type` specifies how a generic class template is to be customized to form a specific template class.

35. The parameter `Type` is mentioned in every class header and member function definition.

36. Suppose `cType` is a class template and `func` is a member function of `cType`. The heading of the function definition of `func` is:

```
template <class Type>
funcType cType<Type>::func(parameters)
```

where `funcType` is the type of the function, such as `void`.

37. Suppose `cType` is a class template, which can take `int` as a parameter. The statement:

```
cType<int> x;
```

declares `x` to be an object of type `cType`, and the type passed to the `class` `cType` is `int`.

EXERCISES

1. Mark the following statements as true or false.

    a. In C++, all operators can be overloaded for user-defined data types.

    b. In C++, operators cannot be redefined for built-in types.

    c. The function that overloads an operator is called the operator function.

    d. C++ allows users to create their own operators.

    e. The precedence of an operator cannot be changed, but its associativity can be changed.

    f. Every instance of an overloaded function has the same number of parameters.

    g. It is not necessary to overload relational operators for classes that have only `int` member variables.

    h. The member function of a `class` template is a function template.

    i. When writing the definition of a `friend` function, the keyword `friend` must appear in the function heading.

    j. Templates provide the capability for software reuse.

    k. The function heading of the operator function to overload the pre-increment operator `(++)` and the post-increment operator `(++)` is the same because both operators have the same symbols.

2. What is a `friend` function?

3. Suppose that the operator `<<` is to be overloaded for a user-defined `class` `mystery`. Why must `<<` be overloaded as a `friend` function?

4. Suppose that the binary operator `+` is overloaded as a member function for a `class` `strange`. How many parameters does the function `operator+` have?

5. When should a class overload the assignment operator and define the copy constructor?

6. Consider the following declaration:

```
class strange
{
    .
    .
    .
};
```

    a. Write a statement that shows the declaration in the `class` `strange` to overload the operator `>>`.

    b. Write a statement that shows the declaration in the `class` `strange` to overload the operator `=`.

    c. Write a statement that shows the declaration in the `class` `strange` to overload the binary operator `+` as a member function.

    d. Write a statement that shows the declaration in the **class** strange to overload the operator == as a member function.

    e. Write a statement that shows the declaration in the **class** strange to overload the post-increment operator ++ as a member function.

7. Assume the declaration of Exercise 6.

    a. Write a statement that shows the declaration in the **class** strange to overload the binary operator + as a **friend** function.

    b. Write a statement that shows the declaration in the **class** strange to overload the operator == as a **friend** function.

    c. Write a statement that shows the declaration in the **class** strange to overload the post-increment operator ++ as a **friend** function.

8. Find the error(s) in the following code:

```cpp
class mystery                            //Line 1
{
     .
     .
     .
    bool operator<=(mystery);            //Line 2
     .
     .
     .
};

bool mystery::<=(mystery rightObj)       //Line 3
{
     .
     .
     .
}
```

9. Find the error(s) in the following code:

```cpp
class mystery                                  //Line 1
{
     .
     .
     .
    bool operator<=(mystery, mystery);   //Line 2
     .
     .
     .
};
```

10. Find the error(s) in the following code:

```cpp
class mystery                      //Line 1
{
     .
     .
     .
```

```
    friend operator+(mystery);     //Line 2
      //overload binary +
        .
        .
        .
};
```

11. How many parameters are required to overload the pre-increment operator for a class as a member function?

12. How many parameters are required to overload the pre-increment operator for a class as a `friend` function?

13. How many parameters are required to overload the post-increment operator for a class as a member function?

14. How many parameters are required to overload the post-increment operator for a class as a `friend` function?

15. Let $a + ib$ be a complex number. The conjugate of $a + ib$ is $a - ib$, and the absolute value of $a + ib$ is $\sqrt{a^2 + b^2}$. Extend the definition of the `class` `complexType` of the Programming Example: Complex Numbers by overloading the operators ~ and ! as member functions so that ~ returns the conjugate of a complex number and ! returns the absolute value. Also, write the definitions of these operator functions.

16. Redo Exercise 15 so that the operators ~ and ! are overloaded as non-member functions.

17. Find the error(s) in the following code:

```
template <class type>          //Line 1
class strange                  //Line 2
{
        .
        .
        .
};

strange<int> s1;               //Line 3
strange<type> s2;              //Line 4
```

18. Consider the following declaration:

```
template <class type>
class strange
{
        .
        .
        .
private:
    type a;
    type b;
};
```

a. Write a statement that declares `sObj` to be an object of type `strange` such that the **private** member variables `a` and `b` are of type **int**.

b. Write a statement that shows the declaration in the **class** `strange` to overload the operator `==` as a member function.

c. Assume that two objects of type `strange` are equal if their corresponding member variables are equal. Write the definition of the function `operator==` for the **class** `strange`, which is overloaded as a member function.

19. Consider the definition of the following function template:

```
template <class Type>
Type surprise(Type x, Type y)
{
    return x + y;
}
```

What is the output of the following statements?

a. `cout << surprise(5, 7) << endl;`

b. `string str1 = "Sunny";`
   `string str2 = " Day";`
   `cout << surprise(str1, str2) << endl;`

20. Consider the definition of the following function template:

```
template <class Type>
Type funcExp(Type list[], int size)
{
    int j;
    Type x = list[0];
    Type y = list[size - 1];

    for (j = 1; j < (size - 1)/2; j++)
    {
        if (x < list[j])
            x = list[j];
        if (y > list[size - 1 - j])
            y = list[size - 1 - j];
    }

    return x + y;
}
```

Further suppose that you have the following declarations:

```
int list[10] = {5, 3, 2, 10, 4, 19, 45, 13, 61, 11};
string strList[] = {"One", "Hello", "Four", "Three",
                    "How", "Six"};
```

What is the output of the following statements?

a. `cout << funExp(list, 10);`

b. `cout << funExp(strList, 6) << endl;`

21. Write the definition of the function template that swaps the contents of two variables.

22. a. Overload the operator + for the **class** newString to perform string concatenation. For example, if s1 is **"Hello "** and s2 is **"there"**, the statement:

```
s3 = s1 + s2;
```

should assign **"Hello there"** to s3, where s1, s2, and s3 are newString objects.

b. Overload the operator += for the **class** newString to perform the following string concatenation. Suppose that s1 is **"Hello "** and s2 is "there". Then, the statement:

```
s1 += s2;
```

should assign **"Hello there"** to s1, where s1 and s2 are newString objects.

PROGRAMMING EXERCISES

1. a. Write the definitions of the functions to overload the increment, decrement, arithmetic, and relational operators as members of the **class** rectangleType.

b. Write a test program that tests various operations on the **class** rectangleType.

2. a. Write the definitions of the functions to overload the increment, decrement, arithmetic, and relational operators as nonmembers of the **class** rectangleType.

b. Write a test program that tests various operations on the **class** rectangleType.

3. a. Extend the definition of the **class** clockType by overloading the post-increment operator function as a member of the **class** clockType.

b. Write the definition of the function to overload the post-increment operator for the **class** clockType as defined in part a.

4. a. The increment and relational operators in the **class** clockType are overloaded as member functions. Rewrite the definition of the **class** clockType so that these operators are overloaded as nonmember functions. Also, overload the post-increment operator for the **class** clockType as a nonmember.

b. Write the definitions of the member functions of the **class** clockType as designed in part a.

c. Write a test program that tests various operations on the class as designed in parts a and b.

5. a. Extend the definition of the **class** `complexType` so that it performs the subtraction and division operations. Overload the operators subtraction and division for this class as member functions.

   If (a, b) and (c, d) are complex numbers,

   $(a, b) - (c, d) = (a - c, b - d)$.

   If (c, d) is nonzero,

   $(a, b) / (c, d) = ((ac + bd) / (c^2 + d^2), (-ad + bc) / (c^2 + d^2))$.

   b. Write the definitions of the functions to overload the operators - and / as defined in part a.

   c. Write a test program that tests various operations on the **class** `complexType`. Format your answer with two decimal places.

6. a. Rewrite the definition of the **class** `complexType` so that the arithmetic and relational operators are overloaded as nonmember functions.

   b. Write the definitions of the member functions of the **class** `complexType` as designed in part a.

   c. Write a test program that tests various operations on the **class** `complexType` as designed in parts a and b. Format your answer with two decimal places.

7. a. Extend the definition of the **class** `newString` as follows:

   i. Overload the operators + and += to perform the string concatenation operations.

   ii. Add the function `length` to return the length of the string.

   b. Write the definition of the function to implement the operations defined in part a.

   c. Write a test program to test various operations on the `newString` objects.

8. a. Rewrite the definition of the **class** `newString` as defined and extended in Programming Exercise 7, so that the relational operators are overloaded as nonmember functions.

   b. Write the definition of the **class** `newString` as designed in part a.

   c. Write a test program that tests various operations on the **class** `newString`.

9. Rational fractions are of the form a / b, where a and b are integers and $b \neq 0$. In this exercise, by "fractions" we mean rational fractions. Suppose a / b and c / d are fractions. Arithmetic operations on fractions are defined by the following rules:

$$a/b + c/d = (ad + bc)/bd$$

$$a/b - c/d = (ad - bc)/bd$$

$$a/b \times c/d = ac/bd$$

$$(a/b)/(c/d) = ad/bc, \text{ where } c/d \neq 0.$$

Fractions are compared as follows: *a / b op c / d* if *ad op bc*, where *op* is any of the relational operations. For example, *a / b < c / d* if *ad < bc*.

Design a **class**—say, `fractionType`—that performs the arithmetic and relational operations on fractions. Overload the arithmetic and relational operators so that the appropriate symbols can be used to perform the operation. Also, overload the stream insertion and stream extraction operators for easy input and output.

Write a C++ program that, using the **class** `fractionType`, performs operations on fractions.

Among other things, test the following: Suppose **x**, **y**, and **z** are objects of type `fractionType`. If the input is **2/3**, the statement:

```
cin >> x;
```

should store 2/3 in **x**. The statement:

```
cout << x + y << endl;
```

should output the value of **x + y** in fraction form. The statement:

```
z = x + y;
```

should store the sum of **x** and **y** in **z** in fraction form. Your answer need not be in the lowest terms.

10. Recall that in C++ there is no check on an array index out of bounds. However, during program execution, an array index out of bounds can cause serious problems. Also, in C++ the array index starts at 0.

Design and implement the **class** `myArray` that solves the array index out of bounds problem, and also allows the user to begin the array index starting at any integer, positive or negative. Every object of type `myArray` is an array of type `int`. During execution, when accessing an array component, if the index is out of bounds, the program must terminate with an appropriate error message. Consider the following statements:

```
myArray<int> list(5);            //Line 1
myArray<int> myList(2, 13);       //Line 2
myArray<int> yourList(-5, 9);     //Line 3
```

The statement in Line 1 declares `list` to be an array of 5 components, the component type is `int`, and the components are: `list[0]`, `list[1]`, ..., `list[4]`; the statement in Line 2 declares `myList` to be an array of 11 components, the component type is `int`, and the components are:

`myList[2]`, `myList[3]`, ..., `myList[12]`; the statement in Line 3 declares `yourList` to be an array of 14 components, the component type is `int`, and the components are: `yourList[-5]`, `yourList[-4]`, ..., `yourList[0]`, ..., `yourList[8]`. Write a program to test the **class** `myArray`.

11. Programming Exercise 10 processes only **int** arrays. Redesign the **class** `myArray` using class templates so that the **class** can be used in any application that requires arrays to process data.

12. Design a class to perform various matrix operations. A matrix is a set of numbers arranged in rows and columns. Therefore, every element of a matrix has a row position and a column position. If A is a matrix of 5 rows and 6 columns, we say that the matrix A is of the size 5×6 and sometimes denote it as $A_{5 \times 6}$. Clearly, a convenient place to store a matrix is in a two-dimensional array. Two matrices can be added and subtracted if they have the same size. Suppose $A = [a_{ij}]$ and $B = [b_{ij}]$ are two matrices of the size $m \times n$, where a_{ij} denotes the element of A in the ith row and the jth column, and so on. The sum and difference of A and B are given by:

$$A + B = [a_{ij} + b_{ij}]$$

$$A - B = [a_{ij} - b_{ij}]$$

The multiplication of A and B $(A \star B)$ is defined only if the number of columns of A is the same as the number of rows of B. If A is of the size $m \times n$ and B is of the size $n \times t$, then $A \star B = [c_{ik}]$ is of the size $m \times t$ and the element c_{ik} is given by the formula:

$$c_{ik} = a_{i1}b_{1k} + a_{i2}b_{2k} + \cdots + a_{in}b_{nk}$$

Design and implement a **class** `matrixType` that can store a matrix of any size. Overload the operators **+**, **−**, and **★** to perform the addition, subtraction, and multiplication operations, respectively, and overload the operator **<<** to output a matrix. Also, write a test program to test various operations on the matrices.

13. **a.** In Programming Exercise 1 in Chapter 11, we defined a **class** `romanType` to implement Roman numbers in a program. In that exercise, we also implemented a function, `romanToDecimal`, to convert a Roman number into its equivalent decimal number.

   Modify the definition of the **class** `romanType` so that the member variables are declared as **protected**. Use the **class** `newString`, as designed in Programming Exercise 7, to manipulate strings. Furthermore, overload the stream insertion and stream extraction operators for easy input and output. The stream insertion operator outputs the Roman number in the Roman format.

Also, include a member function, `decimalToRoman`, that converts the decimal number (the decimal number must be a positive integer) to an equivalent Roman number format. Write the definition of the member function `decimalToRoman`.

For simplicity, we assume that only the letter `I` can appear in front of another letter, and that it appears only in front of the letters `V` and `X`. For example, `4` is represented as `IV`, `9` is represented as `IX`, `39` is represented as `XXXIX`, and `49` is represented as `XXXXIX`. Also, `40` will be represented as `XXXX`, `190` will be represented as `CLXXXX`, and so on.

b. Derive a **class** `extRomanType` from the **class** `romanType` to do the following: In the **class** `extRomanType`, overload the arithmetic operators `+`, `-`, `*`, and `/` so that arithmetic operations can be performed on Roman numbers. Also, overload the pre- and post-increment and decrement operators as member functions of the **class** `extRomanType`.

To add (subtract, multiply, or divide) Roman numbers, add (subtract, multiply, or divide, respectively) their decimal representations and then convert the result to the Roman number format. For subtraction, if the first number is smaller than the second number, output a message saying that, "`Because the first number is smaller than the second, the numbers cannot be subtracted`". Similarly, for division, the numerator must be larger than the denominator. Use similar conventions for the increment and decrement operators.

c. Write the definitions of the functions to overload the operators described in part b.

d. Test your **class** `extRomanType` on the following program. (Include the appropriate header files.)

```cpp
int main()
{
    extRomanType num1("XXXIV");
    extRomanType num2("XV");
    extRomanType num3;

    cout << "Num1 = " << num1 << endl;
    cout << "Num2 = " << num2 << endl;
    cout << "Num1 + Num2 = " << num1 + num2 << endl;
    cout << "Num1 * Num2 = " << num1 * num2 << endl;

    cout << "Enter two numbers in Roman format: ";
    cin >> num1 >> num2;
    cout << endl;

    cout << "Num1 = " << num1 << endl;
    cout << "Num2 = " << num2 << endl;
```

```
            num3 = num2 * num1;
            cout << "Num3 = " << num3 << endl;

            cout << "--num3: " << --num3 << endl;
            cout << "++num3: " << ++num3 << endl;

            return 0;
        }
```

14. Write the definitions of the member functions of the **class**es `arrayListType` and `unorderedArrayListType` that are not given in this chapter. Also, write a program to test your functions.

15. Write the definition of the **class template** `orderedArrayList`, derived from the **class** `arrayListType`, to implement an ordered list. As in Chapter 13, add the function `insert` in this class. Provide the definitions of the nonabstract functions. Also, write a program to test your class.

16. **(Unordered Sets)** Redo Programming Exercise 10 of Chapter 13 using templates.

17. **(Ordered Sets)** Redo Programming Exercise 11 of Chapter 13 using templates.

18. **(Stock Market)** Write a program to help a local stock-trading company automate its systems. The company invests only in the stock market. At the end of each trading day, the company would like to generate and post the listing of its stocks so that investors can see how their holdings performed that day. We assume that the company invests in, say, 10 different stocks. The desired output is to produce two listings, one sorted by stock symbol and another sorted by percent gain from highest to lowest.

    The input data is provided in a file in the following format:

    ```
    symbol openingPrice closingPrice todayHigh todayLow
    prevClose volume
    ```

    For example, the sample data is:

    ```
    MSMT 112.50 115.75 116.50 111.75 113.50 6723823
    CBA 67.50 75.50 78.75 67.50 65.75 378233
    .
    .
    .
    ```

    The first line indicates that the stock symbol is `MSMT`, today's opening price was `112.50`, the closing price was `115.75`, today's high price was `116.50`, today's low price was `111.75`, yesterday's closing price was `113.50`, and the number of shares currently being held is `6723823`.

The listing sorted by stock symbols must be of the following form:

```
*********    First Investor's Heaven   **********
*********        Financial Report         **********
Stock                  Today                      Previous   Percent
Symbol   Open      Close    High     Low       Close      Gain         Volume
------   ------    ------   ------   ------    ---------  -------      -------
   ABC   123.45    130.95   132.00   125.00    120.50      8.67%        10000
  AOLK    80.00     75.00    82.00    74.00     83.00     -9.64%         5000
  CSCO   100.00    102.00   105.00    98.00    101.00      0.99%        25000
   IBD    68.00     71.00    72.00    67.00     75.00     -5.33%        15000
  MSET   120.00    140.00   145.00   140.00    115.00     21.74%        30920
Closing Assets: $9628300.00
_*_*_*_*_*_*_*_*_*_*_*_*_*_*_*_*_*_*_*_*_*_*_*_*_*
```

Develop this programming exercise in two steps. In the first step (part a), design and implement a stock object. In the second step (part b), design and implement an object to maintain a list of stocks.

a. (Stock Object) Design and implement the stock object. Call the class that captures the various characteristics of a stock object stockType.

The main components of a stock are the stock symbol, stock price, and number of shares. Moreover, we need to output the opening price, high price, low price, previous price, and the percent gain/loss for the day. These are also all the characteristics of a stock. Therefore, the stock object should store all this information.

Perform the following operations on each stock object:

i. Set the stock information.

ii. Print the stock information.

iii. Show the different prices.

iv. Calculate and print the percent gain/loss.

v. Show the number of shares.

a.1. The natural ordering of the stock list is by stock symbol. Overload the relational operators to compare two stock objects by their symbols.

a.2. Overload the insertion operator, <<, for easy output.

a.3. Because the data is stored in a file, overload the stream extraction operator, >>, for easy input.

For example, suppose infile is an ifstream object and the input file was opened using the object infile. Further suppose that myStock is a stock object. Then, the statement:

```
infile >> myStock;
```

reads the data from the input file and stores it in the object `myStock`. (Note that this statement reads and stores the data in the relevant components of `myStock`.)

b. Now that you have designed and implemented the `class stockType` to implement a stock object in a program, it is time to create a list of stock objects.

Let us call the class to implement a list of stock objects `stockListType`.

The `class stockListType` must be derived from the `class unorderedArrayListType`, which you designed and implemented in Programming Exercise 14 (of this chapter). However, the `class stockListType` is a very specific class, designed to create a list of stock objects. Therefore, the `class stockListType` is no longer a template.

The following statement derives the `class stockListType` from the `class unorderedArrayListType`:

```
class stockListType: public unorderedArrayListType<stockType>
{
    member list
};
```

The member variables to hold the list elements, the length of the list, and the `max listSize` were declared as `protected` in the `class listType`. Therefore, these members can be directly accessed in the `class stockListType`. Also, add a function to sort the stock list by the stock symbol.

Because the company also requires you to produce the list ordered by the percent gain/loss, you need to sort the stock list by this component. However, you are not to physically sort the list by the component percent gain/loss. Instead, you will provide a logical ordering with respect to this component.

To do so, add a member variable, an array, to hold the indices of the stock list ordered by the component percent gain/loss. Call this array `sortIndicesGainLoss`. When printing the list ordered by the component percent gain/loss, use the array `sortIndicesGainLoss` to print the list. The elements of the array `sortIndicesGainLoss` will tell which component of the stock list to print next.

c. Write a program that uses these two classes to automate the company's analysis of stock data.

EXCEPTION HANDLING

IN THIS CHAPTER, YOU WILL:

- Learn what an exception is
- Learn how to handle exceptions within a program
- See how a `try`/`catch` block is used to handle exceptions
- Become familiar with C++ exception classes
- Learn how to create your own exception classes
- Discover how to throw and rethrow an exception
- Explore stack unwinding

An exception is an occurrence of an undesirable situation that can be detected during program execution. For example, division by zero is an exception. Similarly, trying to open an input file that does not exist is an exception, as is an array index that goes out of bounds.

Until now, we have dealt with certain exceptions by using either an `if` statement or the `assert` function. For instance, in Examples 5-3 and 5-4, before dividing `sum` by `counter` or `count`, we checked whether `counter` or `count` was nonzero. Similarly, in the Programming Example `newString` (Chapter 14), we used the `assert` function to determine whether the array index is within bounds.

On the other hand, there were places where we simply ignored the exception. For instance, while determining a substring in a string (Chapter 8), we never checked whether the starting position of the substring was within range. Also, we did not handle the array index out-of-bounds exception. However, in all these cases, if exceptions occurred during program execution, either we included code to terminate the program or the program terminated with an appropriate error message. For instance, if we opened an input file in the function `main` and the input file did not exist, we terminated the function `main` and so the program was terminated.

There are situations when an exception occurs, but you don't want the program to simply ignore the exception and terminate. For example, a program that monitors stock performance should not automatically sell if the account balance goes below a certain level. It should inform the stockholder and request an appropriate action. Similarly, a program that monitors a patient's heartbeat cannot be terminated if the blood pressure goes very high. A program that monitors a satellite in space cannot be terminated if there is a temporary power failure in some section of the satellite.

The code to handle exceptions depends on the type of application you develop. One common way to provide exception-handling code is to add exception-handling code at the point where an error can occur. This technique allows the programmer reading the code to see the exception-handling code together with the actual code and to determine whether the error-checking code is properly implemented. The disadvantage of this approach is that the program can become cluttered with exception-handling code, which can make understanding and maintaining the program difficult. This can distract the programmer from ensuring that the program functions correctly.

Handling Exceptions within a Program

In Chapter 3, we noted that if you try to input invalid data into a variable, the input stream enters the fail state and so an exception occurs. This occurs, for example, if you try to input a letter into an `int` variable. Chapter 3 also showed how to clear and restore the input stream. Chapter 4 introduced the `assert` function and explained how to use it to avoid certain unforeseeable errors, such as division by zero. Even though the function `assert` can check whether an expression meets the required condition(s), if the conditions are not met, it terminates the program. As indicated in the previous section, situations occur where, if something goes wrong, the program should not be simply terminated.

This section discusses how to handle exceptions. However, first we offer some examples that show what can happen if an exception is not handled. We also review some of the ways to handle exceptions.

The program in Example 15-1 shows what happens when division by zero occurs and the problem is not addressed.

EXAMPLE 15-1

```cpp
#include <iostream>

using namespace std;

int main()
{
    int dividend, divisor, quotient;                //Line 1

    cout << "Line 2: Enter the dividend: ";         //Line 2
    cin >> dividend;                                //Line 3
    cout << endl;                                   //Line 4

    cout << "Line 5: Enter the divisor: ";          //Line 5
    cin >> divisor;                                 //Line 6
    cout << endl;                                   //Line 7

    quotient = dividend / divisor;                  //Line 8
    cout << "Line 9: Quotient = " << quotient
         << endl;                                   //Line 9

    return 0;                                        //Line 10
}
```

Sample Run 1:

```
Line 2: Enter the dividend: 12

Line 5: Enter the divisor: 5

Line 9: Quotient = 2
```

Sample Run 2:

```
Line 2: Enter the dividend: 24

Line 5: Enter the divisor: 0
```

```
abcfgh.exe has encountered a problem and needs to close. We are sorry
for the inconvenience.
```

In Sample Run 1, the value of `divisor` is nonzero and so no exception occurs. The program calculates and outputs the quotient and terminates normally.

In Sample Run 2, the value entered for `divisor` is 0. The statement in Line 8 divides `dividend` by the divisor. However, the program does not check whether `divisor` is 0 before dividing `dividend` by `divisor`. So the program crashes with the message shown. Notice that the error message is platform independent, that is, SDK dependent. Some SDKs might not give this error message and simply hang.

Next, consider Example 15-2. This is the same program as in Example 15-1, except that in Line 8 the program checks whether `divisor` is zero.

EXAMPLE 15-2

```cpp
#include <iostream>

using namespace std;

int main()
{
    int dividend, divisor, quotient;                    //Line 1

    cout << "Line 2: Enter the dividend: ";             //Line 2
    cin >> dividend;                                    //Line 3
    cout << endl;                                       //Line 4

    cout << "Line 5: Enter the divisor: ";              //Line 5
    cin >> divisor;                                     //Line 6
    cout << endl;                                       //Line 7

    if (divisor != 0)                                   //Line 8
    {
        quotient = dividend / divisor;                  //Line 9
        cout << "Line 10: Quotient = " << quotient
            << endl;                                    //Line 10
    }
    else                                                //Line 11
        cout << "Line 12: Cannot divide by zero."
            << endl;                                    //Line 12

    return 0;                                           //Line 13
}
```

Sample Run 1:

```
Line 2: Enter the dividend: 12

Line 5: Enter the divisor: 5

Line 10: Quotient = 2
```

Sample Run 2:

```
Line 2: Enter the dividend: 24

Line 5: Enter the divisor: 0

Line 12: Cannot divide by zero.
```

In Sample Run 1, the value of `divisor` is nonzero and so no exception occurs. The program calculates and outputs the quotient and terminates normally.

In Sample Run 2, the value entered for `divisor` is 0. In Line 8, the program checks whether `divisor` is 0. Because `divisor` is 0, the expression in the `if` statement fails and so the `else` part executes, which outputs the third line of the sample run.

The program in Example 15-3 uses the function `assert` to determine whether the divisor is zero. If the divisor is zero, the function `assert` terminates the program with an error message.

EXAMPLE 15-3

```cpp
#include <iostream>
#include <cassert>

using namespace std;

int main()
{
    int dividend, divisor, quotient;                //Line 1

    cout << "Line 2: Enter the dividend: ";         //Line 2
    cin >> dividend;                                //Line 3
    cout << endl;                                   //Line 4

    cout << "Line 5: Enter the divisor: ";          //Line 5
    cin >> divisor;                                 //Line 6
    cout << endl;                                   //Line 7

    assert(divisor != 0);                           //Line 8
    quotient = dividend / divisor;                  //Line 9

    cout << "Line 10: Quotient = " << quotient
         << endl;                                   //Line 10

    return 0;                                        //Line 11
}
```

Sample Run 1:

```
Line 2: Enter the dividend: 26

Line 5: Enter the divisor: 7

Line 10: Quotient = 3
```

Sample Run 2:

Line 2: Enter the dividend: `24`

Line 5: Enter the divisor: `0`

Assertion failed: divisor != 0, file c:\chapter 15 source code\ch15_exp3.cpp, line 19

In Sample Run 1, the value of `divisor` is nonzero and so no exception occurs. The program calculates and outputs the quotient and terminates normally.

In Sample Run 2, the value entered for `divisor` is 0. In Line 8, the function `assert` checks whether `divisor` is nonzero. Because `divisor` is 0, the expression in the `assert` statement evaluates to **false**, and the function `assert` terminates the program with the error message shown in the third line of the output.

C++ Mechanisms of Exception Handling

Examples 15-1 through 15-3 show what happens when an exception occurs in a program and is not processed. This section describes how to include the necessary code to handle exceptions within a program.

try/catch Block

The statements that may generate an exception are placed in a **try** block. The **try** block also contains statements that should not be executed if an exception occurs. The **try** block is followed by one or more **catch** blocks. A **catch** block specifies the type of exception it can catch and contains an exception handler.

The general syntax of the **try/catch** block is:

```
try
{
    //statements
}
catch (dataType1 identifier)
{
    //exception handling code
}
.
.
.
catch (dataTypen identifier)
{
    //exception handling code
}
.
.
.
catch (...)
{
    //exception handling code
}
```

Suppose there is a statement that can generate an exception, for example, division by 0. Usually, before executing such a statement, we check whether certain conditions are met. For example, before performing the division, we check whether the divisor is non–zero. If the conditions are not met, we typically generate an exception, which in C++ terminology is called throwing an exception. This is typically done using the **throw** statement, which we will explain shortly. We will show what is typically thrown to generate an exception.

Let us now note the following about **try/catch** blocks:

- If no exception is thrown in a **try** block, all **catch** blocks associated with that **try** block are ignored and program execution resumes after the last **catch** block.

- If an exception is thrown in a **try** block, the remaining statements in that **try** block are ignored. The program searches the **catch** blocks in the order they appear after the **try** block and looks for an appropriate exception handler. If the type of thrown exception matches the parameter type in one of the **catch** blocks, the code of that **catch** block executes and the remaining **catch** blocks after this **catch** block are ignored.

- The last **catch** block that has an ellipses (three dots) is designed to catch any type of exception.

Consider the following **catch** block:

```
catch (int x)
{
    //exception handling code
}
```

In this **catch** block:

- The identifier **x** acts as a parameter. In fact, it is called a **catch** block parameter.

- The data type **int** specifies that this **catch** block can catch an exception of type **int**.

- A **catch** block can have *at most* one **catch** block parameter.

Essentially, the **catch** block parameter becomes a place holder for the value thrown. In this case, **x** becomes a place holder for any thrown value that is of type **int**. In other words, if the thrown value is caught by this **catch** block, then the thrown value is stored in the **catch** block parameter. This way, if the exception handling code wants to do something with that value, it can be accessed via the **catch** block parameter.

Suppose in a **catch** block heading only the data type is specified, that is, there is no **catch** block parameter. The thrown value then *may not* be accessible in the **catch** block exception handling code.

THROWING AN EXCEPTION

In order for an exception to occur in a **try** block and be caught by a **catch** block, the exception must be thrown in the **try** block. The general syntax to **throw** an exception is:

```
throw expression;
```

where **expression** is a constant value, variable, or object. The object being thrown can be either a specific object or an anonymous object. It follows that in C++ an *exception is a value*.

In C++, **throw** is a reserved word.

Example 15-4 illustrates how to use a **throw** statement.

EXAMPLE 15-4

Suppose we have the following declaration:

```
int num = 5;
string str = "Something is wrong!!!";
```

throw expression	**Effect**
`throw 4;`	The constant value 4 is thrown.
`throw x;`	The value of the variable **x** is thrown.
`throw str;`	The object **str** is thrown.
`throw string("Exception found!");`	An anonymous **string** object with the string **"Exception found!"** is thrown.

ORDER OF catch BLOCKS

A **catch** block can catch either all exceptions of a specific type or all types of exceptions. The heading of a **catch** block specifies the type of exception it handles. As noted previously, the **catch** block that has an ellipses (three dots) is designed to catch any type of exception. Therefore, if we put this **catch** block first, then this **catch** block can catch all types of exceptions.

Suppose that an exception occurs in a **try** block and is caught by a **catch** block. The remaining **catch** blocks associated with that **try** block are then ignored. Therefore, you should be careful about the order in which you list **catch** blocks following a **try** block. For example, consider the following sequence of **try/catch** blocks:

```
try                     //Line 1
{
    //statements
}
catch (...)             //Line 2
{
    //statements
}
catch (int x)           //Line 3
{
    //statements
}
```

Suppose that an exception is thrown in the **try** block. Because the **catch** block in Line 2 can catch exceptions of all types, the **catch** block in Line 3 cannot be reached. For this sequence of **try/catch** blocks, some compilers might, in fact, give a syntax error (check your compiler's documentation).

In a sequence of **try/catch** blocks, if the **catch** block with an ellipses (in the heading) is needed, then it should be the last **catch** block of that sequence.

USING **try/catch** BLOCKS IN A PROGRAM

Next, we provide examples that illustrate how a **try/catch** block might appear in a program.

A common error that might occur when performing numeric calculations is division by zero with integer values. If, during program execution, division by zero occurs with integer values and is not addressed by the program, the program might terminate with an error message or simply hang. Example 15-5 shows how to handle division by zero exceptions.

EXAMPLE 15-5

This example illustrates how to catch and handle division by zero exceptions. It also shows how a **try/catch** block might appear in a program.

```cpp
#include <iostream>

using namespace std;

int main()
{
    int dividend, divisor, quotient;                    //Line 1

    try                                                 //Line 2
    {
        cout << "Line 3: Enter the dividend: ";         //Line 3
        cin >> dividend;                                //Line 4
        cout << endl;                                   //Line 5

        cout << "Line 6: Enter the divisor: ";          //Line 6
        cin >> divisor;                                 //Line 7
        cout << endl;                                   //Line 8

        if (divisor == 0)                               //Line 9
            throw 0;                                    //Line 10

        quotient = dividend / divisor;                  //Line 11

        cout << "Line 12: Quotient = " << quotient
             << endl;                                   //Line 12
    }
    catch (int)                                         //Line 13
```

```cpp
    {
        cout << "Line 14: Division by 0." << endl;   //Line 14
    }

    return 0;                                          //Line 15
}
```

Sample Run 1: In this sample run, the user input is shaded.

```
Line 3: Enter the dividend: 17

Line 6: Enter the divisor: 8

Line 12: Quotient = 2
```

Sample Run 2: In this sample run, the user input is shaded.

```
Line 3: Enter the dividend: 34

Line 6: Enter the divisor: 0

Line 14: Division by 0.
```

This program works as follows. The statement in Line 1 declares the `int` variables `dividend`, `divisor`, and `quotient`. The `try` block starts at Line 2. The statement in Line 3 prompts the user to enter the value for the dividend; the statement in Line 4 stores this number in the variable `dividend`. The statement in Line 6 prompts the user to enter the value for the divisor, and the statement in Line 7 stores this number in the variable `divisor`. The statement in Line 9 checks whether the value of `divisor` is 0. If the value of `divisor` is 0, the statement in Line 10 throws the constant value 0. The statement in Line 11 calculates the quotient and stores it in `quotient`. The statement in Line 12 outputs the value of `quotient`.

The `catch` block starts in Line 13 and catches an exception of type `int`.

In Sample Run 1, the program does not throw any exception.

In Sample Run 2, the entered value of `divisor` is 0. Therefore, the statement in Line 10 throws 0, which is caught by the `catch` block starting in Line 13. The statement in Line 14 outputs the appropriate message.

The program in Example 15-6 is the same as the program in Example 15-5, except that the `throw` statement throws the value of the variable `divisor`.

EXAMPLE 15-6

Consider the following code:

```cpp
#include <iostream>

using namespace std;
```

```cpp
int main()
{
    int dividend, divisor, quotient;                //Line 1

    try                                             //Line 2
    {
        cout << "Line 3: Enter the dividend: ";     //Line 3
        cin >> dividend;                            //Line 4
        cout << endl;                               //Line 5

        cout << "Line 6: Enter the divisor: ";      //Line 6
        cin >> divisor;                             //Line 7
        cout << endl;                               //Line 8

        if (divisor == 0)                           //Line 9
            throw divisor;                          //Line 10

        quotient = dividend / divisor;              //Line 11

        cout << "Line 12: Quotient = " << quotient
             << endl;                               //Line 12
    }
    catch (int x)                                   //Line 13
    {
        cout << "Line 14: Division by " << x
             << endl;                               //Line 14
    }

    return 0;                                        //Line 15
}
```

Sample Run 1: In this sample run, the user input is shaded.

```
Line 3: Enter the dividend: 14

Line 6: Enter the divisor: 5

Line 12: Quotient = 2
```

Sample Run 2: In this sample run, the user input is shaded.

```
Line 3: Enter the dividend: 23

Line 6: Enter the divisor: 0

Line 14: Division by 0
```

This program works the same way as the program in Example 15-5.

The program in Example 15-7 illustrates how to handle division by zero, division by a negative integer, and input failure exceptions. It also shows how to throw and catch an object. This program is similar to the programs in Examples 15-5 and 15-6.

EXAMPLE 15-7

```cpp
#include <iostream>
#include <string>

using namespace std;

int main()
{
    int dividend, divisor = 1, quotient;         //Line 1

    string inpStr
        = "The input stream is in the fail state.";  //Line 2

    try                                          //Line 3
    {
        cout << "Line 4: Enter the dividend: ";  //Line 4
        cin >> dividend;                         //Line 5
        cout << endl;                            //Line 6

        cout << "Line 7: Enter the divisor: ";   //Line 7
        cin >> divisor;                          //Line 8
        cout << endl;                            //Line 9

        if (divisor == 0)                        //Line 10
            throw divisor;                       //Line 11
        else if (divisor < 0)                    //Line 12
            throw string("Negative divisor.");   //Line 13
        else if (!cin)                           //Line 14
            throw inpStr;                        //Line 15

        quotient = dividend / divisor;           //Line 16

        cout << "Line 17: Quotient = " << quotient
             << endl;                            //Line 17
    }
    catch (int x)                                //Line 18
    {
        cout << "Line 19: Division by " << x
             << endl;                            //Line 19
    }
    catch (string s)                             //Line 20
    {
        cout << "Line 21: " << s << endl;        //Line 21
    }

    return 0;                                     //Line 22
}
```

Sample Run 1: In this sample run, the user input is shaded.

```
Line 4: Enter the dividend: 23

Line 7: Enter the divisor: 6

Line 17: Quotient = 3
```

Sample Run 2: In this sample run, the user input is shaded.

```
Line 4: Enter the dividend: 34

Line 7: Enter the divisor: -6

Line 21: Negative divisor.
```

Sample Run 3: In this sample run, the user input is shaded.

```
Line 4: Enter the dividend: 34

Line 7: Enter the divisor: g

Line 21: The input stream is in the fail state.
```

In this program, the statements in Lines 1 and 2 declare the variables used in the program. Notice that the `string` object `inpStr` is also initialized.

The statements in Lines 4 through 9 input the data into the variables `dividend` and `divisor`. The statement in Line 10 checks whether `divisor` is 0; the statement in Line 12 checks whether `divisor` is negative; and the statement in Line 14 checks whether the standard input stream is in the fail state.

The statement in Line 11 throws the variable `divisor`; the statement in Line 13 throws an anonymous string object with the string `"Negative divisor."`; and the statement in Line 15 throws the object `inpStr`.

The `catch` block in Line 18 catches an exception of type `int`, and the `catch` block in Line 20 catches an exception of type `string`. If the exception is thrown by the statement in Line 11, it is caught and processed by the `catch` block in Line 18. If the exception is thrown by the statements in Lines 13 or 15, it is caught and processed by the `catch` block in Line 20.

In Sample Run 1, the program does not encounter any problems. In Sample Run 2, division by a negative number occurs. In Sample Run 3, the standard input stream enters the fail state.

Using C++ Exception Classes

C++ provides support to handle exceptions via a hierarchy of classes. The `class` `exception` is the base of the classes designed to handle exceptions. Among others, this class contains the function `what`. The function `what` returns a string containing an appropriate message. All derived classes of the **class** exception override the function **what** to issue their own error messages.

Two classes are immediately derived from the **class** exception: logic_error and runtime_error. Both these classes are defined in the header file stdexcept.

To deal with logical errors in a program, such as a string subscript out of range or an invalid argument to a function call, several classes are derived from the **class** logic_error. For example, the **class** invalid_argument is designed to deal with illegal arguments used in a function call. The **class** out_of_range deals with the string subscript out of range error. If a length greater than the maximum allowed for a string object is used, the **class** length_error deals with this error. For example, recall that every string object has a maximum length (see Chapter 8). If a length larger then the maximum length allowed for a string is used, then the length_error exception is generated. If the operator **new** cannot allocate memory space, this operator throws a bad_alloc exception.

The **class** runtime_error is designed to deal with errors that can be detected only during program execution. For example, to deal with arithmetic overflow and underflow exceptions, the **class**es overflow_error and underflow_error are derived from the **class** runtime_error.

Examples 15-8 and 15-9 illustrate how C++'s exception classes are used to handle exceptions in a program.

The program in Example 15-8 shows how to handle the exceptions out_of_range and length_error. Notice that in this program these exceptions are thrown by the string functions substr and the string concatenation operator +. Because the exceptions are thrown by these functions, we do not include any **throw** statement in the **try** block.

EXAMPLE 15-8

```cpp
#include <iostream>
#include <string>

using namespace std;

int main()
{
    string sentence;                                    //Line 1
    string str1, str2, str3;                            //Line 2

    try                                                 //Line 3
    {
        sentence = "Testing string exceptions!";        //Line 4
        cout << "Line 5: sentence = " << sentence
             << endl;                                   //Line 5
        cout << "Line 6: sentence.length() = "
             << static_cast<int>(sentence.length())
             << endl;                                   //Line 6
```

```cpp
    str1 = sentence.substr(8, 20);              //Line 7
    cout << "Line 8: str1 = " << str1
         << endl;                                //Line 8

    str2 = sentence.substr(28, 10);             //Line 9
    cout << "Line 10: str2 = " << str2
         << endl;                                //Line 10

    str3 = "Exception handling. " + sentence;   //Line 11
    cout << "Line 12: str3 = " << str3
         << endl;                                //Line 12

}
catch (out_of_range re)                         //Line 13
{
    cout << "Line 14: In the out_of_range "
         << "catch block: " << re.what()
         << endl;                                //Line 14
}
catch (length_error le)                         //Line 15
{
    cout << "Line 16: In the length_error "
         << "catch block: " << le.what()
         << endl;                                //Line 16
}

    return 0;                                    //Line 17
}
```

Sample Run:

```
Line 5: sentence = Testing string exceptions!
Line 6: sentence.length() = 26
Line 8: str1 = string exceptions!
Line 14: In the out_of_range catch block: invalid string position
```

In this program, the statement in Line 7 uses the function `substr` to determine a substring in the string object `sentence`. The length of the string sentence is 26. Because the starting position of the substring is 8, which is less than 26, no exception is thrown. However, in the statement in Line 9, the starting position of the substring is 28, which is greater than 26 (the length of `sentence`). Therefore, the function `substr` throws an `out_of_range` exception, which is caught and processed by the `catch` block in Line 13. Notice that in the statement in Line 14, the object `re` uses the function `what` to return the error message, `invalid string position`.

The program in Example 15-9 illustrates how to handle the exception `bad_alloc` thrown by the operator `new`.

EXAMPLE 15-9

```cpp
#include <iostream>

using namespace std;

int main()
{
    int *list[100];                              //Line 1

    try                                          //Line 2
    {
        for (int i = 0; i < 100; i++)            //Line 3
        {
            list[i] = new int[50000000];         //Line 4
            cout << "Line 4: Created list[" << i
                 << "] of 50000000 components."
                 << endl;                        //Line 5
        }
    }
    catch (bad_alloc be)                         //Line 6
    {
        cout << "Line 7: In the bad_alloc catch "
             << "block: " << be.what() << "."
             << endl;                            //Line 7
    }

    return 0;                                    //Line 8
}
```

Sample Run:

```
Line 4: Created list[0] of 50000000 components.
Line 4: Created list[1] of 50000000 components.
Line 4: Created list[2] of 50000000 components.
Line 4: Created list[3] of 50000000 components.
Line 4: Created list[4] of 50000000 components.
Line 4: Created list[5] of 50000000 components.
Line 4: Created list[6] of 50000000 components.
Line 4: Created list[7] of 50000000 components.
Line 7: In the bad_alloc catch block: bad allocation.
```

The preceding program works as follows. The statement in Line 1 declares `list` to be an array of 100 pointers. The body of the **for** loop in Line 3 is designed to execute 100 times. For each iteration of the **for** loop, the statement in Line 4 uses the operator **new** to allocate an array of 50000000 components of type **int**. As shown in the sample run, the operator **new** is able to create eight arrays of 50000000 components each. In the ninth iteration, the operator **new** is unable to create the array and throws a `bad_alloc` exception. This exception is caught and processed by the **catch** block in Line 6. Notice that the expression `be.what()` returns the string `bad_alloc`. (Moreover, the string returned by `be.what()` is SDK dependent. Some SDKs might return the string `bad_alloc`.) After the statement in Line 7 executes, control exits the `try`/`catch` block and the statement in Line 8 terminates the program.

Creating Your Own Exception Classes

Whenever you create your own classes or write programs, exceptions are likely to occur. As you have seen, C++ provides numerous exception classes to deal with these situations. However, it does not provide all the exception classes you will ever need. Therefore, C++ enables programmers to create their own exception classes to handle both the exceptions not covered by C++'s exception classes, as well as their own exceptions. This section describes how to create your own exception classes.

C++ uses the same mechanism to process the exceptions that you define as for built-in exceptions. However, you must throw your own exceptions using the `throw` statement.

In C++, any class can be considered an exception class. Therefore, an exception class is simply a class. It need not be inherited from the `class` `exception`. What makes a class an exception is how you use it.

The exception class that you define can be very simple in the sense that it does not contain any members. For example, the following code can be considered an exception class:

```cpp
class dummyExceptionClass
{
};
```

The program in Example 15-10 uses a user-defined class (with no members) to throw an exception.

EXAMPLE 15-10

```cpp
#include <iostream>

using namespace std;

class divByZero
{};

int main()
{
    int dividend, divisor, quotient;              //Line 1
```

```cpp
    try                                         //Line 2
    {
        cout << "Line 3: Enter the dividend: ";  //Line 3
        cin >> dividend;                         //Line 4
        cout << endl;                            //Line 5

        cout << "Line 6: Enter the divisor: ";   //Line 6
        cin >> divisor;                          //Line 7
        cout << endl;                            //Line 8

        if (divisor == 0)                        //Line 9
            throw divByZero();                   //Line 10

        quotient = dividend / divisor;           //Line 11
        cout << "Line 12: Quotient = " << quotient
            << endl;                             //Line 12
    }
    catch (divByZero)                            //Line 13
    {
        cout << "Line 14: Division by zero!"
            << endl;                             //Line 14
    }

    return 0;                                    //Line 15
}
```

Sample Run 1: In this sample run, the user input is shaded.

```
Line 3: Enter the dividend: 34

Line 6: Enter the divisor: 5

Line 12: Quotient = 6
```

Sample Run 2: In this sample run, the user input is shaded.

```
Line 3: Enter the dividend: 56

Line 6: Enter the divisor: 0

Line 14: Division by zero!
```

The preceding program works as follows. If the user enters 0 for the divisor, the statement in Line 10 throws an anonymous object of the **class** divByZero. The **class** divByZero has no members, and so we cannot really do anything with the thrown object. Therefore, in the **catch** block in Line 13, we specify only the data type name without the parameter name. The statement in Line 14 outputs the appropriate error message.

Let us again consider the statement **throw** divByZero(); in Line 10. Notice that in this statement divByZero is the name of the class, the expression divByZero() creates an anonymous object of this class, and the **throw** statement throws the object.

The exception **class** `divByZero` designed and used in Example 15-10 has no members. Next, we illustrate how to create exception classes with members.

If you want to include members in your exception class, you typically include constructors and the function `what`. Consider the following definition of the **class** `divisionByZero`:

```cpp
#include <iostream>
#include <string>

using namespace std;

class divisionByZero                              //Line 1
{                                                 //Line 2
public:                                           //Line 3
    divisionByZero()                              //Line 4
    {
        message = "Division by zero";             //Line 5
    }                                             //Line 6

    divisionByZero(string str)                    //Line 7
    {                                             //Line 8
        message = str;                            //Line 9
    }                                             //Line 10

    string what()                                 //Line 11
    {                                             //Line 12
        return message;                           //Line 13
    }                                             //Line 14

private:                                          //Line 15
    string message;                               //Line 16
};                                                //Line 17
```

The definition of the **class** `divisionByZero` contains two constructors: the default constructor, and the constructor with parameters. The default constructor stores the string `"Division by zero"` in an object. The constructor with parameters allows users to create their own error messages. The function `what` is used to return the string stored in the object.

NOTE In the definition of the **class** `divisionByZero`, the constructors can also be written as:

```cpp
divisionByZero() : message("Division by zero"){}
divisionByZero(string str) : message(str){}
```

The program in Example 15-11 uses the preceding class to throw an exception.

EXAMPLE 15-11

```cpp
#include <iostream>
#include "divisionByZero.h"

using namespace std;

int main()
{
    int dividend, divisor, quotient;                //Line 1

    try                                             //Line 2
    {
        cout << "Line 3: Enter the dividend: ";     //Line 3
        cin >> dividend;                            //Line 4
        cout << endl;                               //Line 5

        cout << "Line 6: Enter the divisor: ";      //Line 6
        cin >> divisor;                             //Line 7
        cout << endl;                               //Line 8

        if (divisor == 0)                           //Line 9
            throw divisionByZero();                 //Line 10

        quotient = dividend / divisor;              //Line 11
        cout << "Line 12: Quotient = " << quotient
             << endl;                               //Line 12
    }
    catch (divisionByZero divByZeroObj)             //Line 13
    {
        cout << "Line 14: In the divisionByZero "
             << "catch block: "
             << divByZeroObj.what() << endl;        //Line 14
    }

    return 0;                                       //Line 15
}
```

Sample Run 1: In this sample run, the user input is shaded.

```
Line 3: Enter the dividend: 34

Line 6: Enter the divisor: 5

Line 12: Quotient = 6
```

Sample Run 2: In this sample run, the user input is shaded.

```
Line 3: Enter the dividend: 56

Line 6: Enter the divisor: 0

Line 14: In the divisionByZero catch block: Division by zero
```

In this program, the statement in Line 10 throws an object (exception) of the **class** **divisionByZero** if the user enters 0 for the **divisor**. This thrown exception is caught and processed by the **catch** block in Line 13. The parameter **divByZeroObj** in the **catch** block catches the value of the thrown object and then uses the function **what** to return the string stored in the object. The statement in Line 14 outputs the appropriate error message.

The program in Example 15-12 is similar to the program in Example 15-11. Here, the thrown object is still an anonymous object, but the error message is specified by the user (see the statement in Line 10).

EXAMPLE 15-12

```cpp
#include <iostream>
#include "divisionByZero.h"

using namespace std;

int main()
{
    int dividend, divisor, quotient;                         //Line 1

    try                                                      //Line 2
    {
        cout << "Line 3: Enter the dividend: ";              //Line 3
        cin >> dividend;                                     //Line 4
        cout << endl;                                        //Line 5

        cout << "Line 6: Enter the divisor: ";               //Line 6
        cin >> divisor;                                      //Line 7
        cout << endl;                                        //Line 8

        if (divisor == 0)                                    //Line 9
            throw divisionByZero("Found division by zero");  //Line 10

        quotient = dividend / divisor;                       //Line 11
        cout << "Line 12: Quotient = " << quotient
             << endl;                                        //Line 12
    }
    catch (divisionByZero divByZeroObj)                      //Line 13
    {
        cout << "Line 14: In the divisionByZero "
             << "catch block: "
             << divByZeroObj.what() << endl;                 //Line 14
    }

    return 0;                                                //Line 15
}
```

Sample Run 1: In this sample run, the user input is shaded.

```
Line 3: Enter the dividend: 34

Line 6: Enter the divisor: 5

Line 12: Quotient = 6
```

Sample Run 2: In this sample run, the user input is shaded.

```
Line 3: Enter the dividend: 56

Line 6: Enter the divisor: 0

Line 14: In the divisionByZero catch block: Found division by zero
```

This program works the same way as the program in Example 15-11. The details are left as an exercise for you.

In the programs in Examples 15-11 and 15-12, the data manipulation is done in the function `main`. Therefore, the exception is thrown, caught, and processed in the function `main`. The program in Example 15-13 uses the user-defined function `doDivision` to manipulate the data. Therefore, the exception is thrown, caught, and processed in the function `doDivision`.

EXAMPLE 15-13

```cpp
#include <iostream>
#include "divisionByZero.h"

using namespace std;

void doDivision();

int main()
{
    doDivision();                                      //Line 1

    return 0;                                          //Line 2
}

void doDivision()
{
    int dividend, divisor, quotient;                   //Line 3

    try
    {
        cout << "Line 4: Enter the dividend: ";        //Line 4
        cin >> dividend;                               //Line 5
        cout << endl;                                  //Line 6
```

```cpp
        cout << "Line 7: Enter the divisor: ";      //Line 7
        cin >> divisor;                             //Line 8
        cout << endl;                               //Line 9

        if (divisor == 0)                           //Line 10
            throw divisionByZero();                 //Line 11

        quotient = dividend / divisor;              //Line 12
        cout << "Line 13: Quotient = " << quotient
            << endl;                                //Line 13
    }
    catch (divisionByZero divByZeroObj)             //Line 14
    {
        cout << "Line 15: In the function "
            << "doDivision: "
            << divByZeroObj.what() << endl;         //Line 15
    }
}
```

Sample Run 1: In this sample run, the user input is shaded.

```
Line 4: Enter the dividend: 34

Line 7: Enter the divisor: 5

Line 13: Quotient = 6
```

Sample Run 2: In this sample run, the user input is shaded.

```
Line 4: Enter the dividend: 56

Line 7: Enter the divisor: 0

Line 15: In the function doDivision: Division by zero
```

Rethrowing and Throwing an Exception

When an exception occurs in a `try` block, control immediately passes to one of the `catch` blocks. Typically, a `catch` block either handles the exception or partially processes the exception and then rethrows the same exception, or rethrows another exception in order for the calling environment to handle the exception. The `catch` block in Examples 15-4 through 15-13 handles the exception. The mechanism of rethrowing or throwing an exception is quite useful in cases when a `catch` block catches the exception, but the `catch` block cannot handle the exception, or if the `catch` block decides that the exception should be handled by the calling block or environment. This allows the programmer to provide the exception handling code all in one place.

To rethrow or throw an exception, we use the `throw` statement. The general syntax to rethrow an exception caught by a `catch` block is:

```cpp
throw;
```

(in this case, the same exception is rethrown) or:

```
throw expression;
```

where **expression** is a constant value, variable, or object. The object being thrown can be either a specific object or an anonymous object.

A function specifies the exceptions it throws (to be handled somewhere) in its heading using the **throw** clause. For example, the following function specifies that it throws exceptions of type **int**, **string**, and **divisionByZero**, where **divisionByZero** is the class, as defined previously.

```
void exmpThrowExcep(int x) throw (int, string, divisionByZero)
{
    .
    .
    .
    //include the appropriate throw statements
    .
    .
    .
}
```

The program in Example 15-14 further explains how a function specifies the exception it throws.

EXAMPLE 15-14

```
#include <iostream>
#include "divisionByZero.h"

using namespace std;

void doDivision() throw (divisionByZero);

int main()
{
    try                                             //Line 1
    {
        doDivision();                               //Line 2
    }
    catch (divisionByZero divByZeroObj)             //Line 3
    {
        cout << "Line 4: In main: "
             << divByZeroObj.what() << endl;        //Line 4
    }

    return 0;                                        //Line 5
}
```

```cpp
void doDivision() throw (divisionByZero)
{
    int dividend, divisor, quotient;                    //Line 6

    try                                                 //Line 7
    {
        cout << "Line 8: Enter the dividend: ";         //Line 8
        cin >> dividend;                                //Line 9
        cout << endl;                                   //Line 10

        cout << "Line 11: Enter the divisor: ";         //Line 11
        cin >> divisor;                                 //Line 12
        cout << endl;                                   //Line 13

        if (divisor == 0)                               //Line 14
            throw divisionByZero("Found division by 0!"); //Line 15

        quotient = dividend / divisor;                  //Line 16
        cout << "Line 17: Quotient = " << quotient
            << endl;                                    //Line 17
    }
    catch (divisionByZero)                              //Line 18
    {
        throw;                                          //Line 19
    }
}
```

Sample Run 1: In this sample run, the user input is shaded.

```
Line 8: Enter the dividend: 34

Line 11: Enter the divisor: 5

Line 17: Quotient = 6
```

Sample Run 2: In this sample run, the user input is shaded.

```
Line 8: Enter the dividend: 56

Line 11: Enter the divisor: 0

Line 4: In main: Found division by 0!
```

In this program, if the value of **divisor** is 0, the statement in Line 15 throws an exception of type **divisionByZero**, which is an anonymous object of this class, with the message string:

```
"Found division by 0!"
```

The statement in Line 19, in the **catch** block, throws the same exception value, which in this case is an object.

In Sample Run 1, no exception is thrown.

Let us see what happens in Sample Run 2. The function `main` calls the function `doDivision` in the `try` block. In the function `doDivision`, the value of `divisor` is 0, and so the statement in Line 15 throws an exception. The exception is caught by the `catch` block in Line 18. The statement in Line 19 rethrows the same exception. In other words, the `catch` block catches and rethrows the same exception. Therefore, the function call statement in Line 2 results in throwing an exception. This exception is caught and processed by the `catch` block in Line 3.

EXAMPLE 15-15

```cpp
#include <iostream>
#include "divisionByZero.h"

using namespace std;

void doDivision() throw (divisionByZero);

int main()
{
    try                                                //Line 1
    {
        doDivision();                                  //Line 2
    }
    catch (divisionByZero divByZeroObj)                //Line 3
    {
        cout << "Line 4: In main: "
             << divByZeroObj.what() << endl;           //Line 4
    }

    return 0;                                           //Line 5
}

void doDivision() throw (divisionByZero)
{
    int dividend, divisor, quotient;                   //Line 6

    try                                                //Line 7
    {
        cout << "Line 8: Enter the dividend: ";        //Line 8
        cin >> dividend;                               //Line 9
        cout << endl;                                  //Line 10

        cout << "Line 11: Enter the divisor: ";        //Line 11
        cin >> divisor;                                //Line 12
        cout << endl;                                  //Line 13

        if (divisor == 0)                              //Line 14
            throw divisionByZero();                    //Line 15
```

```cpp
        quotient = dividend / divisor;                //Line 16
        cout << "Line 17: Quotient = " << quotient
            << endl;                                  //Line 17
    }
    catch (divisionByZero)                            //Line 18
    {
        throw
          divisionByZero("Division by zero found!");  //Line 19
    }
}
```

Sample Run 1: In this sample run, the user input is shaded.

```
Line 8: Enter the dividend: 34

Line 11: Enter the divisor: 5

Line 17: Quotient = 6
```

Sample Run 2: In this sample run, the user input is shaded.

```
Line 8: Enter the dividend: 56

Line 11: Enter the divisor: 0

Line 4: In main: Division by zero found!
```

This program works the same way as the program in Example 15-14. The only difference is that here, the **catch** block in Line 18 rethrows a different exception value, that is, object.

The programs in Examples 15-14 and 15-15 illustrate how a function can rethrow the same exception, or throw another exception for the calling function to handle. This mechanism is quite useful because it allows a program to handle all the exceptions in one location, rather than spreading the exception handling code throughout the program.

Exception Handling Techniques

When an exception occurs in a program, the programmer usually has three choices: terminate the program, include code in the program to recover from the exception, or log the error and continue. The following sections discuss each of these situations.

Terminate the Program

In some cases, it is best to let the program terminate when an exception occurs. Suppose you have written a program that inputs data from a file. If the input file does not exist when the program executes, then there is no point in continuing with the program. In this case, the program can output an appropriate error message and terminate.

Fix the Error and Continue

In other cases, you will want to handle the exception and let the program continue. Suppose that you have a program that takes as input an integer. If a user inputs a letter in place of a number, the input stream will enter the fail state. This is a situation where you can include the necessary code to keep prompting the user to input a number until the entry is valid. The program in Example 15-16 illustrates this situation.

EXAMPLE 15-16

```cpp
#include <iostream>
#include <string>

using namespace std;

int main()
{
    int number;                                     //Line 1
    bool done = false;                              //Line 2

    string str =
        "The input stream is in the fail state.";   //Line 3

    do                                              //Line 4
    {                                               //Line 5
        try                                         //Line 6
        {                                           //Line 7
            cout << "Line 8: Enter an integer: ";   //Line 8
            cin >> number;                          //Line 9
            cout << endl;                           //Line 10

            if (!cin)                               //Line 11
                throw str;                          //Line 12

            done = true;                            //Line 13
            cout << "Line 14: Number = " << number
                << endl;                            //Line 14
        }                                           //Line 15
        catch (string messageStr)                   //Line 16
        {                                           //Line 17
            cout << "Line 18: " << messageStr
                << endl;                            //Line 18
            cout << "Line 19: Restoring the "
                << "input stream." << endl;         //Line 19
            cin.clear();                            //Line 20
            cin.ignore(100, '\n');                  //Line 21
        }                                           //Line 22
    }
    while (!done);                                  //Line 23

    return 0;                                       //Line 24
}
```

Sample Run: In this sample run, the user input is shaded.

```
Line 8: Enter an integer: r5

Line 18: The input stream is in the fail state.
Line 19: Restoring the input stream.
Line 8: Enter an integer: d45

Line 18: The input stream is in the fail state.
Line 19: Restoring the input stream.
Line 8: Enter an integer: hw3

Line 18: The input stream is in the fail state.
Line 19: Restoring the input stream.
Line 8: Enter an integer: 48

Line 14: Number = 48
```

This program prompts the user to enter an integer. If the input is invalid, the standard input stream enters the fail state. In the `try` block, the statement in Line 12 throws an exception, which is a string object. Control passes to the `catch` block, and the exception is caught and processed. The statement in Line 20 restores the input stream to its good state, and the statement in Line 21 clears the rest of the input from the line. The `do...while` loop continues to prompt the user until the user inputs a valid number.

Log the Error and Continue

The program that terminates when an exception occurs usually assumes that this termination is reasonably safe. However, if your program is designed to run a nuclear reactor or continuously monitor a satellite, it cannot be terminated if an exception occurs. These programs should report the exception, but the program must continue to run.

For example, consider a program that analyzes an airline's ticketing transactions. Because numerous ticketing transactions occur each day, a program is run at the end of each day to validate that day's transactions. This type of program would take an enormous amount of time to process the transactions and use exceptions to identify any erroneous entries. Instead, when an exception occurs, the program should write the exception into a file and continue to analyze the transactions.

Stack Unwinding

The examples given in this chapter show how to catch and process an exception. In particular, you learned how to catch and process an exception in the same block, as well as process the caught exception in the calling environment.

When an exception is thrown in, say, a function, the function can do the following:

- Do nothing.
- Partially process the exception and throw the same exception or a new exception.
- Throw a new exception.

In each of these cases, the function-call stack is unwound so that the exception can be caught in the next `try`/`catch` block. When the function call stack is unwound, the function in which the exception was not caught and/or rethrown terminates, and the memory for its local variables is destroyed. The stack unwinding continues until either a `try`/`catch` handles the exception, or the program does not handle the exception. If the program does not handle the exception, then the function `terminate` is called to terminate the program.

Examples 15-17 and 15-18 illustrate how the exceptions are propagated. For this, let us define the following exception class:

```cpp
#include <string>

using namespace std;

class myException
{
public:
    myException()
    {
        message = "Something is wrong!";
    }

    myException(string str)
    {
        message = str;
    }

    string what()
    {
        return message;
    }

private:
    string message;
};
```

NOTE In the definition of the `class` myException, the constructors can also be written as follows:

```cpp
        myException() : message("Something is wrong!"){}
        myException(string str) : message(str){}
```

The program in Example 15-17 illustrates how exceptions thrown in a function get processed in the calling environment.

EXAMPLE 15-17

```cpp
#include <iostream>
#include "myException.h"

using namespace std;

void functionA() throw (myException);
void functionB() throw (myException);
void functionC() throw (myException);

int main()
{
    try
    {
        functionA();
    }
    catch (myException me)
    {
        cout << me.what() << " Caught in main." << endl;
    }

    return 0;
}

void functionA() throw (myException)
{
    functionB();
}

void functionB()   throw (myException)
{
    functionC();
}

void functionC() throw (myException)
{
    throw myException("Exception generated in function C.");
}
```

Sample Run:

```
Exception generated in function C. Caught in main.
```

In this program, the function `main` calls `functionA`, `functionA` calls `functionB`, and `functionB` calls `functionC`. The function `functionC` creates and throws an exception of type `myException`. The functions `functionA` and `functionB` do not process the exception thrown by `functionC`.

The function `main` calls `functionA` in the **try** block and catches the exception thrown by `functionC`. The parameter `me` in the **catch** block heading catches the value of the exception and then uses the function `what` to return the string stored in that object. The output statement in the **catch** block outputs the appropriate message.

The program in Example 15-18 is similar to the program in Example 15-17. Here, the exception is caught and processed by the immediate calling environment.

EXAMPLE 15-18

```cpp
#include <iostream>
#include "myException.h"

using namespace std;

void functionA();
void functionB();
void functionC() throw (myException);

int main()
{
    try
    {
        functionA();
    }
    catch (myException e)
    {
        cout << e.what() << " Caught in main." << endl;
    }

    return 0;
}

void functionA()
{
    functionB();
}

void functionB()
{
    try
    {
        functionC();
    }
    catch (myException me)
    {
        cout << me.what() << " Caught in functionB." << endl;
    }
}
```

```
void functionC() throw (myException)
{
    throw myException("Exception generated in function C.");
}
```

Sample Run:

```
Exception generated in function C. Caught in functionB.
```

In this program, the exception is caught and processed by `functionB`. Even though the function `main` contains the `try/catch` block, the `try` block does not throw any exceptions because the exception thrown by `functionC` is caught and processed by `functionB`.

QUICK REVIEW

1. An exception is an occurrence of an undesirable situation that can be detected during program execution.

2. Some typical ways of dealing with exceptions are to use an `if` statement or the `assert` function.

3. The function `assert` can check whether an expression meets the required condition(s). If the conditions are not met, it terminates the program.

4. The `try/catch` block is used to handle exceptions within a program.

5. Statements that may generate an exception are placed in a `try` block. The `try` block also contains statements that should not be executed if an exception occurs.

6. The `try` block is followed by one or more `catch` blocks.

7. A `catch` block specifies the type of exception it can catch and contains an exception handler.

8. If the heading of a `catch` block contains...(ellipses) in place of parameters, then this `catch` block can catch exceptions of all types.

9. If no exceptions are thrown in a `try` block, all `catch` blocks associated with that `try` block are ignored and program execution resumes after the last `catch` block.

10. If an exception is thrown in a `try` block, the remaining statements in the `try` block are ignored. The program searches the `catch` blocks, in the order they appear after the `try` block, and looks for an appropriate exception handler. If the type of the thrown exception matches the parameter type in one of the `catch` blocks, then the code in that `catch` block executes and the remaining `catch` blocks after this `catch` block are ignored.

11. The data type of the `catch` block parameter specifies the type of exception that the `catch` block can catch.

12. A `catch` block can have, at most, one `catch` block parameter.

13. If only the data type is specified in a `catch` block heading, that is, if there is no `catch` block parameter, then the thrown value may not be accessible in the `catch` block exception handling code.

14. In order for an exception to occur in a `try` block and be caught by a `catch` block, the exception must be thrown in the `try` block.

15. The general syntax to `throw` an exception is:

```
throw expression;
```

where `expression` is a constant value, variable, or object. The object being thrown can be either a specific object or an anonymous object.

16. C++ provides support to handle exceptions via a hierarchy of classes.

17. The `class` `exception` is the base class of the exception classes provided by C++.

18. The function `what` returns the string containing the exception object thrown by C++'s built-in exception classes.

19. The `class` `exception` is contained in the header file `exception`.

20. The two classes that are immediately derived from the `class` `exception` are `logic_error` and `runtime_error`. Both these classes are defined in the header file `stdexcept`.

21. The `class` `invalid_argument` is designed to deal with illegal arguments used in a function call.

22. The `class` `out_of_range` deals with the string subscript `out_of_range` error.

23. If a length greater than the maximum allowed for a string object is used, the `class` `length_error` deals with the error that occurs when a length greater than the maximum size allowed for the object being manipulated is used.

24. If the operator `new` cannot allocate memory space, this operator throws a `bad_alloc` exception.

25. The `class` `runtime_error` is designed to deal with errors that can be detected only during program execution. For example, to deal with arithmetic overflow and underflow exceptions, the classes `overflow_error` and `underflow_error` are derived from the `class` `runtime_error`.

26. A `catch` block typically handles the exception or partially processes the exception, and then either rethrows the same exception or rethrows another exception in order for the calling environment to handle the exception.

27. C++ enables programmers to create their own exception classes to handle both the exceptions not covered by C++'s exception classes, as well as their own exceptions.

28. C++ uses the same mechanism to process the exceptions you define as for built-in exceptions. However, you must throw your own exceptions using the `throw` statement.

29. In C++, any class can be considered an exception class. It need not be inherited from the `class` exception. What makes a class an exception is how it is used.

30. The general syntax to rethrow an exception caught by a `catch` block is:

```
throw;
```

(in this case, the same exception is rethrown) or:

```
throw expression;
```

where `expression` is a constant value, variable, or object. The object being thrown can be either a specific object or an anonymous object.

31. A function specifies the exceptions it throws in its heading using the `throw` clause.

32. When an exception is thrown in a function, the function can do the following: Do nothing; Partially process the exception and throw the same exception or a new exception; Throw a new exception. In each of these cases, the function-call stack is unwound so that the exception can be caught in the next `try`/`catch` block. The stack unwinding continues until a `try`/`catch` handles the exception or if the program does not handle the exception.

33. If the program does not handle the exception, then the function `terminate` is called to terminate the program.

EXERCISES

1. Mark the following statements as true or false.

   a. The order in which `catch` blocks are listed is not important.

   b. An exception can be caught either in the function where it occurred, or in any of the functions that led to the invocation of this method.

   c. One way to handle an exception is to print an error message and exit the program.

   d. All exceptions need to be reported to avoid compilation errors.

2. Consider the following C++ code:

```
int lowerLimit;
    .
    .
    .
try
{
    cout << "Entering the try block." << endl;
```

```cpp
        if (lowerLimit < 100)
            throw exception("Lower limit violation.");

        cout << "Exiting the try block." << endl;
    }
    catch (exception eObj)
    {
        cout << "Exception: " << eObj.what() << endl;
    }
    cout << "After the catch block" << endl;
```

What is the output if:

a.   the value of `lowerLimit` is 50?

b.   the value of `lowerLimit` is 150?

3.   Consider the following C++ code:

```cpp
int lowerLimit;
int divisor;
int result;

try
{
    cout << "Entering the try block." << endl;

    if (divisor == 0)
        throw 0;
    if (lowerLimit < 100)
        throw string("Lower limit violation.");

    result = lowerLimit / divisor;
    cout << "Exiting the try block." << endl;
}
catch (int x)
{
    cout << "Exception: " << x << endl;
    result = 120;
}
catch (string str)
{
    cout << "Exception: " << str << endl;
}

cout << "After the catch block" << endl;
```

What is the output if:

a.   The value of `lowerLimit` is 50 and the value of `divisor` is 10?

b.   The value of `lowerLimit` is 50 and the value of `divisor` is 0?

c.   The value of `lowerLimit` is 150 and the value of `divisor` is 10?

d.   The value of `lowerLimit` is 150 and the value of `divisor` is 0?

4. Define an exception **class** called `tornadoException`. The class should have two constructors, including the default constructor. If the exception is thrown with the default constructor, the method **what** should return `"Tornado: Take cover immediately!"`. The other constructor has a single parameter, say, m, of the **int** type. If the exception is thrown with this constructor, the method **what** should return `"Tornado: m miles away; and approaching!"`

5. Write a C++ program to test the **class** `tornadoException` specified in Exercise 4.

6. Suppose the exception **class** `myException` is defined as follows:

```cpp
class myException
{
public:
    myException()
    {
        message = "myException thrown!";
        cout << "Immediate attention required!"
            << endl;
    }

    myException(string msg)
    {
        message = msg;
        cout << "Attention required!" << endl;
    }

    string what()
    {
        return message;
    }

private:
    string message;
}
```

Suppose that in a user program, the **catch** block has the following form:

```cpp
catch (myException mE)
{
    cout << mE.what() << endl;
}
```

What output will be produced if the exception is thrown with the default constructor? Also, what output will be produced if the exception is thrown with the constructor with parameters with the following actual parameter?

`"May Day, May Day"`

PROGRAMMING EXERCISES

1. Write a program that prompts the user to enter a length in feet and inches and outputs the equivalent length in centimeters. If the user enters a negative number or a nondigit number, throw and handle an appropriate exception and prompt the user to enter another set of numbers.

2. Redo Programming Exercise 6 of Chapter 8 so that your program handles exceptions such as division by zero.

RECURSION

IN THIS CHAPTER, YOU WILL:

- Learn about recursive definitions
- Explore the base case and the general case of a recursive definition
- Discover what is a recursive algorithm
- Learn about recursive functions
- Explore how to use recursive functions to implement recursive algorithms

In previous chapters, to devise solutions to problems, we used the most common technique, called iteration. For certain problems, however, using the iterative technique to obtain the solution is quite complicated. This chapter introduces another problem-solving technique, called recursion, and provides several examples demonstrating how recursion works.

Recursive Definitions

The process of solving a problem by reducing it to smaller versions of itself is called **recursion**. Recursion is a very powerful way to solve certain problems for which the solution would otherwise be very complicated. Let us consider a problem that is familiar to most everyone.

In mathematics, the factorial of an integer is defined as follows:

$$0! = 1 \tag{16-1}$$

$$n! = n \times (n - 1)! \quad \text{if} \quad n > 0 \tag{16-2}$$

In this definition, $0!$ is defined to be 1, and if n is an integer greater than 0, first we find $(n - 1)!$ and then multiply it by n. To find $(n - 1)!$, we apply the definition again. If $(n - 1) > 0$, then we use Equation 16-2; otherwise, we use Equation 16-1. Thus, for an integer n greater than 0, $n!$ is obtained by first finding $(n - 1)!$ (that is, $n!$ is reduced to a smaller version of itself) and then multiplying $(n - 1)!$ by n.

Let us apply this definition to find $3!$. Here, $n = 3$. Because $n > 0$, we use Equation 16-2 to obtain:

$$3! = 3 \times 2!$$

Next, we find $2!$ Here, $n = 2$. Because $n > 0$, we use Equation 16-2 to obtain:

$$2! = 2 \times 1!$$

Now to find $1!$, we again use Equation 16-2 because $n = 1 > 0$. Thus:

$$1! = 1 \times 0!$$

Finally, we use Equation 16-1 to find $0!$, which is 1. Substituting $0!$ into $1!$ gives $1! = 1$. This gives $2! = 2 \times 1! = 2 \times 1 = 2$, which, in turn, gives $3! = 3 \times 2! = 3 \times 2 = 6$.

The solution in Equation 16-1 is direct—that is, the right side of the equation contains no factorial notation. The solution in Equation 16-2 is given in terms of a smaller version of itself. The definition of the factorial given in Equations 16-1 and 16-2 is called a **recursive definition**. Equation 16-1 is called the **base case** (that is, the case for which the solution is obtained directly); Equation 16-2 is called the **general case**.

Recursive definition: A definition in which something is defined in terms of a smaller version of itself.

From the previous example (factorial), it is clear that:

1.   Every recursive definition must have one (or more) base cases.
2.   The general case must eventually be reduced to a base case.
3.   The base case stops the recursion.

The concept of recursion in computer science works similarly. Here we talk about recursive algorithms and recursive functions. An algorithm that finds the solution to a given problem by reducing the problem to smaller versions of itself is called a **recursive algorithm**. The recursive algorithm must have one or more base cases, and the general solution must eventually be reduced to a base case.

A function that calls itself is called a **recursive function**. That is, the body of the recursive function contains a statement that causes the same function to execute again before completing the current call. Recursive algorithms are implemented using recursive functions.

Next, let us write the recursive function that implements the factorial function:

```
int fact(int num)
{
    if (num == 0)
        return 1;
    else
        return num * fact(num - 1);
}
```

Figure 16-1 traces the execution of the following statement:

```
cout << fact(4) << endl;
```

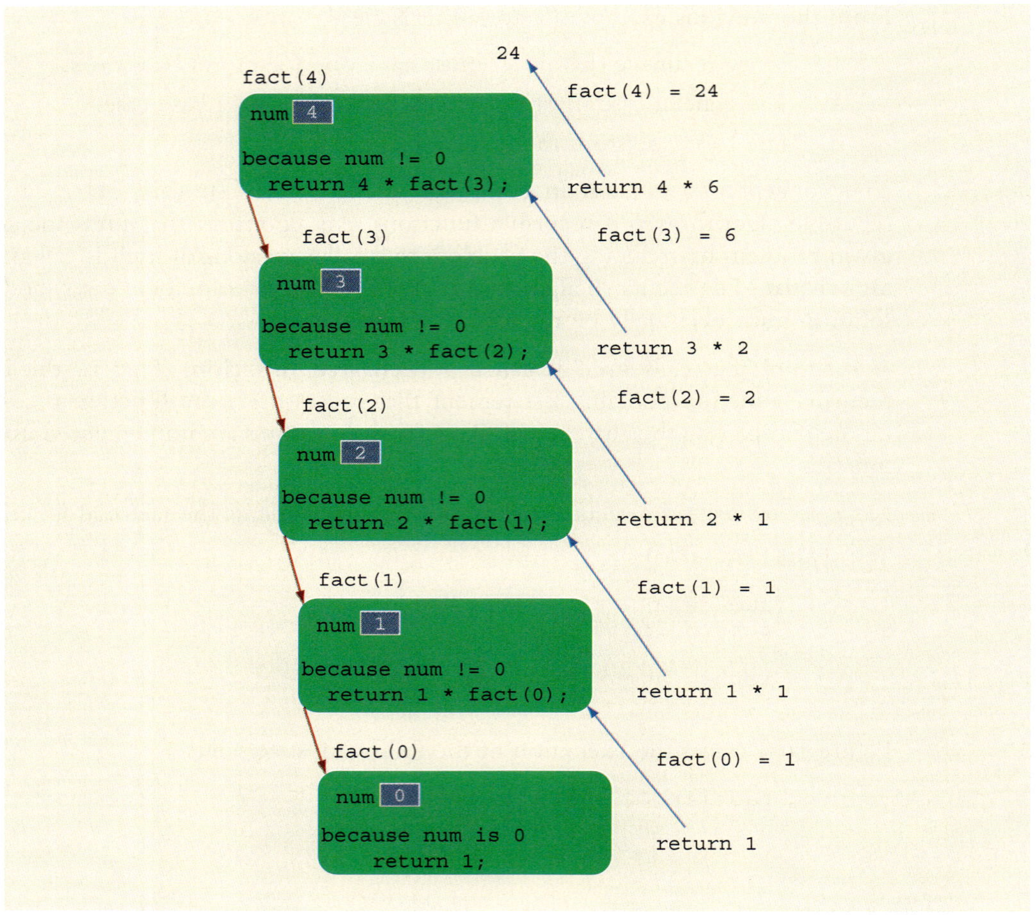

FIGURE 16-1 Execution of `fact(4)`

The output of the previous `cout` statement is:

24

In Figure 16-1, the down arrow represents the successive calls to the function `fact`, and the upward arrows represent the values returned to the caller, that is, the calling function.

Let us note the following from the preceding example, involving the factorial function:

- Logically, you can think of a recursive function as having an unlimited number of copies of itself.

- Every call to a recursive function—that is, every recursive call—has its own code and its own set of parameters and local variables.

- After completing a particular recursive call, control goes back to the calling environment, which is the previous call. The current (recursive) call must execute completely before control goes back to the previous call. The execution in the previous call begins from the point immediately following the recursive call.

Direct and Indirect Recursion

A function is called **directly recursive** if it calls itself. A function that calls another function and eventually results in the original function call is said to be **indirectly recursive**. For example, if a function A calls a function B and function B calls function A, then function A is indirectly recursive. Indirect recursion can be several layers deep. For example, suppose that function A calls function B, function B calls function C, function C calls function D, and function D calls function A. Function A is then indirectly recursive.

Indirect recursion requires the same careful analysis as direct recursion. The base cases must be identified and appropriate solutions to them must be provided. However, tracing through indirect recursion can be tedious. You must, therefore, exercise extra care when designing indirect recursive functions. For simplicity, the problems in this book involve only direct recursion.

A recursive function in which the last statement executed is the recursive call is called a **tail recursive function**. The function `fact` is an example of a tail recursive function.

Infinite Recursion

Figure 16-1 shows that the sequence of recursive calls eventually reached a call that made no further recursive calls. That is, the sequence of recursive calls eventually reached a base case. On the other hand, if every recursive call results in another recursive call, then the recursive function (algorithm) is said to have infinite recursion. In theory, infinite recursion executes forever. Every call to a recursive function requires the system to allocate memory for the local variables and formal parameters. The system also saves this information so that after completing a call, control can be transferred back to the right caller. Therefore, because computer memory is finite, if you execute an infinite recursive function on a computer, the function executes until the system runs out of memory and results in an abnormal termination of the program.

Recursive functions (algorithms) must be carefully designed and analyzed. You must make sure that every recursive call eventually reduces to a base case. This chapter provides several examples that illustrate how to design and implement recursive algorithms.

To design a recursive function, you must do the following:

    a.   Understand the problem requirements.

    b.   Determine the limiting conditions. For example, for a list, the limiting condition is the number of elements in the list.

c.   Identify the base cases and provide a direct solution to each base case.

d.   Identify the general cases and provide a solution to each general case in terms of smaller versions of itself.

Problem Solving Using Recursion

Examples 16-1 through 16-3 illustrate how recursive algorithms are developed and implemented in C++ using recursive functions.

EXAMPLE 16-1: LARGEST ELEMENT IN AN ARRAY

In Chapter 9, we used a loop to find the largest element in an array. In this example, we use a recursive algorithm to find the largest element in an array. Consider the list given in Figure 16-2.

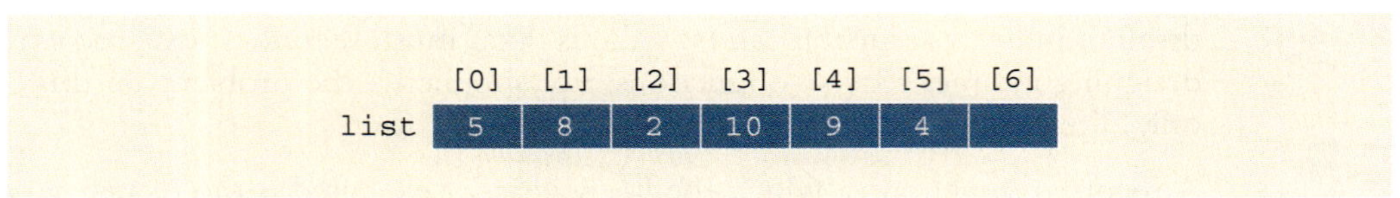

FIGURE 16-2   `list` with six elements

The largest element in the list in Figure 16-2 is 10.

Suppose `list` is the name of the array containing the list elements. Also, suppose that `list[a]...list[b]` stands for the array elements `list[a]`, `list[a + 1]`, ..., and `list[b]`. For example, `list[0]...list[5]` represents the array elements `list[0]`, `list[1]`, `list[2]`, `list[3]`, `list[4]`, and `list[5]`. Similarly, `list[1]...list[5]` represents the array elements `list[1]`, `list[2]`, `list[3]`, `list[4]`, and `list[5]`. To write a recursive algorithm to find the largest element in `list`, let us think in terms of recursion.

If `list` is of length 1, then `list` has only one element, which is the largest element. Suppose the length of `list` is greater than 1. To find the largest element in `list[a]...list[b]`, we first find the largest element in `list[a + 1]...list[b]` and then compare this largest element with `list[a]`. That is, the largest element in `list[a]...list[b]` is given by:

```
maximum(list[a], largest(list[a + 1]...list[b]))
```

Let us apply this formula to find the largest element in the list shown in Figure 16-2. This list has six elements, given by `list[0]...list[5]`. Now the largest element in `list` is:

```
maximum(list[0], largest(list[1]...list[5]))
```

That is, the largest element in `list` is the maximum of `list[0]` and the largest element in `list[1]...list[5]`. To find the largest element in `list[1]...list[5]`, we use the same formula again because the length of this list is greater than 1. The largest element in `list[1]...list[5]` is then:

```
maximum(list[1], largest(list[2]...list[5]))
```

and so on. We see that every time we use the preceding formula to find the largest element in a sublist, the length of the sublist in the next call is reduced by one. Eventually, the sublist is of length 1, in which case the sublist contains only one element, which is the largest element in the sublist. From this point onward, we backtrack through the recursive calls. This discussion translates into the following recursive algorithm, which is presented in pseudocode:

```
Base Case: The size of the list is 1
              The only element in the list is the largest element

General Case: The size of the list is greater than 1
        To find the largest element in list[a]...list[b]

        a. Find the largest element in list[a + 1]...list[b]
           and call it max
        b. Compare the elements list[a] and max
           if (list[a] >= max)
               the largest element in list[a]...list[b] is list[a]
           otherwise
               the largest element in list[a]...list[b] is max
```

This algorithm translates into the following C++ function to find the largest element in an array:

```cpp
int largest(const int list[], int lowerIndex, int upperIndex)
{
    int max;

    if (lowerIndex == upperIndex) //size of the sublist is one
        return list[lowerIndex];
    else
    {
        max = largest(list, lowerIndex + 1, upperIndex);

        if (list[lowerIndex] >= max)
            return list[lowerIndex];
        else
            return max;
    }
}
```

Consider the `list` given in Figure 16-3.

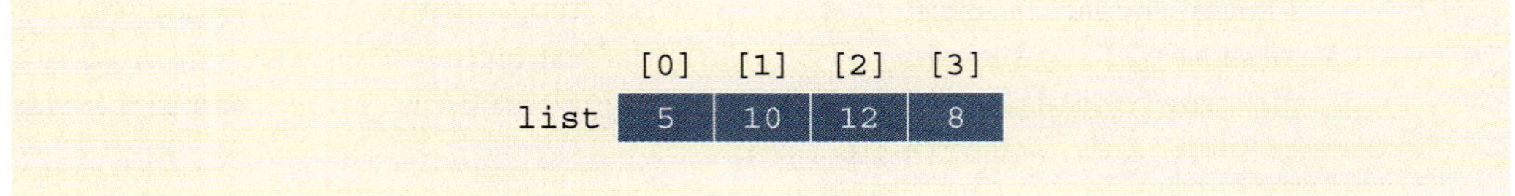

FIGURE 16-3 `list` with four elements

Let us trace the execution of the following statement:

```
cout << largest(list, 0, 3) << endl;
```

Here `upperIndex` = 3 and the list has four elements. Figure 16-4 traces the execution of `largest(list, 0, 3)`.

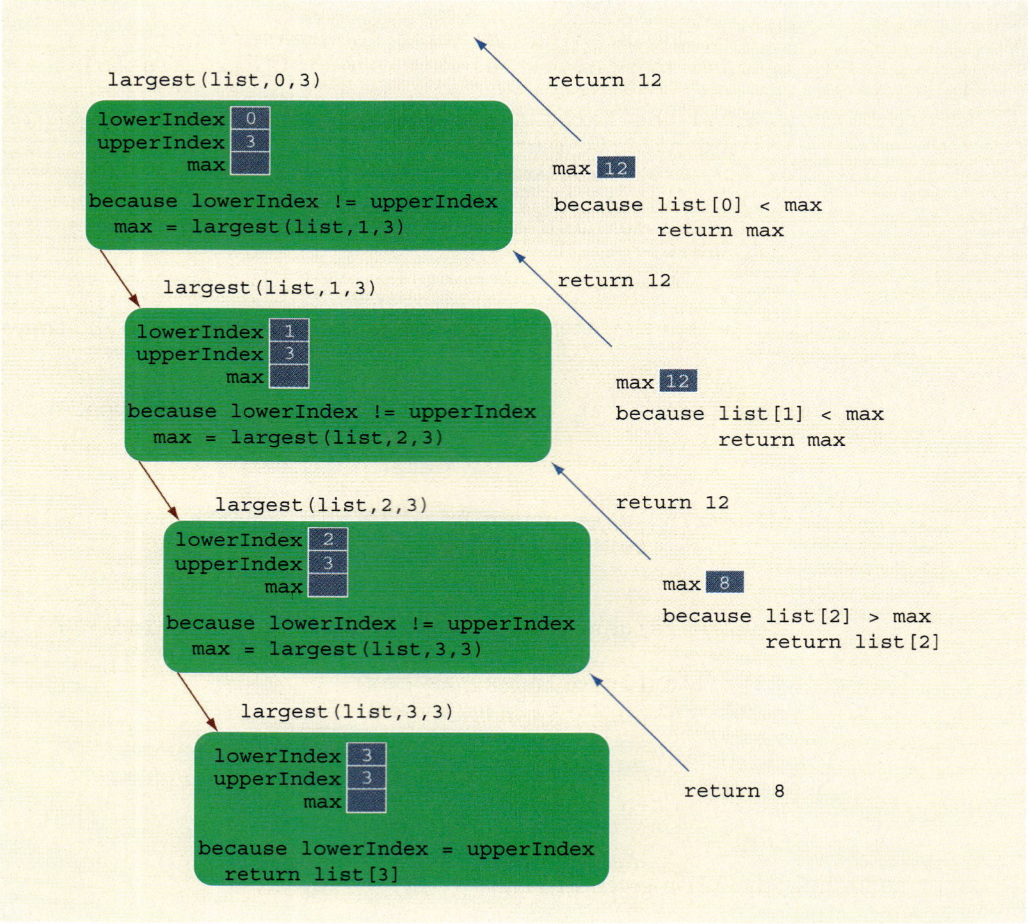

FIGURE 16-4 Execution of `largest(list, 0, 3)`

The value returned by the expression `largest(list, 0, 3)` is 12, which is the largest element in `list`.

The following C++ program uses the function `largest` to determine the largest element in a list:

```cpp
//Largest Element in an Array

#include <iostream>

using namespace std;

int largest(const int list[], int lowerIndex, int upperIndex);

int main()
{
    int intArray[10] = {23, 43, 35, 38, 67, 12, 76, 10, 34, 8};

    cout << "The largest element in intArray: "
         << largest(intArray, 0, 9);
    cout << endl;

    return 0;
}

int largest(const int list[], int lowerIndex, int upperIndex)
{
    int max;

    if (lowerIndex == upperIndex) //size of the sublist is one
        return list[lowerIndex];
    else
    {
        max = largest(list, lowerIndex + 1, upperIndex);

        if (list[lowerIndex] >= max)
            return list[lowerIndex];
        else
            return max;
    }
}
```

Sample Run:

```
The largest element in intArray: 76
```

EXAMPLE 16-2: FIBONACCI NUMBER

In Chapter 5, we designed a program to determine the desired Fibonacci number. In this example, we write a recursive function, `rFibNum`, to determine the desired Fibonacci number. The function `rFibNum` takes as parameters three numbers representing the first two numbers of the Fibonacci sequence and a number n, the desired nth Fibonacci number. The function `rFibNum` returns the nth Fibonacci number in the sequence.

Recall that the third Fibonacci number is the sum of the first two Fibonacci numbers. The fourth Fibonacci number in a sequence is the sum of the second and third Fibonacci numbers. Therefore, to calculate the fourth Fibonacci number, we add the second Fibonacci number and the third Fibonacci number (which is itself the sum of the first two Fibonacci numbers). The following recursive algorithm calculates the nth Fibonacci number, where a denotes the first Fibonacci number, b the second Fibonacci number, and n the nth Fibonacci number:

$$rFibNum(a,b,n) = \begin{cases} a & \text{if } n = 1 \\ b & \text{if } n = 2 \\ rFibNum(a,b,n-1) + rFibNum(a,b,n-2) & \text{if } n > 2. \end{cases} \quad (16\text{-}3)$$

Suppose that we want to determine:

```
rFibNum(2, 5, 4)
```

Here, $a = 2$, $b = 5$, and $n = 4$. That is, we want to determine the fourth Fibonacci number of the sequence whose first number is 2 and whose second number is 5. Because n is 4 > 2,

1. `rFibNum(2, 5, 4) = rFibNum(2, 5, 3) + rFibNum(2, 5, 2)`

   Next, we determine `rFibNum(2, 5, 3)` and `rFibNum(2, 5, 2)`. Let us first determine `rFibNum(2, 5, 3)`. Here, $a = 2$, $b = 5$, and n is 3. Because n is 3,

   1.a. `rFibNum(2, 5, 3) = rFibNum(2, 5, 2) + rFibNum(2, 5, 1)`

   This statement requires us to determine `rFibNum(2, 5, 2)` and `rFibNum(2, 5, 1)`. In `rFibNum(2, 5, 2)`, $a = 2$, $b = 5$, and $n = 2$. Therefore, from the definition given in Equation 16–3, it follows that:

   1.a.1. `rFibNum(2, 5, 2) = 5`

   To find `rFibNum(2, 5, 1)`, note that $a = 2$, $b = 5$, and $n = 1$. Therefore, by the definition given in Equation 16–3,

   1.a.2. `rFibNum(2, 5, 1) = 2`

   We substitute the values of `rFibNum(2, 5, 2)` and `rFibNum(2, 5, 1)` into (1.a) to get:

   `rFibNum(2, 5, 3) = 5 + 2 = 7`

Next, we determine `rFibNum(2, 5, 2)`. As in (1.a.1), `rFibNum(2, 5, 2) = 5`. We can substitute the values of `rFibNum(2, 5, 3)` and `rFibNum(2, 5, 2)` into (1) to get:

`rFibNum(2, 5, 4) = 7 + 5 = 12`

The following recursive function implements this algorithm:

```cpp
int rFibNum(int a, int b, int n)
{
    if (n == 1)
        return a;
    else if (n == 2)
        return b;
    else
        return rFibNum(a, b, n - 1) + rFibNum(a, b, n - 2);
}
```

Let us trace the execution of the following statement:

```cpp
cout << rFibNum(2, 3, 5) << endl;
```

In this statement, the first number is 2, the second number is 3, and we want to determine the 5th Fibonacci number of the sequence. Figure 16-5 traces the execution of the expression `rFibNum(2,3,5)`. The value returned is 13, which is the 5th Fibonacci number of the sequence whose first number is 2 and second number is 3.

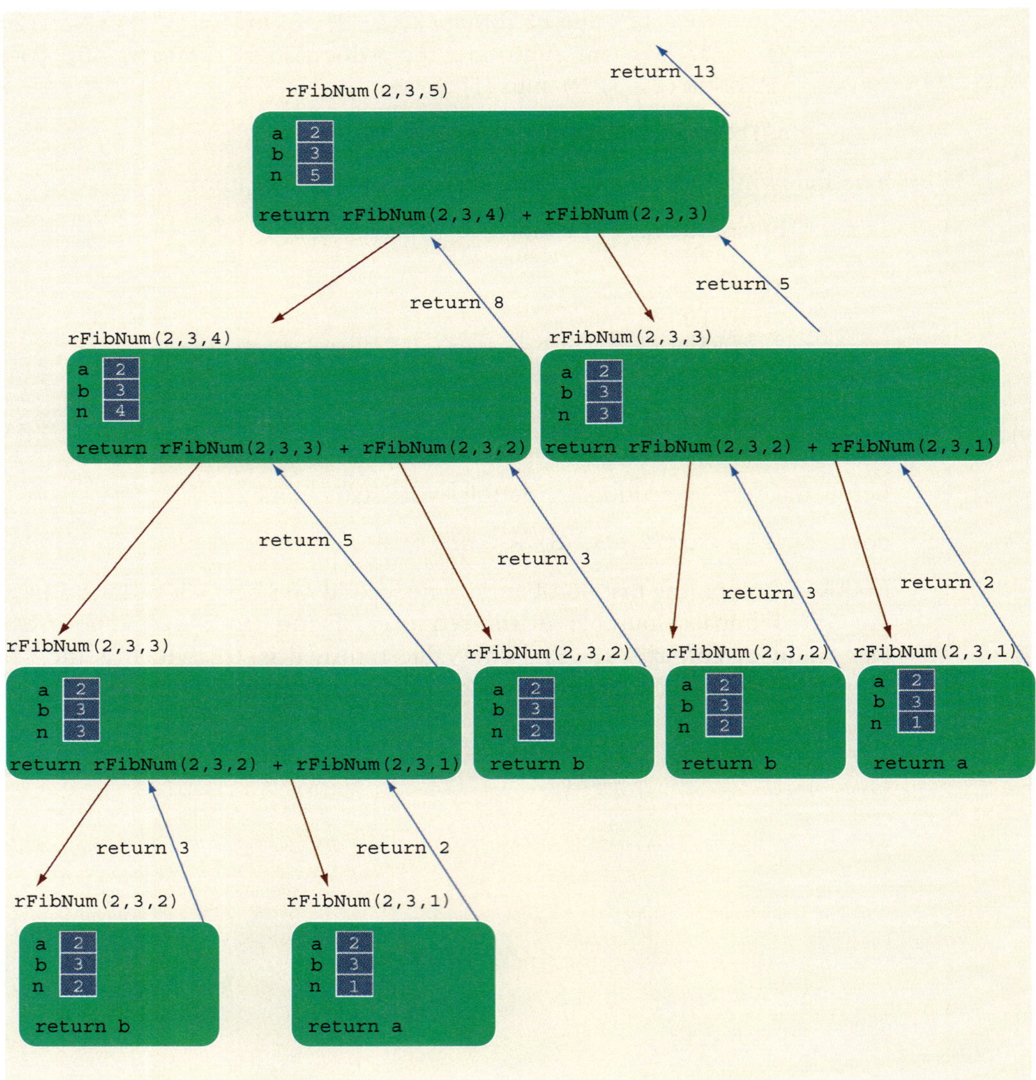

FIGURE 16-5 Execution of rFibNum(2, 3, 5)

The following C++ program uses the function **rFibNum**:

```cpp
//Chapter 16: Fibonacci Number

#include <iostream>

using namespace std;
```

```cpp
int rFibNum(int a, int b, int n);

int main()
{
    int firstFibNum;
    int secondFibNum;
    int nth;

    cout << "Enter the first Fibonacci number: ";
    cin >> firstFibNum;
    cout << endl;

    cout << "Enter the second Fibonacci number: ";
    cin >> secondFibNum;
    cout << endl;

    cout << "Enter the position of the desired Fibonacci number: ";
    cin >> nth;
    cout << endl;

    cout << "The Fibonacci number at position " << nth
         << " is: " << rFibNum(firstFibNum, secondFibNum, nth)
         << endl;

    return 0;
}

int rFibNum(int a, int b, int n)
{
    if (n == 1)
        return a;
    else if (n == 2)
        return b;
    else
        return rFibNum(a, b, n - 1) + rFibNum(a, b, n - 2);
}
```

Sample Runs: In these sample runs, the user input is shaded.

Sample Run 1

```
Enter the first Fibonacci number: 2

Enter the second Fibonacci number: 5

Enter the position of the desired Fibonacci number: 6

The Fibonacci number at position 6 is: 31
```

Sample Run 2

```
Enter the first Fibonacci number: 3

Enter the second Fibonacci number: 4

Enter the position of the desired Fibonacci number: 6

The Fibonacci number at position 6 is: 29
```

Sample Run 3

```
Enter the first Fibonacci number: 12

Enter the second Fibonacci number: 18

Enter the position of the desired Fibonacci number: 15

The Fibonacci number at position 15 is: 9582
```

EXAMPLE 16-3: TOWER OF HANOI

In the nineteenth century, a game called the Tower of Hanoi became popular in Europe. This game represents work that is underway in the temple of Brahma. At the creation of the universe, priests in the temple of Brahma were supposedly given three diamond needles, with one needle containing 64 golden disks. Each golden disk is slightly smaller than the disk below it. The priests' task is to move all 64 disks from the first needle to the third needle. The rules for moving the disks are as follows:

1. Only one disk can be moved at a time.
2. The removed disk must be placed on one of the needles.
3. A larger disk cannot be placed on top of a smaller disk.

The priests were told that once they had moved all the disks from the first needle to the third needle, the universe would come to an end.

Our objective is to write a program that prints the sequence of moves needed to transfer the disks from the first needle to the third needle. Figure 16-6 shows the Tower of Hanoi problem with three disks.

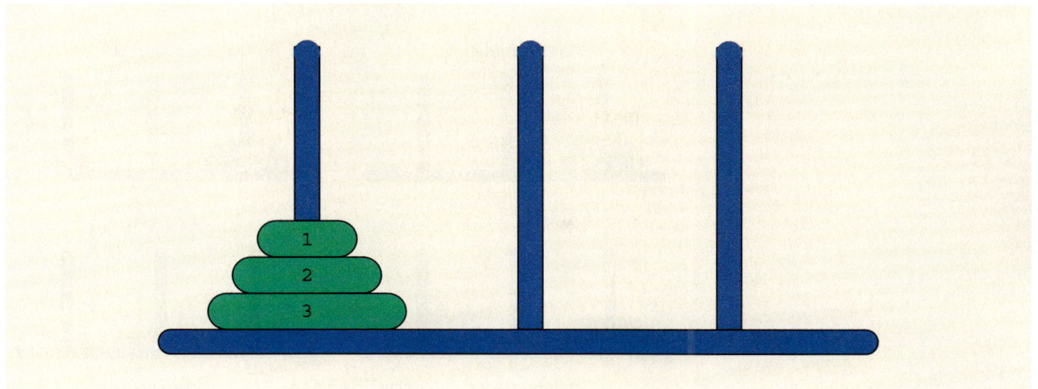

FIGURE 16-6 Tower of Hanoi problem with three disks

As before, we think in terms of recursion. Let us first consider the case when the first needle contains only one disk. In this case, the disk can be moved directly from needle 1 to needle 3. So let us consider the case when the first needle contains only two disks. In this case, first we move the first disk from needle 1 to needle 2, and then we move the second disk from needle 1 to needle 3. Finally, we move the first disk from needle 2 to needle 3. Next, we consider the case when the first needle contains three disks, and then generalize this to the case of 64 disks (in fact, to an arbitrary number of disks).

Suppose that needle 1 contains three disks. To move disk number 3 to needle 3, the top two disks must first be moved to needle 2. Disk number 3 can then be moved from needle 1 to needle 3. To move the top two disks from needle 2 to needle 3, we use the same strategy as before. This time we use needle 1 as the intermediate needle. Figure 16-7 shows a solution to the Tower of Hanoi problem with three disks.

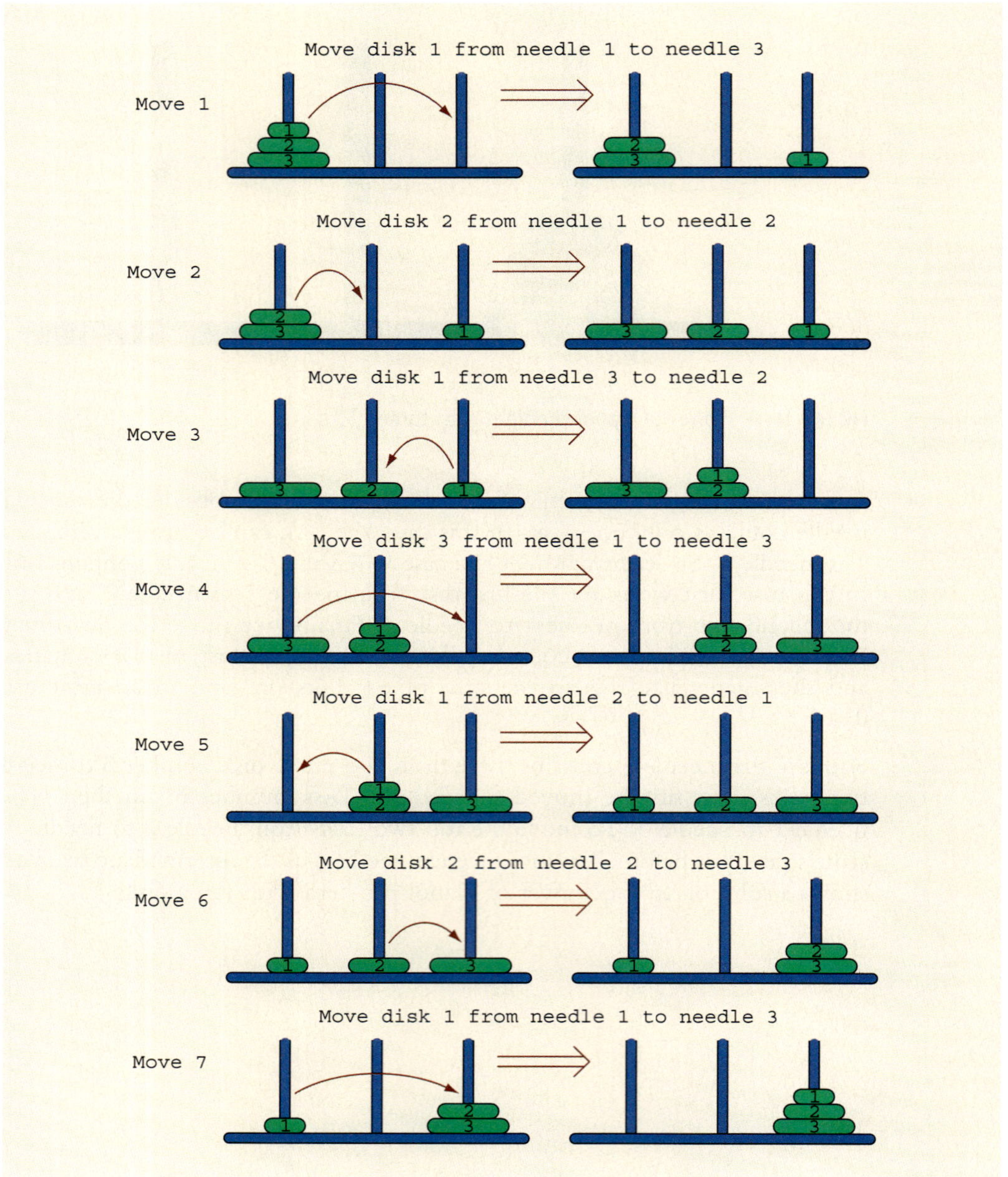

FIGURE 16-7   Solution to Tower of Hanoi problem with three disks

Let us now generalize this problem to the case of 64 disks. To begin, the first needle contains all 64 disks. Disk number 64 cannot be moved from needle 1 to needle 3 unless the top 63 disks are on the second needle. So first we move the top 63 disks from needle 1 to needle 2, and then we move disk number 64 from needle 1 to needle 3. Now the top

63 disks are all on needle 2. To move disk number 63 from needle 2 to needle 3, we first move the top 62 disks from needle 2 to needle 1, and then we move disk number 63 from needle 2 to needle 3. To move the remaining 62 disks, we use a similar procedure. This discussion translates into the following recursive algorithm given in pseudocode. Suppose that needle 1 contains n disks, where $n \geq 1$.

1. Move the top $n - 1$ disks from needle 1 to needle 2, using needle 3 as the intermediate needle.

2. Move disk number n from needle 1 to needle 3.

3. Move the top $n - 1$ disks from needle 2 to needle 3, using needle 1 as the intermediate needle.

This recursive algorithm translates into the following C++ function:

```cpp
void moveDisks(int count, int needle1, int needle3, int needle2)
{
    if (count > 0)
    {
        moveDisks(count - 1, needle1, needle2, needle3);

        cout << "Move disk " << count << " from " << needle1
             << " to " << needle3 << "." << endl;

        moveDisks(count - 1, needle2, needle3, needle1);
    }
}
```

Tower of Hanoi: Analysis

Let us determine how long it would take to move all 64 disks from needle 1 to needle 3. If needle 1 contains 3 disks, then the number of moves required to move all 3 disks from needle 1 to needle 3 is $2^3 - 1 = 7$. Similarly, if needle 1 contains 64 disks, then the number of moves required to move all 64 disks from needle 1 to needle 3 is $2^{64} - 1$. Because $2^{10} = 1024 \approx 1000 = 10^3$, we have:

$$2^{64} = 2^4 \times 2^{60} \approx 2^4 \times 10^{18} = 1.6 \times 10^{19}$$

The number of seconds in one year is approximately 3.2×10^7. Suppose the priests move one disk per second and they do not rest. Now:

$$1.6 \times 10^{19} = 5 \times 3.2 \times 10^{18} = 5 \times (3.2 \times 10^7) \times 10^{11} = (3.2 \times 10^7) \times (5 \times 10^{11})$$

The time required to move all 64 disks from needle 1 to needle 3 is roughly 5×10^{11} years. It is estimated that our universe is about 15 billion years old (1.5×10^{10}). Also, $5 \times 10^{11} = 50 \times 10^{10} \approx 33 \times (1.5 \times 10^{10})$. This calculation shows that our universe would last about 33 times as long as it already has.

Assume that a computer can generate 1 billion (10^9) moves per second. Then the number of moves that the computer can generate in one year is:

$$(3.2 \times 10^7) \times 10^9 = 3.2 \times 10^{16}$$

So the computer time required to generate 2^{64} moves is:

$$2^{64} \approx 1.6 \times 10^{19} = 1.6 \times 10^{16} \times 10^3 = (3.2 \times 10^{16}) \times 500$$

Thus, it would take about 500 years for the computer to generate 2^{64} moves at the rate of 1 billion moves per second.

Recursion or Iteration?

In Chapter 5, we designed a program to determine a desired Fibonacci number. That program used a loop to perform the calculation. In other words, the programs in Chapter 5 used an iterative control structure to repeat a set of statements. More formally, **iterative control structures** use a looping structure, such as `while`, `for`, or `do...while`, to repeat a set of statements. In Example 16-2, we designed a recursive function to calculate a Fibonacci number. From the examples here, it follows that in recursion a set of statements is repeated by having the function call itself. Moreover, a selection control structure is used to control the repeated calls in recursion.

Similarly, in Chapter 9, we used an iterative control structure (a `for` loop) to determine the largest element in a list. In this chapter, we use recursion to determine the largest element in a list. In addition, this chapter began by designing a recursive function to find the factorial of a non-negative integer. Using an iterative control structure, we can also write an algorithm to find the factorial of a non-negative integer. The only reason to give a recursive solution to a factorial problem is to illustrate how recursion works.

We thus see that there are usually two ways to solve a particular problem—iteration and recursion. The obvious question is which method is better—iteration or recursion? There is no simple answer. In addition to the nature of the problem, the other key factor in determining the best solution method is efficiency.

Example 6-7 (Chapter 7), while tracing the execution of the problem, showed us that whenever a function is called, memory space for its formal parameters and (automatic) local variables is allocated. When the function terminates, that memory space is then deallocated.

This chapter, while tracing the execution of recursive functions, also shows us that every (recursive) call has its own set of parameters and (automatic) local variables. That is, every (recursive) call requires the system to allocate memory space for its formal parameters and (automatic) local variables, and then deallocate the memory space when the function exits. Thus, there is overhead associated with executing a (recursive) function both in terms of memory space and computer time. Therefore, a recursive function executes more slowly than its iterative counterpart. On slower computers, especially those with limited memory space, the (slow) execution of a recursive function would be visible.

Today's computers, however, are fast and have inexpensive memory. Therefore, the execution of a recursion function is not noticeable. Keeping the power of today's computers in mind, the choice between the two alternatives—iteration or recursion—depends on the nature of the problem. Of course, for problems such as mission control systems, efficiency is absolutely critical and, therefore, the efficiency factor would dictate the solution method.

As a general rule, if you think that an iterative solution is more obvious and easier to understand than a recursive solution, use the iterative solution, which would be more efficient. On the other hand, problems exist for which the recursive solution is more obvious or easier to construct, such as the Tower of Hanoi problem. (In fact, it turns out that it is difficult to construct an iterative solution for the Tower of Hanoi problem.) Keeping the power of recursion in mind, if the definition of a problem is inherently recursive, then you should consider a recursive solution.

PROGRAMMING EXAMPLE: Converting a Number from Binary to Decimal

In Chapter 1, we explained that the language of a computer, called machine language, is a sequence of 0s and 1s. When you press the key **A** on the keyboard, 01000001 is stored in the computer. Also, you know that the collating sequence of **A** in the ASCII character set is **65**. In fact, the binary representation of **A** is 01000001 and the decimal representation of **A** is **65**.

The numbering system we use is called the decimal system, or base 10 system. The numbering system that the computer uses is called the binary system, or base 2 system. In this and the next programming example, we discuss how to convert a number from base 2 to base 10 and from base 10 to base 2.

Binary to Decimal To convert a number from base 2 to base 10, we first find the weight of each bit in the binary number. The weight of each bit in the binary number is assigned from right to left. The weight of the rightmost bit is 0. The weight of the bit immediately to the left of the rightmost bit is 1, the weight of the bit immediately to the left of it is 2, and so on. Consider the binary number 1001101. The weight of each bit is as follows:

```
Weight  6  5  4  3  2  1  0
        1  0  0  1  1  0  1
```

We use the weight of each bit to find the equivalent decimal number. For each bit, we multiply the bit by 2 to the power of its weight and then we add all of the numbers. For the above binary number, the equivalent decimal number is:

$$1 \times 2^6 + 0 \times 2^5 + 0 \times 2^4 + 1 \times 2^3 + 1 \times 2^2 + 0 \times 2^1 + 1 \times 2^0$$
$$= 64 + 0 + 0 + 8 + 4 + 0 + 1$$
$$= 77$$

To write a program that converts a binary number into the equivalent decimal number, we note two things: (1) the weight of each bit in the binary number must be known, and (2) the weight is assigned from right to left. Because we do not know in advance how many bits are in the binary number, we must process the bits from right to left. After processing a bit, we can add 1 to its weight, giving the weight of the bit immediately to the left of it. Also, each bit must be extracted from the binary number and multiplied by 2 to the power of its weight. To extract a bit, we can use the mod operator. Consider the following recursive algorithm, which is given in pseudocode:

```
if (binaryNumber > 0)
{
    bit = binaryNumber % 10;         //extract the rightmost bit
    decimal = decimal + bit * power(2, weight);
    binaryNumber = binaryNumber / 10; //remove the rightmost
                                      //bit

    weight++;
    convert the binaryNumber into decimal
}
```

This algorithm assumes that the memory locations `decimal` and `weight` have been initialized to 0 before using the algorithm. This algorithm translates to the following C++ recursive function:

```cpp
void binToDec(int binaryNumber, int& decimal, int& weight)
{
    int bit;

    if (binaryNumber > 0)
    {
        bit = binaryNumber % 10;
        decimal = decimal
                    + bit * static_cast<int>(pow(2, weight));
        binaryNumber = binaryNumber / 10;
        weight++;
        binToDec(binaryNumber, decimal, weight);
    }
}
```

In this function, both `decimal` and `weight` are reference parameters. The actual parameters corresponding to these parameters are initialized to 0. After extracting the rightmost bit, this function updates the decimal number and the weight of the next bit. Suppose `decimalNumber` and `bitWeight` are `int` variables. Consider the following statements:

```
decimalNumber = 0;
bitWeight = 0;
binToDec(1101, decimalNumber, bitWeight);
```

Figure 16-8 traces the execution of the last statement, that is, `binToDec(1101, decimalNumber, bitWeight);`. It shows the content of the variables `decimalNumber` and `bitWeight` next to each function call.

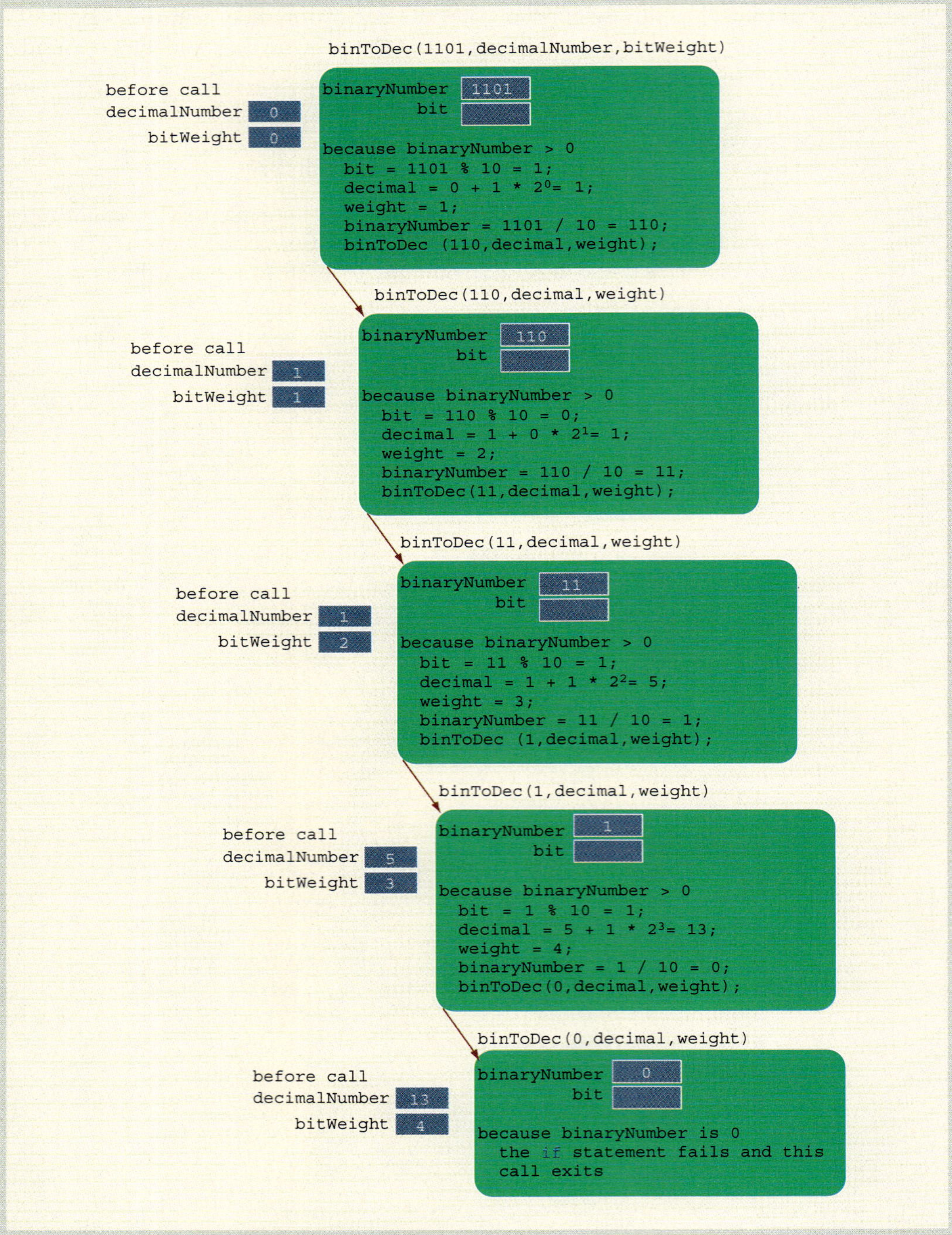

FIGURE 16-8 Execution of `binToDec(1101, decimalNumber, bitWeight);`

In Figure 16-8, each down arrow represents the successive function call. Because the last statement of the function `binToDec` is a function call, after this statement executes, nothing happens. After the statement:

```cpp
binToDec(1101, decimalNumber, bitWeight);
```

executes, the value of the variable `decimalNumber` is 13.

The following C++ program tests the function `binToDec`:

```cpp
//Chapter 16: Program - Binary to Decimal

#include <iostream>
#include <cmath>

using namespace std;

void binToDec(int binaryNumber, int& decimal, int& weight);

int main()
{
    int decimalNum;
    int bitWeight;
    int binaryNum;

    decimalNum = 0;
    bitWeight = 0;

    cout << "Enter number in binary: ";
    cin >> binaryNum;
    cout << endl;

    binToDec(binaryNum, decimalNum, bitWeight);
    cout << "Binary " << binaryNum << " = " << decimalNum
         << " decimal" << endl;

    return 0;
}

void binToDec(int binaryNumber, int& decimal, int& weight)
{
    int bit;

    if (binaryNumber > 0)
    {
        bit = binaryNumber % 10;
        decimal = decimal
                    + bit * static_cast<int>(pow(2, weight));
```

```
                binaryNumber = binaryNumber / 10;
                weight++;
                binToDec(binaryNumber, decimal, weight);
        }
}
```

Sample Run: In this sample run, the user input is shaded.

```
Enter a number in binary: 11010110

Binary 11010110 = 214 decimal
```

PROGRAMMING EXAMPLE: Converting a Number from Decimal to Binary

The previous programming example discussed and designed a program to convert a number from a binary representation to a decimal format—that is, from base 2 to base 10. This programming example discusses and designs a program that uses recursion to convert a non-negative integer in decimal format—that is, base 10—into the equivalent binary number—that is, base 2. First, we define some terms.

Let x be an integer. We call the remainder of x after division by 2 the **rightmost bit** of x.

Thus, the rightmost bit of 33 is 1 because 33 % 2 is 1, and the rightmost bit of 28 is 0 because 28 % 2 is 0.

We first illustrate the algorithm to convert an integer in base 10 to the equivalent number in binary format with the help of an example.

Suppose we want to find the binary representation of 35. First, we divide 35 by 2. The quotient is 17 and the remainder—that is, the rightmost bit of 35—is 1. Next, we divide 17 by 2. The quotient is 8 and the remainder—that is, the rightmost bit of 17— is 1. Next, we divide 8 by 2. The quotient is 4 and the remainder—that is, the rightmost bit of 8—is 0. We continue this process until the quotient becomes 0.

The rightmost bit of 35 cannot be printed until we have printed the rightmost bit of 17. The rightmost bit of 17 cannot be printed until we have printed the rightmost bit of 8, and so on. Thus, the binary representation of 35 is the binary representation of 17 (that is, the quotient of 35 after division by 2), followed by the rightmost bit of 35.

Thus, to convert an integer *num* in base 10 into the equivalent binary number, we first convert the quotient *num* / 2 into an equivalent binary number, and then append the rightmost bit of *num* to the binary representation of *num* / 2.

This discussion translates into the following recursive algorithm, where `binary(num)` denotes the binary representation of num:

1. `binary(num) = num` if num = 0.
2. `binary(num) = binary(num / 2)` followed by num % 2 if num > 0.

The following recursive function implements this algorithm:

```cpp
void decToBin(int num, int base)
{
    if (num > 0)
    {
        decToBin(num / base, base);
        cout << num % base;
    }
}
```

Figure 16-9 traces the execution of the following statement:

```cpp
decToBin(13, 2);
```

where num is 13 and base is 2.

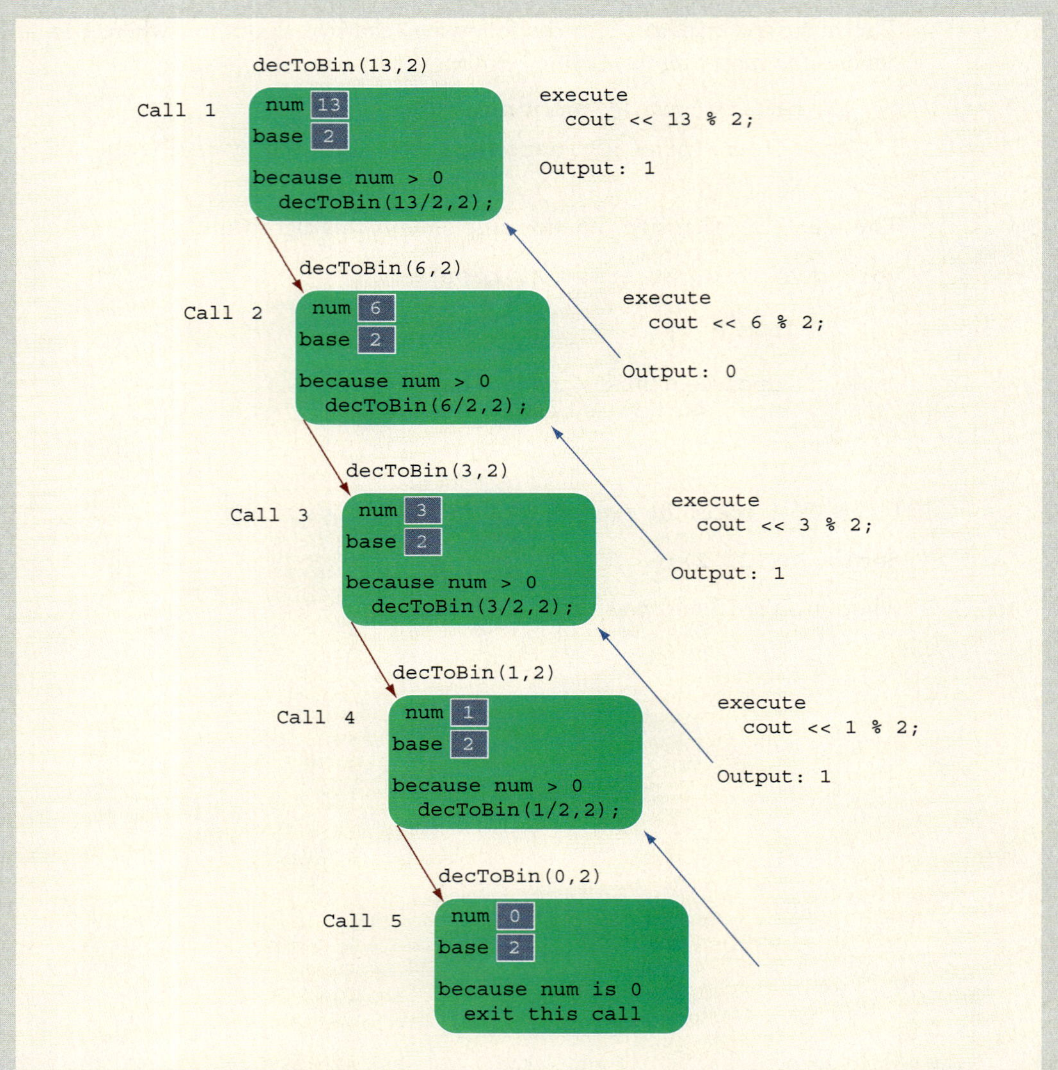

FIGURE 16-9 Execution of decToBin(13, 2)

Because the **if** statement in call 5 fails, this call does not print anything. The first output is produced by call 4, which prints 1; the second output is produced by call 3, which prints 1; the third output is produced by call 2, which prints 0; and the fourth output is produced by call 1, which prints 1. Thus, the output of the statement:

```
decToBin(13, 2);
```

is:

```
1101
```

The following C++ program tests the function decToBin:

```cpp
//Chapter 16: Program - Decimal to Binary

#include <iostream>

using namespace std;

void decToBin(int num, int base);

int main()
{
    int decimalNum;
    int base;

    base = 2;

    cout << "Enter number in decimal: ";
    cin >> decimalNum;
    cout << endl;

    cout << "Decimal " << decimalNum << " = ";
    decToBin(decimalNum, base);
    cout << " binary" << endl;

    return 0;
}

void decToBin(int num, int base)
{
    if (num > 0)
    {
        decToBin(num / base, base);
        cout << num % base;
    }
}
```

Sample Run: In this sample run, the user input is shaded.

```
Enter a number in decimal: 57

Decimal 57 = 111001 binary
```

QUICK REVIEW

1. The process of solving a problem by reducing it to smaller versions of itself is called recursion.

2. A recursive definition defines a problem in terms of smaller versions of itself.

3. Every recursive definition has one or more base cases.

4. A recursive algorithm solves a problem by reducing it to smaller versions of itself.

5. Every recursive algorithm has one or more base cases.

6. The solution to the problem in a base case is obtained directly.

7. A function is called recursive if it calls itself.

8. Recursive algorithms are implemented using recursive functions.

9. Every recursive function must have one or more base cases.

10. The general solution breaks the problem into smaller versions of itself.

11. The general case must eventually be reduced to a base case.

12. The base case stops the recursion.

13. While tracing a recursive function:

    - Logically, you can think of a recursive function as having an unlimited number of copies of itself.

    - Every call to a recursive function—that is, every recursive call—has its own code and its own set of parameters and local variables.

    - After completing a particular recursive call, control goes back to the calling environment, which is the previous call. The current (recursive) call must execute completely before control goes back to the previous call. The execution in the previous call begins from the point immediately following the recursive call.

14. A function is called directly recursive if it calls itself.

15. A function that calls another function and eventually results in the original function call is said to be indirectly recursive.

16. A recursive function in which the last statement executed is the recursive call is called a tail recursive function.

17. To design a recursive function, you must do the following:

    a. Understand the problem requirements.

    b. Determine the limiting conditions. For example, for a list, the limiting condition is the number of elements in the list.

    c. Identify the base cases and provide a direct solution to each base case.

    d. Identify the general cases and provide a solution to each general case in terms of smaller versions of itself.

EXERCISES

1. Mark the following statements as true or false.

   a. Every recursive definition must have one or more base cases.

   b. Every recursive function must have one or more base cases.

   c. The general case stops the recursion.

   d. In the general case, the solution to the problem is obtained directly.

   e. A recursive function always returns a value.

2. What is a base case?

3. What is a recursive case?

4. What is direct recursion?

5. What is indirect recursion?

6. What is tail recursion?

7. Consider the following recursive function:

```cpp
int mystery(int number)                          //Line 1
{
    if (number == 0)                             //Line 2
        return number;                           //Line 3
    else                                         //Line 4
        return(number + mystery(number - 1));    //Line 5
}
```

   a. Identify the base case.

   b. Identify the general case.

   c. What valid values can be passed as parameters to the function `mystery`?

   d. If `mystery(0)` is a valid call, what is its value? If not, explain why.

   e. If `mystery(5)` is a valid call, what is its value? If not, explain why.

   f. If `mystery(-3)` is a valid call, what is its value? If not, explain why.

8. Consider the following recursive function:

```cpp
void funcRec(int u, char v)                      //Line 1
{
    if (u == 0)                                  //Line 2
        cout << v;                               //Line 3
    else if (u == 1)                             //Line 4
        cout << static_cast<char>
                (static_cast<int>(v) + 1);       //Line 5
    else                                         //Line 6
        funcRec(u - 1, v);                       //Line 7
}
```

Answer the following questions:

a. Identify the base case.

b. Identify the general case.

c. What is the output of the following statement?

```
funcRec(5, 'A');
```

9. Consider the following recursive function:

```cpp
void exercise(int x)
{
    if (x > 0 && x < 10)
    {
        cout << x << " ";
        exercise(x + 1);
    }
}
```

What is the output of the following statements?

a. exercise(0);

b. exercise(5);

c. exercise(10);

d. exercise(-5);

10. Consider the following function:

```cpp
int test(int x, int y)
{
    if (x == y)
        return x;
    else if (x > y)
        return (x + y);
    else
        return test(x + 1, y - 1);
}
```

What is the output of the following statements?

a. cout << test(5, 10) << endl;

b. cout << test(3, 9) << endl;

11. Consider the following function:

```cpp
int func(int x)
{
    if (x == 0)
        return 2;
    else if (x == 1)
        return 3;
    else
        return (func(x - 1) + func(x - 2));
}
```

What is the output of the following statements?

a. `cout << func(0) << endl;`

b. `cout << func(1) << endl;`

c. `cout << func(2) << endl;`

d. `cout << func(5) << endl;`

12. Suppose that `intArray` is an array of integers, and `length` specifies the number of elements in `intArray`. Also, suppose that `low` and `high` are two integers such that $0 <= $ `low` $ < $ `length`, $0 <= $ `high` $ < $ `length`, and `low` $ < $ `high`. That is, `low` and `high` are two indices in `intArray`. Write a recursive definition that reverses the elements in `intArray` between `low` and `high`.

13. Write a recursive algorithm to multiply two positive integers m and n using repeated addition. Specify the base case and the recursive case.

14. Consider the following problem: How many ways can a committee of four people be selected from a group of 10 people? There are many other similar problems, where you are asked to find the number of ways to select a set of items from a given set of items. The general problem can be stated as follows: Find the number of ways r different things can be chosen from a set of n items, where r and n are non-negative integers and $r \leq n$. Suppose $C(n, r)$ denotes the number of ways r different things can be chosen from a set of n items. Then $C(n, r)$ is given by the following formula:

$$C(n,r) = \frac{n!}{r!(n-r)!}$$

where the exclamation point denotes the factorial function. Moreover, $C(n, 0) = C(n, n) = 1$. It is also known that $C(n, r) = C(n - 1, r - 1) + C(n - 1, r)$.

a. Write a recursive algorithm to determine $C(n, r)$. Identify the base case(s) and the general case(s).

b. Using your recursive algorithm, determine $C(5, 3)$ and $C(9, 4)$.

PROGRAMMING EXERCISES

1. Write a recursive function that takes as a parameter a non-negative integer and generates the following pattern of stars. If the non-negative integer is 4, then the pattern generated is:

```
****
***
**
*
*
**
***
****
```

   Also, write a program that prompts the user to enter the number of lines in the pattern and uses the recursive function to generate the pattern. For example, specifying 4 as the number of lines generates the above pattern.

2. Write a recursive function to generate a pattern of stars, such as the following:

```
*
**
***
****
****
***
**
*
```

   Also, write a program that prompts the user to enter the number of lines in the pattern and uses the recursive function to generate the pattern. For example, specifying 4 as the number of lines generates the above pattern.

3. Write a recursive a function to generate the following pattern of stars:

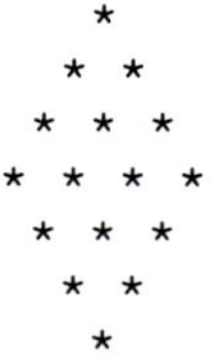

   Also, write a program that prompts the user to enter the number of lines in the pattern and uses the recursive function to generate the pattern. For example, specifying 4 as the number of lines generates the above pattern.

4. Write a recursive function, `vowels`, that returns the number of vowels in a string. Also, write a program to test your function.

5. Write a recursive function that finds and returns the sum of the elements of an `int` array. Also, write a program to test your function.

6. A palindrome is a string that reads the same both forward and backward. For example, the string **"madam"** is a palindrome. Write a program that uses a recursive function to check whether a string is a palindrome. Your program must contain a value-returning recursive function that returns **true** if the string is a palindrome and **false** otherwise. Do not use any global variables; use the appropriate parameters.

7. Write a program that uses a recursive function to print a string backward. Do not use any global variables; use the appropriate parameters.

8. Write a recursive function, **reverseDigits**, that takes an integer as a parameter and returns the number with the digits reversed. Also, write a program to test your function.

9. Write a recursive function, **power**, that takes as parameters two integers x and y such that x is nonzero and returns x^y. You can use the following recursive definition to calculate x^y. If $y \geq 0$,

$$power(x, y) = \begin{cases} 1 & \text{if } y = 0 \\ x & \text{if } y = 1 \\ x \times power(x, y - 1) & \text{if } y > 1. \end{cases}$$

If $y < 0$,

$$power(x, y) = \frac{1}{power(x, -y)}.$$

Also, write a program to test your function.

10. (**Greatest Common Divisor**) Given two integers x and y, the following recursive definition determines the greatest common divisor of x and y, written gcd(x,y):

$$gcd(x, y) = \begin{cases} x & \text{if } y = 0 \\ gcd(y, x \% y) & \text{if } y \neq 0 \end{cases}$$

Note: In this definition, % is the mod operator.

Write a recursive function, **gcd**, that takes as parameters two integers and returns the greatest common divisor of the numbers. Also, write a program to test your function.

11. Write a recursive function to implement the recursive algorithm of Exercise 12 (reversing the elements of an array between two indices). Also, write a program to test your function.

12. Write a recursive function to implement the recursive algorithm of Exercise 13 (multiplying two positive integers using repeated addition). Also, write a program to test your function.

13. Write a recursive function to implement the recursive algorithm of Exercise 14 (determining the number of ways to select a set of things from a given set of things). Also, write a program to test your function.

14. In the Programming Example, Converting a Number from Decimal to Binary, given in this chapter, you learned how to convert a decimal number into the equivalent binary number. Two more number systems, octal (base 8) and hexadecimal (base 16), are of interest to computer scientists. In fact, in C++, you can instruct the computer to store a number in octal or hexadecimal.

    The digits in the octal number system are 0, 1, 2, 3, 4, 5, 6, and 7. The digits in the hexadecimal number system are 0, 1, 2, 3, 4, 5, 6, 7, 8, 9, A, B, C, D, E, and F. So A in hexadecimal is 10 in decimal, B in hexadecimal is 11 in decimal, and so on.

    The algorithm to convert a positive decimal number into an equivalent number in octal (or hexadecimal) is the same as discussed for binary numbers. Here, we divide the decimal number by 8 (for octal) and by 16 (for hexadecimal). Suppose a_b represents the number a to the base b. For example, 75_{10} means 75 to the base 10 (that is decimal), and 83_{16} means 83 to the base 16 (that is, hexadecimal). Then:

    $$753_{10} = 1361_8$$
    $$753_{10} = 2F1_{16}$$

    The method of converting a decimal number to base 2, or 8, or 16 can be extended to any arbitrary base. Suppose you want to convert a decimal number n into an equivalent number in base b, where b is between 2 and 36. You then divide the decimal number n by b as in the algorithm for converting decimal to binary.

    Note that the digits in, say, base 20, are 0, 1, 2, 3, 4, 5, 6, 7, 8, 9, A, B, C, D, E, F, G, H, I, and J.

    Write a program that uses a recursive function to convert a number in decimal to a given base b, where b is between 2 and 36. Your program should prompt the user to enter the number in decimal and in the desired base.

    Test your program on the following data:

    9098 and base 20
    692 and base 2
    753 and base 16

15. The function `sqrt` from the header file `cmath` can be used to find the square root of a nonnegative real number. Using Newton's method, you can also write an algorithm to find the square root of a non-negative real number within a given tolerance as follows: Suppose x is a non-negative real number, a is the approximate square root of x, and *epsilon* is the tolerance. Start with $a = x$;

a. If $|a^2 - x| \leq$ *epsilon*, then *a* is the square root of *x* within the tolerance; otherwise:

b. Replace *a* with $(a^2 + x) / (2a)$ and repeat Step a

where $|a^2 - x|$ denotes the absolute value of $a^2 - x$.

Write a recursive function to implement this algorithm to find the square root of a non-negative real number. Also, write a program to test your function.

LINKED LISTS

IN THIS CHAPTER, YOU WILL:

- Learn about linked lists
- Become aware of the basic properties of linked lists
- Explore the insertion and deletion operations on linked lists
- Discover how to build and manipulate a linked list
- Learn how to construct a doubly linked list

You have already seen how data is organized and processed sequentially using an array, called a *sequential list*. You have performed several operations on sequential lists, such as sorting, inserting, deleting, and searching. You also found that if data is not sorted, then searching for an item in the list can be very time-consuming, especially with large lists. Once the data is sorted, you can use a binary search and improve the search algorithm. However, in this case, insertion and deletion become time-consuming, especially with large lists, because these operations require data movement. Also, because the array size must be fixed during execution, new items can be added only if there is room. Thus, there are limitations on when you organize data in an array.

This chapter helps you to overcome some of these problems. Chapter 13 showed how memory (variables) can be dynamically allocated and deallocated using pointers. This chapter uses pointers to organize and process data in lists, called **linked lists**. Recall that when data is stored in an array, memory for the components of the array is contiguous—that is, the blocks are allocated one after the other. However, as we will see, the components (called nodes) of a linked list need not be contiguous.

Linked Lists

A linked list is a collection of components, called **nodes.** Every node (except the last node) contains the address of the next node. Thus, every node in a linked list has two components: one to store the relevant information (that is, data), and one to store the address, called the **link**, of the next node in the list. The address of the first node in the list is stored in a separate location, called the **head** or **first**. Figure 17-1 is a pictorial representation of a node.

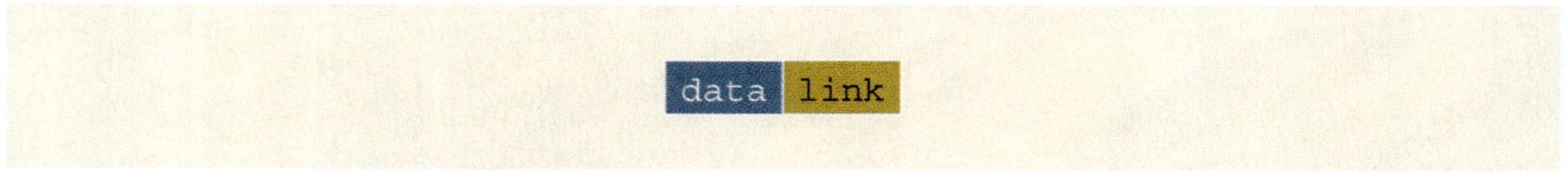

FIGURE 17-1 Structure of a node

Linked list: A list of items, called **nodes**, in which the order of the nodes is determined by the address, called the **link**, stored in each node.

The list in Figure 17-2 is an example of a linked list.

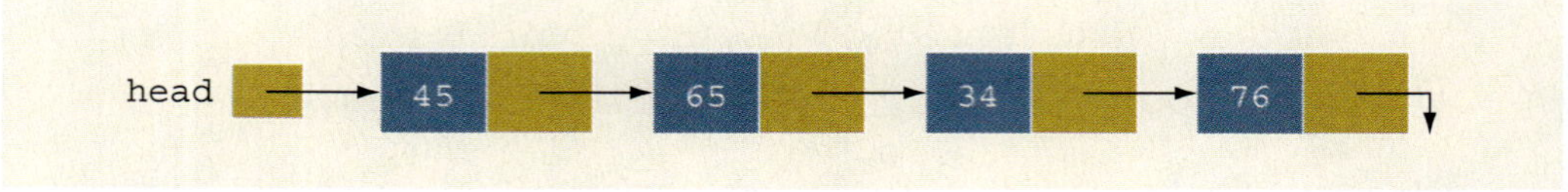

FIGURE 17-2 Linked list

The arrow in each node indicates that the address of the node to which it is pointing is stored in that node. The down arrow in the last node indicates that this link field is NULL.

For a better understanding of this notation, suppose that the first node is at memory location 1200, and the second node is at memory location 1575. We thus have Figure 17-3.

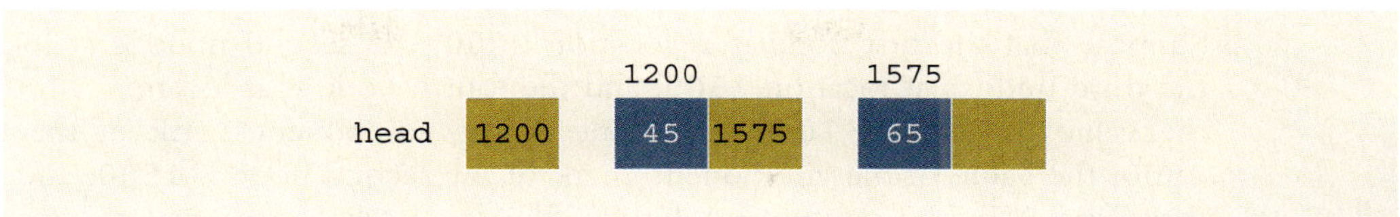

FIGURE 17-3 Linked list and values of the links

The value of the head is 1200, the data part of the first node is 45, and the link component of the first node contains 1575, the address of the second node. If no confusion arises, then we will use the arrow notation whenever we draw the figure of a linked list.

For simplicity and for the ease of understanding and clarity, Figures 17-3 through 17-6 use decimal integers as the values of memory addresses. However, in computer memory, the memory addresses are in binary.

Because each node of a linked list has two components, we need to declare each node as a `class` or `struct`. The data type of each node depends on the specific application—that is, what kind of data is being processed. However, the link component of each node is a pointer. The data type of this pointer variable is the node type itself. For the previous linked list, the definition of the node is as follows. (Suppose that the data type is `int`.)

```
struct nodeType
{
    int info;
    nodeType *link;
};
```

The variable declaration is:

```
nodeType *head;
```

Linked Lists: Some Properties

To help you better understand the concept of a linked list and a node, some important properties of linked lists are described next.

Consider the linked list in Figure 17-4.

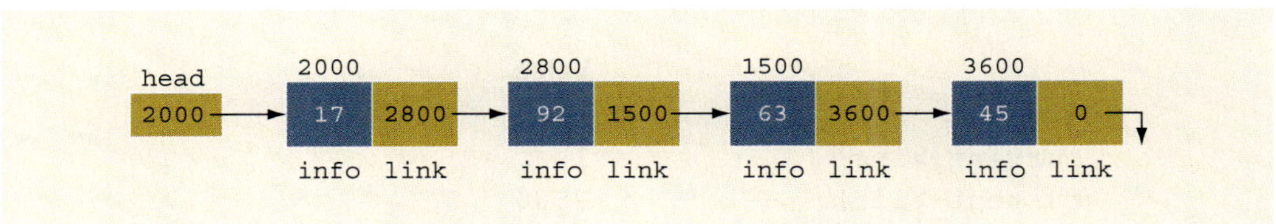

FIGURE 17-4 Linked list with four nodes

This linked list has four nodes. The address of the first node is stored in the pointer head. Each node has two components: info, to store the info, and link, to store the address of the next node. For simplicity, we assume that info is of type int.

Suppose that the first node is at location 2000, the second node is at location 2800, the third node is at location 1500, and the fourth node is at location 3600. Therefore, the value of head is 2000, the value of the component link of the first node is 2800, the value of the component link of the second node is 1500, and so on. Also, the value 0 in the component link of the last node means that this value is NULL, which we indicate by drawing a down arrow. The number at the top of each node is the address of that node. The following table shows the values of head and some other nodes in the list shown in Figure 17-4.

	Value	Explanation
head	2000	
head->info	17	Because head is 2000 and the info of the node at location 2000 is 17
head->link	2800	
head->link->info	92	Because head->link is 2800 and the info of the node at location 2800 is 92

Suppose that current is a pointer of the same type as the pointer head. Then, the statement:

```
current = head;
```

copies the value of head into current (see Figure 17-5).

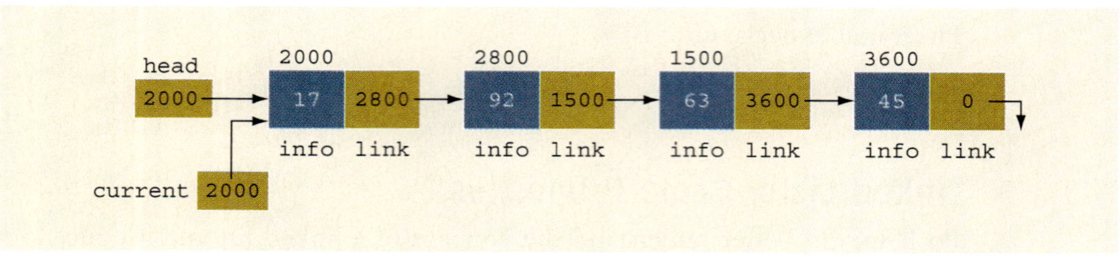

FIGURE 17-5   Linked list after the statement current = head; executes

Clearly, in Figure 17-5:

	Value
current	2000
current->info	17
current->link	2800
current->link->info	92

Now consider the statement:

```
current = current->link;
```

This statement copies the value of `current->link`, which is 2800, into `current`. Therefore, after this statement executes, `current` points to the second node in the list. (When working with linked lists, we typically use these types of statements to advance a pointer to the next node in the list.) See Figure 17-6.

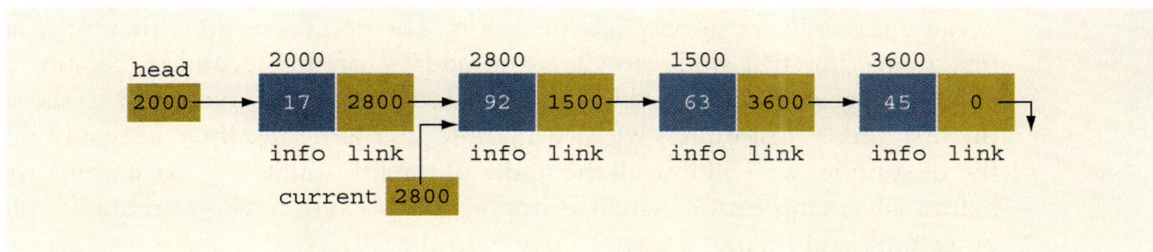

FIGURE 17-6 List after the statement `current = current->link;` executes

In Figure 17-6:

	Value
`current`	2800
`current->info`	92
`current->link`	1500
`current->link->info`	63

Finally, note that in Figure 17-6:

	Value
`head->link->link`	1500
`head->link->link->info`	63
`head->link->link->link`	3600
`head->link->link->link->info`	45
`current->link->link`	3600
`current->link->link->info`	45
`current->link->link->link`	0 (that is, NULL)
`current->link->link->link->info`	Does not exist

From now on, when working with linked lists, we will use only the arrow notation.

TRAVERSING A LINKED LIST

The basic operations of a linked list are as follows: search the list to determine whether a particular item is in the list, insert an item in the list, and delete an item from the list. These operations require the list to be traversed. That is, given a pointer to the first node of the list, we must step through the nodes of the list.

Suppose that the pointer `head` points to the first node in the list, and the link of the last node is NULL. We cannot use the pointer `head` to traverse the list because if we use `head` to traverse the list, we would lose the nodes of the list. This problem occurs because the links are in only one direction. The pointer `head` contains the address of the first node, the first node contains the address of the second node, the second node contains the address of the third node, and so on. If we move `head` to the second node, the first node is lost (unless we save a pointer to this node). If we keep advancing `head` to the next node, we will lose all the nodes of the list (unless we save a pointer to each node before advancing `head`, which is impractical because it would require additional computer time and memory space to maintain the list).

Therefore, we always want `head` to point to the first node. It now follows that we must traverse the list using another pointer of the same type. Suppose that `current` is a pointer of the same type as `head`. The following code traverses the list:

```
current = head;

while (current != NULL)
{
    //Process the current node
    current = current->link;
}
```

For example, suppose that `head` points to a linked list of numbers. The following code outputs the data stored in each node:

```
current = head;

while (current != NULL)
{
    cout << current->info << " ";
    current = current->link;
}
```

ITEM INSERTION AND DELETION

This section discusses how to insert an item into, and delete an item from, a linked list. Consider the following definition of a node. (For simplicity, we assume that the `info` type is `int`. The next section, which discusses linked lists as an abstract data type (ADT) using templates, uses the generic definition of a node.)

```cpp
struct nodeType
{
    int info;
    nodeType *link;
};
```

We will use the following variable declaration:

```cpp
nodeType *head, *p, *q, *newNode;
```

INSERTION

Consider the linked list shown in Figure 17-7.

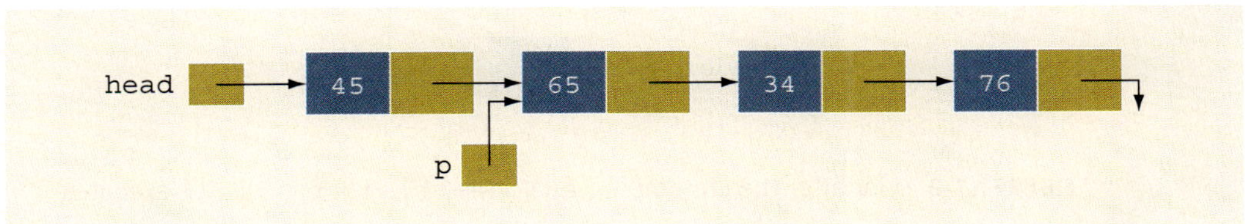

FIGURE 17-7 Linked list before item insertion

Suppose that p points to the node with `info` 65, and a new node with `info` 50 is to be created and inserted after p. The following statements create and store 50 in the `info` field of a new node:

```cpp
newNode = new nodeType;    //create newNode
newNode->info = 50;        //store 50 in the new node
```

The first statement (that is, `newNode = new nodeType;`) creates a node somewhere in memory and stores the address of the newly created node in `newNode`. The second statement (that is, `newNode->info = 50;`) stores 50 in the `info` field of the new node (see Figure 17-8).

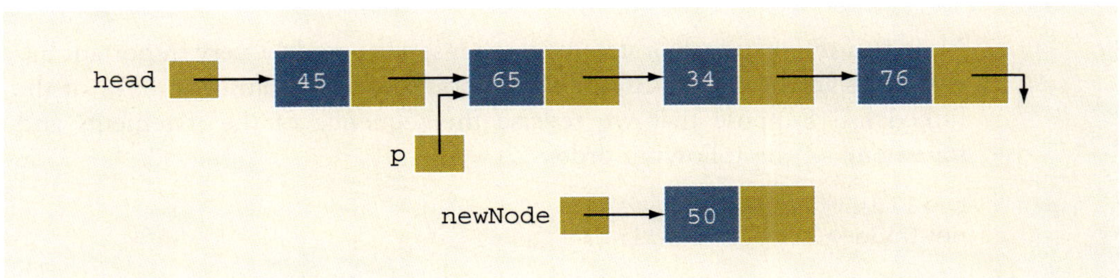

FIGURE 17-8 Create `newNode` and store 50 in it

The following statements insert the node in the linked list at the required place:

```
newNode->link = p->link;
p->link = newNode;
```

After the first statement (that is, `newNode->link = p->link;`) executes, the resulting list is as shown in Figure 17-9.

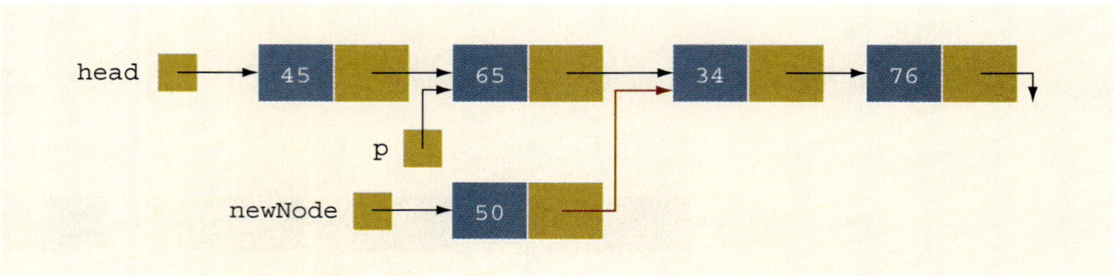

FIGURE 17-9 List after the statement `newNode->link = p->link;` executes

After the second statement (that is, `p->link = newNode;`) executes, the resulting list is as shown in Figure 17-10.

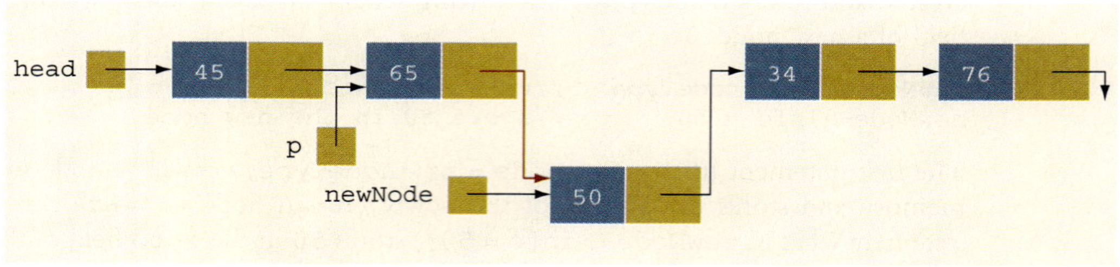

FIGURE 17-10 List after the statement `p->link = newNode` executes

Note that the sequence of statements to insert the node is very important because to insert `newNode` in the list we use only one pointer, `p`, to adjust the links of the node of the linked list. Suppose that we reverse the sequence of the statements and execute the statements in the following order:

```
p->link = newNode;
newNode->link = p->link;
```

Figure 17-11 shows the resulting list after these statements execute.

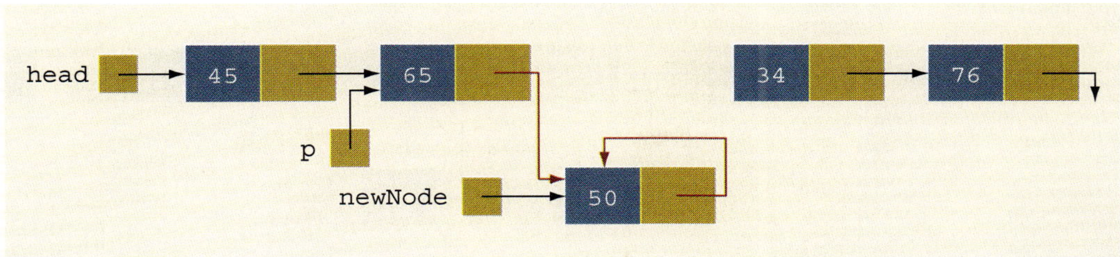

FIGURE 17-11 List after the execution of the statement p->link = newNode; followed by the execution of the statement newNode->link = p->link;

From Figure 17-11, it is clear that **newNode** points back to itself and the remainder of the list is lost.

Using two pointers, we can simplify the insertion code somewhat. Suppose **q** points to the node with **info** 34 (see Figure 17-12).

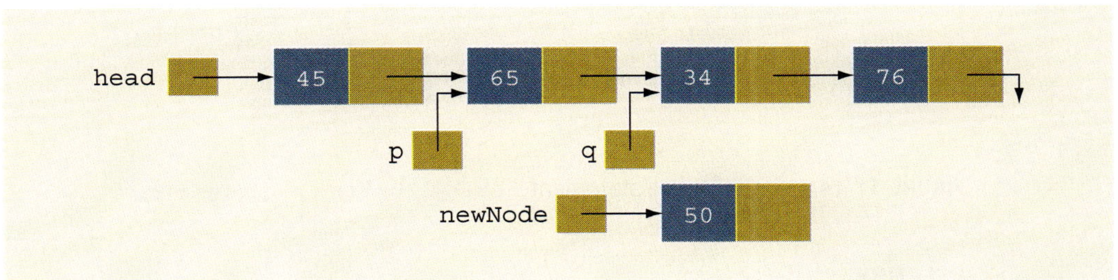

FIGURE 17-12 List with pointers p and q

The following statements insert **newNode** between **p** and **q**:

```
newNode->link = q;
p->link = newNode;
```

The order in which these statements execute does not matter. To illustrate this, suppose that we execute the statements in the following order:

```
p->link = newNode;
newNode->link = q;
```

After the statement p->link = newNode; executes, the resulting list is as shown in Figure 17-13.

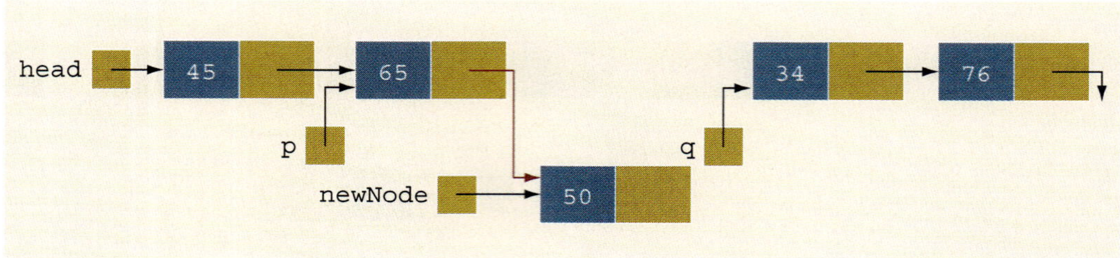

FIGURE 17-13 List after the statement `p->link = newNode;` executes

Because we have a pointer, q, pointing to the remaining list, the remaining list is not lost. After the statement **newNode->link = q;** executes, the list is as shown in Figure 17-14.

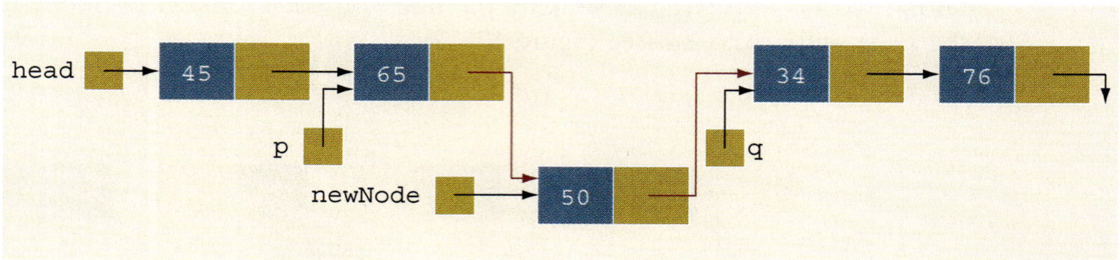

FIGURE 17-14 List after the statement `newNode->link = q;` executes

DELETION

Consider the linked list shown in Figure 17-15.

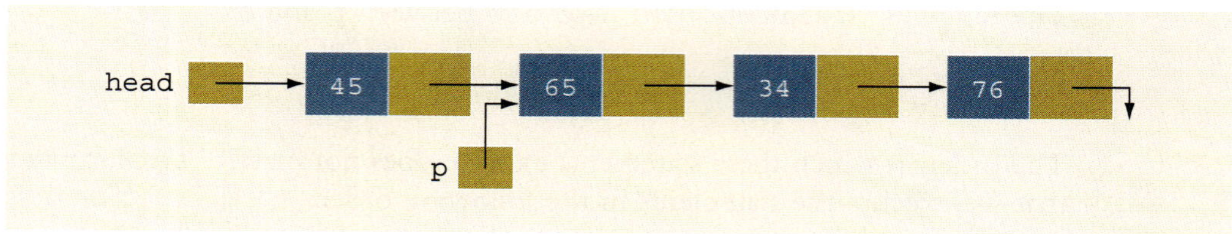

FIGURE 17-15 Node to be deleted is with `info 34`

Suppose that the node with **info 34** is to be deleted from the list. The following statement removes the node from the list:

```
p->link = p->link->link;
```

Figure 17-16 shows the resulting list after the preceding statement executes.

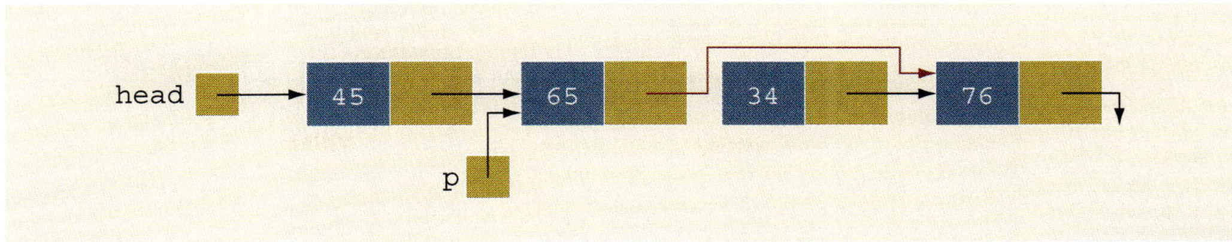

FIGURE 17-16 List after the statement p->link = p->link->link; executes

From Figure 17-16, it is clear that the node with **info** 34 is removed from the list. However, the memory is still occupied by this node and this memory is inaccessible; that is, this node is dangling. To deallocate the memory, we need a pointer to this node. The following statements delete the node from the list and deallocate the memory occupied by this node:

```
q = p->link;
p->link = q->link;
delete q;
```

After the statement q = p->link; executes, the list is as shown in Figure 17-17.

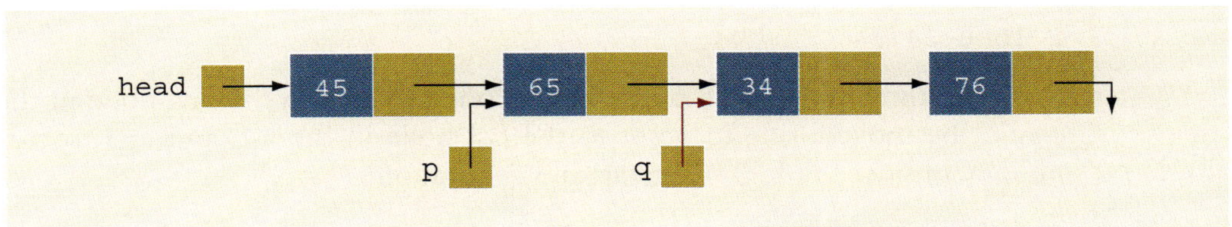

FIGURE 17-17 List after the statement q = p->link; executes

After the statement **p->link = q->link;** executes, the resulting list is as shown in Figure 17-18.

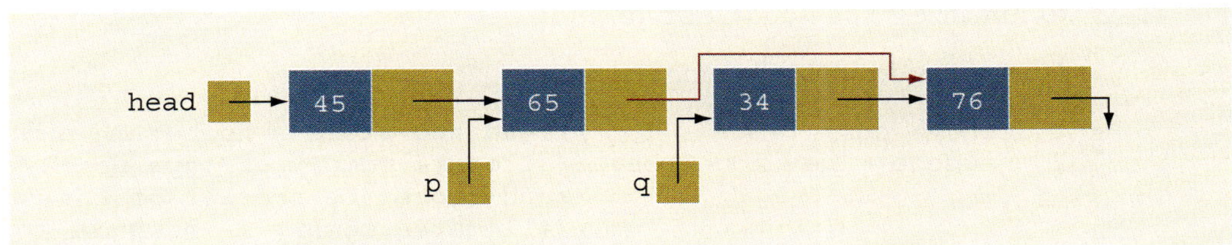

FIGURE 17-18 List after the statement p->link = q->link; executes

After the statement **delete** q; executes, the list is as shown in Figure 17-19.

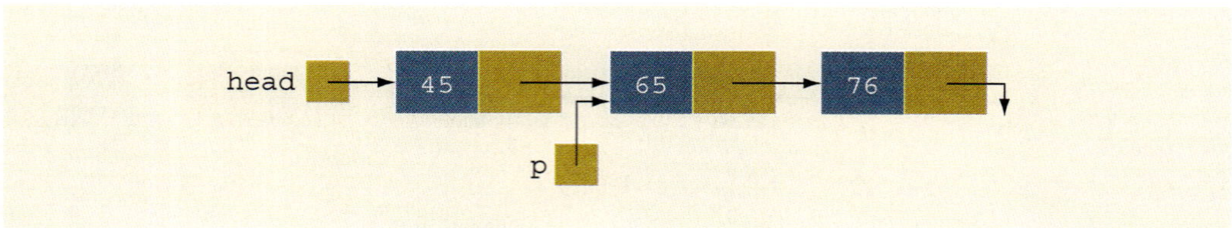

FIGURE 17-19 List after the statement `delete` q; executes

Building a Linked List

Now that we know how to insert a node in a linked list, let us see how to build a linked list. First, we consider a linked list in general. If the data we read is unsorted, the linked list will be unsorted. Such a list can be built in two ways: forward and backward. In the forward manner, a new node is always inserted at the end of the linked list. In the backward manner, a new node is always inserted at the beginning of the list. We will consider both cases.

BUILDING A LINKED LIST FORWARD

Suppose that the nodes are in the usual `info-link` form and `info` is of type `int`. Let us assume that we process the following data:

```
2 15 8 24 34
```

We need three pointers to build the list: one to point to the first node in the list, which cannot be moved; one to point to the last node in the list; and one to create the new node. Consider the following variable declaration:

```
nodeType *first, *last, *newNode;
int num;
```

Suppose that `first` points to the first node in the list. Initially, the list is empty, so both `first` and `last` are NULL. Thus, we must have the statements:

```
first = NULL;
last = NULL;
```

to initialize `first` and `last` to NULL.

Next, consider the following statements:

```
1   cin >> num;                //read and store a number in num
2   newNode = new nodeType;    //allocate memory of type nodeType
                               //and store the address of the
                               //allocated memory in newNode
3   newNode->info = num;       //copy the value of num into the
                               //info field of newNode
4   newNode->link = NULL;      //initialize the link field of
                               //newNode to NULL
```

```
5  if (first == NULL)          //if first is NULL, the list is empty;
                               //make first and last point to newNode

   {
5a     first = newNode;
5b     last = newNode;
   }
6  else                        //list is not empty
   {
6a     last->link = newNode;   //insert newNode at the end of the list
6b     last = newNode;         //set last so that it points to the
                               //actual last node in the list

   }
```

Let us now execute these statements. Initially, both `first` and `last` are NULL. Therefore, we have the list as shown in Figure 17-20.

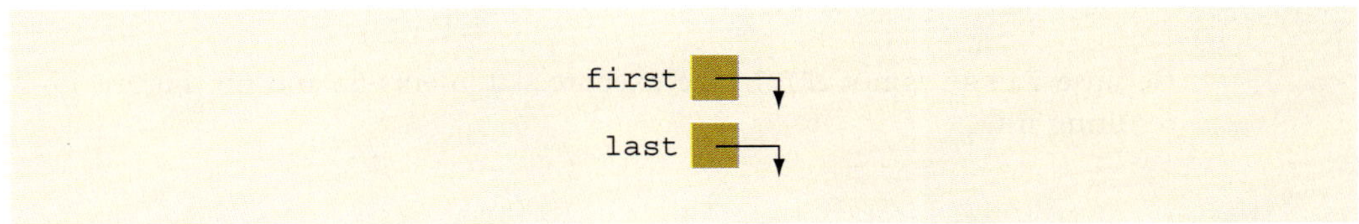

FIGURE 17-20 Empty list

After statement 1 executes, `num` is 2. Statement 2 creates a node and stores the address of that node in `newNode`. Statement 3 stores 2 in the `info` field of `newNode`, and statement 4 stores NULL in the link field of `newNode` (see Figure 17-21).

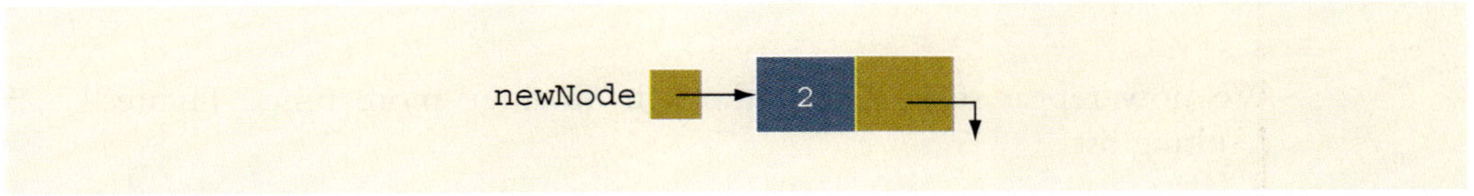

FIGURE 17-21 `newNode` with `info` 2

Because `first` is NULL, we execute statements 5a and 5b. Figure 17-22 shows the resulting list.

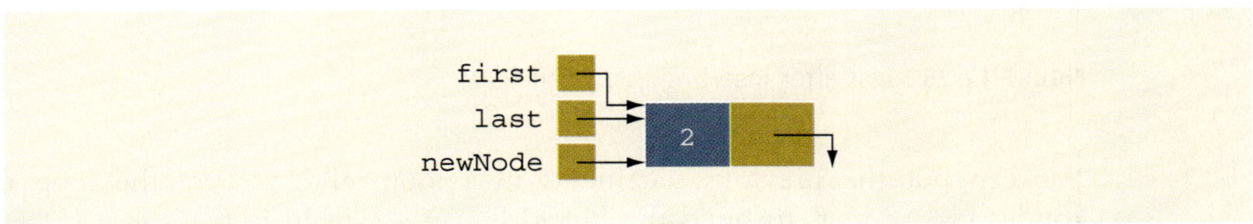

FIGURE 17-22 List after inserting `newNode` in it

We now repeat statements 1 through 6b. After statement 1 executes, num is 15. Statement 2 creates a node and stores the address of this node in newNode. Statement 3 stores 15 in the info field of newNode, and statement 4 stores NULL in the link field of newNode (see Figure 17-23).

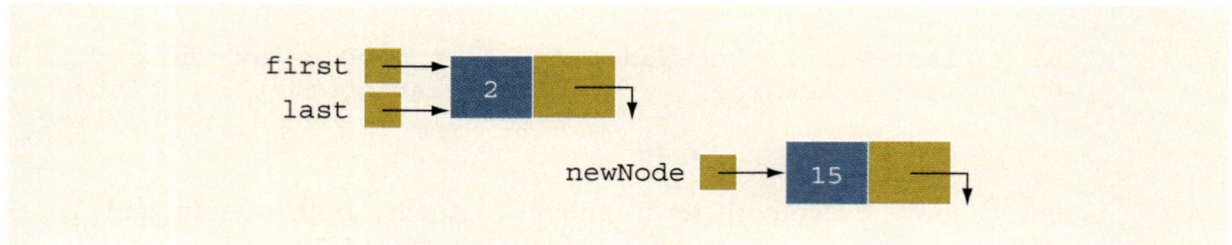

FIGURE 17-23 List and newNode with info 15

Because first is not NULL, we execute statements 6a and 6b. Figure 17-24 shows the resulting list.

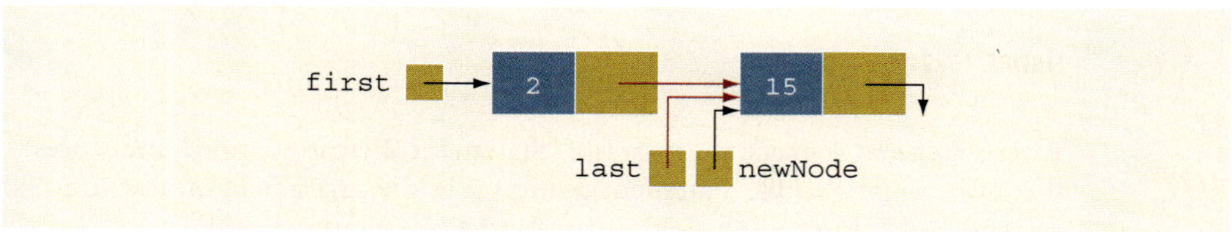

FIGURE 17-24 List after inserting newNode at the end

We now repeat statements 1 through 6b three more times. Figure 17-25 shows the resulting list.

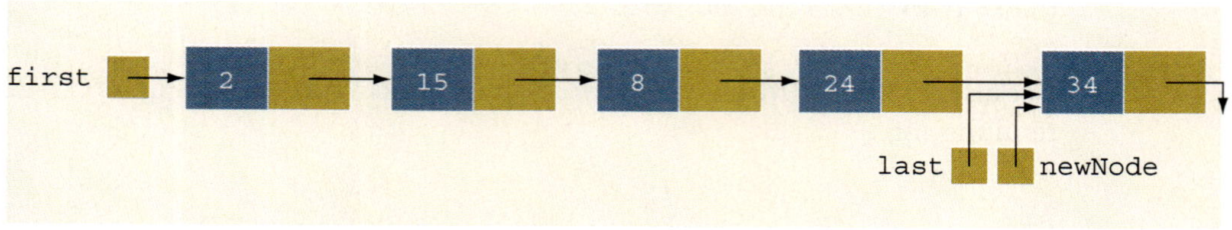

FIGURE 17-25 List after inserting 8, 24, and 34

We can put the previous statements in a loop, and execute the loop until certain conditions are met, to build the linked list. We can, in fact, write a C++ function to build a linked list.

Suppose that we read a list of integers ending with `-999`. The following function, `buildListForward`, builds a linked list (in a forward manner) and returns the pointer of the built list:

```
nodeType* buildListForward()
{
    nodeType *first, *newNode, *last;
    int num;

    cout << "Enter a list of integers ending with -999."
         << endl;
    cin >> num;
    first = NULL;

    while (num != -999)
    {
        newNode = new nodeType;
        newNode->info = num;
        newNode->link = NULL;

        if (first == NULL)
        {
            first = newNode;
            last = newNode;
        }
        else
        {
            last->link = newNode;
            last = newNode;
        }
        cin >> num;
    } //end while

    return first;
} //end buildListForward
```

BUILDING A LINKED LIST BACKWARD

Now we consider the case of building a linked list backward. For the previously given data—2, 15, 8, 24, and 34—the linked list is as shown in Figure 17-26.

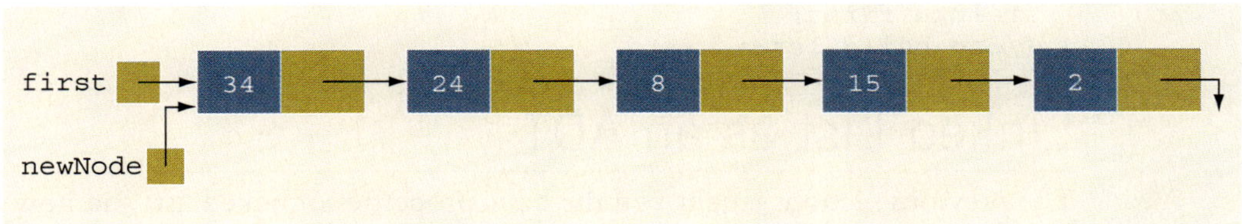

FIGURE 17-26 List after building it backward

Because the new node is always inserted at the beginning of the list, we do not need to know the end of the list, so the pointer `last` is not needed. Also, after inserting the new node at the beginning, the new node becomes the first node in the list. Thus, we need to update the value of the pointer `first` to correctly point to the first node in the list. We see, then, that we need only two pointers to build the linked list: one to point to the list, and one to create the new node. Because initially the list is empty, the pointer `first` must be initialized to `NULL`. In pseudocode, the algorithm is:

1. Initialize `first` to `NULL`.

2. For each item in the list,

    a. Create the new node, `newNode`.

    b. Store the item in `newNode`.

    c. Insert `newNode` before `first`.

    d. Update the value of the pointer `first`.

The following C++ function builds the linked list backward and returns the pointer of the built list:

```cpp
nodeType* buildListBackward()
{
    nodeType *first, *newNode;
    int num;

    cout << "Enter a list of integers ending with -999."
         << endl;
    cin >> num;
    first = NULL;

    while (num != -999)
    {
        newNode = new nodeType;     //create a node
        newNode->info = num;        //store the data in newNode
        newNode->link = first;      //put newNode at the beginning
                                    //of the list
        first = newNode;            //update the head pointer of
                                    //the list, that is, first
        cin >> num;                 //read the next number
    }

    return first;
} //end buildListBackward
```

Linked List as an ADT

The previous sections taught you the basic properties of linked lists and how to construct and manipulate them. Because a linked list is a very important data structure, rather than discuss specific lists such as a list of integers or a list of strings, this section discusses linked lists as an abstract data type (ADT). Using templates, this section gives a generic definition of linked lists, which is then used in the next section and later in this book. The programming example at the end of this chapter also uses this generic definition of linked lists.

The basic operations on linked lists are:

1. Initialize the list.
2. Determine whether the list is empty.
3. Print the list.
4. Find the length of the list.
5. Destroy the list.
6. Retrieve the `info` contained in the first node.
7. Retrieve the `info` contained in the last node.
8. Search the list for a given item.
9. Insert an item in the list.
10. Delete an item from the list.
11. Make a copy of the linked list.

In general, there are two types of linked lists—sorted lists, whose elements are arranged according to some criteria, and unsorted lists, whose elements are in no particular order. The algorithms to implement the operations search, insert, and remove slightly differ for sorted and unsorted lists. Therefore, we will define the **class linkedListType** to implement the basic operations on a linked list as an **abstract class**. Using the principal of inheritance, we, in fact, will derive two **class**es—unorderedLinkedList and orderedLinkedList—from the **class linkedListType**.

Objects of the **class unorderedLinkedList** would arrange list elements in no particular order, that is, these lists may not be sorted. On the other hand, objects of the **class orderedLinkedList** would arrange elements according to some comparison criteria, usually less than or equal to. That is, these lists will be in ascending order. Moreover, after inserting an element into or removing an element from an ordered list, the resulting list will be ordered.

If a linked list is unordered, we can insert a new item at either the end or the beginning. Furthermore, you can build such a list in either a forward manner or a backward manner. The function **buildListForward** inserts the new item at the end, whereas the function **buildListBackward** inserts the new item at the beginning. To accommodate both operations, we will write two functions: **insertFirst** to insert the new item at the beginning of the list, and **insertLast** to insert the new item at the end of the list. Also, to make the algorithms more efficient, we will use two pointers in the list: **first**, which points to the first node in the list, and **last**, which points to the last node in the list.

Structure of Linked List Nodes

Recall that each node of a linked list must store the data as well as the address for the next node in the list (except the last node of the list). Therefore, the node has two member variables. To simplify operations such as insert and delete, we define the class to implement the node of a linked list as a `struct`. The definition of the `struct` nodeType is:

```
//Definition of the node

template <class Type>
struct nodeType
{
    Type info;
    nodeType<Type> *link;
};
```

NOTE The class to implement the node of a linked list is declared as a `struct`. Programming Exercise 9, at the end of this chapter, asks you to redefine the class to implement the nodes of a linked list so that the member variables of the `class` nodeType are `private`.

Member Variables of the `class` linkedListType

To maintain a linked list we use two pointers—`first` and `last`. The pointer `first` points to the first node in the list, and `last` points to the last node in the list. We also keep a count of the number of nodes in the list. Therefore, the `class` linkedListType has three member variables, as follows:

```
protected:
    int count;      //variable to store the number of
                    //elements in the list
    nodeType<Type> *first; //pointer to the first node
                           //of the list
    nodeType<Type> *last;  //pointer to the last node
                           //of the list
```

Linked List Iterators

One of the basic operations performed on a list is to process each node of the list. This requires the list to be traversed, starting at the first node. Moreover, a specific application requires each node to be processed in a very specific way. A common technique to accomplish this is to provide an iterator. So what is an iterator? An **iterator** is an object that produces each element of a container, such as a linked list, one element at a time. The two most common operations on iterators are ++ (the increment operator) and * (the dereferenceing operator). The increment operator advances the iterator to the next node in the list, while the dereferencing operator returns the info of the current node.

Note that an iterator is an object. So we need to define a class, which we will call `linkedListIterator`, to create iterators to objects of the `class` linkedListType. The iterator class would have one member variable pointing to (the current) node.

```
template <class Type>
class linkedListIterator
{
public:
    linkedListIterator();
      //Default constructor
      //Postcondition: current = NULL;

    linkedListIterator(nodeType<Type> *ptr);
      //Constructor with a parameter.
      //Postcondition: current = ptr;

    Type operator*();
      //Function to overload the dereferencing operator *.
      //Postcondition: Returns the info contained in the node.

    linkedListIterator<Type> operator++();
      //Overload the pre-increment operator.
      //Postcondition: The iterator is advanced to the next
      //               node.

    bool operator==(const linkedListIterator<Type>& right) const;
      //Overload the equality operator.
      //Postcondition: Returns true if this iterator is equal to
      //               the iterator specified by right,
      //               otherwise it returns false.

    bool operator!=(const linkedListIterator<Type>& right) const;
      //Overload the not equal to operator.
      //Postcondition: Returns true if this iterator is not equal
      //               to the iterator specified by right,
      //               otherwise it returns false.

private:
    nodeType<Type> *current; //pointer to point to the current
                             //node in the linked list
};
```

Figure 17-27 shows the UML class diagram of the **class** linkedListIterator.

```
linkedListIterator<Type>

-*current: nodeType<Type>

+linkedListIterator()
+linkedListIterator(nodeType<Type>)
+operator*(): Type
+operator++(): linkedListIterator<Type>
+operator==(const linkedListIterator<Type>&) const: bool
+operator!=(const linkedListIterator<Type>&) const: bool
```

FIGURE 17-27 UML class diagram of the **class** linkedListIterator

The definitions of the functions of the **class** `linkedListIterator` are:

```cpp
template <class Type>
linkedListIterator<Type>::linkedListIterator()
{
    current = NULL;
}

template <class Type>
linkedListIterator<Type>::
                    linkedListIterator(nodeType<Type> *ptr)
{
    current = ptr;
}

template <class Type>
Type linkedListIterator<Type>::operator*()
{
    return current->info;
}

template <class Type>
linkedListIterator<Type> linkedListIterator<Type>::operator++()
{
    current = current->link;

    return *this;
}

template <class Type>
bool linkedListIterator<Type>::operator==
                (const linkedListIterator<Type>& right) const
{
    return (current == right.current);
}

template <class Type>
bool linkedListIterator<Type>::operator!=
                (const linkedListIterator<Type>& right) const
{
    return (current != right.current);
}
```

Now that we have defined the classes to implement the node of a linked list and an iterator to a linked list, next we describe the **class** `linkedListType` to implement the basis properties of a linked list.

The following abstract class defines the basic properties of a linked list as an ADT.

```cpp
template <class Type>
class linkedListType
{
public:
    const linkedListType<Type>& operator=
                            (const linkedListType<Type>&);
      //Overload the assignment operator.
```

```cpp
void initializeList();
   //Initialize the list to an empty state.
   //Postcondition: first = NULL, last = NULL, count = 0;

bool isEmptyList() const;
   //Function to determine whether the list is empty.
   //Postcondition: Returns true if the list is empty,
   //               otherwise it returns false.

void print() const;
   //Function to output the data contained in each node.
   //Postcondition: none

int length() const;
   //Function to return the number of nodes in the list.
   //Postcondition: The value of count is returned.

void destroyList();
   //Function to delete all the nodes from the list.
   //Postcondition: first = NULL, last = NULL, count = 0;

Type front() const;
   //Function to return the first element of the list.
   //Precondition: The list must exist and must not be
   //              empty.
   //Postcondition: If the list is empty, the program
   //               terminates; otherwise, the first
   //               element of the list is returned.

Type back() const;
   //Function to return the last element of the list.
   //Precondition: The list must exist and must not be
   //              empty.
   //Postcondition: If the list is empty, the program
   //               terminates; otherwise, the last
   //               element of the list is returned.

virtual bool search(const Type& searchItem) const = 0;
   //Function to determine whether searchItem is in the list.
   //Postcondition: Returns true if searchItem is in the
   //               list, otherwise the value false is
   //               returned.

virtual void insertFirst(const Type& newItem) = 0;
   //Function to insert newItem at the beginning of the list.
   //Postcondition: first points to the new list, newItem is
   //               inserted at the beginning of the list,
   //               last points to the last node in the list,
   //               and count is incremented by 1.

virtual void insertLast(const Type& newItem) = 0;
   //Function to insert newItem at the end of the list.
   //Postcondition: first points to the new list, newItem
   //               is inserted at the end of the list,
   //               last points to the last node in the list,
   //               and count is incremented by 1.
```

```cpp
    virtual void deleteNode(const Type& deleteItem) = 0;
      //Function to delete deleteItem from the list.
      //Postcondition: If found, the node containing
      //               deleteItem is deleted from the list.
      //               first points to the first node, last
      //               points to the last node of the updated
      //               list, and count is decremented by 1.

    linkedListIterator<Type> begin();
      //Function to return an iterator at the begining of the
      //linked list.
      //Postcondition: Returns an iterator such that current is
      //               set to first.

    linkedListIterator<Type> end();
      //Function to return an iterator one element past the
      //last element of the linked list.
      //Postcondition: Returns an iterator such that current is
      //               set to NULL.

    linkedListType();
      //default constructor
      //Initializes the list to an empty state.
      //Postcondition: first = NULL, last = NULL, count = 0;

    linkedListType(const linkedListType<Type>& otherList);
      //copy constructor

    ~linkedListType();
      //destructor
      //Deletes all the nodes from the list.
      //Postcondition: The list object is destroyed.

protected:
    int count;    //variable to store the number of
                  //elements in the list
    nodeType<Type> *first; //pointer to the first node of the list
    nodeType<Type> *last;  //pointer to the last node of the list

private:
    void copyList(const linkedListType<Type>& otherList);
      //Function to make a copy of otherList.
      //Postcondition: A copy of otherList is created and
      //               assigned to this list.
};
```

Figure 17-28 shows the UML class diagram of the **class** linkedListType.

```
                    linkedListType<Type>

#count: int
#*first: nodeType<Type>
#*last: nodeType<Type>

+operator=(const linkedListType<Type>&):
                        const linkedListType<Type>&
+initializeList(): void
+isEmptyList() const: bool
+print() const: void
+length() const: int
+destroyList(): void
+front() const: Type
+back() const: Type
+search(const Type&) const = 0: bool
+insertFirst(const Type&) = 0: void
+insertLast(const Type&) = 0: void
+deleteNode(const Type&) = 0: void
+begin(): linkedListIterator<Type>
+end(): linkedListIterator<Type>
+linkedListType()
+linkedListType(const linkedListType<Type>&)
+~linkedListType()
-copyList(const linkedListType<Type>&): void
```

FIGURE 17-28 UML class diagram of the **class** `linkedListType`

Note that, typically, in the UML diagram the name of an abstract class and abstract function is shown in italics.

The instance variables `first` and `last`, as defined earlier, of the **class** `linkedListType` are **protected**, not **private**, because as noted previously, we will derive the **class**es `unorderedLinkedList` and `orderedLinkedList` from the **class** `linkedListType`. Because each of the **class**es `unorderedLinkedList` and `orderedLinkedList` will provide separate definitions of the functions `search`, `insertFirst`, `insertLast`, and `deleteNode`, and because these functions would access the instance variable, to provide direct access to the instance variables, the instance variables are declared as **protected**.

The definition of the **class** `linkedListType` includes a member function to overload the assignment operator. For classes that include pointer data members, the assignment operator must be explicitly overloaded (see Chapters 13 and 14). For the same reason, the definition of the class also includes a copy constructor.

Notice that the definition of the **class** `linkedListType` contains the member function `copyList`, which is declared as a **private** member. This is due to the fact that this function is used only to implement the copy constructor and overload the assignment operator.

Next, we write the definitions of the nonabstract functions of the **class** `LinkedListClass`.

The list is empty if `first` is `NULL`. Therefore, the definition of the function `isEmptyList` to implement this operation is as follows:

```cpp
template <class Type>
bool linkedListType<Type>::isEmptyList() const
{
    return (first == NULL);
}
```

DEFAULT CONSTRUCTOR

The default constructor, `linkedListType`, is quite straightforward. It simply initializes the list to an empty state. Recall that when an object of the `linkedListType` type is declared and no value is passed, the default constructor is executed automatically:

```cpp
template <class Type>
linkedListType<Type>::linkedListType() //default constructor
{
    first = NULL;
    last = NULL;
    count = 0;
}
```

DESTROY THE LIST

The function `destroyList` deallocates the memory occupied by each node. We traverse the list starting from the first node and deallocate the memory by calling the operator `delete`. We need a temporary pointer to deallocate the memory. Once the entire list is destroyed, we must set the pointers `first` and `last` to `NULL` and `count` to 0:

```cpp
template <class Type>
void linkedListType<Type>::destroyList()
{
    nodeType<Type> *temp;     //pointer to deallocate the memory
                              //occupied by the node
    while (first != NULL)     //while there are nodes in the list
    {
        temp = first;         //set temp to the current node
        first = first->link;  //advance first to the next node
        delete temp;          //deallocate the memory occupied by temp
    }

    last = NULL;  //initialize last to NULL; first has already
                  //been set to NULL by the while loop
    count = 0;
}
```

INITIALIZE THE LIST

The function `initializeList` initializes the list to an empty state. Note that the default constructor or the copy constructor has already initialized the list when the list object was declared. This operation, in fact, reinitializes the list to an empty state, and so it must delete the nodes (if any) from the list. This task can be accomplished by using the `destroyList` operation, which also resets the pointers `first` and `last` to `NULL` and sets `count` to 0:

```cpp
template <class Type>
void linkedListType<Type>::initializeList()
{
    destroyList(); //if the list has any nodes, delete them
}
```

Print the List

The member function `print` prints the data contained in each node. To do so we must traverse the list, starting at the first node. Because the pointer `first` always points to the first node in the list, we need another pointer to traverse the list. (If we use `first` to traverse the list, the entire list will be lost.)

```cpp
template <class Type>
void linkedListType<Type>::print() const
{
    nodeType<Type> *current; //pointer to traverse the list

    current = first;     //set current so that it points to
                         //the first node
    while (current != NULL) //while more data to print
    {
        cout << current->info << " ";
        current = current->link;
    }
}//end print
```

Length of a List

The length of a linked list (that is, how many nodes are in the list) is stored in the variable `count`. Therefore, this function returns the value of this variable:

```cpp
template <class Type>
int linkedListType<Type>::length() const
{
    return count;
}
```

Retrieve the Data of the First Node

The function `front` returns the `info` contained in the first node, and its definition is straightforward:

```cpp
template <class Type>
Type linkedListType<Type>::front() const
{
    assert(first != NULL);

    return first->info; //return the info of the first node
}//end front
```

Notice that if the list is empty, the `assert` statement terminates the program. Therefore, before calling this function, check to see whether the list is nonempty.

Retrieve the Data of the Last Node

The function `back` returns the `info` contained in the last node, and its definition is straightforward:

```cpp
template <class Type>
Type linkedListType<Type>::back() const
{
    assert(last != NULL);

    return last->info; //return the info of the last node
}//end back
```

Notice that if the list is empty, the `assert` statement terminates the program. Therefore, before calling this function, check to see whether the list is nonempty.

Begin and End

The function `begin` returns an iterator to the first node in the linked list, and the function `end` returns an interator to one past the last node in the linked list. Their definitions are:

```cpp
template <class Type>
linkedListIterator<Type> linkedListType<Type>::begin()
{
    linkedListIterator<Type> temp(first);

    return temp;
}
```

```cpp
template <class Type>
linkedListIterator<Type> linkedListType<Type>::end()
{
    linkedListIterator<Type> temp(NULL);

    return temp;
}
```

Copy the List

The function `copyList` makes an identical copy of a linked list. Therefore, we traverse the list to be copied, starting at the first node. Corresponding to each node in the original list, we:

    a.   Create a node, and call it `newNode`.

    b.   Copy the `info` of the node (in the original list) into `newNode`.

    c.   Insert `newNode` at the end of the list being created.

The definition of the function `copyList` is:

```cpp
template <class Type>
void linkedListType<Type>::copyList
                    (const linkedListType<Type>& otherList)
{
    nodeType<Type> *newNode; //pointer to create a node
    nodeType<Type> *current; //pointer to traverse the list

    if (first != NULL) //if the list is nonempty, make it empty
        destroyList();

    if (otherList.first == NULL) //otherList is empty
    {
        first = NULL;
        last = NULL;
        count = 0;
    }
    else
    {
        current = otherList.first; //current points to the
                                   //list to be copied
        count = otherList.count;

            //copy the first node
        first = new nodeType<Type>;   //create the node
        first->info = current->info; //copy the info
        first->link = NULL;          //set the link field of
                                     //the node to NULL
        last = first;                //make last point to the
                                     //first node
        current = current->link;     //make current point to
                                     //the next node

            //copy the remaining list
        while (current != NULL)
        {
            newNode = new nodeType<Type>;   //create a node
            newNode->info = current->info; //copy the info
            newNode->link = NULL;          //set the link of
                                           //newNode to NULL
```

```
            last->link = newNode;   //attach newNode after last
            last = newNode;         //make last point to
                                    //the actual last node
         current = current->link;   //make current point
                                    //to the next node
      }//end while
   }//end else
}//end copyList
```

Destructor

The destructor deallocates the memory occupied by the nodes of a list when the class object goes out of scope. Because memory is allocated dynamically, resetting the pointers `first` and `last` does not deallocate the memory occupied by the nodes in the list. We must traverse the list, starting at the first node, and delete each node in the list. The list can be destroyed by calling the function `destroyList`. Therefore, the definition of the destructor is:

```
template <class Type>
linkedListType<Type>::~linkedListType() //destructor
{
    destroyList();
}
```

Copy Constructor

Because the **class** `linkedListType` contains pointer data members, the definition of this class contains the copy constructor. Recall that, if a formal parameter is a value parameter, the copy constructor provides the formal parameter with its own copy of the data. The copy constructor also executes when an object is declared and initialized using another object. (For more information, see Chapter 13.)

The copy constructor makes an identical copy of the linked list. This can be done by calling the function `copyList`. Because the function `copyList` checks whether the original is empty by checking the value of `first`, we must first initialize the pointer `first` to NULL before calling the function `copyList`.

The definition of the copy constructor is:

```
template <class Type>
linkedListType<Type>::linkedListType
                    (const linkedListType<Type>& otherList)
{
    first = NULL;
    copyList(otherList);
}//end copy constructor
```

Overloading the Assignment Operator

The definition of the function to overload the assignment operator for the `class` `linkedListType` is similar to the definition of the copy constructor. We give its definition for the sake of completeness:

```cpp
        //overload the assignment operator
template <class Type>
const linkedListType<Type>& linkedListType<Type>::operator=
                         (const linkedListType<Type>& otherList)
{
    if (this != &otherList) //avoid self-copy
    {
        copyList(otherList);
    }//end else

    return *this;
}
```

Unordered Linked Lists

As described in the preceding section, we derive the `class` `unorderedLinkedList` from the abstract `class` `linkedListType` and implement the operations `search`, `insertFirst`, `insertLast`, and `deleteNode`.

The following class defines an unordered linked list as an ADT:

```cpp
template <class Type>
class unorderedLinkedList: public linkedListType<Type>
{
public:
    bool search(const Type& searchItem) const;
      //Function to determine whether searchItem is in the list.
      //Postcondition: Returns true if searchItem is in the
      //               list, otherwise the value false is
      //               returned.

    void insertFirst(const Type& newItem);
      //Function to insert newItem at the beginning of the list.
      //Postcondition: first points to the new list, newItem is
      //               inserted at the beginning of the list,
      //               last points to the last node in the
      //               list, and count is incremented by 1.

    void insertLast(const Type& newItem);
      //Function to insert newItem at the end of the list.
      //Postcondition: first points to the new list, newItem
      //               is inserted at the end of the list,
      //               last points to the last node in the
      //               list, and count is incremented by 1.
```

```cpp
    void deleteNode(const Type& deleteItem);
      //Function to delete deleteItem from the list.
      //Postcondition: If found, the node containing
      //               deleteItem is deleted from the list.
      //               first points to the first node, last
      //               points to the last node of the updated
      //               list, and count is decremented by 1.
};
```

Figure 17-29 shows a UML class diagram of the **class** unorderedLinkedList and the inheritance hierarchy.

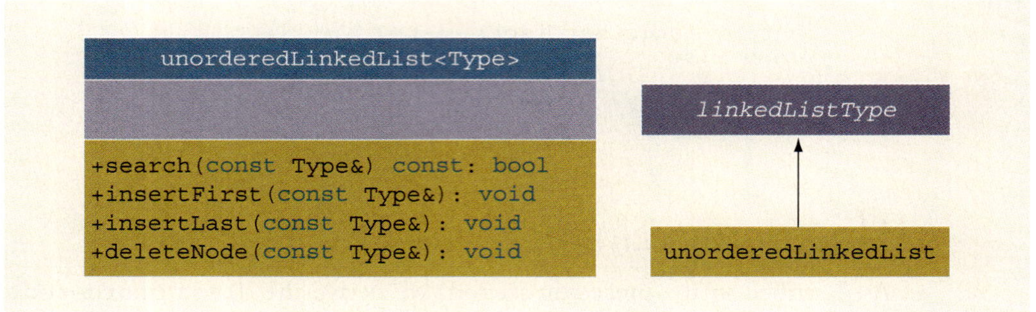

FIGURE 17-29   UML class diagram of the **class** unorderedLinkedList and inheritance hierarchy

Next, we give the definitions of the member functions of the **class** unorderedLinkedList.

Search the List

The member function **search** searches the list for a given item. If the item is found, it returns **true**; otherwise, it returns **false**. Because a linked list is not a random-access data structure, we must sequentially search the list, starting from the first node.

This function has the following steps:

1. Compare the search item with the current node in the list. If the info of the current node is the same as the search item, stop the search; otherwise, make the next node the current node.

2. Repeat Step 1 until either the item is found or no more data is left in the list to compare with the search item.

```cpp
template <class Type>
bool unorderedLinkedList<Type>::
                  search(const Type& searchItem) const
{
    nodeType<Type> *current; //pointer to traverse the list
    bool found = false;
```

```cpp
    current = first; //set current to point to the first
                     //node in the list
    while (current != NULL && !found)     //search the list
        if (current->info == searchItem) //searchItem is found
            found = true;
        else
            current = current->link; //make current point to
                                     //the next node

    return found;
}//end search
```

> **NOTE** The function `search` can also be written as:
>
> ```cpp
> template <class Type>
> bool unorderedLinkedList<Type>::search(const Type& searchItem)
>     const
> {
>     nodeType<Type> *current; //pointer to traverse the list
>
>     current = first; //set current to point to the first
>                      //node in the list
>
>     while (current != NULL)                 //search the list
>         if (current->info == searchItem)    //searchItem is found
>             return true;
>         else
>             current = current->link; //make current point to
>                                      //the next node
>
>     return false; //searchItem is not in the list, return false
> }//end search
> ```

Insert the First Node

The function `insertFirst` inserts the new item at the beginning of the list—that is, before the node pointed to by `first`. The steps needed to implement this function are as follows:

1. Create a new node.
2. Store the new item in the new node.
3. Insert the node before `first`.
4. Increment count by 1.

```cpp
template <class Type>
void unorderedLinkedList<Type>::insertFirst(const Type& newItem)
{
    nodeType<Type> *newNode; //pointer to create the new node
```

```
    newNode = new nodeType<Type>; //create the new node
    newNode->info = newItem;    //store the new item in the node
    newNode->link = first;      //insert newNode before first
    first = newNode;            //make first point to the
                                //actual first node

    count++;                    //increment count

    if (last == NULL)   //if the list was empty, newNode is also
                        //the last node in the list
        last = newNode;
}//end insertFirst
```

Insert the Last Node

The definition of the member function `insertLast` is similar to the definition of the
member function `insertFirst`. Here, we insert the new node after `last`. Essentially,
the function `insertLast` is:

```
template <class Type>
void unorderedLinkedList<Type>::insertLast(const Type& newItem)
{
    nodeType<Type> *newNode; //pointer to create the new node

    newNode = new nodeType<Type>; //create the new node
    newNode->info = newItem;    //store the new item in the node
    newNode->link = NULL;    //set the link field of newNode
                                //to NULL

    if (first == NULL)   //if the list is empty, newNode is
                        //both the first and last node
    {
        first = newNode;
        last = newNode;
        count++;            //increment count
    }
    else    //the list is not empty, insert newNode after last
    {
        last->link = newNode; //insert newNode after last
        last = newNode; //make last point to the actual
                        //last node in the list
        count++;            //increment count
    }
}//end insertLast
```

DELETE A NODE

Next, we discuss the implementation of the member function `deleteNode`, which
deletes a node from the list with a given `info`. We need to consider several cases:

Case 1: The list is empty.

Case 2: The first node is the node with the given `info`. In this case, we need to adjust
the pointer `first`.

Case 3: The node with the given `info` is somewhere in the list. If the node to be deleted is the last node, then we must adjust the pointer `last`.

Case 4: The list does not contain the node with the given `info`.

If `list` is empty, we can simply print a message indicating that the list is empty. If `list` is not empty, we search the list for the node with the given `info` and, if such a node is found, we delete this node. After deleting the node, `count` is decremented by 1. In pseudocode, the algorithm is:

```
if list is empty
    Output(cannot delete from an empty list);
else
{
    if the first node is the node with the given info
        adjust the head pointer, that is, first, and deallocate
        the memory;
    else
    {
        search the list for the node with the given info
        if such a node is found, delete it and adjust the
        values of last (if necessary) and count.
    }
}
```

Case 1: The list is empty.

If the list is empty, output an error message as shown in the pseudocode.

Case 2: The list is not empty. The node to be deleted is the first node.

This case has two scenarios: `list` has only one node, and `list` has more than one node. Consider the list with one node, as shown in Figure 17-30.

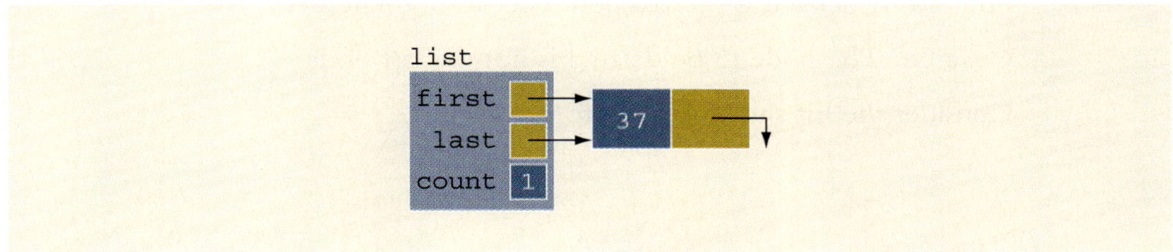

FIGURE 17-30 `list` with one node

Suppose that we want to delete 37. After deletion, the list becomes empty. Therefore, after deletion, both `first` and `last` are set to NULL and `count` is set to 0.

Now consider the list of more than one node, as shown in Figure 17-31.

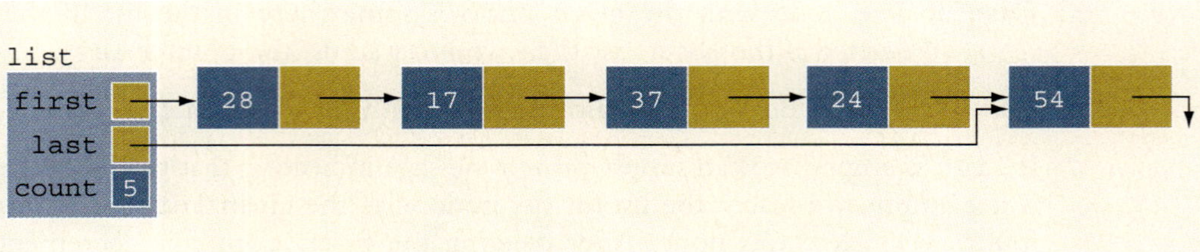

FIGURE 17-31 `list` with more than one node

Suppose that the node to be deleted is 28. After deleting this node, the second node becomes the first node. Therefore, after deleting this node the value of the pointer `first` changes; that is, after deletion, `first` contains the address of the node with `info` 17 and count is decremented by 1. Figure 17-32 shows the list after deleting 28.

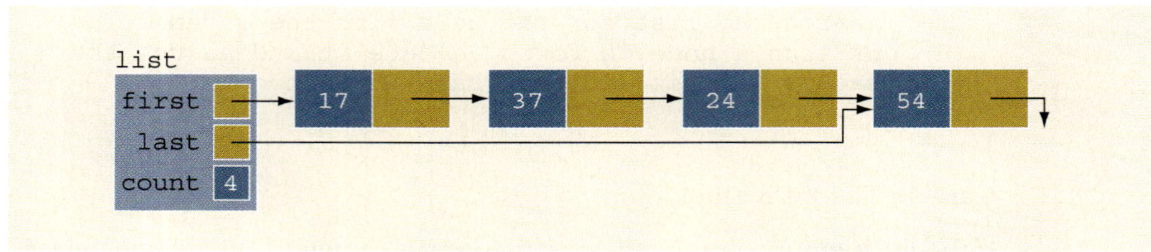

FIGURE 17-32 `list` after deleting node with `info` 28

Case 3: The node to be deleted is not the first node, but is somewhere in the list.

This case has two subcases: (a) the node to be deleted is not the last node, and (b) the node to be deleted is the last node. Let us illustrate both cases.

Case 3a: The node to be deleted is not the last node.

Consider the list shown in Figure 17-33.

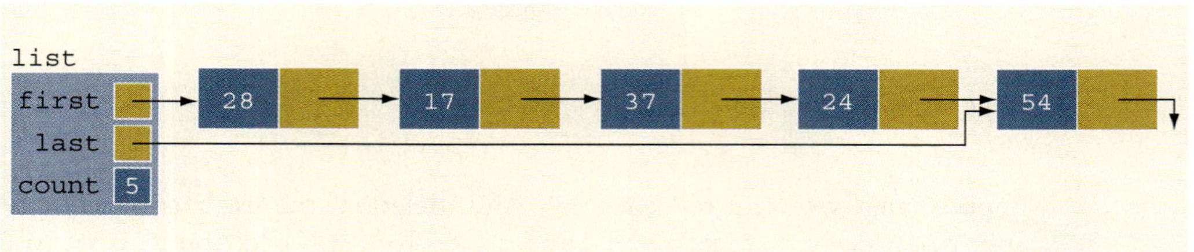

FIGURE 17-33 `list` before deleting 37

Suppose that the node to be deleted is 37. After deleting this node, the resulting list is as shown in Figure 17-34. (Notice that the deletion of 37 does not require us to change the values of `first` and `last`. The link field of the previous node—that is, 17—changes. After deletion, the node with `info` 17 contains the address of the node with 24.)

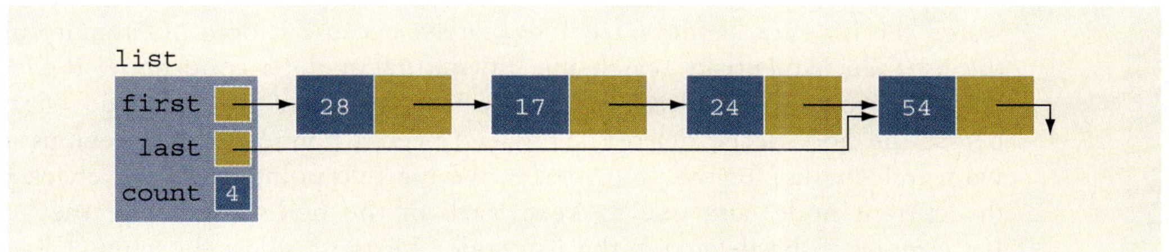

FIGURE 17-34 `list` after deleting 37

Case 3b: The node to be deleted is the last node.

Consider the list shown in Figure 17-35. Suppose that the node to be deleted is 54.

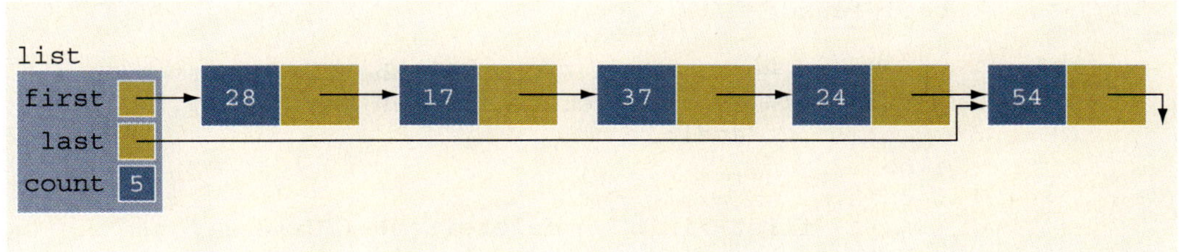

FIGURE 17-35 `list` before deleting 54

After deleting 54, the node with `info` 24 becomes the last node. Therefore, the deletion of 54 requires us to change the value of the pointer `last`. After deleting 54, `last` contains the address of the node with `info` 24. Also, `count` is decremented by 1. Figure 17-36 shows the resulting list.

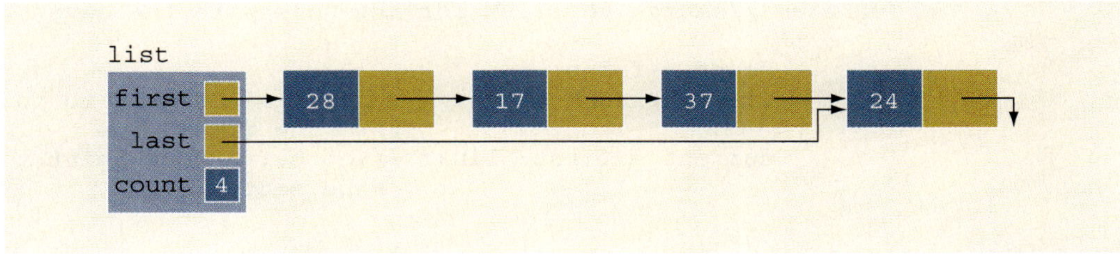

FIGURE 17-36 `list` after deleting 54

Case 4: The node to be deleted is not in the list. In this case, the list requires no adjustment. We simply output an error message, indicating that the item to be deleted is not in the list.

From cases 2, 3, and 4, it follows that the deletion of a node requires us to traverse the list. Because a linked list is not a random-access data structure, we must sequentially search the list. We handle Case 1 separately, because it does not require us to traverse the list. We sequentially search the list, starting at the second node. If the node to be deleted is in the middle of the list, we need to adjust the link field of the node just before the node to be deleted. Thus, we need a pointer to the previous node. When we search the list for the given `info`, we use two pointers: one to check the `info` of the current node, and one to keep track of the node just before the current node. If the node to be deleted is the last node, we must adjust the pointer `last`.

The definition of the function `deleteNode` is:

```cpp
template <class Type>
void unorderedLinkedList<Type>::deleteNode(const Type& deleteItem)
{
    nodeType<Type> *current; //pointer to traverse the list
    nodeType<Type> *trailCurrent; //pointer just before current
    bool found;

    if (first == NULL)     //Case 1; the list is empty.
        cout << "Cannot delete from an empty list."
            << endl;
    else
    {
        if (first->info == deleteItem) //Case 2
        {
            current = first;
            first = first->link;
            count--;

            if (first == NULL)     //the list has only one node
                last = NULL;

            delete current;
        }
        else //search the list for the node with the given info
        {
            found = false;
            trailCurrent = first;  //set trailCurrent to point
                                   //to the first node
            current = first->link; //set current to point to
                                   //the second node
```

```cpp
        while (current != NULL && !found)
        {
            if (current->info != deleteItem)
            {
                trailCurrent = current;
                current = current-> link;
            }
            else
                found = true;
        }//end while

        if (found)  //Case 3; if found, delete the node
        {
            trailCurrent->link = current->link;
            count--;

            if (last == current)    //node to be deleted
                                    //was the last node
                last = trailCurrent; //update the value
                                     //of last
            delete current;   //delete the node from the list
        }
        else
            cout << "The item to be deleted is not in "
                 << "the list." << endl;
    }//end else
  }//end else
}//end deleteNode
```

Header File of the Unordered Linked List

For the sake of completeness, we will show how to create the header file that defines the **class** unorderedListType and the operations on such lists. (We assume that the definition of the **class** linkedListType and the definitions of the functions to implement the operations are in the header file linkedlist.h.)

```cpp
#ifndef H_UnorderedLinkedList
#define H_UnorderedLinkedList

#include "linkedList.h"

using namespace std;

template <class Type>
class unorderedLinkedList: public linkedListType<Type>
{
public:
    bool search(const Type& searchItem) const;
      //Function to determine whether searchItem is in the list.
      //Postcondition: Returns true if searchItem is in the
      //               list, otherwise the value false is
      //               returned.
```

```cpp
    void insertFirst(const Type& newItem);
      //Function to insert newItem at the beginning of the list.
      //Postcondition: first points to the new list, newItem is
      //               inserted at the beginning of the list,
      //               last points to the last node in the
      //               list, and count is incremented by 1.

    void insertLast(const Type& newItem);
      //Function to insert newItem at the end of the list.
      //Postcondition: first points to the new list, newItem
      //               is inserted at the end of the list,
      //               last points to the last node in the
      //               list, and count is incremented by 1.

    void deleteNode(const Type& deleteItem);
      //Function to delete deleteItem from the list.
      //Postcondition: If found, the node containing
      //               deleteItem is deleted from the list.
      //               first points to the first node, last
      //               points to the last node of the updated
      //               list, and count is decremented by 1.
};

//Place the definitions of the functions search,
//insertFirst, insertLast, and deleteNode here.
    .
    .
    .
#endif
```

> **NOTE** The Web site accompanying this book contains several programs illustrating how to use the **class** `unorderedLinkedList`.

Ordered Linked Lists

The preceding section described the operations on an unordered linked list. This section deals with ordered linked lists. As noted earlier, we derive the **class** `orderedLinkedList` from the **class** `linkedListType` and provide the definitions of the abstract functions `insertFirst`, `insertLast`, `search`, and `deleteNode` to take advantage of the fact that the elements of an ordered linked list are arranged using some ordering criteria. For simplicity, we assume that elements of an ordered linked list are arranged in ascending order.

Because the elements of an ordered linked list are in order, we include the function `insert` to insert an element in an ordered list at the proper place.

The following class defines an ordered linked list as an ADT:

```cpp
template <class Type>
class orderedLinkedList: public linkedListType<Type>
{
public:
```

```cpp
bool search(const Type& searchItem) const;
  //Function to determine whether searchItem is in the list.
  //Postcondition: Returns true if searchItem is in the list,
  //               otherwise the value false is returned.

void insert(const Type& newItem);
  //Function to insert newItem in the list.
  //Postcondition: first points to the new list, newItem
  //               is inserted at the proper place in the
  //               list, and count is incremented by 1.

void insertFirst(const Type& newItem);
  //Function to insert newItem at the beginning of the list.
  //Postcondition: first points to the new list, newItem is
  //               inserted at the proper place in the list,
  //               last points to the last node in the
  //               list, and count is incremented by 1.

void insertLast(const Type& newItem);
  //Function to insert newItem at the end of the list.
  //Postcondition: first points to the new list, newItem is
  //               inserted at the proper place in the list,
  //               last points to the last node in the
  //               list, and count is incremented by 1.

void deleteNode(const Type& deleteItem);
  //Function to delete deleteItem from the list.
  //Postcondition: If found, the node containing
  //               deleteItem is deleted from the list;
  //               first points to the first node of the
  //               new list, and count is decremented by 1.
  //               If deleteItem is not in the list, an
  //               appropriate message is printed.
};
```

Figure 17-37 shows a UML class diagram of the **class** orderedLinkedList and the inheritance hierarchy.

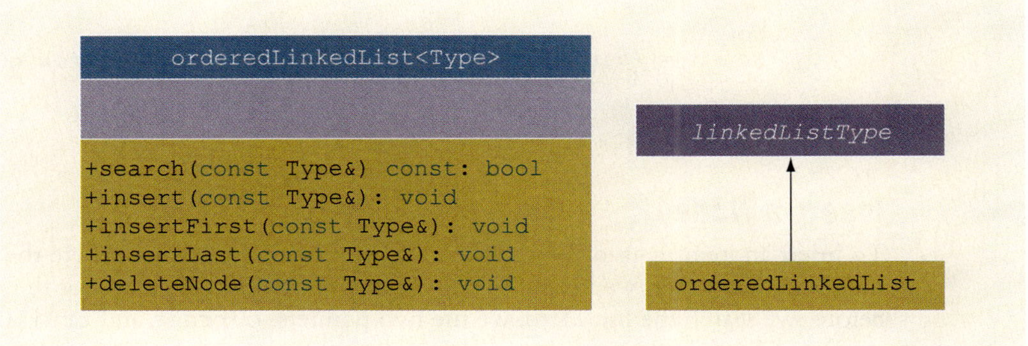

FIGURE 17-37 UML class diagram of the **class** orderedLinkedList and the inheritance hierarchy

Next, we give the definitions of the member functions of the **class** orderedLinkedList.

Search the List

First, we discuss the search operation. The algorithm to implement the search operation is similar to the search algorithm for general lists discussed earlier. Here, because the list is sorted, we can improve the search algorithm somewhat. As before, we start the search at the first node in the list. We stop the search as soon as we find a node in the list with `info` greater than or equal to the search item, or we have searched the entire list.

The following steps describe this algorithm:

1. Compare the search item with the current node in the list. If the `info` of the current node is greater than or equal to the search item, stop the search; otherwise, make the next node the current node.

2. Repeat Step 1 until either an item in the list that is greater than or equal to the search item is found, or no more data is left in the list to compare with the search item.

Note that the loop does not explicitly check whether the search item is equal to an item in the list. Thus, after the loop executes, we must check whether the search item is equal to the item in the list:

```cpp
template <class Type>
bool orderedLinkedList<Type>::
                        search(const Type& searchItem) const
{
    bool found = false;
    nodeType<Type> *current; //pointer to traverse the list

    current = first;  //start the search at the first node

    while (current != NULL && !found)
        if (current->info >= searchItem)
            found = true;
        else
            current = current->link;

    if (found)
        found = (current->info == searchItem); //test for equality

    return found;
}//end search
```

Insert a Node

To insert an item in an ordered linked list, we first find the place where the new item is supposed to go, then we insert the item in the list. To find the place for the new item, as before, we search the list. Here, we use two pointers, `current` and `trailCurrent`, to search the list. The pointer `current` points to the node whose `info` is being compared with the item to be inserted, and `trailCurrent` points to the node just before `current`. Because the list is in order, the search algorithm is the same as before. The following cases arise:

Case 1: The list is initially empty. The node containing the new item is the only node and thus the first node in the list.

Case 2: The new item is smaller than the smallest item in the list. The new item goes at the beginning of the list. In this case, we need to adjust the list's head pointer—that is, `first`. Also, `count` is incremented by 1.

Case 3: The item is to be inserted somewhere in the list.

3a: The new item is larger than all the items in the list. In this case, the new item is inserted at the end of the list. Thus, the value of `current` is `NULL` and the new item is inserted after `trailCurrent`. Also, `count` is incremented by 1.

3b: The new item is to be inserted somewhere in the middle of the list. In this case, the new item is inserted between `trailCurrent` and `current`. Also, `count` is incremented by 1.

The following statements can accomplish both cases 3a and 3b. Assume `newNode` points to the new node:

```
trailCurrent->link = newNode;
newNode->link = current;
```

Let us next illustrate these cases.

Case 1: The list is empty.

Consider the list shown in Figure 17-38.

FIGURE 17-38 Empty `list`

Suppose that we want to insert 27 in the list. To accomplish this task, we create a node, copy 27 into the node, set the link of the node to `NULL`, and make `first` point to the node. Figure 17-39 shows the resulting list.

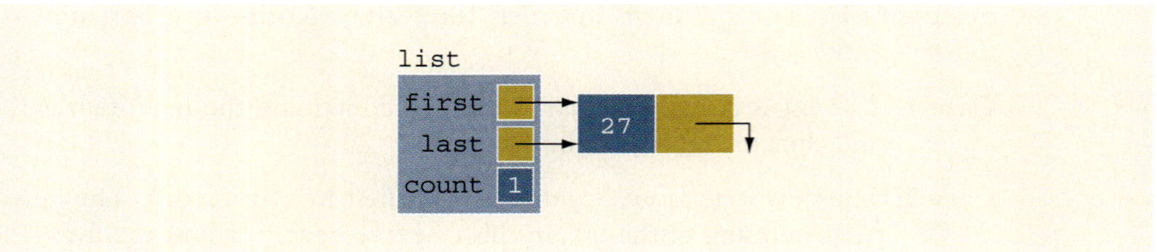

FIGURE 17-39 `list` after inserting 27

Notice that, after inserting 27, the values of both `first` and `count` change.

Case 2: The list is not empty, and the item to be inserted is smaller than the smallest item in the list. Consider the list shown in Figure 17-40.

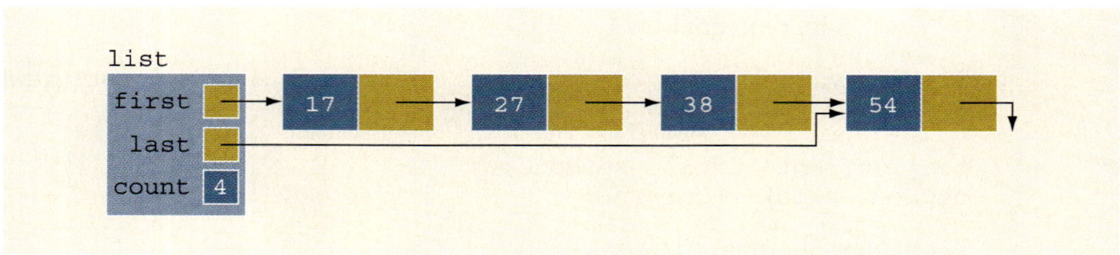

FIGURE 17-40 Nonempty `list` before inserting 10

Suppose that 10 is to be inserted. After inserting 10 in the list, the node with `info` 10 becomes the first node of `list`. This requires us to change the value of `first`. Also, `count` is incremented by 1. Figure 17-41 shows the resulting list.

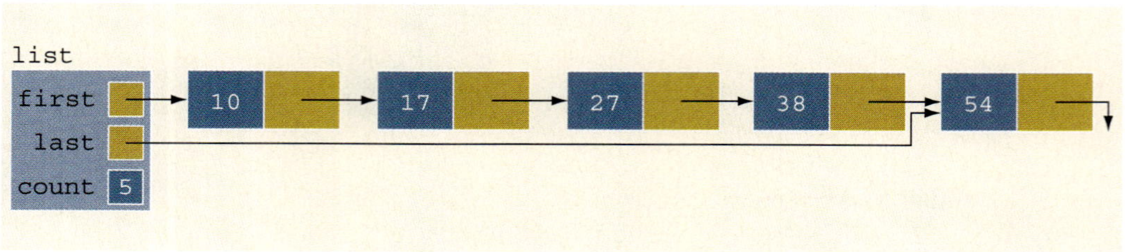

FIGURE 17-41 `list` after inserting 10

Case 3: The list is not empty, and the item to be inserted is larger than the first item in the list. As indicated previously, this case has two scenarios.

Case 3a: The item to be inserted is larger than the largest item in the list; that is, it goes at the end of the list. Consider the list shown in Figure 17-42.

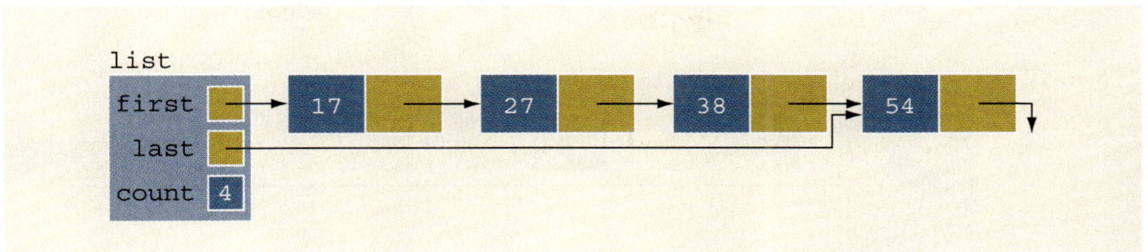

FIGURE 17-42 `list` before inserting 65

Suppose that we want to insert 65 in the list. After inserting 65, the resulting list is as shown in Figure 17-43.

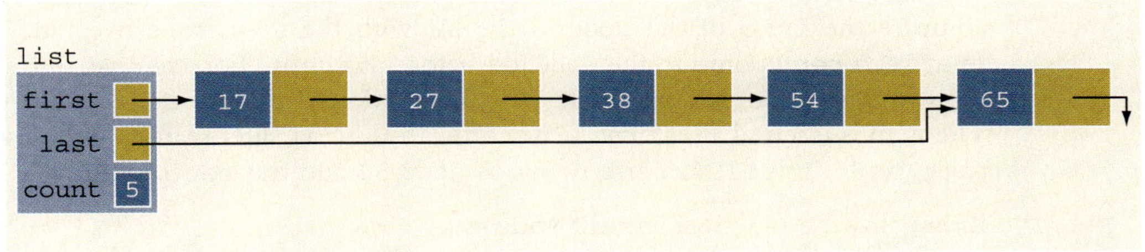

FIGURE 17-43 `list` after inserting 65

Case 3b: The item to be inserted goes somewhere in the middle of the list. Consider the list shown in Figure 17-44.

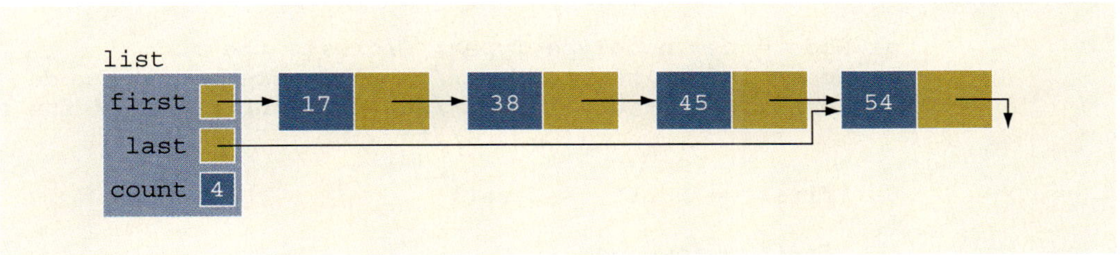

FIGURE 17-44 `list` before inserting 27

Suppose that we want to insert 27 in this list. Clearly, 27 goes between 17 and 38, which would require the link of the node with `info` 17 to be changed. After inserting 27, the resulting list is as shown in Figure 17-45.

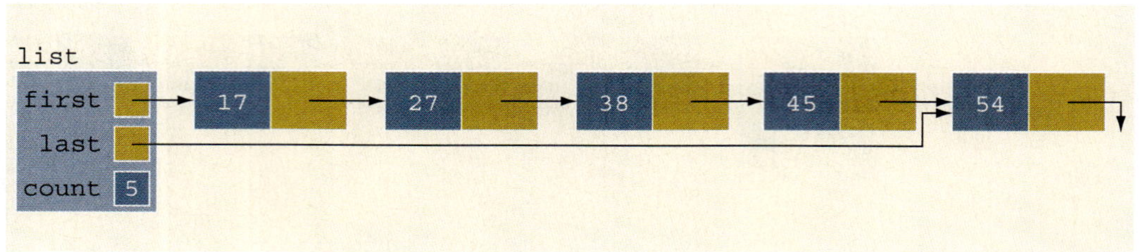

FIGURE 17-45 `list` after inserting 27

From Case 3, it follows that we must first traverse the list to find the place where the new item is to be inserted. It also follows that we should traverse the list with two pointers— say, `current` and `trailCurrent`. The pointer `current` is used to traverse the list and compare the `info` of the node in the list with the item to be inserted. The pointer `trailCurrent` points to the node just before `current`. For example, in Case 3b, when the search stops, `trailCurrent` points to node 17 and `current` points to node 38. The item is inserted after `trailCurrent`. In Case 3a, after searching the list to find the place for 65, `trailCurrent` points to node 54 and `current` is NULL.

Essentially, the function `insertNode` is as follows:

```cpp
template <class Type>
void orderedLinkedList<Type>::insert(const Type& newItem)
{
    nodeType<Type> *current;       //pointer to traverse the list
    nodeType<Type> *trailCurrent;  //pointer just before current
    nodeType<Type> *newNode;       //pointer to create a node

    bool found;

    newNode = new nodeType<Type>;  //create the node
    newNode->info = newItem;        //store newItem in the node
    newNode->link = NULL;           //set the link field of the node
                                    //to NULL

    if (first == NULL)    //Case 1
    {
        first = newNode;
        last = newNode;
        count++;
    }
```

```cpp
        else
        {
            current = first;
            found = false;

            while (current != NULL && !found)  //search the list
                if (current->info >= newItem)
                    found = true;
                else
                {
                    trailCurrent = current;
                    current = current->link;
                }

            if (current == first)        //Case 2
            {
                newNode->link = first;
                first = newNode;
                count++;
            }
            else                         //Case 3
            {
                trailCurrent->link = newNode;
                newNode->link = current;

                if (current == NULL)
                    last = newNode;

                count++;
            }
        }//end else
}//end insert
```

Insert First and Insert Last

The function `insertFirst` inserts the new item at the beginning of the list. However, because the resulting list must be sorted, the new item must be inserted at the proper place. Similarly, the function `insertLast` must insert the new item at the proper place. We, therefore, use the function `insertNode` to insert the new item at its proper place. The definitions of these functions are:

```cpp
template <class Type>
void orderedLinkedList<Type>::insertFirst(const Type& newItem)
{
    insert(newItem);
}//end insertFirst

template <class Type>
void orderedLinkedList<Type>::insertLast(const Type& newItem)
{
    insert(newItem);
}//end insertLast
```

Note that, in reality, the functions `insertFirst` and `insertLast` do not apply to ordered linked lists because the new item must be inserted at the proper place in the list. However, you must provide its definition as these functions are declared as abstract in the parent class.

Delete a Node

To delete a given item from an ordered linked list, first we search the list to see whether the item to be deleted is in the list. The function to implement this operation is the same as the delete operation on general linked lists. Here, because the list is sorted, we can somewhat improve the algorithm for ordered linked lists.

As in the case of `insertNode`, we search the list with two pointers, `current` and `trailCurrent`. Similar to the operation `insertNode`, several cases arise:

Case 1: The list is initially empty. We have an error. We cannot delete from an empty list.

Case 2: The item to be deleted is contained in the first node of the list. We must adjust the head pointer of the list—that is, `first`.

Case 3: The item to be deleted is somewhere in the list. In this case, `current` points to the node containing the item to be deleted, and `trailCurrent` points to the node just before the node pointed to by `current`.

Case 4: The list is not empty, but the item to be deleted is not in the list.

After deleting a node, `count` is decremented by 1. The definition of the function `deleteNode` is:

```cpp
template <class Type>
void orderedLinkedList<Type>::deleteNode(const Type& deleteItem)
{
    nodeType<Type> *current; //pointer to traverse the list
    nodeType<Type> *trailCurrent; //pointer just before current
    bool found;

    if (first == NULL) //Case 1
        cout << "Cannot delete from an empty list." << endl;
    else
    {
        current = first;
        found = false;

        while (current != NULL && !found)   //search the list
            if (current->info >= deleteItem)
                found = true;
            else
            {
                trailCurrent = current;
                current = current->link;
            }
```

```cpp
    if (current == NULL)     //Case 4
        cout << "The item to be deleted is not in the "
             << "list." << endl;
    else
        if (current->info == deleteItem) //the item to be
                                         //deleted is in the list
        {
            if (first == current)        //Case 2
            {
                first = first->link;

                if (first == NULL)
                    last = NULL;

                delete current;
            }
            else                                 //Case 3
            {
                trailCurrent->link = current->link;

                if (current == last)
                    last = trailCurrent;

                delete current;
            }
            count--;
        }
        else                                 //Case 4
            cout << "The item to be deleted is not in the "
                 << "list." << endl;
    }
}//end deleteNode
```

Header File of the Ordered Linked List

For the sake of completeness, we will show how to create the header file that defines the `class` orderedListType, as well as the operations on such lists. (We assume that the definition of the `class` linkedListType and the definitions of the functions to implement the operations are in the header file linkedlist.h.)

```cpp
#ifndef H_orderedListType
#define H_orderedListType

#include "linkedList.h"

using namespace std;

template <class Type>
class orderedLinkedList: public linkedListType<Type>
{
public:
    bool search(const Type& searchItem) const;
        //Function to determine whether searchItem is in the list.
```

```
    //Postcondition: Returns true if searchItem is in the list,
    //                otherwise the value false is returned.

void insert(const Type& newItem);
   //Function to insert newItem in the list.
   //Postcondition: first points to the new list, newItem
   //                is inserted at the proper place in the
   //                list, and count is incremented by 1.

void insertFirst(const Type& newItem);
   //Function to insert newItem at the beginning of the list.
   //Postcondition: first points to the new list, newItem is
   //                inserted at the proper place in the list,
   //                last points to the last node in the
   //                list, and count is incremented by 1.

void insertLast(const Type& newItem);
   //Function to insert newItem at the end of the list.
   //Postcondition: first points to the new list, newItem is
   //                inserted at the proper place in the list,
   //                last points to the last node in the
   //                list, and count is incremented by 1.

void deleteNode(const Type& deleteItem);
   //Function to delete deleteItem from the list.
   //Postcondition: If found, the node containing
   //                deleteItem is deleted from the list;
   //                first points to the first node of the
   //                new list, and count is decremented by 1.
   //                If deleteItem is not in the list, an
   //                appropriate message is printed.
};

//Place the definitions of the functions search, insert,
//insertfirst, insertLast, and deleteNode here.
   .
   .
   .
#endif
```

The following program tests various operations on an ordered linked list:

```
//Program to test the various operations on an ordered linked list

#include <iostream>
#include "orderedLinkedList.h"

using namespace std;

int main()
{
    orderedLinkedList<int> list1, list2;          //Line 1
    int num;                                       //Line 2
```

```cpp
    cout << "Line 3: Enter numbers ending "
         << "with -999." << endl;                    //Line 3
    cin >> num;                                       //Line 4
    while (num != -999)                               //Line 5
    {
        list1.insert(num);                            //Line 6
        cin >> num;                                   //Line 7
    }

    cout << endl;                                     //Line 8

    cout << "Line 9: list1: ";                        //Line 9
    list1.print();                                    //Line 10
    cout << endl;                                     //Line 11

    list2 = list1; //test the assignment operator Line 12

    cout << "Line 13: list2: ";                       //Line 13
    list2.print();                                    //Line 14
    cout << endl;                                     //Line 15

    cout << "Line 16: Enter the number to be "
         << "deleted: ";                              //Line 16
    cin >> num;                                       //Line 17
    cout << endl;                                     //Line 18

    list2.deleteNode(num);                            //Line 19

    cout << "Line 20: After deleting "
         << num << ", list2: " << endl;               //Line 20
    list2.print();                                    //Line 21
    cout<<endl;                                       //Line 22

    return 0;
}
```

Sample Run: In this sample run, the user input is shaded.

```
Line 3: Enter numbers ending with -999.
23 65 34 72 12 82 36 55 29 -999

Line 9: list1: 12 23 29 34 36 55 65 72 82
Line 13: list2: 12 23 29 34 36 55 65 72 82
Line 16: Enter the number to be deleted: 34

Line 20: After deleting 34, list2:
12 23 29 36 55 65 72 82
```

The preceding output is self-explanatory. The details are left as an exercise for you.

NOTE Notice that the function `insert` does not check whether the item to be inserted is already in the list, that is, it does not check for duplicates. Programming Exercise 8 at the end of this chapter asks you to revise the definition of the function `insert`, so that before inserting the item, it checks whether it is already in the list. If the item to be inserted is already in the list, the function outputs an appropriate error message. In other words, duplicates are not allowed.

Print a Linked List in Reverse Order (Recursion Revisited)

The nodes of an ordered list (as constructed previously) are in ascending order. Certain applications, however, might require the data to be printed in descending order, which means that we must print the list backward. We now discuss the function `reversePrint`. Given a pointer to a list, this function prints the elements of the list in reverse order.

Consider the linked list shown in Figure 17-46.

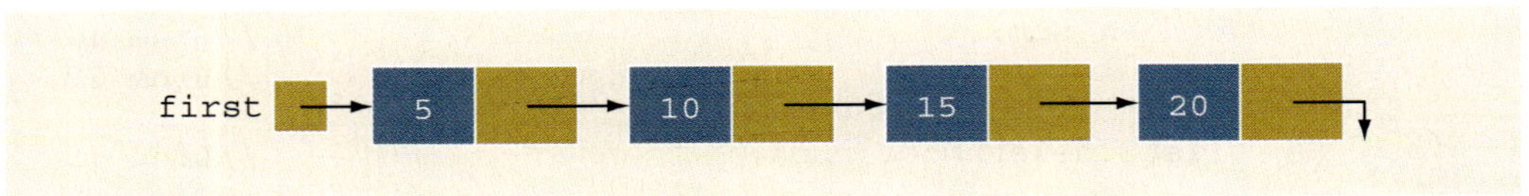

FIGURE 17-46   Linked list

For the list in Figure 17-46, the output should be in the following form:

```
20 15 10 5
```

Because the links are in only one direction, we cannot traverse the list backward starting from the last node. Let us see how we can effectively use recursion to print the list in reverse order.

Let us think in terms of recursion. We cannot print the `info` of the first node until we have printed the remainder of the list (that is, the tail of the first node). Similarly, we cannot print the `info` of the second node until we have printed the tail of the second node, and so on. Every time we consider the tail of a node, we reduce the size of the list by 1. Eventually, the size of the list will be reduced to zero, in which case the recursion will stop. Let us first write the algorithm in pseudocode. (Suppose that `current` is a pointer to a linked list.)

```cpp
if (current != NULL)
{
    reversePrint(current->link);    //print the tail
    cout << current->info << endl; //print the node
}
```

Here, we do not see the base case; it is hidden. The list is printed only if the pointer to the list is not NULL. Also, in the body of the **if** statement the recursive call is on the tail of the list. Because eventually the tail of the list will be empty, the **if** statement in the next call will fail and the recursion will stop. Also, note that statements (for example, printing the `info` of the node) appear after the recursive call; thus, when the transfer comes back to the calling function, we must execute the remaining statements. Recall that the function exits only after the last statement executes. (By the "last statement" we do not mean the physical last statement, but rather the logical last statement.)

Let us write the previous function in C++ and then apply it to a list:

```cpp
template <class Type>
void linkedListType<Type>::reversePrint
                        (nodeType<Type> *current) const
{
    if (current != NULL)
    {
        reversePrint(current->link);    //print the tail
        cout << current->info << " "; //print the node
    }
}
```

Consider the statement:

```cpp
reversePrint(first);
```

where **first** is a pointer of type **nodeType<Type>**.

Let us trace the execution of this statement, which is a function call, for the list shown in Figure 17–46. Because the formal parameter is a value parameter, the value of the actual parameter is passed to the formal parameter. See Figure 17–47.

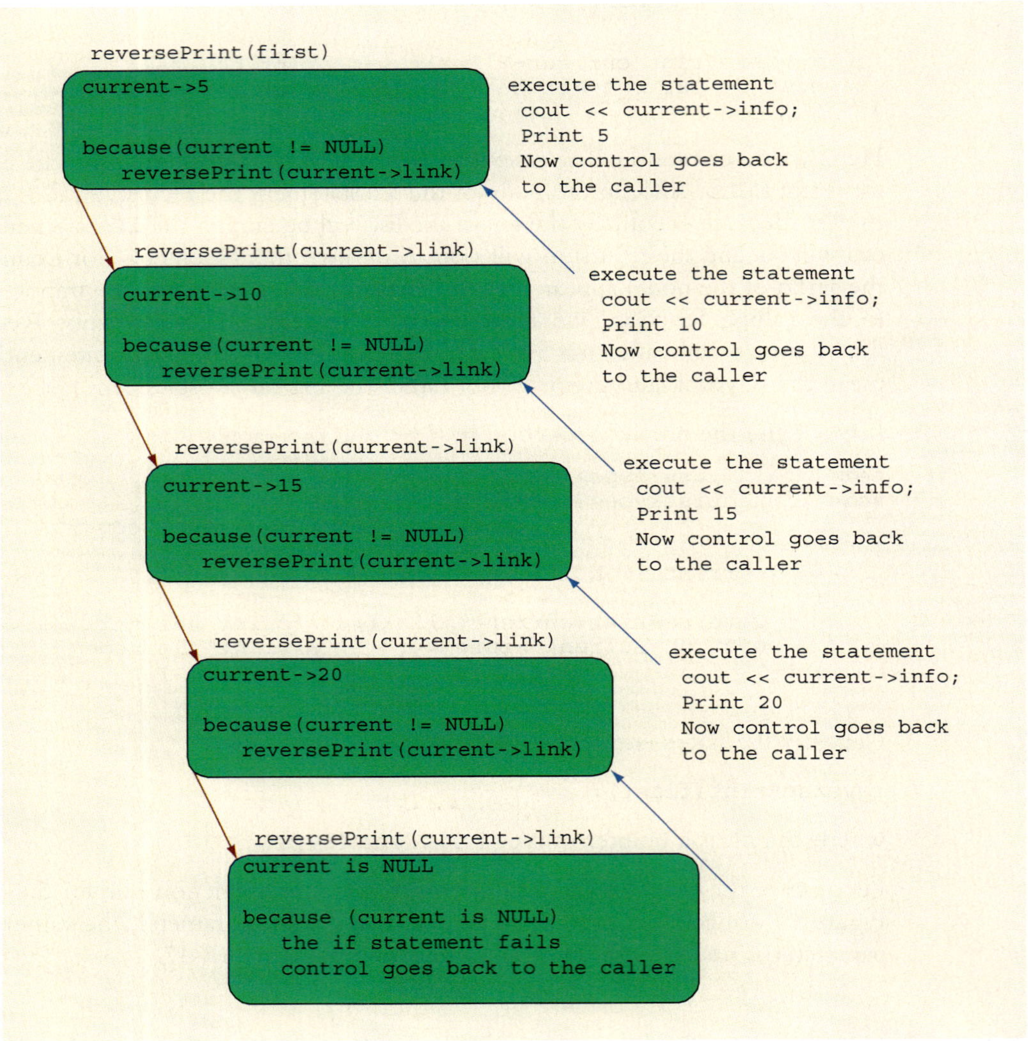

FIGURE 17-47 Execution of the statement `reversePrint(first);`

printListReverse

Now that we have written the function **reversePrint**, we can write the definition of the function **printListReverse**. Its definition is:

```cpp
template <class Type>
void linkedListType<Type>::printListReverse() const
{
    reversePrint(first);
    cout << endl;
}
```

Doubly Linked Lists

A doubly linked list is a linked list in which every node has a next pointer and a back pointer. In other words, every node contains the address of the next node (except the last node), and every node contains the address of the previous node (except the first node) (see Figure 17-48).

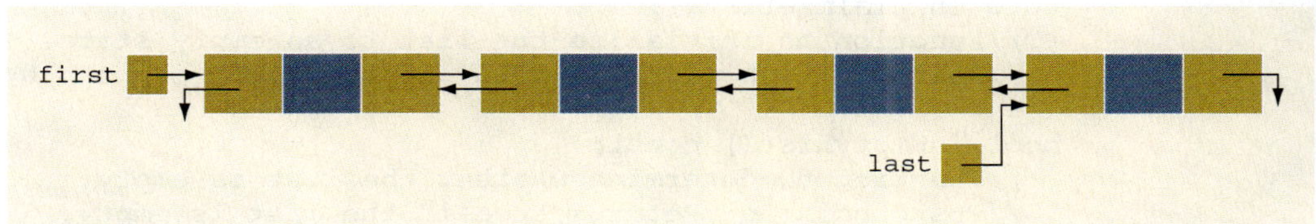

FIGURE 17-48 Doubly linked list

A doubly linked list can be traversed in either direction. That is, we can traverse the list starting at the first node or, if a pointer to the last node is given, we can traverse the list starting at the last node.

As before, the typical operations on a doubly linked list are:

1. Initialize the list.
2. Destroy the list.
3. Determine whether the list is empty.
4. Search the list for a given item.
5. Retrieve the first element of the list.
6. Retrieve the last element of the list.
7. Insert an item in the list.
8. Delete an item from the list.
9. Find the length of the list.
10. Print the list.
11. Make a copy of the doubly linked list.

Next, we describe these operations for an ordered doubly linked list. The following class defines a doubly linked list as an ADT:

```cpp
//Definition of the node
template <class Type>
struct nodeType
{
    Type info;
    nodeType<Type> *next;
    nodeType<Type> *back;
};
```

```cpp
template <class Type>
class doublyLinkedList
{
public:
    const doublyLinkedList<Type>& operator=
                              (const doublyLinkedList<Type> &);
      //Overload the assignment operator.

    void initializeList();
      //Function to initialize the list to an empty state.
      //Postcondition: first = NULL; last = NULL; count = 0;

    bool isEmptyList() const;
      //Function to determine whether the list is empty.
      //Postcondition: Returns true if the list is empty,
      //               otherwise returns false.

    void destroy();
      //Function to delete all the nodes from the list.
      //Postcondition: first = NULL; last = NULL; count = 0;

    void print() const;
      //Function to output the info contained in each node.

    void reversePrint() const;
      //Function to output the info contained in each node
      //in reverse order.

    int length() const;
      //Function to return the number of nodes in the list.
      //Postcondition: The value of count is returned.

    Type front() const;
      //Function to return the first element of the list.
      //Precondition: The list must exist and must not be empty.
      //Postcondition: If the list is empty, the program
      //               terminates; otherwise, the first
      //               element of the list is returned.

    Type back() const;
      //Function to return the last element of the list.
      //Precondition: The list must exist and must not be empty.
      //Postcondition: If the list is empty, the program
      //               terminates; otherwise, the last
      //               element of the list is returned.

    bool search(const Type& searchItem) const;
      //Function to determine whether searchItem is in the list.
      //Postcondition: Returns true if searchItem is found in
      //               the list, otherwise returns false.
```

```
    void insert(const Type& insertItem);
      //Function to insert insertItem in the list.
      //Precondition: If the list is nonempty, it must be in
      //              order.
      //Postcondition: insertItem is inserted at the proper place
      //               in the list, first points to the first
      //               node, last points to the last node of the
      //               new list, and count is incremented by 1.

    void deleteNode(const Type& deleteItem);
      //Function to delete deleteItem from the list.
      //Postcondition: If found, the node containing deleteItem
      //               is deleted from the list; first points
      //               to the first node of the new list, last
      //               points to the last node of the new list,
      //               and count is decremented by 1; otherwise
      //               an appropriate message is printed.

    doublyLinkedList();
      //default constructor
      //Initializes the list to an empty state.
      //Postcondition: first = NULL; last = NULL; count = 0;

    doublyLinkedList(const doublyLinkedList<Type>& otherList);
      //copy constructor
    ~doublyLinkedList();
      //destructor
      //Postcondition: The list object is destroyed.

protected:
    int count;
    nodeType<Type> *first; //pointer to the first node
    nodeType<Type> *last;  //pointer to the last node

private:
    void copyList(const doublyLinkedList<Type>& otherList);
      //Function to make a copy of otherList.
      //Postcondition: A copy of otherList is created and
      //               assigned to this list.
};
```

We leave the UML class diagram of the `class` doublyLinkedList as an exercise for you.

The functions to implement the operations of a doubly linked list are similar to the ones discussed earlier. Here, because every node has two pointers, `back` and `next`, some of the operations require the adjustment of two pointers in each node. For the insert and delete operations, because we can traverse the list in either direction, we use only one pointer to traverse the list. Let us call this pointer `current`. We can set the value of `trailCurrent` by using both the `current` pointer and the `back` pointer of the node pointed to by `current`. We give the definition of each function here, with four exceptions. Definitions of the functions `copyList`, the copy constructor, overloading the assignment operator, and the destructor are left as exercises for you. (See Programming Exercise 11 at the end of this chapter.) Moreover, the function `copyList` is used only to implement the copy constructor and overload the assignment operator.

Default Constructor

The default constructor initializes the doubly linked list to an empty state. It sets `first` and `last` to NULL and count to 0:

```cpp
template <class Type>
doublyLinkedList<Type>::doublyLinkedList()
{
    first= NULL;
    last = NULL;
    count = 0;
}
```

isEmptyList

This operation returns **true** if the list is empty, otherwise it returns **false**. The list is empty if the pointer `first` is NULL:

```cpp
template <class Type>
bool doublyLinkedList<Type>::isEmptyList() const
{
    return (first == NULL);
}
```

Destroy the List

This operation deletes all the nodes in the list, leaving the list in an empty state. We traverse the list starting at the first node and then delete each node. Furthermore, count is set to 0:

```cpp
template <class Type>
void doublyLinkedList<Type>::destroy()
{
    nodeType<Type> *temp; //pointer to delete the node

    while (first != NULL)
    {
        temp = first;
        first = first->next;
        delete temp;
    }

    last = NULL;
    count = 0;
}
```

Initialize the List

This operation reinitializes the doubly linked list to an empty state. This task can be done by using the operation `destroy`. The definition of the function `initializeList` is:

```cpp
template <class Type>
void doublyLinkedList<Type>::initializeList()
{
    destroy();
}
```

Length of the List

The length of a linked list (that is, how many nodes are in the list) is stored in the variable `count`. Therefore, this function returns the value of this variable:

```cpp
template <class Type>
int doublyLinkedList<Type>::length() const
{
    return count;
}
```

Print the List

The function `print` outputs the `info` contained in each node. We traverse the list, starting from the first node:

```cpp
template <class Type>
void doublyLinkedList<Type>::print() const
{
    nodeType<Type> *current; //pointer to traverse the list

    current = first;  //set current to point to the first node

    while (current != NULL)
    {
        cout << current->info << "  ";   //output info
        current = current->next;
    }//end while
}//end print
```

Reverse Print the List

This function outputs the `info` contained in each node in reverse order. We traverse the list in reverse order, starting from the last node. Its definition is:

```cpp
template <class Type>
void doublyLinkedList<Type>::reversePrint() const
{
    nodeType<Type> *current; //pointer to traverse
                             //the list
```

```cpp
    current = last;   //set current to point to the
                      //last node

    while (current != NULL)
    {
        cout << current->info << "  ";
        current = current->back;
    }//end while
}//end reversePrint
```

Search the List

The function `search` returns `true` if `searchItem` is found in the list, otherwise it returns `false`. The search algorithm is exactly the same as the search algorithm for an ordered linked list:

```cpp
template <class Type>
bool doublyLinkedList<Type>::
                        search(const Type& searchItem) const
{
    bool found = false;
    nodeType<Type> *current; //pointer to traverse the list

    current = first;

    while (current != NULL && !found)
        if (current->info >= searchItem)
            found = true;
        else
            current = current->next;

    if (found)
        found = (current->info == searchItem); //test for
                                               //equality

    return found;
}//end search
```

First and Last Elements

The function `front` returns the first element of the list, and the function `back` returns the last element of the list. If the list is empty, both functions terminate the program. Their definitions are:

```cpp
template <class Type>
Type doublyLinkedList<Type>::front() const
{
    assert(first != NULL);

    return first->info;
}
```

```cpp
template <class Type>
Type doublyLinkedList<Type>::back() const
{
    assert(last != NULL);

    return last->info;
}
```

INSERT A NODE

Because we are inserting an item in a doubly linked list, the insertion of a node in the list requires the adjustment of two pointers in certain nodes. As before, we find the place where the new item is supposed to be inserted, create the node, store the new item, and adjust the link fields of the new node and other particular nodes in the list. There are four cases:

Case 1: Insertion in an empty list

Case 2: Insertion at the beginning of a nonempty list

Case 3: Insertion at the end of a nonempty list

Case 4: Insertion somewhere in a nonempty list

Both cases 1 and 2 require us to change the value of the pointer `first`. Cases 3 and 4 are similar. After inserting an item, `count` is incremented by 1. Next, we show Case 4.

Consider the doubly linked list shown in Figure 17-49.

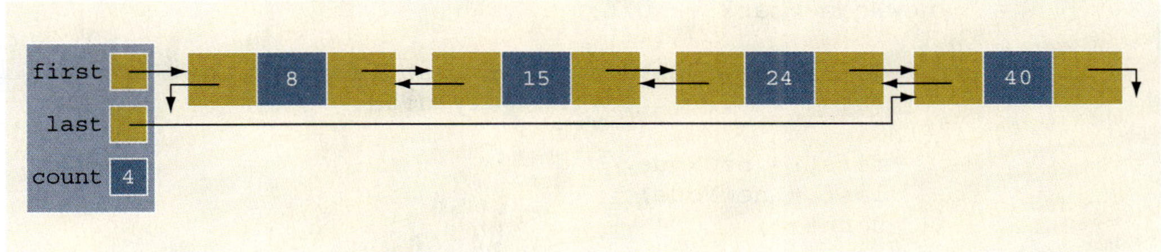

FIGURE 17-49   Doubly linked list before inserting 20

Suppose that 20 is to be inserted in the list. After inserting 20, the resulting list is as shown in Figure 17-50.

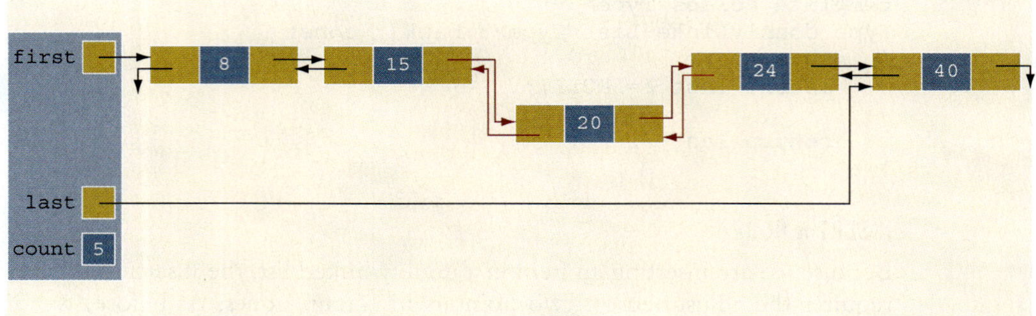

FIGURE 17-50 Doubly linked list after inserting 20

From Figure 17–50, it follows that the `next` pointer of node 15, the `back` pointer of node 24, and both the `next` and `back` pointers of node 20 need to be adjusted.

The definition of the function `insert` is:

```cpp
template <class Type>
void doublyLinkedList<Type>::insert(const Type& insertItem)
{
    nodeType<Type> *current;        //pointer to traverse the list
    nodeType<Type> *trailCurrent;   //pointer just before current
    nodeType<Type> *newNode;        //pointer to create a node
    bool found;

    newNode = new nodeType<Type>;   //create the node
    newNode->info = insertItem;      //store the new item in the node
    newNode->next = NULL;
    newNode->back = NULL;

    if (first == NULL)  //if the list is empty, newNode is
                        //the only node
    {
        first = newNode;
        last = newNode;
        count++;
    }
    else
    {
        found = false;
        current = first;

        while (current != NULL && !found)  //search the list
            if (current->info >= insertItem)
                found = true;
            else
            {
                trailCurrent = current;
                current = current->next;
            }
```

```
        if (current == first) //insert newNode before first
        {
            first->back = newNode;
            newNode->next = first;
            first = newNode;
            count++;
        }
        else
        {

                //insert newNode between trailCurrent and current
            if (current != NULL)
            {
                trailCurrent->next = newNode;
                newNode->back = trailCurrent;
                newNode->next = current;
                current->back = newNode;
            }
            else
            {
                trailCurrent->next = newNode;
                newNode->back = trailCurrent;
                last = newNode;
            }

            count++;
        }//end else
    }//end else
}//end insert
```

DELETE A NODE

This operation deletes a given item (if found) from the doubly linked list. As before, we first search the list to see whether the item to be deleted is in the list. The search algorithm is the same as before. Similar to the `insertNode` operation, this operation (if the item to be deleted is in the list) requires the adjustment of two pointers in certain nodes. The delete operation has several cases:

Case 1: The list is empty.

Case 2: The item to be deleted is in the first node of the list, which would require us to change the value of the pointer `first`.

Case 3: The item to be deleted is somewhere in the list.

Case 4: The item to be deleted is not in the list.

After deleting a node, `count` is decremented by 1. Let us demonstrate Case 3. Consider the list shown in Figure 17-51.

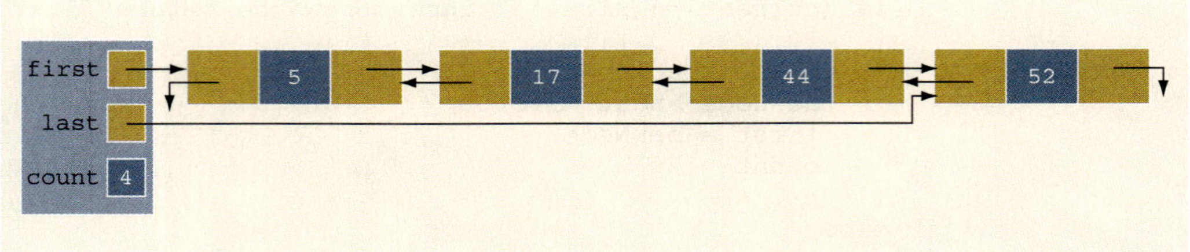

FIGURE 17-51 Doubly linked list before deleting 17

Suppose that the item to be deleted is 17. First we search the list with two pointers and find the node with `info` 17, and then adjust the link field of the affected nodes (see Figure 17-52).

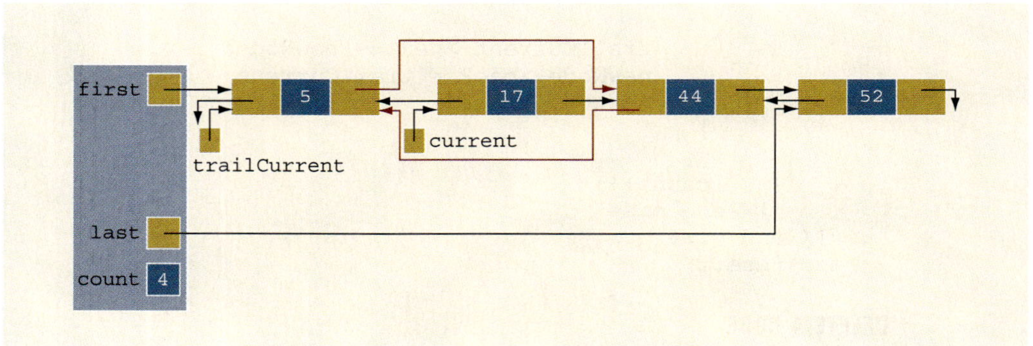

FIGURE 17-52 List after adjusting the links of the nodes before and after the node with `info` 17

Next, we delete the node pointed to by `current` (see Figure 17-53).

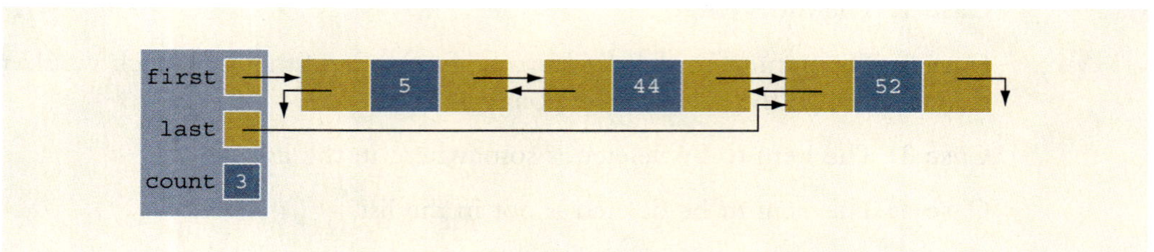

FIGURE 17-53 List after deleting the node with `info` 17

The definition of the function `deleteNode` is:

```cpp
template <class Type>
void doublyLinkedList<Type>::deleteNode(const Type& deleteItem)
{
    nodeType<Type> *current; //pointer to traverse the list
    nodeType<Type> *trailCurrent; //pointer just before current

    bool found;

    if (first == NULL)
        cout << "Cannot delete from an empty list." << endl;
    else if (first->info == deleteItem) //node to be deleted is
                                        //the first node
    {
        current = first;
        first = first->next;

        if (first != NULL)
            first->back = NULL;
        else
            last = NULL;

        count--;

        delete current;
    }
    else
    {
        found = false;
        current = first;

        while (current != NULL && !found)  //search the list
            if (current->info >= deleteItem)
                found = true;
            else
                current = current->next;

        if (current == NULL)
            cout << "The item to be deleted is not in "
                 << "the list." << endl;
        else if (current->info == deleteItem) //check for
                                              //equality
        {
            trailCurrent = current->back;
            trailCurrent->next = current->next;

            if (current->next != NULL)
                current->next->back = trailCurrent;

            if (current == last)
                last = trailCurrent;

            count--;
            delete current;
        }
```

```
        else
            cout << "The item to be deleted is not in list."
                 << endl;
    }//end else
}//end deleteNode
```

Circular Linked Lists

A linked list in which the last node points to the first node is called a **circular linked list**. Figures 17-54 through 17-56 show various circular linked lists.

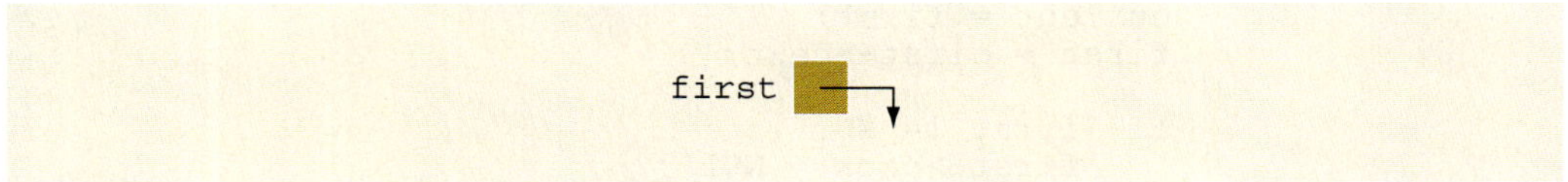

FIGURE 17-54 Empty circular linked list

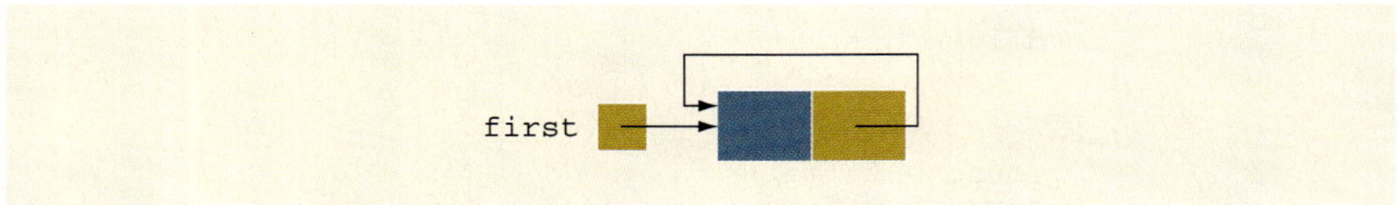

FIGURE 17-55 Circular linked list with one node

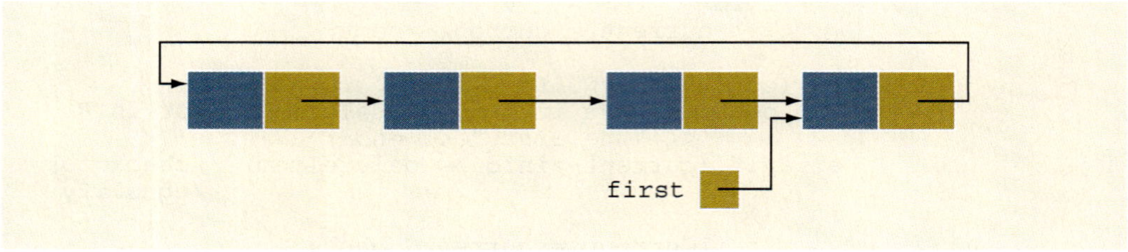

FIGURE 17-56 Circular linked list with more than one node

In a circular linked list with more than one node, as in Figure 17-56, it is convenient to make the pointer **first** point to the last node of the list. Then, by using **first**, you can access both the first and the last node of the list. For example, **first** points to the last node and **first->link** points to the first node.

As before, the usual operations on a circular list are:

1. Initialize the list (to an empty state).
2. Determine if the list is empty.
3. Destroy the list.
4. Print the list.
5. Find the length of the list.
6. Search the list for a given item.
7. Insert an item in the list.
8. Delete an item from the list.
9. Copy the list.

We leave it as an exercise for you to design a class to implement a sorted circular linked list. (See Programming Exercise 13 at the end of this chapter.)

PROGRAMMING EXAMPLE: Video Store

For a family or an individual, a favorite place to go on weekends or holidays is to a video store to rent movies. A new video store in your neighborhood is about to open. However, it does not have a program to keep track of its videos and customers. The store managers want someone to write a program for their system so that the video store can function. The program should be able to perform the following operations:

1. Rent a video; that is, check out a video.
2. Return, or check in, a video.
3. Create a list of videos owned by the store.
4. Show the details of a particular video.
5. Print a list of all the videos in the store.
6. Check whether a particular video is in the store.
7. Maintain a customer database.
8. Print a list of all the videos rented by each customer.

Let us write a program for the video store. This example further illustrates the object-oriented design methodology and, in particular, inheritance and overloading.

The programming requirement tells us that the video store has two major components: videos and customers. We will describe these two components in detail. We also need to maintain two lists:

- a list of all the videos in the store
- a list of all the store's customers
- lists of the videos currently rented by the customers

We will develop the program in two parts. In Part 1, we design, implement, and test the video component. In Part 2, we design and implement the customer component, which is then added to the video component developed in Part 1. That is, after completing Parts 1 and 2, we can perform all the operations listed previously.

PART 1:
VIDEO
COMPONENT

Video Object

This is the first stage, wherein we discuss the video component. The common things associated with a video are:

- name of the movie
- names of the stars
- name of the producer
- name of the director
- name of the production company
- number of copies in the store

From this list, we see that some of the operations to be performed on a video object are:

1. Set the video information—that is, the title, stars, production company, and so on.
2. Show the details of a particular video.
3. Check the number of copies in the store.
4. Check out (that is, rent) the video. In other words, if the number of copies is greater than zero, decrement the number of copies by one.
5. Check in (that is, return) the video. To check in a video, first we must check whether the store owns such a video and, if it does, increment the number of copies by one.
6. Check whether a particular video is available—that is, check whether the number of copies currently in the store is greater than zero.

The deletion of a video from the video list requires that the list be searched for the video to be deleted. Thus, we need to check the title of a video to find out which video is to be deleted from the list. For simplicity, we assume that two videos are the same if they have the same title.

The following class defines the video object as an ADT:

```cpp
#include <iostream>
#include <string>
```

```cpp
using namespace std;

class videoType
{
    friend ostream& operator<< (ostream&, const videoType&);

public:
    void setVideoInfo(string title, string star1,
                      string star2, string producer,
                      string director, string productionCo,
                      int setInStock);
      //Function to set the details of a video.
      //The member variables are set according to the
      //parameters.
      //Postcondition: videoTitle = title; movieStar1 = star1;
      //       movieStar2 = star2; movieProducer = producer;
      //       movieDirector = director;
      //       movieProductionCo = productionCo;
      //       copiesInStock = setInStock;

    int getNoOfCopiesInStock() const;
      //Function to check the number of copies in stock.
      //Postcondition: The value of copiesInStock is returned.

    void checkOut();
      //Function to rent a video.
      //Postcondition: The number of copies in stock is
      //               decremented by one.

    void checkIn();
      //Function to check in a video.
      //Postcondition: The number of copies in stock is
      //               incremented by one.

    void printTitle() const;
      //Function to print the title of a movie.

    void printInfo() const;
      //Function to print the details of a video.
      //Postcondition: The title of the movie, stars,
      //               director, and so on are displayed
      //               on the screen.

    bool checkTitle(string title);
      //Function to check whether the title is the same as the
      //title of the video.
      //Postcondition: Returns the value true if the title
      //               is the same as the title of the video;
      //               false otherwise.
```

```cpp
    void updateInStock(int num);
      //Function to increment the number of copies in stock by
      //adding the value of the parameter num.
      //Postcondition: copiesInStock = copiesInStock + num;

    void setCopiesInStock(int num);
      //Function to set the number of copies in stock.
      //Postcondition: copiesInStock = num;

    string getTitle() const;
      //Function to return the title of the video.
      //Postcondition: The title of the video is returned.

    videoType(string title = "", string star1 = "",
              string star2 = "", string producer = "",
              string director = "", string productionCo = "",
              int setInStock = 0);
      //constructor
      //The member variables are set according to the
      //incoming parameters. If no values are specified, the
      //default values are assigned.
      //Postcondition: videoTitle = title; movieStar1 = star1;
      //               movieStar2 = star2;
      //               movieProducer = producer;
      //               movieDirector = director;
      //               movieProductionCo = productionCo;
      //               copiesInStock = setInStock;

      //Overload the relational operators.
    bool operator==(const videoType&) const;
    bool operator!=(const videoType&) const;

private:
    string videoTitle;   //variable to store the name
                         //of the movie
    string movieStar1;   //variable to store the name
                         //of the star
    string movieStar2;   //variable to store the name
                         //of the star
    string movieProducer; //variable to store the name
                          //of the producer
    string movieDirector; //variable to store the name
                          //of the director
    string movieProductionCo; //variable to store the name
                              //of the production company
    int copiesInStock;   //variable to store the number of
                         //copies in stock
};
```

We leave the UML diagram of the **class** videoType as an exercise for you.

For easy output, we will overload the output stream insertion operator, <<, for the `class` videoType.

Next, we write the definitions of each function in the `class` videoType. The definitions of these functions, as given below, are quite straightforward and easy to follow:

```cpp
void videoType::setVideoInfo(string title, string star1,
                             string star2, string producer,
                             string director,
                             string productionCo,
                             int setInStock)
{
    videoTitle = title;
    movieStar1 = star1;
    movieStar2 = star2;
    movieProducer = producer;
    movieDirector = director;
    movieProductionCo = productionCo;
    copiesInStock = setInStock;
}

void videoType::checkOut()
{
    if (getNoOfCopiesInStock() > 0)
        copiesInStock--;
    else
        cout << "Currently out of stock" << endl;
}

void videoType::checkIn()
{
    copiesInStock++;
}

int videoType::getNoOfCopiesInStock() const
{
    return copiesInStock;
}

void videoType::printTitle() const
{
    cout << "Video Title: " << videoTitle << endl;
}

void videoType::printInfo() const
{
    cout << "Video Title: " << videoTitle << endl;
    cout << "Stars: " << movieStar1 << " and "
         << movieStar2 << endl;
```

```cpp
    cout << "Producer: " << movieProducer << endl;
    cout << "Director: " << movieDirector << endl;
    cout << "Production Company: " << movieProductionCo
        << endl;
    cout << "Copies in stock: " << copiesInStock
        << endl;
}

bool videoType::checkTitle(string title)
{
    return(videoTitle == title);
}

void videoType::updateInStock(int num)
{
    copiesInStock += num;
}

void videoType::setCopiesInStock(int num)
{
    copiesInStock = num;
}

string videoType::getTitle() const
{
    return videoTitle;
}

videoType::videoType(string title, string star1,
                     string star2, string producer,
                     string director,
                     string productionCo, int setInStock)
{
    setVideoInfo(title, star1, star2, producer, director,
                 productionCo, setInStock);
}

bool videoType::operator==(const videoType& other) const
{
    return (videoTitle == other.videoTitle);
}

bool videoType::operator!=(const videoType& other) const
{
    return (videoTitle != other.videoTitle);
}

ostream& operator<< (ostream& osObject, const videoType& video)
{
    osObject << endl;
    osObject << "Video Title: " << video.videoTitle << endl;
```

```cpp
    osObject << "Stars: " << video.movieStar1 << " and "
             << video.movieStar2 << endl;
    osObject << "Producer: " << video.movieProducer << endl;
    osObject << "Director: " << video.movieDirector << endl;
    osObject << "Production Company: "
             << video.movieProductionCo << endl;
    osObject << "Copies in stock: " << video.copiesInStock
             << endl;
    osObject << "_______________________________________"
             << endl;

    return osObject;
}
```

Video List This program requires us to maintain a list of all the videos in the store. We also should be able to add a new video to our list. In general, we would not know how many videos are in the store, and adding or deleting a video from the store would change the number of videos in the store. Therefore, we will use a linked list to create a list of videos (see Figure 17-57).

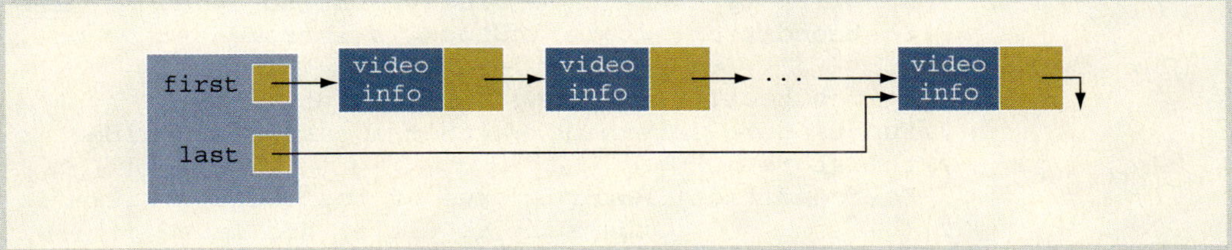

FIGURE 17-57 videoList

Earlier in this chapter, we defined the **class** unorderedLinkedList to create a linked list of objects. We also defined the basic operations such as insertion and deletion of a video in the list. However, some operations are very specific to the video list, such as check out a video, check in a video, set the number of copies of a video, and so on. These operations are not available in the **class** unorderedLinkedList. We will, therefore, derive a **class** videoListType from the **class** unorderedLinkedList and add these operations.

The definition of the **class** videoListType is:

```cpp
#include <string>
#include "unorderedLinkedList.h"
#include "videoType.h"

using namespace std;
```

```cpp
class videoListType:public unorderedLinkedList<videoType>
{
public:
    bool videoSearch(string title) const;
      //Function to search the list to see whether a
      //particular title, specified by the parameter title,
      //is in the store.
      //Postcondition: Returns true if the title is found,
      //               and false otherwise.

    bool isVideoAvailable(string title) const;
      //Function to determine whether a copy of a particular
      //video is in the store.
      //Postcondition: Returns true if at least one copy of the
      //               video specified by title is in the store,
      //               and false otherwise.

    void videoCheckOut(string title);
      //Function to check out a video, that is, rent a video.
      //Postcondition: copiesInStock is decremented by one.

    void videoCheckIn(string title);
      //Function to check in a video returned by a customer.
      //Postcondition: copiesInStock is incremented by one.

    bool videoCheckTitle(string title) const;
      //Function to determine whether a particular video is in
      //the store.
      //Postcondition: Returns true if the video's title is
      //               the same as title, and false otherwise.

    void videoUpdateInStock(string title, int num);
      //Function to update the number of copies of a video
      //by adding the value of the parameter num. The
      //parameter title specifies the name of the video for
      //which the number of copies is to be updated.
      //Postcondition: copiesInStock = copiesInStock + num;

    void videoSetCopiesInStock(string title, int num);
      //Function to reset the number of copies of a video.
      //The parameter title specifies the name of the video
      //for which the number of copies is to be reset, and the
      //parameter num specifies the number of copies.
      //Postcondition: copiesInStock = num;

    void videoPrintTitle() const;
      //Function to print the titles of all the videos in
      //the store.
```

```
private:
    void searchVideoList(string title, bool& found,
                         nodeType<videoType>* &current) const;
        //This function searches the video list for a
        //particular video, specified by the parameter title.
        //Postcondition: If the video is found, the parameter
        //               found is set to true, otherwise it is set
        //               to false. The parameter current points
        //               to the node containing the video.
};
```

Note that the **class** `videoListType` is derived from the **class** `unorderedLinkedList` via a **public** inheritance. Furthermore, `unorderedLinkedList` is a class template and we have passed the **class** `videoType` as a parameter to this class. That is, the **class** `videoListType` is not a template. Because we are now dealing with a very specific data type, the **class** `videoListType` is no longer required to be a template. Thus, the `info` type of each node in the linked list is now `videoType`. Through the member functions of the **class** `videoType`, certain members—such as `videoTitle` and `copiesInStock` of an object of type `videoType`—can now be accessed.

The definitions of the functions to implement the operations of the **class** `videoListType` are given next.

The primary operations on the video list are to check in a video and to check out a video. Both operations require the list to be searched and the location of the video being checked in or checked out to be found in the video list. Other operations, such as determining whether a particular video is in the store, updating the number of copies of a video, and so on, also require the list to be searched. To simplify the search process, we will write a function that searches the video list for a particular video. If the video is found, it sets a parameter `found` to **true** and returns a pointer to the video so that check-in, check-out, and other operations on the video object can be performed. Note that the function `searchVideoList` is a **private** data member of the **class** `videoListType` because it is used only for internal manipulation. First, we describe the search procedure.

Consider the node of the video list shown in Figure 17-58.

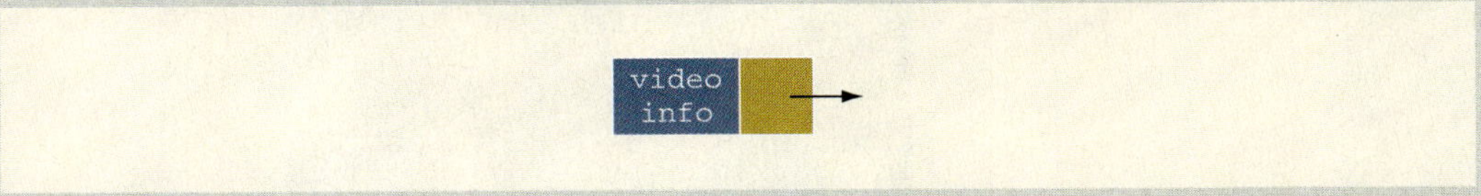

FIGURE 17-58   Node of a video list

The component `info` is of type `videoType` and contains the necessary information about a video. In fact, the component `info` of the node has seven members: `videoTitle, movieStar1, movieStar2, movieProducer, movieDirector,` movieProductionCo, and copiesInStock. (See the definition of the **class** videoType.) Therefore, the node of a video list has the form shown in Figure 17-59.

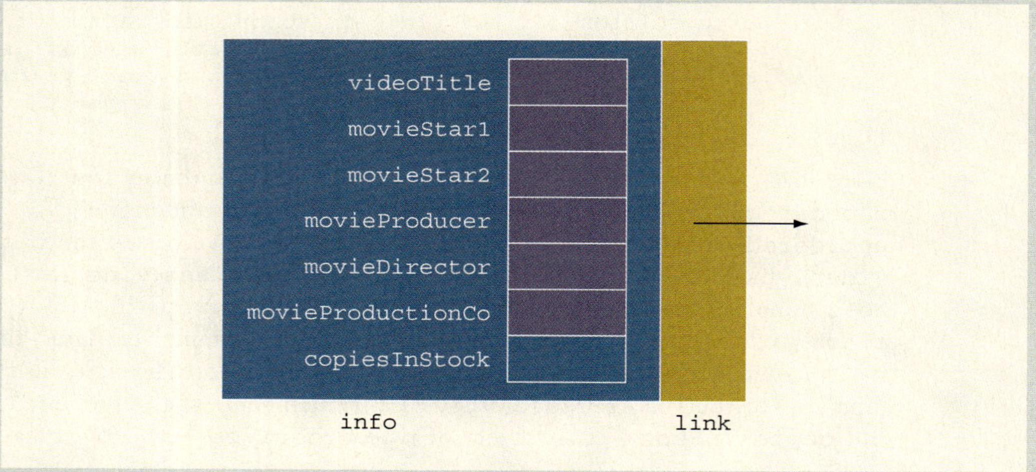

FIGURE 17-59 Video list node showing components of info

These member variables are all **private** and cannot be accessed directly. The member functions of the **class** videoType will help us in checking and/or setting the value of a particular component.

Suppose a pointer—say, current—points to a node in the video list (see Figure 17-60).

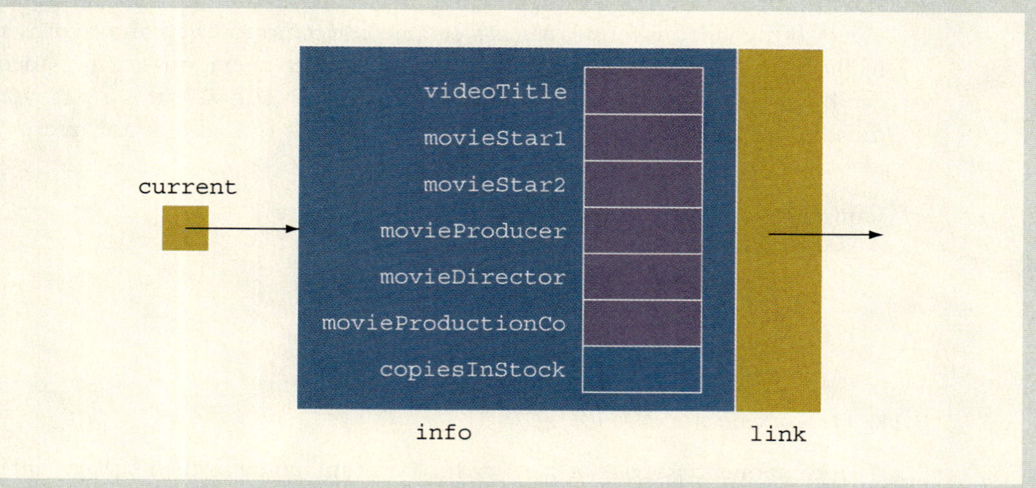

FIGURE 17-60 Pointer current and video list node

Now:

```
current->info
```

refers to the `info` part of the node. Suppose that we want to know whether the title of the video stored in this node is the same as the title specified by the variable `title`. The expression:

```
current->info.checkTitle(title)
```

is `true` if the title of the video stored in this node is the same as the title specified by the parameter `title`, and `false` otherwise. (Note that the member function `checkTitle` is a value-returning function. See its declaration in the `class` `videoType`.)

As another example, suppose that we want to set `copiesInStock` of this node to 10. Because `copiesInStock` is a `private` member, it cannot be accessed directly. Therefore, the statement:

```
current->info.copiesInStock = 10;   //illegal
```

is incorrect and will generate a compile-time error. We have to use the member function `setCopiesInStock` as follows:

```
current->info.setCopiesInStock(10);
```

Now that we know how to access a member variable of a video stored in a node, let us describe the algorithm to search the video list:

```
while (not found)
    if the title of the current video is the same as the desired
        title, stop the search
    else
        check the next node
```

The following function definition performs the desired search:

```
void videoListType::searchVideoList(string title, bool& found,
                        nodeType<videoType>* &current) const
{
    found = false;   //set found to false

    current = first; //set current to point to the first node
                     //in the list

    while (current != NULL && !found)      //search the list
        if (current->info.checkTitle(title)) //the item is found
            found = true;
        else
            current = current->link; //advance current to
                                     //the next node
}//end searchVideoList
```

If the search is successful, the parameter `found` is set to `true` and the parameter `current` points to the node containing the video `info`. If it is unsuccessful, `found` is set to `false` and `current` will be NULL.

The definitions of the other functions of the `class` `videoListType` follow:

```cpp
bool videoListType::isVideoAvailable(string title) const
{
    bool found;
    nodeType<videoType> *location;

    searchVideoList(title, found, location);

    if (found)
        found = (location->info.getNoOfCopiesInStock() > 0);
    else
        found = false;

    return found;
}

void videoListType::videoCheckIn(string title)
{
    bool found = false;
    nodeType<videoType> *location;

    searchVideoList(title, found, location);   //search the list

    if (found)
        location->info.checkIn();
    else
        cout << "The store does not carry " << title
             << endl;
}

void videoListType::videoCheckOut(string title)
{
    bool found = false;
    nodeType<videoType> *location;

    searchVideoList(title, found, location);   //search the list

    if (found)
        location->info.checkOut();
    else
        cout << "The store does not carry " << title
             << endl;
}
```

```cpp
bool videoListType::videoCheckTitle(string title) const
{
    bool found = false;
    nodeType<videoType> *location;

    searchVideoList(title, found, location); //search the list

    return found;
}

void videoListType::videoUpdateInStock(string title, int num)
{
    bool found = false;
    nodeType<videoType> *location;

    searchVideoList(title, found, location); //search the list

    if (found)
        location->info.updateInStock(num);
    else
        cout << "The store does not carry " << title
             << endl;
}

void videoListType::videoSetCopiesInStock(string title, int num)
{
    bool found = false;
    nodeType<videoType> *location;

    searchVideoList(title, found, location);

    if (found)
        location->info.setCopiesInStock(num);
    else
        cout << "The store does not carry " << title
             << endl;
}

bool videoListType::videoSearch(string title) const
{
    bool found = false;
    nodeType<videoType> *location;

    searchVideoList(title, found, location);

    return found;
}
```

```cpp
void videoListType::videoPrintTitle() const
{
    nodeType<videoType>* current;

    current = first;
    while (current != NULL)
    {
        current->info.printTitle();
        current = current->link;
    }
}
```

PART 2: CUSTOMER COMPONENT

Customer Object

The customer object stores information about a customer, such as the first name, last name, account number, and a list of videos rented by the customer.

Every customer is a person. We have already designed the **class** personType in Example 11-9 (Chapter 11) and described the necessary operations on the name of a person. Therefore, we can derive the **class** customerType from the **class** personType and add the additional members that we need. First, however, we must redefine the **class** personType to take advantage of the new features of object-oriented design that you have learned, such as operator overloading, and then derive the **class** customerType.

Recall that the basic operations on an object of type personType are:

1. Print the name.
2. Set the name.
3. Show the first name.
4. Show the last name.

Similarly, the basic operations on an object of type customerType are:

1. Print the name, account number, and the list of rented videos.
2. Set the name and the account number.
3. Rent a video; that is, add the rented video to the list.
4. Return a video; that is, delete the rented video from the list.
5. Show the account number.

The details of implementing the customer component are left as an exercise for you. (See Programming Exercise 14 at the end of this chapter.)

Main Program

We will now write the main program to test the video object. We assume that the necessary data for the videos are stored in a file. We will open the file and create the list of videos owned by the video store. The data in the input file is in the following form:

```
video title (that is, the name of the movie)
movie star1
movie star2
movie producer
movie director
movie production co.
number of copies
.
.
.
```

We will write a function, `createVideoList`, to read the data from the input file and create the list of videos. We will also write a function, `displayMenu`, to show the different choices—such as check in a movie or check out a movie—that the user can make. The algorithm of the function `main` is:

1. Open the input file.
   If the input file does not exist, exit the program.
2. Create the list of videos (`createVideoList`).
3. Show the menu (`displayMenu`).
4. While not done
   Perform various operations.

Opening the input file is straightforward. Let us describe Steps 2 and 3, which are accomplished by writing two separate functions: `createVideoList` and `displayMenu`.

createVideoList This function reads the data from the input file and creates a linked list of videos. Because the data will be read from a file, and the input file was opened in the function `main`, we pass the input file pointer to this function. We also pass the video list pointer, declared in the function `main`, to this function. Both parameters are reference parameters. Next, we read the data for each video and then insert the video in the list. The general algorithm is:

    a. Read the data and store it in a video object.

    b. Insert the video in the list.

    c. Repeat steps a and b for each video's data in the file.

displayMenu This function informs the user what to do. It contains the following output statements:

Select one of the following:

    1. To check whether the store carries a particular video

    2. To check out a video

3. To check in a video

4. To check whether a particular video is in stock

5. To print only the titles of all the videos

6. To print a list of all the videos

9. To exit

In pseudocode, Step 4 (of the main program) is:

```
a. get choice
b.
    while (choice != 9)
    {
        switch (choice)
        {
        case 1:
            a. get the movie name
            b. search the video list
            c. if found, report success
               else report "failure"
            break;
        case 2:
            a. get the movie name
            b. search the video list
            c. if found, check out the video
               else report "failure"
            break;
        case 3:
            a. get the movie name
            b. search the video list
            c. if found, check in video
               else report "failure"
            break;
        case 4:
            a. get the movie name
            b. search the video list
            c. if found
                  if number of copies > 0
                      report "success"
                  else
                      report "currently out of stock"
               else report "failure"
            break;
        case 5:
            print the titles of the videos
            break;
        case 6:
            print all the videos in the store
            break;
        default: bad selection
        } //end switch
```

```cpp
        displayMenu();
        get choice;
}//end while
```


**PROGRAM
LISTING**

```cpp
#include <iostream>
#include <fstream>
#include <string>
#include "videoType.h"
#include "videoListType.h"

using namespace std;

void createVideoList(ifstream& infile,
                     videoListType& videoList);
void displayMenu();

int main()
{
    videoListType videoList;
    int choice;
    char ch;
    string title;

    ifstream infile;

        //open the input file
    infile.open("a:\\videoDat.txt");
    if (!infile)
    {
        cout << "The input file does not exist. "
             << "The program terminates!!!" << endl;
        return 1;
    }

        //create the video list
    createVideoList(infile, videoList);
    infile.close();

        //show the menu
    displayMenu();
    cout << "Enter your choice: ";
    cin >> choice;       //get the request
    cin.get(ch);
    cout << endl;

        //process the requests
    while (choice != 9)
    {
        switch (choice)
```

```cpp
    {
case 1:
        cout << "Enter the title: ";
        getline(cin, title);
        cout << endl;

        if (videoList.videoSearch(title))
            cout << "The store carries " << title
                 << endl;
        else
            cout << "The store does not carry "
                 << title << endl;
        break;

case 2:
        cout << "Enter the title: ";
        getline(cin, title);
        cout << endl;

        if (videoList.videoSearch(title))
        {
            if (videoList.isVideoAvailable(title))
            {
                videoList.videoCheckOut(title);
                cout << "Enjoy your movie: "
                     << title << endl;
            }
            else
                cout << "Currently " << title
                     << " is out of stock." << endl;
        }
        else
            cout << "The store does not carry "
                 << title << endl;
        break;

case 3:
        cout << "Enter the title: ";
        getline(cin, title);
        cout << endl;

        if (videoList.videoSearch(title))
        {
            videoList.videoCheckIn(title);
            cout << "Thanks for returning "
                 << title << endl;
        }
        else
            cout << "The store does not carry "
                 << title << endl;
        break;
```

```cpp
        case 4:
            cout << "Enter the title: ";
            getline(cin, title);
            cout << endl;

            if (videoList.videoSearch(title))
            {
                if (videoList.isVideoAvailable(title))
                    cout << title << " is currently in "
                        << "stock." << endl;
                else
                    cout << title << " is currently out "
                        << "of stock." << endl;
            }
            else
                cout << "The store does not carry "
                    << title << endl;
            break;

        case 5:
            videoList.videoPrintTitle();
            break;

        case 6:
            videoList.print();
            break;

        default:
            cout << "Invalid selection." << endl;
        }//end switch

        displayMenu();        //display menu

        cout << "Enter your choice: ";
        cin >> choice;        //get the next request
        cin.get(ch);
        cout << endl;
    }//end while

    return 0;
}

void createVideoList(ifstream& infile,
                     videoListType& videoList)
{
    string title;
    string star1;
    string star2;
    string producer;
    string director;
    string productionCo;
```

```cpp
    char ch;
    int inStock;

    videoType newVideo;

    getline(infile, title);

    while (infile)
    {
        getline(infile, star1);
        getline(infile, star2);
        getline(infile, producer);
        getline(infile, director);
        getline(infile, productionCo);
        infile >> inStock;
        infile.get(ch);
        newVideo.setVideoInfo(title, star1, star2, producer,
                              director, productionCo, inStock);
        videoList.insertFirst(newVideo);

        getline(infile, title);
    }//end while
}//end createVideoList

void displayMenu()
{
    cout << "Select one of the following:" << endl;
    cout << "1: To check whether the store carries a "
         << "particular video." << endl;
    cout << "2: To check out a video." << endl;
    cout << "3: To check in a video." << endl;
    cout << "4: To check whether a particular video is "
         << "in stock." << endl;
    cout << "5: To print only the titles of all the videos."
         << endl;
    cout << "6: To print a list of all the videos." << endl;
    cout << "9: To exit" << endl;
}//end displayMenu
```

QUICK REVIEW

1. A linked list is a list of items, called nodes, in which the order of the nodes is determined by the address, called a link, stored in each node.

2. The pointer to a linked list—that is, the pointer to the first node in the list—is stored in a separate location, called the head or first.

3. A linked list is a dynamic data structure.

4. The length of a linked list is the number of nodes in the list.

5. Item insertion and deletion from a linked list does not require data movement; only the pointers are adjusted.

6. A (single) linked list is traversed in only one direction.

7. The search on a linked list is sequential.

8. The first (or head) pointer of a linked list is always fixed, pointing to the first node in the list.

9. To traverse a linked list, the program must use a pointer different than the head pointer of the list, initialized to the first node in the list.

10. In a doubly linked list, every node has two links: one points to the next node, and one points to the previous node.

11. A doubly linked list can be traversed in either direction.

12. In a doubly linked list, item insertion and deletion require the adjustment of two pointers in a node.

13. A linked list in which the last node points to the first node is called a circular linked list.

EXERCISES

1. Mark the following statements as true or false.

   a. In a linked list, the order of the elements is determined by the order in which the nodes were created to store the elements.

   b. In a linked list, memory allocated for the nodes is sequential.

   c. A single linked list can be traversed in either direction.

   d. In a linked list, nodes are always inserted either at the beginning or the end because a linked link is not a random-access data structure.

Consider the linked list shown in Figure 17-61. Assume that the nodes are in the usual `info-link` form. Use this list to answer Exercises 2 through 7. If necessary, declare additional variables. (Assume that `list`, `p`, `s`, `A`, and `B` are pointers of type `nodeType`.)

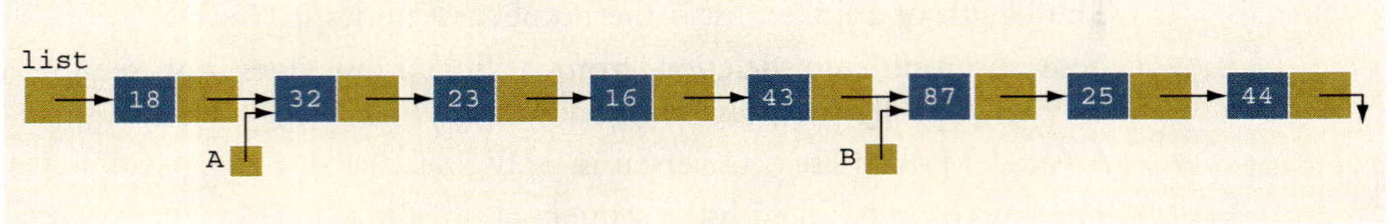

FIGURE 17-61   Linked list for Exercises 2 through 7

2.   What is the output of each of the following C++ statements?

  a.   `cout << list->info;`

  b.   `cout << A->info;`

  c.   `cout << B->link->info;`

  d.   `cout << list->link->link->info`

3.   What is the value of each of the following relational expressions?

  a.   `list->info >= 18`

  b.   `list->link == A`

  c.   `A->link->info == 16`

  d.   `B->link == NULL`

  e.   `list->info == 18`

4.   Mark each of the following statements as valid or invalid. If a statement is
invalid, explain why.

  a.   `A = B;`

  b.   `list->link = A->link;`

  c.   `list->link->info = 45;`

  d.   `*list = B;`

  e.   `*A = *B;`

  f.   `B = A->link->info;`

  g.   `A->info = B->info;`

  h.   `list = B->link->link;`

  i.   `B = B->link->link->link;`

5.   Write C++ statements to do the following.

  a.   Make A point to the node containing `info` 23.

  b.   Make `list` point to the node containing 16.

  c.   Make B point to the last node in the list.

  d.   Make `list` point to an empty list.

  e.   Set the value of the node containing 25 to 35.

f. Create and insert the node with `info` 10 after the node pointed to by A.

g. Delete the node with `info` 23. Also, deallocate the memory occupied by this node.

6. What is the output of the following C++ code?

```
p = list;

while (p != NULL)
    cout << p->info << " ";
    p = p->link;
cout << endl;
```

7. If the following C++ code is valid, show the output. If it is invalid, explain why.

a.
```
s = A;
p = B;
s->info = B;
p = p->link;
cout << s->info << " " << p->info << endl;
```

b.
```
p = A;
p = p->link;
s = p;
p->link = NULL;
s = s->link;
cout << p->info << " " << s->info << endl;
```

8. Show what is produced by the following C++ code. Assume the node is in the usual `info-link` form with the `info` of type `int`. (`list` and `ptr` are pointers of type `nodeType`.)

a.
```
list = new nodeType;
list->info = 10;
ptr = new nodeType;
ptr->info = 13;
ptr->link = NULL;
list->link = ptr;
ptr = new nodeType;
ptr->info = 18;
ptr->link = list->link;
list->link = ptr;
cout << list->info << " " << ptr->info << " ";
ptr = ptr->link;
cout << ptr->info << endl;
```

b.
```
list = new nodeType;
list->info = 20;
ptr = new nodeType;
```

```
    ptr->info = 28;
    ptr->link = NULL;
    list->link = ptr;
    ptr = new nodeType;
    ptr->info = 30;
    ptr->link = list;
    list = ptr;
    ptr = new nodeType;
    ptr->info = 42;
    ptr->link = list->link;
    list->link = ptr;
    ptr = list;
    while (ptr != NULL)
    {
        cout << ptr->info << endl;
        ptr = ptr->link;
    }
```

9. Consider the following C++ statements. (The **class** unorderedLinkedList is as defined in this chapter.)

```
unorderedLinkedList<int> list;

list.insertFirst(15);
list.insertLast(28);
list.insertFirst(30);
list.insertFirst(2);
list.insertLast(45);
list.insertFirst(38);
list.insertLast(25);
list.deleteNode(30);
list.insertFirst(18);
list.deleteNode(28);
list.deleteNode(12);
list.print();
```

What is the output of this program segment?

10. Suppose the input is:

```
18 30 4 32 45 36 78 19 48 75 -999
```

What is the output of the following C++ code? (The **class** unorderedLinkedList is as defined in this chapter.)

```
unorderedLinkedList<int> list;
unorderedLinkedList<int> copyList;
int num;

cin >> num;
while (num != -999)
{
    if (num % 5 == 0 || num % 5 == 3)
        list.insertFirst(num);
```

```
    else
        list.insertLast(num);
    cin >> num;
}

list.print();
cout << endl;

copyList = list;

copyList.deleteNode(78);
copyList.deleteNode(35);

cout << "Copy List = ";
copyList.print();
cout << endl;
```

11. Draw the UML diagram of the **class** `doublyLinkedList` as discussed in this chapter.

12. Draw the UML diagram of the **class** `videoType` of the Video Store programming example.

13. Draw the UML diagram of the **class** `videoListType` of the Video Store programming example.

PROGRAMMING EXERCISES

1. (**Online Address Book revisited**) Programming Exercise 6 in Chapter 12 could handle a maximum of only 500 entries. Using linked lists, redo the program to handle as many entries as required. Add the following operations to your program:

    a. Add or delete a new entry to the address book.

    b. When the program terminates, write the data in the address book to a disk.

2. Extend the **class** `linkedListType` by adding the following operations:

    a. Find and delete the node with the smallest `info` in the list. (Delete only the first occurrence and traverse the list only once.)

    b. Find and delete all occurrences of a given `info` from the list. (Traverse the list only once.)

    Add these as abstract functions in the **class** `linkedListType` and provide the definitions of these functions in the **class** `unorderedLinkedList`. Also, write a program to test these functions.

3. Extend the **class** `linkedListType` by adding the following operations:

   a. Write a function that returns the info of the kth element of the linked list. If no such element exists, terminate the program.

   b. Write a function that deletes the kth element of the linked list. If no such element exists, output an appropriate message.

   Provide the definitions of these functions in the **class** `linkedListType`. Also, write a program to test these functions. (Use either the **class** `unorderedLinkedList` or the **class** `orderedLinkedList` to test your function.)

4. (**Printing a single linked list backward**) Include the functions `reversePrint` and `recursiveReversePrint`, as discussed in this chapter, to the class **class** `linkedListType`. Also, write a program function to print a (single) linked list backward. (Use either the **class** `unorderedLinkedList` or the **class** `orderedLinkedList` to test your function.)

5. (**Dividing a linked list into two sublists of almost equal sizes**)

   a. Add the operation `divideMid` to the **class** `linkedListType` as follows:

```
void divideMid(linkedListType<Type> &sublist);
  //This operation divides the given list into two sublists
  //of (almost) equal sizes.
  //Postcondition: first points to the first node and last
  //               points to the last node of the first
  //               sublist.
  //               sublist.first points to the first node
  //               and sublist.last points to the last node
  //               of the second sublist.
```

   Consider the following statements:

```
unorderedLinkedList<int> myList;
unorderedLinkedList<int> subList;
```

   Suppose `myList` points to the list with elements 34 65 27 89 12 (in this order). The statement:

```
myList.divideMid(subList);
```

   divides `myList` into two sublists: `myList` points to the list with the elements 34 65 27, and `subList` points to the sublist with the elements 89 12.

   b. Write the definition of the function template to implement the operation `divideMid`. Also, write a program to test your function.

6. **(Splitting a linked list, at a given node, into two sublists)**

   a. Add the following operation to the **class** linkedListType:

```
void divideAt(linkedListType<Type> &secondList,
              const Type& item);
  //Divide the list at the node with the info item into two
  //sublists.
   //Postcondition: first and last point to the first and
   //               last nodes of the first sublist.
   //               secondList.first and secondList.last
   //               point to the first and last nodes of the
   //               second sublist.
```

   Consider the following statements:

```
unorderedLinkedList<int> myList;
unorderedLinkedList<int> otherList;
```

   Suppose myList points to the list with the elements:

```
34 65 18 39 27 89 12
```

   (in this order). The statement:

```
myList.divideAt(otherList, 18);
```

   divides myList into two sublists: myList points to the list with the elements 34 65, and otherList points to the sublist with the elements 18 39 27 89 12.

   b. Write the definition of the function template to implement the operation divideAt. Also, write a program to test your function.

7. a. Add the following operation to the **class** orderedLinkedList:

```
void mergeLists(orderedLinkedList<Type> &list1,
                orderedLinkedList<Type> &list2);
  //This function creates a new list by merging the
  //elements of list1 and list2.
  //Postcondition: first points to the merged list
  //               list1 and list2 are empty
```

   Consider the following statements:

```
orderedLinkedList<int> newList;
orderedLinkedList<int> list1;
orderedLinkedList<int> list2;
```

   Suppose list1 points to the list with the elements 2 6 7, and list2 points to the list with the elements 3 5 8. The statement:

```
newList.mergeLists(list1, list2);
```

creates a new linked list with the elements in the order 2 3 5 6 7 8, and the object `newList` points to this list. Also, after the preceding statement executes, `list1` and `list2` are empty.

b. Write the definition of the function template `mergeLists` to implement the operation `mergeLists`.

8. The function `insert` of the **class** `orderedLinkedList` does not check if the item to be inserted is already in the list; that is, it does not check for duplicates. Rewrite the definition of the function `insert` so that, before inserting the item, it checks whether the item to be inserted is already in the list. If the item to be inserted is already in the list, the function outputs an appropriate error message. Also, write a program to test your function.

9. In this chapter, the class to implement the nodes of a linked list is defined as a **struct**. The following rewrites the definition of the **struct** `nodeType` so that it is declared as a class and the member variables are private:

```cpp
template <class Type>
class nodeType
{
public:
    const nodeType<Type>& operator=(const nodeType<Type>&);
      //Overload the assignment operator.

    void setInfo(const Type& elem);
      //Function to set the info of the node.
      //Postcondition: info = elem;

    Type getInfo() const;
      //Function to return the info of the node.
      //Postcondition: The value of info is returned.

    void setLink(nodeType<Type> *ptr);
      //Function to set the link of the node.
      //Postcondition: link = ptr;

    nodeType<Type>* getLink() const;
      //Function to return the link of the node.
      //Postcondition: The value of link is returned.

    nodeType();
      //Default constructor
      //Postcondition: link = NULL;

    nodeType(const Type& elem, nodeType<Type> *ptr);
      //Constructor with parameters
      //Sets info point to the object elem points to, and
      //link is set to point to the object ptr points to.
      //Postcondition: info = elem; link = ptr
```

```
nodeType(const nodeType<Type> &otherNode);
  //Copy constructor
~nodeType();
  //Destructor

private:
    Type info;
    nodeType<Type> *link;
};
```

Write the definitions of the member functions of the **class** nodeType. Also, write a program to test your class.

10. Programming Exercise 9 asks you to redefine the class to implement the nodes of a linked list so that the instance variables are **private**. Therefore, the **class** linkedListType and its derived **class**es unorderedLinkedList and orderedLinkedList can no longer directly access the instance variables of the **class** nodeType. Rewrite the definitions of these classes so that they use the member functions of the **class** nodeType to access the info and link fields of a node. Also, write programs to test various operations of the classes unorderedLinkedList and orderedLinkeList.

11. Write the definitions of the function copyList, the copy constructor, and the function to overload the assignment operator for the **class** doublyLinkedList.

12. Write a program to test various operations of the **class** doublyLinkedList.

13. (**Circular linked lists**) This chapter defined and identified various operations on a circular linked list.

    a. Write the definitions of the **class** circularLinkedList and its member functions. (You may assume that the elements of the circular linked list are in ascending order.)

    b. Write a program to test various operations of the class defined in (a).

14. (**Video Store programming example**)

    a. Complete the design and implementation of the **class** customerType defined in the Video Store programming example.

    b. Design and implement the **class** customerListType to create and maintain a list of customers for the video store.

15. (**Video Store programming example**) Complete the design and implementation of the video store program. In other words, write a program that uses the classes designed in the Video Store programming example and in Programming Exercise 14 to make a video store operational.

STACKS AND QUEUES

IN THIS CHAPTER, YOU WILL:

- Learn about stacks
- Examine various stack operations
- Learn how to implement a stack as an array
- Learn how to implement a stack as a linked list
- Discover stack applications
- Learn how to use a stack to remove recursion
- Learn about queues
- Examine various queue operations
- Learn how to implement a queue as an array
- Learn how to implement a queue as a linked list
- Discover queue applications

This chapter discusses two very useful data structures, stacks and queues. Both stacks and queues have numerous applications in computer science.

Stacks

Suppose that you have a program with several functions. To be specific, suppose that you have functions A, B, C, and D in your program. Now suppose that function A calls function B, function B calls function C, and function C calls function D. When function D terminates, control goes back to function C; when function C terminates, control goes back to function B; and when function B terminates, control goes back to function A. During program execution, how do you think the computer keeps track of the function calls? What about recursive functions? How does the computer keep track of the recursive calls? In Chapter 17, we designed a recursive function to print a linked list backward. What if you want to write a nonrecursive algorithm to print a linked list backward?

This section discusses the data structure called the **stack**, which the computer uses to implement function calls. You can also use stacks to convert recursive algorithms into nonrecursive algorithms, especially recursive algorithms that are not tail recursive. Stacks have numerous applications in computer science. After developing the tools necessary to implement a stack, we will examine some applications of stacks.

A stack is a list of homogeneous elements in which the addition and deletion of elements occurs only at one end, called the **top** of the stack. For example, in a cafeteria, the second tray in a stack of trays can be removed only if the first tray has been removed. For another example, to get to your favorite computer science book, which is underneath your math and history books, you must first remove the math and history books. After removing these books, the computer science book becomes the top book—that is, the top element of the stack. Figure 18-1 shows some examples of stacks.

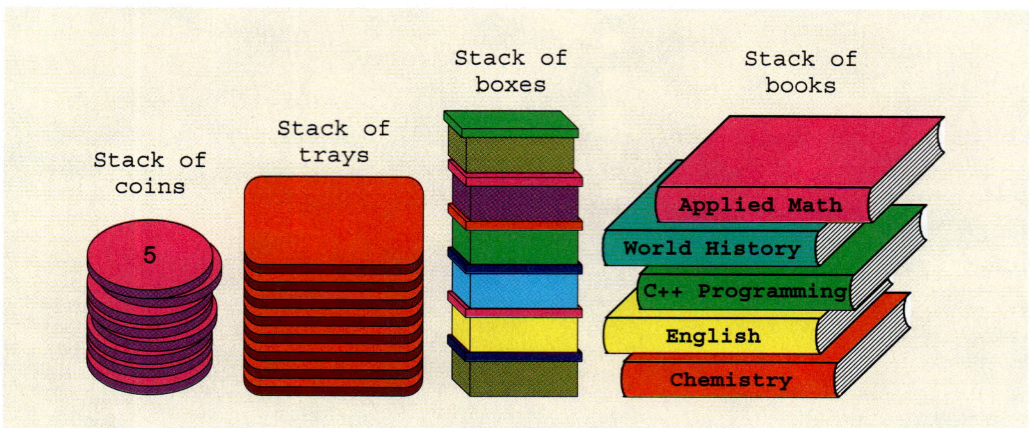

FIGURE 18-1 Various types of stacks

The elements at the bottom of the stack have been in the stack the longest. The top element of the stack is the last element added to the stack. Because the elements are added and removed from one end (that is, the top), it follows that the item that is added last will be removed first. For this reason, a stack is also called a **Last In First Out (LIFO)** data structure.

Stack: A data structure in which the elements are added and removed from one end only; a Last In First Out (LIFO) data structure.

Now that you know what a stack is, let us see what kinds of operations can be performed on a stack. Because new items can be added to the stack, we can perform the add operation, called **push**, to add an element onto the stack. Similarly, because the top item can be retrieved and/or removed from the stack, we can perform the operation **top** to retrieve the top element of the stack, and the operation **pop** to remove the top element from the stack.

The push, top, and pop operations work as follows: Suppose there are boxes lying on the floor that need to be stacked on a table. Initially, all of the boxes are on the floor and the stack is empty (see Figure 18-2).

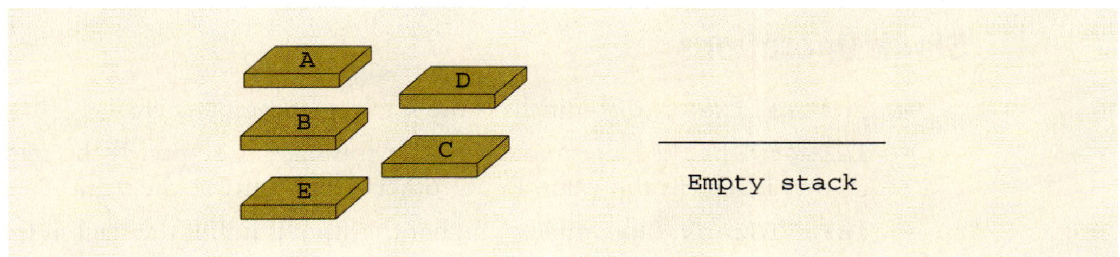

FIGURE 18-2 Empty stack

First, we push box **A** onto the stack. After the push operation, the stack is as shown in Figure 18-3(a).

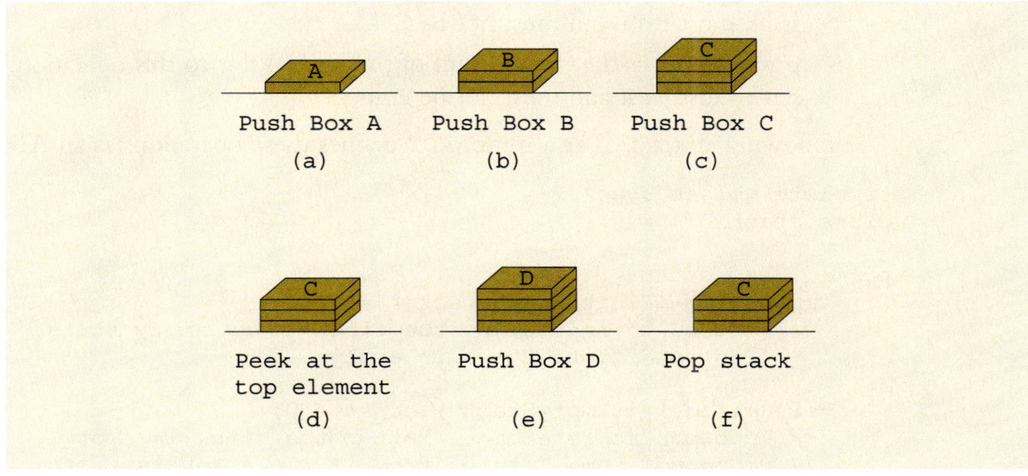

FIGURE 18-3 Stack operations

We then push box B onto the stack. After this push operation, the stack is as shown in Figure 18-3(b). Next, we push box C onto the stack. After this push operation, the stack is as shown in Figure 18-3(c). Next, we look, that is, peek, at the top element of the stack. After this operation, the stack is unchanged and shown in Figure 18-3(d). We then push box D onto the stack. After this push operation, the stack is as shown in Figure 18-3(e). Next, we pop the stack. After the pop operation, the stack is as shown in Figure 18-3(f).

An element can be removed from the stack only if there is something in the stack, and an element can be added to the stack only if there is room. The two operations that immediately follow from push, top, and pop are **isFullStack** (checks whether the stack is full) and **isEmptyStack** (checks whether the stack is empty). Because a stack keeps changing as we add and remove elements, the stack must be empty before we first start using it. Thus, we need another operation, called **initializeStack**, which initializes the stack to an empty state. Therefore, to successfully implement a stack, we need at least these six operations, which are described in the next section. We might also need other operations on a stack, depending on the specific implementation.

Stack Operations

- **initializeStack**: initializes the stack to an empty state.

- **isEmptyStack**: Determines whether the stack is empty. If the stack is empty, it returns the value **true**; otherwise, it returns the value **false**.

- **isFullStack**: Determines whether the stack is full. If the stack is full, it returns the value **true**; otherwise, it returns the value **false**.

- **push**: Adds a new element to the top of the stack. The input to this operation consists of the stack and the new element. Prior to this operation, the stack must exist and must not be full.

- **top**: Returns the top element of the stack. Prior to this operation, the stack must exist and must not be full.

- **pop**: Removes the top element of the stack. Prior to this operation, the stack must exist and must not be empty.

The following abstract **class stackADT** defines these operations as an ADT:

```cpp
template <class Type>
class stackADT
{
public:
    virtual void initializeStack() = 0;
        //Method to initialize the stack to an empty state.
        //Postcondition: Stack is empty.

    virtual bool isEmptyStack() const = 0;
        //Function to determine whether the stack is empty.
        //Postcondition: Returns true if the stack is empty,
        //               otherwise returns false.
```

```cpp
virtual bool isFullStack() const = 0;
  //Function to determine whether the stack is full.
  //Postcondition: Returns true if the stack is full,
  //                  otherwise returns false.

virtual void push(const Type& newItem) = 0;
  //Function to add newItem to the stack.
  //Precondition: The stack exists and is not full.
  //Postcondition: The stack is changed and newItem
  //                  is added to the top of the stack.

virtual Type top() const = 0;
  //Function to return the top element of the stack.
  //Precondition: The stack exists and is not empty.
  //Postcondition: If the stack is empty, the program
  //                  terminates; otherwise, the top element
  //                  of the stack is returned.

virtual void pop() = 0;
  //Function to remove the top element of the stack.
  //Precondition: The stack exists and is not empty.
  //Postcondition: The stack is changed and the top
  //                  element is removed from the stack.
};
```

Figure 18-4 shows the UML class diagram of the **class** stackADT.

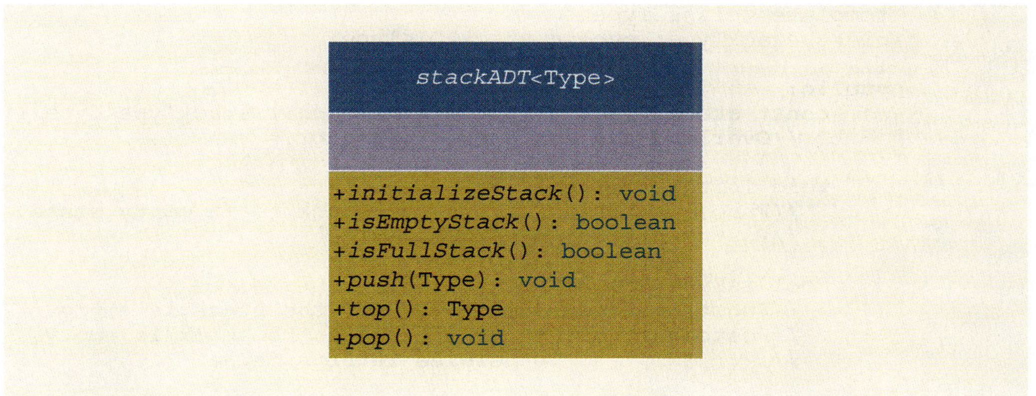

FIGURE 18-4   UML class diagram of the **class** stackADT

We now consider the implementation of our abstract stack data structure. Because all the elements of a stack are of the same type, a stack can be implemented as either an array or a linked structure. Both implementations are useful and are discussed in this chapter.

Implementation of Stacks as Arrays

Because all the elements of a stack are of the same type, you can use an array to implement a stack. The first element of the stack can be put in the first array slot, the second element of the stack in the second array slot, and so on. The top of the stack is the index of the last element added to the stack.

In this implementation of a stack, stack elements are stored in an array, and an array is a random access data structure; that is, you can directly access any element of the array. However, by definition, a stack is a data structure in which the elements are accessed (popped or pushed) at only one end—that is, a Last In First Out data structure. Thus, a stack element is accessed only through the top, not through the bottom or middle. This feature of a stack is extremely important and must be recognized in the beginning.

To keep track of the top position of the array, we can simply declare another variable, called `stackTop`.

The following `class`, `stackType`, implements the functions of the abstract `class` `stackADT`. By using a pointer, we can dynamically allocate arrays, so we will leave it for the user to specify the size of the array (that is, the stack size). We assume that the default stack size is 100. Because the `class` `stackType` has a pointer member variable (the pointer to the array to store the stack elements), we must overload the assignment operator and include the copy constructor and destructor. Moreover, we give a generic definition of the stack. Depending on the specific application, we can pass the stack element type when we declare a stack object:

```cpp
template <class Type>
class stackType: public stackADT<Type>
{
public:
    const stackType<Type>& operator=(const stackType<Type>&);
      //Overload the assignment operator.

    void initializeStack();
      //Function to initialize the stack to an empty state.
      //Postcondition: stackTop = 0;

    bool isEmptyStack() const;
      //Function to determine whether the stack is empty.
      //Postcondition: Returns true if the stack is empty,
      //               otherwise returns false.

    bool isFullStack() const;
      //Function to determine whether the stack is full.
      //Postcondition: Returns true if the stack is full,
      //               otherwise returns false.

    void push(const Type& newItem);
      //Function to add newItem to the stack.
      //Precondition: The stack exists and is not full.
      //Postcondition: The stack is changed and newItem
      //               is added to the top of the stack.
```

```
Type top() const;
  //Function to return the top element of the stack.
  //Precondition: The stack exists and is not empty.
  //Postcondition: If the stack is empty, the program
  //                terminates; otherwise, the top element
  //                of the stack is returned.

void pop();
  //Function to remove the top element of the stack.
  //Precondition: The stack exists and is not empty.
  //Postcondition: The stack is changed and the top
  //                element is removed from the stack.


stackType(int stackSize = 100);
  //Constructor
  //Create an array of the size stackSize to hold
  //the stack elements. The default stack size is 100.
  //Postcondition: The variable list contains the base
  //                address of the array, stackTop = 0, and
  //                maxStackSize = stackSize.

stackType(const stackType<Type>& otherStack);
  //Copy constructor

~stackType();
  //Destructor
  //Remove all the elements from the stack.
  //Postcondition: The array (list) holding the stack
  //                elements is deleted.

private:
    int maxStackSize; //variable to store the maximum stack size
    int stackTop;     //variable to point to the top of the stack
    Type *list;       //pointer to the array that holds the
                      //stack elements

    void copyStack(const stackType<Type>& otherStack);
      //Function to make a copy of otherStack.
      //Postcondition: A copy of otherStack is created and
      //                assigned to this stack.
};
```

Figure 18-5 shows the UML class diagram of the **class** stackType.

```
                        stackType<Type>

-maxStackSize: int
-stackTop: int
-*list: Type

+operator=(const stackType<Type>&):
                         const stackType<Type>&
+initializeStack(): void
+isEmptyStack() const: bool
+isFullStack() const: bool
+push(const Type&): void
+top() const: Type
+pop(): void
-copyStack(const stackType<Type>&): void
+stackType(int = 100)
+stackType(const stackType<Type>&)
+~stackType()
```

FIGURE 18-5 UML class diagram of the **class** stackType

NOTE Because C++ arrays begin with the index 0, we need to distinguish between the value of stackTop and the array position indicated by stackTop. If stackTop is 0, the stack is empty; if stackTop is nonzero, then the stack is nonempty and the top element of the stack is given by stackTop – 1.

Notice that the function copyStack is included as a **private** member. This is because we want to use this function only to implement the copy constructor and overload the assignment operator. To copy a stack into another stack, the program can use the assignment operator.

Figure 18-6 shows this data structure, wherein stack is an object of type stackType. Note that stackTop can range from 0 to maxStackSize. If stackTop is nonzero, then stackTop – 1 is the index of the stackTop element of the stack. Suppose that maxStackSize = 100.

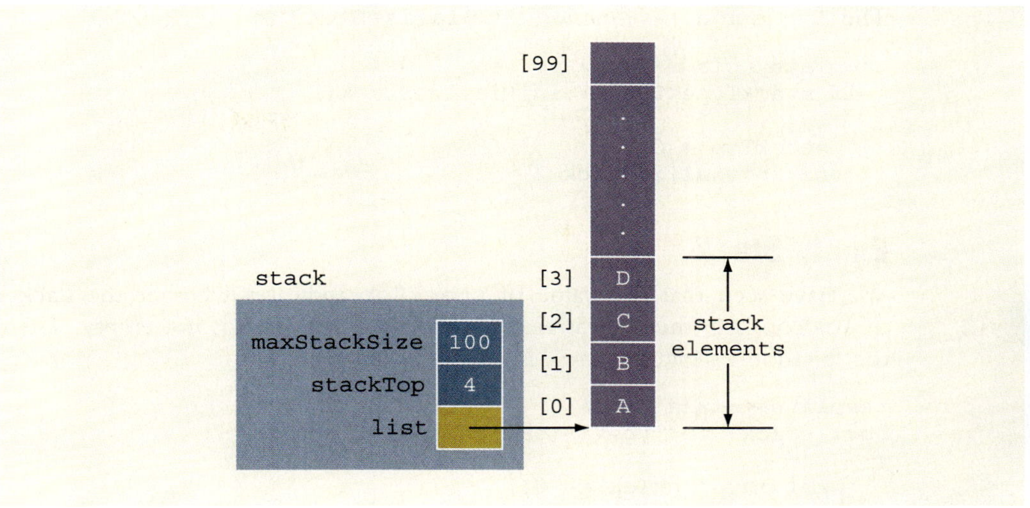

FIGURE 18-6 Example of a stack

Note that the pointer list contains the base address of the array (holding the stack elements)—that is, the address of the first array component. Next, we discuss how to implement the member functions of the **class** stackType.

Initialize Stack

Let us consider the initializeStack operation. Because the value of stackTop indicates whether the stack is empty, we can simply set stackTop to 0 to initialize the stack (see Figure 18-7).

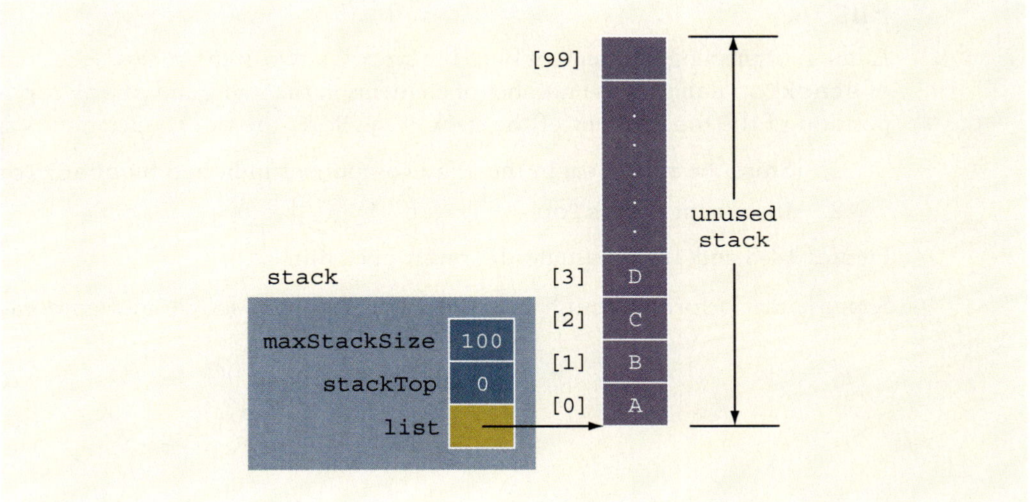

FIGURE 18-7 Empty stack

The definition of the function `initializeStack` is:

```cpp
template <class Type>
void stackType<Type>::initializeStack()
{
    stackTop = 0;
}//end initializeStack
```

Empty Stack

We have seen that the value of `stackTop` indicates whether the stack is empty. If `stackTop` is 0, the stack is empty; otherwise, the stack is not empty. The definition of the function `isEmptyStack` is:

```cpp
template <class Type>
bool stackType<Type>::isEmptyStack() const
{
    return(stackTop == 0);
}//end isEmptyStack
```

Full Stack

Next, we consider the operation `isFullStack`. It follows that the stack is full if `stackTop` is equal to `maxStackSize`. The definition of the function `isFullStack` is:

```cpp
template <class Type>
bool stackType<Type>::isFullStack() const
{
    return (stackTop == maxStackSize);
} //end isFullStack
```

Push

Adding, or pushing, an element onto the stack is a two-step process. Recall that the value of `stackTop` indicates the number of elements in the stack, and `stackTop – 1` gives the position of the top element of the stack. Therefore, the `push` operation is as follows:

1.   Store the `newItem` in the array component indicated by `stackTop`.

2.   Increment `stackTop`.

Figures 18-8 and 18-9 illustrate the `push` operation.

Suppose that before the `push` operation, the stack is as shown in Figure 18-8.

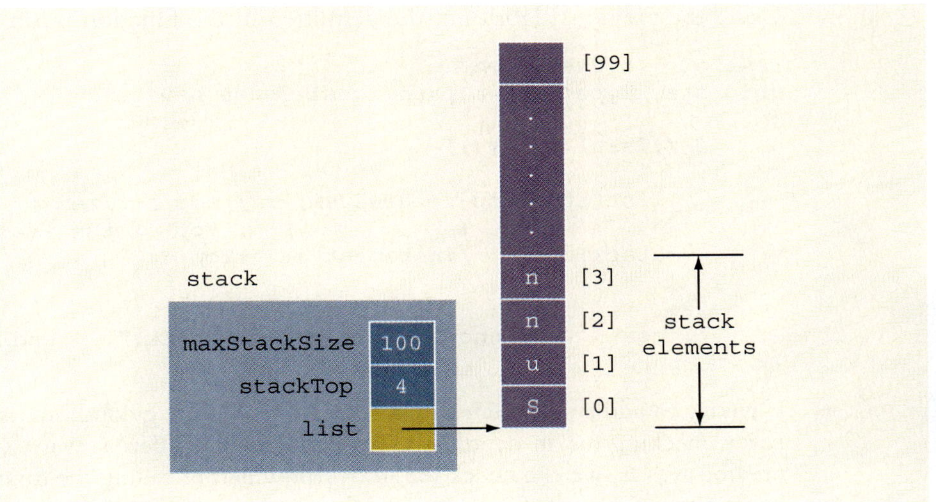

FIGURE 18-8 Stack before pushing y

Assume `newItem` is `'y'`. After the `push` operation, the stack is as shown in Figure 18-9.

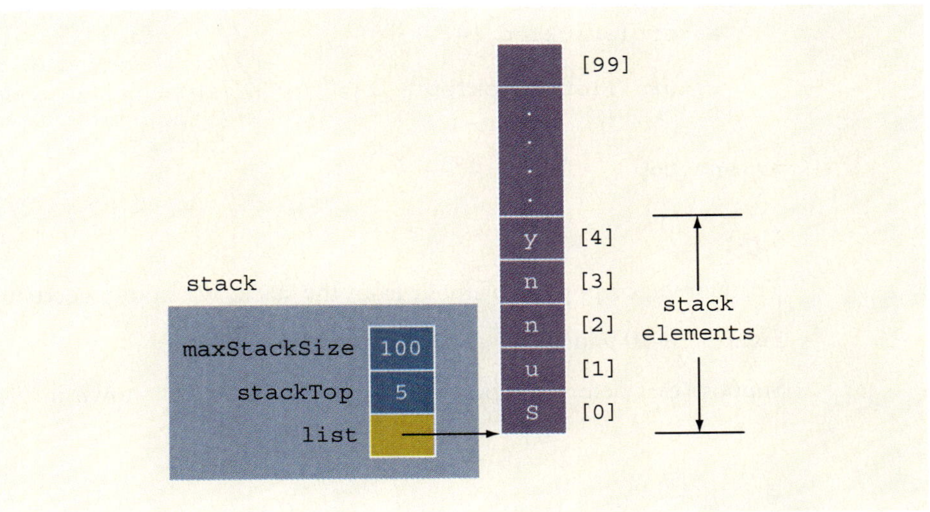

FIGURE 18-9 Stack after pushing y

Using the previous algorithm, the definition of the function push is:

```cpp
template <class Type>
void stackType<Type>::push(const Type& newItem)
{
    if (!isFullStack())
    {
        list[stackTop] = newItem;    //add newItem to the
                                     //top of the stack
        stackTop++; //increment stackTop
    }
    else
        cout << "Cannot add to a full stack." << endl;
}//end push
```

If we try to add a new item to a full stack, the resulting condition is called an **overflow**. Error checking for an overflow can be handled in different ways. One way is as shown previously. Or, we can check for an overflow before calling the function push, as shown next (assuming stack is an object of type stackType):

```cpp
if (!stack.isFullStack())
    stack.push(newItem);
```

Return the Top Element

The operation top returns the top element of the stack. Its definition is:

```cpp
template <class Type>
Type stackType<Type>::top() const
{
    assert(stackTop != 0);        //if stack is empty,
                                  //terminate the program

    return list[stackTop - 1];    //return the element of the
                                  //stack indicated by
                                  //stackTop - 1
}//end top
```

Pop

To remove, or pop, an element from the stack, we simply decrement stackTop by 1. Figures 18-10 and 18-11 illustrate the pop operation.

Suppose that before the pop operation, the stack is as shown in Figure 18-10.

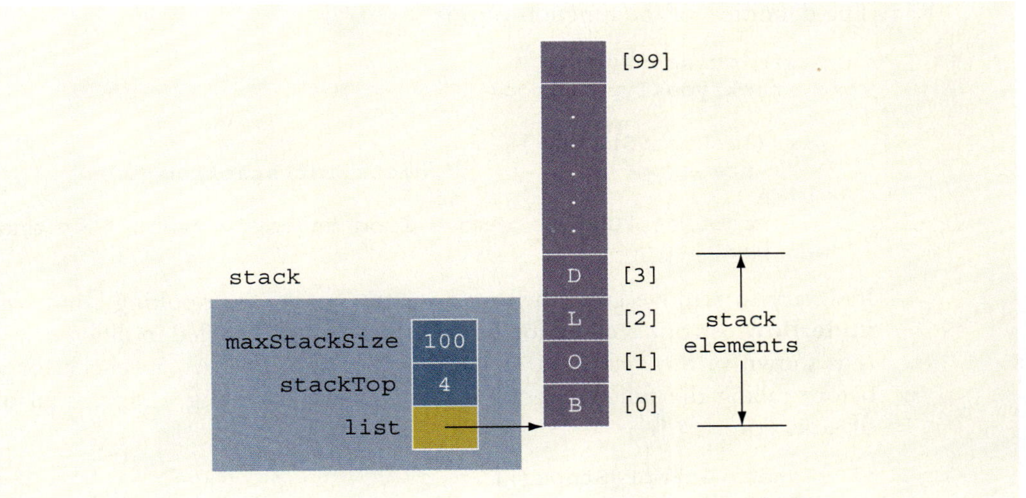

FIGURE 18-10 Stack before popping D

After the **pop** operation, the stack is as shown in Figure 18–11.

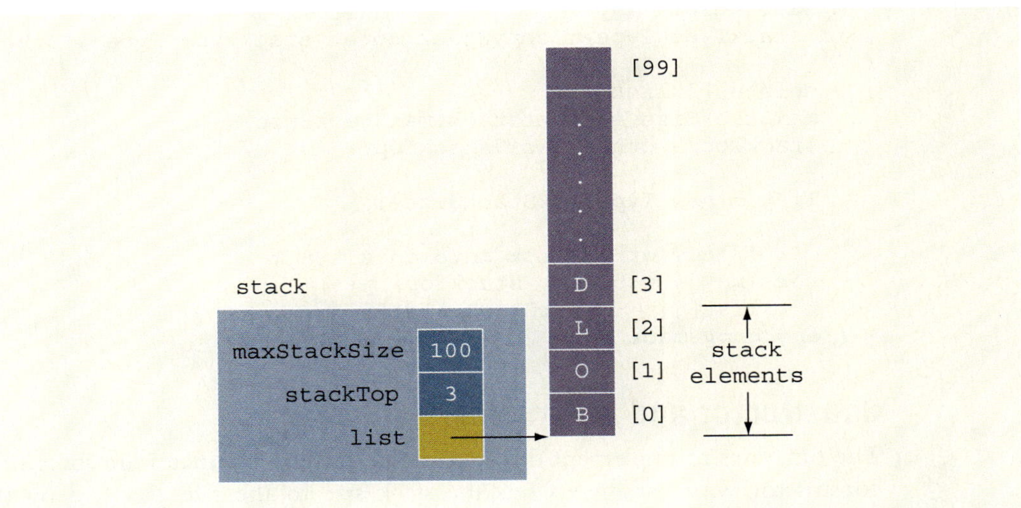

FIGURE 18-11 Stack after popping D

The definition of the function pop is:

```cpp
template <class Type>
void stackType<Type>::pop()
{
    if (!isEmptyStack())
        stackTop--;                 //decrement stackTop
    else
        cout << "Cannot remove from an empty stack." << endl;
}//end pop
```

If we try to remove an item from an empty stack, the resulting condition is called an **underflow**. Error checking for an underflow can be handled in different ways. One way is as shown in the definition of the function pop. Or we can check for an underflow before calling the function pop, as shown next (assuming stack is an object of type stackType):

```cpp
if (!stack.isEmptyStack())
    stack.pop();
```

Copy Stack

The function copyStack makes a copy of a stack. The stack to be copied is passed as a parameter to the function copyStack. We will, in fact, use this function to implement the copy constructor and overload the assignment operator. The definition of this function is:

```cpp
template <class Type>
void stackType<Type>::copyStack(const stackType<Type>& otherStack)
{
    delete [] list;
    maxStackSize = otherStack.maxStackSize;
    stackTop = otherStack.stackTop;

    list = new Type[maxStackSize];

        //copy otherStack into this stack
    for (int j = 0; j < stackTop; j++)
        list[j] = otherStack.list[j];
} //end copyStack
```

Constructor and Destructor

The functions to implement the constructor and the destructor are straightforward. The constructor with parameters sets the stack size to the size specified by the user, sets stackTop to 0, and creates an appropriate array in which to store the stack elements. If the user does not specify the size of the array in which to store the stack elements, the constructor uses the default value, which is 100, to create an array of size 100. The destructor simply deallocates the memory occupied by the array (that is, the stack) and sets stackTop to 0. The definitions of the constructor and destructor are:

```cpp
template <class Type>
stackType<Type>::stackType(int stackSize)
{
    if (stackSize <= 0)
    {
        cout << "Size of the array to hold the stack must "
             << "be positive." << endl;
        cout << "Creating an array of size 100." << endl;

        maxStackSize = 100;
    }
    else
        maxStackSize = stackSize;     //set the stack size to
                                      //the value specified by
                                      //the parameter stackSize

    stackTop = 0;                     //set stackTop to 0
    list = new Type[maxStackSize];    //create the array to
                                      //hold the stack elements
}//end constructor

template <class Type>
stackType<Type>::~stackType() //destructor
{
    delete [] list; //deallocate the memory occupied
                    //by the array
}//end destructor
```

Copy Constructor

The copy constructor is called when a stack object is passed as a (value) parameter to a function. It copies the values of the member variables of the actual parameter into the corresponding member variables of the formal parameter. Its definition is:

```cpp
template <class Type>
stackType<Type>::stackType(const stackType<Type>& otherStack)
{
    list = NULL;

    copyStack(otherStack);
}//end copy constructor
```

Overloading the Assignment Operator (=)

Recall that for classes with pointer member variables, the assignment operator must be explicitly overloaded. The definition of the function to overload the assignment operator for the class stackType is:

```cpp
template <class Type>
const stackType<Type>& stackType<Type>::operator=
                       (const stackType<Type>& otherStack)
```

```cpp
{
    if (this != &otherStack)  //avoid self-copy
        copyStack(otherStack);

    return *this;
} //end operator=
```

Stack Header File

Now that you know how to implement the stack operations, you can put the definitions of the class and the functions to implement the stack operations together to create the stack header file. For the sake of completeness, we next describe the header file. (To save space, only the definition of the class is shown; no documentation is provided.) Suppose that the name of the header file containing the definition of the **class** stackType is myStack.h. We will refer to this header file in any program that uses a stack.

```cpp
//Header file: myStack.h

#ifndef H_StackType
#define H_StackType

#include <iostream>
#include <cassert>

#include "stackADT.h"

using namespace std;

template <class Type>
class stackType: public stackADT<Type>
{
public:
    const stackType<Type>& operator=(const stackType<Type>&);

    void initializeStack();

    bool isEmptyStack() const;

    bool isFullStack() const;

    void push(const Type& newItem);

    Type top() const;

    void pop();

    stackType(int stackSize = 100);

    stackType(const stackType<Type>& otherStack);

    ~stackType();
```

```cpp
private:
    int maxStackSize; //variable to store the maximum stack size
    int stackTop;     //variable to point to the top of the stack
    Type *list;       //pointer to the array that holds the
                      //stack elements

    void copyStack(const stackType<Type>& otherStack);
};

template <class Type>
void stackType<Type>::initializeStack()
{
    stackTop = 0;
}//end initializeStack

template <class Type>
bool stackType<Type>::isEmptyStack() const
{
    return (stackTop == 0);
}//end isEmptyStack

template <class Type>
bool stackType<Type>::isFullStack() const
{
    return (stackTop == maxStackSize);
} //end isFullStack

template <class Type>
void stackType<Type>::push(const Type& newItem)
{
    if (!isFullStack())
    {
        list[stackTop] = newItem;    //add newItem to the
                                     //top of the stack
        stackTop++; //increment stackTop
    }
    else
        cout << "Cannot add to a full stack." << endl;
}//end push

template <class Type>
Type stackType<Type>::top() const
{
    assert(stackTop != 0);        //if stack is empty,
                                  //terminate the program
    return list[stackTop - 1];    //return the element of the
                                  //stack indicated by
                                  //stackTop - 1
}//end top

template <class Type>
void stackType<Type>::pop()
{
    if (!isEmptyStack())
        stackTop--;                   //decrement stackTop
    else
        cout << "Cannot remove from an empty stack." << endl;
}//end pop
```

```cpp
template <class Type>
stackType<Type>::stackType(int stackSize)
{
    if (stackSize <= 0)
    {
        cout << "Size of the array to hold the stack must "
             << "be positive." << endl;
        cout << "Creating an array of size 100." << endl;

        maxStackSize = 100;
    }
    else
        maxStackSize = stackSize;       //set the stack size to
                                        //the value specified by
                                        //the parameter stackSize

    stackTop = 0;                       //set stackTop to 0
    list = new Type[maxStackSize];      //create the array to
                                        //hold the stack elements
}//end constructor

template <class Type>
stackType<Type>::~stackType()  //destructor
{
    delete [] list;  //deallocate the memory occupied
                     //by the array
}//end destructor

template <class Type>
void stackType<Type>::copyStack(const stackType<Type>& otherStack)
{
    delete [] list;
    maxStackSize = otherStack.maxStackSize;
    stackTop = otherStack.stackTop;

    list = new Type[maxStackSize];

        //copy otherStack into this stack
    for (int j = 0; j < stackTop; j++)
        list[j] = otherStack.list[j];
} //end copyStack


template <class Type>
stackType<Type>::stackType(const stackType<Type>& otherStack)
{
    list = NULL;

    copyStack(otherStack);
}//end copy constructor

template <class Type>
const stackType<Type>& stackType<Type>::operator=
                            (const stackType<Type>& otherStack)
{
    if (this != &otherStack) //avoid self-copy
        copyStack(otherStack);
```

```
        return *this;
} //end operator=

#endif
```

EXAMPLE 18-1

Before we give a programming example, let us first write a simple program that uses the
`class stackType` and tests some of the stack operations. Among others, we will test
the assignment operator and the copy constructor. The program and its output are as
follows:

```
//Program to test the various operations of a stack

#include <iostream>
#include "myStack.h"

using namespace std;

void testCopyConstructor(stackType<int> otherStack);

int main()
{
    stackType<int> stack(50);
    stackType<int> copyStack(50);
    stackType<int> dummyStack(100);

    stack.initializeStack();
    stack.push(23);
    stack.push(45);
    stack.push(38);
    copyStack = stack;   //copy stack into copyStack

    cout << "The elements of copyStack: ";

    while (!copyStack.isEmptyStack())   //print copyStack
    {
        cout << copyStack.top() << " ";
        copyStack.pop();
    }
    cout << endl;

    copyStack = stack;
    testCopyConstructor(stack);   //test the copy constructor

    if (!stack.isEmptyStack())
        cout << "The original stack is not empty." << endl
             << "The top element of the original stack: "
             << copyStack.top() << endl;

    dummyStack = stack;   //copy stack into dummyStack
```

```cpp
    cout << "The elements of dummyStack: ";

    while (!dummyStack.isEmptyStack())   //print dummyStack
    {
        cout << dummyStack.top() << " ";
        dummyStack.pop();
    }
    cout << endl;

    return 0;
}

void testCopyConstructor(stackType<int> otherStack)
{
    if (!otherStack.isEmptyStack())
        cout << "otherStack is not empty." << endl
             << "The top element of otherStack: "
             << otherStack.top() << endl;
}
```

Sample Run:

```
The elements of copyStack: 38 45 23
otherStack is not empty.
The top element of otherStack: 38
The original stack is not empty.
The top element of the original stack: 38
The elements of dummyStack: 38 45 23
```

It is recommended that you do a walk-through of this program.

PROGRAMMING EXAMPLE: Highest GPA

In this example, we write a C++ program that reads a data file consisting of each student's GPA followed by the student's name. The program then prints the highest GPA and the names of all the students who received that GPA. The program scans the input file only once. Moreover, we assume that there is a maximum of 100 students in the class.

Input The program reads an input file consisting of each student's GPA, followed by the student's name. Sample data is:

```
3.5 Bill
3.6 John
2.7 Lisa
3.9 Kathy
3.4 Jason
3.9 David
3.4 Jack
```

Output The highest GPA and all the names associated with the highest GPA. For example, for the above data, the highest GPA is `3.9` and the students with that GPA are `Kathy` and `David`.

PROBLEM ANALYSIS AND ALGORITHM DESIGN

We read the first GPA and the name of the student. Because this data is the first item read, it is the highest GPA so far. Next, we read the second GPA and the name of the student. We then compare this (second) GPA with the highest GPA so far. Three cases arise:

1. The new GPA is greater than the highest GPA so far. In this case, we:

   a. Update the value of the highest GPA so far.

   b. Initialize the stack—that is, remove the names of the students from the stack.

   c. Save the name of the student having the highest GPA so far in the stack.

2. The new GPA is equal to the highest GPA so far. In this case, we add the name of the new student to the stack.

3. The new GPA is smaller than the highest GPA so far. In this case, we discard the name of the student having this grade.

We then read the next GPA and the name of the student, and repeat Steps 1 through 3. We continue this process until we reach the end of the input file.

From this discussion, it is clear that we need the following variables:

```cpp
double GPA;            //variable to hold the current GPA
double highestGPA;     //variable to hold the highest GPA
string name;           //variable to hold the name of the student
stackType<string> stack(100); //object to implement the stack
```

The preceding discussion translates into the following algorithm:

1. Declare the variables and initialize stack.

2. Open the input file.

3. If the input file does not exist, exit the program.

4. Set the output of the floating-point numbers to a fixed decimal format with a decimal point and trailing zeroes. Also, set the precision to two decimal places.

5. Read the GPA and the student name.

6. `highestGPA = GPA;`

7. `while` (not end of file)

    {

       7.1. `if` (GPA > highestGPA)

           {

              7.1.1. `clearstack(stack);`

              7.1.2. `push(stack, student name);`

              7.1.3. `highestGPA = GPA;`

           }

       7.2. `else`

            `if` (GPA is equal to highestGPA)

               `push(stack, student name);`

       7.3. Read GPA and student name;

    }

8. Output the highest GPA.

9. Output the names of the students having the highest GPA.

```cpp
//Program Highest GPA

#include <iostream>
#include <iomanip>
#include <fstream>
#include <string>

#include "myStack.h"

using namespace std;

int main()
{
        //Step 1
    double GPA;
    double highestGPA;
    string name;

    stackType<string> stack(100);

    ifstream infile;

    infile.open("a:\\HighestGPAData.txt");          //Step 2

    if (!infile)                                    //Step 3
    {
        cout << "The input file does not "
             << "exist. Program terminates!"
```

```cpp
                    << endl;
        return 1;
    }

    cout << fixed << showpoint;                      //Step 4
    cout << setprecision(2);                         //Step 4

    infile >> GPA >> name;                           //Step 5

    highestGPA = GPA;                                //Step 6

    while (infile)                                   //Step 7
    {
        if (GPA > highestGPA)                        //Step 7.1
        {
            stack.initializeStack();                 //Step 7.1.1

            if (!stack.isFullStack())                //Step 7.1.2
                stack.push(name);

            highestGPA = GPA;                         //Step 7.1.3
        }
        else if (GPA == highestGPA)                  //Step 7.2
            if (!stack.isFullStack())
                stack.push(name);
            else
            {
                cout << "Stack overflows. "
                     << "Program terminates!"
                     << endl;
                return 1;   //exit program
            }
        infile >> GPA >> name;                       //Step 7.3
    }

    cout << "Highest GPA = " << highestGPA
         << endl;                                    //Step 8
    cout << "The students holding the "
         << "highest GPA are:" << endl;

    while (!stack.isEmptyStack())                    //Step 9
    {
        cout << stack.top() << endl;
        stack.pop();
    }

    cout << endl;

    return 0;
}
```

Sample Run:

Input File (a:HighestGPAData.txt)

```
3.4  Randy
3.2  Kathy
2.5  Colt
3.4  Tom
3.8  Ron
3.8  Mickey
3.6  Peter
3.5  Donald
3.8  Cindy
3.7  Dome
3.9  Andy
3.8  Fox
3.9  Minnie
2.7  Gilda
3.9  Vinay
3.4  Danny
```

Output

```
Highest GPA = 3.90
The students holding the highest GPA are:
Vinay
Minnie
Andy
```

Note that the names of the students with the highest GPA are output in the reverse order, relative to the order they appear in the input, due to the fact that top element of the stack is the last element added to the stack.

Linked Implementation of Stacks

Because an array size is fixed, in the array (linear) representation of a stack, only a fixed number of elements can be pushed onto the stack. If in a program the number of elements to be pushed exceeds the size of the array, the program may terminate in an error. We must overcome these problems.

We have seen that by using pointer variables we can dynamically allocate and deallocate memory, and by using linked lists we can dynamically organize data (such as an ordered list). Next, we will use these concepts to implement a stack dynamically.

Recall that in the linear representation of a stack, the value of `stackTop` indicates the number of elements in the stack, and the value of `stackTop - 1` points to the top item in the stack. With the help of `stackTop`, we can do several things: find the top element, check whether the stack is empty, and so on.

Similar to the linear representation, in a linked representation `stackTop` is used to locate the top element in the stack. However, there is a slight difference. In the former case, `stackTop` gives the index of the array. In the latter case, `stackTop` gives the address (memory location) of the top element of the stack.

The following class implements the functions of the abstract **class** `stackADT`:

```cpp
//Definition of the node
template <class Type>
struct nodeType
{
    Type info;
    nodeType<Type> *link;
};

template <class Type>
class linkedStackType: public stackADT<Type>
{
public:
    const linkedStackType<Type>& operator=
                            (const linkedStackType<Type>&);
      //Overload the assignment operator.

    bool isEmptyStack() const;
      //Function to determine whether the stack is empty.
      //Postcondition: Returns true if the stack is empty;
      //               otherwise returns false.

    bool isFullStack() const;
      //Function to determine whether the stack is full.
      //Postcondition: Returns false.

    void initializeStack();
      //Function to initialize the stack to an empty state.
      //Postcondition: The stack elements are removed;
      //               stackTop = NULL;

    void push(const Type& newItem);
      //Function to add newItem to the stack.
      //Precondition: The stack exists and is not full.
      //Postcondition: The stack is changed and newItem
      //               is added to the top of the stack.

    Type top() const;
      //Function to return the top element of the stack.
      //Precondition: The stack exists and is not empty.
      //Postcondition: If the stack is empty, the program
      //               terminates; otherwise, the top
      //               element of the stack is returned.
```

```
    void pop();
      //Function to remove the top element of the stack.
      //Precondition: The stack exists and is not empty.
      //Postcondition: The stack is changed and the top
      //               element is removed from the stack.

    linkedStackType();
      //Default constructor
      //Postcondition: stackTop = NULL;

    linkedStackType(const linkedStackType<Type>& otherStack);
      //Copy constructor

    ~linkedStackType();
      //Destructor
      //Postcondition: All the elements of the stack are
      //               removed from the stack.

private:
    nodeType<Type> *stackTop; //pointer to the stack

    void copyStack(const linkedStackType<Type>& otherStack);
      //Function to make a copy of otherStack.
      //Postcondition: A copy of otherStack is created and
      //               assigned to this stack.
};
```

NOTE In this linked implementation of stacks, the memory to store the stack elements is allocated dynamically. Logically, the stack is never full. The stack is full only if we run out of memory space. Therefore, in reality, the function `isFullStack` does not apply to linked implementation of stacks. However, the **class** `linkedStackType` must provide the definition of the function `isFullStack`, because it is defined in the parent abstract **class** `stackADT`.

We leave the UML class diagram of the **class** `linkedStackType` as an exercise for you. (See Exercise 22 at the end of this chapter.)

EXAMPLE 18-2

Empty stack: Suppose that `stack` is an object of type `linkedStackType` (see Figure 18-12).

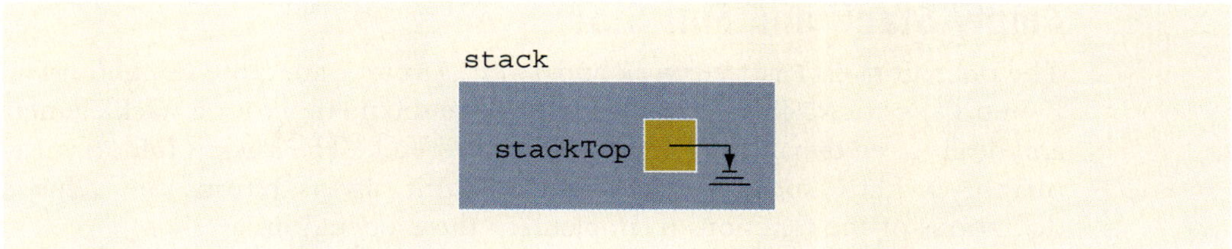

FIGURE 18-12 Empty linked stack

Nonempty stack (see Figure 18–13).

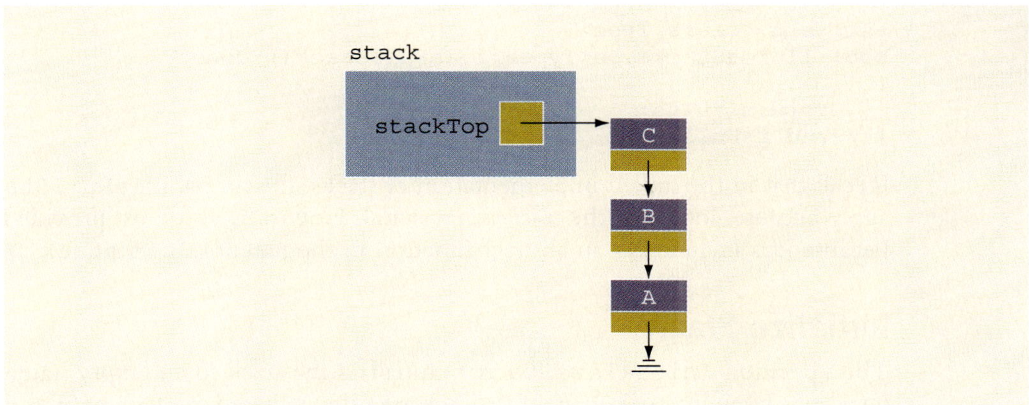

FIGURE 18-13 Nonempty linked stack

In Figure 18–13, the top element of the stack is C; that is, the last element pushed onto the stack is C.

Next, we discuss the definitions of the functions to implement the operations of a linked stack.

Default Constructor

The first operation that we consider is the default constructor. The default constructor initializes the stack to an empty state when a stack object is declared. Thus, this function sets `stackTop` to NULL. The definition of this function is:

```cpp
template <class Type>
linkedStackType<Type>::linkedStackType()
{
    stackTop = NULL;
}
```

Empty Stack and Full Stack

The operations `isEmptyStack` and `isFullStack` are quite straightforward. The stack is empty if `stackTop` is `NULL`. Also, because the memory for a stack element is allocated and deallocated dynamically, the stack is never full. (The stack is full only if we run out of memory.) Thus, the function `isFullStack` always returns the value **false**. The definitions of the functions to implement these operations are:

```
template <class Type>
bool linkedStackType<Type>::isEmptyStack() const
{
    return (stackTop == NULL);
} //end isEmptyStack

template <class Type>
bool linkedStackType<Type>:: isFullStack() const
{
    return false;
} //end isFullStack
```

Recall that in the linked implementation of stacks, the function `isFullStack` does not apply because, logically, the stack is never full. However, you must provide its definition because it is included as an abstract function in the parent **class** `stackADT`.

Initialize Stack

The operation `initializeStack` reinitializes the stack to an empty state. Because the stack may contain some elements and we are using a linked implementation of a stack, we must deallocate the memory occupied by the stack elements and set `stackTop` to `NULL`. The definition of this function is:

```
template <class Type>
void linkedStackType<Type>:: initializeStack()
{
    nodeType<Type> *temp; //pointer to delete the node

    while (stackTop != NULL)  //while there are elements in
                              //the stack
    {
        temp = stackTop;       //set temp to point to the
                               //current node
        stackTop = stackTop->link;  //advance stackTop to the
                                    //next node
        delete temp;      //deallocate memory occupied by temp
    }
} //end initializeStack
```

Next, we consider the `push`, `top`, and `pop` operations. From Figure 18-13, it is clear that the `newElement` will be added (in the case of `push`) at the beginning of the linked list pointed to by `stackTop`. In the case of `pop`, the node pointed to by `stackTop` will be removed. In both cases, the value of the pointer `stackTop` is updated. The operation `top` returns the `info` of the node that `stackTop` is pointing to.

Push

Consider the stack shown in Figure 18-14.

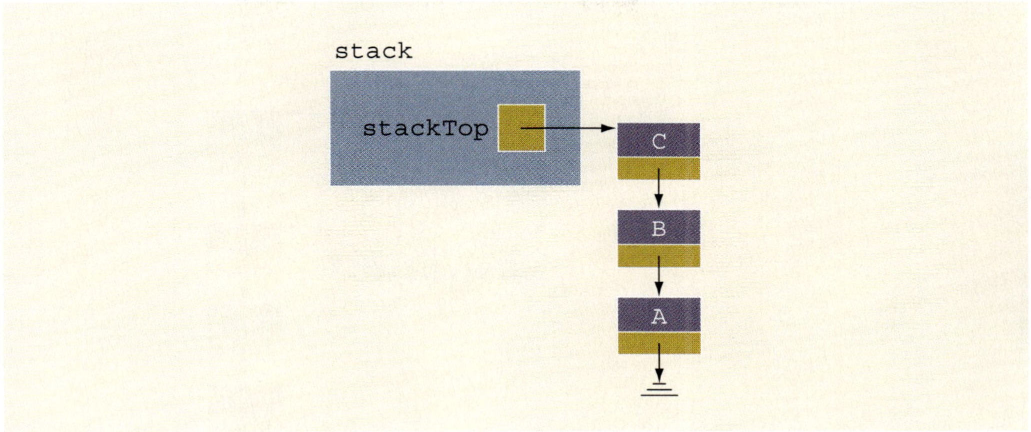

FIGURE 18-14 Stack before the `push` operation

Assume that the new element to be pushed is `'D'`. First, we allocate memory for the new node. We then store `'D'` in the new node and insert the new node at the beginning of the list. Finally, we update the value of `stackTop`. The statements:

```
newNode = new nodeType<Type>; //create the new node
newNode->info = newElement;
```

create a node, store the address of the node into the variable `newNode`, and store `newElement` into the `info` field of `newNode`. Thus, we have the situation shown in Figure 18-15.

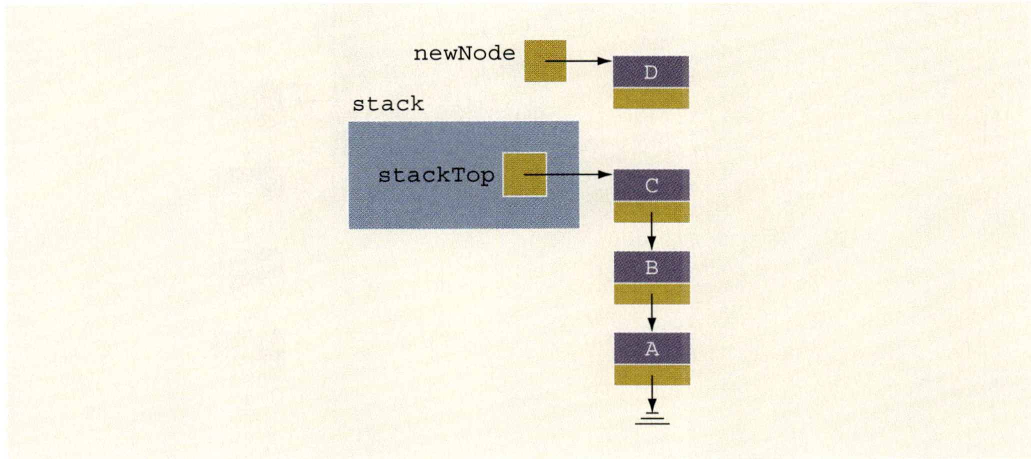

FIGURE 18-15 Stack and `newNode`

The statement:

```
newNode->link = stackTop;
```

inserts **newNode** at the top of the stack, as shown in Figure 18-16.

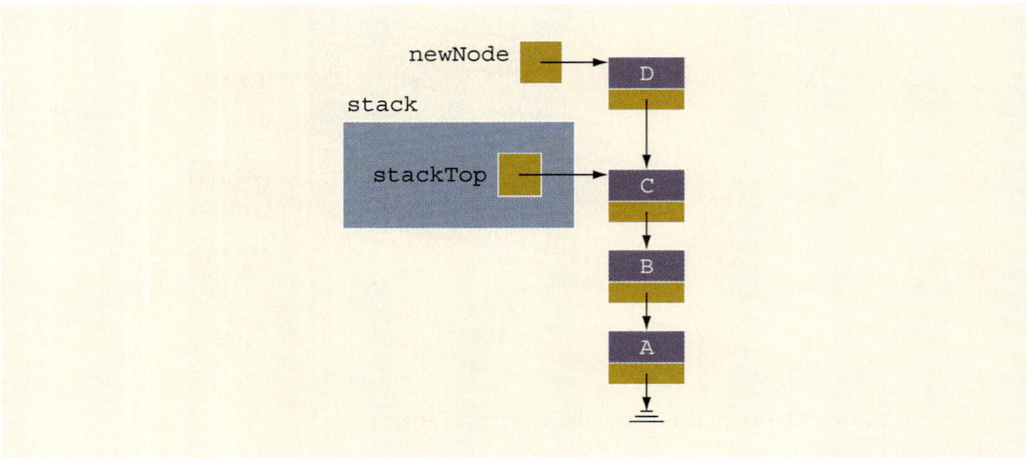

FIGURE 18-16 Stack after the statement `newNode->link = stackTop;` executes

Finally, the statement:

```
stackTop = newNode;
```

updates the value of **stackTop**, which results in Figure 18-17.

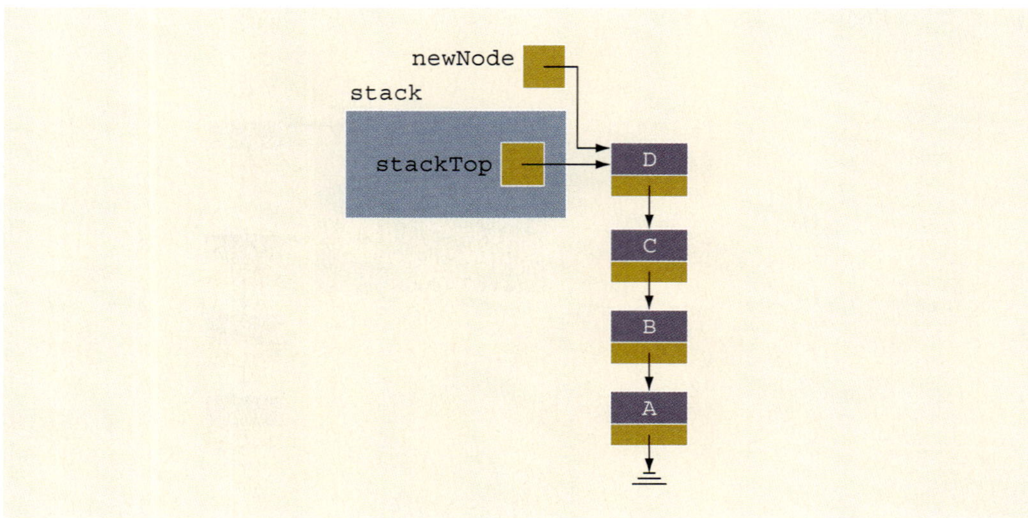

FIGURE 18-17 Stack after the statement `stackTop = newNode;` executes

The definition of the function **push** is:

```cpp
template <class Type>
void linkedStackType<Type>::push(const Type& newElement)
{
    nodeType<Type> *newNode;   //pointer to create the new node

    newNode = new nodeType<Type>; //create the node

    newNode->info = newElement; //store newElement in the node
    newNode->link = stackTop; //insert newNode before stackTop
    stackTop = newNode;         //set stackTop to point to the
                                //top node
} //end push
```

We do not need to check whether the stack is full before we push an element onto the stack because in this implementation, logically, the stack is never full.

Return the Top Element

The operation to return the top element of the stack is quite straightforward. Its definition is:

```cpp
template <class Type>
Type linkedStackType<Type>::top() const
{
    assert(stackTop != NULL); //if stack is empty,
                              //terminate the program
    return stackTop->info;    //return the top element
}//end top
```

Pop

Now we consider the **pop** operation, which removes the top element of the stack. Consider the stack shown in Figure 18-18.

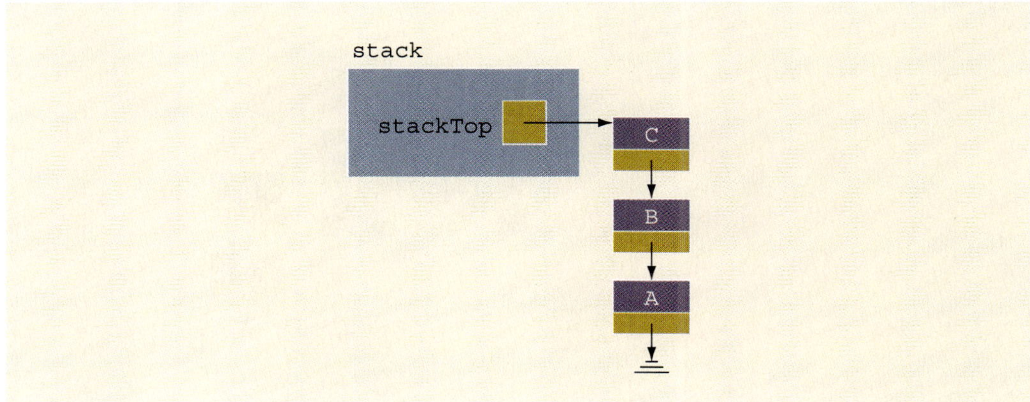

FIGURE 18-18   Stack before the pop operation

The statement:

```
temp = stackTop;
```

makes `temp` point to the top of the stack, and the statement:

```
stackTop = stackTop->link;
```

makes the second element of the stack become the top element of the stack. We then have the situation shown in Figure 18-19.

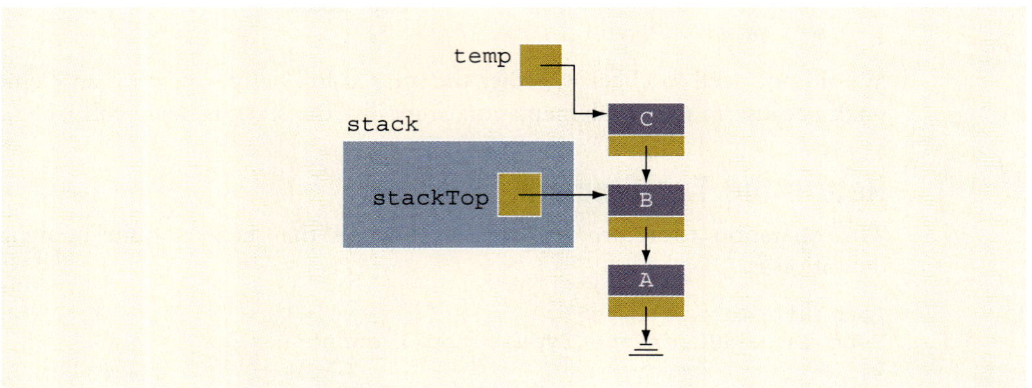

FIGURE 18-19 Stack after the statement `stackTop = stackTop->link;` executes

Finally, the statement:

```
delete temp;
```

deallocates the memory pointed to by `temp`. Figure 18-20 shows the resulting stack.

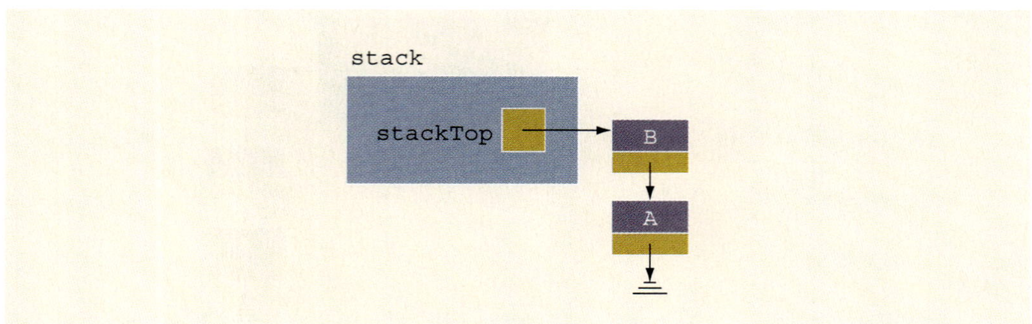

FIGURE 18-20 Stack after the statement **delete** `temp;` executes

The definition of the function pop is:

```
template <class Type>
void linkedStackType<Type>::pop()
{
    nodeType<Type> *temp;    //pointer to deallocate memory

    if (stackTop != NULL)
    {
        temp = stackTop;   //set temp to point to the top node

        stackTop = stackTop->link;   //advance stackTop to the
                                     //next node
        delete temp;     //delete the top node
    }
    else
        cout << "Cannot remove from an empty stack." << endl;
}//end pop
```

Copy Stack

The function copyStack makes an identical copy of a stack. Its definition is similar to
the definition of copyList for linked lists, given in Chapter 17. The definition of the
function copyStack is:

```
template <class Type>
void linkedStackType<Type>::copyStack
                    (const linkedStackType<Type>& otherStack)
{
    nodeType<Type> *newNode, *current, *last;

    if (stackTop != NULL) //if stack is nonempty, make it empty
        initializeStack();

    if (otherStack.stackTop == NULL)
        stackTop = NULL;
    else
    {
        current = otherStack.stackTop;   //set current to point
                                         //to the stack to be copied

            //copy the stackTop element of the stack
        stackTop = new nodeType<Type>;   //create the node

        stackTop->info = current->info; //copy the info
        stackTop->link = NULL;   //set the link field of the
                                 //node to NULL
        last = stackTop;         //set last to point to the node
        current = current->link;     //set current to point to
                                     //the next node
```

```
            //copy the remaining stack
        while (current != NULL)
        {
            newNode = new nodeType<Type>;

            newNode->info = current->info;
            newNode->link = NULL;
            last->link = newNode;
            last = newNode;
            current = current->link;
        }//end while
    }//end else
} //end copyStack
```

Constructors and Destructors

We have already discussed the default constructor. To complete the implementation of the stack operations, next we give the definitions of the functions to implement the copy constructor and the destructor, and to overload the assignment operator. (These functions are similar to those discussed for linked lists in Chapter 17.)

```
    //copy constructor
template <class Type>
linkedStackType<Type>::linkedStackType(
                    const linkedStackType<Type>& otherStack)
{
    stackTop = NULL;
    copyStack(otherStack);
}//end copy constructor

    //destructor
template <class Type>
linkedStackType<Type>::~linkedStackType()
{
    initializeStack();
}//end destructor
```

Overloading the Assignment Operator (=)

The definition of the function to overload the assignment operator for the `class` `linkedStackType` is:

```
template <class Type>
const linkedStackType<Type>& linkedStackType<Type>::operator=
                    (const linkedStackType<Type>& otherStack)
{
    if (this != &otherStack)  //avoid self-copy
        copyStack(otherStack);

    return *this;
}//end operator=
```

The definition of a stack, and the functions to implement the stack operations discussed previously, are generic. Also, as in the case of an array representation of a stack, in the linked representation of a stack we must put the definition of the stack, and the functions to implement the stack operations, together in a (header) file. A client's program can include this header file via the `include` statement.

Example 18-3 illustrates how a `linkedStack` object is used in a program.

EXAMPLE 18-3

We assume that the definition of the `class linkedStackType`, and the functions to implement the stack operations, are included in the header file `"linkedStack.h"`.

```cpp
//This program tests various operations of a linked stack

#include <iostream>
#include "linkedStack.h"

using namespace std;

void testCopy(linkedStackType<int> OStack);

int main()
{
    linkedStackType<int> stack;
    linkedStackType<int> otherStack;
    linkedStackType<int> newStack;

        //Add elements into stack
    stack.push(34);
    stack.push(43);
    stack.push(27);

        //Use the assignment operator to copy the elements
        //of stack into newStack
    newStack = stack;

    cout << "After the assignment operator, newStack: "
         << endl;

        //Output the elements of newStack
    while (!newStack.isEmptyStack())
    {
        cout << newStack.top() << endl;
        newStack.pop();
    }

        //Use the assignment operator to copy the elements
        //of stack into otherStack
    otherStack = stack;
```

```cpp
    cout << "Testing the copy constructor." << endl;

    testCopy(otherStack);

    cout << "After the copy constructor, otherStack: " << endl;

    while (!otherStack.isEmptyStack())
    {
        cout << otherStack.top() << endl;
        otherStack.pop();
    }

    return 0;
}

    //Function to test the copy constructor
void testCopy(linkedStackType<int> OStack)
{
    cout << "Stack in the function testCopy:" << endl;

    while (!OStack.isEmptyStack())
    {
        cout << OStack.top() << endl;
        OStack.pop();
    }
}
```

Sample Run:

```
After the assignment operator, newStack:
27
43
34
Testing the copy constructor.
Stack in the function testCopy:
27
43
34
After the copy constructor, otherStack:
27
43
34
```

Stack as Derived from the `class` unorderedLinkedList

If we compare the push function of the stack with the `insertFirst` function
discussed for general lists in Chapter 17, we see that the algorithms to implement these
operations are similar. A comparison of other functions—such as `initializeStack`

and `initializeList`, `isEmptyList` and `isEmptyStack`, and so on—suggests that the `class linkedStackType` can be derived from the `class linkedListType`. Moreover, the functions `pop` and `isFullStack` can be implemented as in the previous section. Note that the `class linkedListType` is an abstract and does not implement all the operations. However, the `class unorderedLinkedListType` is derived from the the `class linkedListType` and provides the definitions of the abstract functions of the `class linkedListType`. Therefore, we can derive the `class linkedStackType` from the `class unorderedLinkedListType`.

Next, we define the `class linkedStackType` that is derived from the `class unorderedLinkedList`. The definitions of the functions to implement the stack operations are also given:

```cpp
#include <iostream>
#include "unorderedLinkedList.h"

using namespace std;

template <class Type>
class linkedStackType: public unorderedLinkedList<Type>
{
public:
    void initializeStack();
    bool isEmptyStack() const;
    bool isFullStack() const;
    void push(const Type& newItem);
    Type top() const;
    void pop();
};

template <class Type>
void linkedStackType<Type>::initializeStack()
{
    unorderedLinkedList<Type>::initializeList();
}

template <class Type>
bool linkedStackType<Type>::isEmptyStack() const
{
    return unorderedLinkedList<Type>::isEmptyList();
}

template <class Type>
bool linkedStackType<Type>::isFullStack() const
{
    return false;
}

template <class Type>
void linkedStackType<Type>::push(const Type& newElement)
{
    unorderedLinkedList<Type>::insertFirst(newElement);
}
```

```
template <class Type>
Type linkedStackType<Type>::top() const
{
    return unorderedLinkedList<Type>::front();
}

template <class Type>
void linkedStackType<Type>::pop()
{
    nodeType<Type> *temp;

    temp = first;
    first = first->link;
    delete temp;
}
```

Application of Stacks: Postfix Expressions Calculator

The usual notation for writing arithmetic expressions (the notation we learned in elementary school) is called **infix** notation, in which the operator is written between the operands. For example, in the expression $a + b$, the operator $+$ is between the operands a and b. In infix notation, the operators have precedence. That is, we must evaluate expressions from left to right, and multiplication and division have higher precedence than do addition and subtraction. If we want to evaluate the expression in a different order, we must include parentheses. For example, in the expression $a + b \star c$, we first evaluate $\star$ using the operands b and c, and then we evaluate $+$ using the operand a and the result of $b \star c$.

In the early 1920s, the Polish mathematician Jan Lukasiewicz discovered that if operators were written before the operands (**prefix** or **Polish** notation; for example, $+\ a\ b$), the parentheses can be omitted. In the late 1950s, the Australian philosopher and early computer scientist Charles L. Hamblin proposed a scheme in which the operators *follow* the operands (postfix operators), resulting in the **Reverse Polish** notation. This has the advantage that the operators appear in the order required for computation.

For example, the expression:

$a + b \star c$

in a postfix expression is:

$a\ b\ c \star +$

The following example shows various infix expressions and their equivalent postfix expressions.

EXAMPLE 18-4

Infix Expression	Equivalent Postfix Expression
$a + b$	$a\ b +$
$a + b * c$	$a\ b\ c * +$
$a * b + c$	$a\ b * c +$
$(a + b) * c$	$a\ b + c *$
$(a - b) * (c + d)$	$a\ b - c\ d + *$
$(a + b) * (c - d / e) + f$	$a\ b + c\ d\ e / - * f +$

Shortly after Lukasiewicz's discovery, it was realized that postfix notation had important applications in computer science. In fact, many compilers now first translate arithmetic expressions into some form of postfix notation and then translate this postfix expression into machine code. Postfix expressions can be evaluated using the following algorithm:

Scan the expression from left to right. When an operator is found, back up to get the required number of operands, perform the operation, and continue.

Consider the following postfix expression:

6 3 + 2 * =

Let us evaluate this expression using a stack and the previous algorithm. (In the following discussion, we list the postfix expression after each step. The shading indicates the part of the expression that has been processed.)

6 3 + 2 * =

1. Read the first symbol, 6, which is a number. Push the number onto the stack (see Figure 18-21).

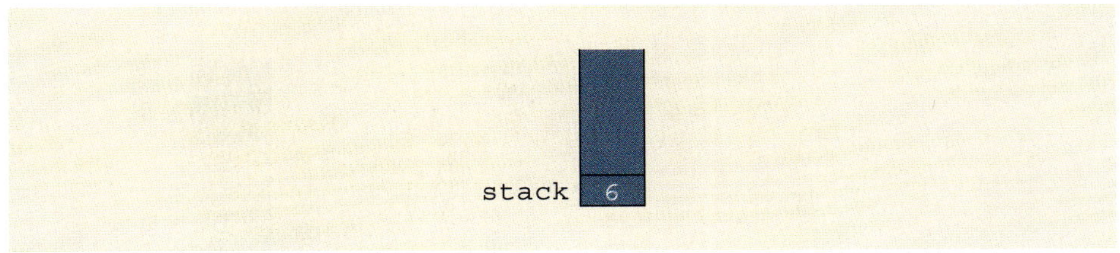

FIGURE 18-21   Stack after pushing 6

6 3 + 2 * =

2. Read the next symbol, 3, which is a number. Push the number onto the stack (see Figure 18-22).

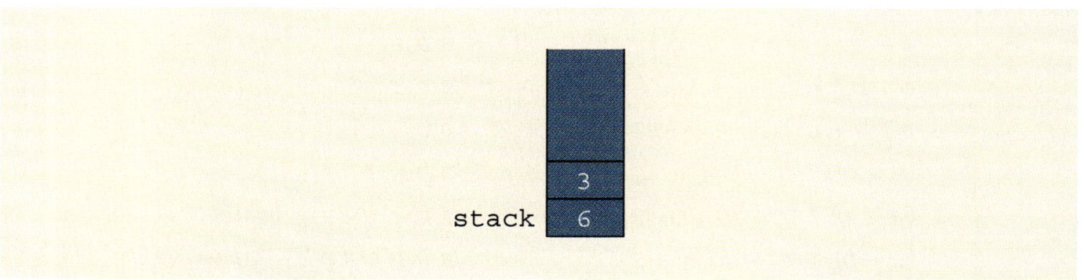

FIGURE 18-22 Stack after pushing 3

`6 3 + 2 * =`

3. Read the next symbol, +, which is an operator. Because an operator requires two operands to be evaluated, pop the stack twice. Perform the operation and put the result back onto the stack (see Figure 18-23).

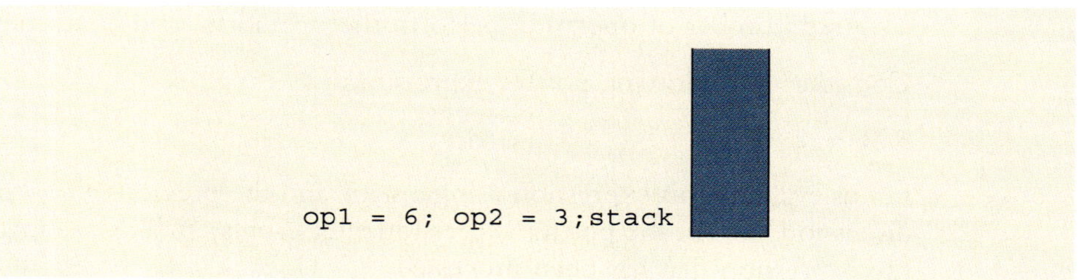

FIGURE 18-23 Stack after popping twice

Perform the operation: `op1 + op2 = 6 + 3 = 9.`

Push the result onto the stack (see Figure 18-24).

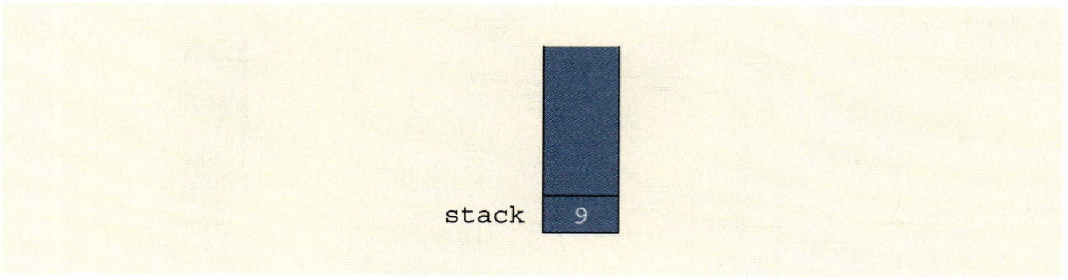

FIGURE 18-24 Stack after pushing the result of `op1 + op2`, which is 9

`6 3 + 2 * =`

4. Read the next symbol, 2, which is a number. Push the number onto the stack (see Figure 18-25).

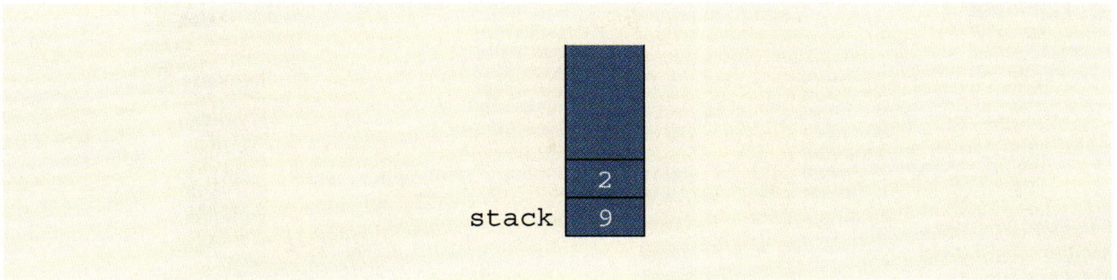

FIGURE 18-25 Stack after pushing 2

6 3 + 2 * =

5. Read the next symbol, *, which is an operator. Because an operator requires two operands to be evaluated, pop the stack twice. Perform the operation and put the result back onto the stack (see Figures 18-26 and 18-27).

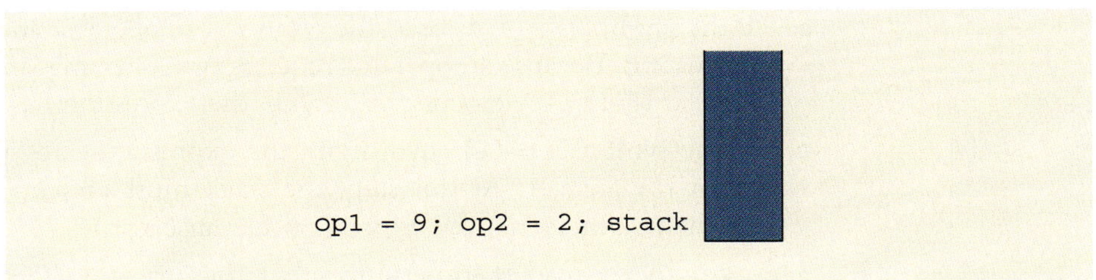

FIGURE 18-26 Stack after popping twice

Perform the operation: op1 * op2 = 9 * 2 = 18.

Push the result onto the stack (see Figure 18-27).

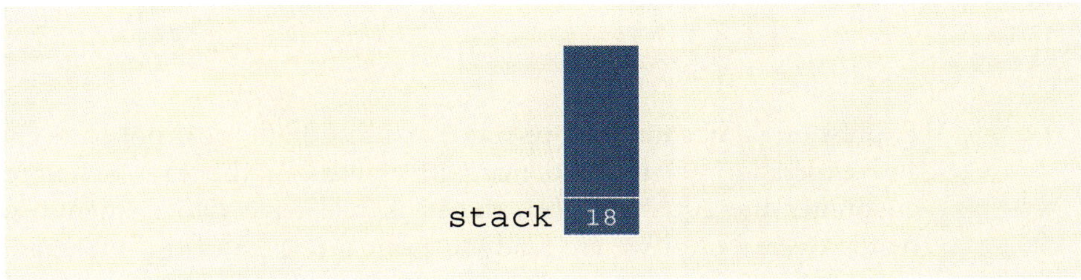

FIGURE 18-27 Stack after pushing the result of op1 * op2, which is 18

6 3 + 2 * =

6.   Scan the next symbol, =, which is the equal sign, indicating the end of the expression. Therefore, print the result. The result of the expression is in the stack, so pop and print are as shown in Figure 18-28.

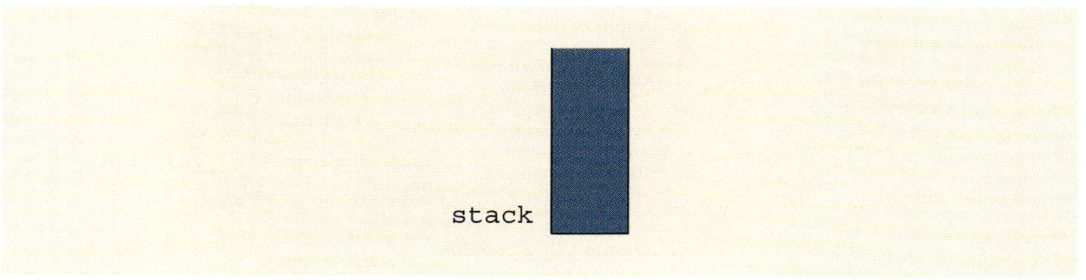

FIGURE 18-28   Stack after popping the element

The value of the expression 6 3 + 2 * = 18.

From this discussion, it is clear that when we read a symbol other than a number, the following cases arise:

1.   The symbol we read is one of the following: +, -, *, /, or =.

a.   If the symbol is +, -, *, or /, the symbol is an operator and so we must evaluate it. Because an operator requires two operands, the stack must have at least two elements; otherwise, the expression has an error.

b.   If the symbol is = (an equal sign), the expression ends and we must print the answer. At this step, the stack must contain exactly one element; otherwise, the expression has an error.

2.   The symbol we read is something other than +, -, *, /, or =. In this case, the expression contains an illegal operator.

It is also clear that when an operand (number) is encountered in an expression, it is pushed onto the stack because the operator comes after the operands.

Consider the following expressions:

a.   7 6 + 3 ; 6 - =

b.   14 + 2 3 * =

c.   14 2 3 + =

Expression (a) has an illegal operator, expression (b) does not have enough operands for +, and expression (c) has too many operands. In the case of expression (c), when we encounter the equal sign (=), the stack will have two elements, and this error cannot be discovered until we are ready to print the value of the expression.

To make the input easier to read, we assume that the postfix expressions are in the following form:

#6 #3 + #2 * =

The symbol # precedes each number in the expression. If the symbol scanned is #, then the next input is a number (that is, an operand). If the symbol scanned is not #, then it is either an operator (may be illegal) or an equal sign (indicating the end of the expression). Furthermore, we assume that each expression contains only the +, -, *, and / operators.

This program outputs the entire postfix expression together with the answer. If the expression has an error, the expression is discarded. In this case, the program outputs the expression together with an appropriate error message. Because an expression may contain an error, we must clear the stack before processing the next expression. Also, the stack must be initialized; that is, the stack must be empty.

Main Algorithm

Following the previous discussion, the main algorithm in pseudocode is:

```
Read the first character
while not the end of input data
{
    a. initialize the stack
    b. process the expression
    c. output result
    d. get the next expression
}
```

To simplify the complexity of the function `main`, we write four functions: `evaluateExpression`, `evaluateOpr`, `discardExp`, and `printResult`. The function `evaluateExpression`, if possible, evaluates the expression and leaves the result in the stack. If the postfix expression is error free, the function `printResult` outputs the result. The function `evaluateOpr` evaluates an operator, and the function `discardExp` discards the current expression if there is any error in the expression.

Function `evaluateExpression`

The function `evaluateExpression` evaluates each postfix expression. Each expression ends with the symbol =. The general algorithm is:

```
while (ch is not = '=') //process each expression
                        //= marks the end of an expression
{
    switch (ch)
    {
    case '#':
        read a number
        output the number;
        push the number onto the stack;
        break;
     default:
        assume that ch is an operation
        evaluate the operation;
    } //end switch
```

```
if no error was found, then
{
    read next ch;
    output ch;
}
else
    Discard the expression
} //end while
```

From this algorithm, it follows that this method has five parameters—one to access the input file, one to access the output file, one to access the stack, one to pass a character of the expression, and one to indicate whether there is an error in the expression. The definition of this function is:

```cpp
void evaluateExpression(ifstream& inpF, ofstream& outF,
                        stackType<double>& stack,
                        char& ch, bool& isExpOk)
{
    double num;

    while (ch != '=')
    {
        switch (ch)
        {
        case '#':
            inpF >> num;
            outF << num << " ";
            if (!stack.isFullStack())
                stack.push(num);
            else
            {
                cout << "Stack overflow. "
                     << "Program terminates!" << endl;
                exit(0);   //terminate the program
            }

            break;
        default:
            evaluateOpr(outF, stack, ch, isExpOk);
        }//end switch

        if (isExpOk) //if no error
        {
            inpF >> ch;
            outF << ch;

            if (ch != '#')
                outF << " ";
        }
```

```
            else
                discardExp(inpF, outF, ch);
        } //end while (!= '=')
}
```

Note that the function **exit** terminates the program.

Function `evaluateOpr`

This function (if possible) evaluates an expression. Two operands are needed to evaluate
an operation, and operands are saved in the stack. Therefore, the stack must contain at
least two numbers. If the stack contains fewer than two numbers, then the expression
has an error. In this case, the entire expression is discarded and an appropriate message
is printed. This function also checks for any illegal operations. In pseudocode, this
function is:

```
if stack is empty
{
    error in the expression
    set expressionOk to false
}
else
{
    retrieve the top element of stack into op2
    pop stack
    if stack is empty
    {
        error in the expression
        set expressionOk to false
    }
    else
    {
        retrieve the top element of stack into op1
        pop stack

            //If the operation is legal, perform the
            //operation and push the result onto the stack.
        switch (ch)
        {
        case '+':
            //Perform the operation and push the result
            //onto the stack.
            stack.push(op1 + op2);
            break;
        case '-':
            //Perform the operation and push the result
            //onto the stack.
            stack.push(op1 - op2);
            break;
```

```
    case '*':
           //Perform the operation and push the
           //result onto the stack.
         stack.push(op1 * op2);
         break;
    case '/':
           //If (op2 != 0), perform the operation and
           //push the result onto the stack.
         stack.push(op1 / op2);

           //Otherwise, report the error.
           //Set expressionOk to false.
         break;
    otherwise operation is illegal
       {
           output an appropriate message;
           set expressionOk to false
       }
    } //end switch
}
```

Following this pseudocode, the definition of the function `evaluateOpr` is:

```cpp
void evaluateOpr(ofstream& out, stackType<double>& stack,
                char& ch, bool& isExpOk)
{
    double op1, op2;

    if (stack.isEmptyStack())
    {
        out << " (Not enough operands)";
        isExpOk = false;
    }
    else
    {
        op2 = stack.top();
        stack.pop();

        if (stack.isEmptyStack())
        {
            out << " (Not enough operands)";
            isExpOk = false;
        }
        else
        {
            op1 = stack.top();
            stack.pop();

            switch (ch)
            {
            case '+':
                stack.push(op1 + op2);
                break;
```

```cpp
            case '-':
                stack.push(op1 - op2);
                break;
            case '*':
                stack.push(op1 * op2);
                break;
            case '/':
                if (op2 != 0)
                    stack.push(op1 / op2);
                else
                {
                    out << " (Division by 0)";
                    isExpOk = false;
                }
                break;
            default:
                out << " (Illegal operator)";
                isExpOk = false;
        }//end switch
    } //end else
  } //end else
} //end evaluateOpr
```

Function `discardExp`

This function is called whenever an error is discovered in the expression. It reads and writes the input data only until the input is `'='`, the end of the expression. The definiton of this function is:

```cpp
void discardExp(ifstream& in, ofstream& out, char& ch)
{
    while (ch != '=')
    {
        in.get(ch);
        out << ch;
    }
} //end discardExp
```

Function `printResult`

If the postfix expression contains no errors, the function `printResult` prints the result; otherwise, it outputs an appropriate message. The result of the expression is in the stack, and the output is sent to a file. Therefore, this function must have access to the stack and the output file. Suppose that no errors were encountered by the method `evaluateExpression`. If the stack has only one element, then the expression is error free and the top element of the stack is printed. If either the stack is empty or it has more than one element, then there is an error in the postfix expression. In this case, this method outputs an appropriate error message. The definition of this method is:

```cpp
void printResult(ofstream& outF, stackType<double>& stack,
                 bool isExpOk)
{
    double result;

    if (isExpOk) //if no error, print the result
    {
        if (!stack.isEmptyStack())
        {
            result = stack.top();
            stack.pop();

            if (stack.isEmptyStack())
                outF << result << endl;
            else
                outF << " (Error: Too many operands)" << endl;
        } //end if
        else
            outF << " (Error in the expression)" << endl;
    }
    else
        outF << " (Error in the expression)" << endl;

    outF << "_______________________________________"
         << endl << endl;
} //end printResult
```

PROGRAM LISTING
```cpp
//Postfix Calculator

#include <iostream>
#include <iomanip>
#include <fstream>
#include "mystack.h"

using namespace std;

void evaluateExpression(ifstream& inpF, ofstream& outF,
                        stackType<double>& stack,
                        char& ch, bool& isExpOk);
void evaluateOpr(ofstream& out, stackType<double>& stack,
                 char& ch, bool& isExpOk);
void discardExp(ifstream& in, ofstream& out, char& ch);
void printResult(ofstream& outF, stackType<double>& stack,
                 bool isExpOk);

int main()
{
    bool expressionOk;
    char ch;
    stackType<double> stack(100);
    ifstream infile;
    ofstream outfile;
```

```
infile.open("a:\\RpnData.txt");

if (!infile)
{
    cout << "Cannot open the input file. "
         << "Program terminates!" << endl;
    return 1;
}

outfile.open("a:\\RpnOutput.txt");

outfile << fixed << showpoint;
outfile << setprecision(2);

infile >> ch;
while (infile)
{
    stack.initializeStack();
    expressionOk = true;
    outfile << ch;

    evaluateExpression(infile, outfile, stack, ch,
                       expressionOk);
    printResult(outfile, stack, expressionOk);
    infile >> ch; //begin processing the next expression
} //end while

infile.close();
outfile.close();

return 0;

} //end main
//Place the definitions of the function evaluateExpression,
//evaluateOpr, discardExp, and printResult as described
//previously here.
```

Sample Run:

Input File

```
#35 #27 + #3 * =
#26 #28 + #32 #2 ; - #5 / =
#23 #30 #15 * / =
#2 #3 #4 + =
#20 #29 #9 * ; =
#25 #23 - + =
#34 #24 #12 #7 / * + #23 - =
```

Output

```
#35.00 #27.00 + #3.00 * = 186.00
```

```
#26.00 #28.00 + #32.00 #2.00 ; (Illegal operator) - #5 / = (Error in the expression)
```

#23.00 #30.00 #15.00 * / = 0.05

#2.00 #3.00 #4.00 + = (Error: Too many operands)

#20.00 #29.00 #9.00 * ; (Illegal operator) = (Error in the expression)

#25.00 #23.00 - + (Not enough operands) = (Error in the expression)

#34.00 #24.00 #12.00 #7.00 / * + #23.00 - = 52.14

Removing Recursion: Nonrecursive Algorithm to Print a Linked List Backward

In Chapter 17, we used recursion to print a linked list backward. In this section, you will learn how a stack can be used to design a nonrecursive algorithm to print a linked list backward.

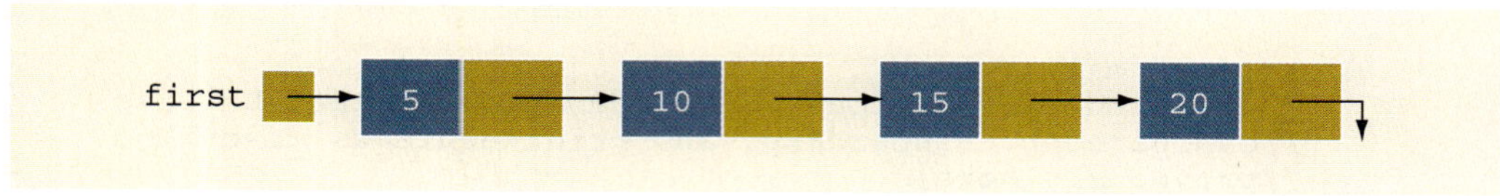

FIGURE 18-29 Linked list

Consider the linked list shown in Figure 18-29.

To print the list backward, first we need to get to the last node of the list, which we can do by traversing the linked list starting at the first node. However, once we are at the last node, how do we get back to the previous node, especially given that links go in only one direction? You can again traverse the linked list with the appropriate loop termination condition, but this approach might waste a considerable amount of computer time, especially if the list is very large. Moreover, if we do this for every node in the list, the program might execute very slowly. Next, we show how to use a stack effectively to print the list backward.

After printing the `info` of a particular node, we need to move to the node immediately behind this node. For example, after printing 20, we need to move to the node with `info 15`. Thus, while initially traversing the list to move to the last node, we must save a pointer to each node. For example, for the list in Figure 18-29, we must save a pointer to each of the nodes with `info 5`, `10`, and `15`. After printing `20`, we go back to the node with `info 15`; after printing `15`, we go back to the node with `info 10`, and so on. From this, it follows that we must save pointers to each node in a stack, so as to implement the Last In First Out principle.

Because the number of nodes in a linked list is usually not known, we will use the linked implementation of a stack. Suppose that `stack` is an object of type `linkedListType`, and `current` is a pointer of the same type as the pointer `first`. Consider the following statements:

```
current = first;                //Line 1

while (current != NULL)         //Line 2
{
    stack.push(current);        //Line 3
    current = current->link;    //Line 4
}
```

After the statement in Line 1 executes, `current` points to the first node (see Figure 18-30).

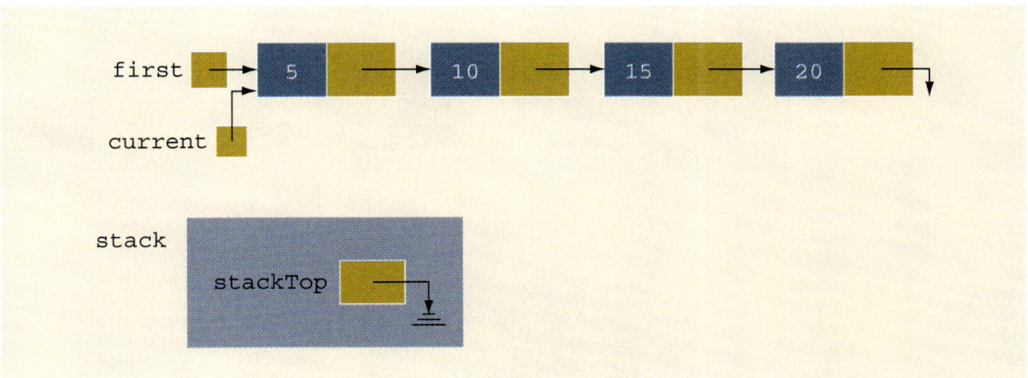

FIGURE 18-30   List after the statement `current = first;` executes

Because `current` is not NULL, the statements in Lines 3 and 4 execute (see Figure 18-31).

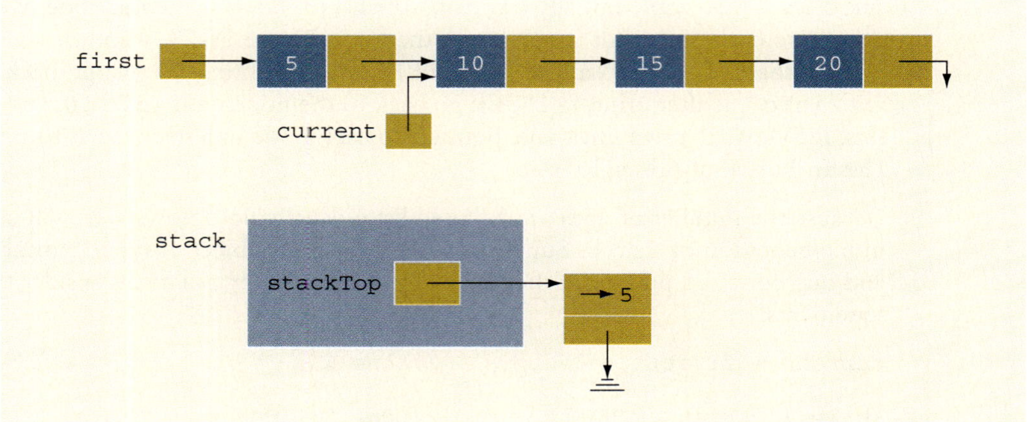

FIGURE 18-31 List and stack after the statements `stack.push(current);` and `current = current->link;` execute

After the statement in Line 4 executes, the loop condition, in Line 2, is reevaluated. Because `current` is not NULL, the loop condition evaluates to **true**, so the statements in Lines 3 and 4 execute (see Figure 18-32).

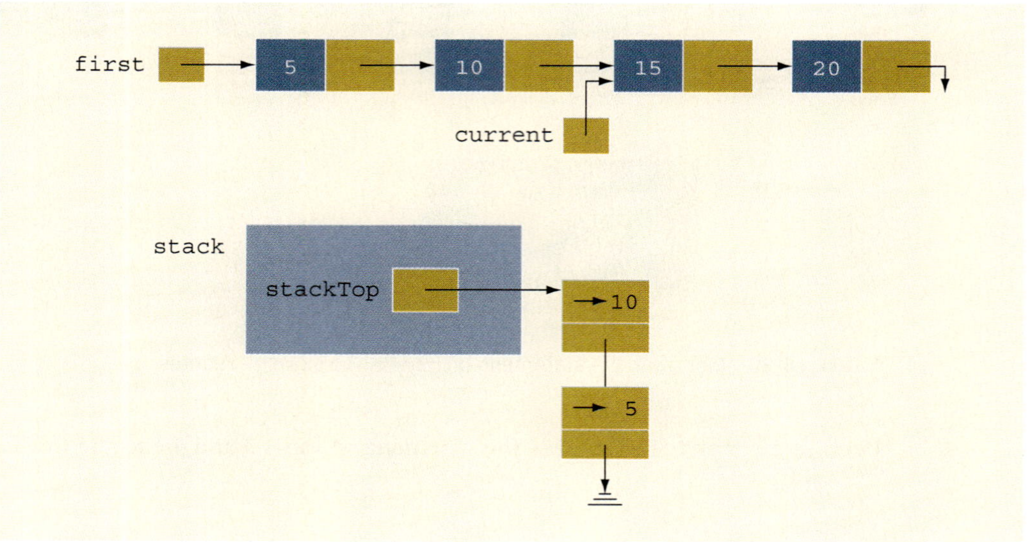

FIGURE 18-32 List and stack after the statements `stack.push(current);` and `current = current->link;` execute

After the statement in Line 4 executes, the loop condition, in Line 2, is evaluated again. Because `current` is not NULL, the loop condition evaluates to **true**, so the statements in Lines 3 and 4 execute (see Figure 18-33).

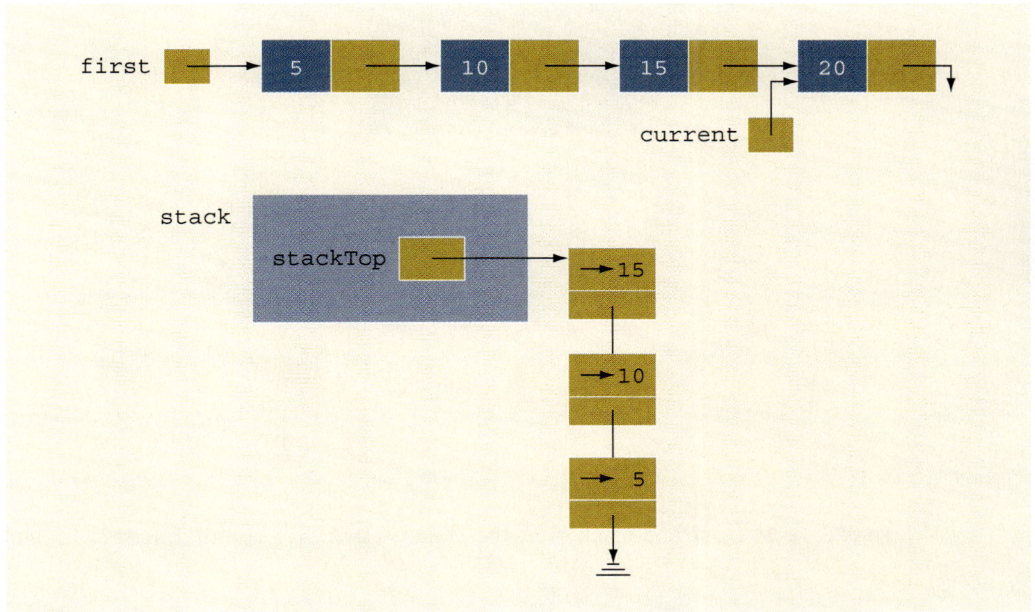

FIGURE 18-33 List and stack after the statements `stack.push(current);` and `current = current->link;` execute

After the statement in Line 4 executes, the loop condition, in Line 2, is evaluated again. Because `current` is not NULL, the loop condition evaluates to **true**, so the statements in Lines 3 and 4 execute (see Figure 18-34).

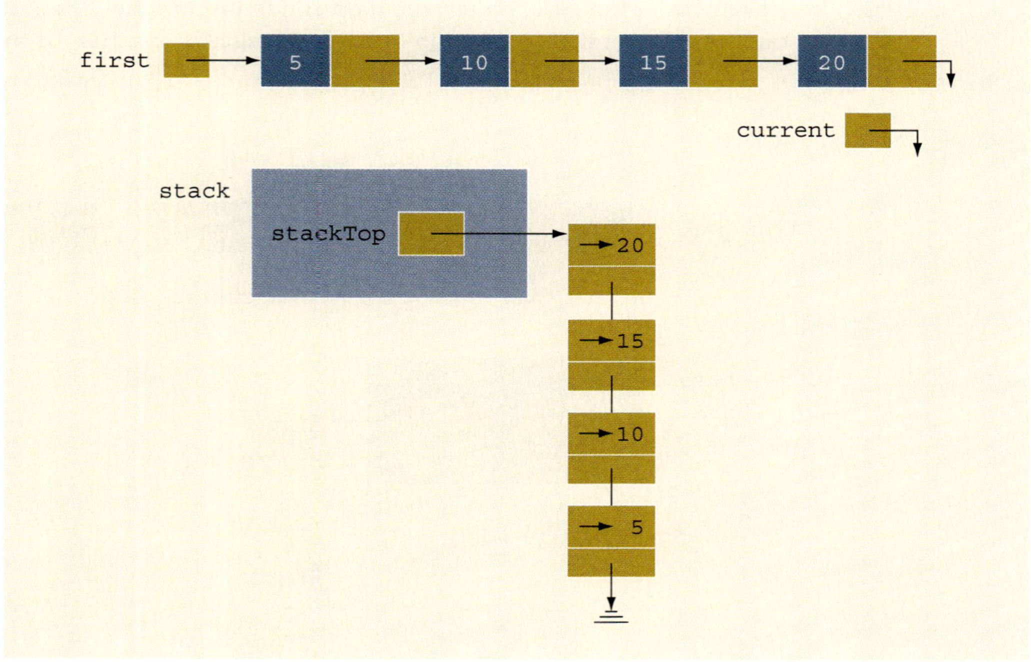

FIGURE 18-34 List and stack after the statements `stack.push(current);` and `current = current->link;` execute

After the statement in Line 4 executes, the loop condition, in Line 2, is evaluated again. Because `current` is NULL, the loop condition evaluates to **false** and the **while** loop, in Line 2, terminates. From Figure 18-34, it follows that a pointer to each node in the linked list is saved in the stack. The top element of the stack contains a pointer to the last node in the list, and so on. Let us now execute the following statements:

```
while (!stack.isEmptyStack())          //Line 5
{
    current = stack.top();             //Line 6
    stack.pop();                       //Line 7
    cout << current->info << " ";      //Line 8
}
```

The loop condition in Line 5 evaluates to **true** because the stack is nonempty. Therefore, the statements in Lines 6, 7, and 8 execute. After the statement in Line 6 executes, `current` points to the last node. The statement in Line 7 removes the top element of the stack (see Figure 18-35).

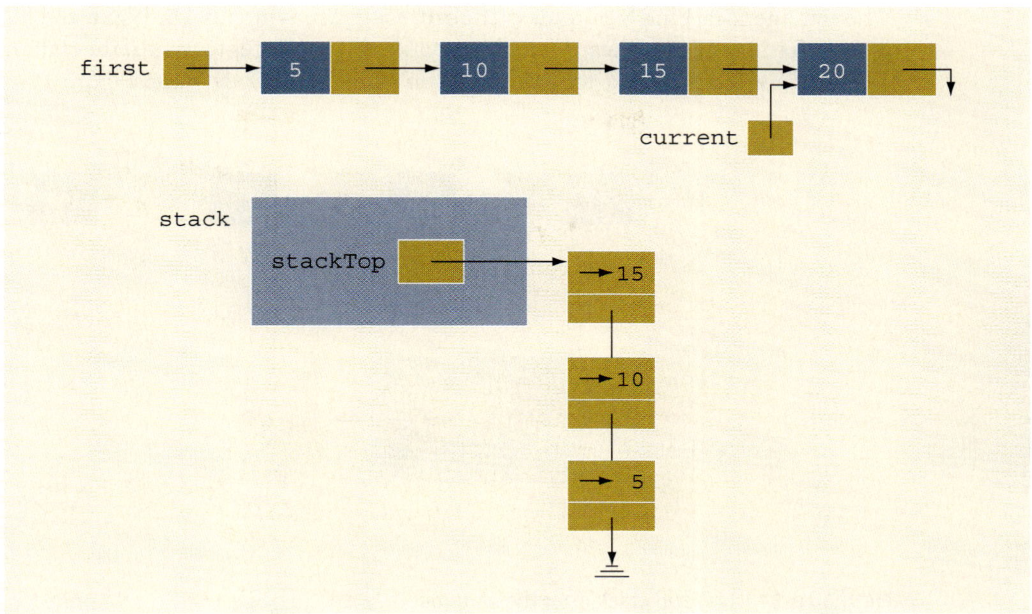

FIGURE 18-35   List and stack after the statements `current = stack.top();` and `stack.pop();` execute

The statement in Line 8 outputs `current->info`, which is 20. Next, the loop condition in Line 5 is evaluated. Because the loop condition evaluates to **true**, the statements in Lines 6, 7, and 8 execute. After the statements in Lines 6 and 7 execute, Figure 18–36 results.

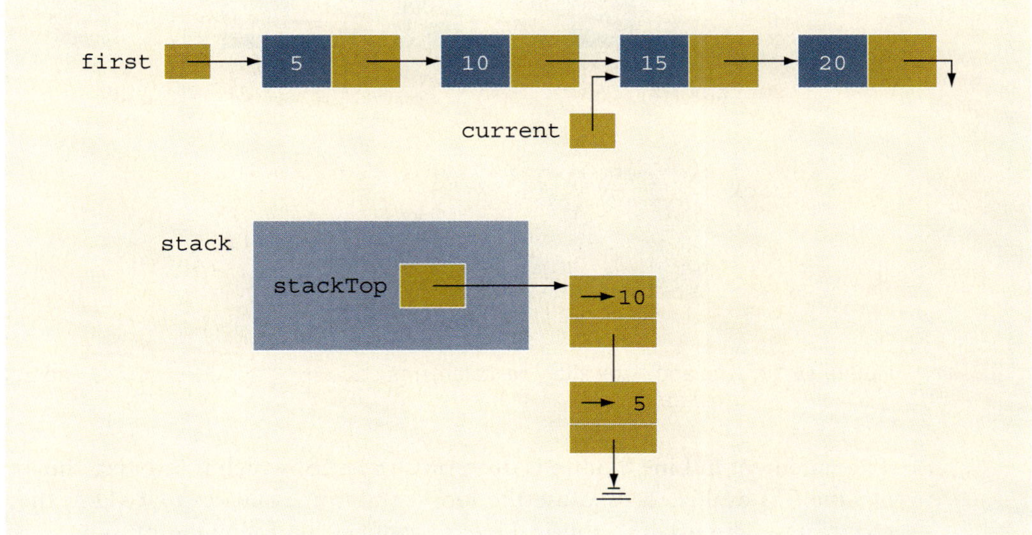

FIGURE 18-36   List and stack after the statements `current = stack.top();` and `stack.pop();` execute

The statement in Line 8 outputs `current->info`, which is 15. Next, the loop condition in Line 5 is evaluated. Because the loop condition evaluates to **true**, the statements in Lines 6, 7, and 8 execute. After the statements in Lines 6 and 7 execute, Figure 18–37 results.

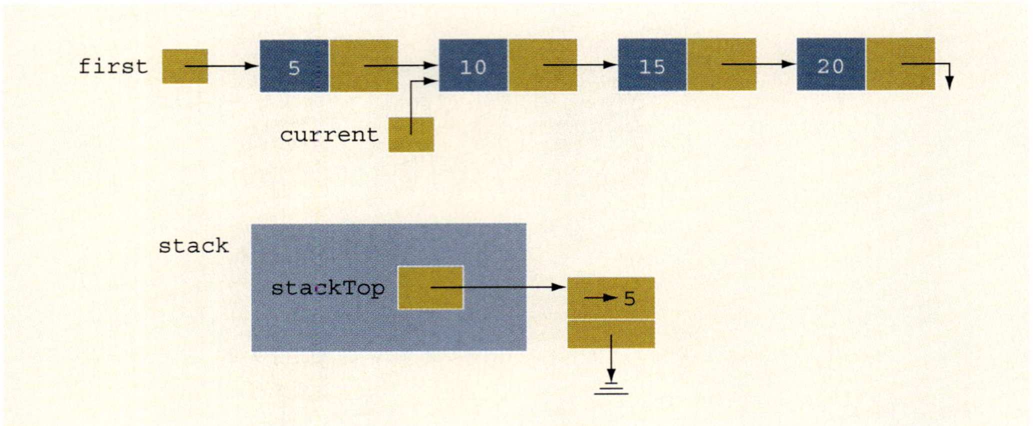

FIGURE 18-37 List and stack after the statements `current = stack.top();` and `stack.pop();` execute

The statement in Line 8 outputs `current->info`, which is 10. Next, the loop condition in Line 5 is evaluated. Because the loop condition evaluates to **true**, the statements in Lines 6, 7, and 8 execute. After the statements in Lines 6 and 7 execute, Figure 18–38 results.

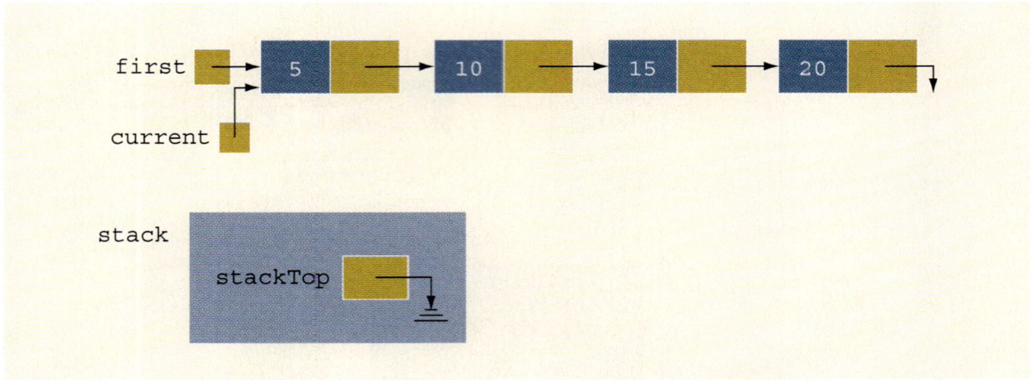

FIGURE 18-38 List and stack after the statements `current = stack.top();` and `stack.pop();` execute

The statement in Line 8 outputs `current->info`, which is 5. Next, the loop condition in Line 5 is evaluated. Because the loop condition evaluates to **false**, the **while** loop terminates. The **while** loop in Line 5 produces the following output:

```
20 15 10 5
```

Queues

This section discusses another important data structure, called a **queue**. The notion of a queue in computer science is the same as the notion of the queues to which you are accustomed in everyday life. There are queues of customers in a bank or in a grocery store, and queues of cars waiting to pass through a tollbooth. Similarly, because a computer can send a print request faster than a printer can print, a queue of documents is often waiting to be printed at a printer. The general rule to process elements in a queue is that the customer at the front of the queue is served next and that when a new customer arrives, he or she stands at the end of the queue. That is, a queue is a First In First Out data structure.

Queues have numerous applications in computer science. Whenever a system is modeled on the First In First Out principle, queues are used. At the end of this section, we will discuss one of the most widely used applications of queues, computer simulation. First, however, we need to develop the tools necessary to implement a queue. The next few sections discuss how to design classes to implement queues as an ADT.

A queue is a set of elements of the same type in which the elements are added at one end, called the **back** or **rear**, and deleted from the other end, called the **front**. For example, consider a line of customers in a bank, wherein the customers are waiting to withdraw/ deposit money or to conduct some other business. Each new customer gets in the line at the rear. Whenever a teller is ready for a new customer, the customer at the front of the line is served.

The rear of the queue is accessed whenever a new element is added to the queue, and the front of the queue is accessed whenever an element is deleted from the queue. As in a stack, the middle elements of the queue are inaccessible, even if the queue elements are stored in an array.

Queue: A data structure in which the elements are added at one end, called the rear, and deleted from the other end, called the front; a First In First Out (FIFO) data structure.

Queue Operations

From the definition of queues, we see that the two key operations are add and delete. We call the add operation **addQueue** and the delete operation **deleteQueue**. Because elements can be neither deleted from an empty queue nor added to a full queue, we need two more operations to successfully implement the **addQueue** and **deleteQueue** operations: **isEmptyQueue** (checks whether the queue is empty) and **isFullQueue** (checks whether a queue is full).

We also need an operation, **initializeQueue**, to initialize the queue to an empty state. Moreover, to retrieve the first and last elements of the queue, we include the operations **front** and **back**, as described in the following list. Some of the queue operations are:

- **initializeQueue**: Initializes the queue to an empty state.

- **isEmptyQueue**: Determines whether the queue is empty. If the queue is empty, it returns the value **true**; otherwise, it returns the value **false**.

- **isFullQueue**: Determines whether the queue is full. If the queue is full, it returns the value **true**; otherwise, it returns the value **false**.

- **front**: Returns the front, that is, the first element of the queue. Input to this operation consists of the queue. Prior to this operation, the queue must exist and must not be empty.

- **back**: Returns the last element of the queue. Input to this operation consists of the queue. Prior to this operation, the queue must exist and must not be empty.

- **addQueue**: Adds a new element to the rear of the queue. Input to this operation consists of the queue and the new element. Prior to this operation, the queue must exist and must not be full.

- **deleteQueue**: Removes the front element from the queue. Input to this operation consists of the queue. Prior to this operation, the queue must exist and must not be empty.

As in the case of a stack, a queue can be stored in an array or in a linked structure. We will consider both implementations. Because elements are added at one end and removed from the other end, we need two pointers to keep track of the front and rear of the queue, called **queueFront** and **queueRear**.

The following abstract **class** queueADT defines these operations as an ADT:

```cpp
template <class Type>
class queueADT
{
public:
    virtual bool isEmptyQueue() const = 0;
      //Function to determine whether the queue is empty.
      //Postcondition: Returns true if the queue is empty,
      //               otherwise returns false.

    virtual bool isFullQueue() const = 0;
      //Function to determine whether the queue is full.
      //Postcondition: Returns true if the queue is full,
      //               otherwise returns false.

    virtual void initializeQueue() = 0;
      //Function to initialize the queue to an empty state.
      //Postcondition: The queue is empty.
```

```cpp
virtual Type front() const = 0;
   //Function to return the first element of the queue.
   //Precondition: The queue exists and is not empty.
   //Postcondition: If the queue is empty, the program
   //               terminates; otherwise, the first
   //               element of the queue is returned.

virtual Type back() const = 0;
   //Function to return the last element of the queue.
   //Precondition: The queue exists and is not empty.
   //Postcondition: If the queue is empty, the program
   //               terminates; otherwise, the last
   //               element of the queue is returned.

virtual void addQueue(const Type& queueElement) = 0;
   //Function to add queueElement to the queue.
   //Precondition: The queue exists and is not full.
   //Postcondition: The queue is changed and queueElement
   //               is added to the queue.

virtual void deleteQueue() = 0;
   //Function to remove the first element of the queue.
   //Precondition: The queue exists and is not empty.
   //Postcondition: The queue is changed and the first
   //               element is removed from the queue.
};
```

We leave it as an exercise for you to draw the UML class diagram of the `class` queueADT.

Implementation of Queues as Arrays

Before giving the definition of the class to implement a queue as an ADT, we need to decide how many member variables are needed to implement the queue. Of course, we need an array to store the queue elements, the variables `queueFront` and `queueRear` to keep track of the first and last elements of the queue, and the variable `maxQueueSize` to specify the maximum size of the queue. Thus, we need at least four member variables.

Before writing the algorithms to implement the queue operations, we need to decide how to use `queueFront` and `queueRear` to access the queue elements. How do `queueFront` and `queueRear` indicate that the queue is empty or full? Suppose that `queueFront` gives the index of the first element of the queue, and `queueRear` gives the index of the last element of the queue. To add an element to the queue, first we advance `queueRear` to the next array position and then add the element to the position that `queueRear` is pointing to. To delete an element from the queue, first we retrieve the element that `queueFront` is pointing to and then advance `queueFront` to the next element of the queue. Thus, `queueFront` changes after each `deleteQueue` operation and `queueRear` changes after each `addQueue` operation.

Let us see what happens when `queueFront` changes after a `deleteQueue` operation and `queueRear` changes after an `addQueue` operation. Assume that the array to hold the queue elements is of size 100.

Initially, the queue is empty. After the operation:

```
addQueue(Queue, 'A');
```

the array is as shown in Figure 18-39.

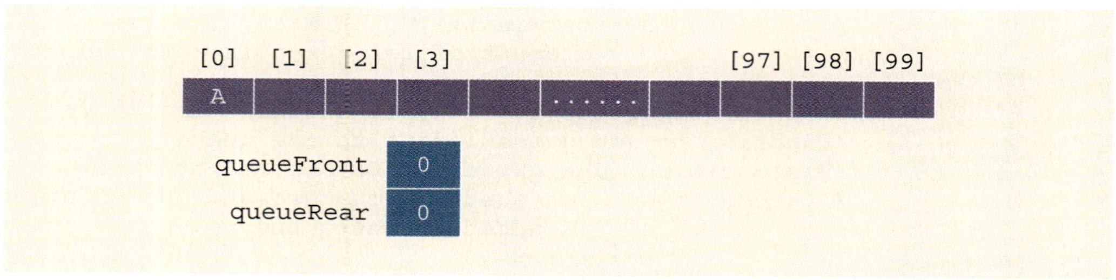

FIGURE 18-39   Queue after the first `addQueue` operation

After two more `addQueue` operations:

```
addQueue(Queue, 'B');
addQueue(Queue, 'C');
```

the array is as shown in Figure 18-40.

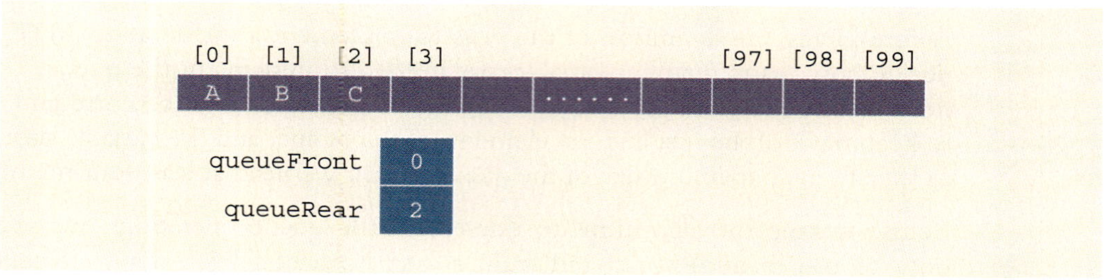

FIGURE 18-40   Queue after two more `addQueue` operations

Now consider the `deleteQueue` operation:

```
deleteQueue();
```

After this operation, the array containing the queue is as shown in Figure 18-41.

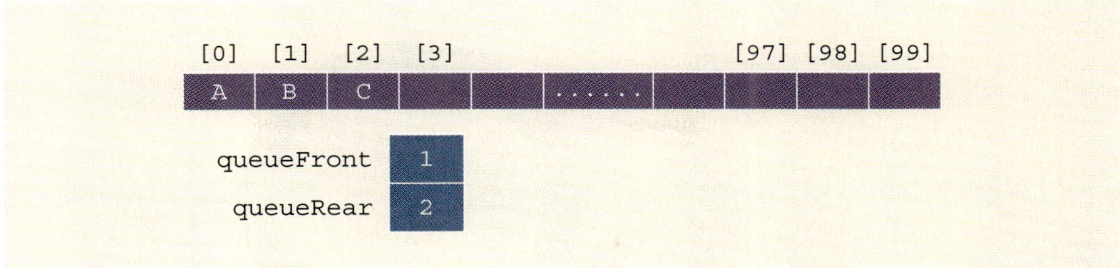

FIGURE 18-41 Queue after the `deleteQueue` operation

Will this queue design work? Suppose `A` stands for adding (that is, `addQueue`) an element to the queue, and `D` stands for deleting (that is, `deleteQueue`) an element from the queue. Consider the following sequence of operations:

`AAADADADADADADADADA...`

This sequence of operations would eventually set the index `queueRear` to point to the last array position, giving the impression that the queue is full. However, the queue has only two or three elements and the front of the array is empty (see Figure 18-42).

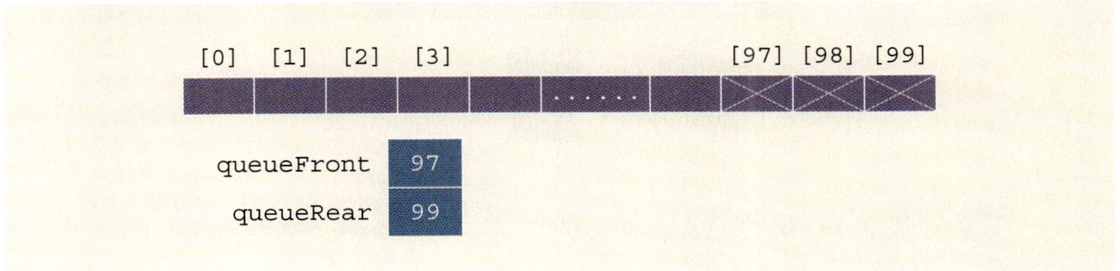

FIGURE 18-42 Queue after the sequence of operations `AAADADADADADA...`

One solution to this problem is that when the queue overflows to the rear (that is, `queueRear` points to the last array position), we can check the value of the index `queueFront`. If the value of `queueFront` indicates that there is room in the front of the array, then when `queueRear` gets to the last array position, we can slide all of the queue elements toward the first array position. This solution is good if the queue size is very small; otherwise, the program may execute more slowly.

Another solution to this problem is to assume that the array is circular—that is, the first array position immediately follows the last array position (see Figure 18-43).

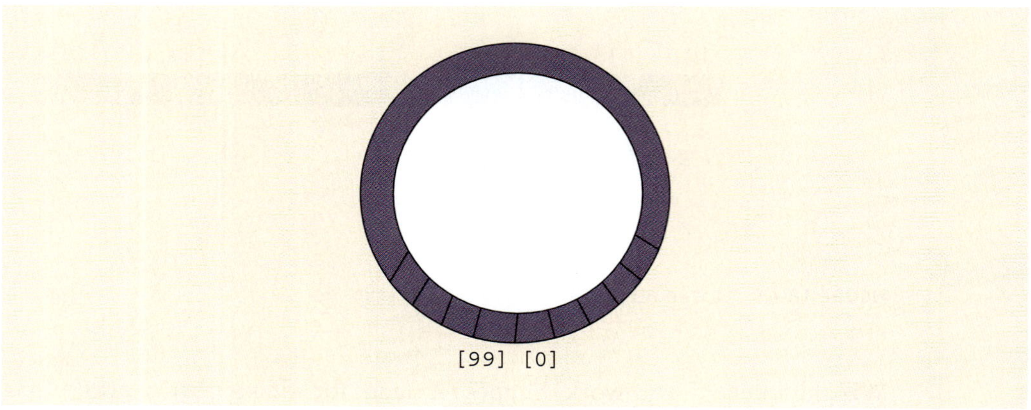

FIGURE 18-43   Circular queue

We will consider the array containing the queue to be circular, although we will draw the figures of the array holding the queue elements as before.

Suppose that we have the queue as shown in Figure 18-44.

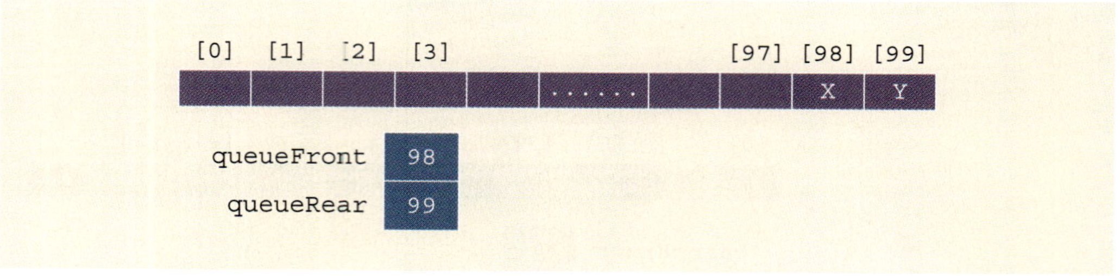

FIGURE 18-44   Queue with two elements at positions 98 and 99

After the operation:

`addQueue(Queue, 'Z');`

the queue is as shown in Figure 18-45.

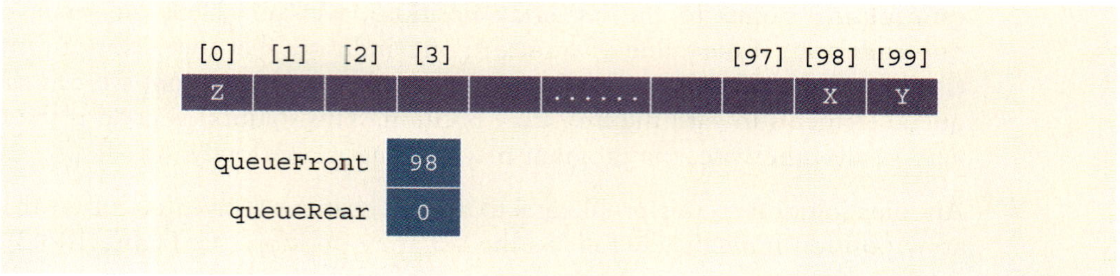

FIGURE 18-45   Queue after one more `addQueue` operation

Because the array containing the queue is circular, we can use the following statement to advance `queueRear` (`queueFront`) to the next array position:

```
queueRear = (queueRear + 1) % maxQueueSize;
```

If `queueRear < maxQueueSize - 1`, then `queueRear + 1 <= maxQueueSize - 1` and so `(queueRear + 1) % maxQueueSize = queueRear + 1`. If `queueRear == maxQueueSize - 1` (that is, `queueRear` points to the last array position), `queueRear + 1 == maxQueueSize` and so `(queueRear + 1) % maxQueueSize = 0`. In this case, `queueRear` will be set to 0, which is the first array position.

This queue design seems to work well. Before we write the algorithms to implement the queue operations, consider the following two cases.

Case 1: Suppose that after certain operations, the array containing the queue is as shown in Figure 18-46.

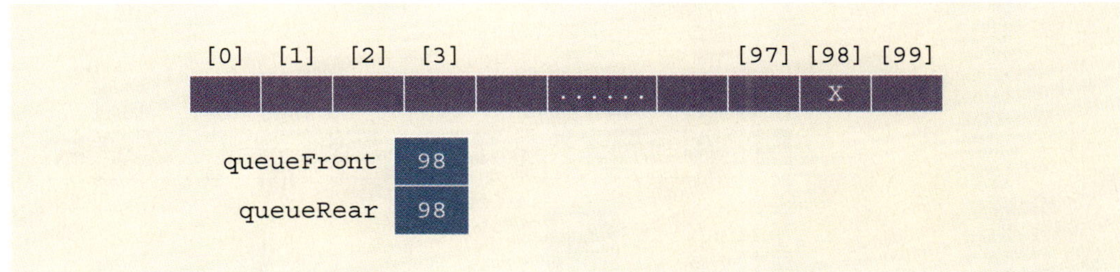

FIGURE 18-46   Queue with one element

After the operation:

```
deleteQueue();
```

the resulting array is as shown in Figure 18-47.

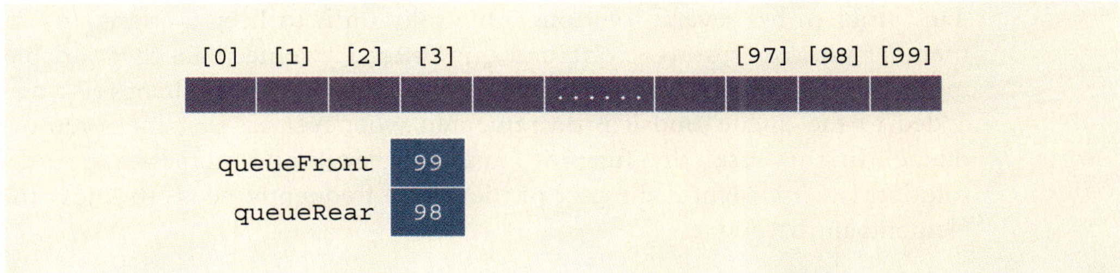

FIGURE 18-47   Queue after the `deleteQueue` operation

Case 2: Let us now consider the queue shown in Figure 18-48.

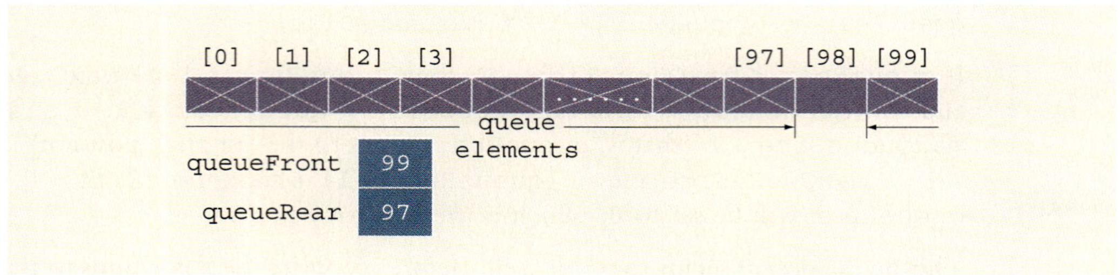

FIGURE 18-48   Queue with 99 elements

After the operation:

```
addQueue(Queue, 'Z');
```

the resulting array is as shown in Figure 18-49.

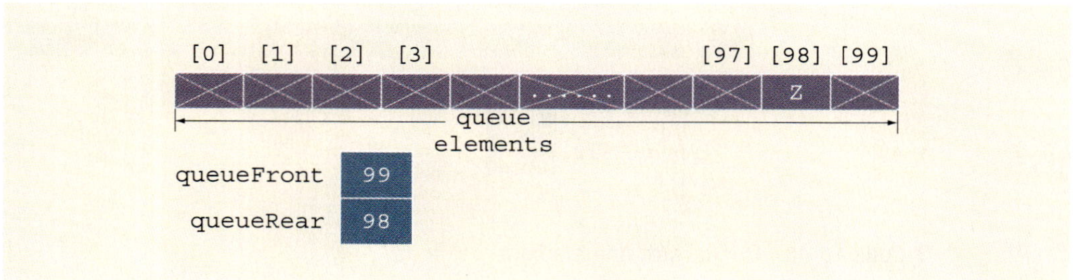

FIGURE 18-49   Queue after the addQueue operation; it is full

The arrays in Figures 18-47 and 18-49 have identical values for queueFront and queueRear. However, the resulting array in Figure 18-47 represents an empty queue, whereas the resulting array in Figure 18-49 represents a full queue. This latest queue design has brought up another problem of distinguishing between an empty and a full queue.

This problem has several solutions. One solution is to keep a count. In addition to the member variables queueFront and queueRear, we need another variable, count, to implement the queue. The value of count is incremented whenever a new element is added to the queue, and it is decremented whenever an element is removed from the queue. In this case, the function initializeQueue initializes count to 0. This solution is very useful if the user of the queue frequently needs to know the number of elements in the queue.

Another solution is to let queueFront indicate the index of the array position *preceding* the first element of the queue, rather than the index of the (actual) first element itself. In this case, assuming `queueRear` still indicates the index of the last element in the queue, the queue is empty if `queueFront == queueRear`. In this solution, the slot indicated by the index `queueFront` (that is, the slot preceding the first true element) is reserved. The queue will be full if the next available space is the special reserved slot indicated by `queueFront`. Finally, because the array position indicated by `queueFront` is to be kept empty, if the array size is, say, `100`, then 99 elements can be stored in the queue (see Figure 18-50).

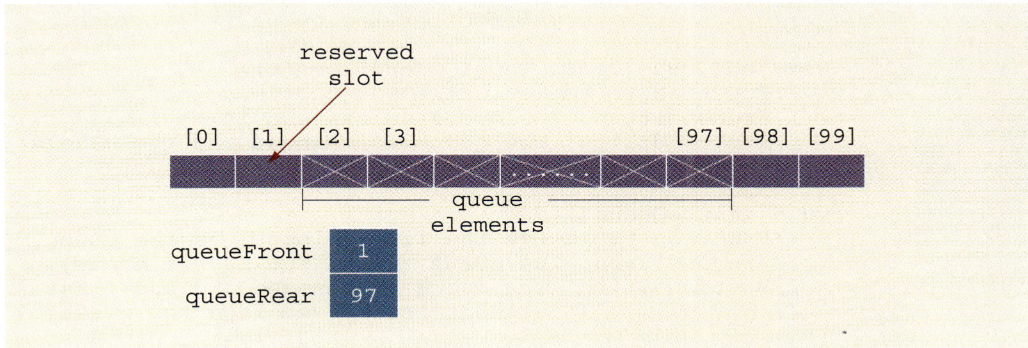

FIGURE 18-50   Array to store the queue elements with a reserved slot

Let us implement the queue using the first solution. That is, we use the variable `count` to indicate whether the queue is empty or full.

The following class implements the functions of the abstract `class` `queueADT`. Because arrays can be allocated dynamically, we will leave it for the user to specify the size of the array to implement the queue. The default size of the array is `100`.

```cpp
template <class Type>
class queueType: public queueADT<Type>
{
public:
    const queueType<Type>& operator=(const queueType<Type>&);
      //Overload the assignment operator.

    bool isEmptyQueue() const;
      //Function to determine whether the queue is empty.
      //Postcondition: Returns true if the queue is empty,
      //               otherwise returns false.

    bool isFullQueue() const;
      //Function to determine whether the queue is full.
      //Postcondition: Returns true if the queue is full,
      //               otherwise returns false.

    void initializeQueue();
      //Function to initialize the queue to an empty state.
      //Postcondition: The queue is empty.
```

```
    Type front() const;
      //Function to return the first element of the queue.
      //Precondition: The queue exists and is not empty.
      //Postcondition: If the queue is empty, the program
      //                  terminates; otherwise, the first
      //                  element of the queue is returned.
    Type back() const;
      //Function to return the last element of the queue.
      //Precondition: The queue exists and is not empty.
      //Postcondition: If the queue is empty, the program
      //                  terminates; otherwise, the last
      //                  element of the queue is returned.

    void addQueue(const Type& queueElement);
      //Function to add queueElement to the queue.
      //Precondition: The queue exists and is not full.
      //Postcondition: The queue is changed and queueElement
      //                  is added to the queue.

    void deleteQueue();
      //Function to remove the first element of the queue.
      //Precondition: The queue exists and is not empty.
      //Postcondition: The queue is changed and the first
      //                  element is removed from the queue.

    queueType(int queueSize = 100);
      //Constructor

    queueType(const queueType<Type>& otherQueue);
      //Copy constructor

    ~queueType();
      //Destructor

private:
    int maxQueueSize; //variable to store the maximum queue size
    int count;        //variable to store the number of
                      //elements in the queue
    int queueFront;   //variable to point to the first
                      //element of the queue
    int queueRear;    //variable to point to the last
                      //element of the queue
    Type *list;       //pointer to the array that holds
                      //the queue elements
};
```

We leave the UML class diagram of the `class` queueType as an exercise for you. (See Exercise 24 at the end of this chapter.)

Next, we consider the implementation of the queue operations.

EMPTY QUEUE AND FULL QUEUE

As discussed earlier, the queue is empty if count == 0, and the queue is full if count == maxQueueSize. So the functions to implement these operations are:

```cpp
template <class Type>
bool queueType<Type>::isEmptyQueue() const
{
    return (count == 0);
} //end isEmptyQueue

template <class Type>
bool queueType<Type>::isFullQueue() const
{
    return (count == maxQueueSize);
} //end isFullQueue
```

INITIALIZE QUEUE

This operation initializes a queue to an empty state. The first element is added at the first array position. Therefore, we initialize `queueFront` to 0, `queueRear` to `maxQueueSize - 1`, and count to 0. See Figure 18-51.

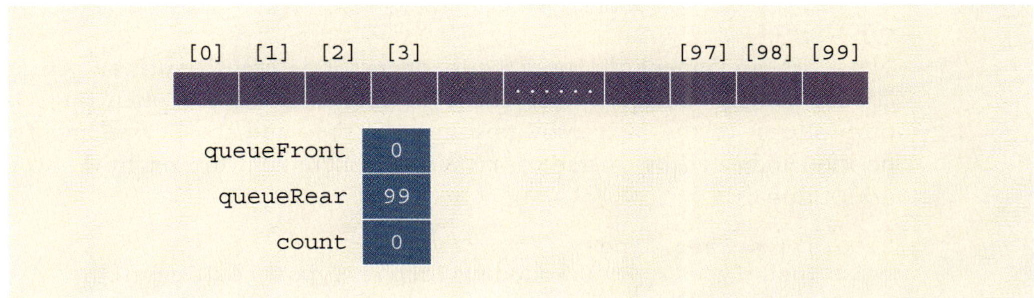

FIGURE 18-51 Empty queue

The definition of the function `initializeQueue` is:

```cpp
template <class Type>
void queueType<Type>::initializeQueue()
{
    queueFront = 0;
    queueRear = maxQueueSize - 1;
    count = 0;
} //end initializeQueue
```

FRONT

This operation returns the first element of the queue. If the queue is nonempty, the element of the queue indicated by the index `queueFront` is returned; otherwise, the program terminates.

```
template <class Type>
Type queueType<Type>::front() const
{
    assert(!isEmptyQueue());
    return list[queueFront];
} //end front
```

BACK

This operation returns the last element of the queue. If the queue is nonempty, the element of the queue indicated by the index `queueRear` is returned; otherwise the program terminates.

```
template <class Type>
Type queueType<Type>::back() const
{
    assert(!isEmptyQueue());
    return list[queueRear];
} //end back
```

addQueue

Next, we implement the `addQueue` operation. Because `queueRear` points to the last element of the queue, to add a new element to the queue, we first advance `queueRear` to the next array position and then add the new element to the array position indicated by `queueRear`. We also increment `count` by 1. So the function `addQueue` is:

```
template <class Type>
void queueType<Type>::addQueue(const Type& newElement)
{
    if (!isFullQueue())
    {
        queueRear = (queueRear + 1) % maxQueueSize; //use the
                                //mod operator to advance queueRear
                                //because the array is circular
        count++;
        list[queueRear] = newElement;
    }
    else
        cout << "Cannot add to a full queue." << endl;
} //end addQueue
```

deleteQueue

To implement the `deleteQueue` operation, we access the index `queueFront`. Because `queueFront` points to the array position containing the first element of the queue, in order to remove the first queue element we decrement `count` by 1 and advance `queueFront` to the next queue element. So the function `deleteQueue` is:

```cpp
template <class Type>
void queueType<Type>::deleteQueue()
{
    if (!isEmptyQueue())
    {
        count--;
        queueFront = (queueFront + 1) % maxQueueSize; //use the
                            //mod operator to advance queueFront
                            //because the array is circular

    }
    else
        cout << "Cannot remove from an empty queue" << endl;
} //end deleteQueue
```

CONSTRUCTORS AND DESTRUCTORS

To complete the implementation of the queue operations, we next consider the implementation of the constructor and the destructor. The constructor gets the `maxQueueSize` from the user, sets the variable `maxQueueSize` to the value specified by the user, and creates an array of size `maxQueueSize`. If the user does not specify the queue size, the constructor uses the default value, which is 100, to create an array of size 100. The constructor also initializes `queueFront` and `queueRear` to indicate that the queue is empty. The definition of the function to implement the constructor is:

```cpp
template <class Type>
queueType<Type>::queueType(int queueSize)
{
    if (queueSize <= 0)
    {
        cout << "Size of the array to hold the queue must "
             << "be positive." << endl;
        cout << "Creating an array of size 100." << endl;

        maxQueueSize = 100;
    }
    else
        maxQueueSize = queueSize;       //set maxQueueSize to
                                        //queueSize

    queueFront = 0;                     //initialize queueFront
    queueRear = maxQueueSize - 1;       //initialize queueRear
    count = 0;
    list = new Type[maxQueueSize];      //create the array to
                                        //hold the queue elements
} //end constructor
```

The array to store the queue elements is created dynamically. Therefore, when the queue object goes out of scope, the destructor simply deallocates the memory occupied by the array that stores the queue elements. The definition of the function to implement the destructor is:

```cpp
template <class Type>
queueType<Type>::~queueType()
{
    delete [] list;
}
```

The implementation of the copy constructor and overloading the assignment operator are left as exercises for you. (The definitions of these functions are similar to those discussed for linked lists and stacks.)

Linked Implementation of Queues

Because the size of the array to store the queue elements is fixed, only a finite number of queue elements can be stored in the array. Also, the array implementation of the queue requires the array to be treated in a special way together with the values of the indices `queueFront` and `queueRear`. The linked implementation of a queue simplifies many of the special cases of the array implementation and, because the memory to store a queue element is allocated dynamically, the queue is never full. This section discusses the linked implementation of a queue.

Because elements are added at one end and removed from the other end, we need to know the front of the queue and the rear of the queue. Thus, we need two pointers, **queueFront** and **queueRear**, to maintain the queue. The following class imlements the functions of the abstract `class queueADT`:

```cpp
//Definition of the node
template <class Type>
struct nodeType
{
    Type info;
    nodeType<Type> *link;
};

template <class Type>
class linkedQueueType: public queueADT<Type>
{
public:
    const linkedQueueType<Type>& operator=
                    (const linkedQueueType<Type>&);
      //Overload the assignment operator.

    bool isEmptyQueue() const;
      //Function to determine whether the queue is empty.
      //Postcondition: Returns true if the queue is empty,
      //                 otherwise returns false.

    bool isFullQueue() const;
      //Function to determine whether the queue is full.
      //Postcondition: Returns true if the queue is full,
      //                 otherwise returns false.
```

```cpp
    void initializeQueue();
      //Function to initialize the queue to an empty state.
      //Postcondition: queueFront = NULL; queueRear = NULL

    Type front() const;
      //Function to return the first element of the queue.
      //Precondition: The queue exists and is not empty.
      //Postcondition: If the queue is empty, the program
      //                terminates; otherwise, the first
      //                element of the queue is returned.

    Type back() const;
      //Function to return the last element of the queue.
      //Precondition: The queue exists and is not empty.
      //Postcondition: If the queue is empty, the program
      //                terminates; otherwise, the last
      //                element of the queue is returned.

    void addQueue(const Type& queueElement);
      //Function to add queueElement to the queue.
      //Precondition: The queue exists and is not full.
      //Postcondition: The queue is changed and queueElement
      //                is added to the queue.

    void deleteQueue();
      //Function  to remove the first element of the queue.
      //Precondition: The queue exists and is not empty.
      //Postcondition: The queue is changed and the first
      //                element is removed from the queue.

    linkedQueueType();
      //Default constructor

    linkedQueueType(const linkedQueueType<Type>& otherQueue);
      //Copy constructor

    ~linkedQueueType();
      //Destructor

private:
    nodeType<Type> *queueFront; //pointer to the front of
                                //the queue
    nodeType<Type> *queueRear;  //pointer to the rear of
                                //the queue
};
```

The UML class diagram of the **class** linkedQueueType is left as an exercise for you. (See Exercise 25 at the end of this chapter.)

Next, we write the definitions of the functions of the **class** linkedQueueType.

EMPTY AND FULL QUEUE

The queue is empty if queueFront is NULL. Memory to store the queue elements is allocated dynamically. Therefore, the queue is never full and so the function to implement the `isFullQueue` operation returns the value **false**. (The queue is full only if we run out of memory.)

```cpp
template <class Type>
bool linkedQueueType<Type>::isEmptyQueue() const
{
    return (queueFront == NULL);
} //end

template <class Type>
bool linkedQueueType<Type>::isFullQueue() const
{
    return false;
} //end isFullQueue
```

Note that in reality, in the linked implementation of queues, the function `isFullQueue` does not apply because, logically, the queue is never full. However, you must provide its definition because it is included as an abstract function in the parent **class** `queueADT`.

INITIALIZE QUEUE

The operation `initializeQueue` initializes the queue to an empty state. The queue is empty if there are no elements in the queue. Note that the constructor initializes the queue when the queue object is declared. So this operation must remove all the elements, if any, from the queue. Therefore, this operation traverses the list containing the queue starting at the first node, and it deallocates the memory occupied by the queue elements. The definition of this function is:

```cpp
template <class Type>
void linkedQueueType<Type>::initializeQueue()
{
    nodeType<Type> *temp;

    while (queueFront!= NULL)   //while there are elements left
                                //in the queue
    {
        temp = queueFront;   //set temp to point to the
                             //current node
        queueFront = queueFront->link;   //advance first to
                                         //the next node
        delete temp;    //deallocate memory occupied by temp
    }

    queueRear = NULL;   //set rear to NULL
} //end initializeQueue
```

`addQueue`, `front`, `back`, AND `deleteQueue` OPERATIONS

The `addQueue` operation adds a new element at the end of the queue. To implement this operation, we access the pointer `queueRear`.

If the queue is nonempty, the operation `front` returns the first element of the queue and so the element of the queue indicated by the pointer `queueFront` is returned. If the queue is empty, the function `front` terminates the program.

If the queue is nonempty, the operation `back` returns the last element of the queue and so the element of the queue indicated by the pointer `queueRear` is returned. If the queue is empty, the function `back` terminates the program. Similarly, if the queue is nonempty, the operation `deleteQueue` removes the first element of the queue, and so we access the pointer `queueFront`.

The definitions of the functions to implement these operations are:

```cpp
template <class Type>
void linkedQueueType<Type>::addQueue(const Type& newElement)
{
    nodeType<Type> *newNode;

    newNode = new nodeType<Type>;    //create the node

    newNode->info = newElement; //store the info
    newNode->link = NULL;   //initialize the link field to NULL

    if (queueFront == NULL) //if initially the queue is empty
    {
        queueFront = newNode;
        queueRear = newNode;
    }
    else          //add newNode at the end
    {
        queueRear->link = newNode;
        queueRear = queueRear->link;
    }
}//end addQueue

template <class Type>
Type linkedQueueType<Type>::front() const
{
    assert(queueFront != NULL);
    return queueFront->info;
} //end front

template <class Type>
Type linkedQueueType<Type>::back() const
{
    assert(queueRear!= NULL);
    return queueRear->info;
} //end back
```

```cpp
template <class Type>
void linkedQueueType<Type>::deleteQueue()
{
    nodeType<Type> *temp;

    if (!isEmptyQueue())
    {
        temp = queueFront;  //make temp point to the
                            //first node
        queueFront = queueFront->link; //advance queueFront

        delete temp;      //delete the first node

        if (queueFront == NULL) //if after deletion the
                                //queue is empty
            queueRear = NULL;   //set queueRear to NULL
    }
    else
        cout << "Cannot remove from an empty queue" << endl;
}//end deleteQueue
```

The definition of the default constructor is:

```cpp
template<class Type>
linkedQueueType<Type>::linkedQueueType()
{
    queueFront = NULL; //set front to null
    queueRear = NULL;  //set rear to null
} //end default constructor
```

When the queue object goes out of scope, the destructor destroys the queue; that is, it deallocates the memory occupied by the elements of the queue. The definition of the function to implement the destructor is similar to the definition of the function `initializeQueue`. Also, the functions to implement the copy constructor and overload the assignment operators are similar to the corresponding functions for stacks. Implementing these operations is left as an exercise for you.

EXAMPLE 18-5

The following program tests various operations on a queue. It uses the **class** linkedQueueType to implement a queue.

```cpp
//Test Program linked queue

#include <iostream>
#include "linkedQueue.h"

using namespace std;
```

```cpp
int main()
{
    linkedQueueType<int> queue;
    int x, y;

    queue.initializeQueue();
    x = 4;
    y = 5;
    queue.addQueue(x);
    queue.addQueue(y);
    x = queue.front();
    queue.deleteQueue();
    queue.addQueue(x + 5);
    queue.addQueue(16);
    queue.addQueue(x);
    queue.addQueue(y - 3);

    cout << "Queue Elements: ";

    while (!queue.isEmptyQueue())
    {
        cout << queue.front() << " ";
        queue.deleteQueue();
    }

    cout << endl;

    return 0;
}
```

Sample Run:

```
Queue Elements:  5 9 16 4 2
```

Queue Derived from the `class` `unorderedLinkedListType`

From the definitions of the functions to implement the queue operations, it is clear that the linked implementation of a queue is similar to the implementation of a linked list created in a forward manner (see Chapter 17). The `addQueue` operation is similar to the operation `insertFirst`. Likewise, the operations `initializeQueue` and `initializeList`, and `isEmptyQueue` and `isEmptyList`, are similar. The `deleteQueue` operation can be implemented as before. The pointer `queueFront` is the same as the pointer `first`, and the pointer `queueRear` is the same as the pointer `last`. This correspondence suggests that we can derive the class to implement the queue from the `class` `linkedListType` (see Chapter 17). Note that the `class` `linkedListType` is an abstract and does not implement all the operations. However, the `class` `unorderedLinkedListType` is derived from the the `class` `linkedListType` and provides the definitions of the abstract functions of the the `class` `linkedListType`. Therefore, we can derive the `class` `linkedQueueType` from the `class` `unorderedLinkedListType`.

We leave it as exercise for you to write the definition of the **class** `linkedQueueType` that is derived from the **class** `unorderedLinkedListType`. See Programming Exercise 16 at the end of this chapter

Application of Queues: Simulation

A technique in which one system models the behavior of another system is called **simulation**. For example, physical simulators include wind tunnels used to experiment with the design of car bodies and flight simulators used to train airline pilots. Simulation techniques are used when it is too expensive or dangerous to experiment with real systems. You can also design computer models to study the behavior of real systems. (We will describe some real systems modeled by computers shortly.)

Simulating the behavior of an expensive or dangerous experiment using a computer model is usually less expensive than using the real system, and a good way to gain insight without putting human life in danger. Moreover, computer simulations are particularly useful for complex systems where it is difficult to construct a mathematical model. For such systems, computer models can retain descriptive accuracy. In computer simulations, the steps of a program are used to model the behavior of a real system. Let us consider one such problem.

The manager of a local movie theater is hearing complaints from customers about the length of time they have to wait in line to buy tickets. The theater currently has only one cashier. Another theater is preparing to open in the neighborhood and the manager is afraid of losing customers. The manager wants to hire enough cashiers so that a customer does not have to wait too long to buy a ticket, but does not want to hire extra cashiers on a trial basis and potentially waste time and money. One thing that the manager would like to know is the average time a customer has to wait for service. The manager wants someone to write a program to simulate the behavior of the theater.

In computer simulation, the objects being studied are usually represented as data. For the theater problem, some of the objects are the customers and the cashier. The cashier serves the customers and we want to determine a customer's average waiting time. Actions are implemented by writing algorithms, which in a programming language are implemented with the help of functions. Thus, functions are used to implement the actions of the objects. In C++, we can combine the data and the operations on that data into a single unit with the help of classes. Thus, objects can be represented as classes. The member variables of the class describe the properties of the objects, and the function members describe the actions on that data. This change in simulation results can also occur if we change the values of the data or modify the definitions of the functions (that is, modify the algorithms implementing the actions). The main goal of a computer simulation is to either generate results showing the performance of an existing system or predict the performance of a proposed system.

In the theater problem, when the cashier is serving a customer, the other customers must wait. Because customers are served on a first come, first served basis and queues are an effective way to implement a First In First Out system, queues are important data structures for use in computer simulations. This section examines computer simulations in which queues are the basic data structure. These simulations model the behavior of systems, called **queuing systems**, in which queues of objects are waiting to be served by various servers. In other words, a queuing system consists of servers and queues of objects waiting to be served. We deal with a variety of queuing systems on a daily basis. For example, a grocery store and a banking system are both queuing systems. Furthermore, when you send a print request to a networked printer that is shared by many people, your print request goes in a queue. Print requests that arrived before your print request are usually completed before yours. Thus, the printer acts as the server when a queue of documents is waiting to be printed.

Designing a Queuing System

In this section, we describe a queuing system that can be used in a variety of applications, such as a bank, grocery store, movie theater, printer, or a mainframe environment in which several people are trying to use the same processors to execute their programs. To describe a queuing system, we use the term **server** for the object that provides the service. For example, in a bank, a teller is a server; in a grocery store or movie theater, a cashier is a server. We will call the object receiving the service the **customer**, and the service time—the time it takes to serve a customer—the **transaction time**.

Because a queuing system consists of servers and a queue of waiting objects, we will model a system that consists of a list of servers and a waiting queue holding the customers to be served. The customer at the front of the queue waits for the next available server. When a server becomes free, the customer at the front of the queue moves to the free server to be served.

When the first customer arrives, all servers are free and the customer moves to the first server. When the next customer arrives, if a server is available, the customer immediately moves to the available server; otherwise, the customer waits in the queue. To model a queuing system, we need to know the number of servers, the expected arrival time of a customer, the time between the arrivals of customers, and the number of events affecting the system.

Let us again consider the movie theater system. The performance of the system depends on how many servers are available, how long it takes to serve a customer, and how often a customer arrives. If it takes too long to serve a customer and customers arrive frequently, then more servers are needed. This system can be modeled as a time-driven simulation. In a **time-driven simulation**, the clock is implemented as a counter and the passage of, say, one minute can be implemented by incrementing the counter by 1. The simulation is run for a fixed amount of time. If the simulation needs to be run for 100 minutes, the counter starts at 1 and goes up to 100, which can be implemented by using a loop.

For the simulation described in this section, we want to determine the average wait time for a customer. To calculate the average wait time for a customer, we need to add the waiting time of each customer and then divide the sum by the number of customers who have arrived. When a customer arrives, he or she goes to the end of the queue and the customer's waiting time begins. If the queue is empty and a server is free, the customer is served immediately and so this customer's waiting time is zero. On the other hand, if a customer arrives and either the queue is nonempty or all the servers are busy, the customer must wait for the next available server and, therefore, this customer's waiting time begins. We can keep track of the customer's waiting time by using a timer for each customer. When a customer arrives, the timer is set to 0, which is incremented after each time unit.

Suppose that, on average, it takes five minutes for a server to serve a customer. When a server becomes free and the waiting customer's queue is nonempty, the customer at the front of the queue proceeds to begin the transaction. Thus, we must keep track of the time a customer is with a server. When the customer arrives at a server, the transaction time is set to five and is decremented after each time unit. When the transaction time becomes zero, the server is marked free. Hence, the two objects needed to implement a time-driven computer simulation of a queuing system are the customer and the server.

Next, before designing the main algorithm to implement the simulation, we design classes to implement each of the two objects: *customer* and *server*.

Customer

Every customer has a customer number, arrival time, waiting time, transaction time, and departure time. If we know the arrival time, waiting time, and transaction time, we can determine the departure time by adding these three times. Let us call the class to implement the customer object `customerType`. It follows that the **class** `customerType` has four member variables: the `customerNumber`, `arrivalTime`, `waitingTime`, and `transactionTime`, each of the data type `int`. The basic operations that must be performed on an object of type `customerType` are as follows: set the customer's number, arrival time, and waiting time; increment the waiting time by one time unit; return the waiting time; return the arrival time; return the transaction time; and return the customer number. The following **class**, `customerType`, implements the customer as an ADT:

```
class customerType
{
public:
    customerType(int cN = 0, int arrvTime = 0, int wTime = 0,
                 int tTime = 0);
      //Constructor to initialize the instance variables
      //according to the parameters
      //If no value is specified in the object declaration,
      //the default values are assigned.
      //Postcondition: customerNumber = cN;
      //               arrivalTime = arrvTime;
      //               waitingTime = wTime;
      //               transactionTime = tTime
```

```cpp
    void setCustomerInfo(int customerN = 0, int inTime = 0,
                         int wTime = 0, int tTime = 0);
      //Function to initialize the instance variables.
      //Instance variables are set according to the parameters.
      //Postcondition: customerNumber = customerN;
      //               arrivalTime = arrvTime;
      //               waitingTime = wTime;
      //               transactionTime = tTime;

    int getWaitingTime() const;
      //Function to return the waiting time of a customer.
      //Postcondition: The value of waitingTime is returned.

    void setWaitingTime(int time);
      //Function to set the waiting time of a customer.
      //Postcondition: waitingTime = time;

    void incrementWaitingTime();
      //Function to increment the waiting time by one time unit.
      //Postcondition: waitingTime++;

    int getArrivalTime() const;
      //Function to return the arrival time of a customer.
      //Postcondition: The value of arrivalTime is returned.

    int getTransactionTime() const;
      //Function to return the transaction time of a customer.
      //Postcondition: The value of transactionTime is returned.

    int getCustomerNumber() const;
      //Function to return the customer number.
      //Postcondition: The value of customerNumber is returned.

private:
    int customerNumber;
    int arrivalTime;
    int waitingTime;
    int transactionTime;
};
```

Figure 18-52 shows the UML class diagram of the **class** customerType.

```
customerType
-------------------------------------------------
-customerNumber: int
-arrivalTime: int
-waitingTime: int
-transactionTime: int
-------------------------------------------------
+setCustomerInfo(int = 0, int = 0, int = 0,
                 int = 0): void
+getWaitingTime() const: int
+setWaitingTime(int): void
+incrementWaitingTime(): void
+getArrivalTime() const: int
+getTransactionTime() const: int
+getCustomerNumber() const: int
+customerType(int = 0, int = 0, int = 0,
              int = 0)
```

FIGURE 18-52 UML class diagram of the **class** customerType

The definitions of the member functions of the **class** customerType follow easily from their descriptions. Next, we give the definitions of the member functions of the **class** customerType.

The function setCustomerInfo uses the values of the parameters to initialize customerNumber, arrivalTime, waitingTime, and transactionTime. The definition of setCustomerInfo is:

```
void customerType::setCustomerInfo(int customerN, int arrvTime,
                                   int wTime, int tTime)
{
    customerNumber = customerN;
    arrivalTime = arrvTime;
    waitingTime = wTime;
    transactionTime = tTime;
}
```

The definition of the constructor is similar to the definition of the function setCustomerInfo. It uses the values of the parameters to initialize customerNumber, arrivalTime, waitingTime, and transactionTime. To make debugging easier, we use the function setCustomerInfo to write the definition of the constructor, which is given next, as follows:

```
customerType::customerType(int customerN, int arrvTime,
                            int wTime, int tTime)
{
    setCustomerInfo(customerN, arrvTime, wTime, tTime);
}
```

The function `getWaitingTime` returns the current waiting time. The definition of the function `getWaitingTime` is:

```
int customerType::getWaitingTime() const
{
    return waitingTime;
}
```

The function `incrementWaitingTime` increments the value of `waitingTime`. Its definition is:

```
void customerType::incrementWaitingTime()
{
    waitingTime++;
}
```

The definitions of the functions `setWaitingTime`, `getArrivalTime`, `getTransactionTime`, and `getCustomerNumber` are left as an exercise for you.

Server

At any given time unit, the server is either busy serving a customer or is free. We use a `string` variable to set the status of the server. Every server has a timer and, because the program might need to know which customer is served by which server, the server also stores the information of the customer being served. Thus, three member variables are associated with a server: the `status`, the `transactionTime`, and the `currentCustomer`. Some of the basic operations that must be performed on a server are as follows: check whether the server is free; set the server as free; set the server as busy; set the transaction time (that is, how long it takes to serve the customer); return the remaining transaction time (to determine whether the server should be set to free); if the server is busy after each time unit, decrement the transaction time by one time unit; and so on. The following `class`, `serverType`, implements the server as an ADT:

```
class serverType
{
public:
    serverType();
      //Default constructor
      //Sets the values of the instance variables to their default
      //values.
      //Postcondition: currentCustomer is initialized by its
      //               default constructor; status = "free"; and
      //               the transaction time is initialized to 0.
```

```cpp
    bool isFree() const;
      //Function to determine if the server is free.
      //Postcondition: Returns true if the server is free,
      //               otherwise returns false.

    void setBusy();
      //Function to set the status of the server to busy.
      //Postcondition: status = "busy";

    void setFree();
      //Function to set the status of the server to "free".
      //Postcondition: status = "free";

    void setTransactionTime(int t);
      //Function to set the transaction time according to the
      //parameter t.
      //Postcondition: transactionTime = t;

    void setTransactionTime();
      //Function to set the transaction time according to
      //the transaction time of the current customer.
      //Postcondition:
      //   transactionTime = currentCustomer.transactionTime;

    int getRemainingTransactionTime() const;
      //Function to return the remaining transaction time.
      //Postcondition: The value of transactionTime is returned.

    void decreaseTransactionTime();
      //Function to decrease the transactionTime by 1 unit.
      //Postcondition: transactionTime--;

    void setCurrentCustomer(customerType cCustomer);
      //Function to set the info of the current customer
      //according to the parameter cCustomer.
      //Postcondition: currentCustomer = cCustomer;

    int getCurrentCustomerNumber() const;
      //Function to return the customer number of the current
      //customer.
      //Postcondition: The value of customerNumber of the
      //               current customer is returned.

    int getCurrentCustomerArrivalTime() const;
      //Function to return the arrival time of the current
      //customer.
      //Postcondition: The value of arrivalTime of the current
      //               customer is returned.

    int getCurrentCustomerWaitingTime() const;
      //Function to return the current waiting time of the
      //current customer.
```

```
    //Postcondition: The value of transactionTime is
    //                returned.

int getCurrentCustomerTransactionTime() const;
    //Function to return the transaction time of the
    //current customer.
    //Postcondition: The value of transactionTime of the
    //                current customer is returned.

private:
    customerType currentCustomer;
    string status;
    int transactionTime;
};
```

Figure 18-53 shows the UML class diagram of the **class** serverType.

```
                        serverType
-currentCustomer: customerType
-status: string
-transactionTime: int

+isFree() const: bool
+setBusy(): void
+setFree(): void
+setTransactionTime(int): void
+setTransactionTime(): void
+getRemainingTransactionTime() const: int
+decreaseTransactionTime(): void
+setCurrentCustomer(customerType): void
+getCurrentCustomerNumber() const: int
+getCurrentCustomerArrivalTime() const: int
+getCurrentCustomerWaitingTime() const: int
+getCurrentCustomerTransactionTime() const: int
+serverType()
```

FIGURE 18-53 UML class diagram of the **class** serverType

The definitions of some of the member functions of the **class** serverType are:

```
serverType::serverType()
{
    status = "free";
    transactionTime = 0;
}
```

```cpp
bool serverType::isFree() const
{
    return (status == "free");
}

void serverType::setBusy()
{
    status = "busy";
}

void serverType::setFree()
{
    status = "free";
}

void serverType::setTransactionTime(int t)
{
    transactionTime = t;
}

void serverType::setTransactionTime()
{
    int time;

    time = currentCustomer.getTransactionTime();

    transactionTime = time;
}

void serverType::decreaseTransactionTime()
{
    transactionTime--;
}
```

We leave the definitions of the functions `getRemainingTransactionTime`, `setCurrentCustomer`, `getCurrentCustomerNumber`, `getCurrentCustomerArrivalTime`, `getCurrentCustomerWaitingTime`, and `getCurrentCustomerTransactionTime` as an exercise for you.

Because we are designing a simulation program that can be used in a variety of applications, we need to design two more classes: one to create and process a list of servers, and one to create and process a queue of waiting customers. The next two sections describe each of these classes.

Server List

A server list is a set of servers. At any given time, a server is either free or busy. For the customer at the front of the queue, we need to find a server in the list that is free. If all the servers are busy, then the customer must wait until one of the servers becomes free. Thus, the class that implements a list of servers has two member variables: one to store the number of servers and one to maintain a list of servers. Using dynamic arrays, depending on the number of servers specified by the user, a list of servers is created during program execution. Some of the operations that must be performed on a server list are as follows: return the server number of a free server; when a customer gets ready to do business and a server is available, set the server to busy; when the simulation ends, some of the servers might still be busy, so return the number of busy servers; after each time unit, reduce the `transactionTime` of each busy server by one time unit; and if the `transactionTime` of a server becomes zero, set the server to free. The following `class`, `serverListType`, implements the list of servers as an ADT:

```cpp
class serverListType
{
public:
    serverListType(int num = 1);
      //Constructor to initialize a list of servers
      //Postcondition: numOfServers = num
      //               A list of servers, specified by num,
      //               is created and each server is
      //               initialized to "free".

    ~serverListType();
      //Destructor
      //Postcondition: The list of servers is destroyed.

    int getFreeServerID() const;
      //Function to search the list of servers.
      //Postcondition: If a free server is found, returns
      //               its ID; otherwise, returns -1.

    int getNumberOfBusyServers() const;
      //Function to return the number of busy servers.
      //Postcondition: The number of busy servers is returned.

    void setServerBusy(int serverID, customerType cCustomer,
                       int tTime);
      //Function to set a server as busy.
      //Postcondition: The server specified by serverID is set
      //               to "busy", to serve the customer
      //               specified by cCustomer, and the
      //               transaction time is set according to the
      //               parameter tTime.

    void setServerBusy(int serverID, customerType cCustomer);
      //Function to set a server as busy.
      //Postcondition: The server specified by serverID is set
      //               to "busy", to serve the customer
      //               specified by cCustomer.

    void updateServers(ostream& outFile);
      //Function to update the status of a server.
      //Postcondition: The transaction time of each busy
```

```
//                      server is decremented by one unit. If
//                      the transaction time of a busy server
//                      is reduced to zero, the server is set
//                      to "free". Moreover, if the actual
//                      parameter corresponding to outFile is
//                      cout, a message indicating which customer
//                      has been served is printed on the screen,
//                      together with the customer's departing
//                      time. Otherwise, the output is sent to
//                      a file specified by the user.

private:
    int numOfServers;
    serverType *servers;
};
```

Figure 18-54 shows the UML class diagram of the **class** serverListType.

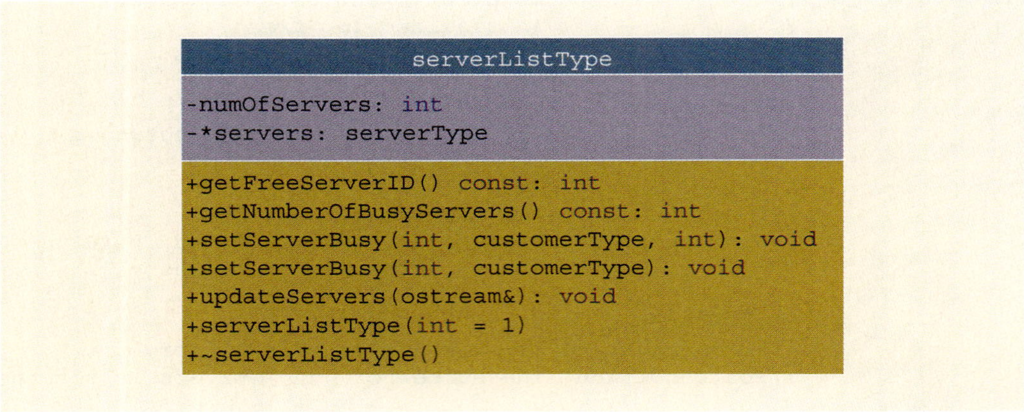

FIGURE 18-54 UML class diagram of the **class** serverListType

Following are the definitions of the member functions of the **class** serverListType.
The definitions of the constructor and destructor are straightforward:

```
serverListType::serverListType(int num)
{
    numOfServers = num;
    servers = new serverType[num];
}

serverListType::~serverListType()
{
    delete [] servers;
}
```

The function `getFreeServerID` searches the list of servers. If a free server is found, it returns the server's ID; otherwise, the value `-1` is returned, which indicates that all the servers are busy. The definition of this function is:

```cpp
int serverListType::getFreeServerID() const
{
    int serverID = -1;

    int i;

    for (i = 0; i < numOfServers; i++)
        if (servers[i].isFree())
        {
            serverID = i;
            break;
        }

    return serverID;
}
```

The function `getNumberOfBusyServers` searches the list of servers and determines and returns the number of busy servers. The definition of this function is:

```cpp
int serverListType::getNumberOfBusyServers() const
{
    int busyServers = 0;

    int i;

    for (i = 0; i < numOfServers; i++)
        if (!servers[i].isFree())
            busyServers++;

    return busyServers;
}
```

The function `setServerBusy` sets a server to busy. This function is overloaded. The `serverID` of the server that is set to busy is passed as a parameter to this function. One function sets the server's transaction time according to the parameter `tTime`; the other function sets it by using the transaction time stored in the object `cCustomer`. The transaction time is later needed to determine the average wait time. The definitions of these functions are:

```cpp
void serverListType::setServerBusy(int serverID,
                                   customerType cCustomer,
                                   int tTime)
{
    servers[serverID].setBusy();
    servers[serverID].setTransactionTime(tTime);
    servers[serverID].setCurrentCustomer(cCustomer);
}
```

```cpp
void serverListType::setServerBusy(int serverID,
                                        customerType cCustomer)
{
    int time;

    time = cCustomer.getTransactionTime();

    servers[serverID].setBusy();
    servers[serverID].setTransactionTime(time);
    servers[serverID].setCurrentCustomer(cCustomer);
}
```

The definition of the function `updateServers` is quite straightforward. Starting at the first server, it searches the list of servers for busy servers. When a busy server is found, its `transactionTime` is decremented by 1. If the `transactionTime` reduces to zero, the server is set to `free`. If the `transactionTime` of a busy server reduces to zero, then the transaction of the customer being served by the server is complete. If the actual parameter corresponding to `outFile` is cout, a message indicating which customer has been served is printed on the screen, together with the customer's departing time. Otherwise, the output is sent to a file specified by the user. The definition of this function is as follows:

```cpp
void serverListType::updateServers(ostream& outFile)
{
    int i;

    for (i = 0; i < numOfServers; i++)
        if (!servers[i].isFree())
        {
            servers[i].decreaseTransactionTime();

            if (servers[i].getRemainingTransactionTime() == 0)
            {
                outFile << "From server number " << (i + 1)
                        << " customer number "
                        << servers[i].getCurrentCustomerNumber()
                        << "\n     departed at time unit "
                        << servers[i].
                             getCurrentCustomerArrivalTime()
                          + servers[i].
                             getCurrentCustomerWaitingTime()
                          + servers[i].
                             getCurrentCustomerTransactionTime()
                        << endl;
                servers[i].setFree();
            }
        }
}
```

Waiting Customers Queue

When a customer arrives, he or she goes to the end of the queue. When a server becomes available, the customer at the front of the queue leaves to conduct the transaction. After each time unit, the waiting time of each customer in the queue is incremented by 1. The ADT `queueType` designed in this chapter has all the operations needed to implement a queue, except the operation of incrementing the waiting time of each customer in the queue by one time unit. We will derive a `class`, `waitingCustomerQueueType`, from the `class` `queueType` and add the additional operations to implement the customer queue. The definition of the `class` `waitingCustomerQueueType` is as follows:

```
class waitingCustomerQueueType: public queueType<customerType>
{
public:
    waitingCustomerQueueType(int size = 100);
      //Constructor
      //Postcondition: The queue is initialized according to
      //               the parameter size. The value of size
      //               is passed to the constructor of queueType.

    void updateWaitingQueue();
      //Function to increment the waiting time of each
      //customer in the queue by one time unit.
};
```

Notice that the `class` `waitingCustomerQueueType` is derived from the `class` `queueType`, which implements the queue in an array. You can also derive it from the `class` `linkedQueueType`, which implements the queue in a linked list. We leave the details as an exercise for you.

The definitions of the member functions are given next. The definition of the constructor is as follows:

```
waitingCustomerQueueType::waitingCustomerQueueType(int size)
                        :queueType<customerType>(size)
{
}
```

The function `updateWaitingQueue` increments the waiting time of each customer in the queue by one time unit. The `class` `waitingCustomerQueueType` is derived from the `class` `queueType`. Because the member variables of `queueType` are `private`, the function `updateWaitingQueue` cannot directly access the elements of the queue. The only way to access the elements of the queue is to use the `deleteQueue` operation. After incrementing the waiting time, the element can be put back into the queue by using the `addQueue` operation.

The `addQueue` operation inserts the element at the end of the queue. If we perform the `deleteQueue` operation followed by the `addQueue` operation for each element of the queue, then eventually the front element again becomes the front element. Given that each `deleteQueue` operation is followed by an `addQueue` operation, how do we determine that all the elements of the queue have been processed? We cannot use the `isEmptyQueue` or `isFullQueue` operations on the queue, because the queue will never be empty or full.

One solution to this problem is to create a temporary queue. Every element of the original queue is removed, processed, and inserted into the temporary queue. When the original queue becomes empty, all of the elements in the queue are processed. We can then copy the elements from the temporary queue back into the original queue. However, this solution requires us to use extra memory space, which could be significant. Also, if the queue is large, extra computer time is needed to copy the elements from the temporary queue back into the original queue. Let us look into another solution.

In the second solution, before starting to update the elements of the queue, we can insert a dummy customer with a wait time of, say, -1. During the update process, when we arrive at the customer with the wait time of -1, we can stop the update process without processing the customer with the wait time of -1. If we do not process the customer with the wait time of -1, this customer is removed from the queue and, after processing all the elements of the queue, the queue will contain no extra elements. This solution does not require us to create a temporary queue, so we do not need extra computer time to copy the elements back into the original queue. We will use this solution to update the queue. Therefore, the definition of the function `updateWaitingQueue` is:

```cpp
void waitingCustomerQueueType::updateWaitingQueue()
{
    customerType cust;

    cust.setWaitingTime(-1);
    int wTime = 0;

    addQueue(cust);

    while (wTime != -1)
    {
        cust = front();
        deleteQueue();

        wTime = cust.getWaitingTime();
        if (wTime == -1)
            break;
        cust.incrementWaitingTime();
        addQueue(cust);
    }
}
```

Main Program

To run the simulation, we first need to get the following information:

- The number of time units the simulation should run. Assume that each time unit is one minute.

- The number of servers.

- The amount of time it takes to serve a customer—that is, the transaction time.

- The approximate time between customer arrivals.

These pieces of information are called simulation parameters. By changing the values of these parameters, we can observe the changes in the performance of the system. We can write a function, `setSimulationParameters`, to prompt the user to specify these values. The definition of this function is:

```cpp
void setSimulationParameters(int& sTime, int& numOfServers,
                             int& transTime,
                             int& tBetweenCArrival)
{
    cout << "Enter the simulation time: ";
    cin >> sTime;
    cout << endl;

    cout << "Enter the number of servers: ";
    cin >> numOfServers;
    cout << endl;

    cout << "Enter the transaction time: ";
    cin >> transTime;
    cout << endl;

    cout << "Enter the time between customer arrivals: ";
    cin >> tBetweenCArrival;
    cout << endl;
}
```

When a server becomes free and the customer queue is nonempty, we can move the customer at the front of the queue to the free server to be served. Moreover, when a customer starts the transaction, the waiting time ends. The waiting time of the customer is added to the total waiting time. The general algorithm to start the transaction (supposing that `serverID` denotes the ID of the free server) is:

1. Remove the customer from the front of the queue.

   ```cpp
   customer = customerQueue.front();
   customerQueue.deleteQueue();
   ```

2. Update the total wait time by adding the current customer's wait time to the previous total wait time.

   ```cpp
   totalWait = totalWait + customer.getWaitingTime();
   ```

3.   Set the free server to begin the transaction.

```
serverList.setServerBusy(serverID, customer, transTime);
```

To run the simulation, we need to know the number of customers arriving at a given time unit and how long it takes to serve the customer. We use the Poisson distribution from statistics, which says that the probability of y events occurring at a given time is given by the formula:

$$P(y) = \frac{\lambda^y e^{-\lambda}}{y!}, y = 0, 1, 2, \ldots,$$

where λ is the expected value that y events occur at that time. Suppose that, on average, a customer arrives every four minutes. During this four-minute period, the customer can arrive at any one of the four minutes. Assuming an equal likelihood of each of the four minutes, the expected value that a customer arrives in each of the four minutes is, therefore, $1 / 4 = .25$. Next, we need to determine whether or not the customer actually arrives at a given minute.

Now $P(0) = e^{-\lambda}$ is the probability that no event occurs at a given time. One of the basic assumptions of the Poisson distribution is that the probability of more than one outcome occurring in a short time interval is negligible. For simplicity, we assume that only one customer arrives at a given time unit. Thus, we use $e^{-\lambda}$ as the cutoff point to determine whether a customer arrives at a given time unit. Suppose that, on average, a customer arrives every four minutes. Then, $\lambda = 0.25$. We can use an algorithm to generate a number between 0 and 1. If the value of the number generated is $> e^{-0.25}$, we can assume that the customer arrived at a particular time unit. For example, suppose that $rNum$ is a random number such that $0 \leq rNum \leq 1$. If $rNum > e^{-0.25}$, the customer arrived at the given time unit.

We now describe the function `runSimulation` to implement the simulation. Suppose that we run the simulation for 100 time units and customers arrive at time units 93, 96, and 100. The average transaction time is 5 minutes—that is, 5 time units. For simplicity, assume that we have only one server and the server becomes free at time unit 97, and that all customers arriving before time unit 93 have been served. When the server becomes free at time unit 97, the customer arriving at time unit 93 starts the transaction. Because the transaction of the customer arriving at time unit 93 starts at time unit 97 and it takes 5 minutes to complete a transaction, when the simulation loop ends, the customer arriving at time unit 93 is still at the server. Moreover, customers arriving at time units 96 and 100 are in the queue. For simplicity, we assume that when the simulation loop ends, the customers at the servers are considered served. The general algorithm for this function is:

1.   Declare and initialize the variables, such as the simulation parameters, customer number, clock, total and average waiting times, number of customers arrived, number of customers served, number of customers left in the waiting queue, number of customers left with the servers, `waitingCustomersQueue`, and a list of servers.

2. The main loop is:

```
for (clock = 1; clock <= simulationTime; clock++)
{
```

    2.1. Update the server list to decrement the transaction time of each busy server by one time unit.

    2.2. If the customer's queue is nonempty, increment the waiting time of each customer by one time unit.

    2.3. If a customer arrives, increment the number of customers by 1 and add the new customer to the queue.

    2.4. If a server is free and the customer's queue is nonempty, remove a customer from the front of the queue and send the customer to the free server.

```
}
```

3. Print the appropriate results. Your results must include the number of customers left in the queue, the number of customers still with servers, the number of customers arrived, and the number of customers who actually completed a transaction.

Once you have designed the function `runSimulation`, the definition of the function `main` is simple and straightforward because the function `main` calls only the function `runSimulation`.

When we tested our version of the simulation program, we generated the following results. (The program was executed two times.) We assumed that the average transaction time is 5 minutes and that, on average, a customer arrives every 4 minutes, and we used a random number generator to generate a number between 0 and 1 to decide whether a customer arrived at a given time unit.

Sample Runs:

Sample Run 1:

```
Customer number 1 arrived at time unit 4
Customer number 2 arrived at time unit 8
From server number 1 customer number 1
     departed at time unit 9
Customer number 3 arrived at time unit 9
Customer number 4 arrived at time unit 12
From server number 1 customer number 2
     departed at time unit 14
From server number 1 customer number 3
     departed at time unit 19
Customer number 5 arrived at time unit 21
From server number 1 customer number 4
     departed at time unit 24
From server number 1 customer number 5
     departed at time unit 29
```

```
Customer number 6 arrived at time unit 37
Customer number 7 arrived at time unit 38
Customer number 8 arrived at time unit 41
From server number 1 customer number 6
        departed at time unit 42
Customer number 9 arrived at time unit 43
Customer number 10 arrived at time unit 44
From server number 1 customer number 7
        departed at time unit 47
Customer number 11 arrived at time unit 49
Customer number 12 arrived at time unit 51
From server number 1 customer number 8
        departed at time unit 52
Customer number 13 arrived at time unit 52
Customer number 14 arrived at time unit 53
Customer number 15 arrived at time unit 54
From server number 1 customer number 9
        departed at time unit 57
Customer number 16 arrived at time unit 59
From server number 1 customer number 10
        departed at time unit 62
Customer number 17 arrived at time unit 66
From server number 1 customer number 11
        departed at time unit 67
Customer number 18 arrived at time unit 71
From server number 1 customer number 12
        departed at time unit 72
From server number 1 customer number 13
        departed at time unit 77
Customer number 19 arrived at time unit 78
From server number 1 customer number 14
        departed at time unit 82
From server number 1 customer number 15
        departed at time unit 87
Customer number 20 arrived at time unit 90
From server number 1 customer number 16
        departed at time unit 92
Customer number 21 arrived at time unit 92
From server number 1 customer number 17
        departed at time unit 97

The simulation ran for 100 time units
Number of servers: 1
Average transaction time: 5
Average arrival time difference between customers: 4
Total waiting time: 269
Number of customers that completed a transaction: 17
Number of customers left in the servers: 1
The number of customers left in queue: 3
Average waiting time: 12.81
************** END SIMULATION *************
```

Sample Run 2:

```
Customer number 1 arrived at time unit 4
Customer number 2 arrived at time unit 8
From server number 1 customer number 1
        departed at time unit 9
```

```
Customer number 3 arrived at time unit 9
Customer number 4 arrived at time unit 12
From server number 2 customer number 2
     departed at time unit 13
From server number 1 customer number 3
     departed at time unit 14
From server number 2 customer number 4
     departed at time unit 18
Customer number 5 arrived at time unit 21
From server number 1 customer number 5
     departed at time unit 26
Customer number 6 arrived at time unit 37
Customer number 7 arrived at time unit 38
Customer number 8 arrived at time unit 41
From server number 1 customer number 6
     departed at time unit 42
From server number 2 customer number 7
     departed at time unit 43
Customer number 9 arrived at time unit 43
Customer number 10 arrived at time unit 44
From server number 1 customer number 8
     departed at time unit 47
From server number 2 customer number 9
     departed at time unit 48
Customer number 11 arrived at time unit 49
Customer number 12 arrived at time unit 51
From server number 1 customer number 10
     departed at time unit 52
Customer number 13 arrived at time unit 52
Customer number 14 arrived at time unit 53
From server number 2 customer number 11
     departed at time unit 54
Customer number 15 arrived at time unit 54
From server number 1 customer number 12
     departed at time unit 57
From server number 2 customer number 13
     departed at time unit 59
Customer number 16 arrived at time unit 59
From server number 1 customer number 14
     departed at time unit 62
From server number 2 customer number 15
     departed at time unit 64
Customer number 17 arrived at time unit 66
From server number 1 customer number 16
     departed at time unit 67
From server number 2 customer number 17
     departed at time unit 71
Customer number 18 arrived at time unit 71
From server number 1 customer number 18
     departed at time unit 76
Customer number 19 arrived at time unit 78
From server number 1 customer number 19
     departed at time unit 83
Customer number 20 arrived at time unit 90
Customer number 21 arrived at time unit 92
From server number 1 customer number 20
     departed at time unit 95
```

```
From server number 2 customer number 21
      departed at time unit 97

The simulation ran for 100 time units
Number of servers: 2
Average transaction time: 5
Average arrival time difference between customers: 4
Total waiting time: 20
Number of customers that completed a transaction: 21
Number of customers left in the servers: 0
The number of customers left in queue: 0
Average waiting time: 0.95
************** END SIMULATION **************
```

QUICK REVIEW

1. A stack is a data structure in which the items are added and deleted from one end only.

2. A stack is a Last In First Out (LIFO) data structure.

3. The basic operations on a stack are as follows: push an item onto the stack, pop an item from the stack, retrieve the top element of the stack, initialize the stack, check whether the stack is empty, and check whether the stack is full.

4. A stack can be implemented as an array or a linked list.

5. The middle elements of a stack should not be accessed directly.

6. Stacks are restricted versions of arrays and linked lists.

7. Postfix notation does not require the use of parentheses to enforce operator precedence.

8. In postfix notation, the operators are written after the operands.

9. Postfix expressions are evaluated according to the following rules:

   a. Scan the expression from left to right.

   b. If an operator is found, back up to get the required number of operands, evaluate the operator, and continue.

10. A queue is a data structure in which the items are added at one end and removed from the other end.

11. A queue is a First In First Out (FIFO) data structure.

12. The basic operations on a queue are as follows: add an item to the queue, remove an item from the queue, retrieve the first or last element of the queue, initialize the queue, check whether the queue is empty, and check whether the queue is full.

13. A queue can be implemented as an array or a linked list.

14. The middle elements of a queue should not be accessed directly.

15. Queues are restricted versions of arrays and linked lists.

EXERCISES

1. Consider the following statements:

```cpp
stackType<int> stack;
int x, y;
```

Show what is output by the following segment of code:

```cpp
x = 4;
y = 0;
stack.push(7);
stack.push(x);
stack.push(x + 5);
y = stack.top();
stack.pop();
stack.push(x + y);
stack.push(y - 2);
stack.push(3);
x = stack.top();
stack.pop();

cout << "x = " << x << endl;
cout << "y = " << y << endl;

while (!stack.isEmptyStack())
{
    cout << stack.top() << endl;
    stack.pop();
}
```

2. Consider the following statements:

```cpp
stackType<int> stack;
int x;
```

Suppose that the input is:

```
14 45 34 23 10 5 -999
```

Show what is output by the following segment of code:

```cpp
stack.push(5);

cin >> x;

while (x != -999)
{
    if (x % 2 == 0)
    {
        if (!stack.isFullStack())
            stack.push(x);
    }
    else
        cout << "x = " << x << endl;
    cin >> x;
}
```

```cpp
    cout << "Stack Elements: ";

    while (!stack.isEmptyStack())
    {
        cout << " " << stack.top();
        stack.pop();
    }
    cout << endl;
```

3. Evaluate the following postfix expressions:

   a. 8 2 + 3 * 16 4 / - =

   b. 12 25 5 1 / / * 8 7 + - =

   c. 70 14 4 5 15 3 / * - - / 6 + =

   d. 3 5 6 * + 13 - 18 2 / + =

4. Convert the following infix expressions to postfix notations:

   a. (A + B) * (C + D) - E

   b. A - (B + C) * D + E / F

   c. ((A + B) / (C - D) + E) * F - G

   d. A + B * (C + D) - E / F * G + H

5. Write the equivalent infix expression for the following postfix expressions.

   a. A B * C +

   b. A B + C D - *

   c. A B - C - D *

6. What is the output of the following program?

```cpp
#include <iostream>
#include <string>
#include "myStack.h"

using namespace std;

template <class type>
void mystery(stackType<type>& s, stackType<type>& t);

int main()
{
    stackType<string> s1;
    stackType<string> s2;

    string list[] = {"Winter", "Spring", "Summer", "Fall",
                     "Cold", "Warm", "Hot"};

    for (int i = 0; i < 7; i++)
        s1.push(list[i]);
```

```cpp
        mystery(s1, s2);

        while (!s2.isEmptyStack())
        {
            cout << s2.top() << " ";
            s2.pop();
        }
        cout << endl;
}

template <class type>
void mystery(stackType<type>& s, stackType<type>& t)
{
        while (!s.isEmptyStack())
        {
            t.push(s.top());
            s.pop();
        }
}
```

7. What is the output of the following program?

```cpp
#include <iostream>
#include <string>
#include "myStack.h"

using namespace std;

void mystery(stackType<int>& s, stackType<int>& t);

int main()
{
        int list[] = {5, 10, 15, 20, 25};

        stackType<int> s1;
        stackType<int> s2;

        for (int i = 0; i < 5; i++)
            s1.push(list[i]);

        mystery(s1, s2);

        while (!s2.isEmptyStack())
        {
            cout << s2.top() << " ";
            s2.pop();
        }
        cout << endl;
}
```

```cpp
void mystery(stackType<int>& s, stackType<int>& t)
{
    while (!s.isEmptyStack())
    {
        t.push(2 * s.top());
        s.pop();
    }
}
```

8. Write the definition of the function template `printListReverse`, that uses a stack to print a linked list in reverse order. Assume that this function is a member of the **class** `linkedListType`, designed in Chapter 17.

9. Write the definition of the method `second` that takes as a parameter a stack object and returns the second element of the stack. The original stack remains unchanged.

10. Consider the following statements:

```cpp
queueType<int> queue;
int x, y;
```

Show what is output by the following segment of code:

```cpp
x = 4;
y = 5;
queue.addQueue(x);
queue.addQueue(y);
x = queue.front();
queue.deleteQueue();
queue.addQueue(x + 5);
queue.addQueue(16);
queue.addQueue(x);
queue.addQueue(y - 3);

cout << "Queue Elements: ";
while (!queue.isEmptyQueue())
{
    cout << queue.front() << " ";
    queue.deleteQueue();
}
cout << endl;
```

11. Consider the following statements:

```cpp
stackType<int> stack;
queueType<int> queue;
int x;
```

Suppose the input is:

```
15 28 14 22 64 35 19 32 7 11 13 30 -999
```

Show what is written by the following segment of code:

```cpp
stack.push(0);
queue.addQueue(0);
cin >> x;
```

```cpp
while (x != -999)
{
    switch (x % 4)
    {
    case 0:
        stack.push(x);
        break;
    case 1:
        if (!stack.isEmptyStack())
        {
            cout << "Stack Element = " << stack.top()
                << endl;
            stack.pop();
        }
        else
            cout << "Sorry, the stack is empty." << endl;
            break;
    case 2:
        queue.addQueue(x);
        break;
    case 3:
        if (!queue.isEmptyQueue())
        {
            cout << "Queue Element = " << queue.front()
                << endl;
            queue.deleteQueue();
        }
        else
            cout << "Sorry, the queue is empty." << endl;
        break;
    } //end switch

    cin >> x;
} //end while

cout << "Stack Elements: ";
while (!stack.isEmptyStack())
{
    cout << stack.top() << " ";
    stack.pop();
}

cout << endl;

cout << "Queue Elements: ";
while (!queue.isEmptyQueue())
{
    cout << queue.front() << " ";
    queue.deleteQueue();
}
cout << endl;
```

12. What does the following function do?

```
void mystery(queueType<int>& q)
{
    stackType<int> s;

    while (!q.isEmptyQueue())
    {
        s.push(q.front());
        q.deleteQueue();
    }

    while (!s.isEmptyStack())
    {
        q.addQueue(2 * s.top());
        s.pop();
    }
}
```

13. Suppose that queue is a queueType object and the size of the array implementing queue is 100. Also, suppose that the value of queueFront is 50 and the value of queueRear is 99.

    a. What are the values of queueFront and queueRear after adding an element to queue?

    b. What are the values of queueFront and queueRear after removing an element from queue?

14. Suppose that queue is a queueType object and the size of the array implementing queue is 100. Also, suppose that the value of queueFront is 99 and the value of queueRear is 25.

    a. What are the values of queueFront and queueRear after adding an element to queue?

    b. What are the values of queueFront and queueRear after removing an element from queue?

15. Suppose that queue is a queueType object and the size of the array implementing queue is 100. Also, suppose that the value of queueFront is 25 and the value of queueRear is 75.

    a. What are the values of queueFront and queueRear after adding an element to queue?

    b. What are the values of queueFront and queueRear after removing an element from queue?

16. Suppose that queue is a queueType object and the size of the array implementing queue is 100. Also, suppose that the value of queueFront is 99 and the value of queueRear is 99.

    a. What are the values of queueFront and queueRear after adding an element to queue?

b. What are the values of `queueFront` and `queueRear` after removing an element from `queue`?

17. Suppose that `queue` is implemented as an array with the special reserved slot, as described in this chapter. Also, suppose that the size of the array implementing `queue` is 100. If the value of `queueFront` is 50, what is the position of the first `queue` element?

18. Suppose that `queue` is implemented as an array with the special reserved slot, as described in this chapter. Suppose that the size of the array implementing `queue` is 100. Also, suppose that the value of `queueFront` is 74 and the value of `queueRear` is 99.

   a. What are the values of `queueFront` and `queueRear` after adding an element to `queue`?

   b. What are the values of `queueFront` and `queueRear` after removing an element from `queue`? Also, what is the position of the removed `queue` element?

19. Write a function template, `reverseStack`, that takes as a parameter a stack object and uses a queue object to reverse the elements of the stack.

20. Write a function template, `reverseQueue`, that takes as a parameter a queue object and uses a stack object to reverse the elements of the queue.

21. Add the operation `queueCount` to the **class** `queueType` (the array implementation of queues), which returns the number of elements in the queue. Write the definition of the function template to implement this operation.

22. Draw the UML class diagram of the **class** `linkedStackType`.

23. Draw the UML class diagram of the **class** `queueADT`.

24. Draw the UML class diagram of the **class** `queueType`.

25. Draw the UML class diagram of the **class** `linkedQueueType`

PROGRAMMING EXERCISES

1. Two stacks of the same type are the same if they have the same number of elements and their elements at the corresponding positions are the same. Overload the relational operator `==` for the **class** `stackType` that returns **true** if two stacks of the same type are the same, **false** otherwise. Also, write the definition of the function template to overload this operator.

2. Repeat Exercise 1 for the **class** `linkedStackType`.

3. a. Add the following operation to the **class** stackType:

```
void  reverseStack(stackType<Type> &otherStack);
```

This operation copies the elements of a stack in reverse order onto another stack.

Consider the following statements:

```
stackType<int> stack1;
stackType<int> stack2;
```

The statement:

```
stack1.reverseStack(stack2);
```

copies the elements of stack1 onto stack2 in reverse order. That is, the top element of stack1 is the bottom element of stack2, and so on. The old contents of stack2 are destroyed and stack1 is unchanged.

  b. Write the definition of the function **template** to implement the operation reverseStack.

4. Repeat Exercises 3a and 3b for the **class** linkedStackType.

5. Write a program that takes as input an arithmetic expression. The program outputs whether the expression contains matching grouping symbols. For example, the arithmetic expressions {25 + (3 − 6) * 8} and 7 + 8 * 2 contain matching grouping symbols. However, the expression 5 + { (13 + 7) / 8 − 2 * 9 does not contain matching grouping symbols.

6. Write a program that uses a stack to print the prime factors of a positive integer in descending order.

7. The Programming Example, Converting a Number from Binary to Decimal, in Chapter 16, uses recursion to convert a binary number into an equivalent decimal number. Write a program that uses a stack to convert a binary number into an equivalent decimal number.

8. The Programming Example, Converting a Number from Decimal to Binary, in Chapter 16, contains a program that uses recursion to convert a decimal number into an equivalent binary number. Write a program that uses a stack to convert a decimal number into an equivalent binary number.

9. **(Infix to Postfix)** Write a program that converts an infix expression into an equivalent postfix expression.

The rules to convert an infix expression into an equivalent postfix expression are as follows:

Suppose infx represents the infix expression and pfx represents the postfix expression. The rules to convert infx into pfx are as follows:

a. Initialize `pfx` to an empty expression and also initialize the stack.

b. Get the next symbol, `sym`, from `infx`.

    b.1. If `sym` is an operand, append `sym` to `pfx`.

    b.2. If `sym` is (, push `sym` into the stack.

    b.3. If `sym` is), pop and append all the symbols from the stack until the most recent left parentheses. Pop and discard the left parentheses.

    b.4. If `sym` is an operator:

        b.4.1. Pop and append all the operators from the stack to `pfx` that are above the most recent left parentheses and have precedence greater than or equal to `sym`.

        b.4.2. Push `sym` onto the stack.

c. After processing `infx`, some operators might be left in the stack. Pop and append to `pfx` everything from the stack.

In this program, you will consider the following (binary) arithmetic operators: +, -, *, and /. You may assume that the expressions you will process are error-free.

Design a class that stores the infix and postfix strings. The class must include the following operations:

- **getInfix**: Stores the infix expression.

- **showInfix**: Outputs the infix expression.

- **showPostfix**: Outputs the postfix expression.

Some other operations that you might need are:

- **convertToPostfix**: Converts the infix expression into a postfix expression. The resulting postfix expression is stored in `pfx`.

- **precedence**: Determines the precedence between two operators. If the first operator is of higher or equal precedence than the second operator, it returns the value **true**; otherwise, it returns the value **false**.

Include the constructors and destructors for automatic initialization and dynamic memory deallocation.

Test your program on the following expressions:

a. A + B - C;

b. (A + B) * C;

c. (A + B) * (C - D);

d. A + ((B + C) * (E - F) - G) / (H - I);

e. A + B * (C + D) - E / F * G + H;

For each expression, your answer must be in the following form:

```
Infix Expression: A + B - C;
Postfix Expression: A B + C -
```

10. Write the definitions of the functions to overload the assignment operator and copy constructor for the **class** queueType. Also, write a program to test these operations.

11. Write the definitions of the functions to overload the assignment operator and copy constructor for the **class** linkedQueueType. Also, write a program to test these operations.

12. This chapter describes the array implementation of queues that use a special array slot, called the reserved slot, to distinguish between an empty and a full queue. Write the definition of the class and the definitions of the function members of this queue design. Also, write a test program to test various operations on a queue.

13. Write the definition of the function moveNthFront that takes as a parameter a positive integer, n. The function moves the nth element of the queue to the front. The order of the remaining elements remains unchanged. For example, suppose:

    queue = {5, 11, 34, 67, 43, 55} and n = 3.

    After a call to the function moveNthFront:

    queue = {34, 5, 11, 67, 43, 55}.

    Add this function to the **class** queueType. Also, write a program to test your method.

14. Write a program that reads a line of text, changes each uppercase letter to lowercase, and places each letter both in a queue and onto a stack. The program should then verify whether the line of text is a palindrome (a set of letters or numbers that is the same whether read forward or backward).

15. The implementation of a queue in an array, as given in this chapter, uses the variable count to determine whether the queue is empty or full. You can also use the variable count to return the number of elements in the queue. (See Exercise 11.) On the other hand, **class** linkedQueueType does not use such a variable to keep track of the number of elements in the queue. Redefine the **class** linkedQueueType by adding the variable count to keep track of the number of elements in the queue. Modify the definitions of the functions addQueue and deleteQueue as necessary. Add the function queueCount to return the number of elements in the queue. Also, write a program to test various operations of the class you defined.

16. Write the definition of the **class** linkedQueueType, which is derived from the **class** unorderedLinkedList, as explained in this chapter. Also, write a program to test various operations of this class.

17. a. Write the definitions of the functions `setWaitingTime`, `getArrivalTime`, `getTransactionTime`, and `getCustomerNumber` of the **class** `customerType` defined in the section Application of Queues: Simulation.

b. Write the definitions of the functions `getRemainingTransactionTime`, `setCurrentCustomer`, `getCurrentCustomerNumber`, `getCurrentCustomerArrivalTime`, `getCurrentCustomerWaitingTime`, and `getCurrentCustomerTransactionTime` of the **class** `serverType` defined in the section Application of Queues: Simulation.

c. Write the definition of the function `runSimulation` to complete the design of the computer simulation program (see the section Application of Queues: Simulation). Test run your program for a variety of data. Moreover, use a random number generator to decide whether a customer arrived at a given time unit.

SEARCHING AND SORTING ALGORITHMS

IN THIS CHAPTER, YOU WILL:

- Learn the various search algorithms
- Explore how to implement the sequential and binary search algorithms
- Discover how the sequential and binary search algorithms perform
- Become aware of the lower bound on comparison-based search algorithms
- Learn the various sorting algorithms
- Explore how to implement the bubble, selection, insertion, quick, and merge sorting algorithms
- Discover how the sorting algorithms discussed in this chapter perform

Chapters 13 and 14 described how to organize data into computer memory using an array and how to perform basic operations on that data. Chapter 17 described how to organize data using linked lists. The most important operation that can be performed on a list is the search algorithm. Using the search algorithm, you can do the following:

- Determine whether a particular item is in the list.
- If the data is specially organized (e.g., sorted), find the location in the list where a new item can be inserted.
- Find the location of an item to be deleted.

The search algorithm's performance, therefore, is crucial. If the search is slow, it takes a large amount of computer time to accomplish your task; if the search is fast, you can accomplish your task quickly.

In the first part of this chapter, we describe the search algorithms: sequential search and binary search. Certain search algorithms work only on sorted data. Therefore, the second half of this chapter discusses various sorting algorithms.

Searching and Sorting Algorithms

The searching and sorting algorithms that we describe are generic. Because searching and sorting require comparisons of data, the algorithms should work on the type of data that provide appropriate functions to compare data items. Now data can be organized with the help of an array or a linked list. You can create an array of data items, or you can use the `class unorderedLinkedList` to organize data. The algorithms that we describe should work on either organization. Consequently, we will write the function templates to implement a particular algorithm. All algorithms described in this chapter, with the exception of the merge sort algorithms, are for array-based lists. Because of storage issues and some other overheads, merge sort works better for linked lists. Therefore, after describing the merge sort algorithm, we will add it as a function to the `class unorderedLinkedList`. We will also show how to use the searching and sorting algorithms on objects of the `class unorderedArrayListType`. Moreover, we will place all the array-based searching and sorting functions in the header file `searchSortAlgorithms.h`. Therefore, if you need to use a particular searching and/or sorting function designed in this chapter, your program can include this header file and use that function.

Search Algorithms

Chapters 13, 14, and 17 described how to implement the sequential search algorithm. This chapter discusses other search algorithms and analyzes them. Analysis of the algorithms enables programmers to decide which algorithm to use for a specific application. Before exploring these algorithms, let us make the following observations.

Associated with each item in a data set is a special member that uniquely identifies the item in the data set. For example, if you have a data set consisting of student records, then the student ID uniquely identifies each student in a particular school. This unique member of the item is called the **key** of the item. The keys of the items in the data set are used in such operations as searching, sorting, inserting, and deleting. For instance, when we search the data set for a particular item, we compare the key of the item for which we are searching with the keys of the items in the data set.

When analyzing searching and sorting algorithms, the key comparisons refer to comparing the key of the search item with the key of an item in the list. The number of key comparisons refers to the number of times the key of the search item (in algorithms such as searching and sorting) is compared with the keys of the items in the list.

Sequential Search

The sequential search (also called a linear search) on array-based lists was described in Chapters 13 and 14, and the sequential search on linked lists was covered in Chapter 17. The sequential search works the same for both array-based and linked lists. The search always starts at the first element in the list and continues until either the item is found in the list or the entire list is searched.

Because we are interested in the performance of the sequential search (that is, the analysis of this type of search), for easy reference and the sake of completeness we provide the sequential search algorithm for array-based lists (as described in Chapters 13 and 14). If the search item is found, its index (that is, its location in the array) is returned. If the search is unsuccessful, –1 is returned. Note that the following sequential search does not require the list elements to be in any particular order:

```cpp
template <class elemType>
int seqSearch(const elemType list[], int length,
              const elemType& item)
{
    int loc;
    bool found = false;

    for (loc = 0; loc < length; loc++)
    {
        if (list[loc] == searchItem)
        {
            found = true;
            break;
        }
    }

    if (found)
        return loc;
    else
        return -1;
} //end seqSearch
```

NOTE The sequential search algorithm, as given here, uses an iterative control structure (the `for` loop) to compare the search item with the list elements. You can also write a recursive algorithm to implement the sequential search algorithm. (See Programming Exercise 1 at the end of this chapter.)

SEQUENTIAL SEARCH ANALYSIS

This section analyzes the performance of the sequential search algorithm in both the worst case and the average case.

The statements before and after the loop are executed only once and hence require very little computer time. The statements in the `for` loop are the ones that are repeated several times. For each iteration of the loop, the search item is compared with an element in the list, and a few other statements are executed, including some other comparisons. Clearly, the loop terminates as soon as the search item is found in the list. Therefore, execution of the other statements in the loop is directly related to the outcome of the key comparison. Also, different programmers might implement the same algorithm differently, although the number of key comparisons would typically be the same. The speed of a computer can also easily affect the time an algorithm takes to perform, but it, of course, does not affect the number of key comparisons required.

Therefore, when analyzing a search algorithm, we count the number of key comparisons because this number gives us the most useful information. Furthermore, the criteria for counting the number of key comparisons can be applied equally well to other search algorithms.

Suppose that L is a list of length n. We want to determine the number of key comparisons made by the sequential search when the list L is searched for a given item.

If the search item is not in the list, we then compare the search item with every element in the list, making n comparisons. This is an unsuccessful case.

Suppose that the search item is in the list. Then, the number of key comparisons depends on where in the list the search item is located. If the search item is the first element of L, we make only one key comparison. This is the best case. On the other hand, if the search item is the last element in the list, the algorithm makes n comparisons. This is the worst case. The best and worst cases are not likely to occur every time we apply the sequential search on L, so it would be more helpful if we could determine the average behavior of the algorithm. That is, we need to determine the average number of key comparisons the sequential search algorithm makes in the successful case.

To determine the average number of comparisons in the successful case of the sequential search algorithm:

1. Consider all possible cases.
2. Find the number of comparisons for each case.
3. Add the number of comparisons and divide by the number of cases.

If the search item, called the **target**, is the first element in the list, one comparison is required. If the target is the second element in the list, two comparisons are required. Similarly, if the target is the *k*th element in the list, *k* comparisons are required. We assume that the target can be any element in the list; that is, all list elements are equally likely to be the target. Suppose that there are *n* elements in the list. The following expression gives the average number of comparisons:

$$\frac{1 + 2 + \cdots + n}{n}$$

It is known that:

$$1 + 2 + \cdots + n = \frac{n(n + 1)}{2}$$

Therefore, the following expression gives the average number of comparisons made by the sequential search in the successful case:

$$\frac{1 + 2 + \cdots + n}{n} = \frac{1}{n}\frac{n(n + 1)}{2} = \frac{n + 1}{2}$$

This expression shows that, on average, a successful sequential search searches half the list. It thus follows that if the list size is 1,000,000, on average, the sequential search makes 500,000 comparisons. As a result, the sequential search is not efficient for large lists.

Binary Search

As you can see, the sequential search is not efficient for large lists because, on average, it searches half the list. We, therefore, describe another search algorithm, called the **binary search**, which is very fast. However, a binary search can be performed only on sorted lists. We, therefore, assume that the list is sorted. Later in this chapter, we describe several sorting algorithms.

The binary search algorithm uses the "divide and conquer" technique to search the list. First, the search item is compared with the middle element of the list. If the search item is less than the middle element of the list, we restrict the search to the first half of the list; otherwise, we search the second half of the list.

Consider the sorted list of `length = 12` in Figure 19-1.

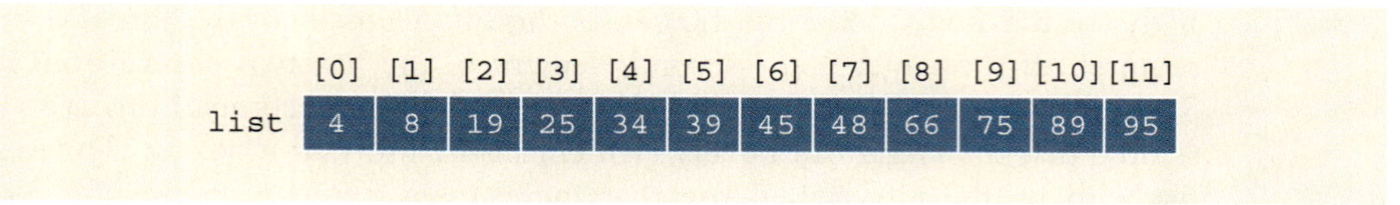

FIGURE 19-1 List of length 12

Suppose that we want to determine whether 75 is in the list. Initially, the entire list is the search list (see Figure 19-2).

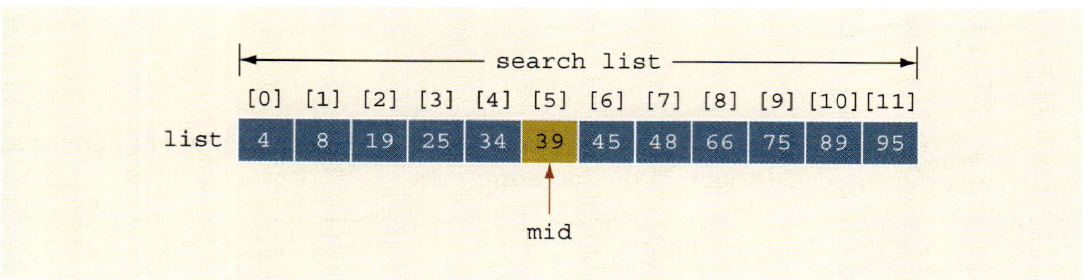

FIGURE 19-2 Search list, `list[0]...list[11]`

First, we compare 75 with the middle element in this list, `list[5]` (which is 39). Because 75 ≠ `list[5]` and 75 > `list[5]`, we then restrict our search to the list `list[6]...list[11]`, as shown in Figure 19-3.

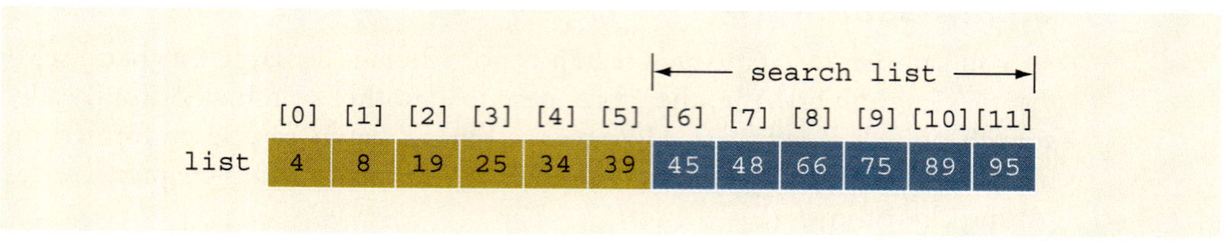

FIGURE 19-3 Search list, `list[6]...list[11]`

This process is now repeated on the list `list[6]...list[11]`, which is a list of `length = 6`.

Because we need to determine the middle element of the list frequently, the binary search algorithm is typically implemented for array-based lists. To determine the middle element of the list, we add the starting index, `first`, and the ending index, `last`, of the search list and then divide by 2 to calculate its index. That is:

$$mid = \frac{first + last}{2}.$$

Initially, `first = 0` and `last = length − 1` (this is because an array index in C++ starts at 0 and `length` denotes the number of elements in the list).

The following C++ function implements the binary search algorithm. If the item is found in the list, its location is returned; if the search item is not in the list, −1 is returned:

```cpp
template <class elemType>
int binarySearch(const elemType list[], int length,
                 const elemType& item)
{
    int first = 0;
    int last = length - 1;
    int mid;

    bool found = false;

    while (first <= last && !found)
    {
        mid = (first + last) / 2;

        if (list[mid] == item)
            found = true;
        else if (list[mid] > item)
            last = mid - 1;
        else
            first = mid + 1;
    }

    if (found)
        return mid;
    else
        return -1;
} //end binarySearch
```

In the binary search algorithm, each time through the loop we make two key comparisons. The only exception is in the successful case; the last time through the loop, only one key comparison is made.

NOTE   The binary search algorithm, as given in this chapter, uses an iterative control structure (the `while` loop) to compare the search item with the list elements. You can also write a recursive algorithm to implement the binary search algorithm. (See Programming Exercise 2 at the end of this chapter.)

Example 19-1 further illustrates how the binary search algorithm works.

EXAMPLE 19-1

Consider the list given in Figure 19-4.

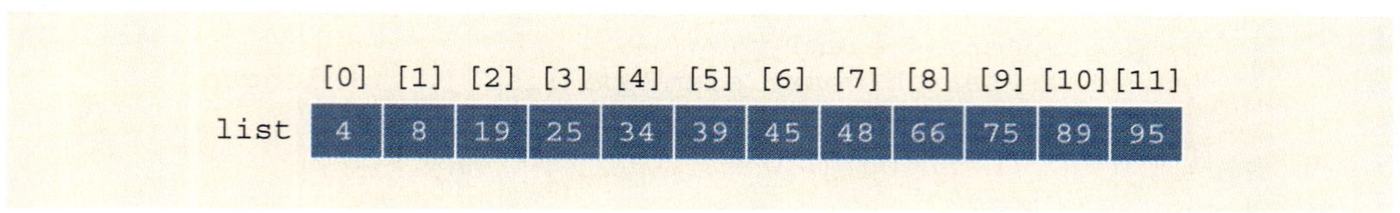

FIGURE 19-4 Sorted list for a binary search

The size of this list is 12; that is, the length is 12. Suppose that we are searching for item 89. Table 19–1 shows the values of `first`, `last`, and `middle` each time through the loop. It also shows the number of times the item is compared with an element in the list each time through the loop.

TABLE 19-1 Values of `first`, `last`, and `middle` and the Number of Comparisons for Search Item 89

Iteration	first	last	mid	list[mid]	Number of comparisons
1	0	11	5	39	2
2	6	11	8	66	2
3	9	11	10	89	1 (found is true)

The item is found at `location` 10, and the total number of comparisons is 5.

Next, let us search the list for item 34. Table 19-2 shows the values of `first`, `last`, and `middle` each time through the loop. It also shows the number of times the item is compared with an element in the list each time through the loop.

TABLE 19-2 Values of `first`, `last`, and `middle` and the Number of Comparisons for Search Item `34`

Iteration	first	last	mid	list[mid]	Number of comparisons
1	0	11	5	39	2
2	0	4	2	19	2
3	3	4	3	25	2
4	4	4	4	34	1 (found is true)

The item is found at `location` 4, and the total number of comparisons is 7.

Let us now search for item 22, as shown in Table 19-3.

TABLE 19-3 Values of `first`, `last`, and `middle` and the Number of Comparisons for Search Item `22`

Iteration	first	last	mid	list[mid]	Number of comparisons
1	0	11	5	39	2
2	0	4	2	19	2
3	3	4	3	25	2
4	3	2	the loop stops (because `first` > `last`)		

This is an unsuccessful search. The total number of comparisons is 6.

Example 19-2 illustrates how to use the binary search algorithm in a program.

EXAMPLE 19-2

```cpp
#include <iostream>
#include "searchSortAlgorithms.h"

using namespace std;

int main()
{
    int intList[] = {2, 16, 34, 45, 53,
                    56, 69, 70, 75, 96};        //Line 1

    int pos;                                    //Line 2

    pos = binarySearch(intList, 10, 45);        //Line 3

    if (pos != -1)                              //Line 4
        cout << "Line 5: " << 45
            << " found at position "
            << pos << endl;                     //Line 5
    else                                        //Line 6
        cout << "Line 7: " << 45
            << " is not in intList " << endl;   //Line 7
    return 0;
}
```

Sample Run:

```
Line 5: 45 found at position 3
```

The preceding program works as follows. The statement in Line 1 creates the array `intList`. (Note that the array `intList` is sorted.) The statement in Line 2 declares `pos` to be an `int` variable. The statement in Line 3 uses the binary search algorithm to determine whether 45 is in `intList`. Note that the array `intList`, its lengths, and the search item, which is 45, are passed as parameters to the function `binarySearch`. The statements in Lines 4 to 7 output the result of the search, which is successful.

Performance of Binary Search

Suppose that `L` is a sorted list of 1000 elements, and you want to determine whether `x` is in `L`. Because `L` is sorted, you can apply the binary search algorithm to search for `x`. Suppose that `L` is as shown in Figure 19-5.

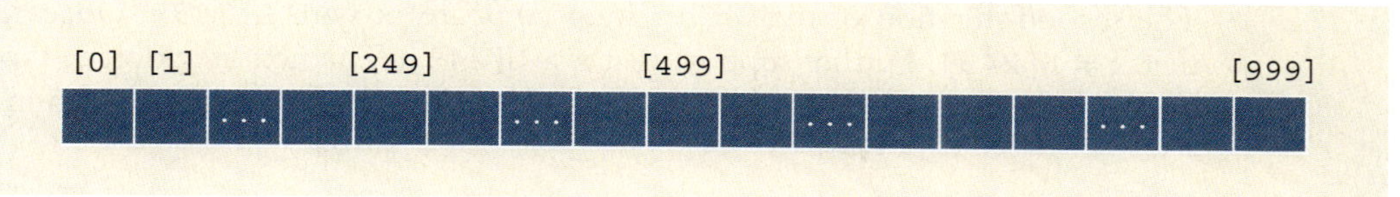

FIGURE 19-5   List L

The first iteration of the **while** loop searches for **x** in L[0]...L[999], which is a list of 1000 items. This iteration of the **while** loop compares **x** with L[499] (see Figure 19-6).

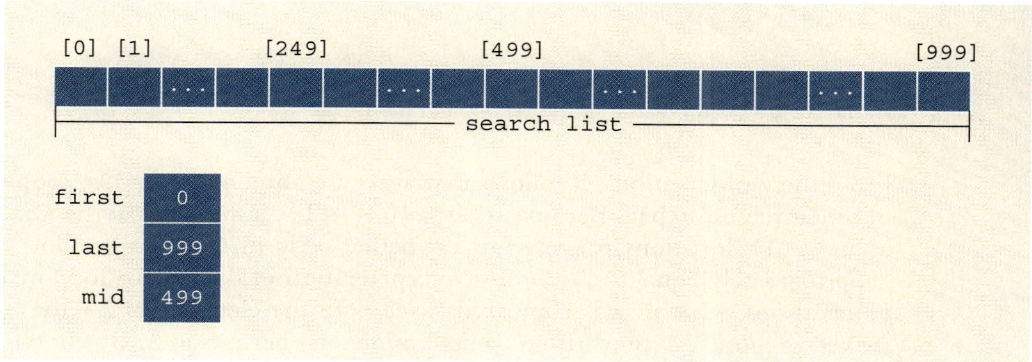

FIGURE 19-6   Search list

Suppose that $x \neq$ L[499]. If $x <$ L[499], then the next iteration of the **while** loop looks for **x** in L[0]...L[498]; otherwise, the **while** loop looks for **x** in L[500]...L[999]. Suppose that $x <$ L[499]. Then, the next iteration of the **while** loop looks for **x** in L[0]...L[498], which is a list of 499 items, as shown in Figure 19-7.

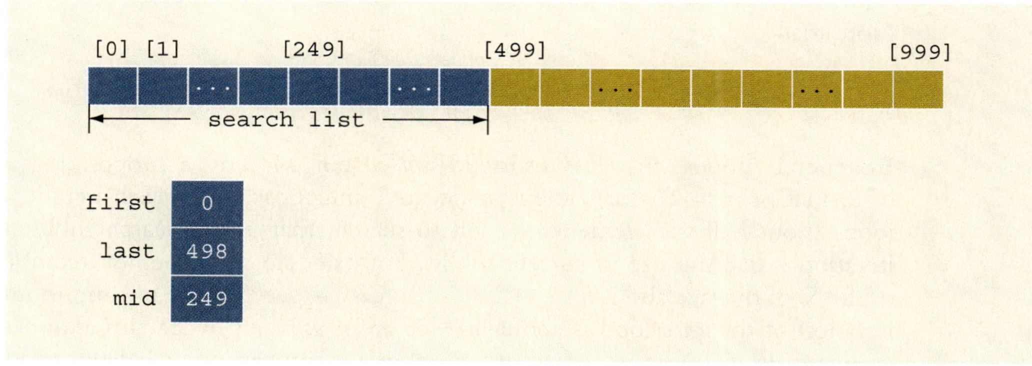

FIGURE 19-7   Search list after the first iteration

The second iteration of the `while` loop compares x with L[249]. Once again, suppose that x ≠ L[249]. Further suppose that x > L[249]. The next iteration of the `while` loop searches for x in L[250]...L[498], which is a list of 249 items, as shown in Figure 19-8.

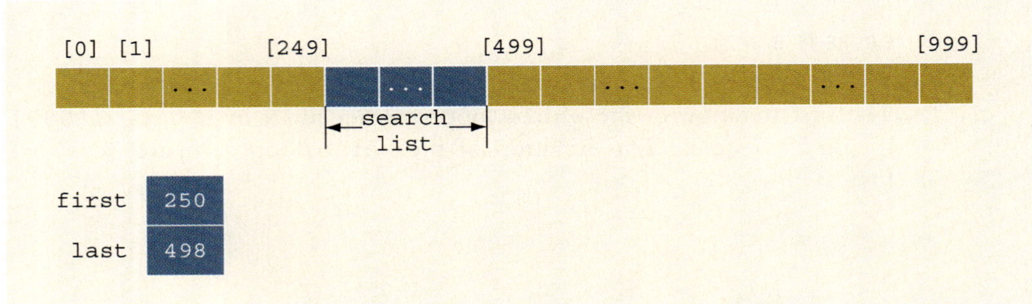

FIGURE 19-8   Search list after the second iteration

From these observations, it follows that every iteration of the `while` loop cuts the size of the search list in half. Because $1000 \approx 1024 = 2^{10}$, it follows that the `while` loop has, at most, 11 iterations to determine whether x is in L. (The symbol $\approx$ stands for "approximately equal to.") Because every iteration of the `while` loop makes two key comparisons—that is, x is compared twice with the elements of L—the binary search makes, at most, 22 comparisons to determine whether x is in L. By contrast, recall that the sequential search, on average, makes 500 comparisons to determine whether x is in L.

To have a better idea of how fast a binary search is as compared to a sequential search, suppose that L is of size 1,000,000. Because $1,000,000 \approx 1,048,576 = 2^{20}$, it follows that the `while` loop in a binary search has, at most, 21 iterations to determine whether an element is in L. Every iteration of the `while` loop makes two item (that is, key) comparisons. Therefore, to determine whether an element is in L, a binary search makes, at most, 42 item comparisons. By contrast, the sequential search, on average, makes 500,000 item (key) comparisons to determine whether an element is in L.

Note that:

$$40 = 2 \times 20 = 2 \times \log_2 2^{20} = 2 \times \log_2(1048576) \approx 2 \times \log_2(1000000)$$

In general, suppose that L is a sorted list of size n. Moreover, suppose that n is a power of 2, that is, $n = 2^m$, for some non-negative integer m. After each iteration of the `for` loop, about half the elements are left to search, that is, the search sublist for the next iteration is half the size of current sublist. For example, after the *first* iteration, the search sublist is of the size about $n/2 = 2^{m-1}$. It is easy to see that the maximum number of the iteration of the `for` loop is about $m + 1$. Also, $m = \log_2 n$. Each iteration makes 2 key comparisons. Thus, the maximum number of comparisons to determine whether an element x is in L is $2(m + 1) = 2(\log_2 n + 1) = 2\log_2 n + 2$.

In the case of a successful search, it can be shown that for a list of length n, on average, a binary search makes $2\log_2 n - 3$ key comparisons. In the case of an unsuccessful search, it can be shown that for a list of length n, a binary search makes approximately $2\log_2 n$ key comparisons.

Binary Search Algorithm and the `class` `orderedArrayListType`

The `class` `orderedArrayListType`, designed in Chapter 14, does not contain the binary search algorithm. Now that you know how to implement the binary search algorithm, you can learn how to use it in the `class` `orderedArrayListType`.

To use the binary search algorithm within the `class` `orderedArrayListType`, we add the function `binSearch` to this class and call the functions `binarySearch` with the appropriate parameters:

```cpp
#include "arrayListType.h"
#include "searchSortAlgorithms.h"

template <class elemType>
class orderedArrayListType: public arrayListType<elemType>
{
public:
    void insertAt(int location, const elemType& insertItem);
    void insertEnd(const elemType& insertItem);
    void replaceAt(int location, const elemType& repItem);
    int seqSearch(const elemType& searchItem) const;
    void insert(const elemType& insertItem);
    void remove(const elemType& removeItem);

    int binSearch(const elemType& removeItem);

    orderedArrayListType(int size = 100);
        //Constructor
};
```

The definition of the member function `binSearch` is:

```cpp
template <class elemType>
int orderedArrayListType<elemType>::
                    binSearch(const elemType& item) const
{
    return binarySearch(list, length, item);
}
```

Asymptotic Notation: Big-O Notation

Just as a problem is analyzed before writing the algorithm and the computer program, after an algorithm is designed, it should also be analyzed. Usually, there are various ways to design a particular algorithm. Certain algorithms take very little computer time to execute, while others take a considerable amount of time. Consider the following examples.

EXAMPLE 19-3

Consider the following algorithm (assume that all variables are properly declared):

```cpp
cout << "Enter the first number: ";               //Line 1
cin >> num1;                                        //Line 2
cout << endl;                                        //Line 3

cout << "Enter the second number: ";              //Line 4
cin >> num2;                                         //Line 5
cout << endl;                                        //Line 6


if (num1 >= num2)                                   //Line 7
    max = num1;                                      //Line 8
else                                                //Line 9
    max = num2;                                      //Line 10

cout << "The maximum number is: " << max << endl; //Line 11
```

Lines 1 to 6 each have one operation, << or >>. Line 7 has one operation, >=. Either Line 8 or Line 9 executes; each has one operation. There are three operations, <<, in Line 11. Therefore, the total number of operations executed in the preceding code is $6 + 1 + 1 + 3 = 11$. In this algorithm, the number of operations executed is fixed.

EXAMPLE 19-4

Consider the following algorithm:

```cpp
cout << "Enter positive integers ending with -1"
     << endl;                                       //Line 1

count = 0                                            //Line 2
sum = 0;                                             //Line 3

cin >> num;                                          //Line 4

while (num != -1)                                    //Line 5
{
    sum = sum + num;                                 //Line 6
    count++;                                         //Line 7
    cin >> num;                                      //Line 8
}
```

```cpp
cout << "The sum of the numbers is: " << sum
     << endl;                                        //Line 9

if (count != 0)                                       //Line 10
   average = sum / count;                             //Line 11
else                                                  //Line 12
   average = 0;                                       //Line 13

cout << "The average is: " << average << endl;        //Line 14
```

This algorithm has five operations (Lines 1 through 4) before the **while** loop. Similarly, there are nine or eight operations after the **while** loop, depending on whether Line 11 or Line 13 executes.

Line 5 has one operation, and four operations within the **while** loop (Lines 6 through 8). Thus, Lines 5 through 8 have five operations. If the **while** loop executes 10 times, these five operations execute 10 times, plus one extra operation is executed at Line 5 to terminate the loop. Therefore, the number of operations executed from Lines 5 through 8 is 51.

If the **while** loop executes 10 times, the total number of operations executed is:

$$5 \times 10 + 1 + 5 + 9 \text{ or } 5 \times 10 + 1 + 5 + 8$$

that is:

$$5 \times 10 + 15 \text{ or } 5 \times 10 + 14$$

We can generalize it to the case when the **while** loop executes n times. If the **while** loop executes n times, the number of operations executed is:

$$5n + 15 \text{ or } 5n + 14$$

In these expressions, for very large values of n, the term $5n$ becomes the dominating term and the terms 15 and 14 become negligible.

Usually, in an algorithm, certain operations are dominant. For example, in the algorithm in Example 19-4, to add numbers, the dominant operation is in Line 6. Similarly, in a search algorithm, because the search item is compared with the items in the list, the dominant operations would be comparison, that is, the relational operation. Therefore, in the case of a search algorithm, we count the number of comparisons.

Suppose that an algorithm performs $f(n)$ basic operations to accomplish a task, where n is the size of the problem. Suppose that you want to determine whether an item is in a list and that the size of the list is n. To determine whether the item is in the list, there are various algorithms. However, the basic method is to compare the item with the items in the list. Therefore, the performance of the algorithm depends on the number of comparisons.

Thus, in the case of a search, n is the size of the list and $f(n)$ becomes the count function, that is, $f(n)$ gives the number of comparisons done by the search algorithm. Suppose that, on a particular computer, it takes c units of computer time to execute one operation. Thus, the computer time it would take to execute $f(n)$ operations is $cf(n)$. Clearly, the constant c depends on the speed of the computer and, therefore, varies from computer to computer. However, $f(n)$, the number of basic operations, is the same on each computer. If we know how the function $f(n)$ grows as the size of the problem grows, we can determine the efficiency of the algorithm. Consider Table 19-4.

TABLE 19-4 Growth Rate of Various Functions

n	$\log_2 n$	$n\log_2 n$	n^2	2^n
1	0	0	1	2
2	1	2	2	4
4	2	8	16	16
8	3	24	64	256
16	4	64	256	65536
32	5	160	1024	4294967296

Table 19-4 shows how certain functions grow as the parameter n (the problem size) grows. Suppose that the problem size is doubled. From Table 19-4, it follows that if the number of basic operations is a function of $f(n) = n^2$, the number of basic operations is quadrupled. If the number of basic operations is a function of $f(n) = 2^n$, then the number of basic operations is squared. However, if the number of operations is a function of $f(n) = \log_2 n$, the change in the number of basic operations is insignificant.

Suppose that a computer can execute 1 billion steps per second. Table 19-5 shows the time that computer takes to execute $f(n)$ steps.

TABLE 19-5 Time for $f(n)$ Instructions on a Computer That Executes 1 Billion Instructions per Second

n	$f(n) = n$	$f(n) = \log_2 n$	$f(n) = n\log_2 n$	$f(n) = n^2$	$f(n) = 2^n$
10	0.01μs	0.003μs	0.033μs	0.1μs	1μs
20	0.02μs	0.004μs	0.086μs	0.4μs	1ms
30	0.03μs	0.005μs	0.147μs	0.9μs	1s
40	0.04μs	0.005μs	0.213μs	1.6μs	18.3min
50	0.05μs	0.006μs	0.282μs	2.5μs	13 days
100	0.10μs	0.007μs	0.664μs	10μs	4×10^{13} years
1000	1.00μs	0.010μs	9.966μs	1ms	
10000	10μs	0.013μs	130μs	100ms	
100000	0.10ms	0.017μs	1.67ms	10s	
1000000	1 ms	0.020μs	19.93ms	16.7m	
10000000	0.01s	0.023μs	0.23s	1.16 days	
100000000	0.10s	0.027μs	2.66s	115.7 days	

In Table 19-5, $1\mu s = 10^{-6}$ seconds and $1ms = 10^{-3}$ seconds.

Figure 19-9 shows the growth rate of functions in Table 19-5.

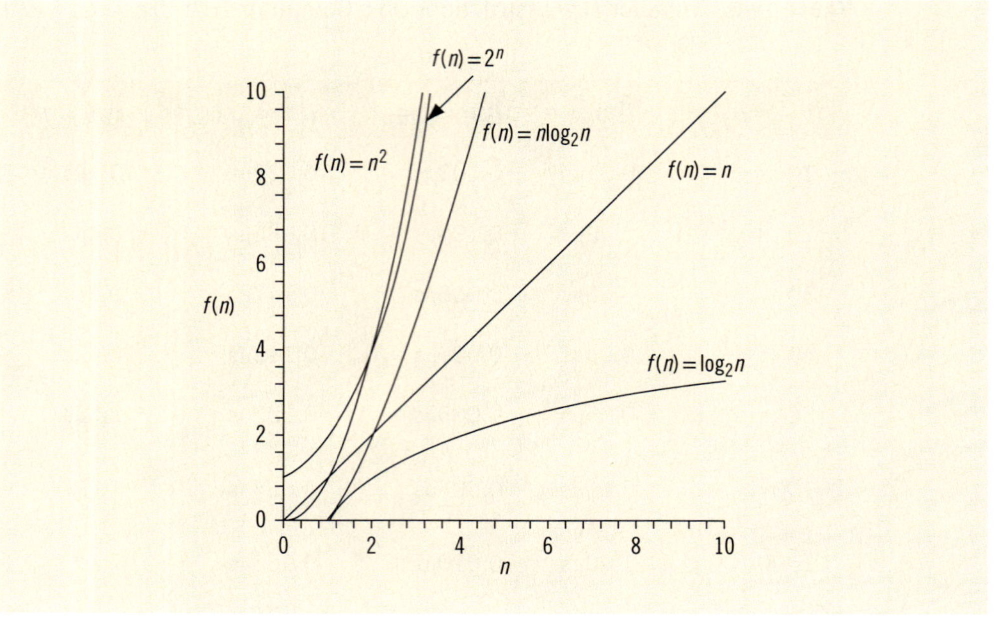

FIGURE 19-9 Growth rate of various functions

The remainder of this section develops a notation that shows how a function $f(n)$ grows as n increases without bound. That is, we develop a notation that is useful in describing the behavior of the algorithm, which gives us the most useful information about the algorithm. First, we define the term "asymptotic."

Let f be a function of n. By the term **asymptotic** we mean the study of the function f as n becomes larger and larger without bound.

Consider the functions $g(n) = n^2$ and $f(n) = n^2 + 4n + 20$. Clearly, the function g does not contain any linear term, that is, the coefficient of n in g is zero. Consider Table 19-6.

TABLE 19-6 Growth Rate of n^2 and $n^2 + 4n + 20$

n	$g(n) = n^2$	$f(n) = n^2 + 4n + 20$
10	100	160
50	2500	2720
100	10000	10420
1000	1000000	1004020
10000	100000000	100040020

Clearly, as n becomes larger and larger the term $4n + 20$ in $f(n)$ becomes insignificant, and the term n^2 becomes the dominant term. For large values of n, we can predict the behavior of $f(n)$ by looking at the behavior of $g(n)$. In the algorithm analysis, if the complexity of a function can be described by the complexity of a quadratic function without the linear term, we say that the function is of $O(n^2)$, called Big-O of n^2.

Let f and g be real-valued functions. Assume that f and g are non-negative, that is, for all real numbers n, $f(n) \geq 0$ and $g(n) \geq 0$.

Definition: We say that $f(n)$ is **Big-O** of $g(n)$, written $f(n) = O(g(n))$, if there exist positive constants c and n_0 such that:

$f(n) \leq cg(n)$ for all $n \geq n_0$.

EXAMPLE 19-5

Let $f(n) = a$, where a is a non-negative real number and $n \geq 0$. Note that f is a constant function.

Now:

$f(n) = a \leq a \cdot 1$ for all $n \geq a$.

Let $c = a$, $n_0 = a$, and $g(n) = 1$. Then, $f(n) \leq cg(n)$ for all $n \geq n_0$. It now follows that $f(n) = O(g(n)) = O(1)$.

From Example 19-5, it follows that if f is a non-negative constant function, then f is $O(1)$.

EXAMPLE 19-6

Let $f(n) = 2n + 5$, $n \geq 0$. Note that:

$f(n) = 2n + 5 \leq 2n + n = 3n$ for all $n \geq 5$.

Let $c = 3$, $n_0 = 5$, and $g(n) = n$. Then, $f(n) \leq cg(n)$ for all $n \geq 5$. It now follows that $f(n) = O(g(n)) = O(n)$.

EXAMPLE 19-7

Let $f(n) = n^2 + 3n + 2$, $g(n) = n^2$, $n \geq 0$. Note that:

$3n + 2 \leq n^2$ for all $n \geq 4$.

This implies that:

$$f(n) = n^2 + 3n + 2 \leq n^2 + n^2 \leq 2n^2 = 2g(n) \text{ for all } n \geq 4.$$

Let $c = 2$ and $n_0 = 4$. Then, $f(n) \leq cg(n)$ for all $n \geq 4$. It now follows that $f(n) = O(g(n)) = O(n^2)$.

In general, we can prove the following theorem. We state the theorem without proof.

Theorem: Let $f(n)$ be a non-negative real-valued function such that:

$$f(n) = a_m n^m + a_{m-1} n^{m-1} + \cdots + a_1 n + a_0,$$

where a_i's are real numbers, $a_m \neq 0$, $n \geq 0$, and m is a non-negative integer. Then:

$$f(n) = O(n^m).$$

In Example 19-8, we use the preceding theorem to establish the Big-O of certain functions.

EXAMPLE 19-8

In the following, $f(n)$ is a non-negative real-valued function:

Function	Big-O
$f(n) = an + b$, where a and b are real numbers and a is nonzero.	$f(n) = O(n)$.
$f(n) = n^2 + 5n + 1$	$f(n) = O(n^2)$
$f(n) = 4n^6 + 3n^3 + 1$	$f(n) = O(n^6)$
$f(n) = 10n^7 + 23$	$f(n) = O(n^7)$
$f(n) = 6n^{15}$	$f(n) = O(n^{15})$

EXAMPLE 19-9

Suppose that $f(n) = 2\log_2 n + a$, where a is a real number. It can be shown that $f(n) = O(\log_2 n)$.

EXAMPLE 19-10

Consider the following code, where m and n are `int` variables and their values are non-negative:

```cpp
for (int i = 0; i < m; i++)            //Line 1
    for (int j = 0; j < n; j++)        //Line 2
        cout << i * j << endl;         //Line 3
```

This code contains nested **for** loops. The outer **for** loop, at Line 1, executes m times. For each iteration of the outer loop, the inner loop, at Line 2, executes n times. For each iteration of the inner loop, the output statement in Line 3 executes. It follows that the total number of iterations of the nested **for** loop is mn. So the number of times the statement in Line 3 executes is mn. It follows that this algorithm is $O(mn)$. Note that if $m = n$, then this algorithm is $O(n^2)$.

Table 19-7 shows some common Big-O functions that appear in the algorithm analysis. Let $f(n) = O(g(n))$, where n is the problem size.

TABLE 19-7   Some Big-O Functions That Appear in Algorithm Analysis

Function $g(n)$	Growth rate of $f(n)$
$g(n) = 1$	The growth rate is constant and so does not depend on n, the size of the problem.
$g(n) = \log_2 n$	The growth rate is a function of $\log_2 n$. Because a logarithm function grows slowly, the growth rate of the function f is also slow.
$g(n) = n$	The growth rate is linear. The growth rate of f is directly proportional to the size of the problem.
$g(n) = n\log_2 n$	The growth rate is faster than the linear algorithm.
$g(n) = n^2$	The growth rate of such functions increases rapidly with the size of the problem. The growth rate is quadrupled when the problem size is doubled.
$g(n) = 2^n$	The growth rate is exponential. The growth rate is squared when the problem size is doubled.

NOTE   It can be shown that:

$$O(1) \le O(\log_2 n) \le O(n) \le O(n\log_2 n) \le O(n^2) \le O(2^n).$$

Using the notations developed in this section, we can conclude that the algorithm in Example 19-3 is of order $O(1)$, and the algorithm in Example 19-4 is of $O(n)$. Table 19-8 summarizes the algorithm analysis of the search algorithms discussed earlier.

TABLE 19-8 Number of Comparisons for a List of Length n

Algorithm	Successful search	Unsuccessful search
Sequential search	$\frac{n+1}{2} = \frac{1}{2}n + \frac{1}{2} = O(n)$	$n = O(n)$
Binary search	$2\log_2 n - 3 = O(\log_2 n)$	$2\log_2 n = O(\log_2 n)$

Lower Bound on Comparison-Based Search Algorithms

Sequential and binary search algorithms search the list by comparing the target element with the list elements. For this reason, these algorithms are called **comparison–based search algorithms**. Earlier sections of this chapter showed that a sequential search is of the order n, and a binary search is of the order $\log_2 n$, where n is the size of the list. The obvious question is: Can we devise a search algorithm that has an order less than $\log_2 n$? Before we answer this question, first we obtain the lower bound on the number of comparisons for the comparison-based search algorithms.

Theorem: Let L be a list of size $n > 1$. Suppose that the elements of L are sorted. If $\mathrm{SRH}(n)$ denotes the minimum number of comparisons needed, in the worst case, by using a comparison-based algorithm to recognize whether an element x is in L, then $\mathrm{SRH}(n) \geq \log_2(n + 1)$.

Corollary: The binary search algorithm is an optimal worst-case algorithm for solving search problems by the comparison method.

From these results, it follows that if we want to design a search algorithm that is of an order less than $\log_2 n$, then it cannot be comparison-based.

Sorting Algorithms

There are several sorting algorithms in the literature. In this chapter, we discuss some of the commonly used sorting algorithms. To compare their performance, we also provide some analysis of these algorithms. These sorting algorithms can be applied to either array-based lists or linked lists. We will specify whether the algorithm being developed is for array-based lists or linked lists.

Sorting a List: Bubble Sort

Many sorting algorithms are available in the literature. This section describes the sorting algorithm called the **bubble sort**, to sort a list.

Suppose `list[0...n - 1]` is a list of n elements, indexed 0 to n - 1. We want to rearrange, that is, sort, the elements of `list` in increasing order. The bubble sort algorithm works as follows:

In a series of n - 1 iterations, the successive elements `list[index]` and `list[index + 1]` of the list are compared. If `list[index]` is greater than `list[index + 1]`, then the elements `list[index]` and `list[index + 1]` are swapped.

It follows that the smaller elements move toward the top and the larger elements move toward the bottom.

In the first iteration, we consider the `list[0...n - 1]`. As you will see after the first iteration, the largest element of the list is moved to the last position, which is position n − 1, in the list. In the second iteration, we consider the `list[0...n - 2]`. After the second iteration, the second largest element in the list is moved to the position n − 2, which is second to the last position in the list. In the third iteration, we consider the `list[0...n - 3]`, and so on. As you will see, after each iteration, the size of the unsorted portion of the list shrinks.

Consider the `list[0...4]` of five elements, as shown in Figure 19-10.

                               list

                    list[0]   10
                    list[1]   7
                    list[2]   19
                    list[3]   5
                    list[4]   16

FIGURE 19-10   List of five elements

Iteration 1:   Sort `list[0...4]`. Figure 19-11 shows how the elements of `list` get rearranged in the first iteration.

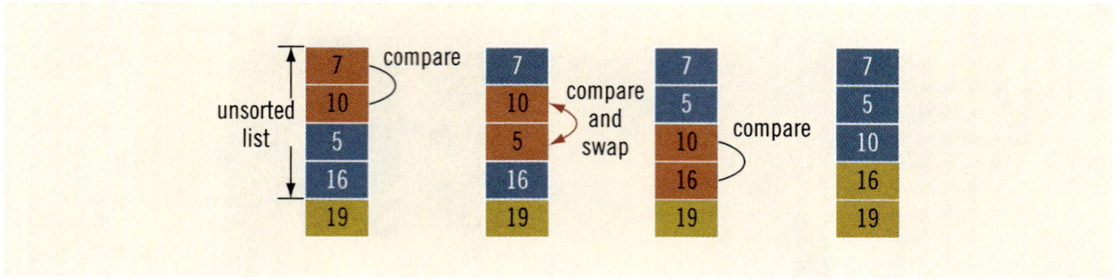

FIGURE 19-11 Elements of `list` during the first iteration

Notice that in the first diagram of Figure 19-11, `list[0]` > `list[1]`. Therefore, `list[0]` and `list[1]` are swapped. In the second diagram, `list[1]` and `list[2]` are compared. Because `list[1]` < `list[2]`, they do not get swapped. The third diagram of Figure 19-11 compares `list[2]` with `list[3]`; because `list[2]` > `list[3]`, `list[2]` is swapped with `list[3]`. Then, in the fourth diagram, we compare `list[3]` with `list[4]`. Because `list[3]` > `list[4]`, `list[3]` and `list[4]` are swapped.

After the first iteration, the largest element is at the last position. Therefore, in the next iteration, we consider the `list[0...3]`.

Iteration 2: Sort `list[0...3]`. Figure 19-12 shows how the elements of `list` get rearranged in the second iteration.

FIGURE 19-12 Elements of `list` during the second iteration

The elements are compared and swapped as in the first iteration. Here, only the list elements `list[0]` through `list[3]` are considered. After the second iteration, the last two elements are in the right place. Therefore, in the next iteration, we consider `list[0...2]`.

Iteration 3: Sort `list[0...2]`. Figure 19-13 shows how the elements of `list` get rearranged in the third iteration.

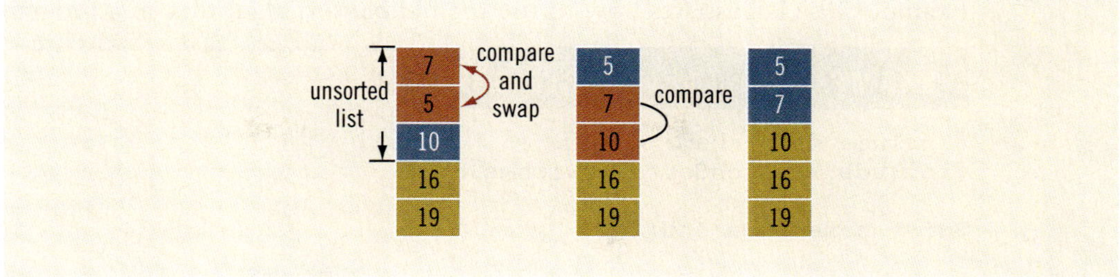

FIGURE 19-13 Elements of `list` during the third iteration

After the third iteration, the last three elements are in the right place. Therefore, in the next iteration, we consider `list[0...1]`.

Iteration 4: Sort `list[0...1]`. Figure 19-14 shows how the elements of `list` get rearranged in the fourth iteration.

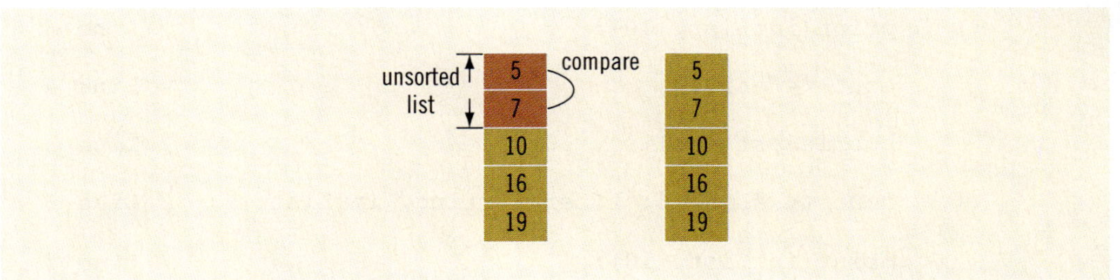

FIGURE 19-14 Elements of `list` during the fourth iteration

After the fourth iteration, `list` is sorted.

The following C++ function implements the bubble sort algorithm:

```cpp
template <class elemType>
void bubbleSort(elemType list[], int length)
{
    for (int iteration = 1; iteration < length; iteration++)
    {
        for (int index = 0; index < length - iteration;
                        index++)
        {
            if (list[index] > list[index + 1])
            {
                elemType temp = list[index];
                list[index] = list[index + 1];
                list[index + 1] = temp;
            }
        }
    }
} //end bubbleSort
```

Example 19-11 illustrates how to use the bubble sort algorithm in a program.

EXAMPLE 19-11 (BUBBLE SORT)

```cpp
#include <iostream>
#include "searchSortAlgorithms.h"

using namespace std;

template <class elemType>
void print(elemType list[], int length);

int main()
{
    int intList[] = {2, 56, 34, 25, 73,
                     46, 89, 10, 5, 16};          //Line 1

    cout << "Line 2: Before sorting, intList: ";  //Line 2

    print(intList, 10);                           //Line 3

    cout << endl;                                 //Line 4

    bubbleSort(intList, 10);                      //Line 5

    cout << "Line 6: After sorting, intList: ";   //Line 6

    print(intList, 10);                           //Line 7

    return 0;
}


template <class elemType>
void print(elemType list[], int length)
{
    for (int i = 0; i < length; i++)
        cout << list[i] << " ";

    cout << endl;
}
```

Sample Run:

```
Line 2: Before sorting, intList: 2 56 34 25 73 46 89 10 5 16

Line 6: After sorting, intList: 2 5 10 16 25 34 46 56 73 89
```

The statement in Line 1 declares and initializes intList to be an array of 10 components of type **int**. The statement in Line 3 outputs the values of the array intList
before sorting this array. The statement in Line 5 uses the function bubbleSort to sort

`list`. Notice that both `intList` and its length (the number of elements) are passed as parameters to the function `bubbleSort`. The statement in Line 7 outputs the sorted `intList`.

Analysis: Bubble Sort

In the case of search algorithms, our only concern was with the number of key (item) comparisons. A sorting algorithm makes key comparisons and also moves the data. Therefore, in analyzing the sorting algorithm, we look at the number of key comparisons as well as the number of data movements.

Suppose a list L of length n is to be sorted using bubble sort. Consider the function `bubbleSort` as given in this chapter. This function contains nested **for** loops. Because L is of length n, the outer loop executes $n - 1$ times. For each iteration of the outer loop, the inner loop executes a certain number of times. Let us consider the first iteration of the outer loop. During the first iteration of the outer loop, the number of iterations of the inner loop is $n - 1$. So there are $n - 1$ comparisons. Similarly, during the second iteration of the outer loop, the number of iterations of the inner loop is $n - 2$, and so on. Thus, the total number of comparisons is:

$$(n - 1) + (n - 2) + \cdots + 2 + 1 = \frac{n(n - 1)}{2} = \frac{1}{2}n^2 - \frac{1}{2}n = O(n^2).$$

In the worst case, the body of the **if** statement always executes. So in the worst case, the number of assignments is:

$$3\frac{n(n - 1)}{2} = \frac{3}{2}n^2 - \frac{3}{2}n = O(n^2).$$

If the list is already sorted, which is the best case, the number of assignments is 0. It can be shown that, on average, bubble sort makes about $\frac{n(n - 1)}{4}$ item assignments. However, the number of comparisons for the bubble sort, as given in this chapter, is always $\frac{n(n - 1)}{2}$.

Therefore, to sort a list of size 1000, bubble sort makes about 500,000 key comparisons and about 250,000 item assignments. The next section presents the selection sort algorithm that reduces the number of item assignments.

NOTE Exercise 5 at the end of this chapter gives a version of the bubble sort algorithm in which the number of comparisons in the best case is $O(n)$.

Bubble Sort Algorithm and the `class` `unorderedArrayListType`

The **class** unorderedArrayListType, designed in Chapter 14, does not contain any sorting algorithm. Now that you know how to implement the bubble sort algorithm, you can learn how to use it in the **class** unorderedArrayListType.

To use the binary search algorithm within the **class** unorderedArrayListType, we add the function `sort` to this class and call the functions `bubbleSort` with the appropriate parameters. (Note that we have also added the function to use the binary search algorithm.)

```cpp
template <class elemType>
class unorderedArrayListType: public arrayListType<elemType>
{
public:
    void insertAt(int location, const elemType& insertItem);
    void insertEnd(const elemType& insertItem);
    void replaceAt(int location, const elemType& repItem);
    int seqSearch(const elemType& searchItem) const;
    void remove(const elemType& removeItem);

    void sort();
    int binSearch(const elemType& item) const;

    unorderedArrayListType(int size = 100);
      //Constructor
};
```

The definition of the member functions `binSearch` and `sort` are:

```cpp
template <class elemType>
int unorderedArrayListType<elemType>::
                    binSearch(const elemType& item) const
{
    return binarySearch(list, length, item);
}

template <class elemType>
void unorderedArrayListType<elemType>::sort()
{
    selectionSort(list, length);
}
```

We leave it as an exercise for you to write a program to test the member functions `sort` and `binSearch`.

Selection Sort: Array-Based Lists

The selection sort algorithm sorts a list by selecting the smallest element in the unsorted portion of the list and then moving this smallest element to the top of the unsorted list. The first time, we locate the smallest item in the entire list; the second time, we locate the smallest item in the list starting from the second element in the list, and so on. The selection sort algorithm described here is designed for array-based lists.

For example, suppose that you have the list as shown in Figure 19-15.

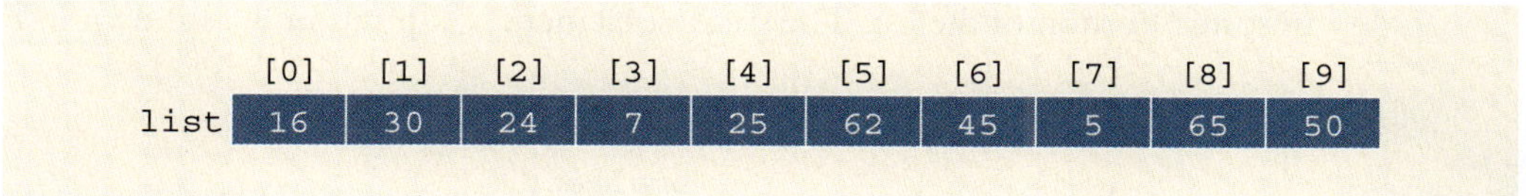

FIGURE 19-15 List of 10 elements

Initially, the entire list is unsorted. So we find the smallest item in the list, which is at position 7, as shown in Figure 19-16.

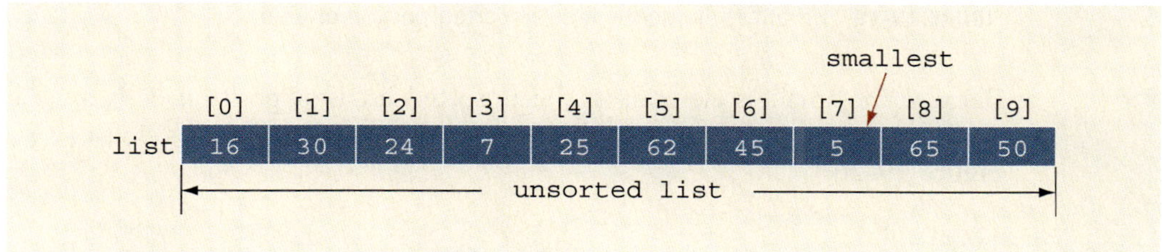

FIGURE 19-16 Smallest element of the unsorted list

Because this is the smallest item, it must be moved to position 0. We, therefore, swap 16 (that is, `list[0]`) with 5 (that is, `list[7]`), as shown in Figure 19-17.

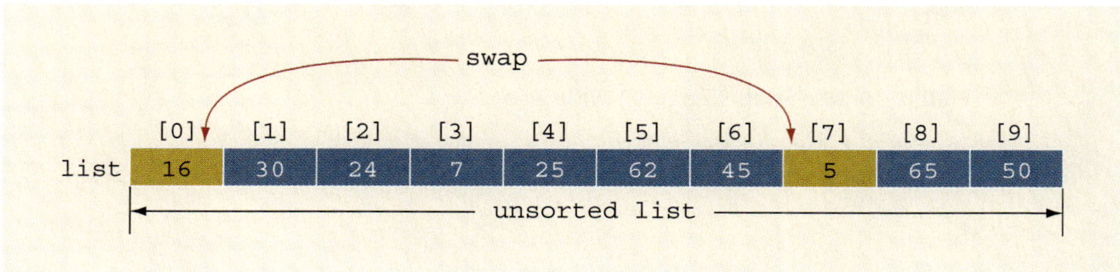

FIGURE 19-17 Swap elements `list[0]` and `list[7]`

Figure 19-18 shows the list after swapping these elements.

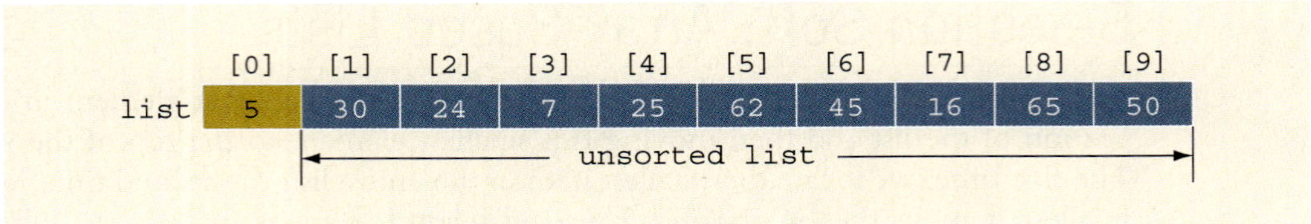

FIGURE 19-18 List after swapping `list[0]` and `list[7]`

Now the unsorted list is `list[1]...list[9]`. Next, we find the smallest element in the unsorted portion of the list. The smallest element is at position 3, as shown in Figure 19-19.

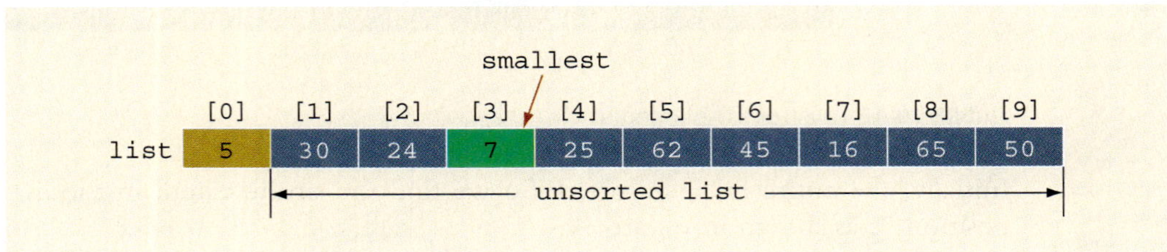

FIGURE 19-19 Smallest element in the unsorted portion of `list`

Because the smallest element in the unsorted list is at position 3, it must be moved to position 1. That is, we swap 7 (that is, `list[3]`) with 30 (that is, `list[1]`), as shown in Figure 19-20.

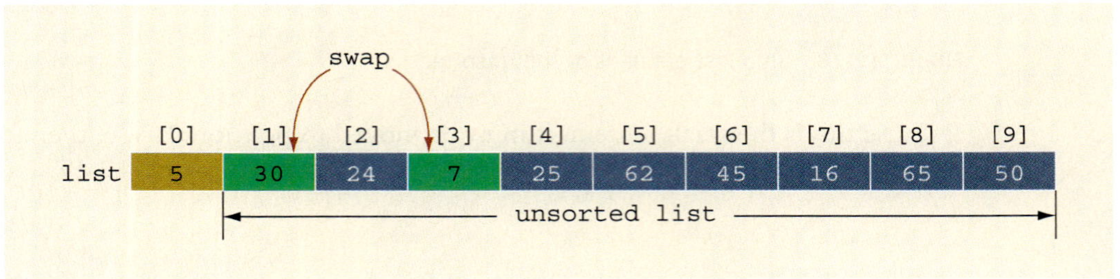

FIGURE 19-20 Swap `list[1]` with `list[3]`

After swapping `list[1]` with `list[3]`, Figure 19-21 shows the resulting list.

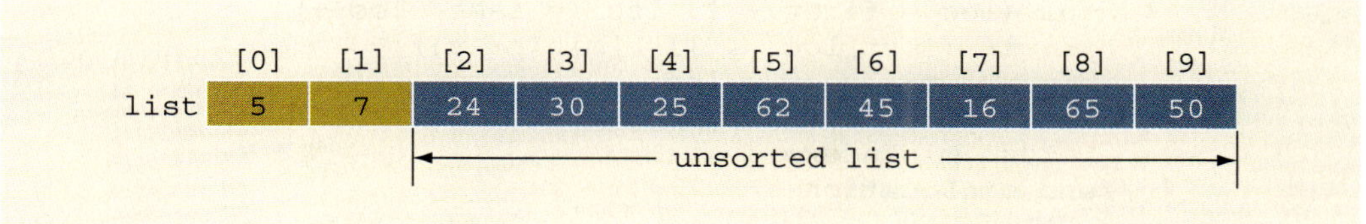

FIGURE 19-21 `list` after swapping `list[1]` with `list[3]`

Now the unsorted list is `list[2]...list[9]`. We repeat this process of finding the position of the smallest element in the unsorted portion of the list and moving it to the beginning of the unsorted portion of the list. The selection sort algorithm thus involves the following steps in the unsorted portion of the list:

> a. Find the location of the smallest element.
>
> b. Move the smallest element to the beginning of the unsorted list.

Initially, the entire list, `list[0]...list[length - 1]`, is the unsorted list. After executing steps a and b once, the unsorted list is `list[1]...list[length - 1]`. After executing steps a and b a second time, the unsorted list is `list[2]...list[length - 1]`, and so on. We can keep track of the unsorted portion of the list and repeat steps a and b, with the help of a **for** loop, as follows:

```
for (int index = 0; index < length - 1; index++)
{
    a. Find the location, smallestIndex, of the smallest element in
       list[index]...list[length - 1].
    b. Swap the smallest element with list[index]. That is, swap
       list[smallestIndex] with list[index].
}
```

The first time through the loop, we locate the smallest element in `list[0]...list[length - 1]` and swap this smallest element with `list[0]`. The second time through the loop, we locate the smallest element in `list[1]...list[length - 1]` and swap this smallest element with `list[1]`, and so on. This process continues until the length of the unsorted list is 1. (Note that a list of length 1 is sorted.) It, therefore, follows that to implement the selection sort algorithm, we need to implement steps a and b within a loop.

Given the starting index, `first`, and the ending index, `last`, of the list, the following C++ function returns the index of the smallest element in `list[first]...list[last]`:

```
template <class elemType>
int minLocation(elemType list[], int first, int last)
{
    int loc, minIndex;

    minIndex = first;
```

```
    for (loc = first + 1; loc <= last; loc++)
        if (list[loc] < list[minIndex])
            minIndex = loc;

    return minIndex;
} //end minLocation
```

Given the locations in the list of the elements to be swapped, the following C++ function, `swap`, swaps those elements:

```
template <class elemType>
void swap(elemType list[], int first, int second)
{
    elemType temp;

    temp = list[first];
    list[first] = list[second];
    list[second] = temp;
} //end swap
```

We can now complete the definition of the function `selectionSort`:

```
template <class elemType>
void selectionSort(elemType list[], int length)
{
    int loc, minIndex;

    for (loc = 0; loc < length; loc++)
    {
        minIndex = minLocation(list, loc, length - 1);
        swap(list, loc, minIndex);
    }
} //end selectionSort
```

We leave it as an exercise for you to write a program to test the selection sort algorithm. (See Programming Exercise 6 at the end of this chapter.)

1. A selection sort can also be implemented by selecting the largest element in the unsorted portion of the list and moving it to the bottom of the list. You can easily implement this form of selection sort by altering the `if` statement in the function `minLocation` and passing the appropriate parameters to both the corresponding function and the function `swap` (when these functions are called in the function `selectionSort`).

2. A selection sort can also be applied to linked lists. The general algorithm is the same, and the details are left as an exercise for you. See Programming Exercise 7 at the end of this chapter.

Analysis: Selection Sort

Suppose that a list L of length n is to be sorted using the selection sort algorithm. The function `swap` does three item assignments and is executed $n - 1$ times. Hence, the number of item assignments is $3(n - 1) = O(n)$.

The key comparisons are made by the function `minLocation`. For a list of length k, the function `minLocation` makes $k - 1$ key comparisons. Also, the function `minLocation` is executed $n - 1$ times (by the function `selectionSort`). The first time, the function `minLocation` finds the index of the smallest key item in the entire list and, therefore, makes $n - 1$ comparisons. The second time, the function `minLocation` finds the index of the smallest element in the sublist of length $n - 1$ and so makes $n - 2$ comparisons, and so on. Hence, the number of key comparisons is as follows:

$$
\begin{aligned}
(n - 1) + (n - 2) + \cdots + 2 + 1 &= \frac{n(n - 1)}{2} \\
&= \frac{1}{2}n^2 - \frac{1}{2}n \\
&= \frac{1}{2}n^2 + O(n) \\
&= O(n^2).
\end{aligned}
$$

It thus follows that if $n = 1000$, the number of key comparisons the selection sort algorithm makes is:

$$
\frac{1}{2}(1000)^2 - \frac{1}{2}(1000) = 499500 \approx 500000.
$$

Note that the selection sort algorithm does not depend on the initial arrangement of the data. The number of comparisons is always $O(n^2)$ and the number of assignments is $O(n)$. In general, this algorithm is good only for small lists because $O(n^2)$ grows rapidly as n grows. However, if data movement is expensive and the number of comparisons is not, then this algorithm could be a better choice over other algorithms.

Insertion Sort: Array-Based Lists

The previous section described and analyzed the selection sort algorithm. It was shown that if $n = 1000$, the number of key comparisons is approximately 500,000, which is quite high. This section describes the sorting algorithm called the **insertion sort**, which tries to improve—that is, reduce—the number of key comparisons.

The insertion sort algorithm sorts the list by moving each element to its proper place in the sorted portion of the list. Consider the list given in Figure 19-22.

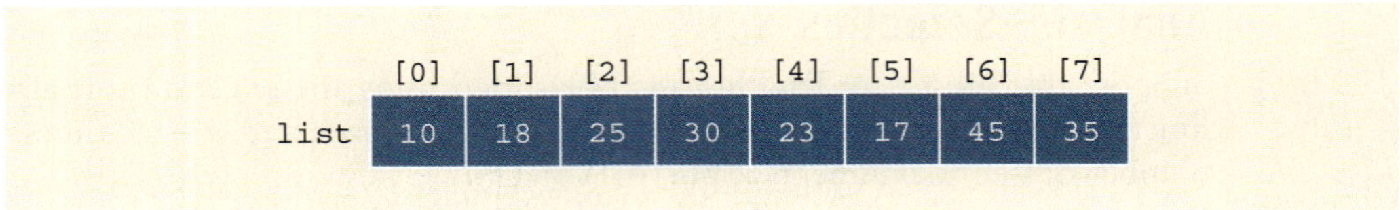

FIGURE 19-22 `list`

The length of the list is 8. In this list, the elements `list[0]`, `list[1]`, `list[2]`, and `list[3]` are in order. That is, `list[0]...list[3]` is sorted (see Figure 19-23).

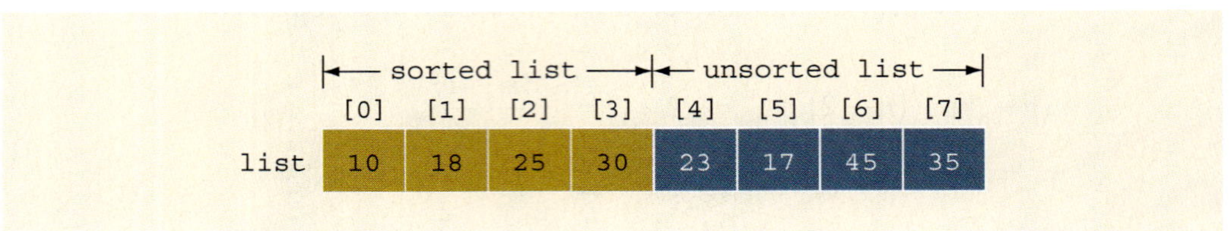

FIGURE 19-23 Sorted and unsorted portion of `list`

Next, we consider the element `list[4]`, the first element of the unsorted list. Because `list[4] < list[3]`, we need to move the element `list[4]` to its proper location. It thus follows that element `list[4]` should be moved to `list[2]` (see Figure 19-24).

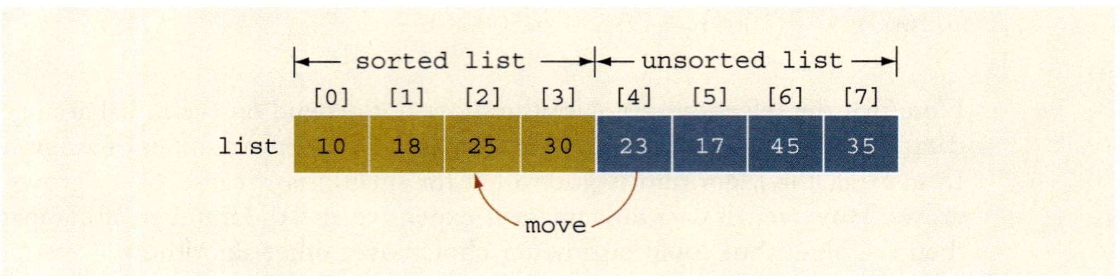

FIGURE 19-24 Move `list[4]` into `list[2]`

To move `list[4]` into `list[2]`, first we copy `list[4]` into `temp`, a temporary memory space (see Figure 19-25).

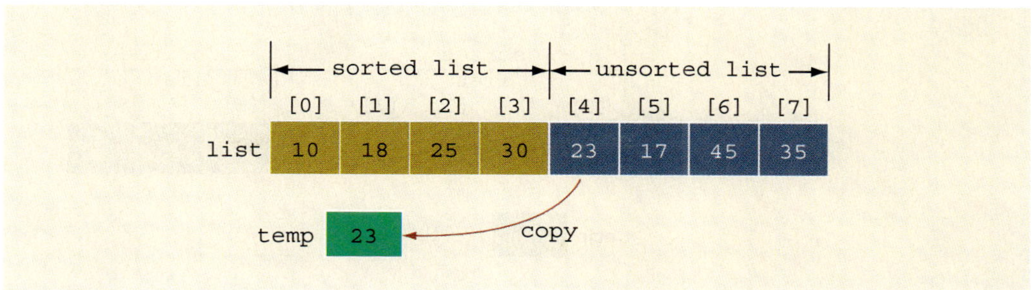

FIGURE 19-25 Copy `list[4]` into `temp`

Next, we copy `list[3]` into `list[4]` and then `list[2]` into `list[3]` (see Figure 19-26).

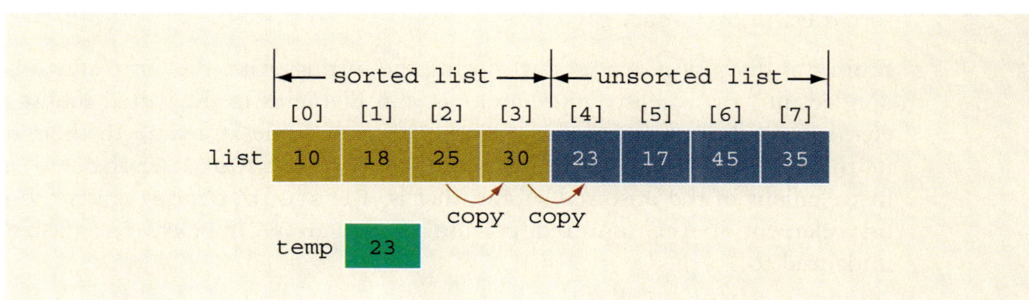

FIGURE 19-26 List before copying `list[3]` into `list[4]` and then `list[2]` into `list[3]`

After copying `list[3]` into `list[4]` and `list[2]` into `list[3]`, the list is as shown in Figure 19-27.

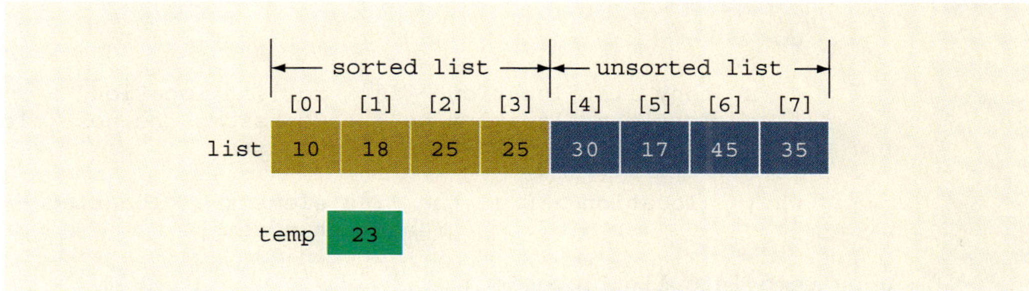

FIGURE 19-27 List after copying `list[3]` into `list[4]` and then `list[2]` into `list[3]`

We now copy temp into `list[2]`. Figure 19-28 shows the resulting list.

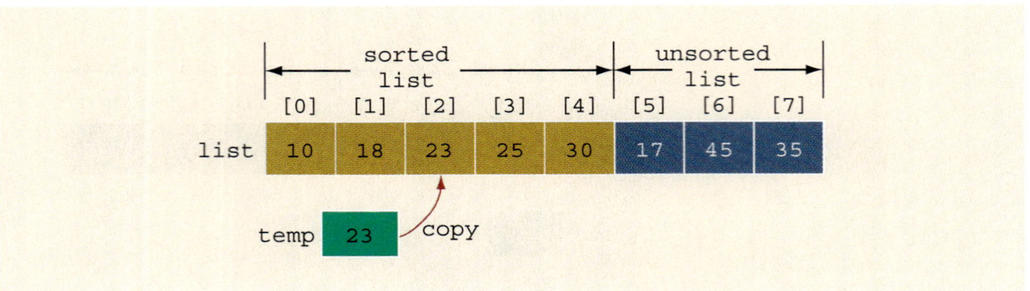

FIGURE 19-28 List after copying `temp` into `list[2]`

Now `list[0]...list[4]` is sorted and `list[5]...list[7]` is unsorted. We repeat this process on the resulting list by moving the first element of the unsorted list into the sorted list in the proper place.

From this discussion, we see that during the sorting phase the array containing the list is divided into two sublists, *sorted* and *unsorted*. Elements in the sorted sublist are in order; elements in the unsorted sublist are to be moved one at a time to their proper places in the sorted sublist. We use an index—say, `firstOutOfOrder`—to point to the first element in the unsorted sublist; that is, `firstOutOfOrder` gives the index of the first element in the unsorted portion of the array. Initially, `firstOutOfOrder` is initialized to 1.

This discussion translates into the following pseudo-code algorithm:

```
for (firstOutOfOrder = 1; firstOutOfOrder < length; firstOutOfOrder++)
  if (list[firstOutOfOrder] is less than list[firstOutOfOrder - 1])
  {
      copy list[firstOutOfOrder] into temp

      initialize location to firstOutOfOrder

      do
      {
          a. copy list[location - 1] into list[location]
          b. decrement location by 1 to consider the next element
             of the sorted portion of the array
      }
      while (location > 0 && the list element at location - 1 is
                             greater than temp)
  }
copy temp into list[location]
```

Let us trace the execution of this algorithm on the list given in Figure 19-29.

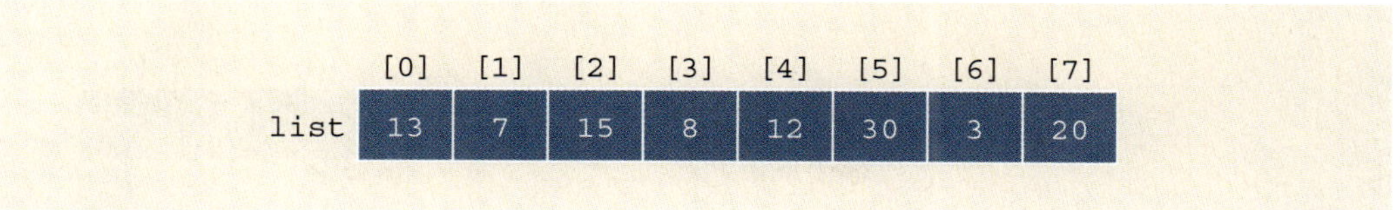

FIGURE 19-29 Unsorted list

The length of this list is 8; that is, `length = 8`. We initialize `firstOutOfOrder` to 1 (see Figure 19–30).

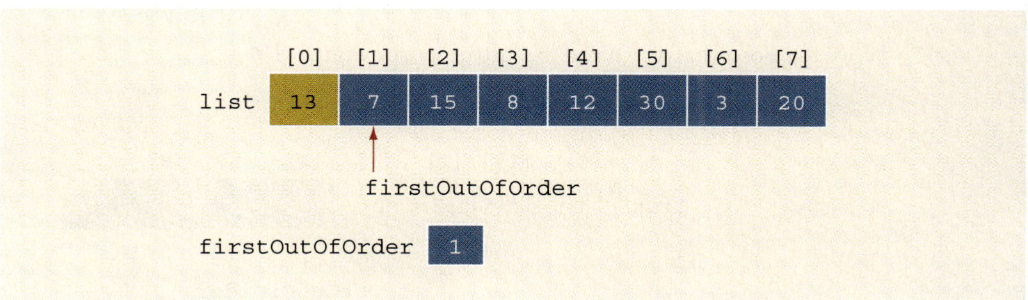

FIGURE 19-30 `firstOutOfOrder = 1`

Because `list[firstOutOfOrder] = 7`, `list[firstOutOfOrder - 1] = 13`, and 7 < 13, the expression in the **if** statement evaluates to **true**. So, we execute the body of the **if** statement:

```
temp = list[firstOutOfOrder] = 7
location = firstOutOfOrder = 1
```

Next, we execute the **do...while** loop:

```
list[1] = list[0] = 13 (copy list[0] into list[1])
location = 0           (decrement location)
```

The **do...while** loop terminates because `location` is 0. We copy `temp` into `list[location]`—that is, into `list[0]`.

Figure 19-31 shows the resulting list.

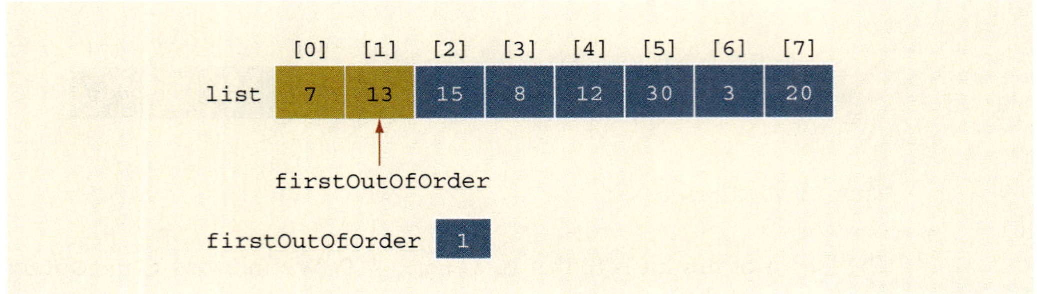

FIGURE 19-31 List after the first iteration of the insertion sort algorithm

Now suppose that we have the list given in Figure 19-32.

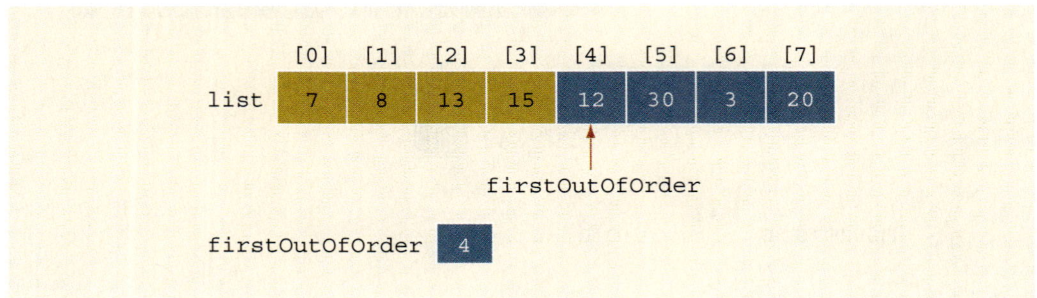

FIGURE 19-32 First out-of-order element is at position 4

Here, `list[0]...list[3]`, or the elements `list[0]`, `list[1]`, `list[2]`, and `list[3]`, are in order. Now `firstOutOfOrder = 4`. Because `list[4] < list[3]`, the element `list[4]`, which is 12, needs to be moved to its proper location.

As before:

```
temp = list[firstOutOfOrder] = 12
location = firstOutOfOrder  =  4
```

First, we copy `list[3]` into `list[4]` and decrement `location` by 1. Then, we copy `list[2]` into `list[3]` and again decrement `location` by 1. Now the value of `location` is 2. At this point, the list is as shown in Figure 19-33.

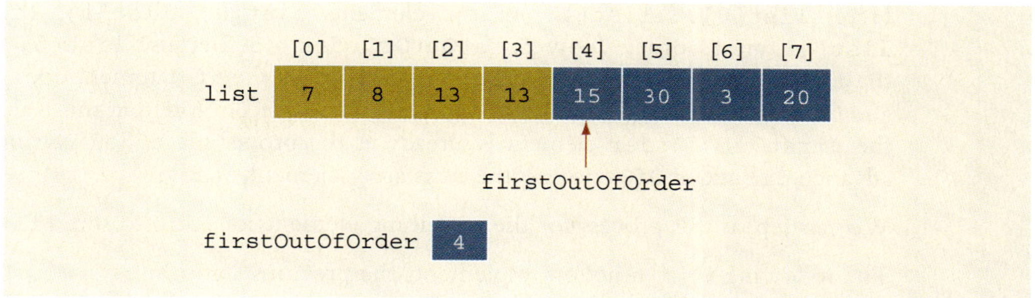

FIGURE 19-33 List after copying `list[3]` into `list[4]` and then `list[2]` into `list[3]`

Because `list[1] < temp`, the **do...while** loop terminates. At this point, `location` is 2, so we copy `temp` into `list[2]`. That is:

`list[2] = temp = 12`

Figure 19-34 shows the resulting list.

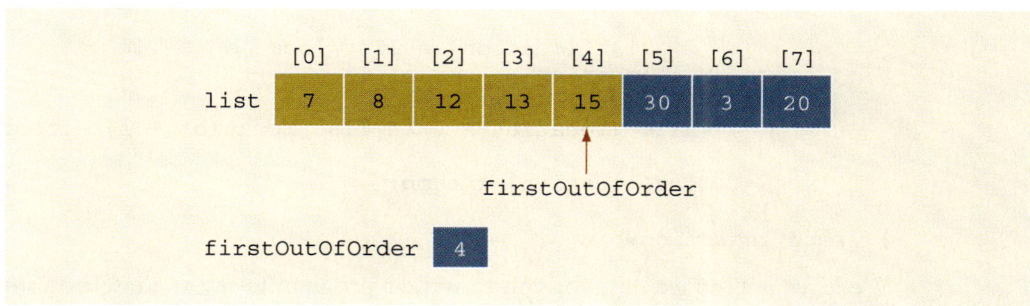

FIGURE 19-34 List after copying `temp` into `list[2]`

Next, suppose that we have the list given in Figure 19-35.

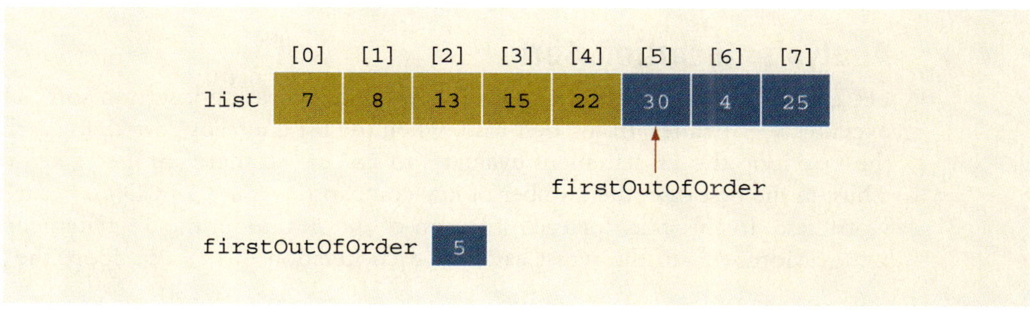

FIGURE 19-35 First out-of-order element is at position 5

Here, `list[0]...list[4]`, or the elements `list[0]`, `list[1]`, `list[2]`, and `list[4]`, are in order. Now `firstOutOfOrder = 5`. Because `list[5] > list[4]`, the `if` statement evaluates to **false**. So, the body of the `if` statement does not execute, and the next iteration of the `for` loop, if any, takes place. Note that this is the case when the `firstOutOfOrder` element is already at the proper place. So, we simply need to advance `firstOutOfOrder` to the next array element, if any.

We can repeat this process for the remaining elements of `list` to sort `list`.

The following C++ function implements the previous algorithm:

```cpp
template <class elemType>
void insertionSort(elemType list[], int length)
{
    for (int firstOutOfOrder = 1; firstOutOfOrder < length;
                                  firstOutOfOrder++)
        if (list[firstOutOfOrder] < list[firstOutOfOrder - 1])
        {
            elemType temp = list[firstOutOfOrder];
            int location = firstOutOfOrder;

            do
            {
                list[location] = list[location - 1];
                location--;
            }
            while (location > 0 && list[location - 1] > temp);

            list[location] = temp;
        }
} //end insertionSort
```

We leave it as an exercise for you to write a program to test the insertion sort algorithm. (See Programming Exercise 8 at the end of this chapter.)

NOTE An insertion sort can also be applied to linked lists. The general algorithm is the same, and the details are left as an exercise for you. See Programming Exercise 9 at the end of this chapter.

Analysis: Insertion Sort

Let L be a list of length n. Suppose L is to be sorted using insertion sort. The `for` loop executes $n - 1$ times. In the best case, when the list is already sorted, for each iteration of the `for` loop the `if` statement evaluates to **false**, so there are $n - 1$ key comparisons. Thus, in the best case, the number of key comparisons is $n - 1 = O(n)$. Let us consider the worst case. In this case, for each iteration of the `for` loop, the `if` statement evaluates to **true**. Moreover, in the worst case, for each iteration of the `for` loop, the `do...while` loop executes `firstOutOfOrder - 1` times. It follows that in the worst case, the number of key comparisons is:

$$1 + 2 + \cdots + (n - 1) = n(n - 1)/2 = O(n^2).$$

It can be shown that the average number of key comparisons and the average number of item assignments in an insertion sort algorithm are:

$$\frac{1}{4}n^2 + O(n) = O(n^2)$$

Table 19-9 summarizes the behavior of the bubble sort, selection sort, and insertion sort algorithms.

TABLE 19-9 Average Case Behavior of the Bubble Sort, Selection Sort, and Insertion Sort Algorithms for a List of Length n

Algorithm	Number of comparisons	Number of swaps
Bubble sort	$\dfrac{n(n - 1)}{2} = O(n^2)$	$\dfrac{n(n - 1)}{4} = O(n^2)$
Selection sort	$\dfrac{n(n - 1)}{2} = O(n^2)$	$3(n - 1) = O(n)$
Insertion sort	$\dfrac{1}{4}n^2 + O(n) = O(n^2)$	$\dfrac{1}{4}n^2 + O(n) = O(n^2)$

Lower Bound on Comparison-Based Sort Algorithms

In the previous sections, we discussed the selection and insertion sort algorithms, and noted that the average-case behavior of these algorithms is $O(n^2)$. Both of these algorithms are comparison-based; that is, the lists are sorted by comparing their respective keys. Before discussing any additional sorting algorithms, let us discuss the best-case scenario for comparison-based sorting algorithms.

We can trace the execution of a comparison-based algorithm by using a graph called a **comparison tree**. Let L be a list of n distinct elements, where $n > 0$. For any j and k, where $1 \le j \le n$, $1 \le k \le n$, either $L[j] < L[k]$ or $L[j] > L[k]$. Because each comparison of the keys has two outcomes, the comparison tree is a **binary tree**. While drawing this figure, we draw each comparison as a circle, called a **node**. The node is labeled as $j{:}k$, representing the comparison of $L[j]$ with $L[k]$. If $L[j] < L[k]$, follow the left branch; otherwise, follow the right branch. Figure 19-36 shows the comparison tree for a list of length 3. (In Figure 19-36, the rectangle, called a **leaf**, represents the final ordering of the nodes.)

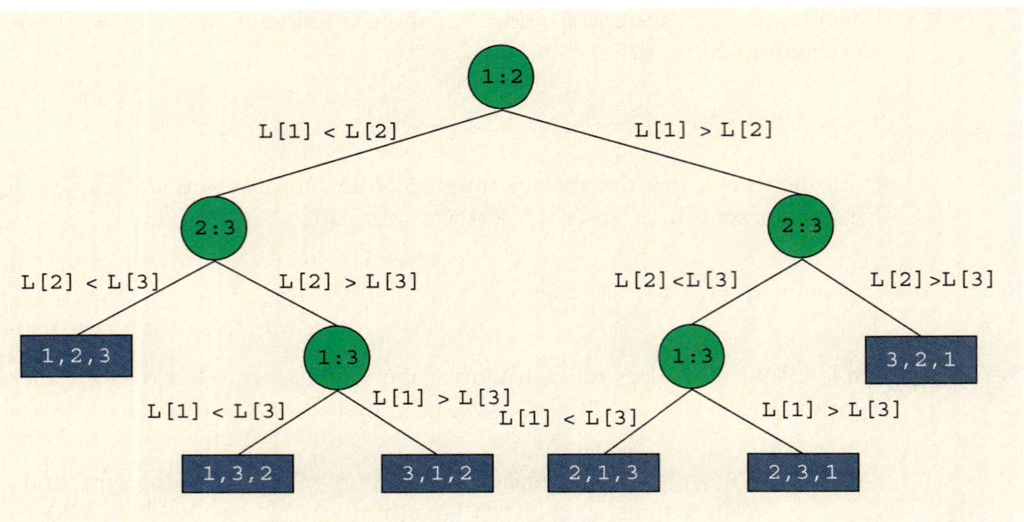

FIGURE 19-36 Comparison tree for sorting three items

We call the top node in the figure the **root** node. The straight line that connects the two nodes is called a **branch**. A sequence of branches from a node, x, to another node, y, is called a **path** from x to y.

Associated with each path from the root to a leaf is a unique permutation of the elements of L. This uniqueness follows because the sort algorithm only moves the data and makes comparisons. Furthermore, the data movement on any path from the root to a leaf is the same regardless of the initial inputs. For a list of n elements, $n > 0$, there are $n!$ different permutations. Any one of these $n!$ permutations might be the correct ordering of L. Thus, the comparison tree must have at least $n!$ leaves.

Now let us consider the worst case for all comparison-based sorting algorithms. We state the following result without proof.

Theorem: Let L be a list of n distinct elements. Any sorting algorithm that sorts L by comparison of the keys only, in its worst case, makes at least $O(n\log_2 n)$ key comparisons.

As analyzed in the previous sections, both the selection and insertion sort algorithms are of the order $O(n^2)$. The remainder of this chapter discusses sorting algorithms that, on average, are of the order $O(n\log_2 n)$.

Quick Sort: Array-Based Lists

In the previous section, we noted that the lower bound on comparison-based algorithms is $O(n\log_2 n)$. The sorting algorithms bubble sort, selection sort, and insertion sort, discussed earlier in this chapter, are $O(n^2)$. In this and the next two sections, we discuss sorting algorithms that are of the order $O(n\log_2 n)$. The first algorithm is the quick sort algorithm.

The quick sort algorithm uses the divide-and-conquer technique to sort a list. The list is partitioned into two sublists, which are then sorted and combined into one list in such a way so that the combined list is sorted. Thus, the general algorithm is:

```
if (the list size is greater than 1)
{
    a. Partition the list into two sublists, say lowerSublist and
       upperSublist.
    b. Quick sort lowerSublist.
    c. Quick sort upperSublist.
    d. Combine the sorted lowerSublist and sorted upperSublist.
}
```

After partitioning the list into two sublists called `lowerSublist` and `upperSublist`, the sublists are sorted using the quick sort algorithm. In other words, we use *recursion* to implement the quick sort algorithm.

The quick sort algorithm described here is for array-based lists. The algorithm for linked lists can be developed in a similar manner and is left as an exercise for you.

In the quick sort algorithm, the list is partitioned in such way that combining the sorted `lowerSublist` and `upperSublist` is trivial. Therefore, in a quick sort, all the sorting work is done in partitioning the list. Because all the sorting work occurs during the partitioning of the list, we first describe the partition procedure in detail.

To partition the list into two sublists, first we choose an element of the list called **pivot**. The `pivot` is used to divide the list into two sublists: `lowerSublist` and `upperSublist`. The elements in `lowerSublist` are smaller than `pivot`, and the elements in `upperSublist` are greater than or equal to `pivot`. For example, consider the list in Figure 19-37.

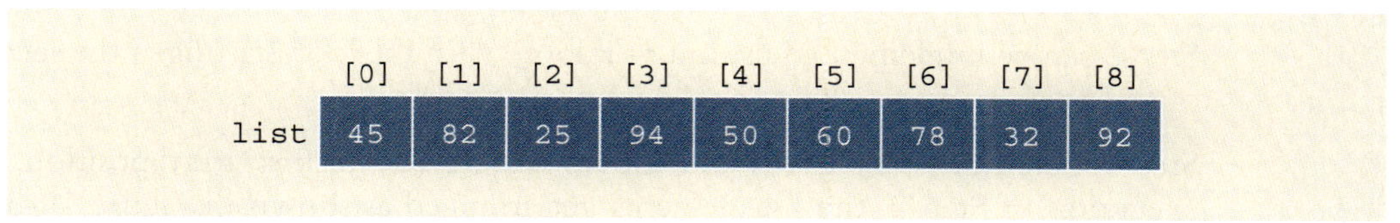

FIGURE 19-37 `list` before the partition

There are several ways to determine **pivot**. However, `pivot` is chosen so that, it is hoped, `lowerSublist` and `upperSublist` are of nearly equal size. For illustration purposes, let us choose the middle element of the list as `pivot`. The partition procedure that we describe partitions this list using `pivot` as the middle element, in our case 50, as shown in Figure 19-38.

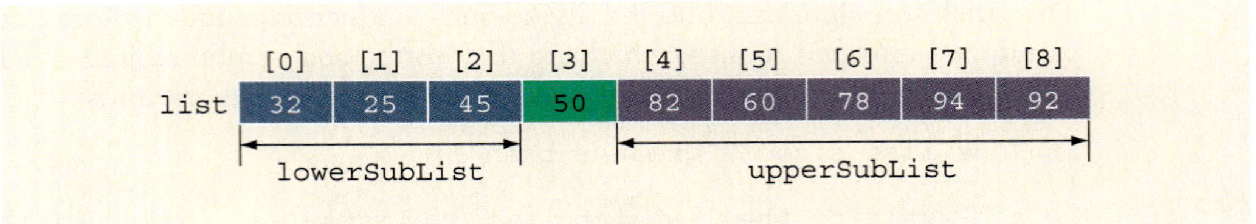

FIGURE 19-38 `list` after the partition

From Figure 19-38, it follows that after partitioning `list` into `lowerSublist` and `upperSublist`, pivot is in the right place. Thus, after sorting `lowerSublist` and `upperSublist`, combining the two sorted sublists is trivial.

The partition algorithm is as follows (we assume that `pivot` is chosen as the middle element of the list):

1.   Determine `pivot`, and swap `pivot` with the first element of the list.

     Suppose that the index `smallIndex` points to the last element less than `pivot`. The index `smallIndex` is initialized to the first element of the list.

2.   For the remaining elements in the list (starting at the second element):

     If the current element is less than pivot,

   a.   Increment `smallIndex`.

   b.   Swap the current element with the array element pointed to by `smallIndex`.

3.   Swap the first element, that is, `pivot`, with the array element pointed to by `smallIndex`.

Step 2 can be implemented using a **for** loop, with the loop starting at the second element of the list.

Step 1 determines the pivot and moves `pivot` to the first array position. During the execution of Step 2, the list elements get arranged as shown in Figure 19-39. (Suppose the name of the array containing the list elements is `list`.)

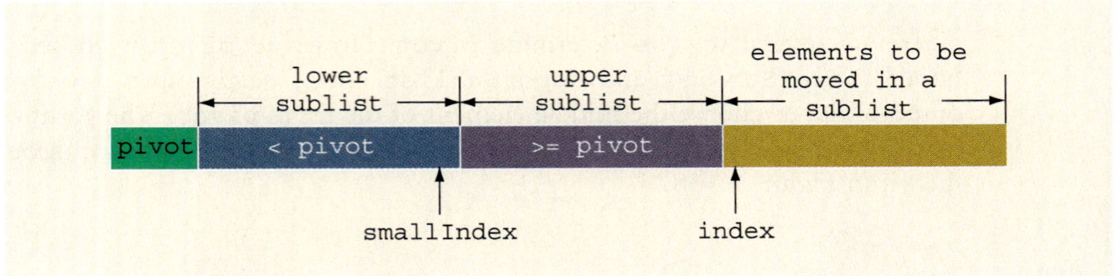

FIGURE 19-39 List during the execution of Step 2

As shown in Figure 19–39, `pivot` is in the first array position. Elements in the lower sublist are less than `pivot`; elements in the upper sublist are greater than or equal to `pivot`. The variable `smallIndex` contains the index of the last element of the lower sublist; the variable `index` contains the index of the next element that needs to be moved, either in the lower sublist or in the upper sublist. As explained in Step 2, if the next element of the list (that is, `list[index]`) is less than `pivot`, we advance `smallIndex` to the next array position and swap `list[index]` with `list[smallIndex]`. Next, we illustrate Step 2.

Suppose that the list is as given in Figure 19–40.

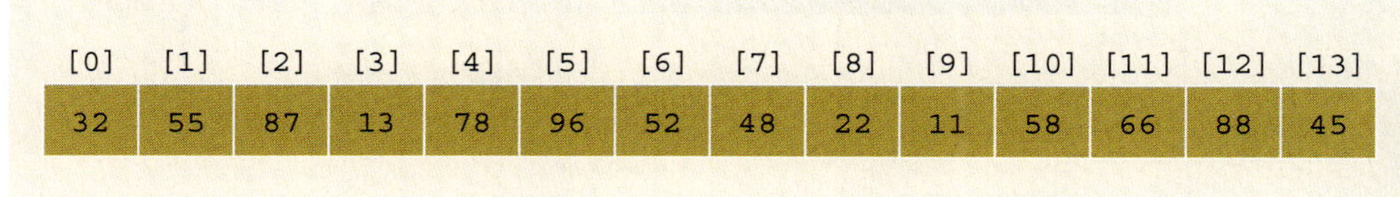

FIGURE 19-40   List before sorting

Step 1 requires us to determine the `pivot` and swap it with the first array element. For the list in Figure 19–40, the middle element is at the position $(0 + 13) / 2 = 6$. That is, `pivot` is at position 6. Therefore, after swapping `pivot` with the first array element, the list is as shown in Figure 19–41. (Notice that in Figure 19–41, 52 is swapped with 32.)

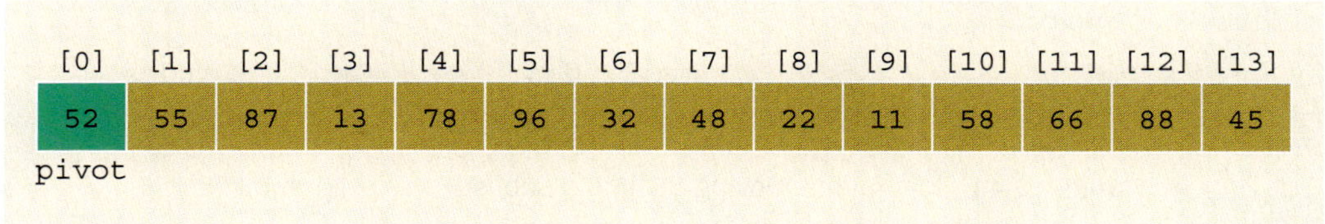

FIGURE 19-41   List after moving `pivot` to the first array position

Suppose that after executing Step 2 a few times, the list is as shown in Figure 19–42.

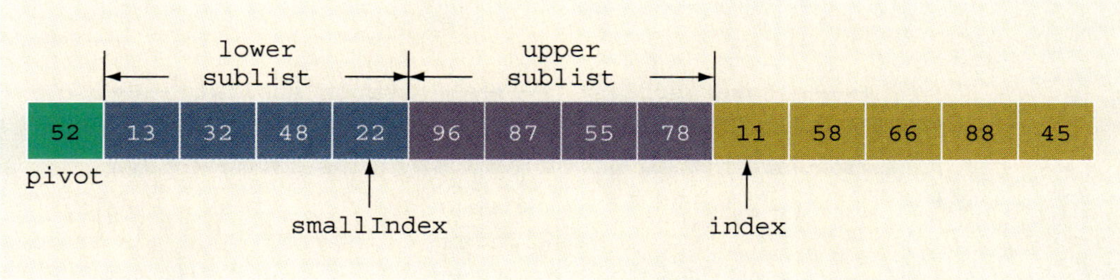

FIGURE 19-42   List after a few iterations of Step 2

As shown in Figure 19-42, the next element of the list that needs to be moved into a sublist is indicated by `index`. Because `list[index] < pivot`, we need to move the element `list[index]` into the lower sublist. To do so, we first advance `smallIndex` to the next array position and then swap `list[smallIndex]` with `list[index]`. The resulting list is as shown in Figure 19-43. (Notice that 11 is swapped with 96.)

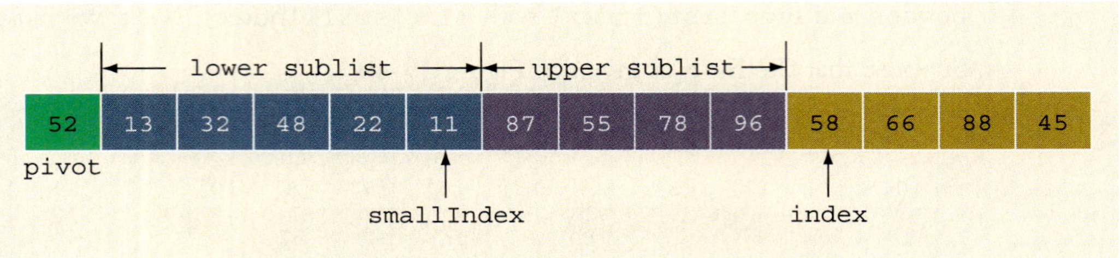

FIGURE 19-43   List after moving 11 into the lower sublist

Now consider the list in Figure 19-44.

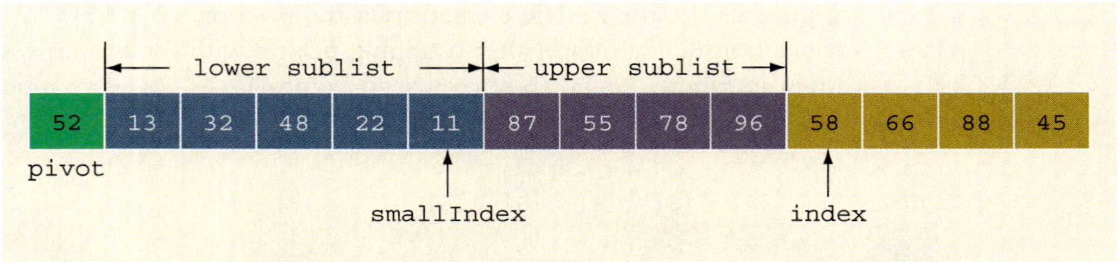

FIGURE 19-44   List before moving 58 into a sublist

For the list in Figure 19-44, `list[index]` is 58, which is greater than `pivot`. Therefore, `list[index]` is to be moved into the upper sublist. This is accomplished by leaving 58 at its position and increasing the size of the upper sublist by one, to the next array position. After moving 58 into the upper sublist, the list is shown in Figure 19-45.

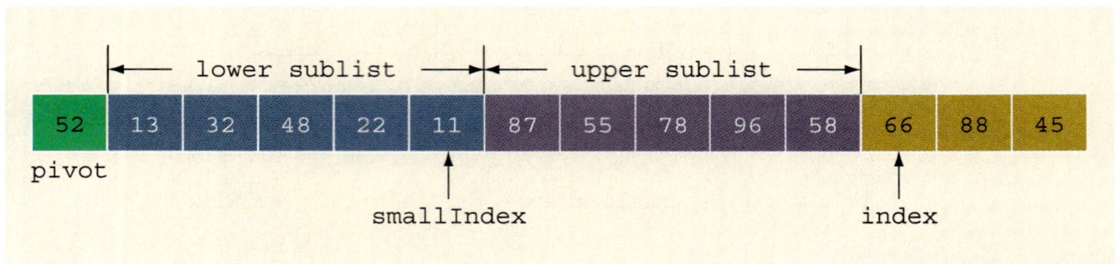

FIGURE 19-45   List after moving 58 into the upper sublist

After moving the elements that are less than `pivot` into the lower sublist and elements that are greater than `pivot` into the upper sublist (that is, after completely executing Step 2). Figure 19-46 shows the resulting list.

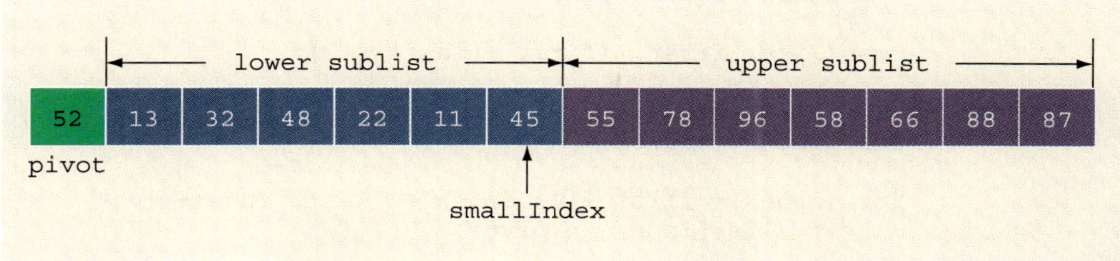

FIGURE 19-46   List elements after arranging into the lower sublist and upper sublist

Next, we execute Step 3 and move 52, `pivot`, to the proper position in the list. This is accomplished by swapping 52 with 45. The resulting list is as shown in Figure 19-47.

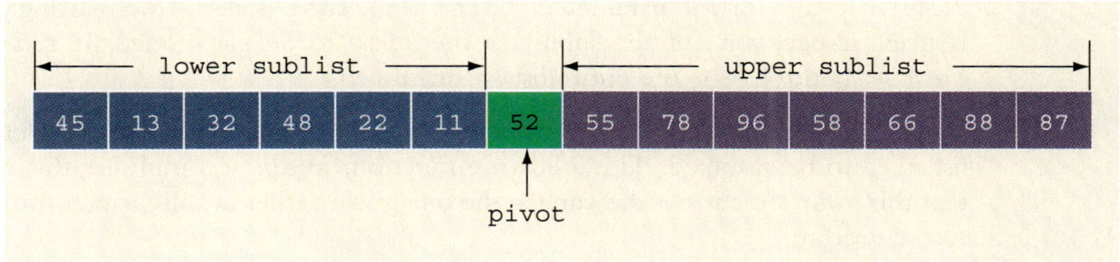

FIGURE 19-47   List after swapping 52 with 45

As shown in Figure 19-47, Steps 1, 2, and 3 in the preceding algorithm partition the list into two sublists. The elements less than `pivot` are in the lower sublist; the elements greater than or equal to `pivot` are in the upper sublist.

To partition the list into the lower and upper sublists, we need to keep track of only the last element of the lower sublist and the next element of the list that needs to be moved into either the lower sublist or the upper sublist. In fact, the upper sublist is between the two indices `smallIndex` and `index`.

We now write the function, `partition`, to implement the preceding partition algorithm. After rearranging the elements of the list, the function `partition` returns the location of `pivot` so that we can determine the starting and ending locations of the sublists. The definition of the function `partition` is:

```cpp
template <class elemType>
int partition(elemType list[], int first, int last)
{
    elemType pivot;

    int index, smallIndex;

    swap(list, first, (first + last) / 2);

    pivot = list[first];
    smallIndex = first;

    for (index = first + 1; index <= last; index++)
        if (list[index] < pivot)
        {
            smallIndex++;
            swap(list, smallIndex, index);
        }

    swap(list, first, smallIndex);

    return smallIndex;
} //end partition
```

Note that the formal parameters `first` and `last` specify the starting and ending indices, respectively, of the sublist of the `list` to be partitioned. If `first` = 0 and `last` = length − 1, the entire list is partitioned.

As you can see from the definition of the function `partition`, certain elements of the list need to be swapped. The following function, `swap`, accomplishes this task. (Notice that this **swap** function is the same as the one given earlier in this chapter for the selection sort algorithm.)

```cpp
template <class elemType>
void swap(elemType list[], int first, int second)
{
    elemType temp;

    temp = list[first];
    list[first] = list[second];
    list[second] = temp;
} //end swap
```

Once the list is partitioned into `lowerSublist` and `upperSublist`, we again apply the quick sort function to sort the two sublists. Because both sublists are sorted using the same quick sort algorithm, the easiest way to implement this algorithm is to use recursion. Therefore, this section gives the recursive version of the quick sort algorithm. As explained previously, after rearranging the elements of the list, the function `partition` returns the index of `pivot` so that the starting and ending indices of the sublists can be determined.

Given the starting and ending indices of a list, the following function, `recQuickSort`, implements the recursive version of the quick sort algorithm:

```cpp
template <class elemType>
void recQuickSort(elemType list[], int first, int last)
{
    int pivotLocation;

    if (first < last)
    {
        pivotLocation = partition(list, first, last);
        recQuickSort(list, first, pivotLocation - 1);
        recQuickSort(list, pivotLocation + 1, last);
    }
} //end recQuickSort
```

Finally, we write the quick sort function, `quickSort`, that calls the function `recQuickSort` on the original list:

```cpp
template <class elemType>
void quickSort(elemType list[], int length)
{
    recQuickSort(list, 0, length - 1);
} //end quickSort
```

We leave it as an exercise for you to write a program to test the quick sort algorithm. See Programming Exercise 10 at the end of this chapter.

Analysis: Quick Sort

The general analysis of the quick sort algorithm is beyond the scope of this book. However, let us determine the number of comparisons in the worst case. Suppose that L is a list of n elements, $n \geq 0$. In quick sort, all the sorting work is done by the function `partition`. From the definition of the function `partition`, it follows that to partition a list of length k, the function `partition` makes $k - 1$ key comparisons. Also, in the worst case, after partition, one sublist is of length $k - 1$ and the other sublist is of length 0.

It follows that in the worst case, the first call of the function `partition` makes $n - 1$ key comparisons. In the second call, the function `partition` partitions a list of length $n - 1$, so it makes $n - 2$ key comparisons, and so on. We can now conclude that to sort a list of length n, in the worst case, the total number of key comparisons made by quick sort is:

$$(n - 1) + (n - 2) + \cdots + 2 + 1 = n(n - 1)/2 = O(n^2).$$

Table 19-10 summarizes the behavior of the quick sort algorithm for a list of length n.

TABLE 19-10 Analysis of the Quick Sort Algorithm for a List of Length n

	Number of comparisons	Number of swaps
Average case	$(1.39)n\log_2 n + O(n) = O(n\log_2 n)$	$(0.69)n\log_2 n + O(n) = O(n\log_2 n)$
Worst case	$\dfrac{n^2}{2} - \dfrac{n}{2} = O(n^2)$	$\dfrac{n^2}{2} + \dfrac{3n}{2} - 2 = O(n^2)$

Merge Sort: Linked List-Based Lists

In the previous section, we described the quick sort algorithm and stated that the average-case behavior of a quick sort is $O(n\log_2 n)$. However, the worst-case behavior of a quick sort is $O(n^2)$. This section describes the sorting algorithm whose behavior is always $O(n\log_2 n)$.

Like the quick sort algorithm, the merge sort algorithm uses the divide-and-conquer technique to sort a list. A merge sort algorithm also partitions the list into two sublists, sorts the sublists, and then combines the sorted sublists into one sorted list. This section describes the merge sort algorithm for linked list-based lists. We leave it for you to develop the merge sort algorithm for array-based lists, which can be done by using the techniques described for linked lists.

The merge sort and the quick sort algorithms differ in how they partition the list. As discussed earlier, a quick sort first selects an element in the list, called `pivot`, and then partitions the list so that the elements in one sublist are less than `pivot` and the elements in the other sublist are greater than or equal to `pivot`. By contrast, a merge sort divides the list into two sublists of nearly equal size. For example, consider the list whose elements are as follows:

```
list: 35   28   18   45   62   48   30   38
```

The merge sort algorithm partitions this list into two sublists as follows:

```
first sublist: 35   28   18   45
second sublist: 62   48   30   38
```

The two sublists are sorted using the same algorithm (that is, a merge sort) used on the original list. Suppose that we have sorted the two sublists. That is, suppose that the lists are now as follows:

```
first sublist: 18   28   35   45
second sublist: 30   38   48   62
```

Next, the merge sort algorithm combines, that is, merges, the two sorted sublists into one sorted list.

Figure 19-48 further illustrates the merge sort process.

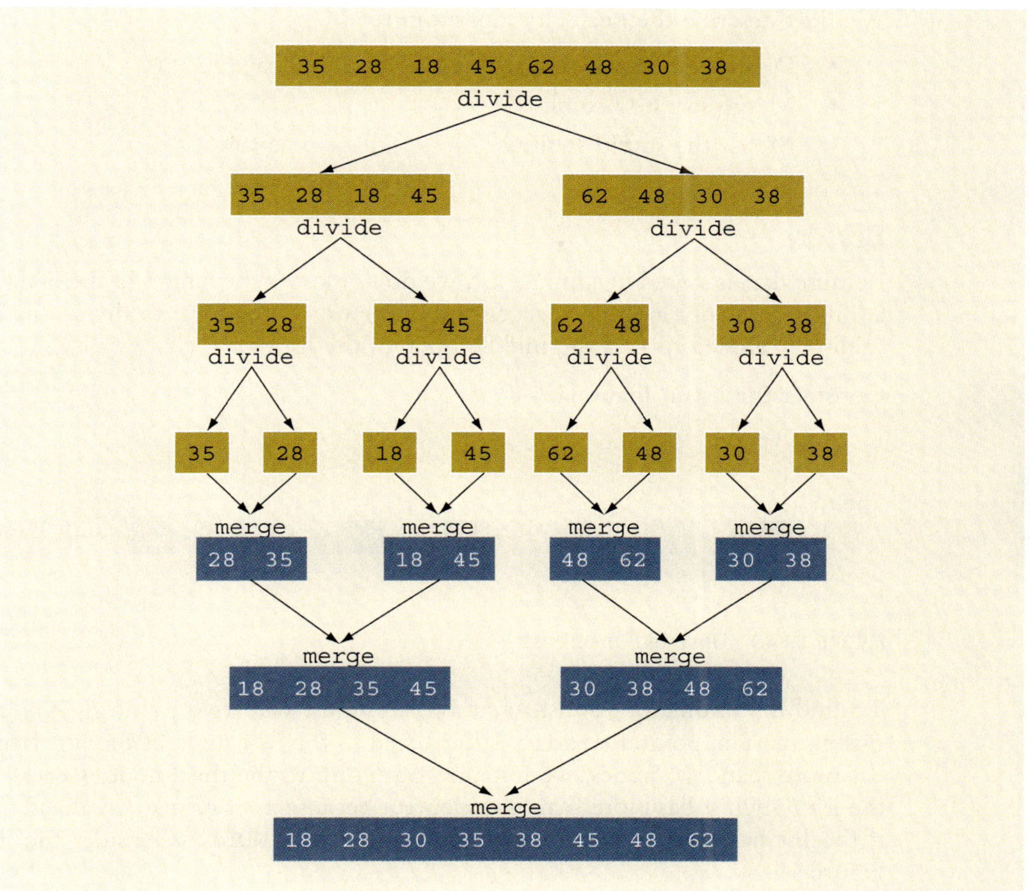

FIGURE 19-48   Merge sort algorithm

From Figure 19-48, it is clear that in the merge sort algorithm, most of the sorting work is done in merging the sorted sublists.

The general algorithm for the merge sort is as follows:

```
if the list is of a size greater than 1
{
    a. Divide the list into two sublists.
    b. Merge sort the first sublist.
    c. Merge sort the second sublist.
    d. Merge the first sublist and the second sublist.
}
```

As remarked previously, after dividing the list into two sublists—the first sublist and the second sublist—the two sublists are sorted using the merge sort algorithm. In other words, we use recursion to implement the merge sort algorithm.

We next describe the necessary algorithm to:

- Divide the list into two sublists of nearly equal size.
- Merge sort both sublists.
- Merge the sorted sublists.

Divide

Because data is stored in a linked list, we do not know the length of the list. Furthermore, a linked list is not a random access data structure. Therefore, to divide the list into two sublists, we need to find the middle node of the list.

Consider the list in Figure 19-49.

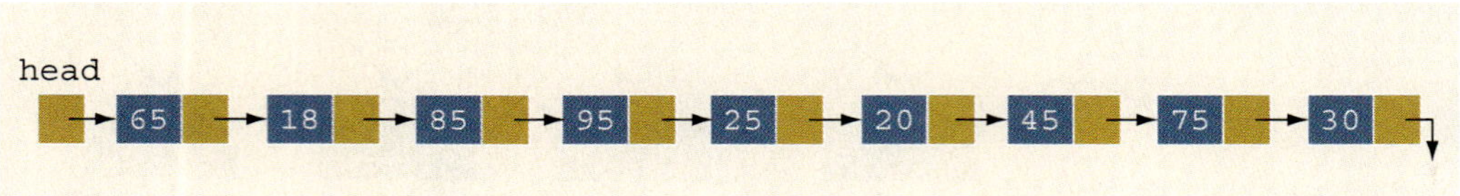

FIGURE 19-49   Unsorted linked list

To find the middle of the list, we traverse the list with two pointers—say, `middle` and `current`. The pointer `middle` is initialized to the first node of the list. Because this list has more than two nodes, we initialize `current` to the third node. (Recall that we sort the list only if it has more than one element because a list of size 1 is already sorted. Also, if the list has only two nodes, we set `current` to NULL.) Consider the list shown in Figure 19-50.

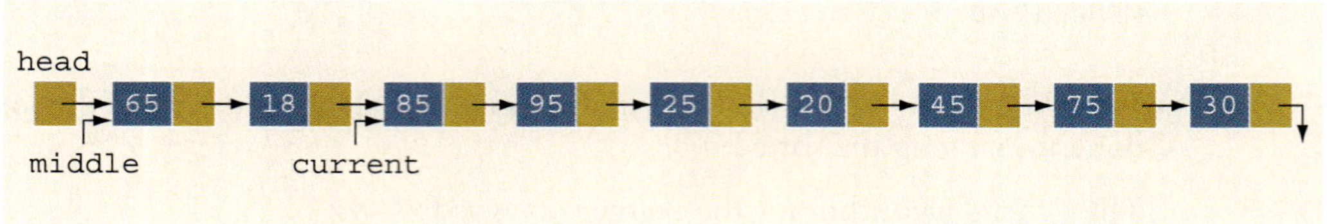

FIGURE 19-50   `middle` and `current` before traversing the list

Every time we advance `middle` by one node, we advance `current` by one node. After advancing `current` by one node, if `current` is not NULL, we again advance `current` by one node. That is, for the most part, every time `middle` advances by one node, `current` advances by two nodes. Eventually, `current` becomes NULL and `middle` points to the last node of the first sublist. For example, for the list in Figure 19-50, when `current` becomes NULL, `middle` points to the node with `info` 25 (see Figure 19-51).

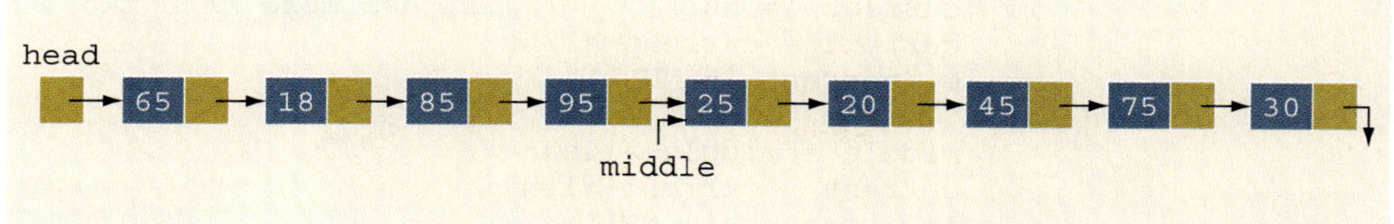

FIGURE 19-51 `middle` after traversing the list

It is now easy to divide the list into two sublists. First, using the link of `middle`, we assign a pointer to the node following `middle`. Then, we set the link of `middle` to NULL. Figure 19-52 shows the resulting sublists.

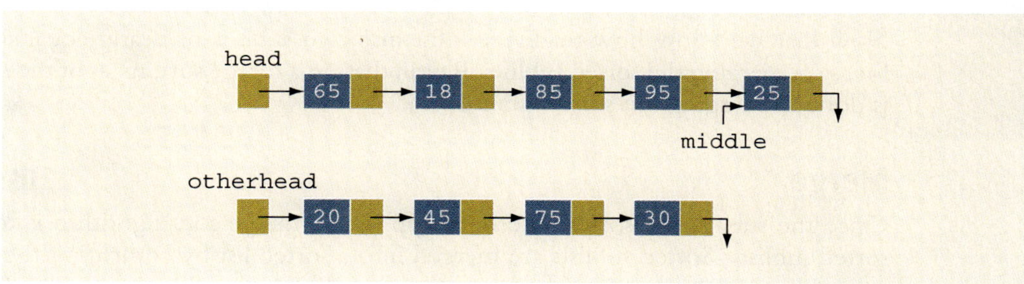

FIGURE 19-52 List after dividing it into two lists

This discussion translates into the following C++ function, `divideList`:

```cpp
template <class Type>
void unorderedLinkedList<Type>::
             divideList(nodeType<Type>* first1,
                        nodeType<Type>* &first2)
{
    nodeType<Type>* middle;
    nodeType<Type>* current;

    if (first1 == NULL)      //list is empty
        first2 = NULL;
    else if (first1->link == NULL)  //list has only one node
        first2 = NULL;
    else
    {
        middle = first1;
        current = first1->link;
```

```cpp
        if (current != NULL)      //list has more than two nodes
            current = current->link;
        while (current != NULL)
        {
            middle = middle->link;
            current = current->link;
            if (current != NULL)
                current = current->link;
        } //end while

        first2 = middle->link;  //first2 points to the first
                                //node of the second sublist
        middle->link = NULL;    //set the link of the last node
                                //of the first sublist to NULL
    } //end else
} //end divideList
```

Now that we know how to divide a list into two sublists of nearly equal size, next we focus on merging the sorted sublists. Recall that, in a merge sort, most of the sorting work is done in merging the sorted sublists.

Merge

Once the sublists are sorted, the next step in the merge sort algorithm is to merge the sorted sublists. Sorted sublists are merged into a sorted list by comparing the elements of the sublists and then adjusting the pointers of the nodes with the smaller `info`. Let us illustrate this procedure on the sublists shown in Figure 19-53. Suppose that `first1` points to the first node of the first sublist, and `first2` points to the first node of the second sublist.

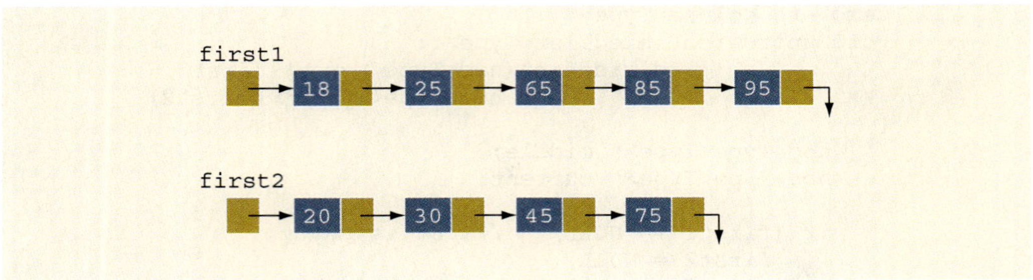

FIGURE 19-53 Sublists before merging

We first compare the `info` of the first node of each sublist to determine the first node of the merged list. We set `newHead` to point to the first node of the merged list. We also use the pointer `lastMerged` to keep track of the last node of the merged list. The pointer of the first node of the sublist with the smaller node, then advances to the next node of that sublist. Figure 19-54 shows the sublist of Figure 19-53 after setting `newHead` and `lastMerged` and advancing `first1`.

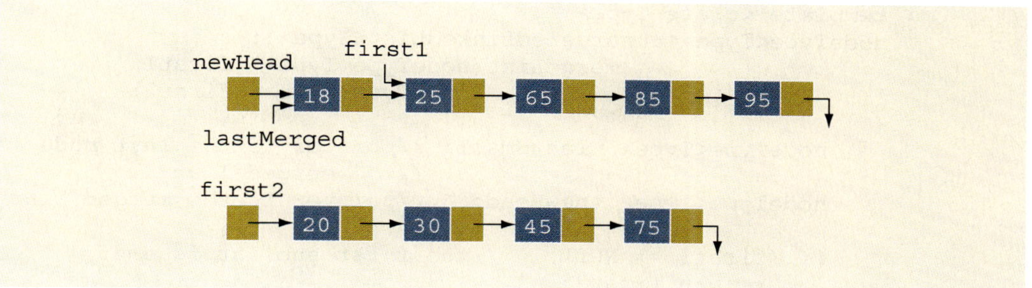

FIGURE 19-54 Sublists after setting `newHead` and `lastMerged` and advancing `first1`

In Figure 19-54, `first1` points to the first node of the first sublist that is yet to be merged with the second sublist. So, we again compare the nodes pointed to by `first1` and `first2`, and adjust the link of the smaller node and the last node of the merged list so as to move the smaller node to the end of the merged list. For the sublists shown in Figure 19-54, after adjusting the necessary links, we have Figure 19-55.

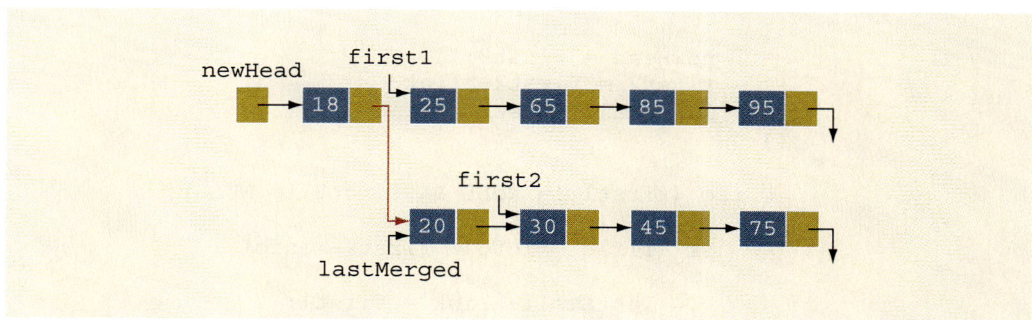

FIGURE 19-55 Merged list after putting the node with `info` 20 at the end of the merged list

We continue this process for the remaining elements of both sublists. Every time we move a node to the merged list, we advance either `first1` or `first2` to the next node. Eventually, either `first1` or `first2` becomes NULL. If `first1` becomes NULL, the first sublist is exhausted first, and so we attach the remaining nodes of the second sublist at the end of the partially merged list. If `first2` becomes NULL, the second sublist is exhausted first, and so we attach the remaining nodes of the first sublist at the end of the partially merged list.

Following this discussion, we can now write the C++ function, `mergeList`, to merge the two sorted sublists. The pointers of the first nodes of the sublists are passed as parameters to the function `mergeList`:

```cpp
template <class Type>
nodeType<Type>* unorderedLinkedList<Type>::
                 mergeList(nodeType<Type>* first1,
                           nodeType<Type>* first2)
{
    nodeType<Type> *lastSmall; //pointer to the last node of
                               //the merged list
    nodeType<Type> *newHead;   //pointer to the merged list

    if (first1 == NULL)    //the first sublist is empty
        return first2;
    else if (first2 == NULL)    //the second sublist is empty
        return first1;
    else
    {
        if (first1->info < first2->info) //compare the
                                         //first nodes
        {
            newHead = first1;
            first1 = first1->link;
            lastSmall = newHead;
        }
        else
        {
            newHead = first2;
            first2 = first2->link;
            lastSmall = newHead;
        }

        while (first1 != NULL && first2 != NULL)
        {
            if (first1->info < first2->info)
            {
                lastSmall->link = first1;
                lastSmall = lastSmall->link;
                first1 = first1->link;
            }
            else
            {
                lastSmall->link = first2;
                lastSmall = lastSmall->link;
                first2 = first2->link;
            }
        } //end while

        if (first1 == NULL) //first sublist is exhausted first
            lastSmall->link = first2;
        else                //second sublist is exhausted first
            lastSmall->link = first1;

        return newHead;
    }
}//end mergeList
```

Finally, we write the recursive merge sort function, `recMergeSort`, which uses the `divideList` and `mergeList` functions to sort a list. The pointer of the first node of the list to be sorted is passed as a parameter to the function `recMergeSort`:

```
template <class Type>
void unorderedLinkedList<Type>::recMergeSort(
                                    nodeType<Type>* &head)
{
    nodeType<Type> *otherHead;

    if (head != NULL)   //if the list is not empty
        if (head->link != NULL)   //if the list has more than
                                  //one node
        {
            divideList(head, otherHead);
            recMergeSort(head);
            recMergeSort(otherHead);
            head = mergeList(head, otherHead);
        }
} //end recMergeSort
```

We can now give the definition of the function `mergeSort`, which should be included as a `public` member of the `class` `unorderedLinkedList`. (Note that the functions `divideList`, `merge`, and `recMergeSort` can be included as `private` members of the `class` `unorderedLinkedList` because these functions are used only to implement the function `mergeSort`.) The function `mergeSort` calls the function `recMergeSort` and passes `first` to this function. It also sets `last` to point to the last node of the list. The definition of the function `mergeSort` is:

```
template <class Type>
void unorderedLinkedList<Type>::mergeSort()
{
    recMergeSort(first);

    if (first == NULL)
        last = NULL;
    else
    {
        last = first;
        while (last->link != NULL)
            last = last->link;
    }
} //end mergeSort
```

We leave it as an exercise for you to write a program to test the merge sort algorithm. See Programming Exercise 13 at the end of this chapter.

Analysis: Merge Sort

Suppose that L is a list of n elements, where $n > 0$. Suppose that n is a power of 2, that is, $n = 2^m$ for some non-negative integer m, so that we can divide the list into two sublists, each of size:

$$\frac{n}{2} = \frac{2^m}{2} = 2^{m-1}$$

Moreover, each sublist can also be divided into two sublists of the same size. Each call to the function **recMergeSort** makes two recursive calls to the function **recMergeSort**, and each call divides the sublist into two sublists of the same size. Suppose that $m = 3$, that is, $n = 2^3 = 8$. So, the length of the original list is 8. The first call to the function **recMergeSort** divides the original list into two sublists, each of size 4. The first call then makes two recursive calls to the function **recMergeSort**. Each of these recursive call divides each sublist, of size 4, into two sublists, each of size 2. We now have four sublists, each of size 2. The next set of recursive calls divides each sublist, of size 2, into sublists of size 1. So, we now have eight sublists, each of size 1. It follows that the exponent 3 in 2^3 indicates the level of the recursion (see Figure 19-56).

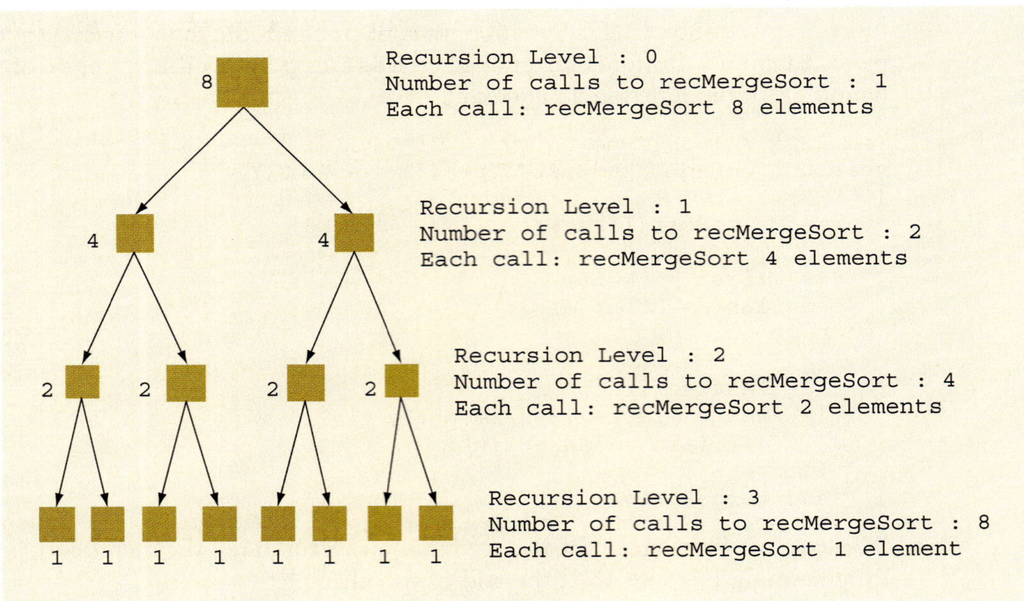

FIGURE 19-56   Levels of recursion levels to recMergeSort for a list of length 8

Let us consider the general case when $n = 2^m$. Note that the number of recursion levels is m. Also, note that to merge a sorted list of size s with a sorted list of size t, the maximum number of comparisons is $s + t - 1$.

Consider the function `mergeList`, which merges two sorted lists into a sorted list. Note that this is where the actual work (comparisons and assignments) is done. The initial call to the function `recMergeSort`, at level 0, produces two sublists, each of the size $n/2$. To merge these two lists, after they are sorted, the maximum number of comparisons is:

$$\frac{n}{2} + \frac{n}{2} - 1 = n - 1 = O(n).$$

At level 1, we merge two sets of sorted lists, where each sublist is of the size $n/4$. To merge two sorted sublists, each of the size $n/4$, we need, at most:

$$\frac{n}{4} + \frac{n}{4} - 1 = \frac{n}{2} - 1$$

comparisons. Thus, at level 1 of the recursion, the number of comparisons is $2(n/2 - 1) = n - 2 = O(n)$. In general, at level k of the recursion, there are a total of 2^k calls to the function `mergeList`. Each of these call merge two sublists, each of the size $n/2^{k+1}$, which requires a maximum of $n/2^k - 1$ comparisons. Thus, at level k of the recursion, the maximum number of comparisons is:

$$2^k\left(\frac{n}{2^k} - 1\right) = n - 2^k = O(n).$$

It now follows that the maximum number of comparisons at each level of the recursion is $O(n)$. Because the number of levels of the recursion is m, the maximum number of comparisons made by the merge sort algorithms is $O(nm)$. Now $n = 2^m$ implies that $m = \log_2 n$. Hence, the maximum number of comparisons made by the merge sort algorithm is $O(n \log_2 n)$.

If $W(n)$ denotes the number of key comparisons in the worst case to sort L, then $W(n) = O(n \log_2 n)$.

Let $A(n)$ denote the number of key comparisons in the average case. In the average case, during merge, one of the sublists will exhaust before the other list. From this, it follows that, on average, when merging two sorted sublists of combined size n, the number of comparisons will be less than $n - 1$. On average, it can be shown that the number of comparisons for merge sort is given by the following equation: If n is a power of 2, $A(n) = n \log_2 n - 1.25n = O(n \log_2 n)$. This is also a good approximation when n is not a power of 2.

NOTE We can also obtain an analysis of the merge sort algorithm by constructing and solving certain equations as follows. As noted before, in merge sort, all the comparisons are made in the procedure `mergeList`, which merges two sorted sublists. If one sublist is of size s and the other sublist is of size t, then merging these lists would require, at most, $s + t - 1$ comparisons in the worst case. Hence:

$$W(n) = W(s) + W(t) + s + t - 1$$

Note that $s = n / 2$ and $t = n / 2$. Suppose that $n = 2^m$. Then, $s = 2^{m-1}$ and $t = 2^{m-1}$. It follows that $s + t = n$. Hence:

$$W(n) = W(n/2) + W(n/2) + n - 1 = 2W(n/2) + n - 1, n > 0$$

Also:

$$W(1) = 0$$

It is known that when n is a power of 2, $W(n)$ is given by the following equation:

$$W(n) = n \log_2 n - (n - 1) = O(n \log_2 n)$$

NOTE **(Heap Sort)** This chapter also discusses the heap sort algorithm. This algorithm and its related exercises are available at the Web site accompanying this book.

PROGRAMMING EXAMPLE: Election Results

The presidential election for the student council of your local university is about to be held. The chair of the election committee wants to computerize the voting and has asked you to write a program to analyze the data and report the winner.

The university has four major divisions, and each division has several departments. For the election, the four divisions are labeled as region 1, region 2, region 3, and region 4. Each department in each division handles its own voting and reports the votes received by each candidate to the election committee. The voting is reported in the following form:

```
firstName lastName regionNumber numberOfVotes
```

The election committee wants the output in the following tabular form:

```
-----------------------Election Results--------------------
                                    Votes
    Candidate Name     Region1  Region2  Region3  Region4   Total
------------------     -------  -------  -------  -------  ------
Sheila   Bower             23       70      133      267     493
Danny    Dillion           25       71      156       97     349
Lisa     Fisher           110      158        0        0     268
Greg     Goldy             75       34      134        0     243
Peter    Lamba            285       56        0       46     387
Mickey   Miller           112      141      156       67     476

Winner: Sheila Bower, Votes Received: 493

Total votes polled: 2216
```

The names of the candidates must be in alphabetical order in the output.

For this program, we assume that six candidates are seeking the student council's president post. This program can be enhanced to handle any number of candidates.

The data are provided in two files. One file, `candData.txt`, consists of the names of the candidates seeking the president's post. The names of the candidates in this file are in no particular order. In the second file, `voteData.txt`, each line consists of the voting results in the following form:

```
firstName lastName regionNumber numberOfVotes
```

Each line in the file `voteData.txt` consists of the candidate's name, the region number, and the number of votes received by the candidate in that region. There is one entry per line. For example, the input file containing the voting data looks like the following:

```
Greg Goldy 2 34
Mickey Miller 1 56
Lisa Fisher 2 56
Peter Lamba 1 78
Danny Dillion 4 29
Sheila Bower 4 78
  .
  .
  .
```

The first line indicates that `Greg Goldy` received 34 votes from region 2.

Input   Two files: One containing the candidates' names and the other containing the voting data, as described previously

Output   The election results in a tabular form, as described previously, and the winner's name

PROBLEM ANALYSIS AND ALGORITHM DESIGN

From the output, it is clear that the program must organize the voting data by region and calculate the total votes received by each candidate and polled for the election overall. Furthermore, the names of the candidates must appear in alphabetical order.

The main component of this program is a candidate. Therefore, first we will design the `class` `candidateType` to implement a candidate object. Moreover, in this program, we use an array of `candidateType` object to implement the list of candidates.

The main component of this program is a candidate. Therefore, first we design the `class` `candidateType` to implement a candidate object. Every candidate has a name and receives votes. Because there are four regions, we can use an array of four components. In Example 11-9 (Chapter 11), we designed the `class` `personType` to implement the name of a person. Recall that an object of type `personType` can store the first name and the last name. Now that we have discussed operator overloading, we redesign the `class` `personType` and define the relational operators so that the names of two people can be compared. We will also overload the assignment operator for easy assignment and use the stream extraction and insertion operators for input/output. Because every candidate is a person, we will derive the `class` `candidateType` from the `class` `personType`.

personType

The `class` `personType` implements the first name and last name of a person. Therefore, the `class` `personType` has two member variables: `firstName`, to store the first name, and `lastName`, to store the last name. We declare these as protected so that the definition of the `class` `personType` can be easily extended to accommodate the requirements of a specific application needed to implement a person's name. The definition of the `class` `personType` is given next:

```cpp
#include <string>

using namespace std;

class personType
{
    friend istream& operator>>(istream&, personType&);
    friend ostream& operator<<(ostream&, const personType&);

public:
    void setName(string first, string last);
      //Function to set firstName and lastName according
      //to the parameters.
      //Postcondition: firstName = first; lastName = last
```

```
    string getFirstName() const;
      //Function to return the first name.
      //Postcondition: The value of firstName is returned.

    string getLastName() const;
      //Function to return the last name.
      //Postcondition: The value of lastName is returned.

    personType(string first = "", string last = "");
      //Constructor
      //Sets firstName and lastName according to the
      //parameters. The default values of the parameters are
      //empty strings.
      //Postcondition: firstName = first; lastName = last

        //overload the relational operators
    bool operator==(const personType& right) const;
    bool operator!=(const personType& right) const;
    bool operator<=(const personType& right) const;
    bool operator<(const personType& right) const;
    bool operator>=(const personType& right) const;
    bool operator>(const personType& right) const;

protected:
    string firstName; //variable to store the first name
    string lastName;  //variable to store the last name
};
```

We now give the definitions of the functions to implement the various operations of the `class personType`.

The definitions of the member functions `setName`, `getFirstName`, `getLastName`, and the constructors are the same as those given in Chapter 11. We, therefore, consider the definitions of the functions to overload the relational and stream operators.

The names of two people are the same if their first and last names are the same. Therefore, the definition of the function to overload the equality operator is:

```
bool personType::operator==(const personType& right) const
{
    return (firstName == right.firstName
            && lastName == right.lastName);
}
```

The names of two people are different if either their first or last names are different. Therefore, the definition of the function to overload the not equal to operator is:

```
bool personType::operator!=(const personType& right) const
{
    return (firstName != right.firstName
         || lastName != right.lastName);
}
```

Similarly, the definitions of the functions to overload the remaining relational operators are:

```cpp
bool personType::operator<=(const personType& right) const
{
    return (lastName <= right.lastName ||
            (lastName == right.lastName &&
             firstName <= right.firstName));
}

bool personType::operator<(const personType& right) const
{
    return (lastName < right.lastName ||
            (lastName == right.lastName &&
             firstName < right.firstName));
}

bool personType::operator>=(const personType& right) const
{
    return (lastName >= right.lastName ||
            (lastName == right.lastName &&
             firstName >= right.firstName));
}

bool personType::operator>(const personType& right) const
{
    return (lastName > right.lastName ||
            (lastName == right.lastName &&
             firstName > right.firstName));
}
```

The definitions of the functions to overload the stream extraction and insertion operators are given next:

```cpp
istream& operator>>(istream& isObject, personType& pName)
{
    isObject >> pName.firstName >> pName.lastName;

    return isObject;
}

ostream& operator<<(ostream& osObject, const personType& pName)
{
    osObject << pName.firstName << " " << pName.lastName;

    return osObject;
}
```

Candidate As remarked previously, the main component of this program is candidate. Every candidate has a name and can receive votes. Because there are four regions, we can use an array of four components to store the votes received.

There are six candidates. Therefore, we declare a list of six candidates of type `candidateType`. This chapter extended the `class` `unorderedArrayListType` by illustrating how to include the searching and sorting algorithms developed in this chapter. We will use this class to maintain the list of candidates. This list of candidates will be sorted and searched. Therefore, we must define (that is, overload) the assignment and relational operators for the `class` `candidateType` because these operators are used by the searching and sorting algorithms.

Data in the file containing the candidates' data consists of only the names of the candidates. Therefore, in addition to overloading the assignment operator so that the value of one object can be assigned to another object, we also overload the assignment operator for the `class` `candidateType`, so that only the name (of the `personType`) of the candidate can be assigned to a candidate object. That is, we overload the assignment operator twice: once for objects of type `candidateType`, and another for objects of types `candidateType` and `personType`:

```cpp
#include <string>
#include "personType.h"

const int NO_OF_REGIONS = 4;

class candidateType: public personType
{
public:
    const candidateType& operator=(const candidateType&);
        //Overload the assignment operator for objects of the
        //type candidateType

    const candidateType& operator=(const personType&);
        //Overload the assignment operator for objects so that
        //the value of an object of type personType can be
        //assigned to an object of type candidateType

    void updateVotesByRegion(int region, int votes);
        //Function to update the votes of a candidate for a
        //particular region.
        //Postcondition: Votes for the region specified by
        //               the parameter are updated by adding
        //               the votes specified by the parameter
        //               votes.

    void setVotes(int region, int votes);
        //Function to set the votes of a candidate for a
        //particular region.
        //Postcondition: Votes for the region specified by
```

```cpp
    //               the parameter region are set to the votes
    //               specified by the parameter votes.

    void calculateTotalVotes();
      //Function to calculate the total votes received by a
      //candidate.
      //Postcondition: The votes in each region are added
      //               and assigned to totalVotes.

    int getTotalVotes() const;
      //Function to return the total votes received by a
      //candidate.
      //Postcondition: The value of totalVotes is returned.

    void printData() const;
      //Function to output the candidate's name, the votes
      //received in each region, and the total votes received.

    candidateType();
      //Default constructor.
      //Postcondition: Candidate's name is initialized to
      //               blanks, the number of votes in each
      //               region, and the total votes are
      //               initialized to 0.

        //Overload the relational operators.
    bool operator==(const candidateType& right) const;
    bool operator!=(const candidateType& right) const;
    bool operator<=(const candidateType& right) const;
    bool operator<(const candidateType& right) const;
    bool operator>=(const candidateType& right) const;
    bool operator>(const candidateType& right) const;

private:
    int votesByRegion[NO_OF_REGIONS];    //array to store the
                                         //votes received in
                                         //each region
    int totalVotes; //variable to store the total votes
};
```

Figure 19-57 shows the UML diagram of the `class` candidateType.

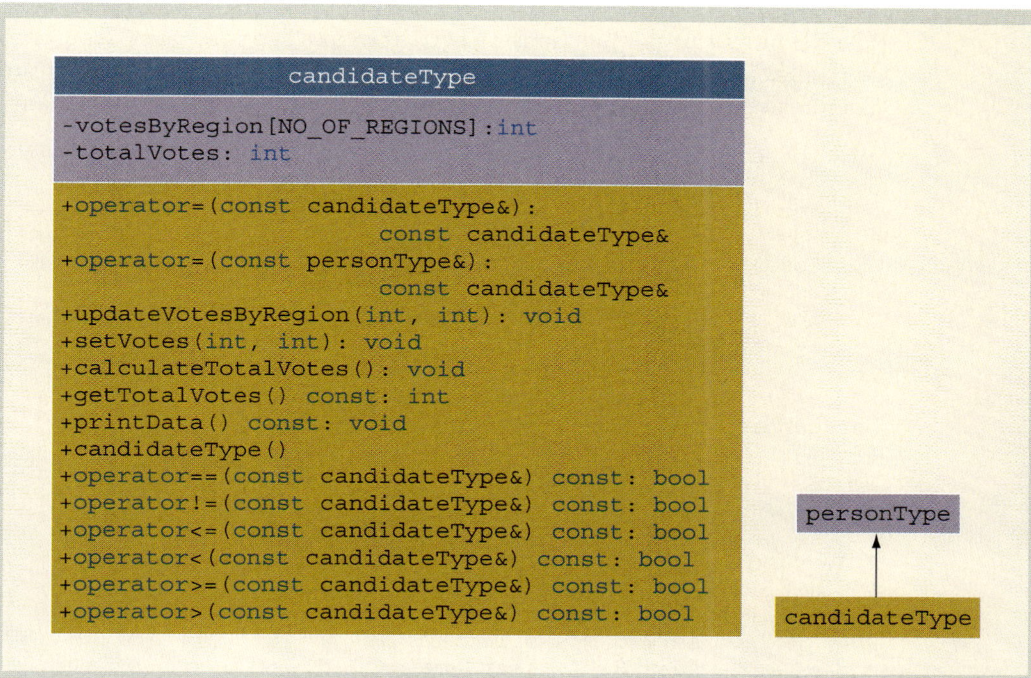

FIGURE 19-57   UML class diagram of **class** candidateType

The definitions of the functions of the **class** candidateType are given next.

To set the votes of a particular region, the region number and the number of votes are passed as parameters to the function **setVotes**. Because an array index starts at 0, region 1 corresponds to the array component at position 0, and so on. Therefore, to set the value of the correct array component, 1 is subtracted from the region. The definition of the function **setVotes** is:

```
void candidateType::setVotes(int region, int votes)
{
    votesByRegion[region - 1] = votes;
}
```

To update the votes for a particular region, the region number and the number of votes for that region are passed as parameters. The votes are then added to the region's previous value. The definition of the function updateVotesByRegion is:

```
void candidateType::updateVotesByRegion(int region, int votes)
{
    votesByRegion[region - 1] = votesByRegion[region - 1]
                                    + votes;
}
```

The definitions of the functions `calculateTotalVotes`, `getTotalVotes`, `printData`, the default constructor, and `getName` are quite straightforward and are given next:

```cpp
void candidateType::calculateTotalVotes()
{
    int i;

    totalVotes = 0;

    for (i = 0; i < NO_OF_REGIONS; i++)
        totalVotes += votesByRegion[i];
}

int candidateType::getTotalVotes() const
{
    return totalVotes;
}

void candidateType::printData() const
{
    cout << left
         << setw(8) << firstName << " "
         << setw(8) << lastName << " ";

    cout << right;
    for (int i = 0; i < NO_OF_REGIONS; i++)
        cout << setw(8) << votesByRegion[i] << " ";
    cout << setw(7) << totalVotes << endl;
}

candidateType::candidateType()
{
    for (int i = 0; i < NO_OF_REGIONS; i++)
        votesByRegion[i] = 0;

    totalVotes = 0;
}
```

To overload the relational operators for the **class** `candidateType`, the names of the candidates are compared. For example, two candidates are the same if they have the same name. The definitions of these functions are similar to the definitions of the functions to overload the relational operators for the **class** `personType` and are given next:

```cpp
bool candidateType::operator==(const candidateType& right) const
{
    return (firstName == right.firstName
            && lastName == right.lastName);
}
```

```cpp
bool candidateType::operator!=(const candidateType& right) const
{
    return (firstName != right.firstName
         || lastName != right.lastName);
}

bool candidateType::operator<=(const candidateType& right) const
{
    return (lastName <= right.lastName ||
           (lastName == right.lastName &&
            firstName <= right.firstName));
}

bool candidateType::operator<(const candidateType& right) const
{
    return (lastName < right.lastName ||
           (lastName == right.lastName &&
            firstName < right.firstName));
}

bool candidateType::operator>=(const candidateType& right) const
{
    return (lastName >= right.lastName ||
           (lastName == right.lastName &&
            firstName >= right.firstName));
}

bool candidateType::operator>(const candidateType& right) const
{
    return (lastName > right.lastName ||
           (lastName == right.lastName &&
            firstName > right.firstName));
}

const candidateType& candidateType::operator=
                                  (const candidateType& right)
{
    if (this != &right)  // avoid self-assignment
    {
        firstName = right.firstName;
        lastName = right.lastName;

        for (int i = 0; i < NO_OF_REGIONS; i++)
            votesByRegion[i] = right.votesByRegion[i];

        totalVotes = right.totalVotes;
    }

    return *this;
}
```

```cpp
const candidateType& candidateType::operator=
                              (const personType& right)
{
    firstName = right.getFirstName();
    lastName = right.getLastName();

    return *this;
}
```

MAIN PROGRAM Now that the `class` `candidateType` has been designed and implemented, we focus on designing the main program.

Because there are six candidates, we create a list, `candidateList`, containing six components of type `candidateType`. The first thing that the program should do is read each candidate's name from the file `candData.txt` into the list `candidateList`. Then, we sort `candidateList`.

The next step is to process the voting data from the file `voteData.txt`, which holds the voting data. After processing the voting data, the program should calculate the total votes received by each candidate and print the data, as shown previously. Thus, the general algorithm is:

1. Read each candidate's name into `candidateList`.
2. Sort `candidateList`.
3. Process the voting data.
4. Calculate the total votes received by each candidate.
5. Print the results.

The following statement creates the object `candidateList` of type

```cpp
unorderedArrayListType<candidateType> candidateList(NO_OF_CANDIDATES);
```

Figure 19-58 shows the object `candidateList`. Every component of the array `list` is an object of type `candidateType`.

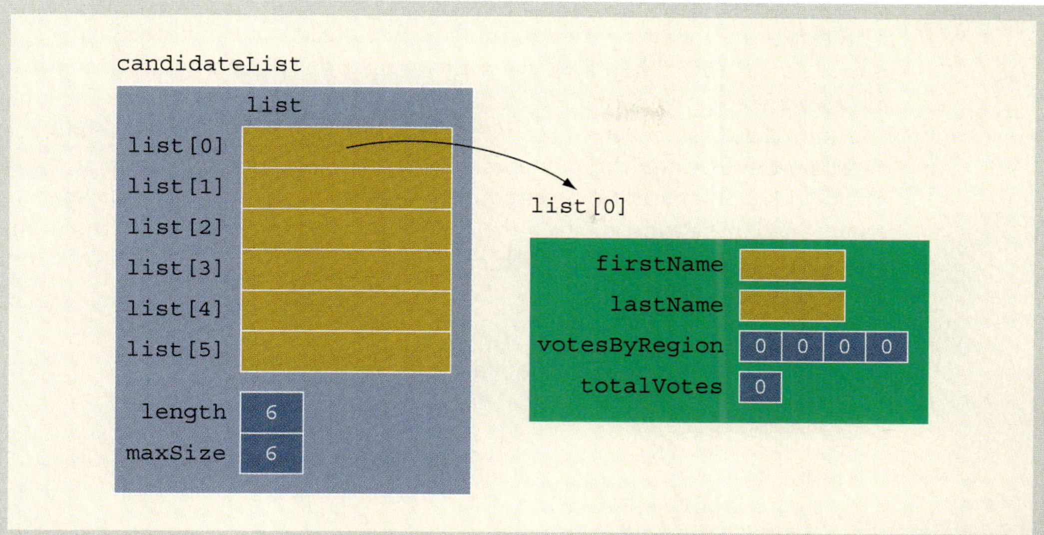

FIGURE 19-58 candidateList

In Figure 19-58, the array **votesByRegion** and the variable **totalVotes** are initialized to 0 by the default constructor of the **class candidateType**. To save space, whenever needed, we will draw the object **candidateList**, as shown in Figure 19-59.

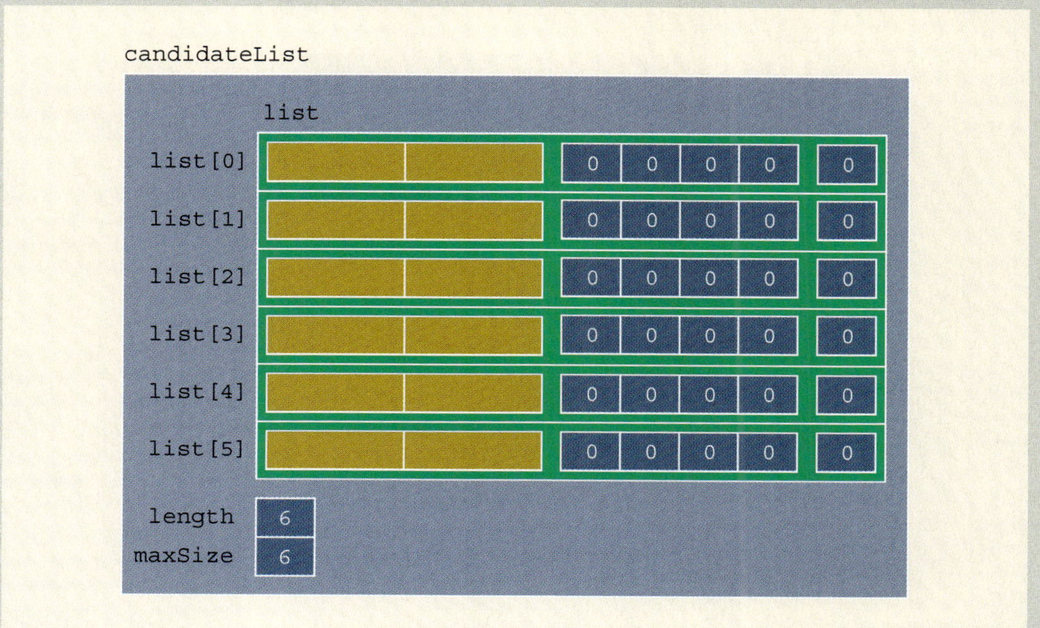

FIGURE 19-59 candidateList

fillNames The first thing that the program must do is to read the candidates' names into `candidateList`. Therefore, we write a function to accomplish this task. The file `candData.txt` is opened in the function `main`. The name of the input file and `candidateList` are, therefore, passed as parameters to the function `fillNames`. Because the member variable `list` of the object `candidateList` is `protected`, it cannot be accessed directly. We, therefore, create an object `temp` of type `candidateType` to store the candidates' names, and use the function `insertEnd` (of list) to store each candidate's name in the object `candidateList`. The definition of the function `fillNames` follows:

```cpp
void fillNames(ifstream& inFile,
               unorderedArrayListType<candidateType>& cList)
{
    string firstN;
    string lastN;
    int i;
    candidateType temp;

    for (i = 0; i < NO_OF_CANDIDATES; i++)
    {
        inFile >> firstN >> lastN;
        temp.setName(firstN, lastN);
        cList.insertEnd(temp);
    }
}
```

Figure 19-60 shows the object `candidateList` after a call to the function `fillNames`.

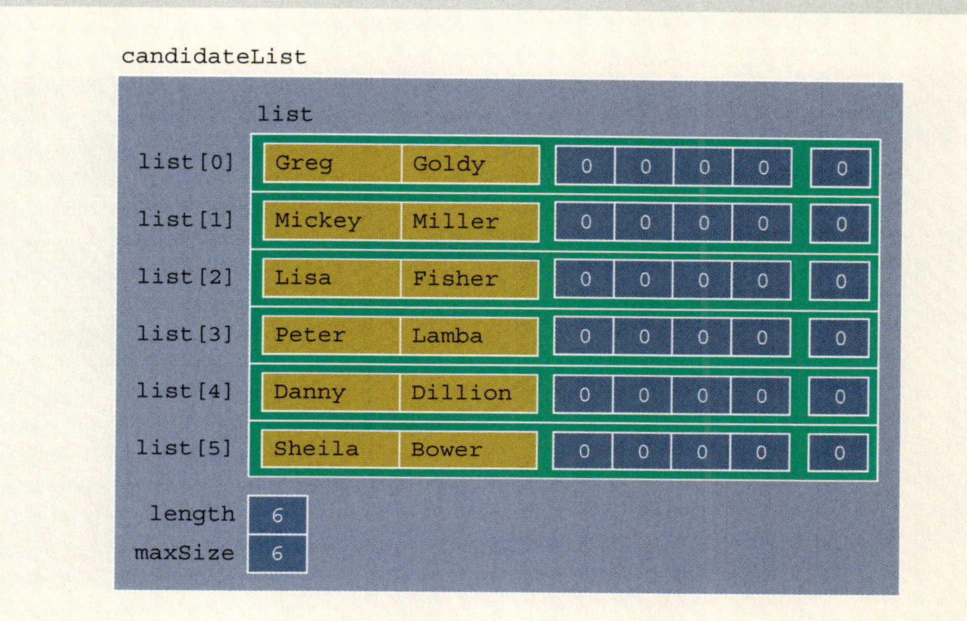

FIGURE 19-60   Object `candidateList` after a call to the function `fillNames`

Sort Names   After reading the candidates' names, we next sort the array list of the object `candidateList` using any of the (array-based) sorting algorithms discussed in this chapter. Because `candidateList` is an object of type `unorderedArrayListType`, we use the member function `sort` to sort `candidateList`. (For illustration purposes, we use selection sort in the function `sort`. In fact, you can use any array-based sorting algorithm discussed in this chapter.) The following statement accomplishes this task:

```
candidateList.sort();
```

After this statement executes, `candidateList` is as shown in Figure 19-61.

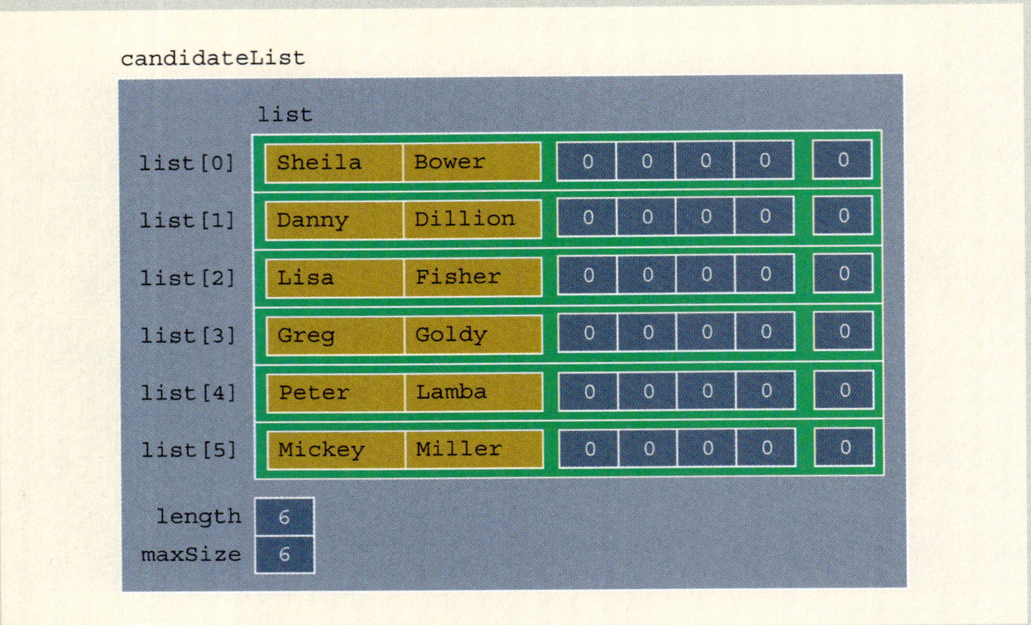

FIGURE 19-61   Object `candidateList` after the statement `candidateList.sort();` executes

Process Voting Data

Processing the voting data is quite straightforward. Each entry in the file `voteData.txt` is of the form:

`firstName lastName regionNumber numberOfVotes`

After reading an entry from the file `voteData.txt`, we locate the row in the array `list` (of the object `candidateList`) corresponding to the specific candidate and update the entry specified by `regionNumber`.

The component `votesByRegion` is a `private` member of each component of the array `list`. Moreover, `list` is a `private` member of `candidateList`. The only way we can update the votes of a candidate is to make a copy of that candidate's record into a temporary object, update the object, and then copy the temporary object back into `list` by replacing the old value with the new value of the temporary object. We can use the member function `retrieveAt` to make a copy of the candidate whose votes need to be updated. After updating the temporary object, we can use the member function `replaceAt` to copy the temporary object back into the list. Suppose the next entry read is:

`Lisa Fisher 2 35`

This entry says that `Lisa Fisher` received 35 votes from region 2. Suppose that before processing this entry, `candidateList` is as shown in Figure 19-62.

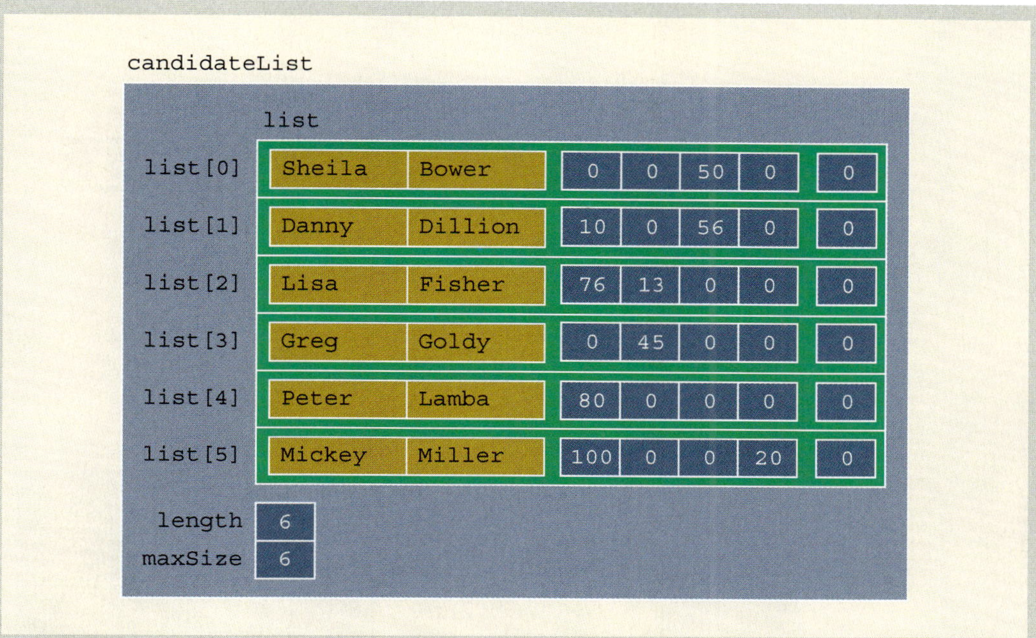

FIGURE 19-62 Object `candidateList` before processing entry `Lisa Fisher 2 35`

We make a copy of the row corresponding to **Lisa Fisher** (see Figure 19-63).

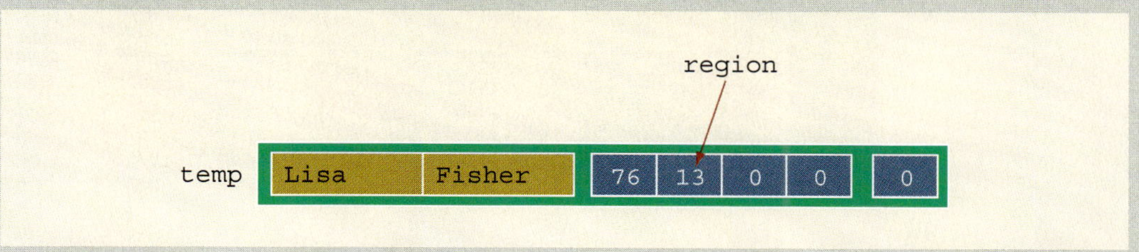

FIGURE 19-63 Object `temp`

Next, the following statement updates the voting data for region 2. (Here, **region** = 2 and **votes** = 35.)

```
temp.updateVotesByRegion(region, votes);
```

After this statement executes, the object **temp** is as shown in Figure 19-64.

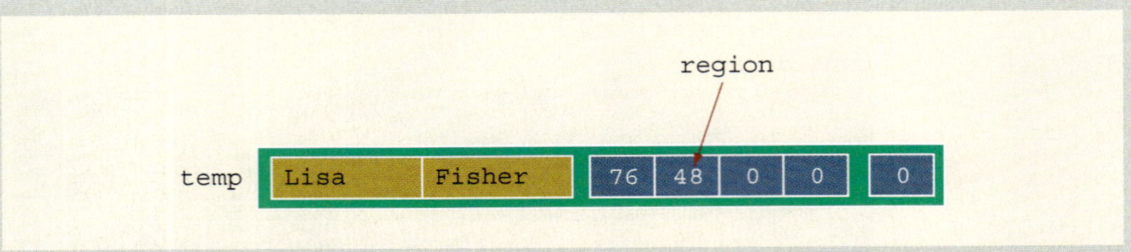

FIGURE 19-64 Object `temp` after `temp.updateVotesByRegion(region,votes);` executes

Now we copy the object **temp** into **list** (see Figure 19-65).

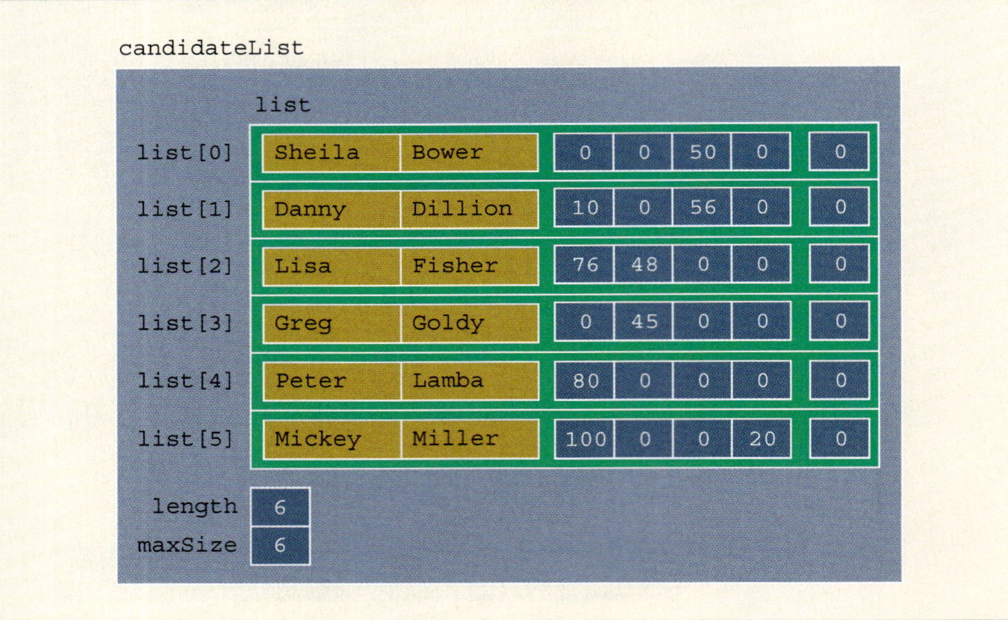

FIGURE 19-65 `candidateList` after copying `temp`

Because the member **list** of **candidateList** is sorted, we can use the binary search algorithm to find the row position in **list** corresponding to the candidate whose votes need to be updated. Essentially, the definition of the function **processVotes** is

```
void processVotes(ifstream& inFile,
                  unorderedArrayListType<candidateType>& cList)
{
    string firstN;
    string lastN;
    int region;
```

```
for (int index = 0; index < length - iteration; index++)
{
    if (list[index] > list[index + 1])
    {
        elemType temp = list[index];
        list[index] = list[index + 1];
        list[index + 1] = temp;
        isSorted = false;
    }
}
}
```

6. Sort the following list using the selection sort algorithm as discussed in this chapter. Show the list after each iteration of the outer **for** loop.

   36, 55, 17, 35, 63, 85, 12, 48, 3, 66

7. Assume the following list of keys:

   5, 18, 21, 10, 55, 20

   The first three keys are in order. To move 10 to its proper position using the insertion sort algorithm as described in this chapter, exactly how many key comparisons are executed?

8. Assume the following list of keys:

   7, 28, 31, 40, 5, 20

   The first four keys are in order. To move 5 to its proper position using the insertion sort algorithm as described in this chapter, exactly how many key comparisons are executed?

9. Assume the following list of keys:

   28, 18, 21, 10, 25, 30, 12, 71, 32, 58, 15

   This list is to be sorted using the insertion sort algorithm as described in this chapter for array-based lists. Show the resulting list after six passes of the sorting phase—that is, after six iterations of the **for** loop.

10. Recall the insertion sort algorithm (contiguous version) as discussed in this chapter. Assume the following list of keys:

    18, 8, 11, 9, 15, 20, 32, 61, 22, 48, 75, 83, 35, 3

    Exactly how many key comparisons are executed to sort this list using the insertion sort algorithm?

11. Both the merge sort and quick sort algorithms sort a list by partitioning it. Explain how the merge sort algorithm differs from the quick sort algorithm in partitioning the list.

12. Assume the following list of keys:

    16, 38, 54, 80, 22, 65, 55, 48, 64, 95, 5, 100, 58, 25, 36

This list is to be sorted using the quick sort algorithm as discussed in this chapter. Use `pivot` as the middle element of the list.

    a.   Give the resulting list after one call to the partition procedure.

    b.   Give the resulting list after two calls to the partition procedure.

13.   Assume the following list of keys:

    18, 40, 16, 82, 64, 67, 57, 50, 37, 47, 72, 14, 17, 27, 35

This list is to be sorted using the quick sort algorithm as discussed in this chapter. Use `pivot` as the median of the `first`, `last`, and `middle` elements of the list.

    a.   What is the pivot?

    b.   Give the resulting list after one call to the partition procedure.

PROGRAMMING EXERCISES

1.   (**Recursive sequential search**) The sequential search algorithm given in this chapter is nonrecursive. Write and implement a recursive version of the sequential search algorithm.

2.   (**Recursive binary search**) The binary search algorithm given in this chapter is nonrecursive. Write and implement a recursive version of the binary search algorithm. Also, write a program to test your algorithm.

3.   Write the definition of the function `seqOrdSearch` to implement a version of the sequential search algorithm for ordered lists. Also, write a program to test it.

4.   Write a program to find the number of comparisons using `binarySearch` and the sequential search algorithm as follows:

Suppose `list` is an array of 1000 elements.

    a.   Use a random number generator to fill `list`.

    b.   Use any sorting algorithm to sort list.

    c.   Search list for some items as follows:

        i.   Use the binary search algorithm to search the list. (You may need to modify the algorithm given in this chapter to count the number of comparisons.)

        ii.   Use the binary search algorithm to search the list, switching to a sequential search when the size of the search list reduces to less than 15. (Use the sequential search algorithm for a sorted list.)

    d.   Print the number of comparisons for Steps c.i and c.ii. If the item is found in the list, then print its position.

5. **(Modified Bubble Sort)** Write a complete C++ function template to implement the modified bubble sort algorithm given in Exercise 5 of this chapter. Call this function `modifiedBubbleSort`. Also, write a program to test your function.

6. Write a program to test the selection sort algorithm for array-based lists as given in this chapter.

7. Write and test a version of the selection sort algorithm for linked lists.

8. Write a program to test the insertion sort algorithm for array-based lists as given in this chapter.

9. Write and test a version of the insertion sort algorithm for linked lists.

10. Write a program to test the quick sort algorithm for array-based lists as given in this chapter.

11. **(C. A. R. Hoare)** Let L be a list of size n. The quick sort algorithm can be used to find the kth smallest item in L, where $0 \leq k \leq n - 1$, without completely sorting L. Write and implement a C++ function, *kThSmallestItem*, that uses a version of the quick sort algorithm to determine the kth smallest item in L without completely sorting L.

12. Sort an array of 10,000 elements using the quick sort algorithm as follows:

    a. Sort the array using `pivot` as the middle element of the array.

    b. Sort the array using `pivot` as the median of the first, last, and middle elements of the array.

    c. Sort the array using `pivot` as the middle element of the array. However, when the size of any sublist reduces to less than 20, sort the sublist using an insertion sort.

    d. Sort the array using `pivot` as the median of the first, last, and middle elements of the array. When the size of any sublist reduces to less than 20, sort the sublist using an insertion sort.

    e. Calculate and print the CPU time for each of the preceding four steps.

    To find the current CPU time, declare a variable, say, `x`, of type `clock_t`. The statement `x = clock();` stores the current CPU time in `x`. You can check the CPU time before and after a particular phase of a program. Then, to find the CPU time for that particular phase of the program, subtract the before time from the after time. Moreover, you must include the header file `ctime` to use the data type `clock_t` and the function clock. Use a random number generator to initially fill the array.

13. Write a program to test the merge sort algorithm for linked lists as given in this chapter.

14. Write and test a version of the merge sort algorithm for array-based lists.

15. Write the definitions of the function `printResults` of the Election Results programming example. Also, write a program to produce the output shown in the sample run of this programming example.

16. In the Election Results programming example, the **class** `candidateType` contains a function `calculateTotalVotes`, which calculates the total number of votes received by a candidate. After processing the voting data, this function calculates the total number of votes for a candidate. The function `updateVotesByRegion` (of the **class** `candidateType`) updates only the number of votes for a particular region. Modify the definition of this function so that it also updates the total number of votes received by the candidate. By doing so, the function `addVotes` in the main program is no longer needed. Modify and run your program with the modified definition of the function `updateVotesByRegion`.

17. In the Election Results programming example, the object `candidateList` of type `unorderedArrayListType` is declared to process the voting data. The operations of inserting a candidate's data and updating and retrieving the votes were somewhat complicated. To update the candidates' votes, copy each candidate's data from `candidateList` into a temporary object of type `candidateType`, update the temporary object, and then replace the candidate's data with the temporary object. This is because the member variable `list` is a **protected** member of `candidateList`, and each component of `list` is a private member. In this exercise, you are to modify the Election Results programming example to simplify the accessing of a candidate's data. Derive the **class** `candidateListType` from the **class** `unorderedArayListType` as follows:

```
class candidateListType:
              public unorderedArrayListType<candidateType>
{
public:
    candidateListType(int size = 0);
      //constructor
    void processVotes(string fName, string lName, int region,
                      int votes);
      //Function to update the number of votes for
      //a particular candidate for a particular region.
      //The name of the candidate, the region number, and
      //the number of votes are passed as parameters.
    void addVotes();
      //Function to find the total number of votes
      //received by each candidate.
    void printResult();
      //Function to output the voting data.
};
```

Because the **class** `candidateListType` is derived from the **class** `unorderedArrayListType`, and `list` is a **protected** member of the **class** `unorderedArrayListType` (inherited from the **class** `arrayListType`), `list` can be directly accessed by a member of the **class** `candidateListType`.

Write the definitions of the member functions of the **class** `candidateListType`. Rewrite and run your program using the **class** `candidateListType`.

BINARY TREES

IN THIS CHAPTER, YOU WILL:

- Learn about binary trees
- Explore various binary tree traversal algorithms
- Learn how to organize data in a binary search tree
- Learn how to insert and delete items in a binary search tree
- Explore nonrecursive binary tree traversal algorithms

When data is being organized, a programmer's highest priority is to organize it in such a way that item insertion, deletion, and lookups (searches) are fast. You have already seen how to store and process data in an array. Because an array is a random-access data structure, if the data is properly organized (say, sorted), then we can use a search algorithm, such as a binary search, to effectively find and retrieve an item from the list. However, we know that storing data in an array has its limitations. For example, item insertion (especially if the array is sorted) and item deletion can be very time-consuming, especially if the list size is very large, because each of these operations requires data movement. To speed up item insertion and deletion, we used linked lists. Item insertion and deletion in a linked list do not require any data movement; we simply adjust some of the links in the list. However, one of the drawbacks of linked lists is that they must be processed sequentially. That is, to insert or delete an item, or simply to search the list for a particular item, we must begin our search at the first node in the list. As you know, a sequential search is good only for very small lists because the average search length of a sequential search is half the size of the list.

Binary Trees

This chapter discusses how to organize data dynamically so that item insertion, deletion, and lookups are more efficient.

We first introduce some definitions to facilitate our discussion.

Definition: A **binary tree**, T, is either empty or such that:

  i. T has a special node called the **root** node;

  ii. T has two sets of nodes, L_T and R_T, called the **left subtree** and **right subtree** of T, respectively; and

  iii. L_T and R_T are binary trees.

Suppose that T is a binary tree with the root node A. Let L_A denote the left subtree of A and R_A denote the right subtree of A. Now L_A and R_A are binary trees. Suppose that B is the root node of L_A and C is the root node of R_A. B is called the **left child** of A; C is called the **right child** of A. Moreover, A is called the **parent** of B and C.

A binary tree can be shown pictorially. In the diagram of a binary tree, each node of the binary tree is represented as a circle and the circle is labeled by the node. The root node of the binary tree is drawn at the top. The left child of the root node (if any) is drawn below and to the left of the root node. Similarly, the right child of the root node (if any) is drawn below and to the right of the root node. Children are connected to the parent by an arrow from the parent to the child. An arrow is usually called a **directed edge** or a **directed branch** (or simply a **branch**) (see Figure 20-1). Because the root node, B, of L_A is already drawn, we apply the same (recursive) procedure to draw the remaining parts of L_A. R_A is drawn similarly. If a node has no left child, for example, we draw an arrow from the node to the left, ending with three stacked lines. That is, three lines at the end of an arrow indicate that the subtree is empty.

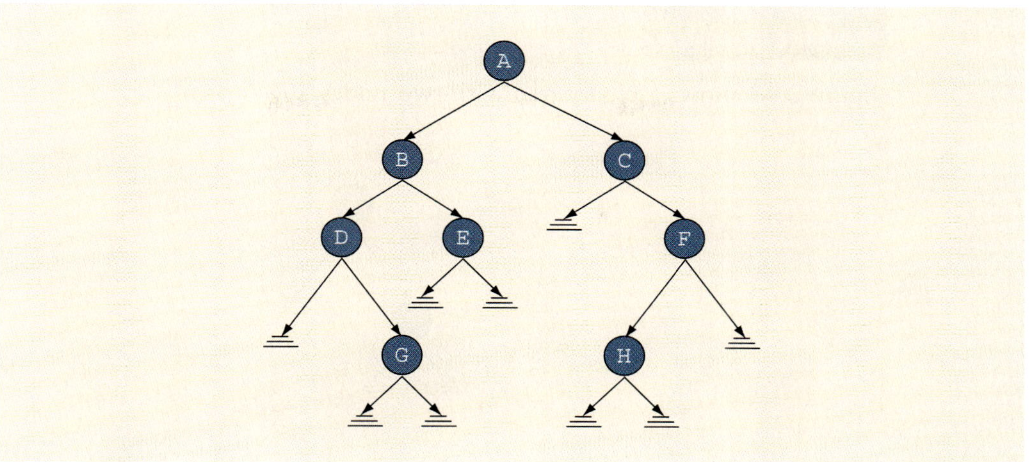

FIGURE 20-1 Binary tree

In Figure 20-1, the root node of this binary tree is A. The left subtree of the root node, which we denote by L_A, is the set $L_A = \{B, D, E, G\}$ and the right subtree of the root node, which we denote by R_A, is the set $R_A = \{C, F, H\}$. The root node of the left subtree of A—that is, the root node of L_A—is node B. The root node of R_A is C, and so on. Clearly, L_A and R_A are binary trees. Because three lines at the end of an arrow mean that the subtree is empty, it follows that the left subtree of D is empty. Also, note that for node F, the left child is H and node F has no right child.

Examples 20-1 to 20-5 show nonempty binary trees.

EXAMPLE 20-1

Figure 20-2 shows a binary tree with one node.

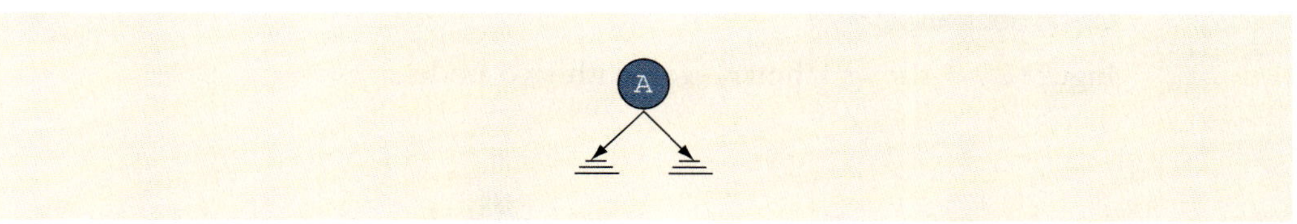

FIGURE 20-2 Binary tree with one node

In the binary tree of Figure 20-2:

The root node of the binary tree = A.

L_A = empty

R_A = empty

EXAMPLE 20-2

Figure 20-3 shows a binary tree with two nodes.

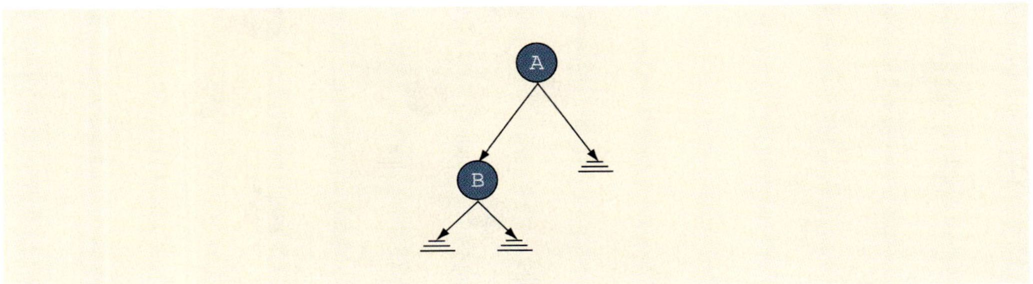

FIGURE 20-3   Binary tree with two nodes; the right subtree of the root node is empty

In the binary tree of Figure 20-3:

The root node of the binary tree = **A**.

$L_A = \{B\}$

$R_A = $ empty

The root node of $L_A = $ **B**.

$L_B = $ empty

$R_B = $ empty

EXAMPLE 20-3

Figure 20-4 shows a binary tree with two nodes.

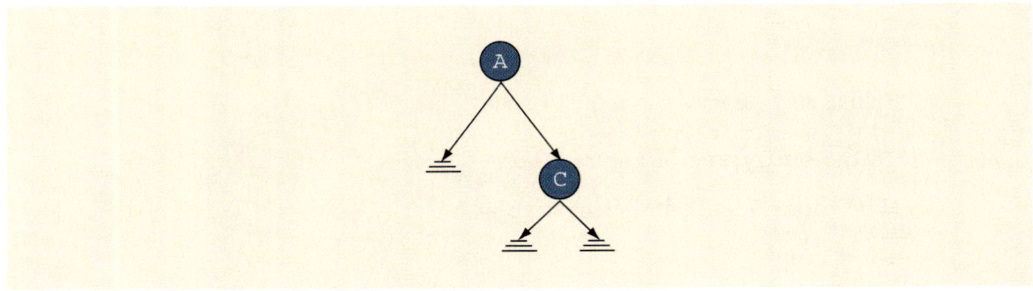

FIGURE 20-4   Binary tree with two nodes; the left subtree of the root node is empty

In the binary tree of Figure 20-4:

The root node of the binary tree = A.

L_A = empty

R_A = {C}

The root node of R_A = C.

L_C = empty

R_C = empty

EXAMPLE 20-4

Figure 20-5 shows a binary tree with three nodes.

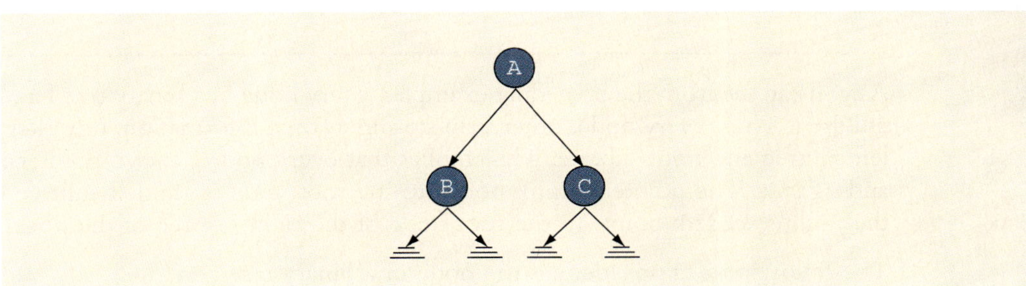

FIGURE 20-5 Binary tree with three nodes

In the binary tree of Figure 20-5:

The root node of the binary tree = A.

L_A = {B}

R_A = {C}

The root node of L_A = B.

L_B = empty

R_B = empty

The root node of R_A = C.

L_C = empty

R_C = empty

EXAMPLE 20-5

Figure 20-6 shows other cases of nonempty binary trees with three nodes.

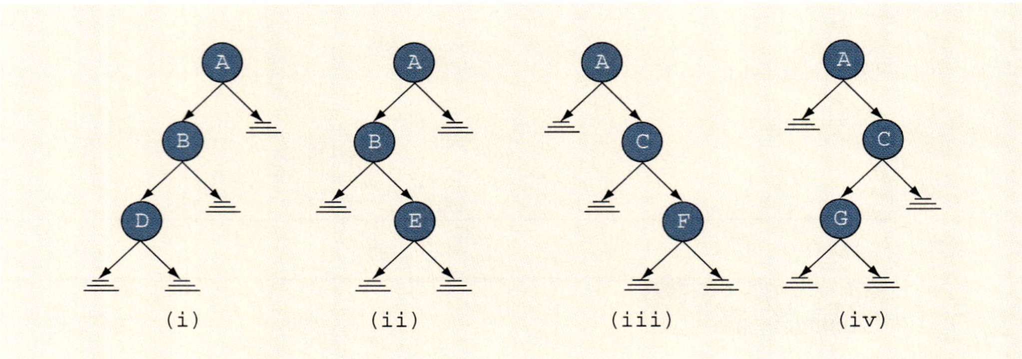

(i)   (ii)   (iii)   (iv)

FIGURE 20-6 Various binary trees with three nodes

As you can see from the preceding examples, every node in a binary tree has, at most, two children. Thus, every node, other than storing its own information, must keep track of its left subtree and right subtree. This implies that every node has two pointers, say, `lLink` and `rLink`. The pointer `lLink` points to the root node of the left subtree of the node; the pointer `rLink` points to the root node of the right subtree of the node.

The following **struct** defines the node of a binary tree:

```
template <class elemType>
struct nodeType
{
    elemType info;
    nodeType<elemType> *lLink;
    nodeType<elemType> *rLink;
};
```

From the definition of the node, it is clear that for each node:

1.   The data is stored in `info`.

2.   A pointer to the left child is stored in `lLink`.

3.   A pointer to the right child is stored in `rLink`.

Furthermore, a pointer to the root node of the binary tree is stored outside the binary tree in a pointer variable, usually called the **root**, of type `nodeType`. Thus, in general, a binary tree looks like the diagram in Figure 20-7.

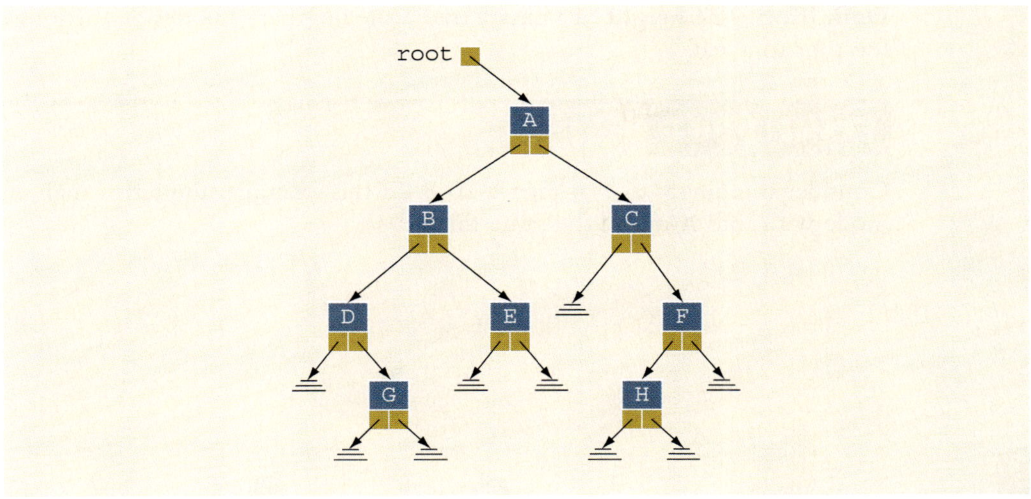

FIGURE 20-7 Binary tree

For simplicity, we will continue to draw binary trees as before. That is, we will use circles to represent nodes and left and right arrows to represent links. As before, three lines at the end of an arrow mean that the subtree is empty.

Before we leave this section, let us define a few terms.

A node in a binary tree is called a **leaf** if it has no left and right children. Let U and V be two nodes in the binary tree T. U is called the **parent** of V if there is a branch from U to V. A **path** from a node X to a node Y in a binary tree is a sequence of nodes $X_0, X_1, \ldots, X_n$ such that:

    i. $X = X_0, X_n = Y$

    ii. X_{i-1} is the parent of X_i for all $i = 1, 2, \ldots, n$. That is, there is a branch from X_0 to X_1, X_1 to X_2, $\ldots$, X_{i-1} to X_i, $\ldots$, X_{n-1} to X_n.

If $X_0, X_1, \ldots, X_n$ is a path from node X to node Y, sometimes we denote it by $X = X_0 - X_1 - \cdots - X_{n-1} - X_n = Y$ or simply $X - X_1 - \cdots - X_{n-1} - Y$.

Because the branches go only from a parent to its children, from the previous discussion it is clear that in a binary tree, there is a unique path from the root to every node in the binary tree.

Definition: The **length** of a path in a binary tree is the number of branches on that path.

Definition: The **level** of a node in a binary tree is the number of branches on the path from the root to the node.

Clearly, the level of the root node of a binary tree is 0, and the level of the children of the root node is 1.

Definition: The **height** of a binary tree is the number of nodes on the longest path from the root to a leaf.

Consider the binary tree of Figure 20-8. In this example, the terms such as node **A** and (node with info **A**) mean the same thing.

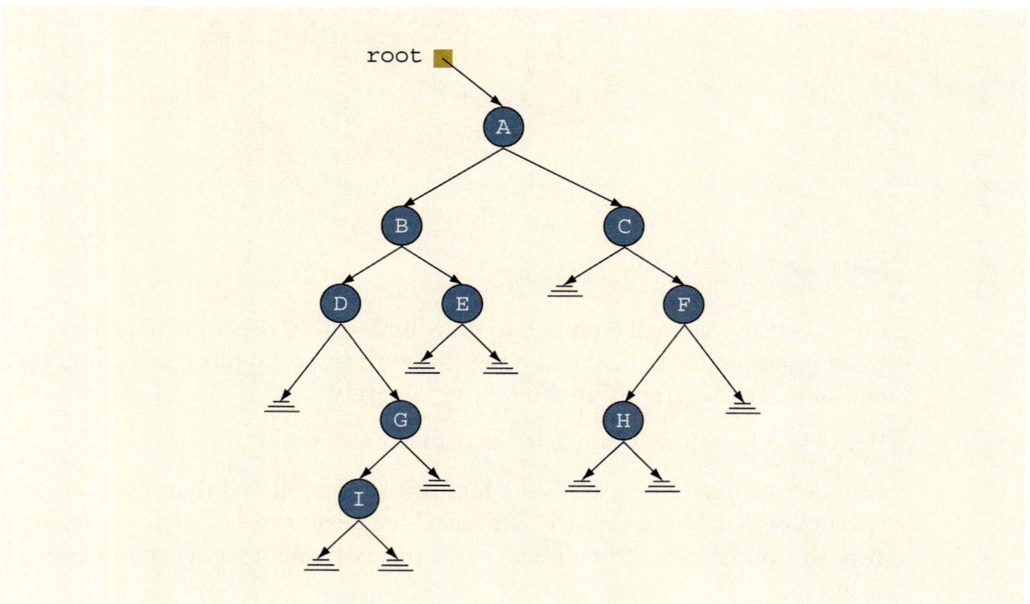

FIGURE 20-8 Binary tree

In this binary tree, the nodes **I**, **E**, and **H** have no left and right children. So, the nodes **I**, **E**, and **H** are leaves.

There is a branch from node **A** to node **B**. So, node **A** is the parent of node **B**. Similarly, node **A** is the parent of node **C**, node **B** is the parent of nodes **D** and **E**, node **C** is the parent of node **F**, node **D** is the parent of node **G**, and so on.

A–B–D–G is a path from node **A** to node **G**. Because there are three branches on this path, the length of this path is 3. Similarly, **B–D–G–I** is a path from node **B** to node **I**.

There are three leaves in this binary tree, which are **I**, **E**, and **H**. Also, the paths from root to these leaves are: **A–B–D–G–I**, **A–B–E**, and **A–C–F–H**. Clearly, the longest path from root to a leaf is **A–B–D–G–I**. The number of nodes on this path is 5. Hence, the height of the binary tree is 5.

Suppose that a pointer, `p`, to the root node of a binary tree is given. We next describe a C++ function, `height`, to find the height of the binary tree. The pointer to the root node is passed as a parameter to the function height.

If the binary tree is empty, then the height is 0. Suppose that the binary tree is nonempty. To find the height of the binary tree, we first find the height of the left subtree and the height of the right subtree. We then take the maximum of these two heights and add 1 to find the height of the binary tree. To find the height of the left (right) subtree, we apply the same procedure because the left (right) subtree is a binary tree. Therefore, the general algorithm to find the height of a binary tree is as follows. Suppose `height(p)` denotes the height of the binary tree with root `p`:

```
if (p is NULL)
    height(p) = 0
else
    height(p) = 1 + max(height(p->lLink), height(p->rLink))
```

Clearly, this is a recursive algorithm. The following function implements this algorithm:

```cpp
template <class elemType>
int height(nodeType<elemType> *p)
{
    if (p == NULL)
        return 0;
    else
        return 1 + max(height(p->lLink), height(p->rLink));
}
```

The definition of the function `height` uses the function `max` to determine the larger of two integers. The function `max` can be easily implemented.

Similarly, we can implement algorithms to find the number of nodes and number of leaves in a binary tree.

Copy Tree

One useful operation on binary trees is to make an identical copy of a binary tree. A binary tree is a dynamic data structure; that is, memory for the nodes of a binary tree is allocated and deallocated during program execution. Therefore, if we use just the value of the pointer of the root node to make a copy of a binary tree, we get a shallow copy of the data. To make an identical copy of a binary tree, we need to create as many nodes as there are in the binary tree to be copied. Moreover, in the copied tree, these nodes must appear in the same order as they are in the original binary tree.

Given a pointer to the root node of a binary tree, we next describe a function that makes a copy of a given binary tree. This function is also quite useful in implementing the copy constructor and overloading the assignment operator, as described later in this chapter (see "Implementing Binary Trees"):

```cpp
template <class elemType>
void copyTree(nodeType<elemType>* &copiedTreeRoot,
              nodeType<elemType>* otherTreeRoot)
{
    if (otherTreeRoot == NULL)
        copiedTreeRoot = NULL;
    else
    {
        copiedTreeRoot = new nodeType<elemType>;
        copiedTreeRoot->info = otherTreeRoot->info;
        copyTree(copiedTreeRoot->lLink, otherTreeRoot->lLink);
        copyTree(copiedTreeRoot->rLink, otherTreeRoot->rLink);
    }
} //end copyTree
```

We will use the function `copyTree` when we overload the assignment operator and implement the copy constructor.

Binary Tree Traversal

The item insertion, deletion, and lookup operations require that the binary tree be traversed. Thus, the most common operation performed on a binary tree is to traverse the binary tree, or visit each node of the binary tree. As you can see from the diagram of a binary tree, the traversal must start at the root node because there is a pointer to the root node of the binary tree. For each node, we have two choices:

- Visit the node first.
- Visit the subtrees first.

These choices lead to three commonly used traversals of a binary tree:

- Inorder traversal
- Preorder traversal
- Postorder traversal

INORDER TRAVERSAL

In an inorder traversal, the binary tree is traversed as follows:

1. Traverse the left subtree.
2. Visit the node.
3. Traverse the right subtree.

PREORDER TRAVERSAL

In a preorder traversal, the binary tree is traversed as follows:

1. Visit the node.
2. Traverse the left subtree.
3. Traverse the right subtree.

POSTORDER TRAVERSAL

In a postorder traversal, the binary tree is traversed as follows:

1. Traverse the left subtree.
2. Traverse the right subtree.
3. Visit the node.

Clearly, each of these traversal algorithms is recursive.

The listing of the nodes produced by the inorder traversal of a binary tree is called the **inorder sequence**. The listing of the nodes produced by the preorder traversal is called the **preorder sequence**, and the listing of the nodes produced by the postorder traversal is called the **postorder sequence**.

Before giving the C++ code for each of these traversals, let us illustrate the inorder traversal of the binary tree in Figure 20-9. For simplicity, we assume that visiting a node means to output the data stored in the node. In the section "Binary Tree Traversal and Functions as Parameters," we explain how to modify the binary tree traversal algorithms so that by using a function, the user can specify the action to be performed on a node when the node is visited.

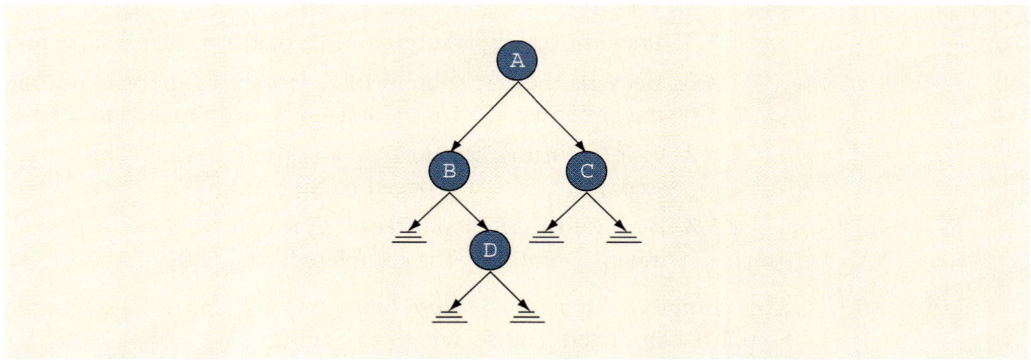

FIGURE 20-9 Binary tree for an inorder traversal

A pointer to the binary tree in Figure 20-9 is stored in the pointer variable `root` (which points to the node with info A). Therefore, we start the traversal at A.

1. Traverse the left subtree of A; that is, traverse L_A = {B, D}.
2. Visit A.
3. Traverse the right subtree of A; that is, traverse R_A = {C}.

Now we cannot do Step 2 until we have finished Step 1.

1. Traverse the left subtree of A; that is, traverse L_A = {B, D}. Now L_A is a binary tree with the root node B. Because L_A is a binary tree, we apply the inorder traversal criteria to L_A.

   1.1. Traverse the left subtree of B; that is, traverse L_B = empty.

   1.2. Visit B.

   1.3. Traverse the right subtree of B; that is, traverse R_B = {D}.

   As before, first we complete Step 1.1 before going to Step 1.2.

   1.1. Because the left subtree of B is empty, there is nothing to traverse. Step 1.1 is completed, so we proceed to Step 1.2.

   1.2. Visit B. That is, output B on an output device. Clearly, the first node printed is B. This completes Step 1.2, so we proceed to Step 1.3.

   1.3. Traverse the right subtree of B; that is, traverse R_B = {D}. Now R_B is a binary tree with the root node D. Because R_B is a binary tree, we apply the inorder traversal criteria to R_B.

      1.3.1. Traverse the left subtree of D; that is, traverse L_D = empty.

      1.3.2. Visit D.

      1.3.3. Traverse the right subtree of D; that is, traverse R_D = empty.

      1.3.1. Because the left subtree of D is empty, there is nothing to traverse. Step 1.3.1 is completed, so we proceed to Step 1.3.2.

      1.3.2. Visit D. That is, output D on an output device. This completes Step 1.3.2, so we proceed to Step 1.3.3.

      1.3.3. Because the right subtree of D is empty, there is nothing to traverse. Step 1.3.3 is completed.

   This completes Step 1.3. Because Steps 1.1, 1.2, and 1.3 are completed, Step 1 is completed, and so we go to Step 2.

2. Visit A. That is, output A on an output device. This completes Step 2, so we proceed to Step 3.

3. Traverse the right subtree of A; that is, traverse R_A = {C}. Now R_A is a binary tree with the root node C. Because R_A is a binary tree, we apply the inorder traversal criteria to R_A.

   3.1. Traverse the left subtree of C; that is, traverse L_C = empty.

   3.2. Visit C.

   3.3. Traverse the right subtree of C; that is, traverse R_C = empty.

   3.1. Because the left subtree of C is empty, there is nothing to traverse. Step 3.1 is completed.

3.2. Visit C. That is, output C on an output device. This completes Step 3.2, so we proceed to Step 3.3.

3.3. Because the right subtree of C is empty, there is nothing to traverse. Step 3.3 is completed.

This completes Step 3, which, in turn, completes the traversal of the binary tree.

Clearly, the inorder traversal of the previous binary tree outputs the nodes in the following order:

Inorder sequence: B D A C

Similarly, the preorder and postorder traversals output the nodes in the following order:

Preorder sequence: A B D C

Postorder sequence: D B C A

As you can see from the walk-through of the inorder traversal, after visiting the left subtree of a node, we must come back to the node itself. The links are only in one direction; that is, the parent node points to the left and right children, but there is no pointer from each child to the parent. Therefore, before going to a child, we must somehow save a pointer to the parent node. A convenient way to do this is to write a recursive inorder function because in a recursive call after completing a particular call, the control goes back to the caller. (Later, we will discuss how to write nonrecursive traversal functions.) The recursive definition of the function to implement the inorder traversal algorithms is:

```
template <class elemType>
void inorder(nodeType<elemType> *p) const
{
    if (p != NULL)
    {
        inorder(p->lLink);
        cout << p->info << " ";
        inorder(p->rLink);
    }
}
```

To do the inorder traversal of a binary tree, the root node of the binary tree is passed as a parameter to the function `inorder`. For example, if `root` points to the root node of the binary tree, a call to the function `inorder` is:

```
inorder(root);
```

Similarly, we can write the functions to implement the preorder and postorder traversals. The definitions of these functions are given next:

```cpp
template <class elemType>
void preorder(nodeType<elemType> *p) const
{
    if (p != NULL)
    {
        cout << p->info << " ";
        preorder(p->lLink);
        preorder(p->rLink);
    }
}

template <class elemType>
void postorder(nodeType<elemType> *p) const
{
    if (p != NULL)
    {
        postorder(p->lLink);
        postorder(p->rLink);
        cout << p->info << " ";
    }
}
```

NOTE This section described the binary tree traversal algorithms inorder, preorder, and post-order. If you want to make a copy of a binary tree while preserving the structure of the binary tree, you can use preorder traversal. To delete all the nodes of a binary tree, you can use the postorder traversal. Later in this chapter, we discuss binary search trees. The inorder traversal of a binary search tree visits the nodes in sorted order.

NOTE In addition to the inorder, preorder, and postorder traversals, a binary tree can also be traversed **level-by-level**, also known as **breadth-first traversal**. In Chapter 21, we discuss graphs. A binary tree is also a graph. We discuss how to implement breadth-first traversal algorithms for graphs. You can modify that algorithm to do a breadth-first traversal of binary trees.

Implementing Binary Trees

The preceding sections described various operations that can be performed on a binary tree, as well as the functions to implement these operations. This section describes binary trees as an abstract data type (ADT). Before designing the class to implement a binary tree as an ADT, let us list the various operations that are typically performed on a binary tree.

1. Determine whether the binary tree is empty.

2. Search the binary tree for a particular item.

3. Insert an item in the binary tree.

4. Delete an item from the binary tree.

5. Find the height of the binary tree.

6. Find the number of nodes in the binary tree.

7. Find the number of leaves in the binary tree.

8. Traverse the binary tree.

9. Copy the binary tree.

The item search, insertion, and deletion operations all require the binary tree to be traversed. However, because the nodes of a binary tree are in no particular order, these algorithms are not very efficient on arbitrary binary trees. That is, no criteria exist to guide the search on these binary trees, as we will see in the next section. Therefore, we will discuss these algorithms when we discuss special binary trees.

The following class defines binary trees as an ADT. The definition of the node is the same as before. However, for the sake of completeness and easy reference, we give the definition of the node followed by the definition of the class:

```cpp
    //Definition of the Node
template <class elemType>
struct nodeType
{
    elemType info;
    nodeType<elemType> *lLink;
    nodeType<elemType> *rLink;
};


    //Definition of the class
template <class elemType>
class binaryTreeType
{
public:
    const binaryTreeType<elemType>& operator=
                (const binaryTreeType<elemType>&);
      //Overload the assignment operator.

    bool isEmpty() const;
      //Function to determine whether the binary tree is empty.
      //Postcondition: Returns true if the binary tree is empty;
      //               otherwise, returns false.

    void inorderTraversal() const;
      //Function to do an inorder traversal of the binary tree.
      //Postcondition: Nodes are printed in inorder sequence.

    void preorderTraversal() const;
      //Function to do a preorder traversal of the binary tree.
      //Postcondition: Nodes are printed in preorder sequence.

    void postorderTraversal() const;
      //Function to do a postorder traversal of the binary tree.
      //Postcondition: Nodes are printed in postorder sequence.
```

```cpp
    int treeHeight() const;
      //Function to determine the height of a binary tree.
      //Postcondition: Returns the height of the binary tree.

    int treeNodeCount() const;
      //Function to determine the number of nodes in a
      //binary tree.
      //Postcondition: Returns the number of nodes in the
      //               binary tree.

    int treeLeavesCount() const;
      //Function to determine the number of leaves in a
      //binary tree.
      //Postcondition: Returns the number of leaves in the
      //               binary tree.

    void destroyTree();
      //Function to destroy the binary tree.
      //Postcondition: Memory space occupied by each node
      //               is deallocated.
      //               root = NULL;

    virtual bool search(const elemType& searchItem) const = 0;
      //Function to determine if searchItem is in the binary
      //tree.
      //Postcondition: Returns true if searchItem is found in
      //               the binary tree; otherwise, returns
      //               false.

    virtual void insert(const elemType& insertItem) = 0;
      //Function to insert insertItem in the binary tree.
      //Postcondition: If there is no node in the binary tree
      //               that has the same info as insertItem, a
      //               node with the info insertItem is created
      //               and inserted in the binary search tree.

    virtual void deleteNode(const elemType& deleteItem) = 0;
      //Function to delete deleteItem from the binary tree
      //Postcondition: If a node with the same info as
      //               deleteItem is found, it is deleted from
      //               the binary tree.
      //               If the binary tree is empty or
      //               deleteItem is not in the binary tree,
      //               an appropriate message is printed.

    binaryTreeType(const binaryTreeType<elemType>& otherTree);
      //Copy constructor

    binaryTreeType();
      //Default constructor

    ~binaryTreeType();
      //Destructor
```

```cpp
protected:
    nodeType<elemType>  *root;

private:
    void copyTree(nodeType<elemType>* &copiedTreeRoot,
                  nodeType<elemType>* otherTreeRoot);
      //Makes a copy of the binary tree to which
      //otherTreeRoot points.
      //Postcondition: The pointer copiedTreeRoot points to
      //               the root of the copied binary tree.

    void destroy(nodeType<elemType>* &p);
      //Function to destroy the binary tree to which p points.
      //Postcondition: Memory space occupied by each node, in
      //               the binary tree to which p points, is
      //               deallocated.
      //               p = NULL;

    void inorder(nodeType<elemType> *p) const;
      //Function to do an inorder traversal of the binary
      //tree to which p points.
      //Postcondition: Nodes of the binary tree, to which p
      //               points, are printed in inorder sequence.

    void preorder(nodeType<elemType> *p) const;
      //Function to do a preorder traversal of the binary
      //tree to which p points.
      //Postcondition: Nodes of the binary tree, to which p
      //               points, are printed in preorder
      //               sequence.

    void postorder(nodeType<elemType> *p) const;
      //Function to do a postorder traversal of the binary
      //tree to which p points.
      //Postcondition: Nodes of the binary tree, to which p
      //               points, are printed in postorder
      //               sequence.

    int height(nodeType<elemType> *p) const;
      //Function to determine the height of the binary tree
      //to which p points.
      //Postcondition: Height of the binary tree to which
      //               p points is returned.

    int max(int x, int y) const;
      //Function to determine the larger of x and y.
      //Postcondition: Returns the larger of x and y.

    int nodeCount(nodeType<elemType> *p) const;
      //Function to determine the number of nodes in
      //the binary tree to which p points.
      //Postcondition: The number of nodes in the binary
      //               tree to which p points is returned.
```

```
    int leavesCount(nodeType<elemType> *p) const;
      //Function to determine the number of leaves in
      //the binary tree to which p points.
      //Postcondition: The number of leaves in the binary
      //               tree to which p points is returned.
};
```

We leave the UML class diagram of the **class** `binaryTreeType` as an exercise for you. See Exercise 17 at the end of this chapter.

The functions `search`, `insert`, and `deleteNode` are declared as abstract in the definition of the **class** `binaryTreeType`. This is because, in this section, we are discussing arbitrary binary trees. Implementing these operations for arbitrary binary trees is inefficient, if not impossible, as we will discuss in the section "Binary Search Trees." Because the **class** `binaryTreeType` contains abstract functions, this **class** is an abstract class. So, you can not create objects of this **class**. In the section "Binary Search Tree," we will derive a class from the **class** `binaryTreeType` and provide the definitions of these functions.

Note that the definition of the **class** `binaryTreeType` contains the statement to overload the assignment operator, copy constructor, and destructor. This is because the **class** `binaryTreeType` contains pointer member variables. Recall that for classes with pointer member variables, we must explicitly overload the assignment operator, include the copy constructor, and include the destructor.

The definition of the **class** `binaryTreeType` contains several member functions that are **private** members of the class. These functions are used to implement the **public** member functions of the **class**. For example, to do an inorder traversal, the function `inorderTraversal` calls the function `inorder` and passes the pointer `root` as a parameter to this function. Moreover, the pointer `root` is declared as a **protected** member so that we can later derive special binary trees.

Next, we give the definitions of the nonabstract member functions of the **class** `binaryTreeType`.

The binary tree is empty if `root` is NULL. So the definition of the function `isEmpty` is:

```
template <class elemType>
bool binaryTreeType<elemType>::isEmpty() const
{
    return (root == NULL);
}
```

The default constructor initializes the binary tree to an empty state; that is, it sets the pointer `root` to NULL. Therefore, the definition of the default constructor is:

```
template <class elemType>
binaryTreeType<elemType>::binaryTreeType()
{
    root = NULL;
}
```

The definitions of the other functions are:

```
template <class elemType>
void binaryTreeType<elemType>::inorderTraversal() const
{
    inorder(root);
}

template <class elemType>
void binaryTreeType<elemType>::preorderTraversal() const
{
    preorder(root);
}

template <class elemType>
void binaryTreeType<elemType>::postorderTraversal() const
{
    postorder(root);
}

template <class elemType>
int binaryTreeType<elemType>::treeHeight() const
{
    return height(root);
}

template <class elemType>
int binaryTreeType<elemType>::treeNodeCount() const
{
    return nodeCount(root);
}

template <class elemType>
int binaryTreeType<elemType>::treeLeavesCount() const
{
    return leavesCount(root);
}


template <class elemType>
void binaryTreeType<elemType>::inorder
                                (nodeType<elemType> *p) const
{
    if (p != NULL)
    {
        inorder(p->lLink);
        cout << p->info << " ";
        inorder(p->rLink);
    }
}
```

```cpp
template <class elemType>
void binaryTreeType<elemType>::preorder
                            (nodeType<elemType> *p) const
{
    if (p != NULL)
    {
        cout << p->info << " ";
        preorder(p->lLink);
        preorder(p->rLink);
    }
}

template <class elemType>
void binaryTreeType<elemType>::postorder
                            (nodeType<elemType> *p) const
{
    if (p != NULL)
    {
        postorder(p->lLink);
        postorder(p->rLink);
        cout << p->info << " ";
    }
}

template<class elemType>
int binaryTreeType<elemType>::height
                            (nodeType<elemType> *p) const
{
    if (p == NULL)
        return 0;
    else
        return 1 + max(height(p->lLink), height(p->rLink));
}

template <class elemType>
int binaryTreeType<elemType>::max(int x, int y) const
{
    if (x >= y)
        return x;
    else
        return y;
}
```

The definitions of the functions `nodeCount` and `leavesCount` are left as exercises for you. See Programming Exercises 1 and 2 at the end of this chapter.

Next, we give the definitions of the functions `copyTree`, `destroy`, and `destroyTree`, the copy constructor, and the destructor. We also overload the assignment operator.

The definition of the function `copyTree` is the same as before; here, this function is a member of the **class** `binaryTreeType`:

```cpp
template <class elemType>
void binaryTreeType<elemType>::copyTree
                      (nodeType<elemType>* &copiedTreeRoot,
                       nodeType<elemType>* otherTreeRoot)
{
    if (otherTreeRoot == NULL)
        copiedTreeRoot = NULL;
    else
    {
        copiedTreeRoot = new nodeType<elemType>;
        copiedTreeRoot->info = otherTreeRoot->info;
        copyTree(copiedTreeRoot->lLink, otherTreeRoot->lLink);
        copyTree(copiedTreeRoot->rLink, otherTreeRoot->rLink);
    }
} //end copyTree
```

To destroy a binary tree, for each node, first we destroy its left subtree, then its right
subtree, and then the node itself. We must use the operator **delete** to deallocate the
memory occupied by the node. The definition of the function `destroy` is:

```cpp
template <class elemType>
void  binaryTreeType<elemType>::destroy(nodeType<elemType>* &p)
{
    if (p != NULL)
    {
        destroy(p->lLink);
        destroy(p->rLink);
        delete p;
        p = NULL;
    }
}
```

To implement the function `destroyTree`, we use the function `destroy` and pass the
root node of the binary tree to the function `destroy`. The definition of the function
`destroyTree` is:

```cpp
template <class elemType>
void  binaryTreeType<elemType>::destroyTree()
{
    destroy(root);
}
```

Recall that when a class object is passed by value, the copy constructor copies the value of
the actual parameters into the formal parameters. Because the **class** `binaryTreeType`
has pointer member variables and a pointer is used to create dynamic memory, we must
provide the definition of the copy constructor to avoid the shallow copying of data. The
definition of the copy constructor, given next, uses the function `copyTree` to make an
identical copy of the binary tree that is passed as a parameter:

```cpp
    //copy constructor
template <class elemType>
binaryTreeType<elemType>::binaryTreeType
                (const binaryTreeType<elemType>& otherTree)
{
    if (otherTree.root == NULL) //otherTree is empty
        root = NULL;
    else
        copyTree(root, otherTree.root);
}
```

The definition of the destructor is quite straightforward. When the object of type
`binaryTreeType` goes out of scope, the destructor deallocates the memory occupied
by the nodes of the binary tree. The definition of the destructor uses the function
`destroy` to accomplish this task:

```cpp
    //Destructor
template <class elemType>
binaryTreeType<elemType>::~binaryTreeType()
{
    destroy(root);
}
```

Next, we discuss the definition of the function to overload the assignment operator. To
assign the value of one binary tree to another binary tree, we make an identical copy of
the binary tree to be assigned by using the function `copyTree`. The definition of the
function to overload the assignment operator is:

```cpp
    //Overload the assignment operator
template <class elemType>
const binaryTreeType<elemType>& binaryTreeType<elemType>::
        operator=(const binaryTreeType<elemType>& otherTree)
{
    if (this != &otherTree) //avoid self-copy
    {
        if (root != NULL)    //if the binary tree is not empty,
                             //destroy the binary tree
            destroy(root);

        if (otherTree.root == NULL) //otherTree is empty
            root = NULL;
        else
            copyTree(root, otherTree.root);
    }//end else

    return *this;
}
```

Binary Search Trees

Now that you know the basic operations on a binary tree, this section discusses a special type of binary tree, called the binary search tree.

Consider the binary tree in Figure 20-10.

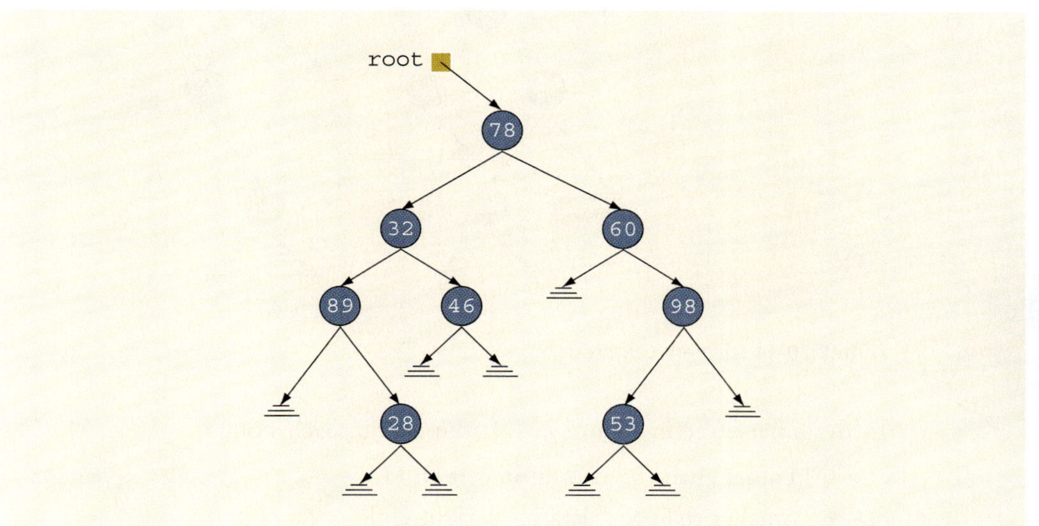

FIGURE 20-10 Arbitrary binary tree

Suppose that we want to determine whether 53 is in the binary tree. To do so, we can use any of the previous traversal algorithms to visit each node and compare the search item with the data stored in the node. However, this could require us to traverse a large part of the binary tree, so the search will be slow. The reason that we need to visit each node in the binary tree until either the item is found or we have traversed the entire binary tree is that no criteria exist to guide our search. This case is like an arbitrary linked list, where we must start our search at the first node and continue looking at each node until either the item is found or the entire list is searched.

On the other hand, consider the binary tree in Figure 20-11.

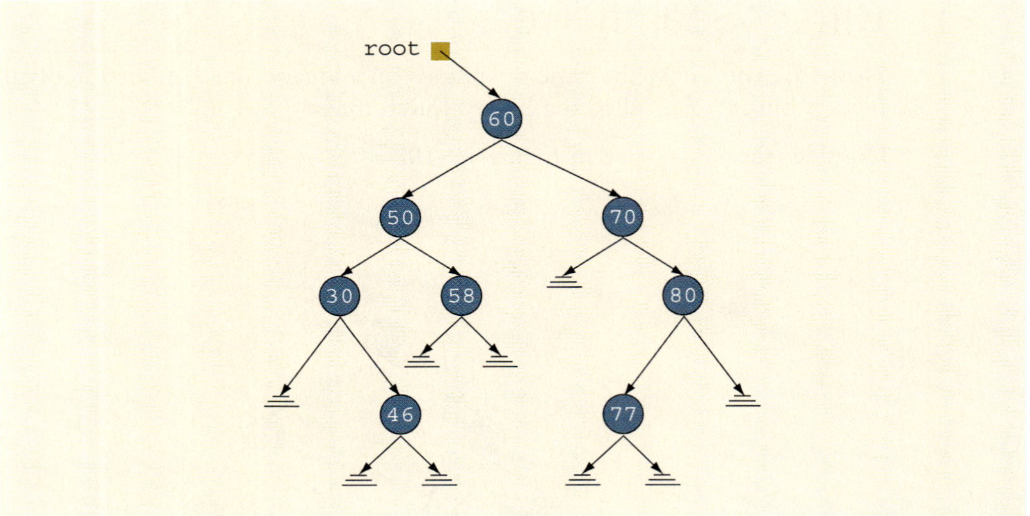

FIGURE 20-11 Binary search tree

In the binary tree in Figure 20-11, the data in each node is:

- Larger than the data in its left child
- Smaller than the data in its right child

The binary tree in Figure 20-11 has some order to its nodes. Suppose that we want to determine whether 58 is in this binary tree. As before, we must start our search at the root node. We compare 58 with the data in the root node; that is, we compare 58 with 60. Because 58 ≠ 60 and 58 < 60, it is guaranteed that 58 will not be in the right subtree of the root node. Therefore, if 58 is in the binary tree, then it must be in the left subtree of the root node. We follow the left pointer of the root node and go to the node with info 50. We now apply the same criteria at this node. Because 58 > 50, we must follow the right pointer of this node and go to the node with info 58. At this node, we find 58.

This example shows that every time we move down to a child, we eliminate one of the subtrees of the node from our search. If the binary tree is nicely constructed, then the search is very similar to the binary search on arrays.

The binary tree given in Figure 20-11 is a special type of binary tree, called a binary search tree. (In the following definition, by the term key of the node we mean the key of the data item that uniquely identifies the item.)

Definition: A **binary search tree**, T, is either empty or:

i. T has a special node called the **root** node;

ii. T has two sets of nodes, L_T and R_T, called the left subtree and right subtree of T, respectively;

iii.   The key in the root node is larger than every key in the left subtree and smaller than every key in the right subtree; and

iv. L_T and R_T are binary search trees.

The following operations are typically performed on a binary search tree:

1.   Determine whether the binary search tree is empty.

2.   Search the binary search tree for a particular item.

3.   Insert an item in the binary search tree.

4.   Delete an item from the binary search tree.

5.   Find the height of the binary search tree.

6.   Find the number of nodes in the binary search tree.

7.   Find the number of leaves in the binary search tree.

8.   Traverse the binary search tree.

9.   Copy the binary search tree.

Clearly, every binary search tree is a binary tree. The height of a binary search tree is determined in the same way as the height of a binary tree. Similarly, the operations to find the number of nodes, to find the number of leaves, and to do inorder, preorder, and postorder traversals of a binary search tree are the same as those for a binary tree. Therefore, we can inherit all of these operations from the binary tree. That is, we can extend the definition of the binary tree by using the principle of inheritance and hence define the binary search tree.

The following class defines a binary search tree as an ADT by extending the definition of the binary tree:

```cpp
template <class elemType>
class bSearchTreeType: public binaryTreeType<elemType>
{
public:
    bool search(const elemType& searchItem) const;
      //Function to determine if searchItem is in the binary
      //search tree.
      //Postcondition: Returns true if searchItem is found in
      //               the binary search tree; otherwise,
      //               returns false.

    void insert(const elemType& insertItem);
      //Function to insert insertItem in the binary search tree.
      //Postcondition: If there is no node in the binary search
      //               tree that has the same info as
      //               insertItem, a node with the info
      //               insertItem is created and inserted in the
      //               binary search tree.

    void deleteNode(const elemType& deleteItem);
      //Function to delete deleteItem from the binary search tree
```

```
    //Postcondition: If a node with the same info as deleteItem
    //                is found, it is deleted from the binary
    //                search tree.
    //                If the binary tree is empty or deleteItem
    //                is not in the binary tree, an appropriate
    //                message is printed.

private:
    void deleteFromTree(nodeType<elemType>* &p);
    //Function to delete the node to which p points is
    //deleted from the binary search tree.
    //Postcondition: The node to which p points is deleted
    //               from the binary search tree.
};
```

We leave it as an exercise for you to draw the UML class diagram of the `class` `bSearchTreeType` and the inheritance hierarchy. See Exercise 18 at the end of this chapter.

Next, we describe each of these operations.

SEARCH

The function `search` searches the binary search tree for a given item. If the item is found in the binary search tree, it returns `true`; otherwise, it returns `false`. Because the pointer `root` points to the root node of the binary search tree, we must begin our search at the root node. Furthermore, because `root` must always point to the root node, we need a pointer—say, `current`—to traverse the binary search tree. The pointer `current` is initialized to `root`.

If the binary search tree is nonempty, we first compare the search item with the info in the root node. If they are the same, we stop the search and return `true`. Otherwise, if the search item is smaller than the info in the node, we follow `lLink` to go to the left subtree; otherwise, we follow `rLink` to go to the right subtree. We repeat this process for the next node. If the search item is in the binary search tree, our search ends at the node containing the search item; otherwise, the search ends at an empty subtree. Thus, the general algorithm is:

```
if root is NULL
    Cannot search an empty tree, returns false.
else
{
    current = root;
    while (current is not NULL and not found)
       if (current->info is the same as the search item)
          set found to true;
       else
          if (current->info is greater than the search item)
             follow the lLink of current
           else
             follow the rLink of current
}
```

This pseudocode algorithm translates into the following C++ function:

```cpp
template <class elemType>
bool bSearchTreeType<elemType>::search
                    (const elemType& searchItem) const
{
    nodeType<elemType> *current;
    bool found = false;

    if (root == NULL)
        cout << "Cannot search an empty tree." << endl;
    else
    {
        current = root;

        while (current != NULL && !found)
        {
            if (current->info == searchItem)
                found = true;
            else if (current->info > searchItem)
                current = current->lLink;
            else
                current = current->rLink;
        }//end while
    }//end else

    return found;
}//end search
```

INSERT

After inserting an item in a binary search tree, the resulting binary tree must be a binary search tree. To insert a new item, first we search the binary search tree and find the place where the new item is to be inserted. The search algorithm is similar to the search algorithm of the function search. Here, we traverse the binary search tree with two pointers—a pointer, say, current, to check the current node and a pointer, say, trailCurrent, pointing to the parent of current. Because duplicate items are not allowed, our search must end at an empty subtree. We can then use the pointer trailCurrent to insert the new item at the proper place. The item to be inserted, insertItem, is passed as a parameter to the function insert. The general algorithm is:

a. Create a new node and copy insertItem into the new node. Also set lLink and rLink of the new node to NULL.

b.
```cpp
if the root is NULL, the tree is empty, so make root point to
the new node.
else
{
    current = root;
    while (current is not NULL)      //search the binary tree
```

```
            {
                 trailCurrent = current;
                 if (current->info is the same as the insertItem)
                    Error: Cannot insert duplicate
                    exit
                 else
                    if (current->info > insertItem)
                       Follow lLink of current
                    else
                       Follow rLink of current
            }

         //insert the new node in the binary tree

         if (trailCurrent->info > insertItem)
            make the new node the left child of trailCurrent
         else
            make the new node the right child of trailCurrent
      }
```

This pseudocode algorithm translates into the following C++ function:

```cpp
template <class elemType>
void bSearchTreeType<elemType>::insert
                (const elemType& insertItem)
{
    nodeType<elemType> *current; //pointer to traverse the tree
    nodeType<elemType> *trailCurrent; //pointer behind current
    nodeType<elemType> *newNode;  //pointer to create the node

    newNode = new nodeType<elemType>;
    newNode->info = insertItem;
    newNode->lLink = NULL;
    newNode->rLink = NULL;

    if (root == NULL)
        root = newNode;
    else
    {
        current = root;

        while (current != NULL)
        {
            trailCurrent = current;

            if (current->info == insertItem)
            {
                cout << "The item to be inserted is already ";
                cout << "in the tree -- duplicates are not "
                     << "allowed." << endl;
                return;
            }
            else if (current->info > insertItem)
                current = current->lLink;
```

```cpp
        else
            current = current->rLink;
    }//end while

    if (trailCurrent->info > insertItem)
        trailCurrent->lLink = newNode;
    else
        trailCurrent->rLink = newNode;
    }
}//end insert
```

DELETE

As before, first we search the binary search tree to find the node to be deleted. To help you better understand the delete operation, before describing the function to delete an item from the binary search tree, let us consider the binary search tree in Figure 20-12.

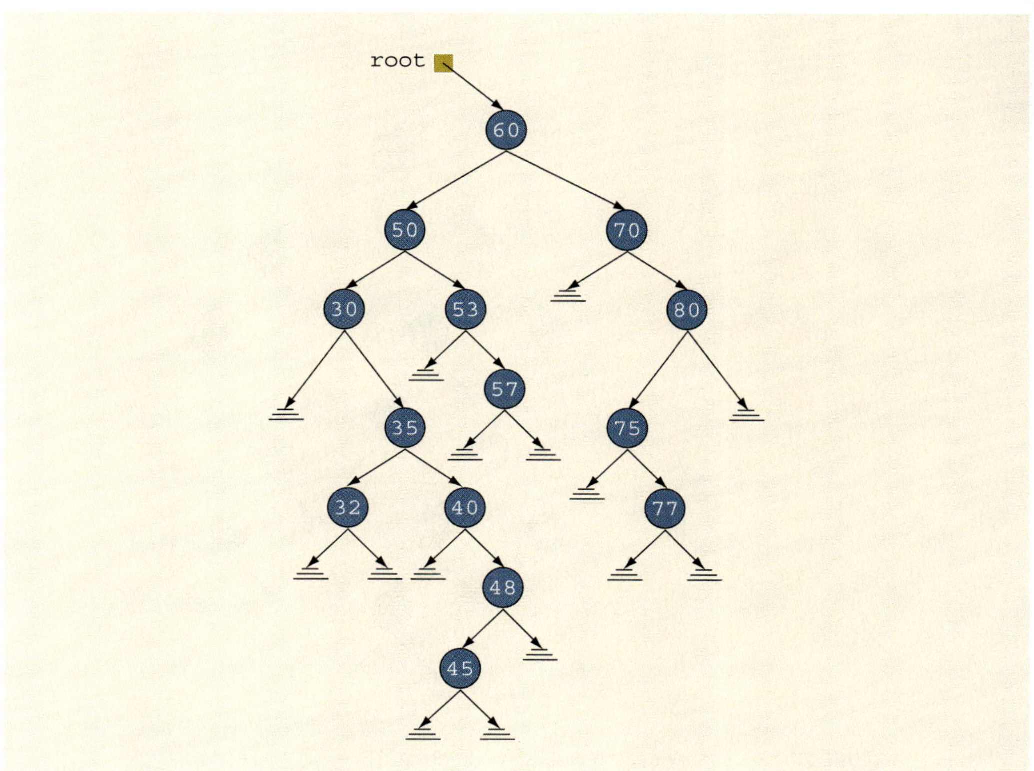

FIGURE 20-12 Binary search tree before deleting a node

After deleting the desired item (if it exists in the binary search tree), the resulting tree must be a binary search tree. The delete operation has four cases, as follows:

1. The node to be deleted has no left and right subtrees; that is, the node to be deleted is a leaf.

2. The node to be deleted has no left subtree; that is, the left subtree is empty, but it has a nonempty right subtree.

3. The node to be deleted has no right subtree; that is, the right subtree is empty, but it has a nonempty left subtree.

4. The node to be deleted has nonempty left and right subtrees.

Case 1: Suppose that we want to delete 45 from the binary search tree in Figure 20-12. We search the binary tree and arrive at the node containing 45. Because this node is a leaf and is the left child of its parent, we can simply set the `lLink` of the parent node to `NULL` and deallocate the memory occupied by this node. After deleting this node, the resulting binary search tree is as shown in Figure 20-13.

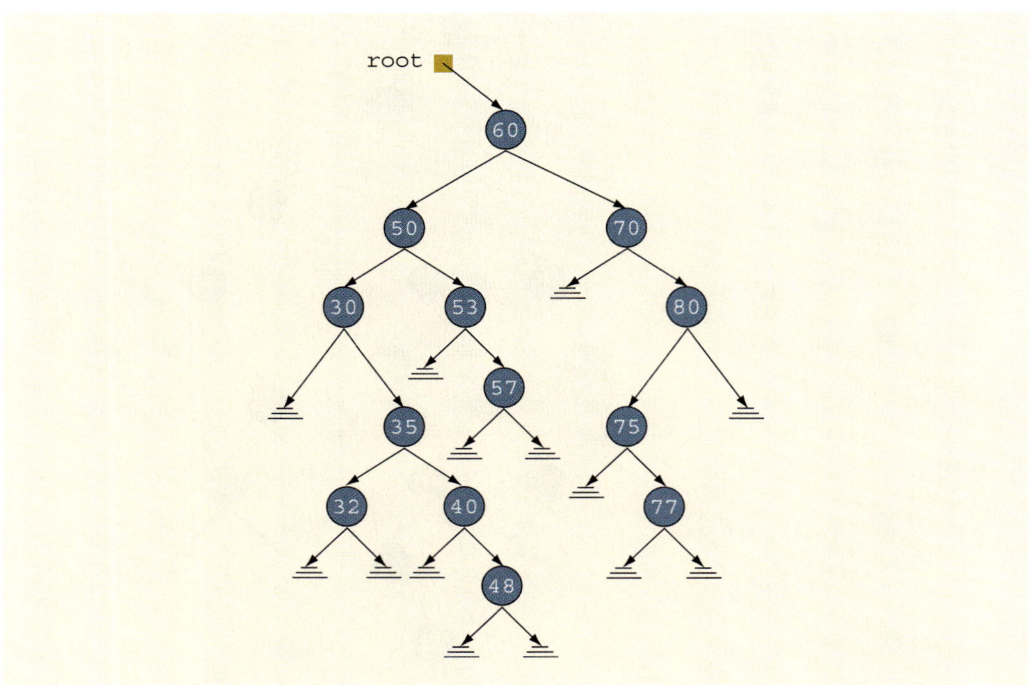

FIGURE 20-13 Binary search tree after deleting 45

Case 2: Suppose that we want to delete 30 from the binary search tree in Figure 20-12. In this case, the node to be deleted has no left subtree. Because 30 is the left child of its parent node, we make the `lLink` of the parent node point to the right child of 30 and then deallocate the memory occupied by 30. Figure 20-14 shows the resulting binary tree.

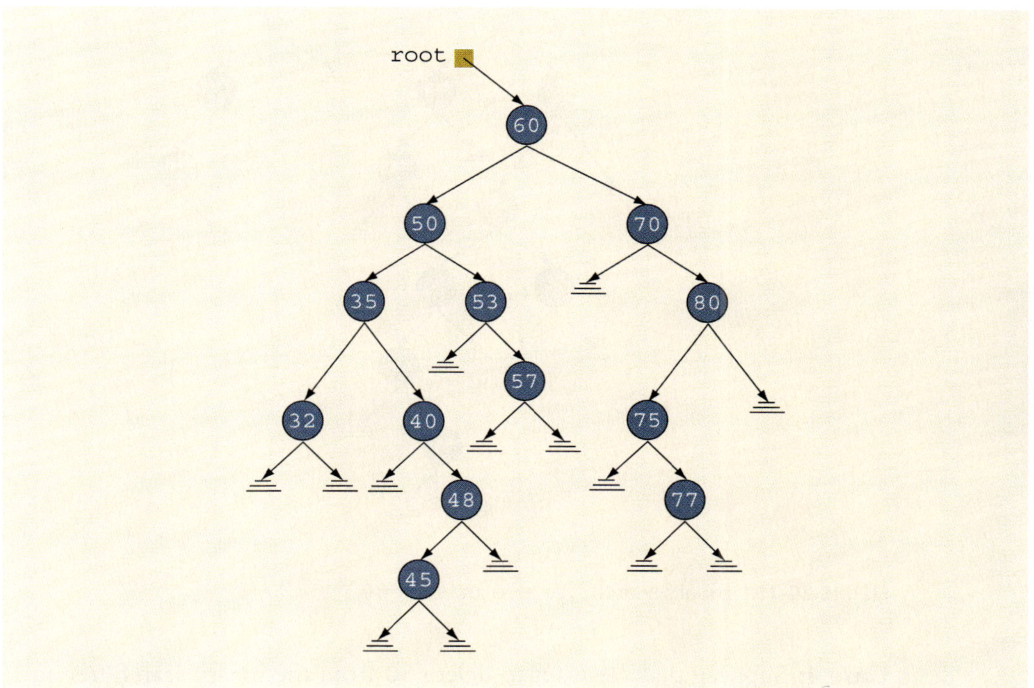

FIGURE 20-14 Binary search tree after deleting 30

Case 3: Suppose that we want to delete 80 from the binary search tree of Figure 20-12. The node containing 80 has no right child and is the right child of its parent. Thus, we make the `rLink` of the parent of 80—that is, 70—point to the left child of 80. Figure 20-15 shows the resulting binary tree.

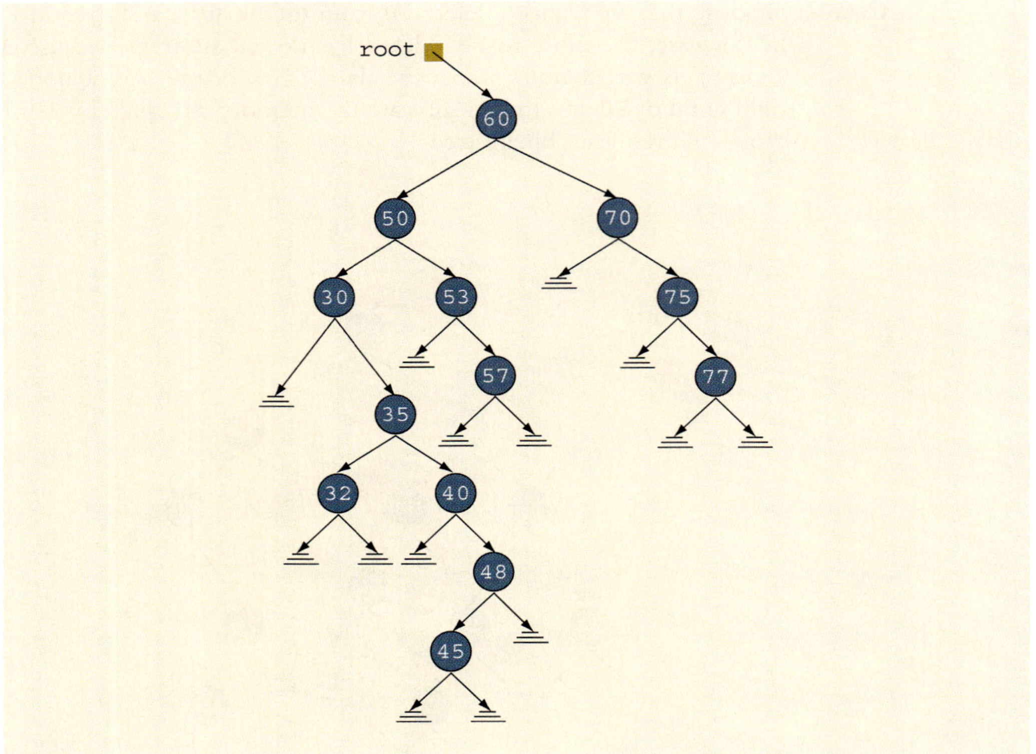

FIGURE 20-15 Binary search tree after deleting 80

Case 4: Suppose that we want to delete 50 from the binary search tree in Figure 20-12. The node with info 50 has a nonempty left subtree and a nonempty right subtree. In this case, we first reduce this case to either Case 2 or Case 3 as follows. To be specific, suppose that we reduce it to Case 3—that is, the node to be deleted has no right subtree. For this case, we find the immediate predecessor of 50 in this binary tree, which is 48. This is done by first going to the left child of 50 and then locating the rightmost node of the left subtree of 50. To do so, we follow the `rLink` of the nodes. Because the binary search tree is finite, we eventually arrive at a node that has no right subtree; see Figure 20-16.

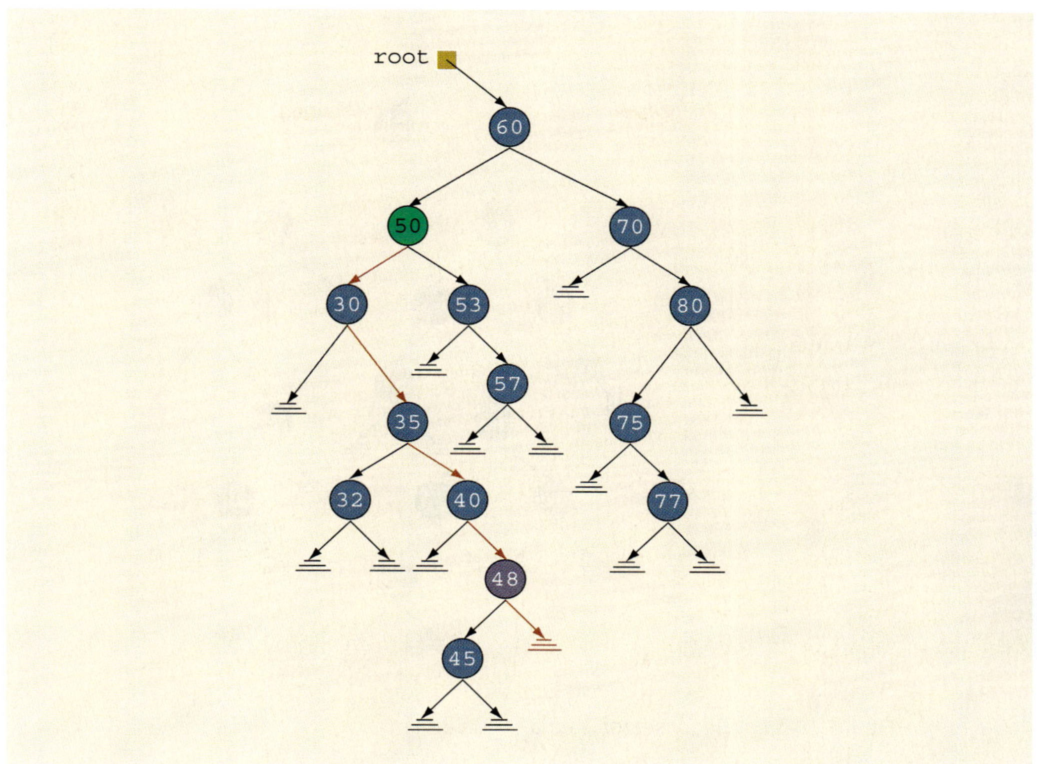

FIGURE 20-16 Binary search tree with a node, 48, that has no right subtree

Next, we swap the info in the node to be deleted with the info of its immediate predecessor. In this case, we swap 48 with 50. This reduces to the case where the node to be deleted has no right subtree. We now apply Case 3 to delete the node. (Note that because we will delete the immediate predecessor from the binary tree, we, in fact, copy only the info of the immediate predecessor into the node to be deleted.) After deleting 50 from the binary search tree in Figure 20-12, the resulting binary tree is as shown in Figure 20-17.

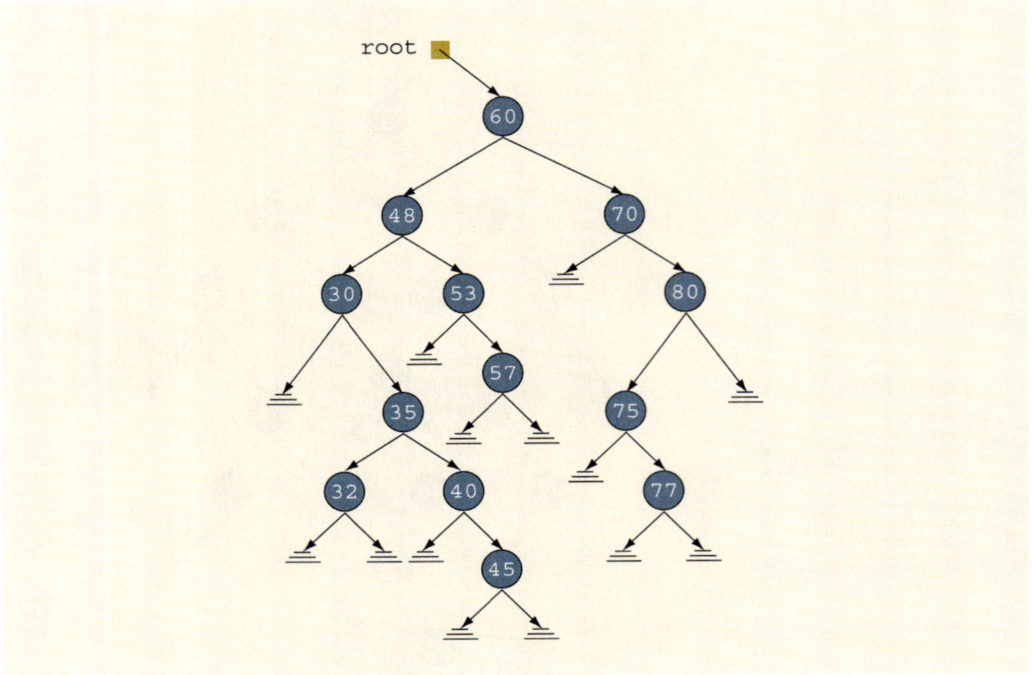

FIGURE 20-17 Binary search tree after deleting 50

In each case, we clearly see that the resulting binary tree is again a binary search tree. From this discussion, it follows that to delete an item from the binary search tree, we must do the following:

1. Find the node containing the item (if any) to be deleted.
2. Delete the node.

We accomplish the second step by a separate function, which we will call `deleteFromTree`. Given a pointer to the node to be deleted, this function deletes the node by taking into account the previous four cases.

From the preceding examples, it is clear that whenever we delete a node from the binary tree, we adjust one of the pointers of the parent node. Because the adjustment has to be made in the parent node, we must call the function `deleteFromTree` by using an appropriate pointer of the parent node. For example, suppose that the node to be deleted is 35, which is the right child of its parent node. Suppose that `trailCurrent` points to the node containing 30, the parent node of 35. A call to the function `deleteFromTree` is:

```
deleteFromTree(trailCurrent->rLink);
```

Of course, if the node to be deleted is the root node, then the call to the function `deleteFromTree` is:

```
deleteFromTree(root);
```

We now define the C++ function `deleteFromTree`:

```cpp
template <class elemType>
void bSearchTreeType<elemType>::deleteFromTree
                                (nodeType<elemType>* &p)
{
    nodeType<elemType> *current; //pointer to traverse the tree
    nodeType<elemType> *trailCurrent;  //pointer behind current
    nodeType<elemType> *temp;        //pointer to delete the node

    if (p == NULL)
        cout << "Error: The node to be deleted is NULL."
             << endl;
    else if (p->lLink == NULL && p->rLink == NULL)
    {
        temp = p;
        p = NULL;
        delete temp;
    }
    else if (p->lLink == NULL)
    {
        temp = p;
        p = temp->rLink;
        delete temp;
    }
    else if (p->rLink == NULL)
    {
        temp = p;
        p = temp->lLink;
        delete temp;
    }
    else
    {
        current = p->lLink;
        trailCurrent = NULL;

        while (current->rLink != NULL)
        {
            trailCurrent = current;
            current = current->rLink;
        }//end while

        p->info = current->info;

        if (trailCurrent == NULL) //current did not move;
                                  //current == p->lLink; adjust p
            p->lLink = current->lLink;
        else
            trailCurrent->rLink = current->lLink;

        delete current;
    }//end else
} //end deleteFromTree
```

2
0

Next, we describe the function `deleteNode`. The function `deleteNode` first searches the binary search tree to find the node containing the item to be deleted. The item to be deleted, `deleteItem`, is passed as a parameter to the function. If the node containing `deleteItem` is found in the binary search tree, the function `deleteNode` calls the function `deletefromTree` to delete the node. The definition of the function `deleteNode` is given next:

```cpp
template <class elemType>
void bSearchTreeType<elemType>::deleteNode
                                (const elemType& deleteItem)
{
    nodeType<elemType> *current; //pointer to traverse the tree
    nodeType<elemType> *trailCurrent; //pointer behind current
    bool found = false;

    if (root == NULL)
        cout << "Cannot delete from an empty tree."
                << endl;
    else
    {
        current = root;
        trailCurrent = root;

        while (current != NULL && !found)
        {
            if (current->info == deleteItem)
                found = true;
            else
            {
                trailCurrent = current;

                if (current->info > deleteItem)
                    current = current->lLink;
                else
                    current = current->rLink;
            }
        }//end while

        if (current == NULL)
            cout << "The item to be deleted is not in the tree."
                    << endl;
        else if (found)
        {
            if (current == root)
                deleteFromTree(root);
            else if (trailCurrent->info > deleteItem)
                deleteFromTree(trailCurrent->lLink);
            else
                deleteFromTree(trailCurrent->rLink);
        }
```

```
      else
        cout << "The item to be deleted is not in the tree."
                << endl;
   }
} //end deleteNode
```

Binary Search Tree: Analysis

Let T be a binary search tree with n nodes, where $n > 0$. Suppose that we want to determine whether an item, x, is in T. The performance of the search algorithm depends on the shape of T. Let us first consider the worst case. In the worst case, T is linear. That is, the T is one of the forms shown in Figure 20-18.

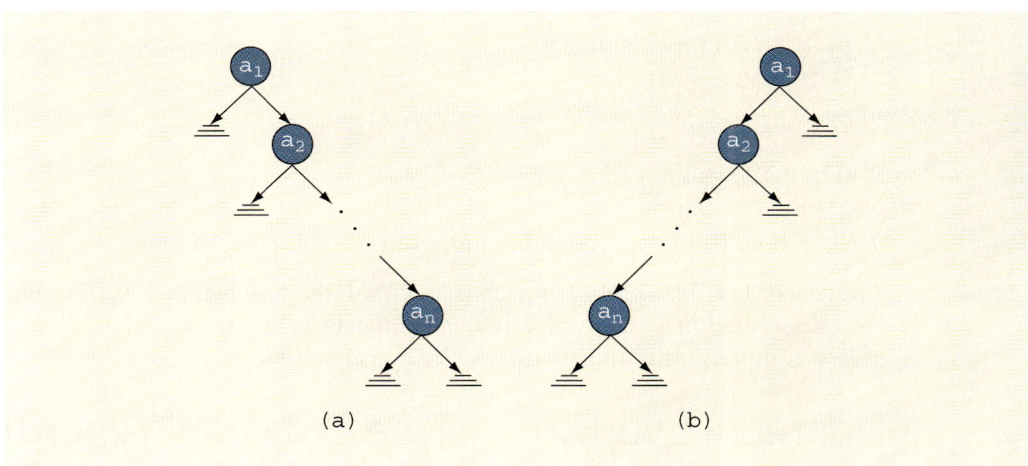

FIGURE 20-18   Linear binary search trees

Because T is linear, the performance of the search algorithm on T is the same as its performance on a linear list. Therefore, in the successful case, on average, the search algorithm makes $\frac{n+1}{2} = O(n)$ key comparisons. In the unsuccessful case, it makes n comparisons.

Let us now consider the average-case behavior. In the successful case, the search would end at a node. Because there are n items, there are $n!$ possible orderings of the keys. We assume that all $n!$ orderings of the keys are possible. Let $S(n)$ denote the number of comparisons in the average successful case, and let $U(n)$ denote the number of comparisons in the average unsuccessful case.

The number of comparisons required to determine whether x is in T is one more than the number of comparisons required to insert x in T. Furthermore, the number of comparisons required to insert x in T is the same as the number of comparisons made in the unsuccessful search, reflecting that x is not in T. From this, it follows that:

$$S(n) = 1 + \frac{U(0) + U(1) + \ldots + U(n-1)}{n} \qquad (20\text{-}1)$$

It is also known that:

$$S(n) = \left(1 + \frac{1}{n}\right)U(n) - 3 \qquad (20\text{-}2)$$

Solving equations (20-1) and (20-2), it can be shown that:

$$U(n) \approx 2.77\log_2 n = O(\log_2 n)$$

and:

$$S(n) \approx 2.77\log_2 n = O(\log_2 n)$$

We can now formulate the following result.

Theorem: Let T be a binary search tree with n nodes, where $n > 0$. The average number of nodes visited in a search of T is approximately $1.39\log_2 n = O(\log_2 n)$, and the number of key comparisons is approximately $2.77\log_2 n = O(\log_2 n)$.

Nonrecursive Binary Tree Traversal Algorithms

The previous sections described how to do the following:

- Traverse a binary tree using the inorder, preorder, and postorder methods.
- Construct a binary tree.
- Insert an item in the binary tree.
- Delete an item from the binary tree.

The traversal algorithms—inorder, preorder, and postorder—discussed earlier are recursive. Because traversing a binary tree is a fundamental operation, this section discusses the nonrecursive inorder, preorder, and postorder traversal algorithms.

Nonrecursive Inorder Traversal

In the inorder traversal of a binary tree, for each node, the left subtree is visited first, then the node, and then the right subtree. It follows that in an inorder traversal, the first node visited is the leftmost node of the binary tree. For example, in the binary tree in Figure 20-19, the leftmost node is the node with info 28.

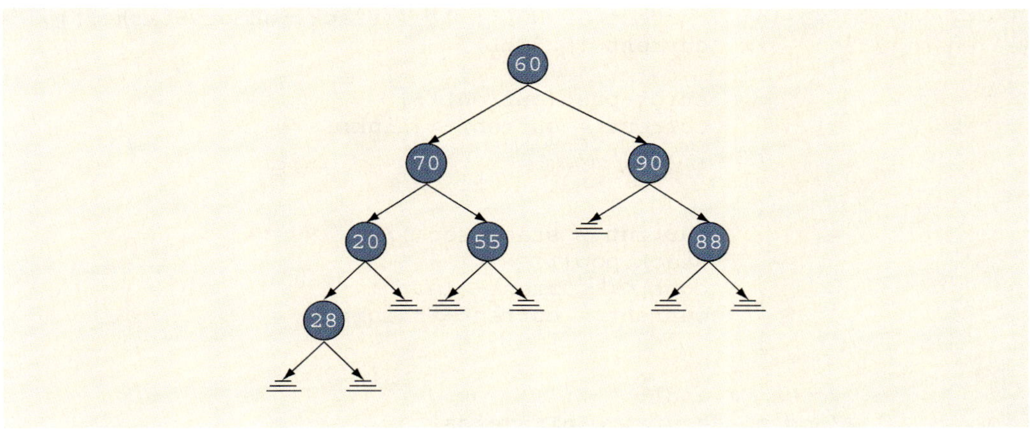

FIGURE 20-19 Binary tree; the leftmost node is 28

To get to the leftmost node of the binary tree, we start by traversing the binary tree at the root node and then follow the left link of each node until the left link of a node becomes null. From this point, we back up to the parent node, visit the node, and then move to the right node. Because links go in only one direction, to get back to a node, we must save a pointer to the node before moving to the child node. Moreover, the nodes must be backtracked in the order they were traversed. It follows that while backtracking, the nodes must be visited in a last–in first–out manner. This can be done by using a stack. We, therefore, save a pointer to a node in a stack. The general algorithm is as follows:

```
1.  current = root; //start traversing the binary tree at the root node

2.  while (current is not NULL or stack is nonempty)
        if (current is not NULL)
        {
            push current onto stack;
            current = current->lLink;
        }
        else
        {
            current = stack.top();
            pop stack;
            visit current;              //visit the node
            current = current->rLink;   //move to the right child
        }
```

The following function implements the nonrecursive inorder traversal of a binary tree:

```cpp
template <class elemType>
void binaryTreeType<elemType>::nonRecursiveInTraversal() const
{
    stackType<nodeType<elemType>*> stack;
    nodeType<elemType> *current;
    current = root;
```

```
    while ((current != NULL) || (!stack.isEmptyStack()))
        if (current != NULL)
        {
            stack.push(current);
            current = current->lLink;
        }
        else
        {
            current = stack.top();
            stack.pop();
            cout << current->info << " ";
            current = current->rLink;
        }

    cout << endl;
} //end nonRecursiveInTraversal
```

Nonrecursive Preorder Traversal

In a preorder traversal of a binary tree, for each node, first the node is visited, then the left subtree is visited, and then the right subtree is visited. As in the case of an inorder traversal, after visiting a node and before moving to the left subtree, we must save a pointer to the node so that after visiting the left subtree, we can visit the right subtree. The general algorithm is as follows:

```
1.  current = root;   //start the traversal at the root node

2.  while (current is not NULL or stack is nonempty)
    if (current is not NULL)
    {
        visit current node;
        push current onto stack;
        current = current->lLink;
    }
    else
    {
        current = stack.top();
        pop stack;
        current = current->rLink; //move to the right child
    }
```

The following function implements the nonrecursive preorder traversal algorithm:

```
template <class elemType>
void binaryTreeType<elemType>::nonRecursivePreTraversal() const
{
    stackType<nodeType<elemType>*> stack;
    nodeType<elemType> *current;

    current = root;
```

```
   while ((current != NULL) || (!stack.isEmptyStack()))
       if (current != NULL)
       {
           cout << current->info << " ";
           stack.push(current);
           current = current->lLink;
       }
       else
       {
           current = stack.top();
           stack.pop();
           current = current->rLink;
       }

   cout << endl;
} //end nonRecursivePreTraversal
```

Nonrecursive Postorder Traversal

In a postorder traversal of a binary tree, for each node, first the left subtree is visited, then the right subtree is visited, and then the node is visited. As in the case of an inorder traversal, in a postorder traversal, the first node visited is the leftmost node of the binary tree. Because—for each node—the left and right subtrees are visited before visiting the node, we must indicate to the node whether the left and right subtrees have been visited. After visiting the left subtree of a node and before visiting the node, we must visit its right subtree. Therefore, after returning from a left subtree, we must tell the node that the right subtree needs to be visited, and after visiting the right subtree, we must tell the node that it can now be visited. To do this, other than saving a pointer to the node (to get back to the right subtree and to the node itself), we also save an integer value of 1 before moving to the left subtree and an integer value of 2 before moving to the right subtree. Whenever the stack is popped, the integer value associated with that pointer is popped as well. This integer value tells whether the left and right subtrees of a node have been visited.

The general algorithm is:

```
   1.  current = root; //start the traversal at the root node

   2.  v = 0;

   3.  if current is NULL
           The binary tree is empty

   4.  if current is not NULL

       a.  push current onto stack;

       b.  push 1 onto stack;

       c.  current = current->lLink;

       d.  while (stack is not empty)
               if (current is not NULL and v is 0)
               {
                   push current and 1 onto stack;
```

```
            current = current->lLink;
    }
    else
    {
        assign the top element of stack to current and v;
        pop stack;
        if (v == 1)
        {
            push current and 2 onto stack;
            current = current->rLink;
            v = 0;
        }
        else
            visit current;
    }
```

We will use two (parallel) stacks: one to save a pointer to a node and another to save the integer value (1 or 2) associated with this pointer. We leave it as an exercise for you to write the definition of a C++ function to implement the preceding postorder traversal algorithm. See Programming Exercise 6 at the end of this chapter.

Binary Tree Traversal and Functions as Parameters

Suppose that you have stored employee data in a binary search tree, and at the end of the year pay increases or bonuses are to be awarded to each employee. This task requires that each node in the binary search tree be visited and that the salary of each employee be updated. The preceding sections discussed various ways to traverse a binary tree. However, in these traversal algorithms—inorder, preorder, and postorder—whenever we visited a node, for simplicity and for illustration purposes, we output only the data contained in each node. How do we use a traversal algorithm to visit each node and update the data in each node? One way to do so is to first create another binary search tree in which the data in each node is the updated data of the original binary search tree, and then destroy the old binary search tree. This would require extra computer time and perhaps extra memory, and, therefore, is not efficient. Another solution is to write separate traversal algorithms to update the data. This solution requires you to frequently modify the definition of the class implementing the binary search tree. However, if the user can write an appropriate function to update the data of each employee and then pass the function as a parameter to the traversal algorithms, we can considerably enhance the program's flexibility. This section describes how to pass functions as parameters to other functions.

In C++, a function name without any parentheses is considered a pointer to the function. To specify a function as a formal parameter to another function, we specify the function type, followed by the function name as a pointer, followed by the parameter types of the function. For example, consider the following statements:

```
void fParamFunc1(void (*visit) (int));        //Line 1
void fParamFunc2(void (*visit) (elemType&));   //Line 2
```

The statement in Line 1 declares `fParamFunc1` to be a function that takes as a parameter any **void** function that has one value parameter of type **int**. The statement in Line 2 declares `fParamFunc2` to be a function that takes as a parameter any **void** function that has one reference parameter of type `elemType`.

We can now rewrite, say, the inorder traversal function of the **class** `binaryTreeType`. Alternatively, we can overload the existing inorder traversal functions. To further illustrate function overloading, we will overload the inorder traversal functions. Therefore, we include the following statements in the definition of the **class** `binaryTreeType`:

```
void inorderTraversal(void (*visit) (elemType&)) const;
   //Function to do an inorder traversal of the binary tree.
   //The parameter visit, which is a function, specifies
   //the action to be taken at each node.
   //Postcondition: The action specified by the function
   //                visit is applied to each node of the
   //                binary tree.

void inorder(nodeType<elemType> *p,
             void (*visit) (elemType&)) const;
   //Function to do an inorder traversal of the binary tree
   //starting at the node specified by the parameter p.
   //The parameter visit, which is a function, specifies the
   //action to be taken at each node.
   //Postcondition: The action specified by the function visit
   //                is applied to each node of the binary tree
   //                to which p points.
```

The definitions of these functions are as follows:

```
template <class elemType>
void binaryTreeType<elemType>::inorderTraversal
                        (void (*visit) (elemType& item)) const
{
    inorder(root, *visit);
}


template <class elemType>
void binaryTreeType<elemType>::inorder(nodeType<elemType>* p,
                        void (*visit) (elemType& item)) const
{
    if (p != NULL)
    {
        inorder(p->lLink, *visit);
        (*visit) (p->info);
        inorder(p->rLink, *visit);
    }
}
```

The statement:

```
(*visit) (p->info);
```

in the definition of the function `inorder` makes a call to the function with one reference parameter of type `elemType` pointed to by the pointer `visit`.

Example 20-7 further illustrates how functions are passed as parameters to other functions.

EXAMPLE 20-7

This example shows how to pass a user-defined function as a parameter to the binary tree traversal algorithms. For illustration purposes, we show how to use only the inorder traversal function.

The following program uses the **class** bSearchTreeType, which is derived from the **class** binaryTreeType, to build the binary tree. The traversal functions are included in the **class** binaryTreeType, which are then inherited by the **class** bSearchTreeType:

```cpp
#include <iostream>
#include "binarySearchTree.h"

using namespace std;

void print(int& x);
void update(int& x);

int main()
{
    bSearchTreeType<int> treeRoot;                      //Line 1

    int num;                                            //Line 2

    cout << "Line 3: Enter numbers ending "
         << "with -999." << endl;                       //Line 3
    cin >> num;                                         //Line 4

    while (num != -999)                                 //Line 5
    {
        treeRoot.insert(num);                           //Line 6
        cin >> num;                                     //Line 7
    }

    cout << endl
         << "Line 8: Tree nodes in inorder: ";          //Line 8
    treeRoot.inorderTraversal(print);                   //Line 9
    cout << endl << "Line 10: Tree Height: "
         << treeRoot.treeHeight()
         << endl << endl;                               //Line 10

    cout << "Line 11: ******* Update Nodes "
         << "*******" << endl;                          //Line 11
    treeRoot.inorderTraversal(update);                  //Line 12
```

```cpp
    cout << "Line 13: Tree nodes in inorder "
         << "after the update: " << endl
         << "                 ";                    //Line 13
    treeRoot.inorderTraversal(print);              //Line 14
    cout << endl << "Line 15: Tree Height: "
         << treeRoot.treeHeight() << endl;          //Line 15

    return 0;                                       //Line 16
}

void print(int& x)                                 //Line 17
{
    cout << x << " ";                              //Line 18
}

void update(int& x)                                //Line 19
{
    x = 2 * x;                                     //Line 20
}
```

Sample Run: In this sample run, the user input is shaded.

```
Line 3: Enter numbers ending with -999.
56 87 23 65 34 45 12 90 66 -999

Line 8: Tree nodes in inorder: 12 23 34 45 56 65 66 87 90
Line 10: Tree Height: 4

Line 11: ******* Update Nodes *******
Line 13: Tree nodes in inorder after the update:
        24 46 68 90 112 130 132 174 180
Line 15: Tree Height: 4
```

This program works as follows. The statement in Line 1 declares `treeRoot` to be a binary search tree object, in which the data in each node is of type `int`. The statements in Lines 4 through 7 build the binary search tree. The statement in Line 9 uses the member function `inorderTraversal` of `treeRoot` to traverse the binary search tree `treeRoot`. The parameter to the function `inorderTraversal`, in Line 9, is the function `print` (defined at Line 17). Because the function `print` outputs the value of its argument, the statement in Line 9 outputs the data of the nodes of the binary search tree `treeNode`. The statement in Line 10 outputs the height of the binary search tree.

The statement in Line 12 uses the member function `inorderTraversal` to traverse the binary search tree `treeRoot`. In Line 12, the actual parameter of the function `inorderTraversal` is the function `update` (defined at Line 19). The function `update` doubles the value of its argument. Therefore, the statement in Line 12 updates the data of each node of the binary search tree by doubling the value. The statements in Lines 14 and 15 output the nodes and the height of the binary search tree.

PROGRAMMING EXAMPLE: Video Store (Revisited)

In Chapter 17, we designed a program to help a video store automate its video rental process. That program used an (unordered) linked list to keep track of the video inventory in the store. Because the search algorithm on a linked list is sequential and the list is fairly large, the search could be time-consuming. In this chapter, you learned how to organize data into a binary tree. If the binary tree is nicely constructed (that is, it is not linear), then the search algorithm can be improved considerably. Moreover, in general, item insertion and deletion in a binary search tree are faster than in a linked list. We will, therefore, redesign the video store program so that the video inventory can be maintained in a binary tree. As in Chapter 17, we leave the design of the customer list in a binary tree as exercises for you.

Video Object In Chapter 17, a linked list was used to maintain a list of videos in the store. Because the linked list was unordered, to see whether a particular video was in stock, the sequential search algorithm used the equality operator for comparison. However, in the case of a binary tree, we need other relational operators for the search, insertion, and deletion operations. We will, therefore, overload all of the relational operators. Other than this difference, the `class` `videoType` is the same as before. However, we give its definition for the sake of completeness:

```cpp
class videoType
{
    friend ostream& operator<< (ostream&, const videoType&);

public:
    void setVideoInfo(string title, string star1,
                      string star2, string producer,
                      string director, string productionCo,
                      int setInStock);
    //Function to set the details of a video.
    //The member variables are set according to the
    //parameters.
    //Postcondition: videoTitle = title; movieStar1 = star1;
    //               movieStar2 = star2;
    //               movieProducer = producer;
    //               movieDirector = director;
    //               movieProductionCo = productionCo;
    //               copiesInStock = setInStock;

    int getNoOfCopiesInStock() const;
    //Function to check the number of copies in stock.
    //Postcondition: The value of copiesInStock is returned.

    void checkOut();
    //Function to rent a video.
    //The number of copies in stock is decremented by one.
    //Postcondition: copiesInStock--;
```

```cpp
    void checkIn();
        //Function to check in a video.
        //The number of copies in stock is incremented by one.
        //Postcondition: copiesInStock++;

    void printTitle() const;
        //Function to print the title of a movie.

    void printInfo() const;
        //Function to print the details of a video.
        //Postcondition: The title of the movie, stars, director,
        //               and so on are output on the screen.

    bool checkTitle(string title);
        //Function to check whether the title is the same as the
        //title of the video.
        //Postcondition: Returns the value true if the title is
        //               the same as the title of the video, and
        //               false otherwise.

    void updateInStock(int num);
        //Function to increment the number of copies in stock by
        //adding the value of the parameter num.
        //Postcondition: copiesInStock = copiesInStock + num;

    void setCopiesInStock(int num);
        //Function to set the number of copies in stock.
        //Postcondition: copiesInStock = num;

    string getTitle() const;
        //Function to return the title of the video.
        //Postcondition: The title of the video is returned.

    videoType(string title = "", string star1 = "",
              string star2 = "", string producer = "",
              string director = "", string productionCo = "",
              int setInStock = 0);
        //Constructor
        //The member variables are set according to the incoming
        //parameters. If no values are specified, the default
        //values are assigned.
        //Postcondition: videoTitle = title; movieStar1 = star1;
        //               movieStar2 = star2;
        //               movieProducer = producer;
        //               movieDirector = director;
        //               movieProductionCo = productionCo;
        //               copiesInStock = setInStock;


        //Overload relational operators
    bool operator==(const videoType&) const;
    bool operator!=(const videoType&) const;
```

```cpp
    bool operator<(const videoType&) const;
    bool operator<=(const videoType&) const;
    bool operator>(const videoType&) const;
    bool operator>=(const videoType&) const;

private:
    string videoTitle;    //variable to store the name
                          //of the movie
    string movieStar1;    //variable to store the name
                          //of the star
    string movieStar2;    //variable to store the name
                          //of the star
    string movieProducer; //variable to store the name
                          //of the producer
    string movieDirector; //variable to store the name
                          //of the director
    string movieProductionCo; //variable to store the name
                              //of the production company
    int copiesInStock;    //variable to store the number of
                          //copies in stock
};
```

The definitions of the member functions of the **class** videoType are the same as in
Chapter 17. Because, here, we are overloading all of the relational operators, we give
only the definitions of these member functions:

```cpp
    //Overload the relational operators
bool videoType::operator==(const videoType& right) const
{
    return (videoTitle == right.videoTitle);
}

bool videoType::operator!=(const videoType& right) const
{
    return (videoTitle != right.videoTitle);
}

bool videoType::operator<(const videoType& right) const
{
    return (videoTitle < right.videoTitle);
}

bool videoType::operator<=(const videoType& right) const
{
    return (videoTitle <= right.videoTitle);
}

bool videoType::operator>(const videoType& right) const
{
    return (videoTitle > right.videoTitle);
}
```

```
bool videoType::operator>=(const videoType& right) const
{
    return (videoTitle >= right.videoTitle);
}
```

Video List The video list is maintained in a binary search tree. Therefore, we derive the `class` `videoListType` from the `class` `bSearchTreeType`. The definition of the `class` `videoListType` is as follows:

```
class videoBinaryTree: public bSearchTreeType<videoType>
{
public:
    bool videoSearch(string title);
      //Function to search the list to see whether a
      //particular title, specified by the parameter title,
      //is in the store.
      //Postcondition: Returns true if the title is found,
      //               and false otherwise.

    bool isVideoAvailable(string title);
      //Function to determine whether a copy of a particular
      //video is in the store.
      //Postcondition: Returns true if at least one copy of
      //               the video specified by title is in the
      //               store, and false otherwise.

    void videoCheckIn(string title);
      //Function to check in a video returned by a customer
      //Postcondition: copiesInStock is incremented by one.

    void videoCheckOut(string title);
      //Function to check out a video, that is, rent a video.
      //Postcondition: copiesInStock is decremented by one.

    bool videoCheckTitle(string title) const;
      //Function to determine whether a particular video is in
      //the store.
      //Postcondition: Returns true if the video's title is
      //               the same as title, and false otherwise.

    void videoUpdateInStock(string title, int num);
      //Function to update the number of copies of a video
      //by adding the value of the parameter num. The
      //parameter title specifies the name of the video for
      //which the number of copies is to be updated.
      //Postcondition: copiesInStock = copiesInStock + num;

    void videoSetCopiesInStock(string title, int num);
      //Function to reset the number of copies of a video.
      //The parameter title specifies the name of the video
```

```cpp
           //for which the number of copies is to be reset, and
           //the parameter num specifies the number of copies.
           //Postcondition: copiesInStock = num;

    void videoPrintTitle() const;
       //Function to print the titles of all the videos in
       //the store.

private:
    void searchVideoList(string title, bool& found,
                          nodeType<videoType>* &current) const;
       //This function searches the video list for a
       //particular video, specified by the parameter title.
       //If the video is found, the parameter found is set to
       //true, otherwise false; the parameter current points
       //to the node containing the video.

    void inorderTitle(nodeType<videoType> *p)   const;
       //This function prints the titles of all the videos
       //in stock.
};
```

The definitions of the member functions `isVideoAvailable`, `videoCheckIn`, `videoCheckOut`, `videoCheckTitle`, `videoUpdateInStock`, `videoSetCopiesInStock`, and `videoSearch` of the `class` `videoBinaryTree` are similar to the definitions of these functions given in Chapter 17. The only difference is that, here, these are members of the `class` `videoBinaryTree`. You can find the complete definitions of these functions on the Web site that accompanies this book. Next, we discuss the definitions of the remaining functions of the `class` `videoBinaryTree`.

The function `searchVideoList` uses a search algorithm similar to the search algorithm for a binary search tree given earlier in this chapter. It returns `true` if the search item is found in the list. It also returns a pointer to the node containing the search item. The definition of this function is as follows:

```cpp
void videoBinaryTree::searchVideoList(string title,
                          bool& found,
                          nodeType<videoType>* &current) const
{
    found = false;

    videoType temp;

    temp.setVideoInfo(title, "", "", "", "", "", 0);

    if (root == NULL)  //tree is empty
        cout << "Cannot search an empty list. " << endl;
```

```cpp
        else
        {
            current = root; //set current point to the root node
                            //of the binary tree
            found = false;  //set found to false

            while (current != NULL && !found) //search the tree
                if (current->info == temp)     //item is found
                    found = true;
                else if (current->info > temp)
                    current = current->lLink;
                else
                    current = current->rLink;
    } //end else
} //end searchVideoList
```

Given a pointer to the root node of the binary tree containing the videos, the function `inorderTitle` uses the inorder traversal algorithm to print the titles of the videos. Notice that this function outputs only the video titles. The definition of this function is as follows:

```cpp
void videoBinaryTree::inorderTitle
                        (nodeType<videoType> *p) const
{
    if (p != NULL)
    {
        inorderTitle(p->lLink);
        p->info.printTitle();
        inorderTitle(p->rLink);
    }
}
```

The function `videoPrintTitle` uses the function `inorderTitle` to print the titles of all videos in the store. The definition of this function is:

```cpp
void videoBinaryTree::videoPrintTitle() const
{
    inorderTitle(root);
}
```

MAIN PROGRAM The main program is the same as before. Here, we give only the listing of this program. We assume that the name of the header file containing the definition of the `class videoBinaryTree` is `videoBinaryTree.h`, and so on:

```cpp
#include <iostream>
#include <fstream>
#include <string>
#include "binarySearchTree.h"
#include "videoType.h"
#include "videoBinaryTree.h"
```

```cpp
using namespace std;

void createVideoList(ifstream& infile,
                     videoBinaryTree& videoList);
void displayMenu();

int main()
{
    videoBinaryTree  videoList;
    int choice;
    string title;

    ifstream infile;

    infile.open("a:\\videoDat.txt");
    if (!infile)
    {
        cout << "The input file does not exist. "
             << "Program terminates!!"<< endl;
        return 1;
    }

    createVideoList(infile, videoList);
    infile.close();

    displayMenu();                  //show the menu
    cout << "Enter your choice: ";
    cin >> choice;                  //get the request
    cin.ignore(100, '\n');          //ignore the remaining
                                    //characters in the line

    cout << endl;

    while (choice != 9)
    {
        switch (choice)
        {
        case 1:
            cout << "Enter the title: ";
            getline(cin, title);
            cout << endl;

            if (videoList.videoSearch(title))
                cout << "The store carries " << title << endl;
            else
                cout << "The store does not carry " << title
                     << endl;
            break;

        case 2:
            cout << "Enter the title: ";
            getline(cin, title);
            cout << endl;
```

```cpp
if (videoList.videoSearch(title))
{
    if (videoList.isVideoAvailable(title))
    {
        videoList.videoCheckOut(title);
        cout << "Enjoy your movie: " << title
            << endl;
    }
    else
        cout << "Currently " << title
            << " is out of stock." << endl;
}
else
    cout << "The store does not carry " << title
        << endl;
break;

case 3:
    cout << "Enter the title: ";
    getline(cin, title);
    cout << endl;

    if (videoList.videoSearch(title))
    {
        videoList.videoCheckIn(title);
        cout << "Thanks for returning " << title
            << endl;
    }
    else
        cout << "The store does not carry " << title
            << endl;
    break;

case 4:
    cout << "Enter the title: ";
    getline(cin, title);
    cout << endl;

    if (videoList.videoSearch(title))
    {
        if (videoList.isVideoAvailable(title))
            cout << title << " is currently in "
                << "stock." << endl;
        else
            cout << title << " is currently out "
                << "of stock." << endl;
    }
    else
        cout << "The store does not carry " << title
            << endl;
    break;
```

```cpp
        case 5:
            videoList.videoPrintTitle();
            break;

        case 6:
            videoList.inorderTraversal();
            break;

        default: cout << "Invalid selection." << endl;
        }//end switch

        displayMenu();              //display the menu
        cout << "Enter your choice: ";
        cin >> choice;                  //get the next request
        cin.ignore(100, '\n');  //ignore the remaining
                                //characters in the line

        cout << endl;
    }//end while

    return 0;
}

void createVideoList(ifstream& infile,
                     videoBinaryTree& videoList)
{
    string title;
    string star1;
    string star2;
    string producer;
    string director;
    string productionCo;
    int inStock;

    videoType newVideo;

    getline(infile, title);

    while (infile)
    {
        getline(infile, star1);
        getline(infile, star2);
        getline(infile, producer);
        getline(infile, director);
        getline(infile, productionCo);
        infile >> inStock;
        infile.ignore(100, '\n');
        newVideo.setVideoInfo(title, star1, star2, producer,
                              director, productionCo, inStock);
        videoList.insert(newVideo);
```

```
            getline(infile, title);
        }//end while
    }//end createVideoList

void displayMenu()
{
        cout << "Select one of the following:" << endl;
        cout << "1: To check whether the store carries a "
             << "particular video." << endl;
        cout << "2: To check out a video." << endl;
        cout << "3: To check in a video." << endl;
        cout << "4: To check whether a particular video is "
             << "in stock." << endl;
        cout << "5: To print only the titles of all the videos."
             << endl;
        cout << "6: To print a list of all the videos." << endl;
        cout << "9: To exit" << endl;
}
```

QUICK REVIEW

1. A binary tree is either empty or it has a special node called the root node. If the tree is nonempty, the root node has two sets of nodes, called the left and right subtrees, such that the left and right subtrees are also binary trees.

2. The node of a binary tree has two links in it.

3. A node in the binary tree is called a leaf if it has no left and right children.

4. A node U is called the parent of a node V if there is a branch from U to V.

5. A path from a node X to a node Y in a binary tree is a sequence of nodes $X_0, X_1, \ldots, X_n$ such that (a) $X = X_0$, $X_n = Y$, and (b) X_{i-1} is the parent of X_i for all $i = 1, 2, \ldots, n$. That is, there is branch from X_0 to X_1, X_1 to X_2, $\ldots, X_{i-1}$ to $X_i, \ldots, X_{n-1}$ to X_n.

6. The length of a path in a binary tree is the number of branches on that path.

7. The level of a node in a binary tree is the number of branches on the path from the root to the node.

8. The level of the root node of a binary tree is 0, and the level of the children of the root node is 1.

9. The height of a binary tree is the number of nodes on the longest path from the root to a leaf.

10. In an inorder traversal, the binary tree is traversed as follows:

    a. Traverse the left subtree.

    b. Visit the node.

    c. Traverse the right subtree.

11. In a preorder traversal, the binary tree is traversed as follows:

   a. Visit the node.

   b. Traverse the left subtree.

   c. Traverse the right subtree.

12. In a postorder traversal, the binary tree is traversed as follows:

   a. Traverse the left subtree.

   b. Traverse the right subtree.

   c. Visit the node.

13. A binary search tree T is either empty or:

   i. T has a special node called the *root* node;

   ii. T has two sets of nodes, L_T and R_T, called the left subtree and the right subtree of T, respectively;

   iii. The key in the root node is larger than every key in the left subtree and smaller than every key in the right subtree; and

   iv. L_T and R_T are binary search trees.

14. To delete a node from a binary search tree that has both left and right nonempty subtrees, first its immediate predecessor is located, then the predecessor's info is copied into the node, and finally the predecessor is deleted.

EXERCISES

1. Mark the following statements as true or false.

   a. A binary tree must be nonempty.

   b. The level of the root node is 0.

   c. If a tree has only one node, the height of this tree is 0 because the number of levels is 0.

   d. The inorder traversal of a binary tree always outputs the data in ascending order.

2. There are 14 different binary trees with four nodes. Draw all of them.

   The binary tree of Figure 20-20 is to be used for Exercises 3 through 8.

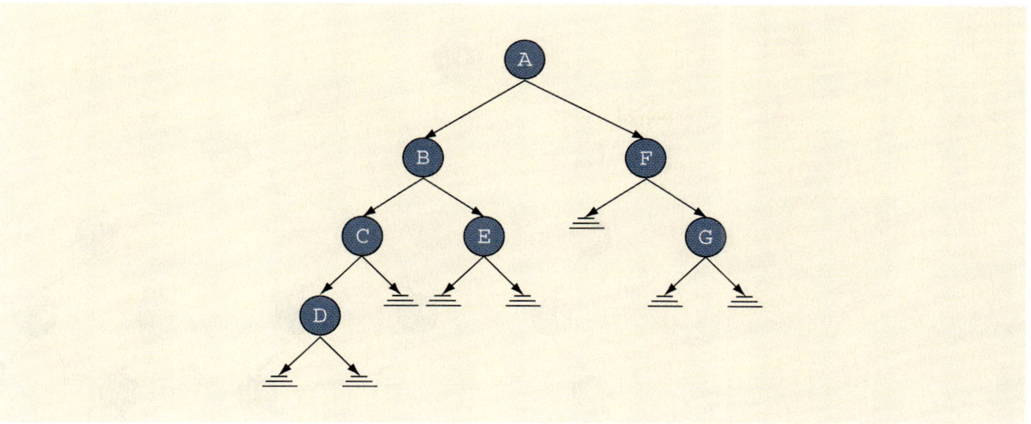

FIGURE 20-20   Figure for Exercises 3 to 8

3. Find L_A, the node in the left subtree of A.

4. Find R_A, the node in the right subtree of A.

5. Find R_B, the node in the right subtree of B.

6. List the nodes of this binary tree in an inorder sequence.

7. List the nodes of this binary tree in a preorder sequence.

8. List the nodes of this binary tree in a postorder sequence.

The binary tree of Figure 20-21 is to be used for Exercises 9 through 13.

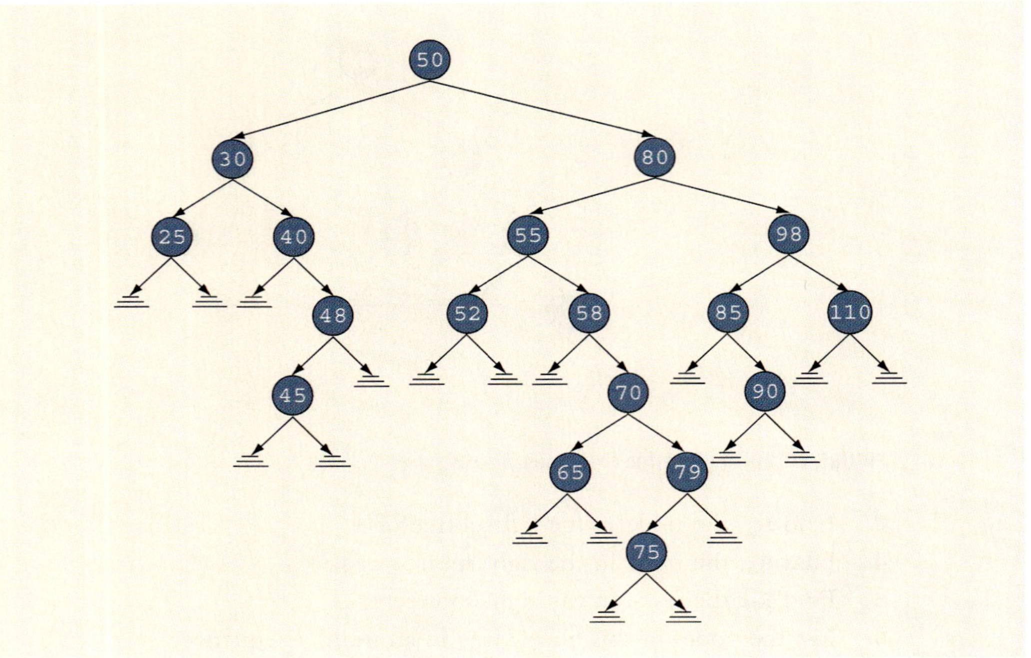

FIGURE 20-21   Figure for Exercises 9 to 13

9. List the path from the node with info 80 to the node with info 79.

10. A node with info 35 is to be inserted in the tree. List the nodes that are visited by the function `insert` to insert 35. Redraw the tree after inserting 35.

11. Delete node 52 and redraw the binary tree.

12. Delete node 40 and redraw the binary tree.

13. Delete nodes 80 and 58 in that order. Redraw the binary tree after each deletion.

14. Suppose that you are given two sequences of elements corresponding to the inorder sequence and the preorder sequence. Prove that it is possible to reconstruct a unique binary tree.

15. The following lists the nodes in a binary tree in two different orders:

```
preorder:    ABCDEFGHIJKLM
inorder:     CEDFBAHJIKGML
```

Draw the binary tree.

16. Given the nodes of a binary tree in the preorder sequence and the postorder sequence, show that it may not be possible to reconstruct the binary tree.

17. Draw the UML class diagram of the **class** binaryTreeType.

18. Draw the UML class diagram of the **class** bSearchTreeType. Also, show the inheritance hierarchy.

PROGRAMMING EXERCISES

1. Write the definition of the function, `nodeCount`, that returns the number of nodes in the binary tree. Add this function to the **class** `binaryTreeType` and create a program to test this function.

2. Write the definition of the function, `leavesCount`, that takes as a parameter a pointer to the root node of a binary tree and returns the number of leaves in a binary tree. Add this function to the **class** `binaryTreeType` and create a program to test this function.

3. Write a function, `swapSubtrees`, that swaps all of the left and right subtrees of a binary tree. Add this function to the **class** `binaryTreeType` and create a program to test this function.

4. Write a function, `singleParent`, that returns the number of nodes in a binary tree that have only one child. Add this function to the **class** `binaryTreeType` and create a program to test this function. (*Note*: first, create a binary search tree.)

5. Write a program to test various operations on a binary search tree.

6. a. Write the definition of the function to implement the nonrecursive postorder traversal algorithm.

   b. Write a program to test the nonrecursive inorder, preorder, and post-order traversal algorithms. (*Note*: first, create a binary search tree.)

7. Write a version of the preorder traversal algorithm in which a user–defined function can be passed as a parameter to specify the visiting criteria at a node. Also, write a program to test your function.

8. Write a version of the postorder traversal algorithm in which a user–defined function can be passed as a parameter to specify the visiting criteria at a node. Also, write a program to test your function.

9. (**Video Store Program**) In Programming Exercise 14 in Chapter 17, you were asked to design and implement a class to maintain customer data in a linked list. Because the search on a linked list is sequential and, therefore, can be time-consuming, design and implement the **class** `customerBTreeType` so that this customer data can be stored in a binary search tree. The **class** `customerBTreeType` must be derived from the **class** `bSearchTreeType`, as designed in this chapter.

10. (**Video Store Program**) Using classes to implement the video data, video list data, customer data, and customer list data, as designed in this chapter and in Programming Exercise 9, design and complete the program to put the video store into operation.

CHAPTER

21

GRAPHS

IN THIS CHAPTER, YOU WILL:

- Learn about graphs
- Become familiar with the basic terminology of graph theory
- Discover how to represent graphs in computer memory
- Explore graphs as ADTs
- Examine and implement various graph traversal algorithms
- Learn how to implement the shortest path algorithm
- Examine and implement the minimal spanning tree algorithm

In previous chapters, you learned various ways to represent and manipulate data. This chapter discusses how to implement and manipulate graphs, which have numerous applications in computer science.

Introduction

In 1736, the following problem was posed. In the town of Königsberg (now called Kaliningrad), the river Pregel (Pregolya) flows around the island Kneiphof and then divides into two branches (see Figure 21-1).

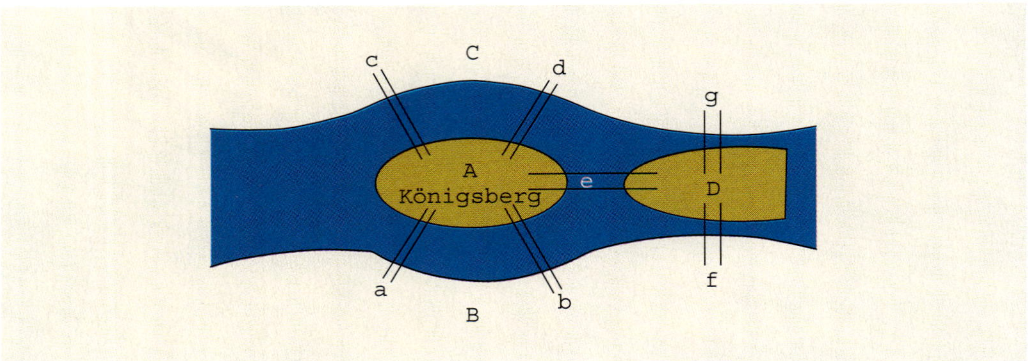

FIGURE 21-1 Königsberg bridge problem

The river has four land areas (*A*, *B*, *C*, *D*), as shown in the figure. These land areas are connected using seven bridges, as shown in Figure 21-1. The bridges are labeled *a*, *b*, *c*, *d*, *e*, *f*, and *g*. The Königsberg bridge problem is as follows: Starting at one land area, is it possible to walk across all the bridges exactly once and return to the starting land area? In 1736, Euler represented the Königsberg bridge problem as a graph, as shown in Figure 21-2, and answered the question in the negative. This marked (as recorded) the birth of graph theory.

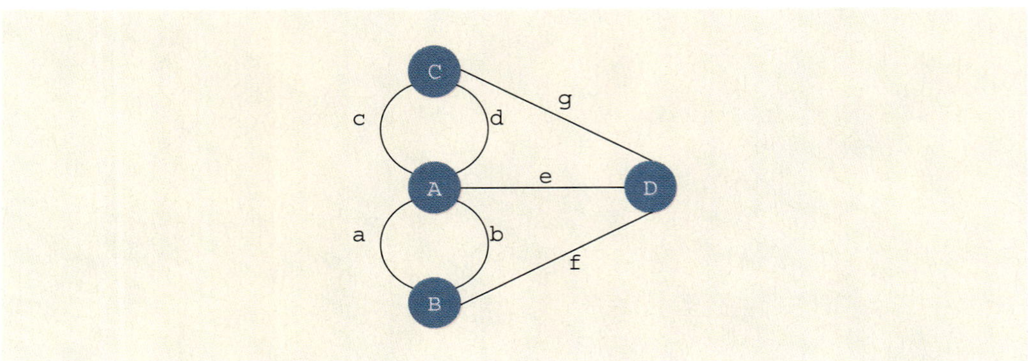

FIGURE 21-2 Graph representation of Königsberg bridge problem

Over the past 200 years, graph theory has been applied to a variety of applications. Graphs are used to model electrical circuits, chemical compounds, highway maps, and so on. They are also used in the analysis of electrical circuits, finding the shortest route, project planning, linguistics, genetics, social science, and so forth. In this chapter, you learn about graphs and their applications in computer science.

Graph Definitions and Notations

To facilitate and simplify our discussion, we borrow a few definitions and terminology from set theory. Let X be a set. If a is an element of X, then we write $a \in X$. (The symbol "$\in$" means "belongs to.") A set Y is called a **subset** of X if every element of Y is also an element of X. If Y is a subset of X, we write $Y \subseteq X$. (The symbol "$\subseteq$" means "is a subset of.") The **intersection** of sets A and B, written $A \cap B$, is the set of all the elements that are in A and B; that is, $A \cap B = \{x \mid x \in A \text{ and } x \in B\}$. (The symbol "$\cap$" means "intersection.") The **union** of sets A and B, written $A \cup B$, is the set of all the elements that are in A or in B; that is, $A \cup B = \{x \mid x \in A \text{ or } x \in B\}$. (The symbol "$\cup$" means "union." Moreover, note that $x \in A \cup B$ means x is in A or x is in B or x is in both A and B. Also, the symbol "$\mid$" is read as "such that.")

For sets A and B, the set $A \times B$ is the set of all the ordered pairs of elements of A and B; that is, $A \times B = \{(a, b) \mid a \in A, b \in B\}$.

A **graph** G is a pair, $G = (V, E)$, where V is a finite nonempty set, called the set of **vertices** of G, and $E \subseteq V \times V$. That is, the elements of E are the pair of elements of V. E is called the set of **edges**.

Let $V(G)$ denote the set of vertices and $E(G)$ denote the set of edges of a graph G. If the elements of $E(G)$ are ordered pairs, G is called a **directed graph** or **digraph**; otherwise, G is called an **undirected graph**. In an undirected graph, the pairs (u, v) and (v, u) represent the same edge. If (u, v) is an edge in a directed graph, then sometimes the vertex u is called the **origin** of the edge, and the vertex v is called the **destination**.

Let G be a graph. A graph H is called a **subgraph** of G if $V(H) \subseteq V(G)$ and $E(H) \subseteq E(G)$; that is, every vertex of H is a vertex of G, and every edge in H is an edge in G.

A graph can be shown pictorially. The vertices are drawn as circles, and a label inside the circle represents the vertex. In an undirected graph, the edges are drawn using lines. In a directed graph, the edges are drawn using arrows. Moreover, in a directed graph, the tail of a pictorial directed edge is the origin, and the head is the destination.

EXAMPLE 21-1

Figure 21-3 shows some examples of undirected graphs.

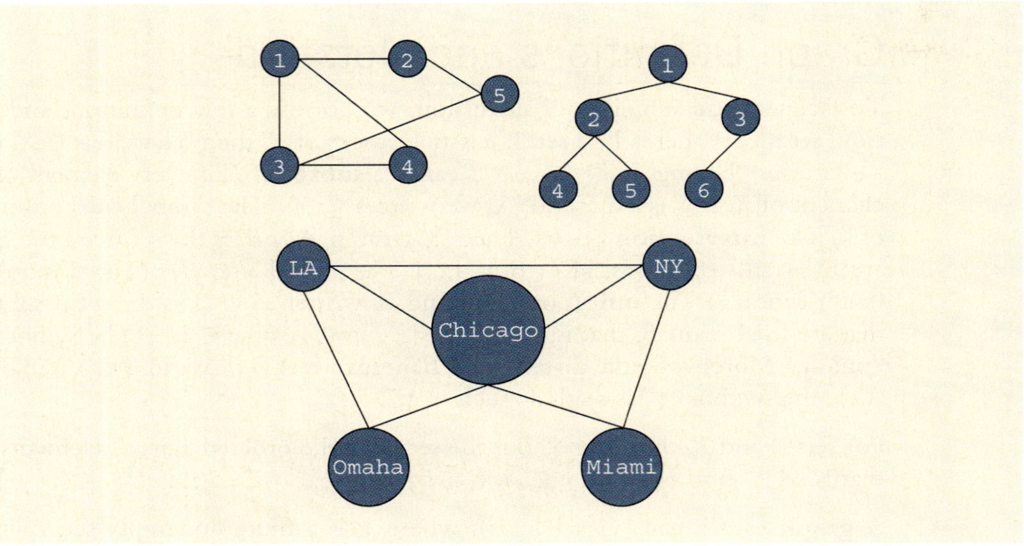

FIGURE 21-3 Various undirected graphs

EXAMPLE 21-2

Figure 21–4 shows some examples of directed graphs.

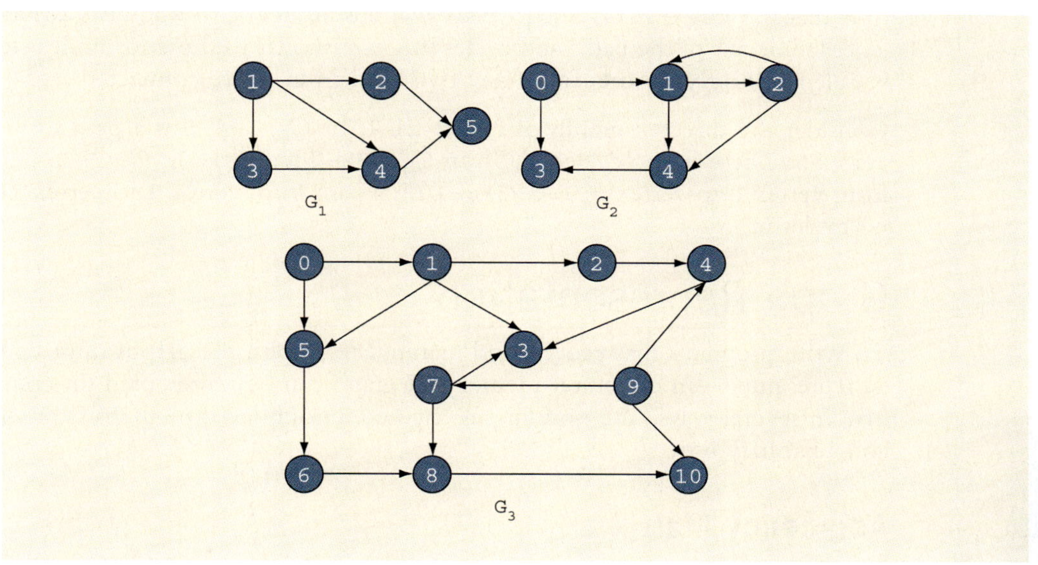

FIGURE 21-4 Various directed graphs

For the graphs of Figure 21–4, we have:

$V(G_1) = \{1, 2, 3, 4, 5\}$

$E(G_1) = \{(1, 2), (1, 4), (2, 5), (3, 1), (3, 4), (4, 5)\}$

$V(G_2) = \{0, 1, 2, 3, 4,\}$

$E(G_2) = \{(0, 1), (0, 3), (1, 2), (1, 4), (2, 1), (2, 4), (4, 3)\}$

$V(G_3) = \{0, 1, 2, 3, 4, 5, 6, 7, 8, 9, 10\}$

$E(G_3) = \{(0, 1), (0, 5), (1, 2), (1, 3), (1, 5), (2, 4), (4, 3), (5, 6), (6, 8), (7, 3), (7, 8), (8, 10), (9, 4), (9, 7), (9, 10)\}$

Let G be an undirected graph. Let u and v be two vertices in G. Then, u and v are called **adjacent** if there is an edge from one to the other; that is, $(u, v) \in E(G)$. Let $e = (u, v)$ be an edge in G. We then say that edge e is **incident** on the vertices u and v. An edge incident on a single vertex is called a **loop**. If two edges, e_1 and e_2, are associated with the same pair of vertices, then e_1 and e_2 are called **parallel edges**. A graph is called a **simple graph** if it has no loops and no parallel edges. There is a **path** from u to v if there is a sequence of vertices $u_1, u_2, \ldots, u_n$ such that $u = u_1$, $u_n = v$, and (u_i, u_{i+1}) is an edge for all $i = 1, 2, \ldots, n - 1$. Vertices u and v are called **connected** if there is a path from u to v. A **simple path** is a path in which all the vertices, except possibly the first and last vertices, are distinct. A **cycle** in G is a simple path in which the first and last vertices are the same. G is called **connected** if there is a path from any vertex to any other vertex. A maximal subset of connected vertices is called a **component** of G.

Let G be a directed graph, and let u and v be two vertices in G. If there is an edge from u to v, that is, $(u, v) \in E(G)$, then we say that u is **adjacent to** v and v is **adjacent from** u. The definitions of the paths and cycles in G are similar to those for undirected graphs. G is called **strongly connected** if any two vertices in G are connected.

Consider the directed graphs of Figure 21-4. In G_1, 1–4–5 is a path from vertex 1 to vertex 5. There are no cycles in G_1. In G_2, 1–2–1 is a cycle. In G_3, 0–1–2–4–3 is a path from vertex 0 to vertex 3; 1–5–6–8–10 is a path from vertex 1 to vertex 10. There are no cycles in G_3.

Graph Representation

To write programs that process and manipulate graphs, the graphs must be stored—that is, represented—in computer memory. A graph can be represented (in computer memory) in several ways. We now discuss two commonly used methods: adjacency matrices and adjacency lists.

Adjacency Matrix

Let G be a graph with n vertices, where $n > 0$. Let $V(G) = \{v_1, v_2, \ldots, v_n\}$. The **adjacency matrix** A_G of G is a two-dimensional $n \times n$ matrix such that the (i, j)th entry of A_G is 1 if there is an edge from v_i to v_j; otherwise, the (i, j)th entry is zero. That is:

$$A_G(i,j) = \begin{cases} 1 & \text{if } (v_i, v_j) \in E(G) \\ 0 & \text{otherwise} \end{cases}$$

In an undirected graph, if $(v_i, v_j) \in E(G)$, then $(v_j, v_i) \in E(G)$, so $A_G(i, j) = 1 = A_G(j, i)$. It follows that the adjacency matrix of an undirected graph is symmetric.

EXAMPLE 21-3

Consider the directed graphs of Figure 21-4. The adjacency matrices of the directed graphs G_1, G_2, and G_3 are as follows:

$$A_{G_1} = \begin{bmatrix} 0 & 1 & 0 & 1 & 0 \\ 0 & 0 & 0 & 0 & 1 \\ 1 & 0 & 0 & 1 & 0 \\ 0 & 0 & 0 & 0 & 1 \\ 0 & 0 & 0 & 0 & 0 \end{bmatrix}$$

$$A_{G_2} = \begin{bmatrix} 0 & 1 & 0 & 1 & 0 \\ 0 & 0 & 1 & 0 & 1 \\ 0 & 1 & 0 & 0 & 1 \\ 0 & 0 & 0 & 0 & 0 \\ 0 & 0 & 0 & 1 & 0 \end{bmatrix}$$

$$A_{G_3} = \begin{matrix} 0 \\ 1 \\ 2 \\ 3 \\ 4 \\ 5 \\ 6 \\ 7 \\ 8 \\ 9 \\ 10 \end{matrix} \begin{bmatrix} 0 & 1 & 0 & 0 & 0 & 1 & 0 & 0 & 0 & 0 & 0 \\ 0 & 0 & 1 & 1 & 0 & 1 & 0 & 0 & 0 & 0 & 0 \\ 0 & 0 & 0 & 0 & 1 & 0 & 0 & 0 & 0 & 0 & 0 \\ 0 & 0 & 0 & 0 & 0 & 0 & 0 & 0 & 0 & 0 & 0 \\ 0 & 0 & 0 & 1 & 0 & 0 & 0 & 0 & 0 & 0 & 0 \\ 0 & 0 & 0 & 0 & 0 & 0 & 1 & 0 & 0 & 0 & 0 \\ 0 & 0 & 0 & 0 & 0 & 0 & 0 & 0 & 1 & 0 & 0 \\ 0 & 0 & 0 & 1 & 0 & 0 & 0 & 0 & 1 & 0 & 0 \\ 0 & 0 & 0 & 0 & 0 & 0 & 0 & 0 & 0 & 0 & 1 \\ 0 & 0 & 0 & 0 & 1 & 0 & 0 & 1 & 0 & 0 & 1 \\ 0 & 0 & 0 & 0 & 0 & 0 & 0 & 0 & 0 & 0 & 0 \end{bmatrix}$$

Adjacency Lists

Let G be a graph with n vertices, where $n > 0$. Let $V(G) = \{v_1, v_2, \ldots, v_n\}$. In the adjacency list representation, corresponding to each vertex, v, there is a linked list such that each node of the linked list contains the vertex, u, such that $(v, u) \in E(G)$. Because there are n nodes, we use an array, A, of size n, such that $A[i]$ is a reference variable pointing to the first node of the linked list containing the vertices to which v_i is adjacent. Clearly, each node has two components, say `vertex` and `link`. The component `vertex` contains the index of the vertex adjacent to vertex i.

EXAMPLE 21-4

Consider the directed graphs of Figure 21-4. Figure 21-5 shows the adjacency list of the directed graph G_2.

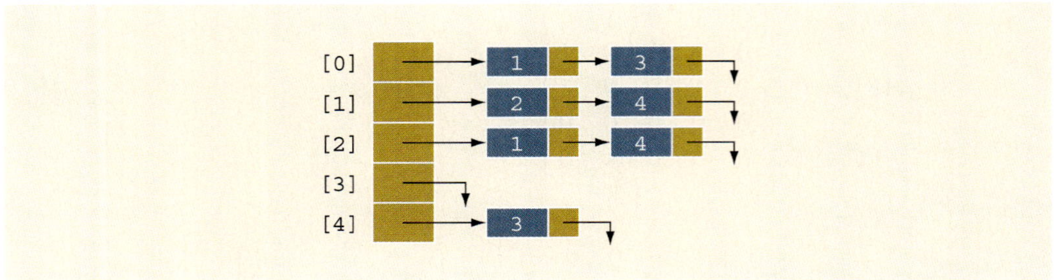

FIGURE 21-5 Adjacency list of graph G_2 of Figure 21-4

Figure 21-6 shows the adjacency list of the directed graph G_3.

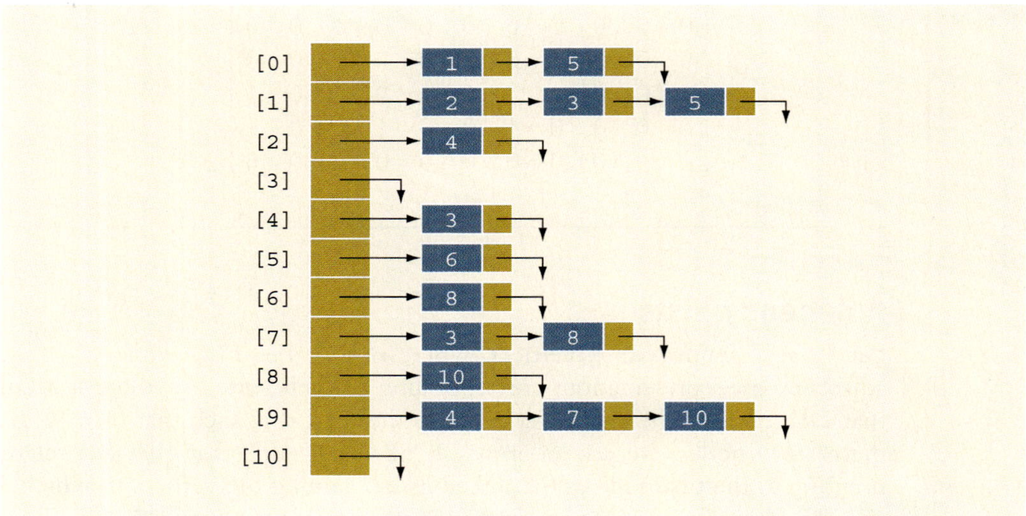

FIGURE 21-6 Adjacency list of graph G_3 of Figure 21-4

Operations on Graphs

Now that you know how to represent graphs in computer memory, the next obvious step is to learn the basic operations on a graph. The operations commonly performed on a graph are as follows:

1. Create the graph. That is, store the graph in computer memory using a particular graph representation.

2. Clear the graph. This operation makes the graph empty.

3. Determine whether the graph is empty.

4. Traverse the graph.

5. Print the graph.

We will add more operations on a graph when we discuss a specific application or a particular graph later in this chapter.

How a graph is represented in computer memory depends on the specific application. For illustration purposes, we use the adjacency list (linked list) representation of graphs. Therefore, for each vertex, v, the vertices adjacent to v (in a directed graph, also called the **immediate successors**) are stored in the linked list associated with v.

To manage the data in a linked list, we use the `class unorderedLinkedList`, discussed in Chapter 17.

The labeling of the vertices of a graph depends on a specific application. If you are dealing with the graph of cities, you could label the vertices by the names of the cities. However, to write algorithms to manipulate a graph as well as to simplify the algorithm, there must be some ordering to the vertices. That is, we must specify the first vertex, the second vertex, and so on. Therefore, for simplicity, throughout this chapter we assume that the n vertices of the graphs are numbered 0, 1, ..., $n - 1$. Moreover, it follows that the class we will design to implement the graph algorithm will *not* be a template.

Graphs as ADTs

In this section, we describe the class to implement graphs as an abstract data type (ADT) and provide the definitions of the functions to implement the operations on a graph.

The following class defines a graph as an ADT:

```cpp
class graphType
{
public:
    bool isEmpty() const;
      //Function to determine whether the graph is empty.
      //Postcondition: Returns true if the graph is empty;
      //               otherwise, returns false.

    void createGraph();
      //Function to create a graph.
      //Postcondition: The graph is created using the
      //               adjacency list representation.

    void clearGraph();
      //Function to clear graph.
      //Postcondition: The memory occupied by each vertex
      //               is deallocated.

    void printGraph() const;
      //Function to print graph.
      //Postcondition: The graph is printed.
```

```cpp
    void depthFirstTraversal();
      //Function to perform the depth first traversal of
      //the entire graph.
      //Postcondition: The vertices of the graph are printed
      //               using depth first traversal algorithm.

    void dftAtVertex(int vertex);
      //Function to perform the depth first traversal of
      //the graph at a node specified by the parameter vertex.
      //Postcondition: Starting at vertex, the vertices are
      //               printed using depth first traversal
      //               algorithm.

    void breadthFirstTraversal();
      //Function to perform the breadth first traversal of
      //the entire graph.
      //Postcondition: The vertices of the graph are printed
      //               using breadth first traversal algorithm.

    graphType(int size = 0);
      //Constructor
      //Postcondition: gSize = 0; maxSize = size;
      //               graph is an array of pointers to linked
      //               lists.

    ~graphType();
      //Destructor
      //The storage occupied by the vertices is deallocated.

protected:
    int maxSize;      //maximum number of vertices
    int gSize;        //current number of vertices
    unorderedLinkedList<int> *graph; //array to create
                                     //adjacency lists

private:
    void dft(int v, bool visited[]);
      //Function to perform the depth first traversal of
      //the graph at a node specified by the parameter vertex.
      //This function is used by the public member functions
      //depthFirstTraversal and dftAtVertex.
      //Postcondition: Starting at vertex, the vertices are
      //               printed using depth first traversal
      //               algorithm.
};
```

We leave the UML class diagram of the **class** graphType as an exercise.

The definitions of the functions of the **class** graphType are discussed next.

A graph is empty if the number of vertices is zero—that is, if gSize is 0. Therefore, the definition of the function isEmpty is:

```
bool graphType::isEmpty() const
{
    return (gSize == 0);
}
```

The definition of the function `createGraph` depends on how the data is input into the program. For illustration purposes, we assume that the data to the program is input from a file. The user is prompted for the input file. The data in the file appears in the following form:

```
5
0 2 4 ... -999
1 3 6 8 ... -999
...
```

The first line of input specifies the number of vertices in the graph. The first entry in the remaining lines specifies the vertex, and all of the remaining entries in the line (except the last) specify the vertices that are adjacent to the vertex. Each line ends with the number -999.

Using these conventions, the definition of the function `createGraph` is:

```
void graphType::createGraph()
{
    ifstream infile;
    char fileName[50];

    int index;
    int vertex;
    int adjacentVertex;

    if (gSize != 0)  //if the graph is not empty, make it empty
        clearGraph();

    cout << "Enter input file name: ";
    cin >> fileName;
    cout << endl;

    infile.open(fileName);

    if (!infile)
    {
        cout << "Cannot open input file." << endl;
        return;
    }

    infile >> gSize;    //get the number of vertices

    for (index = 0; index < gSize; index++)
    {
        infile >> vertex;
        infile >> adjacentVertex;
```

```cpp
        while (adjacentVertex != -999)
        {
            graph[vertex].insertLast(adjacentVertex);
            infile >> adjacentVertex;
        } //end while
    } // end for

    infile.close();
} //end createGraph
```

The function `clearGraph` empties the graph by deallocating the storage occupied by each linked list and then setting the number of vertices to zero:

```cpp
void graphType::clearGraph()
{
    int index;

    for (index = 0; index < gSize; index++)
        graph[index].destroyList();

    gSize = 0;
} //end clearGraph
```

The definition of the function `printGraph` is given next:

```cpp
void graphType::printGraph() const
{
    int index;

    for (index = 0; index < gSize; index++)
    {
        cout << index << " ";
        graph[index].print();
        cout << endl;
    }

    cout << endl;
} //end printGraph
```

The definitions of the constructor and the destructor are:

```cpp
    //Constructor
graphType::graphType(int size)
{
    maxSize = size;
    gSize = 0;
    graph = new unorderedLinkedList<int>[size];
}


    //Destructor
graphType::~graphType()
{
    clearGraph();
}
```

Graph Traversals

Processing a graph requires the ability to traverse the graph. This section discusses the graph traversal algorithms.

Traversing a graph is similar to traversing a binary tree, except that traversing a graph is a bit more complicated. Recall that a binary tree has no cycles. Also, starting at the root node, we can traverse the entire tree. On the other hand, a graph might have cycles and we might not be able to traverse the entire graph from a single vertex (for example, if the graph is not connected). Therefore, we must keep track of the vertices that have been visited. We must also traverse the graph from each vertex (that has not been visited) of the graph. This ensures that the entire graph is traversed.

The two most common graph traversal algorithms are the **depth first traversal** and **breadth first traversal**, which are described next. For simplicity, we assume that when a vertex is visited, its index is output. Moreover, each vertex is visited only once. We use the `bool` array `visited` to keep track of the visited vertices.

Depth First Traversal

The **depth first traversal** is similar to the preorder traversal of a binary tree. The general algorithm is:

```
for each vertex, v, in the graph
    if v is not visited
        start the depth first traversal at v
```

Consider the graph G_3 of Figure 21-4. It is shown here again as Figure 21-7 for easy reference.

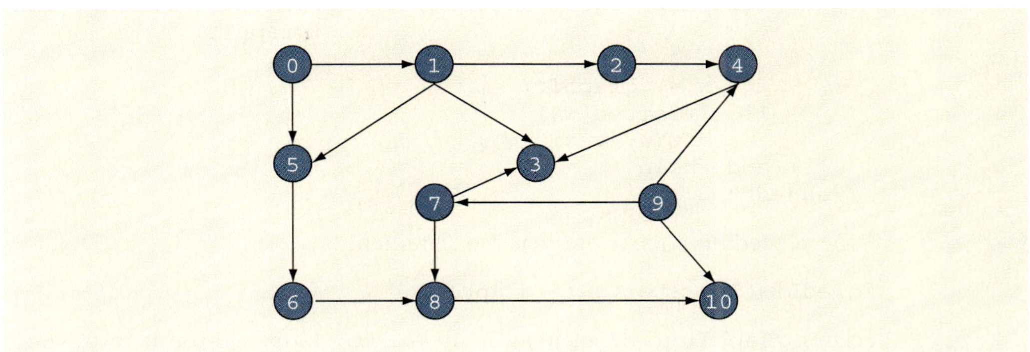

FIGURE 21-7 Directed graph G_3

A depth first ordering of the vertices of the graph G_3 in Figure 21-7 is:

0 1 2 4 3 5 6 8 10 7 9

For the graph of Figure 21-7, the depth first search starts at the vertex 0. After visiting all the vertices that can be reached starting at the vertex 0, the depth first search starts at the next vertex that is not visited. There is a path from the vertex 0 to every other vertex except the vertices 7 and 9. Therefore, when the depth first search starts at the vertex 0, all the vertices except 7 and 9 are visited before these vertices. After completing the depth first search that started at the vertex 0, the depth first search starts at the vertex 7 and then at the vertex 9. Note that there is no path from the vertex 7 to the vertex 9. Therefore, after completing the depth first search that started at the vertex 7, the depth first search starts at the vertex 9.

The general algorithm to do a depth first traversal *at a given node, v,* is:

1. Mark node **v** as visited

2. Visit the node

3. **for** each vertex u adjacent to v
      if u is not visited
          start the depth first traversal at u

Clearly, this is a recursive algorithm. We use a recursive function, `dft`, to implement this algorithm. The vertex at which the depth first traversal is to be started, and the **bool** array `visited`, are passed as parameters to this function:

```cpp
void graphType::dft(int v, bool visited[])
{
    visited[v] = true;
    cout << " " << v << " ";   //visit the vertex

    linkedListIterator<int> graphIt;

        //for each vertex adjacent to v
    for (graphIt = graph[v].begin(); graphIt != graph[v].end();
                                     ++graphIt)
    {
        int w = *graphIt;
        if (!visited[w])
            dft(w, visited);
    } //end while
} //end dft
```

In the preceding code, note that the statement:

```cpp
linkedListIterator<int> graphIt;
```

declares `graphIt` to be an iterator. In the **for** loop, we use it to traverse a linked list (adjacency list) to which the pointer `graph[v]` points. Next, let us look at the statement:

```cpp
int w = *graphIt;
```

The expression `*graphIt` returns the label of the vertex, adjacent to the vertex **v**, to which `graphIt` points.

Next, we give the definition of the function `depthFirstTraversal` to implement the depth first traversal of the graph:

```cpp
void graphType::depthFirstTraversal()
{
    bool *visited; //pointer to create the array to keep
                   //track of the visited vertices
    visited = new bool[gSize];

    int index;

    for (index = 0; index < gSize; index++)
        visited[index] = false;

        //For each vertex that is not visited, do a depth
        //first traverssal
    for (index = 0; index < gSize; index++)
        if (!visited[index])
            dft(index,visited);
    delete [] visited;
} //end depthFirstTraversal
```

The function `depthFirstTraversal` performs a depth first traversal of the entire graph. The definition of the function `dftAtVertex`, which performs a depth first traversal at a given vertex, is as follows:

```cpp
void graphType::dftAtVertex(int vertex)
{
    bool *visited;

    visited = new bool[gSize];

    for (int index = 0; index < gSize; index++)
        visited[index] = false;

    dft(vertex, visited);

    delete [] visited;
} // end dftAtVertex
```

Breadth First Traversal

The **breadth first traversal** of a graph is similar to traversing a binary tree level by level (the nodes at each level are visited from left to right). All the nodes at any level, i, are visited before visiting the nodes at level $i + 1$.

A breadth first ordering of the vertices of the graph G_3 (Figure 21-7) is:

```
0  1  5  2  3  6  4  8  10  7  9
```

For the graph G_3, we start the breadth traversal at vertex 0. After visiting the vertex 0, next we visit the vertices that are directly connected to it and are not visited, which are 1 and 5. Next, we visit the vertices that are directly connected to 1 and are not visited, which are 2 and 3. After this, we visit the vertices that are directly connected to 5 and are not visited, which, in this instance, is the single vertex 6. After this, we visit the vertices that are directly connected to 2 and are not visited, and so on.

As in the case of the depth first traversal, because it might not be possible to traverse the entire graph from a single vertex, the breadth first traversal also traverses the graph from each vertex that is not visited. Starting at the first vertex, the graph is traversed as much as possible; we then go to the next vertex that has not been visited. To implement the breadth first search algorithm, we use a queue. The general algorithm is:

a.   `for` each vertex `v` in the graph
      `if` v is not visited
         add v to the `queue` `//start the breadth first search at v`

b.   Mark v as `visited`

c.   `while` the `queue` is not empty

    c.1.   Remove vertex u from the `queue`

    c.2.   Retrieve the vertices adjacent to u

    c.3.   `for` each vertex `w` that is adjacent to u

        `if` w is not visited

        c.3.1.   Add `w` to the `queue`

        c.3.2.   Mark `w` as `visited`

The following C++ function, `breadthFirstTraversal`, implements this algorithm:

```cpp
void graphType::breadthFirstTraversal()
{
    linkedQueueType<int> queue;

    bool *visited;
    visited = new bool[gSize];

    for (int ind = 0; ind < gSize; ind++)
        visited[ind] = false; //initialize the array
                              //visited to false

    linkedListIterator<int> graphIt;

    for (int index = 0; index < gSize; index++)
        if (!visited[index])
        {
            queue.addQueue(index);
            visited[index] = true;
            cout << " " << index << " ";
```

```cpp
        while (!queue.isEmptyQueue())
        {
            int u = queue.front();
            queue.deleteQueue();

            for (graphIt = graph[u].begin();
                 graphIt != graph[u].end(); ++graphIt)
            {
                int w = *graphIt;
                if (!visited[w])
                {
                    queue.addQueue(w);
                    visited[w] = true;
                    cout << " " << w << " ";
                }
            }
        } //end while
    }

    delete [] visited;
} //end breadthFirstTraversal
```

As we continue to discuss graph algorithms, we will be writing C++ functions to implement specific algorithms, and so we will derive (using inheritance) new classes from the **class** graphType.

Shortest Path Algorithm

The graph theory has many applications. For example, we can use graphs to show how different chemicals are related or to show airline routes. They can also be used to show the highway structure of a city, state, or country. The edges connecting two vertices can be assigned a non-negative real number, called the **weight of the edge**. If the graph represents a highway structure, the weight can represent the distance between two places or the travel time from one place to another. Such graphs are called **weighted graphs**.

Let G be a weighted graph. Let u and v be two vertices in G, and let P be a path in G from u to v. The **weight of the path** P is the sum of the weights of all the edges on the path P, which is also called the **weight** of v from u via P.

Let G be a weighted graph representing a highway structure. Suppose that the weight of an edge represents the travel time. For example, to plan monthly business trips, a salesperson wants to find the **shortest path** (that is, the path with the smallest weight) from her or his city to every other city in the graph. Many such problems exist in which we want to find the shortest path from a given vertex, called the **source**, to every other vertex in the graph.

This section describes the **shortest path algorithm**, also called a **greedy algorithm**, developed by Dijkstra.

Let G be a graph with n vertices, where $n > 0$. Let $V(G) = \{v_1, v_2, \ldots, v_n\}$. Let W be a two-dimensional $n \times n$ matrix such that:

$$W(i,j) = \begin{cases} w_{ij} & \text{if } (v_i, v_j) \text{ is an edge in } G \text{ and } w_{ij} \text{ is the weight of the edge } (v_i, v_j) \\ \infty & \text{if there is no edge from } v_i \text{ to } v_j \end{cases}$$

The input to the program is the graph and the weight matrix associated with the graph. To make inputting the data easier, we extend the definition of the **class graphType** (using inheritance), and add the function **createWeightedGraph** to create the graph and the weight matrix associated with the graph. Let us call this **class weightedGraphType**. The functions to implement the shortest path algorithm will also be added to this class:

```cpp
class weightedGraphType: public graphType
{
public:
    void createWeightedGraph();
        //Function to create the graph and the weight matrix.
        //Postcondition: The graph using adjacency lists and
        //               its weight matrix is created.

    void shortestPath(int vertex);
        //Function to determine the weight of a shortest path
        //from vertex, that is, source, to every other vertex
        //in the graph.
        //Postcondition: The weight of the shortest path from
        //               vertex to every other vertex in the
        //               graph is determined.

    void printShortestDistance(int vertex);
        //Function to print the shortest weight from vertex
        //to the other vertex in the graph.
        //Postcondition: The weight of the shortest path from
        //               vertex to every other vertex in the
        //               graph is printed.

    weightedGraphType(int size = 0);
        //Constructor
        //Postcondition: gSize = 0; maxSize = size;
        //               graph is an array of pointers to linked
        //               lists.
        //               weights is a two-dimensional array to
        //               store the weights of the edges.
        //               smallestWeight is an array to store the
        //               smallest weight from source to vertices.

    ~weightedGraphType();
        //Destructor
        //The storage occupied by the vertices and the arrays
        //weights and smallestWeight is deallocated.
```

```
protected:
    double **weights;      //pointer to create weight matrix
    double *smallestWeight; //pointer to create the array to
                            //store the smallest weight from
                            //source to vertices
};
```

We leave the UML class diagram of the **class** `weightedGraphType` and the inheritance hierarchy as an exercise. The definition of the function `createWeightedGraph` is also left as an exercise for you. Next, we describe the shortest path algorithm.

Shortest Path

Given a vertex, say, `vertex` (that is, a source), this section describes the shortest path algorithm.

The general algorithm is:

1. Initialize the array `smallestWeight` so that:

    `smallestWeight[u] = weights[vertex, u]`

2. Set `smallestWeight[vertex] = 0`.

3. Find the vertex, `v`, that is closest to `vertex` for which the shortest path has not been determined.

4. Mark `v` as the (next) vertex for which the smallest weight is found.

5. For each vertex `w` in `G`, such that the shortest path from `vertex` to `w` has not been determined and an edge `(v, w)` exists, if the weight of the path to `w` via `v` is smaller than its current weight, update the weight of `w` to the weight of `v` + the weight of the edge `(v, w)`.

Because there are n vertices, Steps 3 through 5 are repeated $n - 1$ times.

Example 21-5 illustrates the shortest path algorithm. (We use the **bool** array `weightFound` to keep track of the vertices for which the smallest weight from the source vertex has been found. If the smallest weight for a vertex, from the source, has been found, then this vertex's corresponding entry in the array `weightFound` is set to **true**; otherwise, the corresponding entry is **false**.)

EXAMPLE 21-5

Let G be the graph shown in Figure 21-8.

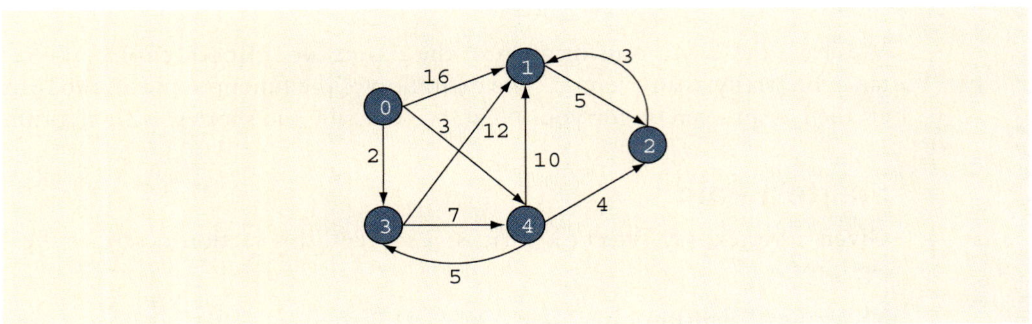

FIGURE 21-8 Weighted graph G

Suppose that the source vertex of G is 0. The graph shows the weight of each edge. After Steps 1 and 2 execute, the resulting graph is as shown in Figure 21-9.

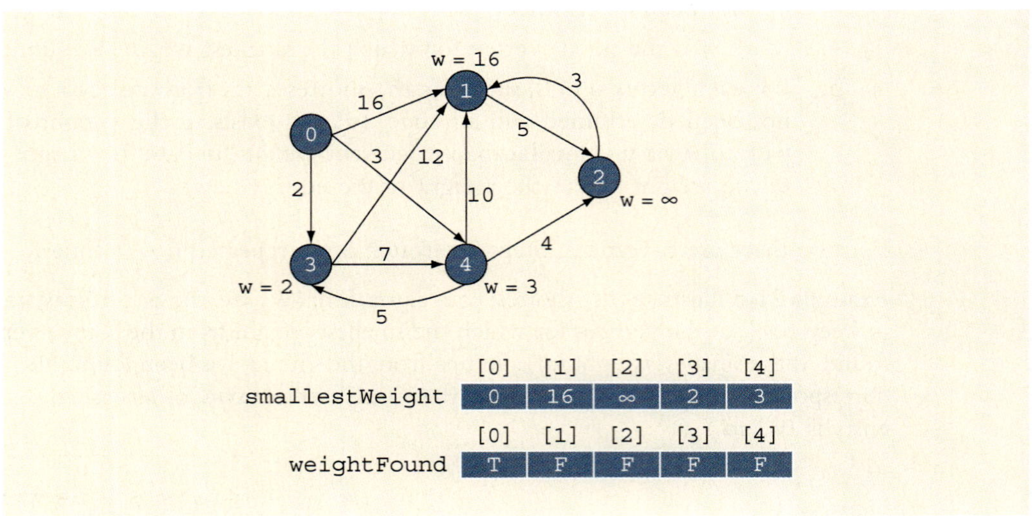

FIGURE 21-9 Graph after Steps 1 and 2 execute

Iteration 1 of Steps 3 to 5: At Step 3, we select a vertex that is closest to the vertex 0 and for which the shortest path has not been found. We do this by finding a vertex in the array **smallestWeight** that has the smallest weight and its corresponding entry in the array **weightFound** is **false**. Therefore, in this iteration, we select the vertex 3. At Step 4, we mark **weightFound[3]** as **true**. Next, at Step 5, we consider vertices 1 and 4 because these are the vertices for which there is an edge from the vertex 3, and the shortest part from 0 to these vertices has not been found. We then check if the path from the vertex 0 to the vertices 1 and 4 via the vertex 3 can be improved. The weight of the path `0-3-1` from 0 to 1 is less than the weight of the path `0-1`. So we update `smallestWeight[1]` to 14. The weight of the path `0-3-4`, which is 2 + 7 = 9, is greater than the weight of the path `0-4`, which is 3. So we do not update the weight of the vertex 4. Figure 21-10 shows the resulting graph. (The dotted arrow shows the shortest path from the source—that is, from 0—to the vertex.)

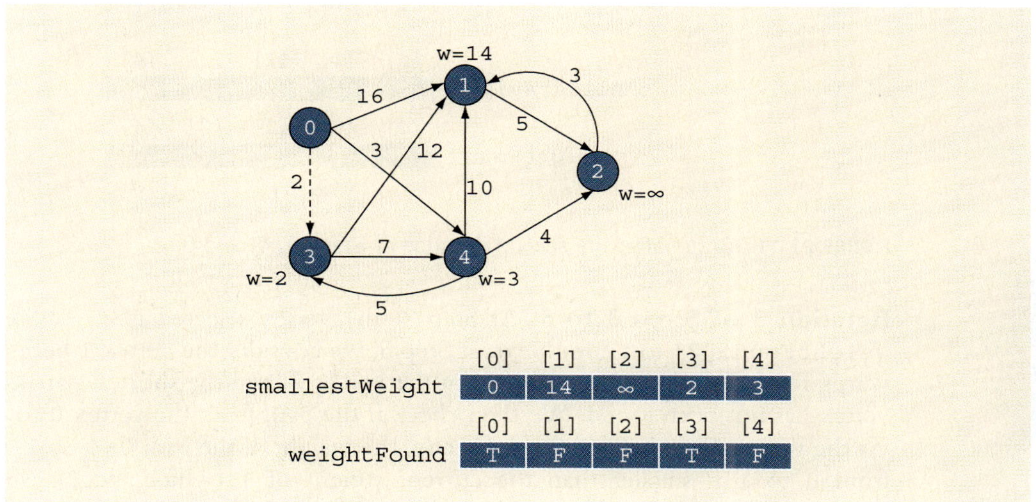

FIGURE 21-10   Graph after the first iteration of Steps 3, 4, and 5

Iteration 2 of Steps 3 to 5: At Step 3, we select vertex 4 because this is the vertex in the array `smallestWeight` that has the smallest weight, and its corresponding entry in the array `weightFound` is `false`. Next, we execute Steps 4 and 5. At Step 4, we set `weightFound[4]` to `true`. At Step 5, we consider vertices 1 and 2 because these are the vertices for which there is an edge from the vertex 4, and the shortest path from 0 to these vertices has not been found. We then check if the path from the vertex 0 to the vertices 1 and 2 via the vertex 4 can be improved. Clearly, the weight of the path `0-4-1`, which is 13, is smaller than the current weight of 1, which is 14. So we update `smallestWeight[1]`. Similarly, we update `smallestWeight[2]`. Figure 21-11 shows the resulting graph.

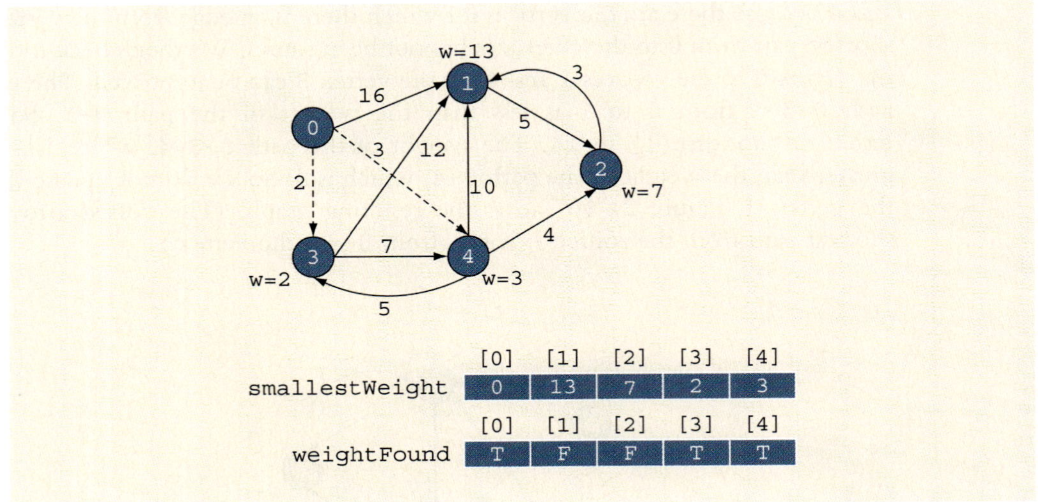

	[0]	[1]	[2]	[3]	[4]
smallestWeight	0	13	7	2	3

	[0]	[1]	[2]	[3]	[4]
weightFound	T	F	F	T	T

FIGURE 21-11   Graph after the second iteration of Steps 3, 4, and 5

Iteration 3 of Steps 3 to 5: At Step 3, the vertex selected is 2. At Step 4, we set `weightFound[2]` to **true**. Next, at Step 5, we consider the vertex 1 because this is the vertex for which there is an edge from the vertex 2, and the shortest part from 0 to this vertex has not been found. We then check if the path from the vertex 0 to the vertex 1 via the vertex 2 can be improved. Clearly, the weight of the path 0–4–2–1, which is 10, from 0 to 1 is smaller than the current weight of 1 (which is 13). So we update `smallestWeight[1]`. Figure 21-12 shows the resulting graph.

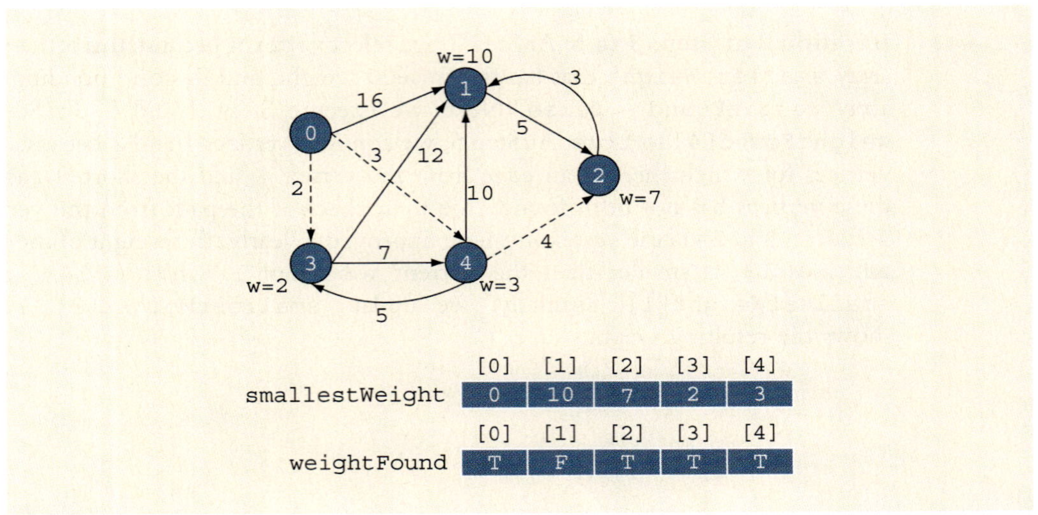

	[0]	[1]	[2]	[3]	[4]
smallestWeight	0	10	7	2	3

	[0]	[1]	[2]	[3]	[4]
weightFound	T	F	T	T	T

FIGURE 21-12   Graph after the third iteration of Steps 3, 4, and 5

Iteration 4 of Steps 3 to 5: At Step 3, the vertex 1 is selected and at Step 4 `weightFound[1]` is set to **true**. In this iteration, the action of Step 5 is null because the shortest path from the vertex 0 to every other vertex in the graph has been determined. Figure 21-13 shows the final graph.

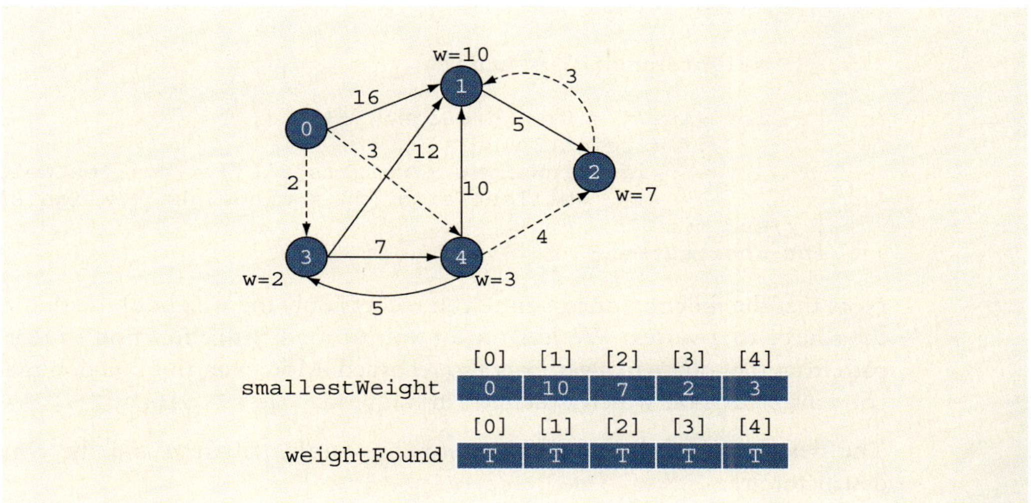

FIGURE 21-13   Graph after the fourth iteration of Steps 3, 4, and 5

The following C++ function, `shortestPath`, implements the previous algorithm:

```cpp
void weightedGraphType::shortestPath(int vertex)
{
    for (int j = 0; j < gSize; j++)
        smallestWeight[j] = weights[vertex][j];

    bool *weightFound;
    weightFound = new bool[gSize];

    for (int j = 0; j < gSize; j++)
        weightFound[j] = false;

    weightFound[vertex] = true;
    smallestWeight[vertex] = 0;

    for (int i = 0; i < gSize - 1; i++)
    {
        double minWeight = DBL_MAX;
        int v;
```

```cpp
        for (int j = 0; j < gSize; j++)
            if (!weightFound[j])
                if (smallestWeight[j] < minWeight)
                {
                    v = j;
                    minWeight = smallestWeight[v];
                }

        weightFound[v] = true;

        for (int j = 0; j < gSize; j++)
            if (!weightFound[j])
                if (minWeight + weights[v][j] < smallestWeight[j])
                    smallestWeight[j] = minWeight + weights[v][j];
    } //end for
} //end shortestPath
```

Note that the function `shortestPath` records only the weight of the shortest path from
the source to a vertex. We leave it for you to modify this function so that the shortest
path from the source to a vertex is also recorded. Moreover, this function used the named
constant `DBL_MAX`, which is defined in the header file `cfloat`.

The definitions of the function `printShortestDistance` and the constructor and
destructor are:

```cpp
void weightedGraphType::printShortestDistance(int vertex)
{
    cout << "Source Vertex: " << vertex << endl;
    cout << "Shortest Distance from Source to each Vertex."
         << endl;
    cout << "Vertex  Shortest_Distance" << endl;

    for (int j = 0; j < gSize; j++)
        cout << setw(4) << j << setw(12) << smallestWeight[j]
             << endl;
    cout << endl;
} //end printShortestDistance

    //Constructor
weightedGraphType::weightedGraphType(int size)
                :graphType(size)
{
    weights = new double*[size];

    for (int i = 0; i < size; i++)
        weights[i] = new double[size];

    smallestWeight = new double[size];
}
```

```
    //Destructor
weightedGraphType::~weightedGraphType()
{
    for (int i = 0; i < gSize; i++)
        delete [] weights[i];

    delete [] weights;
    delete smallestWeight;
}
```

Minimal Spanning Tree

Consider the graph of Figure 21-14, which represents the airline connections of a company between seven cities. The number on each edge represents some cost factor of maintaining the connection between the cities.

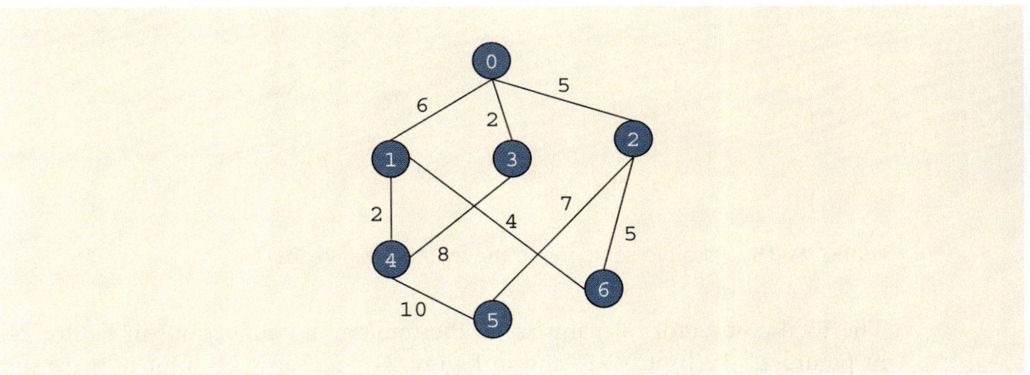

FIGURE 21-14 Airline connections between cities and the cost factor of maintaining the connections

Due to financial hardship, the company needs to shut down the maximum number of connections and still be able to fly from one city to another (the flights need not be direct). The graphs of Figure 21-15(a), (b), and (c) shows three different solutions.

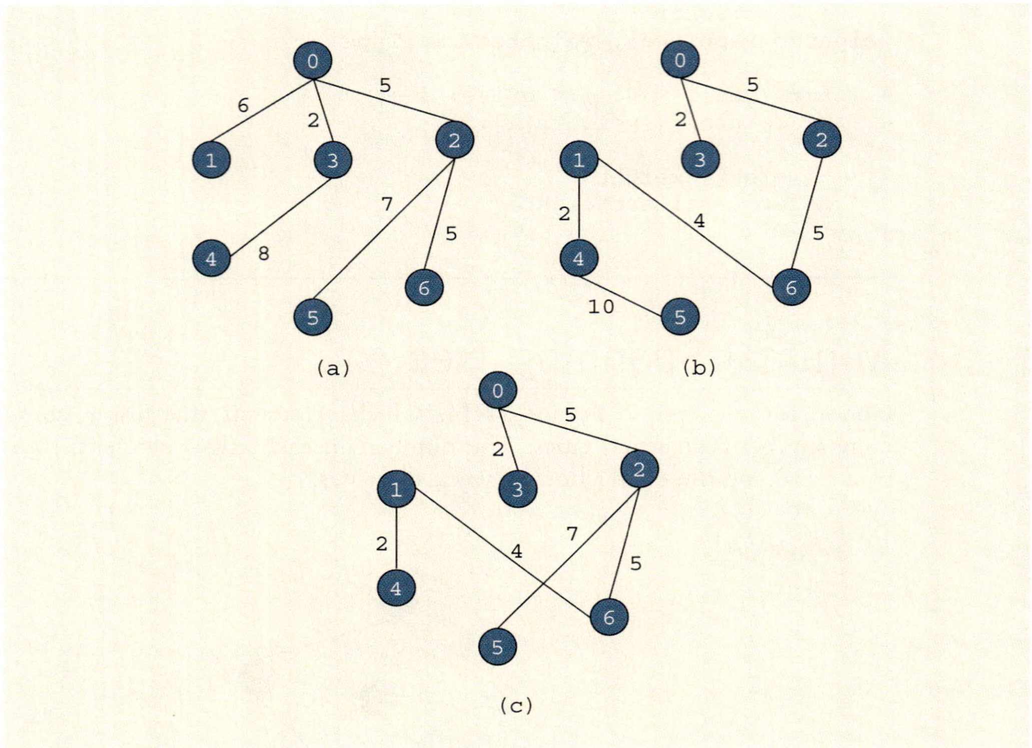

FIGURE 21-15 Possible solutions to the graph of Figure 21-14

The total cost factor of maintaining the remaining connections in Figure 21-15(a) is 33, in Figure 21-15(b) it is 28, and in Figure 21-15(c) it is 25. Out of these three solutions, obviously, the desired solution is the one shown by the graph of Figure 21-15(c) because it gives the lowest cost factor. The graphs of Figure 21-15 are called spanning trees of the graph of Figure 21-14.

Let us note the following from the graphs of Figure 21-15. Each of the graphs is a subgraph of the graph of Figure 21-14, and there is a unique path from a node to any other node. Such graphs are called trees. There are many other situations where, given a weighted graph, we need to determine a graph with the smallest weight, such as in Figure 21-15. In this section, we give an algorithm to determine such graphs. However, first we introduce some terminology.

A (**free**) **tree** T is a simple graph such that if u and v are two vertices in T, then there is a unique path from u to v. A tree in which a particular vertex is designated as a root is called a **rooted tree**. If a weight is assigned to the edges in T, T is called a **weighted tree**. If T is a weighted tree, the **weight** of T, denoted by $W(T)$, is the sum of the weights of all the edges in T.

A tree T is called a **spanning tree** of graph G if T is a subgraph of G such that $V(T) = V(G)$, that is, all the vertices of G are in T.

Suppose G denotes the graph of Figure 21-14. Then, the graphs of Figure 21-15 show three spanning trees of G. Let us note the following theorem.

Theorem: A graph G has a spanning tree if and only if G is connected.

From this theorem, it follows that in order to determine a spanning tree of a graph, the graph must be connected.

Let G be a weighted graph. A **minimal spanning tree** of G is a spanning tree with the minimum weight.

Prim's algorithm and Kruskal's algorithm are two well-known algorithms that can be used to find the minimal spanning tree of a graph. This section discusses Prim's algorithm to find a minimal spanning tree. The interested reader can find the Kruskal's algorithm in the discrete structures book or a data structures book listed in Appendix H.

Prim's algorithm builds the tree iteratively by adding edges until a minimal spanning tree is obtained. We start with a designated vertex, which we call the source vertex. At each iteration, a new edge that does not complete a cycle is added to the tree.

Let G be a weighted graph such that $V(G) = \{v_0, v_1, \ldots, v_{n-1}\}$, where n, the number of vertices, is positive. Let v_0 be the source vertex. Let T be the partially built tree. Initially, $V(T)$ contains the source vertex and $E(T)$ is empty. At the next iteration, a new vertex that is not in $V(T)$ is added to $V(T)$, such that an edge exists from a vertex in T to the new vertex so that the corresponding edge has the smallest weight. The corresponding edge is added to $E(T)$.

The general form of Prim's algorithm is as follows. (Let n be the number of vertices in G.)

1. Set V(T) = {source}

2. Set E(T) = empty

3. `for i = 1 to n`

    3.1. `minWeight = infinity;`

    3.2. `for j = 1 to n`

```
         if vj is in V(T)
            for k = 1 to n
               if vk is not in T and weight[vj, vk] < minWeight
               {
                   endVertex = vk;
                   edge = (vj, vk);
                   minWeight = weight[vj, vk];
               }
```

    3.3. `V(T) = V(T) ∪ {endVertex};`

    3.4. `E(T) = E(T) ∪ {edge};`

Let us illustrate Prim's algorithm using the graph G of Figure 21–16 (which is same as the graph of Figure 21–14).

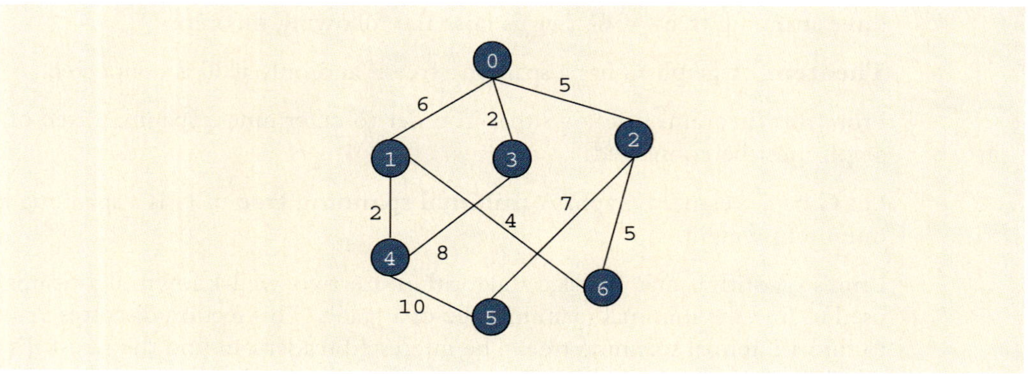

FIGURE 21-16 Weighted graph G

Let N denote the set of vertices of G that are not in T. Suppose that the source vertex is 0. After Steps 1 and 2 execute, $V(T)$, $E(T)$, and N are as shown in Figure 21–17.

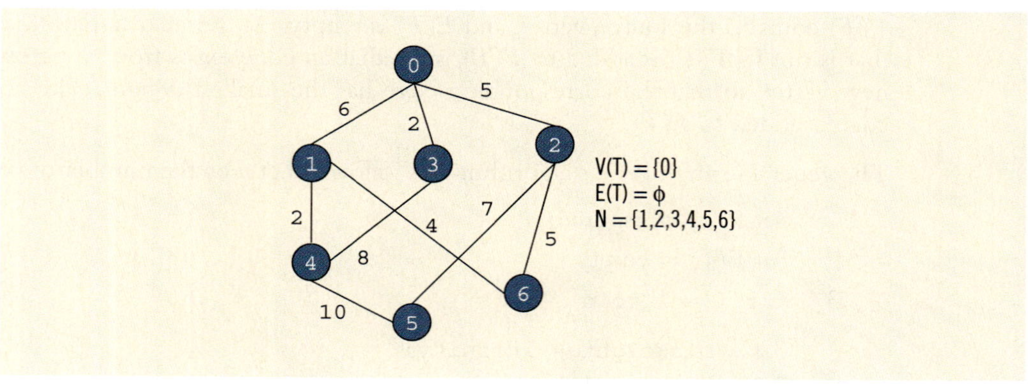

FIGURE 21-17 Graph G, $V(T)$, $E(T)$, and N after Steps 1 and 2 execute

Step 3.2 checks the following edges:

Edge	Weight of the Edge
(0,1)	6
(0,2)	5
(0,3)	2

Clearly, the edge $(0,3)$ has the smallest weight. Therefore, vertex 3 is added to $V(T)$ and the edge $(0,3)$ is added to $E(T)$. Figure 21–18 shows the resulting graph, $V(T)$, $E(T)$, and N. (The dotted line shows the edge in T.)

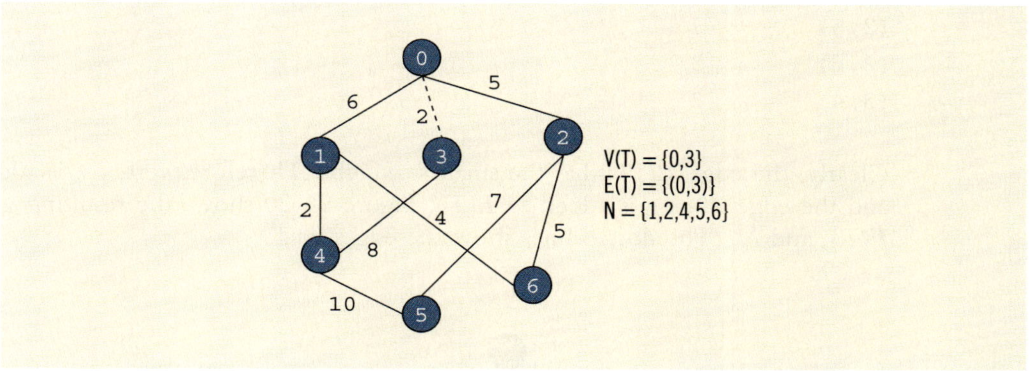

FIGURE 21-18 Graph G, $V(T)$, $E(T)$, and N after the first iteration of Step 3

Next, Step 3.2 checks the following edges:

Edge	Weight of the Edge
(0,1)	6
(0,2)	5
(3,4)	8

Clearly, the edge $(0,2)$ has the smallest weight. Therefore, vertex 2 is added to $V(T)$ and the edge $(0,2)$ is added to $E(T)$. Figure 21–19 shows the resulting graph, $V(T)$, $E(T)$, and N.

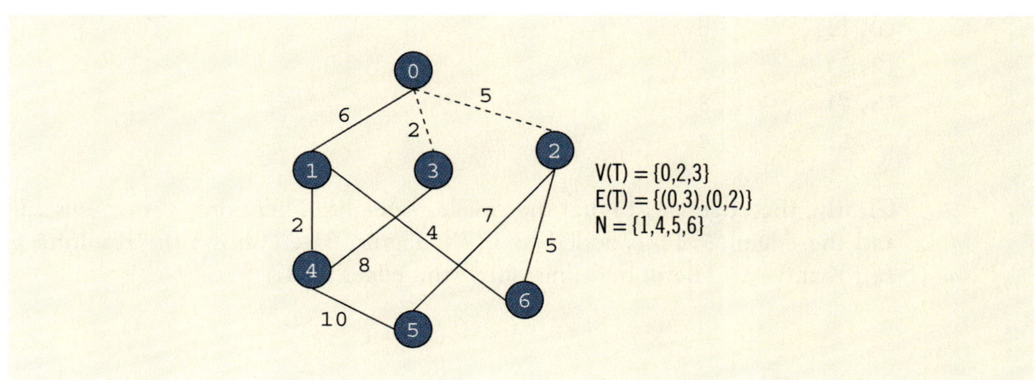

FIGURE 21-19 Graph G, $V(T)$, $E(T)$, and N after the second iteration of Step 3

At the next iteration, Step 3.2 checks the following edges:

Edge	Weight of the Edge
(0,1)	6
(2,5)	7
(2,6)	5
(3,4)	8

Clearly, the edge (2,6) has the smallest weight. Therefore, vertex 6 is added to $V(T)$ and the edge (2,6) is added to $E(T)$. Figure 21-20 shows the resulting graph, $V(T)$, $E(T)$, and N. (The dotted lines show the edges in T.)

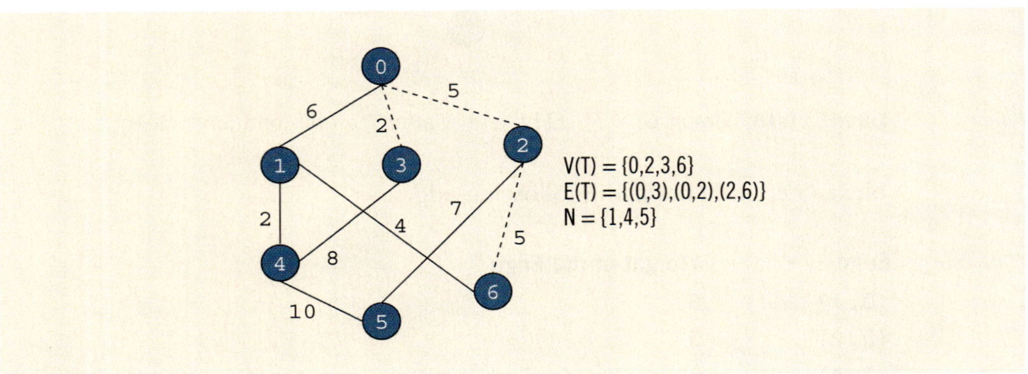

FIGURE 21-20 Graph *G*, *V(T)*, *E(T)*, and *N* after the third iteration of Step 3

At the next iteration, Step 3.2 checks the following edges:

Edge	Weight of the Edge
(0,1)	6
(2,5)	7
(3,4)	8
(6,1)	4

Clearly, the edge (6,1) has the smallest weight. Therefore, vertex 1 is added to $V(T)$ and the edge (6,1) is added to $E(T)$. Figure 21-21 shows the resulting graph, $V(T)$, $E(T)$, and N. (The dotted lines show the edges in T.)

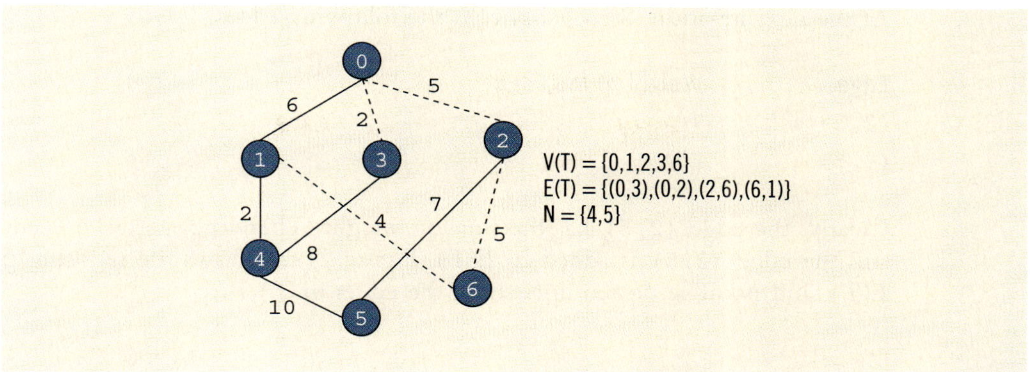

FIGURE 21-21   Graph *G*, *V*(*T*), *E*(*T*), and *N* after the fourth iteration of Step 3

At the next iteration, Step 3.2 checks the following edges:

Edge	Weight of the Edge
(1,4)	2
(2,5)	7
(3,4)	8

Clearly, the edge (1,4) has the smallest weight. Therefore, vertex 4 is added to *V*(*T*) and the edge (1,4) is added to *E*(*T*). Figure 21-22 shows the resulting graph, *V*(*T*), *E*(*T*), and *N*. (The dotted lines show the edges in *T*.)

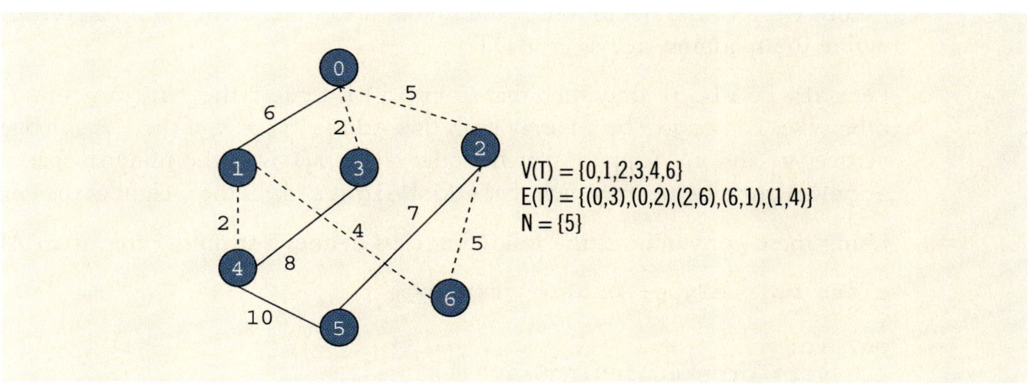

FIGURE 21-22   Graph *G*, *V*(*T*), *E*(*T*), and *N* after the fifth iteration of Step 3

At the next iteration, Step 3.2 checks the following edges:

Edge	Weight of the Edge
(2,5)	7
(4,5)	10

Clearly, the edge (2,5) has the smallest weight. Therefore, vertex 5 is added to $V(T)$ and the edge (2,5) is added to $E(T)$. Figure 21-23 shows the resulting graph, $V(T)$, $E(T)$, and N. (The dotted lines show the edges in T.)

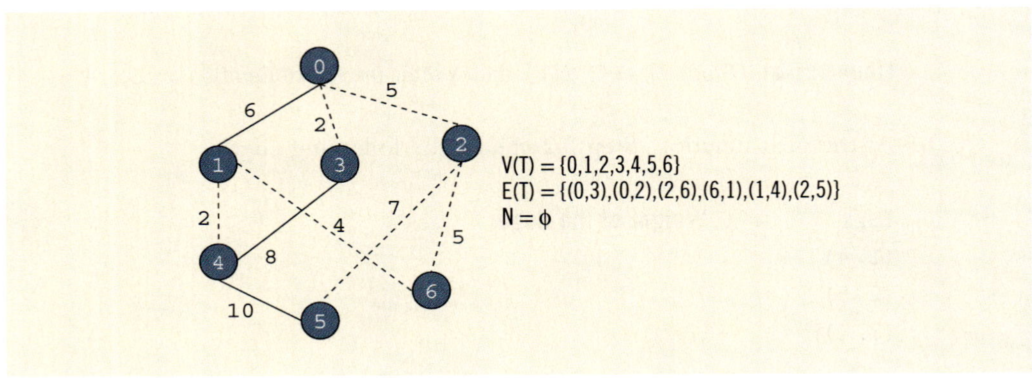

FIGURE 21-23 Graph G, $V(T)$, $E(T)$, and N after the sixth iteration of Step 3

The dotted lines show a minimal spanning tree of G of weight 25.

Before we give the definition of the function to implement Prim's algorithm, let us first define the spanning tree as an ADT.

Let `mstv` be a **bool** array such that `mstv [j]` is **true** if the vertex v_i is in T, and **false** otherwise. Let `edges` be an array such that `edges[j] = k`, if there is an edge connecting vertices v_j and v_k. Suppose that the edge (v_i, v_j) is in the minimal spanning tree. Let `edgeWeights` be an array such that `edgeWeights[j]` is the weight of the edge (v_i, v_j).

Using these conventions, the following class defines a spanning tree as an ADT:

```
class msTreeType: public graphType
{
public:
    void createSpanningGraph();
      //Function to create the graph and the weight matrix.
      //Postcondition: The graph using adjacency lists and
      //                its weight matrix is created.

    void minimalSpanning(int sVertex);
      //Function to create a minimal spanning tree with
      //root as sVertex.
```

```cpp
    // Postcondition: A minimal spanning tree is created.
    //                The weight of the edges is also
    //                saved in the array edgeWeights.

  void printTreeAndWeight();
    //Function to output the edges of the minimal
    //spanning tree and the weight of the minimal
    //spanning tree.
    //Postcondition: The edges of a minimal spanning tree
    //               and their weights are printed.

  msTreeType(int size = 0);
    //Constructor
    //Postcondition: gSize = 0; maxSize = size;
    //               graph is an array of pointers to linked
    //               lists.
    //               weights is a two-dimensional array to
    //               store the weights of the edges.
    //               edges is an array to store the edges
    //               of a minimal spanning tree.
    //               egdeWeight is an array to store the
    //               weights of the edges of a minimal
    //               spanning tree.

  ~msTreeType();
    //Destructor
    //The storage occupied by the vertices and the arrays
    //weights, edges, and edgeWeights is deallocated.

protected:
    int source;
    double **weights;
    int *edges;
    double *edgeWeights;
};
```

We leave the UML class diagram of the **class** `msTreeType` and the inheritance hierarchy
as an exercise. The definition of the function `createSpanningGraph` is also left as an
exercise for you. This function creates the graph and the weight matrix associated with
the graph.

The following C++ function, `minimalSpanning`, implements Prim's algorithm, as
described previously:

```cpp
void msTreeType::minimalSpanning(int sVertex)
{
    int startVertex, endVertex;
    double minWeight;

    source = sVertex;

    bool *mstv;
    mstv = new bool[gSize];
```

```cpp
    for (int j = 0; j < gSize; j++)
    {
        mstv[j] = false;
        edges[j] = source;
        edgeWeights[j] = weights[source][j];
    }

    mstv[source] = true;
    edgeWeights[source] = 0;

    for (int i = 0; i < gSize - 1; i++)
    {
        minWeight = DBL_MAX;

        for (int j = 0; j < gSize; j++)
            if (mstv[j])
                for (int k = 0; k < gSize; k++)
                    if (!mstv[k] && weights[j][k] < minWeight)
                    {
                        endVertex = k;
                        startVertex = j;
                        minWeight = weights[j][k];
                    }

        mstv[endVertex] = true;
        edges[endVertex] = startVertex;
        edgeWeights[endVertex] = minWeight;
    } //end for
} //end minimalSpanning
```

The definition of the function `minimalSpanning` contains three nested `for` loops. Therefore, in the worst case, Prim's algorithm given in this section is of the order $O(n^3)$. It is possible to design Prim's algorithm so that it is of the order $O(n^2)$; Programming Exercise 5 at the end of this chapter asks you to do this.

The definition of the function `printTreeAndWeight` is:

```cpp
void msTreeType::printTreeAndWeight()
{
    double treeWeight = 0;

    cout << "Source Vertex: " << source << endl;
    cout << "Edges    Weight" << endl;

    for (int j = 0; j < gSize; j++)
    {
        if (edges[j] != j)
        {
            treeWeight = treeWeight + edgeWeights[j];
            cout << "("<<edges[j] << ", " << j << ")       "
                 << edgeWeights[j] << endl;
        }

    }
```

```cpp
    cout << endl;
    cout << "Minimal Spanning Tree Weight: "
         << treeWeight << endl;
} //end printTreeAndWeight
```

The definitions of the constructor and the destructor are as follows:

```cpp
msTreeType::msTreeType(int size)
          :graphType(size)
{
    weights = new double*[size];

    for (int i = 0; i < size; i++)
        weights[i] = new double[size];

    edges  = new int[size];

    edgeWeights = new double[size];
}


    //Destructor
msTreeType::~msTreeType()
{
    for (int i = 0; i < gSize; i++)
        delete [] weights[i];

    delete [] weights;
    delete [] edges;
    delete edgeWeights;
}
```

NOTE **(Topological Ordering)** This chapter also discusses topological ordering. The necessary material is in the file TopologicalOrder.pdf. This file is on the Web site accompanying this book.

QUICK REVIEW

1. A graph G is a pair, $G = (V, E)$, where V is a finite nonempty set, called the set of vertices of G, and $E \subseteq V \times V$, called the set of edges.

2. In an undirected graph $G = (V, E)$, the elements of E are unordered pairs.

3. In a directed graph $G = (V, E)$, the elements of E are ordered pairs.

4. Let G be a graph. A graph H is called a subgraph of G if every vertex of H is a vertex of G and every edge in H is an edge in G.

5. Two vertices u and v in an undirected graph are called adjacent if there is an edge from one to the other.

6. Let $e = (u, v)$ be an edge in an undirected graph G. The edge e is said to be incident on the vertices u and v.

7. An edge incident on a single vertex is called a loop.

8. In an undirected graph, if two edges e_1 and e_2 are associated with the same pair of vertices, then e_1 and e_2 are called parallel edges.

9. A graph is called a simple graph if it has no loops and no parallel edges.

10. A path from a vertex u to a vertex v is a sequence of vertices $u_1, u_2, \ldots, u_n$ such that $u = u_1$, $u_n = v$, and (u_i, u_{i+1}) is an edge for all $i = 1, 2, \ldots, n-1$.

11. The vertices u and v are called connected if there is a path from u to v.

12. A simple path is a path in which all the vertices, except possibly the first and last vertices, are distinct.

13. A cycle in G is a simple path in which the first and last vertices are the same.

14. An undirected graph G is called connected if there is a path from any vertex to any other vertex.

15. A maximal subset of connected vertices is called a component of G.

16. Suppose that u and v are vertices in a directed graph G. If there is an edge from u to v, that is, $(u, v) \in E$, we say that u is adjacent to v and v is adjacent from u.

17. A directed graph G is called strongly connected if any two vertices in G are connected.

18. Let G be a graph with n vertices, where $n > 0$. Let $V(G) = \{v_1, v_2, \ldots, v_n\}$. The adjacency matrix A_G is a two-dimensional $n \times n$ matrix such that the (i, j)th entry of A_G is 1 if there is an edge from v_i to v_j; otherwise, the (i, j)th entry is zero.

19. In an adjacency list representation, corresponding to each vertex v is a linked list such that each node of the linked list contains the vertex u, and $(v, u) \in E(G)$.

20. The depth first traversal of a graph is similar to the preorder traversal of a binary tree.

21. The breadth first traversal of a graph is similar to the level-by-level traversal of a binary tree.

22. The shortest path algorithm gives the shortest distance for a given node to every other node in the graph.

23. In a weighted graph, every edge has a non-negative weight.

24. The weight of the path P is the sum of the weights of all the edges on the path P, which is also called the weight of v from u via P.

25. A (free) tree T is a simple graph such that if u and v are two vertices in T, there is a unique path from u to v.

26. A tree in which a particular vertex is designated as a root is called a rooted tree.

27. Suppose *T* is a tree. If a weight is assigned to the edges in *T*, *T* is called a weighted tree.

28. If *T* is a weighted tree, the weight of *T*, denoted by $W(T)$, is the sum of the weights of all the edges in *T*.

29. A tree *T* is called a spanning tree of graph *G* if *T* is a subgraph of *G* such that $V(T) = V(G)$, that is, if all the vertices of *G* are in *T*.

EXERCISES

Use the graph in Figure 21-24 for Exercises 1 through 4.

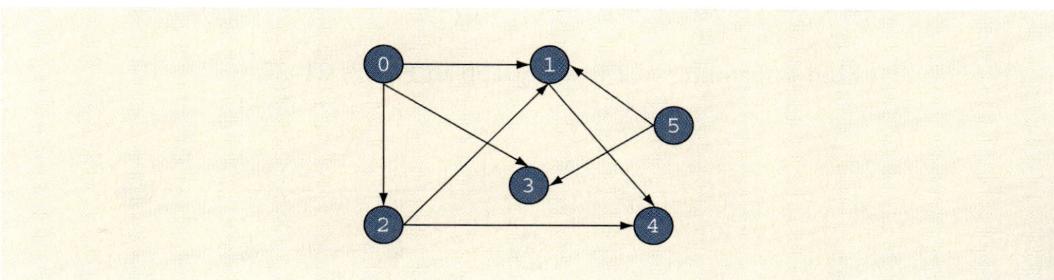

FIGURE 21-24 Graph for Exercises 1 through 4

1. Find the adjacency matrix of the graph.
2. Draw the adjacency list of the graph.
3. List the nodes of the graph in a depth first traversal.
4. List the nodes of the graph in a breadth first traversal.
5. Find the weight matrix of the graph in Figure 21-25.

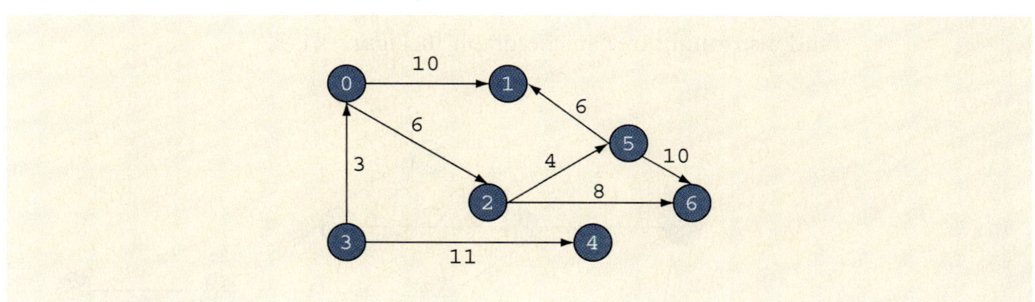

FIGURE 21-25 Graph for Exercise 5

6. Consider the graph in Figure 21-26. Find the shortest distance from node 0 to every other node in the graph.

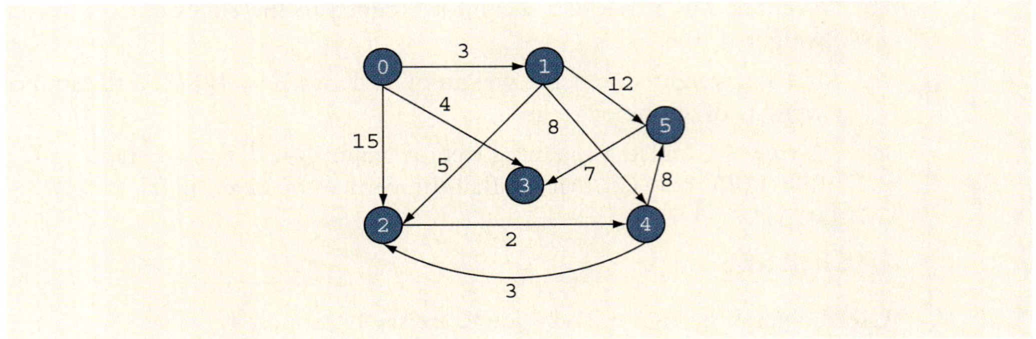

FIGURE 21-26 Graph for Exercise 6

7. Find a spanning tree in the graph in Figure 21-27.

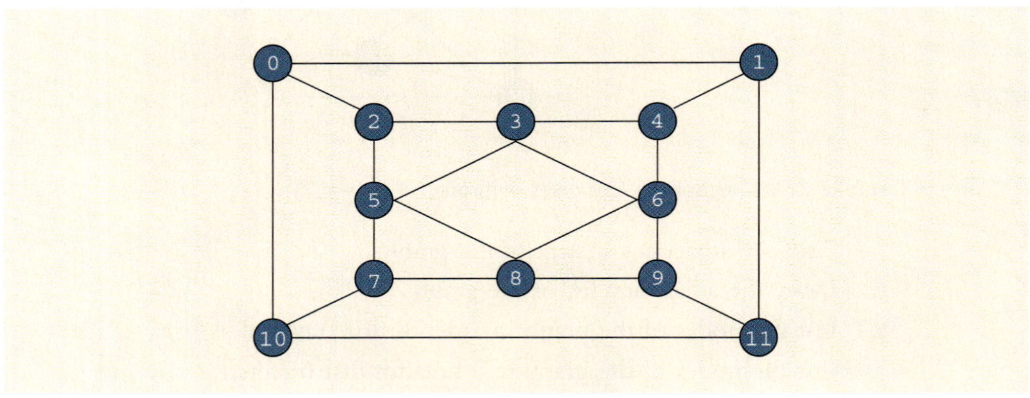

FIGURE 21-27 Graph for Exercise 7

8. Find a spanning tree in the graph in Figure 21-28.

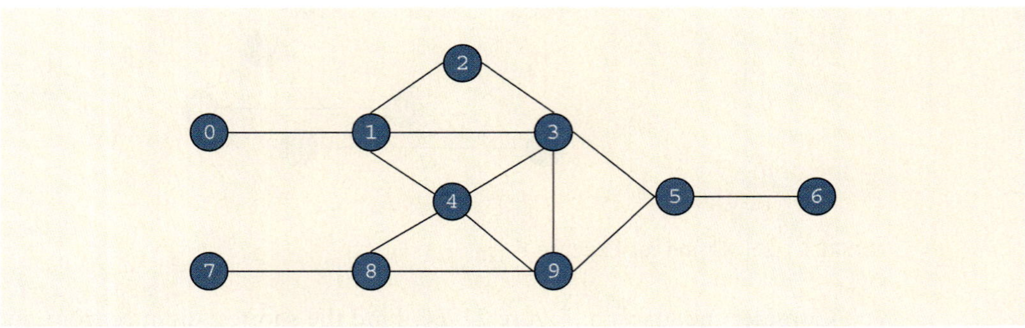

FIGURE 21-28 Graph for Exercise 8

9. Find the minimal spanning tree for the graph in Figure 21-29, using the algorithm given in this chapter.

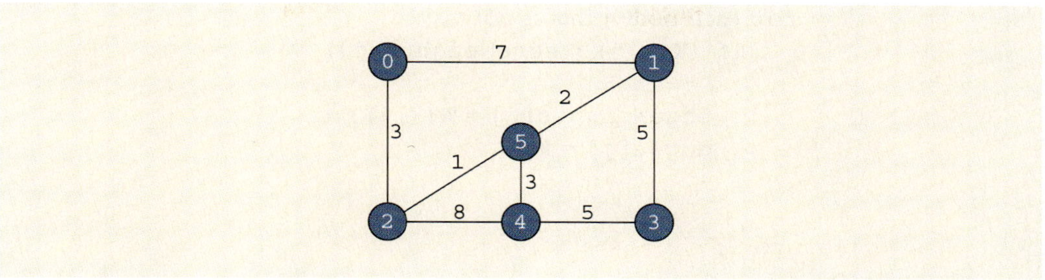

FIGURE 21-29 Graph for Exercise 9

PROGRAMMING EXERCISES

1. Write a program that outputs the nodes of a graph in a depth first traversal.

2. Write a program that outputs the nodes of a graph in a breadth first traversal.

3. Write a program that outputs the shortest distance from a given node to every other node in the graph.

4. Write a program that outputs the minimal spanning tree for a given graph.

5. The algorithm to determine the minimal spanning tree given in this chapter is of the order $O(n^3)$. The following is an alternative to Prim's algorithm that is of the order $O(n^2)$.

Input: A connected weighted graph $G = (V, E)$ of n vertices, numbered $0, 1, \ldots, n - 1$; starting with vertex s, with a weight matrix of W

Output: The minimal spanning tree

```
Prim2 (G, W, n, s)
Let T = (V, E), where E = φ.
for (j = 0; j < n; j++)
{
    edgeWeights[j] = W(s,j);
    edges[j] = s;
    visited[s] = false;
}
edgeWeights[s] = 0;
visited[s] = true;
while (not all nodes are visited)
{
    Choose the node that is not visited and has the smallest weight, and call it k.
```

```
    visited[k] = true;
    E = E ∪ {(k, edges[k])}
    V = V ∪ {k}
    for each node j that is not visited
        if (W(k,j) < edgeWeights[j])
        {
           edgeWeights[j] = W(k,j);
           edges[j] = k;
        }
}
return T;
```

Write a definition of the function `Prim2` to implement this algorithm, and also add this function to the `class msTreeType`. Furthermore, write a program to test this version of Prim's algorithm.

STANDARD TEMPLATE LIBRARY (STL)

IN THIS CHAPTER, YOU WILL:

- Learn about the Standard Template Library (STL)
- Become familiar with the three basic components of the STL: containers, iterators, and algorithms
- Explore how various containers are used to manipulate data in a program
- Learn how iterators are used
- Learn about various generic algorithms

Chapter 14 introduced and examined templates in detail. With the help of class templates, we developed (and used) a generic code to process lists. For example, we used the `class listType` to process a list of integers and a list of strings. In Chapters 17 and 18, we studied the three most important data structures: linked lists, stacks, and queues. In these chapters, using class templates, we developed generic code to process linked lists. In addition, using the second principle of object-oriented programming (OOP), we developed generic code to process ordered lists. Furthermore, in Chapter 18, we used class templates to develop generic code to implement stacks and queues. Along the way, you saw that a template is a powerful tool that promotes code reuse.

ANSI/ISO Standard C++ is equipped with a Standard Template Library (STL). Among other things, the STL provides class templates to process lists (contiguous or linked), stacks, and queues. This chapter discusses many important features of the STL and shows how to use the tools provided by the STL in a program.

Components of the STL

The main objective of a program is to manipulate data and generate results. Achieving this goal requires the ability to store data into computer memory, access a particular piece of data, and write algorithms to manipulate the data.

For example, if all data items are of the same type and we have some idea of the number of data items, we could use an array to store the data. We can then use an index to access a particular component of the array. Using a loop and the array index, we can step through the elements of the array. Algorithms, such as those for initializing the array, sorting, and searching, are used to manipulate the data stored in an array. On the other hand, if we do not want to be concerned about the size of the data, we can use a linked list to process it. If the data needs to be processed in a Last In First Out (LIFO) manner, we can use a stack. Similarly, if the data needs to be processed in a First In First Out (FIFO) manner, we can use a queue.

The STL is equipped with these features to effectively manipulate data. More formally, the STL has three main components:

- Containers
- Iterators
- Algorithms

Containers and iterators are class templates. Iterators are used to step through the elements of a container. Algorithms are used to manipulate data. The following sections discuss each of these components in detail.

Container Types

Containers are used to manage objects of a given type. The STL containers are classified into three categories, as follows:

- Sequence containers (also called sequential containers)
- Associative containers
- Container adapters

Sequence Containers

Every object in a sequence container has a specific position. The three predefined sequence containers are:

- vector
- deque
- list

Before discussing container types in general, let us first briefly describe the sequence container `vector`. We do so because vector containers are similar to arrays and thus can be processed like arrays. Also, with the help of vector, containers we can describe several properties that are common to all containers. In fact, all containers use the same names for the common operations. Of course, there are operations that are specific to a container, which will be discussed when describing a specific container.

Sequence Container: `vector`

A vector container stores and manages its objects in a dynamic array. Because an array is a random access data structure, the elements of a vector can be accessed randomly. Item insertion in the middle or beginning of an array is time-consuming, especially if the array is large. However, inserting an item at the end is quite fast.

The name of the class that implements the vector container is `vector`. (Recall that containers are class templates.) The name of the header file containing the `class vector` is `vector`. Thus, to use a vector container in a program, the program must include the following statement:

```
#include <vector>
```

Furthermore, to define an object of type `vector`, we must specify the type of the object because the `class vector` is a class template. For example, the statement:

```
vector<int> intList;
```

declares `intList` to be a vector and the component type to be `int`. Similarly, the statement:

```
vector<string> stringList;
```

declares `stringList` to be a vector container and the component type to be `string`.

DECLARING VECTOR OBJECTS

The **class** vector contains several constructors, including the default constructor. Therefore, a vector container can be declared and initialized several ways. Table 22-1 describes how a vector container of a specific type can be declared and initialized.

TABLE 22-1 Various Ways to Declare and Initialize a Vector Container

Statement	Effect
`vector<elemType> vecList;`	Creates the empty vector container `vecList`. (The default constructor is invoked.)
`vector<elemType> vecList(otherVecList);`	Creates the vector container `vecList` and initializes `vecList` to the elements of the vector `otherVecList`. `vecList` and `otherVecList` are of the same type.
`vector<elemType> vecList(size);`	Creates the vector container `vecList` of size `size`. `vecList` is initialized using the default constructor.
`vector<elemType> vecList(n, elm);`	Creates the vector container `vecList` of size n. `vecList` is initialized using n copies of the element `elm`.
`vector<elemType> vecList(beg, end);`	Creates the vector container `vecList`. `vecList` is initialized to the elements in the range `[beg, end)`, that is, all the elements in the range `beg...end-1`. Both `beg` and `end` are pointers, called iterators in STL terminology. (Later in this chapter, we explain how iterators are used.)

Now that we know how to declare a vector sequence container, let us discuss how to manipulate the data stored in a vector container. In order to manipulate the data in a vector container, we must know the following basic operations:

- Item insertion
- Item deletion
- Stepping through the elements of a vector container

The elements in a vector container can be accessed directly by using the operations given in Table 22-2. The name of the function is shown in bold.

TABLE 22-2 Operations to Access the Elements of a Vector Container

Expression	Description
`vecList.at(index)`	Returns the element at the position specified by `index`.
`vecList[index]`	Returns the element at the position specified by `index`.
`vecList.front()`	Returns the first element. (Does not check whether the container is empty.)
`vecList.back()`	Returns the last element. (Does not check whether the container is empty.)

From Table 22-2, it follows that the elements in a vector can be processed just as they can in an array. See Example 22-1. (Recall that in C++, arrays start at location 0. Similarly, the first element in a vector container is at location 0.)

EXAMPLE 22-1

Consider the following statement, which declares `intList` to be a vector container of size 5 and the element type is `int`:

```
vector<int> intList(5);
```

You can use a loop, such as the following, to store elements into `intList`:

```
for (int j = 0; j < 5; j++)
    intList[j] = j;
```

Similarly, you can use a `for` loop to output the elements of `intList`.

The **class** vector also contains member functions that can be used to find the number of elements currently in the container, the maximum number of elements that can be inserted into a container, and so on. Table 22-3 describes some of these operations. The name of the function is shown in bold. (Suppose that vecCont is a vector container.)

TABLE 22-3 Operations to Determine the Size of a Vector Container

Expression	Description
vecCont.**capacity**()	Returns the maximum number of elements that can be inserted into the container vecCont without reallocation.
vecCont.**empty**()	Returns **true** if the container vecCont is empty, **false** otherwise.
vecCont.**size**()	Returns the number of elements currently in the container vecCont.
vecCont.**max_size**()	Returns the maximum number of elements that can be inserted into the container vecCont.

The **class** vector also contains member functions that can be used to manipulate the data, as well as insert and delete items, in a vector container. Suppose that vecList is a container of type vector. Item insertion and deletion in vecList are accomplished using the operations given in Table 22-4. These operations are implemented as member functions of the **class** vector and are shown in bold. Table 22-4 also shows how these operations are used.

TABLE 22-4 Various Operations on a Vector Container

Statement	Effect
`vecList.clear()`	Deletes all the elements from the container.
`vecList.erase(position)`	Deletes the element at the position specified by `position`.
`vecList.erase(beg, end)`	Deletes all the elements starting at `beg` until `end-1`.
`vecList.insert(position, elem)`	A copy of `elem` is inserted at the position specified by `position`. The position of the new element is returned.
`vecList.insert(position, n, elem)`	n copies of `elem` are inserted at the position specified by `position`.
`vecList.insert(position, beg, end)`	A copy of the elements, starting at `beg` until `end-1`, is inserted into `vecList` at the position specified by `position`.
`vecList.push_back(elem)`	A copy of `elem` is inserted into `vecList` at the end.
`vecList.pop_back()`	Deletes the last element.
`vecList.resize(num)`	Changes the number of elements to `num`. If `size()` increases, the default constructor creates the new elements.
`vecList.resize(num, elem)`	Changes the number of elements to `num`. If `size()` increases, the new elements are copies of `elem`.

NOTE   In Table 22-4, the identifiers `position`, `beg`, and `end` in STL terminology are called iterators. An iterator is just like a pointer. In general, iterators are used to step through the elements of a container. In other words, with the help of an iterator, we can walk through the elements of a container and process them one at a time. Because iterators are an integral part of the STL, they are discussed in the section "Iterators" located later in this chapter.

Example 22-1 used a `for` loop and the array subscripting operator, `[]`, to access the elements of `intList`. We declare `intList` to be a vector object of size 5. Does this mean that we can store only five elements in `intList`? The answer is no. We can, in fact, add more elements to `intList`. However, because when we declared `intList` we specified the size to be 5, in order to add elements past position 4, we use the function `push_back`. Furthermore, if we initially declare a vector object and do not specify its size, then to add elements to the vector object we use the function `push_back`. Example 22-2 explains how to use the function `push_back`.

EXAMPLE 22-2

The following statement declares `intList` to be a vector object of size 0:

```
vector<int> intList;
```

To add elements to `intList`, we can use the function `push_back` as follows:

```
intList.push_back(34);
intList.push_back(55);
```

After these statements execute, the size of `intList` is 2 and:

```
intList = {34, 55}
```

In Example 22-2, because `intList` is declared to be of size 0, we use the function `push_back` to add elements to `intList`. However, we can also use the `resize` function to increase the size of `intList` and then use the array subscripting operator. For example, suppose that `intList` is declared as in Example 22-2. Then, the following statement sets the size of `intList` to 10:

```
intList.resize(10);
```

Similarly, the following statement increases the size of `intList` by 10:

```
intList.resize(intList.size() + 10);
```

However, at times, the `push_back` function is more convenient because it does not need to know the size of the vector; it simply adds the elements at the end.

Next, we describe how to declare an iterator in a vector container.

DECLARING AN ITERATOR TO A VECTOR CONTAINER

The `class` vector contains a `typedef` iterator, which is declared as a `public` member. An iterator to a vector container is declared using the `typedef` iterator. For example, the statement:

```
vector<int>::iterator intVecIter;
```

declares `intVecIter` to be an iterator in a vector container of type `int`.

Because `iterator` is a **typedef** defined inside the **class** vector, we must use the container name (which is `vector`), the container element type, and the scope resolution operator to use the **typedef** `iterator`.

The expression:

```
++intVecIter
```

advances the iterator `intVecIter` to the next element in the container, and the expression:

```
*intVecIter
```

returns the element at the current iterator position.

Note that these operations are the same as the operations on pointers, discussed in Chapter 13. Recall that when used as a unary operator, `*` is called the dereferencing operator.

We now discuss how to use an iterator in a vector container to manipulate the data stored in the vector container.

Suppose that we have the following statements:

```
vector<int> intList;                //Line 1
vector<int>::iterator intVecIter;   //Line 2
```

The statement in Line 1 declares `intList` to be a vector container, and the element type is `int`. The statement in Line 2 declares `intVecIter` to be an iterator in a vector container whose element type is `int`.

CONTAINERS AND THE FUNCTIONS `begin` AND `end`

Every container has the member functions **begin** and **end**. The function `begin` returns the position of the first element in the container; the function `end` returns the position of one past the last element in the container. Also, these functions have no parameters.

After the following statement executes:

```
intVecIter = intList.begin();
```

the iterator `intVecIter` points to the first element in the container `intList`.

The following **for** loop outputs the elements of `intList` to the standard output device:

```
for (intVecIter = intList.begin(); intVecIter != intList.end();
                        ++intVecIter)
    cout << *intVecIter << " ";
```

Example 22-3 shows how the function `insert` works with vector objects.

EXAMPLE 22-3

Consider the following statements:

```cpp
int intArray[7] = {1, 3, 5, 7, 9, 11, 13};      //Line 1
vector<int> vecList(intArray, intArray + 7};    //Line 2
vector<int>::iterator intVecIter;               //Line 3
```

The statement in Line 2 declares and initializes the vector container `vecList`. Now consider the following statements:

```cpp
intVecIter = vecList.begin();           //Line 4
++intVecIter;                           //Line 5
vecList.insert(intVecIter, 22);         //Line 6
```

The statement in Line 4 initializes the iterator `intVecIter` to the first element of `vecList`; the statement in Line 5 advances `intVecIter` to the second element of `vecList`. The statement in Line 6 inserts 22 at the position specified by `intVecIter`. After the statement in Line 6 executes, `vecList = {1, 22, 3, 5, 7, 9, 11, 13}`. Notice that the size of the container also increases.

The following example illustrates how to use a vector container in a program and how to process the elements in a vector container.

EXAMPLE 22-4

```cpp
#include <iostream>
#include <vector>

using namespace std;

int main()
{
    vector<int> intList;                        //Line 1
    int i;                                      //Line 2

    intList.push_back(13);                      //Line 3
    intList.push_back(75);                      //Line 4
    intList.push_back(28);                      //Line 5
    intList.push_back(35);                      //Line 6

    cout << "Line 7: List elements: ";          //Line 7
    for (i = 0; i < 4; i++)                      //Line 8
        cout << intList[i] << " ";              //Line 9
    cout << endl;                               //Line 10

    for (i = 0; i < 4; i++)                      //Line 11
        intList[i] *= 2;                        //Line 12
```

```cpp
    cout << "Line 13: List elements: ";          //Line 13
    for (i = 0; i < 4; i++)                       //Line 14
        cout << intList[i] << " ";                //Line 15
    cout << endl;                                 //Line 16

    vector<int>::iterator listIt;                 //Line 17

    cout << "Line 18: List elements: ";           //Line 18
    for (listIt = intList.begin();
            listIt != intList.end(); ++listIt)    //Line 19
        cout << *listIt << " ";                   //Line 20
    cout << endl;                                 //Line 21

    listIt = intList.begin();                     //Line 22
    ++listIt;                                     //Line 23
    ++listIt;                                     //Line 24

        //Insert 88 at the position specified
        //by listIt
    intList.insert(listIt, 88);                   //Line 25

    cout << "Line 25: List elements: ";           //Line 26
    for (listIt = intList.begin();
            listIt != intList.end(); ++listIt)    //Line 27
        cout << *listIt << " ";                   //Line 28
    cout << endl;                                 //Line 29

    return 0;
}
```

Sample Run:

```
Line 7: List elements:  13 75 28 35
Line 13: List elements:  26 150 56 70
Line 18: List elements:  26 150 56 70
Line 25: List elements:  26 150 88 56 70
```

The statement in Line 1 declares a vector container (or vector for short), `intList`, of type `int`. The statement in Line 2 declares i to be an `int` variable. The statements in Lines 3 through 6 use the operation `push_back` to insert four numbers—13, 75, 28, and 35—into `intList`. The statements in Lines 8 and 9 use the `for` loop and the array subscripting operator, `[]`, to output the elements of `intList`. In the output, see the line marked Line 7, which contains the output of Lines 7 through 10. The statements in Lines 11 and 12 use a `for` loop to double the value of each element of `intList`; the statements in Lines 14 and 15 output the elements of `intList`. In the output, see the line marked Line 13, which contains the output of Lines 13 through 16.

The statement in Line 17 declares `listIt` to be a vector iterator that processes any vector container whose elements are of type `int`. Using the iterator `listIt`, the statements in Lines 19 and 20 output the elements of `intList`. After the statement in Line 22 executes, `listIt` points to the first element of `intList`. The statements in Lines 23 and 24 advance `listIt` twice; after these statements execute, `listIt` points to the third element of `intList`. The statement in Line 25 inserts 88 into `intList` at the position specified by the iterator `listIt`. Because `listIt` points to the component at position 2 (the third element of `intList`), 88 is inserted at position 2 in `intList`; that is, 88 becomes the third element of `intList`. The statements in Lines 27 and 28 output the modified `intList`.

Member Functions Common to All Containers

The previous section discussed vector containers. This section discusses operations that are common to all containers. For example, every container class has the default constructor, several constructors with parameters, the destructor, a function to insert an element into a container, and so on.

Recall that a class encapsulates data, and operations on that data, into a single unit. Because every container is a class, several operations are directly defined for a container and are provided as part of the definition of the class. Also, recall that the operations to manipulate the data are implemented with the help of functions and are called member functions of the class. Table 22-5 describes the member functions that are common to all containers; that is, these functions are included as members of the class template implementing the container.

Suppose `ct`, `ct1`, and `ct2` are containers of the same type. In Table 22-5, the name of the function is shown in bold. This table also shows how a function is called.

TABLE 22-5 Operations Common to All Containers

Member function	Description
Default constructor	Initializes the object to an empty state.
Constructor with parameters	In addition to the default constructor, every container has constructors with parameters. We will describe these constructors when we discuss a specific container.
Copy constructor	Executes when an object is passed as a parameter by value and when an object is declared and initialized using another object of the same type.
Destructor	Executes when the object goes out of scope.
`ct.empty()`	Returns `true` if container `ct` is empty, `false` otherwise.
`ct.size()`	Returns the number of elements currently in container `ct`.

TABLE 22-5 Operations Common to All Containers (continued)

Member function	Description
`ct.max_size()`	Returns the maximum number of elements that can be inserted in container `ct`.
`ct1.swap(ct2)`	Swaps the elements of containers `ct1` and `ct2`.
`ct.begin()`	Returns an iterator to the first element into container `ct`.
`ct.end()`	Returns an iterator to the position after the last element into container `ct`.
`ct.rbegin()`	Reverse begin. Returns a pointer to the last element into container `ct`. This function is used to process the elements of `ct` in reverse.
`ct.rend()`	Reverse end. Returns a pointer to the position before the first element into container `ct`.
`ct.insert(position,elem)`	Inserts `elem` into container `ct` at the position specified by `position`. Note that, here, `position` is an iterator.
`ct.erase(beg, end)`	Deletes all the elements between `beg...end−1` from container `ct`. Both `beg` and `end` are iterators.
`ct.clear()`	Deletes all the elements from the container. After a call to this function, container `ct` is empty.
Operator functions	
`ct1 = ct2;`	Copies the elements of `ct2` into `ct1`. After this operation, the elements in both containers are the same.
`ct1 == ct2`	Returns `true` if containers `ct1` and `ct2` are equal, `false` otherwise.
`ct1 != ct2`	Returns `true` if containers `ct1` and `ct2` are not equal, `false` otherwise.

NOTE Because these operations are common to all containers, when discussing a specific container, to save space, these operations will not be listed again.

Member Functions Common to Sequence Containers

The previous section described the member functions that are common to all containers. In addition to these member functions, Table 22-6 describes the member functions that are common to all sequence containers, that is, containers of type `vector`, `deque`, and `list`. The name of the function is shown in bold. (Suppose that `seqCont` is a sequence container.)

TABLE 22-6 Member Functions Common to All Sequence Containers

Expression	Description
seqCont.**insert**(position, elem)	A copy of `elem` is inserted at the position specified by the iterator `position`. The position of the new element is returned.
seqCont.**insert**(position, n, elem)	n copies of `elem` are inserted at the position specified by the iterator `position`.
seqCont.**insert**(position, beg, end)	A copy of the elements, starting at beg until end−1, are inserted into seqCont at the position specified by the iterator `position`. Also, beg and end are iterators.
seqCont.**push_back**(elem)	A copy of `elem` is inserted into seqCont at the end.
seqCont.**pop_back**()	Deletes the last element.
seqCont.**erase**(position)	Deletes the element at the position specified by the iterator `position`.
seqCont.**erase**(beg, end)	Deletes all the elements starting at beg until end−1. Both beg and end are iterators.
seqCont.**clear**()	Deletes all the elements from the container.
seqCont.**resize**(num)	Changes the number of elements to num. If `size()` grows, the new elements are created by their default constructor.
seqCont.**resize**(num, elem)	Changes the number of elements to num. If `size()` grows, the new elements are copies of `elem`.

The `copy` Algorithm

Example 22-4 used a `for` loop to output the elements of a vector container. The STL provides a convenient way to output the elements of a container with the help of the function `copy`. The function `copy` is provided as a part of the generic algorithm and can be used with any container type. Because we frequently need to output the elements of a container, before continuing with our discussion of containers, let us describe this function.

The function `copy` does more than output the elements of a container. In general, it allows us to copy the elements from one place to another. For example, to output the elements of a vector or to copy the elements of a vector into another vector, we can use the function `copy`. The prototype of the function template `copy` is:

```
template <class inputIterator, class outputIterator>
outputIterator copy(inputIterator first1, inputIterator last,
                    outputIterator first2);
```

The parameter `first1` specifies the position from which to begin copying the elements; the parameter `last` specifies the end position. The parameter `first2` specifies where to copy the elements. Therefore, the parameters `first1` and `last` specify the source; parameter `first2` specifies the destination.

Note that the elements within the range `first1...last-1` are copied.

The definition of the function template `copy` is contained in the header file `algorithm`. Thus, to use the function `copy`, the program must include the statement:

```
#include <algorithm>
```

The function `copy` works as follows. Consider the following statement:

```
int intArray[] = {5, 6, 8, 3, 40, 36, 98, 29, 75};
```

This statement creates an array `intArray` of nine components. Here, `intArray[0] = 5`, `intArray[1] = 6`, and so on.

The statement:

```
vector<int> vecList(9);
```

creates an empty container of nine components of type `vector` and the element type `int`.

Recall that the array name, `intArray`, is actually a pointer and contains the base address of the array. Therefore, `intArray` points to the first component of the array, `intArray + 1` points to the second component of the array, and so on.

Now consider the statement:

```
copy(intArray, intArray + 9, vecList.begin());
```

This statement copies the elements starting at the location `intArray`, which is the first component of the array `intArray`, until `intArray + 9 - 1` (that is, `intArray + 8`), which is the last element of the array `intArray`, into the container `vecList`. (Note that, here, `first1` is `intArray`, `last` is `intArray + 9`, and `first2` is `vecList.begin()`.) After the previous statement executes:

```
vecList = {5, 6, 8, 3, 40, 36, 98, 29, 75}
```

Next, consider the statement:

```
copy(intArray + 1, intArray + 9, intArray);
```

Here, `first1` is `intArray + 1`; that is, `first1` points to the location of the second element of the array `intArray`, and `last` is `intArray + 9`. Also, `first2` is `intArray`; that is, `first2` points to the location of the first element of the array `intArray`. Therefore, the second array element is copied into the first array component, the third array element into the second array component, and so on. After the preceding statement executes:

```
intArray = {6, 8, 3, 40, 36, 98, 29, 75, 75}
```

Clearly, the elements of the array `intArray` are shifted to the left by one position.

Now consider the statement:

```
copy(vecList.rbegin() + 2, vecList.rend(), vecList.rbegin());
```

Recall that the function `rbegin` (reverse begin) returns a pointer to the last element into a container; it is used to process the elements of a container in reverse. Therefore, `vecList.rbegin() + 2` returns a pointer to the third-to-last element into the container `vecList`. Similarly, the function `rend` (reverse end) returns a pointer to the first element into a container. The previous statement shifts the elements of the container `vecList` to the right by two positions. After the previous statement executes, the container `vecList` is:

```
vecList = {5, 6, 5, 6, 8, 3, 40, 36, 98}
```

Example 22-5 shows the effect of the preceding statements using a C++ program. Before discussing Example 22-5, let us describe a special type of iterators, called **ostream iterators**. These iterators work well with the function `copy` to copy the elements of a container to an output device.

THE `ostream` ITERATOR AND THE FUNCTION `copy`

One way to output the contents of a container is to use a **for** loop, the function `begin` to initialize the **for** loop control variable, and the function `end` to set the limit. Alternatively, the function `copy` can be used to output the elements of a container. In this case, an iterator of type `ostream` specifies the destination. (`ostream` iterators are discussed in detail later in this chapter.) When we create an iterator of type `ostream`, we also specify the type of element that the iterator will output.

The following statement illustrates how to create an `ostream` iterator of type **int**:

```
ostream_iterator<int> screen(cout, " ");        //Line A
```

This statement creates `screen` to be an `ostream` iterator with the element type `int`. The iterator `screen` has two arguments: the object `cout` and a space. Thus, the iterator `screen` is initialized using the object `cout`. When this iterator outputs elements, they are separated by a space.

The statement:

```
copy(intArray, intArray + 9, screen);
```

outputs the elements of `intArray` on the screen.

Similarly, the statement:

```
copy(vecList.begin(), vecList.end(), screen);
```

outputs the elements of the container `vecList` on the screen.

We will frequently use the function `copy` to output the elements of a container by using an `ostream` iterator. Also, until we discuss `ostream` iterators in detail, we will use statements similar to Line A to create an `ostream` iterator.

Of course, we can directly specify an `ostream` iterator in the function `copy`. For example, the statement (shown previously):

```
copy(vecList.begin(), vecList.end(), screen);
```

is equivalent to the statement:

```
copy(vecList.begin(), vecList.end(),
                ostream_iterator<int>(cout, " "));
```

Finally, the statement:

```
copy(vecList.begin(), vecList.end(),
                ostream_iterator<int>(cout, ", "));
```

outputs the elements of `vecList` with a comma and space between them.

Example 22-5 shows how to use the function `copy` and an ostream iterator in a program.

EXAMPLE 22-5

```cpp
#include <algorithm>
#include <vector>
#include <iterator>
#include <iostream>

using namespace std;

int main()
{
    int intArray[] = {5, 6, 8, 3, 40,
                    36, 98, 29, 75};            //Line 1
```

```cpp
    vector<int> vecList(9);                              //Line 2

    ostream_iterator<int> screen(cout, " ");             //Line 3

    cout << "Line 4: intArray: ";                        //Line 4
    copy(intArray, intArray + 9, screen);                //Line 5
    cout << endl;                                         //Line 6

    copy(intArray, intArray + 9, vecList.begin());       //Line 7

    cout << "Line 8: vecList: ";                         //Line 8
    copy(vecList.begin(), vecList.end(), screen);        //Line 9
    cout << endl;                                         //Line 10

    copy(intArray + 1, intArray + 9, intArray);          //Line 11

    cout << "Line 12: After shifting the elements "
         << "one position to the left, " << endl
         << "            intArray: ";                     //Line 12

    copy(intArray, intArray + 9, screen);                //Line 13

    cout << endl;                                         //Line 14

    copy(vecList.rbegin() + 2, vecList.rend(),
                              vecList.rbegin());          //Line 15
    cout << "Line 16: After shifting the elements "
         << "down by two positions, "<< endl
         << "            vecList: ";                      //Line 16

    copy(vecList.begin(), vecList.end(), screen);        //Line 17

    cout << endl;                                         //Line 18

    return 0;
}
```

Sample Run:

```
Line 4: intArray: 5 6 8 3 40 36 98 29 75
Line 8: vecList: 5 6 8 3 40 36 98 29 75
Line 12: After shifting the elements one position to the left,
        intArray: 6 8 3 40 36 98 29 75 75
Line 16: After shifting the elements down by two positions,
        vecList: 5 6 5 6 8 3 40 36 98
```

Sequence Container: `deque`

This section describes the **deque** sequence containers. The term `deque` stands for double-ended queue. Deque containers are implemented as dynamic arrays in such a way that the elements can be inserted at both ends. Thus, a `deque` can expand in either direction. Elements can also be inserted in the middle. Inserting elements in the beginning or at the end is fast; inserting elements in the middle, however, is time-consuming because the elements in the queue need to be shifted.

The name of the class defining the `deque` containers is `deque`. The definition of the `class` deque, and the functions to implement the various operations on a `deque` object, are also contained in the header file `deque`. Therefore, to use a `deque` container in a program, the program must include the following statement:

```
#include <deque>
```

The `class` deque contains several constructors. Thus, a `deque` object can be initialized in various ways when it is declared, as described in Table 22-7.

TABLE 22-7 Various Ways to Declare a `deque` Object

Statement	Description
`deque<elementType> deq;`	Creates an empty `deque` container deq. (The default constructor is invoked.)
`deque<elementType> deq(otherDeq);`	Creates the `deque` container deq and initializes it to the elements of `otherDeq`; deq and `otherDeq` are of the same type.
`deque<elementType> deq(size);`	Creates the `deque` container deq of size `size`. deq is initialized using the default constructor.
`deque<elementType> deq(n, elm);`	Creates the `deque` container deq of size n. deq is initialized using n copies of the element `elm`.
`deque<elementType> deq(beg, end);`	Creates the `deque` container deq. deq is initialized to the elements in the range `[beg, end)`, that is, all elements in the range `beg...end-1`. Both beg and end are iterators.

In addition to the operations that are common to all containers (Table 22-6), Table 22-8 describes the operations that can be used to manipulate the elements of a **deque** container. The name of the function implementing the operations is shown in bold. Each statement also shows how to use a particular function. Suppose that **deq** is a **deque** container.

TABLE 22-8 Various Operations that Can Be Performed on a deque Object

Expression	Description
deq.**assign**(n,elem)	Assigns n copies of **elem**.
deq.**assign**(beg, end)	Assigns all the elements in the range beg...end-1.
deq.**push_front**(elem)	Inserts **elem** at the beginning of **deq**.
deq.**pop_front**()	Removes the first element from **deq**.
deq.**at**(index)	Returns the element at the position specified by **index**.
deq[index]	Returns the element at the position specified by **index**.
deq.**front**()	Returns the first element. (Does not check whether the container is empty.)
deq.**back**()	Returns the last element. (Does not check whether the container is empty.)

Example 22-6 illustrates how to use a **deque** container in a program.

EXAMPLE 22-6

```cpp
//deque Example
#include <iostream>
#include <deque>
#include <algorithm>
#include <iterator>

using namespace std;
```

```cpp
int main()
{
    deque<int> intDeq;                                  //Line 1
    ostream_iterator<int> screen(cout, " ");            //Line 2

    intDeq.push_back(13);                               //Line 3
    intDeq.push_back(75);                               //Line 4
    intDeq.push_back(28);                               //Line 5
    intDeq.push_back(35);                               //Line 6

    cout << "Line 7: intDeq: ";                         //Line 7
    copy(intDeq.begin(), intDeq.end(), screen);         //Line 8
    cout << endl;                                        //Line 9

    intDeq.push_front(0);                               //Line 10
    intDeq.push_back(100);                              //Line 11

    cout << "Line 12: After adding two more "
         << "elements, one at the front " << endl
         << "              and one at the back, intDeq: "; //Line 12
    copy(intDeq.begin(), intDeq.end(), screen);         //Line 13
    cout << endl;                                        //Line 14

    intDeq.pop_front();                                 //Line 15
    intDeq.pop_front();                                 //Line 16

    cout << "Line 17: After removing the first "
         << "two elements, " << endl
         << "            intDeq: ";                     //Line 17
    copy(intDeq.begin(), intDeq.end(), screen);         //Line 18
    cout << endl;                                        //Line 19

    intDeq.pop_back();                                  //Line 20
    intDeq.pop_back();                                  //Line 21

    cout << "Line 22: After removing the last "
         << "two elements, " << endl
         << "            intDeq = ";                    //Line 22
    copy(intDeq.begin(), intDeq.end(), screen);         //Line 23
    cout << endl;                                        //Line 24

    deque<int>::iterator  deqIt;                        //Line 25

    deqIt = intDeq.begin();                             //Line 26
    ++deqIt;                      //deqIt points to the
                                  //second element      //Line 27

    intDeq.insert(deqIt, 444);    //Insert 444 at the
                                  //location deqIt       //Line 28
```

```cpp
    cout << "Line 29: After inserting 444, "
         << "intDeq:   ";                                //Line 29
    copy(intDeq.begin(), intDeq.end(), screen);          //Line 30
    cout << endl;                                         //Line 31

    intDeq.assign(2, 45);                                //Line 32

    cout << "Line 33: After assigning two "
         << "copies of 45, intDeq: ";                    //Line 33
    copy(intDeq.begin(), intDeq.end(), screen);          //Line 34
    cout << endl;                                         //Line 35

    intDeq.push_front(-10);                              //Line 36
    intDeq.push_back(-999);                              //Line 37

    cout << "Line 38: After inserting two "
         << "elements, one at the front " << endl
         << "            and one at the back, intDeq: "; //Line 38
    copy(intDeq.begin(), intDeq.end(), screen);          //Line 39
    cout << endl;                                         //Line 40

    return 0;
}
```

Sample Run:

```
Line 7: intDeq: 13 75 28 35
Line 12: After adding two more elements, one at the front
         and one at the back, intDeq: 0 13 75 28 35 100
Line 17: After removing the first two elements,
         intDeq: 75 28 35 100
Line 22: After removing the last two elements,
         intDeq = 75 28
Line 29: After inserting 444, intDeq:   75 444 28
Line 33: After assigning two copies of 45, intDeq: 45 45
Line 38: After inserting two elements, one at the front
         and one at the back, intDeq: -10 45 45 -999
```

The statement in Line 1 declares a `deque` container `intDeq` of type `int`; that is, all the elements of `intDeq` are of type `int`. The statement in Line 2 declares `screen` to be an `ostream` iterator initialized to the standard output device. The statements in Lines 3 through 6 use the `push_back` operation to insert four numbers—13, 75, 28, and 35—into `intDeq`. The statement in Line 8 outputs the elements of `intDeq`. In the output, see the line marked Line 7, which contains the output of the statements in Lines 7 through 9.

The statement in Line 10 inserts 0 at the beginning of `intDeq`; the statement in Line 11 inserts 100 at the end of `intDeq`. The statement in Line 13 outputs the modified `intDeq`.

The statements in Lines 15 and 16 use the function `pop_front` to remove the first two elements of `intDeq`; the statement in Line 18 outputs the modified `intDeq`. The statements in Lines 20 and 21 use the function **pop_back** to remove the last two elements of **intDeq**, and the statement in Line 23 outputs the modified **intDeq**.

The statement in Line 25 declares **deqIt** to be a **deque** iterator that processes all **deque** containers whose elements are of type **int**. After the statement in Line 26 executes, **deqIt** points to the first element of **intDeq**. The statement in Line 27 advances **deqIt** to the next element of **intDeq**. The statement in Line 28 inserts **444** into **intDeq** at the position specified by **deqIt**. The statement in Line 30 outputs **intDeq**.

The statement in Line 32 assigns two copies of **45** to **intDeq**. After the statement in Line 32 executes, the old elements of **intDeq** are removed and **intDeq** now contains only two copies of **45**. The output of the statement in Line 34 illustrates this. In the output, see the line marked Line 33, which contains the output of the statements in Lines 33 through 35 of the program.

The meaning of the remaining statements is self-explanatory.

Sequence Container: **list**

This section describes the sequence container **list**. List containers are implemented as doubly linked lists. Thus, every element in a list points to both its immediate predecessor and its immediate successor (except the first and last elements). Recall that a linked list is not a random access data structure, such as an array. Therefore, to access, say, the fifth element in the list, we must first traverse the first four elements.

The name of the class containing the definition of the **class list** is **list**. The definition of the **class list**, and the definitions of the functions to implement the various operations on a list, are contained in the header file **list**. Therefore, to use **list** in a program, the program must include the following statement:

```
#include <list>
```

Like other container classes, the **class list** contains several constructors. Thus, a **list** object can be initialized in several ways when it is declared, as described in Table 22-9.

TABLE 22-9 Various Ways to Declare a `list` Object

Statement	Description
`list<elementType> listCont;`	Creates the empty `list` container `listCont`. (The default constructor is invoked.)
`list<elementType> listCont(otherList);`	Creates the `list` container `listCont` and initializes it to the elements of `otherList`. `listCont` and `otherList` are of the same type.
`list<elementType> listCont(size);`	Creates the `list` container `listCont` of size `size`. `listCont` is initialized using the default constructor.
`list<elementType> listCont(n, elm);`	Creates the `list` container `listCont` of size n. `listCont` is initialized using n copies of the element `elm`.
`list<elementType> listCont(beg, end);`	Creates the `list` container `listCont`. `listCont` is initialized to the elements in the range `[beg, end)`, that is, all the elements in the range `beg...end−1`. Both `beg` and `end` are iterators.

Table 22-5 described the operations that are common to all containers. Table 22-6 described the operations that are common to all sequence containers. In addition to these common operations, Table 22-10 describes the operations that are specific to a `list` container. The name of the function implementing the operation is shown in bold.

In Table 22-10, `listCont` is a container of type `list`.

TABLE 22-10 Various Operations Specific to a `list` Container

Expression	Description
listCont.**assign**(n, elem)	Assigns n copies of `elem`.
listCont.**assign**(beg, end)	Assigns all the elements in the range `beg...end-1`. Both beg and end are iterators.
listCont.**push_front**(elem)	Inserts `elem` at the beginning of `listCont`.
listCont.**pop_front**()	Removes the first element from `listCont`.
listCont.**front**()	Returns the first element. (Does not check whether the container is empty.)
listCont.**back**()	Returns the last element. (Does not check whether the container is empty.)
listCont.**remove**(elem)	Removes all the elements that are equal to `elem`.
listCont.**remove_if**(oper)	Removes all the elements for which `oper` is `true`.
listCont.**unique**()	If the consecutive elements in `listCont` have the same value, removes the duplicates.
listCont.**unique**(oper)	If the consecutive elements in `listCont` have the same value, removes the duplicates, for which `oper` is `true`.

TABLE 22-10 Various Operations Specific to a `list` Container (continued)

Expression	Description
listCont1.**splice**(pos, listCont2)	All the elements of listCont2 are moved to listCont1 before the position specified by the iterator pos. After this operation, listCont2 is empty.
listCont1.**splice**(pos, listCont2, pos2)	All the elements starting at pos2 of listCont2 are moved to listCont1 before the position specified by the iterator pos.
listCont1.**splice**(pos, listCont2, beg, end)	All the elements in the range beg...end-1 of listCont2 are moved to listCont1 before the position specified by the iterator pos. Both beg and end are iterators.
listCont.**sort**()	The elements of listCont are sorted. The sort criteria is <.
listCont.**sort**(oper)	The elements of listCont are sorted. The sort criteria is specified by oper.
listCont1.**merge**(listCont2)	Suppose that the elements of listCont1 and listCont2 are sorted. This operation moves all the elements of listCont2 into listCont1. After this operation, the elements in listCont1 are sorted. Moreover, after this operation, listCont2 is empty.

TABLE 22-10 Various Operations Specific to a `list` Container (continued)

Expression	Description
listCont1**.merge**(listCont2, oper)	Suppose that the elements of `listCont1` and `listCont2` are sorted according to the sort criteria `oper`. This operation moves all the elements of `listCont2` into `listCont1`. After this operation, the elements in `listCont1` are sorted according to the sort criteria `oper`.
listCont**.reverse**()	The elements of `listCont` are reversed.

Example 22-7 illustrates how to use the various operations on a list container.

EXAMPLE 22-7

```cpp
//List Container Example

#include <iostream>
#include <list>
#include <iterator>
#include <algorithm>

using namespace std;

int main()
{
    list<int> intList1, intList2, intList3, intList4;    //Line 1

    ostream_iterator<int> screen(cout, " ");             //Line 2

    intList1.push_back(23);                              //Line 3
    intList1.push_back(58);                              //Line 4
    intList1.push_back(58);                              //Line 5
    intList1.push_back(58);                              //Line 6
    intList1.push_back(36);                              //Line 7
    intList1.push_back(15);                              //Line 8
    intList1.push_back(93);                              //Line 9
    intList1.push_back(98);                              //Line 10
    intList1.push_back(58);                              //Line 11
```

```cpp
    cout << "Line 12: intList1: ";                      //Line 12
    copy(intList1.begin(), intList1.end(), screen);     //Line 13
    cout << endl;                                        //Line 14

    intList2 = intList1;                                 //Line 15

    cout << "Line 16: intList2: ";                       //Line 16
    copy(intList2.begin(), intList2.end(), screen);      //Line 17
    cout << endl;                                        //Line 18

    intList1.unique();                                   //Line 19

    cout << "Line 20: After removing the consecutive "
         << "duplicates," << endl
         << "              intList1: ";                  //Line 20
    copy(intList1.begin(), intList1.end(), screen);      //Line 21
    cout << endl;                                        //Line 22

    intList2.sort();                                     //Line 23

    cout << "Line 24: After sorting, intList2: ";        //Line 24
    copy(intList2.begin(), intList2.end(), screen);      //Line 25
    cout << endl;                                        //Line 26

    intList3.push_back(13);                              //Line 27
    intList3.push_back(23);                              //Line 28
    intList3.push_back(25);                              //Line 29
    intList3.push_back(136);                             //Line 30
    intList3.push_back(198);                             //Line 31

    cout << "Line 32: intList3: ";                       //Line 32
    copy(intList3.begin(), intList3.end(), screen);      //Line 33
    cout << endl;                                        //Line 34

    intList4.push_back(-2);                              //Line 35
    intList4.push_back(-7);                              //Line 36
    intList4.push_back(-8);                              //Line 37

    cout << "Line 38: intList4: ";                       //Line 38
    copy(intList4.begin(), intList4.end(), screen);      //Line 39
    cout << endl;                                        //Line 40

    intList3.splice(intList3.begin(), intList4);         //Line 41

    cout << "Line 42: After moving the elements of "
         << "intList4 into intList3," << endl
         << "              intList3: ";                  //Line 42
    copy(intList3.begin(), intList3.end(), screen);      //Line 43
    cout << endl;                                        //Line 44

    intList3.sort();                                     //Line 45
```

```cpp
    cout << "Line 46: After sorting, intList3: ";      //Line 46
    copy(intList3.begin(), intList3.end(), screen);    //Line 47
    cout << endl;                                       //Line 48

    intList2.merge(intList3);                           //Line 49

    cout << "Line 50: After merging intList2 and "
         << "intList3, intList2: " << endl
         << "          ";                               //Line 50
    copy(intList2.begin(), intList2.end(), screen);    //Line 51
    cout << endl;                                       //Line 52

    intList2.unique();                                  //Line 53

    cout << "Line 54: After removing the consecutive "
         << "duplicates, intList2: " << endl
         << "          ";                               //Line 54
    copy(intList2.begin(), intList2.end(), screen);    //Line 55
    cout << endl;                                       //Line 56

    return 0;
}
```

Sample Run:

```
Line 12: intList1: 23 58 58 58 36 15 93 98 58
Line 16: intList2: 23 58 58 58 36 15 93 98 58
Line 20: After removing the consecutive duplicates,
         intList1: 23 58 36 15 93 98 58
Line 24: After sorting, intList2: 15 23 36 58 58 58 58 93 98
Line 32: intList3: 13 23 25 136 198
Line 38: intList4: -2 -7 -8
Line 42: After moving the elements of intList4 into intList3,
         intList3: -2 -7 -8 13 23 25 136 198
Line 46: After sorting, intList3: -8 -7 -2 13 23 25 136 198
Line 50: After merging intList2 and intList3, intList2:
         -8 -7 -2 13 15 23 23 25 36 58 58 58 58 93 98 136 198
Line 54: After removing the consecutive duplicates, intList2:
         -8 -7 -2 13 15 23 25 36 58 93 98 136 198
```

For the most part, the output of the preceding program is straightforward. The statements in Lines 3 through 11 insert the element numbers 23, 58, 58, 58, 36, 15, 93, 98, and 58 (in that order) into `intList1`. The statement in Line 15 copies the elements of `intList1` into `intList2`. After this statement executes, `intList1` and `intList2` are identical. The statement in Line 19 removes any consecutive occurrences of the same elements. For example, the number 58 appears consecutively three times. The operation `unique` removes two occurrences of 58. Note that this operation has no effect on the 58 that appears at the end of `intList1`.

The statement in Line 23 sorts `intList2`. The statements in Lines 27 through 31 insert 13, 23, 25, 136, and 198 into `intList3`. Similarly, the statements in Lines 35 through 37 insert -2, -7, and -8 into `intList4`. The statement in Line 41 uses the operation `splice` to move the elements of `intList4` to the beginning of `intList3`. After the `splice` operation, `intList4` is empty. The statement in Line 45 sorts `intList3`, and the statement in Line 49 merges `intList2` and `intList3` into `intList2`. After the `merge` operation, `intList3` is empty. The meanings of the remaining statements are similar.

Examples 22-5 through 22-7 further clarify that iterators are important to efficiently process the elements of a container. Before describing associative containers, let us discuss iterators in some detail.

Iterators

Iterators are similar to pointers. In general, an iterator points to the elements of a container (sequence or associative). Thus, with the help of iterators, we can successively access each element of a container.

The two most common operations on iterators are `++` (the increment operator) and `*` (the dereferencing operator). Suppose that `cntItr` is an iterator into a container. The statement:

```
++cntItr;
```

advances `cntItr` so that it points to the next element in the container. Similarly, the statement:

```
*cntItr;
```

gives access to the element of the container pointed to by `cntItr`.

Types of Iterators

There are five types of iterators:

- Input iterators
- Output iterators
- Forward iterators
- Bidirectional iterators
- Random access iterators

The following sections describe these iterators.

INPUT ITERATORS

Input iterators, with read access, step forward element-by-element; consequently, they return the values element-by-element. These iterators are provided for reading data from an input stream.

Suppose `inputIterator` is an input iterator. Table 22-11 describes the operations on `inputIterator`.

TABLE 22-11 Operations on an Input Iterator

Expression	Effect
`*inputIterator`	Gives access to the element to which `inputIterator` points.
`inputIterator->member`	Gives access to the member of the element.
`++inputIterator`	Moves forward, returns the new position (pre-increment).
`inputIterator++`	Moves forward, returns the old position (post-increment).
`inputIt1 == inputIt2`	Returns `true` if the two iterators are the same, and `false` otherwise.
`inputIt1 != inputIt2`	Returns `true` if the two iterators are not the same, and `false` otherwise.

OUTPUT ITERATORS

Output iterators, with write access, step forward element-by-element. These iterators are provided for writing data to an output stream. They are also used as inserters.

Suppose `outputIterator` is an output iterator. Table 22-12 describes the operations on `outputIterator`.

TABLE 22-12 Operations on an Output Iterator

Expression	Effect
`*outputIterator = value;`	Writes the value at the position specified by `outputIterator`.
`++outputIterator`	Moves forward, returns the new position (pre-increment).
`outputIterator++`	Moves forward, returns the old position (post-increment).

NOTE Output iterators cannot be used to iterate over a range twice. Thus, if we write data at the same position twice, there is no guarantee that the new value will replace the old value.

FORWARD ITERATORS

Forward iterators combine all of the functionality of input iterators and almost all of the functionality of output iterators. Suppose `forwardIterator` is a forward iterator. Table 22-13 describes the operations on `forwardIterator`.

TABLE 22-13   Operations on a Forward Iterator

Expression	Effect
`*forwardIterator`	Gives access to the element to which `forwardIterator` points.
`forwardIterator->member`	Gives access to the member of the element.
`++forwardIterator`	Moves forward, returns the new position (pre-increment).
`forwardIterator++`	Moves forward, returns the old position (post-increment).
`forwardIt1 == forwardIt2`	Returns `true` if the two iterators are same, and `false` otherwise.
`forwardIt1 != forwardIt2`	Returns `true` if the two iterators are not same, and `false` otherwise.
`forwardIt1 = forwardIt2`	Assignment

NOTE   A forward iterator can refer to the same element in the same collection and process the same element more than once.

BIDIRECTIONAL ITERATORS

Bidirectional iterators are forward iterators that can also iterate backward over the elements. Suppose `biDirectionalIterator` is a bidirectional iterator. The operations defined for forward iterators (Table 22-13) are also applicable to bidirectional iterators. To step backward, the decrement operations are also defined for `biDirectionalIterator`. Table 22-14 shows additional operations on a bidirectional iterator.

TABLE 22-14 Additional Operations on a Bidirectional Iterator

Expression	Effect
`--biDirectionalIterator`	Moves backward, returns the new position (predecrement).
`biDirectionalIterator--`	Moves backward, returns the old position (postdecrement).

NOTE Bidirectional iterators can be used with containers of type `vector`, `deque`, `list`, `set`, `multiset`, `map`, and `multimap`.

RANDOM ACCESS ITERATORS

Random access iterators are bidirectional iterators that can randomly process the elements of a container. These iterators can be used with containers of types `vector`, `deque`, `string`, as well as arrays. The operations defined for bidirectional iterators (for example, Tables 22-13 and 22-14) are also applicable to random access iterators. Table 22-15 describes the additional operations that are defined for random access iterators. Suppose `rAccessIterator` is a random access iterator.

TABLE 22-15 Additional Operations on a Random Access Iterator

Expression	Effect
`rAccessIterator[n]`	Accesses the nth element.
`rAccessIterator += n`	Moves `rAccessIterator` forward n elements if n >= 0 and backward if n < 0.
`rAccessIterator -= n`	Moves `rAccessIterator` backward n elements if n >= 0 and forward if n < 0.
`rAccessIterator + n`	Returns the iterator of the next nth element.
`n + rAccessIterator`	Returns the iterator of the next nth element.
`rAccessIterator - n`	Returns the iterator of the previous nth element.
`rAccessIt1 - rAccessIt2`	Returns the distance between the iterators `rAccessIt1` and `rAccessIt2`.

TABLE 22-15   Additional Operations on a Random Access Iterator (continued)

Expression	Effect
rAccessIt1 < rAccessIt2	Returns **true** if rAccessIt1 is before rAccessIt2, and **false** otherwise.
rAccessIt1 <= rAccessIt2	Returns **true** if rAccessIt1 is before or equal to rAccessIt2, and **false** otherwise.
rAccessIt1 > rAccessIt2	Returns **true** if rAccessIt1 is after rAccessIt2, and **false** otherwise.
rAccessIt1 >= rAccessIt2	Returns **true** if rAccessIt1 is after or equal to rAccessIt2, and **false** otherwise.

Figure 22-1 shows the iterator hierarchy.

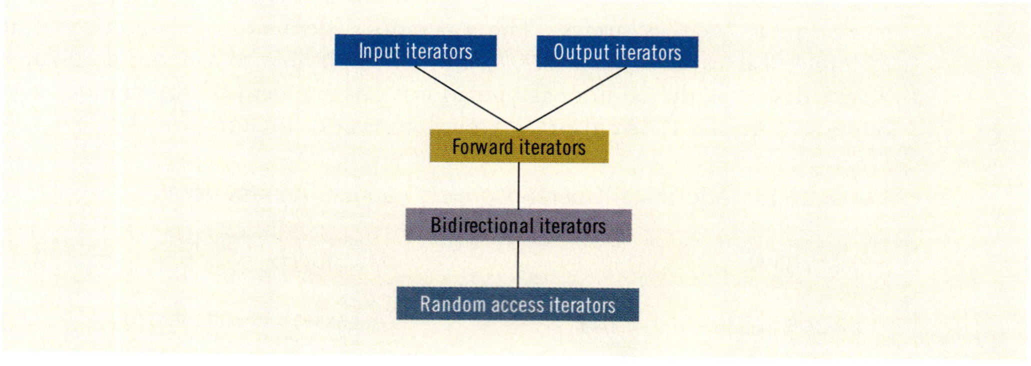

FIGURE 22-1   Iterator hierarchy

Now that you know the different types of iterators, next we describe how to declare an iterator into a container.

typedef ITERATOR

Every container (sequence or associative) contains a **typedef** iterator. Thus, an iterator into a container is declared using the **typedef** iterator. For example, the statement:

```
vector<int>::iterator intVecIter;
```

declares intVecIter to be an iterator into a vector container of type **int**.

Because iterator is a **typedef** defined inside a container (that is, a class) such as vector, we must use the appropriate container name, container element type, and the scope resolution operator to use the **typedef** iterator.

typedef CONST_ITERATOR

Because an iterator works like a pointer, with the help of an iterator into a container and the dereferencing operator, *, we can modify the elements of the container. However, if a container is declared as **const**, then we must prevent the iterator from modifying the elements of the container, especially accidentally. To handle this situation, every container contains another **typedef** const_iterator. For example, the statement:

```
vector<int>::const_iterator intConstVecIt;
```

declares `intConstVecIt` to be an iterator into a `vector` container whose elements are of type `int`. The iterator `intConstVecIt` is used to process the elements of those vector containers that are declared as constant vector containers of type `vector<int>`.

An iterator of type `const_iterator` is a read-only iterator.

typedef REVERSE_ITERATOR

Every container also contains the **typedef** reverse_iterator. An iterator of this type is used to iterate through the elements of a container in reverse.

typedef CONST_REVERSE_ITERATOR

An iterator of this type is a read-only iterator and is used to iterate through the elements of a container in reverse. It is required if the container is declared as **const**, and we need to iterate through the elements of the container in reverse.

In addition to the previous four **typedef**s, several other **typedef**s are common to all containers and are described in Table 22-16.

TABLE 22-16 Various **typedef**s Common to All Containers

typedef	Effect
difference_type	The type of result from subtracting two iterators referring to the same container.
pointer	A pointer to the type of elements stored in the container.
reference	A reference to the type of elements stored in the container.
const_reference	A constant reference to the type of elements stored in the container. A constant reference is read-only.
size_type	The type used to count the elements in a container. This type is also used to index through sequence containers, except `list` containers.
value_type	The type of container elements.

Stream Iterators

Another useful set of iterators are `stream` iterators—`istream` iterators and `ostream` iterators. This section describes both types of iterators.

istream_iterator

The `istream` iterator is used to input data into a program from an input stream. The `class` `istream_iterator` contains the definition of an input stream iterator. The general syntax to use an `istream` iterator is:

```
istream_iterator<Type> isIdentifier(istream&);
```

where `Type` is either a built-in type or a user-defined class type, for which an input iterator is defined. The identifier `isIdentifier` is initialized using the constructor whose argument is either an `istream` class object, such as `cin`, or any publicly defined `istream` subtype, such as `ifstream`.

ostream_iterator

The `ostream` iterators are used to output data from a program into an output stream. These iterators were defined earlier in this chapter. We review them here for the sake of completeness.

The `class` `ostream_iterator` contains the definition of an output stream iterator. The general syntax to use an `ostream` iterator is:

```
ostream_iterator<Type> osIdentifier(ostream&);
```

or

```
ostream_iterator<Type> osIdentifier(ostream&, char* deLimit);
```

where `Type` is either a built-in type or a user-defined class type, for which an output iterator is defined. The identifier `osIdentifier` is initialized using the constructor whose argument is either an `ostream` class object, such as `cout`, or any publicly defined `ostream` subtype, such as `ofstream`. In the second form used to declare an `ostream` iterator, by using the second argument (`deLimit`) of the initializing constructor, we can specify a character separating the output.

Associative Containers

This section discusses associative containers. Elements in an associative container are automatically sorted according to some ordering criteria. The default ordering criterion is the relational operator < (less than). Users also have the option of specifying their own ordering criterion.

Because elements in an associative container are sorted automatically, when a new element is inserted into the container, it is inserted at the proper place. A convenient and fast way to implement this type of data structure is to use a binary search tree. This is, in fact, how associative containers are implemented. Thus, every element in the container has a parent node (except the root node) and, at most, two children. For each element, the key in the parent node is larger than the key in the left child and smaller than the key in the right child.

The predefined associative containers in the STL are:

- Sets
- Multisets
- Maps
- Multimaps

This book discusses only the associative containers `set` and `multiset`.

Associative Containers: `set` and `multiset`

As described earlier, both the containers `set` and `multiset` automatically sort their elements according to some sort criteria. The default sorting criterion is the relational operator < (less than); that is, the elements are arranged in ascending order. The user can also specify other sorting criteria. For user-defined data types, such as classes, the relational operators must be overloaded properly.

The only difference between the containers `set` and `multiset` is that the container `multiset` allows duplicates; the container `set` does not.

The name of the class defining the container `set` is `set`; the name of the class defining the container `multiset` is `multiset`. The name of the header file containing the definitions of the classes `set` and `multiset`, and the definitions of the functions to implement the various operations on these containers, is `set`. Thus, to use any of these containers, the program must include the following statement:

```
#include <set>
```

Declaring `set` or `multiset` Associative Containers

The classes `set` and `multiset` contain several constructors to declare and initialize containers of these types. This section discusses the various ways that these types of associative containers are declared and initialized. Table 22-17 describes how a `set/multiset` container of a specific type can be declared and initialized.

TABLE 22-17 Various Ways to Declare a Set/Multiset Container

Statement	Effect
`ctType<elmType> ct;`	Creates an empty set/multiset container, `ct`. The sort criterion is <.
`ctType<elmType, sortOp> ct;`	Creates an empty set/multiset container, `ct`. The sort criterion is specified by `sortOp`.
`ctType<elmType> ct(otherCt);`	Creates a set/multiset container, `ct`. The elements of `otherCt` are copied into `ct`. The sort criterion is <. Both `ct` and `otherCt` are of the same type.
`ctType<elmType, sortOp> ct(otherCt);`	Creates a set/multiset container, `ct`. The elements of `otherCt` are copied into `ct`. The sort criterion is specified by `sortOp`. Both `ct` and `otherCt` are of the same type. Note that the sort criteria of `ct` and `otherCt` must be the same.
`ctType<elmType> ct(beg, end);`	Creates a set/multiset container, `ct`. The elements starting at the position `beg` until the position `end−1` are copied into `ct`. Both `beg` and `end` are iterators.
`ctType<elmType, sortOp> ct(beg, end);`	Creates a set/multiset container, `ct`. The elements starting at the position `beg` until the position `end−1` are copied into `ct`. Both `beg` and `end` are iterators. The sort criterion is specified by `sortOp`.

If you want to use sort criteria other than the default, you must specify this option when the container is declared. For example, consider the following statements:

```
set<int> intSet;                                    //Line 1
set<int, greater<int> > otherIntSet;                //Line 2
multiset<string> stringMultiSet;                    //Line 3
multiset<string, greater<string> > otherStringMultiSet;  //Line 4
```

The statement in Line 1 declares `intSet` to be an empty set container, the element type is `int`, and the sort criterion is the default sort criterion. The statement in Line 2 declares `otherIntSet` to be an empty set container, the element type is `int`, and the sort criterion is greater-than. That is, the elements in the container `otherIntSet` will be arranged in descending order. The statements in Lines 3 and 4 have similar conventions.

The statements in Lines 2 and 4 illustrate how to specify the descending sorting criterion.

NOTE In the statements in Lines 2 and 4, note the space between the two > symbols—that is, the space between `greater<int>` and `>`. This space is important because `>>` is also a shift operator in C++.

Item Insertion and Deletion from `set/multiset`

Suppose that `ct` is of type either `set` or `multiset`. Table 22-18 describes the operations that can be used to insert or delete elements from a set. It also illustrates how to use these operations. The name of the function is shown in bold.

TABLE 22-18 Operations to Insert or Delete Elements from a Set

Expression	Effect
`ct.insert(elem)`	Inserts a copy of `elem` into `ct`. In the case of sets, it also returns whether the insert operation succeeded.
`ct.insert(position, elem)`	Inserts a copy of `elem` into `ct`. The position where `elem` is inserted is returned. The first parameter, `position`, hints where to begin the search for `insert`. The parameter `position` is an iterator.
`ct.insert(beg, end);`	Inserts a copy of all the elements into `ct` starting at the position `beg` until `end-1`. Both `beg` and `end` are iterators.

TABLE 22-18   Operations to Insert or Delete Elements from a Set (continued)

Expression	Effect
`ct.erase(elem);`	Deletes all the elements with the value `elem`. The number of deleted elements is returned.
`ct.erase(position);`	Deletes the element at the position specified by the iterator `position`. No value is returned.
`ct.erase(beg, end);`	Deletes all the elements starting at the position `beg` until the position `end−1`. Both `beg` and `end` are iterators. No value is returned.
`ct.clear();`	Deletes all the elements from the container `ct`. After this operation, the container `ct` is empty.

Example 22-8 shows the various operations on a `set`/`multiset` container.

EXAMPLE 22-8

```cpp
#include <iostream>
#include <set>
#include <string>
#include <iterator>
#include <algorithm>

using namespace std;

int main()
{
    set<int> intSet;                                //Line 1
    set<int, greater<int> > intSetA;                //Line 2

    set<int, greater<int> >::iterator intGtIt;      //Line 3

    ostream_iterator<int> screen(cout, " ");        //Line 4

    intSet.insert(16);                              //Line 5
    intSet.insert(8);                               //Line 6
    intSet.insert(20);                              //Line 7
    intSet.insert(3);                               //Line 8

    cout << "Line 9: intSet: ";                     //Line 9
    copy(intSet.begin(), intSet.end(), screen);     //Line 10
    cout << endl;                                   //Line 11

    intSetA.insert(36);                             //Line 12
    intSetA.insert(84);                             //Line 13
```

```cpp
intSetA.insert(30);                                     //Line 14
intSetA.insert(39);                                     //Line 15
intSetA.insert(59);                                     //Line 16
intSetA.insert(238);                                    //Line 17
intSetA.insert(156);                                    //Line 18

cout << "Line 19: intSetA: ";                           //Line 19
copy(intSetA.begin(), intSetA.end(), screen);           //Line 20
cout << endl;                                           //Line 21

intSetA.erase(59);                                      //Line 22

cout << "Line 23: After removing 59, intSetA: ";        //Line 23
copy(intSetA.begin(), intSetA.end(), screen);           //Line 24
cout << endl;                                           //Line 25

intGtIt = intSetA.begin();                              //Line 26
++intGtIt;                                              //Line 27
++intGtIt;                                              //Line 28
++intGtIt;                                              //Line 29

intSetA.erase(intGtIt);                                 //Line 30

cout << "Line 31: After removing the fourth "
     << "element, " << endl
     << "            intSetA: ";                        //Line 31
copy(intSetA.begin(), intSetA.end(), screen);           //Line 32
cout << endl;                                           //Line 33


set<int, greater<int> >  intSetB(intSetA);              //Line 34

cout << "Line 35: intSetB: ";                           //Line 35
copy(intSetB.begin(), intSetB.end(), screen);           //Line 36
cout << endl;                                           //Line 37

intSetB.clear();                                        //Line 38

cout << "Line 39: After removing all elements, "
     << endl << "            intSetB: ";                //Line 39
copy(intSetB.begin(), intSetB.end(), screen);           //Line 40
cout << endl;                                           //Line 41

multiset<string, greater<string> > namesMultiSet;       //Line 42
multiset<string, greater<string> >::iterator iter;      //Line 43

ostream_iterator<string> pScreen(cout, " ");            //Line 44

namesMultiSet.insert("Donny");                          //Line 45
namesMultiSet.insert("Zippy");                          //Line 46
namesMultiSet.insert("Goofy");                          //Line 47
namesMultiSet.insert("Hungry");                         //Line 48
```

```
namesMultiSet.insert("Goofy");                          //Line 49
namesMultiSet.insert("Donny");                          //Line 50

cout << "Line 51: namesMultiSet: ";                     //Line 51
copy(namesMultiSet.begin(), namesMultiSet.end(),
     pScreen);                                          //Line 52
cout << endl;                                           //Line 53

return 0;
}
```

Sample Run:

```
Line 9: intSet: 3 8 16 20
Line 19: intSetA: 238 156 84 59 39 36 30
Line 23: After removing 59, intSetA: 238 156 84 39 36 30
Line 31: After removing the fourth element,
         intSetA: 238 156 84 36 30
Line 35: intSetB: 238 156 84 36 30
Line 39: After removing all the elements,
         intSetB:
Line 51: namesMultiSet: Zippy Hungry Goofy Goofy Donny Donny
```

The statement in Line 1 declares `intSet` to be a `set` container. The statement in Line 2 declares `intSetA` to be a set container whose elements are to be arranged in descending order. The statement in Line 3 declares `intGtIt` to be a `set` iterator. The iterator `intGtIt` can process the elements of any set container whose elements are of type `int` and arranged in descending order. The statement in Line 4 declares `screen` to be an `ostream` iterator that outputs the elements of any container whose elements are of type `int`.

The statements in Lines 5 through 8 insert `16`, `8`, `20`, and `3` into `intSet`, and the statement in Line 10 outputs the elements of `intSet`. In the output, see the line marked Line 9; it contains the output of the statements in Lines 9 through 11.

The statements in Lines 12 through 18 insert `36`, `84`, `30`, `39`, `59`, `238`, and `156` into `intSetA`, and the statement in Line 20 outputs the elements of `intSetA`. In the output, see the line marked Line 19. It contains the output of the statements in Lines 19 through 21. Notice that the elements of `intSetA` appear in descending order.

The statement in Line 22 removes `59` from `intSetA`. After the statement in Line 26 executes, `intGtIt` points to the first element of `intSetA`. The statement in Line 27 advances `intGtIt` to the next element of `intSetA`. After the statement in Line 29 executes, `intGtIt` points to the fourth element of `intSetA`. The statement in Line 30 removes the element of `intSetA` pointed to by `intGtIt`. The meanings of the statements in Lines 34 through 41 are similar.

The statement in Line 42 declares `namesMultiSet` to be a container of type `multiset`. The elements in `namesMultiSet` are of type `string` and are arranged in descending order. The statement in Line 43 declares `iter` to be a `multiset` iterator.

The statements in Lines 45 through 50 insert `Donny`, `Zippy`, `Goofy`, `Hungry`, `Goofy`, and `Donny` into `namesMultiSet`. The statement in Line 52 outputs the elements of `namesMultiSet`.

Container Adapters

The previous sections discussed several types of containers. In addition to the containers that work in a general framework, the STL provides containers to accommodate special situations. These containers, called **container adapters**, are adapted standard STL containers to work in a specific environment. The three container adapters are:

- Stacks
- Queues
- Priority queues

Container adapters do not support any type of iterator. That is, iterators cannot be used with these types of containers. The next two sections describe two types of container adapters: stack and queue.

Stack

Chapter 18 discussed the data structure stack in detail. Because a stack is an important data structure, the STL provides a class to implement a stack in a program. The name of the class defining a stack is `stack`; the name of the header file containing the definition of the `class` stack is `stack`. Table 22-19 defines the various operations supported by the stack container class.

TABLE 22-19 Various Operations on a `stack` Object

Operation	Description
`size`	Returns the actual number of elements in the stack.
`empty`	Returns `true` if the stack is empty, `false` otherwise.
`push(item)`	Inserts a copy of `item` onto the stack.
`top`	Returns the top element of the stack but does not remove the element from the stack. This operation is implemented as a value-returning function.
`pop`	Removes the top element of the stack.

In addition to the operations `size`, `empty`, `push`, `top`, and `pop`, the stack container class provides relational operators to compare two stacks. For example, the relational operator `==` can be used to determine whether two stacks are identical.

The program in Example 22-9 illustrates how to use the stack container class.

EXAMPLE 22-9

```cpp
#include <iostream>
#include <stack>

using namespace std;

int main()
{
    stack<int> intStack;                                //Line 1

    intStack.push(16);                                  //Line 2
    intStack.push(8);                                   //Line 3
    intStack.push(20);                                  //Line 4
    intStack.push(3);                                   //Line 5

    cout << "Line 6: The top element of intStack: "
         << intStack.top() << endl;                     //Line 6

    intStack.pop();                                     //Line 7

    cout << "Line 8: After the pop operation, "
         << "the top element of intStack: "
         << intStack.top() << endl;                     //Line 8

    cout << "Line 9: intStack elements: ";              //Line 9

    while (!intStack.empty())                           //Line 10
    {
        cout << intStack.top() << " ";                  //Line 11
        intStack.pop();                                 //Line 12
    }

    cout << endl;                                       //Line 13

    return 0;
}
```

Sample Run:

```
Line 6: The top element of intStack: 3
Line 8: After the pop operation, the top element of intStack: 20
Line 9: intStack elements: 20 8 16
```

The preceding output is self-explanatory. The details are left as an exercise for you.

Queue

Chapter 18 discussed the data structure queue in detail. Because a queue is an important data structure, the STL provides a class to implement queues in a program. The name of the class defining the queue is `queue`, and the name of the header file containing the definition of the **class** `queue` is `queue`. Table 22-20 defines the various operations supported by the queue container class.

TABLE 22-20 Various Operations on a `queue` Object

Operation	Description
`size`	Returns the actual number of elements in the queue.
`empty`	Returns **true** if the queue is empty, **false** otherwise.
`push(item)`	Inserts a copy of `item` into the queue.
`front`	Returns the next—that is, first—element in the queue, but does not remove the element from the queue. This operation is implemented as a value-returning function.
`back`	Returns the last element in the queue but does not remove the element from the queue. This operation is implemented as a value-returning function.
`pop`	Removes the next element in the queue.

In addition to the operations `size`, `empty`, `push`, `front`, `back`, and `pop`, the queue container class provides relational operators to compare two stacks. For example, the relational operator `==` can be used to determine whether two stacks are identical.

The program in Example 22-10 illustrates how to use the queue container class.

EXAMPLE 22-10

```cpp
#include <iostream>
#include <queue>

using namespace std;

int main()
{
    queue<int> intQueue;                               //Line 1

    intQueue.push(26);                                 //Line 2
    intQueue.push(18);                                 //Line 3
```

```cpp
    intQueue.push(50);                                      //Line 4
    intQueue.push(33);                                      //Line 5

    cout << "Line 6: The front element of intQueue: "
         << intQueue.front() << endl;                       //Line 6

    cout << "Line 7: The last element of intQueue: "
         << intQueue.back() << endl;                        //Line 7

    intQueue.pop();                                         //Line 8

    cout << "Line 9: After the pop operation, "
         << "the front element of intQueue: "
         << intQueue.front() << endl;                       //Line 9

    cout << "Line 10: intQueue elements: ";                 //Line 10

    while (!intQueue.empty())                               //Line 11
    {
        cout << intQueue.front() << " ";                    //Line 12
        intQueue.pop();                                     //Line 13
    }

    cout << endl;                                           //Line 14

    return 0;
}
```

Sample Run:

```
Line 6: The front element of intQueue: 26
Line 7: The last element of intQueue: 33
Line 9: After the pop operation, the front element of intQueue: 18
Line 10: intQueue elements: 18 50 33
```

The preceding output is self-explanatory. The details are left as an exercise for you.

Containers, Associated Header Files, and Iterator Support

The previous sections discussed various types of containers. Recall that every container is a class. The definition of the class implementing a specific container is contained in the header file. Table 22-21 describes the container, its associated header file, and the type of iterator supported by the container.

TABLE 22-21 Containers, Their Associated Header Files, and the Type of Iterator Supported by Each Container

Sequence containers	Associated header file	Type of iterator support
vector	<vector>	Random access
deque	<deque>	Random access
list	<list>	Bidirectional
Associative containers	**Associated header file**	**Type of iterator support**
map	<map>	Bidirectional
multimap	<map>	Bidirectional
set	<set>	Bidirectional
multiset	<set>	Bidirectional
Adapters	**Associated header file**	**Type of iterator support**
stack	<stack>	No iterator support
queue	<queue>	No iterator support
priority queue	<queue>	No iterator support

Algorithms

Several operations can be defined for a container. Some of the operations are very specific to a container and, therefore, are provided as part of the container definition (that is, as member functions of the class implementing the container). However, several operations—such as **find**, **sort**, and **merge**—are common to all containers. These operations are provided as generic algorithms and can be applied to all containers, as well as the built-in array type. The algorithms are bound to a particular container through an iterator pair.

The generic algorithms are contained in the header file **algorithm**. This section describes several of these algorithms and shows how to use them in a program. Because algorithms are implemented with the help of functions, in this section, the terms *function* and *algorithm* mean the same thing.

STL Algorithm Classification

In earlier sections, you applied various operations on a sequence container, such as `clear`, `sort`, `merge`, and so on. However, those algorithms were tied to a specific container in terms of the members of a specific class. All those algorithms and a few others are also available in more general forms, called **generic algorithms**, and can be applied in a variety of situations. This section discusses some of these generic algorithms.

The STL contains algorithms that look only at the elements in a container and that move the elements of a container. It also has algorithms that can perform specific calculations, such as finding the sum of the elements of a numeric container. In addition, the STL contains algorithms for basic set theory operations, such as set union and intersection. You have already encountered some of the generic algorithms, such as the `copy` algorithm. This algorithm copies the elements from a given range of elements to another place, such as another container or the screen. The algorithms in the STL can be classified into the following categories:

- Nonmodifying algorithms
- Modifying algorithms
- Numeric algorithms
- Heap algorithms

The next four sections describe these algorithms. Most of the generic algorithms are contained in the header file `algorithm`. Certain algorithms, such as the numeric algorithms, are contained in the header file `numeric`.

NONMODIFYING ALGORITHMS

Nonmodifying algorithms do not modify the elements of the container; they merely investigate the elements. Table 22-22 lists the nonmodifying algorithms.

TABLE 22-22 Nonmodifying Algorithms

adjacent_find	find_end	max
binary_search	find_first_of	max_element
count	find_if	min
count_if	for_each	min_element
equal	includes	search
equal_range	lower_bound	search_n
find	mismatch	upper_bound

MODIFYING ALGORITHMS

Modifying algorithms, as the name implies, modify the elements of the container by rearranging, removing, or changing the values of the elements. Table 22-23 lists the modifying algorithms.

TABLE 22-23 Modifying Algorithms

copy	prev_permutation	rotate_copy
copy_backward	random_shuffle	set_difference
fill	remove	set_intersection
fill_n	remove_copy	set_symmetric_difference
generate	remove_copy_if	set_union
generate_n	remove_if	sort
inplace_merge	replace	stable_partition
iter_swap	replace_copy	stable_sort
merge	replace_copy_if	swap
next_permutation	replace_if	swap_ranges
nth_element	reverse	transform
partial_sort	reverse_copy	unique
partial_sort_copy	rotate	unique_copy
partition		

Modifying algorithms that change the order of the elements, not their values, are also called mutating algorithms. For example, `next_permutation`, `partition`, `prev_permutation`, `random_shuffle`, `reverse`, `reverse_copy`, `rotate`, `rotate_copy`, and `stable_partition` are mutating algorithms.

NUMERIC ALGORITHMS

Numeric algorithms are designed to perform numeric calculations on the elements of a container. Table 22-24 lists these algorithms.

TABLE 22-24   Numeric Algorithms

accumulate	inner_product
adjacent_difference	partial_sum

HEAP ALGORITHMS

A special type of sorting algorithm, called the heap sort algorithm, is used to sort the data stored in an array. In the heap sort algorithm, the array containing the data is viewed as a binary tree. Thus, a heap is a form of binary tree represented as an array. In a heap, the first element is the largest element, and the element at the *i*th position (if it exists) is larger than the elements at positions $2i$ and $2i + 1$ (if they exist). In the heap sort algorithm, first the array containing the data is converted into a heap, and then the array is sorted using a special type of sorting algorithm. Table 22-25 lists the basic algorithms required by the heap sort algorithm.

TABLE 22-25   Heap Algorithms

make_heap	push_heap
pop_heap	sort_heap

Most of the STL algorithms are explained later in this chapter. For the most part, the function prototypes of these algorithms are given along with a brief explanation of what each algorithm does. You then learn how to use these algorithms with the help of a C++ program. The STL algorithms are very powerful and accomplish amazing results. Furthermore, they have been made general, in the sense that other than using the natural operations to manipulate containers, they allow the user to specify the manipulating criteria. For example, the natural sorting order is ascending, but the user can specify criteria to sort the container in descending order. Thus, every algorithm is typically implemented with the help of overloaded functions. Before starting to describe these algorithms, we discuss **function objects**, which allow the user to specify the manipulating criteria.

Function Objects

To make the generic algorithms flexible, the STL usually provides two forms of an algorithm using the mechanism of function overloading. The first form of an algorithm uses the natural operation to accomplish this goal. In the second form, the user can specify criteria based on which algorithm processes the elements. For example, the algorithm `adjacent_find` searches the container and returns the position of the first two elements that are equal. In the second form of this algorithm, we can specify criteria (say, less than) to look for the first two elements, such that the second element is less than the first element.

These criteria are passed as a function object. More formally, a **function object** contains a function that can be treated as a function using the function call operator, `()`. In fact, a function object is a class template that overloads the function call operator, `operator()`.

In addition to allowing you to create your own function objects, the STL provides arithmetic, relational, and logical function objects, which are described in Table 22-26. The STL's function objects are contained in the header file `functional`.

TABLE 22-26 Arithmetic STL Function Objects

Function object name	Description

`plus<Type>`	`plus<int> addNum;`
	`int sum = addNum(12, 35);`
	The value of sum is 47.

`minus<Type>`	`minus<int> subtractNum;`
	`int difference = subtractNum(56, 35);`
	The value of `difference` is 21.

`multiplies<Type>`	`multiplies<int> multiplyNum;`
	`int product = multiplyNum(6, 3);`
	The value of `product` is 18.

`divides<Type>`	`divides<int> divideNum;`
	`int quotient = divideNum(16, 3);`
	The value of `quotient` is 5.

`modulus<Type>`	`modulus<int> remainder;`
	`int rem = remainder(16, 7);`
	The value of `rem` is 2.

`negate<Type>`	`negate<int> num;`
	`int opposite = num(-25);`
	The value of `opposite` is 25.

Example 22-11 shows how to use the STL's function objects.

EXAMPLE 22-11

```
#include <string>
#include <algorithm>
#include <numeric>
#include <iterator>
#include <vector>
#include <functional>
```

```cpp
using namespace std;

int funcAdd(plus<int>, int, int);

int main()
{
    plus<int> addNum;                                      //Line 1
    int num = addNum(34, 56);                              //Line 2

    cout << "Line 3: num = " << num << endl;               //Line 3

    plus<string> joinString;                               //Line 4

    string str1 = "Hello ";                                //Line 5
    string str2 = "There";                                 //Line 6

    string str = joinString(str1, str2);                   //Line 7

    cout << "Line 8: str = " << str << endl;               //Line 8

    cout << "Line 9: Sum of 34 and 26 = "
         << funcAdd(addNum, 34, 26) << endl;               //Line 9


    int list[8] = {1, 2, 3, 4, 5, 6, 7, 8};                //Line 10

    vector<int>  intList(list, list + 8);                  //Line 11
    ostream_iterator<int> screenOut(cout, " ");            //Line 12

    cout << "Line 13: intList: ";                          //Line 13
    copy(intList.begin(), intList.end(), screenOut);       //Line 14
    cout << endl;                                           //Line 15

        //accumulate function
    int sum = accumulate(intList.begin(),
                         intList.end(), 0);                //Line 16

    cout << "Line 17: Sum of the elements of "
         << "intList = " << sum << endl;                   //Line 17

    int product = accumulate(intList.begin(),
                             intList.end(),
                             1, multiplies<int>());        //Line 18

    cout << "Line 19: Product of the elements of "
         << "intList = " << product << endl;               //Line 19

    return 0;
}
```

```
int funcAdd(plus<int> sum, int x, int y)
{
    return sum(x, y);
}
```

Sample Run:

```
Line 3: num = 90
Line 8: str = Hello There
Line 9: Sum of 34 and 26 = 60
Line 13: intList: 1 2 3 4 5 6 7 8
Line 17: Sum of the elements of intList = 36
Line 19: Product of the elements of intList = 40320
```

Table 22-27 describes the relational STL function objects.

TABLE 22-27   Relational STL Function Objects

Function object name	Description

equal_to<Type>	Returns `true` if the two arguments are equal, and `false` otherwise. For example,
	`equal_to<int> compare;`
	`bool isEqual = compare(5, 5);`
	The value of `isEqual` is `true`.

not_equal_to<Type>	Returns `true` if the two arguments are not equal, and `false` otherwise. For example,
	`not_equal_to<int> compare;`
	`bool isNotEqual = compare(5, 6);`
	The value of `isNotEqual` is `true`.

greater<Type>	Returns `true` if the first argument is greater than the second argument, and `false` otherwise. For example,
	`greater<int> compare;`
	`bool isGreater = compare(8, 5);`
	The value of `isGreater` is `true`.

greater_equal<Type>	Returns `true` if the first argument is greater than or equal to the second argument, and `false` otherwise. For example,
	`greater_equal<int> compare;`
	`bool isGreaterEqual = compare(8, 5);`
	The value of `isGreaterEqual` is `true`.

TABLE 22-27   Relational STL Function Objects (continued)

Function object name	Description

less<Type>	Returns **true** if the first argument is less than the second argument, and **false** otherwise. For example,
	`less<int> compare;`
	`bool isLess = compare(3, 5);`
	The value of `isLess` is `true`.

less_equal<Type>	Returns **true** if the first argument is less than or equal to the second argument, and **false** otherwise. For example,
	`less_equal<int> compare;`
	`bool isLessEqual = compare(8, 15);`
	The value of `isLessEqual` is `true`.

The STL relational function objects can also be applied to containers, as shown next. The STL algorithm `adjacent_find` searches a container and returns the position in the container where the two elements are equal. This algorithm has a second form that allows the user to specify the comparison criteria. For example, consider the following vector, `vecList`:

```
vecList = {2, 3, 4, 5, 1, 7, 8, 9};
```

The elements of `vecList` are supposed to be in ascending order. To see if the elements are out of order, we can use the algorithm `adjacent_find` as follows:

```
intItr = adjacent_find(vecList.begin(), vecList.end(),
                       greater<int>());
```

where `intItr` is an iterator of the `vector` type. The function `adjacent_find` starts at the position `vecList.begin()`—that is, at the first element of `vecList`—and looks for the first set of consecutive elements such that the first element is greater than the second. The function returns a pointer to element 5, which is stored in `intItr`.

The program in Example 22-12 further illustrates how to use the relational function objects.

EXAMPLE 22-12

This example shows how the relational STL function objects work:

```
#include <iostream>
#include <string>
#include <algorithm>
#include <iterator>
#include <vector>
#include <functional>
```

```cpp
using namespace std;

int main()
{
    equal_to<int> compare;                              //Line 1
    bool isEqual = compare(6, 6);                        //Line 2

    cout << "Line 3: isEqual = " << isEqual << endl;     //Line 3

    greater<string> greaterStr;                          //Line 4

    string str1 = "Hello";                               //Line 5
    string str2 = "There";                               //Line 6

    if (greaterStr(str1, str2))                          //Line 7
        cout << "Line 8: \"" << str1 << "\" is "
             << "greater than \"" << str2 << "\""
             << endl;                                    //Line 8
    else                                                 //Line 9
        cout << "Line 10: \"" << str1 << "\" is "
             << "not greater than \"" << str2
             << "\"" << endl;                            //Line 10

    int temp[8] = {2, 3, 4, 5, 1, 7, 8, 9};              //Line 11

    vector<int> vecList(temp, temp + 8);                 //Line 12
    vector<int>::iterator intItr1, intItr2;              //Line 13
    ostream_iterator<int> screen(cout, " ");             //Line 14

    cout << "Line 15: vecList: ";                        //Line 15
    copy(vecList.begin(), vecList.end(), screen);        //Line 16
    cout << endl;                                        //Line 17

    intItr1 = adjacent_find(vecList.begin(),
                            vecList.end(),
                            greater<int>());             //Line 18
    intItr2 = intItr1 + 1;                               //Line 19

    cout << "Line 20: In vecList, the first set of "
         << "out-of-order elements is: " << *intItr1
         << " " << *intItr2 << endl;                     //Line 20
    cout << "Line 21: In vecList, the first out-of-"
         << "order element is at position "
         << vecList.end() - intItr2 << endl;             //Line 21

    return 0;
}
```

Sample Run:

```
Line 3: isEqual = 1
Line 10: "Hello" is not greater than "There"
Line 15: vecList: 2 3 4 5 1 7 8 9
Line 20: In vecList, the first set of out-of-order elements is: 5 1
Line 21: In vecList, the first out-of-order element is at position 4
```

Table 22-28 describes the logical STL function objects.

TABLE 22-28 Logical STL Function Objects

Function object name	Effect
`logical_not<Type>`	Returns `true` if its operand evaluates to `false`; otherwise, it returns `false`. This is a unary function object.
`logical_and<Type>`	Returns `true` if both of its operands evaluate to `true`; otherwise, it returns `false`. This is a binary function object.
`logical_or<Type>`	Returns `true` if at least one of its operands evaluates to `true`; otherwise, it returns `false`. This is a binary function object.

PREDICATES

Predicates are special types of function objects that return Boolean values. There are two types of predicates—unary and binary. Unary predicates check a specific property for a single argument; binary predicates check a specific property for a pair—that is, two arguments. Predicates are typically used to specify searching or sorting criteria. In the STL, a predicate must always return the same result for the same value. Therefore, the functions that modify their internal states *cannot* be considered predicates.

Insert Iterator

Consider the following statements:

```cpp
int list[5] = {1, 3, 6, 9, 12};  //Line 1
vector<int> vList;               //Line 2
```

The statement in Line 1 declares and initializes `list` to be an array of 5 components. The statement in Line 2 declares `vList` to be a vector. Because no size is specified for `vList`, no memory space is reserved for the elements of `vList`. Now suppose that we want to copy the elements of `list` into `vList`. The statement:

```cpp
copy(list, list + 8, vList.begin());
```

will not work because no memory space is allocated for the elements of `vList`, and the `copy` function uses the assignment operator to copy the elements from the source to the destination. One solution to this problem is to use a **for** loop to step through the elements of `list` and use the function `push_back` of `vList` to copy the elements of `list`. However, there is a better solution, which is convenient and applicable whenever no memory space is allocated at the destination. The STL provides three iterators, called **insert iterators**, to insert the elements at the destination: `back_inserter`, `front_inserter`, and `inserter`.

- **`back_inserter`**: This inserter uses the `push_back` operation of the container in place of the assignment operator. The argument to this iterator is the container itself. For example, for the preceding problem, we can copy the elements of `list` into `vList` by using `back_inserter` as follows:

      copy(list, list + 5, back_inserter(vList));

- **`front_inserter`**: This inserter uses the `push_front` operation of the container in place of the assignment operator. The argument to this iterator is the container itself. Because the `vector` class does not support the `push_front` operation, this iterator *cannot* be used for the `vector` container.

- **`inserter`**: This inserter uses the container's `insert` operation in place of the assignment operator. There are two arguments to this iterator: the first argument is the container itself; the second argument is an iterator to the container specifying the position at which the insertion should begin.

The program in Example 22-13 illustrates the effect of inserters on a container.

EXAMPLE 22-13

```cpp
//Inserters

#include <iostream>
#include <algorithm>
#include <iterator>
#include <vector>
#include <list>

using namespace std;

int main()
{
    int temp[8] = {1, 2, 3, 4, 5, 6, 7, 8};          //Line 1

    vector<int> vecList1;                             //Line 2
    vector<int> vecList2;                             //Line 3

    ostream_iterator<int> screenOut(cout, " ");      //Line 4

    copy(temp, temp + 8, back_inserter(vecList1));    //Line 5
```

```cpp
    cout << "Line 6: vecList1: ";                          //Line 6
    copy(vecList1.begin(), vecList1.end(),
         screenOut);                                       //Line 7
    cout << endl;                                          //Line 8

    copy(vecList1.begin(), vecList1.end(),
         inserter(vecList2, vecList2.begin()));            //Line 9

    cout << "Line 10: vecList2: ";                         //Line 10
    copy(vecList2.begin(), vecList2.end(),
                          screenOut);                      //Line 11
    cout << endl;                                          //Line 12

    list<int> tempList;                                    //Line 13

    copy(vecList2.begin(), vecList2.end(),
         front_inserter(tempList));                        //Line 14

    cout << "Line 15: tempList: ";                         //Line 15
    copy(tempList.begin(), tempList.end(),
                          screenOut);                      //Line 16
    cout << endl;                                          //Line 17

    return 0;
}
```

Sample Run:

```
Line 6: vecList1: 1 2 3 4 5 6 7 8
Line 10: vecList2: 1 2 3 4 5 6 7 8
Line 15: tempList: 8 7 6 5 4 3 2 1
```

STL Algorithms

The following sections describe most of the STL algorithms. For each algorithm, we give
the function prototypes, a brief description of what the algorithm does, and a program
showing how to use it. In the function prototypes, the parameter types indicate for which
type of container the algorithm is applicable. For example, if a parameter is of type
`randomAccessIterator`, then the algorithm is applicable only on random access type
containers, such as vectors. Throughout, we use abbreviations such as `outputItr` to
mean output iterator, `inputItr` to mean input iterator, `forwardItr` to mean forward
iterator, and so on.

The Functions `fill` and `fill_n`

The function `fill` is used to fill a container with elements; the function `fill_n` is used
to fill in the next n elements. The element that is used as a filling element is passed as a
parameter to these functions. Both of these functions are defined in the header file
`algorithm`. The prototypes of these functions are:

```cpp
template <class forwardItr, class Type>
void fill(forwardItr first, forwardItr last, const Type& value);

template <class forwardItr, class size, class Type>
void fill_n(forwardItr first, size n, const Type& value);
```

The first two parameters of the function `fill` are forward iterators specifying the starting and ending positions of the container; the third parameter is the filling element. The first parameter of the function `fill_n` is a forward iterator that specifies the starting position of the container, the second parameter specifies the number of elements to be filled, and the third parameter specifies the filling element. The program in Example 22-14 illustrates how to use these functions.

EXAMPLE 22-14

```cpp
//STL functions fill and fill_n

#include <iostream>
#include <algorithm>
#include <iterator>
#include <vector>

using namespace std;

int main()
{
    vector<int>  vecList(8);                            //Line 1
    ostream_iterator<int> screen(cout, " ");            //Line 2

    fill(vecList.begin(), vecList.end(), 2);            //Line 3

    cout << "Line 4: After filling vecList "
         << "with 2s: ";                                //Line 4
    copy(vecList.begin(), vecList.end(), screen);       //Line 5
    cout << endl;                                       //Line 6

    fill_n(vecList.begin(), 3, 5);                      //Line 7

    cout << "Line 8: After filling the first three "
         << "elements with 5s: "
         << endl << "           ";                      //Line 8
    copy(vecList.begin(), vecList.end(), screen);       //Line 9
    cout << endl;                                       //Line 10

    return 0;
}
```

Sample Run:

```
Line 4: After filling vecList with 2s: 2 2 2 2 2 2 2 2
Line 8: After filling first three elements with 5s:
        5 5 5 2 2 2 2 2
```

The statements in Lines 1 and 2 declare `vecList` to be a sequence container of size 8 and `screen` to be an `ostream` iterator initialized to `cout` with the delimit character space. The statement in Line 3 uses the function `fill` to fill `vecList` with 2; that is, all eight elements of `vecList` are set to 2. Recall that `vecList.begin()` returns an iterator to the first element of `vecList`, and `vecList.end()` returns an iterator to one past the last element of `vecList`. The statement in Line 5 outputs the elements of `vecList` using the `copy` function. The statement in Line 7 uses the function `fill_n` to store 5 in the elements of `vecList`. The first parameter of `fill_n` is `vecList.begin()`, which specifies the starting position to begin copying. The second parameter of `fill_n` is 3, which specifies the number of elements to be filled. The third parameter, 5, specifies the filling character. Therefore, 5 is copied into the first three elements of `vecList`. The statement in Line 9 outputs the elements of `vecList`.

The Functions `generate` and `generate_n`

The functions `generate` and `generate_n` are used to generate elements and fill a sequence. These functions are defined in the header file `algorithm`. The prototypes of these functions are:

```
template <class forwardItr, class function>
void generate(forwardItr first, forwardItr last, function gen);

template <class forwardItr, class size, class function>
void generate_n(forwardItr first, size n, function gen);
```

The function `generate` fills a sequence in the range `first...last-1`, with successive calls to the function `gen()`. The function `generate_n` fills a sequence in the range `first...first+n-1`—that is, starting at position `first`, with n successive calls to the function `gen()`. Note that `gen` can also be a pointer to a function. Moreover, if `gen` is a function, it must be a value-returning function without parameters. The program in Example 22-15 illustrates how to use these functions.

EXAMPLE 22-15

```
//STL Functions generate and generate_n

#include <iostream>
#include <algorithm>
#include <iterator>
#include <vector>

using namespace std;

int nextNum();
```

```cpp
int main()
{
    vector<int>  vecList(8);                            //Line 1

    ostream_iterator<int> screen(cout, " ");            //Line 2

    generate(vecList.begin(), vecList.end(), nextNum);  //Line 3

    cout << "Line 4: vecList after filling with "
         << "numbers: ";                                //Line 4

    copy(vecList.begin(), vecList.end(), screen);       //Line 5
    cout << endl;                                        //Line 6

    generate_n(vecList.begin(), 3, nextNum);            //Line 7

    cout << "Line 8: vecList after filling the "
         << "first three elements " << endl
         << "            with the next number: ";        //Line 8

    copy(vecList.begin(), vecList.end(), screen);       //Line 9
    cout << endl;                                        //Line 10

    return 0;
}

int nextNum()
{
    static int n = 1;

    return n++;
}
```

Sample Run:

```
Line 4: vecList after filling with numbers: 1 2 3 4 5 6 7 8
Line 8: vecList after filling the first three elements
        with the next number: 9 10 11 4 5 6 7 8
```

This program contains a value-returning function, nextNum, which contains a **static** variable n initialized to 1. A call to this function returns the current value of n and then increments the value of n. Therefore, the first call of nextNum returns 1, the second call returns 2, and so on.

The statements in Lines 1 and 2 declare vecList to be a sequence container of size 8 and screen to be an ostream iterator initialized to cout with the delimit character space. The statement in Line 3 uses the function generate to fill vecList by successively calling the function nextNum. Notice that after the statement in Line 3 executes, the value of the **static** variable n of nextNum is 9. The statement in Line 5 outputs the elements of vecList. The statement in Line 7 calls the function generate_n to fill the first three elements of vecList by calling the function nextNum three times. The starting position is `vecList.begin()`, which is the first element of `vecList`, and the number of elements to be filled is 3, given by the second parameter of `generate_n` (see Line 7). The statement in Line 9 outputs the elements of `vecList`.

The Functions `find`, `find_if`, `find_end`, and `find_first_of`

The functions `find`, `find_if`, `find_end`, and `find_first_of` are used to find the elements in a given range. These functions are defined in the header file `algorithm`. The prototypes of the functions `find` and `find_if` are:

```
template <class inputItr, class size, class Type>
inputItr find(inputItr first, inputItr last,
            const Type& searchValue);


template <class inputItr, class unaryPredicate>
inputItr find_if(inputItr first, inputItr last, unaryPredicate op);
```

The function `find` searches the range of elements `first...last-1` for the element `searchValue`. If `searchValue` is found in the range, the function returns the position in the range where `searchValue` is found; otherwise, it returns `last`. The function `find_if` searches the range of elements `first...last-1` for the element for which `op(rangeElement)` is `true`. If an element satisfying `op(rangeElement)` is `true` is found, it returns the position in the given range where such an element is found; otherwise, it returns `last`.

The program in Example 22-16 illustrates how to use the functions `find` and `find_if`.

EXAMPLE 22-16

```cpp
//STL Functions find and find_if

#include <iostream>
#include <cctype>
#include <algorithm>
#include <iterator>
#include <vector>

using namespace std;

int main()
{
    char cList[10] = {'a', 'i', 'C', 'd', 'e',
                      'f', 'o', 'H', 'u', 'j'};        //Line 1

    vector<char> charList(cList, cList + 10);          //Line 2
```

```cpp
    ostream_iterator<char> screen(cout, " ");          //Line 3

    cout << "Line 4: Character list: ";                //Line 4
    copy(charList.begin(), charList.end(), screen);     //Line 5
    cout << endl;                                        //Line 6

    vector<char>::iterator position;                    //Line 7

        //find
    position = find(charList.begin(),
                    charList.end(), 'd');               //Line 8

    if (position != charList.end())                     //Line 9
        cout << "Line 10: The element is found at "
             << "position "
             << (position - charList.begin())
             << endl;                                    //Line 10
    else                                                //Line 11
        cout << "Line 12: The element is not in "
             << "the list." << endl;                    //Line 12

        //find_if
    position = find_if(charList.begin(),
                       charList.end(), isupper);        //Line 13

    if (position != charList.end())                     //Line 14
        cout << "Line 15: The first uppercase "
             << "letter is found at position "
             << (position - charList.begin())
             << endl;                                    //Line 15
    else                                                //Line 16
        cout << "Line 17: The element is not in "
             << "the list." << endl;                    //Line 17

    return 0;
}
```

Sample Run:

```
Line 4: Character list: a i C d e f o H u j
Line 10: The element is found at position 3
Line 15: The first uppercase letter is found at position 2
```

The statement in Line 1 creates and initializes a character array, cList, of 10 components. The statement in Line 2 creates the vector container charList and initializes it
using the character array cList. The statement in Line 3 creates an ostream iterator.
The statement in Line 5 outputs charList. (In the output, the line marked Line 4
contains the output of Lines 4 through 6 of the program.) The statement in Line 7
declares the iterator position of type vector<char>. The statement in Line 8
searches charList for the first occurrence of 'd' and returns an iterator, which is
stored in position. The statements in Line 9 through 12 output the result of the search.
Because 'd' is the fourth character in charList, its position is 3. (In the output, see the

line marked Line 10.) The statement in Line 13 uses the function `find_if` to find the first uppercase character in `charList`. Note that the function `isupper` from the header file `cctype` is passed as the third parameter to the function `find_if` (see Line 13). The statements in Lines 14 through 17 output the result of the search. The first uppercase character in `charList` is `'C'`, which is the third element of `charList`; its position is 2. (In the output, see the line marked Line 15.)

Next, we describe the functions `find_end` and `find_first_of`. Both of these functions have two forms. The prototypes of the function `find_end` are:

```
template <class forwardItr1, class forwardItr2>
forwardItr1 find_end(forwardItr1 first1, forwardItr1 last1,
                 forwardItr2 first2, forwardItr2 last2);

template <class forwardItr1, class forwardItr2,
        class binaryPredicate>
forwardItr1 find_end(forwardItr1 first1, forwardItr1 last1,
                 forwardItr2 first2, forwardItr2 last2,
                 binaryPredicate op);
```

Both forms of the function `find_end` search the range `first1...last1-1` for the last occurrence as a subrange of the range `first2...last2-1`. If the search is successful, the function returns the position in `first1..last1-1` where the match occurs; otherwise, it returns `last1`. That is, the function `find_end` returns the position of the last element in the range `first1...last1-1` where the range `first2...last2-1` is a subrange of `first1...last1-1`. In the first form, the elements are compared for equality; in the second form, the comparison `op(elementFirstRange, elementSecondRange)` must be `true`.

The prototypes of the function `find_first_of` are:

```
template <class forwardItr1, class forwardItr2>
forwardItr1 find_first_of(forwardItr1 first1, forwardItr1 last1,
                   forwardItr2 first2, forwardItr2 last2);

template <class forwardItr1, class forwardItr2,
        class binaryPredicate>
forwardItr1 find_first_of(forwardItr1 first1, forwardItr1 last1,
                   forwardItr2 first2, forwardItr2 last2,
                   binaryPredicate op);
```

The first form returns the position, within the range `first1...last1-1`, of the first element of `first2...last2-1` that is also in the range `first1...last1-1`. The second form returns the position, within the range `first1...last1-1`, of the first element of `first2...last2-1` for which `op(elemRange1, elemRange2)` is `true`. If no match is found, both forms return `last1-1`.

The program in Example 22-17 illustrates how to use the functions `find_end` and `find_first_of`.

EXAMPLE 22-17

```cpp
//STL Functions find_end and find_first_of

#include <iostream>
#include <algorithm>
#include <iterator>
#include <vector>

using namespace std;

int main()
{
    int list1[10] = {12, 34, 56, 21, 34,
                     78, 34, 56, 12, 25};          //Line 1
    int list2[2] = {34, 56};                       //Line 2
    int list3[3] = {56, 21, 35};                   //Line 3
    int list4[5] = {33, 48, 21, 34, 73};           //Line 4

    vector<int>::iterator location;                //Line 5

    ostream_iterator<int> screenOut(cout, " ");    //Line 6

    cout << "Line 7: list1: ";                     //Line 7
    copy(list1, list1 + 10, screenOut);            //Line 8
    cout << endl;                                  //Line 9

    cout << "Line 10: list2: ";                    //Line 10
    copy(list2, list2 + 2, screenOut);             //Line 11
    cout << endl;                                  //Line 12

        //find_end
    location = find_end(list1, list1+10,
                        list2, list2 + 2);          //Line 13

    if (location != list1 + 10)                     //Line 14
        cout << "Line 15: list2 is found in list 1. "
             << "The last occurrence of \n            "
             << "list2 in list 1 is at position "
             << (location - list1) << endl;         //Line 15
    else                                            //Line 16
        cout << "Line 17: list2 is not in list1."
             << endl;                               //Line 17

    cout << "Line 18: list3: ";                     //Line 18
    copy(list3, list3 + 3, screenOut);              //Line 19
    cout << endl;                                   //Line 20

    location = find_end(list1, list1 + 10,
                        list3, list3 + 3);           //Line 21
```

```cpp
    if (location != list1 + 10)                         //Line 22
        cout << "Line 23: list3 is found in list 1. "
            << "The last occurrence of list3 in "
            << endl << "list 1 is at position "
            << (location - list1) << endl;              //Line 23
    else                                                //Line 24
        cout << "Line 25: list3 is not in list1."
            << endl;                                    //Line 25

        //find_first_of
    cout << "Line 26: list4: ";                         //Line 26
    copy(list4, list4 + 5, screenOut);                  //Line 27
    cout << endl;                                       //Line 28

    location = find_first_of(list1, list1 + 10,
                             list4, list4 + 5);          //Line 29

    if (location != list1 + 10)                         //Line 30
        cout << "Line 31: The first element "
            << *location << " of list4 is found in "
            << endl << "        list 1 at position "
            << (location - list1) << endl;              //Line 31
    else                                                //Line 32
        cout << "Line 33: No element of list4 is "
            << "in list1." << endl;                     //Line 33

    return 0;
}
```

Sample Run:

```
Line 7: list1: 12 34 56 21 34 78 34 56 12 25
Line 10: list2: 34 56
Line 15: list2 is found in list 1. The last occurrence of
        list2 in list 1 is at position 6
Line 18: list3: 56 21 35
Line 25: list3 is not in list1.
Line 26: list4: 33 48 21 34 73
Line 31: The first element 34 of list4 is found in
        list 1 at position 1
```

The statements in Lines 1 through 4 create and initialize the `int` arrays `list1`, `list2`, `list3`, and `list4`. The statements in Lines 5 and 6 declare the `vector` and `ostream` iterators. The statements in Lines 8 and 11 output the values of `list1` and `list2`. (In the output, see the lines marked Line 7 and Line 10.) The statement in Line 13 uses the function `find_end` to find the last occurrence of `list2`, as a subsequence, within `list1`. The last occurrence of `list2` in `list1` starts at position 6 (that is, at the seventh element). The statements in Lines 14 through 17 output the result of the search. (In the output, see Line 15.) The statement in Line 19 outputs `list3`. The statement in Line 21 uses the function `find_end` to find the last occurrence of `list3`, as a subsequence, within `list1`. Because `list3` does not appear as a subsequence in `list1`, it is an unsuccessful search.

The statement in Line 27 outputs `list4`. The statement in Line 29 uses the function `find_first_of` to find the position in `list1` where the first element of `list4` is also an element of `list1`. The first element of `list4`, which is also an element of `list1`, is 34. Its position in `list1` is 1, the second element of `list1`. The statements in Lines 30 through 33 output the result of the search. (In the output, see Line 31.)

The Functions `remove`, `remove_if`, `remove_copy`, and `remove_copy_if`

The function **remove** is used to remove certain elements from a sequence, and the function `remove_if` is used to remove elements from a sequence by using some criteria. The function `remove_copy` copies the elements of a sequence into another sequence by excluding certain elements of the first sequence. Similarly, the function `remove_copy_if` copies the elements of a sequence into another sequence by excluding certain elements, using some criteria, of the first sequence. These functions are defined in the header file `algorithm`.

The prototypes of the functions **remove** and `remove_if` are:

```
template <class forwardItr, class Type>
forwardItr remove(forwardItr first, forwardItr last,
                  const Type& value);


template <class forwardItr, class unaryPredicate>
forwardItr remove_if(forwardItr first, forwardItr last,
                     unaryPredicate op);
```

The function **remove** removes each occurrence of a given element in the range `first...last-1`. The element to be removed is passed as the third parameter to this function. The function `remove_if` removes those elements, in the range `first...last-1`, for which the `op(element)` is **true**. Both of these functions return `forwardItr`, which points to the position after the last element of the new range of elements. These functions do not modify the size of the container; in fact, the elements are moved to the beginning of the container. For example, if the sequence is {3, 7, 2, 5, 7, 9} and the element to be removed is 7, then after removing 7, the resulting sequence is {3, 2, 5, 9, 9, 9}. The function returns a pointer to element 9 (which is after 5).

The program in Example 22-18 further illustrates the importance of this returned `forwardItr`. (See Lines 8, 10, 12, and 14.)

Let us now look at the prototypes of the functions `remove_copy` and `remove_copy_if`:

```
template <class inputItr, class outputItr, class Type>
outputItr remove_copy(inputItr first1, inputItr last1,
                      outputItr destFirst, const Type& value);
```

```cpp
template <class inputItr, class outputItr, class unaryPredicate>
outputItr remove_copy_if(inputItr first1, inputItr last1,
                         outputItr destFirst,
                         unaryPredicate op);
```

The function `remove_copy` copies all the elements in the range `first1...last1-1`, except the elements specified by value, into the sequence starting at the position `destFirst`. Similarly, the function `remove_copy_if` copies all the elements in the range `first1...last1-1`, except the elements for which `op(element)` is `true`, into the sequence starting at the position `destFirst`. Both of these functions return an `outputItr`, which points to the position after the last element copied.

The program in Example 22-18 shows how to use the functions `remove`, `remove_if`, `remove_copy`, and `remove_copy_if`.

EXAMPLE 22-18

```cpp
//STL Functions remove, remove_if, remove_copy, and
//                   remove_copy_if

#include <iostream>
#include <cctype>
#include <algorithm>
#include <iterator>
#include <vector>

using namespace std;

bool lessThanEqualTo50(int num);

int main()
{
    char cList[10] = {'A', 'a', 'A', 'B', 'A',
                      'c', 'D', 'e', 'F', 'A'};       //Line 1

    vector<char> charList(cList, cList + 10);         //Line 2
    vector<char>::iterator lastElem, newLastElem;     //Line 3

    ostream_iterator<char> screen(cout, " ");         //Line 4

    cout << "Line 6: Character list: ";               //Line 5
    copy(charList.begin(), charList.end(), screen);   //Line 6
    cout << endl;                                     //Line 7

        //remove
    lastElem = remove(charList.begin(),
                  charList.end(), 'A');               //Line 8

    cout << "Line 9: Character list after "
         << "removing A: ";                           //Line 9
```

```cpp
    copy(charList.begin(), lastElem, screen);               //Line 10
    cout << endl;                                            //Line 11

        //remove_if
    newLastElem = remove_if(charList.begin(),
                            lastElem, isupper);              //Line 12
    cout << "Line 13: Character list after "
         << "removing the uppercase " << endl
         << "             letters: ";                        //Line 13
    copy(charList.begin(), newLastElem, screen);            //Line 14
    cout << endl;                                            //Line 15

    int list[10] = {12, 34, 56, 21, 34,
                    78, 34, 55, 12, 25};                    //Line 16

    vector<int>  intList(list, list + 10);                  //Line 17
    vector<int>::iterator endElement;                       //Line 18

    ostream_iterator<int> screenOut(cout, " ");            //Line 19

    cout << "Line 20: intList: ";                           //Line 20
    copy(intList.begin(), intList.end(), screenOut);        //Line 21
    cout << endl;                                            //Line 22

    vector<int> temp1(10);                                  //Line 23

        //remove_copy
    endElement = remove_copy(intList.begin(),
                             intList.end(),
                             temp1.begin(), 34);            //Line 24

    cout << "Line 25: temp1 list after copying "
         << "all the elements of intList "
         << endl << "             except 34: ";             //Line 25
    copy(temp1.begin(), endElement, screenOut);            //Line 26
    cout << endl;                                            //Line 27

    vector<int> temp2(10, 0);                               //Line 28

        //remove_copy_if
    remove_copy_if(intList.begin(), intList.end(),
                   temp2.begin(), lessThanEqualTo50);       //Line 29

    cout << "Line 30: temp2 after copying all the "
         << "elements of intList except " << endl
         << "             numbers less than 50: ";          //Line 30
    copy(temp2.begin(), temp2.end(), screenOut);           //Line 31
    cout << endl;                                            //Line 32

    return 0;
}
```

```
bool lessThanEqualTo50(int num)
{
    return (num <= 50);
}
```

Sample Run:

```
Line 6: Character list: A a A B A c D e F A
Line 9: Character list after removing A: a B c D e F
Line 13: Character list after removing the uppercase
        letters: a c e
Line 20: intList: 12 34 56 21 34 78 34 55 12 25
Line 25: temp1 list after copying all the elements of intList
        except 34: 12 56 21 78 55 12 25
Line 30: temp2 after copying all the elements of intList except
        numbers less than 50: 56 78 55 0 0 0 0 0 0 0
```

The statement in Line 2 creates a vector list, `charList`, of type `char` and initializes `charList` using the array `cList` created in Line 1. The statement in Line 2 declares two vector iterators, `lastElem` and `newLastElem`. The statement in Line 4 declares an `ostream` iterator, `screen`. The statement in Line 6 outputs the value of `charList`. The statement in Line 8 uses the function `remove` to remove all occurrences of `'A'` from `charList`. The function returns a pointer to one past the last element of the new range, which is stored in `lastElem`. The statement in Line 10 outputs the elements in the new range. (Note that the statement in Line 10 outputs the elements in the range `charList.begin()...lastElem-1`.) The statement in Line 12 uses the function `remove_if` to remove the uppercase letters from the list `charList` and stores the pointer returned by the function `remove_if` in `newLastElem`. The statement in Line 14 outputs the elements in the new range.

The statement in Line 17 creates a vector, `intList`, of type `int` and initializes `intList` using the array `list`, created in Line 16. The statement in Line 21 outputs the elements of `intList`. The statement in Line 24 copies all the elements, except the occurrences of 34, of `intList` into `temp1`. The list `intList` is not modified. The statement in Line 26 outputs the elements of `temp1`. The statement in Line 28 creates a vector, `temp2`, of type `int` of 10 components and initializes all the elements of `temp2` to 0. The statement in Line 29 uses the function `remove_copy_if` to copy those elements of `intList` that are greater than 50. The statement in Line 31 outputs the elements of `temp2`.

The Functions `replace`, `replace_if`, `replace_copy`, and `replace_copy_if`

The function `replace` is used to replace all occurrences, within a given range, of a given element with a new value. The function `replace_if` is used to replace the values of the elements, within a given range, satisfying certain criteria with a new value. The prototypes of these functions are:

```cpp
template <class forwardItr, class Type >
void replace(forwardItr first, forwardItr last,
             const Type& oldValue, const Type& newValue);

template <class forwardItr, class unaryPredicate, class Type>
void replace_if(forwardItr first, forwardItr last,
                unaryPredicate op, const Type& newValue);
```

The function `replace` replaces all the elements in the range `first...last-1` whose values are equal to `oldValue` with the value specified by `newValue`. The function `replace_if` replaces all the elements in the range `first...last-1`, for which `op(element)` is `true`, with the value specified by `newValue`.

The function `replace_copy` is a combination of `replace` and `copy`. Similarly, the function `replace_copy_if` is a combination of `replace_if` and `copy`. Let us first look at the prototypes of the functions `replace_copy` and `replace_copy_if`:

```cpp
template <class inputItr, class outputItr, class Type>
outputItr replace_copy(forwardItr first, forwardItr last,
                       outputItr destFirst,
                       const Type& oldValue,
                       const Type& newValue);

template <class forwardItr, class outputItr,
          class unaryPredicate, class Type>
outputItr replace_copy_if(forwardItr first, forwardItr last,
                          outputItr destFirst,
                          unaryPredicate op,
                          const Type& newValue);
```

The function `replace_copy` copies all the elements in the range `first...last-1` into the container starting at `destFirst`. If the value of an element in this range is equal to `oldValue`, it is replaced by `newValue`. The function `replace_copy_if` copies all the elements in the range `first...last-1` into the container starting at `destFirst`. If, for any element in this range, `op(element)` is `true`, at the destination its value is replaced by `newValue`. Both of these functions return an `outputItr` (a pointer) positioned one past the last element copied at the destination.

The program in Example 22-19 shows how to use the functions `replace`, `replace_if`, `replace_copy`, and `replace_copy_if`.

EXAMPLE 22-19

```cpp
//STL Functions replace, replace_if, replace_copy, and
//               replace_copy_if

#include <iostream>
#include <cctype>
#include <algorithm>
#include <iterator>
#include <vector>
```

```cpp
using namespace std;

bool lessThanEqualTo50(int num);

int main()
{
    char cList[10] = {'A', 'a', 'A', 'B', 'A',
                      'c', 'D', 'e', 'F', 'A'};        //Line 1

    vector<char>  charList(cList, cList + 10);         //Line 2

    ostream_iterator<char> screen(cout, " ");          //Line 3

    cout << "Line 4: Character list: ";                //Line 4
    copy(charList.begin(), charList.end(), screen);    //Line 5
    cout << endl;                                      //Line 6

        //replace
    replace(charList.begin(), charList.end(),
            'A', 'Z');                                 //Line 7

    cout << "Line 8: Character list after replacing "
         << "A with Z: " << endl
         << "           ";                             //Line 8
    copy(charList.begin(), charList.end(), screen);    //Line 9
    cout << endl;                                      //Line 10

        //replace_if
    replace_if(charList.begin(), charList.end(),
               isupper, '*');                          //Line 11
    cout << "Line 12: Character list after "
         << "replacing the uppercase  " << endl
         << "             letters with *: ";           //Line 12
    copy(charList.begin(), charList.end(), screen);    //Line 13
    cout << endl;                                      //Line 14

    int list[10] = {12, 34, 56, 21, 34,
                    78, 34, 55, 12, 25};               //Line 15

    vector<int>  intList(list, list + 10);             //Line 16

    ostream_iterator<int> screenOut(cout, " ");        //Line 17

    cout << "Line 18: intList: ";                      //Line 18
    copy(intList.begin(), intList.end(), screenOut);   //Line 19
    cout << endl;                                      //Line 20

    vector<int> temp1(10);                             //Line 21

        //replace_copy
    replace_copy(intList.begin(), intList.end(),
                 temp1.begin(), 34, 0);                //Line 22
```

```cpp
    cout << "Line 23: temp1 list after copying "
        << "intList and " << endl
        << "              replacing 34 with 0: ";      //Line 23
    copy(temp1.begin(), temp1.end(), screenOut);        //Line 24
    cout << endl;                                        //Line 25

    vector<int> temp2(10);                               //Line 26

        //replace_copy_if
    replace_copy_if(intList.begin(), intList.end(),
            temp2.begin(), lessThanEqualTo50, 50);   //Line 27

    cout << "Line 28: temp2 after copying intList "
        << "and replacing any " << endl
        << "              numbers less than 50 "
        << "with 50: " << endl << "              ";      //Line 28
    copy(temp2.begin(), temp2.end(), screenOut);         //Line 29
    cout << endl;                                         //Line 30

    return 0;
}

bool lessThanEqualTo50(int num)
{
    return (num <= 50);
}
```

Sample Run:

```
Line 4: Character list: A a A B A c D e F A
Line 8: Character list after replacing A with Z:
        Z a Z B Z c D e F Z
Line 12: Character list after replacing the uppercase
        letters with *: * a * * * c * e * *
Line 18: intList: 12 34 56 21 34 78 34 55 12 25
Line 23: temp1 list after copying intList and
        replacing 34 with 0: 12 0 56 21 0 78 0 55 12 25
Line 28: temp2 after copying intList and replacing any
        numbers less than 50 with 50:
        50 50 56 50 50 78 50 55 50 50
```

The statement in Line 2 creates a vector list, charList, of type **char** and initializes charList using the array cList created in Line 1. The statement in Line 3 declares an ostream iterator, screen. The statement in Line 5 outputs the value of charList. The statement in Line 7 uses the function **replace** to replace all occurrences of **'A'** with **'Z'** in charList. The statement in List 9 outputs the elements of charList. In the output, the line marked Line 8 contains the outputs of Lines 8 through 10. The statement in Line 11 uses the function **replace_if** to replace the uppercase letters with **'*'** in the list charList. The statement in Line 13 outputs the elements of charList. In the output, the line marked Line 12 contains the output of Lines 12 through 14.

The statement in Line 16 creates a vector, `intList`, of type `int` and initializes `intList` using the array `list`, created in Line 15. The statement in Line 19 outputs the elements of `intList`. The statement in Line 21 declares a vector `temp1` of type `int`. The statement in Line 22 copies all the elements of `intList` and replaces 34 with 0. The list `intList` is not modified. The statement in Line 24 outputs the elements of `temp1`. The statement in Line 26 creates a vector, `temp2`, of type `int`, of 10 components. The statement in Line 27 uses the function `replace_copy_if` to copy the elements of `intList` and replaces all the elements less than 50 with 50. The statement in Line 29 outputs the elements of `temp2`. In the output, the line marked Line 28 contains the output of Lines 28 through 30.

The Functions `swap`, `iter_swap`, and `swap_ranges`

The functions `swap`, `iter_swap`, and `swap_ranges` are used to swap elements. These functions are defined in the header file `algorithm`. The prototypes of these functions are:

```cpp
template <class Type>
void swap(Type& object1, Type& object2);


template <class forwardItr1, class forwardItr2>
void iter_swap(forwardItr1 first, forwardItr2 second);


template <class forwardItr1, class forwardItr2>
forwardItr2 swap_ranges(forwardItr1 first1, forwardItr1 last1,
                        forwardItr2 first2);
```

The function `swap` swaps the values of `object1` and `object2`. The function `iter_swap` swaps the values to which the iterators `first` and `second` point.

The function `swap_ranges` swaps the elements of the range `first1...last1-1` with the consecutive elements starting at position `first2`. It returns the iterator of the second range positioned one past the last element swapped. The program in Example 22-20 illustrates how to use these functions.

EXAMPLE 22-20

```cpp
//STL functions swap, iter_swap, and swap_ranges

#include <iostream>
#include <algorithm>
#include <vector>
#include <iterator>

using namespace std;
```

```cpp
int main()
{
    char cList[10] = {'A', 'B', 'C', 'D', 'F',
                      'G', 'H', 'I', 'J', 'K'};        //Line 1

    vector<char> charList(cList, cList + 10);          //Line 2
    vector<char>::iterator  charItr;                   //Line 3

    ostream_iterator<char> screen(cout, " ");          //Line 4

    cout << "Line 5: Character list: ";                //Line 5
    copy(charList.begin(), charList.end(), screen);    //Line 6
    cout << endl;                                       //Line 7

    swap(charList[0], charList[1]);                    //Line 8

    cout << "Line 9: Character list after swapping "
         << "the first and second  " << endl
         << "             elements: ";                 //Line 9
    copy(charList.begin(), charList.end(), screen);    //Line 10
    cout << endl;                                       //Line 11

    iter_swap(charList.begin() + 2,
              charList.begin() + 3);                   //Line 12

    cout << "Line 13: Character list after swapping "
         << "the third and fourth " << endl
         << "             elements: ";                 //Line 13

    copy(charList.begin(), charList.end(), screen);    //Line 14
    cout << endl;                                       //Line 15

    charItr = charList.begin() + 4;                    //Line 16
    iter_swap(charItr, charItr + 1);                   //Line 17

    cout << "Line 18: Character list after swapping "
         << "the fifth and sixth " << endl
         << "             elements: ";                 //Line 18
    copy(charList.begin(), charList.end(), screen);    //Line 19
    cout << endl;                                       //Line 20

    int list[10] = {1, 2, 3, 4, 5, 6, 7, 8, 9, 10};    //Line 21

    vector<int> intList(list, list + 10);              //Line 22

    ostream_iterator<int> screenOut(cout, " ");        //Line 23

    cout << "Line 24: intList: ";                      //Line 24
    copy(intList.begin(), intList.end(), screenOut);   //Line 25
    cout << endl;                                       //Line 26
```

```cpp
        //swap_ranges
    swap_ranges(intList.begin(), intList.begin() + 4,
            intList.begin() + 5);                       //Line 27

    cout << "Line 28: intList after swapping the first "
        << "four elements " << endl
        << "          with four elements starting at "
        << "the sixth element " << endl
        << "          of intList: ";                    //Line 28
    copy(intList.begin(), intList.end(), screenOut);    //Line 29
    cout << endl;                                        //Line 30

    swap_ranges(list, list + 10, intList.begin());      //Line 31

    cout << "Line 32: list and intList after "
        << "swapping their elements " << endl;          //Line 32
    cout << "Line 33: list: ";                          //Line 33
    copy(list, list+10, screenOut);                     //Line 34
    cout << endl;                                        //Line 35
    cout << "List 36: intList: ";                       //Line 36
    copy(intList.begin(), intList.end(), screenOut);    //Line 37
    cout << endl;                                        //Line 38

    return 0;
}
```

Sample Run:

```
Line 5: Character list: A B C D F G H I J K
Line 9: Character list after swapping the first and second
        elements: B A C D F G H I J K
Line 13: Character list after swapping the third and fourth
         elements: B A D C F G H I J K
Line 18: Character list after swapping the fifth and sixth
         elements: B A D C G F H I J K
Line 24: intList: 1 2 3 4 5 6 7 8 9 10
Line 28: intList after swapping the first four elements
         with four elements starting at the sixth element
         of intList: 6 7 8 9 5 1 2 3 4 10
Line 32: list and intList after swapping their elements
Line 33: list: 6 7 8 9 5 1 2 3 4 10
List 36: intList: 1 2 3 4 5 6 7 8 9 10
```

The statement in Line 2 creates the vector `charList` and initializes it using the array `cList` declared in Line 1. The statement in Line 6 outputs the values of `charList`. The statement in Line 8 swaps the first and second elements of `charList`. The statement in Line 12, using the function `iter_swap`, swaps the third and fourth elements of `charList`. (Recall that the position of the first element in `charList` is 0.) After the statement in Line 16 executes, `charItr` points to the fifth element of `charList`. The statement in Line 17 uses the iterator `charItr` to swap the fifth and sixth elements of `charList`. The statement in Line 19 outputs the values of the elements of `charList`.

(In the output, the line marked Line 18 contains the output of Lines 18 through 20 of the program.)

The statement in Line 22 creates the vector `intList` and initializes it using the array declared in Line 21. The statement in Line 25 outputs the values of the elements of `intList`. The statement in Line 27 uses the function `swap_ranges` to swap the first four elements of `intList` with the four elements of `intList`, starting at the sixth element of `intList`. The statement in Line 29 outputs the elements of `intList`. (In the output, the line marked Line 28 contains the output of Lines 28 through 30 of the program.)

The statement in Line 31 swaps the elements of the array `list` with the elements of the vector `intList`. The statement in Line 34 outputs the elements of the array `list`, and the statement in Line 37 outputs `intList`.

The Functions `search`, `search_n`, `sort`, and `binary_search`

The functions `search`, `search_n`, `sort`, and `binary_search` are used to search and sort elements. These functions are defined in the header file `algorithm`.

The prototypes of the function `search` are:

```
template <class forwardItr1, class forwardItr2>
forwardItr1 search(forwardItr1 first1, forwardItr1 last1,
                forwardItr2 first2, forwardItr2 last2);

template <class forwardItr1, class forwardItr2,
        class binaryPredicate>
forwardItr1 search(forwardItr1 first1, forwardItr1 last1,
                forwardItr2 first2, forwardItr2 last2,
                binaryPredicate op);
```

Given two ranges of elements, `first1...last1-1` and `first2...last2-1`, the function `search` searches the first element in the range `first1...last1-1` where the range `first2...last2-1` occurs as a subrange of `first1...last1-1`. The first form makes the equality comparison between the elements of the two ranges. For the second form, the comparison `op(elemFirstRange, elemSecondRange)` must be `true`. If a match is found, the function returns the position in the range `first1...last1-1` where the match occurs; otherwise, the function returns `last1`.

The prototypes of the function `search_n` are:

```
template <class forwardItr, class size, class Type>
forwardItr search_n(forwardItr first, forwardItr last,
                size count, const Type& value);
```

```cpp
template <class forwardItr, class size, class Type,
          class binaryPredicate>
forwardItr search_n(forwardItr first, forwardItr last,
                    size count, const Type& value,
                    binaryPredicate op);
```

Given a range of elements `first...last-1`, the function `search_n` searches count consecutive occurrences of `value`. The first form returns the position in the range `first...last-1` where a subsequence of `count` consecutive elements have values equal to `value`. The second form returns the position in the range `first...last-1` where a subsequence of `count` consecutive elements exists for which `op(elemRange, value)` is `true`. If no match is found, both forms return `last`.

The prototypes of the function `sort` are:

```cpp
template <class randomAccessItr>
void sort(randomAccessItr first, randomAccessItr last);
```

```cpp
template <class randomAccessItr, class compare>
void sort(randomAccessItr first, randomAccessItr last,
          compare op);
```

The first form of the `sort` function reorders the elements in the range `first...last-1` in ascending order. The second form reorders the elements according to the criteria specified by `op`.

The prototypes of the function `binary_search` are:

```cpp
template <class forwardItr, class Type>
bool binary_search(forwardItr first, forwardItr last,
                   const Type& searchValue);
```

```cpp
template <class forwardItr, class Type, class compare>
bool binary_search(forwardItr first, forwardItr last,
                   const Type& searchValue, compare op);
```

The first form returns `true` if `searchValue` is found in the range `first...last-1`, and `false` otherwise. The second form uses a function object, `op`, that specifies the search criteria.

Example 22-21 illustrates how to use these searching and sorting functions.

EXAMPLE 22-21

```cpp
//STL Functions search, search_n, sort, and binary_search

#include <iostream>
#include <algorithm>
#include <iterator>
#include <vector>
```

```cpp
using namespace std;

int main()
{
    int intList[15] = {12, 34, 56, 34, 34,
                       78, 38, 43, 12, 25,
                       34, 56, 62, 5, 49};         //Line 1

    vector<int>  vecList(intList, intList + 15);    //Line 2
    int list[2] = {34, 56};                         //Line 3

    vector<int>::iterator location;                 //Line 4

    ostream_iterator<int> screenOut(cout, " ");     //Line 5

    cout << "Line 6: vecList: ";                    //Line 6
    copy(vecList.begin(), vecList.end(), screenOut); //Line 7
    cout << endl;                                    //Line 8

    cout << "Line 9: list: ";                        //Line 9
    copy(list, list + 2, screenOut);                 //Line 10
    cout << endl;                                     //Line 11

        //search
    location = search(vecList.begin(), vecList.end(),
                      list, list + 2);               //Line 12

    if (location != vecList.end())                   //Line 13
        cout << "Line 14: list found in vecList. "
             << "The first occurrence of " << endl
             << "            list in vecList is at "
             << "the position "
             << (location - vecList.begin()) << endl; //Line 14
    else                                              //Line 15
        cout << "Line 16: list is not in vecList."
             << endl;                                 //Line 16

        //search_n
    location = search_n(vecList.begin(),
                    vecList.end(), 2, 34);            //Line 17

    if (location != vecList.end())                    //Line 18
        cout << "Line 19: two consecutive "
             << "occurrences of 34 found in " << endl
             << "            vecList at the position "
             << (location - vecList.begin()) << endl; //Line 19
    else                                              //Line 20
        cout << "Line 21: vecList does not contain "
             << "two consecutive occurrences of 34."
             << endl;                                 //Line 21

        //sort
    sort(vecList.begin(), vecList.end());             //Line 22
```

```cpp
    cout << "Line 23: vecList after sorting:"
        << endl << "              ";              //Line 23
    copy(vecList.begin(), vecList.end(), screenOut);  //Line 24
    cout << endl;                                 //Line 25

        //binary_search
    bool found;                                   //Line 26

    found = binary_search(vecList.begin(),
                        vecList.end(), 78);       //Line 27

    if (found)                                    //Line 28
        cout << "Line 29: 78 found in vecList."
            << endl;                              //Line 29
    else                                          //Line 30
        cout << "Line 31: 78 not in vecList."
            << endl;                              //Line 31

    return 0;
}
```

Sample Run:

```
Line 6: vecList: 12 34 56 34 34 78 38 43 12 25 34 56 62 5 49
Line 9: list: 34 56
Line 14: list found in vecList. The first occurrence of
        list in vecList is at the position 1
Line 19: two consecutive occurrences of 34 found in
        vecList at the position 3
Line 23: vecList after sorting:
        5 12 12 25 34 34 34 34 38 43 49 56 56 62 78
Line 29: 78 found in vecList.
```

The statement in Line 2 creates a vector, `vecList`, and initializes it using the array `intList` created in Line 1. The statement in Line 3 creates an array, `list`, of 2 components and initializes `list`. The statement in Line 7 outputs `vecList`. The statement in Line 12 uses the function `search`, and searches `vecList` to find the position (of the first occurrence) in `vecList` where `list` occurs as a subsequence. The statements in Lines 13 through 16 output the result of the search; see the line marked Line 14 in the output.

The statement in Line 17 uses the function `search_n` to find the position in `vecList` where two consecutive instances of 34 occur. The statements in Lines 18 through 21 output the result of the search.

The statement in Line 22 uses the function `sort` to sort `vecList`. The statement in Line 24 outputs `vecList`. In the output, the line marked Line 23 contains the output of the statements in Lines 23 through 25.

The statement in Line 27 uses the function `binary_search` to search `vecList`. The statements in Lines 28 through 31 output the search result.

The Functions `adjacent_find`, `merge`, and `inplace_merge`

The algorithm `adjacent_find` is used to find the first occurrence of consecutive elements that meet certain criteria. The prototypes of the functions implementing this algorithm are:

```
template <class forwardItr>
forwardItr adjacent_find(forwardItr first, forwardItr last);

template <class forwardItr, class binaryPredicate>
forwardItr adjacent_find(forwardItr first, forwardItr last,
                         binaryPredicate op);
```

The first form of `adjacent_find` uses the equality criteria; that is, it looks for the first consecutive occurrences of the same element. In the second form, the algorithm returns an iterator to the element in the range `first...last-1` for which `op(elem, nextElem)` is `true`, where `elem` is an element in the range `first...last-1` and `nextElem` is an element in this range next to `elem`. If no matching elements are found, both algorithms return `last`.

The algorithm `merge` merges the sorted lists. The result is a sorted list. Both lists must be sorted according to the same criteria. For example, both lists should be in either ascending or descending order. The prototypes of the functions to implement the merge algorithms are:

```
template <class inputItr1, class inputItr2, class outputItr>
outputItr merge(inputItr1 first1, inputItr1 last1,
                inputItr2 first2, inputItr2 last2,
                outputItr destFirst);

template <class inputItr1, class inputItr2,
          class outputItr, class binaryPredicate>
outputItr merge(inputItr1 first1, inputItr1 last1,
                inputItr2 first2, inputItr2 last2,
                outputItr destFirst, binaryPredicate op);
```

Both forms of the algorithm `merge` merge the elements of the sorted ranges `first1...last1-1` and `first2...last2-1`. The destination range, beginning with the iterator `destFirst`, contains the merged elements. The first form uses the less-than operator, `<`, for ordering the elements. The second form uses the binary predicate `op` to order the elements; that is, `op(elemRange1, elemRange2)` must be `true`. Both forms return the position after the last copied element in the destination range. Moreover, the source ranges are not modified and the destination range should not overlap with the source ranges.

The algorithm `inplace_merge` is used to combine the sorted consecutive sequences. The prototypes of the functions implementing this algorithm are:

```
template <class biDirectionalItr>
void inplace_merge(biDirectionalItr first,
                   biDirectionalItr middle,
                   biDirectionalItr last);

template <class biDirectionalItr, class binaryPredicate>
void inplace_merge(biDirectionalItr first,
                   biDirectionalItr middle,
                   biDirectionalItr last,
                   binaryPredicate op);
```

Both forms merge the sorted consecutive sequences `first...middle-1` and `middle...last-1`. The merged elements overwrite the two ranges beginning at `first`. The first form uses the less-than criterion to merge the two consecutive sequences. The second form uses the binary predicate `op` to merge the sequences; that is, for the elements of the two sequences, `op(elemSeq1, elemSeq2)` must be `true`. For example, suppose that:

```
vecList = {1, 3, 5, 7, 9, 2, 4, 6, 8}
```

where `vecList` is a vector container. Further suppose that `vecItr` is a vector iterator pointing to element 2. Then, after the execution of the statement:

```
inplace_merge(vecList.begin(), vecItr, vecList.end());
```

the elements in `vecList` are in the following order:

```
vecList = {1, 2, 3, 4, 5, 6, 7, 8, 9}
```

The program in Example 22-22 illustrates how these algorithms work.

EXAMPLE 22-22

```
//STL Functions adjacent_find, merge, and inplace_merge

#include <iostream>
#include <functional>
#include <algorithm>
#include <iterator>
#include <vector>
#include <list>

using namespace std;

int main()
{
    int list1[10] = {1, 3, 5, 7, 9, 0, 2, 4, 6, 8};    //Line 1
    int list2[10] = {0, 1, 1, 2, 3, 4, 4, 5, 6, 6};    //Line 2

    int list3[5] = {0, 2, 4, 6, 8};                    //Line 3
    int list4[5] = {1, 3, 5, 7, 9};                    //Line 4
```

```cpp
list<int> intList(list2, list2 + 10);              //Line 5
list<int>::iterator listItr;                       //Line 6

vector<int> vecList(list1, list1 + 10);            //Line 7
vector<int>::iterator     intItr;                  //Line 8

ostream_iterator<int> screen(cout, " ");           //Line 9

cout << "Line 10: intList : ";                     //Line 10
copy(intList.begin(), intList.end(), screen);      //Line 11
cout << endl;                                       //Line 12

    //adjacent_find
listItr = adjacent_find(intList.begin(),
                        intList.end());             //Line 13

if (listItr != intList.end())                       //Line 14
    cout << "Line 15: Adjacent equal "
         << "elements are found " << endl
         << "             The first set of "
         << "adjacent equal elements: "
         << *listItr << endl;                       //Line 15
else                                                //Line 16
    cout << "Line 17: No adjacent equal "
         << "element found" << endl;                //Line 17

intList.clear();                                    //Line 18

    //merge
merge(list3, list3 + 5, list4, list4 + 5,
    back_inserter(intList));                        //Line 19

cout << "Line 20: intList after merging list3 "
     << "and " << "list4:\n"
     << "             ";                            //Line 20
copy(intList.begin(), intList.end(), screen);      //Line 21
cout << endl;                                       //Line 22

    //adjacent_find; second form
intItr = adjacent_find(vecList.begin(),
                       vecList.end(),
                       greater<int>());             //Line 23

cout << "Line 24: Last element of first "
     << "sorted sublist: " << *intItr << endl;      //Line 24
intItr++;                                           //Line 25
cout << "Line 26: First element of second "
     << "sorted sublist: " << *intItr << endl;      //List 26

cout << "Line 27: vecList before "
     << "inplace_merge: ";                          //Line 27
copy(vecList.begin(), vecList.end(), screen);      //Line 28
cout << endl;                                       //Line 29
```

```cpp
        //inplace_merge
    inplace_merge(vecList.begin(), intItr,
              vecList.end());                       //Line 30

    cout << "Line 31: vecList after inplace_merge: "; //Line 31
    copy(vecList.begin(), vecList.end(), screen);     //Line 32
    cout << endl;                                     //Line 33

    return 0;
}
```

Sample Run:

```
Line 10: intList : 0 1 1 2 3 4 4 5 6 6
Line 15: Adjacent equal elements are found
         The first set of adjacent equal elements: 1
Line 20: intList after merging list3 and list4:
         0 1 2 3 4 5 6 7 8 9
Line 24: Last element of first sorted sublist: 9
Line 26: First element of second sorted sublist: 0
Line 27: vecList before inplace_merge: 1 3 5 7 9 0 2 4 6 8
Line 31: vecList after inplace_merge: 0 1 2 3 4 5 6 7 8 9
```

The statement in Line 5 creates an `intList` of type `list<int>` and initializes `intList` using `list2`. Thus, `intList` is a linked list. The statement in Line 7 creates the vector `vecList` of type `int` and initializes it using `list1`. The statement in Line 11 outputs `intList`. The statement in Line 13 uses the function `adjacent_find` to find the position of the (first set of) consecutive identical elements. The function returns a pointer to the first set of consecutive elements, which is stored in `listItr`. The statements in Lines 14 through 17 output those consecutive identical elements, if any are found. Notice that the statement in Line 15 outputs `*listItr`—the contents of the memory space to which `listItr` is pointing.

The statement in Line 18 clears `intList`, by deleting all the elements of `intList`. The statement in Line 19 uses the function `merge` to merge `list3` and `list4`. The third parameter of the function `merge`, in Line 19, is a call to `back_inserter`, which places the merged list into `intList`. After the statement in Line 19 executes, `intList` contains the merged list. The statement in Line 21 outputs `intList`. In the output, see the line marked Line 20, which contains the output of the statements in Lines 20 through 22.

Notice that `vecList` is {1, 3, 5, 7, 9, 0, 2, 4, 6, 8}, which contains two sorted subsequences. The statement in Line 23 uses the second form of the function `adjacent_find` to find the starting position of the second subsequence. Notice that the third parameter of the function `adjacent_find` is the binary predicate `greater`, which returns the position in `vecList` where the first element is greater than the second element. The returned position is stored in the iterator `intItr`, which now points to element 9. The statement in Line 25 advances `intItr` to point to element 0, which is the first element of the second subsequence. The statement in Line 30 uses the function `inplace_merge` and the iterator `intItr` to merge the sorted subsequences of `vecList`. Notice that `vecList` contains the resulting sequence. In the output, the line marked Line 27 contains the output of the statements in Lines 27 through 29; the line marked Line 31 contains the output of the statements in Lines 31 through 33.

The Functions `reverse`, `reverse_copy`, `rotate`, and `rotate_copy`

The algorithm `reverse` reverses the order of the elements in a given range. The prototype of the function to implement the algorithm `reverse` is:

```
template <class biDirectionalItr>
void reverse(biDirectionalItr first, biDirectionalItr last);
```

The elements in the range `first...last-1` are reversed. For example, if `vecList = {1, 2, 5, 3, 4}`, then the elements in reverse order are `vecList = {4, 3, 5, 2, 1}`.

The algorithm `reverse_copy` reverses the elements of a given range while copying into a destination range. The source is not modified. The prototype of the function implementing the algorithm `reverse_copy` is:

```
template <class biDirectionalItr, class outputItr>
outputItr reverse_copy(biDirectionalItr first,
                       biDirectionalItr last,
                       outputItr destFirst);
```

The elements in the range `first...last-1` are copied in the reverse order at the destination, beginning with `destFirst`. The function also returns the position one past the last element copied at the destination.

The algorithm `rotate` rotates the elements of a given range. Its prototype is:

```
template <class forwardItr>
void rotate(forwardItr first, forwardItr newFirst,
            forwardItr last);
```

The elements in the range `first...newFirst-1` are moved to the end of the range. The element specified by `newFirst` becomes the first element of the range. For example, suppose that:

```
vecList = {3, 5, 4, 0, 7, 8, 2, 5}
```

and the iterator `vecItr` points to 0. Then, after the statement:

```
rotate(vecList.begin(), vecItr, vecList.end());
```

executes, `vecList` is as follows:

```
vecList = {0, 7, 8, 2, 5, 3, 5, 4}
```

The algorithm `rotate_copy` is a combination of `rotate` and `copy`. That is, the elements of the source are copied at the destination in a rotated order. The source is not modified. The prototype of the function implementing this algorithm is:

```
template <class forwardItr, class outputItr>
outputItr rotate_copy(forwardItr first, forwardItr middle,
                      forwardItr last,
                      outputItr destFirst);
```

The elements in the range `first...last-1` are copied into the destination range beginning with `destFirst` in the rotated order, so that the element specified by `middle` in the range `first...last-1` becomes the first element of the destination. The function also returns the position one past the last element copied at the destination.

The algorithms `reverse`, `reverse_copy`, `rotate`, and `rotate_copy` are contained in the header file `algorithm`. The program in Example 22-23 illustrates how to use these algorithms.

EXAMPLE 22-23

```cpp
//STL Functions: reverse, reverse_copy, rotate, and rotate_copy

#include <iostream>
#include <algorithm>
#include <iterator>
#include <list>

using namespace std;

int main()
{
    int temp[10] = {1, 3, 5, 7, 9, 0, 2, 4, 6, 8};         //Line 1

    list<int> intList(temp, temp + 10);                    //Line 2
    list<int> resultList;                                  //List 3
    list<int>::iterator listItr;                           //Line 4

    ostream_iterator<int> screen(cout, " ");               //Line 5

    cout << "Line 6: intList: ";                           //Line 6
    copy(intList.begin(), intList.end(), screen);          //Line 7
    cout << endl;                                          //Line 8

        //reverse
    reverse(intList.begin(), intList.end());               //Line 9

    cout << "Line 10: intList after reversal: ";           //Line 10
    copy(intList.begin(), intList.end(), screen);          //Line 11
    cout << endl;                                          //Line 12
```

```cpp
    //reverse_copy
reverse_copy(intList.begin(), intList.end(),
           back_inserter(resultList));                 //Line 13

cout << "Line 14: resultList: ";                       //Line 14
copy(resultList.begin(), resultList.end(),
     screen);      //Line 15
cout << endl;                                          //Line 16

listItr = intList.begin();                             //Line 17
listItr++;                                             //Line 18
listItr++;                                             //Line 19

cout << "Line 20: intList before rotating: ";          //Line 20
copy(intList.begin(), intList.end(), screen);          //Line 21
cout << endl;                                          //Line 22

    //rotate
rotate(intList.begin(), listItr, intList.end());       //Line 23

cout << "Line 24: intList after rotating: ";           //Line 24
copy(intList.begin(), intList.end(), screen);          //Line 25
cout << endl;                                          //Line 26

    //rotate_copy
resultList.clear();                                    //Line 27

rotate_copy(intList.begin(), listItr,
           intList.end(),
           back_inserter(resultList));                 //Line 28

cout << "Line 29: intList after rotating and "
     << "copying:\n"
     << "            ";                                //Line 29
copy(intList.begin(), intList.end(), screen);          //Line 30
cout << endl;                                          //Line 31

cout << "Line 32: resultList after rotating "
     << "and copying:\n"
     << "            ";                                //Line 32
copy(resultList.begin(), resultList.end(),
     screen);                                          //Line 33
cout << endl;                                          //Line 34

resultList.clear();                                    //Line 35

rotate_copy(intList.begin(),
           find(intList.begin(), intList.end(), 6),
           intList.end(),
           back_inserter(resultList));                 //Line 36
```

```cpp
    cout << "Line 37: resultList after rotating and "
         << "copying:\n"
         << "            ";                              //Line 37
    copy(resultList.begin(), resultList.end(), screen); //Line 38
    cout << endl;                                        //Line 39

    return 0;
}
```

Sample Run:

```
Line 6: intList: 1 3 5 7 9 0 2 4 6 8
Line 10: intList after reversal: 8 6 4 2 0 9 7 5 3 1
Line 14: resultList: 1 3 5 7 9 0 2 4 6 8
Line 20: intList before rotating: 8 6 4 2 0 9 7 5 3 1
Line 24: intList after rotating: 4 2 0 9 7 5 3 1 8 6
Line 29: intList after rotating and copying:
         4 2 0 9 7 5 3 1 8 6
Line 32: resultList after rotating and copying:
         0 9 7 5 3 1 8 6 4 2
Line 37: resultList after rotating and copying:
         6 4 2 0 9 7 5 3 1 8
```

The Functions `count`, `count_if`, `max`, `max_element`, `min`, `min_element`, and `random_shuffle`

The algorithm `count` counts the occurrences of a given value in a given range. The prototype of the function implementing this algorithm is:

```cpp
template <class inputItr, class type>
iterator_traits<inputItr>:: difference_type
     count(inputItr first, inputItr last, const Type& value);
```

The function `count` returns the number of times the value specified by the parameter `value` occurs in the range `first...last-1`.

The algorithm `count_if` counts the occurrences of a given value in a given range, satisfying a certain criterion. The prototype of the function implementing this algorithm is:

```cpp
template <class inputItr, class unaryPredicate>
iterator_traits<inputItr>::difference_type
    count_if(inputItr first, inputItr last, unaryPredicate op);
```

The function `count_if` returns the number of elements in the range `first...last-1` for which `op(elemRange)` is `true`.

The algorithm `max` is used to determine the maximum of two values. It has two forms, as shown by the following prototypes:

```
template <class Type>
const Type& max(const Type& aVal, const Type& bVal);

template <class Type, class compare>
const Type& max(const Type& aVal, const Type& bVal, compare comp);
```

In the first form, the greater-than operator associated with `Type` is used. The second form uses the comparison operation specified by `comp`.

The algorithm `max_element` is used to determine the largest element in a given range. This algorithm has two forms, as shown by the following prototypes:

```
template <class forwardItr>
forwardItr max_element(forwardItr first, forwardItr last);

template <class forwardItr, class compare>
forwardItr max_element(forwardItr first, forwardItr last,
                       compare comp);
```

The first form uses the greater-than operator associated with the data type of the elements in the range `first...last-1`. In the second form, the comparison operation specified by `comp` is used. Both forms return an iterator to the element containing the largest value in the range `first...last-1`.

The algorithm `min` is used to determine the minimum of two values. It has two forms, as shown by the following prototypes:

```
template <class Type>
const Type& min(const Type& aVal, const Type& bVal);

template <class Type, class compare>
const Type& min(const Type& aVal, const Type& bVal, compare comp);
```

In the first form, the less-than operator associated with `Type` is used. In the second form, the comparison operation specified by `comp` is used.

The algorithm `min_element` is used to determine the smallest element in a given range. This algorithm has two forms, as shown by the following prototypes:

```
template <class forwardItr>
forwardItr min_element(forwardItr first, forwardItr last);

template <class forwardItr, class compare>
forwardItr min_element(forwardItr first, forwardItr last,
                       compare comp);
```

The first form uses the less-than operator associated with the data type of the elements in the range `first...last-1`. The second form uses the comparison operation specified by `comp`. Both forms return an iterator to the element containing the smallest value in the range `first...last-1`.

The algorithm `random_shuffle` is used to randomly order the elements in a given range. There are two forms of this algorithm, as shown by the following prototypes:

```cpp
template <class randomAccessItr>
void random_shuffle(randomAccessItr first,
                    randomAccessItr last);

template <class randomAccessItr, class randomAccessGenerator>
void random_shuffle(randomAccessItr first,
                    randomAccessItr last,
                    randomAccessGenerator rand);
```

The first form reorders the elements in the range `first...last-1` using a uniform distribution random number generator. The second form reorders the elements in the range `first...last-1` using a random number-generating function object or a pointer to a function.

Example 22-24 illustrates how to use these functions.

EXAMPLE 22-24

```cpp
//STL Functions count, count_if, min_element,
//                max_element, random_shuffle

#include <iostream>
#include <cctype>
#include <algorithm>
#include <iterator>
#include <vector>

using namespace std;

void doubleNum(int num);

int main()
{
    char cList[10] = {'Z', 'a', 'Z', 'B', 'Z',
                      'c', 'D', 'e', 'F', 'Z'};           //Line 1

    vector<char>  charList(cList, cList + 10);            //Line 2

    ostream_iterator<char> screen(cout, " ");            //Line 3

    cout << "Line 4: charList: ";                        //Line 4
    copy(charList.begin(), charList.end(), screen);      //Line 5
    cout << endl;                                        //Line 6

        //count
    int noOfZs = count(charList.begin(),
                       charList.end(), 'Z');             //Line 7
```

```cpp
    cout << "Line 8: Number of Zs in charList = "
         << noOfZs << endl;                                 //Line 8

        //count_if
    int noOfUpper = count_if(charList.begin(),
                             charList.end(), isupper);  //Line 9

    cout << "Line 10: Number of uppercase letters "
         << "in charList = " << noOfUpper << endl;      //Line 10

    int list[10] = {12, 34, 56, 21, 34,
                    78, 34, 55, 12, 25};                //Line 11

    ostream_iterator<int> screenOut(cout, " ");         //Line 12

    cout << "Line 13: list: ";                          //Line 13
    copy(list, list + 10, screenOut);                   //Line 14
    cout << endl;                                        //Line 15

        //max_element
    int *maxLoc = max_element(list, list + 10);         //Line 16

    cout << "Line 17: Largest element in list = "
         << *maxLoc << endl;                             //Line 17

        //min_element
    int *minLoc = min_element(list, list + 10);         //Line 18

    cout << "Line 19: Smallest element in list = "
         << *minLoc << endl;                             //Line 19

        //random_shuffle
    random_shuffle(list, list + 10);                    //Line 20

    cout << "Line 21: list after random shuffle:\n"
         << "              ";                            //Line 21
    copy(list, list + 10, screenOut);                   //Line 22
    cout << endl;                                        //Line 23

    return 0;
}

void doubleNum(int num)
{
    cout << 2 * num << " ";
}
```

Sample Run:

```
Line 4: charList: Z a Z B Z c D e F Z
Line 8: Number of Zs in charList = 4
Line 10: Number of uppercase letters in charList = 7
Line 13: list: 12 34 56 21 34 78 34 55 12 25
```

```
Line 17: Largest element in list = 78
Line 19: Smallest element in list = 12
Line 21: list after random shuffle:
         12 34 25 56 12 78 55 21 34 34
```

The preceding output is self-explanatory. The details are left as an exercise for you.

The Functions `for_each` and `transform`

The algorithm `for_each` is used to access and process each element in a given range by applying a function, which is passed as a parameter. The prototype of the function implementing this algorithm is:

```
template <class inputItr, class function>
function for_each(inputItr first, inputItr last, function func);
```

The function specified by the parameter `func` is applied to each element in the range `first...last-1`. The function `func` can modify the element. The returned value of the function `for_each` is usually ignored.

The algorithm `transform` has two forms. The prototypes of the functions implementing this algorithm are:

```
template <class inputItr, class outputItr,
          class unaryOperation>
outputItr transform(inputItr first, inputItr last,
                    outputItr destFirst,
                    unaryOperation op);

template <class inputItr1, class inputItr2,
          class outputItr, class binaryOperation>
outputItr transform(inputItr1 first1, inputItr1 last,
                    inputItr2 first2,
                    outputItr destFirst,
                    binaryOperation bOp);
```

The first form of the function `transform` has four parameters. This function creates a sequence of elements at the destination, beginning with `destFirst`, by applying the unary operation `op` to each element in the range `first1...last-1`. This function returns the position one past the last element copied at the destination.

The second form of the function `transform` has five parameters. This function creates a sequence of elements by applying the binary operation `bOp`—that is, `bOp(elemRange1, elemRange2)`—to the corresponding elements in the range `first1...last1-1` and the range beginning with `first2`. The resulting sequence is placed at the destination beginning with `destFirst`. The function returns the position one element past the last element copied at the destination.

Example 22-25 illustrates how to use these functions.

EXAMPLE 22-25

```cpp
//STL Functions for_each and transform

#include <iostream>
#include <cctype>
#include <algorithm>
#include <iterator>
#include <vector>

using namespace std;

void doubleNum(int& num);

int main()
{
    char cList[5] = {'a', 'b', 'c', 'd', 'e'};         //Line 1

    vector<char>  charList(cList, cList + 5);           //Line 2

    ostream_iterator<char> screen(cout, " ");           //Line 3

    cout << "Line 4: cList: ";                          //Line 4
    copy(charList.begin(), charList.end(), screen);     //Line 5
    cout << endl;                                       //Line 6

        //transform
    transform(charList.begin(), charList.end(),
              charList.begin(), toupper);               //Line 7

    cout << "Line 8: cList after changing all "
         << "lowercase letters to \n"
         << "            uppercase: ";                  //Line 8
    copy(charList.begin(), charList.end(), screen);     //Line 9
    cout << endl;                                       //Line 10

    int list[7] = {2, 8, 5, 1, 7, 11, 3};              //Line 11

    ostream_iterator<int> screenOut(cout, " ");         //Line 12

    cout << "Line 13: list: ";                          //Line 13
    copy(list, list + 7, screenOut);                    //Line 14
    cout << endl;                                       //Line 15

    cout << "Line 16: The effect of for_each "
         << "function:\n            ";                  //Line 16

        //for_each
    for_each(list, list + 7, doubleNum);                //Line 17
    cout << endl;                                       //Line 18
```

```cpp
    cout << "Line 19: list after a call to "
         << "for_each function:\n                  ";      //Line 19
    copy(list, list + 7, screenOut);                        //Line 20
    cout << endl;                                           //Line 21

    return 0;
}

void doubleNum(int& num)
{
    num = 2 * num;

    cout << num << " ";
}
```

Sample Run:

```
Line 4: cList: a b c d e
Line 8: cList after changing all lowercase letters to
        uppercase: A B C D E
Line 13: list: 2 8 5 1 7 11 3
Line 16: The effect of for_each function:
         4 16 10 2 14 22 6
Line 19: list after a call to for_each function:
         4 16 10 2 14 22 6
```

The statement in Line 7 uses the function `transform` to change every lowercase letter of `charList` into its uppercase counterpart. The statement in Line 9 outputs the elements of `charList`. In the output, the line marked Line 8 contains the output of the statements in Lines 8 through 10 in the program. Notice that the fourth parameter of the function `transform` (in Line 7) is the function `toupper` from the header file `cctype`.

The statement in Line 17 calls the function `for_each` to process each element in the list using the function `doubleNum`. The function `doubleNum` has a reference parameter, num, of type `int`. Moreover, this function doubles the value of num and then outputs the value of num. Because num is a reference parameter, the value of the actual parameter is changed. In the output, the line marked Line 16 contains the output produced by the `cout` statement in the function `doubleNum`, which is passed as the third parameter of the function `for_each` (see Line 17). The statement in Line 20 outputs the values of the elements of `list`. In the output, Line 19 contains the output of the statements in Lines 19 through 20.

The Functions `includes`, `set_intersection`, `set_union`, `set_difference`, and `set_symmetric_difference`

This section describes the set theory operations `includes` (subset), `set_intersection`, `set_union`, `set_difference`, and `set_symmetric_difference`. All of these algorithms assume that the elements within each given range are already sorted.

The algorithm `includes` determines whether the elements in one range appear in another range. This function has two forms, as shown by the following prototypes:

```
template <class inputItr1, class inputItr2>
bool includes(inputItr1 first1, inputItr1 last1,
          inputItr2 first2, inputItr2 last2);

template <class inputItr1, class inputItr2,
          class binaryPredicate>
bool includes(inputItr1 first1, inputItr1 last1,
          inputItr2 first2, inputItr2 last2,
          binaryPredicate op);
```

Both forms of the function `includes` assume that the elements in the ranges `first1...last1-1` and `first2...last2-1` are sorted according to the same sorting criterion. The function returns **true** if all the elements in the range `first2...last2-1` are also in `first1...last1-1`. In other words, the function returns **true** if `first1...last1-1` contains all the elements in the range `first2...last2-1`. The first form assumes that the elements in both ranges are in ascending order. The second form uses the operation op to determine the ordering of the elements.

Example 22-26 illustrates how the function `includes` works.

EXAMPLE 22-26

```cpp
//STL function includes
//This function assumes that the elements in the given ranges
//are ordered according to some sorting criteria

#include <iostream>
#include <algorithm>

using namespace std;

int main()
{
    char setA[5] = {'A', 'B', 'C', 'D', 'E'};          //Line 1
    char setB[10] = {'A', 'B', 'C', 'D', 'E',
                     'F', 'I', 'J', 'K', 'L'};          //Line 2
    char setC[5] = {'A', 'E', 'I', 'O', 'U'};          //Line 3

    ostream_iterator<char> screen(cout, " ");          //Line 4
```

```cpp
    cout << "Line 5: setA: ";                          //Line 5
    copy(setA, setA + 5, screen);                      //Line 6
    cout << endl;                                       //Line 7

    cout << "Line 8: setB: ";                          //Line 8
    copy(setB, setB + 10, screen);                     //Line 9
    cout << endl;                                       //Line 10

    cout << "Line 11: setC: ";                         //Line 11
    copy(setC, setC + 5, screen);                      //Line 12
    cout << endl;                                       //Line 13

    if (includes(setB, setB + 10, setA, setA + 5))     //Line 14
        cout << "Line 15: setA is a subset of "
             << "setB." << endl;                        //Line 15
    else                                                //Line 16
        cout << "Line 17: setA is not a subset "
             << "of setB." << endl;                     //Line 17

    if (includes(setB, setB + 10, setC, setC + 5))     //Line 18
        cout << "Line 19: setC is a subset of "
             << "setB." << endl;                        //Line 19
    else                                                //Line 20
        cout << "Line 21: setC is not a subset "
             << "of setB." << endl;                     //Line 21

    return 0;
}
```

Sample Run:

```
Line 5: setA: A B C D E
Line 8: setB: A B C D E F I J K L
Line 11: setC: A E I O U
Line 15: setA is a subset of setB
Line 21: setC is not a subset of setB
```

The preceding output is self-explanatory. The details are left as exercise for you.

The algorithm `set_intersection` is used to find the elements that are common to two ranges of elements. This algorithm has two forms, as shown by the following prototypes:

```cpp
template <class inputItr1, class inputItr2,
          class outputItr>
outputItr set_intersection(inputItr1 first1, inputItr1 last1,
                           inputItr2 first2, inputItr2 last2,
                           outputItr destFirst);
```

```
template <class inputItr1, class inputItr2,
          class outputItr, class binaryPredicate>
outputItr set_intersection(inputItr1 first1, inputItr1 last1,
                           inputItr2 first2, inputItr2 last2,
                           outputItr destFirst,
                           binaryPredicate op);
```

Both forms create a sequence of sorted elements that are common to two sorted ranges, `first1...last1-1` and `first2...last2-1`. The created sequence is placed in the container beginning with `destFirst`. Both forms return an iterator positioned one past the last element copied at the destination range. The first form assumes that the elements are in ascending order; the second form assumes that both ranges are sorted using the operation specified by op. The elements in the source ranges are not modified.

Suppose that:

```
setA[5] = {2, 4, 5, 7, 8};
setB[7] = {1, 2, 3, 4, 5, 6, 7};
setC[5] = {2, 5, 8, 8, 15};
setD[6] = {1, 4, 4, 6, 7, 12};
setE[7] = {2, 3, 4, 4, 5, 6, 10};
```

Then:

```
AintersectB = {2, 4, 5, 7}
AintersectC = {2, 5, 8}
DintersectE = {4, 4, 6}
```

Notice that because 8 appears only once in `setA`, 8 appears only once in `AintersectC`, even though 8 appears twice in `setC`. However, because 4 appears twice in both `setD` and `setE`, 4 also appears twice in `DintersectE`.

The algorithm `set_union` is used to find the elements that are contained in two ranges of elements. This algorithm has two forms, as shown by the following prototypes:

```
template <class inputItr1, class inputItr2,
          class outputItr>
outputItr set_union(inputItr1 first1, inputItr1 last1,
                    inputItr2 first2, inputItr2 last2,
                    outputItr destFirst);
```

```
template <class inputItr1, class inputItr2,
          class outputItr, class binaryPredicate>
outputItr set_union(inputItr1 first1, inputItr1 last1,
                    inputItr2 first2, inputItr2 last2,
                    outputItr result,
                    binaryPredicate op);
```

Both forms create a sequence of sorted elements that appear in either two sorted ranges, `first1...last1-1` or `first2...last2-1`. The created sequence is placed in the container beginning with `destFirst`. Both forms return an iterator positioned one past the last element copied at the destination range. The first form assumes that the elements are in ascending order. The second form assumes that both ranges are sorted using the operation specified by op. The elements in the source ranges are not modified.

Suppose that you have setA, setB, setC, setD, and setE as defined previously. Then:

```
AunionB = {1, 2, 3, 4, 5, 6, 7, 8}
AunionC = {2, 4, 5, 7, 8, 8, 15}
BunionD = {1, 2, 3, 4, 4, 5, 6, 7, 12}
DunionE = {1, 2, 3, 4, 4, 5, 6, 7, 10, 12}
```

Notice that because 8 appears twice in setC, it appears twice in AunionC. Because 4 appears twice in setD and setE, 4 appears twice in DunionE.

Example 22-27 illustrates how the functions set_union and set_intersection work.

EXAMPLE 22-27

```cpp
//STL set theory functions set_union and set_intersection
//These functions assume that the elements in the given ranges
//are ordered according to some sorting criteria

#include <iostream>
#include <algorithm>

using namespace std;

int main()
{
    int setA[5] = {2, 4, 5, 7, 8};                 //Line 1
    int setB[7] = {1, 2, 3, 4, 5, 6, 7};           //Line 2
    int setC[5] = {2, 5, 8, 8, 15};                //Line 3
    int setD[6] = {1, 4, 4, 6, 7, 12};             //Line 4

    int AunionB[10];                               //Line 5
    int AunionC[10];                               //Line 6
    int BunionD[15];                               //Line 7
    int AintersectB[10];                           //Line 8
    int AintersectC[10];                           //Line 9

    int *lastElem;                                 //Line 10

    ostream_iterator<int> screen(cout, " ");       //Line 11

    cout << "Line 12: setA = ";                    //Line 12
    copy(setA, setA + 5, screen);                  //Line 13
    cout << endl;                                  //Line 14

    cout << "Line 15: setB = ";                    //Line 15
    copy(setB, setB + 7, screen);                  //Line 16
    cout << endl;                                  //Line 17
```

```cpp
    cout << "Line 18: setC = ";                        //Line 18
    copy(setC, setC + 5, screen);                      //Line 19
    cout << endl;                                       //Line 20

    cout << "Line 21: setD = ";                        //Line 21
    copy(setD, setD + 6, screen);                      //Line 22
    cout << endl;                                       //Line 23

    lastElem = set_union(setA, setA + 5,
                         setB, setB + 7,
                         AunionB);                      //Line 24

    cout << "Line 25: Set AunionB: ";                  //Line 25
    copy(AunionB, lastElem, screen);                   //Line 26
    cout << endl;                                       //Line 27

    lastElem = set_union(setA, setA + 5,
                         setC, setC + 5,
                         AunionC);                      //Line 28

    cout << "Line 29: Set AunionC: ";                  //Line 29
    copy(AunionC, lastElem, screen);                   //Line 30
    cout << endl;                                       //Line 31

    lastElem = set_union(setB, setB + 7,
                         setD, setD + 6,
                         BunionD);                      //Line 32

    cout << "Line 33: Set BunionD: ";                  //Line 33
    copy(BunionD, lastElem, screen);                   //Line 34
    cout << endl;                                       //Line 35

    lastElem = set_intersection(setA, setA + 5,
                                setB, setB + 7,
                                AintersectB);           //Line 36

    cout << "Line 37: Set AintersectB: ";              //Line 37
    copy(AintersectB, lastElem, screen);               //Line 38
    cout << endl;                                       //Line 39

    lastElem = set_intersection(setA, setA + 5,
                                setC, setC + 5,
                                AintersectC);           //Line 40

    cout << "Line 41: Set AintersectC: ";              //Line 41
    copy(AintersectC, lastElem, screen);               //Line 42
    cout << endl;                                       //Line 43

    return 0;
}
```

Sample Run:

```
Line 12: setA = 2 4 5 7 8
Line 15: setB = 1 2 3 4 5 6 7
Line 18: setC = 2 5 8 8 15
Line 21: setD = 1 4 4 6 7 12
Line 25: Set AunionB: 1 2 3 4 5 6 7 8
Line 29: Set AunionC: 2 4 5 7 8 8 15
Line 33: Set BunionD: 1 2 3 4 4 5 6 7 12
Line 37: Set AintersectB: 2 4 5 7
Line 41: Set AintersectC: 2 5 8
```

The preceding output is self-explanatory. The details are left as an exercise for you.

The algorithm `set_difference` is used to find the elements in one range of elements that do not appear in another range of elements. This algorithm has two forms, as shown by the following prototypes:

```
template <class inputItr1, class inputItr2,
          class outputItr>
outputItr set_difference(inputItr1 first1, inputItr1 last1,
                         inputItr2 first2, inputItr2 last2,
                         outputItr destFirst);

template <class inputItr1, class inputItr2,
          class outputItr, class binaryPredicate>
outputItr set_difference(inputItr1 first1, inputItr1 last1,
                         inputItr2 first2, inputItr2 last2,
                         outputItr destFirst,
                         binaryPredicate op);
```

Both forms create a sequence of sorted elements that are in the sorted range `first1...last1-1` but not in the sorted range `first2...last2-1`. The created sequence is placed in the container beginning with `destFirst`. Both forms return an iterator positioned one past the last element copied at the destination range. The first form assumes that the elements are in ascending order. The second form assumes that both ranges are sorted using the operation specified by op. The elements in the source ranges are not modified.

Suppose that:

```
setA = {2, 4, 5, 7, 8}
setC = {1, 5, 6, 8, 15}
setD = {2, 5, 5, 6, 9}
setE = {1, 5, 7, 9, 12}
```

Then:

```
AdifferenceC = {2, 4, 7}
DdifferenceE = {2, 5, 6}
```

Because 5 appears twice in `setD` but only once in `setE`, 5 appears once in `DdifferenceE`.

The algorithm `set_symmetric_difference` has two forms, as shown by the following prototypes:

```
template <class inputItr1, class inputItr2,
         class outputItr>
outputItr set_symmetric_difference(inputItr1 first1,
                                   inputItr1 last1,
                                   inputItr2 first2,
                                   inputItr2 last2,
                                   outputItr destFirst);

template <class inputItr1, class inputItr2,
         class outputItr, class binaryPredicate>
outputItr set_symmetric_difference(inputItr1 first1,
                                   inputItr1 last1,
                                   inputItr2 first2,
                                   inputItr2 last2,
                                   outputItr destFirst,
                                   binaryPredicate op);
```

Both forms create a sequence of sorted elements that are in the sorted range `first1...last1-1` but not in `first2...last2-1`, or elements that are in the sorted range `first2...last2-1` but not in `first1...last1-1`. In other words, the sequence of elements created by `set_symmetric_difference` contain the elements that are in `range1_difference_range2` union `range2_difference_range1`. The created sequence is placed in the container beginning with `destFirst`. Both forms return an iterator positioned one past the last element copied at the destination range. The first form assumes that the elements are in ascending order. The second form assumes that both ranges are sorted using the operation specified by `op`. The elements in the source ranges are not modified. It can be shown that the sequence created by `set_symmetric_difference` contains elements that are in `range1_union_range2` but not in `range1_intersection_range2`.

Suppose that:

```
setB = {3, 4, 5, 6, 7, 8, 10}
setC = {1, 5, 6, 8, 15}
setD = {2, 5, 5, 6, 9}
```

Notice that `BdifferenceC = {3, 4, 7, 10}` and `CdifferenceB = {1, 15}`. Therefore:

```
BsymDiffC = {1, 3, 4, 7, 10, 15}
```

Now `DdifferenceC = {2, 5, 9}` and `CdifferenceD = {1, 8, 15}`. Therefore:

```
DsymDiffC = {1, 2, 5, 8, 9, 15}
```

Example 22-28 illustrates how the functions `set_difference` and `set_symmetric_difference` work.

EXAMPLE 22-28

```cpp
//STL set theory functions: set_difference and
//                           set_symmetric_difference.
//These functions assume that the elements in the given
//ranges are ordered according to some sorting criteria.

#include <iostream>
#include <algorithm>

using namespace std;

int main()
{
    int setA[5] = {2, 4, 5, 7, 8};                          //Line 1
    int setB[7] = {3, 4, 5, 6, 7, 8, 10};                   //Line 2
    int setC[5] = {1, 5, 6, 8, 15};                         //Line 3

    int AdifferenceC[5];                                    //Line 4
    int BsymDiffC[10];                                      //Line 5

    int *lastElem;                                          //Line 6

    ostream_iterator<int> screen(cout, " ");                //Line 7

    cout << "Line 8: setA = ";                              //Line 8
    copy(setA, setA + 5, screen);                           //Line 9
    cout << endl;                                           //Line 10

    cout << "Line 11: setB = ";                             //Line 11
    copy(setB, setB + 7, screen);                           //Line 12
    cout << endl;                                           //Line 13

    cout << "Line 14: setC = ";                             //Line 14
    copy(setC, setC + 5, screen);                           //Line 15
    cout << endl;                                           //Line 16


    lastElem = set_difference(setA, setA + 5,
                              setC, setC + 5,
                              AdifferenceC);                //Line 17

    cout << "Line 18: AdifferenceC: ";                      //Line 18
    copy(AdifferenceC, lastElem, screen);                   //Line 19
    cout << endl;                                           //Line 20

    lastElem = set_symmetric_difference(setB, setB + 7,
                                        setC, setC + 5,
                                        BsymDiffC);         //Line 21
```

```cpp
    cout << "Line 22: BsymDiffC: ";          //Line 22
    copy(BsymDiffC, lastElem, screen);       //Line 23
    cout << endl;                            //Line 24

    return 0;
}
```

Sample Run:

```
Line 8: setA = 2 4 5 7 8
Line 11: setB = 3 4 5 6 7 8 10
Line 14: setC = 1 5 6 8 15
Line 18: AdifferenceC: 2 4 7
Line 22: BsymDiffC: 1 3 4 7 10 15
```

The preceding output is self-explanatory. The details are left as an exercise for you.

The Functions `accumulate`, `adjacent_difference`, `inner_product`, and `partial_sum`

The algorithms `accumulate`, `adjacent_difference`, `inner_product`, and `partial_sum` are numerical functions and thus manipulate numeric data. Each of these functions has two forms. The first form uses the natural operation to manipulate the data. For example, the algorithm `accumulate` finds the sum of all the elements in a given range. In the second form, we can specify the operation to be applied to the elements of the range. For example, rather than add the elements of a given range, we can specify the multiplication operation to the algorithm `accumulate` to multiply the elements of the range. Next, we give the prototype of each of these algorithms followed by a brief explanation. The algorithms are contained in the header file `numeric`:

```cpp
template<class inputItr, class Type>
Type accumulate(inputItr first, inputItr last, Type init);

template<class inputItr, class Type, class binaryOperation>
Type accumulate(inputItr first, inputItr last,
                Type init, binaryOperation op);
```

The first form of the algorithm `accumulate` adds all the elements, to an initial value specified by the parameter `init`, in the range `first...last-1`. For example, if the value of `init` is 0, the algorithm returns the sum of all the elements. In the second form, we can specify a binary operation, such as multiplication, to be applied to the elements of the range. For example, if the value of `init` is 1 and the binary operation is multiplication, the algorithm returns the products of the elements of the range.

Next, we describe the algorithm `adjacent_difference`. Its prototypes are:

```cpp
template <class inputItr, class outputItr>
outputItr adjacent_difference(inputItr first, inputItr last,
                              outputItr destFirst);
```

```
template <class inputItr, class outputItr,
          class binaryOperation>
outputItr adjacent_difference(inputItr first, inputItr last,
                              outputItr destFirst,
                              binaryOperation op);
```

The first form creates a sequence of elements in which the first element is the same as the first element in the range `first...last-1`, and all other elements are the differences of the current and previous elements. For example, if the range of elements is:

```
{2, 5, 6, 8, 3, 7}
```

then the sequence created by the function `adjacent_difference` is:

```
{2, 3, 1, 2, -5, 4}
```

The first element is the same as the first element in the original range. The second element is equal to the second element in the original range minus the first element in the original range. Similarly, the third element is equal to the third element in the original range minus the second element in the original range, and so on.

In the second form of `adjacent_difference`, the binary operation `op` is applied to the elements in the range. The resulting sequence is copied at the destination specified by `destFirst`. For example, if the sequence is {2, 5, 6, 8, 3, 7} and the operation is multiplication, the resulting sequence is {2, 10, 30, 48, 24, 21}.

Both forms return an iterator positioned one past the last element copied at the destination.

The algorithm `inner_product` is used to manipulate the elements of two ranges. The prototypes of this algorithm are:

```
template <class inputItr1, class inputItr2, class Type>
Type inner_product(inputItr1 first1, inputItr1 last,
                   inputItr2 first2, Type init);
```

```
template <class inputItr1, class inputItr2, class Type
          class binaryOperation1, class binaryOperation2>
Type inner_product(inputItr1 first1, inputItr1 last,
                   inputItr2 first2, Type init,
                   binaryOperation1 op1, binaryOperation2 op2);
```

The first form multiplies the corresponding elements in the range `first1...last-1` and the range of elements starting with `first2`. The products of the elements are then added to the value specified by the parameter `init`. To be specific, suppose that `elem1` ranges over the first range and `elem2` ranges over the second range starting with `first2`. The first form computes:

```
init = init + elem1 * elem2
```

for all the corresponding elements. For example, suppose that the two ranges are {2, 4, 7, 8} and {1, 4, 6, 9}, and that `init` is 0. The function computes and returns:

```
0 + 2 * 1 + 4 * 4 + 7 * 6 + 8 * 9 = 132
```

In the second form, the default addition can be replaced by the operation specified by op1, and the default multiplication can be replaced by the operation specified by op2. This form, in fact, computes:

```
init = init op1 (elem1 op2 elem2);
```

The algorithm `partial_sum` has two forms, as shown by the following prototypes:

```
template <class inputItr, class outputItr>
outputItr partial_sum(inputItr first, inputItr last,
                  outputItr destFirst);

template <class inputItr, class outputItr,
        class binaryOperation>
outputItr partial_sum(inputItr first, inputItr last,
                  outputItr destFirst, binaryOperation op);
```

The first form creates a sequence of elements in which each element is the sum of all the previous elements in the range `first...last-1` up to the position of the element. For example, the first element of the new sequence is the same as the first element in the range `first...last-1`, the second element is the sum of the first two elements in the range `first...last-1`, the third element of the new sequence is the sum of the first three elements in the range `first...last-1`, and so on. For example, for the sequence of elements:

```
{1, 3, 4, 6}
```

the function `partial_sum` generates the following sequence:

```
{1, 4, 8, 14}
```

In the second form, the default addition can be replaced by the operation specified by op. For example, if the sequence is:

```
{1, 3, 4, 6}
```

and the operation is multiplication, the function `partial_sum` generates the following sequence:

```
{1, 3, 12, 72}
```

The created sequence is copied at the destination specified by `destFirst` and returns an iterator positioned one past the last copied element at the destination.

Example 22-29 illustrates how the functions of this section work.

EXAMPLE 22-29

```cpp
//Numeric algorithms: accumulate, adjacent_difference,
//                    inner_product, and partial_sum

#include <iostream>
#include <algorithm>
#include <numeric>
#include <iterator>
#include <vector>
#include <functional>

using namespace std;

void print(vector<int>  vList);

int main()
{
    int list[8] = {1, 2, 3, 4, 5, 6, 7, 8};                //Line 1

    vector<int> vecList(list, list + 8);                   //Line 2
    vector<int>    newVList(8);                             //Line 3

    cout << "Line 4: vecList: ";                           //Line 4
    print(vecList);                                        //Line 5

        //accumulate function
    int sum = accumulate(vecList.begin(),
                        vecList.end(), 0);                 //Line 6

    cout << "Line 7: Sum of the elements of "
        << "vecList = " << sum << endl;                    //Line 7

    int product = accumulate(vecList.begin(),
                        vecList.end(),
                        1, multiplies<int>());             //Line 8

    cout << "Line 9: Product of the elements of "
        << "vecList = " << product << endl;               //Line 9

        //adjacent_difference function
    adjacent_difference(vecList.begin(),
                        vecList.end(),
                        newVList.begin());                 //Line 10

    cout << "Line 11: newVList: ";                         //Line 11
    print(newVList);                                       //Line 12

    adjacent_difference(vecList.begin(), vecList.end(),
                        newVList.begin(),
                        multiplies<int>());                //Line 13
```

```cpp
    cout << "Line 14: newVList: ";                          //Line 14
    print(newVList);                                        //Line 15

        //inner_product function
    sum = inner_product(vecList.begin(), vecList.end(),
                        newVList.begin(), 0);               //Line 16

    cout << "Line 17: Inner product of vecList "
         << "and newVList: " << sum << endl;                //Line 17

    sum = inner_product(vecList.begin(), vecList.end(),
                        newVList.begin(), 0,
                        plus<int>(), minus<int>());          //Line 18

    cout << "Line 19: Inner product of vecList and "
         << "newVList, using - for *: "
         << sum << endl;                                    //Line 19

        //partial_sum function
    partial_sum(vecList.begin(), vecList.end(),
            newVList.begin());                              //Line 20

    cout << "Line 21: newVList with partial sum : ";  //Line 21
    print(newVList);                                        //Line 22

        //partial_sum: the default + is replaced by *
    partial_sum(vecList.begin(), vecList.end(),
            newVList.begin(), multiplies<int>()); //Line 23

    cout << "Line 24: newVList with partial "
         << "multiplication: " << endl
         << "            ";                                 //Line 24
    print(newVList);                                        //Line 25

    return 0;
}

void print(vector<int>  vList)
{
    ostream_iterator<int> screenOut(cout, " ");            //Line 26

    copy(vList.begin(), vList.end(), screenOut);           //Line 27
    cout << endl;                                          //Line 28
}
```

Sample Run:

```
Line 4: vecList: 1 2 3 4 5 6 7 8
Line 7: Sum of the elements of vecList = 36
Line 9: Product of the elements of vecList = 40320
Line 11: newVList: 1 1 1 1 1 1 1 1
Line 14: newVList: 1 2 6 12 20 30 42 56
```

```
Line 17: Inner product of vecList and newVList: 1093
Line 19: Inner product of vecList and newVList, using - for *: -133
Line 21: newVList with partial sum: 1 3 6 10 15 21 28 36
Line 24: newVList with partial multiplication:
         1 2 6 24 120 720 5040 40320
```

The preceding output is self-explanatory. The details are left as an exercise for you.

QUICK REVIEW

1. The three main components of the STL are containers, iterators, and algorithms.

2. STL containers are class templates.

3. Iterators are used to step through the elements of a container.

4. Algorithms are used to manipulate the elements in a container.

5. The main categories of containers are sequence containers, associative containers, and container adapters.

6. The three predefined sequence containers are `vector`, `deque`, and `list`.

7. A vector container stores and manages its objects in a dynamic array.

8. Because an array is a random access data structure, elements of a vector can be accessed randomly.

9. The name of the class that implements the vector container is `vector`.

10. Item insertion in a vector container is accomplished by using the operations `insert` and `push_back`.

11. Item deletion in a vector container is accomplished by using the operations `pop_back`, `erase`, and `clear`.

12. An iterator to a vector container is declared using the `typedef` iterator, which is declared as a `public` member of the `class` vector.

13. Member functions common to all containers are the default constructor, constructors with parameters, the copy constructor, the destructor, `empty`, `size`, `max_size`, `swap`, `begin`, `end`, `rbegin`, `rend`, `insert`, `erase`, `clear`, and the relational operator functions.

14. The member function `begin` returns an iterator to the first element into the container.

15. The member function `end` returns an iterator to one past the last element into the container.

16. In addition to the member functions listed in item 14 above, the other member functions common to all sequence containers are `insert`, `push_back`, `pop_back`, `erase`, `clear`, and `resize`.

17. The `copy` algorithm is used to copy the elements in a given range to another place.

18. The function `copy`, using an `ostream` iterator, can also be used to output the elements of a container.

19. When we create an iterator of type `ostream`, we also specify the type of element that the iterator will output.

20. Deque containers are implemented as dynamic arrays in such a way that the elements can be inserted at both ends of the array.

21. A `deque` can expand in either direction.

22. The name of the class containing the definition of the `class` deque is `deque`.

23. In addition to the operations that are common to all containers, other operations that can be used to manipulate the elements of a `deque` are `assign`, `push_front`, `pop_front`, `at`, the array subscripting operator `[]`, `front`, and `back`.

24. List containers are implemented as doubly linked lists. Thus, every element in the list points to its immediate predecessor and its immediate successor (except the first and last elements).

25. The name of the class containing the definition of the `class` list is `list`.

26. In addition to the operations that are common to sequence containers, other operations that can be used to manipulate the elements in a list container are `assign`, `push_front`, `pop_front`, `front`, `back`, `remove`, `remove_if`, `unique`, `splice`, `sort`, `merge`, and `reverse`.

27. The five categories of iterators are input, output, forward, bidirectional, and random access iterator.

28. Input iterators are used to input data from an input stream.

29. Output iterators are used to output data to an output stream.

30. A forward iterator can refer to the same element in the same collection and process the same element more than once.

31. Bidirectional iterators are forward iterators that can also iterate backward over the elements.

32. Bidirectional iterators can be used with containers of type `list`, `set`, `multiset`, `multimap`, `map`, and `multimap`.

33. Random access iterators are bidirectional iterators that can randomly process the elements of a container.

34. Random access iterators can be used with containers of type `vector`, `dequeue`, `string`, as well as arrays.

35. Elements in an associative container are automatically sorted according to some various ordering criteria. The default ordering criterion is the relational operator less-than, `<`.

36. The predefined associative containers in the STL are `set`, `multiset`, `map`, and `multimap`.

37. Containers of the type `set` do not allow duplicates.

38. Containers of the type `multiset` allow duplicates.

39. The name of the class defining the container `set` is `set`.

40. The name of the class defining the container `multiset` is `multiset`.

41. The name of the header file containing the definition of the `class`es `set` and `multiset`, and the definitions of the functions to implement the various operations on these containers, is `set`.

42. The operations `insert`, `erase`, and `clear` can be used to insert or delete elements from sets.

43. Most of the generic algorithms are contained in the header file `algorithm`.

44. The main categories of STL algorithms are nonmodifying, modifying, numeric, and heap.

45. Nonmodifying algorithms do not modify the elements of the container.

46. Modifying algorithms modify the elements of the container by rearranging, removing, and/or changing the values of the elements.

47. Modifying algorithms that change the order of the elements, not their values, are also called mutating algorithms.

48. Numeric algorithms are designed to perform numeric calculations on the elements of a container.

49. A function object is a class template that overloads the function call operator, `operator()`.

50. The predefined arithmetic function objects are `plus`, `minus`, `multiplies`, `divides`, `modulus`, and `negate`.

51. The predefined relational function objects are `equal_to`, `not_equal_to`, `greater`, `greater_equal`, `less`, and `less_equal`.

52. The predefined logical function objects are `logical_not`, `logical_and`, and `logical_or`.

53. Predicates are special types of function objects that return Boolean values.

54. Unary predicates check a specific property for a single argument; binary predicates check a specific property for a pair—that is, two arguments.

55. Predicates are typically used to specify a searching or sorting criteria.

56. In the STL, a predicate must always return the same result for the same value.

57. The functions that modify their internal states cannot be considered predicates.

58. The STL provides three iterators—`back_inserter`, `front_inserter`, and `inserter`—called insert iterators, to insert the elements at the destination.

59. The `back_inserter` uses the `push_back` operation of the container in place of the assignment operator.

60. The `front_inserter` uses the `push_front` operation of the container in place of the assignment operator.

61. Because the vector class does not support the `push_front` operation, this iterator cannot be used for the vector container.

62. The `inserter` iterator uses the container's `insert` operation in place of the assignment operator.

63. The function `fill` is used to fill a container with elements, and the function `fill_n` is used to fill in the next n elements.

64. The functions `generate` and `generate_n` are used to generate elements and fill a sequence.

65. The functions `find`, `find_if`, `find_end`, and `find_first_of` are used to find the elements in a given range.

66. The function `remove` is used to remove certain elements from a sequence.

67. The function `remove_if` is used to remove elements from a sequence using a specified criterion.

68. The function `remove_copy` copies the elements in a sequence into another sequence by excluding certain elements from the first sequence.

69. The function `remove_copy_if` copies the elements in a sequence into another sequence by excluding certain elements, using a specified criterion, from the first sequence.

70. The functions `swap`, `iter_swap`, and `swap_ranges` are used to swap elements.

71. The functions `search`, `search_n`, `sort`, and `binary_search` are used to search elements.

72. The function `adjacent_find` is used to find the first occurrence of consecutive elements satisfying a certain criterion.

73. The algorithm `merge` merges two sorted lists.

74. The algorithm `inplace_merge` is used to combine two sorted, consecutive sequences.

75. The algorithm `reverse` reverses the order of the elements in a given range.

76. The algorithm `reverse_copy` reverses the elements in a given range while copying into a destination range. The source is not modified.

77. The algorithm `rotate` rotates the elements in a given range.

78. The algorithm `rotate_copy` copies the elements of the source at the destination in a rotated order.

79. The algorithm `count` counts the occurrences of a given value in a given range.

80. The algorithm `count_if` counts the occurrences of a given value in a given range, satisfying a certain criterion.

81. The algorithm `max` is used to determine the maximum of two values.

82. The algorithm `max_element` is used to determine the largest element in a given range.

83. The algorithm `min` is used to determine the minimum of two values.

84. The algorithm `min_element` is used to determine the smallest element in a given range.

85. The algorithm `random_shuffle` is used to randomly order the elements in a given range.

86. The algorithm `for_each` is used to access and process each element in a given range by applying a function, which is passed as a parameter.

87. This function `transform` creates a sequence of elements by applying certain operations to each element in a given range.

88. The algorithm `includes` determines whether the elements of one range appear in another range.

89. The algorithm `set_intersection` is used to find the elements that are common to two ranges of elements.

90. The algorithm `set_union` is used to find the elements that are contained in two ranges of elements.

91. The algorithm `set_difference` is used to find the elements in one range of elements that do not appear in another range of elements.

92. Given two ranges of elements, the algorithm `set_symmetric_difference` determines the elements that are in the first range but not the second range, or the elements that are in the second range but not the first range.

93. The algorithms `accumulate`, `adjacent_difference`, `inner_product`, and `partial_sum` are numerical functions and manipulate numeric data.

EXERCISES

1. What are the three main components of the STL?

2. What is the difference between an STL container and an STL iterator?

3. What is the difference between an STL container and an STL algorithm?

4. What is the difference between a set and a multiset?

5. What is an STL function object?

6. Suppose that `vecList` is a `vector` container and:

   ```
   vecList = {12, 16, 8, 23, 40, 6, 18, 9, 75}
   ```

   Show `vecList` after the following statement executes:

   ```
   copy(vecList.begin() + 2, vecList.end(), vecList.begin());
   ```

7. Suppose that `vecList` is a `vector` container and:

   ```
   vecList = {12, 16, 8, 23, 40, 6, 18, 9, 75}
   ```

   Show `vecList` after the following statement executes:

   ```
   copy(vecList.rbegin() + 3, vecList.rend(), vecList.rbegin());
   ```

8. Suppose that `intList` is a `list` container and:

   ```
   intList = {3, 23, 23, 43, 56, 11, 11, 23, 25}
   ```

   Show `intList` after the following statement executes:

   ```
   intList.unique();
   ```

9. Suppose that `intList1` and `intList2` are `list` containers and:

   ```
   intList1 = {3, 58, 78, 85, 6, 15, 93, 98, 25}
   intList2 = {5, 24, 16, 11, 60, 9}
   ```

   Show `intList` after the following statement executes:

   ```
   intList1.splice(intList1.begin(),intList2);
   ```

10. Suppose that `charList` is a `vector` container and:

    ```
    charList = {a, A, B, b, c, d, A, e, f, K}
    ```

    Further suppose that:

    ```
    lastElem = remove_if(charList.begin(), charList.end(), islower);
    ostream_iterator<char> screen(cout, " ");
    ```

    where `lastElem` is a `vector` iterator into a `vector` container of type `char`. What is the output of the following statement?

    ```
    copy(charList.begin(), lastElem, screen);
    ```

11. Suppose that `intList` is a `vector` container and:

    ```
    intList = {18, 24, 24, 5, 11, 56, 27, 24, 2, 24}
    ```

    Furthermore, suppose that:

    ```
    vector<int>::iterator lastElem;
    ostream_iterator<int> screen(cout, " ");
    vector<int> otherList(10);
    lastElem = remove_copy(intList.begin(), intList.end(),
                           otherList.begin(), 24);
    ```

    What is the output of the following statement?

    ```
    copy(otherList.begin(), lastElem, screenOut);
    ```

12. Suppose that `intList` is a `vector` container and:

    ```
    intList = {2, 4, 6, 8, 10, 12, 14, 16}
    ```

    What is the value of `result` after the following statement executes?

    ```
    result = accumulate(intList.begin(), intList.end(), 0);
    ```

13. Suppose that `intList` is a `vector` container and:

    ```
    intList = {2, 4, 6, 8, 10, 12, 14, 16}
    ```

    What is the value of `result` after the following statement executes?

    ```
    result = accumulate(intList.begin(), intList.end(),
                        0, multiplies<int>());
    ```

14. Suppose that `setA`, `setB`, `setC`, and `setD` are defined as follows:

    ```
    int setA[] = {3, 4, 5, 8, 9, 12, 14};
    int setB[] = {2, 3, 4, 5, 6, 7, 8};
    int setC[] = {2, 5, 5, 9};
    int setD[] = {4, 4, 4, 6, 7, 12};
    ```

    Further suppose that you have the following declarations:

    ```
    int AunionB[10];
    int AunionC[9];
    int BunionD[10];
    int AintersectB[4];
    int AintersectC[2];
    ```

    What is stored in `AunionB`, `AunionC`, `BunionD`, `AintersectB`, and `AintersectC` after the following statements execute?

    ```
    set_union(setA, setA + 7, setB, setB + 7, AunionB);
    set_union(setA, setA + 7, setC, setC + 4, AunionC);
    set_union(setB, setB + 7, setD, setD + 6, BunionD);
    set_intersection(setA, setA + 7, setB, setB + 7, AintersectB);
    set_intersection(setA, setA + 7, setC, setC + 4, AintersectC);
    ```

PROGRAMMING EXERCISES

1. Redo the Video Store programming example of Chapter 17 so that it uses the STL `class` `list` to process a list of videos.

2. Redo Programming Exercise 9 of Chapter 17 so that it uses the STL `class` `list` to process the list of videos rented by the customer and the list of store members.

3. Redo Programming Exercise 10 of Chapter 17 so that it uses the STL `class` `list` to process the list of videos owned by the store, the list of videos rented by each customer, and the list of store members.

4. Redo the Postfix Expression Calculator program of Chapter 18 so that it uses the STL `class` `stack` to evaluate the postfix expressions.

5. Redo Programming Exercise 9 of Chapter 18 so that it uses the STL `class` `stack` to convert the infix expressions to postfix expressions.

6. Redo the simulation program of Chapter 18 so that it uses the STL `class` queue to maintain the list of waiting customers.

7. Write a program to play the Card Guessing Game. Your program must give the user the following choices:

   a. Guess only the face value of the card.

   b. Guess only the suit of the card.

   c. Guess both the face value and suit of the card.

   Before the start of the game, create a deck of cards. Before each guess, use the function `random_shuffle` to randomly shuffle the deck.

Reserved Words

and	and_eq	asm	auto
bitand	bitor	bool	break
case	catch	char	class
compl	const	const_cast	continue
default	delete	do	double
dynamic_cast	else	enum	explicit
export	extern	false	float
for	friend	goto	if
include	inline	int	long
mutable	namespace	new	not
not_eq	operator	or	or_eq
private	protected	public	register
reinterpret_cast	return	short	signed
sizeof	static	static_cast	struct
switch	template	this	throw
true	try	typedef	typeid
typename	union	unsigned	using
virtual	void	volatile	wchar_t
while	xor	xor_eq	

OPERATOR PRECEDENCE

The following table shows the precedence (highest to lowest) and associativity of the operators in C++.

Operator	Associativity
:: (binary scope resolution)	Left to right
:: (unary scope resolution)	Right to left
()	Left to right
[] -> .	Left to right
++ -- (as postfix operators)	Right to left
`typeid` `dynamic_cast`	Right to left
`static_cast` `const_cast`	Right to left
`reinterpret_cast`	Right to left
++ -- (as prefix operators) ! + (unary) - (unary)	Right to left
~ & (address of) * (dereference)	Right to left
`new` `delete` `sizeof`	Right to left
->* -- .*	Left to right
* / %	Left to right
+ -	Left to right
<< >>	Left to right
< <= > >=	Left to right
== !=	Left to right
&	Left to right
^	Left to right
|	Left to right
&&	Left to right

Operator	Associativity
`||`	Left to right
`?:`	Right to left
`=` `+=` `-=` `*=` `/=` `%=`	Right to left
`<<=` `>>=` `&=` `|=` `^=`	Right to left
`throw`	Right to left
`,` (the sequencing operator)	Left to right

ASCII (American Standard Code for Information Interchange)

The following table shows the ASCII character set.

ASCII										
	0	1	2	3	4	5	6	7	8	9
0	nul	soh	stx	etx	eot	enq	ack	bel	bs	ht
1	lf	vt	ff	cr	so	si	dle	dc1	dc2	dc3
2	dc4	nak	syn	etb	can	em	sub	esc	fs	gs
3	rs	us	b̲	!	"	#	$	%	&	'
4	(	)	*	+	,	-	.	/	0	1
5	2	3	4	5	6	7	8	9	:	;
6	<	=	>	?	@	A	B	C	D	E
7	F	G	H	I	J	K	L	M	N	O
8	P	Q	R	S	T	U	V	W	X	Y
9	Z	[	\	]	^	_	`	a	b	c
10	d	e	f	g	h	i	j	k	l	m
11	n	o	p	q	r	s	t	u	v	w
12	x	y	z	{	|	}	~	del		

The numbers 0–12 in the first column specify the left digit(s), and the numbers 0–9 in the second row specify the right digit of each character in the ASCII data set. For example, the character in the row marked 6 (the number in the first column) and the column marked 5 (the number in the second row) is A. Therefore, the character at position 65 (which is the 66th character) is A. Moreover, the character b̲ at position 32 represents the space character.

The first 32 characters, that is, the characters at positions 00–31 and at position 127 are nonprintable characters. The following table shows the abbreviations and meanings of these characters.

nul	null character	ff	form feed	can	cancel
soh	start of header	cr	carriage return	em	end of medium
stx	start of text	so	shift out	sub	substitute
etx	end of text	si	shift in	esc	escape
eot	end of transmission	dle	data link escape	fs	file separator
enq	enquiry	dc1	device control 1	gs	group separator
ack	acknowledge	dc2	device control 2	rs	record separator
bel	bell	dc3	device control 3	us	unit separator
bs	back space	dc4	device control 4	b	space
ht	horizontal tab	nak	negative acknowledge	del	delete
lf	line feed	syn	synchronous idle		
vt	vertical tab	etb	end of transmitted block		

EBCDIC (Extended Binary Coded Decimal Interchange Code)

The following table shows some of the characters in the EBCDIC character set.

EBCDIC										
	0	1	2	3	4	5	6	7	8	9
6					b					
7						.	<	(	+	|
8	&									
9	!	$	*	)	;	¬	-	/		
10								,	%	_
11	>	?								
12		`	:	#	@	'	=	"		a
13	b	c	d	e	f	g	h	i		

EBCDIC									
14						j	k	l	m	n
15	o	p	q	r						
16		~	s	t	u	v	w	x	y	z
17										
18	[	]								
19				A	B	C	D	E	F	G
20	H	I								J
21	K	L	M	N	O	P	Q	R		
22							S	T	U	V
23	W	X	Y	Z						
24	0	1	2	3	4	5	6	7	8	9

The numbers 6–24 in the first column specify the left digit(s), and the numbers 0–9 in the second row specify the right digits of the characters in the EBCDIC data set. For example, the character in the row marked 19 (the number in the first column) and the column marked 3 (the number in the second row) is A. Therefore, the character at position 193 (which is the 194th character) is A. Moreover, the character b at position 64 represents the space character. The preceding table does not show all the characters in the EBCDIC character set. In fact, the characters at positions 00–63 and 250–255 are nonprintable control characters.

Operator Overloading

The following table lists the operators that can be overloaded.

Operators that can be overloaded							
+	–	*	/	%	^	&	|
!	&&	||	=	==	<	<=	>
>=	!=	+=	-=	*=	/=	%=	^=
|=	&=	<<	>>	>>=	<<=	++	–
->*	,	->	[]	()	~	new	delete

The following table lists the operators that cannot be overloaded.

Operators that cannot be overloaded				
.	.*	::	?:	sizeof

ADDITIONAL C++ TOPICS

Binary (Base 2) Representation Of a Non-Negative Integer

Converting a Base 10 Number to a Binary Number (Base 2)

Chapter 1 remarked that A is the 66th character in the ASCII character set, but its position is 65 because the position of the first character is 0. Furthermore, the binary number 1000001 is the binary representation of 65. The number system that we use daily is called the **decimal number system** or **base 10 system**. The number system that the computer uses is called the **binary number system** or **base 2 system**. In this section, we describe how to find the binary representation of a non-negative integer and vice versa.

Consider 65. Note that:

$$65 = 1 \times 2^6 + 0 \times 2^5 + 0 \times 2^4 + 0 \times 2^3 + 0 \times 2^2 + 0 \times 2^1 + 1 \times 2^0$$

Similarly:

$$711 = 1 \times 2^9 + 0 \times 2^8 + 1 \times 2^7 + 1 \times 2^6 + 0 \times 2^5 + 0 \times 2^4 + 0 \times 2^3 + 1 \times 2^2 +$$
$$1 \times 2^1 + 1 \times 2^0$$

In general, if m is a non-negative integer, then m can be written as:

$$m = a_k \times 2^k + a_{k-1} \times 2^{k-1} + a_{k-2} \times 2^{k-2} + \cdots + a_1 \times 2^1 + a_0 \times 2^0,$$

for some non-negative integer k, and where $a_i = 0$ or 1, for each $i = 0, 1, 2, \ldots, k$. The binary number $a_k a_{k-1} a_{k-2} \ldots a_1 a_0$ is called the **binary** or **base 2 representation** of m. In this case, we usually write:

$$m_{10} = \left(a_k a_{k-1} a_{k-2} \cdots a_1 a_0\right)_2$$

and say that m to the base 10 is $a_k a_{k-1} a_{k-2} \ldots a_1 a_0$ to the base 2.

For example, for the integer 65, $k = 6$, $a_6 = 1$, $a_5 = 0$, $a_4 = 0$, $a_3 = 0$, $a_2 = 0$, $a_1 = 0$, $a_0 = 1$. Thus, $a_6 a_5 a_4 a_3 a_2 a_1 a_0 = 1000001$, so the binary representation of 65 is 1000001, that is:

$$65_{10} = \left(1000001\right)_2.$$

If no confusion arise, then we write $(1000001)_2$ as 1000001_2.

Similarly, for the number 711, $k = 9$, $a_9 = 1$, $a_8 = 0$, $a_7 = 1$, $a_6 = 1$, $a_5 = 0$, $a_4 = 0$, $a_3 = 0$, $a_2 = 1$, $a_1 = 1$, $a_0 = 1$. Thus:

$$711_{10} = 1011000111_2.$$

It follows that to find the binary representation of a non-negative, we need to find the coefficients, which is 0 or 1, of various powers of 2. However, there is an easy algorithm, described next, that can be used to find the binary representation of a non-negative integer. First, note that:

$$0_{10} = 0_2, 1_{10} = 1_2, 2_{10} = 10_2, 3_{10} = 11_2, 4_{10} = 100_2, 5_{10} = 101_2, 6_{10} = 110_2,$$

and $7_{10} = 111_2$.

Let us consider the integer 65. Note that $65 / 2 = 32$ and $65 \% 2 = 1$, where $\%$ is the mod operator. Next, $32 / 2 = 16$, and $32 \% 2 = 0$, and so on. It can be shown that $a_0 = 65 \% 2 = 1$, $a_1 = 32 \% 2 = 0$, and so on. We can show this continuous division and obtaining the remainder with the help of Figure E-1.

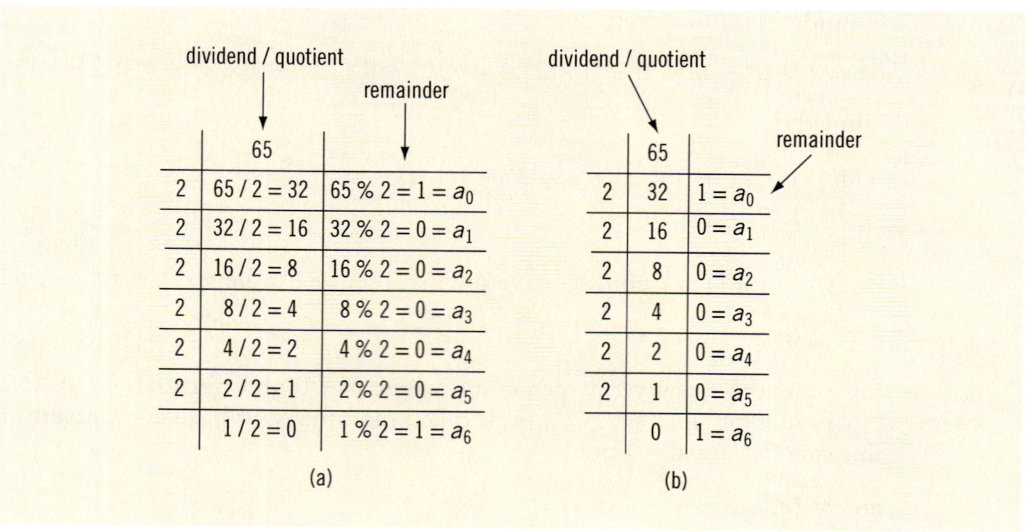

FIGURE E-1   Determining the binary representation of 65

Notice that in Figure E-1(a), starting at the second row, the second column contains the quotient when the number in the previous row is divided by 2 and the third column contains the remainder of that division. For example, in the second row, $65 / 2 = 32$, and $65 \% 2 = 1$. In the third row, $32 / 2 = 16$ and $32 \% 2 = 0$, and so. For each row, the number in the second column is divided by 2, the quotient is written in the next row, below the current row, and the remainder in the third column. When using a figure, such as E-1, to find the binary representation of a non-negative integer, typically, we show only the quotients and remainders as in Figure E-1(b). You can write the binary representation of the number starting with the last remainder in the third column, followed by the second last remainder, and so on. Thus:

$65_{10} = 1000001_2$.

Next, consider the number 711. Figure E-2 shows the quotients and the remainders.

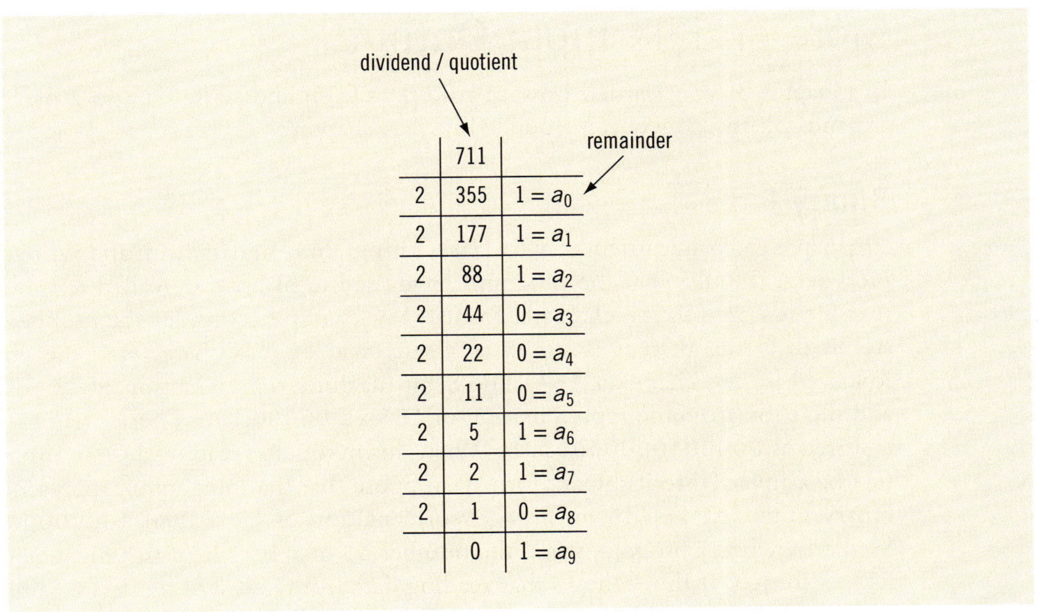

FIGURE E-2 Determining the binary representation of 711

From Figure E-2, it follows that:

$711_{10} = 1011000111_2$.

Converting a Binary Number (Base 2) to Base 10

To convert a number from base 2 to base 10, we first find the weight of each bit in the binary number. The weight of each bit in the binary number is assigned from right to left. The weight of the rightmost bit is 0. The weight of the bit immediately to the left of the rightmost bit is 1, the weight of the bit immediately to the left of it is 2, and so on. Consider the binary number 1001101. The weight of each bit is as follows:

```
weight  6  5  4  3  2  1  0
           1  0  0  1  1  0  1
```

We use the weight of each bit to find the equivalent decimal number. For each bit, we multiply the bit by 2 to the power of its weight and then we add all of the numbers. For the above binary number, the equivalent decimal number is:

$$1 \times 2^6 + 0 \times 2^5 + 0 \times 2^4 + 1 \times 2^3 + 1 \times 2^2 + 0 \times 2^1 + 1 \times 2^0$$

$$= 64 + 0 + 0 + 8 + 4 + 0 + 1$$

$$= 77.$$

More on File Input/Output

In Chapter 3, you learned how to read data from and write data to a file. This section expands on the concepts introduced in that chapter.

Binary Files

In Chapter 3, you learned how to make a program read data from and write data to a file. However, the files that the programs have used until now are called text files. Data in a text file is stored in the character format. For example, consider the number 45. If 45 is stored in a file, then it is stored as a sequence of two characters—the character `'4'` followed by the character `'5'`. The 8-bit machine representation of `'4'` is `00000100` and the 8-bit machine representation of `'5'` is `00000101`. Therefore, in a text file, 45 is stored as `0000010000000101`. When this number is read by a C++ program, it must first be converted to its binary format. Suppose that the integers are represented as 16-bit binary numbers. The 16-bit binary representation of 45 is then `0000000000101101`. Similarly, when a program stores the number 45 in a text file, it first must be converted to its text format. It thus follows that reading data from and writing data to a text file is not efficient, because the data must be converted from the text to the binary format and vice versa.

On the other hand, when data is stored in a file in the binary format, reading and writing data is faster because no time is lost in converting the data from one format to another format. Such files are called binary files. More formally, **binary files** are files in which data is stored in the binary format. Data in a text file is also called **formatted data**, and in a binary file it is called **raw data**.

C++ allows a programmer to create binary files. This section explains how to create binary files and also how to read data from binary files.

To create a binary file, the file must be opened in the binary mode. Suppose `outFile` is an `ofstream` variable (object). Consider the following statement:

```
outFile.open("employee.dat", ios::binary);
```

This statement opens the file `employee.dat`. Data in this file will be written in its binary format. Therefore, the file opening mode `ios::binary` specifies that the file is opened in the binary mode.

Next, you use the stream function `write` to write data to the file `employee.dat`. The syntax to use the function `write` is:

```
fileVariableName.write(reinterpret_cast<const char *> (buffer),
                        sizeof(buffer));
```

where `fileVariableName` is the object used to open the output file, and the first argument `buffer` specifies the starting address of the location in memory where the data is stored. The expression `sizeof(buffer)` specifies the size of the data, in bytes, to be written.

For example, suppose num is an `int` variable. The following statement writes the value of num in the binary format to the file associated with `outFile`:

```
outFile.write(reinterpret_cast<const char *> (&num),
             sizeof(num));
```

Similarly, suppose `empSalary` is an array of, say, 100 components and the component type is `double`. The following statement writes the entire array to the file associated with `outFile`:

```
outFile.write(reinterpret_cast<const char *> (empSalary),
             sizeof(empSalary));
```

Next, let us discuss how to read data from a binary file. The operation of reading data from a binary file is similar to writing data to a binary file. First, the binary file must be opened. For example, suppose `inFile` is an `ifstream` variable, and a program has already created the binary file `employee.dat`. The following statement opens this file:

```
inFile.open("employee.dat");
```

or:

```
inFile.open("employee.dat", ios::binary);
```

To read data in the binary format, the stream function `read` is used. The syntax to use the function `read` is:

```
fileVariableName.read(reinterpret_cast<char *> (buffer),
                       sizeof(buffer));
```

The first argument `buffer` specifies the starting address of the location in memory where the data is to be stored. The expression `sizeof(buffer)` specifies the size of the data, in bytes, to be read.

The program in the following example further explains how to create binary files and read data from a binary file.

EXAMPLE E-1

```cpp
//Creating and reading binary files

#include <iostream>
#include <fstream>

using namespace std;

struct studentType
{
    char firstName[15];
    char lastName[15];
    int ID;
};

int main()
{
        //create and initialize an array of students' IDs
    int studentIDs[5] = {111111, 222222, 333333,
                         444444, 555555};                 //Line 1

        //declare and initialize the struct newStudent
    studentType newStudent = {"John", "Wilson",
                             777777};                      //Line 2

    ofstream outFile;                                      //Line 3

        //open the output file as a binary file
    outFile.open("a:\\ids.dat", ios::binary);              //Line 4

        //write the array in the binary format
    outFile.write(reinterpret_cast<const char *> (studentIDs),
             sizeof(studentIDs));                          //Line 5
        //write the newStudent data in the binary format
    outFile.write(reinterpret_cast<const char *> (&newStudent),
             sizeof(newStudent));                          //Line 6

    outFile.close();   //close the file                    //Line 7

    ifstream inFile;                                       //Line 8
    int arrayID[5];                                        //Line 9
    studentType student;                                   //Line 10

        //open the input file
    inFile.open("a:\\ids.dat");                            //Line 11
```

```cpp
    if (!inFile)                                        //Line 12
    {
        cout << "The input file does not exist. "
            << "The program terminates!!!!" << endl;    //Line 13
        return 1;                                       //Line 14
    }

        //input the data into the array arrayID
    inFile.read(reinterpret_cast<char *> (arrayID),
            sizeof(arrayID));                           //Line 15
        //output the data of the array arrayID
    for (int i = 0; i < 5; i++)                         //Line 16
        cout << arrayID[i] << " ";                      //Line 17
    cout << endl;                                       //Line 18

        //read the student's data
    inFile.read(reinterpret_cast<char *> (&student),
            sizeof(student));                           //Line 19

        //output studentData
    cout << student.ID << " " << student.firstName
        << " " << student.lastName << endl;             //Line 20

    inFile.close();       //close the file              //Line 21

    return 0;                                           //Line 22
}
```

Sample Run:

```
111111 222222 333333 444444 555555
777777 John Wilson
```

The output of the preceding program is self-explanatory. The details are left as an exercise for you.

NOTE   In the program in Example E-1, the statement in Line 2 declares the `struct` variable `newStudent` and also initializes it. Because `newStudent` has three components and we want to initialize all the components, three values are specified in braces separated by commas. In other words, `struct` variables can also be initialized when they are declared.

The program in the following example further explains how to create binary files and then read the data from the binary files.

EXAMPLE E-2

```cpp
//Creating and reading a binary file consisting of
//bank customers' data

#include <iostream>
#include <fstream>
#include <iomanip>

using namespace std;

struct customerType
{
    char firstName[15];
    char lastName[15];
    int ID;
    double balance;
};

int main()
{
    customerType cust;                                      //Line 1
    ifstream inFile;                                        //Line 2
    ofstream outFile;                                       //Line 3

    inFile.open("a:\\customerData.txt");                    //Line 4

    if (!inFile)                                            //Line 5
    {
        cout << "The input file does not exist. "
            << "The program terminates!!!!" << endl;        //Line 6
        return 1;                                           //Line 7
    }

    outFile.open("a:\\customer.dat", ios::binary);          //Line 8

    inFile >> cust.ID >> cust.firstName >> cust.lastName
        >> cust.balance;                                    //Line 9

    while (inFile)                                          //Line 10
    {
        outFile.write(reinterpret_cast<const char *> (&cust),
                    sizeof(cust));                          //Line 11
        inFile >> cust.ID >> cust.firstName >> cust.lastName
            >> cust.balance;                                //Line 12
    }

    inFile.close();                                         //Line 13
    inFile.clear();                                         //Line 14
    outFile.close();                                        //Line 15
```

```cpp
    inFile.open("a:\\customer.dat", ios::binary);       //Line 16

    if (!inFile)                                         //Line 17
    {
        cout << "The input file does not exist. "
             << "The program terminates!!!!" << endl;    //Line 18
        return 1;                                        //Line 19
    }

    cout << left << setw(8) << "ID"
         << setw(16) << "First Name"
         << setw(16) << "Last Name"
         << setw(10) << " Balance" << endl;              //Line 20
    cout << fixed << showpoint << setprecision(2);       //Line 21

        //read and output the data from the binary
        //file customer.dat
    inFile.read(reinterpret_cast<char *> (&cust),
                sizeof(cust));                           //Line 22
    while (inFile)                                       //Line 23
    {
        cout << left << setw(8) << cust.ID
             << setw(16) << cust.firstName
             << setw(16) << cust.lastName
             << right << setw(10) << cust.balance
             << endl;                                    //Line 24
        inFile.read(reinterpret_cast<char *> (&cust),
                    sizeof(cust));                       //Line 25
    }

    inFile.close();      //close the file                //Line 26

    return 0;                                            //Line 27
}
```

Sample Run:

```
ID       First Name      Last Name           Balance
77234    Ashley          White                4563.50
12345    Brad            Smith              128923.45
87123    Lisa            Johnson              2345.93
81234    Sheila          Robinson              674.00
11111    Rita            Gupta               14863.50
23422    Ajay            Kumar               72682.90
22222    Jose            Ramey               25345.35
54234    Sheila          Duffy               65222.00
55555    Tommy           Pitts                 892.85
23452    Salma           Quade                2812.90
32657    Jennifer        Ackerman             9823.89
82722    Steve           Sharma              78932.00
```

Random File Access

In Chapter 3 and the preceding section, you learned how to read data from and write data to a file. More specifically, you used `ifstream` objects to read data from a file and `ofstream` objects to write data to a file. However, the files were read and/or written sequentially. Reading data from a file sequentially does not work very well for a variety of applications. For example, consider a program that processes customers' data in a bank. Typically, there are thousands or even millions of customers in a bank. Suppose we want to access a customer's data from the file that contains such data, say, for an account update. If the data is accessed sequentially, starting from the first position and read until the desired customer's data is found, this process might be extremely time consuming. Similarly, in an airline's reservation system to access a passenger's reservation information sequentially, this might also be very time consuming. In such cases, the data retrieval must be efficient. A convenient way to do this is to be able to read the data randomly from a file, that is, randomly access any record in the file.

In the preceding section, you learned how to use the stream function `read` to read a specific number of bytes, and the function `write` to write a specific number of bytes.

The stream function `seekg` is used to move the read position to any byte in the file. The general syntax to use the function `seekg` is:

```
fileVariableName.seekg(offset, position);
```

The stream function `seekp` is used to move the write position to any byte in the file. The general syntax to use the function `seekp` is:

```
fileVariableName.seekp(offset, position);
```

The `offset` specifies the number of bytes the reading/writing positions are to be moved, and `position` specifies where to begin the offset. The offset can be calculated from the beginning of the file, end of the file, or the current position in the file. Moreover, `offset` is a long integer representation of an offset. Table E-1 shows the values that can be used for `position`.

TABLE E-1 Values of `position`

position	Description
`ios::beg`	The offset is calculated from the beginning of the file.
`ios::cur`	The offset is calculated from the current position of the reading marker in the file.
`ios::end`	The offset is calculated from the end of the file.

EXAMPLE E-3

Suppose you have the following line of text stored in a file, say, `digitsAndLetters.txt`:

`0123456789ABCDEFGHIJKLMNOPQRSTUVWXYZ`

Also, suppose that `inFile` is an `ifstream` object and the file `digitsAndLetters.txt` has been opened using the object `inFile`. One byte is used to store each character of this line of text. Moreover, the position of the first character is 0.

Statement	Explanation
`inFile.seekp(10L, ios::beg);`	Sets the reading position of `inFile` to the 11th byte (character), which is at position 10. That is, it sets the reading position just after the digit 9 or just before the letter A.
`inFile.seekp(5L, ios::cur);`	Moves the reading position of `inFile` five bytes to the right of its current position.
`inFile.seekp(-6L, ios::end);`	Sets the reading position of `inFile` to the 6th byte (character) from the end. That is, it sets the reading position just before the letter U.

The program in the following example further explains how the functions `seekg` and `seekp` work.

EXAMPLE E-4

```cpp
#include <iostream>
#include <fstream>

using namespace std;

int main()
{
    char ch;                                        //Line 1
    ifstream inFile;                                //Line 2

    inFile.open("a:\\digitsAndAlphabet.txt");       //Line 3

    if (!inFile)                                     //Line 4
    {
        cout << "The input file does not exist. "
             << "The program terminates!!!!" << endl;   //Line 5
        return 1;                                   //Line 6
    }
```

```cpp
    inFile.get(ch);                                     //Line 7
    cout << "Line 8: The first byte: " << ch << endl;  //Line 8

        //position the reading marker six bytes to the
        //right of its current position
    inFile.seekg(6L, ios::cur);                         //Line 9
    inFile.get(ch);    //read the character              //Line 10
    cout << "Line 11: Current byte read: " << ch
         << endl;                                       //Line 11

        //position the reading marker seven bytes
        //from the beginning
    inFile.seekg(7L, ios::beg);                         //Line 12
    inFile.get(ch);    //read the character              //Line 13
    cout << "Line 14: Seventh byte from the beginning: "
         << ch << endl;                                 //Line 14

        //position the reading marker 26 bytes
        //from the end
    inFile.seekg(-26L, ios::end);                       //Line 15
    inFile.get(ch);    //read the character              //Line 16
    cout << "Line 17: Byte 26 from the end: " << ch
         << endl;                                       //Line 17

    return 0;                                           //Line 18
}
```

Sample Run:

```
Line 8: The first byte: 0
Line 11: Current byte read: 7
Line 14: Seventh byte from the beginning: 7
Line 17: Byte 26 from the end: A
```

The input file contains the following line of text:

```
0123456789ABCDEFGHIJKLMNOPQRSTUVWXYZ
```

The following program illustrates how the function `seekg` works with `structs`.

EXAMPLE E-5

Suppose `customerType` is a `struct` defined as follows:

```cpp
struct customerType
{
    char firstName[15];
    char lastName[15];
    int ID;
    double balance;
};
```

The program in Example E-2 created the binary file `customer.dat` consisting of certain customers' data. You can use the function `seekg` to move the reading position of this file to any record. Suppose `inFile` is an `ifstream` object used to open the binary file `customer.dat`.

The following statement calculates the size of a `customerType` **struct** and stores it in the variable `custSize`:

```
long custSize = sizeof(cust);
```

We can use the value of the variable `custSize` to move the reading position to a specific record in the file. For example, consider the following statement:

```
inFile.seekg(6 * custSize, ios::beg);
```

This statement moves the reading position just after the sixth customer's record, that is, just before the seventh customer's record.

The following program further illustrates how the function `seekg` works with **struct**s.

EXAMPLE E-6

```cpp
//Reading a file randomly

#include <iostream>
#include <fstream>
#include <iomanip>

using namespace std;

struct customerType
{
    char firstName[15];
    char lastName[15];
    int ID;
    double balance;
};

void printCustData(const customerType& customer);

int main()
{
    customerType cust;                              //Line 1
    ifstream inFile;                                //Line 2

    long custSize = sizeof(cust);                   //Line 3

    inFile.open("a:\\customer.dat", ios::binary);   //Line 4
    if (!inFile)                                    //Line 5
```

```cpp
    {
        cout << "The input file does not exist. "
             << "The program terminates!!!!" << endl;     //Line 6
        return 1;                                          //Line 7
    }

    cout << fixed << showpoint << setprecision(2);         //Line 8

        //randomly read the records and outputs them
    inFile.seekg(6 * custSize, ios::beg);                  //Line 9
    inFile.read(reinterpret_cast<char *> (&cust),
             sizeof(cust));                                //Line 10
    cout << "Seventh customer's data: " << endl;           //Line 11
    printCustData(cust);                                   //Line 12

    inFile.seekg(8 * custSize, ios::beg);                  //Line 13
    inFile.read(reinterpret_cast<char *> (&cust),
             sizeof(cust));                                //Line 14
    cout << "Ninth customer's data: " << endl;             //Line 15
    printCustData(cust);

    inFile.seekg(-8 * custSize, ios::end);                 //Line 16
    inFile.read(reinterpret_cast<char *> (&cust),
             sizeof(cust));                                //Line 17
    cout << "Eighth (from the end) customer's data: "
         << endl;                                          //Line 18
    printCustData(cust);                                   //Line 19

    inFile.close();       //close the file                 //Line 20

    return 0;                                              //Line 21
}

void printCustData(const customerType& customer)
{
    cout << "  ID: " << customer.ID <<endl
         << "  First Name: " << customer.firstName <<endl
         << "  Last Name: " << customer.lastName <<endl
         << "  Account Balance: $" << customer.balance
         << endl;
}
```

Sample Run:

```
Seventh customer's data:
  ID: 22222
  First Name: Jose
  Last Name: Ramey
  Account Balance: $25345.35
Ninth customer's data:
  ID: 55555
  First Name: Tommy
  Last Name: Pitts
```

```
   Account Balance: $892.85
Eighth (from the end) customer's data:
   ID: 11111
   First Name: Rita
   Last Name: Gupta
   Account Balance: $14863.50
```

The program in Example E-6 illustrates how the function `seekg` works. Using the function `seekg`, the reading position in a file can be moved to any location in the file. Similarly, the function `seekp` can be used to move the write position in a file to any location. Furthermore, these functions can be used to create a binary file in which the data is organized according to the values of either a variable or a particular component of a `struct`. For example, suppose there are at most, say, 100 students in a class. Each student has a unique ID in the range 1 to 100. Using the students' IDs, we can create a random access binary file in such a way that in the file a student's data is written at the location specified by its ID. This is like treating the file as an array. The advantage is that, once the file is created, a student's data from the file can be read, directly, using the student's ID. Another advantage is that in the file the data is sorted according to the IDs.

Here, we are assuming that the student IDs are in the range 1 to 100. However, if you use, say, a 3-, 4-, or 5-digit number as a student ID and there are only a few students in the class, the data in the file could be scattered. In other words, a lot of space could be used just to store only a few students' data. In such cases, more advanced techniques are used to organize the data so that it can be accessed efficiently.

The program in Example E-7 illustrates how to use the students' IDs to organize the data in a binary file. The program also shows how to output the file.

EXAMPLE E-7

```cpp
//Creating and reading a random access file.

#include <iostream>
#include <fstream>
#include <iomanip>

using namespace std;

struct studentType
{
    char firstName[15];
    char lastName[15];
    int ID;
    double GPA;
};

void printStudentData(const studentType& student);
```

```cpp
int main()
{
    studentType st;                                     //Line 1
    ifstream inFile;                                    //Line 2
    ofstream outFile;                                   //Line 3

    long studentSize = sizeof(st);                      //Line 4

        //open the input file, which is a text file
    inFile.open("a:\\studentData.txt");                 //Line 5

    if (!inFile)                                         //Line 6
    {
        cout << "The input file does not exist. "
            << "The program terminates!!!!" << endl;    //Line 7
        return 1;                                       //Line 8
    }

        //open a binary output file
    outFile.open("a:\\student.dat", ios::binary);       //Line 9

    inFile >> st.ID >> st.firstName
        >> st.lastName >> st.GPA;                        //Line 10

    while (inFile)                                       //Line 11
    {
        outFile.seekp((st.ID - 1) * studentSize,
                    ios::beg);                           //Line 12
        outFile.write(reinterpret_cast<const char *> (&st),
                    sizeof(st));                         //Line 13
        inFile >> st.ID >> st.firstName
            >> st.lastName >> st.GPA;                    //Line 14
    };

    inFile.close();                                     //Line 15
    inFile.clear();                                     //Line 16
    outFile.close();                                    //Line 17

    cout << left << setw(3) << "ID"
        << setw(16) << "First Name"
        << setw(16) << "Last Name"
        << setw(12) << "Current GPA" << endl;           //Line 18
    cout << fixed << showpoint << setprecision(2);       //Line 19

        //open the input file, which is a binary file
    inFile.open("a:\\student.dat", ios::binary);        //Line 20

    if (!inFile)                                         //Line 21
    {
        cout << "The input file does not exist. "
            << "The program terminates!!!!" << endl;    //Line 22
        return 1;                                       //Line 23
    }
```

```cpp
        //read the data at location 0 in the file
    inFile.read(reinterpret_cast<char *> (&st),
            sizeof(st));                                    //Line 24
    while (inFile)                                          //Line 25
    {
        if (st.ID != 0)                                     //Line 26
            printStudentData(st);                           //Line 27

            //read the data at the current reading position
        inFile.read(reinterpret_cast<char *> (&st),
                sizeof(st));                                //Line 28
    };

    return 0;                                               //Line 29
}


void printStudentData(const studentType& student)
{
    cout << left << setw(3) << student.ID
        << setw(16) << student.firstName
        << setw(16) << student.lastName
        << right << setw(10)<< student.GPA
        << endl;
}
```

Sample Run:

```
ID First Name       Last Name         Current GPA
2  Sheila           Duffy                   4.00
10 Ajay             Kumar                   3.60
12 Ashley           White                   3.90
16 Tommy            Pitts                   2.40
23 Rita             Gupta                   3.40
34 Brad             Smith                   3.50
36 Salma            Quade                   3.90
41 Steve            Sharma                  3.50
45 Sheila           Robinson                2.50
56 Lisa             Johnson                 2.90
67 Jose             Ramey                   3.80
75 Jennifer         Ackerman                4.00
```

The data in the file studentData.txt is as follows:

```
12 Ashley White 3.9
34 Brad Smith 3.5
56 Lisa Johnson 2.9
45 Sheila Robinson 2.5
23 Rita Gupta 3.4
10 Ajay Kumar 3.6
67 Jose Ramey 3.8
2 Sheila Duffy 4.0
16 Tommy Pitts 2.4
```

```
36 Salma Quade 3.9
75 Jennifer Ackerman 4.0
41 Steve Sharma 3.5
```

Naming Conventions of Header Files in ANSI/ISO Standard C++ and Standard C++

The programs in this book are written using ANSI/ISO Standard C++. As indicated in Chapter 1, there are two versions of C++—ANSI/ISO Standard C++ and Standard C++. For the most part, these two standards are the same. The header files in Standard C++ have the extension .h, while the header files in ANSI/ISO Standard C++ have no extension. Moreover, the names of certain header files, such as `math.h`, in ANSI/ISO Standard C++ start with the letter c. The language C++ evolved from C. Therefore, certain header files—such as `math.h`, `stdlib.h`, and `string.h`—were brought from C into C++. The header files—such as `iostream.h`, `iomanip.h`, and `fstream.h`—were specially designed for C++. Recall that when a header file is included in a program, the global identifiers of the header file also become the global identifiers of the program. In ANSI/ISO Standard C++, to take advantage of the `namespace` mechanism, all of the header files were modified so that the identifiers are declared within a `namespace`. Recall that the name of this `namespace` is `std`.

In ANSI/ISO Standard C++, the extension .h of the header files that were specially designed for C++ was dropped. For the header files that were brought from C into C++, the extension .h was dropped and the names of these header files start with the letter c. Following are the names of the most commonly used header files in Standard C++ and ANSI/ISO Standard C++:

Standard C++ Header File Name	ANSI/ISO Standard C++ Header File Name
`assert.h`	`cassert`
`ctype.h`	`cctype`
`float.h`	`cfloat`
`fstream.h`	`fstream`
`iomanip.h`	`iomanip`
`iostream.h`	`iostream`
`limits.h`	`climits`
`math.h`	`cmath`
`stdlib.h`	`cstdlib`
`string.h`	`cstring`

To include a header file, say, `iostream`, the following statement is required:

```
#include <iostream>
```

Furthermore, to use identifiers, such as `cin`, `cout`, `endl`, and so on, the program should use either the statement:

```
using namespace std;
```

or the prefix `std::` before the identifier.

HEADER FILES

The C++ standard library contains many predefined functions, named constants, and specialized data types. This appendix discusses some of the most widely used library routines (and several named constants). For additional explanation and information on functions, named constants, and so on, check your system documentation. The names of the Standard C++ header files are shown in parentheses.

Header File cassert (assert.h)

The following table describes the function **assert**. Its specification is contained in the header file **cassert** (**assert.h**).

assert(expression)	expression is any int expression; expression is usually a logical expression	• If the value of expression is nonzero (true), the program continues to execute. • If the value of expression is 0 (false), execution of the program terminates immediately. The expression, the name of the file containing the source code, and the line number in the source code are displayed.

NOTE To disable all the **assert** statements, place the preprocessor directive **#define** NDEBUG before the directive **#include** <cassert>.

Header File `cctype` (`ctype.h`)

The following table shows various functions from the header file `cctype` (`ctype.h`).

Function Name and Parameters	Parameter(s) Types	Function Return Value
`isalnum(ch)`	ch is a `char` value	Function returns an `int` value as follows: • If ch is a letter or a digit character, that is (`'A'-'Z'`, `'a'-'z'`, `'0'-'9'`), it returns a nonzero value (`true`) • 0 (`false`), otherwise
`iscntrl(ch)`	ch is a `char` value	Function returns an `int` value as follows: • If ch is a control character (in ASCII, a character value 0–31 or 127), it returns a nonzero value (`true`) • 0 (`false`), otherwise
`isdigit(ch)`	ch is a `char` value	Function returns an `int` value as follows: • If ch is a digit (`'0'-'9'`), it returns a nonzero value (`true`) • 0 (`false`), otherwise
`islower(ch)`	ch is a `char` value	Function returns an `int` value as follows: • If ch is lowercase (`'a'-'z'`), it returns a nonzero value (`true`) • 0 (`false`), otherwise
`isprint(ch)`	ch is a `char` value	Function returns an `int` value as follows: • If ch is a printable character, including blank (in ASCII, `' '` through `'~'`), it returns a nonzero value (`true`) • 0 (`false`), otherwise
`ispunct(ch)`	ch is a `char` value	Function returns an `int` value as follows: • If ch is a punctuation character, it returns a nonzero value (`true`) • 0 (`false`), otherwise
`isspace(ch)`	ch is a `char` value	Function returns an `int` value as follows: • If ch is a whitespace character (blank, newline, tab, carriage return, form feed), it returns a nonzero value (`true`) • 0 (`false`), otherwise

Function Name and Parameters	Parameter(s) Types	Function Return Value
`isupper(ch)`	ch is a `char` value	Function returns an `int` value as follows: • If ch is an uppercase letter (`'A'`–`'Z'`), it returns a nonzero value (`true`) • 0 (`false`), otherwise
`tolower(ch)`	ch is a `char` value	Function returns an `int` value as follows: • If ch is an uppercase letter, it returns the ASCII value of the lowercase equivalent of ch • ASCII value of ch, otherwise
`toupper(ch)`	ch is a `char` value	Function returns an `int` value as follows: • If ch is a lowercase letter, it returns the ASCII value of the uppercase equivalent of ch • ASCII value of ch, otherwise

Header File `cfloat` (`float.h`)

In Chapter 2, we listed the largest and smallest values belonging to the floating-point data types. We also remarked that these values are system-dependent. These largest and smallest values are stored in named constants. The header file `cfloat` contains many such named constants. The following table lists some of these constants.

Named Constant	Description
`FLT_DIG`	Approximate number of significant digits in a `float` value
`FLT_MAX`	Maximum positive `float` value
`FLT_MIN`	Minimum positive `float` value
`DBL_DIG`	Approximate number of significant digits in a `double` value
`DBL_MAX`	Maximum positive `double` value
`DBL_MIN`	Minimum positive `double` value
`LDBL_DIG`	Approximate number of significant digits in a `long double` value
`LDBL_MAX`	Maximum positive `long double` value
`LDBL_MIN`	Minimum positive `long double` value

A program similar to the following can print the values of these named constants on your system:

```cpp
#include <iostream>
#include <cfloat>

using namespace std;

int main()
{
    cout << "Approximate number of significant digits "
         << "in a float value " << FLT_DIG << endl;
    cout << "Maximum positive float value " << FLT_MAX
         << endl;
    cout << "Minimum positive float value " << FLT_MIN
         << endl;
    cout << "Approximate number of significant digits "
         << "in a double value " << DBL_DIG << endl;
    cout << "Maximum positive double value " << DBL_MAX
         << endl;
    cout << "Minimum positive double value " << DBL_MIN
         << endl;
    cout << "Approximate number of significant digits "
         << "in a long double value " << LDBL_DIG << endl;
    cout << "Maximum positive long double value " << LDBL_MAX
         << endl;
    cout << "Minimum positive long double value " << LDBL_MIN
         << endl;

    return 0;
}
```

Header File `climits` (`limits.h`)

In Chapter 2, we listed the largest and smallest values belonging to the integral data types. We also remarked that these values are system-dependent. These largest and smallest values are stored in named constants. The header file `climits` contains many such named constants. The following table lists some of these constants.

Named Constant	Description
CHAR_BIT	Number of bits in a byte
CHAR_MAX	Maximum `char` value
CHAR_MIN	Minimum `char` value
SHRT_MAX	Maximum `short` value
SHRT_MIN	Minimum `short` value

Named Constant	Description
INT_MAX	Maximum **int** value
INT_MIN	Minimum **int** value
LONG_MAX	Maximum **long** value
LONG_MIN	Minimum **long** value
UCHAR_MAX	Maximum **unsigned char** value
USHRT_MAX	Maximum **unsigned short** value
UINT_MAX	Maximum **unsigned int** value
ULONG_MAX	Maximum **unsigned long** value

A program similar to the following can print the values of these named constants on your system:

```cpp
#include <iostream>
#include <climits>

using namespace std;

int main()
{
    cout << "Number of bits in a byte " << CHAR_BIT << endl;
    cout << "Maximum char value " << CHAR_MAX << endl;
    cout << "Minimum char value " << CHAR_MIN << endl;
    cout << "Maximum short value " << SHRT_MAX << endl;
    cout << "Minimum short value " << SHRT_MIN << endl;
    cout << "Maximum int value " << INT_MAX << endl;
    cout << "Minimum int value " << INT_MIN << endl;
    cout << "Maximum long value " << LONG_MAX << endl;
    cout << "Minimum long value " << LONG_MIN << endl;
    cout << "Maximum unsigned char value " << UCHAR_MAX
        << endl;
    cout << "Maximum unsigned short value " << USHRT_MAX
        << endl;
    cout << "Maximum unsigned int value " << UINT_MAX << endl;
    cout << "Maximum unsigned long value " << ULONG_MAX
        << endl;

    return 0;
}
```

Header File `cmath` (`math.h`)

The following table shows various math functions.

Function Name and Parameters	Parameter(s) Type	Function Return Value
`acos(x)`	x is a floating-point expression, $-1.0 \leq x \leq 1.0$	Arc cosine of x, a value between 0.0 and π
`asin(x)`	x is a floating-point expression, $-1.0 \leq x \leq 1.0$	Arc sine of x, a value between $-\pi/2$ and $\pi/2$
`atan(x)`	x is a floating-point expression	Arc tan of x, a value between $-\pi/2$ and $\pi/2$
`ceil(x)`	x is a floating-point expression	The smallest whole number $\geq$ x, ("ceiling" of x)
`cos(x)`	x is a floating-point expression, x is measured in radians	Trigonometric cosine of the angle
`cosh(x)`	x is a floating-point expression	Hyperbolic cosine of x
`exp(x)`	x is a floating-point expression	The value e raised to the power of x; (e = 2.718...)
`fabs(x)`	x is a floating-point expression	Absolute value of x
`floor(x)`	x is a floating-point expression	The largest whole number $\leq$ x; ("floor" of x)
`log(x)`	x is a floating-point expression, where x > 0.0	Natural logarithm (base e) of x
`log10(x)`	x is a floating-point expression, where x > 0.0	Common logarithm (base 10) of x
`pow(x,y)`	x and y are floating-point expressions. If x = 0.0, y must be positive; if x $\leq$ 0.0, y must be a whole number.	x raised to the power of y
`sin(x)`	x is a floating-point expression; x is measured in radians	Trigonometric sine of the angle
`sinh(x)`	x is a floating-point expression	Hyperbolic sine of x

Function Name and Parameters	Parameter(s) Type	Function Return Value
sqrt(x)	x is a floating-point expression, where x $\geq$ 0.0	Square root of x
tan(x)	x is a floating-point expression; x is measured in radians	Trigonometric tangent of the angle
tanh(x)	x is a floating-point expression	Hyperbolic tangent of x

Header File cstddef (stddef.h)

Among others, this header file contains the definition of the following symbolic constant:

NULL: The system–dependent null pointer (usually 0)

Header File cstring (string.h)

The following table shows various string functions.

Function Name and Parameters	Parameter(s) Type	Function Return Value
strcat(destStr, srcStr)	destStr and srcStr are null-terminated char arrays; destStr must be large enough to hold the result	The base address of destStr is returned; srcStr, including the null character, is concatenated to the end of destStr
strcmp(str1, str2)	str1 and str2 are null terminated char arrays	The returned value is as follows: • An int value < 0, if str1 < str2 • An int value 0, if str1 = str2 • An int value > 0, if str1 > str2

Function Name and Parameters	Parameter(s) Type	Function Return Value
`strcpy(destStr, srcStr)`	`destStr` and `srcStr` are null-terminated **char** arrays	The base address of `destStr` is returned; `srcStr` is copied into `destStr`
`strlen(str)`	`str` is a null-terminated **char** array	An integer value ≥ 0 specifying the length of the `str` (excluding the `'\0'`) is returned

HEADER FILE `string`

This header file—not to be confused with the header file `cstring`—supplies a programmer-defined data type named `string`. Associated with the `string` type are a data type `string::size_type` and a named constant `string::npos`. These are defined as follows:

`string::size_type`	An unsigned integer type
`string::npos`	The maximum value of type `string::size_type`

Several functions are associated with the `string` type. The following table shows some of these functions. Unless stated otherwise, `str`, `str1`, and `str2` are variables (objects) of type `string`. The position of the first character in a `string` variable (such as `str`) is 0, the second character is 1, and so on.

Function Name and Parameters	Parameter(s) Type	Function Return Value
`str.c_str()`	None	The base address of a null-terminated C-string corresponding to the characters in `str`.
`getline(istreamVar, str)`	`istreamVar` is an input stream variable (of type `istream` or `ifstream`). `str` is a `string` object (variable).	Characters until the newline character are input from `istreamVar` and stored in `str`. (The newline character is read but not stored into `str`.) The value returned by this function is usually ignored.

Function Name and Parameters	Parameter(s) Type	Function Return Value
`str.empty()`	None	Returns `true` if `str` is empty, that is, the number of characters in `str` is zero, `false` otherwise.
`str.length()`	None	A value of type `string::size_type` giving the number of characters in the string.
`str.size()`	None	A value of type `string::size_type` giving the number of characters in the string.
`str.find(strExp)`	`str` is a string object and `strExp` is a string expression evaluating to a string. The string expression, `strExp`, can also be a character.	The `find` function searches `str` to find the first occurrence of the string or the character specified by `strExp`. If the search is successful, the function `find` returns the position in `str` where the match begins. If the search is unsuccessful, the function returns the special value `string::npos`.
`str.substr(pos, len)`	Two unsigned integers, `pos` and `len`. `pos`, represent the starting position (of the substring in `str`), and `len` represents the length (of the substring). The value of `pos` must be less than `str.length()`.	A temporary string object that holds a substring of `str` starting at `pos`. The length of the substring is, at most, `len` characters. If `len` is too large, it means "to the end" of the string in `str`.
`str1.swap(str2);`	One parameter of type `string`. `str1` and `str2` are `string` variables.	The contents of `str1` and `str2` are swapped.

Function Name and Parameters	Parameter(s) Type	Function Return Value
`str.clear();`	None	Removes all the characters from `str`.
`str.erase();`	None	Removes all the characters from `str`.
`str.erase(m);`	One parameter of type `string::size_type`.	Removes all the characters from `str` starting at index m.
`str.erase(m, n);`	Two parameters of type `int`.	Starting at index m, removes the next n characters from `str`. If n > length of `str`, removes all the characters starting at the mth.
`str.insert(m, n, c);`	Parameters m and n are of type `string::size_type`; c is a character.	Inserts n occurrences of the character c at index m into `str`.
`str1.insert(m, str2);`	Parameter m is of type `string::size_type`.	Inserts all the characters of `str2` at index m into `str1`.
`str1.replace(m, n, str2);`	Parameters m and n are of type `string::size_type`.	Starting at index m, replaces the next n characters of `str1` with all the characters of `str2`. If n > length of `str1`, then all the characters until the end of `str1` are replaced.

MEMORY SIZE ON A SYSTEM AND RANDOM NUMBER GENERATOR

A program similar to the following prints the memory size of the built-in data types on your system. (The output of the program shows the size of the built-in data type on which this program was run.)

```cpp
#include <iostream>

using namespace std;

int main()
{
    cout << "Size of char = " << sizeof(char) << endl;
    cout << "Size of int = " << sizeof(int) << endl;
    cout << "Size of short = " << sizeof(short) << endl;
    cout << "Size of unsigned int = " << sizeof(unsigned int)
         << endl;
    cout << "Size of long = " << sizeof(long) << endl;
    cout << "Size of bool = " << sizeof(bool) << endl;
    cout << "Size of float = " << sizeof(float) << endl;
    cout << "Size of double = " << sizeof(double) << endl;
    cout << "Size of long double = " << sizeof(long double)
         << endl;
    cout << "Size of unsigned short = "
         << sizeof(unsigned short) << endl;
    cout << "Size of unsigned long = "
         << sizeof(unsigned long) << endl;

    return 0;
}
```

Sample Run:

```
Size of char = 1
Size of int = 4
Size of short = 2
Size of unsigned int = 4
Size of long = 4
Size of bool = 1
Size of float = 4
Size of double = 8
Size of long double = 8
Size of unsigned short = 2
Size of unsigned long = 4
```

Random Number Generator

To generate a random number, you can use the C++ function `rand`. To use the function `rand`, the program must include the header file `cstdlib`. The header file `cstdlib` also contains the constant `RAND_MAX`. Typically, the value of `RAND_MAX` is 32767. To find the exact value of `RAND_MAX`, check your system's documentation. The function `rand` generates an integer between 0 and `RAND_MAX`. The following program illustrates how to use the function `rand`. It also prints the value of `RAND_MAX`:

```cpp
#include <iostream>
#include <cstdlib>
#include <iomanip>

using namespace std;

int main()
{
    cout << fixed << showpoint << setprecision(5);
      cout << "The value of RAND_MAX: " << RAND_MAX << endl;
    cout << "A random number: " << rand() << endl;
    cout << "A random number between 0 and 9: "
         << rand() % 10 << endl;
    cout << "A random number between 0 and 1: "
         << static_cast<double> (rand())
             / static_cast<double>(RAND_MAX)
         << endl;

    return 0;
}
```

Sample Run:

```
The value of RAND_MAX: 32767
A random number: 41
A random number between 0 and 9: 7
A random number between 0 and 1: 0.19330
```

APPENDIX H
REFERENCES

1. G. Booch, *Object-Oriented Analysis and Design*, Second Edition, Addison-Wesley, 1995.
2. E. Horowitz, S. Sahni, and S. Rajasekaran, *Computer Algorithms C++*, Computer Science Press, 1997.
3. N.M. Josuttis, *The C++ Standard Library: A Tutorial and Reference*, Addison-Wesley, Reading, MA, 1999.
4. D.E. Knuth, *The Art of Computer Programming*, Vols. 1-3, Addison-Wesley, 1973, 1969, 1973.
5. S.B. Lippman and J. Lajoie, *C++ Primer*, Third Edition, Addison-Wesley, Reading, MA, 1998.
6. D.S. Malik and M.K. Sen, *Discrete Mathematical Structures: Theory and Applications*, Course Technology, Boston, MA, 2004.
7. E.M. Reingold and W.J. Hensen, *Data Structures in Pascal*, Little Brown and Company, Boston, MA, 1986.
8. R. Sedgewick, *Algorithms in C*, Third Edition, Addison-Wesley, Reading, MA, Parts 1-4, 1998; Part 5, 2002.
9. B. Stroustrup, *The Design and Evolution of C++*, Addison-Wesley, Reading, MA, 1994.

ANSWERS TO ODD NUMBERED EXERCISES

Chapter 1

1. a. true; b. false; c. false; d. false; e. true; f. false; g. false; h. true; i. true; j. true

3. Fetch and decode instructions, control the flow of information (instructions or data) in and out of main memory, and control the operation of the internal components of the CPU.

5. Screen and printer.

7. Every computer directly understands its own machine language. Therefore, for the computer to execute a program written in a high-level language, the high-level language program must be translated into the computer's machine language.

9. A well-analyzed problem leads to a well-designed algorithm. Moreover, a program that is well analyzed is easier to modify as well as spot and fix errors.

11. To find the weighted average of the four test scores, first you need to know each test score and its weight. Next, you multiply each test score with its weight, and then add these numbers; the sum is then divided by four to get the average. Therefore,

```
1.  Get testScore1, weightTestScore1
2.  Get testScore2, weightTestScore2
3.  Get testScore3, weightTestScore3
4.  Get testScore4, weightTestScore4
5.  sum = testScore1 * weightTestScore1 +
          testScore2 * weightTestScore2 +
          testScore3 * weightTestScore3 +
          testScore4 * weightTestScore4;
6.  average = sum / 4;
```

13. To calculate the selling price of an item, we need to know the original price (the price the store pays to buy) of the item. We can then the use the following formula to find the selling price:

```
sellingPrice = originalPrice + originalPrice * .60
```

The algorithm is as follows:

```
a.  Get originalPrice
b.  Calculate the sellingPrice using the formula:

sellingPrice = originalPrice + originalPrice * .60
```

The information needed to calculate the selling price is the original price and the marked–up percentage.

15. Let *r* denote the radius of the circle. Given the lengths *a*, *b*, and *c*, such that $a + b + c$ is the circumference of the circle, we have $2\pi r = a + b + c$. This implies that $r = (a + b + c) / (2\pi)$. We can now write the algorithm as follows:

   a. Get the values of `a, b, c`
   b. Calculate `r` using the formula:

   ```
   r = (a + b + c) / (2π)
   ```

17. Suppose `averageTestScore` denotes the average test score, `highestScore` denotes the highest test score, `testScore` denotes a test score, `sum` denote the sum of all the test scores, and `count` denotes the number of students in class, and `studentName` denotes the name of a student.

   a. First, you design an algorithm to find the average test score. To find the average test score, first you need to count the number of students in the class and add the test score of each student. You then divide the sum by count to find the average test score. The algorithm to find the average test score is as follows:

   i. Set `sum` and `count` to 0.
   ii. Repeat the following for each student in class.
   1. Get `testScore`
   2. Increment `count` and update the value of `sum` by adding the current test score to `sum`.
   iii. Use the following formula to find the average test score.

   ```
   if (count is 0)
       averageTestScore = 0;
   otherwise
       averageTestScore = sum / count;
   ```

   b. The following algorithm determines and prints the names of all the students whose test score is below the average test score.

   Repeat the following for each student in class:
   i. Get `studentName` and `testScore`
   ii.

   ```
       if (testScore is less than averageTestScore)
           print studentName
   ```

   c. The following algorithm determines the highest test score
   i. Get first student's test score and call it `highestTestScore`.

   ii. Repeat the following for each of the remaining student in class

      1. Get `testScore`

      2.

```
if (testScore is greater than highestTestScore)
    highestTestScore = testScore;
```

d. To print the names of all the students whose test score is the same as the highest test score, compare the test score of each student with the highest test score and if they are equal print the name. The following algorithm accomplishes this. Repeat the following for each student in class:

   i. Get `studentName` and `testScore`

   ii.

```
if (testScore is equal to highestTestScore)
    print studentName
```

You can use the solutions of the subproblems obtained in parts a to d to design the main algorithm as follows:

1. Use the algorithm in part a to find the average test score.

2. Use the algorithm in part b to print the names of all the students whose score is below the average test score.

3. Use the algorithm in part c to find the highest test score.

4. Use the algorithm in part d to print the names of all the students whose test score is the same as the highest test score.

Chapter 2

1. a. false; b. false; c. false; d. true; e. true; f. false; g. true; h. true; i. false; j. true; k. false

3. a, b

5. a. 3

   b. Not possible. Both the operands of the operator `%` must be integers. Because the second operand, `w`, is a floating-point value, the expression is invalid.

   c. Not possible. Both the operands of the operator `%` must be integers. Because the first operand, which is `y + w`, is a floating-point value, the expression is invalid.

   d. `38.5`

   e. `1`

   f. `2`

   g. `2`

   h. `420.0`

7. 7

9. `a` and `c` are valid

11. a. `-10 * a`

    b. `'8'`

    c. `(b * b - 4 * a * c) / (2 * a)`

    d. `(-b + (b * b - 4 * a * c)) / (2 * a)`

13.
```
x = 20
y = 15
z = 6
w = 11.5
t = 4.5
```

15. a. `0.50`; b. `24.50`; c. `37.6`; d. `8.3`; e. `10`; f. `38.75`

17. a and c are correct

19. a. `x *= 2;`

    b. `x += y - 2;`

    c. `sum += num;`

    d. `z *= x + 2;`

    e. `y /= x + 5;`

21.

```
                                  a     b     c
a = (b++) + 3;                    9     7     und
c = 2 * a + (++b);                9     8     26
b = 2 * (++c) - (a++);            10    45    27
```

23. (The user input is shaded.)

```
a = 25
Enter two integers : 20 15

The numbers you entered are 20 and 15
z = 45.5
Your grade is A
The value of a = 65
```

25.

```cpp
#include <iostream>
#include <string>

using namespace std;

const double X = 13.45;
const int Y = 34;
const char BLANK = ' ';

int main()
{
    string firstName, lastName;
    int num;
    double salary;
```

```cpp
    cout << "Enter first name: ";
    cin >> firstName;
    cout << endl;

    cout << "Enter last name: ";
    cin >> lastName;
    cout << endl;

    cout << "Enter a positive integer less than 70: ";
    cin >> num;
    cout << endl;

    salary = num * X;

    cout << "Name: " << firstName << BLANK << lastName << endl;
    cout << "Wages: $" << salary << endl;
    cout << "X = " << X << endl;
    cout << "X + Y = " << X + Y << endl;

    return 0;
}
```

Chapter 3

1. a. true; b. true; c. false; d. false; e. true; f. true

3. a.   `x = 37, y = 86, z = 0.56`

   b.   `x = 37, y = 32, z = 86.56`

   c.   Input failure: `z = 37.0, x = 86,` trying to read the . (period) into `y`.

5. Input failure: Trying to read A into `y`, which is an `int` variable. `x = 46, y = 18,` and `z = 'A'`. The values of `y` and `z` are unchanged.

7. a.   `name = " Mickey Balto", age = 35`

   b.   `name = " ", age = 35`

9.

```cpp
#include <iostream>
#include <fstream>

using namespace std;

int main()
{
    int num1, num2;
    ifstream infile;
    ostream outfile;

    infile.open("input.dat");
    outfile.open("output.dat");

    infile >> num1 >> num2;
```

```
        outfile << "Sum = " << num1 + num2 << endl;

        infile.close();
        outfile.close();

        return 0;
}
```

11. a. Same as before.
     b. The file contains the output produced by the program.
     c. The file contains the output produced by the program. The old contents are erased.
     d. The program would prepare the file and store the output in the file.

Chapter 4

1. a. false; b. false; c. false; d. true; e. false; f. false; g. false; h. false; i. false; j. true

3. 100 200 0

5. Omit the semicolon after `else`. The correct statement is:

```
if (score >= 60)
     cout << "You pass." << endl;
else
     cout << "You fail." << endl;
```

7. 15

9. 96

11.

```
#include <iostream>

using namespace std;
const int one = 5;

int main()
{
    int x, y, w, z;

    z = 9;

    if (z > 10)
    {
        x = 12;
        y = 5;
        w = x + y + one;
    }
    else
```

```
    {
        x = 12;
        y = 4;
        w = x + y + one;
    }

    cout << "w = " << w << endl;

    return 0;
}
```

Chapter 5

1. a. false; b. true; c. false; d. true; e. true; f. true; g. true; h. false

3. 5

5. if ch > 'Z' or ch < 'A'

7. Sum = 158

9. Sum = 158

11. 11 18 25

13. a. 18; b. 14; c. false

15. 2 7 17 37 77 157

17. a. *

    b. infinite loop

    c. infinite loop

    d. ****

    e. ******

    f. ***

19. WHAT IS DONE , OFTEN IS NOT DONE WELL.

21.

```
0 - 24
25 - 49
50 - 74
75 - 99
100 - 124
125 - 149
150 - 174
175 - 200
```

23. a. both; b. do...while; c. while; d. while

25. There is more than one answer to this problem. One solution is:

```
do
{
    cin >> number;
    if (number != -1)
```

```
            total = total + number;
        count++;
    }
    while (number != -1);
```

27. a.

```
    number = 1;
        while (number <= 10)
        {
            cout << setw(3) << number;
            number++;
        }
```

   b.

```
    number = 1;
        do
        {
            cout << setw(3) << number;
            number++;
        }
        while (number <= 10);
```

29. 11 18 25

Chapter 6

1. a. false; b. true; c. true; d. true; e. false

3. a, b, c, e, f, and g are valid. In d, the function call in the output (`cout`) statement requires one more argument.

5. a. 4; `int`

   b. 2; `double`

   c. 4; `char`

   d. The function test requires four actual parameters. The order of the parameters is: `int, char, double, int`.

   e. `cout << test(5, 'z', 7.3, 5) << endl;`

   f. `cout << two(17.5, 18.3) << endl;`

   g. `cout << static_cast<char>(static_cast<int>`
      `                    (three(4, 3, 'A', 17.6)) + 1)`
      `        << endl;`

7. a. i. 125   ii. 432

   b. The function computes x^3, where x is the argument of the function.

9. 1
   2
   6
   24
   120

Chapter 7

1. a. true; b. false; c. true; d. false; e. true; f. false; g. false; h. false; i. true

3. a. A variable declared in the heading of a function definition is called a formal parameter. A variable or expression used in a function call is called an actual parameter.

   b. A value parameter receives a copy of the actual parameter's data. A reference parameter receives the address of the actual parameter.

   c. A variable declared within a function or block is called a local variable. A variable declared outside of every function definition is called a global variable.

5.

```
3 4 20 78
7 3 20 4
7 5 6 2
```

7.

```
#include <iostream>

using namespace std;

void func(int val1, int val2);

int main()
{
        int num1, num2;
 __1__   cout << "Please enter two integers." << endl;
 __2__   cin >> num1 >> num2;
 __3__   func (num1, num2);
 __7__   cout << " The two integers are " << num1
                << ", " << num2 << endl;
 __8__   return 0;
}

void func (int val1, int val2)
{
        int val3, val4;
 __4__   val3 = val1 + val2;
 __5__   val4 = val1 * val2;
 __6__   cout << "The sum and product are " << val3
                << " and " << val4 << endl;
}
```

9.

```
Line 4: In main: num1 = 10, num2 = 20, and t = 15
Line 9: In funOne: a = 15, x = 10, z = 25, and t = 15
Line 11: In funOne: a = 15, x = 15, z = 25, and t = 15
Line 13: In funOne: a = 27, x = 15, z = 25, and t = 27
```

```
Line 15: In funOne: a = 40, x = 15, z = 25, and t = 40
Line 6: In main after funOne: num1 = 15, num2 = 20, and t = 40
```

11. (i), (ii), and (iv) are correct.

Chapter 8

1. a. true; b. false; c. true; d. false; e. false; f. true; g. true; h. true; i. false; j. true; k. false

3. Only a and c are valid.

5. The statement:

```
using namespace std;
```

is missing between Lines 1 and 2.

7. Either include the statement:

```
using namespace aaa;
```

before the function `main` or refer to the identifiers `x` and `y` in `main` as `aaa::x` and `aaa::y`, respectively.

9.

```
Going to the Amusement Park
14
10
musem
ABCDEFGHIJK
11
aBdDEFGHIJK
```

Chapter 9

1. a. true; b. true; c. false; d. false; e. true; f. false; g. false; h. false; i. true; j. false; k. false; l. false

3.

   a. `funcOne(list, 50);`

   b. `cout << funcSum(50, list[3]) << endl;`

   c. `cout << funcSum(list[29], list[9]) << endl;`

   d. `funcTwo(list, Alist);`

5. `list` elements are: `5, 6, 9, 19, 23, 37`

7. a. Invalid; the assignment operator is not defined for C-strings.

   b. Invalid; the relational operators are not defined for C-strings.

   c. Invalid; the assignment operator is not defined for C-strings.

   d. Valid

9.

a. ```
strcpy(str1, "Sunny Day");
```

b.  ```
length = strlen(str1);
```

c. ```
strcpy(str2, name);
```

d.  ```
if (strcmp(str1, str2) <= 0)
    cout << str1 << endl;
else
    cout << str2 << endl;
```

11. List elements: 11 16 21 26 30

13. a. 30; b. 5; c. 6; d. row; e. column

15. a. `beta` is initialized to 0.

b.

```
First row of beta: 0 1 2
Second row of beta: 1 2 3
Third row of beta: 2 3 4
```

c.

```
First row of beta: 0 0 0
Second row of beta: 0 1 2
Third row of beta: 0 2 4
```

d.

```
First row of beta: 0 2 0
Second row of beta: 2 0 2
Third row of beta: 0 2 0
```

Chapter 10

1. a. false; b. false; c. true; d. true; e. true; f. true; g. false

3. a. Invalid; the member `name` of `newEmployee` is a `struct`. Specify the member names to store the value `"John Smith"`. For example,

```
newEmployee.name.first = "John";
newEmployee.name.last = "Smith";
```

b. Invalid; the member `name` of `newEmployee` is a `struct`. There are no aggregate output operations on a `struct`. A correct statement is:

```
cout << newEmployee.name.first << " "
        << newEmployee.name.last << endl;
```

c. Valid

d. Valid

e. Invalid; `employees` is an array. There are no aggregate assignment operations on arrays.

Chapter 11

1. a. false; b. false; c. true; d. false; e. false;
3. a. 6; b. 2; c. 2;
   d.

```
void xClass::func()
{
    u = 10;
    w = 15.3;
}
```

   e.

```
void xClass::print()
{
    cout << u << " " << w << endl;
}
```

   f.

```
xClass::xClass()
{
    u = 0;
    w = 0;
}
```

   g. `x.print();`
   h. `xClass t(20, 35.0);`
5. a.

```
int testClass::sum()
{
    return x + y;
}

void testClass::print() const
{
    cout << "x = " << x << ", y = " << y << endl;
}

testClass::testClass()
{
    x = 0;
    y = 0;
}

testClass::testClass(int a, int b)
{
    x = a;
    y = b;
}
```

b. One possible solution. (We assume that the name of the header file containing the definition of the `class testClass` is `Exercise5Ch12.h`.)

```cpp
#include <iostream.h>
#include "Exercise5Ch12.h"

int main()
{
    testClass one;
    testClass two(4, 5);

    one.print();
    two.print();

    return 0;
}
```

7. a. `personType student("Buddy", "Arora");`

    b. `student.print();`

    c. `student.setName("Susan", "Gilbert");`

9.

    a. `myClass::count = 0;`

    b. `myClass.incrementCount();`

    c. `myClass.printCount();`

    d.

```cpp
int myClass::count = 0;

void myClass::setX(int a)
{
    x = a;
}

void myClass::printX() const
{
    cout << x;
}

void myClass::printCount()
{
    cout << count;
}

void myClass::incrementCount()
{
    count++;
}
```

```
myClass::myClass(int a)
{
    x = a;
}
```

e. `myClass myObject1(5);`

f. `myClass myObject2(3);`

g.

The statements in Lines 1 and 2 are valid.

The statement in Line 3 should be: `myClass::printCount();`.

The statement in Line 4 is invalid because the member function `printX` is not a `static` member of the class, and so cannot be called by using the name of class.

The statement in Line 5 is invalid because `count` is a **private static** member variable of the class.

h.

```
5
2
2
3
14
3
3
```

Chapter 12

1. a. true; b. true; c. true

3. Some of the member variables that can be added to the **class** `employeeType` are: `department, salary, employeeCategory` (such as supervisor and president), and `employeeID`. Some of the member functions are: `setInfo, getSalary, getEmployeeCategory`, and `setSalary`.

5. a. The statement :

```
class bClass public aClass
```

should be:

```
class bClass: public aClass
```

b. Missing semicolon after }.

7.

a.

```
yClass::yClass()
{
    a = 0;
    b = 0;
}
```

b.

```
xClass::xClass()
{
    z = 0;
}
```

c.

```
void yClass::two(int u,  int v)
{
    a = u;
    b = v;
}
```

9. a.

```
void two::setData(int a,  int b,  int c)
{
    one::setData(a,  b);
    z = c;
}
```

b.

```
void two::print() const
{
    one::print();
    cout << z << endl;
}
```

11.

```
In base: x = 7
In derived: x = 3,  y = 8;  x + y = 11
****7
####11
```

Chapter 13

1. a. false; b. false; c. false; d. true; e. true; f. true; g. false; h. false

3.

```
98  98
98  98
```

5. b and c

7. 78 78

9. 4 4 5 7 10 14 19 25 32 40

11. In a shallow copy of data, two or more pointers point to the same memory space. In a deep copy of data, each pointer has its own copy of the data.

13.

```
Array p: 5 7 11 17 25
Array q: 25 17 11 7 5
```

15. The copy constructor makes a copy of the actual variable.

17. Classes with pointer data members should include the destructor, overload the assignment operator, and explicitly provide the copy constructor by including it in the class definition and providing its definition.

19.

```
ClassA x: 4

ClassA x: 6
ClassB y: 10
```

21. Yes.

23.

    a. Because `employeeType` is an abstract class, you cannot instantiate an object of this class. Therefore, this statement is illegal.

    b. This statement is legal.

    c. This statement is legal.

Chapter 14

1. a. false; b. true; c. true; d. false; e. false; f. true; g. false; h. true; i. false; j. true; k. false

3. Because the left operand of `<<` is a stream object, which is not of the type `mystery`.

5. When the class has pointer data members.

7. a. `friend strange operator+(const strange&, const strange&);`

    b. `friend bool operator==(const strange&, const strange&);`

    c. `friend strange operator++(strange&, int);`

9. In Line 2, the word `friend` before the word `bool` is missing. The correct statement is:

```
friend bool operator<=(mystery, mystery); //Line 2
```

11. None.

13. One.

15. Answer to this question is available at the Web site accompanying this book.

17. Error in Line 4. A template instantiation can be for only a built-in type or a user-defined type. The word "`type`" between the angular brackets must be replaced either with a built-in type or a user-defined type.

19. a. `12` b. `Sunny Day`

21.

```
template <class Type>
void swap(Type &x, Type &y)
{
    Type temp;
    temp = x;
    x = y;
    y = temp;
}
```

Chapter 15

1. a. false, b. true, c. true, d. false

3. a.

```
Entering the try block.
Exception: Lower limit violation.
After the catch block
```

   b.

```
Entering the try block.
Exception: 0
After the catch block
```

   c.

```
Entering the try block.
Exiting the try block.
After the catch block
```

   d.

```
Entering the try block.
Exception: 0
After the catch block
```

5. (Assume that the definition of the `class tornadoException` is in the header file `tornadoException.h`.)

```
#include <iostream>
#include "tornadoException.h"

using namespace std;

int main()
{
    int miles;

    try
    {
        cout << "Enter the miles: ";
        cin >> miles;
```

```
        cout << endl;

        if (miles < 5)
            throw tornadoException();
        else
            throw tornadoException(miles);
    }
    catch (tornadoException tE)
    {
        cout << tE.what() << endl;
    }

    return 0;
}
```

Chapter 16

1. a. true; b. true; c. false; d. false; e. false

3. The case in which the solution is defined in terms of smaller versions of itself.

5. A function that calls another function and eventually results in the original function call is said to be indirectly recursive.

7. a. The statements in Lines 2 and 3.
   b. The statements in Lines 4 and 5.
   c. Any non-negative integer.
   d. It is a valid call. The value of `mystery(0)` is 0.
   e. It is a valid call. The value of `mystery(5)` is 15.
   f. It is an invalid call. It will result in infinite recursion.

9. a. It does not produce any output.
   b. 5 6 7 8 9
   c. It does not produce any output.
   d. It does not produce any output.

11. a. 2; b. 3; c. 5; d. 21

13.

$$multiply(m, n) = \begin{cases} 0 & \textit{if } n = 0 \\ m & \textit{if } n = 1 \\ m + multiply(m, n - 1) & \textit{otherwise} \end{cases}$$

The base cases are when $n = 0$ or $n = 1$. The general case is specified by the option otherwise.

Chapter 17

1. a. false; b. false; c. false; d. false
3. a. true; b. true; c. false; d. false; e. true
5. a. `A = A->link;`
   b. `list = A->link->link;`
   c. `B = B->link->link;`
   d. `list = NULL;`
   e. `B->link->info = 35;`
   f.
   ```
   newNode = new nodeType;
   newNode->info = 10;
   newNode->link = A->link;
   A->link = newNode;
   ```
   g.
   ```
   p = A->link;
   A->link = p->link;
   delete p;
   ```
7. a. This is an invalid code. The statement `s->info = B;` is invalid because B is a pointer and `s->info` is an `int`.
   b. This is an invalid code. After the statement `s = s->link;` executes, s is NULL and so `s->info` does not exist.
9.
   ```
   Item to be deleted is not in the list.
   18 38 2 15 45 25
   ```
11. Answer to this question is available at the Web site accompanying this book.
13. Answer to this question is available at the Web site accompanying this book.

Chapter 18

1.
   ```
   x = 3
   y = 9
   7
   13
   4
   7
   ```
3. a. 26; b. 45 ; c. 8; d. 29;
5. a. `A * B + C`
   b. `(A + B) * (C - D)`
   c. `(A - B - C) * D`
7. `10 20 30 40 50`

9.

```cpp
template <class elemType>
elemType second(stackType<elemType> stack)
{
    elemType temp1, temp2;

    if (stack.isEmptyStack())
    {
        cout << "Stack is empty." << endl;
        exit(0); //terminate the program
    }

    temp1 = stack.top();
    stack.pop();

    if (stack.isEmptyStack())
    {
        cout << "Stack has only one element." << endl;
        exit(0); //terminate the program
    }

    temp2 = stack.top();
    stack.push(temp1);

    return temp2;
}
```

11.
```
Queue Element = 0
Queue Element = 14
Queue Element = 22
Sorry, the queue is empty
Sorry, the queue is empty
Stack Element = 32
Stack Elements: 64 28 0
Queue Elements: 30
```

13. a. queueFront = 50; queueRear = 0.

      b. queueFront = 51; queueRear = 99.

15. a. queueFront = 25; queueRear = 76.

      b. queueFront = 26; queueRear = 75.

17. 51

19.

```cpp
template <class Type>
void reverseStack(stackType<Type> &s)
{
    linkedQueueType<Type> q;
    Type elem;
```

```
        while (!s.isEmptyStack())
        {
            elem = s.top();
            s.pop();
            q.addQueue(elem);
        }

        while (!q.isEmptyQueue())
        {
            elem = q.front();
            q.deleteQueue();
            s.push(elem);
        }
    }
```

21.

```
    template <class Type>
    int queueType<Type>::queueCount()
    {
        return count;
    }
```

23. Answer to this question is available at the Web site accompanying this book.

25. Answer to this question is available at the Web site accompanying this book.

Chapter 19

1. a. false; b. true; c. false; d. false

3. a.

Iteration	first	last	mid	list[mid]	No of comparisons
1	0	10	5	55	2
2	0	4	2	17	2
3	0	1	0	2	2
4	1	1	1	10	2
5	2	1	the loop stops, unsuccessful search		

This is an unsuccessful search. The total number of comparisons is 8.

b.

Iteration	`first`	`last`	`mid`	`list[mid]`	No of comparisons
1	0	10	5	55	2
2	0	4	2	17	2
3	3	4	3	45	2
4	4	4	4	49	1 (found is `true`)

The item is found at location 4 and the total number of comparisons is 7.

c.

Iteration	`first`	`last`	`mid`	`list[mid]`	No of comparisons
1	0	10	5	55	2
2	6	10	8	92	2
3	9	10	9	98	1 (found is `true`)

The item is found at location 9 and the total number of comparisons is 5.

d.

Iteration	`first`	`last`	`mid`	`list[mid]`	No of comparisons
1	0	10	5	55	2
2	6	10	8	92	2
3	9	10	9	98	2
4	10	10	10	110	2
5	11	10	the loop stops		

This is an unsuccessful search. The total number of comparisons is 8.

5. Suppose that the list is of length n. Then `length` $= n$. Consider the first iteration of the outer `for` loop, that is, when the value of `iteration = 1`. Now the inner loop executes $n - 1$. Before the execution of the inner `for` loop, the variable `isSorted` is set to `true`, assuming that the list is sorted. If the list is already sorted, then the expression `list[index] > list[index + 1]` in the `if`

statement always evaluates to `false`, so the body of the `if` statement never executes. Because the inner loop executes $n - 1$ times, there are $n - 1$ comparisons. In the second iteration of the outer loop, because the variable `isSorted` is `true`, the loop condition, `(iteration < length) && !isSorted`, evaluates to `false`, so the outer `for` loop terminates. It follows that, if the list is already sorted, the outer `for` loop executes only once. Hence, the total number of comparisons is $n - 1 = O(n)$.

7. 3

9. 10, 12, 18, 21, 25, 28, 30, 71, 32, 58, 15

11. In quick sort the list is partition according to an element, called pivot, of the list. After partition, elements is the first sublist are smaller than the pivot and in the second sublist are larger than the pivot. The merge sort partitions the list by dividing into two sublists of nearly equal size by breaking the list in the middle.

13. a. 35

    b. 18, 16, 40, 14, 17, 35, 57, 50, 37, 47, 72, 82, 64, 67

Chapter 20

1. a. false; b. true; c. false; d. false

3. L_A = {B, C, D, E}

5. R_B = {E}

7. A B C D E F G

9. 80–55–58–70–79

11.

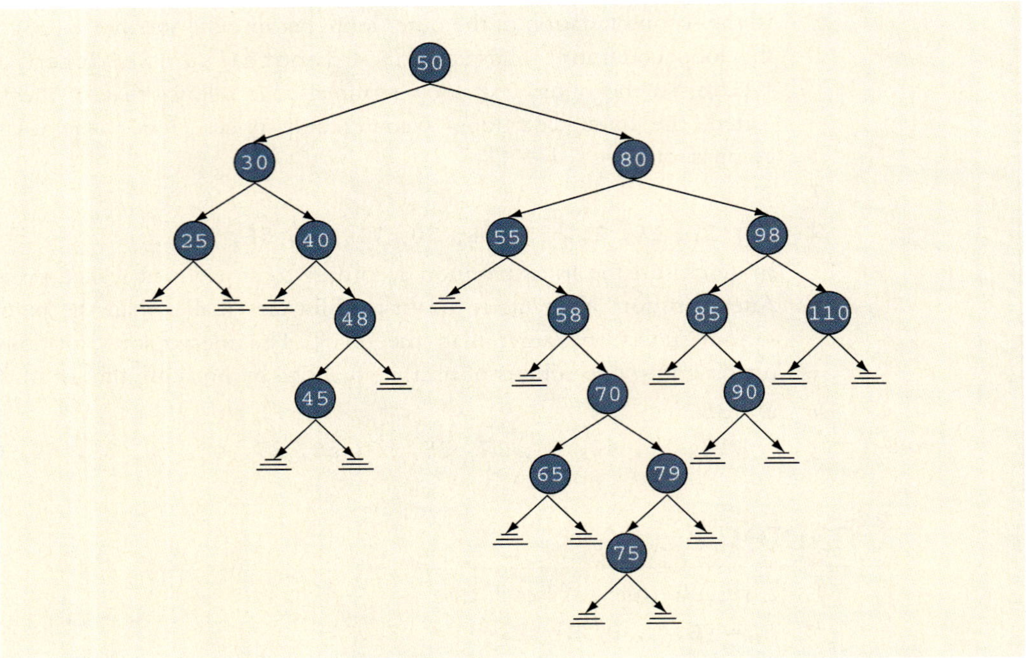

13. Answer to this question is available at the Web site accompanying this book.

15.

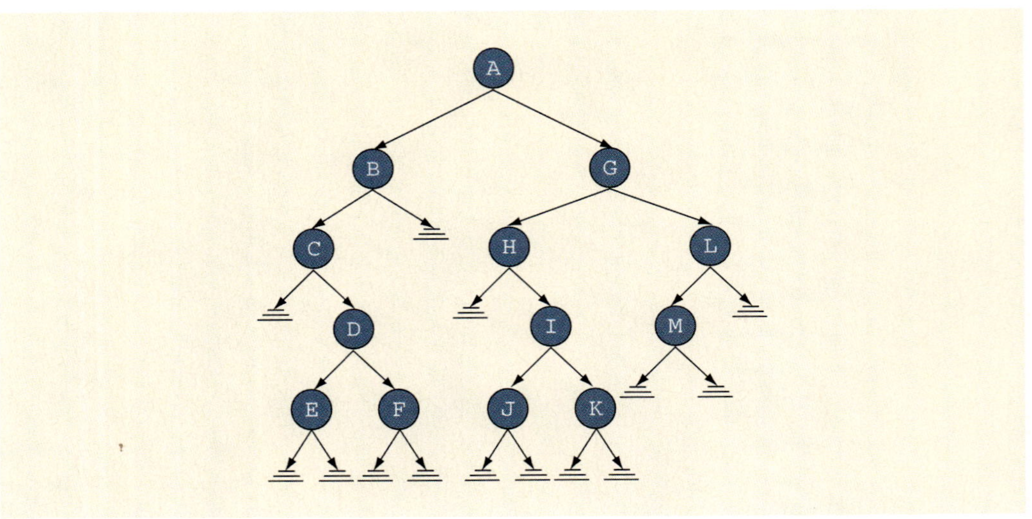

17. Answer to this question is available at the Web site accompanying this book.

Chapter 21

1.
$$\begin{bmatrix} 0 & 1 & 1 & 1 & 0 & 0 \\ 0 & 0 & 0 & 0 & 1 & 0 \\ 0 & 1 & 0 & 0 & 1 & 0 \\ 0 & 0 & 0 & 0 & 0 & 0 \\ 0 & 0 & 0 & 0 & 0 & 0 \\ 0 & 1 & 0 & 1 & 0 & 0 \end{bmatrix}$$

3. 0 1 4 2 3 5

5.
$$\begin{bmatrix} \infty & 10 & 6 & \infty & \infty & \infty & \infty \\ \infty & \infty & \infty & \infty & \infty & \infty & \infty \\ \infty & \infty & \infty & \infty & \infty & 4 & 8 \\ 3 & \infty & \infty & \infty & 11 & \infty & \infty \\ \infty & \infty & \infty & \infty & \infty & \infty & \infty \\ \infty & 6 & \infty & \infty & \infty & \infty & 10 \\ \infty & \infty & \infty & \infty & \infty & \infty & \infty \end{bmatrix}$$

7.

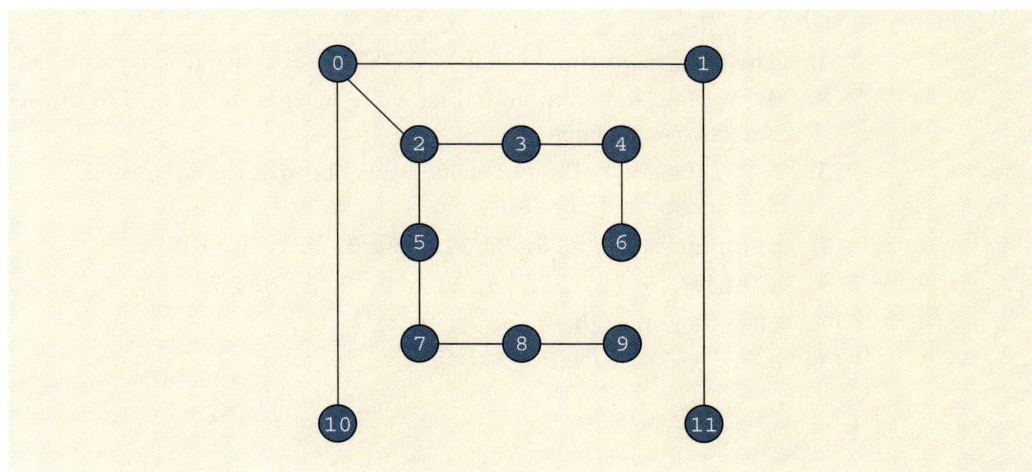

9.

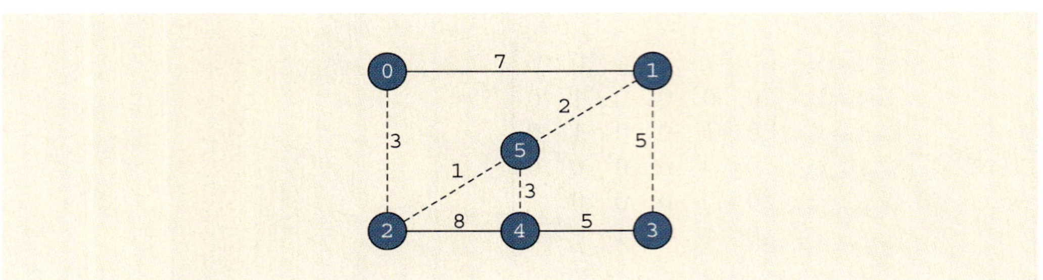


```
Source Vertex: 0
Edges      Weight
(5, 1)      2
(0, 2)      3
(1, 3)      5
(5, 4)      3
(2, 5)      1

Minimal Spanning Tree Weight: 14
```

Chapter 22

1. The three main components of the STL are: containers, iterators, and algorithms.

3. A container is used to store data, while an algorithm is used to manipulate the data stored in a container.

5. A STL function object contains a function that can be treated as a function using the function call operator.

7. `vecList = {12, 16, 8, 12, 16, 8, 23, 40, 6}`

9. `intList1 = {5, 24, 16, 11, 60, 9, 3, 58, 78, 85, 6, 15, 93, 98, 25}`

11. `18 5 11 56 27 2`

13. `0`

INDEX

SYMBOLS

! (not) operator, using, 175

" " (double quotation marks)
    escape sequence, 76
    and strings, 10, 50, 499, 500

(pound sign) and preprocessor
    directives, 12, 78

% (percent sign) and integral data
    type, 40

& (address of) operator, 178, 350,
    356, 486, 735–736, 801–804

&& (and) operator, 176, 178, 182

( ) (parentheses)
    overriding operator precedence
        with, 181
    and peek function, 129
    and precedence in arithmetic
        expressions, 43–44
    and semicolons in if statements,
        187

* (asterisks)
    arithmetic operator, 32, 43–44,
        833–836
    dereferencing operator, 735–742,
        998

+ (plus, addition) operator
    built-in operations on classes, 598
    and operator overloading, 819
    and string data type, 448

++ (increment) operator, 68–70,
    851–857, 998

, (commas) in C++ programs, 32, 85

- (minus, subtraction) operator,
    overloading, 819

-- (decrement) operator, 68–70

. (dot, period)
    member access operator, 555,
        598, 600
    in string variables, 450

/ (slash)
    arithmetic operator, 32, 40, 819
    and code comments, 87

:: (scope resolution) operator, 379, 602

; (semicolons)
    in C++ programs, 32, 75, 85
    in if and if...else structures,
        187
    in for loops, 266

<< (stream insertion) operator, 82,
    135
    and C++ stream classes, 688–689
    and cout, 135
    described, 12
    overloading, 819, 838–840
    using, 59, 70

= (assignment) operator, 56, 170
    built-in operations on classes, 598
    and classes, 599, 762–764
    overloading, 843–851,
        1089–1090, 1108–1110

= = (equality) operator, 170, 182,
    202–203

>> (stream extraction) operator, 116
    and C++ stream classes, 688–689
    and c-strings, 500
    cin and, 117–123
    overloading, 819, 840–843

\ (backslashes)
    escape sequence, 76, 148
    and newline characters, 37

[ ] (array index operator), 447, 448,
    476, 872–873

_ (underscore character), and linkers

_ (underscore character)
    and global identifiers, 441
    and identifiers, linkers, 32, 33

' ' (single quotation marks) and
    entering character data, 76–77,
    122

{} (curly braces)
    in C++ programs, 12, 85
    and compound statements, 191
    and main function, 81

| | (or) operator, 176–178, 182

?: (conditional operator), using,
    203–204

A

abstract classes and pure virtual
    functions, 778–786

abstract data type. *See* ADTs

abstraction, data, 626–628

accessing
    array components, 476–478
    class members, 597–598
    identifiers, 375

accessor and mutator functions class,
    601–602

accumulate function, 1475–1480

action statements described, 185

addFirst function, 371

addition operation symbol (+), 32

addQueue operation, 1131–1143

address of operator (&)
    and classes, 801–804
    described, using, 178, 735–736

addresses of memory cells, 5

adjacency matrix, 1338–1339

adjacent_difference function,
    1475–1480

adjacent_find function,
    1453–1457

ADTs (abstract data types)
    and array-based lists, 788
    binary trees as, 1286–1294
    described, 626–628
    graphs as, 1341–1344
    linked lists as, 996–1009

aggregate operations on arrays,
    485–486

algorithms
    *See also specific algorithm,
        function*
    comparison-based search, 1204
    container operations, 1419–1480
    copy, 1387–1390
    problem-solving using, 14
    recursive, nonrecursive, 947,
        1124–1130, 1310–1314

search, 1184–1204
shortest path, 1349–1357
sorting. *See* sorting algorithms

allocating memory with constants and variables, 51–54

ALU (arithmetic logical unit), 3–4

American National Standard Institution (ANSI), ANSI/ISO standard C++, 24

American Standard Code for Information Interchange (ASCII) character set (table), 1493–1494 and keyboard encoding, 7

ampersand (&)
address of operator, 735–736, 801–804
and `dataType`, 350, 356
and passing arrays, 486

analog signals, 6

analyzing problems for program development, 15–16

and (&&) operator, 176, 178, 182

`and` functions, 244

anonymous data types, 428–429

ANSI/ISO standard C++, 24
`namespace` mechanism, 79
naming conventions of header files, 1516–1517
and Standard Template Library (STL), 1374

answers to odd-numbered exercises, 1533–1558

application programs described, 6

arguments and functions, predefined functions, 123–131

arithmetic
expressions, 10
operations, special symbols for, 32
pointer, 751

arithmetic logical unit (ALU), 3–4

arithmetic operators
and classes, 598
constructing, 40
and floating-point numbers, 42–43
and `int` data type, 420
and operator overloading, 819
and order of precedence, 39–44

overloading as nonmember functions, 836–838

array-based lists
described, 786–794
insertion sorts, 1215–1223
quick sorts, 1224–1232
selection sorts, 1211–1215

array subscript operator ([ ]), 447, 448, 476, 872–873

arrays
base addresses of, 489–492
described, using, 474–476, 492–495
dynamic, 771–757
index out of bounds, 483–484
initialization, part initialization, 484–485
integral data type and array indices, 495–496
linked implementation of queues, 1144–1150
multidimensional, 521–522
parallel, 503–504
as parameters to functions, 486–487
processing one-dimensional, 479–483
processing restrictions, 485–486
of strings, 518–520
two-dimensional, 504–521
vs. `structs`, in `structs`, 559–562

`arraysAsParameter` function, 492

ASCII (American Standard Code for Information Interchange)
character set (table), 1493–1494
collating sequence, and expression evaluation, 172
and keyboard encoding, 7
null, nonprinting, 37

assemblers, assembly languages, 8–9

`assert` function, 873, 1519
for exception handling, 908–912
terminating programs with, 211–213

assigning
expression values to variables, 170
`struct` variables, 556–557

assignment operator (=)
associativity of, 56
built-in operations on classes, 598

and classes, 599, 762–764
described, 170
overloading, 843–851, 1089–1090, 1108–1110
vs. equality operator (= =), 202–203

assignment statements
built-in operations on classes, 598–599
initializing variables in, 63–67
using, 54–56, 89–91

associative containers, 1408–1415

associativity
of arithmetic operators, 44
of logical expressions, 178

asterisks (*)
arithmetic operator, 32, 43–44
dereferencing operator, 736–742

asymptotic notation, 1195–1204

automatic variables, using, 380–382

averages, calculating, 21–22, 156–159, 232–233

B

backslashes (\)
escape sequence, 76, 148
and newline characters, 37

`bad_alloc` exception, 747

base 2 number system, 7–8, 1499–1502

base addresses of arrays, 489

base and general case, recursive definitions, 946

base classes
constructors, header files, 678–687
and derived classes, 668–671
described, 668–669

`BaseAddressOfAnArray.cpp` program, 491

`begin` function, 1006

Bell Laboratories and C language, 24

bidirectional iterators, 1404–1405

big-O notation, 1195–1204

billings, calculating cable company (programming example), 214–219

binary
digits, code described, 6–7
files, 1502–1507
number systems, 7–8
numbers, converting to and from
decimal, 963–971
representation of non-negative
integer, 1499–1502
trees. *See* binary trees
units (table), 6–7

binary operators, 40, 832–838

binary searches, 1187–1195

binary trees
binary search trees, 1295–1310
described, using, 1223,
1274–1286
implementing, 1286–1294
nonrecursive traversal algorithms,
1310–1314
traversal, and functions as
parameters, 1314–1317

`binary_search` function,
1449–1452

binding, types of, 774

bits described, 6–7

blank symbols in C++ programs,
32, 85

`block` statements, using, 191–192

body of function in value-returning
functions, 314–315

`bool` data types, 36, 173, 183–184

Boolean values, expressions and data
types, 37

braces ({})
in C++ programs, 12, 85
and compound statements, 191
and `main` function, 81

breadth-first traversals, 1286,
1347–1349

`break` and `continue` statements,
279–281

`break` statements
and `switch` statements, 205
in `while, for, do...while`
loops, 279–280

bubble sorts, 1205–1210

buffers, clearing, 141

build command, compiling and linking,
class implementation, 634–636

building linked lists, 992–996

bytes, 6–7, 116

C

C++
ANSI/ISO standard, 24
arithmetic operators, precedence,
39–43
case-sensitivity, 32
data types, 34–39
equations in, 9
exception classes, 919–923
exception handling mechanism,
912–919
expressions in, 10, 39–43
increment, decrement operators,
68–70
naming conventions of header files,
1516–1517
and object-oriented design (OOD),
23–24
OOP language, 700
preprocessor directives, 78–79
reserved words, 32, 1489
`string` data type, 50–51
`structs` and `classes`, 628–629
type conversion, 47–50

C++ Builder (Borland), 13–14, 634

C++ programs
See also C++
basics of, 30–33
closing files at termination, 149
creating complete, 80–83
described, 9–12
documenting, 87
input, 51–68
output, 70–77
predefined functions in, 123–131
processing of, 12–14
program failure, 131–133
style and form of, 84–89
terminating with assert function,
211–213

c-strings (character arrays)
arrays of strings and, 519–520
defining class for manipulation,
874–881
described, using, 496–498
string comparison, 498–499

cable company billing (programming
example), 214–219

calculating
See also converting
averages, 21–22
checking account balance
(programming example),
250–259
Fibonacci numbers (programming
example), 259–264
grades, 356–360
monthly paycheck, 18–20
sales tax (example), 17–18
value of coins, 95–98

`callPrint` function, 773–777

candy machine (programming
example), 642–656

`case` labels, 203–204

`cassert` header file, 1519

casting (type conversion), 47–50

`catch, try/catch` blocks,
912–919, 929–933, 935–939

`cctype` header file, 1520–1521

cells, memory, 5, 57–58

centimeters, converting into feet and
inches, 91–94

central processing unit. *See* CPU

`cfloat` header file, 1521–1522

`char` data type, 37

character arrays. *See* c-strings

character sets, ASCII and EBCDIC
(tables), 1493–1495

characters
ASCII sets, 7, 37
and `char` data type, 37
newline, 37
special symbols in C++, 32
in strings, 50
underscore character (_), 32
whitespace, and extraction
operator, 118

checking account balance
calculation (programming
example), 250–259

`cin` function
and extraction operator >>,
117–123
and `get`, 125–126
and `ignore`, 126–128
and `istream` (input stream) data
type, 116–117

and `namespace` mechanism, 79
using, 77

circular linked lists, 1044–1045

class objects, 596, 600–601

`class` reserved word, 593

class templates, 883–885

classes
    abstract, and pure virtual functions,
        778–786
    accessing class members,
        597–598
    accessor and mutator functions,
        601–612
    address of operator (&) and,
        801–804
    assignment operator (=) and, 599
    built-in operations on, 598
    constructors, destructors,
        614–625
    creating exception, 923–933
    described, using, 592–595
    friend functions of, 826–829
    implementation of member
        functions, 601–606
    inheritance. *See* inheritance
    operator overloading, 818–858
    order of `private`, `public`
        members of, 612–614
    and pointer member variables, 771,
        858
    and pointers, peculiarities,
        760–771
    reference parameters and class
        objects, 600–601
    relating by composition,
        693–698
    relating by inheritance, 668–693
    scope, functions and, 600
    `static` members of, 636–642
    `structs` and pointer variables,
        742–745
    UML class diagrams, 595–596
    variable (object) declaration,
        596–597
    and virtual destructors, 778
    vs. `structs`, 628–629

classifying
    data from two files (programming
        example), 392–402
    numbers (programming example),
        270–273

odd and even numbers
    (programming example),
    387–391

`clear` function, using, 133–135

clearing buffers, 141

`clearList` function, 793

`climits` header file, 1522–1523

`clockType` programming example,
    858–866

`close` function, 149

closing files at program termination,
    149

`cmath` file header, 78, 123, 312,
    444, 1524–1525

code
    binary, 6–7
    executable, 633–636
    pseudocode, 196–198
    source. *See* source code

code detection (programming
    example), 522–529

CodeWarrior (Metroworks), 13–14, 634

collating sequences, and `char` data
    type, 37

columns
    and `cout`, 140
    filling with characters, 142
    justifying, 143–145

commands
    See also specific commands
    SDK linking, 14

commas (,) in C++ programs, 32, 85

comments in C++ programs, 61, 87

common input. *See* `cout` function

comparing
    characters, 37
    `if` and `if...else` control
        structures, 195–196
    `struct` variables, 557–558
    using relational operators,
        169–170
    values of different data types, 172

comparison-based search algorithms,
    1204

comparison trees, 1223

compile-time binding, 774

compilers
    and build, rebuild, make
        commands, 634–636
    C++ program processing, 9, 12, 14

complex numbers (programming
    example), 866–872

composition, relating classes by, 668,
    693–698

compound assignment statements,
    89–90

compound (block of) statements,
    using, 191–192

compound operators, 89–90

computer language described, 6–8

computers
    historical overview of, 2–3
    systems elements, 3–6

conditional expressions, using,
    203–204

conditional operator (?:), using,
    203–204

conditional statements in control
    structures, 169

`const` keyword, declaring reference
    parameters with, 356

constant arrays as formal parameters,
    487–489

constants
    allocating memory using, 51–54
    named, 379–380, 1522–1523

constructors
    class, 614–625
    conversion, 878
    copy, 764–771
    of derived and base classes,
        678–686

container adapters, 1415

containers
    associated header files, and iterator
        support, 1418–1419
    associative, 1408–1415
    STL, 1375

`continue` and `break` statements,
    using, 279–281

control structures
    counter-controlled `while` loops,
        236–238

described, 168–169, 259–264
iterative vs. recursive, 962–963
logical (Boolean) operators
    and logical expressions,
    175–204
nested, 281–289
relational operators in, 169–174
repetition. *See* repetition control
    structures
selection. *See* selection control
    structures
`switch` structures, 204–211
terminating programs with `assert`
    function, 211–213
`while` looping structure,
    233–236
control unit (CU) described, 4
conversion constructors, 878
converting
    binary to decimal numbers,
        963–968, 1501–1502
    compound into simple assignments
        statements, 90
    decimal to binary numbers,
        968–971, 1499–1501
    feet and inches into centimeters,
        91–94
    floating-point numbers to integers,
        47–49
`copy` algorithm, 1387–1390
copy (binary) tree, 1281
copy constructor, 764–771
copying binary trees, 1281
`copyList` function, 1007,
    1007–1008
`copyStack` function, 1088,
    1107–1108
`count`, `count_if` functions,
    1460–1464
counter-controlled `while` loops,
    236–238
counting backward, with `for` loop,
    267
cout function
    and `namespace` mechanism, 79
    and `ostream` (input stream) data
        type, 116–117
    and output, 82, 116
    using, 77

.cpp files, 12, 80
CPU (central processing unit), 3–4
creating C++ programs, 80–83
`cstddef` header file, 1525
`cstring` header file, 1525–1528
CU (control unit) described, 4
curly braces ({})
    and compound statements, 191
    and `main` function, 81
`current` pointer, 1020–1025
`customerType` class, 1152–1155
cycle, problem-analysis-coding-
    execution, 14–16

D

dangling pointers, 749
data
    comparing from different files
        (programming example),
        392–402
    in object-oriented design (OOD), 22
    putting into variables, 54–56
data abstraction, abstract data types,
    626–628
data types
    See also specific data type
    anonymous, 428–429
    described, 34–39
    enumeration types, 420–441
    floating-point, 37–39
    and mixed expressions, 45–47
    pointer, 734–735
    simple. *See* simple data types
    simple vs. structured, 474
    use of ampersand (&), 350
`dataType`, ampersand after, 350,
    356
debugging
    exception handling. *See* exception
        handling
    programs with pseudocode,
        196–198
decimal expressions described,
    44–45
decimal numbers
    converting base 10 to binary,
        1499–1501

converting from, to binary,
    963–971
and floating-point data types,
    37–39
decimal systems, 7
decision maker expressions, 185
declaration statements, 51–52,
    81–82
declaring
    arrays, 476–479
    file stream variables, 148
    identifiers, 53, 81
    pointer variables, 734–735
    `struct` variables, 554–559
    variables, 56–62, 81–83
    virtual functions, 774
decrement operators (--) described,
    68–70
deep copy vs. shallow, and pointers,
    760
default constructors, 614–616, 620
definition of function in value-
    returning functions, 315
definitions, recursion, 946–950
`delete` operator, 745–749
`deleteNode` function, 1012–1017
`deleteQueue` operation,
    1131–1143
deleting items from ordered linked
    lists, 1026–1027
depth first traversal, graphs,
    1345–1347
`deque` sequence containers,
    1391–1395
dereferencing operator (*)
    described, using, 736–742
    and linked lists, 998
    and pointers, 735
derived classes
    and base classes, 668–671
    constructors, header files, 678–687
    described, 668–669
    header files of, 685–686
    inheritance, pointers, and virtual
        functions, 771–778
    overriding member functions of
        base classes, 671–678

design, object-oriented. *See* object-oriented design

designing `while` looping structures, 235–236

destructors
class, 625
and dynamic arrays, 761–762
virtual, 778–786

determining end-of-file status, 248

devices
computer input, output, 3, 5–6
I/O (input/output). *See* I/O devices

diagrams
control structure flow of execution (fig.), 168
UML class, 595–596

digital signals, 6

digraphs, 1335

directed edge, branch, binary trees, 1274

directed graphs, 1335–1336

directives, preprocessor, 78–79

`discardExp` function, 1121

displaying program results on standard output device, 135

`divideList` function, 1235

division
of integers, 276–2
operation symbol, 32
by zero, 909–912

documentation using prompt lines, 86–87

documenting your programs, 87

`done` variable, 245

dot (.)
member access operator, 555
in string variables, 450

dot notation between I/O stream variables and I/O functions, 130–131

`double` data type, 38–39

double precision and float values, 39

double quotation marks (" ")
escape sequence, 76

and strings, 50, 499, 500
strings and, 10

`doubleFirst` function, 372

douby linked lists, 1033–1044

`do...while` looping (repetition) structures, 274–276

dynamic arrays, 479
using, 751–754
two-dimensional, 755–757

dynamic binding, 774

dynamic variables, using, 745–749

E

EBCDIC character
encoding, 7–8, 37
set (table), 1494–1495

Eiffel OOP language, 700

election results (programming example), 1242–1264

empty strings, 50

encapsulation principle of OOD, 699

`end` function, 1006

End Of File (EOF)-controlled `while` loops, 247–249, 285, 286

`endl` manipulator, 73, 135

enumeration data types, 34–35, 420–441, 507–512

`enum` data type, 421

EOF (End Of File)-controlled `while` loops, 247–249, 285, 286

`eof` function, using, 248–249

equality operator (= =), 170, 202–203

equations, writing in C++, 9

errors
syntax, 14, 16, 84
syntax, in `if` and `if...else` structures, 189
terminating programs with `assert` function, 211–213

escape sequences, commonly used (table), 76

`evaluateExpression` function, 1117–1119

`evaluateOpr` function, 1119–1121

even numbers, classifying (programming example), 387–391

exception handling
creating exception classes, 923–933
within programs, 908–923
stack unwinding, 935–939
techniques for, 933–935

.exe files, 81

executable code, object implementation, 633–636

executing C++ programs, 16

exercise answers (odd-numbered), 1533–1558

exiting loops with `break`, 279

`expfun` function, 351

expressions
arithmetic, 40
in assignment statements, 54
in C++, 10, 39–43
floating-point, 42–43
logical (Boolean), and logical operators, 173, 175–204
saving and using values of, 50, 56–57
in `while` statements, 249–250

Extended Binary-Coded Decimal Interchange Code. *See* EBCDIC

`extern` reserved word, 379

external variables, 379

extraction operator (>>), 116
and C++ stream classes, 688–689
and c-strings, 500
and `cin`, 117–123
overloading, 819, 840–843

F

`fact` function, 949

fail state
and `clear` function, 133–134
described, 132
input failure and `if` statements, 199–201

failure, input, 122

`false` reserved word and `bool` data type, 37

feet and inches, converting into centimeters, 91–94

Fibonacci numbers
calculating (programming example), 259–264
using with recursive function, 954–958

file input/output described, 147–150

file stream variables, 147

files
binary, 1502–1507
described, 147
determining end-of-file status, 248
header. *See* header files
opening, 150
source, 80

`fill` function, 757

`fill`, `fill_n` functions, 1430–1432

`find`, `find_if`, `find_end`, `find_first_of` functions, 1434–1439

First In First Out (FIFO) data processing, 1374

`first` keyword, 371

`fixed` manipulator, using, 136

flag-controlled `while` loops, 243–244, 249

`float` data type, 38–39

floating-point
`cfloat` header file, 1521–1522
data types described, 37–39
expressions, 44–45
notation, 38

floating-point numbers
comparing for equality, 171–172
converting to integers, 47–49
in mixed expressions, 45–47
and operator overloading, 819

`floor` function, 311, 312

`for` looping (repetition) structures, 264–270

`for` statements, scope of variables declared in, 376

`for_each` algorithm, 1464–1466

formatted and raw data, 1502

formatting output, 135–145

forward iterators, 1404

`friend` functions of classes, 826–829

`funcArrayAsParam` function, 486–487

function calls
described, 123–131
parameters vs. data type, 319

function headers in value-returning functions, 314

function objects, STL, 1422–1428

function overloading, introduction to, 382–384

function prototypes for value-returning functions, 320–324

function templates, 881–883

functions
See also specific function, algorithm
and algorithms, 1419
arrays as parameters to, 486–487
and classes, 600
with default parameters, 384–386
described, 11
and enumeration types, 426–428
friend, 826–829
main. *See* `main` function
math (table), 1524–1525
naming, 346
overloading, 880
predefined. *See* predefined functions
recursive, 947
specifying as formal parameter to other, 1314
standard, 30
STS. *See* Standard Template Library
user-defined. *See* user-defined functions
with value parameters, 354–355

`funcValueParam` function, 355

`funOne` function, 363–375

`funTwo` function, 366–369

G

games
creating number guessing, 244–247
rock, paper, scissors game (programming example), 430–441

`generate`, `generate_n` functions, 1432–1434

generating random numbers, 20

generic algoritms, 1420

`get` function
and `cin`, 125–126
and dot notation, 131

`getline` function, 146, 288

`getScore` function, 356–360

global identifiers, 375, 441–450

global variables, named constants and side effects, 379–382

GPA, calculating highest (programming example), 1094–1098

grade report (programming example), 701–721

graphs
as ADTs, 1341–1344
definitions, notations, 1335–1338
minimal spanning tree, 1357–1367
operations on, 1340–1341
representing in computer memory, 1338–1340
shortest path algorithm, 1349–1357
traversals, 1345–1349

greedy algorithm, 1349

grids of numbers, creating, 283

H

Hamblin, Charles L., 1112

handling exceptions. *See* exception handling

hardware, computer components,
3–6
header files
See also specific header file
`algorithm`, 1419
of class templates, 885
of derived classes, 685–686
derived classes, 686–678
and implementation files,
630–633
multiple inclusions of, 686–687
naming conventions of C++,
1516–1517
and preprocessor directives, 78
stack, 1090–1093
heap algorithms, 1422
hierarchies
C++ stream classes, 688–689
inheritance, 669
high-level programming languages, 9
history
of computers, 2–3
of programming languages, 8–9
horizontal tab character, 37

I

I/O (input/output), 145
devices and I/O streams, 116–123
file, 147–150
input failure, 131–133
operations generally, 116
`putback` and `peek` functions,
128–131
streams and standard I/O devices,
116–123
and `string` data type, 146
on `structs`, 557–558
identifiers
declaring, 53, 79
naming, 85–86
scope of, 375–379
token category, 32–33
`if` and `if...else` control
structures, 184–204
`if` statements, input failure and,
199–201
`ifstream` objects, 1508

`ignore` function and `cin`, 126–128
implementation files, and header
files, 630–633, 885
implicit type coercion, 47
`include` preprocessor directive,
78–79
`includes` function, 1467–1475
increment operator (++)
described, 68–70
and linked lists, 998
overloading, 851–852
indenting program code, 82–83
indices in arrays, 476, 483–484,
495–496
indirection operator (*), 736–742
infinite recursion, 949–950
infix notation, 1112
information hiding, class
implementation details, 629–633
inheritance
base and derived classes,
668–671
C++ stream classes, 688–689
constructors of derived and base
classes, 678–686
OOD principle, 699
overriding base class member
functions, 671–678
pointers, and virtual functions,
771–778
as `public`, `protected`,
`private`, 689–693
`initializeList` function, 1005
`initializeQueue` operation,
1131–1132, 1141, 1146–1149
`initializeStack`, 1083–1084,
1102
initializing
classes and constructors,
622–623
partial initialization during array
declaration, 484–485
pointer variables, 745
`struct` variables, 1505
two-dimensional arrays, 507
variables, 54, 62–68
vector containers, 1376

`inner_product` function,
1475–1480
`inplace_merge` function,
1453–1457
input
in C++ programs, 51–68
of enumeration types, 424–426
failure, 131–133
iterators, 1402–1403
/output. *See* I/O (input/output)
and prompt lines, 86–87
for variable of simple data type
(table), 119
input devices described, 3, 5–6
input failure
and data type errors, 122
and `if` statements, 199–201
input/output (I/O)
binary files, 1502–1507
random file access, 1508–1516
input (`read`) statements and stream
insertion operator (<<), 59
input stream variables, 117
`insert` function, 800–801, 1018
`insert` iterator, 1428–1430
`insertAt` function, 794
`insertEnd` function, 795
`insertFirst` function,
1011–1012, 1025–1026
<< (insertion operator), 82, 135, 501,
688–689
insertion point
on computer screen, 70
and `endl` manipulator, 135
insertion sorts, 1215–1223
`insertLast` function, 1025–1026
instance, class, 596
instruction register (IR) described, 4
`int` data type, 36, 182–183, 420
integers
calculating sums of, 269–270
classifying numbers (programming
example), 270–273
converting floating-point numbers
to, 47–49

in mixed expressions, 45–47
relational operators and simple data types, 171
representing non-negative, 1499–1502

integral data type, 34–35, 495–496

integral expressions described, 44–45

interface files, 630–633

International Standard Organization (ISO), ANSI/ISO standard C++, 24

intersection (U SYMBOL) in graph notation, 1335

`iomanip` header file and `setw` manipulor, 139

`ios::app` option, 150

`iostream` header file, 78, 83, 116, 147

IR (instruction register) described, 4

`isEmptyQueue` operation, 1131–1132, 1140–1141, 1145–1146

`isEmptyStack`, 1084, 1102

`isFullQueue` operation, 1131–1132, 1140–1141, 1145–1146

`isFullStack`, 1084, 1102

`isItemAtEqual` function, 792

ISO standard, ANSI/ISO standard C++, 24

`istream` (input stream) data type, 116

`istream` member function, 123

`istream_iterator`, 1408

iterative control structures, 962–963

iterators, linked list, 998–1004, 998–1005

`iter_swap` function, 1446–1449

J

Java, OOP language, 700

justifying output columns, 143–145

K

keywords, and reserved words, 32

kilobytes (KBs) described, 6–7

Königsberg bridge problem, 1334–1335

L

languages
computer, 6–8
programming, 8–9, 31–32

`larger` function, using, 328–335

Last In First Out (LIFO) data structures, 1077, 1374

leaf
in binary trees, 1279
in comparison trees, 1223

`left` manipulator, using, 143–145

length, determining string, 50–51

`length` function, 124, 125, 450–452

level-by-level binary tree traversals, 1286

libraries
and high-level languages, 12
predefined function, 311–312

LIFO (Last In First Out) data structures, 1077

linear searches, 796

linked implementation of stacks, 1098–1112

linked lists
as ADTs, 996–1009
building, 992–996
circular, 1044–1045
described, properties, 982–992
douby, 1033–1044
and insertion sorts, 1222
ordered, 1018–1030
printing in reverse order, 1030–1032
unordered, 1009–1018

`linkedListType` class, 998–1004

linkers
programs described, 13
and underscore character (_), 33

links, in linked lists, 982

`list` sequence containers, 1395–1402

lists
array-based, 786–794
bubble sorts, 1205–1210
described, 560, 627
linked. *See* linked lists
ordered, 800–801
partitioning, 1225
server, 1158–1162
sets and, 799
unordered, 794–799

loaders, 13

local declarations in value-returning functions, 318

local identifiers, 375

local variables, 360

logging errors, 935

logical (Boolean) operators and logical expressions, 175–204

logical (Boolean) values, 37, 170

`long double` data type, 38–39

loop control variable (LCV), using, 234–235

looping structures. *See* `while` looping structures

loops, 235–236, 480–482

lowercase, and C++'s case-sensitivity, 32

Lukasiewicz, Jan, 1112

M

machine language and programming languages, 8–9

main function
in C++ programs, 10–12, 31, 80–83
definition, and user-defined functions, 386
flow of execution, value-returning functions, 327

main memory (MM) described, 3, 4–5

make command, compiling and linking, class implementation, 634–636

manipulators
output, 135–141
parameterized stream, 144

math functions (table), 1524–1525

maxQueueSize variable, 1143

member access operator (.), 131, 555, 598, 600

member functions. *See specific function*

members of classes, 592

memory
allocating with constants and variables, 51–54
allocation for data types (table), 36
allocation in user-defined functions, 360–375
base addresses of arrays in, 489–492
bits and bytes, 6–7
cell and addresses, 5, 57–58
computer system element, 3, 4–5
representing graphs in, 1338–1340
size on system and random number generator, 1529–1530

memory leaks, avoiding, 748, 749

merge function, 1453–1457

merge sorts, 1232–1242

mergeSort function, 1239

methodologies, programming, 22–24

minimal spanning tree, and graphs, 1357–1367

- (minus) subtraction operator, overloading, 819

mixed expressions, 45–47

mnemonic and assembly languages, 8–9

modifying algorithms, 1421

Modula-2 OOP language, 700

modular programming, 22

modules and functions, 310

money, calculating value of change, 95–98

multidimensional arrays, 521–522, 755

multiplication operator (*), overloading, 833–836

multiple inheritance, 669

multiple line comments, 87

multiplication operator (*), 32, 833–836

multiset containers, 1409–1415

mutator functions, class, 601–612

N

n-dimensional arrays, 521

named constants
described, using, 51–52, 379–380, 1522–1523
global variables and, 379–382

namespace
mechanism, and cin and cout, 79
statement, 83
using namespace std statement, 117

namespace mechanism, 1516

namespace std., 117, 446

namespaces and global identifiers, 441–446

naming
functions, 346
identifiers, 85–86
named constants, 51–52
variables, 53

naming conventions of header files, ANSI/ISO Standard C++, 1516–1517

nested control structures, 281–289

nesting if...else structures, 192–193

new operator, 745–749, 922

newline character, 37, 76–77

newString class (programming example), 874–880

nodes
in binary trees, 1274–1280
in comparison trees, 1223

inserting in ordered linked lists, 1020
linked list structure of, 998
and linked lists, 982–991

non-static member variables, 642

nonmodifying algorithms, 1420

not (!) operator, using, 175

notation
dot, and I/O stream variables and I/O functions, 130–131
graph, 1335–1338
infix, 1112
scientific and floating-point, 38

null
cstddef header file, 1525
pointers, 745
strings described, 50

numbers
calculating Fibonacci (programming example), 259–264
classifying odd, even (programming example), 387–391
classifying (programming example), 270–273
complex (programming example), 866–872
creating grid of (example), 283
finding the larger of two, 328
generating random, 20, 244
representing real, 38–39

numeric algorithms, 1421–1422

O

object-oriented design (OOD)
and object-oriented programming (OOP), 698–701
objects and classes, 592
programming approach described, 22–24

object-oriented programming (OOP), 23–24, 698–701

Object Pascal OOP language, 700

object programs, 12

objects
class, described, 596
function (STL), 1422–1428

in object-oriented programming, 23–24

odd numbers, classifying (programming example), 387–391

`ofstream` objects, 1508

one-dimensional arrays, 479–483

one-way selection statements, 185–187

OOD (object-oriented design), 23–24, 592, 698–701

OOP (object-oriented programming), 23–24, 698–701

`open` statement, opening files, 149

operands in expressions, 40

operating systems, computer system element, 6

operations
aggregate, on arrays, 485–486
algorithms for container, 1419–1480
arithmetic operation symbols, 32
on graphs, 1340–1341
in object-oriented design (OOD), 22–23
on pointer variables, 749–751
on `set/multiset` containers, 1409–1415
stack, 1078–1079
and vector containers, 1377–1384

operator functions including in class definitions, 829–832

operator overloading
See also specific operator
described, using, 819–858
need for, 818–819
specified (table), 1497

`operator` reserved word, 819

operators
See also specific operator
arithmetic, 39–43
cast, 49
compound, 89–90
increment, decrement, 68–70
logical (Boolean), in control structures, 175–204
member access, 131
overloading, 818–858

precedence of (table), 178, 1491–1492
relational, in control structures, 169–174

or (| |) operator, using, 176–177

order of declaring public, private members of classes, 612–614

order of precedence
logical expressions, 177–178
overriding operator, 181

ordered linked lists, 1018–1030

ordered lists, using, 800–801

`orderedArrayListType` class, 1195

ordering, topological, 1367

`ostream` header file, 144

`ostream` iterators, 1388–1390

`ostream` (output stream) data type, 116

`ostream_iterator`, 1408

`ostreamVar` output stream variable, 141, 142, 144

out of bounds, array index, 483–484

output
of C++ programs, 70–77
of c-strings, 501–502
controlling with escape sequences, 76–77
devices, 3, 5–6, 70
of enumeration types, 424–426
and formatting output, 135–141
iterators, 1403
manipulators, 135–141
statements, 10–11, 71
tools for formatting, 141–145

output stream variables, 117

overloading
array index operator ([ ]), 872–873
assignment operator (=), 843–851, 1009, 1089–1090, 1108–1110
binary operators, 832–838
functions, 382–384, 880
operators, 818–858, 1497

`public` members, and derived classes, 676
stream insertion and extraction operators, 838–843
unary operators, 851–857

overriding
base class member functions, 671–678
operator's order of precedence, 181

P

palindrome numbers, returning in value-returning function, 325–327

parallel arrays, 503–504

parameterized stream manipulators, 144

parameterized types, 883

parameters
arrays as parameters to functions, 486–487
of functions, 123, 126
functions with default, 384–386
invoking class constructor with, 617–620
reference. *See* reference parameters
reference variables as, 355–360
value. *See* value parameters
in value-returning functions, 314–316, 321

parametric polymorphism, 699

parentheses (())
overriding operator precedence with, 181
and `peek` function, 129
and precedence in arithmetic expressions, 43–44
and semicolons in if statements, 187

`partial_sum` function, 1475–1480

`partition` function, 1231

partitioning lists, 1225

paths in undirected graphs, 1337

`peek` function, using, 128–131

percent sign (%) and integral data type, 40

period (.)
   member access operator (.), 598
   in string variables, 450

personal computers, elements of, 3–6

pig Latin strings (programming example), 458–464

planning algorithm development, 16

plus (+) addition operator
   built-in operations on classes, 598
   and operator overloading, 819
   and **string** data type, 448

pointer arithmetic, 751

pointer data type and pointer variables, 734–735

pointer member variables, and classes, 858

pointer variables
   classes, **structs** and, 742–745
   functions and pointers, 754
   initializing, 745
   operations on, 749–751

pointers
   and classes, peculiarities, 760–771
   current, **trailCurrent**, 1020–1025
   dangling, 749
   and functions, and return values, 754
   inheritance and virtual functions, 771–778
   shallow vs. deep copy, 758–760

Polish notation, 1112

polymorphism, OOD principle, 699

pop operations, stacks and, 1086–1088, 1105–1107

post-increment operator (++), overloading, 854–857

postfix expressions calculator, 1112–1124

postfix notation, 1112–1117

pound sign (#) and preprocessor directives, 12, 78

pow (power) function, 123, 311, 312, 444

pre-increment operator (++), overloading, 851–853

precedence order
   arithmetic operators, 39–44, 43–44
   logical expressions, 177–178
   operators (table), 178, 1491–1492
   overriding operator, 181

precision and float values, 39

predefined functions, 30, 123–128, 310–313

predefined identifiers, 33

predicates, STL, 1428

prefix notation, 1112

preprocessor directives, 12, 78–79

preprocessors described, 12

print function, 757, 1005

printGrade function, 356–360

printing
   file output, 147
   lines of stars (example), 282
   linked lists, 1030–1032, 1124–1130
   and program output, 135

printResult function, 1121–1124

printStars function, 347–349, 351–353

private members, class, 593–595, 612–614, 629, 689

private reserved word, 593–595

problem-analysis-coding-execution cycle, programming with, 14–16

problem-solving using recursion, 950–962

processing
   arrays using loops, 480–482
   C++ programs, 12–14

program counter (PC), 4

program development
   analyzing problems for, 15–16
   using SDKs, 11, 13

programming
   described, 14, 30
   methodologies described, 22–24

object-oriented. *See* object-oriented programming
   with problem-analysis-coding-execution cycle, 14–16
   structured, modular, 22

programming languages, 8–9, 31–32

programs
   See also software
   application. *See* application programs
   C++. *See* C++ programs
   computer, described, 30
   exception handling within, 908–923
   source, 12
   terminating on exception, 933
   using in **string** data type, 79

prompt lines in documentation, 86–87

protected classes described, 593–595

protected members of classes, 689–693

prototypes, value-returning functions, 320–324

pseudocode, developing, testing, debugging programs with, 196–198

public members, class, 593–595, 612–614, 671, 689

public reserved word, 593–595

pure virtual functions, 779

push operations, stacks and, 1084–1086, 1103–1105

putback function, 128–131

Q

queueFront, **queueRear** variables, 1133, 1143, 1144

queueing system simulations, 1151

queueRear operation, 1142

queues
   described, operations, 1131–1133
   implementation as arrays, 1133–1144
   implementing in programs, 1417–1418

simulation application, 1150–1170

quotation marks
double (" ") and strings in C++, 10, 50, 499, 500
escape sequences, 76–77
single, 71, 122

R

RAM (random access memory), computer system element, 3

`rand` function, 1530

random access iterators, 1405–1407

random access memory (RAM), 3

random file access, 1508–1516

random numbers, generating, 20, 244, 1530

raw and formatted data, 1502

reading
strings, 60–62, 500
texts (programming example), 529–536

real numbers
relational operators and simple data types, 171
representing, 38–39

rebuild command, compiling and linking, class implementation, 634–636

`recMergeSort` function, 1240–1242

records. *See* `structs`

recursion
printing linked lists in reverse order, 1030–1032
problem-solving using, 950–962
recursive definitions, 946–950

redefining base class member functions, 671–678

reference parameters
and class objects, 600–601
manipulating actual parameters, 369–373
in user-defined functions, 360–375
and value-returning functions, 375
in void functions, 350–351

reference variables as parameters, 355–360

references to this book, 1531

registers, instruction (IR), 4

relational operator (<), sorting associative containers, 1408

relational operators
in C++ (table), 170
in control structures, 171–174
described, 169
and enumeration type, 423–424
evaluation order, 184
overloading as nonmember functions, 836–838
and `string` data type, 173–174

`remove`, `remove_if`, `remove_copy`, `remove_copy_if` functions, 1439–1442

`removeAt` function, 792, 797

repetition control structures
`break` and `continue` statements, 279–281
counter-controlled `while` loops, 236–238
described, 168–169, 232–233
`do...while` looping (repetition) structures, 274–276
flag-controlled `while` loops, 243–244
`for` looping structure, 264–270
nested control structures, 281–289
`while` looping structure, 233–236

`replace`, `replace_if`, `replace_copy`, `replace_copy_if` functions, 1442–1446

representation of non-negative integer, 1499–1502

representing ASCII characters, 7–8

reserved words in C++ programs, 32, 1489

rethrowing exceptions, 929–933

`retrieveAt` function, 793

return escape sequence, 76

`return` reserved word, 80

return statements
program output, 200
in value-returning functions, 317–320, 323

Reverse Polish notation, 1112

`reverse`, `reverse_copy` functions, 1457–1460

`reversePrint` function, 1030–1032

`right` manipulator, using, 143–145

rock, paper, scissors game (programming example), 430–431

root node, in comparison trees, 1224

`rotate`, `rotate_copy` functions, 1457–1460

row order form in array processing, 515

rules, syntax and semantic, 31

run-time binding, 774

run-time errors, 920

run-together words
and constants, 52
as identifiers, 86

`runSimulation` class, 1166–1170

S

sales data analysis (programming example), 569–58

sales tax (example), 17–18

saving expression values, 50, 56–57

scientific notation and floating-point notation, 38

scope
class, 600
of identifiers, 375–379
of namespace member, 442

scope resolution operator (::), 379, 602

screen, sending output to, 147

SDKs (software development kits), 12, 13

`search` function, 1298, 1449–1452

search trees, binary, 1295–1310

searching
binary search trees, 1295–1310
binary searches, 1187–1195
ordered linked lists, 1020
search algorithms, 1184–1204

`search_n` function, 1449–1452

`second` keyword, 371

secondary storage, computer system element, 5

secret code detection (programming example), 522–529

`seekp`, `seekg` functions, 1508–1516

selection control structures
described, 168–169
`if` and `if...else` control structures, 184–204

selection sorts, 1211–1222

selector expressions, `switch`, 203–204

semantic rules
in C++ programs, 85
in programming languages, 31

semicolons (;)
in C++ programs, 32, 75, 85
in `if` and `if...else` structures, 187
in `for` loops, 266

sentinel-controlled `while` loops, using, 238–240, 284

sentinel values and EOF-controlled while loops, 247

`seqSearch` function, 562

sequence containers
`deque`, 1391–1395
`list`, 1395–1402
member functions common to, 1386

sequential searches, 796, 1185–1187

server lists, 1158–1162

`serverListType` class, 1159–1162

`serverType` class, 1155

`set` containers, 1409–1415

set theory, and graphs, 1335

`setfill` manipulator, using, 142–143

`set_intersection`, `set_union`, `set_difference`, `set_symmetric_difference` functions, 1467–1475

`setprecision` manipulator, using, 135–136

sets, and lists, 799

`setw` manipulator, 138–140

shallow vs. deep copy, and pointers, 760

short-circuit evaluation, logical expressions, 181–182

shortest path algorithm, 1349–1357

`showpoint` manipulator, using, 136–138

signals, analog and digital, 6

simple assignment statements, 89–90

simple data types
described, 34–37, 474
relational operators and, 171–173
valid input for variable of (table), 119

Simula OOP language, 700

simulations
described, 1150
waiting customers queue, 1163–1164

single inheritance, 669

single line comments
in C++ programs, 87
in `main` function, 61
and output statements, 76–77

single precision and float values, 39

single quotation marks ('') and entering character data, 76–77, 122

`size` function, 452–455

size of arrays, 479, 486

slashes (/)
arithmetic operators, 32, 40, 819
and code comments, 87

Smalltalk OOP language, 700

software
described, 6
development kits. *See* SDKs

`sort` function, 1449–1452

sorting
quick sorts: array-based lists, 1224–1232

sorting algorithms
bubble sorts, 1205–1210
lower bound on comparison-based, 1223–1224
merge sorts, 1232–1242
selection sorts, 1211–1215

source code
C++, 80
described, 12

space bar and blank symbols, 32

`sqrt` (square root) function, 123, 311

`squareFirst` function, 372

stack unwinding, exception handling, 935–939

`stackADT` class, 1080

stacks
container adapters, 1415–1418
described, using, 1076–1079
implementing as arrays, 1080–1094
linked implementation of, 1098–1112
nonrecursive algorithm to print linked list backward, 1124–1130
postfix expressions calculator, 1112–1124

`stackType` class, 1080–1083

Standard C++
described, 24
namespace mechanism, 441
naming conventions of header files, 1516–1517

standard functions in C++ programs, 30

standard input device, putting variables into, 58

standard output devices, 70, 135

Standard Template Library (STL)
components of, 1374–1402
container adapters, 1402–1418
containers, header files, iterator
support, 1418–1430
STL algorithms, function
prototypes, 1430–1480

statement terminators, 85

statements
See also specific statements
action, described, 185
assignment. *See* assignment
statements
conditional, 169
and main function, 80–83
output, 70
prompt lines, 86–87
syntax of, 31

static binding, 774

static members of classes, 636–642

static variables, using, 380–382

static_cast, 49, 67

std prefix, 444–445

stepwise refinement, 22

storage, secondary, 5

storing logical expression values,
183

strcpy, strcmp, strlen functions,
498

stream classes, C++ hierarchy,
688–689

stream insertion operator (<<)
and C++ stream classes,
688–689
and cout, 135
described, 12
overloading, 819, 838–840
using, 59, 70

stream iterators, 1408

stream member functions, 123

stream variables, input and output,
117

streams, IO, and standard I/O devices,
116–123

string data type, 446–450

string data type
arrays of strings, 518
described, 50–51
I/O and, 146
relational operators and, 173–174
specifying input/output files at
execution time, 502–503
using in programs, 79

string variables, logical expression
evaluation (table), 173–174

strings
arrays of, 518
c-strings (character arrays),
496–498
comparing, 498–499
cstring header file, 1525–1528
described, 50, 447
and double quotation marks (" "),
10, 499, 500
as expressions, 11
reading, 60–62
string data type, 446–458

Stroustrup, Bjarne, 24

struct reserved word, 553

struct variables, 557–558, 1505

structs (records)
accessing struct members,
554–554
in arrays, arrays in, 560–564
assignment, 556–557
described, 552–554
input/output, 558
within structs, 565–568
variables and functions, 558–559
vs. arrays, 559
vs. classes, 628–629

structured data types vs. simple data
types, 474

structured design, programming
methodology, 22

structures
control. *See* control structures
LIFO (Last In First Out) data
structures, 1077
queues. *See* queues
stacks. *See* stacks

subgraphs, 1335

subprograms in C++ programs, 30

subscript operator ([ ]), 872–873

subset of, in graph notation, 1335

substr function, 456–458

sumArray function, 492–495

sums
calculating averages and, 232–233
calculating for positive integers,
269–270

swap function, 1215, 1446–1449

swap_ranges function,
1446–1449

switch structures
break statements in, 279
in control structures, 204–211
if...else structures, 243

symbols, special, in C++, 32

syntax
See also specific function
in C++ programs, 12
checking for errors, 14, 16
increment operator (++), 68
program style and form, 84–89
rules, 31
shading in this book, 59
value-returning functions,
316–317

T

tab, escape sequence, 76–77

tab character, horizontal, 37

tail recursion functions, 949

tax, sales (example), 17–18

telephone digits, reading and printing
(example), 240–243

templates
array-based lists, 886–892
function, and class, 881–885

terminating
programs when exceptions occur,
933
programs with assert function,
211–213

terminator, statement, 85

ternary operators, 203

test scores, averaging (example), 156–159

testing
algorithms, 16
programs with pseudocode, 196–198

text
outputting as message, 75–76
reading (programming example), 529–536

text editors in SDKs, 14

`this` pointers and operator overloading, 821–826

`this` reserved word, 821

throwing exceptions, 913–914, 929–933

tilde character (~), class destructors, 625

time-driven simulations, 1151

`time` function, using, 244

tokens
in C++ programs, 31
symbols, identifiers, 32

top-down design described, 22

topological ordering, 1367

Tower of Hanoi problem, 958–962

`trailCurrent` pointer, 1020–1025

transaction time, 1151

`transform` algorithm, 1464–1466

translating pseudocode into C++ programs, 196–198

traversals, graph, 1345–1349

traversing binary trees, 1282–1286

`true` reserved word and `bool` data type, 37

try/catch blocks, 912–919, 929–933, 935–939

Turbo Pascal OOP language, 700

two-dimensional arrays, 504–521, 755–757

two-way selection statements, 187–191

type conversion (casting), 47–50

type of programming, 84–89

`typedef` iterators, 1406–1407

`typedef` statements, 429–430, 520–521

U

UML class diagrams, 595–596, 628

unary operators, overloading, 40, 851–857

underscore character (_)and identifiers, 32, 33, 441

undirected graphs, 1335–1336

Unicode character encoding, 7–8

Unified Modeling Language (UML), class diagrams, 595–596

union symbol in graph notation, 1335

unordered linked lists, 1009–1018

unordered lists, 794–799

`unorderedArrayListType` class, 1184, 1210

`unorderedLinkedList` class, 1110–1112, 1184

`unorderedLinkedListType` class, 1149–1150

`unorderedListType` function, 1017–1018

update expression, using, 266

user-defined functions
described, using, 313–314
value and reference parameters, memory allocation, 360–375
value parameters, 354–360
value-returning functions, 314–327, 375
void functions, 346–353

V

value parameters
and memory allocation in user-defined functions, 354–360
in user-defined functions, 360–375
using, 354–355
in void functions, 350–351

value-returning functions
described, using, 314–326
flow of execution, 327
and reference parameters, 375

values
saving expression, 50, 56–57
sentinels defined, 238–239
walk-throughs, 56

variable (object) declaration, 596–597

variables
allocating memory using, 51–54
arrays of class objects and constructors, 623–625
in assignment statements, 63–67
automatic, 380–382
declaring and initializing, 56–68
declaring for `enum` type, 422, 428
dynamic, 745–749
file stream, 147
global, 379–380, 379–382
initializing, 54
`istream`, `ostream` declarations, 116–117
local, 360
loop control, 234–235
outputting, 73
pointer, and pointer data type, 735–736
putting data into, 54–56
reference parameters and class objects, 600–601
static, 380–382
`struct`, 554–559

vector containers
described, using, 1374–1384
member functions common to, 1384–1385

video store (programming example), 1045–1064, 1318–1327

virtual destructors, classes and, 778

virtual functions
and inheritance and pointers, 771–778
pure, and abstract classes, 778–786

visibility
See also scope
of identifiers, 378

Visual C++, 13–14, 634
Visual Studio .NET, 13–14, 634
void functions, 314, 346–353

W

walk-through and value sequence, 56
warning messages
  See also error messages
  and floating-point numbers, 39
weighted graphs, 1349

weighted trees, 1358
`what` function, 919–923
`while` looping structure
  counter-controlled, 238–240
  EOF (End Of File)-controlled `while`
    loops, 247–249
  finding Fibonacci numbers with,
    259–264
  flag-controlled `while` loops,
    243–244
  sentinel-controlled, 238–240
  using, 233–236

`while` statements
  expressions in, 249–250
  using, 233–236
`whitespace` characters and
  extraction operator (>>), 118
word symbols, tokens, 32
words
  reserved, 32
  run-together, 52, 86
writing c-strings (character arrays),
  500